MW01426922

THE INTERNATIONAL HANDBOOK OF GENDER AND POVERTY

The International Handbook of Gender and Poverty

Concepts, Research, Policy

Edited by

Sylvia Chant

Professor of Development Geography, London School of Economics and Political Science, UK

Edward Elgar
Cheltenham, UK • Northampton, MA, USA

© Sylvia Chant 2010

All rights reserved. No part of this publication may be reproduced, stored in a retrieval system or transmitted in any form or by any means, electronic, mechanical or photocopying, recording, or otherwise without the prior permission of the publisher.

Published by
Edward Elgar Publishing Limited
The Lypiatts
15 Lansdown Road
Cheltenham
Glos GL50 2JA
UK

Edward Elgar Publishing, Inc.
William Pratt House
9 Dewey Court
Northampton
Massachusetts 01060
USA

A catalogue record for this book
is available from the British Library

Library of Congress Control Number: 2009940740

Mixed Sources
Product group from well-managed
forests and other controlled sources
www.fsc.org Cert no. SA-COC-1565
© 1996 Forest Stewardship Council

ISBN 978 1 84844 334 1 (cased)

Printed and bound by MPG Books Group, UK

Contents

List of figures	xiii
List of tables	xiv
List of boxes	xv
List of contributors	xvii
Acknowledgements	xxv
List of abbreviations	xxvii

1 Gendered poverty across space and time: introduction and overview   1
    Sylvia Chant

PART I   CONCEPTS AND METHODOLOGIES FOR GENDERED POVERTY

2 Strategic gendering: one factor in the constituting of novel political economies   29
    Saskia Sassen

3 Subjectivity, sexuality and social inequalities   35
    Henrietta L. Moore

4 Power, privilege and gender as reflected in poverty analysis and development goals   41
    Gerd Johnsson-Latham

5 Gender into poverty won't go: reflections on economic growth, gender inequality and poverty with particular reference to India   47
    Cecile Jackson

6 Advancing the scope of gender and poverty indices: an agenda and work in progress   53
    Thomas Pogge

7 Methodologies for gender-sensitive and pro-poor poverty measures   59
    Sharon Bessell

8 Multidimensional poverty measurement in Mexico and Central America: incorporating rights and equality   65
    Anna Coates

9 Gender, time poverty and Amartya Sen's capability approach: evidence from Guatemala   71
    Sarah Gammage

10 Why is progress in gender equality so slow? An introduction to the 'Social Institutions and Gender' Index   77
    Denis Drechsler and Johannes Jütting

11 Diamonds are a girl's best friend? Experiences with the Gender Action Learning System   84
    Linda Mayoux

vi   *Contents*

PART II   DEBATES ON THE 'FEMINISATION OF POVERTY', AND
         FEMALE-HEADED HOUSEHOLDS

12   The 'feminisation of poverty': a widespread phenomenon?   95
     Marcelo Medeiros and Joana Costa
13   Poor households or poor women: is there a difference?   101
     Gita Sen
14   Globalisation and the need for a 'gender lens': a discussion of dichotomies
     and orthodoxies with particular reference to the 'feminisation of poverty'   105
     Tine Davids and Francien van Driel
15   Towards a (re)conceptualisation of the 'feminisation of poverty':
     reflections on gender-differentiated poverty from The Gambia,
     Philippines and Costa Rica   111
     Sylvia Chant
16   Post-adjustment, post-mitigation, 'post-poverty'? The feminisation of
     family responsibility in contemporary Ghana   117
     Lynne Brydon
17   Female-headed households and poverty in Latin America: state policy in
     Cuba, Puerto Rico and the Dominican Republic   123
     Helen I. Safa
18   Gender, households and poverty in the Caribbean: shadows over
     islands in the sun   129
     Janet Momsen
19   Poverty and female-headed households in post-genocide Rwanda   135
     Marian Koster
20   Between stigmatisation and survival: poverty among migrant and
     non-migrant lone mothers in the Netherlands   141
     Annelou Ypeij
21   Lone mothers, poverty and paid work in the United Kingdom   147
     Jane Millar
22   Urban poverty and gender in advanced economies: the persistence of
     feminised disadvantage   153
     Fran Tonkiss

PART III   GENDER, FAMILY AND LIFECOURSE

23   Gender and household decision-making in developing countries: a review
     of evidence   161
     Agnes R. Quisumbing
24   Linking women's and children's poverty   167
     Ruth Lister
25   Reducing the gender gap in education: the role of wage labour for rural
     women in Mozambique   173
     John Sender

26	Understanding the gender dynamics of Russia's economic transformation: women's and men's experiences of employment, domestic labour and poverty *Sarah Ashwin*	178
27	Gender, poverty and transition in Central Asia *Jane Falkingham and Angela Baschieri*	184
28	Urban poverty, heteronormativity and women's agency in Lima, Peru: family life on the margins *Carolyn H. Williams*	190
29	Youth, gender and work on the streets of Mexico *Gareth A. Jones and Sarah Thomas de Benítez*	195
30	Sexuality, poverty and gender among Gambian youth *Alice Evans*	201
31	Ghettoisation, migration or sexual connection? Negotiating survival among Gambian male youths *Stella Nyanzi*	207
32	Poverty and old age in sub-Saharan Africa: examining the impacts of gender with particular reference to Ghana *Isabella Aboderin*	215
33	Gender, urban poverty and ageing in India: conceptual and policy issues *Penny Vera-Sanso*	220
34	Poverty, gender and old age: pension models in Costa Rica and Chile *Monica Budowski*	226
35	Gender, poverty and pensions in the United Kingdom *Jane Falkingham, Maria Evandrou and Athina Vlachantoni*	232

PART IV GENDER, 'RACE' AND MIGRATION

36	Assessing poverty, gender and well-being in 'Northern' indigenous communities *Janet Hunt*	241
37	Gender and ethnicity in the shaping of differentiated outcomes of Mexico's *Progresa-Oportunidades* conditional cash transfer programme *Mercedes González de la Rocha*	248
38	Gender, poverty, and national identity in afrodescendent and indigenous movements *Helen I. Safa*	254
39	The gendered exclusions of international migration: perspectives from Latin American migrants in London *Cathy McIlwaine*	260
40	Latino immigrants, gender and poverty in the United States *Cecilia Menjívar*	266
41	Culturing poverty? Ethnicity, religion, gender and social disadvantage among South Asian Muslim communities in the United Kingdom *Claire Alexander*	272

viii Contents

42 Gender, occupation, loss and dislocation: a Latvian perspective 278
    Linda McDowell
43 Gender, poverty and migration in Mexico 284
    Haydea Izazola
44 Migration, gender and sexual economies: young female rural–urban
    migrants in Nigeria 290
    Daniel Jordan Smith
45 Internal mobility, migration and changing gender relations: case study
    perspectives from Mali, Nigeria, Tanzania and Vietnam 296
    Cecilia Tacoli
46 Picturing gender and poverty: from 'victimhood' to 'agency'? 301
    Kalpana Wilson

PART V GENDER, HEALTH AND POVERTY

47 Poverty gender and the right to health: reflections with particular
    reference to Chile 309
    Jasmine Gideon
48 Maternal mortality in Latin America: a matter of gender and ethnic
    equality 315
    Anna Coates
49 New labyrinths of solitude: lonesome Mexican migrant men and AIDS 321
    Matthew Gutmann
50 Gender, poverty and AIDS: perspectives with particular reference to
    sub-Saharan Africa 327
    Catherine Campbell and Andrew Gibbs
51 Gender, HIV/AIDS and carework in India: a need for
    gender-sensitive policy 333
    Keerty Nakray
52 Women's smoking and social disadvantage 339
    Hilary Graham

PART VI GENDER, POVERTY AND ASSETS

53 Household wealth and women's poverty: conceptual and methodological
    issues in assessing gender inequality in asset ownership 347
    Carmen Diana Deere
54 Gender, poverty and access to land in cities of the South 353
    Carole Rakodi
55 Power, patriarchy and land: examining women's land rights in Uganda
    and Rwanda 360
    Kate Bird and Jessica Espey
56 Gender, livelihoods and rental housing markets in the Global South:
    the urban poor as landlords and tenants 367
    Sunil Kumar

57	Renegotiating the household: successfully leveraging women's access to housing microfinance in South Africa *Sophie Mills*	373
58	Gender issues and shack/slum dweller federations *Sheela Patel and Diana Mitlin*	379
59	Gender, poverty and social capital: the case of Oaxaca City, Mexico *Katie Willis*	385
60	Moving beyond gender and poverty to asset accumulation: evidence from low-income households in Guayaquil, Ecuador *Caroline Moser*	391
61	Conceptual and practical issues for gender and social protection: lessons from Lesotho *Rachel Slater, Rebecca Holmes, Nicola Jones and Matšeliso Mphale*	399

PART VII GENDER, POVERTY AND WORK

62	Gender, work and poverty in high-income countries *Diane Perrons*	409
63	The extent and origin of the gender pay gap in Europe *Janneke Plantenga and Eva Fransen*	415
64	Women's work, nimble fingers and women's mobility in the global economy *Ruth Pearson*	421
65	Gender, poverty and inequality: the role of markets, states and households *Shahra Razavi and Silke Staab*	427
66	Women's employment, economic risk and poverty *James Heintz*	434
67	Gender and ethical trade: can vulnerable women workers benefit? *Stephanie Barrientos*	440
68	Fraternal capital and the feminisation of labour in South India *Sharad Chari*	446
69	Economic transition and the gender wage gap in Vietnam: 1992–2002 *Amy Y.C. Liu*	452
70	Gender, poverty and work in Cambodia *Katherine Brickell*	458
71	Informality, poverty, and gender: evidence from the Global South *Marty Chen*	463
72	The empowerment trap: gender, poverty and the informal economy in sub-Saharan Africa *Kate Meagher*	472
73	A gendered analysis of decent work deficits in India's urban informal economy: case study perspectives from Surat *Paula Kantor*	478
74	Gender and quality of work in Latin America *Javier Pineda*	484

x Contents

75 Gender inequalities and poverty: a simulation of the likely impacts of reducing labour market inequalities on poverty incidence in Latin America 490
Joana Costa and Elydia Silva

PART VIII GENDERED POVERTY AND POLICY INTERVENTIONS

76 Gender, poverty and aid architecture 497
Gwendolyn Beetham

77 Brand Aid? How shopping has become 'Saving African Women and Children with AIDS' 504
Lisa Ann Richey

78 Sweden to the rescue? Fitting brown women into a poverty framework 510
Katja Jassey

79 Poverty alleviation in a changing policy and political context: the case of PRSPs with particular reference to Nicaragua 516
Sarah Bradshaw and Brian Linneker

80 Gender-responsive budgeting and women's poverty 522
Diane Elson and Rhonda Sharp

81 Reducing gender inequalities in poverty: considering gender-sensitive social programmes in Costa Rica 528
Monica Budowski and Laura Guzmán Stein

82 Is gender inequality a form of poverty? Shifting semantics in Oxfam GB's thinking and practice 535
Nicholas Piálek

83 Tackling poverty: learning together to improve women's rights through partnership – the case of WOMANKIND Worldwide 541
Tina Wallace and Ceri Hayes

84 Millennial woman: the gender order of development 548
Ananya Roy

PART IX MICROFINANCE AND WOMEN'S EMPOWERMENT

85 The housewife and the marketplace: practices of credit and savings from the early modern to modern era 557
Beverly Lemire

86 Money as means or money as end? Gendered poverty, microcredit and women's empowerment in Tanzania 563
Fauzia Mohamed

87 Capitalising on women's social capital: gender and microfinance in Bolivia 569
Kate Maclean

88 'A woman and an empty house are never alone for long': autonomy, control, marriage and microfinance in women's livelihoods in Addis Ababa, Ethiopia 575
Caroline Sweetman

Contents xi

89	Gender and poverty in Egypt: do credit projects empower the marginalised and the destitute? *Iman Bibars*	581
90	Women's empowerment: a critical re-evaluation of a GAD poverty-alleviation project in Egypt *Joanne Sharp, John Briggs, Hoda Yacoub and Nabila Hamed*	587
91	Impacting women through financial services: the Self Help Group Bank Linkage Programme in India and its effects on women's empowerment *Ranjula Bali Swain*	594
92	Microcredit and women's empowerment: understanding the 'impact paradox' with particular reference to South India *Supriya Garikipati*	599
93	Gender and poverty in microfinance: illustrations from Zambia *Irene Banda Mutalima*	606
94	The impact of microcredit programmes on survivalist women entrepreneurs in The Gambia and Senegal *Bart Casier*	612
95	Methodologies for evaluating women's empowerment in poverty alleviation programmes: illustrations from Paraguay and Honduras *Yoko Fujikake*	618

PART X NEW FRONTIERS IN GENDERED POVERTY RESEARCH AND ANALYSIS

96	Women, poverty and disasters: exploring the links through Hurricane Mitch in Nicaragua *Sarah Bradshaw*	627
97	Decentralisation, women's rights and poverty: learning from India and South Africa *Jo Beall*	633
98	Poverty, entitlement and citizenship: vernacular rights cultures in Southern Asia *Sumi Madhok*	638
99	Contradictions in the gender–poverty nexus: reflections on the privatisation of social reproduction and urban informality in South African townships *Faranak Miraftab*	644
100	Gender, neoliberalism and post-neoliberalism: re-assessing the institutionalisation of women's struggles for survival in Ecuador and Venezuela *Amy Lind*	649
101	Who does the counting? Gender mainstreaming, grassroots initiatives and linking women across space and 'race' in Guyana *D. Alissa Trotz*	655
102	Poverty, religion and gender: perspectives from Albania *Claire Brickell*	661

xii *Contents*

103 Sexuality, gender and poverty 667
     Susie Jolly and Andrea Cornwall
104 Masculinity, poverty and the 'new wars' 674
     Jane L. Parpart

Index 681

Figures

6.1	New indices based on a holistic measure of individual (dis)advantage	58
9.1	Time poverty in Guatemala by key characteristics (percentage)	74
10.1	Construction of the OECD Social Institutions and Gender Index (SIGI)	79
10.2	Discrimination in social institutions and women's participation in non-agricultural wage employment	80
11.1	Example of 'Happy Families Diamond' by women entrepreneurs from Uganda	88
25.1	Ratio of sons' and daughters' years of schooling in the MRLS, male principal respondents and divorced and separated (DS) and non-divorced and non-separated (NDS) female principal respondents (Mozambique)	175
35.1	Percentage of men and women of working age contributing to a private pension (UK)	236
52.1	Cigarette smoking among women by socio-economic group, Spain, 1987	341
61.1	Impact pathways of vulnerability to economic and social risk	400
71.1	Segmentation of the informal economy by sex, average earnings and poverty risk	468
71.2	Poverty risk of households by sources of income	469
75.1	The contribution of reducing gender inequalities in the labour market to poverty reduction: selected Latin American countries	493
90.1	Location of Wadi Allaqi	589
93.1	Development paths of microfinance institutions (1980s–2000s)	608
95.1	Schematic matrix of 'empowerment' outcomes for women of the Improving Living Standards Project (ILSP), Paraguay	623

Tables

9.1	The capability index in Guatemala by key characteristics (men and women 12–65 years)	75
18.1	Gender gaps in the Caribbean, 2006 (selected islands)	130
25.1	Education of sons and daughters of female and male principal respondents in the MRLS (Mozambique)	174
27.1	Absolute poverty by gender according to the unitary and different assumptions of collective household model using income and $1.08 PPP a day poverty line (Tajikistan)	187
43.1	Evolution of income by gender in ranks of minimum wages, Mexico, 1990–2008	286
52.1	Social disadvantage and cigarette smoking among women with young children, UK, 2001–2002	342
59.1	Women's use of social networks by socio-economic status, Oaxaca City, Mexico	386
60.1	Asset types by index categories and components	393
60.2	Asset accumulation by headship in Indio Guayas, 1992–2004 (standard deviations above average)	395
63.1	Gender pay gaps in selected European countries	416
67.1	Comparison of employment in selected sectors linked to Global Value Chains	441
69.1	Decomposition of the gender wage gap in Vietnam, 1992–2002	456
70.1	Selected information on human development, poverty and gender in Cambodia	459
73.1	Distribution of sample workers by sex and employment status, Surat, India	481
76.1	The Paris Declaration's five principles, twelve indicators of progress and examples of gender-sensitive indicators	499
92.1	Loan-use by control over loan and source of repayment (N = 397), Andhra Pradesh, India	602

Boxes

11.1	Steps in using the Diamond tool	86
60.1	Definition of the most important capital assets	392
61.1	World Vision Cash and Food Transfers Pilot Project, Lesotho	404
95.1	Sub-projects of the ILSP, Paraguay	621
95.2	Criteria for the evaluation of empowerment	622

Contributors

Isabella Aboderin, BSc (Brist), MSc (Lond), PhD (Brist), Senior Research Fellow, Oxford Institute of Ageing, University of Oxford, UK

Claire Alexander, MA (Oxon), MSt (Oxon), DPhil (Oxon), Reader in Sociology, London School of Economics and Political Science, UK

Sarah Ashwin, BA (Oxon), PhD (Warw), Professor of Industrial Relations, London School of Economics and Political Science, UK

Ranjula Bali Swain, PhL (Uppsala), PhD (Uppsala), Assistant Professor of Economics, Uppsala University, Sweden

Stephanie Barrientos, BA (Kent), PhD (Kent), Senior Lecturer in Global Development, University of Manchester, UK

Angela Baschieri, Laurea (Pisa), PhD (Soton), Lecturer in Demography, London School of Hygiene and Tropical Medicine, UK

Jo Beall, BA (Natal), MA (Natal), PhD (Lond), Deputy Vice-Chancellor, University of Cape Town, South Africa, and Professor of Development Studies, London School of Economics and Political Science, UK

Gwendolyn Beetham, BA (Ohio), MSc (Lond), Doctoral Student, Gender Institute, London School of Economics and Political Science, UK

Sharon Bessell, BA (Tasmania), PhD (Monash), Senior Lecturer in Policy and Governance, Australian National University, Australia

Iman Bibars, BA (American University, Cairo), MA (American University, Cairo), PhD (Sus), Vice President, Ashoka; Regional Director, Ashoka Arab World, and Chairperson, Association for the Development and Enhancement of Women (ADEW), Egypt

Kate Bird, BA (Leic), PGCE (Leic), MSc (Lond), Research Assocate, Overseas Development Institute (ODI), UK

Sarah Bradshaw, BA (Manc), MA (Liv), PhD (Lond), Principal Lecturer in Development Studies, Middlesex University, UK

Claire Brickell, BA (Nott), MA (Leeds), MSc (Lond), Doctoral Student, Department of Geography and Environment, London School of Economics and Political Science, UK

Katherine Brickell, BA (UCL), MSc (Sus) PhD (Lond), British Academy Postdoctoral Fellow, Department of Geography, Royal Holloway, University of London, UK

John Briggs, BA (Lond), PhD (Wales), Professor of Geography, University of Glasgow, UK

Lynne Brydon, MA (Cantab), PhD (Cantab), Head of School of History and Cultures, University of Birmingham, UK

Monica Budowski, BA (Zürich), MA (Zürich), PhD (Zürich), Professor of Sociology, Social Policy and Social Work, University of Fribourg, Switzerland

Catherine Campbell, BA (KwaZulu-Natal), BA (Stellenbosch), MA Res Psych (KwaZulu-Natal), MA Clin Psych (KwaZulu-Natal), PhD (Brist), Professor of Social Psychology, London School of Economics and Political Science, UK

Bart Casier, BA (Gent), MA (Antwerp), MA (Brussels), Programme Advisor, Local Economic Development Programme for Monduli District, TRIAS Regional Office, Arusha, Tanzania

Sylvia Chant, BA (Cantab), PhD (Lond), Professor of Development Geography, London School of Economics and Political Science, UK

Sharad Chari, AB (UC Berkeley), MA (UC Berkeley), PhD (UC Berkeley), Lecturer in Human Geography, London School of Economics and Political Science, UK

Marty Chen, BA (Connecticut College), PhD (Pennsylvania), Lecturer in Public Policy, Harvard Kennedy School, USA, and International Coordinator, Women in Informal Employment: Globalising and Organising (WIEGO) Network, USA

Anna Coates, BA (Soton), MA (Leeds), PhD (Lond), Head, Social Development Unit, Subregional Office for Mexico, Central America, Cuba, the Dominican Republic and Haiti, Economic Commission for Latin America and the Caribbean (ECLAC), Mexico

Andrea Cornwall, BA (Lond), PhD (Lond), Professor of Anthropology and Development, University of Sussex, UK

Joana Costa, BA Econ (PUC-Rio), MSc Econ (UnB), Policy Specialist, Institute of Applied Economic Research, Brazil

Tine Davids, BSc (Utrecht), MSc (Utrecht), Lecturer/Researcher Anthropology and Development Studies, Radboud University, The Netherlands

Carmen Diana Deere, BA (Colorado), MA (Fletcher School of Law and Diplomacy), PhD (UC Berkeley), Professor of Food and Resource Economics and Latin American Studies, University of Florida, USA

Denis Drechsler, BSc (Potsdam), MSc (Wisconsin), Policy Analyst and Communication Coordinator, Economic and Social Development Department, Food and Agriculture Organisation (FAO), Italy

Francien van Driel, BSc (Nijmegen), PhD (Nijmegen), Assistant Professor in Development Studies, Radboud University, The Netherlands

Diane Elson, BA (Oxon), PhD (Manc), Professor of Sociology, University of Essex, UK

Jessica Espey, BA (Oxon), MSc (Lond), Research Officer, Overseas Development Institute (ODI), UK

Maria Evandrou, BSc (Sur), MSc (Essex), Professor of Gerontology, University of Southampton, UK

Alice Evans, BA (Nott), MSc (Lond), Doctoral student in Department of Geography and Environment, London School of Economics and Political Science, UK

Jane Falkingham, BSc Econ (Lond), MSc (Lond), Professor of Demography and International Social Policy, University of Southampton, UK

Eva Fransen, BA (Utrecht), MA (Utrecht), Junior Researcher, Utrecht University School of Economics, The Netherlands

Yoko Fujikake, BA (Ochanomizu), MA (Ochanomizu), PhD (Ochanomizu), Associate Professor of Development Anthropology and Gender and Development, Tokyo Kasei-Gakuin University, Japan

Sarah Gammage, BSc (Lond), MSc (Lond), PhD (The Hague), Social Protection and Development Specialist, Sub-regional Office for the Southern Cone of Latin America, International Labour Organisation (ILO), Chile

Supriya Garikipati, BA (Osmania), MPhil (Cantab), PhD (Cantab), Lecturer in Regional and International Development, University of Liverpool, UK

Andrew Gibbs, BSc (Bath), MSc (Lond), Researcher, Health Economics and HIV/AIDS Research Division (HEARD), University of KwaZulu-Natal, South Africa

Jasmine Gideon, BA (Leeds), MA Econ (Manc), PhD (Manc), Lecturer in Development Studies, Birkbeck College, University of London, UK

Mercedes González de la Rocha, BA (Universidad Iberoamericana), MA (Manc), PhD (Manc), Professor-Senior Researcher, Centro de Investigaciones y Estudios Superiores en Antropología Social (CIESAS), Mexico.

Hilary Graham, BA (York), MA (York), PhD (York), Professor of Health Sciences, University of York, UK

Matthew Gutmann, AB (UC Berkeley), PhD (UC Berkeley), Vice President for International Affairs, Director, Center for Latin American and Caribbean Studies, and Professor of Anthropology, Brown University, USA

Laura Guzmán Stein, BA (New York), MA (Costa Rica), PhD (Arizona), Emerita Professor of Social Work and Gender Studies, Universidad de Costa Rica, Costa Rica

Nabila Hamed, BSc (South Valley), MSc (Mansoura), Doctoral Student, Institute of Pharmacy and Biomedical Science, Strathclyde University, UK

Ceri Hayes, BA (Sheff), MA (Essex), Head of Policy and Advocacy, WOMANKIND Worldwide, UK

James Heintz, BS (Cornell), MS (Minnesota), PhD (Massachusetts), Associate Research Professor, Political Economy Research Institute, University of Massachusetts, USA

Rebecca Holmes, BA (Manc), MA (Sus), Research Officer, Overseas Development Institute, UK

Janet Hunt, BEd (Cantab), M Ed (New England, Aust), PhD (RMIT), Fellow in Aboriginal Economic Policy Research, Australian National University, Australia

Haydea Izazola, BA (UNAM), MA (El Colegio de México), PhD (El Colegio de México), Professor of Population and Environment, Universidad Autónoma Metropolitana-Xochimilco, Mexico

Cecile Jackson, BSc (Lond), PhD (Lond), Professor of Development Studies, University of East Anglia, UK

Katja Jassey, BSc (Stockholm), Consultant, Markatta Film and Antropologi, Sweden

Gerd Johnsson-Latham, BA (Uppsala), Deputy Director, Department for Development Policy, Ministry for Foreign Affairs, Sweden

Susie Jolly, BA (Oxon), MPhil (Sus), Sexuality and Development Programme Convenor, Institute of Development Studies, University of Sussex, UK

Gareth A. Jones, BSc (Lond), PhD (Cantab), Senior Lecturer in Development Geography, London School of Economics and Political Science, UK

Nicola Jones, BA (Canterbury, NZ), PhD (UNC-Chapel Hill), Research Fellow, Overseas Development Institute, UK

Johannes Jütting, Dip (Humboldt), PhD (Humboldt), Senior Economist and Head of Poverty Reduction and Social Development Unit, OECD Development Centre, France

Paula Kantor, BS (Pennsylvania), MA (Sus), PhD (UNC-Chapel Hill), Director, Afghanistan Research and Evaluation Unit, Afghanistan

Marian Koster, BSc (Wageningen), MSc (Wageningen), PhD (Wageningen), Visiting Researcher, Wageningen University, The Netherlands

Sunil Kumar, BArch (Madras), MSc (New Delhi), PhD (Lond), Lecturer in Social Policy and Development, London School of Economics and Political Science, UK

Beverly Lemire, BA (Guelph), MA (Guelph), DPhil (Oxon), Professor of History and Henry Marshall Tory Chair, University of Alberta, Canada

Amy Lind, BA (UC Santa Cruz), PhD (Cornell), Mary Ellen Heintz Associate Professor of Women's, Gender, and Sexuality Studies, University of Cincinnati, USA

Brian Linneker, BA (Leeds), MSc (Lond), PhD (Lond), Senior Research Fellow, Birkbeck College, University of London, UK

Ruth Lister, BA (Essex), MA (Sus), Hon Lld (Manc), Professor of Social Policy, Loughborough University, UK

Amy Y.C. Liu, HonDip (Hong Kong), MA (Washington State), PhD (ANU), Lecturer in International and Development Economics, Australian National University, Australia

Kate Maclean, MA (Edin), PhD (York), Lecturer in Human Geography, King's College London, UK

Sumi Madhok, BA (Delhi) MA (JNU), PhD (Lond), Lecturer in Transnational Gender Studies, London School of Economics and Political Science, UK

Linda Mayoux, BA (Cantab), MA (Cantab), PhD (Cantab), Global Consultant with Women's Empowerment Mainstreaming and Networking (WEMAN) programme, Oxfam Novib, The Netherlands

Linda McDowell, MA (Cantab), PhD (Lond), FBA, Professor of Human Geography, University of Oxford, UK

Cathy McIlwaine, BA (Liv), MA (Liv), PhD (Lond), Reader in Human Geography, Queen Mary, University of London, UK

Kate Meagher, BA (Toronto), MA (Toronto), MPhil (Sus), DPhil (Oxon), Lecturer in Development Studies, London School of Economics and Political Science, UK

Marcelo Medeiros, BSc (UnB), MSc (UnB), PhD (UnB), Policy Specialist, Institute of Applied Economic Research, Brazil

Cecilia Menjívar, BA (Southern California), PhD (California, Davis), Cowden Distinguished Professor of Sociology, Arizona State University, USA

Jane Millar, BA (Sus), MA (Brun), DPhil (York), OBE, Professor of Social Policy, University of Bath, UK

Sophie Mills, BSc Econ (Swansea), PhD (Lond), Housing and Microfinance Specialist, Habitat for Humanity International, South Africa

Faranak Miraftab, BA (Tehran), MArch (Norwegian Institute of Technology), PhD (UC Berkeley), Associate Professor of International Development Planning, University of Illinois, Urbana-Champaign, USA

Diana Mitlin, BA (Manc), MA (Lond), PhD (Lond), Senior Researcher, International Institute for Environment and Development (IIED), UK, and Lecturer, Institute for Development Policy and, Management, University of Manchester, UK

Fauzia Mohamed, BA (UDSM), MA (UDSM), PhD (Lond), Lecturer in Sociology, Open University of Tanzania, Tanzania

Janet Momsen, BA (Oxon), BLitt (Oxon), MSc (McGill), PhD (Lond), Emerita Professor of Geography, University of California, Davis, USA, and Senior Research Associate, Oxford University Centre for the Environment and International Gender Studies, Oxford University, UK

Henrietta L. Moore, BA (Dunelm), PhD (Cantab), William Wyse Professor of Social Anthropology, University of Cambridge, UK, and Director of Culture and Communications Programme, Centre for Global Governance, London School of Economics and Political Science, UK

Caroline Moser, BA (Dunelm), PG Dip (Manc), DPhil (Sus), Professor of Urban Development and Director, Global Urban Research Centre, University of Manchester, UK

Matšeliso Mphale, BA (Lesotho), PhD (Bangor), Lecturer in Geography, National University of Lesotho, Lesotho

Irene Banda Mutalima, Cert CIB (Lond), MA (Leeds), Executive Director of Global Microfinance Network, Switzerland

Keerty Nakray, BA (Mumbai), MSc (Mumbai), MPhil (Mumbai), Doctoral Student in Sociology and Social Policy, Queen's University Belfast, UK

Stella Nyanzi, BA (Makerere), MSc (Lond), MA (Nkumba), PhD (Lond), Medical Anthropologist/ Research Assistant, Law, Gender and Sexuality Research Project, Makerere University, Uganda.

Jane L. Parpart, BA (Brown), MA (Boston), PhD (Boston), Visiting Professor in Gender and Development, University of the West Indies (UWI), St. Augustine, Trinidad and Tobago

Sheela Patel, BSc (Baroda), MA (Tata Institute), Director, Society for the Promotion of Area Resource Centres (SPARC), India, and Chair of the Board of Shack/Slum Dwellers International (SDI), South Africa

Ruth Pearson, BA (Cantab), PhD (Sus), Professor of Development Studies, University of Leeds, UK

Diane Perrons, BSc (Brist), MSc (Brighton), PhD (Brist), Professor of Economic Geography and Gender Studies, London School of Economics and Political Science, UK

Nicholas Piálek, MA (St And), MPhil (Oxon), DPhil (Oxon), Global Gender Advisor, Oxfam GB, UK

Javier Pineda, BSc (Universidad del Valle, Colombia), MSc (CIDE, México), PhD (Dunelm), Lecturer in Development Studies, Universidad de los Andes, Colombia

Janneke Plantenga, BA (Groningen), MA (Groningen), PhD (Groningen), Professor of Economics, Utrecht University School of Economics, The Netherlands

Thomas Pogge, Dip (Hamburg), PhD (Harvard), Leitner Professor of Philosophy and International Affairs, Yale University, USA, Professorial Fellow, Centre for Applied Philosophy and Public Ethics, Australian National University, Australia, and Research Director, Centre for the Study of Mind in Nature, Oslo University, Norway

Agnes R. Quisumbing, BA (De La Salle), PhD (UP), Senior Research Fellow, International Food Policy Research Institute, USA

Carole Rakodi, BA (Manc), Dip TP (Manc), PhD (Wales), Professor of International Urban Development, University of Birmingham, UK

Shahra Razavi, BSc (Lond), MSc (Oxon), DPhil (Oxon), Research Coordinator, Gender and Development, United Nations Research Institute for Social Development (UNRISD), Switzerland

Lisa Ann Richey, BA (Furman), PhD (UNC-Chapel Hill), Professor of International Development Studies, Roskilde University, Denmark

Ananya Roy, BA (Mills College, Oakland), PhD (UC Berkeley), Professor, City and Regional Planning, University of California, Berkeley, USA

Helen I. Safa, BA (Cornell), PhD (Columbia), Professor Emerita of Anthropology and Latin American Studies, University of Florida, USA

Saskia Sassen, PhD (Nôtre Dame), Robert S. Lynd Professor of Sociology, Columbia University, USA

Gita Sen, BA (Poona), MA (Delhi), PhD (Stanford), Professor of Public Policy, Indian Institute of Management, India

John Sender, MA (Oxon), MSc (Lond), PhD (Lond), Emeritus Professor of Economics, School of Oriental and African Studies, University of London, UK

Joanne Sharp, BA (Cantab), MA (Syracuse), PhD (Syracuse), Senior Lecturer in Geography, University of Glasgow, UK

Rhonda Sharp, BEc (New England, Aust), MEc (QLD), PhD (Sydney), Professor of Economics, University of South Australia, Australia

Elydia Silva, BA Econ (Viçosa), MSc Econ (Minas Gerais), Associate Researcher, International Policy Centre for Inclusive Growth (IPC-IG), Brazil

Rachel Slater, BA (Oxon), MA (Manc), PhD (Manc), Research Fellow and Social Protection Programme Leader, Overseas Development Institute (ODI), UK

Daniel Jordan Smith, AB (Harvard), MPH (Johns Hopkins), PhD (Emory), Associate Professor of Anthropology, Brown University, USA

Silke Staab, MA (Cologne), Research Analyst, Gender and Development, United Nations Research Institute for Social Development (UNRISD), Switzerland

Caroline Sweetman, BA (Cantab), MA (E. Anglia), PhD (Leeds), Editor, Gender and Development, Oxfam GB, UK

Cecilia Tacoli, BSc (Rome), MSc (Lond), PhD (Lond), Senior Researcher, International Institute for Environment and Development (IIED), UK

Sarah Thomas de Benítez, BSc (N'cle [UK]), MPP (Princeton), MSc (Lond), PhD (Lond), International Social Policy Consultant, UK

Fran Tonkiss, BA (Adelaide), MA (Lancaster), PhD (Lond), Reader in Sociology, London School of Economics and Political Science, UK

D. Alissa Trotz, BA (York), MPhil (Cantab), PhD (Cantab), Associate Professor, Women and Gender Studies, and Director, Caribbean Studies, New College, University of Toronto, Canada

Penny Vera-Sanso, BA (Lond), PhD (Lond), Lecturer in Development Studies, Birkbeck College, University of London, UK

Athina Vlachantoni, BSc (Lond, MSc (Oxon), PhD (Lond), Lecturer in Gerontology, University of Southampton, UK

Tina Wallace, BA, PhD (Mkerere), Research Associate, International Gender Studies, Queen Elizabeth House, Oxford University, UK

Carolyn H. Williams, BA (Thames V), MA (ISS), PhD (Lond), Freelance Researcher/Consultant, UK

Katie Willis, BA (Oxon), MPhil (Oxon), DPhil (Oxon), Reader in Development Geography, Royal Holloway, University of London, UK

Kalpana Wilson, BA (Sus), MA (Lond), PhD (Lond), Fellow in Transnational Gender Studies, London School of Economics and Political Science, UK

Hoda Yacoub, BSc (Assuit), MSc (South Valley), PhD (Mansoura), Environmental Researcher, Egyptian Environmental Affairs Agency, Egypt

Annelou Ypeij, MA (Utrecht), PhD (Utrecht), Teacher and Researcher of Anthropology and Gender, Centre for Latin American Research and Documentation (CEDLA), The Netherlands

Acknowledgements

This book represents a personally unprecedented feat of international cooperation, and has been an experience through which I have learned a phenomenal amount. In the 13 months from conception to completion of the manuscript, I became privy to up-to-the-minute first-hand research and debate on gendered poverty from a host of specialists with expertise not only in the areas and countries pertinent to my own field interests, but across a much broader spectrum, and from a wide range of disciplinary and professional backgrounds. As each chapter rolled in, my knowledge edged forward, as did my awe at the amount and quality of work related to gender and poverty that was being done. Although I was directly familiar with the work of a substantial number of contributors, and had asked the vast majority of these to write at the earliest stage of the project, as time unfolded some of these invitations led to others by way of recommendation, new connections were made at conferences, workshops and on field trips, and ongoing reading for research and teaching caused me to stumble upon scholarship that I felt had to be represented in the *Handbook*. Although, somewhat inevitably, a few of the originally commissioned chapters fell by the wayside, those included in this volume were received within the space of just a few months in 2009, thereby representing a spread of discussions which between them reflect state-of-the-art thinking on gender and poverty at the close of the first twenty-first century decade. This is not to detract from the fact that some of the richest analyses in the *Handbook* have been based on several years of longitudinal fieldwork and theorisation. Nor, by the same token, is it to divert attention from the fact that no volume can ever be exhaustive or without its caveats. One unintended and regrettable consequence of stringent deadlines coupled with the random events which made it difficult for a number of invited authors to contribute as planned, is some unevenness in geographical coverage. While the spread of papers from Africa, the Americas, Europe, Asia and Australasia more than qualify the *Handbook* as 'international' (with the strong representation of the Global South befitting its majority share of the world population, not to mention income poverty), the Middle East and South Pacific are much less represented than I had originally desired. In light of this it is hoped that the discussions on areas in which these regions are proximate geographically, or which share some features in common, will go some way to compensating for these unavoidable omissions.

Among the major debts I owe in this editorial venture is to Felicity Plester, Commissioning Editor at Edward Elgar. It was Felicity's idea to prepare this *Handbook*; she kindly invited me to edit it and has been infinitely accommodating and patient as the project evolved way beyond its originally envisaged (and contract-stipulated!) limits to more than 100 chapters and over 330 000 words. Also absolutely crucial to the publication process at Elgar have been Caroline Cornish in editorial, and Emma Gribbon in marketing, to whom warm thanks are similarly extended.

At my home institution, the London School of Economics, Lee Mager's editorial and administrative assistance routinely surpassed all expectations, as did the work of Ralph

Kinnear on the index, and that of Alice Evans, who in the final stages of preparing the manuscript during our fortuitously overlapping field trips to The Gambia in July 2009 provided consistently good-natured, efficient and insightful support.

Alice is also included in the massive debt I owe to my 120 contributors, not only for their vital intellectual input, but for their willingness to prioritise my deadlines at the expense of other commitments, and to conform with exacting editorial restrictions on word length and references in the interests of the common good. I am equally grateful to the authors who delivered on – and sometimes ahead of – schedule, as to those who were invited a little later to the feast, but managed to step up to the plate with such amazing alacrity, enthusiasm and attention to detail.

For inspiration and assistance with the cover design, I am, as ever, grateful to Suelle Nachif, who painted '*Mbooloo*' ('Gathering') especially for this *Handbook*, and who advised on my artistic interpretation of his work and its presentation on the jacket. Thanks are also due to my Wolof teacher, Baboucarr Jallow, for his help with the fascinating intricacies of spelling and meaning in a language which continues to prove one of my biggest learning challenges to date.

Last, but not least, many of the named and unnamed above form part of a deeply valued circle of family, friends and colleagues who have supported me through another book-production cycle when I had vowed that my preceding effort – co-written with Cathy McIlwaine with whom I have now enjoyed scholarly collaboration for two decades – would be my 'last for a while'. Aside from Cathy, who true to form produced her contribution to this volume well on time, my husband, Chris Mogridge, deserves special mention for his incomparably enduring and compassionate tolerance, encouragement and inspiration.

Sylvia Chant
October 2009/February 2010

Abbreviations

ADB	Asian Development Bank
ADEW	Association for the Development and Enhancement of Women (Egypt)
ADRA	Adventist Development and Relief Agency (Rwanda)
ADWAC	Agency for the Development of Women and Children (The Gambia)
AEC	Anti-Eviction Campaign (South Africa)
AHRC	Arts and Humanities Research Council (UK)
AIDS	Acquired Immunodeficiency Syndrome
ANANDI	Area Networking and Development Initiatives (India)
ANU	Australian National University
ART	Anti-Retroviral Therapy/Anti-Retroviral treatment
ARV	Anti-Retroviral Medication
ASEAN	Association of Southeast Asian Nations
ASS	Akal Sangharsh Samiti (India)
AU	African Union
AU-Plan	African Union Policy Framework and Plan of Action on Ageing
AUGE	(Plan) Acceso Universal con Garantías Explicítas en Salud (Chile)
AWID	Association for Women's Rights in Development
BBSRC	Biotechnology and Biological Sciences Research Council (UK)
BME	Black and Minority Ethnic (communities) (UK)
BMI	Body Mass Index
BPFA	Beijing Platform for Action
BPL	Below the Poverty Line (India)
BRAC	Bangladesh Rural Advancement Committee
BSP	Basic State Pension (UK)
BWI	Bretton Woods Institutions
CAFTA-DR	Central American Free Trade Area-Dominican Republic
CAWN	Central American Women's Network
CBO	Community-based organisation
CCER	Civil Coordinator (Nicaragua)
CCM	Country Coordinating Mechanism
CCSS	Caja Costarricense de Seguro Social (Costa Rica)
CCT	Conditional Cash Transfer (programmes)
CDD	Community-driven development
CEDAW	Convention on the Elimination of All Forms of Discrimination Against Women
CEO	Chief Executive Officer
CEPIP	Programme for Innovative PhD Research (The Netherlands)
CERES	Research School for Resource Studies for Development (The Netherlands)
CETZAM	Christian Enterprise Trust of Zambia

xxviii *Abbreviations*

CGAP	Consultative Group for Assisting the Poor
CIDA	Canadian International Development Agency
CIDDEF	Centre d'Information et de Documentation sur les Droits de l'Enfant et de la Femme (Algeria)
CIS	Commonwealth of Independent States
CMD	Common Mental Disorder
CMF	Centro Nacional del Desarrollo de la Mujer y de la Familia (Costa Rica)
CMN	Cambodian Men's Network
COESIDA	Consejo Estatal para la Prevención del VIH/SIDA (Mexico)
COHRE	Centre for Housing Rights and Evictions
COMBATS	Community Based Action Teams (Ghana)
CONAPO	Consejo Nacional de Población (Mexico)
CONASOL	Comisión Nacional de Solidaridad y Desarrollo Humano (Costa Rica)
COVAW	Coalition on Violence Against Women (Kenya)
CPD	Coalition of Parties for Democracy (Chile)
CPE	Complex Political Emergency
CPI	Consumer Price Index
CPM	Capability Poverty Measure
CPRC	Chronic Poverty Research Centre
CRE	Commission for Racial Equality (UK)
CreCER	Credit with Rural Education (Bolivia)
CSO	Civil Society Organisation
CSW	Commission on the Status of Women
CT	Cash Transfer
CWB	Community Well-Being Index (Canada)
DAC	Development Assistance Committee (of OECD)
DALYs	Disability Adjusted Life Years
DAWN	Development Alternatives with Women for a New Era
DCLG	Department for Communities and Local Government (UK)
DF	Distrito Federal (Mexico)
DFID	Department for International Development (UK)
DHS	Demographic and Health Survey
DOE	Degrees of Empowerment
DoSFEA	Department of State for Finance and Economic Affairs (The Gambia)
DWP	Department for Work and Pensions (UK)
EAP	Economically-active Population (with reference to employment) *or* East Asia and the Pacific (with reference to region)
EC	European Commission
ECA	Europe and Central Asia
ECLA/ECLAC	Economic Commission for Latin America and the Caribbean
ECO/PN	L'Espace de Concertation et d'Orientation de Pikine Nord (Senegal)
ECERP	Estrategia Reforzada de Crecimiento Económico y Reducción de Pobreza (Nicaragua)
EEM	Empowerment Evaluation Model

EFF	Extended Fund Facility
EmOC	Emergency Obstetric Care
EOI	Export-oriented Industrialisation
EPSRC	Engineering and Physical Sciences Research Council (UK)
EPZ	Export Processing Zone
ERP	Economic Recovery Programme
ESAF	Enhanced Structural Adjustment Facility
ESF	Emergency Social Fund
ESI	Employees' State Insurance
ESRC	Economic and Social Research Council (UK)
ETI	Ethical Trading Initiative
EU	European Union
FAO	Food and Agriculture Organisation
FBDO	Faith-Based Development Organisation
FCW	Federation of Cuban Women
FDI	Foreign Direct Investment
FGD	Focus Group Discussion
FGM	Female Genital Mutilation
FHH	Female-headed Household
FLO	Fairtrade Labelling Organisations International
FMC	Federación de Mujeres Cubanas
FODESAF	Fondo de Desarrollo Social y Asignaciones Familiares (Costa Rica)
FONASA	Fondo Nacional de Salud (Chile)
FPA	Family Planning Association
FSLN	Frente Sandinista de Liberación Nacional (Nicaragua)
FTZ	Free Trade Zone
FWCW	Fourth World Conference on Women
G8	Group of 8 referring to 7 of the world's leading industrialised nations (France, Germany, Italy, Japan, UK, USA, and Canada) plus Russia
GAD	Gender and Development
GADU	Gender and Development Unit (Oxfam GB)
GALCK	Gay and Lesbian Coalition of Kenya
GALS	Gender Action Learning System
GALZ	Gays and Lesbians of Zimbabwe
GAP	Gender Action Plan
GATT	General Agreement on Tariffs and Trade
GBA	Gender Budget Analysis
GDI	Gender-related Development Index
GDP	Gross Domestic Product
GEM	Gender Empowerment Measure
GID	Gender, Institutions and Development
GLSS	Ghana Living Standards Survey (Ghana)
GNI	Gross National Income
GNP	Gross National Product
GOI	Government of India
GRB	Gender-responsive Budgeting

GRO	Grassroots Organisation
GVC	Global Value Chain
GWAR	Guyanese Women Across Race
HAI	HelpAge International
HDI	Human Development Index
HIPC	Heavily Indebted Poor Country
HIV	Human Immunodeficiency Virus
HIVOS	Humanist Institute for Development Co-operation (The Netherlands)
HLF	High Level Forum
HPI	Human Poverty Index
HRP	Home Responsibilities Protection (UK)
HWW	HomeWorkers Worldwide
IADB	Inter American Development Bank
ICCPR	International Covenant of Civil and Political Rights
ICESCR	International Covenant of Economic, Social and Cultural Rights
ICFFD	International Conference on Financing for Development
ICFTC	International Confederation of Free Trade Unions
ICLS	International Conference of Labour Statisticians
ICPD	International Conference on Population and Development
ICT	Information and Communications Technology
ICVP	Increasing Consumption of Vegetables Project (Paraguay)
IDA	Instituto de Desarrollo Agrario (Costa Rica)
IDA	International Development Association
IDP	Internally Displaced Person
IEPD	Instituto de Estudios de Población y Desarrollo (Dominican Republic)
IFAD	International Fund for Agricultural Development
IFC	International Finance Corporation
IFI	International Financial Institution
IFPRI	International Food Policy and Research Institute
IGLHRC	International Gay and Lesbian Human Rights Commission
IGVGD	Income Generating Vulnerable Group Development Programme
IIRIRA	Illegal Immigration Reform and Immigrant Responsibility Act (USA)
ILO	International Labour Organisation
ILSP	Improving Living Standards Project (Paraguay)
IMAS	Instituto Mixto de Ayuda Social (Costa Rica)
IMF	International Monetary Fund
INAC	Indian and Northern Affairs Canada
INAMU	Instituto Nacional de las Mujeres (Costa Rica)
INEGI	Instituto Nacional de Estadística, Geografía e Informática (Mexico)
INSTAT	National Institute of Statistics (Albania)
IPC-IG	International Policy Centre for Inclusive Growth (formerly IPC/ International Poverty Centre)
IPL	International Poverty Line
IPPF	International Planned Parenthood Federation
ISAPRES	Institutos de Salud Previsional (Chile)

ISDR	International Strategy for Disaster Reduction
ISI	Import Substitution Industrialisation
IT	Information Technology
ITUC	International Trade Union Confederation
IUD	Intra-uterine Device
IV	Intravenous
IWD	International Women's Day
IWTC	International Women's Tribune Centre
IWY	International Women's Year
JICA	Japan International Cooperation Agency
JOCV	Japanese Overseas Cooperation Volunteer
JUCONI	Junto Con los Niños y Niñas de México
LAC	Latin America and the Caribbean
LBGTI	Lesbian, Gay, Bisexual, Transgender and Inter-sex
LECD	Less Economically Developed Country
LGBT	Lesbian, Gay, Bisexual and Transgender
LSMS	Living Standards Measurement Survey
MAG	Ministerio de Agricultura y Ganadería (Paraguay)
MDG	Millennium Development Goal
MEDC	More Economically Developed Country
MENA	Middle East and North Africa
MFI	Microfinance Institution
MG3S	Mansholt Graduate School of Social Sciences
MHH	Male-headed household
MICS	Multiple Indicator Cluster Survey
MIGA	Multilateral Investment Guarantee Agency
MIPAA	Madrid International Plan of Action on Ageing
MMR	Maternal Mortality Rate
MNC	Multinational Corporation (or Company)
MOSA	Ministry of Social Affairs (Egypt)
MOWA	Ministry of Women's Affairs (Cambodia)
MRC	Medical Research Council
MRLS	Mozambican Rural Labour Survey
MSI	Multi-stakeholder Initiative
MSM	Men Who Have Sex with Men
NABARD	National Bank for Agricultural and Rural Development
NACO	National AIDS Control Organisation (India)
NACP	National AIDS Control Programme (India)
NAFTA	North American Free Trade Agreement
NBFI	Non-bank Financial Institution
NCEUIS	National Commission for Enterprises in the Unorganised Sector (India)
NCHS	National Center for Health Statistics (USA)
NDNGO	Northern Development Non-governmental Organisation
NGDO	Non-governmental Development Organisation
NGO	Non-governmental Organisation

NHE	New Household Economics
NIC	Newly Industrialising Country
NIDL	New International Division of Labour
NIE	New Institutional Economics
NNGO	Northern NGO or National NGO
NPA	New Poverty Agenda
NPM	New Public Management
NREGA	National Rural Employment Guarantee Act (India)
NSDF	National Slum Dwellers' Federation (India)
NWO	Netherlands Organisation for Scientific Research
ODA	Overseas Development Assistance/Official Development Assistance
OECD	Organisation for Economic Co-operation and Development
ONS	Office of National Statistics (UK)
OPM	Oxford Policy Management (UK)
PADV	Partnership Against Domestic Violence
PAHO	Pan-American Health Organisation
PALS	Participatory Action Learning System
PAMSCAD	Programme of Actions to Mitigate the Social Costs of Adjustment (Ghana)
PASIS	Programa de Pensiones Asistenciales (Chile)
PC	Pension Credit (UK)
PCA	Principal Components Analysis
PCP	Private Consumption Poverty
PD	Paris Declaration (on Aid Effectiveness)
PDS	Public Distribution System (India)
PEP	Poverty-Environment Partnership
PEPFAR	President's Emergency Plan for AIDS Relief (USA)
PEWH	Promotion of Self-managed Enterprises Project of Women in Rural Areas of Honduras
PFP	Productive Family Programme (Egypt)
PHC	Primary Health Care
PL	Poverty Line
PLC	Partido Liberal Contitucionalista (Nicaragua)
PLN	Partido Liberación Nacional (Costa Rica)
PLWHA	People Living With HIV/AIDS
PNCP	Plan Nacional de Combate a la Pobreza (Costa Rica)
PND	Plan Nacional de Desarrollo (Nicaragua)
PNDH	National Plan for Human Development (Nicaragua)
PNS	Plan Nacional de Solidaridad (Costa Rica)
PPA	Participatory Poverty Assessment
PPP	Purchasing Power Parity
PQLI	Physical Quality of Life Index
PREM	Poverty Reduction and Economic Management Network
PRGF	Poverty Reduction and Growth Facility
PRIDE	Promotion of Rural Initiatives and Development Enterprises (Tanzania)
PROGRESA	Programa de Educación, Salud y Alimentación (Mexico)

PRS	Poverty Reduction Strategy
PRSP	Poverty Reduction Strategy Paper/Programme
PUSC	Partido Unidad Social Cristiana (Costa Rica)
PVN	Plan Vida Nueva (Costa Rica)
PWN	Positive Women's Network (India)
RBA	Rights-Based Approach
RLMS	Russian Longitudinal Monitoring Survey
RNC	Regimen No-contributivo (Costa Rica)
RPS	Red de Protección Social (Nicaragua)
S2P	Second State Pension (UK)
SA	South Asia
SAC	Savings and Credit Association (Ethiopia)
SAP	Structural Adjustment Programme
SAPRIN	Structural Adjustment Participatory Review International Network
SC/ST	Scheduled Caste/Scheduled Tribe
SDI	Shack/Slum Dwellers International
SEAGA	Socio-Economic and Gender Analysis
SELFINA	Sero Lease and Finance Company Limited (Tanzania)
SERPS	State Earnings Related Pension Scheme (UK)
SEWA	Self-employed Women's Association (India)
SF	Social Fund
SHG	Self Help Group (India)
SHPA	Self Help Promotion Agent (India)
Sida	Swedish International Development Agency
SIDS	Small Island Developing States
SIGE	Standardised Indicator of Gender Equality
SIGI	Social Institutions and Gender Index
SLA	Sustainable Livelihoods Approach
SLF	Sustainable Livelihoods Framework
SNA	System of National Accounts
SOE	State-owned Enterprise
SPARC	Society for the Promotion of Area Resources
SPHC	Selective Primary Health Care
SPS	Sistema de Pensiones Solidarias (Chile)
SRHH	Sexual and Reproductive Health and Rights
SRI	Socially Responsible Investment
SS	Schutzstaffel (Germany under Third Reich)
SSA	Sub-Saharan Africa
STI	Sexually Transmitted Infection
SUF	Slum Upgrading Facility
SuPen	Superintendencia de Pensiones de Costa Rica
TAC	Treatment Action Campaign (South Africa)
TBA	Traditional Birth Attendant
TFEGE	Taskforce on Education and Gender Equality
TFR	Total Fertility Rate
TGNP	Tanzania Gender Networking Programme

TNC	Transnational Corporation (or Company)
TTR	Three Types of Results
TUC	Trade Union Congress (UK)
UBN	Unmet Basic Needs
UCW	Unpaid Carework
UIS	Urban Informal Sector
UK	United Kingdom
UN	United Nations
UN-DESA	United Nations Department of Economic and Social Affairs
UN-HABITAT	United Nations Human Settlements Programme
UNAIDS	Joint United Nations Programme on HIV/AIDS
UNCHS	United Nations Centre for Human Settlements
UNDAW	United Nations Division for the Advancement of Women
UNDP	United Nations Development Programme
UNDW	United Nations Decade for Women
UNECE	United Nations Economic Commission for Europe
UNESCO	United Nations Economic, Scientific and Cultural Organisation
UNFPA	United Nations Fund for Population Activities
UNGASS	United Nations General Assembly Special Session
UNICEF	United Nations Children's Fund
UNIFEM	United Nations Development Fund for Women
UNMP	United Nations Millennium Project
UNPD	United Nations Population Division
UNPFII	United Nations Permanent Forum on Indigenous Issues
UNSD	United Nations Statistics Division
US/USA	United States/United States of America
USAID	United States Agency for International Development
VAT	Value-added Tax
VAW	Violence Against Women
VCC	Voluntary Code of Conduct
WAD	Women and Development
WB	World Bank
WEDO	Women's Environment and Development Organisation
WEF	World Economic Forum
WFDD	World Faiths Development Dialogue
WFP	World Food Programme
WHO	World Health Organisation
WID	Women in Development
WIEGO	Women in Informal Employment: Globalising and Organising
WILSA	Women in Law in South Africa
WLUML	Women Living Under Muslim Laws
WRI	Women's Research Institute (Indonesia)
WSO	World Summit Outcome
WTO	World Trade Organization
WVI	World Vision International
WWW	Women Working Worldwide

1 Gendered poverty across space and time: introduction and overview[1]
Sylvia Chant

The past 15 years have borne witness not only to the prioritisation of gender inequality and poverty as two of the most challenging barriers to social and economic justice in a globalising world, but also to their progressive intertwining. This is as much the case in policy as in academic arenas, and owes in no small measure to the significance formally attached to addressing women's poverty by the Beijing Platform for Action (BPFA) launched in 1995 at the Fourth World Conference on Women (FWCW). Although for innumerable countries the historical record (albeit anecdotal rather than empirically or statistically rigorous) had suggested that women's economic disadvantage was not new, impetus for the Beijing breakthrough was spawned by a novel globalised assertion: that women were as many as 70 per cent of the world's poor. This categorical and seemingly bona fide statement (at least as intimated by its rapid adoption and circulation in the policy and academic literature) was usually accompanied by the ominous sub-clause that the level was likely to rise (see Chant, 2008; Moghadam, 1997).[2]

The BPFA's ensuing exhortation to eliminate gender bias in poverty worldwide became something of a *cause célèbre* given prior tendencies for poverty analyses to deal in the currency of 'sexless averages' (Johnsson-Latham, 2004: 18), and for gender's common neglect in anti-poverty programmes (UNDP, 2000: 3). Thanks in large measure to Beijing, the period from the mid-1990s onwards has seen an unprecedented number of countries introducing new programmes (or strengthening existing ones) to combat poverty among women. Such interventions both reinforce and are reinforced by the mission statements of institutions representing different world regions. For example, the Asian Development Bank rationalises its call for gendered poverty interventions on grounds that the 'overarching goal of poverty reduction is closely linked to improving the status of women, since equity – especially gender equity – is now recognised as an essential factor in transforming growth to development, and reducing poverty' (ADB, 2002: 135). In turn, the Economic Commission for Latin America and the Caribbean stresses one of its main priorities as identifying 'the characteristics of female poverty and its associated causes' (ECLAC, 2004: 82). At a wider international level, some of the world's poorest countries which have sought debt relief under the HIPC (Heavily Indebted Poor Countries) initiative have been bound in principle, if not necessarily in practice, to 'mainstream gender' in their Poverty Reduction Strategy Papers (PRSPs) (see Bradshaw and Linneker, 2003; Whitehead and Lockwood, 1999). Microfinance schemes in developing nations are also disproportionately directed to women (see Goetz and Sen Gupta, 1996; Mayoux, 2006), as are conditional cash transfer (CCT) programmes, although directing resources *through* women might be a more apposite description for the latter (see Bradshaw, 2008; Molyneux, 2006; also González de la Rocha, 2006a, and below). At a global level, all United Nations (UN) member states are urged both to reduce extreme poverty and to promote gender equality and the empowerment of women, as part and parcel of eight 'universal' goals for the early twenty-first century established by the Millennium Declaration (see Chant, 2007a: ch. 1; Sweetman, 2005). Just a few months before the present *Handbook* was completed, and in response to the global financial crisis which broke in 2008, the Women's Working Group on Financing for Development called upon the UN to (re)position itself as leader in a 'new global development, economic and financial architecture' with the full integration of gender equality and women's rights.[3] And the theme of the five-yearly *World Survey on the Role of Women in Development* of 2009 is 'Women's control over economic resources and access to financial resources, including microfinance' (UN-DESA/UNDAW, 2009). On the surface, at least, the general context for institutional and policy directives to reduce poverty gaps between women and men has never looked so propitious.

Yet the task of converting the goal of reducing gendered poverty into actual results is far from straightforward. Quite apart from the uneasy tensions between market growth and poverty reduction, and the towering barriers to gender justice and rights posed by the new neoliberal world order (see for example, Cornwall et al., 2008a; Cornwall and Molyneux, 2007; Molyneux and Razavi, 2002; Perrons, 2004; Razavi, 2009; Sweetman, 2005), as has become well rehearsed in the feminist literature, gender is not just about women, and poverty is not just about income (see Chant, 1997, 2007a; Fukuda-Parr, 1999; Jackson, 1996). The complex intersections between these two heterogeneous entities accordingly require analysis, assessment and interventions which are fine-tuned to a multiplicity of conceptual, contextual and practical specificities. As Sarah Bradshaw, a contributor to this volume (Chapters 79 and 96), so concisely describes in relation to her work on Nicaragua, women's poverty is 'not only multidimensional but is also "multisectoral . . . [and] . . . is experienced in different ways, at different times and in different "spaces"' (Bradshaw, 2002a: 12). These spaces include, *inter alia*, the home, the community, the labour market, the realm of assets and property ownership, the legal environment, the social policy arena, the political economy, and territories of war, conflict and natural disaster (see for example, Afshar, 2003; Bradshaw, 2002a, 2002b; Chant, 2007b; Clark and Moser, 2001; CLEP, 2008; Deere and Doss, 2006; Enarson and Chakrabarti, 2009; Enarson and Morrow, 1998; Folbre, 1994, 2006; Hart, 1995; Mazurana et al., 2005; Moser, 2007; Parpart and Zalewski, 2008; Razavi and Hassim, 2006; Rodenberg, 2004). Beyond this, gendered poverty is also experienced by men and boys, and is differentially impacted by a whole series of factors such as age, 'race', nationality, sexuality, class, household headship and composition, the marital, fertility and family status of women and men, urban versus rural provenance and residence, migration within and across national borders, availability of public as well as private assets, labour market possibilities in the formal and informal economy, and state social transfers (see Barker et al., 2007; Chant, 2007a; Cornwall et al., 2007, 2008b; Fernández-Kelly and Sassen, 1995; Piper and Roces, 2002; Razavi, 2009; Ruxton, 2009; Tronto, 2002; Vera-Sanso, 2006). Many of these variables not only intersect with gender and poverty, but with one another, and exert diverse influences and outcomes depending on whether one's 'take' on poverty is filtered through the conceptual lens of monetary poverty, capability poverty, social exclusion, and so on; whether it is oriented more to 'objective'/quantitative or 'subjective'/qualitative/participatory measures;[4] and/or is personal, domestic, local, national or global in its subject or spatial orientation. The nuancing of different terminologies to describe the relationships between gender and poverty is also critically important. For example, while the expressions 'gender gaps in poverty', 'gender-specific poverty' or even 'gender-differentiated poverty' commonly imply a particular kind of poverty (largely materially based, and usually focused on income, consumption or financial assets), the term 'gendered poverty' (or perhaps 'gendered poverty burdens'), summons up a broader notion whereby poverty – and gender – are less predetermined and static. The concept of 'gendered poverty' opens up scope for a range of perspectives on the diverse meanings, causes, processes and outcomes embroiled in different forms of privation among women and men, and on their intersections with a host of social, economic, demographic and other cleavages. Although issues of gender gaps in earnings, expenditure and the like remain vitally important elements under this more flexible and dynamic umbrella term, and there is strong evidence for persistent and ubiquitous gender differences in access to economic resources, major doubts have been mooted in the feminist literature about whether income should be pre-eminent in gender-sensitive conceptions of well-being, and whether tackling income poverty is the most effective strategy for solving women's disadvantage. As Johnsson-Latham (2004: 26–7), among others, has contended, income is probably a less 'robust' indicator of women's privation than factors such as access to land, agency in decision-making, legal rights within the family, vulnerability to violence, and (self-)respect and dignity. The primacy routinely accorded to income in poverty assessments may also minimise other practical and potentially measurable, as well as subjectively interpreted and experienced, dimensions of poverty such as 'overwork', 'time deficiency', 'dependency' and 'powerlessness'. As a growing body of research in different geographical contexts has revealed, the latter may be as, if not more, relevant to women's perceptions of disadvantage, and to the 'trade-offs' they are able to make between different aspects of poverty (Blanc-Szanton, 1990; Chant, 1997; Fonseca, 1991; Fukuda-Parr, 1999; Kabeer, 1997; Sen, 1999; Whitehead and Lockwood, 1999). It is something of the multifarious character, causes and consequences of gendered poverty, and how these elements and their interactions might be conceptualised, investigated and measured, which constitutes a primary aim of the present volume.

Also of major importance in this *Handbook* is how policy interventions may address the complexities of gendered poverty in a positive and effective manner. While nation states, non-governmental organisations (NGOs), and bilateral and multilateral agencies are often genuinely well-intentioned in their bids to reduce poverty and promote gender equality – increasingly under the banner of 'empowering women' – a number of pitfalls and unintended consequences are glaringly evident. One is the tendency for a rich body of feminist analysis on gendered poverty to get 'lost in translation' at various stages of policy design and implementation (see Longwe, 1995). Even the coining of guiding rhetoric itself, such as one of the most popularised shorthands, the 'feminisation of poverty',[5] has proved deeply problematic. On one hand this has been quite effective at garnering resources for women (Chant, 2008), and nominally, at least, has served as a 'marching call that impels us to question our assumptions about poverty itself by examining how it is caused, manifested and reduced, and to do this from a gender perspective' (Williams and Lee-Smith, 2000: 1; see also Wennerholm, 2002). Yet, on another hand, the term 'feminisation of poverty' is actually semantically incorrect in respect of its usual referent, namely, a state rather than a process (Chant, 2008; Medeiros and Costa, 2006). Furthermore, the 'feminisation of poverty' construction could be charged with having simplified concepts of both poverty and gender such that some individuals in need are missed, those individuals most associated with the phenomenon (particularly female heads of household) are scapegoated as part and parcel of the 'problem', and issues of major importance in feminised poverty, such as gendered power relations within as well as beyond the household, are glossed over (Chant, 2008; Davids and van Driel, 2001, 2005; Lampietti and Stalker, 2000; Medeiros and Costa, 2008; Molyneux, 2006; Moore, 1994; Quisumbing and McClafferty, 2006; Sen, 2008; Varley, 1996). While a dedicated section of the *Handbook* deals with these issues, it is pertinent here to recall Robert Johnson's (2005) argument that poverty interventions have tended to be rather more preoccupied with addressing the *condition* of poor women (primarily their material circumstances), than their *position* (their place and power within domestic units and in wider society). In turn, steps to improve women's poorer condition have rarely challenged men's condition *or* position (Johnson, 2005: 57, emphasis in original). Notwithstanding the importance of income in helping women to challenge other aspects of inequality, therefore, boosting women's economic status is unlikely to go very far on its own given that the '"feminisation of poverty" is . . . an issue of inequality that extends to the very basis of women's position in economic relations, in access to power and decision-making, and in the domestic sphere. It is emphatically not addressed in a sustainable manner solely by measures to improve the material conditions of women' (ibid.; see also Jackson, 1996; Kabeer, 2003; Sweetman, 2005: 6; UN/UNIFEM, 2003).

Leading on from this, another prevailing concern in the realm of planned interventions is the instrumentalist manner in which anti-poverty initiatives such as microcredit and CCT programmes rely heavily on women as a 'conduit of policy' (Molyneux, 2006, 2007). Through capitalising on women's economic prudence and/or 'voluntary' unpaid labour in the context of assumptions about women's 'traditional' roles as altruistic wives and mothers, such initiatives may simply add to already heavily feminised burdens of poverty-associated labour, time and expenditure (see Bradshaw, 2008; Brickell and Chant, 2010; Chant, 2008; Molyneux, 2007; Roy, 2002; UN/UNIFEM, 2003). As summarised by Stefan de Vylder (2004: 85), the pursuit of gender equality has normally been regarded by the GAD community as an end in itself and from a human rights perspective; yet from the vantage point of stakeholders whose primary interest is in alleviating poverty in general, the incorporation of women into poverty reduction programmes may be driven less by imperatives of social justice than by goals of pragmatism and efficiency (see also Mayoux, 2006).[6]

Accepting the contention that poverty and gender inequality alike are 'morally unacceptable' (Medeiros and Costa, 2008: 115), it is vital that both feature as policy priorities in the twenty-first century. Further, if addressing *gendered poverty* is to be uppermost, it is crucial that more informed and imaginative ways are devised to ensure the attainment of comprehensive, and sustainable, gender justice 'on the ground'. Again, this volume aims to identify some critical ways forward, both in the context of initiatives on the part of institutional stakeholders, as well as those generated by women and men at the grassroots.

Organisation of the *Handbook*

The remainder of this chapter sketches out the organisation of the *Handbook*, which, given its extensive thematic and geographical range, requires some basic navigational guidelines. These guidelines mainly consist of a rationalisation of my choice of subsections, and brief pointers to the topics and highlights in each. I refrain from discussing more than the sparest details of content and argument of individual chapters, just as I adopted a generally light touch to how my authors approached their contributions in the first place. Such a format not only permits a diverse international and multidisciplinary body of experts to speak directly to readers, but minimises what I feel may be a gratuitous second sight, with even more elaborate vignettes still unlikely to do justice to the fine-grained complexities of a huge number of specialist subject areas.

Bearing in mind that the cross-cutting nature of issues, ideas and arguments made dividing the fruits of my editorial endeavour extremely difficult, I settled on ten broad sections, hereafter referred to as 'parts', which as far as possible dovetail with the particular content and context of contributors' chapters, but which should not be read as analytically discrete. Indeed, themes such as the intersectionality of gender with other criteria of social difference, the undervaluation of women's paid and unpaid labour, gendered asset inequalities, power, agency, discrimination, and so on, stretch right across the volume. To signpost some of the more critical links, cross-references are made to other chapters and parts throughout. It should also be noted that the ordering of the sections (and the chapters therein) does not indicate any particular priority in respect of their conceptual, methodological or policy significance, with many of the more area-specific case studies speaking to theoretical debates well beyond place or subject boundaries.

With the above in mind, I chose to begin the volume with a part entitled 'Concepts and Methodologies for Gendered Poverty', in which a set of chapters considers in broad terms how different aspects of gendered poverty might be approached, analysed and measured. Saskia Sassen's opening discussion (Chapter 2), for instance, which has particular resonance for aspects of migration and work dealt with later in the *Handbook*, introduces the importance of 'strategic gendering' to a range of international economic processes past and present, and particularly the 'alternative political economies' associated with the current phase of globalisation. This links with another of Sassen's concepts, the 'feminisation of survival', by which she refers to the increasing significance of women's labour not only in underpinning household livelihoods – across the social spectrum and frequently across borders – but also in sustaining states and global corporations. The inclusion of women's subjective experiences of poverty and exploitation – for example, as migrant or minoritised workers forming part of the 'serving classes' responsible for the 'smooth functioning' of professional households – is one way to unseat a persistent gender-neutrality in analyses of economic globalisation which so often selectively invisibilise labour regimes which are key to its existence and evolution.

The question of subjectivities is taken further by Henrietta Moore (Chapter 3) who stresses how gendered poverty analysis may be enriched not only by taking into account subjective interpretations of poverty and well-being, but by adopting a much more explicit and theoretically informed analysis of gendered subjectivities in ways which depart from naturalised and universalised assumptions about the sites in which these are predominantly configured, such as heterosexual marriage and 'conventional' households. A particular preoccupation in Moore's discussion is that of how social and economic inequalities engage with women's and men's views of morality and selfhood, and how such an approach opens up a more historically and culturally sensitive space in which to analyse the intersections of gender and poverty.

In Gerd Johnsson-Latham's chapter (Chapter 4), attention turns to how power, privilege and gender are reflected in poverty analysis and development goals. Identifying two main schools of thought on the interrelations between gender and poverty – the 'poverty discourse' and the 'gender discourse' – Johnsson-Latham shows how the knowledge and policy prescriptions of the latter (predominantly concerned with gender justice, rights-based approaches, and poverty broadly defined) are often overshadowed by the former (more concerned with economic growth, and monetary poverty) not least in the formulation of the MDGs. To strengthen the knowledge base from which gendered poverty analysis and action take their lead, much more primacy to a Gender and Development (GAD) approach is necessary.

Echoes of these (as well as Moore's) arguments are found in Cecile Jackson's chapter (Chapter 5), which, with particular reference to India, stresses how gender inequality cannot be collapsed to poverty and vice versa. Observing that economic growth rather than poverty is often responsible for increasing gender inequalities, Jackson's discussion foregrounds the need for gender-focused policy which extends beyond targeted interventions to low-income women.

The next cluster of chapters in this part deal with the measurement of gender inequality, in which various types of poverty are implicated. The chapters by Thomas Pogge (Chapter 6) and Sharon Bessell (Chapter 7), for example, reflect on the limitations of existing indicators, such as international poverty lines and the poverty and gender indices developed by the United Nations Development Programme (UNDP), to capture experiences of gendered poverty. Among the suggestions made to improve measures are a more comprehensive range of variables, and the factoring in of information generated through participatory assessments. Examples of some of the more specific issues vital to enhancing the gender-sensitivity of poverty indicators are rights and equality (as discussed in the chapter by Anna Coates, Chapter 8) and time poverty (Sarah Gammage, Chapter 9).

A new measure – the Social Institutions and Gender Index (SIGI) developed at the Organisation for Economic Co-operation and Development (OECD) – is introduced in the chapter by Dennis Drechsler and Johannes Jütting (Chapter 10). Notwithstanding persistent and uneven data gaps, the SIGI attempts to incorporate a far wider range of variables pertinent to gender inequality and poverty than most of its predecessors, including the provisions of national Family Codes, son preference and gender disparities in ownership rights.

The last chapter in this section, by Linda Mayoux (Chapter 11), discusses the 'Gender Action Learning System' (GALS), which aims to elicit the key factors in household poverty. In its application in a range of countries in the Global South, GALS has revealed the centrality of gender inequalities, such as in relation to violence and property rights, to individual privation. As a proven gender-sensitive participatory tool in specific localities, this could be an important addition to more qualitative methodologies for poverty assessment in general.

The second part of the *Handbook* is entitled 'Debates on the "Feminisation of Poverty", and Female-headed Households'. Although it is increasingly recognised that the 'feminisation of poverty' is a lumpen term of little theoretical, explanatory or even descriptive utility, and one whose association with female-headed households is tenuous, despite its origins in relation to Afro-American women and their households in the United States (US) (Pearce, 1978), chapters dealing with one or both these phenomena are grouped here for two interrelated reasons. The first is on account of the historical positioning of discussions of female household headship within expositions (or critiques) of the 'feminisation of poverty'. The second is because the majority of authors in this section make reference to both issues. With this in mind, Part II opens with a discussion by Marcelo Medeiros and Joana Costa (Chapter 12) on the extent to which available statistics corroborate a trend towards a 'feminisation of poverty'. Beyond the conclusion that the evidence for such an assertion is weak, one of the main points in Medeiros's and Costa's discussion revolves around the methodological significance of whether the unit of analysis is the individual or the household. This is also taken up by Gita Sen (Chapter 13), who further echoes some of the issues discussed by Jackson about pockets of gendered poverty (including violence, and 'time tax') within well-off as well as poor (not to mention, male-headed) households.

One of the major downsides of persistent assumptions about the 'feminisation of poverty', and again perhaps most notably its association with female household headship, is the reproduction of heteronormative orthodoxies such as the 'male breadwinner' paradigm. This comes in for close discussion by Tine Davids and Francien van Driel (Chapter 14), who propose the adoption of a multilayered 'gender lens' which minimises essentialist assumptions about women's and men's behaviour, power and agency in a world in which processes of globalisation are often deeply associated with what they denominate as 'false dichotomies'.

Another slant on the 'feminisation of poverty' is presented in my own case study chapter (Chapter 15), which, on the basis of fieldwork in The Gambia, Philippines and Costa Rica, distils a tendency over time towards a 'feminisation of responsibility and/or obligation'. This leads me to advocate that the analytical parameters of the 'feminisation of poverty' are broadened beyond income to include gender-differentiated inputs of labour and time into household livelihoods, as well as taking into account male – as well as female – household headship. These suggestions seem to have resonance in other contexts, with Lynne Brydon (Chapter 16) noting a similar trend towards a 'feminisation of family responsibility' over nearly forty years of longitudinal anthropological observation in Ghana.

The chapters based on comparative work by Helen Safa (Chapter 17) in Cuba, Puerto Rico and the Dominican Republic, and by Janet Momsen (Chapter 18) in various Caribbean islands, transport us to another area of the Global South where female-headed households have a long and comparatively well-documented history. Safa's particular concern is the way in which state policies under socialist and non-socialist regimes have impacted on the formation and viability of female-headed units, whereas Momsen concentrates on factors such as violence and HIV/AIDS which appear to be undermining the relative success traditionally achieved by female-headed households in survival and well-being. Another potential threat for female-headed households comes from war and civil conflict, as explored by Marian Koster (Chapter 19) in the aftermath of the Rwandan genocide of the early 1990s. Like Caroline Moser, whose discussion of asset accumulation in Ecuador is featured later in the volume, Koster finds that female-headed households may not necessarily be income-poor (as is often imagined to be the norm), but face asset vulnerability on account of limited access to land.

The succeeding chapter, by Annelou Ypeij (Chapter 20), traces the experiences of migrant lone mothers of Dutch Caribbean origin as well as those of indigenous nationals in Amsterdam. One of the main patterns highlighted by Ypeij is an intensification of social stigmatisation against lone mothers in receipt of welfare benefits as the Netherlands, like many countries, pares down social expenditure. That state support for lone mothers – and women in general – should not be compromised is further urged in Jane Millar's discussion (Chapter 21) of lone mothers in the UK which identifies, *inter alia*, the critical role played by subsidised childcare in reducing poverty. The UK – along with other European countries, the USA and Canada – also forms a focus in Fran Tonkiss's chapter (Chapter 22) on the advanced economies. Following her discussion of the intersectionality of gender with household headship and composition, 'race', age and space, Tonkiss draws the conclusion that for diverse social groups disadvantage persists in being 'feminised', even if the determination of precise trends remains difficult.

In Part III on 'Gender, Family and Lifecourse' we move into the more general terrain of households and families, taking into consideration different lifecourse phases – ranging from youth to old age – as well as inter- and intra-generational relations. In the first chapter here, Agnes Quisumbing (Chapter 23) sets out a review of gender and household decision-making, paying particular attention to the utility of different theoretical models, and how vital elements such as 'bargaining power', which she sums up as 'a most elusive concept', can be measured and accounted for. Making reference to case studies from different developing countries, Quisumbing emphasises the important influences of social norms and control over resources in intrahousehold allocation, including, again, access to assets.

In respect of intergenerational household dynamics and their relations with poverty, Ruth Lister's discussion of the UK (Chapter 24) pays particular attention to the manifold ways in which women's poverty undermines their perceived and actual capacity to live up to parenting norms, and how raising children, in turn, obstructs their ability to exit poverty. Among the main issues driven home in Lister's chapter is how the responsibility for managing poverty, which usually falls to women, entails hard, complex, time-consuming and exhausting labour burdens, often little alleviated by state support.

A somewhat more specific perspective on the links between women's and children's poverty is provided by John Sender (Chapter 25) on the basis of Mozambique, where he considers the impacts of female wage labour on investments in children's education. As often found in other poor countries, where education is a costly undertaking for parents, girls tend to do better in respect of schooling where their mothers have income in their own right, even where they have to manage without the wage of a male partner.

Households and intra-generational divisions and dynamics – particularly between spouses – are a major interest in Sarah Ashwin's chapter (Chapter 26) on gendered experiences and outcomes of poverty in post-Soviet Russia. Here she concentrates on employment and domestic labour through the years of transition from a centrally planned to a market economy, highlighting continuities in women's attachment to the labour force (mainly as a result of economic need), and men's peripherality to unpaid reproductive labour. The latter obtains even as threats to men's breadwinning position have intensified, which also appear to have provoked a rise in risk-taking behaviour, especially alcoholism. In light of the traumas attached to male marginalisation, and notwithstanding the knock-on effects on women's income- and time-poverty, women's continued responsibility for domestic labour and childcare arguably comprises a rather more positive than usual connotation insofar as it helps them to sustain a sense of 'efficacy, competence and meaning'.

Other post-Soviet states in Central Asia, such as Tajikistan, as discussed by Jane

Falkingham and Angela Baschieri (Chapter 27), reveal similar patterns in women's continued straddling of paid and unpaid work, despite the substantial withdrawal of state support for childcare and parental leave, and a renaissance of Tajik cultural values of male authority. One issue of particular relevance to gendered poverty raised by these authors is the need for assessments of household income which do not assume equality of pooling and allocation.

A somewhat different perspective on household experiences of poverty is presented by Carolyn Williams (Chapter 28) in her discussion of Peru. This chapter draws out some of the links between sexuality, gender and poverty explored in other parts of the volume with particular reference to a close study of family life in Lima's low-income settlements. Here Williams highlights the various forms of discrimination and isolation faced by women on account of their experiences of same-sex desire and relationships, and the strategies they deploy for overcoming the negative effects of not conforming with heterosexual norms.

Also dealing in various degrees with sexuality are the next three chapters in Part III which consider issues around youth. Gareth Jones and Sarah Thomas de Benítez (Chapter 29) explore gender differences in work and life among Mexican streetchildren, finding, among other things, that in spite of their non-normative economic, social and cultural positions male and female street youth often subscribe to dominant gendered ideals of work and caring as part of their survival strategies.

Survival strategies are also key to Alice Evans's (Chapter 30) discussion of sexuality and poverty among young people in The Gambia, where sexual partners are commonly regarded as providers of economic resources, as highlighted for other sub-Saharan African (SSA) countries discussed elsewhere in the *Handbook* by Moore, Campbell and Gibbs, and Jolly and Cornwall. Stella Nyanzi's discussion (Chapter 31) is also on The Gambia and touches upon sexuality, but concentrates more on male youths and particularly their homosocial strategies for survival in a context where high levels of unemployment are associated with widespread aspirations to overseas migration.

The last four chapters in this part consider various aspects of gender and poverty in old age, which has hitherto been a rather neglected issue. The particular focus of Isabella Aboderin's chapter (Chapter 32) is Ghana where she draws the possibly counterintuitive finding that older women tend to fare better than older men on account of their prior and/or ongoing emotional, labour and financial investments in their children. Although Aboderin notes that similar patterns have been found in other countries such as Costa Rica, this is not always the case, as demonstrated by Penny Vera-Sanso (Chapter 33) for Chennai, India, where in addition to filial support (or its erosion), pensions (which include means-tested non-contributory schemes) do relatively little to redress gender inequalities in old age. In Chennai older women appear to be multiply disadvantaged on a number of counts. Not only do more women than men end up destitute because women tend to live longer than men (although premature mortality is often a corollary of their poverty), but because women are less likely to accumulate earnings or pension advantages over the lifecourse, and because of prevailing social perceptions that the old need fewer resources than the young, and women less than men.

Monica Budowski's comparative discussion of multi-pillar pension models in Chile and Costa Rica (Chapter 34), where the decline of normative expectations, and actual practices of family support have made pensions absolutely critical for women and men to survive in later life, reflects *inter alia* on how privileges in pension policies for elderly women (as mandated by recent Chilean reforms), can institutionalise gender differences. By the same token, Jane Falkingham, Maria Evandrou and Athina Vlachantoni (Chapter 35) in relation to the UK, defend the importance of recent moves to acknowledge women's caring responsibilities, even if the low value of disbursements remains a concern.

In Part IV, attention turns to aspects of gendered poverty in which questions of 'race' and migration feature prominently, and often in conjunction with one another given the growing incidence of demographic mobility within and across borders.

On the subject of 'race' per se, the first chapter in this part, by Janet Hunt (Chapter 36), considers questions of how to assess poverty, gender and well-being among indigenous communities of the Global North – particularly Australia, Canada and New Zealand – where different meanings and priorities often hold sway among 'mainstream' and 'marginalised' populations.

Notwithstanding the problems attached to who defines the needs of indigenous peoples and how, Mercedes González de la Rocha's discussion (Chapter 37) finds some interesting and encouraging results for indigenous women of the high-profile Mexican CCT programme *Progresa-Oportunidades*, which, after more than ten years' duration, offers substantial potential for evaluating long-term and sustainable outcomes. Although this programme is not specifically tailored to Mexico's indigenous populations, its cash transfers provide a source of regular income to groups traditionally deprived in terms of schooling and who suffer precarious positioning in the labour market. Moreover, the unprecedented opportunity for indigenous girls to progress with their education is regarded as a vital route to improve well-being in future. These positive findings go somewhat against the grain of other analyses (see earlier), and thereby bring to bear the importance of intersectional analysis and differentiation among women.

Also on Latin America, Helen Safa's second contribution to the *Handbook* (Chapter 38) considers questions of gender, poverty and national identity in the context of a comparative analysis of indigenous and afrodescendent groups in the region. Among Safa's principal findings is the particularly strong social, economic and political role of afrodescendent women. This has not only been forced by conditions of greater racial marginalisation than faced by indigenous populations, but also through wider diasporic movements in which women have participated either as migrants in their own right, or as the managers of remittances.

Interesting gender dynamics of international migration are further pinpointed by Cathy McIlwaine (Chapter 39) in the context of her detailed fieldwork among Latin American migrants in London which reveals a complex and often contradictory tapestry of gender-differentiated 'exclusions'. At one level migrant men deem themselves marginalised by their lack of access to jobs which are routinely associated with the preferential recruitment of women, or because of their consignment to menial, 'feminised', occupations. Yet at another level, men's privileges in respect of legal status, gender divisions of reproductive labour, and questions of social identity, collude to maintain male–female hierarchies.

Questions of women's access to low-wage – and even 'recession-proof' – servile jobs, along with women's disproportionate 'liminal legality', also form a substantial part of Cecilia Menjívar's analysis of Central American migrants to the USA (Chapter 40), wherein she finds that changes in daily practices among women and men do not necessarily destabilise inequitable gender ideologies.

In many senses similar patterns are found by Claire Alexander (Chapter 41) in her study of the UK. Although this discussion mainly focuses on Asian-Muslim young men in the context of the 'war on terror', and their progressive marking as emblematic of 'imagined national, racial and cultural crisis', Alexander also demonstrates the injurious ways in which Asian-Muslim women encounter discrimination in their own 'enclaves' as well as in wider British society which has major implications for their social, political and economic positioning and agency.

The succeeding chapter, by Linda McDowell (Chapter 42), considers from a more historical perspective the gender dynamics of 'race' and international migration from the relatively under-studied context of Latvia, which in the 1940s underwent a 'double' occupation by Soviet and Nazi German armed forces. This gave rise to a variety of movements, including the migration of some young women to the UK. Such displacements not only disrupted conventional lifecourse transitions, but were often associated with significant downward mobility.

The extent to which the forfeit of accepted social norms – and the costs of these – is a corollary of intra-national migration is explored in various degrees in the three chapters in this part which deal primarily with gendered mobility within national borders. The review by Haydea Izazola (Chapter 43), for example, on gender, poverty and migration in Mexico, although touching upon gender-selective international as well as national migration, reports diverse implications for women 'left behind' in source areas. On one hand the latter may benefit from greater income security and enhancement, and even more power and autonomy. However, others are condemned to greater vulnerability, especially where remittances from migrant spouses dry up, often without forewarning.

In the chapter by Daniel Jordan Smith (Chapter 44), on the migration by young Igbo women to the northern Nigerian city of Kano, the contradictory corollaries of – in this case – female-selective migration are highlighted through evidence of trade-offs between moral and material currencies negotiated by young women in their pursuit of pathways out of poverty.

The chapter by Cecilia Tacoli (Chapter 45), which focuses on internal migration not only in Nigeria, but also Mali, Tanzania and Vietnam, reveals how mobility and the move away from 'traditional' rural economies and societal values has increased in recent years. At one level this reflects women's ongoing disadvantage in land acquisition and inheritance in rural areas. However, new patterns are also fuelled by the opening up of spaces for women in urban labour markets, and the drive among young women to assert independence, even if one price to be paid is heavier obligations of support to natal kin.

The final chapter in this part, by Kalpana Wilson (Chapter 46), entitled 'Picturing gender and poverty: from "victimhood" to "agency"', expounds on the changing representation of racial 'minority' women in the Majority World in development discourse and campaign documentation – an issue which also features in the later chapters by Roy, Richey and Jassey.[7]

In Part V, a fairly small, but vital, series of issues relating to 'Gender, Health and Poverty' are addressed from a range of perspectives. In the opening chapter (Chapter 47) Jasmine Gideon discusses gender, poverty and the right to health with particular reference to Chile, one of several countries in the world whose pronounced marketisation and commodification of healthcare carries deep gender implications. For example, in Chile's new neoliberal provision model, women have less 'ability to pay' than men, have to pick

12   *The international handbook of gender and poverty*

up the cudgels for the 'return' of vital reproductive and care services to the home, and on top of this are increasingly having to make ends meet through labour force insertion, predominantly in the informal economy. Over and above the additional strains on women's labour, time and bodies, that few jobs offer prospects of private health insurance poses threats to their well-being.

Anna Coates's second contribution to the *Handbook* (Chapter 48) considers the wider Latin American scenario in specific relation to the reduction of maternal mortality, which has qualified as a goal in its own right on the MDG agenda. Although maternal mortality rates (MMR) are lower in Latin America than other regions of the Global South, at a sub-regional level there are marked inequalities related to poverty and ethnicity, which have been deemed tantamount to a form of gender violence against poor, minority mothers.

Although women are often the main victims of inadequate, class-biased healthcare, a rather different scenario is painted in Matthew Gutmann's chapter (Chapter 49) which branches into one of the biggest contemporary global health issues: HIV/AIDS. Set in the context of the Oaxaca, southern Mexico, where poverty has increasingly driven men to engage in cross-border migration to the USA, Gutmann reveals how this has led to men having the highest rates of HIV infection in the state. Men's exposure to the disease seems to be linked with casual sexual encounters forced by loneliness during their time away from home. The social stigmatisation and inadequate public health responses which greet them on their return do little to improve the situation for migrant men, not to mention the female sexual partners that they infect.

The disadvantaged position of men in respect of treatment, even in contexts such as South Africa where, unlike in Mexico, the drugs used in anti-retroviral therapy (ART) can be purchased at less than market price, is echoed in the chapter by Catherine Campbell and Andrew Gibbs (Chapter 50). Yet in this discussion, we also learn that although, in the heartland of the epidemic in SSA, HIV/AIDS has historically been associated with populations who are 'affluent, educated and mobile', poverty and inequality have begun to transfer new infections to poor young women, often as a result of the socio-economic inequalities associated with 'transactional sex'. Thus while women are more likely to be diagnosed early and to receive treatment – partly because of their greater engagement with healthcare services through pregnancy and children – the majority (60 per cent) of new HIV-cases in the region are female.[8]

Another issue raised by Campbell and Gibbs – that of gender bias in carework for people living with HIV/AIDS (PLWHA) – receives more dedicated treatment by Keerty Nakray (Chapter 51) in the context of India, which is one of the countries outside SSA where new rates of HIV infection are on an alarming rise. The disjunctures between the rights and rewards of women carers in respect of marginalisation and eviction – even when they themselves are ill, and often due to infection by husbands who did not disclose their HIV-positive status – constitute persuasive grounds for policy interventions to recognise and support these new feminised burdens borne by 'housewives', and not just to target groups commonly perceived to be most 'at risk'.

The final chapter in this part, by Hilary Graham (Chapter 52), with particular reference to the UK, deals with a health-related issue – smoking – historically associated with 'risk-taking' activity among elite men, but which is in the process of becoming a major concern among poor women in advanced economies. In Graham's opinion, this requires interventions which go well beyond standard medical anti-smoking campaigns, to those which address social disadvantage and inequality.

The relatively uncharted but immensely significant issue of 'Gender, Poverty and Assets' forms the subject of Part VI. This starts with a chapter from Carmen Diana Deere (Chapter 53), who outlines some of the principal conceptual and methodological factors in assessing gender inequalities in asset ownership. Deere reveals the critical role of these in shedding light on intrahousehold disparities, and how the valuation of assets (in addition to working out the share of this accruing to women who own assets jointly as well as independently) is critical in assessing gender-differentiated poverty. On the basis of her exploration of Latin American data, Deere points out that the biggest asset gap between women and men is land. This is echoed for cities of the Global South more generally in the chapter by Carole Rakodi (Chapter 54), with particular complexities noted here on account of the fact that a major share of land and property ownership is of an 'informal' nature.

Continuing in a similar, although more context-specific vein, is a chapter by Kate Bird and Jessica Espey (Chapter 55) on women's land rights in two 'post-conflict' environments: Uganda and Rwanda. Here they contend that 'gender blindspots' in policies and legislation around land are likely to leave poor women disempowered to change their situations, which echoes Koster's arguments in relation to asset poverty in Rwanda.

Another set of perspectives on questions of land and property is drawn out in Sunil Kumar's chapter on gender, livelihoods and rental housing markets in the Global South (Chapter 56). While Kumar's discussion shows that women are often as disadvantaged in rental tenure as in owner-occupation, he also points up the economic potential for women who are able to let out parts of their dwellings or compounds in contexts where other livelihood opportunities are in limited supply.

Also on the matter of housing, Sophie Mills's discussion of women's access to shelter microfinance in South Africa reveals the potentially transformative personal and public impacts of housing credits directed to women (Chapter 57). Yet although on one hand these can bolster women's bargaining power and 'fallback' position, Mills reminds us that housing may also be a 'problematic asset' insofar as it can imply greater burdens of female responsibility for non-contributing household members.

In another housing-related chapter, Sheela Patel and Diana Mitlin (Chapter 58) report on the critical role of women in 'feminising' the agenda and interventions of grassroots organisations such as the now internationally networked Shack/Slum Dweller Federation. This has not only raised the profile of women's concerns in low-income settlements, but has also led to a more prominent political role for women in local governance.

Turning to other types of 'assets', such as social capital, Katie Willis's chapter (Chapter 59) on Oaxaca City, Mexico, explores the differential access by women (and particularly female-headed households) to this vital resource according to socio-economic status. Willis warns that for poorer women – whose needs are arguably greatest – the supply of social capital is limited both by a combination of lack of contacts and time, such that caution needs to be exercised by development agencies who assume that this can be mobilised by the poor at will.

Caroline Moser's chapter (Chapter 60) looks not only at the importance of social, human, physical and other assets, but also at their accumulation over time, in the context of over thirty years' detailed ethnographic research in a low-income settlement built on reclaimed swampland in Guayaquil, Ecuador. From these inauspicious beginnings, many households have been successful in strengthening their asset portfolios, most recently through international migration among younger generations. Again there is evidence that even if female-headed households may not be income-poor in comparison with male-headed units, their relative asset poverty begs questions about the processes which lead to this outcome.

While Moser's chapter covers an extensive range of assets, so too does the final chapter in this part, by Rachel Slater, Rebecca Holmes, Nicola Jones and Matšeliso Mphale (Chapter 61). On the basis of a pilot study in Lesotho, these authors stress the importance of taking into account social as well as economic vulnerability for shaping social protection measures to reduce gender inequalities and to promote women's empowerment.

The conclusions of Slater et al. are extremely important for Part VII, on 'Gender, Poverty and Work', where we take a detailed look at one of the biggest assets of all households, and perhaps particularly the poor: labour (González de la Rocha, 2006b, 2007; Moser, 1998). Although this section might conceivably have come earlier in the *Handbook*, I chose to place it later on to disrupt something of the tendency for gender inequalities in employment to be given the lion's share of attention in analyses of gender and poverty – mainly through the association with income and pay gaps – when the origins, emanation, character and impacts of gendered poverty occur in so many other forms and spaces. As it is, the diverse discussions in this part serve to highlight that gender inequalities in work and their interrelationships with poverty require analyses which go far beyond cursory treatment of labour markets per se. As summarised by James Heintz in his chapter on women's employment, economic risk and poverty reduction (Chapter 66): 'an exclusive focus on the market relationships that govern employment dynamics ignores non-market activities that have an enormous effect on poverty status, development outcomes, and the production of human potential'. For example, although occupational segmentation and segregation play a major role in accounting for gendered earning differentials, as discussed by Janneke Plantenga and Eva Fransen (Chapter 63) in the context of Europe, and by Amy Liu for Vietnam (Chapter 69), it is impossible to understand why and how employment divisions come about without reference to the embeddedness of gendered processes within global capitalist production and accumulation (as discussed, *inter alia*, by Ruth Pearson, Chapter 64, in relation to the most dynamic sectors of the global economy [including information and communications technology/ICT], by Stephanie Barrientos, Chapter 67, with respect to Global Value Chains, by Sharad Chari, Chapter 68, in relation to the feminisation of industrial labour in one of India's hubs of garment exports, Tiruppur, and by Marty Chen, Chapter 71, and Kate Meagher, Chapter 72 whose chapters touch upon the links between economic globalisation and informal work.

Integral to gender inequalities in different economic sectors – and at different scales – is the interplay of markets with states and households. For example, Katherine Brickell's chapter on Cambodia's post-conflict transition to a market economy (Chapter 70) points to the various tensions posed by women's designation by the state as 'precious gems' in the new economic model, and their roles in managing household poverty burdens, while their paid labour in the emerging tourism sector, and on construction sites, continues to be regarded as secondary to the work of men, and is often a source of conflict within the home. More generally, and with reference to a range of countries in the Global North and Global South, Shahra Razavi and Silke Staab (Chapter 65) indicate how states play a massive role in mediating the links between households and labour markets through programmes of social assistance and fiscal policy (tax and transfers). These are especially relevant to women workers whose degree and type of economic activity is strongly influenced by claims on their unpaid household labour, and its social and symbolic corollaries.

As with this latter contribution, a thread running through most of the chapters in this part is the question of the fundamental factors underpinning persistent labour force divisions. One crucial factor, highlighted, *inter alia*, by Diane Perrons (Chapter 62) in relation to high-income economies, is that the continued bias of unpaid care and reproductive labour towards women, in the absence of effective public support for unpaid carework, not only restrains many women's access to well-paid employment, but also leads to clusters of feminised jobs in areas of the service economy (often in care services per se) which are undervalued and underpaid, both at national and international levels.

Low-paid, part-time, precarious and undervalued work, often on the margins of the formal economy, is a common predicament for women in advanced economies. As the chapters by Perrons and others in this part show, the demands of women's domestic roles frequently force them to prioritise hours and location above occupation and pay, and once they are in the part-time/flexible sector it becomes difficult to escape, with major impacts on their lifetime earnings.[9] Yet in developing regions, where between one-half and three-quarters of the labour force is informally employed, the situation is arguably worse still. Informal employment is generally associated with lower incomes (Heintz, Chapter 66), and as Chen points out, sources of informal work are not only generally more significant than formal jobs, as well as a larger source of employment for women than men, but women are also usually found in the lower echelons of the informal economy. Paramount here, then, is Meagher's question about whether informal employment, so often regarded as a positive means of accommodating women's needs to balance income-generating work with reproductive responsibilities, is a source of 'impoverishment' rather than 'empowerment'.

The issue of employment status – which refers to the degree of autonomy one has in employment, including brokers and intermediaries in subcontracted or self-employment, or what Heintz refers to as the 'quasi labour market' – is also critical here. This is discussed in relation to Colombia and other parts of Latin America with reference to 'quality of work' by Javier Pineda (Chapter 74), and in the context of Surat, India by Paula Kantor (Chapter 73), who explores gender-differentiated deficits in 'decent work' as defined by the International Labour Organisation (ILO) which in 1999 launched its agenda for more and better quality jobs.

The significance of examining the links between gendered labour divisions and poverty in the twenty-first century is arguably more important than ever, when, as Heintz notes, more women are undertaking income-generating activity during an epoch in which increased demands are made on their unpaid work as a result of social expenditure cuts. Yet despite a backdrop of declining access to regular, guaranteed, full-time employment, Heintz cautions against unproblematised connections between the 'feminisation of labour' and the 'feminisation of poverty', even if, as the simulation performed by Joana Costa and Elydia Silva for Latin America (Chapter 75) reveals, a reduction of gender inequalities in the labour market would go a long way to reducing poverty.

Another consideration relevant to this debate is that the links between employment and poverty are not as readily assessed as they may first appear. Corroborating the discussions by Heintz (Chapter 66) and Razavi and Staab (Chapter 65), Chen (Chapter 71) points up how employment is measured at an individual level, whereas poverty is routinely calculated at the household level. Bridging this hiatus, a new technique noted by Chen, devised originally by UNIFEM, is to assess household poverty risk on the basis of the proportion of members employed in different kinds of work. Even then, questions of intrahousehold income pooling, control and resource allocation also need to be more closely scrutinised in order to determine the risk of poverty among different women and men, as further discussed by Meagher (Chapter 72) with reference to sub-Saharan Africa, as well as by Heintz, and by Razavi and Staab.

Given the diverse factors affecting gender divisions in formal and informal employment at different scales, it is no surprise that the policy agendas proposed by authors are extremely heterogeneous. Nevertheless, there is broad consensus that a major step towards rectifying gendered labour market disadvantage and creating more 'decent work' for women in the spirit of ILO directives would be a proper economic valuation of the unpaid work which women routinely perform, and more national recognition and spending on appropriate support facilities for mothers and unpaid carers. From the standpoint that social policies to date have rarely measured up to the task of compensating 'labour market losers' (Chen, Chapter 71; Razavi and Staab, Chapter 65), comprehensive packages, over and above more adequate childcare support, might include the creation or more, better quality, and less gender-segregated job opportunities, gender-sensitive wage policies, more gender-responsive social protection (pensions and so forth), and increased access to credit and training. In the context of informal employment specifically, Chen proposes a '3V' framework encompassing 'Voice, Visibility and Validity', which makes visible the participation of women workers, recognises and validates them, and ensures their better representation in labour market institutions. A parallel discussion in Perrons' chapter on high-income economies with greater levels of regulated employment includes a more extended version of this model based on the work of Damian Grimshaw and Jill Rubery (2007). This identifies five 'V's with rather different nomenclature and referencing points. One of these is *vocation*, which pertains to the tendency for particular kinds of work to be attributed to women's 'natural talents' rather than skills. Another is *variance*, which relates primarily to the over-representation of women in part-time employment which confines them to a narrower range of sectors and occupations.

Questions of working conditions and 'quality of work', will also require the extension of ILO core standards to women engaged in seasonal, casual, homework, migrant labour and contract work in export production. This is a particular focus of Barrientos's chapter (Chapter 67), which also notes the potential pressure that can be brought to bear by consumers in the Global North to protect workers at the lowest end of Global Value Chains (GVCs) in developing nations.

Another potentially critical factor is that employment should feature more prominently in the MDG agenda, which as Chen and Kantor note has until recently remained conspicuous by its absence, notwithstanding one major recommendation by the United Nations Millennium Project's Taskforce on Education and Gender Equality (UNMP/ TFEGE, 2005) that steps are taken to reduce women's reliance on poor quality informal work within the paid economy (Meagher).[10]

Building on some of the policy recommendations made in relation to employment, in Part VIII we move into the broader field of 'Gendered Poverty and Policy Interventions', in which the tensions between genuine bids to promote gender equality and empower women through poverty reduction are arguably among their most visible in the *Handbook*. One issue covered in this part of the volume is aid. This comprises discussions that range from the fleshing out of the possible implications for gender of new forms of 'aid architecture' in the wake of the 2005 Paris Declaration which, *inter alia*, devolves more determination over aid expenditure to recipient states (Gwendolyn Beetham, Chapter 76), to the stranglehold over aid priorities and mediation by people far-removed from the everyday life of their intended beneficiaries (Katja Jassey, Chapter 78 and Lisa Ann Richey, Chapter 77). Both the latter authors reflect on the motives of aid-givers as well as the portrayal of, and outcomes for receivers. While Jassey's discussion explores, *inter alia*, why the policy agenda of the Swedish International Development Agency (Sida) continues to be dominated by 'poor brown women', usually constructed as 'downtrodden helpless victims', Richey's chapter focuses on the new celebrity-driven development initiative 'Product Red™'. The latter sees corporates dedicating a slice of profits from certain of their 'Red-branded' products to the Global Fund to Fight AIDS, Malaria and Tuberculosis. Although the conditions under which Red products are actually elaborated may not always stand up to the test of scrutiny, Richey levels that this initiative has contributed to converting 'consumption into a mechanism for compassion', affording opportunities for 'low cost heroism' to shoppers in the Global North, not to mention the 'stars' who feature in the campaign media.

But policy interventions are not solely driven by external actors: 'poor women' themselves (or through their representation by politically elected individuals and civil society groups) are nominally able to exert more agency in policy initiatives which on the surface require greater and more polycentric 'stakeholder' involvement. Classic examples include gender-responsive budgeting (GRB), which has been road-tested in an increasingly widespread range of countries in the Global North and Global South (Diane Elson and Rhonda Sharp, Chapter 80), and programmes guided by Poverty Reduction Strategy Papers (PRSPs) adopted by poor countries seeking debt relief (Sarah Bradshaw and Brian Linneker, Chapter 79) in which gender is purportedly a 'cross-cutting' issue. Although, as Bradshaw and Linneker point out, the PRSP process has evolved in the context of a 'new era' in which international financial institutions (IFIs) are concerned with poverty as well as growth, and nominally committed to broad-based consultation and consensus, in reality the amount of input by poor women to policy design and delivery is minimal. In turn, the CCT programmes often linked with PRSP initiatives tend to narrowly link women's poverty issues to their roles as mothers (see earlier). While GRB offers a more positive scenario, ensuring greater transparency and accountability in public expenditure, and that at least a proportion of this gets allotted in pro-gender equality and pro-poor ways, Elson and Sharp caution that the amounts are too small to make GRB a stand-alone panacea for poverty. Similar conclusions in relation to the slightly different context of targeted anti-poverty programmes for women and female household heads in Costa Rica are reached by Monica Budowski and Laura Guzmán Stein (Chapter 81), who reiterate the need for a range of interventions to overcome gendered poverty.

Interesting light on gendered poverty interventions is presented from the vantage points of two northern development NGOs (NDNGOs), Oxfam GB (Nicholas Piálek, Chapter 82) and WOMANKIND Worldwide (Tina Wallace and Ceri Hayes, Chapter 83), both of which have a strong commitment to learning from their partners.

While Wallace and Hayes point up how WOMANKIND's work is often compromised by short-termism, and increasing pressure from major donors for demonstrable results (something also emphasised by Jassey in relation to her discussion of Sida), both WOMANKIND and Oxfam have been at the forefront of working with multidimensional concepts of gendered poverty. In the specific case of Oxfam, Piálek traces the evolution of discourses within the organisation from regarding gender inequality as a compounding factor in poverty, to a type of poverty itself, meriting action in its own right.

Touching upon many of the arguments in this section, the concluding chapter by Ananya Roy (Chapter 84), entitled 'Millennial woman: the gender order of development', reinforces the observation that gender has become increasingly 'yoked' to poverty, and discerns what she calls a 'financialisation of the poverty agenda' in which women are often positioned at the forefront. This increasingly entails the depiction in development documentation and imagery of women as happy and productive entrepreneurs (as also described by Wilson in Chapter 46), which are harnessed to the 'technofinancial infrastructure of the new millennium' through microcredit initiatives in their various guises, as discussed in the next and ninth part of the *Handbook*.

I decided to create a separate part on 'Microfinance and Women's Empowerment' because microcredit stands out as one of the most obviously gender-specific types of contemporary policy interventions – particularly in developing countries – and to which the UN has now seen fit to dedicate a special year.[11]

Despite the particular relevance of microfinance to the Global South, Beverly Lemire's opening chapter in Part IX (Chapter 85) draws attention to the centuries' importance of women's roles in underpinning household survival. This has taken the form in Europe, and elsewhere, of women acting as brokers between the household and the market through personal, local and more public thrift and savings initiatives, including the lending of money to one another, and the guaranteeing of loans. The common emphasis in microfinance schemes on group loans is, as Kate Maclean (Chapter 87) discusses in relation to twenty-first century Bolivia, often a perceived and actual way in which microcredit organisations can guard against risk of default and ensure their own survival. Yet to use Maclean's expression 'capitalising on women's social capital', drawing on relationships of support and reciprocity which women are already actively engaged in building, may not be in the best interests of women clients or 'beneficiaries' insofar as it can exert immense pressure upon them to sacrifice their own well-being to keep up repayments. Indeed, the question of whether poor women are necessarily inclined to join forces in their bids to exit poverty is one in which general assumptions are ill-advised. On one hand, Bart Casier's discussion of microfinance in The Gambia and Senegal (Chapter 94) reveals that individual business growth appears to be less important to women recipients of credit than (re)investing the proceeds of entrepreneurial ventures in infrastructure which benefits the community as a whole. However, another scenario is revealed in Caroline Sweetman's discussion of Addis Ababa, Ethiopia (Chapter 88), which raises the issue that strategising for economic advancement beyond women's own households is something of an anathema in this context. As further highlighted by Supriya Garikipati in her discussion of the Self Help Group (SHG) Bank Linkage Programme in India (Chapter 92), women may not actually be in a position to use their loans even for investment in personally-owned assets. Thus while Ranjula Bali Swain's discussion of the same programme (Chapter 91) contends that women who receive credit through the SHG scheme are more 'empowered' than non-clients, Garikipati, in the context of South India, echoing Sweetman's observations in Ethiopia, errs towards the conclusion women's participation can often result in their 'disempowerment', through a hefty 'feminisation of debt' which requires more self-exploitation, and sometimes a widening of gendered gaps in well-being.

Questions of collective versus individual interests aside, a number of chapters in this section such as those of Iman Bibars on Egypt (Chapter 89) and Fauzia Mohamed on Tanzania (Chapter 86), as well as some already mentioned (Casier, and Sweetman, for example) stress how microfinance can make some inroads to reducing poverty – mainly because it allows women to 'smooth-out' fluctuations in household income – but is ineffective at providing a pathway out of gendered poverty. Obstacles here include the small size of loans, insufficient attention on the part of implementing institutions to the gendered structures of constraint which act to limit women's personal autonomy, lack of specialist orientation in enterprise growth, and the fact that there is insufficient dynamism in the local or even macroeconomic contexts in which women operate to allow for truly successful business ventures. These factors are noted not only by Casier for Senegal and The Gambia (Chapter 94), but by Irene Banda Mutalima in relation to Zambia (Chapter 93), who points up the contradictions posed by the poverty-reducing social missions of microfinance institutions (MFIs) and the need for the latter to ensure their own viability in an increasingly competitive context of donor funding. An additional point, raised by Joanne Sharp, John Briggs, Hoda Yacoub and Nabila Hamed (Chapter 90) in the context of microfinance interventions among the Bedouin in southeast Egypt, is that until microcredit projects prove to be successful, they tend to be residualised and to be regarded of little worth by better-off members of the community. Thus, while on balance many MFIs may enjoy high rates of on-time repayments and rich returns on their investments, including capital growth, whether an escape from poverty, and the enhancement of women's individual well-being, form part of this scenario are less assured (Casier, Chapter 94 and Maclean, Chapter 87). The issue of whether microfinance provides a route towards female empowerment also remains a moot point, with Mohamed (Chapter 86), *inter alia*, stressing the need for a range of ancillary interventions such as reforms in education and legal systems.

Last but not least, the question of how women's empowerment may be measured is taken up briefly by Bali Swain (Chapter 91), and in more depth by Yoko Fujikake in the closing chapter of this part (Chapter 95). Introducing her own 'empowerment evaluation' model developed in Paraguay, Fujikake highlights how methodologies and frameworks which give rounded consideration to processes and outcomes may require substantial inputs of time and expenditure on the part of development organisations, as well as to be validated and/or adjusted in other contexts.

The title of the tenth and concluding part of the *Handbook* – 'New Frontiers in Gendered Poverty Research and Analysis' – is not intended to detract from the pioneering nature of many of the preceding discussions (with which there is often considerable overlap), but was chosen partly because the chapters deal explicitly with issues which either represent some of the newest bodies of research on gendered poverty or which are comparatively recent in their appearance on policy agendas.

In Sarah Bradshaw's discussion of disaster relief (Chapter 96), through the lens of

Hurricane Mitch in Nicaragua, it appears that the cart has come somewhat before the horse. Despite relatively little empirical investigation into the gender-differentiated impacts of disaster, assumptions about the comparative poverty of women – and about their roles and dispositions within communities – seem to have led to a 'feminisation of post-disaster responses' in which there appears to have been a co-option of the same kind of 'feminisation of responsibility' logic observed in anti-poverty programmes in general. Moreover, while Bradshaw notes that the allocation of resources to women and female-headed households can secure material gains, this may not necessarily leave them with a greater sense of well-being or self-worth.

A pervasive 'feminisation of responsibility' is also apparent in the context of a clutch of chapters which deal with varying aspects of women's community and public roles in the context of neoliberalism and the 'democratisation' of local and national politics Although the mobilisation of women in defence of household, neighbourhood and, even, city-wide survival was observed during the era of recession and structural adjustment in the 1980s, ongoing processes of decentralisation and the encroaching of new 'rights-based agendas' in local-level governance have been critical in the opening up of new political spaces. In the context of India and South Africa, which Jo Beall (Chapter 97) highlights as among the countries in which most progress has been made towards the representation of women on decision-making bodies, 'presence matters' insofar as this has been associated with greater likelihood that issues of crucial relevance to women's daily lives, such as basic services and infrastructure, are prioritised. This is echoed by Sumi Madhok (Chapter 98) in the context of what she terms 'vernacular rights cultures' in her case study of India, and by Faranak Miraftab (Chapter 99), with reference to contradictions in the 'gender-poverty nexus' in South African townships. However, one major concern, summarised cogently by Beall is that 'the pursuit of decentralisation and women's rights does not become a vehicle for putting a human face on neoliberal preoccupations with privatisation, deregulation and cost recovery at the expense of poor women'. Similar doubts are aired by Amy Lind (Chapter 100) in relation to her (re)assessment of the institutionalisation of women's struggles for survival in the neoliberal (and postneoliberal) contexts of Venezuela and Ecuador. Despite the alternative development paths offered by the more left-wing governments elected in these countries in 1999 and 2006 respectively, and a greater degree of political participation by women, traditional heteronormative maternalist assumptions continue to hold considerable sway. This translates into women's continued framing as the main 'problem-solvers' for poverty in their households and communities, and, more insidiously, as the vanguard in compensating for weak welfare states. A fundamental rethinking of the contemporary family is one of the main ways forward stressed by Lind.

On a more positive note, Alissa Trotz's discussion of the experience of the grassroots women's organisation 'Red Thread' (Chapter 101) echoes some of the more encouraging examples from India and South Africa highlighted in the chapters by Beall, Madhok and Miraftab, whereby women's active involvement not only in protest and demand-making, but also in undertaking surveys which have involved recording the labour performed by women, has been critical in sharpening women's visibility to one another, and fomenting linkages across different 'race' groups in the country.

Another 'new frontier' in gendered poverty analysis is that of religion, with Claire Brickell's chapter on Albania (Chapter 102) pointing up the contradictions posed for women's 'empowerment' by 'external' faith-based organisations (FBDOs), specifically that of an Evangelical Christian charity, in the low-income community of Bathore on the outkirts of the capital, Tirana. While concentrating mainly on the dangers embodied in prescriptions for female empowerment infused with patriarchal religious dictates, Brickell's discussion raises the more general question about how far short-term solutions to addressing women's daily experiences of gendered poverty can go to addressing their underlying causes.

Taking up a theme covered in the context of a number of case studies earlier in the volume (for example, Evans, Lind, Moore, Williams), the chapter by Susie Jolly and Andrea Cornwall (Chapter 103) summarises more generally the increasingly recognised importance of sexuality within discussions of gender, poverty and development. This highlights, *inter alia*, the threats that sexual ill-health present to security, economic growth and human well-being, and how various forms of poverty – broadly-defined – are faced by those whose sexual preferences, practices and pleasures are marginal to dominant norms and forms.

Last but not least, Jane Parpart's closing chapter on 'Masculinity, poverty and the "new wars"' (Chapter 104) speaks to the issue of post-Cold War violence, mainly in the context of fragile sub-Saharan African states. Here conflicts, in which systematic forms of gendered violence – including sexual brutality – are frequently integral, appear to be driven substantially, if not exclusively, by economic inequalities and poverty. Young men are often readily recruited into 'new war' regiments because this is their only way of making a livelihood and garnering some kind of social recognition and stability. Although some women are also admitted into these ranks as 'foot soldiers', their lot is more usually one of abuse and disempowerment. Among one of the biggest priorities for the world at large, therefore, is that attention is paid to the gendered needs and anxieties suffered by women and men, in and out of combat, in the struggle to create a more effective and enduring 'liberal peace'.

A final word
While the chapters introduced above cover most of the main ground appropriate to a benchmark book on the subject of gender and poverty at the end of the first twenty-first century decade, all countries are undergoing new threats as a result of the global financial crisis whose historical recency precludes more than speculative thoughts about the ways that this will impact women and men in the future. On top of this, there is the contentious matter of climate change which is deeply implicated in world economic development and poverty, but until the last few years has been considered mainly from a scientific rather than a social perspective, and has left the possible gender ramifications largely uncharted (see Demetriades and Esplen, 2008). In this current – and potentially cataclysmic – global economic and environmental context, demonstrated so poignantly by the January 2010 earthquake in Haiti and the disturbing surge in sexual violence against women in its aftermath, a number of pressing questions for gender must form part of upcoming academic and policy agendas. For example, how will poor women and men cope with the costs of climate change when it is commonly thought that the poor have less 'adaptive capacity' than wealthier groups, and that although women may be worse affected and perceive and prospectively react differently to men, their often circumscribed powers of negotiation within households and communities may prevent them from exercising

defensive strategies? (ibid.; see also PEP, 2003; Tanner and Mitchell, 2008).[12] How will subsidised microcredit loans to low-income women pan out in a situation in which banks in general struggle to regain profits, as well as trust and confidence? What is to be done vis-à-vis welfare, poverty reduction and environmental protection programmes when the contraction of economic growth undermines the resources conventionally made available through tax and transfers to 'social' expenditure? What new gender dynamics are likely to present themselves in a context in which men have even greater difficulties in fulfilling normative expectations of economic provision, and in which women are likely to receive even less public support for their endeavours to manage poverty burdens within their households and communities? What space is likely to be afforded to the intersections of gender with other crucial issues such as age, sexuality, migrant status, class, and so on, when the prospective 'flattening' of economic growth is likely to plunge the world into a recession of a magnitude not witnessed for several decades, despite an incredible accumulation of wealth on the part of a few? There is already evidence of international remittance income 'drying up' as recession hits vulnerable workers on the margins of economies in the Global North, which, given the hitherto mounting role of private transfers in propping-up survival in southern countries as aid budgets have fallen, bodes ominously for poorer countries in the world.[13] These kinds of questions are not only signalled by a number of contributors to the *Handbook*, but in other contemporary writings, and, as identified earlier, by one of the biggest international feminist networks (DAWN) (see note 3). Does this historical juncture represent, as DAWN and others hope, a new – and potentially productive moment – in which to rethink the operation of global and national economic systems? To what extent does an opportunity now present itself to devise policies which build on the time-honoured attempts of academics, activists and policymakers to create a more just world order in which polarities are evened out, and women and men come to enjoy being part of a global community in which compassion, cooperation and collective responsibility supercede competition? Although many of these issues are too new to the scene to warrant definitive, or maybe even vaguely informed, predictions, this *Handbook* lays some critical foundations and a knowledge base for research and policy which I strongly hope are taken further in the second millennial decade and beyond.

Acknowledgements
I am extremely grateful to Sarah Bradshaw, Gwendolyn Beetham, Bart Casier, Alice Evans, Amy Hause, Lee Mager, Diane Perrons, Cecilia Tacoli and Carolyn Williams for their valuable comments on this chapter.

Notes
1. In the interests of scoping out this *Handbook*, I have flouted my own regulations on word length and a maximum of seven bibliographic items per chapter. These were rigidly imposed on all authors (including in relation to my own case study contribution on the 'feminisation of poverty'). In these restrained circumstances, contributors were encouraged to include in their 'select bibliographies' key sources cited in their chapters in which more fully referenced discussions could be consulted. Although my introductory bibliography here is not quite as 'select' as in the body of the volume, I have adopted a minimalist approach, and apologies are offered to those authors who with freer rein would certainly have been acknowledged. At least a good number of them will find their vital contributions to the field cited elsewhere in the *Handbook*.
2. That the level was likely to rise is extremely doubtful given the tenuous nature of the baseline. Aside from lack of robust empirical evidence, for example, Alain Marcoux (1998a, 1998b) points out that the 70 per

cent share of poverty purportedly borne by women in 1995 is implausible in light of the age distribution of the global population (even at the time of a comparatively more youthful global population), and its household characteristics. Even assuming a priori that being female places persons at a greater risk of being poor, given that the sex of children under 15 is unlikely to have more than a negligible impact on gender differentials in household poverty, only single person and lone parent units could be responsible for the excess of female poverty. Yet there are simply not enough households of this type to give rise to the purported 70/30 ratio of poor women and girls to poor men and boys (see also Klasen, 2004).
3. The Women's Working Group on Financing for Development is coordinated by the Southern-launched international feminist network Development Alternatives with Women for a New Era (DAWN). The Declaration emerging out of their second meeting in New York, held 24–26 April 2009, can be sourced on the website of the Association for Women's Rights in Development: http://www.awid.org/eng (accessed 15 July 2009).
4. See Kabeer (2003: 79ff) for an excellent discussion of different approaches to poverty analysis and measurement. Other useful sources include Chant (2007a: ch. 2), and on urban poverty specifically, Beall and Fox (2009: ch. 4).
5. Many 'shorthands' in the GAD field are discussed by Cornwall and Brock (2005) in the context of 'buzzwords'. See also Cornwall et al. (2007) on 'myths' and 'fables'.
6. I am grateful to Bart Casier for the reaffirmation, based on his extensive experience of development work with NGOs, that the reason why development projects are increasingly channelled through women is because they are deemed to be 'easier to work with' than men or youth.
7. Recent times have seen a massive increase in interest in the political and popular significance of development 'imagery', and the messages conveyed there in about people and poverty in the 'Global South'. As a prime, and up-to-the-minute example, the UNDP's Brasilia-based International Policy Centre for Inclusive Growth (IPC-IG) launched in June 2009 the 'Human Development Global Photography Campaign'. This campaign's website (http://www.ipc-undp.org/photo/), in its own words, encourages visitors and contributors to 'show development through a new lens, depicting examples of people winning the battle against poverty, social exclusion and marginalisation, rather than the usual desolation and despair we see in the media. The campaign aims at showing hope and success of development initiatives, empowering and inspiring people!'. According to a circular email sent on 20 July 2009, the website had received more than 35 000 visitors and 'hundreds of beautiful pictures' since its launch seven weeks earlier.
8. This higher rate could conceivably be a function of more women attending healthchecks, especially when pregnant. I am grateful to Sarah Bradshaw for this observation.
9. In countries of the Global North, such as the UK, where class divisions have widened among men as well as among women, it is interesting that the gender pay gap in the lowest income decile is only 5 per cent compared with 20 per cent in the top decile. This reinforces the significance of intersectionality and class divisions among women, and I am especially grateful on this point to Diane Perrons.
10. In 2008 an additional target was added to MDG1 on eradicating extreme poverty and hunger, namely to 'achieve full and productive employment and decent work for all, including women and young people'. However, since the target (along with its component indicators) is not actually monitored in a gender- (or age-) specific way, and has no timeline (see http://www.mdgmonitor.org/goal1.cfm, accessed 14 February 2010), this clearly begs the question of its potential efficacy in accomplishing purpose.
11. The UN celebrated its first year of Microcredit in 2005.
12. I am particularly grateful to Sarah Bradshaw and Cecilia Tacoli for their pointers on gender, poverty and climate change.
13. Credit is due to Gwendolyn Beetham for raising this issue.

Select bibliography

Afshar, Haleh (ed.) (2003) *Development, Women and War: Feminist Perspectives*, Oxford: Oxfam Professional.
Asian Development Bank (ADB) (2002) *Sociolegal Status of Women in Indonesia, Malaysia, Philippines, and Thailand*, Manila: ADB.
Barker, Gary, Marco Nascimento, Christine Ricardo and Marcio Segundo (2007) 'The individual and the political: PROMUNDO's evolving approaches in engaging young men in transforming masculinities', paper presented at international symposium 'Politicising Masculinities: Beyond the Personal', Dakar, Senegal, 15–18 October, available at: http://www.siyanda.org (accessed 30 January 2008).
Beall, Jo and Sean Fox (2009) *Cities and Development*, London: Routledge.
Blanc-Szanton, Cristina (1990) 'Gender and inter-generational resource allocation among Thai and Sino-Thai households', in Leela Dube and Rajni Palriwala (eds), *Structures and Strategies: Women, Work and Family*, New Delhi: Sage, pp. 79–102.

Bradshaw, Sarah (2002a) *Gendered Poverties and Power Relations: Looking Inside Communities and Households*, Managua: International Cooperation for Development/Embajada de Holanda/Puntos de Encuentro.
Bradshaw, Sarah (2002b) 'Exploring the gender dimensions of reconstruction processes post-Hurricane Mitch', *Journal of International Development*, **14**, 871–9.
Bradshaw, Sarah (2008) 'From structural adjustment to social adjustment: a gendered analysis of conditional cash transfer programmes in Mexico and Nicaragua', *Global Social Policy*, **8** (2), 188–207.
Bradshaw, Sarah and Brian Linneker (2003) *Challenging Women's Poverty: Perspectives on Gender and Poverty Reduction Strategies from Nicaragua and Honduras*, London: Catholic Institute of International Relations.
Brickell, Katherine and Sylvia Chant (2010) 'The unbearable heaviness of being: reflections on female altruism from Cambodia, Philippines, The Gambia and Costa Rica', *Progress in Development Studies*, **10** (2).
Chant, Sylvia (1997) 'Women-headed households: poorest of the poor? Perspectives from Mexico, Costa Rica and the Philippines', *IDS Bulletin*, **28** (3), 26–48.
Chant, Sylvia (2007a) *Gender, Generation and Poverty: Exploring the 'Feminisation of Poverty' in Africa, Asia and Latin America*, Cheltenham, UK and Northampton, MA, USA: Edward Elgar.
Chant, Sylvia (2007b) *Gender, Cities and the Millennium Development Goals in the Global South*, Gender Institute New Series Working Paper, Issue 21, London: London School of Economics, available at: http://www.lse.ac.uk/collections/genderInstitute/pdf/CHANT%20GIWP.pdf (accessed 15 June 2009).
Chant, Sylvia (2008) 'The "feminisation of poverty" and the "feminisation" of anti-poverty programmes: room for revision?', *Journal of Development Studies*, **44** (2), 165–97.
Clark, Fiona and Caroline Moser (eds) (2001) *Victims, Perpetrators or Actors? Gender, Armed Conflict and Political Violence*, London: Zed.
Commission on Legal Empowerment of the Poor (CLEP) (2008) *Making the Law Work for Everyone*, New York: CLEP and United Nations Development Programme, available at: http://www.undp.org/legalempowerment/report/ (accessed 24 June 2009).
Cornwall, Andrea and Karen Brock (2005) *Beyond Buzzwords. 'Poverty Reduction', 'Participation' and 'Empowerment' in Development Policy*, Overarching Concerns, Programme Paper Number 10, Geneva: United Nations Research Institute for Social Development.
Cornwall, Andrea and Maxine Molyneux (eds) (2007) *The Politics of Rights: Dilemmas for Feminist Praxis*, Routledge: London.
Cornwall, Andrea, Sonia Correa and Susie Jolly (eds) (2008a) *Development with a Body: Sexualities, Human Rights and Development*, London: Zed.
Cornwall, Andrea, Justine Gideon and Kalpana Wilson (2008b) 'Introduction. Reclaiming feminism: gender and neoliberalism', *IDS Bulletin*, **39** (6), 1–9.
Cornwall, Andrea, Elizabeth Harrison and Ann Whitehead (2007) 'Introduction: feminisms in development: contradictions, contestations and challenges', in Andrea Cornwall, Elizabeth Harrison and Ann Whitehead (eds), *Feminisms in Development: Contradictions, Contestations and Challenges*, London: Zed, pp. 1–17.
Davids, Tine and Francien van Driel (2001) 'Globalisation and gender: beyond dichotomies', in Frans J. Schuurman (ed.), *Globalisation and Development Studies: Challenges for the 21st Century*, London: Sage, pp. 153–75.
Davids, Tine and Francien van Driel (2005) 'Changing perspectives', in Tine Davids and Francien van Driel (eds), *The Gender Question in Globalisation: Changing Perspectives and Practices*, Aldershot: Ashgate, pp. 1–22.
Deere, Carmen Diana and Cheryl Doss (2006) 'The gender asset gap: what do we know and why does it matter?', *Feminist Economics*, **12** (1), pp. 1–50.
Demetriades, Justine and Emily Esplen (2008) 'The gender dimensions of poverty and climate change adaptation', *IDS Bulletin*, **39** (4), 24–31.
Economic Commission for Latin America and the Caribbean (ECLAC) (2004) *Roads Towards Gender Equity in Latin America and the Caribbean*, Santiago de Chile: ECLAC.
Enarson, Elaine and P.G. Dhar Chakrabarti (eds) (2009) *Women, Gender and Disaster: Global Issues and Initiatives*, New Delhi: Sage.
Enarson, Elaine and Betty Morrow (eds) (1998) *The Gendered Terrain of Disaster: Through Women's Eyes*, Westport, CT: Praeger.
Fernández-Kelly, María Patricia and Saskia Sassen (1995) 'Recasting women in the global economy: internationalisation and changing definitions of gender', in Christine Bose and Edna Acosta-Belén (eds), *Women in the Latin American Development Process*, Philadelphia, PA: Temple University Press, pp. 95–124.
Folbre, Nancy (1994) *Who Pays for the Kids? Gender and the Structures of Constraint*, London: Routledge.
Folbre, Nancy (2006) 'Gender, empowerment, and the care economy', *Journal of Human Development*, **7** (2), 183–99.
Fonseca, Claudia (1991) 'Spouses, siblings and sex-linked bonding: a look at kinship organisation in a Brazilian slum', in Elizabeth Jelin (ed.), *Family, Household and Gender Relations in Latin America*, London: Kegan Paul International/Paris: United Nations Economic, Scientific and Cultural Organisation, pp. 133–60.

Fukuda-Parr, Sakiko (1999) 'What does feminisation of poverty mean? It isn't just lack of income', *Feminist Economics*, **5** (2), 99–103.
Goetz, Anne-Marie and Rina Sen Gupta (1996) 'Who takes the credit? Gender, power and control over loan use in rural credit programmes in Bangladesh', *World Development*, **24** (1), 45–63.
González de la Rocha, Mercedes (2006a) *Procesos Domésticos y Vulnerabilidad: Perspectivas Antropológicas de los Hogares con Oportunidades*, Mexico City: Publicaciones de la Casa Chata.
González de la Rocha, Mercedes (2006b) 'Vanishing assets: cumulative disadvantages among the urban poor', in Patricia Fernández-Kelly and Jon Shefner (eds), *Out of the Shadows: Political Action and the Informal Economy in Latin America*, University Park, PA: Pennsylvania State University Press, pp. 97–124.
González de la Rocha, Mercedes (2007) 'The construction of the myth of survival', *Development and Change*, **38** (1), 45–66.
Grimshaw, Damian and Jill Rubery (2007) *Undervaluing Women's Work*, EOC Working Paper No. 53, Manchester: Equal Opportunities Commission.
Hart, Gillian (1995) 'Gender and household dynamics: recent theories and their implications', in Muhammad Ghulam Quibria (ed.), *Critical Issues in Asian Development*, Oxford: Oxford University Press, pp. 39–74.
Jackson, Cecile (1996) 'Rescuing gender from the poverty trap', *World Development*, **24** (3), 489–504.
Johnson, Robert (2005) 'Not a sufficient condition: the limited relevance of the gender MDG to women's progress', in Caroline Sweetman (ed.), *Gender and the Millennium Development Goals*, Oxford: Oxfam, pp. 56–66.
Johnsson-Latham, Gerd (2004) 'Understanding female and male poverty and deprivation', in Gerd Johnsson-Latham (ed.), *Power and Privileges: Gender Discrimination and Poverty*, Stockholm: Regerinskanliet, pp. 16–45.
Kabeer, Naila (1997) 'Editorial. Tactics and trade-offs: revisiting the links between gender and poverty', *IDS Bulletin*, **28** (3), 1–25.
Kabeer, Naila (2003) *Gender Mainstreaming in Poverty Eradication and the Millennium Development Goals: A Handbook for Policy-makers and Other Stakeholders*, London: Commonwealth Secretariat.
Klasen, Stephan (2004) *Gender-related Indicators of Well-Being*, Discussion Paper No. 102, Goettingen: Georg-August Universität, Ibero-Amerika Institüt für Wirtschaftsforschung, available at: http://www.iai.wiwi.uni-goettingen.de (accessed 20 January 2009).
Lampietti, Julian and Linda Stalker (2000) *Consumption Expenditure and Female Poverty: A Review of the Evidence*, Policy Research Report on Gender and Development, Working Paper Series No. 11, Washington, DC: World Bank, Development Research Group/Poverty Reduction and Economic Management Network.
Longwe, Sara Hlupekile (1995) 'A development agency as a patriarchal cooking pot: the evaporation of policies for women's advancement', in Mandy MacDonald (compiler), *Women's Rights and Development*, Oxford: Oxfam, pp. 18–29.
Marcoux, Alain (1998a) 'How much do we really know about the feminisation of poverty?', *The Brown Journal of World Affairs*, **5** (2), 187–94.
Marcoux, Alain (1998b) 'The feminisation of poverty: claims, facts and data needs', *Population and Development Review*, **24** (1), 131–9.
Mayoux, Linda (2006) *Women's Empowerment through Sustainable Micro-finance: Rethinking 'Best Practice'*, Discussion Paper, Gender and Micro-finance, available at: http://www.genfinance.net (accessed 4 July 2008).
Mazurana, Dyan, Jane Parpart and Angela Raven-Roberts (eds) (2005) *Gender, Conflict and Peacekeeping*, Boulder, CO: Rowman and Littlefield.
Medeiros, Marcelo and Joana Costa (2006) *Poverty Among Women in Latin America: Feminisation or Over-representation?*, Working Paper No. 20, Brasilia: International Poverty Centre.
Medeiros, Marcelo and Joana Costa (2008) 'Is there a feminisation of poverty in Latin America?', *World Development*, **36** (1), 115–27.
Moghadam, Valentine (1997) *The Feminisation of Poverty: Notes on a Concept and Trend*, Women's Studies Occasional Paper No. 2, Normal, IL: Illinois State University.
Molyneux, Maxine (2006) 'Mothers at the service of the New Poverty Agenda: Progresa/Oportunidades, Mexico's conditional transfer programme', *Journal of Social Policy and Administration*, **40** (4), 425–49.
Molyneux, Maxine (2007) *Change and Continuity in Social Protection in Latin America: Mothers at the Service of the State*, Gender and Development Paper 1, Geneva: United Nations Research Institute for Social Development, available at: www.unrisd.org (accessed 31 July 2008).
Molyneux, Maxine and Shahra Razavi (eds) (2002) *Gender Justice, Development and Rights*, Oxford: Oxford University Press.
Moore, Henrietta (1994) *Is There a Crisis in the Family?*, Occasional Paper No. 3, World Summit for Social Development, Geneva: United Nations Research Institute for Social Development, available at: www.unrisd.org (accessed 20 June 2009).
Moser, Caroline (1998) 'The Asset Vulnerability Framework: reassessing urban Poverty Reduction Strategies', *World Development*, **26** (1), 1–19.

Moser, Caroline (ed.) (2007) *Reducing Global Poverty: The Case for Asset Accumulation*, Washington, DC: Brookings Press.

Parpart, Jane and Marysia Zalewski (2008) *Rethinking the Man Question: Sex, Gender and Violence in International Relations*, London: Zed.

Pearce, Diana (1978) 'The feminisation of poverty: women, work and welfare', *The Urban and Social Change Review*, **11**, 23–36.

Perrons, Diane (2004) *Globalisation and Social Change: People and Places in a Divided World*, London: Routledge.

Piper, Nicola and Mina Roces (eds) (2002) *Wife or Worker? Asian Women and Migration*, Boulder, CO: Rowbotham and Littlefield.

Poverty-Environment Partnership (PEP) (2003) *Poverty and Climate Change: Reducing the Vulnerability of the Poor through Adaptation*, New York: PEP, available at: http://www.energyandenvironment.undp.org/undp/index.cfm?module=Library&page=Document&DocumentID=5050 (accessed 5 August 2009).

Quisumbing, Agnes and Bonnie McClafferty (2006) *Using Gender Research in Development*, Washington, DC: International Food Policy Research Institute.

Razavi, Shahra (ed.) (2009) *The Gendered Impacts of Liberalisation: Towards 'Embedded Liberalism'?*, Geneva: United Nations Research Institute for Social Development.

Razavi, Shahra and Shireen Hassim (eds) (2006) *Gender and Social Policy in a Global Context: Uncovering the Global Structures of 'The Social'*, Geneva: United Nations Research Institute for Social Development.

Rodenberg, Birte (2004) *Gender and Poverty Reduction: New Conceptual Approaches in International Development Cooperation*, Reports and Working Papers 4/2004, Bonn: German Development Institute.

Roy, Ananya (2002) *Against the Feminisation of Policy*, Comparative Urban Studies Project Policy Brief, Washington, DC: Woodrow Wilson International Center for Scholars.

Ruxton, Sandy (2009) *Man Made: Men, Masculinities and Equality in Public Policy*, London: The Coalition for Men and Boys.

Sen, Gita (1999) 'Engendering poverty alleviation: challenges and opportunities', *Development and Change*, **30** (3), 685–92.

Sen, Gita (2008) 'Poverty as a gendered experience: the policy implications', *Poverty in Focus*, **13**, 6–7, available at: http://www.undp-povertycentre.org/pub/IPCPovertyInFocus13.pdf (accessed 15 January 2009).

Sweetman, Caroline (2005) 'Editorial', in Caroline Sweetman (ed.), *Gender and the Millennium Development Goals*, Oxford: Oxfam, pp. 2–8.

Tanner, Thomas and Tom Mitchell (2008) 'Introduction: building the case for pro-poor adaptation', *IDS Bulletin*, **39** (4), 1–5.

Tronto, Joan (2002) 'The "nanny" question in feminism', *Hypatia*, **17** (2), 34–51.

United Nations (UN) Country Team/United Nations Fund for Women (UNIFEM) (2003) *To Produce and to Care: How do Women and Men Fare in Securing Well-being and Human Freedoms?*, Manila: UN Country Team/UNIFEM.

United Nations Department for Economic and Social Affairs (UN-DESA)/United Nations Division for the Advancement of Women (UNDAW) (2009) *World Survey on the Role of Women in Development 2009: Women's Control over Economic Resources and Access to Financial Resources, Including Microfinance*, New York: UN-DESA/UNDAW.

United Nations Development Programme (UNDP) (2000) *Overcoming Human Poverty: UNDP Poverty Report 2000*, New York: UNDP, available at: http://www.undp.org/povertyreport/Chapters/chap9.html (accessed 8 July 2009).

United Nations Millennium Project (UNMP)/Task Force on Education and Gender Equality (TFEGE) (2005) *Taking Action: Achieving Gender Equality and Empowering Women*, London: Earthscan, available at: http://www.unmillenniumproject.org/documents/gender (accessed 16 June 2009).

Varley, Ann (1996) 'Women-headed households: some more equal than others?', *World Development*, **24** (3), 505–20.

Vera-Sanso, Penny (2006) 'Experiences in old age: a South Indian example of how functional age is socially structured', *Oxford Development Studies*, **34** (4), 457–72.

Vylder, Stefan de (2004) 'Gender in poverty reduction strategies', in Gerd Johnsson-Latham (ed.), *Power and Privileges: Gender Discrimination and Poverty*, Stockholm: Regerinskanliet, pp. 82–107.

Wennerholm, Carolina Johansson (2002) *The 'Feminisation of Poverty': The Use of a Concept*, Stockholm: Swedish International Development Cooperation Agency.

Whitehead, Ann and Matthew Lockwood (1999) 'Gendering poverty: a review of six World Bank African Poverty Assessments', *Development and Change*, **30** (3), 525–55.

Williams, Chris and Diana Lee-Smith (2000) 'Feminisation of poverty: re-thinking poverty reduction from a gender perspective', *Habitat Debate*, **6** (4), 1–5, available at: http://www.unhabitat.org/HD (accessed 24 July 2008).

PART I

CONCEPTS AND METHODOLOGIES FOR GENDERED POVERTY

2 Strategic gendering: one factor in the constituting of novel political economies
Saskia Sassen

Microlevel social, economic and political conditions have complex interactions with particular macrolevel economic restructuring processes. The interactions focused on here are not generalised and diffuse but partial and particular. For instance, labour migrations are not simply about the survival strategies of migrants and their households. They are also microlevel enactments of larger processes of economic restructuring in sending and receiving countries. These include International Monetary Fund (IMF) and World Bank programmes that have devastated traditional economies in the Global South and forced states to shift growing shares of revenue into debt servicing. And they include the growing demand for a wide range of very low-wage jobs in some of the most advanced, rather than declining or backward, economic sectors in highly developed countries.

The effort here is to lay bare the specific ways in which gendering becomes strategic for the emergence and for the functioning of major restructuring processes and the partial economies that get constituted in this interaction. By 'strategic gendering' I seek to capture not simply the outcomes of gendering, but those processes where gendering is constitutive, where the fact itself of gendering is an enabling condition for particular processes of restructuring. One outcome, albeit partial, is the feminising of survival, not only for households, but also for firms and for governments (Sassen, 2001).

I first examine how strategic gendering has been at work in the constituting of earlier political economies, and next, how it is at work in the current period, one marked by powerful global regulators and vast technical systems.

Strategic gendering in the global division of labour
There is, by now, a fairly long-standing research and theorisation effort engaged in uncovering the role of women in international economic processes.[1] The central effort in the earlier research literature was to balance the almost exclusive and mostly implicit focus on men in international economic development research. In the mainstream development literature, these processes have often, perhaps unwittingly, been represented as neutral when it comes to gender. We can identify at least two phases in the study of gendering in the recent history of economic internationalisation – all processes that continue today.

A first phase focused especially on the implantation, typically by foreign firms, of cash crops and wage labour, in general. The critical analytical variable introduced by feminist scholars was the partial dependence of commercial agriculture on women subsidising the waged labour of men through their household production and subsistence farming. Far from being unconnected, the subsistence sector and the modern capitalist enterprise were shown to be articulated through a gender dynamic; this gender dynamic, in turn, veiled this articulation. It was the 'invisible' work of women producing food and other necessities in the subsistence economy that contributed to maintaining extremely low wages on commercial plantations and mines producing for export. Women in the so-called subsistence sector thereby contributed to the financing of the 'modernised' sector through their largely unmonetised subsistence production. This contrasted sharply with the standard development literature, which represented the subsistence sector as a drain on the modern sector and as an indicator of backwardness. It was not measured in standard economic analyses.

A second phase was the scholarship on the internationalisation of manufacturing production that took off in the 1970s and the feminisation of the proletariat in the developing countries that came with it. The key analytic element in this scholarship was that off-shoring manufacturing jobs from developed economies under pressure of low-cost imports generated a disproportionately female workforce in the poorer countries where those jobs moved. These women had hitherto largely remained outside the industrial economy. In this regard, it is an analysis that also intersected with national issues, such as why women predominate in certain industries, notably, garment and electronics assembly, no matter what the level of development of a country (see also Chari, Chapter 68, this volume; Pearson, Chapter 64, this volume). From the perspective of the world economy, the formation of a feminised offshore proletariat helped firms in the developed countries in their efforts to weaken what had become increasingly strong unions and it helped firms secure competitive prices for the re-imported goods assembled offshore.

Thus, the strategic sites where the international division of labour can be studied from a feminist perspective in these earlier literatures varied across different components of the economy. In the case of export-oriented agriculture, this strategic site is the nexus between subsistence economies and capitalist enterprise, where the former actually subsidise and partly enable the latter. In the case of the internationalisation of manufacturing production, it is the nexus between the dismantling of an established, largely male 'labour aristocracy' in major industries whose gains spread to a large share of the workforce in developed economies, on one hand, and the formation of a low-wage, offshore, largely female proletariat in new and old growth sectors, on the other. Off-shoring and feminising this proletariat has kept it from becoming an empowered workforce, including actual union power, and prevented existing, largely male unionised workforces from becoming stronger. Introducing a gendered understanding of economic processes lays bare these connections – the existence of a gender nexus as an operational reality and an analytic category.

But what about the strategic sites for gendering in today's leading processes of globalisation? In part, at least, a long-standing history of gendering remains a critical variable insofar as both the expansion of commercial export-oriented agriculture and the off-shoring of jobs to low-wage countries continue today. They do so often with new contents and through new economic geographies. Examples are the proliferation of outsourcing activities and China's massive expansion of offshore manufacturing regions since the 1990s. In many, although not all, ways, these developments are predicated on dynamics identified and theorised in that earlier literature. One type of scholarship that uncovers the specifics of the current global phase focuses on transformations in women's subjectivities and in women's notions of community of membership. As did the older development literature, today's literature on economic globalisation tends to assume gender-neutrality. And it tends to proceed as if questions of subjectivity somehow were not part of the diverse workforces involved. Among other publications, a special issue on 'Feminism and Globalisation: The Impact of the Global Economy on Women and Feminist Theory' of the *Indiana Journal of Global Legal Studies* (1996) addresses the effects of economic globalisation on the partial unbundling of sovereignty and what this means for the emergence of cross-border feminist agendas, the place of women and of feminist consciousness in the new Asian mode of implementing advanced global capitalism, and the global spread of a set of core human rights and its power to alter how women themselves understand their position in various potential communities of membership (Nash, 2005; Ong, 1999). Among the richest literatures, and most pertinent to the issues discussed in this chapter, is a feminist scholarship specifically focused on female immigrants, including research on how international migration alters gender patterns and how the formation of transnational households can empower women (Hondagneu-Sotelo, 2003).

Far more specific is the question of strategic gendering in today's leading global economic sectors. Research on the particular instances where gendering is actually strategic for such sectors is still rare (Ehrenreich and Hochschild, 2003). I turn to this next.

Strategic gendering in today's global economy

The cross-border circuits examined in this article are instances in which the role of women, and especially the condition of being a migrant woman, emerges as crucial to the formation of novel economic arrangements, notably, particular components of global cities and of the alternative political economies posited in the preceding section.

The feminising of survival: the formation of an alternative political economy
A mix of major global trends in many of the struggling underdeveloped economies is predicated on strategic gendering as a critical factor. This becomes visible in some of the component trends, notably the formation of alternative survival circuits for individuals, firms and governments on the backs of mostly poor and undervalued women. Thus trafficking in women is not only about traffickers and their victims. It has multiple insertions, from microlevels to macrolevels, in key components of these restructured economies. There is the well-known fact of household survival. Further, trafficking in women for the sex industry feeds into the larger political economy by generating 'entrepreneurial' opportunities for small and large traffickers, and from there on to a whole range of components of the larger tourism industry and various consumer services. Finally, such trafficking feeds government revenues, especially significant when IMF and World Bank adjustment programmes force much government revenue into interest payments to the international system. More generally, immigrants' remittances are a significant source of foreign exchange for several poor countries.

The growing immiseration of governments and whole economies in the Global South has promoted and enabled the proliferation of survival and profit-making activities that involve the migration and trafficking of people. To some extent, these are older processes, which used to be national or regional and today can operate on global scales. The same infrastructure that facilitates cross-border flows of capital, information, and trade is also making possible a whole range of cross-border flows not intended by the framers and designers of the current corporate globalisation of economies. Growing numbers of traffickers and smugglers are making money off the backs of men, women, and children, and

32 *The international handbook of gender and poverty*

many governments are increasingly dependent on their remittances. A key aspect here is that through their work and remittances, migrants enhance the government revenue of deeply indebted countries. The need for traffickers to help in the migration effort also offers new profit-making possibilities to large and small 'entrepreneurs' (besides criminal syndicates) who have seen other opportunities vanish as global firms and markets enter their countries, and to long-time criminals who can now operate their illegal trade globally. These survival circuits are often complex, involving multiple locations and types of actors, and constituting increasingly global chains of traders, traffickers and workers.

One question of concern here is whether there are systemic links between the growing presence of women from developing economies in a variety of global migration and trafficking circuits, on one hand, and the rise in unemployment and debt in those same economies, on the other. There is a large body of data on each of these two major processes, but it does not necessarily address and develop the connection between them. More substantively, we can posit that the following combination of conditions in poor countries has contributed to raising the importance of alternative ways of making a living, making a profit, and securing government revenue: first, the shrinking opportunities for male employment; second. the shrinking opportunities for more traditional forms of profit-making as these countries increasingly accept foreign firms in a widening range of economic sectors and are pressured to develop export industries, and third, the fall in government revenues, partly linked to the first two conditions and to the burden of debt servicing. In many ways, these three conditions are not new. What is different today is their rapid internationalisation and considerable institutionalisation. The evidence for any of these conditions is incomplete and partial, yet there is a growing consensus among experts about their importance in the expansion of alternative survival strategies for households, enterprises, and governments.

I go further and argue that these three conditions are contributing to an alternative political economy (Sassen, 2001), one arising partly from Global North interventions in poor countries and eventually extending back into those same Global North countries but through different circuits (notably, trafficking of women) from those of the earlier interventions. Women from developing or struggling economies play an increasingly important role in the possibility of constituting this alternative political economy, even when this is often not self-evident or visible. This lack of visibility has long marked much of the difficulty in understanding the role of women in development, generally, and it continues today, as I discussed in the preceding section.

Strategic gendering in the global city
Strategic gendering in the global city occurs through both the sphere of production and that of social reproduction (Sassen, 2001). The macrolevel context is the fact that these cities are a crucial infrastructure for the specialised servicing, financing, and management of global economic processes. Everything in this infrastructure needs to function well, including the households of the professional workforce. Gendering becomes strategic in the production sphere because women excel at cultural brokering, at building trust across sharp cultural boundaries and differences (Hindman, 2007). Cultural brokering has emerged as critical because globalising firms and markets continually enter new environments at home and abroad, each with its own specificities.

The critical background variable is that these cities are a crucial infrastructure for the specialised servicing, financing, and management of global economic processes. It means that all key components of this infrastructure need to function like clockwork. The globalising of a firm's or a market's operations entails opening up domains (sectors, countries, the world of consumers) to new kinds of businesses, practices, and norms. This kind of cultural brokering is critical, especially given the mistrust and the resistances that had to be overcome to implement economic globalisation.

Gendering is also strategic for the social reproduction of the high-level professional workforce. There are two reasons for this. One is the growing demand for female professionals and the other is the strong preference among both male and female professionals for living in the city, given long work hours and very demanding responsibilities at work. The result is a proliferation in cities of what I like to refer to as 'the professional household without a "wife"'. What matters here is the *absent* historical-cultural subject of the 'wife' – more precisely, the mix of functions this subject represents. This mix of functions is a critical factor precisely at a time when professional households are crucial to the infrastructure for globalised sectors and need to function like clockwork in a context where 'feeling good and at top of one's form' more often than not includes traditional notions of family life, with children, pets, plants, dinner-at-home included. The demands placed on the top-level professional and managerial workforce in global cities are such that the usual modes of handling household tasks and lifestyle cannot work.

Most of the research on this issue has focused on the return of the serving classes and on the poor working conditions, exploitation and multiple vulnerabilities of these household workers (see Perrons, Chapter 62, this volume). This is a fact. But, analytically, what matters here is the strategic importance of well-functioning professional households for the leading globalised sectors in these cities and, hence, the importance of this new type of serving class. These households have to function like clockwork because the professionals have to function like clockwork. But this takes place precisely at a time marked by the disappearing subject that is the 'wife' in these urbanised professional households – regardless of their demographics: two men, two women, man and woman. The disappearing 'wife' in the urbanised professional household given long work hours and very demanding responsibilities at work becomes potentially a crisis, not just for the household, but for the advanced economic system.

I posit that these households should be reconceptualised as part of the strategic 'infrastructure' of global cities and that the low-wage domestic workers are in fact strategic infrastructure-maintenance workers. In this setting, domestic workers are part of a larger (uncodified) maintenance function of strategic infrastructures for the advanced economic sectors. Thus the social systems represented by these households cannot be understood fully in terms of patriarchy, though that is clearly one dynamic – where the professionals, whether men or women, function as a male subject. Nor can this household be explained simply in terms of the return of the serving classes or the poor working conditions, exploitation and multiple vulnerabilities of these household workers. All three approaches get at critical facts about these households. But, analytically, they do not help in capturing the strategic importance of well-functioning professional households for the leading globalised sectors in global cities, and hence my positing that these household workers are actually maintaining a strategic infrastructure – their workplace is the global corporate economy – and should be valued correspondingly.

For a variety of reasons, immigrant and minoritised women are a favoured source for this type of work. Theirs is a mode of economic incorporation that makes their crucial role invisible; being immigrant or minoritised citizens facilitates breaking the nexus between being workers with an important function in the global information economy, that is, in leading industries, and the opportunity to become an empowered workforce, as has historically been the case in industrialised economies. In this sense, the category 'immigrant women' emerges as the systemic equivalent of the offshore proletariat.

Note
1. It is impossible to include the enormous literature on gendering that allows me to develop this argument. I have discussed this scholarship and the data sources elsewhere (Sassen, 2008).

Select bibliography
Ehrenreich, Barbara and Arlie Hochschild (2003) *Global Woman: Nannies, Maids, and Sex Workers in the New Economy*, New York: Metropolitan.
Hindman, Heather (2007) 'Outsourcing difference: expatriate training and the disciplining of culture', in Saskia Sassen (ed.), *Deciphering the Global: Its Scales, Spaces and Subjects*, New York: Routledge, pp. 153–76.
Hondagneu-Sotelo, Pierrette (ed.) (2003) *Gender and US Immigration: Contemporary Trends*, Los Angeles, CA: University of California Press.
Nash, June (2005) *Social Movements: An Anthropological Reader*, Malden, MA: Blackwell.
Ong, Aihwa (1999) *Flexible Citizenship: The Cultural Logics of Transnationality*, Durham, NC: Duke University Press.
Sassen, Saskia (2001) 'Women's burden: counter-geographies of globalisation and the feminisation of survival', *Journal of International Affairs*, **53** (2), 503–25.
Sassen, Saskia (2008) 'Two stops in today's new global geographies: shaping novel labour supplies and employment regimes', *American Behavioral Scientist*, **52**, 457–96.

3 Subjectivity, sexuality and social inequalities
Henrietta L. Moore

Relationships between poverty and gender are complex. Poverty reduction programmes do not necessarily improve well-being or gender equity. Approaches designed to raise women's incomes, arguing that they are often primarily responsible for maintaining households, have led in some instances to increased vulnerability for women who inhabit multiplex relationships embedded in long-run distributions of power, access and resources. What seems more certain is that changes in income, resources and bargaining strength intersect with new configurations of gendered identities. Research from both Africa and South Asia emphasises the impact of changing ideals of selfhood, masculinity, femininity and morality for individuals struggling to thrive in circumstances of want.

Definitions of poverty have moved away from earlier models based on deficit towards multidimensional models that recognise the shifting character of poverty through historical time and incorporate the views of poor people themselves (see Jackson, Chapter 5, this volume). Recent work on gender and poverty has thus explored notions of agency, voice and empowerment, while acknowledging that such analyses are frequently set in the context of conceptual and policy frameworks that tie women ever more inexorably to the intransigencies of their material, social and political circumstances. Hence the now well-documented transformation of the feminisation of poverty into its other gendered manifestations: the feminisation of survival (Sassen, 2002), policy (Roy, 2002), and responsibility and obligation (Chant, Chapter 15, this volume). Critics of mainstream conceptual frameworks and associated policy initiatives have consistently pointed out that gender disadvantages are part of an overall bundle of interests, and have to be set in complex dynamic interrelations incorporating desired outcomes, notions of well-being and situated capacities and functionings. However, much of this work still looks both to intra-household allocation and to gender relations set within conventional kinship models as the self-evident fulcrums of research and policy providing an unintended congruence between the household as the site of measurement and marital relations as the 'naturalised' site of gender relations. This may appear a surprising claim given the intertwined origins of the feminisation of poverty and debates on female-headed households, but some recent research has drawn attention to the importance of a broader matrix of changing ideals of masculinity and femininity, and processes of subjectification for analysing intersections between constraints, vulnerabilities and aspirations (see Davids and van Driel, Chapter 14, this volume; Williams, Chapter 28, this volume). The result is a potentially productive shift in theoretical perspectives and conceptual frameworks relating to well-being, power and gender.

Well-being and social relationships
Poverty has been extensively studied, but research data on well-being, happiness and life satisfaction in contexts of chronic economic poverty have yet to receive the same level of analytic attention (see Hunt, Chapter 36, this volume; Pineda, Chapter 74, this volume).

Research on Bangladesh, one of the poorest countries in the world, shows that while the very poor do indeed define their well-being around basic subsistence needs, including food intake, income adequacy, housing and health, levels of happiness and life satisfaction are crucially related to the character and quality of social relationships (Camfield et al., 2009). As might be expected, the researchers found that the perception that one's own socio-economic status was equal to or better than others in the community was a significant source of happiness and satisfaction. While the respondents focused on income and the fulfilment of basic needs, having a good socio-economic status demonstrated not only personal capacities, but household strength understood as the perceived association between income and a household's reputation: the ability to look after the household, to satisfy needs, being an important source of a good reputation. Older men considered the ability to meet their own needs and those of their family as a life achievement in itself. Older women linked economic success to their own security, and the success of their sons, on whom many were dependent in old age, to the fact that they had brought their sons up well. Younger men associated income as evidence of personal success and capacity, while younger women saw household income as related to having a good husband who could provide for the family's needs (Camfield et al., 2009: 81–2).

In Bangladesh, people are perceived as constituted through interpersonal, intergenerational and intergroup relationships. Personal satisfactions are thus consistently linked to providing for 'us', to realising one's capacities and fulfilling one's social roles within a matrix of shifting and negotiated relationships. The material and emotional benefits of cooperation and of mutual assistance in times of need were singled out by respondents as significant. Participation and consultation in decision-making were identified as an important indicator of a happy marriage, and young women reported feeling proud when they were respected by their marital families. The quality of the relationships with their wives was also important to both older and younger men. Children in Bangladesh, as elsewhere, are a source of happiness, both in themselves, and through the evidence they provide of parental capacity. Ensuring children have a good upbringing, are educated and successful in life is a vital aspect of the reputation of individual parents and the household as a whole (Camfield et al., 2009: 83–4).

Relationships may be sources of satisfaction and happiness, but they are also constituted through relays of power and inequality, and are important mechanisms for acquiring goods, resources and material benefits. However, as Camfield et al. (2009) have pointed out, intangible and symbolic goods, such as respect, influence and authority are equally important. Such intangible benefits often link households and individual household members to the wider community. Good relationships between household members are seen as evidence of influence and leadership which can be applied potentially in other contexts. The desire to be respected and/or influential beyond the immediate arc of the family and the household, being able to help community members in need and to fulfil religious duties are all important aspects of self and of satisfaction in life (ibid.: 85–6; see also Nyanzi, Chapter 31 this volume).

Gender discourses and gendered subjectivities
It is well recognised that gender discourses are very often about ideals, the proper wife, the dutiful daughter, the perfect partner – and that despite their satisfactions much of the misery relationships engender come from the disparities between these ideals and the

lived reality of life. Well-being and happiness connect not just to the realisation of these ideals, but to a broader sense of doing good, of doing as well as one can, of making a life and making a living in the broadest sense. In this context, ideals of masculinity and femininity and the way they play out in practice always link to notions of the moral self. The term moral here simply refers to an idea of a self that not only acts in ways that are seen as good by others, but is one that realises its purpose and achieves its proper mode of being through striving. Evaluations such as 'he is a good man' engage with morality. All societies have multiple conceptions of moral selfhood, and individuals are frequently engaged in negotiating or managing or enduring the contradictions between them. Among the most salient of these contradictions, but one which is always imagined and experienced in specific historical and cultural inflections, is that between a vision of the moral self constituted in and through social relations and larger spiritual concerns, and the notion of a self understood as properly autonomous and connected to the way specific individuals realise their lives, make choices and act in the circumstances in which they find themselves. These aspects of self should not be imagined as dichotomous nor binary, nor even as separate models, because in most circumstances they are intertwined, since relationships are the means through which autonomy is achieved. Relationships determine how individuals will realise who they are, what they may become and what they will achieve (capabilities and functionings), but they are also the dynamic matrices through which individuals realise values, choices and actions (Camfield et al., 2009: 87–8). What is often missing in accounts of the interrelations between gender and poverty is a theory of gendered subjectivities, of the way people imagine and experience the nature and value of the embodied, gendered self, and of how they orient themselves within a set of relationships that practically and ethically define a complex moral terrain. Specific cultural and historical understandings of the gendered self emerge out of – rather than determine or create – the mechanisms and processes through which individuals reflect on and try to make sense of the challenging and contradictory worlds they inhabit. The gendered self can only be realised in relationships with others, but part of it is also the product of an internal relation to self. Subjectivity is thus about the thoughts, desires, fears, emotions and perceptions experienced by each individual and how they are inserted into, or lived through, the cultural, social, political and economic discourses and formations that configure and effect those modes of thought, aspiration, desire and so on. Reflexivity and human meaning-making ensure gendered subjectivities always have certain historical and cultural shapes, but ones that are animated by the possibility of failure.

Recent work on gendered subjectivities has emphasised that the sites of subjectification in contemporary societies are heterogeneous – the family, school, the workplace, the market, government interventions, health policies, civil society organisations and citizenship programmes, for example – and that gendered identities are not stable, unitary and coherent, but engage with multiple subject positions many of which may be conflicting and contradictory. New possibilities for identifications open up – new frameworks for moral and social order, such as the market and neoliberal reforms – and gendered subjectivities are shaped not only within the family, but through larger-scale processes of economic and political transformation that both undermine and shore up existing cultural understandings (Moore, 2007: Chapter 7). Accession to dominant models of masculinity and femininity is partial, unstable and contradictory, and neither men nor women fully take up dominant gender models (see Moore, 1994: ch. 4; also Brydon, Chapter 16, this volume). In contemporary contexts of social transformation and deepening social, political and economic inequality, cultural explanations for gender roles, subjectivities and practices will have limited explanatory reach if they assume monolithic or unitary gender models. Similarly, analytic approaches which look only to gendered relations within households – and understandings of masculinity and femininity based by default on marital relations – will occlude broader shifts in the transformation of gendered subjectivities (Moore, 1994: ch. 5).

Sexual networks and ties of interdependence
Research on South Africa has emphasised the importance of analysing HIV prevalence rates by combining ethnographic, historical and demographic approaches to gender relations, and focusing on transformations in sexuality and gender relations in the context of a broader political economy of sex, including the post-apartheid government's adoption of neoliberal policies (Hunter, 2006; see also Campbell and Gibbs, Chapter 50, this volume). Recognising the shifting intersections and locations historically of 'race', class, gender and sexuality offers a fresh perspective on constraints, vulnerabilities and aspirations for women and men over time and place. A focus on the political economy of sex reveals that rising unemployment, rapidly declining marital rates and a growth in women's (circular) migration have led not only to rising social inequalities, but to a sexualisation of gender relations, that is to increasing recourse to multiple sexual partners as a mechanism for the redistribution of formal and informal earnings, and other resources (see also Evans, Chapter 30, this volume). The resulting sexual networks are not simply instrumental exchanges of sex for money, but provide frameworks for claims about love, pleasure, identity and care. These networks operate, as the research makes clear, alongside, and not in opposition to, social networks based on kinship, friends, and churches.

Research on sexual networks in rural Malawi emphasises that while transactional sex is widespread and women are indeed often poorer than men, understanding what motivates and sustains particular patterns of gendered behaviour requires a shift in analytic frameworks. Two anomalies require explanation: why women from wealthier groups engage in transactional sex; and why very poor men are willing to pay to collect multiple partners. It is certainly the case that in many contexts in Africa economic exchange has historically been integral to a wide range of sexual relationships, including marriage. If we turn away from the transactions themselves, as Swidler and Watkins (2007) suggest, towards what motivates women and men to engage in concurrent partnerships, then a broader range of analytic explanations become relevant. While men with money can afford more partners, the researchers record that Malawians frequently make a rather different sort of statement, saying of a man with money that 'the money was forcing him to have many partners' (ibid.: 6). This statement makes sense if we see transactional sex as part of a larger system of patron–client relations, ties of asymmetrical interdependence which operate not only at the level of the household, but through broader kinship networks and into civil society organisations and the state, being modern extensions and transformations of older 'wealth in people systems' (see Smith, Chapter 44, this volume). In contemporary African contexts, politics and intimate sexual relations are spoken of using the conjoined metaphor of 'eating'. When particular groups are in power, their followers are spoken of as 'having eaten'. Food and sex serve not only as metaphors for sex and politics, but for power more generally, corruption, violence, extraction and witchcraft, for the potential of all forms of relations to go awry. This powerful composite metaphor connects to the interwoven links between ties of interdependence and the flow of resources which move back and forth along them. Clients need access to resources and patrons need followers to demonstrate their power and prestige. Ties of interdependence can be seen at all levels of African societies, and they provide both opportunities for upward mobility, as well as security in times of trouble when downward mobility is threatened or actual (Swidler and Watkins, 2007: 7). These relationships are infused with power, but contrary to many of the assumptions inherent in poverty eradication policies and theories, it is their rootedness in social inequalities that provides their dynamism. They are also fundamentally redistributive. As the researchers insist, redistribution is not only strategic and instrumental, but is also perceived by local actors as quintessentially moral. Moral obligations are the core of asymmetrical ties of interdependence – such practices as hoarding or failure to help those in need are seen as profoundly anti-social, and may invoke social sanctions, including accusations of witchcraft – and they fan out well beyond the household into broad networks of social relationships which may even intersect with and incorporate aspects of state power.

It is not difficult to understand that a man with resources is obliged to redistribute them, but one might wonder why this has to take place through sexual relationships? We might start from the recognition that multiple conceptions of moral selfhood are at play in these contexts. Even for those with concurrent partners, fidelity continues to be seen as a desirable goal by those involved. Many justifications for having multiple partners are advanced, from economic need to sexual lust and revenge, and some of these justifications gain purchase by referring to or being embedded within other valorised notions of the self, such as the potent male as protector of women or the obedient wife. However, sexual ties of interdependence should be more broadly conceived as an extension of the rights to make claims in contexts where ties of intimacy and care are legitimately connected to demands for material support. The fact that sexual ties are a way of managing future uncertainty, part of the fabric of the social safety net, may explain why they are so multiple and overlapping, as the researchers suggest. Both women and men try not only to secure a 'main' partner, but a series of back-ups, or 'spare tyres' as they are known in the Malawian context, in case things go wrong or the fortunes of the main partner take a downward turn. Multiple sexual partners may be connected to women's economic needs, but where uncertainty is chronic and where personal ties are the major bulwark against future uncertainties, people will need to have those ties in place and in reserve even if they do not immediately need what they can offer. This is why small gifts – 'symbolic luxuries', rather than necessities – can be enough to secure a woman's sexual favours. The issue is not just the immediacy of want or economic need, but the potential threat of unexpected crisis, the fear of unforeseen shortages, the impact of unplanned risk. Such uncertainty and vulnerability is not only about economic poverty, but the awful prospect of the loss of such things as social status, family reputation, personal autonomy and self-esteem (Swidler and Watkins, 2007: 17).

Concluding thoughts
In social systems where differences of power and resources provide the motivation for social connectedness, as well as the dynamic potential for the flexibility and pervasiveness of social relations, gender is one of the major axes of social inequality. The

intersections between gender and poverty have to be analytically and empirically situated within the broader terrain of changing ideals about masculinity and femininity, but also simultaneously connected to theories of gendered subjectification which account for how social and economic inequalities engage with notions of the moral self and its relations to others. This opens up an alternative space for analysing the interrelations and overdeterminations between constraints, vulnerabilities and aspirations as they are imagined and experienced by gendered individuals in specific historical locations.

Select bibliography

Camfield, Laura, Kaneta Choudhury and Jo Devine (2009) 'Well-being, happiness and why relationships matter: evidence from Bangladesh', *Journal of Happiness Studies*, **10**, 71–91.

Hunter, Mark (2006) 'The changing political economy of sex in South Africa: the significance of unemployment and inequalities to the scale of the AIDS pandemic', *Social Science and Medicine*, **64** (3), 689–700.

Moore, Henrietta L. (1994) *A Passion for Difference*, Cambridge: Polity Press.

Moore, Henrietta L. (2007) *The Subject of Anthropology*, Cambridge: Polity Press.

Roy, Ananya (2002) *Against the Feminisation of Policy*, Comparative Urban Studies Project Policy Brief, Washington, DC: Woodrow Wilson International Center for Scholars.

Sassen, Saskia (2002) 'Counter-geographies of globalisation: feminisation of survival', in Kreimild Saunders (ed.), *Feminist Post-Development Thought*, London: Zed, pp. 89–104.

Swidler, Ann and Susan Cotts Watkins (2007) *Ties of Dependence: Aids and Transactional Sex in Rural Malawi*, Los Angeles: California Center for Population Research On-Line Working Paper Series, CCPR-2007-025, available at: http://repositories.cdlib.org/cgi/viewcontent.cgi?article=1306&context=ccpr (accessed 10 June 2009).

4 Power, privilege and gender as reflected in poverty analysis and development goals
Gerd Johnsson-Latham

This chapter focuses on how gender-based power and privileges influence perceptions of what 'development' means, which in turn is a determinant for defining both 'poverty' and ways of measuring and addressing it. The chapter builds on studies and on my own experiences as gender adviser within the Swedish Ministry for Foreign Affairs in regard to development cooperation. I discuss links between power, privilege and gender, and reflect on two separate schools of thought. The first is the dominant poverty discourse, focusing on economic growth and quantitative measurements. The second is gender and development (GAD), which contrary to the dominant discourse exposes structural, asymmetrical power relations between the sexes, and does *not* regard economic growth as a prerequisite for improving women's living conditions. Instead, GAD highlights legal and social barriers, which relate to power structures. Basing my reflections on these two schools of thought, I examine the extent to which the centrepiece in poverty reduction strategies in terms of the Millennium Development Goals (MDGs), notably the third sub-goal, addresses female deprivation and disempowerment.[1] It notes that a global, political consensus on the MDGs at the United Nations (UN) General Assembly in 2000 was attained only at the cost of removing key aspects of women's rights from the MDG package. The chapter concludes by discussing how GAD and exposure of power, privilege and gender can influence the present dominant agenda and make better provision for non-discriminatory development and human well-being by addressing the dilemma of current male bias in many development undertakings.

Power, privilege and gender
While photographs illustrating poverty often feature women, the analysis, strategies and resources aimed at eradicating poverty tend to focus on men (see Wilson, Chapter 46, this volume). From the very start of life in many contexts, power, male privilege and perceptions of gender-specific entitlements result in girls and boys being assigned different sets of rights and privileges. Gender relations assign authority, agency and decision-making power (Kabeer, 2003: 193). Thus, males tend not only to obtain more material resources in terms of food, healthcare and so forth, compared with their sisters, but also to have non-material advantages such as the 'right' to play and have fun. These are key factors in developing boys' self-confidence and perception of having superior 'rights' vis-à-vis females. Gender-based discrimination is expressed from discrimination *de jure* through law texts to stereotypes, norms and codes which *de facto* limit the individual's freedom and distribute resources asymmetrically.

Gender is literally a man-made construction, generally apportioning more power and advantages to men, above all *certain* men. The fact that women all over the world perform most work in the home, without pay, for example, is neither biologically self-evident nor based on physical sexual attributes, but the result of a gender-based distribution of power. The 'reproductive' role assigned to women has decisive consequences in terms of their dependence, power, long working hours for little pay, financial insecurity, and so on, in relation to men, in the family, in the group/clan and in society as a whole.

Men as a group have been able to use their privileged access to resources both in the household and in the public domain to both defend and promote their own interests, often at the expense of women (Kabeer, 2003: xiv). Thus, while attention is often paid to the deprivation of women, a fruitful course might be to look instead at how the gender-based division of labour and rights entails *privileges* for males, in terms of access to resources, sexual rights, greater mobility, influence and voice, agenda-setting and leisure time, and also in terms of the oft-perceived 'right' to use violence against women. This approach would show how male privileges are the problem rather than the shortcomings of women. However, 'development' and poverty strategies seldom challenge gender-based discrimination. Instead they seek remedies for women's 'vulnerability' by means of 'special support', and are designed to 'lift' women closer to the level of men, by reducing gaps in terms of education and income and so on.

One reason might be that gender equality may be threatening to power and privileges of the policymakers themselves (Kabeer, 2003).

Two schools of thought: decisive factors in the way power, privilege and gender are reflected in poverty strategies and development goals

Knowledge about female and male poverty is chiefly to be found in the discourses of two partly overlapping schools of thought which have coexisted for decades among actors in the development cooperation field, albeit on different terms. The *'poverty discourse'*, which has set the tone, is stronger on growth-based policies than on rights-based ones (Kabeer, 2003: 18). It is prestigious and rich in resources. It is embraced by the donor community at large, including the World Bank, the UN, several research bodies and large sections of civil society. It tends to focus on aggregate macro-data and poor people as 'sexless averages'. A key feature of poverty reduction strategies is their strong focus on 'tradeables'. This places men at an advantage, since men get paid for a much larger share of their work than women – the ratio is approximately 2:1 according to the UNDP's *Human Development Report 1997*. This approach leads to a clear but *unexpressed bias towards men*, since resources tend to be allocated to the market and (men's) paid work, while the unpaid contribution of women to human well-being, which is often crucial to family welfare, goes unsupported (de Vylder, 2004). Furthermore, in focusing on economic aspects, policymakers seldom note how research has shown that men often keep substantial parts of their incomes for their own, personal consumption before sharing it with family members (Chant, 2003).

Poverty strategies often disregard the fact that women as a group face non-economic barriers in terms of social constructs (laws, norms, attitudes) which limit their access to land, inheritance, education, employment, carriers, mobility and personal freedom (de Vylder, 2004). This reflects a crucial feature of dominant gender-insensitive analyses, which avoid or hide the existence both of asymmetrical power relations and of *conflicting interests* among groups, for example, between the sexes, ethnic groups and classes. This might be a reflection of preferences among many politicians to rather point at economic growth as a means for creating resources to be distributed instead of requesting powerful groups in societies to share resources with poorer groups.

The other source of knowledge about female and male poverty is the 'gender discourse'. Discussions concerning GAD never primarily emphasise monetary aspects of poverty. Instead, the concept refers to the broad agenda outlined in legal and political documents adopted by the international community, such as CEDAW (the UN Convention on the Elimination of All Forms of Discrimination Against Women) and the Beijing Platform of Action (BPFA) adopted at the fourth UN World Conference on Women in 1995. Gender and development is by no means to be understood as a single school of thought but as a multitude of views, often aimed at *transforming* the dominant discourse on poverty. Gender and development focuses on aspects of ill-being/well-being such as domestic violence, respect, participation in decision-making, reproductive and sexual rights, freedom of movement, the right to custody of one's own children, and empowerment in general. It also focuses on methods for detecting and describing how power structures operate. As a consequence, GAD rarely highlights measurable data on poverty and deprivation since quantified methods fail to assess and address qualitative, power-related social aspects of development and obstacles to women's active participation in agenda-setting at all levels (Johnsson-Latham, 2004).

It is also clear that the gender discourse stems from a different 'dialogue structure' to that of the poverty discourse. The latter is based throughout on the existence of a superior donor, rich in resources and knowledge, who assists weaker recipients. In contrast, the gender discourse recognises that the problems are more or less the same the world over since gender discrimination occurs in *all* countries, and among donors as well as recipients. Interaction between women's rights groups in rich and poor countries thus involves cooperation on equal terms where both partners have the answers, as opposed to the top-down approach prevailing in the dominant poverty dialogue.

A reflection of existing power structures is that the gender discourse is represented in the multilateral architecture by very small organisations, chiefly the UN Division for the Advancement of Women (UNDAW) and the UN Development Fund for Women (UNIFEM), both of which have extremely limited resources and little voice in the overall normative and operative debate on development issues. Over the years, the UNFPA (United Nations Fund for Population Activities) has also been a key actor in promoting women's rights.

Studies conducted by the Development Assistance Committee of the Organisation for Economic Co-operation and Development (OECD/DAC) in 2007 show that resources for gender-related work in development agencies have decreased considerably since 1995. The explanation has often been that gender work has been 'mainstreamed – though few efforts have been taken to measure mainstreaming by means of quantifiable indicators. The picture is confirmed by the Association for Women's Rights in Development (AWID), who by mapping resources earmarked for gender/women in official development assistance (ODA) has concluded that out of US$107 billion in 2006, only 7.5 billion was allocated specifically to gender/women (Clark, 2007).

Privileges and gender as expressed in the formulation of the Millenium Development Goals
The MDGs, adopted in 2001, soon emerged as the internationally most accepted and far-reaching strategy or 'roadmap' for poverty reduction. Prior to the adoption of the goals,

the OECD/DAC had in the late 1990s embraced the notion of numerical and time-bound targets for development, to facilitate the monitoring of progress in this field. However, the OECD/DAC gender group had been critical of the targets under discussion as they were perceived not to reflect gender aspects of development.

The MDGs relate to a number of UN indices aimed at assessing complex aspects of poverty, such as the Human Development Index, the Gender Development Index and the Gender and Empowerment Measurement. The goals should be read in the context of the Millennium Declaration adopted by the UN General Assembly in September 2000, which on the whole highlights gender more than the MDGs and specifically mentions CEDAW.

The overall goal of the MDGs is to halve global poverty by 2015, measured in average income per person per day. The eight interim goals were identified by the UN in consultation with key actors in the global community.

The third sub-goal specifically addressed gender equality, expressed in the form of a target for the elimination of gender disparity in education. Of the 48 original economic and social indicators designed to assess progress on the MDGs, only three refer explicitly to gender equality. These relate to women's educational status, their share in wage employment in the non-agricultural sector, and the proportion of seats they occupy in national parliaments. While other goals, targets and indicators relate to women (for instance, maternal health) they do not explicitly aim at gender equality.

Only a few years before the adoption of the MDGs, several UN World Conferences (Vienna 1993, Cairo 1994 and Beijing 1995) contained ground-breaking political agreements on women's empowerment, expressed in government commitments to address women's land rights and inheritance, action against male violence, and the strengthening of reproductive health and rights for women and adolescent girls. The agreements in Beijing 1995 seem to have taken both women's rights groups and their opponents by surprise. However, instead of paving the way for a more gendered development discourse, the result was that groups strongly influenced by patriarchal values – who claimed religious sanction for their positions – reinforced their lobbying in support of 'traditional family values' and challenged women's claim for control over their own bodies. This was evident at the time of 'Beijing+5', the follow-up to Beijing held in New York in 2000. This, along with the lack of adequate attention paid to gender in the targets set by OECD/DAC in the late 1990s, could explain why the MDGs address gender equality in terms of girls' education instead of targetting more far-reaching but controversial areas such as land rights, male violence and reproductive health and rights. Furthermore, the emphasis was placed on girls' rather than women's voice and rights, and on girls' inferiority (in terms of lack of education) rather than discriminatory structures (Johnsson-Latham, 2004).

It should also be noted that the UNDP in its *Human Development Report 1995* describing women's conditions worldwide shows that the *narrowest gap in terms of gender equality was in the educational arena*. Thus, the problem was not so much gender disparities in education as the fact that even if girls and women had the same educational opportunities as men, they still did not get access to (well-paid) jobs, nor to decision-making bodies, or to influence resource allocation and agenda-setting. Thus, even if men had less education they still enjoyed a number of privileges, especially in respect of political voice and representation, labour market access and domestic rights.

In measuring one of the targets of MDG3, namely, the elimination of gender disparity in primary and secondary education, reports from governments and other actors tend to focus on gaps in terms of the number of school years. The BPFA, however, discusses the quality of education, and how 'education' often helps maintain predominant values and norms such as gender stereotypes, arguing that a focus on legal and functional education to enhance women's rights would be stronger instruments for the empowerment of women and girls. The BPFA also noted that girls' learning is only one part of the gender agenda on education since this also encompasses lifelong education for women's empowerment.

One of the architects behind the MDGs, Jan Vandemoortele, has confirmed that the agreement on the goals in 2001 could only be achieved at the price of removing controversial issues such as reproductive health, since these subjects were unacceptable to the US and to several other countries and actors (especially the Vatican but also several countries with active Catholic churches as well as many Muslim countries). Thus a political choice was made in favour of 'consensus and harmonisation', which in the case of the MDGs (and in several other arenas), was to the disadvantage of women's reproductive rights, access to land, freedom from violence and other key power issues (Johnsson-Latham 2004).

In a study commissioned by the UNDP in 2002 asking whether the MDGs were a feasible proposition, Vandemoortele noted the difficulty of attaining the goals for women and girls in almost all areas, since 'gender becomes a liability', implying that women and girls *inter alia* get less access to income, health services (including prenatal care) and education, and are more likely to be infected by HIV/AIDS. Vandemoortele further stresses that the failure to disaggregate by gender in the vast majority of goals leads to 'a fallacy of misplaced correctness' as average household consumption remains an abstraction for women who have little or no control over how money is spent (Vandemoortele, 2002: 9). Thus, by looking mainly at human 'averages', planners and policymakers acquire an incomplete or incorrect picture of the problems at hand. This in turn may lead to misplaced undertakings and less efficient use of resources.

Since 2001, the MDGs have been partly modified and goal three now includes the concept of 'empowering' women. However, reporting and assessments still focus on girls' education and the MDGs have largely retained their original elements.[2]

Concluding remarks and suggestions
The dominant poverty discourse embraced by major actors in the development community primarily emphasises economic growth and tends to view poor people as sexless averages. By way of contrast, the gender discourse places the focus on gender-based power and privilege, and stresses both legal, social and economic aspects of human well-being.

For decades, the gender discourse has sought to influence the dominant school of thought. Gender and development has generally been 'a step behind', as gender experts have not been in a position to set agendas. Nor has there been any concerted attempt to 'mainstream gender *before* decisions are taken' (as called for by the BPFA). However, gender experts have sought to add gender dimensions in all major areas, such as work on poverty reduction strategies, harmonisation and coordination. Willingness to address these concerns in the World Bank, the UN, the OECD/DAC, and so on, has fluctuated over the years. And while the poverty discourse has paid 'special' (but often limited) attention to 'women's vulnerability', it has seldom focused on non-discriminatory measures aimed at gender equality.

As a result of the above, the general male bias that currently prevails in society makes it difficult to use resources for development and human well-being in an adequate, effective and non-discriminatory manner. A closer blend of the two schools and the greater involvement of women in all stages of the process – setting agendas, defining strategies and allocating resources – would enhance the prospects for overall poverty reduction.

To promote such a merger, action could be initiated by both donors and recipients in a number of ways, including in the form of seminars and joint studies. This is surely crucial to the overarching task of enhancing human well-being in general. It is particularly important at times of global economic distress when the growth-driven approach to development that currently predominates would seem to be in need of revision.

Notes
1. See www.milleniumcampaign.org (accessed 30 March 2009)
2. See www.un.org (accessed 30 March 2009).

Select bibliography

Chant, Sylvia (2003) *New Contributions to the Analysis of Poverty: Methodological and Conceptual Challenges to Understanding Poverty from a Gender Perspective*, Unidad Mujer y Desarrollo, Serie 47, Santiago de Chile: Comisión Económica para América Latina, available at: www.eclac.org (accessed 20 March 2009).

Clark, Cindy (2007) *Where is the Money for Women's Rights?*, Mexico: Association for Women's Rights in Development, available at: http://awid.org (accessed 20 March 2009).

De Vylder, Stefan (2004) 'Gender in poverty strategies', in Gerd Johnsson-Latham (ed.), *Power and Privileges: Gender Discrimination and Poverty: (Interim Studies)*, Stockholm: Ministry for Foreign Affairs, pp. 80–106.

Johnsson-Latham, Gerd (ed.) (2004) *Power and Privileges: Gender Discrimination and Poverty (Main Report and Interim Studies)*, Stockholm: Ministry for Foreign Affairs.

Kabeer, Naila (2003) *Gender Mainstreaming in Poverty Eradication and the Millennium Development Goals: A Handbook for Policy-makers and Other Stakeholders*, London: Commonwealth Secretariat.

Vandemoortele, Jan (2002) *Are the MDG's Feasible?*, New York: UNDP, Bureau for Development Policy.

5 Gender into poverty won't go: reflections on economic growth, gender inequality and poverty with particular reference to India
Cecile Jackson

Discussions of gender and poverty since the 1990s have revolved around the 'feminisation of poverty', and been largely in terms of private consumption poverty (PCP) (see Chant, Chapter 15 this volume). It was argued, *inter alia*, that conventional indicators such as food, incomes, and land could not be used to measure women's poverty in the same ways they are for men, and that poverty reduction programmes could not be expected to automatically improve gender equity (Jackson, 1996). Since then we have seen more analysis of the relationship between economic growth and gender equity, a conceptual shift towards well-being rather than PCP, an opening for a more cultural understanding of the experience of gendered ill-being, and a recognition of how male gender indentities relate to poverty. It is the latter themes which are addressed in this chapter, drawing in particular on evidence from India.

Economic growth and gender
The relationship between gender and poverty is complex and non-linear, and varies with spatial and temporal scales. At a macrolevel, gender inequality seems to reduce economic growth but on the question of how economic growth affects gender equity, there are more mixed views, even if the historical record indicates that growth seems to have reduced gender inequality, since the position of women in developed countries is generally more favourable than in developing countries.

The non-linear relationship between gender and poverty can be thought of as a Kuznets curve, showing inequality relating to household incomes in an inverted 'U' pattern, so that inequality initially rises with rising household income then flattens and falls. A range of studies, however, fail to find the decline in inequality at higher income levels, and posit, accordingly, that there are no grounds for believing that poverty reduction and growth in household incomes will be accompanied by improved intrahousehold equity. On the contrary there may be increased inequality until quite high income levels are achieved.

Oster (2009) finds a similar non-monotonic relationship between gender inequality and access to health, specifically vaccinations in India, and shows how increased access to such health services produces greater gender inequality as families first invest in the health of the favoured gender, boys, thus increasing inequality for some time before further increases in access finally lead to investments in girls and reduced gender inequality.

The implications of these gender and growth links are that rather than expecting poverty reduction to automatically reduce gender inequality it would be more realistic to assume that when economic growth produces rising household incomes, accentuated gender and generational inequalities are likely. A context of successful economic growth, such as contemporary India, would thus suggest a greater need than ever for interventions to address gender inequalities.

What are the implications of the Kuznets relationship for how we see men and masculinities, since men are no longer to be seen as unmarked and gender-free? A rising *household* income may disempower women in terms of bargaining strength (see below), but may also bias relations towards cultural ideals of hegemonic masculinities in ways unfavourable to women. Men with rising incomes may behave in more patriarchal ways, since when poor, they experience an authority deficit. Aspirations to more patriarchal lifestyles, for example, a dependent wife, may be unaffordable and remain latent. Poverty conceals a latent patriarchy, which achieves expression when resource constraints are loosened. The consumption appropriate to an upwardly mobile man, who needs to signal his status with 'things', may well also produce distortions within the household where resources available to other family members are diverted towards the bid for status. The role of a wife in maintaining family honour may be increasingly emphasised, requiring the exercise of control. When a landless man acquires land he also acquires new concerns about the inheritance of sons and new expectations about his responsibility to make good marriages for his daughters. Social mobility entails changed familial relationships, frequently towards greater authority and responsibility of the male household head.

Capabilities and functionings

Private consumption poverty remains a very widely used concept of poverty, often arrived at through per capita estimates from household-level data, and not from individual-level data, thus hiding intrahousehold ill-being. Even with individual data, however, the quantity of consumption of commodities is not a good way to understand, or to measure, women's gender disadvantage. For example, adult physical well-being is assessed by body mass index (BMI) and life expectancy, well-being outcomes which should reflect significant food or health deficits. But when we look at these indicators of individual physical well-being we find, for most of the developing world, little evidence of adult women's gender disadvantage. Food consumption research, in terms of calorie adequacy, does not support the idea that because women are supposed to 'eat least and last' they have greater calorie deficits than men. However, the *quality* of adult women's nutrition is often inferior, entailing micronutrient deficiencies and morbidity, even if neither translates directly to outcomes in terms of BMI and life expectancy. Many of these problems stem from the fact that 'women' are not a homogenous social category. In food adequacy questions, age is a vital element by which gender has to be disaggregated to be meaningful.

The specificity of patterns of gender disadvantage, the difficulty of categorising 'women', and the existence of gender bias across all income levels supports the argument that considering gender bias against women as a *poverty* issue is inappropriate. Amartya Sen's (1985) capabilities approach to well-being moves away from a commodities metric, arguing that commodities cannot be taken to indicate well-being because possessions do not guarantee a state of being, and that what matters is not the commodity but what it allows a person to be or do. Sen distinguishes between 'capabilities' as the potential for beings and doings, and 'functionings' as the achievement of those beings and doings (see also Coates, Chapter 48, this volume). Functionings are thus the achievement of, for instance, a state of adequate nutrition, which can, but does not always, occur, when a person has access to a commodity, food. It is an advance to recognise that what is significant for, say, women's land rights, is not mere possession, but what such possession allows them to be and do. The space between capabilities and functionings, where the conversions from potentials to actualities takes place, is an important one for the workings of gendered cultures which regulate, to some extent, the beings and doings of women. Sen allows us to question assumptions such as if land is good for poor men it is also good for poor women in the same ways, since the conversion of commodities to functionings differs for men and women, and depends on gendered cultural forms and processes (see also Gammage, Chapter 9, this volume).

Women inhabit multiple identities, as members of various social categories relating to age, ethnicity, class, religion, nationality and residence, and have gender interests and disadvantages as only part of their overall bundle of interests and well-being. Outcomes like functionings are measured in relation to actually embodied female individuals – whose functionings are a composite outcome deriving from multiple identities which privilege or exclude in contradictory ways so that extracting the specifically gender-driven disadvantage is extremely difficult. Ultimately, approaches which focus on women as a single category, and on outcomes rather than social relations are poor tools for describing gendered disadvantage, since how capabilities become functionings for women and men depends both on other social identities, such as age and ethnicity, and on social relations, such as conjugality. How commodities become capabilities and functionings is enabled and constrained by household relations. A woman may have the capability (education) for employment, yet the achievement of the functioning 'being employed' may be prevented by a husband, or a mother-in-law, who objects to her working. Or a man may achieve a functioning of 'being healthy' on the basis of caring labour provided by a wife (see Nakray, Chapter 51, this volume). This is not to suggest that gender relations always enable male functionings and always constrain female functionings. Indeed, if they did we would be able to detect the evidence for gender disadvantage more clearly. Gender roles can constrain male functionings, and meeting provider expectations can lead to occupational hazards and morbidity.

The need for a finer grained, more dynamic view of gender and disadvantage as a *social* relation, invokes another strand of Amartya Sen's work, namely, his cooperative–conflict model of intra-household relations developed in the late 1980s. In this, resource allocation outcomes within households are a product of three elements: the degree of self-interest perceived by each party; the degree of perceived contribution to household income, and the differential breakdown positions of different household members. Women tend to be weakened by lower levels of self-interest, lower perception of contributions, and poorer breakdown positions. What, then, might happen to the differential power of husbands and wives when household income, under male control, rises? In the absence of autonomous incomes of women, a husband will strengthen his breakdown position vis-à-vis his wife, since the gap between partners' ability to survive outside the marriage, or contract an equally good marriage, widens, and the power of the wife declines simultaneously. In these diverging breakdown scenarios the greater acceptability of remarriage, or the high-status option of polygyny, for men, and the disapproval of divorce for women, and uncertain support from natal families who may be distant and/or unwilling to accept the ending of an expensive social investment in hypergamous marriages, can mean that the *relative* income gap between husband and wife intensifies patriarchy. By contrast, for poorer men, the imitation of the consumption and social practices of the wealthy is unaffordable, the ideals of hegemonic masculinity too unattainable to influence everyday gender relations, and cooperation in survival-oriented livelihoods entails a much more egalitarian ethos. For a poor man, marriage is relatively costly, more difficult to sustain, and divorce more problematic, and his breakdown position weaker as a consequence.

From a poverty perspective, the cooperative-conflict model suggests the gendered conversions of capabilities to functionings, but more significantly it suggests the possibility that women may face everyday lives in which, despite adequate elementary material functionings, their work is devalued, they face implicit threats of physical violence, curtailed physical mobility and limited exit options. Poverty is revealed to be as much a cultural as a material phenomenon in even the poorest societies, and gendered disadvantage is not more materially based in developing countries, and more cultural in the affluent West. The capabilities framework takes a step towards thinking of gendered ill-being as cultural, in the translations of capabilities to functionings, and in the inclusion of capabilities such as self-respect.

Cultural perspectives on commodities and poverty

Thinking culturally in relation to poverty means seeing commodities not just as quantities of goods and services available for women's consumption, but also as objects expressing and mediating inequality. Consumption is not simply about meeting individual material needs, but is profoundly social, and 'speaks' to others, articulating aspirations, status claims, identities and relationships. For example, the spread and intensification of dowry practices in India needs to be understood in relation to changing desires for the consumer durables which increasingly constitute dowry.

Culture refers to both the meanings which inhere in social life for actors, and the public symbolic forms that shape them. Underestimating how rooted the experience of gendered ill-being is in these forms and meanings leads to thwarted development policy expectations. One of the greatest gender injustices of our time is the force and persistence of son preference in India, driving femicide affecting female foetuses, infants, children and adult women. Where a woman dying a slow death from burns in hospital might be so cowed by patriarchy as to refuse to name her husband as the perpetrator, some extremely powerful forces are at work (Rajan, 1993). Dowry murders, where a wife is threatened to extort dowry payments from her natal family, and harmed, murdered or driven to suicide, very often involve 'accidents' with fire in kitchens. They are not new but increasingly evidenced in the statistics on burn mortalities. In 1998 India was the only country in the world where fire burns figured amongst the leading causes of death: 80 per cent of these are female, and the great majority of women are young, married and rural (Batra, 2003). Rajan (1993: 83) sees the answer to the silence of dying wives in the 'socially sanctioned violence against women that reinforces and is reinforced by the ideology of husband-worship (*pativrata*)'.

The sex ratio problem in India is a good example of both the non-linear, sometimes perverse, relationship between economic growth and gender inequality, and of the importance of culture to understanding the persistence of gender bias. It is in the states which have seen most rapid economic growth that the sex ratio is the most adverse to women. Changing material circumstances affect women's well-being in ways mediated by the cultures of son preference which are enhanced or muted with economic change, in multiple and contradictory directions. Social science explanations of the adverse to women sex ratios in India have converged on 'culture' as the culprit, since explanations based on wage rates, agro-ecosystems, labour force participation, education and other factors fail to account for the observed patterns. Change requires a better understanding of son preference as an enduring cultural form which is *not* simply rational behaviour in the face of differential wage rates.

While the cultural contrasts between North and South India can be overdrawn, as ideal types they capture something of the more intensely patriarchal northern cultures, where the population has been steadily masculinising over many decades, and generally more favourable gender relations of the south, where more balanced sex ratios have been found. Recently, however, we have seen the general growth of foeticide (sex-selective abortion to kill females), and in parts of the south which have been seen as relatively favourable to women there is now a precipitous decline in the sex ratio. Gender cultures are not static, dowry practices spread to new regions, ideals of family composition are refigured, propertied identities are threatened and defended, but the bedrock of son preference mediates the well-being of girls and women across the subcontinent.

Harriss-White (1999) shows how within a state such as Tamil Nadu, which has a relatively favourable overall sex ratio in the context of all-India comparisons, there is a complex intra-state pattern of discrimination not visible in the macro statistics, with the more developed regions displaying more adverse ratios. Once again the reduction of poverty intensifies gender inequality. By focusing on more detailed and long-term studies of particular locations she finds some shocking realities within this state – the lowest sex ratio in her work was a block which showed only 614 girls for every 1000 boys under 6 (ibid.: 135) and 'In certain regions and villages where the culling of girls has never previously been recorded, and in precisely those households that are amassing property, where the ownership of land and non-land moveable property are closely associated, female child deaths are on the increase' (ibid.: 127).

Harriss-White finds strong links to the acquisition and intensification of land relations at the heart of greater bias against girls. And while a recent study finds the practice of daughter elimination across all classes, castes, wealth and education categories in Tamil Nadu, more infanticide is found in poorer households and where women are less educated, but more foeticide, which accounts for 85 per cent of the daughter deficit, among wealthier households and more educated women (Srinivasan and Singh Bedi, 2008). The wealthy and educated express a culture of son preference in different ways to, and more effectively than, the poor, and the strong relationship of birth order with sex ratios, whereby the first child is much less likely to be aborted for being female but later ones are much more likely to be, shows a uniform and enduring culture of gender bias.

Concluding thoughts

If gender inequalities rise with economic growth we should be looking to intervene most vigorously on behalf of women in those social locations where household incomes are on the rise. Furthermore, we should consider alternative forms of policy delivery. For example, a sprinkling of health services across a wide territory may appear to be a fair use of scarce resources, but in terms of gender equity a 'saturation' approach may be better, as proposed, *inter alia*, by Oster (2009: 75):

From a policy perspective . . . non-monotonicity would suggest that if policymakers care directly about the sex ratio, interventions to increase access to health inputs should focus on saturating one area rather than introducing the inputs in a more limited way in all areas. Depending on the magnitude of the effect of vaccinations on mortality, saturating one area versus providing some vaccination to all areas could make a reasonable difference in the gender imbalance in mortality.

Finally, recent gender analysis appears to be confirming the arguments made earlier (Jackson, 1996), that gender bias cannot be assumed to be rooted in poverty and therefore tackled through mainstream anti-poverty approaches, but instead require gender-focused policy. Thus, in relation to daughter elimination in India: 'Measures to ensure daughter survival include implementation of the law, a reworking of prevailing interventions which are based on the notion that daughter elimination is mainly a problem amongst the poor, and an explicit focus on tackling sex selection' (Srinivasan and Singh Bedi, 2008: 985). The last of these will need an engagement with cultural analysis focused on the meanings, desires, symbolic values, compulsions and choices swirling around gender identities and relations in particular times and places.

I conclude that measurements of possessions give an incomplete and distorted perspective on gendered ill-being, which is better tracked through capabilities and functionings, married to a socially relational gender analysis (which includes men and masculinities within its scope) and addresses gender cultures as the drivers of such ill-being. Materialist emphases on the possession of commodities, and the implication that gendered disadvantage will vanish with the snows of poverty, are called into question by the evidence for deep and intensifying bias against women in India in many of the locations, and groups, which have experienced strong poverty reduction. Effective policy needs to confront this challenge.

Select bibliography

Batra, Anil (2003) 'Burn mortality: recent trends and sociocultural determinants in rural India', *Burns*, **29**, 270–75.
Harriss-White, Barbara (1999) 'Gender cleansing: the paradox of development and deteriorating female life chances in Tamil Nadu', in Sunjari Rajan (ed.), *Signposts: Gender issues in Post-independence India*, Delhi: Kali for Women, pp. 125–54.
Jackson, Cecile (1996) 'Rescuing gender from the poverty trap', *World Development*, **24** (3), 489–50.
Oster, Emily (2009) 'Does increased access increase equality? Gender and child health investments in India', *Journal of Development Economics*, **89**, 62–76.
Rajan, Sunjari (1993) *Real and Imagined Women: Gender, Culture and Post-colonialism*, London: Routledge.
Sen, Amartya (1985) *Commodities and Capabilities*, Amsterdam: Elsevier.
Srinivasan, Sharada and Arjun Singh Bedi (2008) 'Daughter elimination in Tamil Nadu, India: a tale of two ratios', *Journal of Development Studies*, **44** (7), 961–90.

6 Advancing the scope of gender and poverty indices: an agenda and work in progress
Thomas Pogge

The World Bank's International Poverty Line (IPL) and the Human and Gender-Related Development Indices of the United Nations Development Programme (UNDP) guide – and often misguide – the efforts of policymakers in governments, non-governmental organisations (NGOs), and international agencies. Political actors use such indices as proxies for the values they purport to measure: devoting certain resources toward effecting the largest achievable reduction in the poverty index, for example, on the assumption that they will thereby have brought about – or be perceived to have brought about – the largest achievable reduction in what makes poverty objectionable. Insofar as an index fails to track, money and human effort go to waste.

This chapter marks the beginning of a major research effort, funded by, among others, the Australian Research Council, Oxfam, and the International Women's Development Agency. Our objective is to reflect critically on how gender equity, development, and poverty have been – and on how they ought to be – measured and tracked across a plurality of diverse natural and social environments. The immediate motivation for this project is dissatisfaction with current ways of measuring poverty, development, and gender equity.

Tracking poverty as the number or proportion of people living below some IPL
The best-known poverty index is a crude headcount index pioneered by the World Bank (hereafter, the Bank), which reports simply, for any population, the percentage of persons living below some international poverty line. This IPL is defined in US dollars of a certain base year – currently US$1.25 per person per day in 2005. Purchasing power parities (PPPs) are used to convert this amount into 2005 currency of any other country, and this country's consumer price index (CPI) is then used to convert the result further into local currency of any other year. In this way, the local cost of the consumption of any person in any country and year can be compared with the IPL.

This procedure has six flaws. First, it indefensibly prioritises people living just below the IPL. Moving such people to just above the IPL is the cheapest and easiest way of reducing the poverty headcount. But why should only moves which cross the IPL count as progress? There evidently is no good reason for ignoring changes in people's economic situation when these occur entirely below the IPL or slightly above it.

Second, the Bank's exclusive focus on income and cost of consumption ignores many other poverty-relevant aspects of a person's situation. Someone who survives by working in a cold climate, which requires additional expenses for staying warm, is poorer than another who can earn the same income without having to bear such extra costs. Also, any plausible measure of poverty must take account of necessary labour time – including here also unpaid work on family food production, housekeeping, and child rearing, which is very predominantly performed by women and girls.

Third, the IPL's US-dollar-denominated starting point is not grounded in any rigorous analysis of the level of resources needed to meet basic human requirements. The current IPL comes to roughly US$10 per person per week in 2009 – or US$42 per month or US$500 per year (see Bureau of Labor Statistics, 2010). A US resident evidently cannot locally purchase even her most minimal requirements so cheaply. This may appear to be no problem because dollars buy more where very poor people actually live. But this thought cannot save the Bank's chosen IPL, because the Bank converts all local currency amounts not at market exchange rates but at PPPs. And the Bank cannot say that, while US$500 annually per person is too little in the US, the PPP equivalent of US$500 in less developed countries is adequate. Making this claim, the Bank would be undermining its entire method, which assumes that PPPs provide suitable conversion rates for comparing incomes and consumption expenditures of poor people worldwide. It is also implausible to claim that a higher IPL would make the eradication of poverty unaffordable: in 2005, the aggregate shortfall of the 1.4 billion people living below the IPL amounted to merely 0.17 per cent of the global product – or about US$76 billion per annum or one-ninth of US military spending (see Center for Defense Information, 2008). If the IPL had been twice as high, fully 3.08 billion people would have been counted as poor – yet even their aggregate shortfall from the higher IPL would have amounted to only 1.13 per cent of the 2005 global product (Pogge, 2010: s. 3.4).

Fourth, the use of general consumption PPPs introduces massive distortions because PPPs are influenced by the prices, in all countries, of many commodities that are not needed to avoid poverty. Thus, the purchasing power assigned to poor-country currencies may be greatly inflated by the inexpensiveness there of services (such as maids and drivers), which poor people neither need nor consume.

Fifth, a CPI is based on the consumption pattern of a country, which differs greatly from that of its poor households. In the CPI, prices of cars and computers may play a much larger role than prices of rice and beans; but for the poor the former are irrelevant and the latter all-important. Food prices have more than doubled in the 2006–08 period, with devastating effects on the poor; but these effects are invisible as long as their spending keeps pace with their national CPI.

Sixth, the Bank's method is not robust with respect to base year. When a year other than 2005 is used to relate all currencies to one another, then the poverty ranking of persons across countries and years is observed to change substantially (Pogge, 2010: s. 4.2). This is unsurprising because PPPs and CPIs are based on very different (international versus national) consumption patterns and thus involve very different notions of equivalency.

The six flaws combine to make existing estimates of the extent, distribution and trend of global income poverty highly unreliable.

Tracking development through the HDI and gender equity through the GDI
The UNDP's Human Development Index (HDI) is meant to measure the degree of development a population enjoys. It is calculated as the average of three components, each normalised to a scale of 0–1. These components are: the national population's *life expectancy at birth*, its *level of education* (adult literacy and school enrolment), and its *gross domestic product (GDP) per capita*. Each country receives a score in each of these

components, and its overall HDI score is then the average of those three scores (UNDP, 2007).

The Gender Development Index (GDI) uses the same three components weighted in the same way. The difference is that each of the component scores is marked down for any gender inequity. To do this, the population is divided into its male and female subpopulations. Each subpopulation is then scored just like the entire population would be scored for HDI purposes. The GDI then uses, in each component, the harmonic mean of the male and female scores. When the male and female scores in some component are equal, then the harmonic mean is simply this equal score. The more unequal they are, the more the harmonic mean sinks below the average, reflecting a penalty for gender inequity.

The HDI/GDI method usefully recognised some development dimensions other than income. Yet there is no reflective justification of its crude aggregation (through normalisation of the index components and the weights then assigned to them). For example, the indices imply that certain trade-offs between income and life expectancy are neutral with regard to development, but these implications are not explored and examined for their plausibility.

The HDI and GDI are gravely defective in other ways as well. The first and most general problem is that both indices are focused on countries and also marketed as standards of achievement for countries. This is a step backward from the World Bank's poverty headcount measure which is focused mainly on the *global* poverty count (though headcounts disaggregated by country and region are also provided). This focus on the global poverty count rightly suggests that what matters is the impoverishment *of individual human beings* and that the responsibility of avoiding such impoverishment is shared worldwide. The HDI and GDI, by contrast, focus on the ranking of countries and thereby sustain the common view – well liked in affluent states – that poor countries themselves bear primary responsibility for their underdevelopment.

The shift in focus away from individuals is most obvious in the first and last components which, together, constitute two-thirds of both indices. Life expectancy is simply averaged across a national population, or across its male and female subpopulations, and all information about its distribution within such (sub)populations is discarded as irrelevant. This is implausible, because inequalities in life expectancy – not merely between men and women, but generally – must be considered relevant for any morally plausible conception of development. Thus an increase in a society's life expectancy cannot be celebrated as development when it derives from a gain to the rich beyond 80 years of age that slightly exceeds losses to the poor under 50.

Analogous thoughts apply also to the last component – more so, because inequalities related to class, 'race', or religion tend to be much greater in income than in life expectancy. The HDI uses gross domestic product per person, which averages over an entire country, while the GDI uses average earned income per person computed separately for the male and female subpopulations. In both cases, internal inequalities are disregarded completely. Thus, the HDI is indifferent between a society's income being heavily concentrated at the top with the poor majority living in life-threatening poverty and this income being widely dispersed with no one compelled to endure severe poverty. A given increase in per capita GDP is considered by the HDI to make the same contribution to development, regardless of whether the vast majority of the population is sharing in this increase or is left behind.

Similarly, what matters for the GDI is the average earned income of females relative to the average earned income of males. It makes no difference to gender-related development, as the GDI conceives it, whether overall gender income parity exists because employment opportunities and pay packages of men and women are roughly equal across all social strata or because male income advantages in the lower nine-tenths of the socio-economic distribution are balanced by female advantages in the top tenth. This is obviously morally implausible.

More importantly, this total neglect of distribution also provides perverse incentives. When policymakers are concerned to improve their country's HDI, they will seek to enlarge its GDP without regard to whether the additional income goes to the rich or to the poor. They may emulate the example of Angola, which achieved huge gains in per capita GDP between 2001 and 2007 by expanding crude oil production, without worrying whether the extra income was earned by foreigners or embezzled by a small ruling clique. Likewise, insofar as policy makers are concerned to reduce their country's gender inequity penalty, they will seek to shift the income distribution in favour of females – but again without regard to whether the additional income goes to rich or to poor women. The GDI thus encourages such policymakers to boost their country's GDI score through policies that double to US$200000 the incomes of 10000 women executives if this is even slightly more convenient to them than it would be to achieve the same US$1 billion female income boost by doubling to US$2000 the incomes of 1 million female domestics. The GDI here values doubling an affluent woman's income *100 times* more highly than doubling a poor women's income – even though poor women have more at stake, in terms of both human needs and gender disadvantage. This evidently wrong conclusion arises from the GDI here giving equal weight to each unit of income rather than to each woman.

The shift in focus away from individuals manifests itself also in how the HDI and GDI aggregate information across the three index components. They do so by first aggregating within each component indicator across the population, and then aggregating the results across these components. This renders both indices insensitive to how different aspects of disadvantage are correlated. This is problematic because disadvantages persons suffer are typically more burdensome and always morally more problematic when they aggravate than when they mitigate one another.

The GDI inherits these problems. And it adds an additional one by discarding information about whether gender inequities aggravate or mitigate each other. The GDI calculates the gender inequity penalty separately in each component and simply adds up the penalties – regardless of whether women are disadvantaged in all three components, say, or each gender is disadvantaged in some.

In order to promote development, governments, international agencies, and NGOs should, other things being equal, prioritise the neediest. Yet, in order to pinpoint those who are in greatest need overall, any multidimensional index must be constructed to aggregate in the opposite order: aggregating first intra-personally across the component indicators, and then aggregating the results across the population.

Toward new indices of development, poverty and gender equity
Today's leading indices of development, poverty and gender equity suffer from one or more of the following deficiencies:

1. Lack of a moral rationale, which results in some aspects of development or gender inequity being selected in preference to others without a sound justification of the former as being of greater constitutive or instrumental importance.
2. False universality – a focus on deprivations (for example, income poverty) that anyone may suffer combined with relative neglect of deprivations that differentially affect persons according to gender, age, and environment.
3. Bias towards the better-off, which manifests itself in
   (a) a focus on indicators that are relevant mostly to the more privileged, such as women in parliament or women in higher education, which matter but are less important than gender inequities burdening much larger numbers of more disadvantaged women and girls, and in
   (b) implausible aggregation that ignores correlations among different aspects of deprivation, for instance, or compares male and female income totals and thereby implicitly gives much greater weight to income inequalities at the top; and
4. Lack of integration, as when several partial indices are presented side by side without any guidance for how to resolve conflicts among them about the ranking of programmes and policies.

Because indices thus flawed provide faulty guidance and incentives to policymakers, it is important to explore the possibility of constructing better indices. This is the point of the project our research group is commencing with NGO personnel from five countries.

We have two broad ideas that serve as a starting point. First, handling distributional issues correctly requires a holistic measure of individual deprivation. An index is supposed to provide summary information about a group. To do so, it must track how group members are doing. This purpose is much better served when the interpersonal aggregation is performed last, after the relevant aspects of each person's situation have been holistically assessed. This is so because the value of any good we might measure – income, education, healthcare, leisure, participation, security, and so on – varies widely with the age and gender of the person who has it and also with the other goods this person has access to. If individual lives are what ultimately matters, then we must attend to these interdependencies. A credible index of development must be sensitive to whether an increase in literacy goes to landowners or the landless, an improvement in medical care goes to children or to the aged, an increase in enrolment to privileged university students or to children in slums, an increase in life expectancy to the elite or to the marginalised, enhanced physical security to males or to females.

The second idea is that a holistic measure of individual deprivation, grounded in a sound conception of basic human needs or requirements or capabilities, can serve within different aggregation exercises. Thus, the poverty of a population, or its level of development, can be defined as the mean level of individual deprivation. And gender inequity in a group can be defined as the mean difference across population fractiles (averaging over male/female ratios as calculated for each fractile).

Obviously, these ideas, as illustrated in Figure 6.1, are rough and preliminary. But they show in general terms at least how better indices might be specified – indices that would support plausible judgements about whether, for instance, World Trade Organization (WTO) globalisation has fostered development or fuelled a 'feminisation of poverty'.

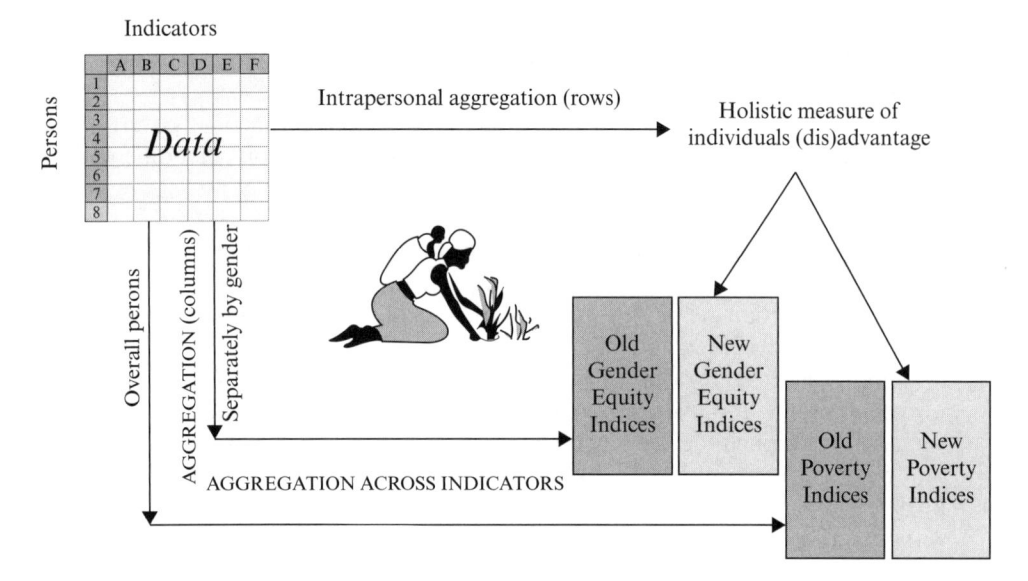

58　*The international handbook of gender and poverty*

Figure 6.1　New indices based on a holistic measure of individual (dis)advantage

Select bibliography

Bureau of Labor Statistics (2010) 'Consumer Price Index', available at: www.bls.gov/data/inflation_calculator.htm (accessed 31 January 2010).

Center for Defense Information (2008) 'What is the "defense" budget?', available at: www.cdi.org/PDFs/What is the Defense Budget.pdf (accessed 31 January 2010).

Pogge, Thomas (2010) *Politics as Usual: What Lies Behind the Pro-Poor Rhetoric*, Cambridge: Polity Press.

UNDP (United Nations Development Programme) (2007) 'Technical note', in UNDP, *Human Development Report 2007/2008* Houndmills: Palgrave Macmillan, pp. 355–61, available at: hdr.undp.org/en/media/HDR_20072008_Tech_Note_1.pdf (accessed 31 January 2010).

7 Methodologies for gender-sensitive and pro-poor poverty measures
Sharon Bessell

This chapter seeks to provide a gender-sensitive critique of both income-based and multidimensional definitions and measures of poverty. The first section examines the ways in which income-based measures are insensitive to the gendered dimensions of poverty. The second section examines multidimensional approaches, suggesting that to date the opportunity to capture and deepen understanding of the various ways in which women and men experience poverty has been missed. The third section outlines existing multi-dimensional measures of poverty, while the final section maps out the ways in which we might conceptualise and operationalise methodologies for gender-sensitive measures of poverty, capable of reflecting the experiences of women and men.

Shortcomings of income-based measures of poverty
Definitions and measurements of poverty have long been heavily contested. Income-based measures, particularly using the US$1 per day poverty threshold, have been criticised as failing to reflect adequately the experience and reality of poverty. Nevertheless, income remains a dominant measure of poverty, as evidenced by the first of the Millennium Development Goals (MDGs). As Harriss-White (2005: 882) notes, there is a degree of arbitrariness about all income-based measures but 'in the absence of consensus, their main value lies in their convenience for statistical analyses of headcounts, of the intensity of the deficit and the shape of distribution, and of the changes in these parameters over time'. As such, they have proven to be remarkably durable. This durability is problematic given the insensitivity of income-based measures to the gendered dimensions of poverty and, in particular, to the ways women's experiences of being poor differ from a 'male standard' of poverty.

Two assumptions underlying income-based measures of poverty are especially troubling. First, there is a tendency to conflate income with the ability to control income. While women may control earned income, the limits on (particularly poor) women's financial autonomy have been well demonstrated. Income-based measures may mask the extent and nature of poverty when women earn an income but have no control over those earnings. While the question of who controls income is acute for women, it is also relevant to the position and well-being of men. Societies that place upon individuals a heavy communal, kinship or clan-based obligation may result in both women and men having limited control over individual income.

Second, and related, is the assumption that income creates equal access and generates equal benefits. Access to education illustrates the point. While lack of financial resources may result in low enrolment or high drop-out rates among poor children, social values around the role of women and the value of formal education for girls are likely to be more significant in explaining disparity between male and female enrolment rates. The problems of assuming that income generates equal benefits are exacerbated when the household is used as the basic unit for poverty measurement, thus ignoring the internal distribution of resources. As many feminist scholars have argued, treating the household as a single entity ignores secondary poverty. In reality, individuals may experience poverty within households that are well-off, while not all those who reside in nominally poor households experience poverty. In societies where gender-based discrimination produces a highly unequal division of household resources, the combination of income-based measures and reliance on the household as the unit of measurement renders invisible the poverty experienced by women and girls (see Quisumbing, Chapter 23, this volume). Ravallion's (1996: 1332–3) argument that a credible approach to poverty measurement must include an indicator of the gender disparities in the intrahousehold distribution of resources has gone largely unheeded in practice.

Beyond these serious shortcomings, income-based measures of poverty fail to capture aspects of poverty that are crucial for poor women. That women and men experience poverty differently is well documented. Longwe (1991) articulates the gendered nature of poverty eloquently, noting that while poverty affects the lives and well-being of both women and men, it becomes a women's issue when women carry the main responsibility for producing the food crop and for the welfare of children; when food and income are not distributed fairly between men and women; and when women do not receive a fair share of the benefits of their labour. Chant (2007) demonstrates the extent to which women shoulder the burden of responsibility within households, with important implications for the ways in which women and men experience poverty. Chant's concept of the 'feminisation of responsibility' is a reminder of the labour and time burdens on poor women and the failure of poverty measures to account for the care economy. Chant argues cogently that it is 'inputs rather than incomes' that are crucial in analysing women's experiences of poverty (ibid.; see also Chant, Chapter 15, this volume).

A shift towards multidimensional definitions of poverty
If income-based measures of poverty fail to capture the gendered nature of poverty, how do multidimensional approaches fare? Based on the idea that poverty impacts on people's lives in complex ways, multidimensional definitions and measures of poverty aim to recognise not only material but also social and human deprivation (see also Coates, Chapter 8, this volume).

In broadening the way poverty is conceptualised, material deprivation is commonly characterised by a lack of goods such as food, water, shelter and clothing, while social deprivation takes the form of familial, social, recreational and educational deficits. Amartya Sen's work has been crucial in a rethinking of poverty, within both the scholarly debates and the world of policy and practice (see also Gammage, Chapter 9, this volume; Jackson, Chapter 5, this volume). Sen emphasises the notion of human capabilities, which are the opportunities to achieve valuable 'functionings' or 'states of being'. Functionings may be either material or social, and extend to being able to take part in community life, engaging in public life without shame, and freedom from violence. Human capabilities approaches have identified the ways in which women are particularly vulnerable to capability poverty. Thus, conceptualisations of poverty have progressively shifted from income alone to more complex understandings, captured under the umbrella term of multidimensional poverty.

Such developments in the conceptualisation of poverty have the potential to provide both definitions and measurements that better reflect the lived experiences of the poor. Yet it is also the case that expanded definitions of poverty have not been adequately operationalised. A notable shortcoming of debates on how the concept of multidimensional poverty might be captured through measurement frameworks is the absence of gender analysis. There is a striking disconnect between the voluminous literature examining the gendered dimensions of poverty and the growing literature on operationalising and measuring multidimensional concepts of poverty. Consideration of gender, or of women's specific experiences of poverty, is too often absent from the latter (Bourguignon and Chakravarty, 2003), or is incorporated as one of several variables (Deutsch and Silber, 2005). Significantly, proposals for the inclusion of data that are currently missing from measures of multidimensional poverty have paid little heed to the importance of gender. This has been the case even when the issues under consideration have strong gendered dimensions, such as agency and empowerment, or violence. The lack of gender analysis within much of the literature on multidimensional poverty creates a context whereby the gender blindness that characterises income-based measures is unlikely to be corrected in multidimensional approaches. This raises the question of how new measures incorporate gender issues.

Gender and multidimensional measures
The United Nations Development Programme (UNDP) has been at the forefront of developing measures of multidimensional poverty, well-being and human development. These include the Human Development Index (HDI) and the Gender-related Development Index (GDI), the Human Poverty Index (HPI) and the Capability Poverty Measure (CPM). The HDI, introduced in 1990 via the *Human Development Report*, aims to measure not poverty but the distinct, if related, concept of human development. It is constructed from three dimensions: (1) longevity (measured by life expectancy at birth), (2) educational attainment (measured by adult literacy and combined primary, secondary and tertiary enrolment ratios), and (3) standard of living (measured by real Gross Domestic Product [GDP] per capita). The 1995 *Human Development Report* introduced the GDI, which uses the same dimensions as the HDI and applies a penalty for gender inequality The GDI is not a measure of the gendered experience of poverty or human development, nor is it a measure of gender inequality. Rather, the GDI adjusts the HDI by applying a welfare penalty on gender gaps (see Pogge, Chapter 6, this volume).

The HPI adopts a dual approach to measuring poverty, one for developing countries (HPI-1) and one for OECD countries (HPI-2). The HPI-1 (most relevant for the discussion here) uses three dimensions: (1) poor survival (measured by the likelihood of dying before the age of 40), (2) exclusion from knowledge (measured by illiteracy), (3) lack of a decent standard of living (measured by the unweighted average of the percentage of the population without access to safe water and the percentage of underweight children for their age). The CPM is a multidimensional poverty tool aiming to capture capabilities, and is based on: (1) living a healthy life (measured by the percentage of children under five who are underweight), (2) having the capability of safe and healthy reproduction (measured by the percentage of births unattended by trained health personnel), and (3) being literate and knowledgeable (measured by the percentage of women aged 15 and above who are illiterate).

These measures do not present poverty or human development as gendered phenomena. The indicators used are not based on sex-disaggregated data (with the exception of the GDI), and consequently reveal nothing of the gendered nature of poverty. Moreover, gender-sensitive dimensions of poverty and associated indicators are conspicuously absent. For example time-burdens, labour inputs, responsibility for household survival and maintenance, personal security and gender-based violence do not feature in any of the measures discussed above. Only the Capability Poverty Measure includes reproductive health.

The interrelationship between gender-based discrimination, poverty and human well-being or development is complex, but fundamentally important. While efforts to measure multidimensional poverty fall short from a gender perspective, so too do efforts to measure gender-based inequality. The UNDP's Gender Empowerment Measure (GEM) represents an important attempt to measure gender equality beyond the experience of poverty, but adopts a narrow interpretation of empowerment based on women's professional engagement. Using Kabeer's (2005: 13) conceptualisation of empowerment as the ability to make choices, the GEM falls short. In essence, the GEM uses professional status and income as proxies for the ability to exercise choice. The GEM does not capture empowerment among women who are in lower status employment or outside the formal labour market. Thus, the GEM provides no insights into the levels of empowerment – or disempowerment – experienced by poor women (see Chant, 2007: 52ff).

Outside the efforts of UNDP, other organisations have sought to measure gaps between men and women. One example is the Global Gender Gap Index developed by the World Economic Forum (WEF) and aiming to measure the gap between women's and men's access to resources and opportunities. The measure has four dimensions: economic participation and opportunity; educational attainment; political empowerment; and health and survival. Like the UNDP measures, the Global Gender Gap Index relies on formal labour force participation and the proportion of women in parliament and senior decision-making and managerial positions. As such, it reflects gender gaps primarily among the non-poor.

Enrolment ratios are a common indicator, used by the HDI, the GDI, the GEM and the Global Gender Gap Index. The information provided by enrolment rates is, however, limited, revealing only whether children are formally enrolled in school, not whether they attend – at all or on a regular basis. Moreover, and importantly from a gender perspective, enrolment rates tell us nothing of the experience of education or of the ways in which gender stereotypes that propagate gender-based disadvantage may be transmitted and reproduced through curricula, learning materials and teachers' attitudes.

While the poverty measures discussed above aim to produce internationally comparative indices, an interesting recent development is the Economic Commission for Africa's African Gender and Development Index, launched in 2004. This index is based on two components: the Gender Status Index and the African Women's Progress Scoreboard. The African Gender Status Index is made up of three dimensions: social power, economic power, and political power. The Gender Status Index overcomes some, but not all, of the problems with global measures. Like many global measures, it relies heavily on indicators of school enrolment, income, employment, managerial positions, seats in parliament and other high-level decision-making positions. Significantly, however, it also includes time use in market activities, as well as in domestic, care and volunteer activities; ownership of property; access to credit; and freedom to dispose of one's own income. Here, the African Gender Status Index expands the measurement paradigm in important ways and draws on data sources, such as time-use surveys, that are often neglected. The second component of the African Gender and Development Index, the African Women's Progress Scoreboard, aims to measure government policy and action on gender equality

At the global level, existing measures reveal something of the gap between men and women in clearly circumscribed areas – particularly education enrolment, literacy, formal employment, high level decision-making and, to some extent, income. They reveal little of the gendered experience of poverty or the ways in which gender-based discrimination and empowerment or disempowerment shape the lives of poor women (or poor men). The African Gender and Development Index provides an example of a regional measure that moves towards a more comprehensive measurement of gender equality/inequality, but it does not focus specifically – or perhaps adequately – on the nexus between gender and poverty.

Gender-sensitive, pro-poor measures of poverty: where now?

In moving towards gender-sensitive, pro-poor measures of poverty, four 'next steps' are worthy of consideration. First, there is a need for measures of poverty to pay greater heed to the lived experiences and priorities of individuals, particularly those for whom poverty is a daily experience. Participatory approaches to understanding poverty have long featured in the gender and development literature. The message is consistent and clear: it is only by listening to the views and priorities of those who are in situations of poverty and subordination that we can develop development strategies (including definitions and measures of poverty) that respond to reality and avoid misinterpreting the lives of the poor. Methodological explanations of measures of poverty tend to focus on technical details rather than providing a justification for the choice of dimensions and indicators. There appears to be a reliance on dimensions and indicators that are developed by experts and driven by the availability of data that are currently and relatively easily collected through large-scale surveys. It could be argued that such approaches may be able to *measure* poverty, and with work could measure gendered experiences of poverty, but are not well equipped to deepen *understanding* of the lived experiences and priorities of poor women and men.

Second, and related, there is a need to bridge the apparent disconnect between the literature on poverty measurement and feminist analyses of poverty, given the potential of the latter to contribute to the identification of dimensions and indicators capable of revealing the gendered nature of poverty.

Third, there is a need for greater emphasis on sex disaggregation in the collection, analysis and reporting of national, sub-national and local level data. Without sex disaggregated data, existing measures of poverty cannot be gender aware.

Finally, rather than relying exclusively on large-scale surveys, there is a need to utilise more responsive and participatory forms of data collection, including qualitative techniques. Such methods are capable of producing additional data necessary to understand how poverty is experienced by women and men, and to reveal the intersection between poverty, gender and other markers of identify, including age, ethnicity and religion.

The four issues identified here are by no means exhaustive, and should be the subject of debate. They may, however, represent tentative but important steps towards the development of poverty measures that value the priorities and experiences of poor men and women and recognise the deeply gendered nature of poverty. As a result, we may be better placed not only to measure, but also to understand the causes, realities and consequences of poverty, and the ways in which it shapes women's and men's lives, choices and chances.

Select bibliography

Bourguignon, François and Satya R. Chakravarty (2003) 'The measurement of multidimensional poverty', *Journal of Economic Inequality*, **1** (1), 25–49.

Chant, Sylvia (2007) *Gender, Generation and Poverty: Exploring the 'Feminisation of Poverty' in Africa, Asia and Latin America*, Cheltenham, UK and Northampton, MA, USA: Edward Elgar.

Deutsch, Joseph and Jacques Silber (2005) 'Measuring multidimensional poverty: an empirical comparison of various approaches', *Review of Income and Wealth*, **51** (1), 145–74.

Harriss-White, Barbara (2005) 'Destitution and the poverty of its politics – with special reference to South Asia', *World Development*, **33** (6), 881–91.

Kabeer, Naila (2005) 'Gender equality and women's empowerment: a critical analysis of the third Millennium Development Goal', *Gender and Development*, **13** (1), 13–24.

Longwe, Sara Hlupekile (1991) 'Gender awareness: the missing element in the Third World Development Project', in Tina Wallace with Candida March (eds), *Changing Perceptions: Writings on Gender and Development*, London: Oxfam, pp. 149–57.

Ravallion, Martin (1997) 'Good and bad growth: the Human Development Reports', *World Development*, **25** (5), 631–8.

8 Multidimensional poverty measurement in Mexico and Central America: incorporating rights and equality
Anna Coates

Why multidimensional poverty?
Prior to the current global financial crisis, Latin America had enjoyed sustained economic growth during recent years, as evidenced by a 5.6 per cent increase in Gross National Product (GNP) in 2006 and 2007.[1] However, despite this growth, poverty rates registered relatively minor decreases, at only 8 per cent over the last decade in Nicaragua, and 9 per cent in Honduras. Furthermore, inequalities within countries continue to pose a considerable challenge, with an average GINI coefficient of 0.57 for Central America in 2007. Given widespread recognition of the failure of macroeconomic policies to achieve sustained economic growth with equity (within the trickledown philosophy of the Washington Consensus), a growing wave of interdisciplinary conceptual frameworks have re-examined the household income and consumption model of 'poverty', drawing heavily on the seminal work of Amartya Sen. In the context of the current world crisis, it is a timely moment to review the basic principles of current poverty measurements applied in Mexico and Central America and the potential to develop measurements that better reflect new conceptual models, particularly given the significance of the common refrain of 'what's measured is what counts' for understanding current development challenges in the region and for formulating public policies.

Current poverty measures
The majority of current poverty calculations in Mexico and Central America are based upon household incomes, and their adequacy for covering essential items of consumption. Internationally, perhaps the best known is the World Bank poverty line, estimated according to the average of the ten lowest poverty lines globally and in relation to Purchasing Power Parity (PPP). The poverty and extreme poverty lines are currently estimated at US$2 and US$1.25 per day. The Economic Commission for Latin America and the Caribbean's (ECLAC) poverty lines are also common reference points and are estimated according to the cost of a basket of basic goods. Households below the extreme poverty line are those that, even devoting 100 per cent of total household income exclusively to buying food, are unable to fulfil the basic nutritional needs of all household members. The poverty line is calculated as the extreme poverty line multiplied by two for urban areas and by approximately 1.75 for rural areas, and covers both dietary and non-dietary requirements. Similarly, the Interamerican Development Bank (IADB) compares per capita income with established poverty lines to determine the proportion of the population living in poverty.

Alternatives to poverty line measurements, grounded in basic needs, include different kinds of goods and household services. Such measures include ECLAC's index of Unmet

Basic Needs (UBN), which includes household quality, overcrowding, running water, basic sanitation, education, medical insurance, electricity and household consumption capacity, and the World Bank's Wealth Index, constructed according to household assets (varying for each country) such as construction materials, access to water and sanitation, television, and so on.

Country-level measures of poverty employ similar methodologies and are based on data from household surveys (conducted with differing regularity) and censuses. Some, such as Guatemala, apply an UBN approach and many, such as Honduras, Nicaragua and Panama, combine a satisfaction of basic needs with an income-based poverty line approach. Mexico, with more sophisticated survey data and methodological approaches, applies a variation of this approach in the production of three poverty lines: 'pobreza alimentaria' (food poverty), 'pobreza de capacidades' (capability poverty), and 'pobreza de patrimonio' (asset poverty). Several countries use basic calorific requirements for survival to constitute basic needs in the case of extreme poverty. In El Salvador, for example, this is calculated as the cost of consuming a minimum of 2200 calories per person and 46 grammes of protein per day within a 'usual diet'.

What current measures fail to tell us

Such measurements of poverty are certainly useful within an economic framework of poverty. However, methodologically as well as conceptually, they contain inherent limitations. For example, while such poverty lines recognise some expenses, they are limited in their potential to adequately represent each household's real expenditure. The cost of basic goods is estimated as a national average, usually only differentiating between urban and rural areas; hence, it is difficult to reflect accurately the inequality experienced by household types and between different populations. Furthermore, it is likely that inequality is underestimated since, in areas with poor coverage of public services and limited social protection, incomes have less significance in real terms (because of the need for more out-of-pocket expenditure for social goods) and such areas often coincide with those where incomes are lowest. This is substantiated by the nature of social protection coverage and social expenditure in the region. Although there are significant differences between countries, social expenditure continues to be regressive due to the predominance of contributory financial systems, with a slight increase for the poorest groups due to targeted poverty reduction programmes. The regressive tendency of social security is yet more marked and highly correlated with formal labour market participation: Central American coverage was 26 per cent overall in 2006, applying to 67.5 per cent of those in formal urban employment but only 10.6 per cent of those informally employed. Indeed, another limitation of poverty lines is their inability to distinguish among the poorest groups in society.

While such criticisms are essentially methodological, they are also associated with broader concerns. What is included, and what is not, in any measurement involves a choice and reflects a partial, and therefore subjective, representation of a truth that in itself implies particular political processes and goals. This raises a number of questions. For example, why focus upon incomes and/or possessions and services? What does this focus reveal – or not – about poverty, equality, development and rights? If we take an alternative approach, would we have a different perspective on poverty and development goals that would allow us to better draw out the role of rights and equality, particularly as related to gender?

Indeed, one criticism of current poverty measurements is their lack of engagement with personal, social, cultural and political factors. This limits the ability to distinguish the significance of incomes and expenses for each individual since there is no recognition of the obstacles that inhibit his or her ability to take full advantage of economic resources to improve personal well-being, an aspect fundamental to full comprehension of the poverty experience and the ability to link poverty to rights. This lack is related, as noted by Sen (1999), to economists' traditional tendency to focus upon the household as the unit of measurement, not taking into account 'intrahousehold' processes (a particular focus of feminist economists and theorists and only recently beginning to impregnate mainstream economic and statistical institutions).

Arguably, the basic needs approach is better able to distinguish between different groups of the extreme poor and is closer to a rights perspective than household income and expenditure measures. Functionally, basic needs are similar to human rights. However, while they illuminate different aspects of poverty in a more integral way, basic needs constitute precisely what the term indicates, the *needs* required for human survival. As such, they can be distinguished from *rights* since, at their heart, *needs* imply a perspective on development related only to immediate physical functionality and key indicators of related living standards, while *rights* comprehend a host of social, political and economic factors which afford possibilities for individual improvement and for full societal participation. Such factors might be measured and compared to the possibilities – or rights – enjoyed by other individuals and groups in society, hence illuminating inequalities. Furthermore, the fulfilment of needs does not necessarily imply government responsibility. In their configuration as needs, they can be operationalised in a purely instrumental manner since, although it may be indirectly implied, the responsibility of the State is not inherent; depending upon differing political stances, the responsibility to fulfill these requirements can be placed on the family itself while the State's *raison d'être* (at least in its democratic configuration) is precisely the assurance of its population's rights. In addition, the level of analysis is again at a household level, which poses problems for understanding the experiences, possibilities and barriers faced by each individual in fulfilling their right not to live in poverty. While there are some rights that are understood at a communal level (for example, the right of a group to practise a particular religion, shared cultural expressions, and so on), rights are inherent, and belong equally, to all human beings, implying a vision that is individual rather than household based.

Thus, what is required is a more integral vision than that employed in current international and regional measurements, expressed in all its complexity and clearly linking poverty and rights within a context of complete and equal development.

Amartya Sen's conceptual framework: capabilities and rights
The theoretical framework developed by Amartya Sen (1999) broadens understanding of how inequality and rights relate to poverty, since it is formulated not only in terms of lack of economic resources (for example, incomes and possessions) but also defines poverty as the lack of capacities and opportunities needed to 'lead the kind of lives [people] have reason to value' (ibid.: 10). The inability to access economic resources is only one component of this, and therefore does not in itself define 'poverty'. In other words, we are accustomed to a limited concept of 'poverty' that emphasises means but not ends. As Sen explains, economic resources combined with other kinds of resources,

are not the *end* of development (if we understand poverty to be the deprivation of capabilities as thus the opposite of development) but the *means*. The goal of development is what an individual experiences of life. Different kinds of resources (economic, social and political) are the instruments required to reach this end; that is, the tools that give us the 'agency' to enable us to determine lives that have value (see also Gammage, Chapter 9, this volume). If, given the lack of any of these resources, we are not able to live a dignified life, we can be considered poor. Thus, poverty and human rights are two sides of the same coin, with the lack of either or both producing inequality.

This perspective does not ignore the importance of macroeconomic and microeconomic contexts, which play a key role in terms of constituting the necessary environment for poverty elimination and fulfilment of human rights. Indeed, the relationship between lack of economic resources and the deficiency of other types of resource, such as individual rights or freedom, can be perceived as bidirectional or even multidirectional, and related to inequality. In brief, this broadened concept recognises the importance of interactions among mutually generative types of resource. Individual rights, such as the right to justice, the right to health, and the right to 'basic needs' such as food and shelter, are as much part of the solution as well as the ultimate aim.

Such an approach does not contradict but rather expands traditional conceptual frameworks and measures, and the poverty reduction strategies to which they give rise. Indeed, by employing strategies to increase household or individual incomes, implications can be multiple. We need to ask *why* we want to improve incomes. Patently, it is not just because we want excluded individuals to be wealthier in terms of economic resources. Although this may be desirable, money itself does not have any inherent value but constitutes the means that enable people to obtain 'liberty' and thus what they need from life (see also Mohamed, Chapter 86, this volume). If, however, there are other obstacles to achieving this end, money itself has limited value. Economic participation and resources need to be combined with the other necessary resources that allow people to fully participate in society and the economy, and hence achieve a dignified life.

Within this framework there is a two-way relationship between, on the one hand, social arrangements to expand individual freedoms and, on the other, the use of individual freedoms 'not only to improve the respective lives but also to make the social arrangements more appropriate and effective' (Sen, 1999: 31). Thus, it is necessary to broaden the concept of poverty and to consider the coverage and access to public services and social protection, among other needs such as rights, personal agency and relational power. At this point, we arguably enter into fields of factors that are not easily, nor objectively, measured and that can be perceived as intangible. However, such factors are important in understanding the difference between the existence of opportunities, as reflected in the measurement of incomes, possessions and services, and individual capacity to utilise these resources to improve life and well-being, and to potentially escape poverty.

Gender equality: rights, relativism and process
The implications for an understanding of equality and specifically for the concept denominated the 'feminisation of poverty' (Chant, 2007, and Chapter 15, this volume; Kabeer, 2003) are clear, as outlined by Sen (1999) in his discussion of women's agency. According to Sen, inequality contributes to, and can also constitute, a form of poverty even in prosperous environments. Thus, a woman who is not 'poor' in terms of economic

resources can be considered 'poor' (in comparison to her male counterpart) because of a lack of other resources (for example, capacities and opportunities) which are, in turn, related to her right to equality and participation in society. In other words, a woman's ability freely to determine her life is restricted by gender norms. For example, if a woman lacks the power to make decisions or gain access to public services such as education or healthcare, or if she does not have full access to economic resources within the household or to credit outside the home, her possibilities and life options will be more limited than a man who may enjoy access to these opportunities.

Nevertheless, the lack of economic resources constitutes a substantial difference with regard to women's life experiences. In situations of extreme poverty, in which survival options are already limited due to the lack of economic resources, any other restriction posed to individual agency exacerbates social and economic marginalisation. In this way, the manner in which women experience poverty is often more arduous and complex than that experienced by men.

This phenomenon is substantiated by data from the Mesoamerican region where women-headed households tend to be over-represented among the extreme poor. For example, in Costa Rica 54.2 per cent of urban households within the indigent strata are headed by women, compared with the 45.8 per cent of indigent urban households headed by men. While such data do not show whether female household heads experience better (or worse) living conditions compared with their counterparts within male-headed households, they do indicate that female-headed households have fewer possibilities to obtain economic resources.[2] Women's economic activity remains low (the rate in Honduras was only 25 per cent in 2004), and is also concentrated in low-paid informal occupations, rather than in technical and professional employment. Despite advances towards gender equality in education, the salary gap continues to be significant (women's wages are 79 per cent of men's wages in the Central American Isthmus), even for those with the same level of education. Besides prejudice and discrimination, one reason is the reproductive burden of women. Fertility rates have decreased in the region; for example, from 6.5 to 4.6 in Guatemala between 1965 and 2005, but remain a challenge particularly for marginalised groups, such as the rural indigenous poor.

Women's experiences of 'poverty' illustrate the difference of this approach to that of current poverty measurements in terms of the necessity to include the broader context of human rights and inequality. Here the process itself becomes as important as the result. Not only can we begin to conceptualise different forms of poverty, not all based in economic factors, but we can also begin to understand that results and processes are interchangeable and that the existence of inequalities performs an important role at various levels. Similarly, the case of gender equality illustrates that absolutes for understanding poverty, fundamental to poverty lines, lose ground to a relative approach in which comparative measures (for example, between groups) gain an increased significance.

Multidimensional poverty: measurement implications
Various attempts to develop multidimensional poverty measures have been made in the Mesoamerican region, most notably, Mexico in response to the 2004 Ley General de Desarrollo Social (Law of Social Development), but also Costa Rica's Índice de Rezago Social (Index of Social Exclusion), and Honduras's 2005 and El Salvador's 1995 and 2005 *Mapas de Pobreza* (Poverty Maps). International bodies, such as the World Bank

and IADB, have also conducted in-depth studies into multidimensional poverty, such as in Guatemala in 2001. Other countries, particularly Cuba, have demonstrated interest in revising current income-based methods in order to more effectively reflect inequality and vulnerability. However, as yet such efforts do not reflect the complexity of poverty, or the interrelationships between different causes, aspects and processes of poverty. Nor do they include more intangible aspects that may require a combination of different methodological approaches, including more qualitative and participatory ones. It is clear that a variety of social, cultural and political processes affect an individual's experience of poverty, understood within a broader conceptual framework, and that these also constitute the result. Required data goes beyond that captured for poverty measurements estimated by income, consumption, possessions and household services. To date, there persists a distinct lack of relevant data in household surveys in the region. In terms of gender inequality, much of this missing information relates to processes and inequalities *within* the household, which is characterised as an unopenable 'blank box' in many surveys.

There is a major need to (re-)evaluate data collection and analysis in order to develop more comprehensive and innovative multidimensional poverty measures in Mexico and Central America, and hence more accurately represent and understand contemporary development contexts. Such measures would put policymakers in a stronger position to devise effective poverty reduction policies and ultimately help states to comply with the protection and promotion of fundamental human rights.

Acknowledgement
I would like to thank Matthew Hammill for data analysis.

Notes
1. All data are drawn from the Economic Commission for Latin America and the Caribbean statistics database – 'CEPALSTAT', available at: http://www.cepal.cl/estadisticas/bases/default.asp?idioma=IN (accessed May 2009).
2. See Chant (2009) for a detailed interrogation of the apparently paradoxical situation whereby income poverty is 'feminising' in Costa Rica, despite a far greater degree of state support for female heads and women in poverty than in most other parts of Mesoamerica, and Latin America and the Global South more generally.

Select bibliography
Chant, Sylvia (2007) *Gender, Generation and Poverty: Exploring the 'Feminisation of Poverty' in Africa, Asia and Latin America*, Cheltenham, UK and Northampton, MA, USA: Edward Elgar.
Chant, Sylvia (2009) 'The "feminisation of poverty" in Costa Rica: to what extent a conundrum?', *Bulletin of Latin American Research*, **28** (1), 19–44.
Kabeer, Naila (2003) *Gender Mainstreaming in Poverty Eradication and the Millennium Development Goals: A Handbook for Policy-makers and Other Stakeholders*, London: Commonwealth Secretariat.
Sen, Amartya (1999) *Development as Freedom*, New York: Anchor Books.

9 Gender, time poverty and Amartya Sen's capability approach: evidence from Guatemala
Sarah Gammage

Time poverty as one dimension of capability poverty
How poverty is defined depends very much upon the purpose for which we wish to enumerate deficits or deficiencies according to the different characteristics that we believe are important for describing well-being. Following Amartya Sen (1999), conventional measures of poverty or deficiency, that focus on per capita household income or consumption and express these in terms of a money metric, miss important dimensions of deficits that affect individual freedoms and well-being. For Sen the foundation of poverty analysis should be the 'substantive freedom' or 'capabilities' that enable an individual to choose a life that she or he values.

A focus on capabilities, especially as part of a multidimensional analysis of poverty, would vary depending on the context, the level and unit of analysis, the information available, and the freedoms considered. As both Alkire (2008) and Sen (1999) identify, there is no single list of capabilities nor a unique array of spheres or dimensions that describe these capabilities, nor techniques to combine these spheres that can be relevant in all circumstances. As a result, one of the strengths of a capability approach is that the researchers can employ multiple analytical techniques and measurements of poverty, selecting those that appear to be most relevant for the analysis they wish to undertake. The challenge in this instance is limiting the relevant dimensions of the capabilities under consideration. Alkire (2008) identifies two main criteria for choosing those dimensions of the relevant capabilities for an analysis of poverty and well-being:

1. That the chosen dimension has *instrumental power*; that is, the dimension contributes to the effective reduction of one or more dimensions of poverty and/or inequality.
2. That the dimensions respond to an intentional result of a project or a specific activity. For example, if a project provides health services then one would expect to document a reduction in those dimensions of poverty associated with lack of access to health services.

This chapter incorporates the notion of time poverty into a multidimensional measurement of poverty in Guatemala that goes beyond a simple money metric. Time is included because it is an important resource that is often distributed inequitably across individuals, especially in the context of scarcity of other resources. It is also especially pertinent to gender, with a marked difference in gender roles and responsibilities observed across the world. Typically, women concentrate in reproductive or unremunerated activities, while men concentrate in productive or remunerated activities. Moreover, women frequently face more restricted access to leisure and work more hours in the sum of productive and reproductive work than do men. Consequently, it is more likely that women experience leisure restrictions or 'time poverty' (Floro, 1995; see also Sen, Chapter 13, this volume; Slater et al., Chapter 61, this volume).

Time poverty can be understood in terms of the lack of adequate time to sleep and rest. As Bardasi and Wodon (2006) highlight, and in direct contrast to consumption or income measures of well-being, where economists assume that 'more is better', time is a limited resource – both across the life of an individual and in a given day. The greater the time dedicated to remunerated or unremunerated work, the less time there is available for other activities such as rest and recreation. Consequently, a person who lacks adequate time to sleep and rest, lives and works in a state of 'time poverty'.

Individual capabilities can be greatly affected by time poverty. If an individual is time-poor this affects not only their present functionings but their future functionings – it limits their ability to rest, to enjoy leisure and recreation, and to invest in expanded capabilities and opportunities acquiring new or more abilities such as formal education. Moreover, experiencing time poverty can contribute to the loss of human capital, compromising an individual's health and undermining their well-being. Given these concerns, I incorporate the dimension of time poverty in the array of functionings relevant for this study.

It is important to note, however, that there are trade-offs between the different dimensions of poverty or well-being. As Bardasi and Wodon (2006) ask in their article, can we consider someone time-poor if their decision to allocate their time means that they have more income in exchange for having less time for unremunerated activities including leisure? These authors argue that we can. Time poverty applies to those individuals who by working longer hours face reduced time for other activities such as leisure and rest. Notwithstanding this claim, being time-poor does not imply that these individuals are in worse conditions in other relevant dimensions of poverty and well-being — just in the time dimension, which may be one of many dimensions chosen to reflect individual well-being.

Multidimensional poverty
Multidimensional poverty measures should be both context- and purpose-specific. There can be many measures of multidimensional poverty or well-being which reflect sufficiency or scarcity enumerated at different levels of aggregation, for example at the level of the individual, the household, or across subjective units of analysis such as the 'community'.

Expressing measures of multidimensional poverty or well-being at any level of aggregation requires a series of steps, first defining the concept of poverty and second applying this concept to identify who is poor. In the current literature there are two approaches to identifying poverty in a multidimensional context (see Alkire and Foster, 2007). One of these approaches is known as the 'union' approach which defines poverty as fulfilling at least one of the multiple dimensions of poverty identified as relevant. For example, we could identify an array of deficits that summarise multidimensional poverty in a particular context that include a lack of adequate nutrition, lack of access to potable water and sewage, as well as the lack of access to adequate housing. If a person or household were found to be in deficit in any one of these dimensions, that person or household would be defined as being in poverty. This approach could be deemed too broad and inclusive, however, and may be considered to 'over-estimate' poverty if not all the dimensions of insufficiency are met.

A second method is the 'intersection' approach which requires that an individual or household be identified as being in deficit in all of the dimensions of poverty to be defined as poor. This methodology could be considered too restrictive and may be deemed to underestimate poverty, particularly if there are many dimensions. Another means of creating a multidimensional measure of poverty is to apply a hybrid approach that selects the intersection of various characteristics of important deficits, but not all those that may be relevant.

One way of avoiding having to apply a union or intersection approach when defining multidimensional poverty is to use factor analysis. Factor analysis looks for correlations between certain characteristics to determine clusters or constellations of characteristics considered to be related to a deficit of capabilities or functionings. The goal of factor analysis is to reduce the number of variables associated with particular qualities or characteristics and detect a structure in the relationship between the remaining variables or dimensions. Principal components analysis (PCA) is a type of factor analysis that seeks to express the most parsimonious relationship that captures the greatest variance with the minimum number of factors.

Multidimensional poverty: an example from Guatemala
To develop and apply a measure of multidimensional poverty, I use the National Household Survey of Living Conditions (*Encuesta Nacional sobre Condiciones de Vida –* ENCOVI) for Guatemala for 2000. This survey includes a module on time use which is nationally representative.

I use a variety of indicators of human capital and time poverty in addition to measures of individual income generated in the labour market to summarise an individual's ability to achieve the lifestyle that they may want. I take various indicators of human capital such as number of years of formal education and whether the individual reports being able to read and write, as a means of measuring current capabilities that describe some of the possibilities for an individual to seek alternative functionings. Individual income is used to describe the income that a person generates which can be used to achieve individual or collective family well-being. The individual is defined as being time-poor if she or he has a cumulative time burden for remunerated and unremunerated work within and beyond the household that exceed 12 hours per day.

As Bardasi and Wodon (2006) point out, establishing a time poverty line can be quite arbitrary. In the literature on income and consumption there are some fundamental guidelines about the lack of income and consumption that translates into the lack of adequate nutrition or the inability to purchase a basket of basic goods deemed essential for survival. Yet it is important to note that these guidelines are typically based on the potential for each individual to achieve the array of goods required for survival without actually determining whether they are in fact acquired by each individual. If we refer to time poverty the arguments that motivate poverty or insufficiency are even less clear, especially when considering the importance of time allocated to recreation and rest above that considered strictly necessary from a health perspective.

Bardasi and Wodon (2006) choose a relative time poverty line that depends on the social context of the country in which the analysis is being conducted and corresponds to 1.5 or 2 times the median for the sum of total hours worked. In the Guatemala example, I use a time-poverty line of 12 hours a day dedicated to the sum of reproductive and

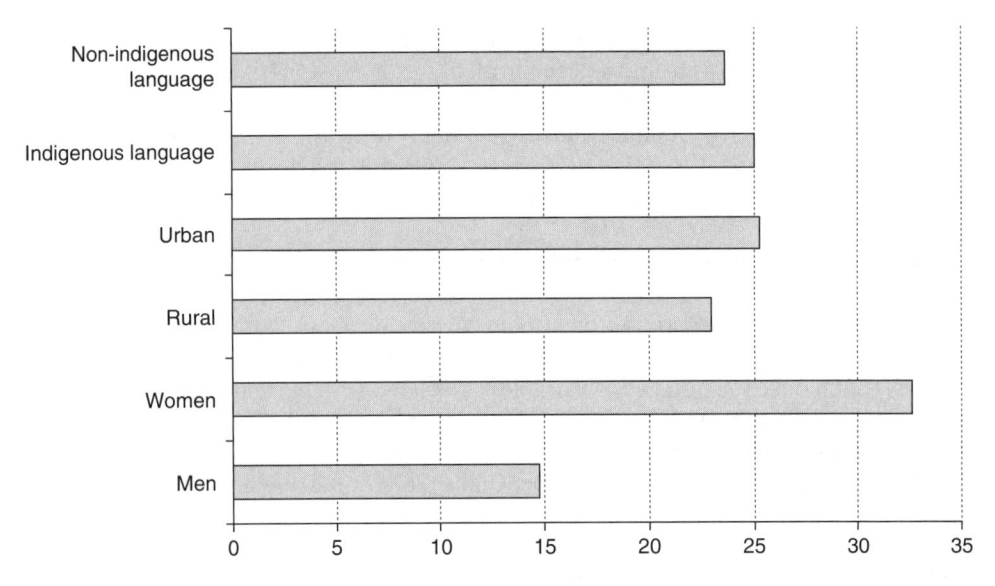

74   *The international handbook of gender and poverty*

Source: ENCOVI (2000).

Figure 9.1   Time poverty in Guatemala by key characteristics (percentage)

productive work. This time poverty line corresponds to a little more than 1.5 times the median and falls within the range of the number of hours suggested by Bardasi and Wodon (2006).

Applying this time poverty line we can analyse the distribution of time poverty by household key characteristics. Figure 9.1 shows that women are much more likely than men to experience time poverty. Individuals who speak an indigenous language at home are slightly more likely to experience time poverty compared with those who speak a non-indigenous language at home. Individuals in urban areas are slightly more likely to experience time poverty than those in rural areas – reflecting the fact that as more women enter the labour market in urban areas their time in paid work increases but their time in unpaid work does not decrease equivalently.

To develop a measure of multidimensional poverty I undertook a principal components analysis to distil a series of factors that summarise the relationship between the variables considered relevant for a multidimensional measure of poverty such as age, the years of formal education completed, whether the individual can read or write, whether the individual is time-poor, or has less than one hour a day for rest and recreation. I also considered whether the individual lives in a rural community, and whether they are unskilled labourers. Finally, I included the individual income that they generate from paid work.

Subsequently I explore the '*factor loadings*', that is, which factors are correlated positively or negatively with the variables being explored. I chose factors that are correlated negatively with time poverty and the limited ability to rest, and positively with age, along with rural residence, literacy and earnings. The collective selection and naming of these as a 'capabilities factor' is because we can assume that this constellation of attributes describes the capabilities that an individual possesses that allow him or her to effect

Table 9.1 The capability index in Guatemala by key characteristics (men and women 12–65 years)

	Men	Women
Urban	0.801	0.646
Rural	0.422	0.206
Non-poor	0.715	0.562
Poor	0.434	0.233
Extremely poor	0.365	0.156
Without piped water	0.387	0.200
Household use of fuelwood	0.481	0.282
Dirt floor	0.384	0.165
Precarious housing	0.367	0.159
Average	0.574	0.396

Note: Poverty is defined using income per capita corrected by the failure to report income using the Comisión para América Latina (CEPAL) methodology and official income poverty lines for Guatemala in 2000.

Source: ENCOVI (2000).

changes in their lives and to achieve the lifestyles that they would wish to have. Someone with fewer capabilities would have more limited ability to choose and realise the lifestyle or level of well-being that they may desire.

This factor is used to create an index of capabilities which is estimated for each individual given their particular characteristics. We can then explore this index to observe its consistency. In an analysis undertaken for household members aged 12 to 65 years for whom there is reliable data on time use, it transpires that, on average, women tend to have a lower capability index than men – reporting a mean of 0.396 as against 0.574 respectively. Similarly, the index of capabilities is higher for those who live in urban areas (0.717) than in rural areas (0.311) which is likely to reflect differences in access to formal education, the ability to read and write, and income-earning opportunities. Finally the capabilities index is lower for the income poor (0.328) and extremely poor (0.254).

Table 9.1 reports the average scores on the capabilities index for men and women aged between 12 and 65 according to key characteristics, including the type of infrastructure and housing to which they have access. It is clear that women score lower in the capabilities index than men. Similarly the capabilities index is lower for those who live in rural as compared to urban areas and for the poor and extremely poor. One salient finding is that where there is no piped water in the house or on the plot of land that the house occupies, women are even more disadvantaged in capabilities. This is hardly surprising, because lack of infrastructure and services – such as piped water or a gas stove – is likely to increase women's load of reproductive work.

Conclusions
This simple exercise illustrates that existing survey instruments can be used to define and analyse measures of multidimensional poverty – even when they are not necessarily designed for this purpose. The index of capabilities that is developed here varies

consistently with other measures of poverty such as the lack of income, or lack of access to infrastructure. But it also captures an important dimension of poverty which may shape individuals' capabilities and opportunities: time poverty.

Women are clearly more time-poor than men across the income distribution. That the capabilities index also varies with key household characteristics such as whether the household has piped water, whether they rely primarily on fuelwood as a source of domestic energy, or whether it has a dirt floor, underscores that capabilities can be shaped by factors such as household infrastructure. Women are clearly more disadvantaged than men by poor household infrastructure or the lack of piped water and less time-consuming energy sources.

These conclusions are not independent of social norms and conventions that dictate women and men's gender roles and responsibilities. In a world where women continue to bear the disproportionate responsibility for social reproduction, the lack of access to services such as piped water or alternatives to biomass fuels and primitive stoves, will increase women's time burdens and has the potential to reduce their capabilities and substantive freedoms to choose other lifestyles and engage in other activities.

These findings point to some key recommendations for reducing capability poverty as it is defined here. Investing in small-scale infrastructure is likely to greatly enhance individual capabilities and as a result improve welfare and well-being.

Finally, it is likely that where individual capabilities are restricted there is a generalised collapse of capabilities at a local or sub-regional level. In further analyses it would be useful to examine the geographic dimensions of capabilities and see whether other measures, such as community and social capital, might be incorporated within the analysis to explore other types of intervention and social programmes that could support the development of expanded capabilities in specific communities and regions.

Acknowledgements
I am grateful to Sylvia Chant, Lourdes Colinas, Flavio Comim, Matthew Hammill, Juan Carlos Moreno Brid and Denise Stanley for their comments on earlier versions of this chapter.

Select bibliography
Alkire, Sabina (2008) *Choosing Dimensions: The Capability Approach and Multidimensional Poverty*, Munich personal RePEc Archive, MPRA Paper No. 8862, 26 May, available at: http://mpra.ub.uni-muenchen.de/8862 (accessed August 2008).
Alkire, Sabina and James Foster (2007) *Counting and Multidimensional Poverty Measurement*, Oxford Working Paper Series No. 7, Oxford Poverty and Human Development Initiative (OPHI).
Bardasi, Elena and Quentin Wodon (2006) 'Measuring time poverty and analysing its determinants: concept and application to Guinea', in Mark Blackden and Quentin Wodon (eds), *Gender, Time Use and Poverty in Sub-Saharan Africa*, World Bank Working Paper No. 73, Washington, DC: World Bank, Washington, pp. 77–95.
Encuesta Nacional sobre Condiciones de Vida (ENCOVI) (2000) *Módulo del Uso de Tiempo, Encuesta Nacional sobre Condiciones de Vida*, Guatemala City: ENCOVI.
Floro, Maria (1995) 'Women's well-being, poverty and work intensity', *Feminist Economics*, **1** (3), 1–25.
Sen, Amartya (1999) *Development as Freedom*, New York: Anchor Books.

10 Why is progress in gender equality so slow? An introduction to the 'Social Institutions and Gender' Index
Denis Drechsler and Johannes Jütting

Introduction

Every year on 8 March, International Women's Day (IWD) reminds the world community of women's achievement in economic, political and social life. In some countries – Russia, Vietnam and Bulgaria, for example – the day is even recognised as a public holiday. With all this attention given to women's empowerment, it might be a good moment to ask how gender equality fares today, almost a century after IWD was first celebrated in 1911.

Beyond doubt, the situation of women has improved considerably over the past decades: access to education is no longer a privilege for boys, the literacy ratio – an indicator of equal advancement in education between boys and girls – is constantly narrowing, signalling that girls are catching up and sometimes even surpassing their male counterparts (Clark, 2003). Other advances can be reported with regard to women's access to basic healthcare, participation in the labour market and representation in national parliaments – all of which are crucial elements in women's social and economic empowerment. Raising awareness of the particular needs of women and attempts to mainstream gender into other policy domains through instruments such as gender-sensitive budgeting gradually seem to be paying off (World Bank, 2001).

What is more, the call for more gender equality has involved actors beyond feminists or human rights activists. The weekly news magazine *The Economist*, for example, has coined the term 'womenomics', highlighting the prominent role of women for economic growth and prosperity. Apart from being a goal in itself, gender equality is now widely perceived as being a key instrument to stimulate and promote sustainable development.

However, digging a little deeper and looking beyond the surface of these undeniable achievements, the picture still looks rather gloomy. Despite various efforts and international declarations, for example the 2000 Millennium Development Goals (MDGs), important gender gaps remain. In many countries, women are still deprived of their full economic, social and political rights and opportunities. Despite having gained access to areas such as healthcare, education and wage employment, women frequently occupy the lower ranks within each domain.

Take the example of economic opportunities. While many countries have experienced stable economic growth over the past decades, often coupled with a strong expansion of the labour market, women mostly find themselves in informal jobs with low and insecure income, insufficient access to social security, and no upward mobility (Standing, 1999; see also Chen, Chapter 71, this volume). Being in informal employment renders women vulnerable to poverty, economic shocks and natural disasters and hence leads to a 'feminisation of poverty' (Jütting and de Laiglesia, 2009; although see also chapters in Part

II, this volume). Similar scenarios emerge in other key areas of gender equality. Despite increased investments in women's access to schools and vocational training, women remain under-represented in higher education, earn significantly less than their male colleagues and barely find themselves in top government or managerial positions (see also Perrons, Chapter 62, this volume).

What are the reasons that, despite economic growth and targeted investments to improve the situation of women, progress in gender equality is so slow? One important, but often ignored factor is people's mindset that is frequently hostile to further advancements in gender equality. In Algeria, for example, a survey by the CIDDEF (Centre d'Information et de Documentation sur les Droits de l'Enfant et de la Femme) published in March 2009 finds that only 16 per cent of the population approves of gender equality and less than 33 per cent agrees that brothers and sisters should have equal access to their parent's inheritance. In Afghanistan, President Hamid Karzaï has recently signed a law that makes it very difficult for women to engage in paid work, pursue an education, and consult a doctor, which could be interpreted as legalising material rape.[1]

Such attitudes based on prevailing norms and traditions are severe impediments to women's social and economic development. However, information on these hidden instances of gender discrimination is scarce and not captured in conventional gender statistics. This chapter presents a new tool to measure gender inequalities based on social institutions and argues that in many countries traditions and social norms are the decisive factors restraining progress in women's empowerment.

The Social Institutions and Gender Index (SIGI): measuring hidden forms of gender discrimination

Existing measures of gender equality focus on outcome variables, such as literacy ratios, maternal mortality rates or employment statistics. The underlying reasons of persisting gender inequalities, however, are not well captured, let alone understood. Several new studies suggest that social institutions play a dominant role in inhibiting women's social and economic development (Jütting et al., 2008; Morrisson and Jütting, 2005). With the launch of the Social Institutions and Development Index (SIGI) in 2009, the Development Centre of the Organisation for Economic Co-operation and Development (OECD) presents a new composite measure to identify and better understand the impact of social institutions on gender equality.

Social institutions, which have often been in existence for centuries, are conceived as long-lasting codes of conduct, norms, traditions and informal family laws that do not change much over time. The SIGI helps to measure social institutions that have an impact on gender equality and correlates them with various inequality outcomes.

The index combines 12 innovative indicators relating to household behaviour and social norms, including such practices as forced marriage and genital mutilation, as well as factors such as freedom of movement and restricted access to inheritance and property. It is composed of five sub-categories (see Figure 10.1) that provide a comprehensive picture of gender inequalities in social institutions.

1. *Family Code*, refers to institutions that influence decision-making power of women within the household, looking at parental authority, inheritance rights, early marriage and polygamy.

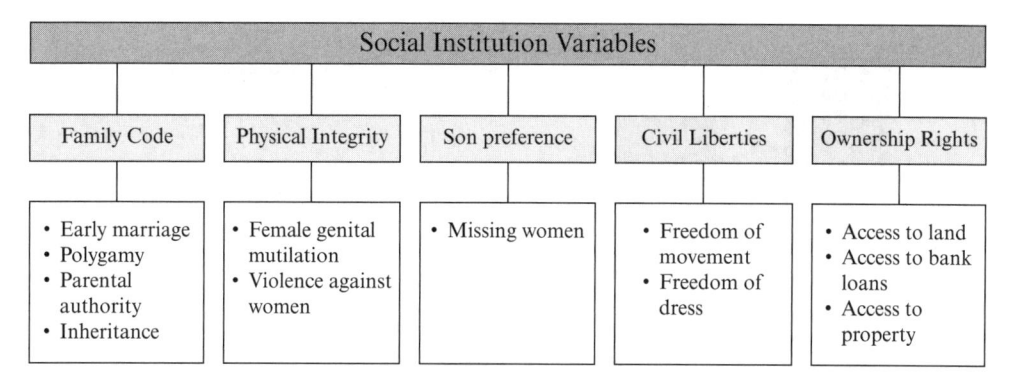

```
                        Social Institution Variables
    ┌──────────────┬──────────────┬──────────────┬──────────────┬──────────────┐
    Family Code   Physical      Son preference  Civil Liberties  Ownership Rights
                  Integrity
```

- Early marriage
- Polygamy
- Parental authority
- Inheritance

- Female genital mutilation
- Violence against women

- Missing women

- Freedom of movement
- Freedom of dress

- Access to land
- Access to bank loans
- Access to property

Source: OECD Development Centre, available at: www.oecd.org (accessed 20 April 2009).

Figure 10.1 Construction of the OECD Social Institutions and Gender Index (SIGI)

2. *Civil Liberties*, captures the social participation of women, including information on women's freedom of movement and freedom of dress.
3. *Physical Integrity*, comprises different indicators on violence against women, for example, the legal protection of women against domestic violence, rape and sexual assault, as well as the prevalence of female genital mutilation.
4. *Son Preference*, based on the 'missing women' concept introduced by Nobel Laureate Amartya Sen in 1990 reflects the economic valuation of women and measures gender bias in mortality due to sex-selective abortions or insufficient care given to baby girls.
5. *Ownership Rights*, covers the access of women to several types of property, for example land, credit and housing.

What does the SIGI show us?

Uneven discrimination through social institutions between regions
The SIGI shows that women in most parts of the world face discrimination based on social institutions. It also highlights important regional differences: for instance, inequalities are particularly pronounced in sub-Saharan Africa, South Asia and the Middle East and North Africa region. Many of the world's worst performers are situated in the belt that stretches from Mali to Pakistan. Sudan, Afghanistan and Sierra Leone are at the bottom of the SIGI ranking, indicating that in these countries social discrimination against women is very strong. By contrast, relatively low inequalities in social institutions can be observed in Latin America, Eastern Europe and Central Asia. Among the 102 countries that are included in the ranking, Paraguay, Croatia and Kazakhstan score best. Both high and low performers can be found in the East Asia and Pacific region. The ranking does not include OECD countries.

Social institutions as principal determinants of persisting gender inequalities
Social institutions are related to a number of gender inequality outcomes. In fact, strong correlations can be observed between the level of discrimination through social institutions and educational attainment as well as women's economic opportunities.

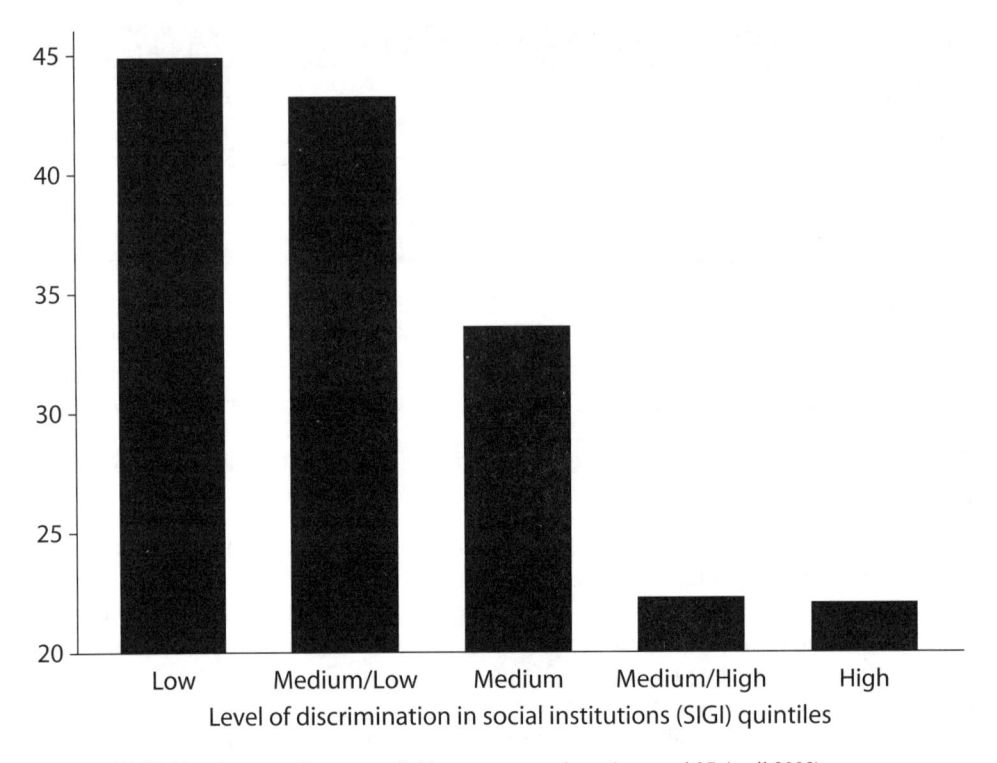

80   *The international handbook of gender and poverty*

Source: OECD Development Centre, available at: www.oecd.org (accessed 27 April 2009).

Figure 10.2   Discrimination in social institutions and women's participation in non-agricultural wage employment

As regards women's educational attainment, social institutions seem to have a negative impact on women's literacy rates relative to men. Countries with low SIGI scores show a ratio of female to male literacy of close to 1, indicating gender equality. The ratio is significantly below 1 in countries where discrimination in social institutions is high.

Among the SIGI indicators, 'early marriage' has a particularly strong effect on this relationship. Marriages at a young age, usually a result of arranged or even forced wedlock, limit women's access to education and discourage them from pursuing a professional career. This is not only detrimental for women, but also has negative consequences for the overall economic development of a country. Several studies find that gender differences in education weaken a country's economic growth potential as lower education for girls reduces the 'talent pool' of a country's labour force. Persisting gender gaps in education also lower women's skills, social competences, health and life expectancy (Klasen, 2002), which not only diminish women's quality of life but the welfare of the entire economy in an intergenerational context.

Another strong correlation can be observed between social institutions and women's participation in non-agricultural wage employment, which has been identified as a key element of women's economic empowerment (see Figure 10.2).

More specifically, women's participation in non-agricultural wage employment is lowest in countries with strong social discrimination. Among the countries which score low in the SIGI ranking, labour force participation is close to 50 per cent, while in countries that show high social discrimination, women's average participation rate is just above 20 per cent. Further analysis shows that women's participation in non-agricultural wage employment is particularly low in countries with high discrimination in the family context (SIGI variables: parental authority, inheritance rights, early marriage and polygamy). Again, women's access to paid jobs is not only crucial for their own personal well-being, but an important driver for the overall economic development of a country. For example, the additional income of an employed woman can increase savings and stimulate consumption. Apart from positively affecting a country's output level, female wage employment also raises women's bargaining power within the household, with positive repercussions on children's education and health.

A strong relationship also exists between the SIGI scores and fertility rates. In particular, violence against women and the prevalence of female genital mutilation (both of which are variables of the SIGI) are associated with a higher number of babies per woman. High fertility, in turn, has negative implications for women's access to education and economic opportunities, which also dampens a country's economic development. Indeed, growth rates appear to be lower in regions where social institutions are to the disadvantage of women.

Finally, social institutions also have a bearing on women's job quality in the agricultural sector, in which traditional attitudes and mindsets are dominant. This impact appears to be particularly strong in Asian countries and the Middle East and North Africa region. The lower the level of discrimination through social institutions, the higher is the proportion of women in wage employment, which is a cornerstone of financial independence and a self-determined life. Moreover, the lower the number of women who have access to land and credit (both constituting sub-indices of the SIGI), the greater the likelihood that women work as contributing family workers, which frequently subjects them to the orders of male relatives and traps them in poor working conditions without income and social protection.

Policy implications

Focusing on social institutions is an important step to understand the root causes of existing gender inequalities. The SIGI analysis shows why progress in achieving sustainable results has been so slow. Development policies have frequently proved inappropriate because they did not recognise prevailing norms and traditions as the driving forces of gender discrimination and consequently failed to incorporate adequate measures to target social institutions. The discussion on how to advance women's educational attainment is a case in point. In order to strengthen women's empowerment, many development experts have called for more funding, to build schools, for instance. Yet, the analytical findings of this chapter suggest that standard policy responses (as in the example of building schools) risk being unsuccessful to contain discrimination as long as traditions prevent girls from attending educational facilities or deprive them of access to land, technology and information. Extra spending, while badly needed, will generate real returns only if the fundamental causes of discrimination are dealt with too.

The fight for gender equality needs to effectively address traditions and social norms. A multilayered approach – including institutional and legal reforms and a better enforcement of existing laws – can gradually work towards changing deep-rooted attitudes and beliefs. Partner countries should take a lead in this, but donors play an important role as well in exchanging lessons learned and sharing knowledge based on their own experiences at home. As a first step, policies should change legal institutions that discriminate against women, such as property rights, inheritance laws, divorce regulations and family codes. Establishing monitoring systems could then help ensure that such changes not only go on paper but also become enforced. At the same time, efforts need to be made to effectively change social attitudes that discriminate against women, for example, by influencing media and communication channels and by initiating information campaigns to win the support of the entire population, including men. The last point is especially crucial. Many reform programmes have failed due to their exclusive focus on women's needs, overlooking the fact that societies based on persistent discrimination generate advantages that men will not sacrifice easily. Effective policies therefore need to consider men's perspective as well and provide incentives for men to engage in the reform process.

From Morocco and Tunisia to some states in southern India, several initiatives can already be identified that have tried to change the institutional frameworks limiting women's opportunities. Although these might be isolated cases, such reform efforts are encouraging and point in the right direction; they also promise positive results. Despite the regional patterns of social discrimination mentioned above, several countries with similar social and cultural backgrounds also show important variation in the SIGI scoring. This suggests that past reforms in these countries have worked and future efforts can be successful if applied properly.

In Tunisia, for example, social discrimination measured by the SIGI is much lower than in its neighbouring countries. This situation can be explained by looking into the country's recent history. Under the leadership of President Habib Bourguiba, the Tunisian government, in 1956, changed the family code and banned discriminatory practices such as polygamy and repudiation, promoted consensual marriage and introduced equal divorce proceedings. The results of these measures can be seen today. At rates of 30 to 50 per cent, women constitute a higher share of judges, physicians and schoolteachers than in all other countries in the Middle East and North Africa region except Israel.

Conclusion
Gender equality is widely perceived as a fundamental human right and is increasingly seen as being crucial for social and economic development. Despite various efforts to improve the situation of women, progress in gender equality is still lagging behind internationally proclaimed objectives. Better measures of gender equality are urgently needed to better understand and effectively address the elements that prevent women's social and economic opportunities. Drawing on results of the SIGI this chapter shows that making sustainable progress in gender equality requires a deep transformation of traditions and social norms. With coherent, sensitive and inclusive strategies, discrimination that denies women their rights and blights the development potential of whole countries can one day be removed for good.

Note

1. See '"Worse than the Taliban" – new law rolls back rights for Afghan women', *Guardian*, 31 March 2009, available at: http://www.guardian.co.uk/world/2009/mar/31/hamid-karzai-afghanistan-law (last accessed 15 October 2009).

Select bibliography

Clark, Rebecca (2003) 'Female literacy rates, information technology and democracy', working paper presented at the Annual Conference of the Canadian Political Science Association (CPSA), Dalhousie University, 30 May–1 June, Halifax, Nova Scotia.
Jütting, Johannes, Christian Morrisson, Jeff Dayton-Johnson and Denis Drechsler (2008) 'Measuring gender (in)equality: the OECD Gender, Institutions and Development Data Base', *Journal of Human Development*, **9** (1), 65–86.
Jütting, Johannes and Juan de Laiglesia (eds) (2009), *Is Informal Normal? Towards More and Better Jobs in Developing Countries*, Paris: Organisation for Economic Co-operation and Development.
Klasen, Stefan (2002) 'Low schooling for girls: slower growth for all?', *World Bank Economic Review*, **16**, 345–73.
Morrison, Christian and Johannes Jütting (2005) 'Women's discrimination in developing countries: a new data set for better policies', *World Development*, **33** (7), 1065–81.
Standing, Guy (1999) 'Global feminisation through flexible labour: a theme revisited', *World Development*, **27** (3), 583–602.
World Bank (2001) *Engendering Development*, Washington, DC: World Bank.

11 Diamonds are a girl's best friend? Experiences with the Gender Action Learning System

Linda Mayoux

There is now overwhelming evidence that gender inequality is a key cause of poverty, and women's empowerment a key strategy for reducing it. Despite statements to this effect in policy documents of most donor agencies and many governments, gender issues are still widely marginalised in most poverty reduction initiatives apart from a few measures targeted to women entrepreneurs or female-headed households. Addressing gender inequalities within households and communities is widely seen as both less important, and more difficult to address, than household-level material poverty and well-being. Such assertions are often based on assumptions about the views of women and men at the community-level, and inevitability of conflict and the need for cultural sensitivity.

This chapter challenges these views based on experience of a methodology called the Gender Action Learning System (GALS) in Uganda, Sudan, India, Pakistan and Peru. The analyses of poverty produced by both women and men clearly show the centrality of gender inequalities to household poverty. Men as well as women, provided they are given sufficient support and space, have identified their own behaviour as key causes of poverty and identified and implemented effective strategies for change which they themselves have undertaken as individuals. These provide a basis for community-led collective action and advocacy for change.

Gender Action Learning System (GALS): methodology overview
GALS is the adaptation of a generic methodology, Participatory Action Learning System (PALS), specifically to analyse and address gender issues.[1] GALS adapts very simple diagramming tools: Diamonds, Road Journeys, Trees and Circles to specific gender issues, contexts and organisational needs. The methodology is based on and continually reinforces underlying principles of equity, inclusion and gender justice and women's human rights as stated in international agreements like the Convention on the Elimination of All Forms of Discrimination Against Women (CEDAW). The tools can be used independently by people who cannot read and write as well as organisational staff and academic researchers to analyse issues and strategise change. Ideally the GALS is a long-term community-led change process alternating individual reflection and planning with group peer learning and planning, progressively building organisational structures for collective action and community-led gender advocacy. The tools can also be used by organisations and researchers to rapidly obtain reliable quantitative information and very rich qualitative information in a more empowering and interesting manner for participants. Using the same tools at different levels of an organisation, where people who cannot read and write are often better at drawing and analysis, serves to increase communication, understanding and respect and challenge power relations between different stakeholders.

The chapter focuses particularly on one tool – 'Diamonds – which can be used to:

1. explore, identify and compare women and men's criteria for gender justice and/or empowerment and/or gendered perceptions of wealth and happiness;
2. rank and prioritise these as issues for individual, collective and organisational action;
3. quantify where participants currently are in relation to each criterion or level;
4. quantify where they started as a rapid impact assessment;
5. plot and quantify where they want to get to after a specified period of time as the basis for planning and monitoring;
6. provoke rich qualitative discussion on all the above, including sensitive issues like power relations, sexuality and violence.

The main steps are summarised in Box 11.1.

The Diamond tool can be used in combination with other GALS tools as part of a longer-term empowerment process, or on its own as a half-day participatory meeting. A common practice has been to give one group or set of groups the question 'What are women/men doing in a happy family and in an unhappy family?', another group the question 'What does a powerful/powerless woman/man look like/do/have?', and yet another group another question 'What does a rich/poor woman/man look like/do/have?' This then enables exploration of differences in perceptions of linkages between women's empowerment, wealth and happiness and/or women's powerlessness, poverty and unhappiness in the household and community. An example of a Happy Families Diamond from Uganda is given in Figure 11.1.

Diamonds have been used not only to look at general criteria for poverty and inequality, but also more specific dimensions of poverty like food security or health, and sensitive issues like gender-based violence, decision-making and property ownership.

Women and men's analyses of poverty and empowerment
Rigorous cross-cultural comparisons of the outcomes of the GALS remains to be done. The focus so far has been more on establishing the methodology as a community-led empowerment process, particularly with women and men who cannot read and write. It has therefore been important not to overload meetings with lots of outsiders taking notes for monitoring or research. This can be done retrospectively using changes marked on the same initial diagrams which always remain as a record.

Nevertheless experience in Uganda, Sudan, Pakistan, India and Peru with poor and very poor women in different types of organisation have identified many common criteria for both the 'ideal situation' and their actual and worst case situations. Regardless of the specific question asked or cultural context, women generally put their own property ownership, earning their own income and respect/love from the husband at the top of the diamond. Women also generally value motherhood highly and have a positive view of certain 'feminine' traits like caring, multitasking and hard working. In Pakistan women's possession of mobile phones was important as a means of maintaining contact with their children, friends and access to outside knowledge of the world – as well as a symbol of wealth. Interestingly 16 per cent of a heavily veiled group of women in Baluchistan considered they were in the empowered category, able to contribute income to the household

BOX 11.1 STEPS IN USING THE DIAMOND TOOL

Diamonds are best used in mixed-sex workshops where women analyse women's situation and men analyse men's, with further subgroups also where possible for comparison of differing views between women and between men. A variant is for one sex to do what they like or dislike about the other sex on a separate diamond. These group outputs are brought together and compared in a common plenary 'Mother Diamond' focusing on 'common human values'. Each group has ideally 10–15 participants with one facilitator and one co-facilitator/rapporteur, both of whom need to have done the exercise before, but neither of whom need to be literate. It requires large wall space, flipcharts, small coloured cards, sticky tape and markers. General facilitation guidelines are given in Mayoux (2009).

Step 1: Individual brainstorming: 'best' and 'worst' cases
Participants are each given two differently coloured sets of three cards and asked to draw or write:

> On cards of one colour the three 'best case' criteria, for example, things you like most about being a woman/man?
> On cards of the other colour the three 'worst case' criteria, for example, things you like least?

Step 2: Sharing, grouping and voting of criteria
Each person presents what is on their cards, placing them on the wall and grouping together similar criteria. Each person then has five votes on best and worst to get ranking.

Step 3: Placing on the diamond: gender analysis
Each group of cards are ranked on the diamond with the groups of 'best' cards with the most votes to the top of the diamond and groups of 'worst' cards with the most votes to the bottom. While this is being done, participants decide the horizontal position criteria seen as currently most unique to each sex on each side, in the columns marked for each sex. Common things go in the middle. And the constant question is whether or not each issue is in fact sex-specific, or a common human issue.

Step 4: Quantification and impact assessment
Each person comes up and puts a mark by the card group which applies to them. This then enables quantification of all the criteria at a glance. Depending on the time available, participants can also mark where they were before an intervention started to provide a basis for quantified impact assessment and qualitative discussion of impacts.

> *Step 5: What do we want to change in future?*
> At the same time participants put an unhappy face by the three things they most want to change from the things at the bottom of the diamond. The issues with the most unhappy faces can then be discussed in more detail if time permits, and taken forward for further analysis through Challenge Action Trees.
>
> It is also possible if time permits for people to put a happy face by the three things they like most and would like to retain/increase.

and gain respect, leading to discussion of very complex entrepreneurship strategies by these women which challenged many of the stereotypes held by the non-governmental organisation (NGO) concerned.

The criteria do differ depending on the organisational context, and the types of activity in which the organisation is involved. For example, tribal women in Area Networking and Development Initiatives (ANANDI) in India, an organisation which focuses specifically on women's empowerment and gender advocacy, focused more on collective and political dimensions for empowerment. The most empowered women were seen as those able to get development funds for the village, who help women overcome violence, are educated and aware of the laws and bring new information for other women. A least empowered woman was one who cannot stand up to the wrong harassment of the forest official (Mayoux and ANANDI, 2005).

On the lower 'worst case' part of all types of diamond and in all contexts women almost invariably cite the issue of violence, having too many children and illiteracy. Quantification here has shown very alarming statistics – in Pakistan 80 per cent of women are subject to serious forms of violence, with 5 per cent at suicidal breaking point (Sardar et al., 2005). In ANANDI a diamond focusing specifically on violence was used with a group of tribal women who initially denied there was any violence in their community. Within two hours they had produced a detailed ranking of different types of violence. Extreme violence was agreed to be 'Beating till you get wounded (bleeding) and you feel like committing suicide is extreme, unbearable violence'. Ranked less severe were cases of being imprisoned in their houses for disobedience and the many forms of violence 'which they have to deal with every day and hence do not call violence' – verbal abuse, fights over money, daily consumption of alcohol by men, minor beating by the husband because the 'meal is not tasty'. Their ideal situation was 'When husband–wife stay together peacefully without any kind of mistrust and suspicion, children go to school, no illness, adequate water, and agriculture produce, neither have to migrate out for work and above all prohibition on liquor and ban on torture would bring peace'. The only women considered in this situation were those with no man in their household or extended family: no husband, father or brother. Five out of the 20 women admitted to having experienced very serious violence just stopping short of murder, which they had never before discussed with anyone (Mayoux and ANANDI, 2005).

In India, Uganda and Sudan, after initial training, diamonds have been used by women's groups without external facilitation to identify the poorest and least empowered women in their community and to develop strategies for their inclusion in the group.

The Diamond has also been used with men in Pakistan and Uganda. In both contexts

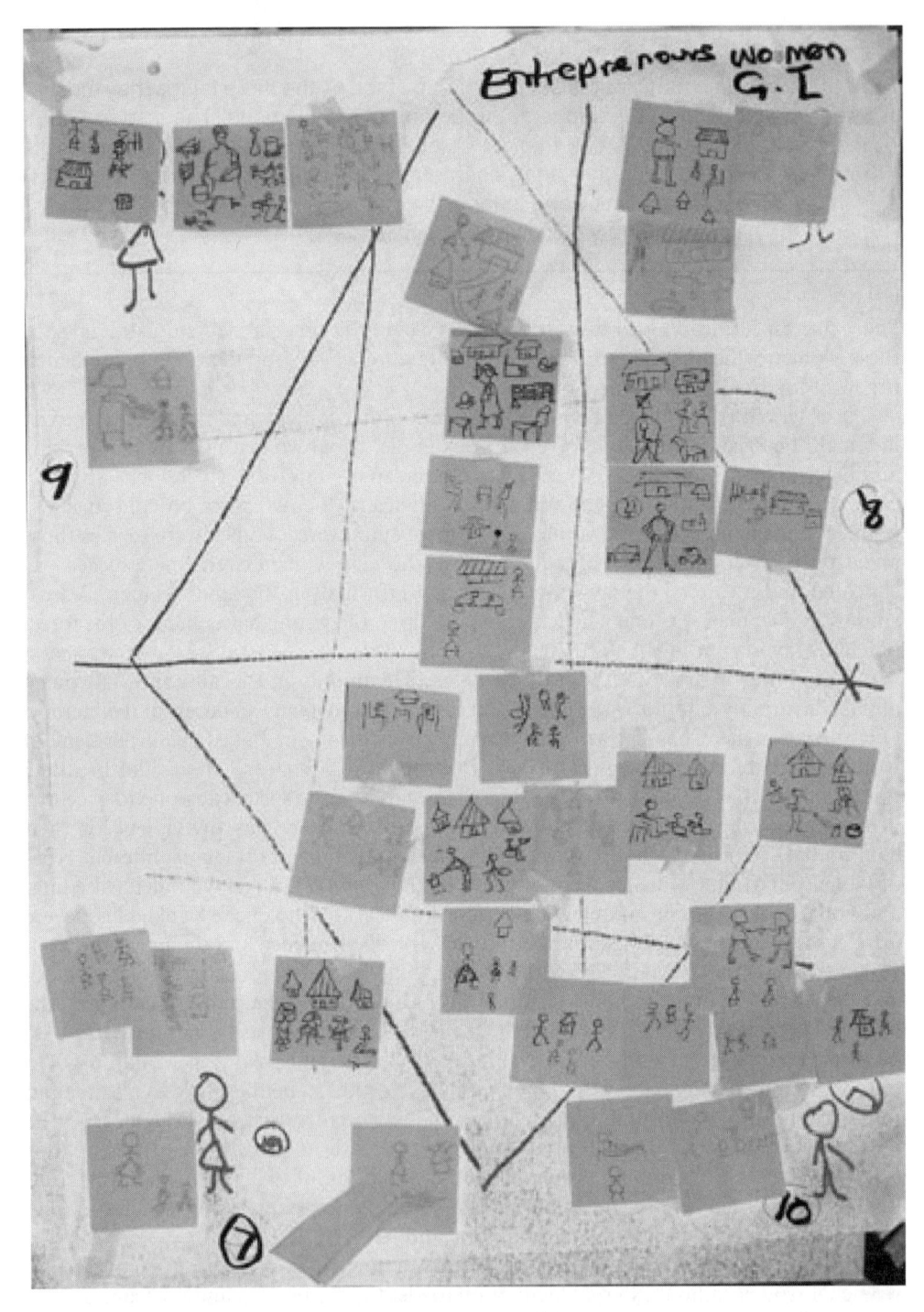

88   *The international handbook of gender and poverty*

Figure 11.1   Example of 'Happy Families Diamond' by women entrepreneurs from Uganda

use of the Diamond and other tools have led to identification of changes which men can make to both increase their own happiness and have greater gender equality in the household. Mutual respect and participation in decision-making was commonly cited by men as an element in both happiness and women's empowerment, along with women's literacy and having few children. In Pakistan men mentioned lack of political representation for disempowered women. Significantly, however, household violence featured much less prominently in any of men's analysis of poverty, empowerment or happiness.

In Uganda, where the PALS methodology originated, most groups are mixed sex and have been using Poverty Diamonds, and also a range of livelihood development tools, without external facilitation to identify poverty levels in their groups and analyse and plan their businesses. A particularly important development in Uganda, continuing on from diamonds, have been Challenge Action Trees where men identify the causes for their own adultery, violence and alcoholism and make commitment to action steps to change – on the understanding that such men are not happy as well as their behaviour damaging their wives and children. Anecdotal information from their wives and others in the community indicate these pledges have often been fulfilled, and that the men are presenting their experience in church to other men and women and to their friends.

In Baluchistan, Pakistan, it was clear that for men the way in which gender issues are presented was important. The group of men asked to discuss 'women's empowerment' walked out of the meeting leaving the facilitator alone. The group asked to discuss women and men's role in 'happy families', on the other hand, had a very engaged and in-depth discussion. Although the focus on men's own happiness was necessary as an entry point, the men still identified a number of issues which mirrored women's priorities as a basis on which both men and women could work. They strongly supported women's literacy and smaller families. Many men felt overburdened by their economic responsibilities and the demands placed upon them by their families, and would like to share this more with their wives. Men wanted to be able to go to the cinema with their wives and move around freely with them. This then led to a discussion of why they felt they could not do this and what they could do to change the situation (Mayoux, 2005). Interestingly, none of the drawings by either women or men showed women veiled, even though they wore *burqa* at the meetings – also challenging external stereotypes.

Conclusions and remaining challenges

The GALS methodology has developed in different ways in the different contexts, and the tools are used in different combinations – because of different initial purposes for which it is used and different organisational experiences and capacities more than because of differences in economic and social context. The methodology is ideally integrated as a more empowering and effective methodology for existing activities –rather than as separate process. This flexibility is a strength, but also makes any written manual or initial training blueprint problematic. It also makes ownership/accreditation issues rather sensitive – over time it is the women and men in communities who lead innovation in the methodology, not development organisations.

The GALS cannot claim to resolve all the contradictions and power inequalities and potential conflict inherent in any participatory process which aims to challenge gender inequality.[2] The aim of the Diamond is to provoke discussion and rapidly identify actions which could lead to rapid tangible valued changes in a short period of time through participants' own actions in their households and communities. This is a means for increasing community ownership of a gender justice peer learning and action process which does not require continual external facilitation to maintain its momentum.

The GALS is not a substitute for in-depth training, but an entry point which provides motivation and highlights demand as well as increasing people's learning skills to benefit from training they receive. In addition to the almost universal demand for enterprise and technical training of various types, demands/actions which have arisen have included women in Sudan deciding to go as a group to government literacy courses they had previously not thought worthwhile, demands in Uganda, Sudan and Pakistan for in-depth women's legal rights training, and in Sudan and Pakistan training on women's rights under Islam. The facilitation process is important. The GALS does not aim to be a consciousness-raising tool with preset gender messages. Facilitation is done 'actively from the back'. The facilitator introduces the activity, but only participants handle the marker or cards. The facilitator's role is to ask questions where these are not raised by participants, particularly on apparent differences/contradictions in opinions, to prevent any one person dominating and make sure everyone's voice is heard. The only 'messages' as such come in the summing-up where the outcomes can be compared with a simplified version of the Convention on the Elimination of All Forms of Discrimination Against Women or some other very simple statement of rights and principles. Through eliciting spontaneous views of gender difference, the GALS provokes discussion of which differences are desirable and which are 'unjust' and generally in and of itself leads to a consensus on common human rights, and the need to ensure that women as well as men enjoy these. Facilitation does not require formal education, but good communication skills and empathy – something which is paradoxically often more difficult for those with conventional training experience than people in communities themselves. In Uganda women entrepreneurs who cannot read and write are the preferred 'trainers' by the community.

Once established for a couple of years, the GALS is potentially a financially and organisationally sustainable change process integrated into other activities (existing livelihood or gender training, savings and credit group meetings, annual general meetings, community fairs and so on) and needing little external facilitation of the methodology itself. The organisation's role becomes one of effectively responding to issues identified as needing external support through integration in their participatory planning process. The GALS therefore does not in any way remove the need for development agencies and governments to be actively committed to gender justice, backed by adequate resources. It increases the respect and voice of very poor people in organisational decision-making and enables external resources to be targeted where they are most needed, based on articulate and informed demand.

Notes
1. The PALS originated with work by the author with Kabarole Research and Resource Centre and their partner organisations in Uganda in 2002. For an overview of this generic methodology see Mayoux (2006). The GALS adaptations with consultancies in Pakistan, India and Sudan are now an integral part of Oxfam Novib's 'Women's Empowerment, Mainstreaming and Networking Process'. The other tools used are described in detail in Mayoux (2008). There are also two websites which may be consulted: www.palsnetwork.info, which is dedicated to the Participatory Action Learning System (including GALS) with multimedia learning materials and core resources, and www.wemanglobal.org, which is the website for Oxfam Novib's Women's Empowerment Mainstreaming and Networking for Gender Justice in Economic Development process. This contains further documents and updates on the GALS methodology and regional processes.

2. For an overview of some of these contradictions and challenges, see Mayoux (1995), which is the starting point of the ideas which eventually led to the GALS.

Select bibliography

Mayoux, Linda (1995) 'Beyond naivety: women, gender inequality and participatory development: some thorny issues', *Development and Change*, **26** (2), 235–58.

Mayoux, Linda (2005) 'Women's empowerment through sustainable micro-finance: organisational gender training, Taraqee Foundation draft report', available at: http://www.genfinance.info/Trainingresources_05/Taraqee_Report_draft.pdf (accessed April 2009).

Mayoux, Linda (2006) 'Road to the foot of the mountain – but reaching for the sun: PALS adventures and challenges', in Karen Brock and Jethro Pettit (eds), *Springs of Participation: Creating and Evolving Methods for Participatory Development*, London: Intermediate Technology Publications, pp. 93–106.

Mayoux, Linda (2008) *Steering Life's Rocky Road – Equal and Together: Gender Action Learning System Core Manual First Draft*, The Hague: Oxfam Novib/Women's Empowerment Mainstreaming and Networking for Gender Justice in Economic Development (WEMAN), available at: http://www.wemanglobal.org (accessed 30 October 2009).

Mayoux, Linda (2009) *Diamond Tree of Dreams: GALS Stage 1 Manual, Draft for Field-testing*, The Hague: Oxfam Novib/WEMAN, available at: http://www.wemanglobal.org (accessed 30 October 2009).

Mayoux, Linda and Area Networking and Development Initiatives (ANANDI) (2005) 'Participatory action learning in practice: experience of Anandi, India', *Journal of International Development*, **17**, 211–42.

Sardar, Farzana, Nasir Mumtaz, Shazreh Hussain and Linda Mayoux (2005) 'Women's and men's views of empowerment: Kashf empowerment diamonds', available at: http://www.genfinance.info/Documents/Kashf%20Empowerment%20Diamonds.pdf (accessed 25 April 2009).

PART II

DEBATES ON THE 'FEMINISATION OF POVERTY', AND FEMALE-HEADED HOUSEHOLDS

12 The 'feminisation of poverty': a widespread phenomenon?

Marcelo Medeiros and Joana Costa

In the process of policymaking accurate information about societal trends can be crucial. The choice of best strategies for action may differ according to this information. Data on the 'feminisation of poverty' is particularly important because it combines two critical issues: gender inequality and poverty. But the two are not synonymous; gender inequality extends beyond the poor and, by its turn, poverty is not exclusive to females. A flawed diagnosis of the facts may end up misguiding policies and making their results inadequate in both areas. On the one hand, emphasising poverty tends to overshadow the debate on gender inequality and, on the other, putting excessive stress on gender issues may lead to inadequate anti-poverty policies.

The question of whether there is a 'feminisation of poverty' depends first and foremost on a definition of the term. To seek an answer for this question this chapter discusses the meaning of different concepts of 'feminisation', argues in favour of one that can be applied to several dimensions of poverty, including income deprivation, and shows that according to this way of defining the phenomenon, there is no empirical evidence of a feminisation of income poverty in several countries of the world.

The numerous meanings of 'feminisation of poverty'
Different definitions may lead to the observation of different phenomena and therefore have different implications in terms of policymaking. For example, a feminisation of *income* poverty is likely to imply policies that differ from those designed to face the feminisation of *time* poverty; the first may require an increase in full-time paid jobs for women, while the latter more access to childcare services to reduce household work.

The concept of feminisation of poverty depends on the meanings of its two components, namely, 'feminisation' and 'poverty'. In studies on the subject, feminisation has been understood as a static phenomenon (or 'end state'), as well as a dynamic process, has compared the gender composition of the poor and the levels of poverty within and between gender groups, and has also associated 'feminine' with women and female-headed households. The notion of poverty in these studies also varies according to the way in which poverty is identified (spaces or dimensions of poverty and poverty thresholds), and aggregated (the measures of poverty). To analyse the broad range of possibilities in more detail let us put it schematically, beginning with poverty.

1. Poverty
Poverty is a concept deeply related to deprivation, but consensus about its definition ends here. There is a tendency nowadays to accept that poverty is different from inequality and it is absolute in terms of what people need or should be able to do but relative in terms of how these needs can be satisfied or these capabilities can be acquired, or, to

use the jargon, poverty is absolute in the space of needs and relative in the space of what is required to satisfy these needs. 'Space' is a concept borrowed from mathematics to reflect the useful notion that a space is composed by many dimensions. Some less mathematical synonyms for space are 'sphere', 'realm' and 'set'.

1.1 Spaces or dimensions of poverty The majority of the statistical studies on the feminisation of poverty have looked at one dimension of poverty, income deprivation. Some others have looked at the satisfaction of basic needs such as potable water, sanitation, and so on. Yet, gender studies would obviously benefit from the analysis of other types of deprivation. Due to the very nature of gender inequalities, the deprivation of non-work time and of certain opportunities and freedoms is clearly a subject that needs further investigation (see also Chant, Chapter 15, this volume).

There is also a tendency to accept that a definition of poverty should reflect the fact that human well-being depends not only on consumption of goods and services but also on other factors such as freedoms, care, respect and social bondings; that is, to accept that human well-being is multidimensional and thus that poverty should be a multidimensional concept. As a consequence of this, income poverty should be viewed as one important dimension of poverty but not as the *sole* dimension. Note that multidimensionality does not require the simultaneous approach of all dimensions at the same time. According to the needs of each case, different dimensions can be analysed separately and later combined.

1.2 Unit of analysis The identification of poverty and therefore its measurement reflects the choice for a unit of analysis. This unit could be, for instance, individuals or families. It is common to talk about poor individuals but this is usually based on information regarding their families, not the individuals only. Perhaps it would be more appropriate, in these cases, to mention individuals in poor households and not simply poor individuals because, from a gender perspective, the distinction does make a difference. The conventional household approach to poverty is an inheritance from income deprivation analysis and is based on the implicit assumption that within a household individuals share equally the resources available to them. Actually, the scarce statistical evidence about this suggests that this assumption is not realistic: there are intrahousehold inequalities in consumption and they tend to be correlated with gender and generational inequalities. This said, two points deserve highlighting. First, it is hard, particularly in developing countries, to proceed otherwise because of the lack of data available to measure intrahousehold inequalities. Second, a bias against women in, say, intrahousehold consumption, does not translate automatically into a feminisation of poverty if the latter is taken as a dynamic concept. Only an increase of this bias over time could become a factor in 'feminisation'. The notion of feminisation as a dynamic concept is discussed below.

1.3 Measure of poverty The choices of the dimensions and of a unit of analysis are part of the process of identification of the poor. The next logical step is known as aggregation and consists in using measures of poverty to determine the level of poverty in a social group.

Measures are also called indices of poverty. Two very common measures of income poverty are, first, the proportion of the poor in the total population, a measure of incidence of poverty also known as the headcount ratio, and, second, the average income the poor need to reach the poverty line, a measure of the intensity of poverty also known as the income gap ratio. However, there are other measures, including some with mathematical properties, that are useful for statistical analysis.

Decisions about the measures of poverty to use are of major importance because different measures can lead to completely different conclusions. Imagine a situation in which a little income is given to those women right below the poverty line and nothing goes to the extremely poor. A large number of women would just cross the poverty line but the extremely poor ones would remain in the same situation. By measures of incidence this society has gone through a huge decrease in female poverty, whereas by measures of intensity poverty remains about the same. Of course, the same study may – perhaps must – compare different measures of poverty.

2. Feminisation

The concept of feminisation has been used with different meanings, some of them being more plausible than others. It has been used to describe both static and dynamic situations, to examine the gender composition of the poor, to compare the levels of poverty between and within gender groups, and to evaluate the conditions of women and of female-headed households.

2.1 Static or dynamic? It does not seem correct to use the term feminisation to describe a static situation such as a higher incidence of poverty among women. The etymology of the term indicates action, thus it implies changes in the levels of poverty. To avoid terminological inconsistencies, static situations should preferably be described using terms such as 'over-representation' – which refers to the higher incidence – or simply 'higher incidence', 'higher intensity' and so forth. Saying that poverty has a female face is different from saying that poverty increasingly has a female face. It is the dynamics implicit in this last idea what characterises feminisation. Put simply, feminisation is not about worst or worse, it is all about worsening.

2.2 Comparison approach There are two basic ways to compare what happens to poverty in different social groups. The first consists in looking at variations in the size of a group among the poor and the second at changes in the levels of poverty inside a group. Both can be used to assess female poverty, but the methodological point of view of these approaches are substantially different. In the first case what matters is the variation in the proportion of, say, women among the poor; in the second the changes in the levels of poverty among women are under analysis. The more precise terminology for the focus at the 'size of a group among the poor' is the analysis of the 'gender composition of the poor'.

There is no doubt about the importance of the gender decomposition for the study of poverty, but in the specific case of the analysis of the feminisation of poverty it has disadvantages as it is subject to variations in both the size of the group and its level of poverty. For example, the impoverishment of female-headed households can be offset by a reduction of the numbers of female-headed households in the population, leaving room for the (wrong) interpretation that there is nothing worsening in the lives of people in female-headed households. This approach was used by Diane Pearce (1978) in her first study about the subject but has been abandoned, and nowadays the statistical studies of feminisation of poverty focus primarily on the changes in the levels of poverty within the gender groups, which is the same as saying that they now compare poverty indexes of gender groups in different moments, not the gender composition of the poor.

2.3 Type of referential A gender group can be formed by women or female-headed households, as we discuss below, but for the sake of brevity let us consider the case of women only. Feminisation is a worsening in the levels of poverty of women. To decide whether poverty is worsening one can either make a 'within group only' comparison or a slightly more complex comparison between groups. There are advantages in using this more complex comparison.

A 'within group only' comparison takes the levels of poverty of the group in a initial period as its baseline reference (or referential). For instance, it compares the levels of poverty among women in one year with the levels of the previous year, ignoring what happened to men. The more complex alternative makes that same first comparison and then contrasts the results with the variation observed in the other gender group. For example, it compares women now to women in a previous period and then contrasts this with the corresponding situations for men.

However, one can easily argue that feminisation is not worsening with respect to women, but worsening with respect to what is happening among men. Suppose the intensity of poverty among men falls while among women it stays the same; women are not worse in absolute terms but undoubtedly are worse in relative terms, thus a feminisation of poverty is taking place. Moreover, suppose poverty increases among both men and women. The two groups become worse in absolute terms. Would it be correct to say that there is an ongoing 'feminisation of poverty' in parallel with a 'masculinisation of poverty'? (see also Chant, Chapter 15, this volume). It is reasonable to reserve the term feminisation of poverty to express the dynamic idea of a relative worsening of women with regard to the situation of men (or female-headed households compared with male-headed households, or even other sorts of gender groups).

2.4 The gender grouping The feminisation of poverty is examined using two types of gender groups, based on the sex of individuals and on the sex of the head of the households. These grouping alternatives deserve a comment. Measures of poverty 'among female-headed households' and 'among women' are not one and the same They both capture a gender dimension of poverty, but in quite distinct ways. They are not mutually exclusive but, because they differ by the unit of analysis and by the population included in each group, they should be interpreted differently (see also Lister, Chapter 24, this volume; Sen, Chapter 13, this volume).

Even though poverty among female-headed households is a gender-related problem it is not a *proxy* for poverty among women. Its gender dimension refers to a bias that determines family composition and has implications for the responsibilities of women in their households. Headship-based indicators aim at representing what happens to specific vulnerable groups of women and their families, thus adopting as their unit of analysis the entire population of the household, irrespectively of sex.

By making a complete separation of men and women as individuals the indicators of poverty among females have a distinct unit of analysis. They set a clear-cut division of sex-based categories, counting or not children as a gendered group in their aggregations. However, because poverty is often measured at the household level, as we have seen above, and because men and women co-reside, female poverty is, by construction of the indicator, intrinsically associated to male poverty and vice versa.

Both grouping alternatives are useful, as long as one keeps in mind that they represent different things. As any other classification system their appropriateness must be assessed instrumentally, that is, in terms of the purposes they will serve to. Neither classification is more or less a gender indicator until the exact meaning of 'gender' is defined by the researcher.

3. A definition of the 'feminisation of poverty'

Taking the discussion above as a starting point we now argue in favour of one specific way of defining feminisation of poverty that can be applied to different concepts of 'feminine' and 'poverty'. Here we are more systematising a diverse debate rather than actually proposing an innovative approach to the problem. We present this discussion in more detail, including mathematical notation, elsewhere (Medeiros and Costa, 2007).

The definition we defend emphasises the dynamic and the relative aspects of feminisation by comparing how the social indicators of gender groups vary over time. It is flexible and can be used when feminisation is interpreted both as 'increasing among women' and 'increasing among female-headed households'. It also has the advantage of distinguishing between the 'feminisation of poverty' as process and a so-called 'over-representation of poverty among women' (Medeiros and Costa, 2007). One can apply it to many dimensions of poverty such as income, basic needs or time deprivation, to mention a few, to different poverty lines and to different statistical measures of poverty – measures of the incidence or of the intensity of poverty, for example.

The feminisation of poverty may be defined as: (a) an increase in the difference in the levels of poverty among women and among men, and (b) an increase in the difference in the levels of poverty among female-headed households and among male- and couple-headed households. By 'difference in the levels of poverty' we mean a comparison by subtraction of the levels in one moment in time with these levels in another moment.

A widespread feminisation of poverty?

Some studies have reviewed the literature on female poverty around the world, regarding both its level and variation over time (see Buvinic and Gupta, 1997; Chant, 2007; Lampietti and Stalker, 2000; Medeiros and Costa, 2007 for further references). In the way we define it, no systematic feminisation of income poverty has been observed in countries in Europe or the Americas in the 1990s and 2000s, and the results obtained tend to be robust to different poverty measures and poverty lines (see Medeiros and Costa, 2007, for a detailed longitudinal study of Latin America). Little is known about the time trends of gender differentials in income poverty in the Middle East, Africa and Asia, and we still depend on a higher geographical coverage to generalise and be assertive about what is happening in the world.

Several studies have found a slightly higher incidence of income poverty among women or female-headed households in some countries, but in many others, this does not occur. A higher incidence of poverty among female-headed households in developing countries in Africa and Latin America is not a common finding. The differentials, when they exist, are usually not very relevant. Therefore, there is no empirical evidence supporting the claims of a worldwide feminisation of income poverty or that income poverty has a female face. On the contrary, the existing evidence seems to reject both assertions.

Notwithstanding, because other dimensions of poverty have different determinants, it is hard to estimate the extent to which these conclusions would hold true for dimensions of poverty other than income or family-consumed goods and services. Poverty understood as the deprivation of education, for example, does not share the same determinants as income deprivation, thus its behaviour can be different to that of income poverty.

Acknowledgements
The authors would like to thank Nanak Kakwani, Eduardo Zepeda, Alejandro Grinspun, Sergei Soares and Fábio Veras for comments and Rafael Osorio, Cristina Queiroz and Luis F. Oliveira for data processing. Marcelo Medeiros would like to thank the Institute for Human Development in New Delhi for support while writing this chapter.

Select bibliography
Buvinic, Mayra and Gita Rao Gupta (1997) 'Female-headed households and female-maintained families: are they worth targetting to reduce poverty in developing countries?', *Economic Development and Cultural Change*, **45** (2), 259–80.
Chant, Sylvia (2007) *Gender, Generation and Poverty: Exploring the 'Feminisation of Poverty' in Africa, Asia and Latin America*, Cheltenham, UK and Northampton, MA, USA: Edward Elgar.
Lampietti, Julian and Linda Stalker (2000) *Consumption Expenditure and Female Poverty: A Review of the Evidence*, Policy Research Report on Gender and Development, Working Paper Series No. 11, Washington, DC: World Bank, Development Research Group/Poverty Reduction and Economic Management Network.
Medeiros, Marcelo and Joana Costa (2007) 'Is there a feminization of poverty in Latin America?', *World Development*, **36** (1), 115–27.
Pearce, Diance (1978) 'The feminization of poverty: women, work and welfare', *Urban and Social Change Review*, **11**, 28–36.

13 Poor households or poor women: is there a difference?
Gita Sen

Introduction
Among the main contributions of feminist economic theory is the recognition that households and the people within them may diverge quite systematically in economic terms. Household averages in wealth, income, spending, consumption, work and leisure can, and often do, mask unequal distributions among household members. What is more, the consequences of this inequality for well-being can be serious. Age, marital status and, perhaps most importantly, gender, embody and reflect power relations that govern who may be poor within a household, and what this poverty implies. The recognition of intrahousehold inequality is critical to understanding who really is poor. This is especially so when poverty is defined not just in terms of money income but along a range of dimensions that include productive assets such as capital, skills and knowledge; nutrition, health and education; time and leisure; and personal autonomy. Looking within the household uncovers the extraordinary extent to which one's economic experiences can differ depending on whether one is a woman or a man, a girl or a boy.

Ironically, even as the need to look within the household gained ground, the idea of the poverty-stricken household, headed by a woman with multiple young, old and possibly ill dependents, reached near iconic status in gender and development policy and activism in the 1990s. Fuelled by the interest in women's economic status and the 'feminisation of poverty' generated by the United Nations (UN) Fourth World Conference on Women in Beijing in 1995, the image of the poor female-headed household captured policy interest and imagination. Typically, this approach fed the perception that female-headed households tend to be poorer than other households. Unfortunately, the evidence base was thin and somewhat ambiguous as has been pointed out in recent years by a number of authors (see Chant, 2008, and Chapter 15 this volume; Medeiros and Costa, Chapter 12, this volume). Not only is the empirical generalisation inaccurate, but a single-minded focus on female-headed households narrows which households we focus on and how we understand what goes on within them. In many ways focusing on female-headed households is of course much simpler, since this avoids having to address the messy complexities posed by gender relations within households (see for example, Chant, 2008; Jackson, 1997).

Poverty . . . and inequality
While some households headed by women may indeed be poor, broadening our vision allows us to recognise that the result of gender inequality within households can be that poverty is not evenly distributed within poor households. In fact, not everyone in a poor household may be equally poor; and some may not be poor at all. Recent work on health and education in India points to the ways in which poor households ration

limited resources among their members (Iyer, 2007) so that not only is there inequality, but even absolute poverty may only be experienced by some. New methodologies for probing reveal that what appear on the surface to be differences in health-seeking behaviour between poor and non-poor households may actually be caused by differences only among women and not among men (Sen et al., 2009). Conversely, there may be poverty lurking in the gendered corners of relatively well-off households as well (Jackson, Chapter 5, this volume). Gender bias and discrimination can operate so that girls and women in well-off households may not receive equal or equitable shares in education and health. The pervasiveness of violence against women across the household economic spectrum has been well noted (WHO, 2005). What is needed therefore is to broaden the scope of the households we analyse to include all households (however headed, poor and non-poor).

Turning our attention from poor households to poor women also leads us to a wider range of issues beyond simply asking whether women or men are poorer in income terms. The poverty that women endure has many dimensions that interact with each other. The ways in which gender norms and values, divisions of assets, work and responsibility, and relations of power and control function make the experience of poverty a profoundly gendered one. These gendered experiences include first, different experiences of poverty for girls versus boys, and women versus men within the household; second, different household responses to resource limitations depending on the gender of the person being affected; third, the presence of deprivation for some members along certain dimensions even in non-poor and well-off households; and fourth, the differential impact of the design and implementation of anti-poverty policies and programmes. Understanding how gender relations work to define the experience of programmes requires focusing on who gets, or has access to, resources; how roles and relationships of work, responsibilities, cooperation, sharing or conflict define both women's and men's living and working conditions within households; how structures and programmes of the state and other actors (private sector, civil society) reinforce or transform those roles and relationships, and how normative frameworks affecting differential entitlements and responsibilities are challenged or reinforced by policies and programmes (see for example, Lind, Chapter 100, this volume; Roy, Chapter 84, this volume).

That resources including both tangible productive assets such as land, and intangible resources like knowledge and networks, are overwhelmingly distributed in favour of men is well known. Equally valid is the proposition that girls and women bear greater work burdens and responsibility for the 'care economy' – the usually unpaid work that goes into the care of human beings. This is well evidenced through large numbers of studies of time-use and qualitative surveys. The carework done by women and girls in the poorest households tends to be extremely time- and drudgery-intensive, but critical to household members' ability to sustain basic daily consumption. As a result, it drastically limits women's choice of compatible income-earning opportunities, their ability to take time off for government programmes, social exchanges or minimal leisure, and their possibilities for acknowledging their own needs for rest, recuperation or healthcare. The gendered impact of poverty not only distinguishes between women and men, but also differentiates how carework burdens and responsibilities are experienced by different women. Evidence suggests that, where such burdens are reinforced by strong gender norms that define the 'good' woman as self-sacrificing, poor women (and to a lesser extent, those who are better-off) are likely to receive much less acknowledgement of or attention to their needs for nutrition or healthcare, not only by other family members but even by themselves.

Responding to poverty
Poor households respond to their poverty in a variety of ways. In doing so, they react not only to insufficiency of average incomes but also to insecurity and risk. Even if household income rises above poverty levels, risk management may dictate behaviours that appear more appropriate to lower income levels, at least until the new higher level becomes more secure. Well known are such responses as increased time spent on work, reduced consumption levels, increases in borrowing, migration, and fostering in or out of household members. Less understood are such strategies as maintenance of socio-economic networks through ceremonies involving consumption (despite the inadequacy of average consumption levels), spreading risk and borrowing potential through taking on multiple jobs, desertion or abandonment of the family, and selective education or rationing of healthcare among family members.

At least three of these responses are gendered, although with variations across cultural and economic contexts. While men may take on more income-earning work (sometimes in order to support their own consumption of items such as tobacco and liquor), women often face difficult time allocation choices between increased income-earning work versus substitution of home-made or freely gathered consumption items (food, clothing, fuel) based on increased unpaid work and time. These tensions are often resolved by sacrificing the leisure, playtime, or education of daughters, who are expected to take on additional carework including kitchen tasks, foraging, and looking after siblings, as well as other responsibilities. Another gendered response is desertion or abandonment of families, a strategy often used by poor men to escape the responsibilities of contributing to household consumption, particularly when their partners or spouses become pregnant. A third phenomenon, noted particularly in South Asia, is selective education and healthcare with sharply lower entitlements for women and girls relative to men and boys. Such differentials in entitlements are reinforced through gendered norms and values that permeate across the economic spectrum. Hence, while they tend to be lower in intensity for better-off households, they do not completely disappear.

Reflections on policy implications
The gendered impacts of poverty and of household responses to impoverishment are often missed in the design of anti-poverty policies and programmes. Women's responsibilities for care fundamentally affect their ability to participate in social programmes , in labour markets, or to derive benefits from household resources. For poor women, time is often the most valuable resource, and poor women's time is so much taken up by caring work that they can remain caught in a vicious circle of poverty. Even worse, social policies often profit from this gendered division of work and its associated norms, thereby reinforcing the gendered norms and roles that are at the root of women's poverty and within-household inequalities. This represents a convenient marriage of new social policies built on downsizing and decentralising the state while ensuring 'community' (largely women's) responsibilities for the success of programmes (see Chant, 2008; Molyneux, 2006; Lind, Chapter 100, this volume). Recent examination of conditional cash transfer

(CCT) programmes through a gender lens reveals that they can make significant additional demands on poor women's time if designed in this way. Although women may be willing to pay this 'time tax' in order to improve their children's health, nutrition or education, it is nonetheless a costly burden and may involve other hidden sacrifices and burdens. The hidden gendered cost of programmes also raises questions about programme sustainability.

How can these insights be used for programme assessment? The collection of more gender-based information can be a way to improve programme functioning. Such information can be used to understand better the way in which the care economy and gendered poverty are affected by and affect social policies. Programme development based on such information can help to ensure that gendered responsibilities for care are not reinforced, as these are at the core of gendered poverty. Such approaches can be complemented by programmes to transform masculinist norms and behaviours in relation to carework and responsibilities. Schools, public education, child and adolescent programmes should direct gender education not only to girls but also to boys and young men. Consistent attention has to be paid to violence against women and girls within households which is often triggered by women's inability to meet all male demands in relation to food, keeping the house clean, taking care of children, sexuality or reproduction. Such change in anti-poverty programmes requires the transformation of mindsets within government bureaucracies towards greater awareness of the gendered consequences of their interventions.

Acknowledgements
Some sections of this chapter draw from an earlier paper by the author that was published in *Poverty in Focus* in 2008 (see Sen, 2008).

Select bibliography
Iyer, Aditi (2007), 'Gender, caste and class in health: compounding and competing inequalities in rural Karnataka, India', unpublished PhD dissertation, Division of Public Health, University of Liverpool.
Chant, Sylvia (2008) 'The "feminisation of poverty" and the "feminisation" of anti-poverty programmes: room for revision?', *Journal of Development Studies*, **44** (2), 165–97.
Jackson, Cecile (1997) 'Post poverty, gender and development', *IDS Bulletin*, **28** (3), 145–55.
Molyneux, Maxine (2006) 'Mothers at the service of the new poverty agenda: Progresa/Oportunidades, Mexico's conditional transfer programme', *Journal of Social Policy and Administration*, **40** (4), 425–49.
Sen, Gita (2008) 'Poverty as a gendered experience: the policy implications', *Poverty in Focus*, **13**, 6–7, available at: http://www.undp-povertycentre.org/pub/IPCPovertyInFocus13.pdf (last accessed 26 June 2009).
Sen, Gita, Aditi Iyer and Chandan Mukherjee (2009) 'A methodology to analyse the intersections of social inequalities in health', *Journal of Human Development and Capabilities*, **10** (3), 397–415.
World Health Organisation (WHO) (2005) *WHO's Multi-country Study on Women's Health and Domestic Violence Against Women*, Geneva: WHO.

14 Globalisation and the need for a 'gender lens': a discussion of dichotomies and orthodoxies with particular reference to the 'feminisation of poverty'
Tine Davids and Francien van Driel

This chapter seeks to problematise and counter a trend in the field of gender and development (GAD) for the production of a series of global orthodoxies that are repeatedly reproduced in debates on globalisation (see Cornwall et al., 2007). We will discuss how 'victim–heroine' and 'global–local' dichotomies seem to inform the analysis of globalisation processes as well as representations of gender. One such orthodoxy is the feminisation of poverty thesis. Without attempting to discuss whether feminisation of poverty actually exists (see Chant, 2007, and Chapter 15, this volume; Medeiros and Costa, 2008, and Chapter 12, this volume), we will deconstruct the feminisation of poverty thesis from the perspective of demonstrating the subtle reproduction of orthodoxies, such as the 'male-breadwinner' paradigm.

In order to (re)instate the representation of women and men as bearers of globalisation and gender, we will argue that we have to go beyond dichotomous thinking and, instead, regard gender as a multidimensional and intersectional analytical concept. This theoretical approach to gendered global–local dynamics – labelled the 'gender lens' – provides us with tools to reveal women's and men's multiple and differentiated agency and space for manoeuvre, rather than encoding essentialist notions of gender both in theories and policies.

The feminisation of poverty deconstructed
Notwithstanding elaborate analysis within gender and development studies aiming to analyse core mechanisms of globalisation from a gender perspective, we found that, in several of the most dominant debates in this field, globalisation itself does not get analysed, but is instead taken for granted (Davids and van Driel, 2005). In such debates, globalisation often appears as a process 'out there' that has a negative impact on women locally. Within these kinds of analyses, women get represented one-dimensionally (see also Chant, Chapter 15, this volume). Both the reduction of gender to women and the top-down approach of globalisation can be found in the 'feminisation of poverty' thesis. Although this thesis has been hotly debated in the academic literature (see other chapters in this part), the weak theoretical and empirical premises on which it has conventionally rested lingers on in the formulation and execution of social policy.

The main reasoning behind the feminisation of poverty thesis is that globalisation has accelerated the feminisation of poverty, mostly reflected in the increasing number of households headed by women. The following step – to the claim that households headed by women, as a category, are the 'poorest of the poor' – is one that, on the surface, is easily made, carrying with it an implicit reproduction of the male-breadwinner paradigm. Female-headed households are not compared with male-headed households in which the male head does not have a partner and takes on domestic labour and unpaid carework. It is assumed that female household heads combine breadwinning and reproductive tasks, and this combination then appears as a deviation from the norm. In connecting female-headed households unproblematically with the feminisation of poverty and by characterising the latter as a result of globalisation and as a global phenomenon, unilinear and universalistic representations of both women and globalisation are formulated and reproduced as global orthodoxies. Instead of deconstructing this essentialist stance on gender relations, the latter is actually reinstated. As a result, women are targeted and, on the back of such clichés, become instruments in the fight against poverty, both nationally and internationally.

The production of orthodoxies: a troublesome trend
The particular representations of gender and globalisation in this debate are, in our view, deeply troublesome, and lead us to question how gender is commonly deployed as an analytical concept. Defining women in their capacities as female heads of households, as both a problem and a solution in relation to poverty and as victims who somehow miraculously change into heroines, rings a familiar bell from the past. When we recall the first feminist debates on Women in Development (WID), the parallels with the present issue become obvious. The debate on the feminisation of poverty still tends to mirror the premise that women are somehow positioned 'outside' the system, suffering its consequences, albeit as outsiders – leaving no room for the idea that women can also be agents, in this case, in globalisation and its attendant social, political and economic changes.

Besides the fact that this seems to bring us back to studying women, instead of studying gender, the way in which power relations are portrayed in globalisation debates also evoke former paradigms of dichotomous thinking in terms of 'oppressors' and 'oppressed'. As in the more Marxist- and socialist-informed Women and Development (WAD) debates (except that globalisation now replaces [patriarchal] capitalism), global orthodoxies such as the 'feminisation of poverty' reproduce the male-breadwinner paradigm and, thus, implicitly, the status quo (see also below). Echoing the thoughts of writers such as Carol Patemen (1989), therefore, who long ago cautioned that addressing women's issues is not the same as engaging with feminist theory, in our view, one-sided and/or dichotomous 'gender analysis' has been largely responsible for a series of reactive and inappropriate universalisms about women and globalisation. Moreover, and again following Pateman, we contend that addressing globalisation in terms of 'women's issues' runs the risk of the latter becoming sidelined or even invisibilised in mainstream theoretical debates on development and globalisation.

Aside from the fact that globalisation itself is often studied more from the perspective of its (assumed) effects, rather than in terms of its intrinsic complexities and multidimensionalities, gender continues quite commonly to get treated not as a set of intersecting and complex power relations, but as a binary phenomenon carrying certain disadvantages for women and women only. What is frequently left unproblematised is that these women are caught in the repetition of a discourse in which gender differences are indirectly represented via an image of femininity in juxtaposition to the male-breadwinner ideal, such that dichotomous representations of men as breadwinners and women as caretakers are reproduced without question. Or, probably, and even more accurately, what is left unquestioned is how practices of household organisation are informed and constituted by notions of masculinity, femininity, heterosexual normativity and the power relations at stake.

Furthermore, questions of whether female-headed households are poorer – and what the causes of their poverty might be – are in general addressed only in economic terms. The fact that female-headed households are often better off emotionally, socially or even financially is not discussed (although see Chant, 2007; Ypeij, Chapter 20, this volume). The same applies to the fact that women within male-headed households can be worse-off, despite the fact that their households are headed by men, because, for example, they may be subject to abuse or lack access to or command over resources. As Jackson (2007: 109) has asserted: 'a nuanced and context-specific understanding of how households embody both separate and shared interests, and both conflict and co-operation, is critical to the workings of gender.[1]

The feminisation of poverty is not the only instance in which these kinds of orthodoxies get reproduced. Different positions on, and analyses of, the relationship between globalisation and gender also display thinking in dichotomies, such as the 'victim versus the heroine', the 'global versus the local', and the 'modern versus the traditional'.[2] Repetition of this kind of binary thinking lies at the heart of the production and reproduction of orthodoxies that sometimes reach mythical proportions (see also Cornwall et al., 2007), and which, as many feminist scholars have cautioned, maintain the status quo. Orthodoxies that produce women as a homogenous category of victims, become narratives and texts and, although unwillingly and partly unconsciously, inform our daily scientific practices of theorising, debating, doing research and formulating policy.

The need for a 'gender lens'

If we are to overcome the view on women as victims of globalisation, we have to answer the question of how women as an objectified category can obtain agency and the means to act. First, in order to grasp globalisation as complex and multifaceted processes and to avoid orthodoxies, the global–local nexus, as a dynamic process, has to be centre stage in understanding the relationship between gender and globalisation. This calls for a gendered reconceptualisation of globalisation, whereby local forms of globalisation are understood not merely as effects, but also as constitutive ingredients in the changing character of wider globalisation processes.

Second, the concept of gender needs to be assessed, in which gender is not synonymous with women but refers to complicated multidimensional processes of discourses and lived realities. Gender, building on established insights of feminist studies, includes different dimensions. These dimensions entail symbolic representations, institutional practices and the positioning of subjects. These three dimensions, although distinguished for analytical purposes, intersect in complex ways in real life.

The symbolic dimension stands for representations, stereotypes, norms, values and images that can solidify into very persistent cultural texts and stereotypes. Although hierarchies are represented in this discursive dimension, often as dichotomies as in 'the woman' and 'the man', 'the homosexual' and 'the heterosexual', 'the global' and 'the local', these hierarchies can also be contradictory and conflicting. Persistent categories are created that are no longer questioned on the one hand, or that are heavily contested on the other, so that the nuanced distinctions among multiple axes of difference disappear.

These ideas, stereotypes, images, differences and hierarchies are reflected in socially institutionalised practices. In this dimension, differences get multiplied, reshaped and reinterpreted and, equally important, performed in different practices such as marriage laws and arrangements, labour regulations and divisions of labour, household composition, and so on. Within this second dimension, the differences articulated at the symbolic dimension are diversified, institutionalised and embodied in the organisation of everyday life. Since social groups coalesce around a variety of circumstances that form the basis of a sense of shared identity, diversification can be based on the intersection of class, gender, 'race', ethnicity, nationality, sexuality, rural/urban, age, religion, among others. In this dimension, intersectionality is performed by people of flesh and blood.

The third dimension is the dimension of subjectivity, in which individuals shape their own identities and juggle all kinds of contradictory and intersecting representations within institutional and practical limits. This dimension refers to the process of identification of individuals and (collective) actors with the multiple identities or aspects of ascribed identities which constrain, but also create, room to manoeuvre. The scope of this room to manoeuvre represents the core of empowerment potentials in specific moments and localities.

The analysis of dynamics between these different dimensions clarifies how discourses get (re)produced, (de)constructed and (re)constructed through real-life experience. Herein also lies the political potency of this analytical approach. Not only does it provide leeway to describe, deconstruct and execute discourse analysis, it seeks to localise and understand the way in which these discourses are negotiated within different practices by acting subjects. In other words, this analytical approach entails difference and diversity, agency and the means to act at the same time. Actors with agency are an intrinsic part of these gendered and globalisation processes, instead of objective onlookers that only play a role when others want them to do so. These are not objective categories of actors marching as automatons through reality, but a diversity of actors with agency who are juggling and struggling. The outcomes of this juggling and struggling are not given; they are diverse and can even be contradictory.

Returning to our deconstruction of the discourse on the feminisation of poverty, with hindsight we can discern that some scholars and institutions saw themselves confronted with a rise of female-headed households and took this phenomenon too much for granted, especially in its links with income poverty. Consequently, these practices were not questioned in relation to the more invisible symbolic and discursive mechanisms at work, or in relation to the individual subjective agency of the women and men involved. In other words, the dynamic and intersecting relationships between the symbolic dimension, the institutional dimension and the subjective dimension were sometimes not fully appreciated. While it may not always be possible in different types of research to analyse the full scope of these multidimensional dynamics, we at least have to be aware of which dimensions are left out and which dynamics tend to become fixed. Within debates on the 'feminisation of poverty', the paradigm of the male breadwinner tends to have become frozen symbolically, thereby forming the basis for the reproduction of orthodoxy.

Leading on from this, freezing or solidifying an equivalence of female-headed households with poverty, while situating the causes of poverty elsewhere (at a supposed global level), implies a neglect of the links and interconnections between different symbolic, subjective and structural processes, as part of embedded (and changing) social practices and meanings in different contexts. Analysing processes of globalisation through a multidimensional 'gender lens' helps to analyse globalisation as a gendered process and to prevent dichotomous thinking in global–local oppositions. If the global is being constantly produced in a ready-made and primordial fashion, so is the local, and so too is gender. Seen from a local perspective, globalisation processes inform the different discourses at stake in the practices of a certain locality. As such, they are always present and articulated within the different representations of gender in a corresponding symbolical dimension. Globalisation processes inform local practices and the dynamic relations between the different dimensions of gender. But the reverse is also true: local notions and representations are always present in global practices and processes. In short, the 'gender lens' can help to analyse globalisation processes as situated practices in which the global and the local are considered to be mutually intrinsic parts.[3]

Concluding remarks
We hope to have made clear that the link between gender and globalisation is all about multiplicity. We therefore argue that the concept of gender offers no universal explanatory causes, as that would suggest some sort of a primordial meaning and content of gender, leading us back to the formulation of a grand old metatheory. Gender only gets meaning in its specific context and discourses and through the performance of specific actors. We need complex and multilayered conceptualisations of gender in order to overcome and avoid rigid and dichotomous thinking. However, this does not mean that we cannot compare and theorise the workings of gender mechanisms, without ascribing a predefined meaning to gender, as often occurs in debates around the feminisation of poverty.

As intimated above, we would like to broaden the analytical scope and power of the concept of gender. The appeal here lies not so much in improving its explanatory potential, as helping to guarantee the conceptualisation of gender as encompassing power structures and discourses, as well as the agency of actual men and women, without being narrowed down to either one. If we would study gender only at an individual subject dimension, narrowing it down to studying women or men for that matter, we would again oversimplify gender, and depoliticise feminist analysis, with all the consequences identified above.

The 'gender lens' will help – if used in a flexible way and, by (re)instating women's and men's agency – to conceptualise globalisation processes, without encoding essentialist notions of gender. This agency need not be confused with the mythical belief in female autonomy or endless flexible survival strategies of poor women as discussed in Cornwall et al. (2007). The analysis of the global–local dynamic defines women's or men's agency not in terms of autonomy but in terms of a limited manoeuvring space. This limited space is the outcome of the dynamics between discourses acted out in practices and the negotiating power and possibilities performed by actors. It therefore leaves room for considering women (just as men) to be bearers of globalisation without losing track of the power relations involved. These power mechanisms are constantly at work, negotiated in all kinds of different practices in which they operate. It depends on the context as to which power relations are privileged based on class, gender, ethnicity or otherwise.

The political power of conceptualising gender as multilayered lies precisely in the awareness that discourses always get deconstructed and reconstructed by real-life experiences. We should seek to understand these momentums of negotiation. Instead of positioning women outside processes of globalisation, it is within the conceptualisation of these momentums of negotiation that women's resistance can be understood.

Notes

1. According to Jackson (2007: 108–9), these intersections are often neglected in the work of major international development and research organisations such as the World Bank and the International Food Policy Research Institute (IFPRI), who are key stakeholders in the persistence of the feminisation of poverty thesis (although see also Quisumbing, Chapter 23, this volume).
2. See Davids and van Driel (2005) for a more complete discussion of different stands on gender and globalisation.
3. For use of a 'gender lens', see the contributions in Davids and van Driel (2005).

Select bibliography

Chant, Sylvia (2007) *Gender, Generation and Poverty, Exploring the 'Feminisation of Poverty' in Africa, Asia and Latin America*, Cheltenham, UK and Northampton, MA, USA: Edward Elgar.

Cornwall, Andrea, Elizabeth Harrison and Ann Whitehead (2007) 'Gender myths and feminist fables: the struggle for interpretative power in gender and development', *Development and Change*, **38** (1), 1–20.

Davids, Tine and Francien van Driel (eds) (2005) *The Gender Question in Globalisation, Changing Perspectives and Practices*, Aldershot: Ashgate.

Jackson, Cecile (2007) 'Resolving risk? Marriage and creative conjugality', *Development and Change*, **38** (1), 107–29.

Medeiros, Marcelo and Joana Costa (2008) 'Is there a feminisation of poverty in Latin America?', *World Development*, **36** (1), 115–27.

Pateman, Carole (1989) *The Disorder of Women*, Stanford, CA: Stanford University Press.

15 Towards a (re)conceptualisation of the 'feminisation of poverty': reflections on gender-differentiated poverty from The Gambia, Philippines and Costa Rica

Sylvia Chant

Based on comparative field research with women and men from different age groups in The Gambia, Philippines and Costa Rica,[1] this chapter reflects on the applicability of the 'feminisation of poverty' to depict contemporary trends in gendered disadvantage. It starts by tracing the evolution and components of this 'pithy and polyvalent phrase' (Molyneux, 2007: 18), and proceeds to a brief a priori critique. This is followed by discussion of evidence for a 'feminisation of poverty' from the three case study countries, from which revisions to the construct are drawn out. The latter include: (1) paying less exclusive attention to incomes in favour of inputs (such as labour and time) into household livelihoods, (2) abandoning the conventional emphasis on female-headed households at the expense of male-headed units, and (3) acknowledging the dynamics of power and obligation around poverty. Such changes would afford the 'feminisation of poverty' greater scope to encapsulate issues of particular relevance for women, especially the burden they shoulder for dealing with poverty. The proposed revisions might, in turn, provide a more fruitful entry point for policy interventions.

The 'feminisation of poverty': origins, evolution and an a priori critique
The 'feminisation of poverty' acquired something of its current status as a global 'orthodoxy' in 1995, when, at the Fourth World Conference on Women, it was asserted that 70 per cent of the world's poor were female, and eradication of the 'persistent and increasing burden of poverty on women' was adopted as one of the twelve arms of the Beijing Platform for Action (BPFA).

In its original incarnation in the late 1970s the 'feminisation of poverty' had been used to describe rising levels of poverty among women in the United States. This process was attributed in part to the mounting incidence of female-headed households, particularly those of Afro-Caribbean descent (see Momsen, Chapter 18, this volume; Moser, Chapter 60, this volume; Tonkiss, Chapter 22, this volume). Faithful in terms of the basic principles of this historically and geographically specific legacy, but much less so data-wise (partly as a result of astounding levels of spatial extrapolation in the post-Beijing era), the (global) 'feminisation of poverty' seems to have become associated with three main tenets. The first is that women are the majority of the world's poor. The second is that the incidence of poverty among women is growing relative to men over time. The third is that women's rising share of poverty is linked with the 'feminisation' of household headship (Chant, 2007: 1).

Each of these tenets, while having a surface self-evidence within the 'feminisation of poverty', is problematic. The first assertion, that women are poorer than men, is static, and therefore anomalous within a construct whose very nomenclature implies dynamism. A pattern of poverty which indicates a female bias may not actually be an outcome of a *trend* for more women to become poor relative to men. Indeed, women in poverty could still outnumber men at a global scale even if poverty was 'masculinising' over a given time period (Chant, 2007: 18). As summarised by Medeiros and Costa (2006: 3):

> the feminisation of poverty should not be confused with the existence of higher levels of poverty among women or female-headed households . . . The term 'feminisation' relates to the way poverty changes over time, whereas 'higher levels' of poverty (which include the so-called 'over-representation'), focuses on a view of poverty at a given moment. Feminisation is a process, 'higher poverty' is a state.

While trend is at least implied in the second tenet of the 'feminisation of poverty', the continued patchiness of sex-disaggregated panel data makes it virtually impossible to establish not only whether women actually are the majority of the world's poor (Rodenberg, 2004: 1), but whether gendered poverty gaps are widening (Johnsson-Latham, 2004: 18). Moreover, where relevant panel data *do* exist, they reveal little systematic tendency to increased poverty among women relative to men (see Chant, 2007: 4–5). For instance, Medeiros and Costa's (2006) detailed quantitative study of Argentina, Bolivia, Brazil, Chile, Colombia, Costa Rica, Mexico and Venezuela between the early 1990s and 2000s found 'no solid evidence of a process of feminisation of poverty in the Latin American region' (ibid.: 13). This conclusion was drawn on the basis of per capita income figures for women and men in general and according to male- and female-household headship, as well as taking into account the incidence, severity and intensity of poverty.[2]

Other studies based on macro- and/or micro-data sets also fail to confirm any consistent linkage between the 'feminisation of poverty' and the 'feminisation' of household headship (Chant, 2007: 104–7). Besides this, concerns have been raised that the blanket association of 'women' with 'female-headed households' (itself a product of the dearth of sex-disaggregated data beyond the household level) detracts from the 'secondary poverty' to which women may be exposed in male-headed units (Davids and van Driel, 2001). A further critical issue is that undue emphasis on income deprives female heads of their 'subject position' and the fact that they might make trade-offs between different aspects of poverty, with material sacrifice potentially being 'preferred over a position of dependence and domination' (ibid.: 164; see also Chant, 2007: 113). As summarised by Rodenberg (2004: 13):

> Women are . . . more often affected, and jeopardised by poverty. Lacking powers of self-control and decision-making powers, women – once having fallen into poverty – have far fewer chances to remedy their situation. This fact, however, should not be understood to imply globally that e.g., a rising number of women-headed households is invariably linked with a rising poverty rate. It is instead advisable to bear in mind that a woman's decision to maintain a household of her own may very well be a voluntary decision – one that may, for instance, serve as an avenue out of a relationship marred by violence. If poverty is understood not only as income poverty but as a massive restriction of choices and options, a step of this kind, not taken in isolation, may also mean an improvement of women's life circumstances.

Leading on from this, my main concerns in this chapter are the implicit (if not explicit) emphasis on incomes in the 'feminisation of poverty' and the arguably misplaced attention accorded to female-headed households.

That the 'feminisation of poverty' has been associated primarily, if not exclusively, with income privation, appears rather at odds with the wider literature on gender and development in which there has been growing support for concepts and measures which address poverty's multidimensionality (for example, asset deficiency, overwork, time poverty, powerlessness and vulnerability), and which, via participatory methods, endeavours to incorporate the 'voices of the poor' themselves (see Deere, Chapter 53, this volume; Gammage, Chapter 9, this volume; Moser, Chapter 60, this volume). The relevance of more holistic and subjective perspectives is not only underlined by critiques of the purported linkages between female headship and poverty, but is also borne out by recent investigation into the 'feminisation of poverty' in The Gambia, the Philippines and Costa Rica.

Evidence for a 'feminisation of poverty' in The Gambia, Philippines and Costa Rica
Although there is no consistent quantitative or qualitative evidence to support a generalised tendency to a 'feminisation' of income poverty in The Gambia, Philippines and Costa Rica, one striking trend discerned across these countries is perhaps best summed up as a 'feminisation of responsibility and/or obligation' (Chant, 2007: 333).[3]

This notion rests on three main observations. The first pertains to *growing gender disparities in the range and amount of labour invested in household livelihoods*. While rising numbers of poor women of all ages are working outside the home, as well as continuing to perform the bulk of unpaid domestic and carework, men are not generally increasing their participation in reproductive labour, despite their diminishing role as sole or chief earners in households. This corroborates findings from wider time-use studies using the '24 hour model' which have found, *inter alia*, that women spend shorter hours in paid work, but more hours in work overall than men, that they simultaneously perform a variety of activities such as child-minding, housework and remunerative labour, and that they have less discretionary time (see Corner, 2002: 7). That growing unevenness in gendered inputs to household livelihoods is occurring in a context where neoliberal restructuring frequently requires greater investments of time and effort in all forms of labour, including self-provisioning, raises major concerns not only about inequality and exploitation, but sustainability.

My second main observation relates to the *persistent and/or growing disparities in women's and men's capacities to negotiate gendered obligations and entitlements in households*. Despite women's progressive movements to the frontline of coping with poverty, they do not seem to have gained any ground for negotiating greater inputs to household incomes or labour on the part of men, let alone reductions in resource-depleting activities which appear to be wedded to normative ideals of masculinity. Regardless of their declining shares of household effort, many men withhold earnings (and/or to appropriate those of wives or other household members), to fund extra-domestic pursuits. These may include fraternising with male companions, drinking, engaging in extra-marital affairs and/or gambling. Recognising that some of these activities may be forced upon men by peer and societal expectations, and not all may be wholly self-oriented and/or without spin-offs for other members of men's families, they leave women few options other than to take up the cudgels for household provisioning, especially where idealised norms of femininity continue to emphasise altruism. Moreover, the activities in which men often engage not only reinforce women's obligations, but can, in the process, exacerbate them. For example, illness or incapacity induced by risk-taking behaviour can deprive household members of economic resources through losses in earnings and medical expenditure. Recourse to, or intensification of, 'traditional' norms of 'masculinity' and 'femininity' may well represent tactical psycho-social steps for all parties where the traditional bedrock of gendered roles, relations and identities is crumbling. Nonetheless, that women are becoming exposed to greater extremes of servitude and vulnerability is a serious matter.

A third distinctive pattern across the case study countries is an *increasing disarticulation between investments/responsibilities and rewards/rights*. While the onus of dealing with poverty is becoming progressively feminised, there is no obvious increase in women's rights and rewards, whether of a material or non-material nature. Gambian, Filipina and Costa Rican women frequently stress that they are working harder in and outside the home. However, seldom, if ever (unless they head their own households), do they claim that this has entitled them to any benefits such as more personal over collective expenditure, more freedom, or licence to pursue goals which might be construed as individualistic. Indeed, in most cases women appear to see no justification to expect or demand more as a result of giving more. This is even the case with young women, who are undoubtedly the biggest beneficiaries of institutional attempts to level the gender playing field in such areas as education and employment. While young women's growing personal asset base might be expected to strengthen their bargaining power and aspirations, potential gains are frequently circumscribed by social and familial constraints. Young women's higher earning capacity, for example, does not necessarily enable them to negotiate new deals within households, but instead can simply expose them to more claims (see Chant, 2007: ch. 4, on The Gambia). Men, on the other hand, despite declining inputs to household livelihoods, are managing to retain their traditional privileges and prerogatives, including the exercise of authority, distancing from the time and labour efforts necessary for household survival, and recourse to resource-draining 'escape routes'. This constitutes a disturbing scenario in which investments are becoming progressively detached from rights and rewards, and perceptibly evolving into new and deeper forms of gender inequality

Whither the 'feminisation of poverty'?
The above findings raise important questions about the relevance of the 'feminisation of poverty', which, in respect of its current referents, does not seem to capture the essence of where poor women's most significant contemporary privations lie. Gendered poverty goes far beyond the question of income, with a broader perspective on poverty also indicating that the 'feminisation' of privation may owe more to the actual and idealised majority position of male household headship (under patriarchal conditions) than a rise in the numbers of households headed by women. On balance, the notion that poverty is 'feminising' might only be sustained if inputs are given as much emphasis as income, with due attention paid to their subjective and objective corollaries. The mounting onus on women to cope with household survival arises not only because they cannot necessarily rely on men and/or do not *expect* to rely on men, but because a growing number seem to be supporting men as well (whether through income or labour contributions). This underlines the argument that poverty is not just about the privation of minimum basic needs, but of opportunities and choices. While

female household heads could conceivably be seen as an extreme case of 'choicelessness' and 'responsibility', in having little option other than to fend for themselves and their dependents, and on potentially weaker grounds given gender discrimination in society at large, this needs to be qualified: (1) because female-headed households do not necessarily lack male members, (2) free of a senior male 'patriarch', female-headed households can become 'enabling spaces' in which there is scope to distribute household tasks and resources more equitably, and (3) women in *male*-headed households may be in the position of supporting not only children, but spouses as well, as an increasing proportion of men seem to be stepping out of the shoes of 'chief breadwinner' into those of 'chief spender'.

If classic conceptualisations of the 'feminisation of poverty' are methodologically and analytically inappropriate in depicting trends in gendered privation, one option would be to abandon existing terminology in favour of something akin to a 'feminisation of responsibility and/or obligation'. A second is that the original term is retained with the proviso that the poverty part of the construct refers not just to income but other, albeit related, privations. The latter is preferable, firstly because the 'feminisation of poverty' is succinct, well known and has already gone some way to 'en-gender' poverty reduction strategies. Secondly, giving poverty a more explicit multidimensional emphasis would bring it more in line with poverty discourses in general. Provided it is made patently clear that poverty is not just about incomes, but inputs, the 'feminisation of poverty' would have greater theoretical and empirical resonance. It would also provide a better basis for policy interventions which, in the process of directing poverty reduction programmes to, and or through, women, can simply add to the disproportionate burdens they are currently carrying, as evidenced by the use of women as a 'conduit for policy' (Molyneux, 2007) in conditional cash transfer programmes (CCTs), micro-credit schemes and targeted programmes for female-headed households (see also Chant, 2007).

In order to establish to what degree poverty is 'feminising', on any grounds, one salient issue for future research is arguably to examine how wealth (and its associated prerogatives and privileges) might be 'masculinising' in a context in which, on paper, gender gaps in capabilities appear to be narrowing. This, in turn, poses challenges to Gender and Development (GAD) policies, in which nominally men and gender relations are implicated, but in practice are all too often sidelined. Only by acting on deeper knowledge of how women's well-being is affected by the social relations of gender within households, as well as within other institutions such as the labour market, are anti-poverty interventions likely to be more effective in eliminating gender bias.

Acknowledgements

Research for this chapter was funded by a Leverhulme Trust Major Research Fellowship (2003–2006) (Award no. F07004R). For field assistance in The Gambia I am indebted to Baba Njie, in the Philippines, to Tessie Sato, Josie Chan and Fe Largado, and in Costa Rica, to Enid Jaén Hernández, Luis Castellón Zelaya and Roberto Rojas.

Notes

1. The project fieldwork comprised individual interviews and focus group discussions with a total of 223 low-income women and men in the case study countries, and 40 consultations with personnel in government departments, non-governmental organisations (NGOs) and in regional offices of international agencies.

Part of the reason for consulting women and men in different age groups was to try to establish whether the 'feminisation of poverty' was a function of factors such as demographic ageing (which often leads to a preponderance of women in older age groups) or whether this phenomenon was affecting women across generational cohorts (see Chant, 2007, for further details).
2. The incidence of poverty measures the proportion of the poor in a given population and is the most commonly used indicator when assessing poverty differentials between women and men, or between female- and male-headed households. The intensity of (income) poverty is measured by the aggregated difference between the observed income of poor populations and the poverty line, while the severity of poverty refers to 'some combination of the incidence and intensity of poverty and inequality among the poor' (Medeiros and Costa, 2006: 20n).
3. Saskia Sassen's concept of a 'feminisation of survival', originally developed in 2001, and discussed in this volume in the context of 'strategic gendering', Chapter 2, is also useful here, especially insofar as it draws attention to the more macrolevel context of gendered performances and subjectivities (see also Roy, Chapter 84, this volume).

Select bibliography

Chant, Sylvia (2007) *Gender, Generation and Poverty: Exploring the 'Feminisation of Poverty' in Africa, Asia and Latin America*, Cheltenham, UK and Northampton, MA, USA: Edward Elgar.

Corner, Lorraine (2002) 'Time use data for policy advocacy and analysis: a gender perspective and some international examples', paper presented at the National Seminar on Applications of Time Use Statistics, UNIFEM Asia-Pacific and Arab States, Regional Programme for Engendering Economic Governance, UNDP Conference Hall, Delhi, 8–9 October, available at: http://www.unifem-ecogovapas/ecogovapas/EEGProjectsActivities/TimeUseMeeting (accessed 10 October 2005).

Davids, Tine and Francien van Driel (2001) 'Globalisation and gender: beyond dichotomies', in Frans J. Schuurman (ed.), *Globalisation and Development Studies: Challenges for the 21st Century*, London: Sage, pp. 153–75.

Johnsson-Latham, Gerd (2004) 'Understanding female and male poverty and deprivation', in Gerd Johnsson-Latham (ed.), *Power and Privileges: Gender Discrimination and Poverty*, Stockholm: Regerinskanliet, pp. 16–45.

Medeiros, Marcelo and Joana Costa (2006) *Poverty Among Women in Latin America: Feminisation or Overrepresentation?*, Working Paper No. 20, Brasilia: International Poverty Centre.

Molyneux, Maxine (2007) *Change and Continuity in Social Protection in Latin America: Mothers at the Service of the State*, Gender and Development Paper 1, Geneva: UNRISD, available at: www.unrisd.org (accessed 31 July 2008).

Rodenberg, Birte (2004) *Gender and Poverty Reduction: New Conceptual Approaches in International Development Cooperation*, Reports and Working Papers 4/2004, Bonn: German Development Institute.

16 Post-adjustment, post-mitigation, 'post-poverty'? The feminisation of family responsibility in contemporary Ghana

Lynne Brydon

In the early 1990s I carried out research in villages and towns in Ghana on the 'grassroots effects of adjustment'.[1] Drawing on experience from previous work in Ghana the aim was to explore ways in which the World Bank and International Monetary Fund (IMF) prescriptions for fiscal stability and economic growth ('stabilisation' and 'adjustment') had affected the lives of people in a range of different communities, or not (Brydon and Legge, 1996). Having had experience of a time 'before' the take-up of World Bank-backed policies, the fieldwork was conducted in several Ghanaian communities, both those my colleague and I already knew, and in others, both urban and rural, to understand and elucidate an 'after' state of affairs. The main focus of research was trying to understand people's lives after about eight years of structural adjustment in Ghana; to find out just what was going on. In addition, I was particularly interested in women's lives: their education, work, family responsibilities, how they managed to make ends meet, and the juggling of responsibilities.

In addition to Ghana being seen, in the late 1980s and early 1990s, as a 'model adjuster,' it was also one of the countries whose progress the World Bank chose to monitor closely. This began in 1987 with the first round of Ghana Living Standards Survey (GLSS), compiled by the Ghana Statistical Service. This was a series of annual large-scale surveys with a rolling population of respondents, and lasted until 1992. In theory, the results of the first round of the GLSS (and possibly subsequent rounds) were available for the work I planned to do: they would provide national and regional socio-economic data with which results could be compared, and this together with previous work and the prospective fieldwork on village and urban lives, on ameliorative programmes and on ideas of economic recovery, should provide indications of grassroots perceptions of adjustment.

With this in mind, the main aim of my chapter is to contextualise changes in women's lives in Ghana, before, during and after adjustment, and its consequences, and to draw out some implications and indications for women's lives and life-chances in terms of both of theory and practice in the early twenty-first century.

I have almost 40 years' experience of working in Ghana and a trend that has become more and more noticeable in fieldwork at everyday/household levels since the mid-twentieth century is the increasing burden of responsibility that women bear for family livelihoods. This trend has recently been singled out by Sylvia Chant (2008) in her work on The Gambia, Philippines and Costa Rica, leading her to propose that the 'feminisation of poverty' might be more appropriately understood as a 'feminisation of responsibility and/or obligation' (see also Chant, Chapter 15, this volume). For this reason the subtitle of my chapter refers to the 'feminisation of family responsibility' which appears to be one of the most salient and growing phenomena contributing to gender inequalities in contemporary Ghana.

Ghana and the road to adjustment

Ghana's adjusting began after years of serious economic decline and two major economic shocks, in 1983. Not only was there drought followed by major bush fires in the dry season of 1982–83 in much of southern Ghana, destroying newly planted, perennial and stored crops, but, in addition, over a million Ghanaian migrants (then, around one-twelfth of the population) were forcibly expelled from Nigeria and most found their way home to Ghana.

Unlike highly indebted countries elsewhere in the world, Ghana's formal economy had ground almost to a halt by the late 1970s because of years of mismanagement (the gold industry had collapsed and cocoa that was produced and harvested might be sold to the government at a fixed and wholly uneconomic price, but, if at all possible, was smuggled over the borders to Ivory Coast and Togo for much better prices), and formal GNP was nugatory. However, this did not mean that there was no economic activity in the country. The informal sector developed and adapted to cope with economic decline: seamstresses unpicked clothes and remade them, hair was styled with minimal chemical input; a market developed in second-hand paper, from books, magazines, newspapers and, even, archival documents, for wrapping goods: petty trading became an even smaller-scale enterprise where tiny amounts of officially priced goods were obtained through patronage networks and sold on an individual basis, allowing the circulation of cash and credit and small-scale profit, and the continuation of urban life.

In rural areas subsistence farming became a reality as supplies of government-controlled and imported tinned foods and wheat flour dried up completely. Soap, matches and batteries, whose import was also under the aegis of the state, became unobtainable, and supplies of fuel, whether petrol/ diesel for transport or kerosene for lamps, were at best erratic, at worst, non-existent. In villages women began to make local soap after years of buying, in order to wash themselves and the family's clothes, and they made rudimentary lamps running on locally produced vegetable oil. Fuel shortages also meant that urban markets sometimes ran out of produce, but at least in southern rural areas there were basic foodstuffs, that is, until the drought and bush fires of 1982–83. Ghanaian women were at the forefront, as is so often reported in the literature, of the coping and juggling that enabled individual, and national, survival in the immediate pre-adjustment period.

Adjustment

Ghana's adjustment packages and the conditions on its obtaining loans from the international financial institutions were typical: stabilise the currency, letting it find its real value in international markets; prune out 'slack' in the state/public sector; promote efficiency in taxation policies and revenue collection; and, more generally, encourage an open market and the conditions attracting inward investment and effective entrepreneurship.

But even after a short time it became clear that adjustment policies, among other problems, had two serious blind spots. First, adjustment policies did not just signal short-term belt-tightening for those who felt their effects: there were possible serious longer-term implications in respect both of child malnutrition and the health of the country more generally, and entrepreneurship seemed to need some kind of kickstart in an economy which was effectively bereft of capital or locally available credit. Second, as became apparent in several studies, the effects of adjustment were not gender-neutral: women seemed to have to bear the brunt of coping with the harsher impacts of the policies (see Elson, 1991, for discussion and references).

Information about women, adjustment, coping and poverty was difficult to obtain. The early rounds of the GLSS contained few data that could be disaggregated by sex. It became apparent by the early 1990s to both Ghanaian statisticians and World Bank staff, that in the 1987–88 round of the GLSS, disaggregation by sex was only possible in relation to 'sex of household head' and, since the term 'household' had not been defined initially, even then, the data were probably not valid or reliable (Brydon and Legge, 1996; also Chant, 2008). It was only with later rounds of the GLSS that disaggregation by sex over a wider range of variables and responses became possible.

Women's lives, women's responsibilities

As noted by Chant (2008) for other parts of the world, women's lives in Ghana had become more complicated and financially more stretched, not only because of the non-gender-neutral impacts of adjustment (and other contemporary economic policies), but also because of a *de facto* increase in women's 'share' of livelihood responsibilities. This happened in Ghana not because anyone sat down and (re)negotiated family roles and responsibilities to the disadvantage of women, but because changes in social and economic conditions have shifted the boundaries around phenomena such as 'obligation' and 'responsibility', and because understandings and expressions of morality, both in cultural and religious terms, have diverged from everyday behaviours and common practices. Baldly stated, where men opt out of their responsibility for payment of what was traditionally considered (traditionally here being taken as the mid-twentieth century) their responsibilities, such as clothes, shoes and school fees, the responsibility tends to be taken on by their wives, ex-wives, girlfriends and even mothers. What were formerly traditionally validated and accepted male responsibilities or obligations to pay for different aspects of family maintenance have been twisted, so that in many instances women have been left with the responsibility for childcare in all of its aspects, including food, health and education. One major question, then, is how the norms of family responsibility have shifted so that the feminisation of family responsibility has appeared and developed and is, *de facto*, accepted.

This appearance and development of the feminisation of family responsibility, now brought to prominence by Chant and others working in a range of contexts, was apparent in my previous work in Ghana from the early 1970s. When I first lived in the village of Amedzofe in the early to mid 1970s, there seemed to be a paradox between the fact that Amedzofe's people were patrilineal and so we should expect the village's social organisation to be based around two- and three-generation household groups in which the middle generation were the sons (and their wives) of male heads of household, and the youngest generation were children of the sons of the household head. My census of the village showed that out of 212 residential groups, 64 had no adult male present, but, in addition, where there were three co-resident generations, then it was more likely than not that the middle generation consisted of daughters, and the youngest generation, of daughters' children (Brydon, 1976). Already, in the early 1970s the complementary moral and social obligations of Amedzofe parents in terms of economic support in relation to childcare seemed to have become much less strongly determined. Women might have children in their late teens and through their twenties, perhaps with one man, perhaps with more, with or without being formally married, and while there is no quantitative evidence of this that I know of, similar family structures and the accommodation of divorced, separated and non-married mothers and their children in both villages and towns in southern Ghana was becoming more commonplace (see, for example, Bukh, 1979). That practice and what 'ought' to be were out of kilter was obvious from field interviews where most women and men stressed the significance of working, with a spouse to take care of their children (Brydon, 1976).

But where young women, married or unmarried, could, they tried to find work, usually away from the village since there were few paying jobs there. Given that food and accommodation have to be bought in urban areas or other migrant destinations, and childcare also paid for, then a popular option with migrant women was to leave children behind with their maternal grandparents in the village, thus contributing to the significant minority of households where there were three generations linked through a woman, whether the woman herself was there or not (Brydon, 1979).

In Amedzofe itself there was also a group of women in their late twenties and early thirties living with their children in family houses in the villages without the presence of an adult male father figure for the children. These women had all lived away in Accra or smaller towns, had worked, had children with actual or potential 'husbands' (those who would at least provide support for them and their children along traditional lines), and had managed to make ends meet for a while, until either the relationship broke up, or both partners had problems finding work in the increasingly crumbling economy of Ghana in the 1970s. The young women had returned home to Amedzofe as the best, or effectively only, economic and social survival option at that time. In the village they had shelter in family houses and access to family land to farm, and so could provide basic sustenance for themselves and their children. Children went to the village schools and there was childcare support in the presence of mothers, aunts, siblings and cousins. In addition, where a relationship had not deteriorated, there might be some cash forthcoming from children's fathers, albeit nothing on a regular basis, to provide support, perhaps for clothes or for funding an informal apprenticeship. But the underlying message here was that social and economic changes in livelihood opportunities and living in other than traditional settings meant that the brunt of bearing obligations for childcare and rearing was shifting towards women, and that women were turning to their own, natal families for help, whatever traditional structural kinship practices dictated.

Studies of poverty and female household headship
While studies from the Caribbean from the 1950s onwards emphasised the central position of women (mothers and grandmothers), most often in the absence of adult males, as a Caribbean phenomenon of 'matrifocality' (see Safa, Chapter 17, this volume), the supposed traditional norms of 'African societies' (*sic*), whether patrilineal or matrilineal, implied that women had husbands and that households had male heads. Indeed, although around 30 per cent of households in Amedzofe were headed by women, those self-same women (as well as women more generally) unequivocally stressed the rectitude of marriage and having children within the marriage (see Brydon, 1976).

Alongside the growing burden of responsibility on Ghanaian women, income poverty was obviously apparent from a range of qualitative data drawn from small-scale studies when their results were read in conjunction with those of later and more gender-sensitive rounds of the GLSS. Brydon and Legge (1996) show the decline in the buying power of money overall in the first half of the 1990s, but with Ghana's see-saw economic trajectory in the late twentieth century, the more than million-fold devaluation in the currency and the liberalisation of the economy, it is impossible to pinpoint income fluctuations relative to gender. In other words, it is difficult to establish a feminisation of poverty as *process* (see Medeiros and Costa, Chapter 12, this volume), although poverty as a feminised state (ibid.) would appear to be much in evidence. Notwithstanding the many problems attached to comparative estimates of household headship and poverty in the bulk of quantitative surveys (see Chant, 2008), GLSS data over several rounds suggest that women on their own or who head family groups tend to be found in disproportionately high numbers in the lower percentiles of population when measured in terms of income and access to resources and capital.

However, somewhat paradoxically, what also came out clearly from these studies was that the health and nutritional status of members of women-headed households tended to be better than that of those from households of both similar and slightly greater incomes where there was at least one adult male. In the absence of men (who might consume more than they contribute to household expenses) and in spite of poverty, women allocate their income more appropriately to care for dependents (see also Aboderin, Chapter 32, this volume). This is perhaps not surprising since in contemporary Ghana, as through the twentieth century, children are the sine qua non of womanhood, and any adult woman should (and most do) give first priority to the care of her children. Are women just better managers with fewer resources, or perhaps this is simply another aspect of the phenomenon of the 'feminisation of responsibility'?

Why do women take on the responsibility for family support when relationships fail? Obviously causes, contributing factors, and economic and social circumstances vary widely across different times and places, but the common denominator is that women pick up the pieces, try at least to build on them, if not run with them, and even, sometimes, make a success of things. Perhaps we can say rather naively that women seem to 'make the best of' living in poverty?

Gender and coping in the twenty-first century

Based on my experience of working in Ghana since the mid-twentieth century, I have shown that women have taken on more and more family responsibility. Whether this is associated with a feminisation of poverty relative to men is impossible to state, but the increase in women's overall responsibilities imply minimally that women have less time both for training and earning. Can a focus on poverty alleviation improve the positions of women? Probably not! As Cecile Jackson (1998) has shown, the assumption that because women are poor and poverty has to be alleviated, by alleviating poverty, gender bias can be addressed, is unfounded. We need to unpick sociocultural and economic conditions underpinning the feminisation of family responsibility to understand the gender implications here. We need to tease out futures for the relationships between reproductive and productive dimensions, and the valorisation of the former (see also Tonkiss, Chapter 22, this volume). Perhaps the credit crunch and the world economic crisis will provide a space to begin to develop new thinking in these directions?

Note

1. This research was funded by the Economic and Social Research Council (Award no. R00023 1989), jointly held with Dr Karen Legge. The main findings are published in Brydon and Legge (1996).

Select bibliography

Brydon, Lynne (1976) 'Status ambiguity in Amedzofe-Avatime: women and men in a changing patrilineal society', unpublished PhD dissertation, Department of Anthropology, University of Cambridge.
Brydon, Lynne (1979) 'Women at work: some changes in family structure in Amedzofe-Avatime', *Africa*, **49** (3), 97–111.
Brydon, Lynne and Karen Legge (1996) *Adjusting Society: The IMF, the World Bank and Ghana*, London: I.B. Tauris.
Bukh, Jette (1979) *The Village Woman in Ghana*, Uppsala: Scandinavian Institute for African Studies.
Chant, Sylvia (2008) 'The "feminisation of poverty" and the "feminisation" of anti-poverty programmes: room for revision?', *Journal of Development Studies*, **44** (2), 165–97.
Elson, Diane (ed.) (1991) *Male Bias in the Development Process*, Manchester: Manchester University Press.
Jackson, Cecile (1998) 'Rescuing gender from the poverty trap', in Cecile Jackson and Ruth Pearson (eds), *Feminist Visions of Development*, London and New York: Routledge, pp. 39–64.

17 Female-headed households and poverty in Latin America: state policy in Cuba, Puerto Rico and the Dominican Republic
Helen I. Safa

Female household headship has long been associated with poverty, primarily because of the lack of a stable male breadwinner. But Chant and others have questioned this automatic assumption, showing that female heads are not always 'the poorest of the poor' (see Chant, 2007, and Chapter 15, this volume; Davids and van Driel, Chapter 14, this volume; Medeiros and Costa, Chapter 13, this volume; Momsen, Chapter 18, this volume). The vulnerability of female-headed households to poverty depends on a number of variables, including their demography (age, marital status) and household composition, their access to employment and other sources of income such as remittances, and state policy, which I shall focus on here.

While Cuba, Puerto Rico and the Dominican Republic share a common historical and cultural background as Spanish colonies that came under strong United States (US) economic control in the early twentieth century, today they differ dramatically in terms of state policy. Cuba's 1959 revolution established a socialist state, while Puerto Rico remained a US colony, and through federal transfers established an advanced welfare state. After years of dictatorship, the Dominican Republic established a democratically elected neoliberal state in 1965, but remains economically dependent on the USA.

These differences in state policy dramatically affect their approach to the poor and female-headed households in particular. In the neoliberal Dominican Republic, the market reigns supreme and the highly indebted state is subsidiary to the private sector, which sees inequality to be 'natural' and inevitable. In a welfare state such as Puerto Rico, however, the state attempts to address market 'inefficiencies' with supplementary state funds to the poor. Socialist Cuba attacked poverty by taking over all of the means of production and virtually eliminating the market to replace it with state systems of distribution and consumption (Espina Prieto, 2008).

All of these policies were affected by the economic crisis of the 1980s, which hit the Caribbean particularly hard due to its long-term dependence on foreign investment and exports. The opening of rival markets, particularly in China, made the Caribbean less competitive and more dependent on cheap labour, while the cost of living increased. This forced greater numbers of women into the labour force in each country, and also increased the proportion of households with female headship.

Women in Cuba now head over one-third of the households, while in the Dominican Republic and Puerto Rico they constitute about 27 per cent. In Cuba and the Dominican Republic, they are primarily young single mothers living in large extended families, while in Puerto Rico, 30 per cent are widows, reflecting the ageing of the Puerto Rican population. These demographic differences also condition the vulnerability of female heads in each country, as we shall see.

State socialism in Cuba

Cuba's economic crisis in the 1990s was due primarily to the break-up of the socialist bloc and the elimination of aid and trade from the former Soviet Union. The period beginning 1989 became known as the 'Special Period', when GDP dropped by 35 per cent, as exports and imports collapsed and nutritional levels declined drastically. A dual economy evolved, including a dynamic or emergent sector based largely on tourism and a traditional sector including most agriculture and manufacturing. A dual currency system benefited those with access to dollars through tourism, remittances, and self-employment in the informal sector.

The Special Period has hit the Afro-Cuban population particularly hard, because they have less access to dollars through remittances (since the émigré population is largely white), and through the new tourist economy, which favours white employees. Shortcomings in public services and particularly the low wage rate in the formal state sector forced the Cuban population to develop survival techniques, in which women played a critical role. However, the state also maintained a high level of social expenditure, particularly through universal free education and health care, which as a percentage of GDP nearly doubles the average for Latin America. Despite growing inequality, the state maintained its policy of universal access, not overtly recognising racial or gender differences among the poor, including female-headed households.

Part of this emphasis on universality can be explained through socialist principles, which place class inequalities above racial or gender differences. But some may also be explained by the Cuban dedication to *la patria* (nation), which grew out of Cuba's long wars of independence in the nineteenth century and its struggle to free itself of US domination in the twentieth (Pérez, 2009). The idea of *la patria* was so all-encompassing, as Pérez (2009: 13) observes, as to 'subordinate all competing identities' (including gender and 'race').

Women did receive considerable attention in the first decades of the revolution, largely through the Federation of Cuban Women (FCW), which promoted women's incorporation into the labour force, raising educational levels, increasing job opportunities for women, and providing generous maternity leaves, and free day care. Female labour force participation increased rapidly, reaching 40.6 per cent in 1993 and also changed qualitatively. Starting in the 1970s as a result of higher educational levels, two-thirds of technical and professional jobs are held by women. But the proportion of households headed by women has grown at an alarming rate, from 14 per cent in 1953 to 28.1 per cent in 1981, to 36 per cent in 1995. This is due, *inter alia*, to: (1) weakened dependence on a male breadwinner, because of women's increasing educational and occupational opportunities, and free social services; (2) the continued importance of the extended family especially among young, single mothers, more important now that public support services have been reduced; (3) a rising rate of consensual unions, particularly among the young, which often results in single mothers; (4) the weakened legitimacy of the colonial dual marriage system whereby legal marriage was confined to the white elite, because of the reduction in class and racial barriers and the growth of inter-racial unions; and (5) granting women in consensual unions equal legal recognition as women in legal marriage, further debilitating the latter's validity. The birthrate has also fallen drastically, to below replacement levels.

During the Special Period, as the problems in keeping a full-time job mounted, women's labour force participation fell to 31.5 per cent by 1995. Men's labour force participation also declined, more precipitously than that of women, but unemployment was more than twice as high for women as for men (10.1 per cent versus 4.4 per cent). Many people withdrew from state jobs because the purchasing power of the state salary in pesos has steeply declined, and instead seek resources in self-employment, the informal economy or remittances. One 2000 study in Havana (Blue, 2004) found that remittances had doubled average household incomes, and this again benefited whites because they have more relatives living abroad. Territorial inequality has also increased as the area surrounding Havana receives a far greater share of remittances and foreign investment. Though salary levels have increased, they are not sufficient to stimulate greater productivity, and most critical observers agree that additional market incentives are needed (Espina Prieto, 2008).

Neoliberalism in the Dominican Republic
There is no public support specifically targeted for female-headed households in the Dominican Republic, which continues to have one of the lowest levels of public social expenditures in Latin America. The economic crisis at the end of the 1990s made public expenditure even more difficult as the value of the Dominican peso dropped along with high inflation. This contributed to a rapid increase in the female labour force participation rate, standing at 37.6 per cent in 2000. Since 1980, it has increased more than that of men, and, as is common in the Caribbean, female heads have a higher rate than either married or single women (Safa, 2002).

Here again the extended family, very prevalent in the Dominican Republic, plays a fundamental role. An analysis of the 1991 national level Demographic and Health Survey (DHS) by the Instituto de Estudios de Población y Desarrollo (IEPD), found that although female heads of household earn less than male heads and have a much higher rate of unemployment, their average household incomes are nearly equal (Safa, 2002). Apparently female heads of household are able to raise their income through the contributions of other family members, particularly subheads, since over half (53 per cent) of households headed by women are extended compared with only 35 per cent of the male-headed households. Many young, single mothers living as subheads go undetected in the census, subsumed in their extended families.

My ethnographic research among Dominican free trade zone workers shows that female heads of household often resist marriage or remarriage and prefer to support themselves if they cannot find a good provider (Safa, 2002). Women increasingly take the initiative in breaking relationships that are unsatisfactory, whereas previously female heads of household were often the result of male abandonment. This reflects not only male irresponsibility, but also increasing male unemployment. Initially men rejected employment in the free trade zones as 'women's work', but since 1980, the percentage of men employed nationally in the free trade zones has more than doubled. Some blame this on the Labour Code of 1992, which gave working women three month's maternity leave at half pay.

As emigration increased, the volume of remittances has grown enormously, more than doubling from 1997 to 2.4 billion in 2003. Women receiving remittances are often forbidden from working in the free trade zones by their absent husbands, seeking to maintain stricter control over their behaviour. In a 1991 comparative study focusing on the capital, Santo Domingo, female-headed and older households were shown to receive more remittance income than other households and were often not working. Remittances constituted nearly 40 per cent of all household income, boosting economic well-being in all strata from the urban poor to professionals.

Remittances, their own low wages, and the extended family appear to be taking the place of the lack of state support for Dominican female-headed households. Exports have declined from the free trade zones, particularly after 2005, as China became the new global competitor. The new Labour Code issued in 1992 has not been enforced, so in the free trade zones few collective bargaining agreements have been signed and implemented. Men are preferred in technical and managerial positions and receive higher salaries (Safa, 2002). Though the Dominican Republic recently entered a new free trade pact with the USA through CAFTA-DR (Central American Free Trade Area – Dominican Republic), the Dominican government is still worried about competition from cheaper wages elsewhere, and is therefore reluctant to enforce workers' rights.

The welfare state in Puerto Rico
In Puerto Rico, the decline in export manufacturing is far more severe. Though Puerto Rico started early and served as a model of export growth for much of the Caribbean (and other parts of the world), decline began in the late 1970s as other countries offered even cheaper wages and more lucrative tax incentives. United States government policies that favoured export manufacturing in other countries in the region, such as the Caribbean Basin Initiative in the 1980s and NAFTA in the 1990s, accelerated this trend.

The decline in production has precipitated a sharp decrease in Puerto Rican garment workers, who as early as 1980, were advancing in age after working in the same plant for 20 to 30 years (Safa, 1995). Some of the older female heads interviewed revealed that when they were younger and raising children on their own, most lived with or relied on the help of extended family members, usually female kin. Like Dominican women, two-thirds of the female heads of household in our Puerto Rican sample said they would prefer not to remarry (Safa, 1995).

Today the percentage of three-generation families has dropped sharply. Nationally, 29 per cent of female heads live alone, much higher than in Cuba or in the Dominican Republic. This partly reflects the high percentage of widows (30 per cent), who in Cuba and the Dominican Republic would normally live with extended families. Nuclearisation is also the result of public policy, which through public housing, social security and other social programmes has stressed the American middle-class nuclear family as the ideal. Structural factors such as rapid urbanisation and migration accelerated this trend.

Federal transfer payments include both earned benefits like social security and unearned benefits, primarily nutritional assistance or food stamps, which increased substantially in the 1970s. This made it easier for female heads to live separately, but many do not work. In 2000, only 35 per cent of Puerto Rican female heads of household were employed (Colón, 2006) and 42 per cent had no one employed in the households (many of whom are widows). That same year, 61 per cent of female heads of households were living below the poverty line, which can be explained by their dependence on federal assistance, low female labour force participation rates, and the absence of support from extended families. Nationally, only 16 per cent of Puerto Rican female-headed households include more than one employed person compared with 39 per cent headed by married couples (Colón, 2006).

Clearly, Puerto Rican female heads of household differ in certain important respects from the profile of Cuban and Dominican female heads outlined above. Many more are widows, and the percentage of single mothers is lower, due partly to a steep decline in consensual unions and the official promotion of legal marriage. Legal marriage was defined as part of the USA's 'civilising mission' in 1898, and was later reinforced by privileging spouses in legal unions through access to federal transfer payments. However, eliminating consensual unions has not brought about marital stability, because the divorce rate is very high. Remittances have also declined as a source of income since more than half the Puerto Rican population now lives on the mainland.

Today the Puerto Rican economy is in crisis. After decades of economic growth and increasing per capita income, since 2006 the economy has contracted 10 per cent, and the public debt has risen to 40 per cent of the budget, higher than any US state. The payroll for public employees grew 10 per cent annually between 2000 and 2005, and now represents 67 per cent of the state budget. The 1996 federal phaseout of Section 936, which accorded US corporations in Puerto Rico special federal tax treatment, was the death blow to Operation Bootstrap and ended the favourable trade terms with the US mainland.

Comparing the consequences of social policy
There are striking similarities between the consequences of state policy in Puerto Rico and Cuba, though these policies are dramatically different in origin. Through its industrialisation programme based on private capital, Puerto Rico sought to bring prosperity to its citizens, but as this collapsed, the population became more dependent on federal transfers, which in 2009 totalled US$11 879 million. The government rather than the private sector became the motor of the economy. In Cuba, the sharp reduction of the private sector also made the state the principal employer. The Special Period forced Cuba to open its markets somewhat, but a dual economy and currency have contributed to the stagnation of state wages, which no longer cover the cost of living.

In both Puerto Rico and Cuba, the incentive to work has been eroded. Clearly this was not the intention of state policy in either case, and was due to the inflexibility of their economic models and an economic crisis which left the government little alternative. It is also possible that the high level of federal transfers to Puerto Rico, starting in the 1970s as Operation Bootstrap deteriorated, was consciously designed to prop up the economy. Puerto Rico's Operation Bootstrap was seen as an alternative economic model in the Caribbean and Latin America to socialist Cuba, a subject that certainly bears further investigation.

Does this mean that both the welfare state as epitomised by Puerto Rico and socialism as practised in Cuba must be seen as flawed social policies? I do not think so. Many factors intervened in both cases to damage these experiments, including the ageing of the Puerto Rican (and to some extent the Cuban) population, accelerated by emigration, and, above all, global changes which reduced the competitiveness of both economies. I think it could be argued that both Puerto Rico and Cuba became too reliant on certain economic models, and failed to make all the necessary shifts as the global economy changed. Puerto Rico became too reliant on federal transfer payments and the public payroll, while Cuba has not fully recognised the need to use market incentives to boost productivity (Espina Prieto, 2008).

The increase in female-headed households has been higher in Cuba than in Puerto Rico, but I would argue this has less to do with economic than cultural factors, such as the Puerto Rican promotion of legal marriage and the nuclear family. Certainly the growth of female-headed households has alarmed the Cuban state, and may be a factor in not assigning them greater priority in public support. The proportion of female-headed households is comparable in the Dominican Republic, where they receive no state support. This comparison suggests that the common assumption in the US that public support increases the percentage of female-headed households, is greatly exaggerated. Rather than reducing public support for female-headed households, as some critics demand, poverty among female heads could be alleviated by facilitating rather than deterring household extension.

Select bibliography

Blue, Sara (2004) 'State policy, economic crisis, gender and family ties: determinants of family remittances to Cuba', *Economic Geography*, **80** (1), 63–8.

Chant, Sylvia (2007) *Gender, Generation and Poverty: Exploring the 'Feminisation of Poverty' in Africa, Asia and Latin America*, Cheltenham, UK and Northampton, MA, USA: Edward Elgar.

Colón, Alice (2006) 'Incremento en la Mujeres Jefas de Familia y Feminización de la Pobreza en Puerto Rico', *Plerus, Revista de la Escuela Graduada de Planificación*, Puerto Rico: Universidad de Puerto Rico, pp. 78–96.

Espina Prieto, Mayra (2008) *Políticas de Atención a la Pobreza y la Desigualdad: Examinando el Rol del Estado en la Experiencia Cubana*, Buenos Aires: Consejo Latinoamericano de Ciencias Sociales/CLACSO-CROP.

Pérez, Louis A. (2009) 'Thinking back on Cuba's future: the logic of *Patria*', *NACLA Report on the Americas*, **42** (2), 12–20.

Safa, Helen I. (1995) *The Myth of the Male Breadwinner: Women and Industrialisation in the Caribbean*, Boulder, CO: Westview Press.

Safa, Helen I. (2002) 'Questioning globalisation: gender and export processing in the Dominican Republic', *Journal of Developing Societies*, **18** (2–3), 11–31.

18 Gender, households and poverty in the Caribbean: shadows over islands in the sun
Janet Momsen

The islands of the Caribbean are the archetype for the 'original incarnation' of the feminisation of poverty and its link to female-headed afrodescendent households in the United States (see Chant, Chapter 15, this volume). However, there is an important distinction between the Caribbean situation and those elsewhere where female-headed households are considered to be a relatively recent phenomenon. The Caribbean, on the other hand, has a tradition of female-headed households and women's involvement in economic activities to support their families and households which pre-dates modernisation by more than a century, stretching back to the days of slavery (Barrow, 1996: 77; see also Safa, Chapter 17, this volume). Female household headship is so well established throughout the region that it has laid the basis for women's independence and is not necessarily associated with poverty. In this chapter I argue, however, that despite regional similarities of colonial history, economic activity and geographical location, political and environmental differences between countries and aspects of intersectionality such as age, class, ethnicity, religion and education shape current gendered life experiences in distinctive ways.

In 1994 at the first United Nations (UN) Global Conference on the Sustainable Development of Small Island Developing States (SIDS) held in Barbados, Caribbean governments highlighted the problems posed by the region's insularity, remoteness, and vulnerability to natural disasters such as hurricanes and seismic activity. The region's leaders pledged to pursue economic, social and environmental development policies that would improve the health, well-being and safety of its citizens, in particular of women, young people and indigenous groups. These promises were short-lived and a decade later little had been achieved and political attitudes had changed. In the new millennium the member states decided to make trade-related issues a priority in order to encourage the integration of the region's small states into the global economy. This shift in priorities showed how economic sustainability has now taken precedence over social issues. The 1994 commitment to gender equity and to recognition of the role and contribution of women has been reduced to noting that women and youth play a key role in promoting sustainable development and should be encouraged in their efforts. In failing to acknowledge how neoliberal trade policies were undermining gendered social policies and contributing to the feminisation of poverty, regional governments, in many cases, reversed the closing of the gender gap and made achieving the Millennium Development Goals (MDGs) more difficult.

The gender gap in the Caribbean
Within the Caribbean there are enormous differences in terms of wealth with the richer islands of Puerto Rico and the Bahamas contrasting with the poverty of Haiti, the

Table 18.1 Gender gaps in the Caribbean, 2006 (selected islands)

	Dominican Republic	Jamaica	Trinidad & Tobago
Total Population (millions)	8.90	2.70	1.30
GDP (PPP) per capita (US$)	7203	4293	14258
Mean age of marriage for women (years)	21	33	27
Fertility Rate (births per woman)	2.73	2.30	1.80
Infant mortality/1000 live births	19	10	13
Length of paid maternity leave (weeks)	12	12	13
Literacy Rate for women (%)	87	86	98
Female to male ratio in tertiary education	1.64	2.29	1.26
Labour force participation of women (%)	46	54	47
Income (female to male ratio)	0.36	0.66	0.46
Women members of parliament (%)	20	12	19

Source: Hausmann et al. (2006).

poorest country in the western hemisphere. Table 18.1 illustrates some of the inter-island similarities and differences in the gender gap in 2006. The Dominican Republic has half the purchasing power per capita income of Trinidad and Tobago but much more than Jamaica, yet all three islands have relatively high levels of literacy and more women than men in tertiary education. Despite the generally high levels of education among women, and their strong labour force participation, wage equality is poor in all three islands. The female to male ratio of income is just over one-third in the Dominican Republic but two-thirds in Jamaica and less than half in Trinidad. These differences are related to the colonial histories of the three islands. The Dominican Republic was a Spanish colony with relatively few slaves, has a dominant Roman Catholic Church and a Hispanic society. Trinidad and Tobago is a country almost equally divided between Afro-Caribbean and Indo-Caribbean people with a history of occupation by Spanish, French and English peoples. Jamaica is predominantly Afro-Caribbean although with a few people of Chinese and East Indian ethnicity and a predominantly British colonial past.

As Wiltshire-Brodber (1988: 142) states: '[T]he dominance of race, colour and class in Caribbean colonial societies, historically made the issue of gender peripheral to an understanding of power, dominance and change'. The East Indians in Trinidad tend to marry younger and have more children than the Afro-Caribbean people but throughout the region about half of all children are born out of wedlock. Even in the Dominican Republic over 39 per cent of households are made up of single mothers with children (see also Safa, Chapter 17, this volume). Despite this reality, the Dominican Republic government, under pressure from the Roman Catholic Church, in 2009 pushed through a draconian abortion law as an amendment to the Constitution making abortion under any circumstances illegal. Currently there are over 100 000 abortions a year in the Dominican Republic as contraceptive use is restricted, and the amendment will make the use of even such methods as the intra-uterine device (IUD) illegal. Although abortion is already illegal in practice the law is not currently enforced but with this amendment abortion will become more clandestine. Currently the only Caribbean country with higher fertility than the Dominican Republic is Haiti. The change in the Constitution can only make the feminisation of poverty worse, as fertility, and infant and maternal mortality rates are likely to increase and more women will be forced to work in the informal economy.

On the other hand, Barbados was one of the first countries in the world to have a government-sponsored programme of contraception and today its Total Fertility Rate (TFR) among women is only 1.5 children.[1] In 2008 the Gender Equity Index of Social Watch[2] of Barbados and the Bahamas was higher than that of any other developing country in the world except for Rwanda, which now has women as over half its members of parliament. The Dominican Republic, despite its marked gender gap in income and state-sponsored decline in women's reproductive power, has more women in parliament than all other Caribbean countries except for Cuba which had 36 per cent female representation in 2007. This may reflect what I have called elsewhere 'patriarchy in absentia', in that, despite large numbers of female-headed households, few women have political power. The Caribbean has generally a matrilocal and matrifocal society but within a patriarchal structure. However, between 2004 and 2008 the Dominican Republic had a bigger statistical increase in gender equity than any other Caribbean country, followed by Cuba, Barbados and Trinidad and Tobago. In Jamaica gender equity declined while in Guyana it remained static over the four years.

Migration, gender and poverty
Female-headed households also predominated in post-slavery periods when male migration affected sex ratios in the population. For example, by 1921 the exodus of men from Barbados, mainly to Panama to assist in the building of the canal, left a sex imbalance of 679 males to every 1000 females. Within the productive and reproductive age groups the proportion was only 526 per 1000 females (Barrow, 1996: 77). Yet these women were not necessarily poor. The money sent back by migrant men to their mothers, girlfriends and wives was often invested by the recipients in land to which they had title so that women became, for a short period at the beginning of the twentieth century, the majority of small landowners (Momsen, 1998), which is quite exceptional at a world scale (see Deere, Chapter 53, this volume).

The prevalence of female-headed households cannot be explained solely with reference to unbalanced sex ratios. In Barbados the sex ratio had evened out by 1990 to 911 men per 1000 females but the proportion of female-headed households remained high at 43.5 per cent. Women's greater longevity, and limited remarriage following widowhood, have also encouraged the formation of female-headed households. But there is also evidence that women are choosing independence and freedom from male dominance suggesting a high level of female economic autonomy and well-being (see Ypeij, Chapter 20, this volume).

Although the Caribbean has long been known as a migration society, it is men who have generally seen their fortune as being found overseas while women have tended to invest in education and a life in their own country. Thus women often become teachers and civil servants at home while raising their children, while men leave them behind and move overseas. However, today women also migrate when young to work or to further their education but may become return migrants earlier than men in order to put their children in school locally.

Remittances from migrants are a very important economic resource, especially for women, so that, as in the islands of the South Pacific, the Caribbean can be said to be a remittance society. When a grandmother looks after her migrant daughter's children, she can be fairly certain of financial support. For many small farmers remittances are a vital supplement to subsistence farming, although in the wealthier islands such as Barbados and Trinidad and Tobago, with increasingly diversified economies, such a role has become much less important in recent years. In old age it appears that women are more likely than men to move overseas to live with their children in comfort, probably reflecting their closer relationship with these children as they were growing up and their sacrifices to educate them and prepare them to earn good incomes as migrants (see also Aboderin, Chapter 32, this volume).

Gender and poverty: context and catastrophe
Both absolute and food-only poverty tends to be more widespread in rural than urban areas (UNDP, 2008). In the anglophone and francophone Caribbean women have equal rights in terms of land ownership and inheritance, although their farms tend to be smaller, more isolated and on less fertile soil than farms belonging to men. Women often farm in order to feed their families rather than to produce for the market, but will sell their excess. The proportion of women small farmers in the islands varies from about one-third to almost two-thirds, but both men and women are usually part-time small farmers and both will have some waged employment, although such opportunities for men are often better paid. In 2002 in St Vincent and the Grenadines, the proportion of female-headed households experiencing food-only poverty in rural areas was 29.8 per cent compared with 18.9 per cent in urban areas (ibid.).

Economic diversification combined with poverty alleviation has become the main development initiative in rural areas of many Caribbean islands to mitigate the effects of globalisation and neoliberal policies (UNDP, 2008). The collapse of markets for the Windward Islands and Jamaican banana industries and the ending of sugar production in St Kitts have affected large segments of rural jobs with few safety nets for the most vulnerable, often female-headed, rural households. The gendered dimension of rural poverty relates to women's unequal access to and control over resources, especially credit and transport, women's multiple household responsibilities, which limit their access to waged jobs, and their dominance of local and regional trade which is poorly supported (UNDP, 2008). However, the new trend to Fair Trade banana production in the Windward Islands does emphasise gender equality. In its encouragement of women as producers as well as leaders of the Fair Trade grower groups, and its provision of training courses, it is empowering rural women in these islands.

Prior to the passage of Hurricane Ivan in 2004, Grenada had the highest incidence of extreme poverty in the Eastern Caribbean. The hurricane resulted in an immediate increase in poverty, and unemployment, estimated at 12.2 per cent in 2002, rose to 18.8 per cent in 2005 (see also Bradshaw, Chapter 96, this volume). Slightly more female-headed households did not own the land on which their houses were built and so were ineligible for rebuilding assistance provided by the United States Agency for International Development (USAID). Damage to the nutmeg and cacao trees meant that jobs in the processing of these crops, mainly done by women, disappeared. Fair Trade banana production has not yet recovered. The poverty rate in Grenada was estimated at 32 per cent in 2002 with 5 per cent living in extreme poverty (UNDP, 2005). While not detracting from the observation that many women in the Caribbean choose female household headship, and are not the 'poorest of the poor', out of the 47 per cent of households in Grenada which are headed by women, 20 per cent are in the poorest quintile compared with only 13 per cent of male-headed households (UNDP, 2005). For urban households 44 per cent of female-headed households are in the poorest 60 per cent of the population while only 18.6 per cent of male-headed households are this poor. Female-headed households also have higher dependency ratios (UNDP, 2005). Following Hurricane Ivan damage to the main economic sectors of agriculture and tourism was so severe that it has made attainment of the MDGs more difficult.

Declining state intervention in social welfare increased pressure on women especially in urban areas, so that during the 1990s slightly more Jamaican households headed by women experienced financial difficulties compared with those headed by men. Women found short-term solutions through informal work and pooling of incomes and care responsibilities through extended families with longer-term solutions of migration and the transnationalisation of social reproduction. Remittances became vital for family survival (see also Pearson, Chapter 64, this volume). In the mid-2000s remittances to the Caribbean were highest to the Dominican Republic and Jamaica. These remittances protected many families from the worst poverty but left children in unstable family situations and contributed to growing domestic violence, especially in urban areas. The decline in remittances as a result of the current financial crisis and the loss of jobs by migrants in the United States of America (USA), Canada and the United Kingdom (UK) will only make the situation worse.

In addition to suffering impoverishment from natural and financial catastrophes, the Caribbean is second only to sub-Saharan Africa in its level of HIV/AIDS infection. The prevalence rate was 1.96 per cent across the region in 2003. HIV/AIDS is the major cause of death for persons aged 25 to 44. Over half the adults with AIDS are women in the Bahamas, Cuba, the Dominican Republic, Guyana, Haiti and Trinidad and Tobago. Barbados began to provide anti-retroviral drugs free of charge to infected individuals in 2002 and this led to a 43 per cent reduction in the number of deaths within a year (UNDP, 2004; see also Campbell and Gibbs, Chapter 50, this volume). As other Caribbean countries implement similar programmes the number of AIDS orphans will decline. Following Hurricane Ivan in Grenada, it was estimated that 1 per cent of the population had AIDS and the number of AIDS orphans was increasing. In the 15–24 age group the United Nations Development Fund for Women (UNIFEM) found that women in the Caribbean are up to six times more likely to contract HIV than men, often as a result of sexual violence.

Conclusion
Outside Haiti, poverty in the Caribbean is not extreme, with fewer than 5 per cent of people in the Eastern Caribbean islands living on less than US$1 a day (UNDP, 2004). Caribbean women are relatively independent and well educated but there is no gender equality in terms of income and wages. Female-headed households make up almost half the region's households and, despite the evidence from post-hurricane Grenada, are not necessarily among the poorest, are not stigmatised and the welfare of children in such households is in many cases better than in nuclear households. However, the region suffers from the related pandemics of violence and HIV/AIDS, both of which tend to

impact women most heavily. In addition, the decline in remittances from migrants in the face of the global financial crisis may have an especially deleterious effect on poor Caribbean women and children.

Notes
1. The Total Fertility Rate is a calculation of the average number of births to women in the reproductive age group (15–49 years).
2. For details of the index, which is based on education, employment and empowerment gaps, see pages, 13–18 of *Social Watch Report 2008*, available at: http://www.socialwatch.org/en/informeImpreso/index.htm (last accessed 14 October 2009).

Select bibliography
Barrow, Christine (1996) *Family in the Caribbean: Themes and Perspectives*, Kingston and Oxford: Ian Randle Publishers and James Currey.
Hausmann, Ricardo, Laura D. Tyson and Saadia Zahidi (2006) *The Global Gender Gap Report* 2006, *Country Profiles*, Geneva: World Economic Forum.
Momsen, Janet H. (1998) 'Gender ideology and land', in Christine Barrow (ed.), *Caribbean Portraits: Essays on Gender Ideologies and Identities*, Kingston: Ian Randle Publishers in association with the Centre for Gender and Development Studies, University of the West Indies, pp. 115–32.
United Nations Development Programme (UNDP) (2004) *The Millennium Development Goals, Barbados and the Eastern Caribbean: A Progress Report*, Trinidad: UNDP.
United Nations Development Programme (UNDP) (2005) *Grenada Core Welfare Indicators Questionnaire (CWIQ) Survey 2005. Basic Report. Key Indicators of Development Performance including an Assessment of the Impact of Hurricane Ivan*, Trinidad: UNDP.
United Nations Development Programme (UNDP) (2008) *Towards a Strategy for Agriculture and Poverty Alleviation in the OECS*, prepared by Rufina Paul, Barbados: UNDP.
Wiltshire-Brodber, Rosina (1988) 'Gender, race and class in the Caribbean', in Patricia Mohammed and Catherine Shepherd (eds), *Gender in Caribbean Development*, Mona, Jamaica, St Augustine, Trinidad and Cave Hill, Barbados: The University of the West Indies Women and Development Studies Project, pp. 142–55.

19 Poverty and female-headed households in post-genocide Rwanda
Marian Koster

Rwanda is one of the most densely populated countries in Africa. It is also one of the poorest, with a GNI per capita of US$230. In 2001, 60 per cent of the total population lived below the poverty line. In the rural areas, where most Rwandans live, this level was as high as 66 per cent. Despite the fact that the proportion of the poor fell to 57 per cent in 2006, the total number of Rwandans living in poverty increased to 5.4 million in that year, compared with 4.8 million in 2001.

As a result of the genocide in 1994, the proportion of female-headed households increased considerably, from 25 per cent in 1991 to 34 per cent in 1996. The majority of these are headed by widows. In the literature on the 'feminisation of poverty', female-headed households are usually depicted as belonging to 'the poorest of the poor' (see Chant, 2004; Tinker, 1990). The assumed poverty of female-headed households is linked to women's disadvantage with respect to 'either assets or activities, or some combination of both, linked to inequalities of access to resources and income-generating opportunities' (Ellis, 2000: 141). However, even when female-headed households are disadvantaged in terms of access to resources like land, livestock, credit, education, and health care, it is not necessarily the case that they are poorer than male-headed households in terms of income (see Chant, 2004, and Chapter 15, this volume).

Empirical evidence of the poverty status of female-headed households in post-genocide Rwanda is scarce but the available evidence suggests that they are indeed poorer than male-headed households. In this chapter, which is based on extensive field research in northeast Rwanda,[1] the assumed relation between poverty and female-headed households is discussed.

Poverty and female headship
To date, a commonly used indicator for poverty is individual or household income. In this chapter, land, the most important productive asset for the majority of (rural) Rwandans, is taken as a proxy for household income. Poverty is multi-causal and multidimensional, and cannot simply be equated with female headship. Nevertheless, prevailing gender relations may explain why some female heads are more vulnerable to poverty than others.

As argued by Chant (2004), the simple equation of female-headed households with poverty is dangerous because it tends to convey the impression that poverty is the result of household characteristics, it diverts attention from wider structures of gender and socio-economic inequality and vulnerabilities, and it leaves the causes and nature of poverty inadequately explored. Whether female-headed households are disadvantaged in comparison to other types of households should form a hypothesis, not an assumption. Even if female-headed households are poorer than those headed by men, this tells us nothing about the causes of their poverty or the vulnerability to poverty.

Female-headed households form a heterogeneous group. To look beyond differences between male- and female-headed households, and to consider differences among female-headed households, may provide us with valuable insights into the causes and nature of poverty. A thorough analysis is needed to show if, and under what circumstances, female-headed households are poorer than male-headed households. Moreover, as articulated by Chant (2004: 21) in relation to her own work on female household headship: 'given the widespread economic inequalities between women and men, it is perhaps *more* important to ask how substantial numbers of female heads succeed in evading the status of "poorest of the poor"' (emphasis in original). To do so, it is necessary to look beyond simple measures of income poverty. There is a need to include social indicators of poverty and to evaluate different vulnerabilities among individuals and groups. In this chapter, it is argued that the missing link between poverty and headship, and between poverty and vulnerability, can be found in household size and composition.

Access to land in post-genocide Rwanda
The large majority of Rwandans (over 90 per cent) depend on agricultural (subsistence) production. In light of the underdevelopment of the non-agricultural sector, land and farming form the main source of income for most households and employment opportunities outside the agricultural sector are few. Over the years, the size of land per farm holding has decreased considerably, from 1.6 hectares in 1983 to 0.72 hectares at present. Apart from small landholdings, the country is characterised by unequal land distribution, insecure land rights, land fragmentation and increasing numbers of landless people.

My own field data reveal that nearly all households interviewed for this study (94.8 per cent) have access to land. However, at 0.59 hectares, the average size of holdings in this study's sample is below the national average. Moreover, 67.9 per cent of the households in the sample fall below the 0.7 hectares threshold – the minimum size of land needed by Rwandan households to sustain a family – and could thus be considered to be the poorest of the poor. The distribution of land in the sample is also highly unequal. The vast majority of households (41.2 per cent) has access to 0.25 hectares of land or less. Together, these households farm less than 7 per cent of the total cultivated area. Given the underdevelopment of off-farm and non-farm employment opportunities in the research area, members of such micro-farms barely survive. Nearly 60 per cent of households have holdings of under 0.5 hectares, representing less than one-fifth of the total cultivated area. Small farmers (owning between 0.5 and 1.0 hectares) constitute almost one-quarter of the sample, having access to 25 per cent of cultivated land. Farmers with more than 1 hectare of land constitute only 16.1 per cent of all households in the sample. However, these households have access to almost half of the cultivated land.

Looking at the difference between male- and female-headed households, the data show that the mean size of male-headed farm holdings in the sample is 0.6 hectares, while the mean size of female-headed farm holdings is 0.56 hectares, a difference that is not statistically significant. However, grouping households headed by women into one category hides real and significant differences among different types of female-headed households. For when further disaggregating the data, I found that the difference between widow- and divorcée-headed households is significant: widow-headed households tend to have much larger landholdings than divorcée-headed households (respectively 0.72 and 0.22 ha). More importantly, none of the widow-headed households in the sample were landless, and relatively few were found among the near landless. In contrast, almost one-third of divorcée-headed households are landless, and more than two-thirds of households have access to less than 0.25 hectares of land. The difference between male- and divorcée-headed households is also significant. These findings clearly show that divorcée-headed households have significantly smaller landholdings than all other types of households and, hence, are poorer.

The finding that widows have nearly as much land as male household heads, and more land than divorcées, is surprising. The literature tends to emphasise that women, and particularly widows, face more constraints with regard to access to land than men, and, thus, are less likely to own land. When women's access to land depends on their relationship with men, female heads of household are particularly vulnerable: as a result of widowhood, divorce, desertion, or male migration, women risk losing access altogether. Indeed, in Rwanda, customary law tends to restrict women's inheritance rights. Widows' rights to land normally consist only of usufruct, and even then, property grabbing by relatives is rampant (see also Rakodi, Chapter 54, this volume).

So why do women, and in particular widows, in the northeast of Rwanda have access to more land than one might otherwise anticipate? In order to answer this question, it is necessary to take a closer look at the processes of land distribution in the research area.

Post-genocide land (re-)distribution in eastern Rwanda

Before the 1970s, the far eastern parts of Rwanda were scarcely populated. Due to population pressure and land shortage, migration to these regions became more common, despite their low agricultural potential. Once the war started in 1990, many people were displaced and forced to live in camps north of Kigali. Others, foremost Tutsi, fled to Uganda. The land these refugees left behind was taken over by those who remained behind, mainly Hutu. Yet after the genocide in 1994, when the Rwandan Patriotic Front gained control over the country, hundreds of thousands of Hutu fled the country, including those who had previously settled in the far eastern parts. At the same time, some 800 000 Rwandan refugees, mostly Tutsi, started to return from exile.

The government encouraged these new arrivals to settle in the east of the country. Problems arose as the latest group of refugees returned in 1996 after the closure of the refugee camps in the Democratic Republic of Congo. Many found their farms occupied by earlier returnees, who had worked the land in the absence of former farm holders and who were reluctant to leave the property they had occupied with the approval of the government. Under the National Habitat Policy, which was introduced in 1996, landowners were nevertheless required to share their landed property with this latest group of refugees.

Key informants have indicated that women benefited from the National Habitat Policy. This is supported by Bigagaza et al., (2002), who claim that the primary beneficiaries of land distribution programmes have been refugees who returned immediately after the genocide (that is, Tutsi) and landless people – among whom relatively many were female-headed households (see also Bird and Espey, Chapter 55, this volume). Pottier (2002) also suggests that victims of genocide, and in particular genocide widows, were at an advantage during the land distribution programmes, as they had a moral claim on land and were also at a psychological advantage over Hutu (in the form of 'ancestral revenge').

Aside from the reshuffling of land among different groups of refugees, more land was reshuffled at the beginning of the twenty-first century when a large marsh in the research area was converted into rice fields by the Adventist Development and Relief Agency (ADRA). Before this conversion, the marsh – which officially belonged to the government – had been used by cattle-owners and farmers. Farmers were re-allowed access to the rice fields on condition that they form farmers' groups, while cattle-owners had to find new grazing fields. Other people in the area were also allowed access to the new rice fields, on the same condition.

The ADRA, responsible for the conversion of the marsh, was very much concerned with the position of women,[2] and encouraged them to organise themselves and claim access to the rice fields. Indeed, many women in the research area did so. However, the poorest of the poor did not profit – simply because they did not have the money to pay the membership fees of the farmers' groups.

Poverty: linking access to land and household composition
So far this chapter has shown that female-headed households are not necessarily poorer than male-headed households, and that widow-headed households have access to considerably more land than is commonly assumed in the literature. But does this imply that female-headed households in northeast Rwanda are less poor than male-headed households? In order to answer this question, it is necessary to look at the relation between the size of landholdings and household composition.

Small landholdings, such as found in Rwanda, are not necessarily problematic. Difficulties arise when there are few other income-earning opportunities and households largely depend upon income gained by farming, as is the case in northeast Rwanda.

The data show that the average size of households in the sample is 5.6. Male-headed households tend to consist of a somewhat larger number of members (5.7) than female-headed households (5.3). Divorcée-headed households consist of the smallest number of people (4.9), but none of the differences is statistically significant. The data also reveal that the average size of landholding per household member in the sample (at 0.13 ha) does not differ between male- and female-headed households. However, among female-headed households large and significant differences can be discerned. Whereas household members of widow-headed households have on average 0.16 hectares land at their disposal, members of divorcée-headed households only have 0.05 hectares. If we assume that the minimum amount of land needed to sustain the average household in Rwanda – consisting of 4.5 persons – is 0.7 hectares, this implies that on average household members need to have access to approximately 0.16 hectares of land. Clearly, only widow-headed households reach this minimum target. Male-headed households, but especially divorcée-headed households, fall far below.

Clearly, it is not only household size that matters but also household composition. Whereas household size can be used as an indicator of the size of a household's potential pool of labour, household composition can tell us more about the quality of that labour pool. The number of dependents in a household has a direct impact on the resources available for livelihood generation and the scope of potential activities. While children may eventually contribute to household income, investments first need to be made in order to raise them to become healthy, knowledgeable, and able human beings. The elderly also strain household resources; for example, in the form of medical treatment when ill, and old-age care arrangements. Unless other household members are available to take over the tasks of the elderly, a household's labour pool is negatively affected when the elderly become less able to perform demanding tasks themselves. The composition of households is thus directly related to potential future livelihood options (see also Brydon, Chapter 16, this volume).

Female-headed households in the sample have a considerably higher dependency ratio than do male-headed households. In particular, divorcée-headed households consist of a high proportion of dependents, mainly as a result of the high number of young children in these households. This implies, first, that divorcée-headed households tend to be the smallest (implying a limited labour pool) and, second, that they also have the smallest effective labour pool (consisting of economically active persons able to contribute to livelihood generation). Female-headed households, and in particular widow-headed households, also consist of a larger proportion of elderly than male-headed households.

Thus, while all three types of household are confronted with constraining care arrangements, the nature of care differs between different types of households. While care of the very young may be as constraining for a household's labour pool as care of the elderly or the ill, the young will grow up and be able to contribute to household welfare at a later stage of a household's lifecourse (see also Aboderin, Chapter 32, this volume; Moser, Chapter 60, this volume). The vulnerability of widow-headed households does not only lie in the immediate care that needs to be provided for the old and the infirm. There is also the inherent risk that remaining household members face when the elderly or the ill pass away. This is especially a risk when these heads of households have taken on the responsibility for grandchildren or young, unrelated children. In contrast, the vulnerability of divorcée-headed households lies in the initial investments they have to make in the raising of young children. In the absence of access to sufficient land and in light of the difficulties of obtaining employment outside the agricultural sector, divorcées experience considerable difficulties. This implies that divorcées do not only belong to the poorest of the poor at present, but that these women, and their children, may also face a bleak future.

Conclusion

The above discussion clearly indicates that it is too much of a simplification to assume that female-headed households in Rwanda belong to the poorest of the poor. In fact, my findings show that even if female-headed households tend to have access to less land than male-headed households, the difference is small and not significant. My data also show that there are large differences among female-headed households. Not all female-headed households are poor, and to depict all households headed by women as poor is a form of improper victimisation. My data do show that divorcée-headed households belong to the poorest of the poor. It is these households that now need to be targeted by policy interventions.

Based on the results presented in this chapter, one might conclude that there is no need for policy interventions targeting female-headed households in Rwanda. But this is not what I would like to argue. Considering the extensive discrimination against women in Rwanda[3] – in terms of access to education, credit and control over resources – it is remarkable that poverty differences between male- and female-headed households in Rwanda are not larger than reported here. However, I do argue that it is incorrect to assume a direct link between headship and poverty (see also Chant, Chapter 15, this volume; Medeiros and Costa, Chapter 12, this volume; Sen, Chapter 13, this volume). Looking beyond conventional indicators of income poverty, household size and composition may form the missing link between headship and poverty. This proposition becomes all the more clear when considering the fact that female-headed households, particularly those with young children and other unproductive household members, are over-represented among the poor whereas they form only the minority of households in the wider population.

Acknowledgements
Research for this chapter was funded by the Research School for Resource Studies for Development (CERES) Programme for Innovative PhD Research (CEPIP) of CERES-Wageningen Research School, The Mansholt Graduate School of Social Sciences (MG3S), and the Netherlands Organisation for Scientific Research (NWO).

Notes
1. Data was collected in Gatsibo district, northeast Rwanda, between September 2003 and January 2008. A mix of qualitative and quantitative methods of data collection was used, including participant observation, selected life history reconstructions, and a household survey. The latter was meant to capture variation in the wider population. A random sample of 136 households was taken, of which 93 were male headed and 43 female headed. To gain a better understanding of the nature of poverty among female-headed households, a further distinction has been made between households headed by widows and those headed by divorced, separated or abandoned women. The sample did not include any households headed by single women, or women who never married (see Koster, 2008, for further details).
2. Personal communication with the Country Director of ADRA-Rwanda, August 2002.
3. Despite the fact that Rwanda has very high female representation in parliament and that gender mainstreaming is promoted in all government policies and programmes, women, and especially rural women, continue to be discriminated against. For example, while women's ownership of land is theoretically promoted by the government, legislative revisions are inadequate to guarantee women's rights (see Koster, 2008).

Select bibliography
Bigagaza, Jean, Carolyne Abong and Cecile Mukarubuga (2002) 'Land scarcity, distribution and conflict in Rwanda', in Jeremy Lind and Kathryn Sturman (eds), *Scarcity and Surfeit: The Ecology of Africa's Conflicts*, Pretoria: Institute for Security Studies, pp. 50–82.
Chant, Sylvia (2004) 'Dangerous equations? How female-headed households became the poorest of the poor: causes, consequences and cautions', *IDS Bulletin*, 35 (4), 19–26.
Ellis, Frank (2000) *Rural Livelihoods and Diversity in Developing Countries*, Oxford: Oxford University Press.
Koster, Marian (2008) *Fragmented Lives: Reconstructing Rural Livelihoods in Post-Genocide Rwanda*, Wageningen: Wageningen University.
Pottier, Johan (2002) *Re-Imagining Rwanda: Conflict, Survival and Disinformation in the Late Twentieth Century*, Cambridge: Cambridge University Press.
Tinker, Irene (1990) *Persistent Inequalities: Women and World Development*, Oxford: Oxford University Press.

20 Between stigmatisation and survival: poverty among migrant and non-migrant lone mothers in the Netherlands
Annelou Ypeij

Remarkable as it may seem for one of the richest welfare states in the world, lone mothers in the Netherlands run a high risk of poverty. Though they may be entitled to social housing and benefits, their allowances are often too low to get by. Yet material deprivation is not the only challenge that lone mothers face. Poverty has many social and cultural dimensions, and for lone mothers this may mean that they are doubly stigmatised: as lone mothers who do not form a household with a man and as welfare recipients who supposedly take advantage of society.

The Netherlands is increasingly becoming a multicultural society with a growing migrant population. This is reflected in the fact that lone mothers are not a homogeneous group. They have diverse cultural backgrounds. This chapter is based on qualitative interviews with almost 70 lone mothers who lived in Amsterdam at the end of the 1990s. They were low skilled and received a welfare allowance or an income from work at the social minimum level (Ypeij, 2009). My sample comprised black lone mothers who migrated to the Netherlands from Surinam and the Netherlands Antilles and white, 'autochthonous' mothers who were born in the Netherlands.[1] While cultural differences among the women are noteworthy, and relate both to their access to social support and some practices of stigmatisation, the women share a class position and – in instances where they were married or cohabited with a man – experiences of dominant or even violent relationships with ex-husbands and boyfriends.

Everyday experiences of stigmatisation and discrimination
Lone mothers have a vulnerable position in Dutch society, especially when they have little education. Public childcare facilities are inadequate for which reason lone mothers are often forced to work in part-time jobs. While low-skilled jobs available to them pay little, women on benefits also have many difficulties making ends meet and as welfare recipients they are subject to severe scrutiny and bureaucratic control. In the 1990s, with the aim of cutting back on expenditure, many Western welfare states implemented welfare reforms along the neoliberal lines (Kingfisher, 2002). For the Netherlands, this means that the alleviation of poverty through raising benefits has become a political taboo: access to benefits is increasingly limited and fraud prevention has become ever more important. In the daily practice of accessing and administering welfare, women respondents were confronted with severe practices of stigmatisation and discrimination. Standard benefit entitlement is based on the economic situation of the married or cohabiting couple. Although single women (and men) have independent access to benefits, fraud prevention requires social sector officials to repeatedly interrogate women about their household composition and love lives. The policy is to visit every lone mother on

benefits at least once to make sure that she is not living with a boyfriend and receiving her benefits undeservingly. Needless to say, the women experienced all this as a very intrusive and unwelcome interference in their private lives. This situation was aggravated by the fact that the Social Services' employees are not always very polite towards lone mothers. They openly question their integrity and often think of them as fraudulent clients who got pregnant in order to obtain benefits and who are solely driven by their wish to profit from society. An employee (who was married) of the Social Services told me:

> Those mothers think they can have children and that they are automatically entitled to benefits. I have children myself, but I do not bother society with them. To have children is my own, private decision. But it happens more and more. Those women have a child and think that society should take care of them.

Lone mothers' benefits can be jeopardised by such discriminatory attitudes and several mothers interviewed had to engage in lengthy legal battles to get what they were entitled to. Prejudiced government bureaucrats do not stand alone in their condemnation of lone mothers. Against the dominant discourse of the nuclear family, lone mothers are considered incomplete and sexually unfulfilled women. As young single women on benefits their love lives become of interest to the entire society. Many people think that lone mothers (and other people on benefits) live off taxpayers' money. If a woman becomes pregnant without having a stable relationship with a man, she should have an abortion instead of burdening society with her benefit claim. If she is divorced, there is still no reason to burden society with it. Why does she not find a job? Children are very much considered to be a private matter for which society in general should not be held responsible. Many neighbours are willing to spy on lone mothers. If a lone mother is seen regularly in the company of a man, she might be cohabiting and her benefits may be improperly received. An anonymous telephone call to the 'snitch line' is viewed as desirable public duty. It will help all taxpayers and prevent the further moral decay of society.

Divergent notions of motherhood and household formation
All the lone mothers in my research experienced stigmatisation and they often complained about their financial difficulties, humiliation and stress. Nevertheless, they did not perceive themselves to be victims. They did their utmost to deal with their situation and were creative in making ends meet (Edin and Lein, 1997; Ypeij, 2009). An important resource for them was their social networks. All women received material, practical and emotional support from family and friends which often implies substantial financial assistance. Nevertheless, a comparison between Afro-Surinamese, Curaçaoan and autochthonous women shows that their networks functioned differently and that this was related to notions of motherhood and family formation. The ways Afro-Surinamese and Curaçaoan women organised their family life shows many characteristics of the so-called matrifocal family system which is common in their places of origin. In this system lone motherhood and female-headed households are frequent phenomena and men may have a more marginal role as husbands and fathers. The vast majority of the Afro-Surinamese and Curaçaoan respondents had never lived together with a man or if they did, then only for a short period. None of them had been married. Nevertheless, to refer to these women as single or lone mothers is rather ethnocentric because of the sharing of parenting and childcare with their female kin. My interviews show that female family members feel

responsible for each other's children and that reciprocal exchange of social support was accepted without question. The women mentioned daughters, cousins, sisters, mothers, aunts and close girlfriends as their main sources of support. A Curaçaoan mother of two described the support she received: 'We help each other, my family and me. My aunt calls me before she goes shopping. My cousin babysits for me. The four of us form a unit: my aunt, my sister, myself and my cousin. If one of us has a problem, we get together. That's how we live.'

Among the autochthonous, white interviewees and their social networks the nuclear family household was given much more importance as the best place to raise children. Forming a household with the father of the children was considered a normal and good thing to do and most interviewed women had been married or lived together with a man in the past. Parenthood was perceived as a deliberate and planned decision. One should only become a mother when the conditions are perfect. In this context, lone motherhood may be considered as something exceptional and a deviation from norms. An interviewee became pregnant when she was 17 despite using contraceptives. This was bad enough, but there was not even a reliable boyfriend around to take care of her. Because she did not want an abortion, her family and friends considered her lone motherhood to be her own fault and did not feel involved. Consequently, the woman received hardly any support from them. Another woman was married to an illegal immigrant from Egypt and had two children with him. He walked out on her the moment he got a residence permit. Her divorce weakened her ties with her family: 'They all think I'm a stupid so-and-so, because I fell for him. They had all warned me: "You can not trust those filthy foreigners." They told me this would happen and now I'd better solve my problems myself.' This does not mean that the autochthonous interviewees did not receive any help at all, but support was often accompanied by either explicit or implicit messages about the women's exceptional situation, their wrongdoing and their failure. In other words, their social networks were offering support while simultaneously stigmatising the women.

Also the flexibility of the boundaries between households is conducive to reciprocal social support (Stack, 1974). The matrifocal households of the Curaçaoan and Afro-Surinamese mothers were much more open entities than those of the autochthonous women (see also Momsen, Chapter 18, this volume; Safa, Chapter 17, this volume). Within the autochthonous nuclear family system domestic units are isolated, fixed and closed. In the overwhelming majority of cases, after their divorce or separation, the interviewed autochthonous women formed a domestic unit exclusively with their children and these units had a far more static composition than those of their Afro-Surinamese and Curaçaoan counterparts. The autochthonous adult siblings of the interviewed women may relate to their sister in a friendly manner, but the exchange of financial support among them is more an exception than a rule. They are raised by the same parents, the reasoning goes, and all had the same opportunities to become financially independent. If one of them has not succeeded in this respect, it is that person's own fault and responsibility. This contrasts rather sharply with the flexible, spontaneous and matter-of-course way of giving and receiving among female kin of the Afro-Surinamese and Curaçaoan women, who feel a strong sense of responsibility towards each other and a willingness to help. Family members, who belong to different households, may form extra-domestic networks (Stack, 1974). An Afro-Surinamese woman with three children explained: 'My mum gives me her debit card. She knows that I will repay any money I withdraw. Her money is my money, and my money is her money; that is how it works.'

The majority of the migrant women had lived in an extended household in the past or did so at the time of the interviews. These households were often formed with the aim of helping somebody out, whether with temporary lodging, childcare responsibilities, or paying off debts.

A new husband? No way!
Though the cultural differences regarding family systems and related reciprocal exchange relations between the black and white women are unmistakable, in their dealings with their boyfriends, ex-husbands and the fathers of their children, the women were more unified. The vast majority of them rejected the idea of forming a household with a male anew. They felt that they were better off without a man in the house. In cases where the women had lived together with a man in the past, often gender inequalities and power relations had been a major issue. But also the women who had never lived together with a man, who were mostly the Afro-Surinamese and Curaçaoan women, could explain perfectly well all the disadvantages of cohabitation.

Gender inequalities and male domination are manifest in various ways, the most obvious being male violence against women. Another manifestation is the gendered division of labour in which women carry considerably more responsibility for caring and household tasks than men. This implies a lot of work for women and a limitation of their personal freedom. A man in the house often means additional work on top of an already exhausting work schedule (see also Chant, Chapter 15, this volume). A third manifestation of gender inequalities is that men may control intrahousehold money flows, which they frequently do, as evidenced in men deciding how much they will give to their wives and girlfriends for the maintenance of the domestic unit. Men may also spend money on themselves in an irresponsible way, or try to control or claim the money of their wives and girlfriends, and demand that the latter account for their expenses. A man in the house may accordingly mean loss of control over finances that are often already stretched to the limit. After divorce or separation, in many cases the women are still not freed from male domination. Through maintenance payments, ex-husbands and ex-boyfriends may try to exercise power over their former wives and girlfriends. Therefore, many women reject maintenance in order to preserve their independence (see also Chant, 1997).

Based on their negative experiences with marriage and cohabitation, a substantial majority of the interviewed women, irrespective of their cultural background, said that they did not want to cohabit with a man anymore (for comparable conclusions about Costa Rica and the Philippines, see Chant, 2007, and on the United States, see Edin and Kefalas, 2005). Although the women's cultural notion on family formation may diverge, all the women shared a comparable discourse on the advantages of living without a husband or boyfriend. It is important to realise that the men in their lives were often men with little education, who were either unemployed, had unstable, low-paying jobs or, as migrants, were discriminated against (see also McIlwaine, Chapter 39, this volume). The marriage market in which these women were active did not give them access to men from the middle class who could offer them financial stability. Instead they were often dating and marrying lower-class men who had a marginalised position in the labour market, and thus were poor, or made a living in an illegal way. Compared with that of men, the position of the women themselves, as lone mothers in a welfare state, was more stable. Although they had little education, had limited access to the job market and were poor, their income and housing were relatively secure because of their benefits and the government's social housing policies. The women's statements about preferring to live alone should therefore be seen in the light of their class position in a welfare society, and that of their potential boyfriends and husbands. If a man cannot bring in money, his dominant behaviour is felt as even more unacceptable. On the other hand, for the men, the women are an attractive party. According to some of the interviewed women men are consciously searching for women who receive benefits and have a house or an apartment. It is not so much love and attraction that leads these men to make passes at women, as the fact that they do not have a roof over their own heads. The women regard this behaviour as the betrayal and misuse of women.

> The men who live in this neighbourhood [Amsterdam Southeast] look for a woman with a house. If a woman has a house, then they move in. They move in for the house. And they do not want to contribute any money. That is why I want to live alone with my two kids. (Curaçaoan women, aged 33, with two children)

It was not without reason that some women yearned for a rich man because that would really make a difference.

Between stigmatisation and survival
The women interviewed experienced gender inequality and stigmatisation on several counts in their everyday lives. The lack of public childcare in combination with the low level of their welfare allowance condemns them to poverty. Social services employees, family members and neighbours may stigmatise them as single mothers or as welfare recipients and their love lives may become subject to bureaucratic questioning, scrutiny and control. Yet despite their stigmatisation for being single and on welfare, they reject the idea of forming a household with a man. The same Dutch welfare state that condemns the women to poverty offers them an escape route from male domination. As singles, the women have independent access to housing and benefits, however low their income level. These benefits allow them to stand up for themselves and become independent from men. The majority of the respondents wish to stay single and reject the meagre advantages offered by marriage or cohabitation. These women's striving for independence and gender equality is an expression of their agency. Even if their benefit dependence may lead to poverty and stigmatisation, they may still be able to survive, and prefer survival on the margins to marriage and male domination (see also Chant, 1997).

In the case of the Afro-Surinamese and Curaçaoan women these findings may not be too surprising when cast in the light of long-standing matrifocal values that the women appreciate and the social support they so matter of factly exchange with each other.

In the case of the autochthonous, white women who endured stigmatisation even in their most intimate social networks and in such a way that it could cut off social and psychological support, these findings are remarkable to say the least. They are not only an indication of the women's self-worth and the strength of their wish for independence, but also of how unhappy they must have felt in the marriages they have left behind.

Note

1. I use the term 'autochthonous' for the white Netherlands-born lone mothers because I consider this more suitable than the terms 'indigenous' or 'native' which often indicate minorities or excluded groups in certain geographical regions. Besides this, the term autochthonous is widely used in the Netherlands.

Select bibliography

Chant, Sylvia (1997) 'Women-headed households: poorest of the poor? Perspectives from Mexico, Costa Rica and the Philippines', *IDS Bulletin*, **28** (3), 26–48.
Chant, Sylvia (2007) *Gender, Generation and Poverty, Exploring the 'Feminisation of Poverty' in Africa, Asia and Latin America*, Cheltenham, UK and Northampton, MA, USA: Edward Elgar.
Edin, Kathryn and Maria Kefalas (2005) *Promises I Can Keep. Why Poor Women Put Motherhood before Marriage*, Berkeley, CA: University of California Press.
Edin, Kathryn and Laura Lein (1997) *Making Ends Meet. How Single Mothers Survive Welfare and Low-Wage Work*, New York: Russell Sage Foundation.
Kingfisher, Catherine (ed.) (2002) *Western Welfare in Decline. Globalisation and Women's Poverty*, Philadelphia, PA: University of Philadelphia Press.
Stack, Carol B. (1974) *All Our Kin. Strategies for Survival in a Black Community*, New York: Harper and Row.
Ypeij, Annelou (2009) *Single Motherhood and Poverty. The Case of the Netherlands*, Amsterdam: Aksant.

21 Lone mothers, poverty and paid work in the United Kingdom

Jane Millar

The risk of income poverty for lone mothers remains high in the UK, despite much policy attention in recent years and a government commitment to end child poverty. This chapter briefly summarises the key evidence on poverty levels and trends for British lone mothers and their children. This is followed by a discussion of current policy and in particular the focus upon employment as the main route out of poverty. This 'work as welfare' agenda raises some particular issues for lone mothers, who not only have to combine paid work with their caring responsibilities but also face a gender-divided labour market in which many women with children work part-time in low-paid jobs. This is a challenge that also faces partnered mothers, but the difficulties are especially acute for lone mothers. The conclusion reflects on current and future policy issues.

Lone mothers are a key group for understanding the gender dimensions of poverty in countries such as the UK, where there is substantial economic inequality in the context of generally high incomes and living standards and well-developed social welfare provisions and infrastructure. In these countries, to a greater or lesser extent, the social divisions of gender, social class, ethnicity, disability and citizenship status remain important determinants of advantage and disadvantage, and of opportunities. Gender inequality in the labour market and in the home means that women are more vulnerable to poverty than men. However, women's poverty tends to be hidden in the family or household because income poverty is usually measured at the family, not the individual, level. This aggregation obscures issues of the distribution of income within the family, as well as the role of women in managing and coping with poverty on a daily basis. Lone mothers are much more visible – they form their own households – and their situations highlight the difficulties that many women face in maintaining economic independence and autonomy.

In the UK lone mothers have a very much higher risk of income poverty than average and they tend to stay poor for long periods of time. This has generally been the case since researchers started collecting regular data on poverty levels and rates. For example, at the turn of the twentieth century, the time of the first systematic poverty studies in Britain, widows – and especially widows with children – were identified as one of the groups most at risk of poverty. Today it is divorced, separated or single mothers, rather than widowed mothers, who make up the majority of lone mothers. But, like the widows of a century ago, these women often struggle to achieve adequate income to support themselves and their children.

There are currently about 1.9 million lone-parent families in the UK, making up about a quarter of all families with children. Official statistics for 2006/2007 show that about half – 49 per cent – of all lone-parent families in the UK are living in income poverty, compared with 21 per cent of couples with children.[1] Income poverty is defined as individuals living in households with income of less than 60 per cent of the median, taking account of household size and after meeting housing costs. Becoming a lone mother is a key risk factor for falling into poverty, with most women who become lone mothers experiencing a fall in income, and for many lone mothers – and their children – this means long-term poverty lasting years rather than months. Many lone mothers spend at least some period of time in receipt of state social security benefits. These provide an essential safety-net of support, but most families in long-term receipt struggle to make ends meet and avoid debt.

Over the past decade, in particular, employment rates for lone mothers have been increasing, and most lone mothers, especially those with older children, say they would prefer to be employed. This reflects a number of factors, including the general rise in labour market participation among women with dependent children, the growth of service sector employment, legislation to outlaw gender discrimination in employment, and the improved provision of services and other measures to support workers with family responsibilities. The two-earner family is now the norm, with almost seven in ten couples with children having both parents in work. However, many mothers work in part-time jobs, which helps them to combine paid work and family care, and these jobs are often low paid and with limited opportunities for advancement. Motherhood continues to exact a pay penalty which, over the lifecourse, can mean a substantial difference in earnings and thus also in pensions. The risk of poverty chases women down the years.

For lone mothers who are the sole earners for their families participation in employment does reduce the risk of poverty, but it does not eliminate it. This can be seen from the data on child poverty. Living with a lone mother, and especially with a lone mother who is not employed, is a high-risk factor for child poverty. In 2006/2007 about 3.8 million children in the UK were living in income poverty (defined as above), including about 1.6 million children in lone-parent families. Just over half (52 per cent) of children in lone-parent families are living in poverty, ranging from 77 per cent if the mother is not employed, to 33 per cent if the mother works part-time (under 30 hours per week) and 16 per cent if she works full-time (see DWP website).

Employment is thus a key factor in understanding poverty among lone parents, and it is therefore not surprising that government policy has become so focused on paid work as the main route out of poverty. The Labour government has set an employment target that 70 per cent of lone parents should be employed by 2010, and has introduced various measures to support this. These include generous tax credits to supplement wages, increases in child care provision, and a work-first labour market programme (the 'New Deal for Lone Parents') to offer advice, information and some training opportunities for non-employed lone mothers receiving social security benefits. These incentives and supports to engage in employment are reinforced by increasingly stringent conditions on benefit receipt. Currently all lone parents with a child aged 12 and above are required to be available for work as a condition of benefit receipt. From 2010 this will apply to all lone parents with a child aged 7 and over. Thus lone mothers are increasingly being treated in the same way as any unemployed person, with little or no account taken of their role as sole carers for their children.

This stress on the importance of paid work for all adults, with and without children, is central to the Labour government's general approach to welfare and social security, and indeed is shared across party political lines. This is justified not only in relation to income poverty and the desire to reduce public expenditure on social security benefits, but also because work is seen as having a wider role in social integration. This view is summarised by the Department for Work and Pensions (2007: 23):

> *Work is good for you*: people who work are better-off financially, better-off in terms of their health and well-being, their self-esteem, and future prospects for themselves and their families. Work promotes choice and independence for people, supports our society and increases community cohesion. . . . Work is also good for society as a whole. Both economic prosperity and fairness dictate that everyone who can work should be expected to do so, especially where people would otherwise be seeking to be supported through taxpayers' money.

Paid work, poverty and living standards: challenges
In the current policy climate, increasing employment for all is promoted not only as the key to reducing poverty and reliance on social security benefits, but also the way to enhance well-being and social inclusion. However, we need to look more closely at the situation and experiences of lone mothers in and out of the labour market in order to understand the implications and limitations of the work-for-all model.

First, not all lone mothers are easily able to engage in the labour market. Employment rates among lone mothers have risen from 42 per cent in 1994 to 56 per cent in 2008. However, employment rates vary with factors such as the age and number of children, family type, level of education and training, receipt of child support payment, extent of work experience, housing tenure, health of parent and children, and age of mother at the birth of first child (Millar and Ridge, 2001). The lone mothers most likely to be employed are older women who are divorced, have school-age children, who worked before they became lone parents, who have some qualifications, are in good health, live in owner-occupied housing, and live outside London. By contrast, the lone mothers who are least likely to be employed are younger women, never married, with young children of pre-school age. Or they are older women, with poor health, or with children in poor health or with disabilities. In either case these are women who have low qualifications and limited employment experience, who may lack confidence in their abilities and have limited knowledge about how to go about finding work.

Some lone mothers have multiple disadvantages in the labour market, for example, they have large families *and* poor health *and* lack qualifications *and* have limited work experience. The New Deal for Lone Parents, which is the main labour market programme to support lone parents into work, has had some success in raising employment rates. But it has proved less effective in helping those with such multiple disadvantages who would require significant support to bring them closer to employability. Over the past ten to 15 years, there has been a steady growth in employment in general in the UK, but unemployment is now rising again and this will certainly have an impact on job opportunities, especially for those already on the margins of the labour market.

Second, although there has been significant investment in childcare services over the past decade, there is still insufficient provision to meet demand and the costs of good quality childcare are high, especially for those on low wages. The national childcare strategy and ten year childcare plan seeks to ensure the provision of 'good quality affordable childcare' for all children aged under 14. Provisions have included free part-time (up to 12.5 hours per week) nursery places for all 3- and 4-year-old children, the expansion of school-based care provision for older children, and the establishment of children's centres. But there is significant variation in availability and quality of care across the country and gaps in provision especially for older children, for care in school holidays, for care that covers atypical working hours, and for care for disabled children. The costs of care are only partially subsidised to parents through the tax credit system, and the system for claiming this support is complex and difficult to access. As Skinner (2005) shows, even where lone mothers have access to childcare, they can find it difficult to coordinate getting younger children to childcare with getting older children to school with travel to work and working-time schedules.

Third, not everyone who works succeeds in getting out of poverty. As noted above, those lone mothers who are in work are often in typically female-dominated service-sector occupations, and are therefore not highly paid. Part-time work (under 30 hours per week) is also quite common, especially among those with younger children, which again means lower incomes. The average hourly wage for women in part-time work in the UK in 2008 was £7.51 (US$11.3), compared with £10.91 (US$ 16.4) for women in full-time jobs and £12.50 (US$18.8) for men in full-time jobs (see National Statistics website). Thus, for many lone mothers, it is not wages alone that provide a route out of poverty since their own earnings are not sufficient to ensure that their families remain out of poverty. Rather it is the total income package of earnings combined with direct state financial transfers, and sometimes with other sources of income such as child support, that enables some lone mothers to avoid poverty in work.

The system of tax credits, introduced in 2003, plays a significant role in this. Tax credits are means-tested on the basis of annual income and provide an important supplement to wages for working lone parents. Over a million lone-parent families are now receiving these. In 2006/2007, a family with two children would have received on average about £135 (US$202.5) per week if they were entitled to both the Working Tax Credit (for low-paid people) and the Child Tax Credit (for families with children). Tax credits have thus transformed the financial rewards of working for lone parents, making part-time jobs with relatively low hourly pay possible. This enables lone mothers to engage in employment in a way that would have been financially impossible a few years ago. But tax credits are not without problems. The administration of tax credits has been plagued by delays and errors and the annual means test has not proved to be the best way to deliver accurate and timely payments.

Fourth, the impact of insecure jobs and insecure income on time for care, health, well-being and family life can be profound. Ridge and Millar (2008) have been following the labour market experiences of a group of 50 lone mothers since the end of 2002. The women were selected for the study at the point when they started working for at least 16 hours per week, and since then there have been three rounds of in-depth interviews with both the mothers and their children (at the final interviews this included 34 families). This qualitative longitudinal methodology has highlighted some of the day-to-day challenges facing these families.

The lone mothers in the study were keen to work in order to improve their income, living standards and quality of life. Over the course of the research most did manage to stay in work, although almost all changed jobs and several experienced some further periods out of work due to unemployment or sickness, or because of changes in childcare or family circumstances. Most relied on family support to help them manage to combine work and care. The women, and their children, were generally positive about working and the impact that this had had upon their lives. But there was also some ambivalence.

Over time their aspirations, especially for financial security in work, came up against the reality of employment in low-paid work. Feeling insecure was a common refrain and was related to several factors including temporary and unstable jobs, changing family circumstances, rising debts, and difficulties with securing tax credits and regular child support payments from the fathers of their children. Most of these lone mothers had a weekly income made up from wages, child benefit, tax credits, and – for some – child support and housing benefit. It was difficult for women to feel financially secure when any one of these elements in their overall income could change in ways that were beyond their control. Thus, while these families were in general achieving incomes above the poverty line, they were nevertheless far from being financially secure.

Conclusion

For lone mothers there is always going to be some tension between employment and care. There are only so many hours in the day and days in the week, and caring and providing for a family alone is a daunting task. Combining work and care, especially when children are older, has become the norm for British mothers whether in lone-parent or two-parent families. Unlike some European countries, the UK has arguably been rather slow to adapt welfare provisions to recognise this. In recent years, however, family policy has become a more significant part of social policy with the extension of measures such as childcare provisions and parental leave, the provision of fiscal support for working families, and encouragement to employers to offer more family-friendly work practices (Williams, 2005). Lone mothers have benefited from these developments and their poverty rates, while still high, have fallen. But alongside the positive support for employment more restrictions have been placed on benefit receipt. Lone mothers are increasingly being required, rather than simply encouraged, to take up employment. Compelling work, without due regard to family circumstances and care needs of children, is unlikely to improve quality of life.

High rates of cohabitation, births outside marriage, separation and divorce mean that lone motherhood is a situation that many women now experience in their lifecourse. The high risk of poverty for lone mothers would be much less if the economic situation of all women was stronger and more secure, so that women who become lone mothers are not already at a disadvantage. One important factor in achieving this would be that the costs of raising children are more equally shared, both within families and between families and society as a whole.

Note

1. See Department for Work and Pensions website at www.dwp.gov.uk/asd/hbai.asp (accessed 9 February 2009)

Select bibliography

Department for Work and Pensions (DWP) (2007) *Ready for Work: Full Employment in Our Generation*, Command 7290, London: The Stationery Office, available at: http://www.dwp.gov.uk/welfarereform/readyforwork/readyforwork.pdf (accessed 20 February 2009).

Millar Jane and Tess Ridge (2001) *Families, Poverty, Work and Care: A Review of the Literature*, Department for Work and Pensions Research Report No. 153, Leeds: Corporate Document Services, available at: http://www.dwp.gov.uk/asd/asd5/rrep153.pdf (accessed 20 February 2009).

Ridge, Tess and Jane Millar (2008) *Work and Well-being Over Time: Lone Mothers and Their Children*,

Department for Work and Pensions Research Report No. 536, London: The Stationery Office, available at: http://www.dwp.gov.uk/asd/asd5/rports2007-2008/rrep536.pdf (accessed 20 February 2009).

Skinner, Christine (2005) 'Co-ordination points: a hidden factor in reconciling work and family life', *Journal of Social Policy*, **34** (1), 99–121.

Williams, Fiona (2005) 'New Labour's family policy', in Martin Powell, Linda Bauld and Karen Clarke (eds), *Social Policy Review No. 17*, Bristol: Policy Press, pp. 289–302.

Websites

Department for Work and Pensions, link to page on Households Below Average Income: www.dwp.gov.uk/asd/hbai.asp

UK Statistics Authority: www.statistics.gov.uk

22 Urban poverty and gender in advanced economies: the persistence of feminised disadvantage
Fran Tonkiss

Recent debates over the 'feminisation of poverty' have been closely concerned with gender and poverty in developing economies, but the original analysis of this problem emerged in the United States (US) in the late 1970s, tracing a systematic and widening poverty gap over time between women and men in the world's largest economy (Pearce, 1978). While the 'feminisation of poverty' has since travelled globally (see Chant, Chapter 15, this volume), my discussion considers the contemporary relevance of such an analysis to advanced economies, and to cities in particular. The rapid urbanisation of the global population, largely in developing contexts, has focused critical attention on poverty conditions in urbanising areas and among urbanising populations. However the link between cities and poverty has a long history, and helps structure gendered patterns of poverty in developed as well as in developing economies. Early debates over the feminisation of poverty in the US were soon qualified to examine the racial and urban dimensions of women's poverty: in the 1980s Diana Pearce modified her original argument to write of the 'feminisation of ghetto poverty' (Pearce, 1983; see also Fuchs, 1986).[1] While this shift emphasised the racialised nature of women's poverty, it also highlighted the way that patterns of poverty played out spatially, notably in certain parts of North American cities. Women's poverty was not only shaped along racial lines: it had a specific geography.

This discussion considers current poverty conditions in advanced economies, examining recent data from Europe and North America. In these settings it is more useful to think about gendered poverty than its 'feminisation', given the way the latter term focuses attention on trends in relative poverty levels between men and women. Evidence from these wealthier economies suggests that, while the gendered poverty gap may be stable or decreasing, women are consistently more likely to live in poverty than are men, and with particular concentrations of poverty in cities.

Explaining gendered poverty
Similar factors help explain the gendering of poverty in developed contexts as in developing economies. Women have lower overall levels of employment; they are more likely to be employed part-time or on temporary contracts, to interrupt their employment to care for children or other family members, and to work at lower wage levels. They accumulate fewer pension rights and other protections. Women are far more likely everywhere to head lone-parent households, and more likely – in developed economies – to live alone in old age (see also Falkingham and Baschieri, Chapter 27, this volume).

How these factors combine to structure gender poverty gaps varies across national settings. An early study using international data by Casper et al., (1994) found that employment and household characteristics were key across their sample, but interacted with demographic and political variables to produce different poverty and inequality outcomes in different countries. In those countries with large gender poverty gaps – notably the Anglo-Saxon liberal market economies (Australia, Canada, the United Kingdom and the USA), as well as Germany – women's employment and parenthood status were the chief factors accounting for differential poverty rates. Meanwhile, the analysis of advanced economies with smaller gender differences in poverty rates highlighted the impact of social and political factors in closing the poverty gap. Sweden's relative equality in respect of gender poverty ratios was seen to be due principally to women's high rate of labour force participation. In Italy, in contrast, relative equality was attributable to high rates of marriage, flattening out the country's gender poverty ratio. While Italy had a higher rate of poverty overall than Sweden, its high marriage rate meant that men and women took a more equal 'share' in poverty, with a gender–poverty ratio close to one. A third point of comparison was found in the Netherlands, where women had significantly lower rates of labour force participation than men, and the country as a whole had a relatively low rate of marriage. In this case, welfare provision provided a safety net against income poverty for all citizens, regardless of their employment or marital status. Casper et al., (1994) traced these patterns to both government policy and social cultures: in Sweden, a specific commitment to gender equality underpinned women's employment rates while robust subsidies for childcare transferred many of these costs from carer/s to the state. In Italy, culture and policy promoted the conjugal family as the primary social and welfare unit; in the Netherlands, a universal welfare safety net protected both women and men against income poverty.

For Casper et al., (1994: 601) these could be read as 'three strategies for minimising gender differences in poverty rates'. Such 'strategies', of course, have broader implications for gender equality outside the measurement of income poverty. While high rates of marriage correlated, in the Italian case, with flat gender–poverty ratios, this measure does not capture the distribution of resources within the household, within which income is assumed to be shared. In the Swedish case, active strategies for gender equality militated against a substantial gender poverty gap, while in the Dutch case, a universalist approach to social security protected both men and women against poverty irrespective of their employment status and household formation.

The European context
While the European Union (EU) includes some of the world's richest nations, poverty remains an issue in European societies. Moreover the picture in the EU has altered with the accession of transitional economies from Central and Eastern Europe after 2004: poverty has not disappeared from the wealthier EU nations, and it is a pronounced problem in many of the accession states.

The European Commission (EC) measures the risk of poverty rates for all member states, analysed in terms of different demographic characteristics. The official poverty measure for European countries is based on the share of the population whose disposable income falls below 60 per cent of the national median. In 2007, national poverty rates ranged from fewer than one in ten of the population in Sweden to more than one in five in Lithuania, Latvia and Poland.

While the risks of poverty varied for different groups across different countries, four groups stood out 'as having a high risk in nearly all countries' (Eurostat, 2008: 10):

1. People of working age living alone with a dependent child or children.
2. People aged over 65, living alone and no longer in paid employment.
3. People of working age living alone and not in paid employment.
4. Households with dependent children where only one parent is in paid employment.

Women are the majority in the first two groups, markedly so in respect of lone-parent households. They are also more likely to live alone after the age of 65 – and women in this group are less likely than men to have worked up to that age. How these patterns of poverty play out varies across different countries, but one striking contrast appears between the old and new member states. Couples with one or more children where only one parent is working form the largest at-risk-of-poverty population in nearly all the accession states. The gender effects of this pattern of poverty are, logically, neutral. It is in the wealthier EU states that the more 'feminised' groups (single parents and seniors) dominate the poverty statistics: in Germany, the United Kingdom, Denmark, Finland and Sweden (see also Ypeij, Chapter 20, this volume, on the Netherlands). This is suggestive of demographic, social and policy differences between older and newer member states, advanced and transitional economies.

Smaller but particularly vulnerable subgroups of the population give a further gender profile to patterns of poverty, insecurity and exclusion: women are more likely to suffer domestic violence or sex trafficking, for instance, while men tend to be over-represented among ex-prisoners and rough sleepers. Some of the most at-risk groups within Europe also have particular spatial patterns of settlement and poverty. This includes refugee and asylum-seeker populations in cities, as well as Roma, Gypsy and Traveller populations living in overcrowded and precarious settlements on urban peripheries, in areas of environmental blight with poor access to running water, sanitation, sewage and electricity.

The North American context
An early response to US analyses of a feminisation of poverty in the second half of the twentieth century is found in Fuchs's (1986) study examining census and population survey data from 1959 to 1984. Fuchs notes that trends towards feminisation were highly uneven over time: while there was evidence of a steady feminisation of poverty in the 1960s, during the 1970s the 'sex mix' of poverty varied up and down, with women's relative share of poverty then decreasing (although remaining higher than men's) by the mid-1980s. Moreover, echoing the work of Pearce (1978), Fuchs argued that an increase in female-headed households with dependent children was the chief factor in trends towards the feminisation of poverty during this period, and held for black American women far more strongly than for white American women.

This work has left its mark on research and debate in the field, but certainly did not conclude it. The downward trend for female poverty rates Fuchs identified to 1984 was halted by an upturn in 1985, and the gender–poverty ratio fluctuated between the mid-1980s and late 1990s, peaking in 1998. Year-on-year declines to 2004 were interrupted by a further spike in 2005. The poverty threshold in the USA has been set since the 1960s by the Federal Poverty Standard, adjusted annually for inflation. This is a measure of absolute income poverty, set at different levels for individuals and families of increasing size. While the Federal Poverty Standard offers a fairly conservative measure – and has not kept pace with increases in real household incomes over time – the USA nonetheless has official poverty rates comparable to those of other wealthy economies where poverty is measured relative to median incomes. Women remain significantly more likely than men to be living below the poverty threshold, with the gender poverty gap increasing for people aged 65 or over, and increasing substantially for lone parents. Being in paid employment markedly decreases the risk of poverty for both men and women, although women in work are still more likely to experience poverty than are working men.

These patterns are acute in family contexts. Married-couple families, with or without dependent children, have relatively low rates of poverty. Where the head of the family is living without a marital partner, rates of poverty rise markedly. However, this effect is gendered. While families headed by a single male householder have a notably higher rate of poverty than the average (13.6 per cent in 2007, compared to 9.8 per cent of all US families), households headed by a single female are drastically more likely to live in poverty (28.3 per cent of these households in 2007).

The early debates over the feminisation of poverty in the USA make it difficult to think about these issues without considering questions of 'race' and ethnicity. Poverty rates in the USA are clearly shaped along racial and ethnic lines. In 2007, non-Hispanic whites had a rate of poverty estimated at 8.2 per cent, while black and Hispanic populations had estimated poverty rates of 24.4 and 21.5 per cent respectively. The pattern of poverty for female-headed households plays out starkly in respect of 'race' and ethnicity. In 2007, people living in households headed by lone black or Hispanic women were almost twice as likely to be living below the poverty line (39.6 per cent) than those living in households headed by non-Hispanic white women (21.4 per cent). The poverty rate for households headed by Asian women was lower again (17.6 per cent). It should be stressed of course that the rates of poverty for all these groups are well above the national poverty rate – living in a household headed by a single female, simply, is a key risk factor for poverty. Indeed, residing in such a household increases the risk of poverty more sharply among white than among black populations. Differential rates of poverty for female-headed households across racial and ethnic categories compound gender and household effects with the racialised structuring of poverty.

Poverty rates are also spatialised. Official estimates for 2008 show that numerous urban areas with a population over 250 000 have significantly higher poverty rates than their state average.[2] Even in states with poverty rates below the national estimate there are marked patterns of urban poverty, where the proportion of households living in poverty in large cities is at least double the estimate for their state: including Cleveland and Cincinnati in Ohio; Miami in Florida; Milwaukee in Wisconsin; Philadelphia in Pennsylvania; and Newark in New Jersey. Trends over the past 50 years suggest a changing geography of poverty in the USA. In 1959, people living in non-metropolitan areas were more than twice as likely to live below the poverty line as those living in metropolitan areas. Since then, the US population has urbanised, with fewer people – and far fewer poor people – living in rural areas. United States metropolitan areas have grown their population share over this period, but not necessarily their poverty share: in the urban context it is noticeably central or 'principal' cities that evince the highest poverty rates.

These complex patterns of gender, 'race' and space are difficult to integrate, but certain North American researchers have traced some of the links. Lichtenwalter's (2005) study in the USA cross-cuts data on urban poverty with that on gender. Her particular interest is in the long-standing correlation between female poverty and lone parenthood. Taking 2000 Census data on the seventy largest US cities, and the urban population aged 18–64, she analyses how far the gender poverty gap can be attributed to single female-headed households, as well as considering gender differences in employment and education. Lichtenwalter found that the proportion of women with incomes below the poverty threshold was higher than that of men in all seventy cities in the sample. Her regression analysis is striking, indicating that occupational segregation is the single largest factor impacting not only on the gender *wage gap* in major US cities, but on the gender poverty gap. For the working-age urban population, she contends, the standard factors for explaining gendered poverty rates – women's labour force participation, earnings inequality and the impact of lone parenthood – appear to operate via women's overrepresentation in low-wage occupations.

The profile for urban poverty in Canada is comparable. As in other advanced economies, the poverty rate for women remains higher than for men. Research based on the 2000 Census found that poverty rates for all Canadians were highest in the major cities, with poverty rates for women rising to more than one in five (CCSD, 2007). Moreover patterns of poverty for men and women varied over the lifecourse. Rates of childhood poverty are similar (and relatively high) for males and females. From the age of 15, however, the poverty gap widens. The risk of poverty for men peaks in their mid-twenties, before declining to its lowest point in middle age: from 55 onwards, men's poverty rates increase, but only gradually, with men in their mid-seventies not much likelier to be poor than men in their mid-fifties. Women's poverty also peaks in the 15–24 age group, before declining into middle age. After age 55, however, women's poverty rate increases sharply, such that old age becomes the key risk factor for women's poverty: women over 75 are twice as likely to be living in poverty in Canada's largest cities as are their male counterparts. Among particularly vulnerable groups, women with disabilities, immigrant and Aboriginal women, and women who are members of 'visible minorities', all had higher poverty rates than either men who were members of these groups, or women who were not. The rate of poverty for Aboriginal women in large Canadian cities was more than twice the poverty rate for non-Aboriginal women. According to the Canadian Council on Social Development (2007: 13): 'While all women are at risk of being poor, some are at greater risk than others' (see also Hunt, Chapter 36, this volume).

Conclusion
Debates over the 'feminisation' of poverty in its strict sense – tracing trends up and down, for better or worse – should not obscure the fact that poverty rates remain persistently gendered in a range of rich as well as in poor nations. Moreover the gendering of poverty compounds the systematic inequalities that impact on certain minority ethnic and migrant populations, or the increased risk of poverty that individuals face at either end of the lifecourse. Cities concentrate these patterns of disadvantage in spatial terms. There is a double edge here: cities afford women enhanced opportunities in labour markets, in education and in access to services, but modes of exclusion from these spheres may bite harder in urban contexts (see also Perrons, Chapter 62, this volume). While women in rural areas tend to have lower incomes than those living in cities, they may also have greater non-market opportunities for consumption and social support.

National data on poverty and inequality indicate the direction in which gender poverty gaps are widening or narrowing, but necessarily disguise inequalities within households that bear not only on the distribution of household income but on access to labour and consumption markets, education and welfare. But there is still a more basic argument to be made concerning women's poverty, in wealthy as in poor countries. Having children, looking after them, getting older – these are simple elements in many women's lives that make them more likely than men to live in poverty. Poverty 'de-feminises' when caring for a child or growing old become facts of life rather than risk factors.

Notes

1. It should be noted that Pearce used the US spelling of 'feminisation' (that is, feminization), as did Fuchs, but UK spellings have been used throughout to conform with the rest of the volume.
2. Data drawn from US Bureau of the Census, Current Population Survey, Annual Social and Economic Supplements, available at: http://www.census.gov/hhes/www/poverty (accessed 15 May 2009).

Select bibliography

Casper, Lynne M., Sara S. McLanahan and Irwin Garfinkel (1994) 'The gender–poverty gap: what we can learn from other countries', *American Sociological Review*, **59** (4), 594–605.

Canadian Council on Social Development (CCSD) (2007) *Age, Gender and Family: Urban Poverty in Canada, 2000*, Ottawa: CCSD, available at: http://www.ccsd.ca/pubs/2007/upp/ (accessed 15 May 2009).

Eurostat (2008) *The Social Situation in the European Union 2007*, Luxembourg: Office for Official Publications of the European Communities, available at: http://epp.eurostat.ec.europa.eu (accessed 13 March 2009).

Fuchs, Victor R. (1986) *The Feminization of Poverty?*, Working Paper No. 1934, Cambridge: National Bureau of Economic Research.

Lichtenwalter, Sara (2005) 'Gender poverty disparity in US cities: evidence exonerating female-headed families', *Journal of Sociology and Social Welfare*, **32** (2), 75–96.

Pearce, Diana (1978) 'The feminization of poverty: women, work and welfare', *The Urban and Social Change Review*, **11**, 23–36.

Pearce, Diana (1983) 'The feminization of ghetto poverty', *Society*, **21** (1), 70–74.

PART III

GENDER, FAMILY AND LIFECOURSE

23 Gender and household decision-making in developing countries: a review of evidence
Agnes R. Quisumbing

Many decisions that affect the well-being of individuals are made within families or households. Although the internally differentiated household was described, analysed, and widely accepted in mainstream anthropology from the mid-1970s, it took at least a decade for mainstream development economists to take notice. Challenges from economists to the traditional model of household behaviour and proposals of alternative models that bear closer resemblance to reality came from studies in the 1980s that suggested that men and women systematically spend income under their control in different ways. Since the 1990s, four factors have contributed to the tremendous growth of research on intrahousehold issues: (1) the development of new models of household decision-making, (2) an increased awareness that paying attention to intrahousehold allocation matters in the design and implementation of development policy, (3) the growing availability of data from developing and developed countries with which to test alternative household models, and (4) the use of qualitative methods, arising from increased collaboration with anthropologists and other social scientists, to understand non-economic dimensions of human behaviour. These studies have contributed to the rejection of the traditional paradigm of the unitary model of household behaviour in favour of the collective model.

Unitary versus collective household models[1]
The unitary model characterises the household as a group of individuals who behave as if they agree on how best to combine time and purchased goods to maximise household welfare. Thus, either all members of the household share the same preferences or a (self-interested or altruistic) dictator makes all the decisions. In contrast, all collective models have two common features: first, they allow different decision-makers to have different preferences and, second, they do not require a unique household welfare index to be interpreted as a utility function, thereby allowing the index to be dependent on prices and incomes as well as 'tastes'. In the collective model, nothing is assumed a priori about the nature of the decision process, that is, it does not directly address the question of how individual preferences lead to a collective choice. If one wishes to give more structure to the decision-making process, two subclasses of collective models emerge, one rooted in cooperative and the other in non-cooperative game theory.

In the cooperative approach, individuals have a choice of remaining single or of forming a household or other grouping. They choose the latter option when the advantages associated with being in a household outweigh those derived from being single. The existence of the household generates a surplus, which will be distributed among its members. Unitary models represent a special case of cooperative collective models where preferences are identical and, as a consequence, resources are pooled.

Within the cooperative subclass are examples that represent household decisions as the outcome of some bargaining process applying the tools of cooperative game theory. In this literature, outside options (also called 'exit options' or 'threat points') are important influences on spouses' bargaining power and hence on intrahousehold welfare. If this approach is correct, one may hope to affect intrahousehold welfare by improving the exit options of disadvantaged groups. Two main categories of outside options have been proposed by the literature, namely, non-cooperation within an existing household – the so-called 'separate spheres' hypothesis – and separation from the household. These exit options are themselves a function of extrahousehold norms such as laws concerning access to common property and prohibitions on women working outside the home.

The second subclass of collective models relies on non-cooperative game theory. While all cooperative models are Pareto efficient, only some non-cooperative models are. The noncooperative approach assumes that individuals cannot enter into binding and enforceable contracts with each other. Instead, an individual's actions are conditional on the actions of others. This conditionality of action implies that not all non-cooperative models are Pareto optimal – that is, a redistribution of resources from one household member to another could still improve overall welfare. In these models, the household is depicted as a site of largely separate gender-specific economies linked by reciprocal claims on members' income, land, goods and labour. Net transfers of income between individuals are the only link between them. Thus, when making decisions, each person takes net transfers as given and chooses the goods that he or she will consume to maximise individual utility, rather than the utility of the household unit. Since differential allocations across household members are consistent with both unitary and collective models, the empirical challenge lies in testing whether or not such differentials are consistent with a unitary model of the household, or with a decision-making process in which different household members have different preferences and varying abilities to enforce these.

Empirical evidence
Because of the paucity of individual-level data on outcomes, particularly in developing countries, early tests of household models were based on household-level outcomes such as expenditure shares (see reviews in Behrman, 1997; Fafchamps and Quisumbing, 2008; Haddad et al., 1997; Schultz, 2001). For example, a study in Côte d'Ivoire found that the share of household cash income earned by women had a positive and significant effect on the budget share for food.[2] Research drawing on Taiwanese data found that women's income share increases expenditure shares of staples and education, and decreases that of alcohol and cigarettes. More recent studies have taken advantage of increasingly available individual-level data both on outcomes and on non-labour income. Studies based on data from Thailand, India, and Brazil reject the pooling of non-labour income in relation to family labour supplies (see the review in Schultz, 2001). Having both household-level and individual data in the same data set also permits more nuanced investigations. A four-country study in Bangladesh, Ethiopia, Indonesia and South Africa found that in Bangladesh and South Africa, increasing the share of assets controlled by women increases educational budget shares. However, whether these gains benefited girls or boys differs across countries – differences driven both by differences in preferences and underlying economic rationales.

Measuring bargaining power

Specification and measurement of bargaining power – a most elusive concept – underlies most of these tests of the collective model. Bargaining power is affected by control over resources, such as assets, by factors that influence the bargaining process, by mobilisation of interpersonal networks, and by basic attitudinal attributes. Economic analyses have tended to focus on economic resources exogenous to labour supply as a major determinant of bargaining power. These include: shares of income earned by women, non-labour income, current assets, inherited assets, assets at marriage, and the public provision of resources to specific household members. The threat of withdrawing both oneself and one's assets from the household grants the owner of those assets some power over household resources. These threats are credible if supported by community norms or divorce laws. All of these measures capture some dimension of bargaining strength, but only the relatively uncommon natural experiments related to public provision of resources are likely to be entirely exogenous to individual and household decisions.

Factors that can influence the bargaining process include legal rights, skills and knowledge, the capacity to acquire information, education, and bargaining skills. Some of these influences are external to the individual (for example, legal rights), but many of them are highly correlated with human capital or education. In some instances, domestic violence can be used to extract resources from spouses or their families, as in the case of dowry-related violence in India. Individuals can also mobilise personal networks to improve their bargaining power. Membership in organisations, access to kin and other social networks, and 'social capital' may positively influence a person's power to affect household decisions. Last, basic attitudinal attributes that affect bargaining power include self-esteem, self-confidence and emotional satisfaction.

Increasingly, economists have turned to ethnographic evidence and methods used by other social scientists to guide the construction of appropriate measures of bargaining power. For example, drawing on anthropological evidence, a study on the rural Philippines used inherited landholdings as a measure of bargaining power since land is usually given as part of the marriage gift. Another study in Indonesia used ethnographic evidence and focus group discussions to identify types of assets women and men bring to marriage and what claims they have on them upon divorce.

Production, risk and uncertainty

While many of the studies discussed above do not reject Pareto-optimality in consumption decisions, Pareto-optimality has been rejected in production and in situations with risk and uncertainty. Pareto-efficiency for a household implies efficiency in consumption as well as in its productive activities. However, in Burkina Faso, plots controlled by women are farmed less intensively than those controlled by men, implying inefficiency in household productive activities. Indeed, productivity gains of 10–20 per cent could be realised if resources were allocated from men's plots to women's plots within the same household.

Other studies from Côte d'Ivoire, Ethiopia and Ghana have found that risk is not shared equally within the household, additional proof that intrahousehold allocation is inefficient. A study in Ethiopia tested whether individual illness shocks affect the evolution of an individual nutrition index, controlling for a variety of confounding factors. While risk is shared efficiently in most of the Ethiopian highlands, poor women in the southern part of the country, where customary laws on settlement at divorce are biased against women, fare worst. A study on Côte d'Ivoire also rejected the hypothesis of complete insurance within households. Conditional on overall levels of expenditure, the composition of household expenditure is sensitive to the gender of the recipient of a 'rainfall shock'. Rainfall shocks associated with high yields of women's crops shift expenditure towards food. However, strong social norms constrain the use of profits from yam cultivation, which is carried out almost exclusively by men. In line with these norms, rainfall-induced fluctuations in income from yams are transmitted to expenditures on education and food, not to expenditures on private goods. Spouses may also look outside the household for insurance mechanisms, such as in Ghana. Women pool their risk with other women in the village while men have a wider and less defined risk pool. Indeed, transfers from the spouse and the extended family are not responsive to shocks, while those from non-family friends are. Interestingly, a study from pastoralist societies in Ethiopia and Kenya suggests not only that shocks matter, but also that *perceptions* of shocks matter. Men and women may differ in their perception of the nature of a shock, the severity of the shock, as well as the appropriate coping mechanisms to be used.

Implications for future research
Three issues emerging from this review highlight areas for future work. First, both social norms and control of resources matter in intrahousehold allocation. Social norms set the context of intrahousehold negotiation over labour and other resources, including the sharing of resources within the household. Second, assets are important: they are not only associated with greater bargaining power but women's control of assets has also been associated with better development outcomes. Third, there is much we do not know about assets – interactions between different types of assets, the ways that men and women obtain access to and control of assets, and the importance of assets beyond tangible physical assets and human capital (see Deere, Chapter 53, this volume). I discuss each of these in turn.

First, the studies on Côte d'Ivoire and Ghana illustrate the importance both of extra-household norms affecting intrahousehold decision-making and the need to learn from other social sciences. In Côte d'Ivoire, the existence of social norms surrounding yam income, even if controlled by men, dictates its disposition toward food, unlike proceeds of cash crops, which are typically spent by the plot owners on private goods. In Ghana, the nature of marital relationships induces women to share risks not with their husbands, but with other non-kin women within the village. Without drawing from previous anthropological work, or knowledge of these social norms, standard economic models would have been hard-pressed to explain these findings.

Second, research conducted at the International Food Policy Research Institute has found that increasing women's control over assets has positive effects on a number of important development outcomes for the household, including food security, child nutrition and education, as well as women's own well-being (see studies in Quisumbing, 2003). In Bangladesh, a higher share of women's assets is associated with higher expenditures on education and better health outcomes for girls. A study using cross-country data found that increases in women's education made the greatest contribution to reducing the rate of child malnutrition, even greater than the contribution from improved agricultural productivity. These gains to household welfare suggest that strengthening women's control of resources need not result in a zero-sum gain. Indeed, if the existing distribution of resources is not Pareto-optimal – that is, if welfare can be improved by redistributing resources from one household member to another – there may be efficiency gains in increasing women's control of resources.

Women's control of tangible assets may also affect the outcomes of household decisions. In the context of a burgeoning HIV/AIDS epidemic, securing women's property and inheritance rights to land can promote women's economic security and thus reduce their vulnerability to domestic violence, unsafe sex and other AIDS-related risk factors. However, titling programmes have, in many cases, decreased rather than increased women's tenure security by strengthening the claims of men without recognising the rights women have had over land under customary systems (although see Rakodi, Chapter 54, this volume).

Finally, there is much we have to learn about assets (Meinzen-Dick and Quisumbing, 2008; see also Deere, Chapter 53, this volume). Recent work highlights the potential interaction between natural capital, especially land and water, physical capital, and other assets much more broadly defined to include access to education, information and institutions in reducing poverty. Gender differences in access to assets at the individual, household and community level are also important. A growing body of literature has documented gender disparities in asset endowments between female- and male-headed households and more recently, within male-headed households. In addition, one of the important sources of economic vulnerability for women is the potential dissolution of their household, through divorce or their husband's death. Depending on marital and inheritance regimes, women may lose access to all of their husband's tangible assets.

At the community level, women's control over assets is often conditioned by governance arrangements, the extent to which they give voice to women, and the political capital of men and women. India's *panchayati raj* programme to devolve resources and authority to elected village-level bodies provided a natural experiment, whereby one-third of bodies were assigned to have women presidents. A well-cited study in India found that those villages with women leaders were more likely to invest in infrastructure (drinking water and roads) related to women's priorities.

Analysis of gendered access to assets at different levels would have important implications for development policy. At the intrahousehold level, analysis would flesh out how different assets contribute to individual well-being; at the household level, how assets controlled by men and women influence household-level welfare outcomes, and at the community or national/subnational level, how policies and laws create the institutional environment for men's and women's ownership and control of assets. Overall there is a need to understand the conditions under which secure access to assets can enhance men's and women's livelihoods and well-being. Such a multi-level approach to understanding gendered access to and control of assets would be better able to provide the basis for integrated policy packages as opposed to isolated, piecemeal reforms that seek to increase one particular type of asset without looking at the complementarity or substitutability among assets.

Moreover, there is a need to expand the definition of assets beyond 'standard' physical and financial assets. The development research community is recognising the importance of collecting information on gendered access to tangible assets, and projects are beginning to do so on a more systematic scale (see Moser, Chapter 60, this volume).

Information on schooling and nutrition is typically collected on a gender-disaggregated basis, but there has been much less work on other aspects of information or social and political capital (see Willis, Chapter 59, this volume). In addition to measurement issues, there are likely to be important differences between types of assets, particularly between many tangible assets such as land or physical capital, and many intangible assets such as human or social capital. Different policies will be needed to encourage the accumulation of these different types of assets, particularly by the poor, and to ensure their gender-equitable distribution.

Acknowledgements
This chapter draws on past work undertaken at the International Food Policy Research Institute (IFPRI) under the multi-country programme on 'Strengthening Development Policy through Gender and Intrahousehold Analysis', particularly work with Marcel Fafchamps and John Maluccio. The discussion of future work on gender and assets borrows liberally from a new research programme on 'Strengthening Women's Assets for Better Development Outcomes' and joint work with Ruth Meinzen-Dick and other IFPRI colleagues.

Notes
1. See Haddad et al. (1997) for a review.
2. Detailed citations can be found in the reviews listed in the select bibliography.

Select bibliography
Behrman, Jere R. (1997) 'Intrahousehold distribution and the family', in Mark R. Rosenzweig and Oded Stark (eds), *Handbook of Population and Family Economics*, vol. 1A, Amsterdam: North-Holland, pp. 125–238.
Fafchamps, Marcel and Agnes R. Quisumbing (2008) 'Household formation and marriage markets in rural areas', in T. Paul Schultz and John A. Strauss (eds), *Handbook of Development Economics*, vol. 4, Amsterdam: North-Holland, pp. 3187–247.
Haddad, Lawrence, John Hoddinott and Harold Alderman (eds) (1997) *Intrahousehold Resource Allocation in Developing Countries: Methods, Models, and Policy*, Baltimore, MD: Johns Hopkins University Press for the International Food Policy Research Institute.
Meinzen-Dick, Ruth S. and Agnes R. Quisumbing (2008) *Strengthening Women's Assets for Better Development Outcomes: A Proposal for a Global Research Programme*, Washington, DC: International Food Policy Research Institute.
Quisumbing, Agnes R. (ed.) (2003) *Household Decisions, Gender, and Development: A Synthesis of Recent Research*, Washington, DC: International Food Policy Research Institute.
Schultz, T. Paul (2001) 'Women's roles in the agricultural household: bargaining and human capital investments', in Bruce L. Gardner and Gordon C. Rausser (eds), *Handbook of Agricultural Economics*, vol. 1A, Amsterdam: North-Holland, pp. 383–456.

24 Linking women's and children's poverty
Ruth Lister

Child poverty is high on the agenda of the British and other European governments. Yet the links between child poverty and women's poverty tend to be overlooked. The first part of this chapter, which is written primarily in the British context, makes some general observations about the gendered nature of poverty from the perspective of women. The second part focuses on some of the ramifications with regard to child poverty. In particular, it discusses the effects of women's role as poverty managers on their parenting and job-seeking capacities and the importance of women's earnings in preventing child poverty. The conclusion draws out some implications for the conceptualisation of poverty and for policy.[1]

The gendered nature of poverty
Poverty is gendered in terms of its incidence, causes and effects. Insofar as it is possible to estimate the numbers of women and men living in income poverty using existing measures, the evidence from the European Union (EU) and the United States (US) shows that, to varying degrees and with the clearest exception of Sweden, women are at greater risk than men. Black and minority ethnic women and disabled women are particularly vulnerable. Longitudinal research in the United Kingdom (UK) also shows that women are more likely than men to suffer longer spells of income poverty and to move in and out of poverty.

The data on incidence tend to be inadequate because, although they purport to count the number of individual women and men in income poverty, they in fact count the number of households in poverty and assume that all members of the households share equally in that income. This is, however, a heroic assumption given the number of studies showing that income is not always shared fairly within the family, to the detriment of women. It is important, therefore, when statistics refer to the number of individual men and women living in poverty, to be clear whether they really do refer to the number of individuals or to the number of individuals living in households counted as poor.

The inadequacy of most statistics means that women's poverty is partly hidden. This is reflected in surveys that ask individuals about their living standards as well as income. Typically they find that low-income women are more likely than men to say they go without basic items and that men tend to be privileged consumers in terms of both everyday commodities such as food and consumer durables such as a car.

Women's hidden poverty reflects their inferior position of power in the gendered division of labour, continued sex discrimination and gender stereotyping, and the realities and ideology of female economic dependence (even if this is only partial in practice). Together these underpin women's position in the labour market, family and welfare state. It is the interaction between the three that determines women's economic status over their lifetimes and that distinguishes the causes of female from male poverty. In particular, the causes of women's poverty are to be found in the private domestic sphere of the family as well as the public sphere of the labour market and welfare state.

The continued power of the gendered division of labour, which means that women continue to take the main responsibility for the everyday care of children, also has implications for the management of poverty. By and large it is women who manage poverty. Managing poverty involves juggling an inadequate income in a constant struggle to make ends meet. A number of studies document how women draw on personal resources of resilience, resourcefulness and skill to maintain this difficult balancing act. In some cases they also draw on social resources that derive from social networks. In others, poverty can be exacerbated by social isolation that can result in 'feeling trapped and depressed' (Women's Budget Group, 2008: 8).

Managing poverty is difficult, time-consuming and tiring work. This means that some women suffer time as well as income poverty. Although recent research in the UK suggests that it is relatively rare for adults of working age to be both time- and income-poor, insofar as they are, women are more likely than men to suffer the double penalty, 'as a result of prevailing norms about the gender division of care' (Burchardt, 2008: 1). In participatory research with women in poverty in three British cities 'feelings of hopelessness and emotional and physical exhaustion were commonly expressed'; in the words of one woman 'poverty means "having to work until 9pm every evening after getting up at 5.45am"' (Women's Budget Group, 2008: 10).

The study also found that 'when asked to discuss what poverty means to them, their children's needs permeated all their experiences, demonstrating women's continuing prioritisation of others' needs' (Women's Budget Group, 2008: 11). This is just one example in a long line of research, historical and contemporary, which illuminates how, in managing poverty, mothers also typically sacrifice their own needs in the interests of protecting other family members, particularly children. Mothers frequently go without food, clothing and warmth in order to mitigate the full impact of poverty on children (and sometimes partners). Both historically and today, women have acted as the shock-absorbers of poverty.

Not only do they absorb the material shocks but they also often try to shield their children from the stigma and 'othering' all too often associated with poverty. 'Othering' refers to the way in which people in poverty are often treated and talked about as if they were 'other' and inferior to the majority non-poor (Lister, 2004). At a workshop run by the Women's Budget Group, women with experience of poverty talked about how their 'children are bullied for being poor and are made to feel inferior' (Women's Budget Group, 2005: 25). They also talked about how they 'feel blamed for being poor and for the poverty of their children' and provided 'powerful accounts of a lack of respect, especially from agencies that showed a lack of understanding, and made inappropriate and incorrect assumptions' (ibid.). The Women's Budget Group's participatory research project underlined the difficulties the women faced in 'remaining resilient in the face of hostility, judgement, pity and shame', in other words in the face of 'othering' (Women's Budget Group, 2008: 8).

Resilience is also difficult to maintain in the face of the hard work of getting by. While some women are able to derive a sense of pride from the ability to get by on an inadequate income, this should not obscure the evidence of the stressful nature of the work involved in managing poverty. It is particularly stressful when getting by is achieved only at the expense of getting into debt and arrears. The combined effect of managing poverty and debt, together with feelings of failure and guilt about the effects on children, takes its toll on women's health – both physical and mental. A number of studies have found that low-income women report higher levels of stress than low-income men and have identified a very high incidence of mental health problems. In some cases this is aggravated by experience of domestic violence.

Nevertheless, such research also demonstrates the extraordinary resilience and resourcefulness that some low-income women display in order to get by in the most difficult circumstances. This resilience also translates into the active contribution that some make towards managing and combating poverty at the community level, with studies conducted in a range of countries revealing the important role that women play as poverty activists.

Some implications for child poverty

The British government's child poverty strategy is couched in terms of a contract between government and parents. Parents are expected to do what they can to improve their own situation through paid work and to do their best for their children's well-being and development. While the strategy tends to be presented in gender-neutral terms, both the job-seeking and parenting responsibilities ascribed to parents have to be understood in the context of the gendered division of labour.

A study of parenting in poverty found that 'in practice, parenting was still a clearly gendered role, in terms of both identity and activity' (Hooper et al., 2007: 39). While there was considerable variation in the extent to which fathers were actively involved in parenting, mothers' roles reflected 'the more tightly prescribed social expectations of motherhood' (ibid.: 40). Although their inability to live up to their own ideals of parenting because of poverty was a source of stress for both fathers and mothers, half of the women in the study also carried the emotional scars of the experience of domestic violence in adult relationships. Abusive relationships had often undermined mothers' confidence in their parenting abilities. Moreover, 'unresolved trauma, ongoing conflict and abuse, mental health problems and the impacts of stigma on self-esteem could all seriously undermine parents' energy for developing the activities with children that contribute to mutually satisfying relationships and their capacity to adopt the authoritative style associated with optimal outcomes for children' (ibid.: 43).

In the findings from participatory research facilitated by the Women's Budget Group (2008: 8), 'poverty was commonly expressed as an inability to be a financially and emotionally supportive parent to children'. This inability was closely bound up with the women's feelings of guilt and lack of self-worth. These and other studies paint a graphic picture of how poverty undermines parenting capacities and how mothers carry much of the strain in their role as poverty managers. The stress of managing poverty can have a damaging impact on mothers' physical and mental health, which in turn adversely affects their morale and overall well-being. This activates a vicious and damaging spiral: as observed earlier, mothers struggle to do their best by their children and to protect them from the full impact of poverty. The cost of doing so in terms of their own health and morale makes it harder to be a good parent and to give their children the kind of childhood and upbringing for which they strive. It can also make it harder to meet the expectations of educational policy of active parental involvement in their children's education. All these factors in turn can make it harder for their children to escape poverty as they grow up. The links are particularly strong for lone mothers but may work in different ways for mothers in couples, particularly where they feel trapped in abusive relationships.

The poor health and low morale associated with managing poverty not only make parenting more difficult but they also damage mothers' ability to seek and find paid work – typically the key route out of poverty in industrialised countries' anti-poverty strategies. There is clear evidence from a number of studies that poor health impedes the ability to get and keep paid work. Low morale too makes effective job-seeking harder. Based on his research with lone mothers, Alan Marsh writes that 'many out-of-work lone parents experience a malign spiral of hardship, poor health and low morale. There is something about this experience that builds up its own barriers to work . . . It is quite hard to contemplate work if you are that demoralised and hard up' (Marsh, 2001: 26–7). He argues that 'the first step in restoring the optimism and the sense of well-being essential to turn the view of even the most disadvantaged lone parent outward towards work, is to improve the present stand of living. Hardship reduces morale and allows little room for the kind of optimism and forward planning' needed for effective job-seeking (ibid.: 32).

The potential earnings of both lone mothers and mothers in couples are important resources in contemporary anti-poverty strategies. Cross-national experience shows that generally lone mothers in paid work are less likely to be in poverty than those out of work and that mothers' earnings play a critical role in keeping many families out of poverty. Moreover, if a family splits up, the mother is less likely to face poverty if she already has the resources (personal and cultural as well as financial) that derive from paid employment. The relatively low rates of employment among Pakistani and Bangladeshi mothers is likely to be a contributory factor in the extremely high levels of child poverty among British Pakistani and Bangladeshi families.

However, both lone mothers and mothers in couples face a labour market that still favours men over women. Occupational segregation, gender pay gaps and a range of barriers to employment such as inflexible hours, inadequate childcare facilities and poor transport links all disadvantage women. Thus anti-poverty strategies that prioritise paid employment need to be gendered strategies, which do not simply improve women's employment rates but also strengthen their position within the labour market, particularly at the lower end.

Women's labour market position means that paid work is not a panacea for the poverty that they and their children experience. Moreover, there is concern in various quarters that too much emphasis on paid work as the route out of poverty and the extension of conditionality to parents of young children risk devaluing the unpaid work involved in caring for children.

Gendering poverty analysis and policy
A gendered analysis of poverty has implications for the conceptualisation and measurement of poverty and for policy. Poverty is ultimately experienced by individuals. Yet where individuals are members of wider households or families, their needs and resources are typically subsumed within those of the latter. Irrespective of the material living standards a woman may enjoy at any one point in time, she is vulnerable to poverty

if she lacks control over resources and the independent means to support herself. From a dynamic perspective, this is particularly important in the event of possible relationship breakdown. To the extent that income is a key element in any definition and measure of poverty, arguably women's poverty should be understood and measured in terms of the income actually available to them. This, however, sets up a methodological challenge that has not yet been resolved, given the difficulties of measuring the incomes received by individuals within households (see also Chen, Chapter 71, this volume; Heintz, Chapter 66, this volume; Razavi and Staab, Chapter 65, this volume).

There is also a tension between this individualistic focus, necessary to the exposure of different aspects of hidden female poverty, and an understanding of this poverty as rooted within women's relationships to other family members (Millar, 2003). If an undifferentiated household analysis is the thesis and an individualised analysis the antithesis, what is needed is a synthesis in which the individual experience of poverty is understood within its relational context.

Such an understanding needs also to take account of the resource of time. A comprehensive understanding of the gendered nature of poverty requires knowledge of how much time and energy women and men each expend on converting income into living standards or, following Amartya Sen, into capabilities and functionings.

Key here is the gendered division of labour, which also has implications for policy. As long as women are disadvantaged in both public and private spheres by the gendered division of labour, they will remain at greater risk of poverty than men. Effective policies to tackle women's (and by extension children's) poverty need to ensure access to an adequate independent income from the labour market and/or the state, through a combination of labour market, welfare services and income maintenance measures.

Among the priorities articulated by the women involved in the Women's Budget Group's participatory research were more generous benefits and free high-quality childcare. The project, which involved women with experience of poverty engaging with policymakers, also made a powerful case for a more participatory approach to policy-making. The lesson learned by the Women's Budget Group from the project has a wider resonance:

> When given the opportunity to come together and share their individual experiences of living in poverty, women are able to articulate the urgency of their situation and the need for both practical and strategic needs to be met. They are the experts on how policy is implemented on the ground, and can help guide the development of policy that is more receptive to their needs and thus more effective. It is important to create opportunities for women with experience of living in poverty to go beyond acting as 'witnesses' to poverty, and engage with decision-makers in a way that recognises this expertise (Women's Budget Group, 2008: 27).

Note
1. This chapter draws substantially on Lister (2004) and Women's Budget Group (2005).

Select bibliography

Burchardt, Tania (2008) *Time and Income Poverty. Findings*, York: Joseph Rowntree Foundation, available at: www.jrf.org.uk (accessed 19 February 2009).
Hooper, Carol, Sarah Gorin, Christie Cabral and Claire Dyson (2007) *Living With Hardship 24/7*, London: Frank Buttle Trust.
Lister, Ruth (2004) *Poverty*, Cambridge: Polity.

Marsh, Alan (2001) 'Helping British lone parents get and keep paid work', in Jane Millar and Karen Rowlingson (eds), *Lone Parents, Employment and Social Policy*, Bristol: Policy Press, pp. 11–36.
Millar, Jane (2003) 'Gender, poverty and social exclusion', *Social Policy and Society*, **23**, 181–8.
Women's Budget Group (2005) *Women's and Children's Poverty: Making the Links*, London: Women's Budget Group, available at www.wbg.org.uk (accessed 14 October 2009).
Women's Budget Group (2008) *Women and Poverty. Experiences, Empowerment and Engagement*, York: Joseph Rowntree Foundation, available at www.jrf.org.uk (accessed 14 October 2009).

25 Reducing the gender gap in education: the role of wage labour for rural women in Mozambique
John Sender

Introduction

Analysis of research results from rural Mozambique offers some important new insights into gender relations and the inter-generational transmission of poverty. The Mozambican Rural Labour Survey (MRLS) underpinned the research and covered many of the poorest rural households in the country.[1] In some of these households, especially in those where women have greater autonomy in making resource allocation decisions, the welfare of young girls (daughters) is less likely to be neglected than in other households. This finding confirms patterns found in the well-established international literature on the determinants of gender gaps in education and in nutrition between sons and daughters (Thomas, 1994: 979). However, the estimates of 'autonomy' in this literature have not considered divorced and separated statuses as unambiguous indicators of women's ability to act independently.

The MRLS contains a remarkably high incidence of divorced, separated and widowed women. The fate of these women is not only important in the context of Mozambique. A great many extremely poor people in sub-Saharan Africa, especially in southern Africa, live in similar rural households that do not receive regular support from a male spouse. In the poorest African households, the ratio of adult males to adult females is relatively low or there are no adult males at all (Sender, 2003).

Many women in the survey told the researchers that they became wage workers following the death of or desertion by their spouse, or said that they left the labour market as soon as they married or began to cohabit.[2] These statements highlight the need to examine interactions between labour market participation and marital status; and the major objective here is to assess the implications of these interactions for rural girls. In much of the literature, the focus is on maternal *education* as predicting the level of child education, particularly the education of girls, rather than on the types of *wage employment* open to women and their effects on girls' schooling. It has been claimed that wage employment for women 'is generally associated with lower levels of education of girls, most often the oldest girl who substitutes for her mother in the domestic division of labour' (Kabeer, 2003: 37). In contrast, the argument here emphasises the positive impact of women's access to decent rural wage employment opportunities, as the basis for investment in their daughters' future.

Results

The women interviewed in the MRLS work in a wide array of occupations and enterprises for very different wages. The relatively weak bargaining power of most of these wage workers, especially casual agricultural workers and domestic servants, means that many of them live on pitiful and irregular wages and receive few, if any, non-wage

Table 25.1 Education of sons and daughters of female and male principal respondents in the MRLS

	Variable	Statistic	Female principal[1] respondents – Divorced/separated	Female principal[1] respondents – Non-divorced/non-separated	Male principal respondents
Children 16 years+	Years of schooling	Mean	4.62	4.25	4.36
		Median	5.00	4.00	4.00
Sons 16 years+[2]	Years of schooling	Mean	5.29	4.89	5.39
		Median	5.00	5.00	5.00
Daughters 16 Years+[3]	Years of schooling	Mean	3.93	3.40	3.23
		Median	4.00	3.00	3.00

Notes:
1. The use of the term 'principal' does not have any connotations of 'headship' since the MRLS did not attempt to identify a household 'head'. Households are defined in terms of economic relationships among members, rather than the narrower residential or sociological relationships commonly used in socio-economic surveys.
2. For female principal respondents, N = 214, for male principal respondents, N = 209.
3. For female principal respondents, N = 334, for male principal respondents, N = 189.

benefits (Cramer et al., 2008). However, the MRLS also shows that some types of employers – typically larger employers with more access to capital – are able to offer decent jobs and much better working conditions to their female workers. Divorced and separated women in the MRLS were much more likely than other women to succeed in finding these decent jobs; and they benefit from the new opportunities for organisation and unionisation that these jobs provide.

Part of the explanation for the fact that so many partnered women are employed in degrading and insecure jobs may be that men (husbands or fathers) forcibly prevent them from working in the better types of job; men fear that women will have better opportunities to meet male co-workers if they commute to work in (large-scale) enterprises offering regular employment. However, despite male coercive behaviour within households and pervasive gender discrimination in rural labour markets, some divorced and separated women can earn enough to escape the most abject poverty and the worst living conditions.

At the same time, divorced and separated women achieve better results in educating their children than do other women. Divorced and separated mothers are especially good at investing in their daughters' education compared to non-divorced/separated mothers and to male wage workers. Thus, in absolute terms, the daughters of divorced and separated women have achieved more schooling (in terms of the mean and median number of years of schooling completed) than the daughters of non-divorced/separated women, as shown in Table 25.1.

The education gap between daughters and sons of divorced and separated mothers is also lower than the corresponding gap between the daughters and sons of non-divorced/separated mothers, that is, divorced and separated mothers favour their sons far less

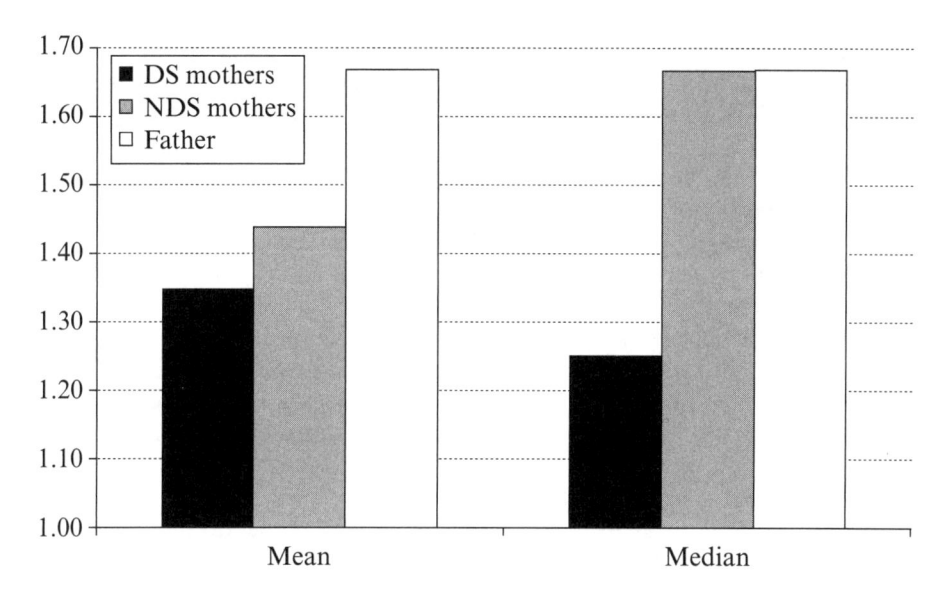

Figure 25.1 Ratio of sons' and daughters' years of schooling in the MRLS, male principal respondents and divorced and separated (DS) and non-divorced and non-separated (NDS) female principal respondents

than non-divorced/separated mothers. Figure 25.1 shows that the size of the gender gap, measured by the ratio of the mean or median years of education achieved by sons compared to daughters, is much higher for non-divorced/separated than divorced and separated mothers.

It is not surprising that the sons of the male principal respondents in the MRLS have had more years of education (a mean of 5.39 years) than other children in the MRLS, since their fathers are more educated and earn higher wages, on average, than female wage workers. It is more surprising that the children of divorced and separated female principal respondents are, on average, better educated than the children of male principal respondents – because the daughters of divorced and separated women boost the average by being significantly better educated than the daughters of male principal respondents (Table 25.1). The median number of years of education completed by the daughters of divorced and separated women is 4.0 years, compared to 3.0 years for the daughters of male principal respondents. Although the sons of divorced and separated women do complete more years of education than their daughters, 5.29 years compared to 3.93 years (equivalent to 35 per cent more years), the sons of male principal respondents are much more privileged, receiving 70 per cent more years of education than the daughters of the principal male respondents. Thus, the size of the gender gap between the education of sons and daughters is particularly large for the children of the male principal respondents, and very much larger than the gender gap for the children of divorced and separated women (Figure 25.1).

Some policy implications
Research focused on divorced, separated and widowed women in rural areas can provide insights into extreme poverty that are directly relevant to policy debates on

poverty reduction in Africa. These policy debates too often tend to focus on expanding funding for microcredit to support self-employment, despite the fact that there is too little evidence in Africa or elsewhere to justify belief in the poverty-reducing impact of these conventional policies (see, for example, Casier, Chapter 94; Garikipati, Chapter 92; Mohamed, Chapter 86 and Sweetman, Chapter 88, this volume). Most donors, non-governmental organisations (NGOs), and government agencies continue to believe as an article of faith that the poverty of rural women can be effectively reduced by efforts to promote and subsidise self-employment on small farms and in microenterprises, rather than wage employment.

In contrast, the evidence and analysis presented here, focused on a sample of the poorest women in Mozambique, suggests that increasing women's access to decently remunerated wage employment, as well as lowering the legislative and social barriers of paternalist coercion within and outside the family, could make a substantial difference to the welfare of these women and their children. Policy interventions are required to improve rural women's prospects in the labour market. Obviously, there is an urgent need for a very substantial increase in the resources devoted to the education of rural girls in sub-Saharan Africa; the intergenerational poverty reduction impact of female education has been widely recognised for some time. Unfortunately, there is little evidence of a commitment to such a policy by donors or the state in Mozambique, or elsewhere in Africa.

There is even less evidence that donors have recognised the need for, or developed effective policies to promote, the massive investments in agribusiness and rural infrastructure required to increase the demand for female wage labour in rural Africa. In fact, the share of official development assistance (and of government public expenditures) devoted to agricultural investments in Africa has remained remarkably small. The World Bank, the most influential donor in Africa, has only very recently recognised that '[m]aking the rural labor market a more effective pathway out of poverty is . . . a major policy challenge that remains poorly understood and sorely neglected in policymaking' (World Bank, 2007: 287). Having recognised this neglect, the task of devising new and powerful incentives (fiscal, credit, infrastructural, and so on) to generate demand for female labour among the types of employer most likely to offer decent working conditions has been ignored. Instead, resources and subsidies continue to be distributed to small 'family farms', to women's microcredit projects, or to the party/bureaucratic/military elite.

Conclusion
Some divorced and separated women appear to have gained in self-confidence not only through schooling, but also as a result of the emancipatory experience of a successful struggle to survive on their wage income without a male partner. As a result, they appreciate that their daughters would be unwise to rely on male support, especially if men continue to restrict women's access to the labour market. Instead, they believe that their daughters' welfare and, less altruistically, their ability to care for them in their old age, will be greater if their daughters remain at school for as long as possible.

Rural wage employment has the potential to provide an escape route from poverty for a new generation of women in Mozambique and elsewhere in Africa. Therefore, it is unfortunate that donors have done so little to develop effective policies to promote the massive investments in agribusiness and rural infrastructure required to increase the demand for female wage labour in rural Africa.

Acknowledgements

This research was funded by the National Directorate of Planning and Budget of the Ministry of Planning and Finance (now Ministry of Planning and Development) in Mozambique.

Notes

1. The MRLS was the first ever large-scale survey of the rural labour market in Mozambique. The methodology was innovative, developed to overcome some of the many limitations of household budget surveys in rural Africa. One element of the survey conducted in 2002–2003 was a detailed questionnaire completed for 2626 people working for wages in the rural areas and small district towns of three provinces in Mozambique. The MRLS was designed and implemented by the author, together with Carlos Oya and Christopher Cramer. Further methodological details are available in the three papers by these authors listed in the select bibliography below.
2. The life histories of Mozambican women are discussed in Sender et al. (2006), while the article by Oya and Sender (2009) provides more information on divorced, separated and widowed women.

Select bibliography

Cramer, Christopher, Carlos Oya and John Sender (2008) 'Lifting the blinkers: a new view of power and poverty in Mozambican labour markets', *Journal of Modern African Studies*, **46** (3), 361–92.

Kabeer, Naila (2003) 'Gender inequality in educational outcomes: a household perspective', in *Education for All (EFA) Global Monitoring Report 2003/4, The Leap to Equality*, Paris: UNESCO.

Oya, Carlos and John Sender (2009) 'Divorced, separated and widowed female workers in rural Mozambique', *Feminist Economics*, **15** (2), 1–31.

Sender, John (2003) 'Rural poverty and gender: analytical frameworks and policy proposals', in Ha-Joon Chang (ed.), *Rethinking Development Economics*, London: Anthem Press, pp. 401–20.

Sender, John, Carlos Oya and Christopher Cramer (2006) 'Women working for wages: putting flesh on the bones of a rural labour market survey in Mozambique', *Journal of Southern African Studies*, **32** (2), 313–34.

Thomas, Duncan (1994) 'Like father, like son; like mother, like daughter', *Journal of Human Resources*, **29** (4), 950–88.

World Bank (2007) *World Development Report 2008: Agriculture for Development*, Washington, DC: World Bank.

26 Understanding the gender dynamics of Russia's economic transformation: women's and men's experiences of employment, domestic labour and poverty
Sarah Ashwin

When Russia launched its programme of economic 'shock therapy' in 1991, commentators were quick to predict that women would be the primary victims of economic reform. It was anticipated that unemployment would have a 'female face', that the wage gap would grow and that female labour participation would fall, trends that were likely to lead to a 'feminisation of poverty'. But despite a deep depression lasting most of the 1990s and a devastating decline in living standards, these predictions proved inaccurate. Indeed, the continuity in gender trends in employment has been notable. Although men have retained their economic advantage, women have maintained their presence in the labour force. Moreover, official figures reveal no significant gender difference in the proportion of men and women living below the 'subsistence minimum' (Russia's poverty line). There is evidence that the task of managing the adjustment of households to new economic conditions has fallen disproportionately on women, but otherwise women's position relative to men has been stable. The paradox is that while men have higher incomes than women, as well as a lighter burden in terms of domestic responsibilities, they have proved less able to 'survive' Russia's transformation in the literal sense of the term. Economic reform has had a dramatic impact on male mortality rates, leading to a gender gap in life expectancy of over 13 years between 1994 and 2006. In light of this, it is difficult to portray women as the 'losers' in Russia's transformation. Rather, the extremity of Russia's economic crisis has revealed the way in which gender inequality harms both men and women.

Did Russia's reform programme increase women's disadvantage?
In contrast to some developing countries where neoliberal reform has pushed women into the labour market as a survival strategy, in Russia high levels of female labour participation were a legacy of the Soviet era. On the eve of reform, these were close to the biological maximum. Predictions that once the obligation to work was lifted women would return to the home were not realised. Both male and female labour participation dropped significantly between 1989 and 1998, but the gender difference in these falls was marginal (Ashwin, 2006: 2). In 2007 women still comprised over 49 per cent of the economically active population. Meanwhile, the expectation that women would make up the majority of the unemployed also failed to transpire. When the Labour Force Survey, using the internationally comparable definition of unemployment, was introduced in Russia in 1992, the male unemployment rate was found marginally to exceed that of females. Since then, the unemployment rates of men and women have been roughly

equal, with the male rate once again marginally exceeding that of women in 2007, at 6 per cent compared with 5.3 per cent.[1]

Although women have managed to maintain their attachment to the labour market, men continue, as in the Soviet era, to enjoy a more favourable position at work. Studies of the wage gap during the transition era suggest that it has remained more or less constant. Given the nature of Soviet official statistics, it was difficult to calculate the level of the wage gap precisely, but in the late Soviet era women were estimated to earn between 60 and 70 per cent of men's wages. This figure still stands at around 66 per cent, with apparent fluctuations resulting from late payment of wages which renders income data unreliable. Whether those affected are kept in the sample or excluded, distortions are unavoidable (Kazakova, 2007). While the wage gap does not seem to have widened significantly, the gender restructuring of employment appears to favour men, with men increasing their presence in the now lucrative, but once female-dominated, spheres of banking and commerce. Meanwhile, women continue to make up the overwhelming majority of employees in the poorly paid 'budget sector' areas of healthcare and education. In Russia there is a widespread assumption that men are superior employees, and this gives them an important advantage at a time when the gender profile of many professions is in flux, as new areas of the economy are opened up and old areas shaken up by economic transformation (for more details see discussion by Kozina and Zhidkova in Ashwin, 2006).

Despite their lower personal incomes, women are not significantly more likely to live in poverty, since the majority of them live in households containing a male earner. The Russian state statistical service (Rosstat) calculates the numbers living below the poverty line on the basis of a household budget survey and in doing so assumes equal sharing within households. These official figures suggest only marginal gender differences in the proportions of men and women living below the poverty line: in 2007 13.8 per cent of women versus 12.8 per cent of men in the 16–30 age group; 14.9 per cent in the 31–54 age group for women compared to 12.6 per cent in the 31–59 cohort for men, and 9.2 per cent for both sexes in the post-retirement cohort (women retire at 55, men at 60).[2] While the official figures are open to criticism on various counts, a World Bank study using different calculations came to similar conclusions (World Bank, 2005). It may be that the assumption of income sharing leads to an underestimation of female poverty, because men may withhold earnings from the household budget. But reliable data suggest that most male and female household members put the vast majority of their income into the household budget (Clarke, 2002: 265). In this sense, it is difficult to make a strong case that there has been a 'feminisation of poverty' in Russia, either in the first meaning associated with the term, that women predominate among the poor, or the second, that poverty increasingly affects women. Indeed, women benefited from the growth Russia experienced since the 1998 crash, as incomes for those in the lowest quartile increased more than for those with higher incomes (Kazakova, 2007: 366). Meanwhile, increases in pension levels improved the position of single retired women who had been at significant risk of poverty in the late Soviet era and the 1990s. Currently, the main risk groups of poverty in Russia are children, those living in rural areas or small towns, the unemployed and those with only primary education (World Bank, 2005: 18–25).

The third tenet associated with the 'feminisation of poverty' thesis is that women's rising share of poverty is linked with the 'feminisation' of household headship (see

Chant, Chapter 15, this volume; Medeiros and Costa, Chapter 12, this volume). But in the Russian case it is misleading to make an automatic link between female-headed households and poverty. This can be illustrated by reference to a careful study of an important subset of women-headed households – those headed by lone mothers (Kanji, 2004). As would be expected, poverty levels for children in these households are higher than for two-parent households. Using data from the Russian Longitudinal Monitoring Survey (RLMS), Kanji (2004: 210) calculates a difference of over 11 percentage points (23.8 versus 35.2) in the child poverty rate, but she also shows a good deal of diversity beneath this figure based on the route into lone motherhood, which shapes access to different resources (such as alimony and widow's pensions). Even within the subgroups of lone mothers there is diversity. The heterogeneity of lone-mother households is illustrated by the fact that 7.5 per cent of children living in them are in the top decile of the whole population welfare distribution, while 16 per cent are in the bottom (ibid.: 219). As Kanji shows, the crude conflation of lone-mother households (and by implication women-headed households in general) does little to further our understanding of poverty.

The broader definition of the feminisation of poverty suggested by Sylvia Chant in Chapter 15 in this volume includes inputs, thus taking account of women's increased responsibility and obligations in ensuring survival. There has been significant research in this area in Russia. It is widely asserted that Russian women have taken primary responsibility for coping with the privations of the reform era. Using the best available survey data (RLMS and the 1998 Institute for Comparative Labour Relations Research [ISITO] Household Survey), Simon Clarke (2002) investigated this proposition. While acknowledging the qualitative evidence suggesting that women were compensating for the failings of men, his analysis found 'no evidence that women have taken over responsibility for bringing in an income from men' (ibid.: 257). It should be stressed that Soviet wage scales were premised on the idea of the dual-income couple, so women's contribution to the household budget has always been important and has become even more so in the reform era. But Clarke's analysis shows that even in households where men were failing to provide, women's employment decisions did not appear to respond to this. In general, in couple-headed households there was very little relationship between income-earning decisions of one partner and the circumstances of the other. In terms of adjustment to new conditions, men were significantly more likely to have sought additional income-earning opportunities, while women were more likely to have reduced spending or asked others for help (ibid.: 258). This is in line with a gender division of labour in which men are seen as primary breadwinners, and women are expected to manage household resources on top of working.

The last points highlight an area in which women have played a leading role, namely, budgeting. Clarke's research shows that the main burden of adjustment to deteriorating economic conditions fell on the expenditure rather than the income side of the household budget. In the majority of couple-headed households, it is women who control the budget, and thus 'we can safely presume that the burden of making ends meet falls predominately on women' (Clarke, 2002: 265). Being responsible for the budget in an era of shrunken household incomes is a worrisome position of responsibility, and qualitative evidence suggests that women often restrict their own consumption to provide for other household members. But although women's roles in household management became more onerous in the economic crisis, the domestic division of labour had been notably unbalanced during the Soviet era. Early Bolshevik plans for a transfer of domestic labour to the public sphere were only realised to a limited degree in the area of childcare, and women's mass entry into paid work was not accompanied by a reallocation of domestic responsibilities. Time budget surveys consistently revealed that women performed the vast majority of domestic labour in the Soviet era, and this has not changed, even in couples where the woman is working and the man is not (Ashwin, 2006: 46). Thus, gender inequality with regard to inputs may have intensified in some cases, but it was largely a Soviet inheritance rather than an outcome of economic crisis.

Russian men in crisis
Women have undoubtedly faced enormous challenges during Russia's transformation. But paradoxically they have proved more resilient than men in the face of economic privation. The changes of the 1990s have had devastating consequences for men. Male life expectancy plummeted, declining from 64.2 in 1989, to a low of 57.4 in 1994. It then recovered to 61.2 in 1998, only to fall back to 58.6 in 2002. In 2005 it was still below 59, approximately 16 years below the European Union (EU) average (Rosstat, 2007: 95). It climbed to 61.4 in 2007, but a 13-year gender gap in life expectancy is projected to persist until at least 2025 (ibid.: 535). Meanwhile, female life expectancy remained more constant, declining from 74.4 in 1989 to a nadir of 71.08 in 1994, followed by a stabilisation at approximately 72 between 1996 and 2005 (ibid.: 95). In 2007 it was 73.9. These trends have important implications for understanding the gender dynamics of poverty, particularly when viewed from the 'capabilities' perspective associated with Amartya Sen and Martha Nussbaum. The first item on Nussbaum's list of ten central capabilities is that of being able to live a life of normal length. There is no doubt that Russian men are currently deprived of this capability.

The gendered nature of deprivation cannot be appreciated without an understanding of why reform has had such a dramatic impact on men. The following section outlines an explanation for this based on the results of a longitudinal qualitative research project which followed 120 men and 120 women between 1998 and 2001 (for more details see Ashwin, 2006). Although it is men who appear to benefit from Russia's unequal gender division of labour, this study found that the reality was more complex. In Russia men's identity is closely connected with work, with their contribution to and status within the household defined by their role as primary breadwinners. This has two key effects. First, given the marginal role that men play in the everyday running of the household, and the underdevelopment of the civic sphere and leisure infrastructure in Russia, it is difficult for them to find meaning and validation outside paid work. This renders them vulnerable to demoralisation when they experience labour market problems. While unemployed or low-earning women also experience psychological discomfort in the face of such difficulties, their pivotal role in the household gives them a strong motivation not to succumb to despair, while also providing a source of meaning and status not dependent on remunerated work.

Second, the fact that men's main role in the household is as breadwinners renders them vulnerable when they lose their position as main earner. Thus, falling wages or unemployment can threaten married men with domestic 'redundancy', and increases their chances of being left by their wives. This is a particular threat when their response to their labour market problems is seen to exacerbate the difficulties of the household – as is the case when men turn to alcohol for solace (of which more below). Meanwhile, when men are excluded from the household it generally accelerates their decline, as both the social support provided by the family and female control in relation to drinking and other risky behaviours are lost.

Men's concentration on employment also shapes the character of their social networks, which tend to be more narrowly focused on work than those of women. While this undoubtedly has positive effects in terms of job search and promotion prospects, it means that men's networks can be rendered vulnerable in the face of changes in employment status. Men who become unemployed or marginalised at work can find themselves cut off from the contacts capable of helping them. This danger is intensified by the fact that perceived equality of status is a more important consideration in mediating relations between men than between women. While women also form important relations at work, alongside this their role as household managers binds them to a web of ongoing exchange relations with family members and female acquaintances. Such relations are unlikely to be disrupted by changes in their labour market status. Conversely, the fragility of men's work-centred networks tends to be revealed precisely in moments of adversity when they are most needed.

Russia's drinking culture adds a lethal element to the cocktail of risks which attend men's marginality in the household. There is little doubt that excessive drinking is predominately a male problem in Russia. Although women's use of alcohol appears to have increased somewhat recently, heavy drinking among women is still culturally proscribed, while it is considered normal among men. In the absence of other means of compensating for or dealing with their labour market problems, men are liable to turn to the treacherous 'medicine' of alcohol. Studies are now beginning to reveal the link between hazardous drinking and economic strain. For example, a recent study by Jukkala et al. (2008) of binge drinking in Moscow found that the odds ratios for binge drinking of men experiencing manifold economic problems were almost twice as high as those for men with few economic difficulties. Significantly, the opposite seemed to be true for women, who were less likely to binge drink when experiencing economic problems. As the authors acknowledge, there is a possibility of reverse causality (alcoholism causing economic difficulties), but the gender difference makes this explanation less likely since it should apply to both sexes. Rather, it seems the social explanation laid out above is more plausible. The consequences for the longevity of men are clear: there is a widespread consensus that alcohol abuse is a major proximate cause of Russia's crisis in premature male mortality.

Conclusion

The continuity in gender relations in Russia in the face of a bruising and radical economic reform programme is striking. The relative economic position of men and women has changed little; if anything, economic crisis served to intensify Soviet trends. The pressure on men to perform as primary breadwinners increased, women's attachment to the labour market was cemented by acute financial need, and women's role as household managers attained extra gravity in an era of shrinking household budgets. An already unbalanced gender division of labour was thus rendered even more so by the privations of reform. Since it is an extreme scenario, the Russian case exposes the implications of unequal inputs on the part of men and women. The most notable lesson is that not only is this pattern of relations bad for women, it is also deeply damaging to men. In a situation in which men and women share the task of breadwinning, and yet women take full responsibility for domestic management, men risk becoming peripheral to the household. A narrow focus on work leaves men exposed at a time of economic decline, and makes adjustment to events such as unemployment or downward mobility very difficult. Russia's drinking culture sharply increases the risks for men in this situation, but though Russia has particular problems with alcohol abuse, masculine cultures endorsing heavy drinking are widespread. Thus, it is likely that it is not only in Russia that male marginality in the household entails serious dangers. The other implication of this is that household management, though often onerous, has hidden benefits, potentially providing a sustaining sense of efficacy, competence and meaning.

Notes

1. Data from the Rosstat website: http://www.gks.ru/bgd/regl/b08_11/IssWWW.exe/Stg/d01/06-01.htm (accessed 10 March 2009).
2. Data from Rosstat website: http://www.gks.ru/bgd/regl/B08_50/IssWWW.exe/Stg/05-02.htm (accessed 10 March 2009).

Select bibliography

Ashwin, Sarah (ed.) (2006) *Adapting to Russia's New Labour Market: Gender and Employment Behaviour*, Abingdon and New York: Routledge.

Clarke, Simon (2002) *Making Ends Meet in Contemporary Russia: Secondary Employment, Subsidiary Agriculture and Social Networks*, Cheltenham, UK and Northampton, MA, USA: Edward Elgar.

Jukkala, Tanya, Ilkka H. Mäkinen, Olga Kislitsyna, Sara Ferlander and Denny Vågero (2008) 'Economic strain, social relations, gender and binge drinking in Moscow', *Social Science and Medicine*, **66**, 663–74.

Kanji, Shireen (2004) 'The route matters: poverty and inequality among lone mother households in Russia', *Feminist Economics*, **10** (2), 207–55.

Kazakova, Elena (2007) 'Wages in a growing Russia: when is a 10 per cent rise in the gender wage gap good news?', *Economics of Transition*, **15** (2), 365–92.

Rosstat (2007) *Demograficheskii Ezhegodnik Rossii*, Moscow: Rosstat.

World Bank (2005) *Russian Federation: Reducing Poverty Through Growth and Social Policy Reform*, Washington, DC: World Bank.

27 Gender, poverty and transition in Central Asia
Jane Falkingham and Angela Baschieri

Introduction

The break-up of the Soviet Union and the subsequent transition to market-led economies were accompanied by a decade of economic and social upheaval on an unprecedented scale. The Central Asian countries of Kyrgyzstan and Tajikistan were already among the poorest of the Soviet Republics and following independence in 1991, Gross Domestic Product (GDP) per capita more than halved, while spending on social services such as health, education and social protection declined even further. During the early 1990s, the proportion of the population in the region living in poverty rose dramatically as inequality widened, real wages fell and unemployment increased. At the end of a decade of transition, an estimated 39 million people living in Central Asia and the Caucasus were living in poverty, of which over 14 million were living in extreme poverty (Falkingham, 2005). In 2003, nearly three-quarters of the populations of Tajikistan (74 per cent) and Kyrgyzstan (70 per cent) were surviving on less than $2.15 PPP (Purchasing Power Parity) a day, along with just under half the population of Uzbekistan (47 per cent) (Alam et al., 2005: table 2, 238–41).

The economic and social transformation of the region has affected women and men in different ways, creating both new opportunities and challenges. For many women in Central Asia, there has been a reversal of the gains in political representation and leadership positions achieved during the Soviet Union with the re-emergence of traditional gender roles (Harris, 2004). Women as primary care providers have also been harder hit by the withdrawal of state support for childcare and parental leave. However, there remains some debate as to whether gender inequality has increased during the post-communist transition in the region.

According to a database published by the United Nations Economic Commission for Europe (UNECE), there has been very little change on many measures. Moreover, recent World Bank poverty assessments in the region have found either negligible gender differentials in poverty or even that female-headed households fare better than those headed by males. For example, in 2003 in Kyrgyzstan 67 per cent of male-headed households were poor as defined by living below $2.15 PPP a day compared with just 36 per cent of female-headed households (Alam et al., 2005: table 2, 238–41). Evidence from Russia suggests that men have experienced greater problems in adapting to the economic and social changes, with male life expectancy falling from 64.2 years in 1989 to a low of 57.5 in 1994. Much of this decline has been attributed to an increase in alcohol consumption, with Russian men consuming up to ten times more alcohol than women (Bobak et al., 1999; see also Ashwin, Chapter 26, this volume). This chapter assesses the impact of transition on women's well-being. Whether it has been beneficial or disadvantageous for women depends in part on the measures used and the methodology applied in constructing those measures.

Women and the labour market

The evidence on whether the economic transition has harmed the position of women in the labour market is mixed. During the Soviet period there was a network of kindergartens for pre-school age children, although the network was not as extensive in Central Asia as elsewhere in the Soviet Union; even in 1989 it is estimated that only 17 per cent of 3–6-year-olds in Tajikistan were enrolled in kindergarten, compared with 31 per cent in the Kyrgyz Republic, 39 per cent in Uzbekistan and 52 per cent in Kazakhstan (Falkingham, 2005). Following independence, enrolment rates among pre-school children collapsed, largely as a result of the closure of enterprise-based (employer-provided) kindergartens. This in turn may be thought to have had a knock-on effect on women's ability to (re-)enter the labour market after having children. However, data from UNECE for Kyrgyzstan suggests that while male economic activity rates fell from 74.5 per cent in 1990 to 68.6 per cent in 2000, those for women remained largely constant, falling just 1.8 percentage points from 58.6 per cent to 56.8 per cent over the same time period. The 2002 World Bank report on 'Gender in Transition' concluded that 'there is no empirical evidence that the treatment of women in the formal labour market has deteriorated' (Paci, 2002: 28), although the report did highlight the need for further research on differentials in wages and the role of the informal sector before reaching any firm conclusion on ruling out the hypothesis of increasing gender inequality.

Worryingly, although overall participation rates appear not to have changed considerably, there are marked variations by age. Looking at economic activity rates amongst young women, there are clear gender downward trends over time. For example, in Kazakhstan in 1990 25.5 per cent of 15–19-year-olds, and 75 per cent of 20–24-years-olds were economically active; by 2007 these rates had fallen to 20.8 per cent and 68.8 per cent respectively. In Tajikistan, only two-fifths of women aged 20–24 were economically active. It is these younger age groups that are hardest hit by the double burden of lack of childcare on the one hand and lack of job opportunities on the other.

Data on the gender pay gap from UNECE suggests that most women still work in lower-paid jobs than men, and that things may be getting worse. In 2000 the difference between average monthly earnings of male employees and female employees as a percentage of the average monthly earnings of men was 38.5 in Kazakhstan, 32.4 in Kyrgyzstan and 56.8 in Tajikistan. This compares with 26.9 in the United Kingdom (UK) and 26.4 in the United States of America (USA). Women tend to work in the public sector and indeed comprise the majority of teachers and doctors in some countries. However these public sector jobs are poorly paid and wages are often in arrears. In contrast, men make up the majority of employees in the new private sector and appear to have been better placed to take advantage of the new opportunities created by the opening up of markets.

Women and poverty

Given the gender differences in pay one might expect to see these reflected in differentials in poverty rates. However as mentioned above, recent studies conducted by the World Bank in the region have found no such differentials. For example the 2004 Tajikistan Poverty Assessment Update found no gender differentials in poverty, despite the fact that the risk of poverty was found to vary by age, region and household size. This was the case regardless of the type of material poverty examined: 24 per cent of women and

23 per cent of men were living in households ranked in the bottom quintile of the distribution of per capita household expenditure (in other words, they were living in relative poverty), and 64 per cent of women and 63 per cent of men lived in a household with a per capita expenditure less than $2.15 PPP a day (that is, they were absolutely poor). However it is important to bear in mind that the standard economic analyses presented in the World Bank Poverty Assessments typically adopt a unitary model of the household, which assumes that all the resources in the household are pooled and that all members share in these pooled resources in equal measure (see Quisumbing, Chapter 23, this volume).

Recent work has questioned how appropriate such a model is within the central Asian context (see Baschieri and Falkingham, 2009). Gender relations in Tajikistan reflect both the country's Soviet legacy, with its strong emphasis on gender equality in the public sphere, and traditional Tajik values where women play a central role in the private sphere of the family. Since independence, traditional cultural and social values have enjoyed a renaissance. Harris (2004) found a strong hierarchy of power relationship across the different actors in Tajik society, with women at the bottom of the power ladder. Men continue to expect to be regarded as the dominant figure and women are often forced by husband, family and community to conform to a specific submissive role (ibid.). This view is supported by data on domestic violence. A study conducted by the Association of Women Scientists of Tajikistan in 1999 interviewed some 1600 women in the capital city of Dushanbe, and across the Republic in Kurgan-Tube, Kulyab, Kofarnihon and Tusunzade, on their understanding and experience of violence. A broad definition of violence was adopted, including physical, psychological and economic violence. Overall the study found that two-thirds (67 per cent) of Tajik women were regularly exposed to some form of violence within the home.

The results of the Tajikistan Multiple Indicator Cluster Survey (MICS) conducted by the United Nations Children's Fund (UNICEF) in 2005 provides further evidence of the submissive role of Tajik women within the family. More than 62 per cent of women reported that a husband is justified in hitting or beating his wife if she fails to tell him when she goes out, if she neglects children or if she argues with him, and more than 50 per cent believe that husband is justified in beating his wife if she refuses sex (see also K. Brickell, Chapter 70, this volume).

In the mid-1980s, Amartya Sen had suggested that the relative bargaining position amongst household members will depend on their perceived contribution to the household. In Tajikistan, just 45 per cent of women aged 16 and over reported themselves as being economically active compared with almost 70 per cent of men, with one-third of all women (32.9 per cent) reporting that they are not in the labour force as they are 'taking care of the home', compared with 6 per cent of men. Of those women who are economically active, nearly three-quarters are employed in agriculture where wages are low and payments in kind frequent, and where often the goods that are produced are consumed within the household. Data on women's use of time also reflects a strongly gendered division of labour within the household, with Tajik women spending significant amounts of time on household tasks on a daily basis. If time contributions to the household are viewed as less valuable than pecuniary contributions, Tajik women may be more likely to be placed in a disadvantaged bargaining position relative to men. Given this context it appears unlikely that the unitary model of the household will reflect the dominant

Table 27.1 Absolute poverty by gender according to the unitary and different assumptions of collective household model using income and $1.08 PPP a day poverty line

	Poverty rate amongst women		Poverty rate amongst men		Poverty rate amongst children	
		95% CI[1]		95% CI		95% CI
1. Unitary household	63.9	61.2–66.6	63.5	60.8–66.3	68.9	66.2–71.6
2. Collective household (men and women pool 50% wage income)[2]	66.1	63.5–68.7	52.7	49.7–55.7	77.6	75.7–80.0
3. Collective household (men and women pool 80% wage income)	64.6	61.9–67.2	58.1	55.3–60.9	72.1	69.4–74.7
4. Collective household (men pool 80% wage income, women pool 80% and share 100% with children)	66.3	63.6–68.9	58.1	55.3–60.9	68.7	66.0–71.4
5. Collective household (men pool 80%, women pool 100% and share with children)	66.7	64.1–69.3	57.4	54.6–60.2	71.5	68.8–74.2

Notes:
1. CI is 95 per cent confidence interval.
2. 45 per cent of total income comes from wage income. The female share in total wage income is 28 per cent.

Source: Authors' own analysis from 2003 data from the Tajikistan Living Standards Survey (TLSS).

form of household behaviour within Tajikistan and thus poverty analysis using such an assumption may be misleading.

Baschieri and Falkingham (2009), using data from the 2003 Tajikistan Living Standards Survey, explore the impact on poverty rates for women and men of moving away from the assumption of equal pooling and sharing of resources. Their main results are shown in Table 27.1. The first line of the table shows levels of absolute poverty among men, women and children using per capita household income as the welfare indicator and an absolute poverty line of $1.08 PPP a day (23.62 Somoni). As noted previously, there appear to be no significant differences between men and women in the likelihood of being poor, although children face a higher risk of poverty than adults.

Under a range of collective models of the household (lines 2–5 in Table 27.1), income is no longer assumed to be equally pooled and shared amongst all members of the household. The critical assumptions in determining the welfare of different members of the household are now the proportion of income pooled by men and women. As a first step we assume that both men and women decide to retain 50 per cent of their wage income and pool 50 per cent (line 2). As wages are considerably higher for men than women, with average (mean) primary wages for men being double those for women ($2.47/54 Somoni versus $1.2/26 Somoni), it is not surprising that moving from the unitary household to

188 *The international handbook of gender and poverty*

a collective household model results in an increase in absolute poverty rates amongst women and children, and a fall amongst men. The changes in the welfare position of men and women are sufficiently large to result in a statistically significant gender gap. Under the unitary model, and using per capita household income as the welfare measure, around 64 per cent of both men and women are absolutely poor; under the collective model, 66 per cent of women are defined as poor compared with 53 per cent of men. These gender differentials directly reflect the differentials in wage income between men and women in the household, which in turn reflect the gendered division of labour within the household, with women being more likely to engage in unpaid family work.

The assumption of individuals only pooling half their wage income is a strong one. In reality in an agricultural society like Tajikistan, where extended families with large numbers of children are the norm, it is unlikely that men or women would want, or be able, to retain as much as half their wage income for their own purposes. A more realistic scenario is to assume women and men retain one-fifth their wage income and pool four-fifths. Under this stronger pooling scenario the gender poverty gap is reduced from 13 percentage points to 7 percentage points. By pooling a greater share of their income, men experience a heightened risk of poverty, while women experience a slight fall. The greatest gainers, however, are children, with poverty rates falling from 78 per cent, under the moderate pooling assumption, to 72 per cent, under the stronger pooling assumption.

So far it is assumed that women do not share their personal 'retained' resources with their children. Thus, children with 'access' only to communal household resources experience much higher rates of poverty than their mothers or fathers. However, this is unlikely to be the case. Assuming that women pool all their income with children in the household (line 4 in Table 27.1) results in the gender and poverty gap between men and women widening, with 66 per cent of women and 69 per cent of children having a per capita income below the poverty line compared to 58 per cent of men.

A final scenario is presented in the last row of Table 27.1, which assumes that women put all their income into the shared household pot and men retain one-fifth of their wage income and pool four-fifths. By women pooling all their income, the poverty rate among women and children increases slightly as all women's resources are now shared with both their children and their menfolk. Moreover poverty among males is reduced yet further as they benefit from the sharing of women's income, with the result that the gender poverty gap is just under ten percentage points. It is worth reiterating that it is assumed that all the other household income except wage income is equally shared by the household members. This is a strong assumption as in reality men rather than women may be managing these resources. Thus the results presented in the last row of Table 27.1 represent only a relatively small step away from the unitary household assumption and probably represent an underestimate of actual gender differentials in welfare in Tajikistan.

Conclusion
Making definitive conclusions on how gender differentials in welfare have changed during transition remains difficult. It is clear that the labour market position and living standards of both women and men have deteriorated. However the answer to who has fared less badly depends on the measures employed and the methodology used. Moving away from the unitary model of the household, where resources are assumed to be shared equally amongst household members and each member of the household is assumed to

enjoy the same level of welfare, has profound implications for any analysis of poverty by gender. Significant gender differentials result even from relatively moderate assumptions concerning male control over resources. If men are assumed to retain just 20 per cent of their wage income for their own use and all other sources of income, including social assistance benefits, remittances and the imputed value of consumption of home production, are equally shared, on average women experience a headcount income poverty rate of ten percentage points higher than men. Children are the most disadvantaged, with poverty rates 14 percentage points higher than adult males. Although the true extent of gender differentials within Central Asia remains uncertain, the message is clear: by utilising the unitary model of household allocation we are in danger of underestimating significant differences in the welfare of men and women. Understanding how resources are allocated within households can profoundly affect policies associated with the design and implementation of development projects. The above analysis highlights the importance of paying greater attention to intrahousehold resource allocation patterns, however difficult that may be. Only then will we begin to get a meaningful picture of how transition has affected the reality of women's lives.

Select bibliography

Alam, Asad, Mamta Murthi, Ruslan Yemtsov, Edmundo Murrugarra, Nora Dudwick, Ellen Hamilton and Erwin Tiongson (2005) *Growth, Poverty and Inequality: Eastern Europe and the Former Soviet Union*, Washington, DC: World Bank.

Baschieri, Angela and Jane Falkingham (2009) 'Gender and poverty: how misleading is the unitary model of household resources? An illustration from Tajikistan', *Global Social Policy*, **9** (1), 43–62.

Bobak, Martin, Martin McKee, Richard Rose and Michael Marmot (1999) 'Alcohol consumption in a national sample of the Russian population', *Addiction*, **94** (4), 857–66.

Falkingham, Jane (2005) 'The end of the rollercoaster? Growth, inequality and poverty in Central Asia and the Caucasus', *Social Policy and Administration*, **39** (4), 340–60.

Harris, Colette (2004) *Control and Subversion: Gender Relationships in Tajikistan*, London and Sterling, VA: Pluto Press.

Paci, Pierella (2002) *Gender in Transition*, Washington, DC: World Bank.

United Nations Economic Commission for Europe (UNECE) Gender Statistics Database, Geneva, available at: http://www.unece.org/stats/gender/database.htm (accessed 30 June 2009).

28 Urban poverty, heteronormativity and women's agency in Lima, Peru: family life on the margins
Carolyn H. Williams

International development, feminist and lesbian, gay, bisexual and transgender (LBGT) action and research have seldom explored expressions and experiences of same-sex sexuality among low-income women in continents such as Africa, Asia, Latin America and the Caribbean (for notable exceptions, see Swarr and Nagar, 2004; Wekker, 2006; Williams, 2009). The masculinities and non-normative sexualities and gender identities of men and male to female transgender in these contexts have, by contrast, been the subject of increasing levels of academic and policy-oriented research (see Aggleton et al., 2005; Gutmann, 2003; Kulick, 1998). Meanwhile the voices of women living in poverty have rarely been heard or documented in terms of their knowledge and experiences of heteronormative inequality and discrimination.

In order to address this lacuna my research has examined the lives of women from different low-income settlements in Lima, Peru. Three of the women I interviewed, Julia and Maria (who had lived together as a couple for 19 years) and Carmen, were aged between 45 and 50. Carmen was a community leader, single and living with her 7-year-old son when we met in 2006. The youngest, Charo, was 18 years old. Charo's partner, Ceci, was 28 years old and was living in a working-class district of central Lima. In this chapter I focus on the women's histories with their families, an aspect of their lives they highlighted as central to their experiences of the pressures and negative effects of heterosexual norms, as well as their efforts to overcome them and create alternative opportunities for their sexual freedom and well-being.

Two decades of partnership against all the odds
As Julia, Maria, Carmen, Charo and Ceci talked about their life histories they provided me with a picture of how they had coped with problems of discrimination and violence due to their sexuality and relationships with women. Their experiences with family members were marked by a complex combination of love, acceptance and support from some, rejection and violence from others, and changing attitudes over time among some who were initially resistant. Julia recalled that when she informed her family that she was only interested in girls, as a teenager in the 1970s, her mother supported her and protected her from the negative response of her siblings. Julia noted that she had always felt '*como un hombrecito*' (like a boy) when she was a child, to such an extent that she felt obliged to leave school when she was 14 because she could no longer bear the 'shame' of wearing a skirt. She found work as a seamstress and spent her spare time playing football with other girls and women, some of whom identified as *lesbiana*, adopting the Spanish version of 'lesbian'. Others identified as *chito*, a term known and used only in the settlements, adopted by women who dress in men's clothes and who express greater masculinity than their *lesbiana* counterparts. When Julia was young and spent her spare time with

her *chito* and *lesbiana* friends away from her family, her siblings' negativity towards her sexuality was limited. However, when she and Maria decided to live together, when they were both in their late twenties, she was forced to deal with serious sibling aggression:

> My brother threatened to report me to the police, until one day I said: 'I'm sick of you, do you want to fight with me? Do it once and for all, but I'm not going to let you hit me'. When I challenged him to a fight, he stopped his threats. But I said to Maria that we should leave my family home. I loved her very much and couldn't let my brother humiliate her. (Julia, 50)

Despite the support of her parents and Julia's courage in facing up to her brother, she and Maria felt they could not stay in Julia's family home, even though Maria had no home to offer as an alternative. Having been abused and rejected as a child by her father and step-mother after her mother died, and without any support from her siblings, Maria had left home as a teenager to marry a man who continued the pattern of violence:

> He used to hit me, he was like a beast, then he raped me, and I got pregnant. I used to say, 'I don't want any more children'. It was one pregnancy after another. Having children and still working was hard. I said to myself, how can I separate? I was afraid, because he always said to me: 'If you leave me, or if I see you with anyone else, I'll kill you.' (Maria, 48)

After having her fifth child Maria met Julia. Maria recounted how she had felt attracted to a woman for the first time in her life, and that she fell in love even though she had never previously considered or desired a relationship with a woman. Unable to cope any longer with the cycle of marital violence, rape and unwanted pregnancies, with Julia and the support of members of a feminist non-governmental organisation (NGO) she decided to leave her husband:

> I told him: 'You know what? I'm with a woman', and he was furious, he hit me, he shouted: 'How is it possible you're with a woman?' So I took the children and went to live with my brother and my sister-in-law, but he came after me and said: 'Your children or your life', so I had to give him the children. I cried, I suffered, it was a terrible blow. Then my brother said that if the children were with their father, his wife didn't want me in the house any more. (Maria, 48)

The aggression from both brothers and Maria's husband, combined with Maria's loss of access to her children, forced Julia and Maria to move away to a new settlement. By then Julia was a skilled seamstress and Maria was working as a cook and cleaner with the feminist NGO where the two had first met. They rented a room and a year later participated in a land invasion nearby in order to take over a small plot of desert land. Over a period of 20 years they built their two-storey house, which was still unfinished when I visited them in 2006. For many years Maria's husband refused her access to their children until the eldest reached 18 and was legally allowed to choose to see her. Gradually Maria regained her relationship with each of her children, who as adults defied their father and severely criticised his cruelty in keeping them apart for so many years. By the time I met the couple all Maria's five children had migrated to northern Spain to seek work. They had slowly come to accept Julia as their mother's partner to such an extent that one of Maria's daughters left her 1-year-old daughter Milagros with both of them when she left for Spain. Maria's children all sent monthly remittances back to Lima so that Julia and Maria could afford to slowly improve their house and bring up Milagros.

When I asked Julia and Maria how they had managed to stay together for 20 years, despite all the problems they had encountered, they both agreed that of central importance for them was the love and support of Julia's mother, and eventually of Maria's children, who, at the time of my fieldwork, were attempting to convince Julia, Maria and Milagros to go and live with them in Spain after so many years of separation.

The life and times of a community leader
Of a similar age to Julia and Maria, Carmen spent her childhood living with her parents and younger brother in a working-class area of central Lima. Carmen recalled how her mother, a teacher, worked hard and endured constant aggression from Carmen's father, until after nine years of marriage her mother demanded a divorce and her father left their home. Before she was a teenager, Carmen's preference for boys' activities had already created difficulties with her father:

> I never played with dolls. I liked books and drawing, football and cycling. I always played with my brother and we used to fight and hit each other as if we were both boys. I remember once my father wanted to take me to see a doctor, he thought it was atrocious what I was like at home. He said: 'I don't know what I'm going to do with this girl, it's like two boys, fighting and playing football.' (Carmen, 48)

Carmen talked of how she resisted the pressure she felt with her family to change these expressions of masculinity, find a boyfriend and get married. Carmen recounted how she fell in love for the first time at 17 with Teresa, a girl from her local Catholic Church group. Their relationship did not last long, however, as members of the group began to suspect them and reported them to the priest who was coordinating the group. The priest challenged them both and threatened to publicly denounce their relationship and cancel their application to go together to the Amazon region to work as missionaries. Teresa capitulated and agreed to go to the Amazon alone, while Carmen's ensuing depression led her father to visit her, and, uncharacteristically, offer her his support:

> When I had that crisis I ended up in the emergency room. My father came to see me. I think he realised what was happening with me. He said: 'your mother is very rigid, but you have to choose to live the life that you want. Sometimes she's not right, nor am I, so you have to be free. Whatever you decide, I will support you.' He didn't say I was lesbian or homosexual, that I liked women, he just said that. (Carmen, 48)

Carmen believed that her father's words of support and acceptance gave her greater confidence to face her anxieties concerning how to live outside the heterosexual norms of her family and community, but her troubles were far from over:

> My mother found out about Teresa and reacted very badly. She threw me out of the house, shouting: 'I can't believe I have a child like that, who is lost like that!', but I wasn't lost, I was quiet and loved to study. But for my mother, so Catholic, it was a great sin. She said: 'Here God's word says that the person that practises those things brings damnation onto the family. I don't want that type of person in my house.' It hurt all the more because it was my mother who said this to me, the one who had given me life. As far as she was concerned, I had physically died. (Carmen, 48)

Carmen's mother expressed the more intolerant beliefs that have dominated the Catholic leadership's discourse in Peru, exemplified by the Archbishop of Lima's recent labelling of homosexuals as 'children of the devil' (Ugarteche, 2001: 308). With no alternative accommodation or income to rent a room, Carmen asked for help at one of the *Comedores* (community soup kitchens) in a Lima settlement where she had been carrying out voluntary work with her church group. One of the women there who she knew well rented her a room in her house and slowly Carmen began to make a new life for herself. Having previously graduated from secondary school, she was qualified to teach the children of the women in the nurseries of the *Comedores* and Glass of Milk grassroots organisations, giving her a small income and a free lunch every day. When we met, 30 years later, Carmen was living in the same neighbourhood with her 7-year-old son. She confirmed that having been forced to separate from her family, she had dedicated her life to community activism and leadership in the *Comedores* and local government, which she considered incompatible with speaking publicly about her sexuality or being part of the local social networks of *chitos* and *lesbianas*. Carmen commented to me that although she had not restored her relationship with her mother, it was crucial to her that her son knew about her sexuality: 'He knows about me [my sexuality], he's fine about it, he's like my best friend.' Changing the norms within her own household had ultimately provided Carmen with the freedom in which her father had encouraged her to believe.

Teenage troubles

Although Charo was an 18-year-old in 2006, three decades after Carmen, Julia and Maria, her relationship with her family as a teenager was proving equally problematic. When we met, Charo was living with her mother and two sisters, since her brother and father were almost always working outside Lima. Similar to Julia, Charo was passionate about playing football and first encountered problems with her family when she began to spend more time with one of her teammates, Ceci:

> My family didn't find out about us at first. Ceci used to go to my house to pick me up. Then, well, I fell in love with her. My sister saw me with Ceci one night and said she thought she looked a bit strange. She said to me: 'why are you hanging out with her?' and I said she was my friend. 'But I don't want to see you with her', she said, and I asked why not, but she just said that, nothing else, without any explanation. (Charo, 18)

Charo recounted how her sisters then began to monitor her movements, forbidding her to go to football training in the evenings which led Charo to lie to them and tell them she was going elsewhere. This strategy helped to limit her sisters' efforts to control her, but although Charo had created some opportunities to see Ceci, they were based on secrecy and concealment at home, leaving her feeling anxious and insecure. When I asked Charo what plans she had for the future, she immediately replied: 'Well, we want to live together. Work and study, she'll work and help me, we'll help each other. But not here, where I live, or in the centre of Lima where Ceci lives' (Charo, 18).

A month after my interview with Charo, Ceci informed me that Charo's sisters and mother had discovered their relationship and had threatened to send Charo away to stay with an aunt outside Lima unless she stopped seeing Ceci. They also prohibited her from working at the Internet shop where she had recently started a new job, taking away her newly found source of income. After these events Charo felt obliged to stay with her family and she distanced herself from Ceci, who was in no position to offer any alternative. Ceci lived in central Lima with her own parents who were both elderly with health problems, relying on her income as a taxi driver to cover their basic needs including medical bills.

The family histories recounted by Julia, Maria, Carmen, Charo and Ceci outline just some of the difficulties faced by girls and women who attempt to resist heterosexual norms in the context of urban poverty in Peru. As teenagers and younger women they all encountered conflict and attempts at control over their sexuality by parents, siblings and male partners. However, by their late forties, Julia, Maria and Carmen were all well established in their own (albeit very modest) homes, having worked hard all their lives to satisfy their basic needs and for freedom from parental, sibling or male partners' pressures to conform. Over the years, Julia and Maria had changed the attitudes of Maria's children to such an extent that they learnt to respect and support Julia and Maria's relationship. Without exception the women emphasised the great importance they attached to their relationships with family members, both emotionally and as the central strategy for survival by helping each other through economic and emotional difficulties.

The examples of problems and struggles highlighted by the Peruvians in my study currently fall outside any of the fields of research, policy and action on gender and poverty, women's empowerment, masculinities, gender equality, gender-based violence, human rights, sexual and reproductive rights and LGBT rights. These fields of discourse and practice are consequently weakened by their normative assumptions of women's sexuality, masculinity and gender identity, while they also reinforce the exclusion and silence of women marginalised by these very norms. Promoting academic and policy-oriented research and dialogue on these three key aspects of women's lives in the context of poverty would enable many other women to speak for the first time about their problems, as well as their strategies for survival and their capacity for creating cultural change in the face of adversity.

Acknowledgements
Research for this chapter was funded by an Economic and Social Research Council Research Fellowship (2005–2008) (Award no. PTA -030-2005-00166). I would also like to thank my PhD supervisors, Professors Henrietta L. Moore and Sylvia Chant at the London School of Economics and Political Science, as well as all the Peruvians who facilitated and contributed to my fieldwork in Lima from November 2005 to July 2006.

Select bibliography
Aggleton, Peter, Kate Wood, Anne Malcolm and Richard Parker (2005) *HIV-Related Stigma, Discrimination and Human Rights Violations. Case Studies of Successful Programmes*, UNAIDS Best Practice Collection, Geneva: UNAIDS.

Gutmann, Matthew C. (ed.) (2003) *Changing Men and Masculinities in Latin America*, Durham, NC: Duke University Press.

Kulick, Don (1998) *Travesti: Sex, Gender, and Culture among Brazilian Transgendered Prostitutes*, Chicago, IL: University of Chicago Press.

Swarr, Amanda Lock and Richa Nagar (2004) 'Dismantling assumptions: interrogating "lesbian" struggles for identity and survival in India and South Africa', *Signs: Journal of Women in Culture and Society*, **29** (2), 491–516.

Ugarteche, Oscar (2001) 'El Movimiento Gay: El silencio de la Resistencia, Perú 1982–1995', in Jorge Bracamonte Allaín (ed.), *De Amores y Luchas. Diversidad Sexual, Derechos Humanos y Ciudadanía*, Lima: Centro de la Mujer Peruana Flora Tristán, pp. 299–314.

Wekker, Gloria (2006) *The Politics of Passion: Women's Sexual Culture in the Afro-Surinamese Diaspora*, New York: Columbia University Press.

Williams, Carolyn H. (2009) 'Sexuality, rights and development: Peruvian feminist connections', unpublished PhD dissertation, Gender Institute, London School of Economics and Political Science.

29 Youth, gender and work on the streets of Mexico
Gareth A. Jones and Sarah Thomas de Benítez

Introduction

Stand at the junction to any major thoroughfare of a Mexican city and one cannot but notice the number and diversity of street-workers. Many, though not all, will be part of the 'informal' sector, possibly selling foodstuffs or clothing, others may be engaged in more obviously illegal activities such as the sale of DVDs (*pirateria*) or goods stolen, smuggled or manufactured without licence (*fayuca*). Some activities may be legal or give the appearance of formality such as those conducted by uniform-clad sellers of mobile phonecards, ice-creams or newspapers. Many activities are services, including cleaning car windscreens, fixing appliances or shining shoes, or entertainment such as acrobats and fire-eaters. Some long-standing services, such as letter-writing and story-telling, have almost faded away, while others such as prostitution are firmly entrenched in street life. Street-work is ever changing with the availability of new products and new technologies, responding to the formulation of new regulations or the possibilities of globalisation. To the sharp eye of artists like Francis Alys, the street economy depicted in his photographic collection '*Ambulantes*' ('Pushing and Pulling') captures the vibrancy of public space. What many academics consider to be the 'underground economy' is conducted in public view even if, as we explore in this chapter, not all dimensions are immediately visible.

The presence of street-workers in Mexican cities has long been a preoccupation of national and city officials, concerned about the effects on public health and security, the protection of guilds and taxation. Business groups have frequently complained at the 'disloyal competition' and negative impacts on the image of the city. Attempts at removals have been met by violence and negotiation, as many traders are organised into associations with links to political parties, and have been highly effective at gaining concessions from politicians. The daily life of traders depends on a range of social and political connections, most obviously with police, market inspectors and local 'bosses' who may be needed to secure a 'patch'. Although often depicted in the literature as individual 'entrepreneurs' street-workers are almost always part of wider social networks, including ethnic groups, the most recognisable of which in central Mexico are the Mazahua from the State of Mexico and Michoacán, who sell food and embroidery. The street-worker also depends on family members whose labour acquiring goods, preparing foods or dealing with authorities may be invisible. 'Public' actions of the street-workers therefore are reliant upon the social reproduction of their labour in the private realm, involving partners, children, other relatives and fictive kin. The notion therefore of an individual trader as datum for 'informality' risks ignoring the complexity of social relations, a point first made by Keith Hart (1973) whose research on the organisation of economic activities critiqued the conventional conceptualisation of a neat transition from unemployment and underemployment to full (and formal) employment as 'absurd' (ibid.: 83). As Hart stressed, economic activity relates to pressures imposed and opportunities exposed by family networks, and access is determined by ethnicity, gender and age. In this chapter we consider, first, how street-work is gendered and, second, how some particular forms of street-work are undertaken by young people. The chapter is based on ethnographic research in the city of Puebla with two groups of young people whose lives are intimately linked with the street and work.

Street lives: gender, age and work
Attempts to understand street-work often rely upon simple two-dimensional analyses that draw a relationship between informality and regulations, tending to regard workers as synonymous with entrepreneurs and their motives and organisation to that of a 'firm'. Accordingly, the decision to work becomes co-joined with either voluntary choice or enforced constraint. As Perry et al. (2007) have argued, for example, women engage in informal work in order to remain close to the physical home and conduct roles as 'mothers'. Street-work, however, challenges this moral economy. Reporting data from early 1970s Mexico City, Arizpe (1977) noted that 40.2 per cent of 'street peddlers' were women, often working at considerable distances from 'home' and, as a later study revealed, many were accompanied by young children whose health is put at risk from poor hygiene and traffic pollution (Hernández et al., 1996). Moreover, many street-workers are young people with no *obvious* connection to parental or familial groups, sometimes depicted as 'streetchildren', at others as part of criminal networks.

From the late nineteenth century, concern at the large number of women and children working on the streets formed an important motive for philanthropic initiatives and an incipient welfare state across Latin America. These institutions often preferred education to labour, although schooling was usually intended to prepare young people for a trade, and supported normative notions of the nuclear family with parental rights dominant over those of children. Beginning with the crisis of the early 1980s, however, both the role and structure of the welfare state in Mexico and the declining ability of the family or wider social networks to serve as 'resources' for survival had led by the twenty-first century to what González de la Rocha (2006: 69) has called a condition of 'radical exclusion'.[1] Young people, especially men, are identified as particularly vulnerable to the difficulties of acquiring anything other than the most precarious of jobs, with those aged 19–23 constituting the group with the highest proportion engaged in the informal sector (Perry et al., 2007). For young people the value of contributing to household budgets and gaining some personal financial space is attractive, whereas the experience of a school system structured around rote learning and discipline, gender-conditioned expectations, and where unhindered movement from education to employment is limited, makes this approach unattractive to some (Giorguli, 2002).

For many young people, working on the streets represents a practical means to support themselves or their families. Although some are on the streets for a range of other motives, including escaping from violence at home or, as many have explained to us, because the streets present opportunities for fun (*cotorreo*), young people have to contend with attitudes that they are idle and lazy, or criminal, while their active negotiation of working opportunities within the street environment is ignored. What they do is rarely understood as work, unless it is with the intention of arguing for the removal of such activities from the immediate area or to 'rehabilitate' the participants to a 'proper' childhood. It remains difficult to convince others that street lives can be socially and economically organised in processes that involve complex arrangements of identity formation, group solidarity and discursive interaction.

Youth in work on the streets of Puebla

Porous boundaries and gender divisions
In the public perception the distinction between children working to accompany parents on the street and those working independently is lost. Academics and agencies may highlight a heuristic difference between children 'on' or 'of' the street or between street-involved and street-living children but in reality the categories overlap. Many children live temporarily on the street and occasionally work; some might sleep on streets while working during the week and return home at weekends; some may work long hours without a parent or carer around but be guided by them. Among the young people encountered in our research, working on a Sunday was very rare, and there would be long stretches of a day when little work as such seemed to be undertaken. Yet of all distinctions perhaps the child–adult cut-off is the most ambiguous, with the idea that 17-year-old children work differently from 18-year-old adults in conditions of poverty and social exclusion as illusory. The picture is further complicated by young people aged between 12 and 29 years in Mexico being classified as 'youth', a category that draws less sympathetic images than 'children' and different government responses. There has been almost no research to consider how youth engage with work on the streets, and how this work is gendered or draws on gendered constructions of roles.

Twenty-five-year-old Amparo has been working in and around Puebla's streets since she was 18. She earns money these days by travelling through the streets – 'clowning' on the buses (her face and that of her 3-year-old son, Juan Alvaro, caked in paint) or, in more stationary mode, washing car windscreens at *Las Jardineras* traffic junction. Clowning or juggling may (rarely) be followed by an opportunity to entertain in a family home at a child's birthday party. More often, particularly now she is in her third pregnancy, Amparo spends the day sitting in a well-shaded spot on the roadside, looking after her son and keeping an eye on her husband and the boy's father, Alvaro, as he washes car windscreens or, after night-fall, breathes fire at the traffic lights.[2] When her mother-in-law finds work at the ailing brick-making factory, Amparo joins the young male 'family' members carrying bricks herself or supervising others at a site near to where they rent a two-room house two bus rides away from her habitual street-working base. Brick-making, although back-breaking, provides a higher daily wage and is closer to home, but openings are scarce and the street is a reliable fall-back, despite its unpredictability of daily earnings and risks of violence. Decisions on whether, where and how to work are taken daily, subject to constantly changing conditions – a sick child, a husband in rehabilitaton or a police cell, eruption of simmering frictions within the nearby street markets – and are constantly reassessed. Amparo, like other young female (and male) inhabitants of Puebla streets, is resourceful in combining her working strategies on and off the street.

Understanding Amparo's role among the Jardineras group shows the importance of uncovering the layers of gendered street-work in Puebla. At one level it would seem that male youth are more prevalent than their female counterparts in activities such as windscreen cleaning, usually undertaken alone or in small groups, and women are more prevalent on stalls selling food on street corners or fruit and vegetables within covered street markets, as well as begging with young babies. Both sexes can, however, earn money from activities including juggling, selling pirated CDs or running errands. Several income-earning activities can be combined over the day, responding to traffic ebbs and flows in windscreen washing and juggling as well as to opportunities to offload surplus goods from market traders and to sell seasonal items. In the Jardineras it is often the women, both Amparo and her mother-in law, who decide how, when and where these combinations take place. At this second level, then, the activities of male youth are likely to be determined by the decisions of wives, mothers and partners.

There is greater complexity still. Nineteen-year-old Isabel has been working on the streets for ten years, during which time she has, among other activities, begged, sold food, carried bags, and touted tickets for football matches. Unusually she has no children or constant partner, but works alone, casually affiliated to a loose cluster of male street-workers who have known each other for several years. Isabel's on-street masculinised behaviour and language mirror those of her colleagues in order to (successfully) assert her right to work on an equal footing. Isabel currently earns her money on the street by juggling, most recently using gasoline-soaked juggling sticks which she sets on fire as part of her routine:

> I've been doing it [using fire] for about two years [. . .] the truth is because, whether you like it or not, they give you a little bit more money for it. Yes, then I take, like, well like today when I've only just started, I've already got like a hundred pesos [. . .] for two hours work.

Although juggling with fire is seen as a male preserve, Isabel has successfully turned the technique into a lucrative source of income for herself. Alongside her street-work she does more traditionally female domestic work, cleaning and tending beds every morning in a house in the Xanenetla neighbourhood. In a friendly pharmacy close to her street base, Isabel changes from domestic attire into hardier, asexual, street clothes. At the start of work Isabel usually looks clean and alert, and unless the temptation to slide into binge drinking and drug use presents itself she makes an effort recognised by both sexes to bodily represent herself as engaged in street-work rather than delinquency (Herrera et al., 2009).

Intrahousehold divisions of labour
We want to draw attention to two patterns of work: the 'on-street family' and the more traditional 'breadwinner-carer' model. Under the *breadwinner-carer model*, young males leave their family homes alone, travelling to carry out street-work in locales such as Las Jardineras or El Boulevard, heading home to their families at the end of the work day, perhaps stopping first to share beers or drugs with friends. These families have a demarcation of roles, in which the young fathers generate and control the family's main income, allocating money to their partners who are absent from the workplace and are responsible for the care of home and children. This model emulates the breadwinner-carer model common in wider Mexican society, while subject to strains of the informal economy in which young men's earnings are unpredictable and largely unaccountable to their female partners. Several young men had ex-partners and offspring to whom they made no financial contributions, but others, such as Manuel, were proud of their headship role and considered street-work the best available option:

Wages now, for the preparation [schooling] we have, which isn't much, we can't find good jobs which cover our needs, see? So you get a job and they're paying you 500 pesos, 600 pesos and you have to work eight hours for that. Here [on street] we more or less earn a little more than that sometimes, sometimes less sometimes more, but it's less time. Sure, a job has its 'pros' because they give you social security, you have a basic wage and you don't run the risks that you do here. So, yes, we'd like that but it doesn't cover our needs. [. . .] I have a son, a five year old. [. . .] you try to give him what you didn't have. So for that [a formal job] isn't enough, because we put our kids into school. [. . .] the costs are greater, and truthfully on 500 pesos a week, that's not enough.

The work roles of an *on-street family* are less clearly demarcated and involve more sharing of financial responsibilities as the commodity and care economies play out in the same space. Divisions of responsibilities are still gender-based, but there is some blurring at the edges. On-street mothers are primarily responsible for childcare but fathers do step in to supervise children and hold babies (although we never saw a father feed a baby or change a nappy), and young parents, such as 19-year-olds Estela and Alfonso, sometimes worked together washing car windscreens. When Estela left Alfonso and their baby girl (ostensibly for a more independent lifestyle, although she soon began living with another young man), baby Jazmín was quickly handed over to Estela's mother to look after, with some support from Alfonso's mother, since Alfonso was not expected by either family to become joint carer and breadwinner for his daughter. On-street families show some flexibility around division of work in unusual circumstances, as women step in temporarily to work on the streets when their partners are ill or imprisoned. Young males, working in close proximity to their partners and children, are expected to be the main breadwinners, but while their earnings remain unpredictable, in this model they are more accountable to their female partners who both witness their earnings and are better placed to negotiate financial allocations than their counterparts off-street. On-street partners may also be better placed to limit young male spending excesses. But these advantages may be offset by higher risks of accident, together with exposure to the sun and pollution, as well as lack of schooling for children.

Conclusion

In the early 1970s Keith Hart made the important point that the urban poor were not unemployed but engaged in informal economic activity. It is an argument that formed the basis for later research into 'survival strategies', livelihoods and asset frameworks, as well as development initiatives such as microfinance. But publics and agencies, national and international, still need some convincing that young people on the streets are engaged in productive activity – and that their patterns of managing caring roles are similar to those of others engaged in survival strategies outside social protection arrangements. Furthermore, studies of 'informality' continue to make distinctions between children and adults, with the former assumed both to be less productive and to be better off in school. Yet young people, despite their apparently non-normative economic, social and cultural positions, often make decisions about work and 'caring' in gendered terms, with an overlay of crossovers determined usually by the women. For families on the streets with young children, the notion that work might be voluntary is clearly an awkward one, and when young people, predominantly males, are engaged in heavy drug use and all are susceptible to violence then decision-making around work is highly constrained. In these circumstances, female partners' decisions to accompany males on to the streets may be eminently sensible, since the home-based carer model provides less negotiating power.

Acknowledgements
Research for this chapter was conducted as part of the project, Being in Public: The Multiple Childhoods of Mexican 'Street' Children, funded by a grant from the UK Economic and Social Research Council (ESRC) (Award number 148-25-0050), and doctoral research by Sarah Thomas de Benítez (2008) 'Square holes for round pegs? Social policy processes and "street" children's experiences: a case study in Puebla City, Mexico' (unpublished PhD Dissertation, London School of Economics).

Notes
1. The much praised social protection programme *Progresa-Oportunidades* which began in 1997 maintains an archetypal family focus with children linked to parents (especially the mother) and imposes schooling as a 'co-responsibility' requirement (see González de la Rocha, Chapter 37, this volume).
2. 'Husband', like 'wife', is a common arrangement neither confirmed in religious ceremony nor registered. Participants often referred to 'family' as both a biological and social unit, since unregistered adoptions and co-habitation are prevalent.

Select bibliography
Arizpe, Lourdes (1977) 'Women in the informal labour sector: the case of Mexico City', *Signs*, **3** (1), 25–37.
Giorguli Saucedo, Silvia (2002) 'Estructuras Familiares y Oportunidades Educativas de los Niños y Niñas en México', *Estudios Demográficos y Urbanos*, **17** (3), 523–46.
González de la Rocha, Mercedes (2006) 'Vanishing assets: cumulative disadvantage among the urban poor', *Annals of the American Academy of Political and Social Science*, **606** (1), 68–94.
Hart, Keith (1973) 'Informal income opportunities and urban employment in Ghana', *Journal of Modern African Studies*, **11** (1), 61–89.
Hernández, Patricia, Alfredo Zetina, Medardo Tapia, Claudia Ortiz and Irma C. Soto (1996) 'Childcare needs of female street vendors in Mexico City', *Health Policy and Planning*, **11** (2), 169–78.
Herrera, Elsa, Gareth A. Jones and Sarah Thomas de Benítez (2009) 'Bodies on the line: identity markers among Mexican street youth', *Children's Geographies*, **7** (1), 67–80.
Perry, Guillermo, William Maloney, Omar Arias, Pablo Fajnzylber, Andrew Mason and Jaime Saavedra-Chanduvi (2007) *Informality: Exit and Exclusion*, Washington, DC: World Bank.

30 Sexuality, poverty and gender among Gambian youth
Alice Evans

Studying sexuality in The Gambia – a poor, predominantly Muslim, country in West Africa – reveals gendered responses to poverty that other routes of inquiry might leave unearthed. Based on consultations undertaken with 44 low-income, predominantly unmarried, young people (28 male, 16 female) in urban communities in and around the capital and major metropolitan area, Banjul,[1] this chapter discusses how sexual strategies are shaped, buffeted and interact with Islamic guidance and pervasive poverty. In particular it considers how social norms and income-generating strategies affect the power dynamics of sexual relationships and attitudes towards sexual pleasure.

Sexual exchange

As noted in The Gambia, and in several other parts of sub-Saharan Africa (see for example, Arnfred, 2006; Campbell and Gibbs, Chapter 50, this volume; Jassey, 2005; Jolly and Cornwall, Chapter 103, this volume; Jones et al., forthcoming; Madise et al., 2007; Undie and Benaya, 2006), the transfer of money and gifts between sexual partners (henceforth, 'sexual exchange') is socially acceptable, even if engaging in sexual relations for the sole purpose of financial benefit is not. While the latter practice is deemed to be widespread, no participant in my survey (see note 1) admitted to having such motivations. Instead, women expressly valued indirect routes to money, and if money was cited as a key benefit, it was made clear that they, unlike 'other girls', did not give sex in return.

However, all male participants maintained that most females *do* 'follow' money: they pursue males for money; evaluate the financial status of those who proposition them; and desert or are unfaithful to those short of funds. In short, as Mohammed (24) put it, 'they don't care for boys unless you get. That is the main problem here in The Gambia between the boys and the girls'.

While female participants did not admit to 'following money', they did openly value routes to money. For example, the vast majority explicitly said they wanted a *caring* partner, in which notions of economic support and appreciation were integral (see also Spronk, 2005, on Kenya). As a mother of two children from an unfaithful husband, Ngneer (aged 24) put it, 'caring is more important than the money; if you care somebody, if you have even single butut [less than one fraction of a US cent] you will share it with the person'.[2] Another indirectly valued trait was that of being 'hard-working, so that we can help each other ... but if he is those mans who used to sit at the Bantaba [tree], drinking attaya [green tea], playing gamble ... they are not like that kind', explained Christian school girl Anna Marie (18) (see also Chant, 2007: ch. 4).

And when women did directly highlight the financial benefits of a relationship, they denied sex was given in return. For example, when, unmarried mother of one and girlfriend of three, Chilel (22) was being mocked for following 'small boys' (men under 35 years old without much money), she insisted that one *does* gives her substantial sums of money. However, she consistently denied that she has sex with him (though Ramatoulie, a 22-year-old hairdresser, later claimed, 'that's a lie'). Soffie (22) likewise denied that she had sex with her 71-year-old 'sugar daddy'. And though Ngneer laughed when I asked her what she thought her boyfriend wanted in return for his gifts, she maintained that 'until you married you are a virgin, you don't have time with your boyfriend'.

For girls, if anyone follows money, it is '*other* girls', as Halimatou (24), a hairdresser, put it. Anna Marie also maintained that 'all my friends, they are serious, they are not like those other guys who used to give themselves to boys' – 'they say, "hey, see that boy, he's having lot of money, I'm going to follow that boy" . . . they not used to be shamed to say that'.

Reasons for sexual exchange
Male motivations for gift-giving include desires to communicate one's love; demonstrate one's abilities to provide financially; actually help one's partner; and, have sex. Another issue is that of masculinity. As Hadim (28), a teacher, who is currently trying to earn enough so that he can provide for, and thereby marry, his fiancée, explained, 'pride will not allow you to be seeing your girlfriend every day or every time and that she needs something and that you cannot at least solve one or two problems of hers [. . .] you will have to give her something to solve her problems'.

Sometimes money is given to encourage, though not strictly pay for, sex. This may be partly explained by the strong social pressure on girls to refrain from pre-marital sexual relations, which creates an obstacle sometimes overcome by financial incentives. For many Gambians, scarcity of money renders any income source desirable (even to parents – some of whom were said to be 'encouraging, lead their children to the bad', as Anna Marie put it). Some female participants also seem to accept money to ensure that they get some long-term benefit from their boyfriends, who were widely portrayed as 'unserious' (unfaithful). Soffie explained,

> This small, small [young and financially weak] boyfriends, she will love them. After, those boys they are going to find another person, every time your heart will break, it's better to find a big [financially strong] boyfriend who will give her, because if she has nobody she will go and have sex with them anyway so it's better for him [that is, her] to have a big boy, it's better than having sex with this small boy, they cannot give her anything, they know that she is no more a virgin, [s]he can go and find a big man who can give her.

But sexual exchange is not only male to female, it goes vice versa – which, in the context of a boyfriend–girlfriend (as opposed to marital) relationship, is judged positively by young men. Loving someone in The Gambian context, as indicated above, partly means, or at least is expressed by, helping them with money. For example, when I asked Ngneer whether her boyfriend loves her, she said, 'yes, he give me a phone, a V3'. Ramatoulie similarly explained that 'if you love somebody you have to spend'.

Reasons for refusing sexual exchange
Not all girls are said to accept money. Hadim explained that some are 'very very good, even if you give them money they will not take it . . . they will feel that you are giving

them the money for them to love you but they will want to show you that you are not there for the money, they love you naturally'. But Omar (27), a cloth trader, then noted a problem: 'they will reject the money in order for you to believe in them, and trust them . . . And then you trust them, you get married, now they will even give you hell'.

Such characterisations may not portray the whole story. Anna Marie explained that she did not follow money because 'when the boy [. . .] keep on giving me money every day, one day he will [. . .] tell me, "I want to sleep with you, you, you eating my money, every time, can't you sleep with me?". You refuse, he'll just force me . . . When they're giving you money they want something in return'. Her worry may be justified. Mustafa explained that 'when you know man give you money every time [. . .] but still she will not give you any chance to have her [. . .] So, some [people], that makes them [the boys] to . . . [rape], because he spend always, she don't spend'.

Reactions to sexual exchange
Male participants detailed that the consequences of not giving money included less frequent meetings, infidelity, and curtailment of the relationship. Three solutions were identified.

One was to satisfy financial requests – prompting Kalifa (17), a student, to steal 600 dalasis [*c*.US$28] from his father. But this option was widely regarded as unfeasible for those on low incomes and also, by some, as unwise. For example, Wally (30), a bartender, expressed concern about mistakenly investing in a girl who you later see 'going with another man'.

To avoid such pitfalls, Ibou (30), a wood-carving finisher, stressed the importance of his partner being 'simple' and not envying the neighbours. The second solution is thus to seek a partner who does not 'follow money'.

Baboulowe (27), a tailor, detailed a third option (practised by '*other* boys'): to accept that one's partner may be unfaithful and adjust one's own commitment accordingly. In this way, he blamed the girls' cash-seeking behaviour for many boys becoming 'playboys' (promiscuous). Note the vicious circle implied by Soffie's aforementioned comment: since boys are unfaithful, it is rational for girls to follow money, in order to ensure some long-term benefit. But, as Baboulowe suggests, the expectation of minimal commitment leads their boyfriends to be unfaithful, with 'back-up' girlfriends. He admitted that there are problems from 'both sides, but a lot of it's happening from the girls'.

Another effect of sexual exchange is parental jealousy and resentment of their sons' girlfriends receiving scarce funds – prompting many to withhold this information from their parents, and one parent to pay a marabout (a witch-doctor) to cause harm to the receiving girlfriend.

Gendered power dynamics

Obedience
Virtually all male participants stressed they wanted a 'serious' (committed, respectful, obedient and long-term) girlfriend. Indeed, all participants, both male and female, maintained that a wife should obey her husband, because of 'the religion' (that is, Islam). Deviation from this rule was interpreted as disloyalty and that, as many young women as well as Francis (34), a Christian wood-carving finisher, put it, 'she don't loves you'.

However, boyfriend–girlfriend relations seem to be less patriarchal than marital relations. For example, most male participants expressed a tolerance and even an appreciation of their girlfriends, but not their wives, earning more or being more educated than them. Similarly, most young men seemed to accept their girlfriends wearing revealing 'European dress' (that is, tight jeans and a low top) in public, but insisted that they would deny this option to wives, who should wear (the more loose-fitting) 'African dress', such as kaftans, shawls and sometimes *hijabs* (head-coverings).

A wife's negotiating power seemed limited. For example, Ngneer said that although she used to ask her husband not to 'stay till late hours', his response was to say 'don't disturb me' – rarely returning earlier (from what later transpired to be sexual liaisons with his ex-wife) (see also Chant, 2007: ch. 4).

Domestic violence and rape
Violence was said, by female participants, to be widespread; inevitable for wives, and likely for girlfriends – even though all male participants maintained that they would not beat their girlfriends or wives. Most participants said that their response would be minimal; echoing Anna Marie's expectation that 'if I do bad thing, if he beat me, I will not saying nothing'. However, Dolly (26) divorced her first husband because he was, 'beating me, very serious', something also found by Chant (2007: ch. 4) in a number of cases.

All male participants and the vast majority of female participants have said that a wife is obliged to have sex with her husband when he wants it. Of the male participants asked, all denied that they would force their girlfriends to have sex with them, but, as previously noted, there are many indications that such practice is prevalent.

Sexual activity

Sexual conservatism and shame
Although men, particularly those 'spending', were said to pressure their partners for sex, there is also strong (but uneven) social pressure on unmarried females and males to maintain their virginity.

Compliance with the latter pressure is enforced through the fear of public and private abuse. Anna Marie detailed, and other participants concurred, that, 'When they sleep with you, they go and sit at the road. When you passing they say, hey, I was having sex with this girl, they will say many things about you'. Also, 'if you get a small problem with your husband, your husband used to say to you, "You, you are not a virgin, by the time I meet you, I don't even see nothing, you go and give yourself to boys", and that will pain you . . . people will hear that, it's not good, it's not good'. It was for these reasons, she said, that she stood up to her previous boyfriend's bullying and called his bluff when he suggested that the alternative to them having sex was that they separate.

There is also pressure on young men to remain virgins or at least to refrain from relationships where marriage was not intended. As such, no male participant said he wanted a short-term relationship – though some admitted to having enjoyed 'fun' relationships in the past.

With such social pressures, participants may not have been entirely truthful. Quite a few participants (both male and female) over the age of 25 maintained that they were virgins, and Halimatou (24) (whose friends assure me that she has been pregnant four times, has had two abortions and is now taking contraceptives) told me that the toddler she currently looks after was conceived the first and only time she has ever had sex. Such concealment was not unusual, since sexuality is a major taboo in The Gambia – rarely openly discussed and even between close friends only through heavily euphemistic language.

Indeed, many people seemed ashamed of sexual activity. Francis, who claims to have had 12 sexual partners, said that some girls ask for the light to be turned off, then, during intercourse, lie motionless, like 'dead fish', with some even covering their eyes. Notably, he, and other young men, expressed a preference for more active participation. Some participants were more adventurous (though, if ever this was revealed it was only done so after several of my visits). For example, Ngneer explained that some women 'used to off the light because they feel ashamed, but me I don't do that, light on!' Ngneer may be in the minority here, or perhaps it just depends on level of experience. Ramatoulie, for instance, detailed that although she could not look at her partner the first time they had sex, 'maybe one month, two month, you cannot feel ashamed', and now 'my man . . . cannot joke with me because of what I used to do, I cannot feel ashamed, no, I used to do anything he want'.

Whose pleasure matters?
Female sexual pleasure is widely regarded, by both genders, as secondary to that of males. Even if many young men expressed that their partners' pleasure was important, the primary focus in actuality was on their own sexual satisfaction. While some took great pride in their (alleged) ability to satisfy their partners, this was largely overshadowed by emphasis on what they themselves coveted. For Momodou, for instance, this was for her to 'suck his dick' and for him to 'take her back' [penetrate from behind], even if he added that, after having sex, partners would say that they liked these activities.

With only one or two exceptions, the focus on male pleasure was echoed by female participants. For example, when I asked Ramatoulie what her favourite sexual position was, she told me that her *man's* favourite was sex from behind. Likewise, when I asked Ngneer whether she told her boyfriend what she liked, she answered, 'my boyfriend tell me'. Similarly, Anna Marie stressed that girls 'want to give the boyfriend pleasure'.

Another issue pertinent to discussions of female sexual pleasure is Female Genital Mutilation (FGM).

Safe sex
All participants were aware of AIDS and some could list, though not detail, a few sexually transmitted infections (STIs). Only one participant said that their school advised unmarried sexual partners to use condoms.

Some said they had used condoms, particularly with those who, as Francis put it, 'can jump from one place to another'. Others explained that they preferred 'natural' or 'raw' sex. Price does not seem to be the limiting factor (condoms are either free or just a few cents), and the shame of obtaining them can be avoided by sending a friend.

No participant said that they would use condoms when married. Young women maintained that they would not request this, even if they suspected their husbands of having an affair, as to do so would be disrespectful. Some said they would ask their spouse to be tested for HIV/AIDS.

For those who become infected, the Gambian President, Yahya Jammeh, claims to cure AIDS at his weekly clinics. Some, but not all, Gambians expressed a belief in his secret herbal remedies.

Conclusion and reflections
This research reveals three major trends. First, the well-being of women and girls is severely constrained by their weak negotiating power and by domestic violence – interpreted by participants to be required and permitted, respectively, by Islam. Second, the limited use of condoms may prove fatal as the price of rice rises, and more girls pursue unsafe income-generating strategies, which may cause spiralling numbers of HIV infections. Third, participants' focus on heterosexual relationship reflects widespread social hostility towards homosexuality, which effectively silenced any discussion on this topic, save for the pronouncement of disgust.

Further research needs to explore the dynamics of sexual relationships within as well as before marriage. In particular, if sex is a means by which young women gain access to resources, how does this pan out with their older counterparts?

Acknowledgements
This chapter owes a great deal to the many Gambians who shared their experiences with me, as well as Charlotte Callens, Sylvia Chant and Nick Day.

Notes
1. The fieldwork was conducted during 2008 as part of a broader project directed by Professor Sylvia Chant, LSE, on youth, sexualities and marriage in The Gambia.
2. All interview quotes are presented verbatim.

Select bibliography
Arnfred, Signe (ed.) (2006) *Re-thinking Sexualities in Africa*, 2nd edn, Uppsala: Nordiska Afrikainstitutet.
Chant, Sylvia (2007) *Gender, Generation and Poverty: Exploring the 'Feminisation of Poverty' in Africa, Asia and Latin America*, Cheltenham, UK and Northampton, MA, USA: Edward Elgar.
Jassey, Katja (2005) 'In the eyes of the beholder: male and female agency in relation to "race", sexuality, love and money', paper presented at the workshop on 'Sex and Gender in Africa: Critical and Feminist Approaches During Nordic Africa Days', Nordic Africa Institute, Uppsala, 30 September–2 October.
Jones, Gareth A., Katherine Brickell, Sylvia Chant and Sarah Thomas de Benítez (forthcoming) *Bringing Youth into Development*, London: Zed.
Madise, Nyovani, Eliya Zulu and James Ciera (2007) 'Is poverty a driver for risky sexual behaviour? Evidence from national surveys of adolescents in four African countries', *African Journal of Reproductive Health*, **11** (3), 83–98.
Spronk, Rachel (2005) 'Female sexuality in Nairobi: flawed or favoured?', *Culture, Health and Sexuality*, **7** (3), 267–77.
Undie, Chi-Chi and Kabwe Benaya (2006) *The State of Knowledge on Sexuality in Africa: A Synthesis of the Literature*, APHRC Working Paper No. 24 Nairobi: African Population and Health Research Centre, available at: www.aphrc.org (accessed 20 March 2008).

31 Ghettoisation, migration or sexual connection? Negotiating survival among Gambian male youths
Stella Nyanzi

Introduction

In The Gambia, successful livelihoods among youths are challenged by unemployment, underemployment, low employability due to limited skills, early school drop-out, high inflation rates and fledging groundnut prices (DoSFEA, 2006: 24; Heintz et al., 2008: 23–9; Jones and Chant, 2009). Important national policy frameworks such as the National Youth Policy 1998–2008 and Poverty Reduction Strategy 2007–2011 highlight the significance of youth unemployment to national development.

In communities, adults and elders complain about contemporary young people suffering from delayed maturity and its disadvantages. Struggling against the current, youths either succumb to apocalyptic pronouncements of a cursed generation, or innovatively resist this marginalisation.

This chapter explores how male youths cope with failing livelihoods by fantasising about exodus, in publicly derided cliques, and examines how they (re)craft values of success amid poverty.

Methods and context

I conducted ethnographic fieldwork between 2003 and 2007 in rural and urban parts of The Gambia. The study aimed at obtaining emic perspectives. Data collection triangulated participant observation, individual interviews, focus group discussions and policy review.

The Gambia is the smallest country in West Africa. The predominantly youthful population is urbanising rapidly. The economy depends on agriculture, tourism and services. Islam is the main religion. The main ethnic groups are Mandinka, Wolof and Fula.

Socialising is a gendered activity in The Gambia, and in this instance I was particularly interested in young men who hung out with other young men in 'the *voos*'.[1,2]

Fashioning the *voos*

The concept of 'the *voo*' – a colloquial term locally defined by male youths as 'a meeting place', 'a joint for hanging out', 'a hideout for chilling with my boys' and 'a place where we are on our own doing our own thing' – was important to locate social spaces in which these youths freely congregated. The *voo* is a social rather than a geographical space, with fluid intangible rules of association, specific criteria of membership and patterns of etiquette. Often, a group of particular male youths congregate around a charcoal-stove brewing *attaya* (Chinese green tea), sit on *togals* or wooden stools, and begin to talk 'boy-talk'. They could meet at a street-corner, backyard quarters of one member, the beach, on a balcony or in the sandy streets between houses. In the *voos*, they are free to be themselves: idle, restless, obscene, angry and daydreaming. Many youths openly smoked marijuana (weed) and/or cigarettes, drank alcohol and shared stories of their sexual exploits. They also shared tips about getting employment, foreign-exchange rates, the latest car models, how to pass a visa interview, groundnut prices, the dominance of Nigerians and Ghanaians in the Gambian economy, the latest football craze, stories of nagging mothers, and so on. Frequently, they exchanged stories about their frustrations of life, fantasies about furnishing themselves a better lifestyle and strategies for attaining this betterment by migrating to the West. In the *voos*, these male youths expressed solidarity and support for each other. While hanging out in the *voos* and daydreaming with like-minded youths about accumulating untold wealth in the West, it is common practice to listen to reggae music, brew and drink *attaya*, and roll up their unkempt hair into dreadlocks. These practices are summed-up as 'Nerves Syndrome'.[3]

To outsiders in society and critics involved in policy-making, sitting in the *voos* is stereotypically constructed as a dangerous pastime, a waste of youthful resources, idleness, illusory daydreaming, stress-inducing activity, an avenue for associating with social misfits and hence learning bad morals. Some parents of urban youths freely expressed discontent:

> They afford money for music cassettes and batteries, but they cannot even buy a small piece of soap for the compound. I don't know where they get this money. (Ma Fatou, Kotu)

> Our youths are useless! They don't want to work. They just sit chatting, chatting, chatting. We call it *wahtan rek* (just go to have a chat)! Better to go and look for a job because the parents who paid school-fees need to start getting some profits out of it. But they just sit chatting away their youthfulness. Allah help us! (Yayi Binta, Serrekunda)

Similar sentiments were expressed by the late director of the Gambian National Youth Service Scheme, Sebastian Njie:

> These young men are crafty. They have a new *barada* (pot for brewing *attaya*), money for *attaya*, sugar and charcoal. But they will not help anyone. They just sit at home, eat food from the common bowl, and fold their hands. Just depending on their elders! Big able-bodied boys who are ready to go off to Babylon whatever which way! It is in these groups where they learn what to do.

Likewise in the public media, at open rallies and in cabinet, policymakers and youth development workers condemn this facet of Gambian youth subculture. 'Hanging in *voos*', 'Nerves Syndrome' and daydreaming about migrating to the West are criticised for encouraging a generation of laziness, promoting youth redundancy, and perpetuating dependency on a few over-burdened adults. Interviews with National Youth Council members revealed that youth policymakers and implementers associate the *voos* with petty crime, antisocial behaviour, juvenile delinquency and introduction to vices such as substance misuse, petty theft, pick-pocketing, hustling tourists, deception, sex tourism, drug or pornography peddling, and pimping. Even President Yahyah Jammeh in his national addresses regularly criticises youths who are idle, chat, drink *attaya* and think that wealth will somehow drop in their laps.

From the ghetto *voos* to Babylon: the role of social networks
Given this widespread opposition, why do youths maintain the *voos*? It was important to capture the youths' own logic, and justifications for frequenting the *voos*.

It is a place where we get ideas about how to do to go to Babylon. Your boys share stories about so-and-so who did this, so-and-so who did that. And you learn from these examples. (Bojang, Talinding)

After the embassy refused me a visa, I was feeling real bad in my heart. I couldn't go anywhere else for comfort but then I went to my boys in the *voo*. We listened to the music of 'Burn down Babylon! Burn down Babylon!' as we puff-puff pass. And my boys consoled me to try again for another visa. *Billahi*! (Swear to God!) I felt the world was alright again. (Marcus, Kotu-Kololi)

For me, meeting the ghetto boys is necessary to maintain contact with others who travelled first. 'Yeah man', they call and say, 'now I am on the metro. Now I am on the escalator. Now I am touching on the snow'. Things like that which we do not have in The Gambia here. So it helps us to prepare for our turn of going. Even it makes you feel closer; much closer to Babylon. (Malick, Kotu)

When I don't hang out with my boys, where do you want me to be? If you stay with girls too much, people say you are like a woman. They call you *gor-jigen* (man-woman). Better to hang out with the boys in the ghetto than to be with the women and girls at home! (Ansumana, Bakoteh)

If you rub shoulders with boys wanting to go to Babylon you get sharpened up and you will go, deh! Definitely. They give you ideas about how to answer those mean officers at the embassy. And they can even connect you to a *Toubab* (white person) for a letter of invitation that you show at the visa office of the embassy. It is good for contacts, contacts, contacts. (Joof, Banjul)

Rather than a site festering with social vice, these urban male cliques were positively discussed by the male youths who participate in them. The *voos* were emically constructed as:

- a networking resource for reaching others of like mind
- a club of belonging where it was acceptable to be themselves
- a space for forging or drawing support and comfort for non-conformist behaviour
- a fertile site where dreams of Babylon were nurtured and experiences shared
- a ground for strategising against multiple systems, for example, the state, family, foreign embassies
- a source of relaxation and leisure, for example, music, games, conversation and daydreaming
- an avenue to vent frustration against self, the older generation and the establishment
- a masculine space where only females 'connected' to male members had temporary access
- a hub for generating or maintaining alternative livelihoods, for example, peddling, pimping, forging immigration documents, and fabricating plight stories to lure tourists.

In their attempts to beat looming poverty, many Gambian youths aspire towards migrating to 'Babylon' (Ebron, 2002; Gaibazzi, 2008; Jones and Chant, 2009; Nyanzi et al., 2005). In focus group discussions, we jointly assessed options available to youths who tried their luck at prosperity by remaining in the country. The lists they mentioned always included cultivation, livestock rearing, wholesale import trade, retail petty trade, the service industry (specifically tourism), teaching and secretarial or computer services. Rarely did they consider professional employment such as law, medicine, nursing, dentistry, veterinary, social work, administration, engineering or architecture. When queried about this, they reasoned that their minimal educational attainment was a limiting factor. Similarly, very seldom did they mention microenterprises, although many Gambian youths are refashioning alternative livelihoods through this route. When I probed about this disjuncture, a common rejoinder was the lack of initial capital to embark on business.

It was interesting that many youths were willing to try their hands at meeting the costs of migrating to the West, and yet found the initial capital of investing in their own small-scale enterprises unaffordable. Families, friends and networks were able to pool resources to facilitate overseas travel (see Shipton, 1995), and yet seemed unable to invest the same resources in (a probably more viable) business in the youth's hometown or homeland. This contrast highlights the constructedness and situatedness of success and youth livelihoods in The Gambia. Shipton's (1995) study reveals the historicity of today's high value that society places on youths migrating to the West in the hope of making wealth. Many stories are recounted of (mostly male youths) risking their lives in illegal trafficking scams, attempting long trips by sea either in pirogues or on the cargo decks of ships, being smuggled in the back of long-distance trucks, travelling by land for many months through various Sahelian countries, sex tourism with the promise of emigration, and cross-generational sex with much older tourists in exchange for visa and air ticket. Narratives of deportation do not discourage them, but rather sharpen their resolve to make it and not get caught in the process.

For youths with ties to kin who can support accessing the much desired West, connections made in the *voos* were not necessary to actualising the aspiration to emigrate. However, for the majority of disillusioned youths, the *voos* offered a stepping stone into a promised land flowing with untold opportunities. Many are the nights when we rehearsed answers and practised potential questions posed at visa sections of different Western embassies, consulates and high commissions. I frequently helped members of different *voos* to fill in application forms for passport or visa applications, or spell-checked a request for an invitation letter. After each embassy visit, we congregated, either to offer solace and comfort, revise strategy, or indeed to celebrate any rare successes. Youth members of a *voo* clique cooperated to support one another's dreams, build on strategies to beat migration systems, and discuss schemes for soliciting monies for travel. Lacking relevant connections to strategically positioned kin or patrons, youths from marginalised sub-population groups often linked up with ghettoised urban youths already embedded into networks of emigration.

Sexual connection as a route out of poverty: sex tourism and arranged marriages
Sexual connection was discussed as a viable route out of poverty by many male and female youths in The Gambia. Rather than seek employment bringing a monthly salary, many youths believed it was more strategic to partner with a wealthier individual who could facilitate travel to the West, or else save the youth from impoverishment. Sexual

liaisons with powerful or wealthy partners were thus widely sought. This sexual connection commonly took the shape of either sex tourism or arranged marriages. While sex tourism was mostly a strategy for the boys, arranged marriages featured largely for the girls.

Young men in The Gambia are widely reputed for offering sexual services to foreigners mainly comprising tourists and expatriates, in exchange for possibilities of foreign travel, a Western work permit, permanent residence or citizenship overseas (see Ebron, 2002; Nyanzi et al., 2005). Instead of feeling shame for this transactional sex, male youths involved in the practice boldly justified it as highly lucrative, a shortcut to prosperity, and even cited examples of wealthy Gambians who succeeded through this avenue. They reasoned that the remittances sent home from such unions are the backbone of diverse local assets, developments and investments.

Family members often contract an arranged marriage for their daughter/son with a family that is wealthy and well respected. Although decried by human rights activists, the justifications for arranged marriages include either the need to keep wealth within a particular family, village or ethnic tribe, or else to link up with a wealthy family in order to absolve one's children of poverty. Arranged marriages are often contracted for young virginal brides, and much older, wealthier men, with established position, social status, family wealth or political acclaim. Many of these older men are already married (sometimes to multiple wives) and with children. Poverty disables the girl to contest these arrangements. Marriages of urban girls are sometimes arranged by their brothers or friends in networks with *semesters* (local word for Gambians who live abroad). Often, these girls have never met the groom, but their families consent because of the hope of exodus to a better life of imagined wealth and prosperity.

'But I cannot dig myself out of poverty': rural boys' perceptions about livelihoods

While *voos* are often presented as an urban phenomenon (see Gaibazzi, 2008), I variously found similar gathering places in the form of *bantabas* (a central place in the village, trading centre or family compound) in rural areas. Often roofed with thatch, and furnished with makeshift seats, the *bantaba* is not only the usual venue for village meetings, but also collects (usually gendered and generation-segregated) cliques of people on an informal basis. For example, in DibbaKunda Fula village, the elders regularly met to listen to Fula fables on radio, chew kola nuts and play cards or a board-game. In Sankalang Wolof, it was often young men who met to talk about football, hunting or the latest cross-border smuggling exploits. In Marakissa, the male elders regularly lay on the log seats after *juma* (prayers at the mosque).

Thus I met with rural male youths either in their compounds, or at the village *bantaba*. Similar to hanging-out in the *voos,* my moments with these young men were spent chatting about everyday life in The Gambia. We talked about girls, growing up, family, culture, tradition, hunting, making money and their frustrations with trying to get a job. We talked about farming, buying seeds, selling produce at the weekly *lumo* (cyclical market) in Farafenni, repairing the family's donkey-cart with a new wheel, fund-raising for a wedding or a naming ceremony. Interestingly, these rural male youths also aspired towards migrating to the Kombos, the heartland of Gambian tourism on the coast. While the dream of many was to get into casual labour in the Kombos, some aspired towards exodus to North America and Europe in order to 'get rich quick'. Often, they requested me to link them to Westerners able to facilitate their emigration. A few were so persistent in their pleas that interaction sometimes proved personally uncomfortable,

> *Me*: But why do you only talk about going to America, whenever you are with me?
> *Cherno*: Because I need to go. Aminata [my anthropological name], Allah must help you to help me to go in America. If that should happen, I will be the happiest man, Billahi, the happiest man.
> *Me*: But what is wrong with Sansakono village?
> *Cherno*: Poverty, Aminata, poverty. We farm groundnuts and rice, but then we do not even get enough fish-money to last the year. We work, sweating so hard here in the provinces, but we do not get plenty money like the people who are over there in America. They work little, but then they have plenty dollars. We cannot hoe ourselves out of this poverty. The hoe will not solve poverty.

This dialogue, recorded early in my fieldwork, captures sentiments frequently expressed by many rural male youths. Parents who believed that wealth and better incomes were located in the capital city, or better still, abroad in the West, shared similar views. Six different parents approached me during this ethnographic fieldwork, with pleas of helping their sons leave the provinces and emigrate to London where they knew my university was. They were testing the potential of their social connection to me to facilitate their children's exodus.

However, not all Gambians believed that emigration to the West was the solution to local poverty. For example, my fieldwork father, an elderly *alkalo* (chief) of a small Fula hamlet in Northbank division was adamant:

> Alkalo Pateh Bah: America . . . [vigorously shakes his head] me, to go to America? Why would I ever want to go to America? What is there that is not here in this village? We have cows and milk. We have rice and couscous, groundnuts and fish. We have our children and grandchildren, our wives and mothers. Me, I have batteries in my radio and I can listen to anyone anywhere. If I want anything (stares directly into my eyes), anything at all, I buy it from the *lumo* or I send for it from Kombos. What do I want in America? My America is right here in this village of Dibbakunda.

Discussion

Although poverty is often conceptualised as belonging to the margins of society, this chapter illustrates that poverty actually does transcend simplistic bounded classifications. Poverty is felt by the youths in this study although they have diverse characters of empowerment: male gender, urbanity, youthful age, relative education, access to the West, and globalisation. Although more educated than their rural counterparts, urban youths cannot get employment because they are not that qualified, and there are no jobs. They fall very short of social expectations on them as young men to become exemplary breadwinners and responsible citizens. Lacking resources (financial, social, technical, geographical) to access immigration documents, they seek the comfort of their clique members, weed and fantasy. They are dependent, redundant and frustrated. They are ostracised by responsible adults, and criticised by policy elites.

Rather than giving up on their dreams of exodus, these young men fan alive their aspirations in the *voos*. They strategise, converse, discuss and link-up with Gambian youths in the diaspora to consult about routes to success. When they fail to make it on their own, they are willing to (and do) exchange their sexual bodies and sexual services for friendship, partnership or marriage that will bring the cherished ticket to North America and Europe. They logically 'marry' their way out of poverty to an imagined better life in the West. Amid idleness, redundancy and unemployment, the *voos* offer an alternative space to refashion meanings of success among these male youths. Extrapolating from the experiences of other Gambian youths who 'made it', the youths in the *voos* build their own pathways to success, however unconventional. The *voos* thus become schools where youthful minds are exercised in their own terms. Youthful energies and potential are released, fashioned and shaped within the *voos*. Value systems of what is right and wrong, success and failure get re-scripted during the time spent in the *voos*. Thus, cultivating groundnuts and rice for subsistence attains meagre importance relative to migrating to an imagined West to strike success. Hanging out in *voos* becomes an integral part of these urban youths because their dreams and values are reinstated by other clique members. Belonging to a *voo* takes on significance as a space in which male youths' sense of security, personhood, value, identity and future is re-established by others, even though the present circumstances of poverty and lack may still abound.

In the absence of government provisioning for disoriented youths, the *voos* are a coping strategy that male youths in The Gambia have fashioned for themselves, to allow them to deal with their multiple frustrations and aggravations. Rather than being new to Gambian society, the *voo* is a male youth generation-specific modification of the *bantaba* concept. Perhaps more accurate is the observation that the unwritten rules of membership and the activities engaged in have changed to suit postmodern Gambia. However the idea of sitting together in age- and gender-specific groups to chat is integral to Gambian social fabric.

Rather than condone these male youth activities, national youth workers, policymakers and programme developers should engage with youths to assess how they can best harness the existing model of *voos* to create safe, productive and legal clubs of association for disoriented male youths. More research is needed to examine why such *voos* prevail, what need they are meeting in contemporary Gambian society, what they are offering to these male youths, how best they can be enhanced as vehicles for conscripting male youths into productive service, and how they can be made safer and thus more accessible to other male youths who do not associate with them for fear of ostracisation by parents and other elders.

Notes

1. In Brikama and Farafenni, boys also referred to 'the ghetto' to describe a similar concept.
2. Elsewhere I discuss the socialising avenues of female youths, such as the 'programmes' (political, cultural or neighbourhood festivities), the home and beauty parlours.
3. Rather than actual psychosis or a diagnosable psychiatric condition, 'Nerves Syndrome' is a local label for a wide repertoire of antisocial behaviour, including seclusion, associating with juvenile delinquents, and idleness, the latter characterised by no desire to seek a steady job, loitering, having heaps of visa application forms, spinning deceitful stories to solicit money for processing travel documents and fares, forging identification papers, smoking weed and blatant rudeness. These phenomena are mainly associated with frustrated male youths who feel thwarted at their failure to achieve the much coveted aspiration of going to 'Babylon' – a term used to describe North America and Europe (see Gaibazzi, 2008).

Select bibliography

Department of State for Finance and Economic Affairs (DoSFEA) (2006) *Poverty Reduction Strategy 2007–2011*, Banjul: DoSFEA.

Ebron, Paula (2002) *Performing Africa*, Princeton, NJ and Oxford: Princeton University Press.
Gaibazzi, Paolo (2008) 'Nerves! Struggling with immobility in The Gambia', paper presented at the European Association of Social Anthropologists Conference 'Mobility, Transnational Connections and Socio-cultural change in Contemporary Africa', Ljubljana, 28–29 April.
Heintz, James, Carlos Oya and Eduardo Zepeda (2008) *Towards an Employment-centred Development Strategy for Poverty Reduction in The Gambia: Macroeconomic and Labour Market Aspects*, Brasilia: International Policy Centre.
Jones, Gareth, A. and Sylvia Chant (2009) 'Globalising initiatives for gender equality and poverty reduction: exploring 'failure' with reference to education and work among urban youth in The Gambia and Ghana', *Geoforum*, **40** (2), 184–96.
Nyanzi, Stella, Ousman Rosenberg-Jallow, Ousman Bah and Susan Nyanzi (2005) '*Bumsters*, big black organs and old white gold: embodied racial myths in sexual relationships of Gambian beach boys', *Culture, Health and Sexuality*, **7** (6), 557–69.
Shipton, Parker (1995) 'How Gambians save: culture and economy at an ethnic crossroads', in Jane Guyer (ed.), *Money Matters: Instability and Values in West and Equatorial Africa*, Portsmouth, NH and London: Heinemann and James Currey, pp. 245–76.

32 Poverty in old age in sub-Saharan Africa: examining the impacts of gender with particular reference to Ghana

Isabella Aboderin

Debates on ageing and poverty in sub-Saharan Africa

In recent years an intensifying debate has focused on the impacts and policy challenges of population ageing in sub-Saharan Africa (SSA). Although SSA's populations will remain the youngest in the world in terms of the share taken by persons aged 60 and over,[1] their absolute number will rise sharply from 42.6 million in 2010 to 160 million by 2050 – a more rapid increase than in any other major world region or any other age-group. Moreover, and contrary to common misconceptions, older persons in SSA can on average expect to live many years beyond 60. According to the latest United Nations Population Division (UNPD) estimates, life expectancy at that age (15 years for men and 17 years for women) is not substantially lower than in other world regions.

The discourse on the implications of ageing in SSA is being driven by a number of dedicated non-governmental organisations (NGOs) and United Nations (UN) agencies (specifically HelpAge International [HAI], the United Nations Fund for Population Activities [UNFPA] and the World Health Organisation [WHO]), and a small corpus of African researchers. It is buttressed by, and takes as reference points, two recently forged international policy frameworks. These are the 2002 UN Madrid International Plan of Action on Ageing (MIPAA) and the 2003 African Union Policy Framework and Plan of Action on Ageing (AU-Plan) (see Aboderin and Ferreira, 2009). A central focus in the instruments and in the debate generally is a concern over a heightened vulnerability of older persons to poverty and consequent deprivation. Within a context of economic hardship, social ills and a lack of formal pension provision[2] in SSA, the particular risk of poverty in old age is seen as a result of the combined impacts of three factors. First, a diminished capacity at older ages to engage in sufficiently paid productive work due to (a) physical, mental and social attributes (for example, very low literacy levels, or age-related chronic disease), and (b) scant employment or other income generating opportunities. Second, a concomitant lack or erosion of savings accumulated during working lives. Third, a weakening of customary family support mechanisms, which have traditionally protected older persons unable to sustain themselves.

In light of the concern about old-age poverty, the MIPAA and the AU-Plan both call on governments to forge policy responses. Specifically, policies are needed to ensure old-age economic security for present and future cohorts of older persons as part of mainstream development efforts. Both plans emphasise two principal approaches to such policy: an institution of comprehensive social pension schemes and/or a strengthening of customary family support systems.

Perspectives on gender and old-age poverty in SSA

As an overarching principle for effective and efficient policy formulation, the MIPAA in particular asserts a need for a clear gender perspective, which recognises the differential impact of ageing on women and men (see Aboderin and Ferreira, 2009). In this vein, the plan and other contributions to the debate explicitly assert a disadvantage of women compared to men in the risk of old-age poverty. The assumption of a greater female economic vulnerability draws directly on the 'feminisation of poverty' notion (see Chant, Chapter 15, this volume; Davids and van Driel, Chapter 14, this volume). It moreover chimes with the idea of a universal disadvantage of older women in comparison to older men that was put forward at the 1994 Third World Conference on Population and Development in Cairo (see Knodel and Ofstedal, 2003). The presumed preponderance of poverty among older women compared with older men is generally seen as a consequence of two sets of influences. The first is older women's greater likelihood of being widowed, separated or divorced (rather than married) and to live alone in old age. These features are believed to make older women more likely to face economic and social adversity. The second set of factors relates to women's cumulative labour market disadvantages over the lifecourse. These include limited opportunities for engagement in paid work, lower salaries, or curtailed career development due to interrupted work histories or family care obligations. Together, these conditions impair women's access to work-related pension schemes and their ability to build resources for retirement (see Knodel and Ofstedal, 2003).

A link between the above circumstances and a resultant female economic disadvantage in old age seems eminently plausible. However, as Knodel and Ofstedal's (2003) trenchant critique makes clear, there is little evidence to corroborate it. Despite the MIPAA's rhetoric on a need for gender sensitivity, there has been little, if any, analysis of how older women's vulnerability to poverty actually differs from that of older men in SSA, and why. Moreover, there are reasons to question the presumed disadvantage of women in the SSA context. First, while older women certainly *are* more likely than older men to be unmarried and to live alone, this does not automatically imply economic disadvantage. Second, the scant sex-disaggregated evidence that exists on old-age poverty in SSA does not show a significantly higher prevalence of poverty among older females compared to males (May, 2003).[3] Finally, one may question whether women's labour market disadvantages in SSA indeed imply a greater female vulnerability to poverty in old age. The overwhelming majority of SSA's working population (both women and men) has typically been engaged in the informal or small-scale private formal sector – with no access to pension schemes, and income levels that foreclose any significant saving opportunities. For the most part, therefore, any earlier labour market advantage older men might have had is unlikely to have translated into significantly greater economic means in old age compared to women. Indeed, a much more important determinant of the level of resources older persons have at their disposal is the amount of family support they receive.

How (or whether) older men and women in SSA societies differ in this respect, and what gendered processes over the lifecourse underlie any differences, remain key questions for systematic empirical inquiry.[4] While comprehensive research is lacking, initial, interesting insights have emerged from an in-depth qualitative investigation into recent shifts in material family support for older persons in urban Ghana (Aboderin, 2006). Drawing on perspectives from three generations of respondents, the study's findings point to a possible *male* disadvantage in receipt of family support.

A male disadvantage? Indications from urban Ghana

An apparent male disadvantage in receipt of old-age support from kin arises within a context of a general decline in family support for older persons in urban Ghana. This decline has occurred against a backdrop of entrenched economic strain since the 1980s, and has manifested on three levels: first, a virtual ceasing of support from extended relatives; second, a reduced level of filial support from adult children; and third, an increased incidence of children who support older parents only minimally or not at all. Two broad interrelated shifts have led to such diminished family support. The first is an erosion of younger generations' resource capacity, coupled with an escalation of their material needs. The second is a change in the normative basis of filial support. Previous generations of adult children largely fulfilled filial support obligations *irrespective* of their feelings towards their parents. Today adult children are making the extent of their assistance dependent on their assessment of parents' earlier 'performance'. In particular, they judge the degree to which parents tried their best to set them up for life by providing for solid formal education and/or professional training. Children who consider parents not to have tried much, do little to help them in old age. In the most extreme cases children withhold all (or almost all) support from parents in 'retaliation' for their neglect in the past. Such retaliation – and the resultant destitution or abandonment of older parents – have become an acknowledged 'social problem' in urban Ghana. Its defining feature is that it affects almost exclusively fathers. Older men, in other words, appear much more vulnerable than older women to a lack of filial support.[5] This reflects the fact that fathers are much more likely than mothers to have shirked earlier parental support duties – typically as a result of pursuing (and spending resources on) additional or alternative conjugal relationships (see also Momsen, Chapter 18, this volume). This basic state of affairs is nothing new, however. Past generations of fathers, too, had multiple conjugal relationships and, in so doing, could neglect responsibilities to children. Yet they suffered no discernible detriment compared to women in receipt of filial support. Why has a male disadvantage appeared in recent times? A gender lens suggests that the emergent vulnerability of older men is the result of continuity in normative masculine roles and behaviours, at the same time as changes in broader family and socio-economic contexts have altered the consequences of, and reactions to, such behaviours.

Continuity in normative male behaviours
Ghanaian custom has continued to confer a particular duty on *fathers* (more than on mothers) to provide for their children's material needs and, especially, their education and/or professional training. At the same time, in having multiple wives, previous and contemporary generations of men have enacted persisting cultural conceptions of masculinity, including dominant norms about male, as opposed to female, sexual behaviours (Allah-Mensah, 2005). However, while men's normative sexual conduct has remained unaltered, its potential impact on children, and their subsequent judgement of it have changed in several crucial ways.

Altered impacts of male sexual behaviours
In a context of growing economic hardship, fathers' pursuit of multiple sexual relationships has become much more likely to result in a critical lack of support, for two main reasons. First, given material resource constraints and escalating needs, fathers often

no longer have sufficient means to cater adequately for their various children. While formerly fathers were mostly able to 'afford' several 'families', they have become increasingly unable to do so. Moreover, extended family influence, which in previous generations compelled 'irresponsible' men to fulfil conjugal and parental duties, has weakened. Second, assistance from extended family members, which was previously able to compensate for any gap in paternal support, in particular for a child's schooling, has become increasingly unavailable. At the same time, the repercussions of lacking paternal support for children have worsened in a context of severe economic and labour market strain. Without a sound educational or professional foundation they are increasingly unable to find sufficiently gainful employment and to 'make it' in life.

Changing reactions to 'male' behaviour
As the consequences of fathers' 'irresponsibility' have become more grave, so have adult children's reactions to earlier paternal negligence. Embittered by the impact on their life chances, adult children today are much more ready than previous generations to judge and retaliate to fathers' polygamous behaviours and resultant parental neglect by withholding filial support. In doing so, children are encouraged by an intensified societal emphasis on child rights, which emerged in the wake of Ghana's ratification of the 1989 UN Convention on the Rights of the Child and the 1990 African Charter on the Rights and Welfare of the Child.

Future and policy implications
A critical question is whether young fathers today are 'adapting' their sexual behaviours to the new intergenerational and structural realities that will likely shape their family support in old age. Indications are that they are not. The incidence of paternal 'irresponsibility' appears to be rising, suggesting that a male disadvantage in receipt of family support will likely persist among future cohorts of older persons. This raises potentially important implications for policy. Above all, it suggests that strategies to strengthen family support must consider differing approaches for older women and men. Policies for the latter may require a focus not only on the adult child–older parent relationship, but also on dynamics earlier in the parent–child relationship. More generally, the initial insights presented here highlight the danger of relying on dominant, a priori assumptions about the links between gender and old-age poverty in SSA societies. They underscore the urgent need for more critical, empirically based analyses of these links as a basis for apposite policy.

Notes
1. The United Nations' definition of 'old age' as 60 years and over is becoming increasingly entrenched in the international discourse. Readers should bear in mind the limitations of this definition, however, including its questionable appropriateness for African settings. The percentage of persons aged 60+ in the SSA population will rise to only 9.1 per cent by 2050 from 4.9 per cent today, compared to increases from currently 10 per cent to 20 per cent and 25 per cent for Asia and Latin America, respectively.
2. Only seven countries in SSA currently provide comprehensive old-age pension schemes: South Africa, Botswana, Lesotho, Mauritius, Namibia, Senegal and Seychelles.
3. Evidence from Latin American and Asian countries similarly fails to show a clear female economic disadvantage in old age (see Chant, 2008, and Chapter 15, this volume; Knodel and Ofstedal, 2003).
4. The lack of such true gender analysis has also been critiqued in Western gerontology (Calasanti, 2004).
5. This echoes findings from Asia as well as parts of Latin America, such as Costa Rica, which suggest that

in some settings older mothers command greater emotional loyalty from adult children than fathers (see Chant, 2008; Knodel and Ofstedal, 2003). It also resonates with Western evidence showing older fathers to experience greater estrangement from children than older mothers (see Calasanti, 2004).

Select bibliography

Aboderin, Isabella (2006) *Intergenerational Support and Old Age in Africa*, Piscataway NJ: Transaction.

Aboderin, Isabella and Monica Ferreira (2009) 'Linking ageing to development agendas in sub-Saharan Africa: challenges and approaches', *Journal of Population Ageing*, **1**, 51–73.

Allah-Mensah, Beatrix (2005) *Women in Politics and Public Life in Ghana*, Accra: Friedrich-Ebert Stiftung.

Calasanti, Toni (2004) 'Feminist gerontology and old men', *Journal of Gerontology: Social Sciences*, **59B**, 305–14.

Chant, Sylvia (2008) *The Curious Question of Feminising Poverty in Costa Rica: The Importance of Gendered Subjectivities*, Gender Institute New Working Paper Series No. 22, London: London School of Economics, available at: http://www.lse.ac.uk/collections/genderInstitute/pdf/curiouschant.pdf (accessed 4 May 2009).

Knodel, John and Ofstedal, Mary Beth (2003) 'Gender and aging in the developing world: where are the men?', *Population and Development Review*, **29**, 677–98.

May, Julian (2003) 'Chronic poverty and older people in South Africa', *Chronic Poverty Research Centre Working Paper No. 25*, Durban: School of Development Studies, University of Natal, available at: http://www.chronicpoverty.org/pubfiles/26Ravallion.pdf (accessed 20 April 2009).

33 Gender, urban poverty and ageing in India: conceptual and policy issues
Penny Vera-Sanso

Old-age poverty is increasingly a developing country issue where the population is ageing at a much faster rate than in developed countries. The World Health Organization (WHO) estimates that by 2050, 80 per cent of the global population aged 60 or more will live in developing economies and India, the second largest population of people aged 60 plus (following China), will have a life expectancy of 70 years. Rapid population ageing raises significant policy issues in countries that have become old before becoming wealthy and where the vast majority of the population cannot save for their old age. With the exception of Nepal, Mauritius, Namibia, Botswana and Bolivia which provide universal pensions, developing country governments expect most, if not all, ageing people to be self-supporting either through work or pension savings (see Budowski, Chapter 34, this volume) or supported by their families (Aboderin, Chapter 32, this volume), often while pursuing policies that make filial support less feasible and self-support less viable. Even when countries, such as India, do provide means-tested, non-contributory pensions, their coverage and value often fall short of need.

This chapter uncovers the conceptual issues underlying policy framing in India that impinge on older people's self-support or support from family or State, demonstrating the latter with a brief review of Indian pension policy. Drawing on the author's collaborative research, it explains why filial support does not meet the needs of the older urban poor in Chennai, the capital of the South Indian state of Tamil Nadu. It identifies the accumulation of disadvantage over the lifecourse as the determining factor in the urban poor's well-being and, by raising the taboo subject of what happens to inadequately supported older people, it identifies age discrimination as a key issue for development policy and social justice. The argument presented below is that despite the duty to provide public assistance for the aged, as stipulated in the Indian Constitution, the Government of India (GOI) considers itself to have limited responsibility for the welfare of the older urban poor, relying instead on filial support and people working into late old age, and has overlooked the mortality implications of poverty in later life.

Concepts and policies I: old age and widow pensions
Article 41 of the Indian Constitution, 1949, stipulates that states should provide a pension to the old and 'other cases of undeserved want'. The ethic of social justice underlying the Constitution has not been borne out in practice. Between 1957 and 1970 only 11 of 15 States and 5 Union Territories, including Tamil Nadu, introduced cash-limited, means-tested, non-contributory pensions for people aged 60 or 65, *despite* a life expectancy at age 5 of under 56 years in 1970. In 1995 the GOI introduced a national scheme providing central funding for old age pensions for men and women aged 65 who were destitute, having neither adult sons nor any other means of subsistence. In 2007 the

surviving adult son bar was removed and entitlement was based on age, 65 years, and *household* income falling below the poverty line (BPL). Yet even with this fundamental revision the old-age pension has not met need.

Instead of focusing on need, pension design has focused on limiting the GOI's burden by curtailing entitlement. It has done this by four means. First, by setting an age threshold that does not take into account life expectancies in the BPL income group, nor the physically depleting nature of manual labour that curtails working lives, nor age discrimination in the context of a youth bulge. The class bias in GOI provision is clear from its pension policy for its permanent employees, including white-collar employees, who retire at 58 or 60 years, not the 65 year threshold for the national pension for people living in BPL households.

A second element in curtailing entitlement comes with the retention of a poverty line based on the 1979 standard of the minimum cost of an adult daily intake of 2100 calories in urban areas. This poverty line does not cover the costs of the most basic needs that would define the narrowest conceptualisation of poverty (a diet that prevents malnutrition, shelter, electricity, healthcare, clothing, and so on). A few figures will elucidate the argument. The Planning Commission declared Rs538 (US$11) per month as the cost of meeting the urban calorific norm of 2100 calories in 2004/2005. Yet only in 2008 was the old age pension raised to Rs400 (US$8.17) per month (the cost split between central and state governments). Further, our random survey of 800 households in six of Chennai's irregular settlements in 2007/2008 found that 30 per cent of households rent and that 97 per cent of households pay substantially *more* than Rs300 (US$6.13) per month. The pension's inability to cover basic needs is demonstrated by older people having little choice but to work for as long as they are able after receipt of the pension. In this context the pension represents a critical *subsidy* to old age livelihoods, *not* a means of supporting people too frail to work – yet income earning disqualifies entitlement.

Having identified a poverty line which denotes severe destitution rather than poverty, a third strategy adopted by the GOI was to set a ceiling on the number of pensions provided. Alam (2006: 230) describes GOI's limiting the number of pensions to 50 per cent of entitlement, that is, 50 per cent of people living in BPL households aged 65 or more, as 'arbitrary'. This is a clear indication that GOI policy continues to rely on an assumption of filial support and on people working through old age. Yet even this 50 per cent provision may not be meeting the needs of the poorest. The failure to reach the poorest, a common feature of non-universal pensions, is reported for North India (HelpAge International, 2003). Initial results from field data in Chennai suggest something similar; that poorer, smaller households may be less able to release someone from income earning or domestic roles to pursue protracted application procedures directly, or to fund an agent to do it for them. In other words, by placing numerical ceilings the GOI has created a situation where additional *de facto* entitlement criteria *exclude* the poorest.

The fourth means for limiting the GOI's burden is delegating responsibility to state governments for match funding and administering the old age pension. While this is the standard format by which central government schemes are implemented, states wishing to pursue other policies have little incentive to progress schemes they have to match fund.

All these strategies can be seen in the second source of public provision for older women, the widows' pension. Until March 2009 this was funded solely by state governments and in several states women who receive a widows' pension continued to do so after reaching 65. In February 2009 funding of a national widows' pension was debated in cabinet. Proposals to make Rs200 (US$4.08) available to *all* 'BPL' widows aged 40–64 from central government funding was charged by the Finance Ministry with making the pension 'open ended' and robbing young widows of the 'enterprise to work'.[1] Amendments were suggested to allow local administrations to determine which widows should receive a pension. In March 2009, a cash-limited, means-tested pension, entitled the 'Indira Gandhi National Widow Pension' was introduced. The beneficiaries are to be identified by the local administration, which is to match and deliver the pension. Once again the coverage, pension sum and implementation strategy will not meet need and access is likely to be mediated by criteria beyond entitlement. Regrettably the newly imposed upper-age threshold may force older widows (including those already receiving pensions under state schemes) back into the pool of people aged 65+, where pension coverage is below half that needed and where the *de facto* criteria of access works against women-headed households.

Concepts and policies II: social and economic development
Chennai is one of India's largest and most economically diversified cities. Its success in drawing foreign direct investment (FDI) is locally attributed to its 'abundant skilled man-power' and its 'business-friendly' and 'congestion-busting' policies. In turn, FDI, increased migration to the city from all over India, large infrastructural projects, and booming confidence in the property market have raised property values and rents throughout the city, including in irregular settlements. The new service industries and expanded manufacturing have increased the number of higher status work locations in shopping malls, offices and residential complexes to which the younger urban poor aspire. The population's large youth bulge has significantly increased the competition for work, leading to rising credentialism and age-discriminating employment practices. To secure their children's future, families need to ensure they minimally pass the year 10 public examinations. Yet, despite Tamil Nadu's comparatively good human development indicators, the rapid progress of the 1980s has stagnated as health and education services are not reaching the poor. Inadequate public sector health and education provision and increasing 'user-pay' policies are increasing the costs of social reproduction borne by families, in part by forcing them into the private sector. It is the rising minimal standards for raising children, the insufficient public provision for social reproduction, inflation of over 10 per cent in food costs, high land values, age discrimination and transformations to urban livelihoods that pose the most immediate challenges to the filial support of parents in old age and to older people's self-support.

The urban poor's livelihoods are threatened by three trends. First, the ongoing displacement of manual trades by new techniques, technologies or products that replace one set of workers by another (see also Chari, Chapter 68, this volume). Second, by the knock-on impact of the global economic slowdown on people servicing those more directly engaged in the global economy, for example from auto drivers to domestic workers and neighbourhood *tiffin* (snack) sellers. Third, by local government's removal of street markets from busy shopping areas and relocation of irregular settlements to sites that make previous livelihoods untenable or less lucrative. The relocation of markets and settlements significantly undermines the capacity of older people to make a living in labour markets marked by age discrimination, as will the proposed limiting of street-trader numbers.

It is the third means, the sweeping away of irregular settlements and the high visibility, informal work of street trading that most clearly reveals the State's conceptualisation of how the urban poor should fit into the 'modern' Indian city. The importance of older women's street vending both to the economy (in terms of distributing agricultural and industrial products) and old-age livelihoods is overlooked in a conceptualisation now widespread in India of the 'global city'. Based on an idealised image of the hyper modern city of free flowing traffic, out-of-town supermarkets and streets reduced to advertising corridors for the movement of people and goods, the model is of a sanitised modern city devoid of poverty and disorder. This vision finds expression in Chennai's local government's beautification and anti-congestion schemes that are designed to attract and retain FDI, the most recent formulation being the restructuring of urban development and financing through the World Bank-funded Jawaharlal Nehru National Urban Renewal Mission, which is predicated on the eviction of irregular settlements and street trading from the city to the extreme urban periphery, that is, from the high-value centre with transport, health, education and other essential services to the unserviced, low-value margins.

These threats to the urban poor's livelihoods, as well as the additional costs forced by relocation to unserviced areas, significantly constrain both older people's capacity to support themselves and younger people's capacity to maintain and care for ageing parents.

Gender and old age
The failure to meet the needs of old age disproportionately affects older women for three reasons. First, wives outlive husbands, both due to women's greater longevity and the age gap between husband and wife. This affords men the safety net of female support in old age but leaves wives and widows in BPL households working deep into old age.[2] Second, as economic positioning in old age is the outcome of advantage/disadvantage accumulated over the lifecourse, women's disadvantages in relation to health, education, property holding, incomes and social benefits mean they enter old age with fewer resources than do men. Third, because female remarriage is stigmatised, widows living in irregular settlements tend to choose more secure but generally less well-paid livelihoods (typically domestic work) that provide some flexibility in order to cover both the income earning and domestic and caring duties normally 'split' between husband and wife. This coverage of 'male' and 'female' roles in household subsistence and reproduction and the lower incomes involved means that widows can be particularly disadvantaged in old age.

Underlying female disadvantage over the lifecourse is the view that females need less than males, a situation compounded by the widespread view that the old need less than younger people. In other words, a hierarchical model of family need operates that leaves 'altruistic grandmothers' at the back of the queue for access to family resources and makes them less able to hold on to their own incomes (Vera-Sanso, 2004). While gender discrimination has a high profile in the research community, age discrimination, as a category of socially institutionalised discrimination is generally not recognised, and is yet to be fully accepted as either a development policy or social justice issue. This lack of interest in old age is graphically seen in the Indian National Family Health Survey which uncovers the health status of female family members up to age 49. Until better evidence is provided it would be fair to assume that female disadvantage in health, property ownership, incomes and so on found among the under-60s is sharpened in old age. At the same time, the casual assumption of frailty and dependence in old age and use of residential proximity as a substitute for investigating actual intergenerational transfers leads to the unwarranted conclusion that filial support is the dominant mode of support for older people for all sections of the population (ibid.; see also Aboderin, Chapter 32, this volume).

Contrary to popular belief, for the majority of women working in the informal economy, old age is not about having needs met by others, but of meeting others' needs, and of increasing vulnerability and deprivation; the latter stages of ageing being a process (rather than a period) in which increasing female deprivation is considered routine, normal and inescapable.

The taboo question
There is virtually total silence on the most important and yet most difficult question to face up to – what happens to older people unable to support themselves and who are unsupported or inadequately supported by State and family? To answer this question we need to extrapolate from data gathered on life expectancies by class and 'racial' difference in a number of different countries and historical periods. The data provides a uniform and entirely logical conclusion that 'where material deprivation is severe, a social gradient in mortality could arise from degrees of absolute deprivation' (Marmot, 2005: 1102). In other words, severe poverty leads to shorter lives and without mitigating policies excess mortality will be concentrated among the poorest. The data also demonstrate that the greatest risk of poverty-induced excess death occurs in the early and middle years (Antonovsky, 1967). Evidence from South Asia indicates that adult socioeconomic positioning in the middle and latter part of adult life, especially downward mobility in old age and widowhood, have significant mortality implications for both men and women, though more so for women (Cain, 1986).

What can this data lend to our understanding of the older urban poor generally and women in particular? First, that their life expectancies will be lower than that of better-off people of equivalent age. Second, their potential familial sources of support are likely to be few (or none) because of excess mortality of their offspring and spouses in the middle years. Third, their potential sources of family support, their middle-aged children, will be fighting off their own mortality or that other consequence of severe poverty, the excess mortality of their own young children.

The answer to the taboo question of what happens to older people unable to support themselves and unsupported or inadequately supported by State and family is: they die.

Conclusion
The central issue for old-age well-being is the routinisation of human suffering; that the institutionalised violence of everyday life for the poor, particularly for women, girls and the aged, is considered normal and inevitable. In choosing to predominantly rely on individual and family solutions to poverty, governments have left unchallenged the institutionalised violence of everyday life that results in a social gradient in mortality.

While political rhetoric and policy discourse, both in India and elsewhere, might appear to challenge these statements, public provision for older people as well as the compartmentalisation of old age and old age policy from all other stages of the lifecourse and from social and economic policies more generally, make it evident that governments see themselves as having very limited responsibility for, and interest in, old-age welfare, especially the welfare of older women.

This ought to, and probably will, change. The interplay between economics and demography will force governments to shift from a negative paradigm of old age to seeing older people as a national resource. Yet the issue is not whether things will change but what form they will take. Will governments take the easy route, improving the wellbeing of a minority of better-off older people while 'harvesting' the opportunities of old age poverty (low wages, unpaid work and the release of assets/property onto the market to buy medical care)? Will they *in*effectively 'challenge' the discrimination against the poor, women and aged people which creates that poverty and the class differential in mortality? Or will they really live up to their rhetoric of well-being and social justice for all?

Acknowledgements

This research is supported by the New Dynamics of Ageing initiative, a multidisciplinary research programme supported by Arts and Humanities Research Council (AHRC), Biotechnology and Biological Sciences Research Council (BBSRC), Engineering and Physical Sciences Research Council (EPSRC), Economic and Social Research Council (ESRC) (RES 352–25–0027) and Medical Research Council (MRC) and conducted with the Centre for Law, Policy and Human Rights Studies, Chennai. I am indebted to Marlia Hussain, Arul George and M.S.W. Henry for their field research and to V. Suresh for comments on an earlier draft of this paper.

Notes

1. See Indian Express (2009), available at: http://www.indianexpress.com/news/cabinet-amends-bpl-widow-pension-plan/419967/ (accessed 21 February 2009).
2. Our 800 household survey (referred to earlier) found that 21 per cent of male household heads aged 24–29 have working wives, but as many as 46 per cent by age 75–79.

Select bibliography

Alam, Moneer (2006) *Ageing in India: Socio-Economic and Health Dimensions*, New Delhi: Academic Foundation.
Antonovsky, Aaron (1967) 'Social class, life expectancy and overall mortality', *The Milbank Memorial Fund Quarterly*, **45** (2), 31–73.
Cain, Mead (1986) 'The consequences of reproductive failure: dependence, mobility, and mortality among the elderly of rural South Asia', *Population Studies*, **40**, 378–88.
HelpAge International (2003) 'Old age pensions in India', *Ageing and Development*, **15** (October), 4.
Marmot, Michael (2005) 'Social determinants of health inequalities', *The Lancet*, **365**, 1099–104.
Vera-Sanso, Penny (2004) '"They don't need it and I can't give it" filial support in South India', in Philip Kreager and Elisabeth Schroeder-Butterfill (eds), *Ageing Without Children: European and Asian Perspectives*, Oxford: Berghahn Books, pp. 77–105.

34 Poverty, gender and old age: pension models in Costa Rica and Chile
Monica Budowski

Introduction

Pensions are important instruments for poverty reduction in old age. Despite pensions accounting for a large proportion of state expenditure, and women's disproportionate longevity, research on pension models rarely treats gender as a core analytical concept. Moreover, old-age poverty and pensions seldom feature on the agendas of women's organisations in the South. These shortcomings are addressed in this chapter when comparing Chile and Costa Rica's multi-pillar pension models from a gender perspective.

Gender equality in old age, and in pension entitlements, requires an analytical framework incorporating two perspectives. The first is the interdependency between state-designed pension models for its citizens and other relevant institutions, such as markets, communities and families. The second comprises the logics of each pillar (individually and as a whole) in multi-pillar pension models.

Pension models reflect a country's endeavour to provide for the contingencies of its citizens. This provision is based on implicit arrangements in other domains, especially gendered divisions of labour which distinguish between remunerated and acknowledged labour market work and unacknowledged housework and carework. This has led to a 'two-track welfare state' in which the 'traditional' family becomes an implicit force 'structuring social policies and reproducing the social division of labour between the sexes' (Sainsbury, 1996: 151). Where traditional forms of gendered divisions of labour prevail, old-age pension models linked to formal labour markets which lack redistributive components can reproduce or aggravate existing gender inequalities. State-implemented pension models may thus highlight dependencies among men and women and specific relationships between citizens and the state.

However, whether pension models are considered equitable or fair varies according to different bodies of literature. Actuarial perspectives emphasise the insurance function of pension systems, whereas social scientific perspectives focus on social citizenship rights, and the distribution of responsibilities between the state, the market and the family. Consequently, notions of equity are associated, on the one hand, with the relationships between financial inputs and outputs, economic feasibility, sustainability, savings and an economic growth logic, or, on the other, with equal opportunities, human needs and rights, resource redistribution, elimination of discrimination and social citizenship. Thus, the notion of equity depends on whether the pension system is considered a 'postponed salary' or a 'citizen right'.

In order to overcome poverty in old age equitably, redistribution and privileges are necessary to counter inequalities resulting from the gendered division of labour at home and in the labour market. However, institutionalising privileges can, paradoxically perhaps, reinforce the gendered division of labour. For this reason, a pragmatic focus on equity might be proposed, notably that gender inequalities are reduced in old age on the basis of policies which incorporate (and ideally harmonise) the views of all relevant stakeholders. Widespread participation renders contrasting situations and conditions visible, turns them into issues of debate and provides the base for future designs and reforms.

The Chilean pension model
Chile introduced the Bismarckian model of occupationally-segmented social insurance schemes in 1924, and then replaced it during the 1970s with the Beveridge model of universal social security coverage.[1] The former was comparatively generous and potentially redistributive although criticised for institutionalising privileges. It was quite gender equitable at the cost of subscribing to a patriarchal gender order in that women were better served as dependents (through marriage) than as workers (Arenas de Mesa and Montecinos, 1999).

After a brief period of universal coverage, Pinochet's reform of 1981, still largely in force today, liberalised and privatised social protection with Law 3500. It reduced the state's responsibility drastically and abolished redistributive elements and employers' contributions.

The model's central pillar is a fully funded for-profit pension scheme based solely on individual capitalisation. It is managed according to an actuarial logic. Employees or self-employed persons pay a defined contribution rate of their wage, commission charges and a premium covering invalidity and survivors' contingencies to a private Pension Fund Administration of their choice. Pension eligibility depends on a minimal contribution equating to at least 20 years (defined contribution). Calculations of benefit levels are based on (gender-differentiated) retirement age, longevity, and individual saving.[2]

These modalities are not conducive for gender equity: capitalisation and benefits depend on personal contributions only, women retire earlier and live longer. Women's lower labour force participation, interrupted labour market trajectories (maternity and care), lower wages for equal work and higher unemployment rates than men accentuate the inequalities in old age as they lead to lower replacement rates and higher risks of not reaching the minimum pension.

The second pillar of the new Chilean pension scheme guarantees a minimum pension at a low level when duration requirements are fulfilled yet savings do not suffice. A third (voluntary) pillar allows for further non-legislated and guaranteed saving.

Despite the caveats of privatisation, a residual model of social assistance (PASIS/ Programa de Pensiones Asistenciales), introduced in 1975, complements the three pillars. It pays a flat rate at a very low benefit level and aims at alleviating poverty among elderly and disabled persons. Eligibility is based on citizenship and means-testing. Here women are over-represented in receiving minimum pension and social assistance (Bertranou et al., 2002).

Apart from the low level of guaranteed minimum income, evidence has increasingly shown that the three pillars of the scheme introduced by Pinochet failed to cover various groups and provide for insured who did not meet eligibility criteria (for example, contributions equivalent to 20 years), among which women and self-employed were again over-represented.

This led the democratic regime of the Coalition of Parties for Democracy (CPD/

Concertación) that came into power in 1991 to remedy some of the negative effects, although it did not change the basic structure of the model. In March of 2008, Law 20.255 created the 'Solidarity Pension Scheme' (SPS/Sistema de Pensiones Solidarias) that replaced the social assistance scheme (PASIS). It builds on a basic non-contributory old-age and invalidity pension (provided after the age of 65 for citizens with more than 20 years of residence in Chile and who belong to the 60 per cent population with the lowest income), and thus includes low-income groups, and other groups not entitled to a minimum pension or a social assistance pension. Gender inequalities were addressed by legislating a minimum wage for domestic workers, a maternity grant for all women having contributed at least once to the pension system, and providing access to pension benefits after divorce. Minimum pensions and social assistance benefits were raised. Further institutional elements contained emphasising information, transparency and citizen participation. These reforms suggest that the state is reconsidering its role and responsibility by reorganising social citizenship status (Mesa-Lago, 2008). Women represented as many as 80 per cent of the applicants for a pension from Chile Solidario between July and November 2008, although originally it had been estimated by the government that they would only constitute 60 per cent.

Despite reforms, the crucial fully funded capitalised pillar based on actuarial logic remains problematic: individual capitalisation hampers gender equity in old age due to women's unequal opportunities within the persistent gendered division of labour in the household and labour market.

Costa Rica's pension model
In Costa Rica in the 1940s, the Catholic Church, the Communist Party and groups of the ruling class cooperated to implement various social institutions, most importantly, the Costa Rican Social Insurance Fund (CCSS/Caja Costarricense de Seguro Social), an insurance for health and pension. This was mandatory for all employed workers earning up to a defined income level. A constitutional amendment was passed in 1961 stipulating universalisation of its services (health and pension) within ten years. It was successively extended to include self-employed workers and the rural population. Originally financed by the state and workers, employers were included in sharing the burden in 1971. This was the most progressive pension model in Latin America at the time and its principal tenets have remained core to social security protection in the country. In 1974 social assistance was introduced and included women as dependants (wives).

The economic crisis in the 1980s led to pension system reforms. Laws to reform the public sector and special pension plans were passed in 1991, 1992 and 1995. These abolished privileges, and/or unified or closed down several single insurance plans, modified eligibility requirements, reduced benefit levels and increased women's retirement age to that of men. The aim was to implement a universal basic insurance for the whole population and to integrate wealthier groups by means of private complementary individual savings schemes. Law 7523 established the multi-pillar system in 2000 regulating entitlements and benefit levels. Reflecting Costa Rica's established pattern of consensual policy-making practices, reforms resulted from constant discussions between governmental actors and stakeholders from various groups: workers, providers and beneficiaries.[3]

Today, the first and central pillar consists of a highly redistributive contributory pension based on collective capitalisation financed by employees, employers and the state. It targets family protection and is mandatory for employed and self-employed. The scheme is progressive, with contributions and benefits being defined, and calculated as the average of the last 240 wages. Eligibility requires 25 years of contribution with earlier retirement as an option. This pillar is conducive to gender equity even if benefits are at a very low level.

The second, individual capitalisation, pillar is mandatory for all employees insured in the first pillar and voluntary for informally or self-employed persons. Individual capitalisation pillars increase existing gender inequalities in the labour market in old age as contributions and benefits are linked tightly. The third pillar relates to voluntary saving. It facilitates early retirement and benefits the wealthy.

Social assistance secures a minimum pension for destitute people. Eligibility depends on having Costa Rican nationality, means-testing, and not receiving income from the other pension pillars. Aside from the fact that this discriminates against non-naturalised Nicaraguan migrants, who are commonly thought to constitute at least 5 per cent of the Costa Rican population, the income level is too low to cover basic needs. In 2000, 20 per cent of all people aged 65 and older received a non-contributory (*Regimen No-contributivo*/RNC) pension among which widows and women are disproportionately represented (Bertranou et al., 2002).

Costa Rica followed a moderate path to reduce structural deficits and liberalised only gradually. Social achievements were maintained to buffer the adjustments (Budowksi and Suter, 2009). Reform pressures did not dismantle the public pension, since this was complemented by private individual savings schemes. However, despite high coverage rates, the benefit levels of social assistance and the crucial redistributive pillar remain low; the recently introduced pillars require further analysis yet point to greater gendered inequalities in old age.

Comparison and conclusion
Chile and Costa Rica differ regarding the structure and development of the labour market, and the political balance of power and the political systems. They have a long-standing but different history of welfare institutions dating back to the 1920s and 1940s respectively. Until the 1970s, both countries improved social protection and population coverage rates successively.

Before its reforms in 1981, Chile's pension programmes covered approximately two-thirds of the economically active, and somewhat more of the employed population. Costa Rica, although economically only weakly developed at that time, managed to cover approximately one-half of the active population. Both countries had a high coverage of women in comparison to most other countries in Latin America. They also managed to balance social and economic goals and achieved a good performance (Segura-Ubiergo, 2007).

Chile and Costa Rica followed different reform paths in the world economic crisis (hitting Chile in 1970s and Costa Rica in the 1980s). Pinochet implemented a radical programme of trade liberalisation and market-oriented reform and redesigned old-age pension as a fully funded individualised capitalisation scheme that was not fundamentally altered even in the 1990s when Chile returned to democracy.

Costa Rica, a democratic country, with executive authority dispersed among various branches of government, did not implement radical reforms; moreover, the moderate reforms were the result of constant negotiations between multiple national and international interest groups, including women's organisations.

In 2000, both countries had high coverage rates of the elderly receiving pensions, and in both women's coverage rate was about ten per cent lower than men's with consequences for dependency on non-contributory pensions (Bertranou et al., 2002).

The Chilean system is more effective and generous than that of Costa Rica, yet despite its recent reforms is less gender-equitable. For one, Chile's dictatorship impacted profoundly on political participation; women's needs were attended to by maternal policies and not in terms of rights. Women remained dependent on their spouses or on the state. The state, however, reduced its responsibility to mitigate contingencies and considered the market the primary provider of welfare. Thus, gendered labour market inequalities impacted strongly in old age. The new democratically elected government has remedied some consequences without substantially reforming the model's structure, even if Bachelet's socialist government's most recent reforms (in 2008) suggest that certain changes are taking place in the way the state–citizenship relation is thought of (for example, in respect of maternity leave, accounting for live births in old-age pension, and enabling divorced women's access to pensions).

Costa Rica designed policy measures on the basis of democratic consensus, targeting inclusion of different population groups. Gender equity, human, women and children's rights were on the feminist agenda, and women's organisations participated in designing the pension reforms. Thus, different life trajectories and experiences of men and women were acknowledged and compensatory benefit levels in the pension scheme accepted. Responsibilities were shared among the state, markets and families/individuals. Nonetheless, gender inequalities remain. The gendered division of labour has not changed, women are over-represented among the poor, and pension coverage remains lower among the poor than the non-poor. By the same token, the reforms of the main pillar are conducive to gender equity in contrast to the recent capitalisation pillar when inequalities in the labour market exist.

Chile is improving transparency, information, education, participation and supervision. Although not mandatory as in Costa Rica, Chile is motivating employers to contribute to pension schemes voluntarily. Self-employed workers in Chile are still not obliged to affiliate as in Costa Rica. Yet since 2008, as in Costa Rica, Chile now also accounts for different life trajectories in old-age pension benefits. In Costa Rica negative impacts for women are that pension age and contribution duration have been raised. In comparison to Chile, wage replacement rates and social assistance are lower.

Substantial differences remain between Chile and Costa Rica: although in Chile the Solidarity Pension Scheme is explicitly targeting (gender) inequalities, has improved coverage of formerly non-entitled population groups, and has increased benefit levels, because old age provision continues to build on private capitalisation it continues to lack redistributive elements that account for structural social inequalities.

In Costa Rica, the contributory old-age and invalidity pension, constituting the core pillar, addresses social inequalities by progressive redistribution and consideration of different social roles. Although this pillar is more gender-equitable than the Chilean one, it disposes of less capital and the pensions provide insufficient means for survival. Consequently, Chile performs better. In both countries the individual capitalisation scheme is contribution-defined and thus reproduces existing inequalities in the labour market.

Both the main pension pillar structures as well as the overall package of pillars still vary considerably: Costa Rica's main pillar is one of collective responsibility and relies on contributions of employees, employers and the state. Chile's main pillar, by contrast, emphasises individual responsibility.

Pension policies in both countries still need to privilege women to counter their lifetime disadvantages at home and in the labour market. Such privileges might not appear beneficial theoretically because they institutionalise gender differences. However, if stakeholders and social actors are involved and participate in reform design, a pragmatic focus considers these to be favourable, as participation enables change in future. Beyond this, and in order to more roundly address women's poverty in old age, policy measures need to focus on all those services and interventions which have recently been cut back at the expense of non-contributory pensions, such as childcare facilities, school meals, housing, and programmes for women's empowerment. The latter substantially counter inequalities in the labour market and may thereby contribute in a major way to reducing inequalities based on the gendered division of labour.

Notes

1. The Bismarckian insurance and redistribution scheme was introduced in Germany in the mid-nineteenth century. Contributions and benefits are closely linked, and financed by workers, employers, and sometimes the state. The Bismarckian model smoothes out lifetime income and provides for the maintenance of social status. The Beveridge model, by contrast, which was introduced in England in the mid-twentieth century, is universal in scope. It focuses on poverty relief, is available to all citizens as a last resort, and there are no links between contributions and benefits since the model is financed by taxpayers.
2. Chile has a lower compulsory retirement age for women; 60 versus 65 for men. As of 2005, women and men at the age of 60 had an estimated additional life expectancy of 23.4 and 19.5 years respectively.
3. These included representatives of the CCSS, the Ministry for Labour and Social Security, the National Institute for Women, the Pension Supervision Bureau (SuPen/Superintendencia de Pensiones de Costa Rica), the Defensory of the Residents, the Ministry of Finance and Economic Planning, the employers' sector, trade unions, and the cooperative and the solidarity movement (see Martínez Franzoni, 2005).

Select bibliography

Arenas De Mesa, Alberto and Veronica Montecinos (1999) 'The privatisation of social security and women's welfare: gender effects of the Chilean reform', *Latin American Research Review*, **34** (3), 7–37.

Bertranou, Fabio, Carmen Solorio and Wouter Van Ginneken (eds) (2002) *Pensiones No Contributivas y Asistenciales: Argentina, Brasil, Chile, Costa Rica y Uruguay*, Santiago de Chile: Organización Internacional de Trabajo.

Budowski, Monica and Christian Suter (2009) 'Lateinamerika als Modernisierungsvorbild? Vom korporatistisch-klientelistischen zum neoliberalen Sozialpolitikmodell', in Peter Fleer and Stephan Scheuzger (eds), *Die Moderne in Lateinamerika. Zentren und Peripherien des Wandels*, Berlin: Vervuert Verlag, pp. 377–404.

Martínez Franzoni, Juliana (2005) *Undécimo Informe sobre el Estado de la Nación en Desarrollo Humano Sostenible. Informe Final*, San José: Estado de la Nación.

Mesa-Lago, Carmelo (2008) 'Social protection in Chile: reforms to improve equity', *International Labour Review*, **147** (4), 377–402.

Sainsbury, Diane (1996) 'Women's and men's social rights: gendering dimensions of welfare states', in Diane Sainsbury (ed.), *Gendering Welfare States*, London: Sage, pp. 150–69.

Segura-Ubiergo, Alex (2007) *The Political Economy of the Welfare State in Latin America*, Cambridge: Cambridge University Press.

35 Gender, poverty and pensions in the United Kingdom
Jane Falkingham, Maria Evandrou and Athina Vlachantoni

Introduction
Across the developed world women are more likely than men to experience poverty in old age as a result of the way their work/life/care patterns interact with the entitlement rules of pension systems (Ginn et al., 2001). The pension problem for women originates in pension structures that were designed to provide pensions directly to men by virtue of their employment record and indirectly to women by virtue of their marital bond to their spouse. However, women's likelihood of being in poverty in old age can be smaller or greater depending on the extent to which pension systems reward, or at least do not penalise, lifecourses that are interrupted and that include periods caring for dependent children or adults (Leitner, 2001). For instance, pension systems that award pensions relative to individuals' employment records can be detrimental to women if they strictly reward long and continuous employment records and do not take caring periods into account. Similarly, pension systems that award flat-rate pensions can be beneficial to many women, as long as these flat-rate benefits are adequate to lift them out of poverty. This chapter provides first, a summary of the issues linking the areas of gender, pension protection and poverty in the developed world; second, an overview of the British pension system and the most recent reforms in this policy field; and third, a set of recommendations for the continuous gender-sensitive design of pension protection in the United Kingdom (UK) and beyond.

Gender, poverty and pensions: an overview of the issues
The feminisation of poverty in old age is likely to occur as a result of the combined effect of behavioural or lifecourse differences on the one hand, and institutional features of modern pension systems (Falkingham and Rake, 1999). This section outlines, first, the areas where differences in men's and women's work/care patterns can impact on their pension accumulation and, second, the ways in which such differentials can be treated by pension systems that operate under different principles of pension entitlement and distribution.

Gender differences in work/care patterns
The main gender differences relevant to work/care patterns fall into five main categories.

1. Women live longer than men Population ageing affects women adversely in that women live longer than men on average, and are therefore more likely to experience the death of their spouse, to live alone in the older old ages and to face a poverty risk for longer in old age.

2. Women tend to work less than men, and often part-time   In spite of increasing rates of labour force participation among women since the 1970s, there remain significant male–female differences in this area. More men than women work, and more men than women work full-time, which impacts on their income throughout their lifecourse and in old age (see below). In the UK, the shorter and often interrupted working lives of women can have an adverse impact on their entitlement to both the basic state pension as well as additional occupational and private pensions.

3. Women tend to provide more care than men   Throughout their lifecourse, women are more likely to provide care to persons in the household or family who need it, be it children or disabled or elderly persons. The indirect effect of caring on pension incomes is dual: on the one hand periods of caring result in lower lifetime earnings and therefore lower pension contributions to private insurance schemes, and on the other hand periods of caring can also jeopardise the carer's entitlement to the basic state pension (see also Tonkiss, Chapter 22, this volume). Recent reforms in the British pension system, as outlined below, have contributed to the better recognition of caring periods towards both the basic state and private pension insurance but still fail to recompense women fully for their caring responsibilities.

4. Women tend to earn less than men   When women do enter the labour market, they are more likely to earn less than their male counterparts, affecting the level of their contributions to private pension insurance. In countries like the UK, where the basic state pension has remained at a low level, it is income from private sources that determines whether or not an individual will face a poverty risk in old age.

5. Women tend to have less access to occupational and private sources of income and to rely more on public sources of income   Fewer women than men contribute to occupational and private pension schemes, and when they do, they tend to contribute smaller amounts than men. These small amounts may still be sufficient to exclude them from means-tested benefits, the so-called 'occupational pensions trap'.

Gender differentials and pension system design
Women's pension incomes are dependent on the complex interaction between their labour market behaviour and the institutional characteristics of any given pension system. Gender differences in work/care patterns are treated differently by different pension systems, and this is why the entitlement structure of pension systems is a crucial determinant of women's pension protection (see also Budowski, Chapter 34, this volume; Vera-Sanso, Chapter 33, this volume). For the purpose of this chapter, the effects of two distinctions between pension systems on gender differentials will be briefly explored: first, the distinction between earnings-related and flat-rate pension systems, and second, the distinction between universal and means-tested benefits provided in old age.

Earnings-related pension schemes, where the pension entitlement is based on the individual's average earnings over a specified period, can be beneficial to women whose employment records approximate the typical male employment records, that is, long, continuous and with increasing earnings. However, women's entitlement in such systems can be hampered by breaks in their employment history, periods of part-time work that often equate with lower earnings, as well as a lower number of contribution years per se, which may not reach the minimum requirement. Conversely, flat-rate pension schemes offer a minimum (or basic) pension that is often tied to a minimum contribution amount, like in the UK, which can guarantee a pension income to women with typical female employment records. Nevertheless, what makes the difference for women's pension incomes in either earnings-related or flat-rate pension schemes is the extent to which periods spent outside the labour market can count towards the qualifying years for the pension entitlement. This is an area where the British pension system has made significant progress following the most recent pension reforms, as the following section demonstrates.

Most countries in the developed world, including the UK, offer means-tested benefits to older people who have not accumulated adequate contributions based on their employment and/or caring records. This is in contrast to universal pension schemes, which can be found in countries like Denmark, Finland and the Netherlands, and which take the duration of residence into account for the pension entitlement rather than a person's work and/or care record, or their individual or their household's income. Given that means-tested benefits constitute the last resort for older people whose income falls below a certain income threshold, it is not surprising that women in the UK have traditionally tended to rely on such benefits as a source of pension income compared to occupational or other private pension income (Falkingham and Rake, 1999).

Women, poverty and pensions in the British context
When the 'New Labour' government came to power in the UK in 1997 an estimated 2.9 million pensioners were living in 'poverty', of whom nearly three-quarters (70 per cent) were female (DWP, 2008). The following decade witnessed a transformation of the pensions landscape, with changes to all parts of the system, from reform of eligibility criteria for the basic state pension through to regulation of occupational and personal pensions and changes in the value and scope of means-tested benefits (Evandrou and Falkingham, 2009). This section outlines the most important reforms to the minimum safety net and the three tiers (basic, earnings-related and private) of pension protection in the UK since New Labour came into power in 1997, and their likely effects on women's prospects of pension entitlement.

The issue of older women's poverty is closely linked with the development of the modern British welfare state. The UK welfare state was constructed on the assumption that women would be largely dependent on their husbands' earnings during their working lives and on their pensions in retirement – the so-called 'breadwinner' model (Land, 1994). In the early 1930s, when Beveridge was developing his proposals, only 10 per cent of married women were in the workforce. Hence, the state pension was designed to provide a basic income for married couples, based on the main earner's contributions, usually the husband's. However, changes in social norms and the decline of marriage as a lifelong contract has made reliance on a husband for income in later life an increasingly unacceptable and risky strategy for women. As argued in the 2004 Report of the Pensions Commission, 'an effective pension system for the future must be one in which the vast majority of women accrue pension entitlements, both state and private, in their own right'.[1]

The first element of the British pension system to be reformed by New Labour was the minimum safety net, which until 1998 had been a unified system of Income Support, providing the same level of benefit to those on low income regards of age. In order to help lift more older people out of poverty and to reward people who saved for their retirement, in 1999 Income Support for people aged 60 and over was replaced by the Minimum Income Guarantee and then in 2003 by the Pension Credit (PC). Pension Credit consists of a guarantee element, payable to those aged 60 and over living on a low income, and a saving element, payable up to a certain threshold to those aged 65 and over with small amounts of savings. The combined value of the Basic State Pension (BSP) and maximum level of PC is now payable at a rate just above 50 per cent of median earnings – in theory, effectively lifting all pensioners out of relative poverty. However, there remain significant problems of take-up of means-tested benefits with many pensioners, especially older women, failing to claim their entitlements. In 2006/2007 between 33 and 41 per cent of entitled pensioners failed to claim the PC they were entitled to.

The first, or basic, tier of pension protection was significantly reformed through the 2007 Pensions Act. The real value of the BSP has fallen continuously since 1979 as a result of being linked with growth in prices rather than earnings. In 2008 it was estimated that the BSP was equivalent to just 16 per cent of national average earnings compared with 24 per cent in 1979 (Evandrou and Falkingham, 2009). The New Labour government has promised that 'subject to affordability and [the government's] fiscal position' the link of the BSP with earnings will be restored between 2012 and 2015. In addition to an improvement to the value of the first-tier pension that will benefit poorer older people more broadly, the 2007 Pensions Act has significantly changed the rules for pension entitlement for carers, many of whom are women. First, the minimum number of qualifying years for the BSP has been reduced to 30 (this used to be 39 years for women and 44 years for men). This will bring full entitlement to many women who previously had only partial entitlement. Second, the system of Home Responsibilities Protection (HRP), introduced in 1978, will be replaced from April 2010 with a system of weekly credits, effectively reducing the number of qualifying years for carers of children or severely disabled persons to 20 years. This means that many carers will now have full entitlement to a BSP.

The second tier of pension protection, which has been particularly important in the British system due to the relatively low value of the BSP, has also been reformed. In 2002, the State Earnings Related Pension Scheme (SERPS) was replaced by the State Second Pension (S2P). The S2P was designed to boost the incomes of the low paid and those with significant caring responsibilities, the majority of whom are women. However, through the 2007 Pensions Act the S2P will be gradually transformed to a secondary flat-rate pension benefit, which in contrast to the BSP, will be indexed to prices and therefore will decrease in real value over time. If the Pension Credit remains linked to earnings and S2P to prices, this means that over time more older women will fall into means-testing during later life despite entering retirement with pension entitlements that lift them out of poverty.

The third and final tier of pension protection, including occupational and other forms of private pension arrangements such as savings, has been one of the most challenging areas of policy-making for New Labour, and one from which women with atypical employment records are the least likely to benefit in pension income terms. As Figure 35.1 shows, fewer women than men contribute to a private pension. The government's 1998 Green Paper described occupational pensions as 'one of the great welfare success

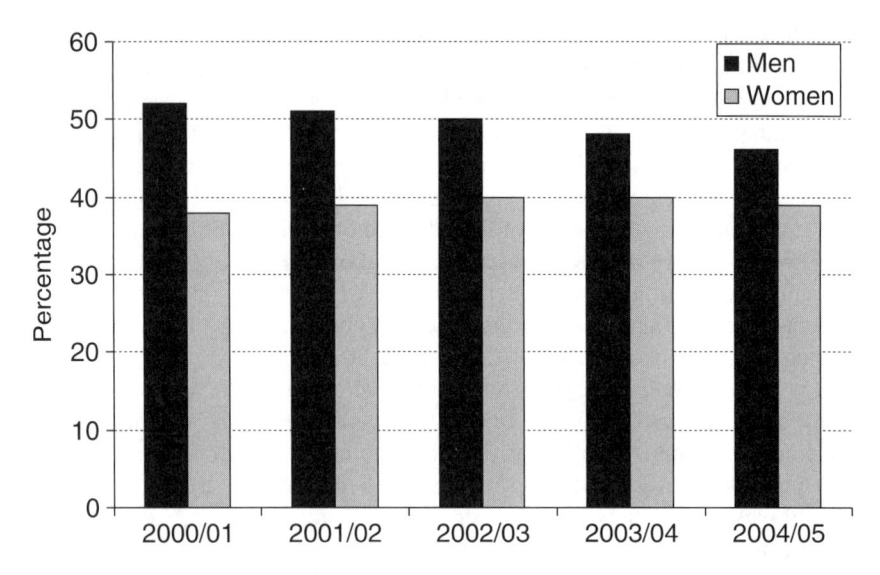

Note: Working age defined as 20 years to State Pension Age (currently 65 for men and 60 for women).

Source: Data drawn from the Department of Work and Pensions' Family Resources Survey 2004/2005, available at: http:www.dwp.gov.uk/asd/frs.2004_5 (accessed 28 June 2009).

Figure 35.1 Percentage of men and women of working age contributing to a private pension

stories of the century'; however when Stakeholder Pensions were introduced in 2001, the take-up was disappointingly low. The government has more recently opted for a 'soft compulsion' approach through the introduction of the 2007 Pensions Act which provides for automatic enrolment into Personal Accounts or an equivalent employer-based scheme with effect from 2012 for all persons aged 22 and over.

What do these recent pension reforms mean for women with typical female lifecourses that often include low earnings and significant periods devoted to persons in need of care? First, New Labour has signalled a commitment to raising the value of the BSP, which, combined with the means-tested and saving-enticing PC, is often the only source of income for women in old age. In addition, the shift to a weekly credit that can contribute towards both the BSP and the S2P is an important recognition of the activity of caring within society that can boost the pension income of carers. Finally, the reforms relating to occupational or other kinds of private pension protection are less likely to benefit those persons in the population with low lifetime incomes, many of whom are women. However, in light of population ageing and changing family structures that result in more older people living alone, the recognition of care provision for older adults, and not based solely on a measure of disability, must be at the centre of future policy planning in the area of pension entitlement.

Women and pensions: a way forward

The history of, and recent reforms in, the British pension system offer a useful framework in examining the key principles of a pension system aimed at balancing the goals of income adequacy, personal choice and reward (or compensation) for a person's contribution to social and/or economic production over their lifecourse. If universality in pension entitlement, based solely on individuals' age and residence, is not a viable policy option, then the recognition of caring responsibilities in entitlements towards first- and second-tier pension protection, as exemplified by the British system, is a fundamental step in the right direction. However, if women's historical reliance on these two tiers is to continue, then the value of benefits in flat-rate systems must be significantly above the poverty line, while the minimum qualifying conditions in earnings-related systems must be relaxed. Otherwise women will continue to face a means-tested old age.

Note

1. This quote comes from page 259 of the first report, which is available at: http://www.webarchive.org.uk/wayback/archive/20070801230000/http://www.pensionscommission.org.uk/publications/2004/annrep/full-report.pdf (accessed 1 July 2009).

Select bibliography

Department for Work and Pensions DWP (2008) *The Pensioner Income Series 2006–07*, London: National Statistics Office.
Evandrou, Maria and Jane Falkingham (2009). 'Pensions and income security in later life', in John Hills, Tom Sefton and Kitty Stewart (eds), *Towards a More Equal Society? Poverty, Inequality and Policy Since 1997*, Bristol: Policy Press, pp. 157–78.
Falkingham, Jane and Katherine Rake (1999) *Partnership in Pensions: Delivering a Secure Retirement for Women?*, Centre for the Analysis of Social Exclusion (CASE) Discussion Paper 24, London: London School of Economics.
Ginn, Jay, Debra Street and Sara Arber (2001) *Women, Work and Pensions: International Issues and Prospects*, Philadelphia, PA: Open University Press.
Leitner, Sigrid (2001) 'Sex discrimination within EU pension systems', *Journal of European Social Policy*, **11** (2), 99–115.
Land, Hilary (1994) 'The demise of the male breadwinner – in practice but not in theory: a challenge for social security', in Sally Baldwin and Jane Falkingham (eds), *Social Security and Social Change: New Challenges to Beveridge*, London: Harvester Wheatsheaf, pp. 100–115.

PART IV

GENDER, 'RACE' AND MIGRATION

36 Assessing poverty, gender and well-being in 'Northern' indigenous communities
Janet Hunt

Indigenous people are among the poorest, most marginalised people in the world. There are some 370 million indigenous people globally, many of whom would be among the billion categorised as the absolute poor. Even in the developed settler state countries such as Australia, New Zealand, Canada and the United States (USA), this marginalisation and relative poverty remains the case (see Tonkiss, Chapter 22, this volume). The social consequences are that in Australia, for example, life expectancy and other social indicators for indigenous people may rank with those of much poorer developing countries, such as Cambodia and Bangladesh. Such countries are 'developed' but within, there are pockets of extreme poverty and marginalisation.

However, there are different perceptions about what development and poverty mean in indigenous communities compared to Western social science measures. Unless we understand these perceptions our efforts to reduce poverty and increase well-being may be misdirected and ultimately unsuccessful. Equally, there may be gendered differences within indigenous communities which are rarely attended to, as the emphasis on the differences in economic and social outcomes between indigenous and non-indigenous populations in such settler societies is the dominant type of analysis. Differences within indigenous populations are rarely explored.

In this chapter I investigate what indigenous people themselves see as important dimensions of their well-being, and how conceptualisations of gender differences in indigenous communities may vary from standard Western measures. I refer briefly to New Zealand efforts to generate Maori measures of well-being, and recent Australian and Canadian efforts to assess gender differences in indigenous communities.

Indigenous people and poverty

Research among indigenous people in western Sydney has revealed that for urban Australian indigenous people, poverty is best defined as having no familial networks to call upon, particularly for shelter and food.[1] Even those who were at income poverty levels at or below the Australian poverty line did not consider themselves to be poor if they were able to call upon extended family or kin networks to provide them with a roof over their head or a feed. Their family or kin network was the critical factor in their own perception of poverty, and access through that network to shelter and food were the important requirements. For these people, poverty was about a lack of kin relationships which could provide for their needs

That indigenous people construct poverty differently from Western measurement dimensions is evident in work being undertaken through the United Nations Permanent Forum on Indigenous Issues (UNPFII). In recognising that existing indicators do not adequately reflect the perspectives and aspirations of indigenous people, the UNPFII convened a series of regional workshops to develop some appropriate global indicators. Apart from the problem of the national scale for which data is usually gathered, and hence its limited practical value for detailed local or regional planning (whether for discrete remote indigenous communities or in mixed regional areas where indigenous people might be in a minority), there is also a problem of the data collected being based simply on the measurement of gaps or deficits in areas such as employment, education, and health (see Taylor, 2006). Such deficit approaches can provide useful advocacy data for champions of indigenous rights, but can simultaneously reinforce negative stereotypes in the settler society of 'failure' in indigenous communities. This can be demoralising and self-fulfilling to indigenous people. Such measures also emphasise goals of statistical equality which reflect the dominant society's priorities rather than adequately accounting for differences in indigenous aspirations.

In particular, indicators such as those being used for the Millennium Development Goals (MDGs) may not include matters of high priority for indigenous people, such as participation in decision-making, access to traditional lands, language maintenance, ability to practice culture and so on, all of which may have a great bearing on the perception of well-being or poverty of an indigenous group. Such indicators are commonly sought by indigenous people across a range of settler states. Indeed indigenous people generally place great emphasis on the non-material, cultural and spiritual aspects of their well-being which are neglected in orthodox measures. The challenge is to find a broad range of social indicators which reflect an indigenous perspective on development and well-being. These may include certain current indicators defined by governments, but would certainly go beyond them to incorporate indicators defined as important by indigenous people themselves.

The work by UNPFII is ongoing, with some proposed indicators available, which cover a number of themes and issues:

1. Security of rights to territories, lands and natural resources.
2. Integrity of indigenous cultural heritage.
3. Respect for identity and non-discrimination.
4. Fate control (self-determination or ability to guide one's destiny).
5. Full, informed and effective participation.
6. Culturally appropriate education.
7. Health.
8. Access to infrastructure and basic services.
9. Extent of external threats.
10. Material well-being.
11. Demographic patterns (UNPFII, 2008).

While implicit to the measurement of poverty is a deficit assumption, the goal of reducing poverty is presumably to increase human well-being – yet research among indigenous people indicates that this requires a more holistic measure than we currently utilise. For example, such a measure would try to capture all the elements of the indigenous concept of well-being discussed above.

The term 'development' of course has very negative connotations for many indigenous people, who are often its victims, as those most negatively affected by mines, dams, and population dispersal for projects of modernisation. They may prefer to function in a 'hybrid economy' (a concept developed by Professor Jon Altman at the Centre for Aboriginal Economic Policy Research at the Australian National University) whereby they generate a living through the intersections of customary activity, state support and the market. Having 'mainstream' employment five days or more per week may not be their measure of success. Rather their abilities to retain social and cultural networks, care for their 'country' (the land and sea for which they are culturally responsible), and retain their cultural practices may be very high priorities in their lives. Development, for many indigenous people, would entail greater security in these dimensions as well as better physical conditions.

For an indigenous person, the concept of *deprivation* might focus more on loss of connection to family and kin, land, language and culture, than on lack of income, important though that might be in the contemporary world. We therefore need to recognise the cultural foundations of any measure we develop, and consider how to develop indicators which can be sensitive to, and cognisant of, the cultural variations in conceptions of poverty and well-being across the world. We also need to be able to develop measures which could be more acceptable to indigenous peoples internationally than existing ones, since these peoples represent a significant subgroup of the population generally considered to be living in poverty at a global scale. This suggests more holistic measures of deprivation (and development) are required.

Work in New Zealand on the Maori Statistics Framework is one valuable initiative in this direction. As Maori have won rights, settled Treaty claims and taken greater control over their own development, the statistical information they require has gone well beyond existing measures. Statistics New Zealand has therefore been working with Maori to develop meaningful indicators to measure progress in Maori development. Understanding Maori well-being to be the goal, and Maori development to be the process to achieve it, these statistics were based on an approach to development consistent with Amartya Sen's capability approach but contextualised by Maori. Thus, by combining Sen's theory and Maori concepts of development, a relevant statistical framework has been drafted. It encompasses 18 'areas of concern' (such as Maori language, Maori knowledge, social connections and attachments, income and expenditure, participation in political decision-making processes), and for each area considers six relevant 'dimensions': sustainability of *Te Ao Maori* (Maori inheritance), social capability, human resource potential, economic self-sufficiency, environmental sustainability and empowerment and enablement (Wereta and Bishop, 2004). This framework represents a valuable effort at measuring indigenous well-being as the goal of development.

Durie (2006) notes that whether measures are universally relevant or Maori-specific, the level of measurement (individual, subgroup, or the whole population) demands different indicators. For individuals, indicators must reflect spiritual, physical, mental and social parameters; for a Maori subgroup (*whānau*), measures should relate to capacities for working together, planning, nurturing and empowering others and transmitting culture; and for the Maori population as a whole, they must be able to measure human well-being *and* resource capacity, including Maori access to and enjoyment of a healthy environment, since central to indigeneity is a world view that human well-being cannot be separated from the natural environment. However, most measures remain at the individual level.

An initial effort at constructing a Community Well-Being Index has been undertaken in Canada, in order to compare First Nation communities with each other and with other Canadian communities. The Community Well-Being (CWB) Index uses four indicators (education, labour force activity, income and housing) and draws on standard census data to calculate a CWB score for all communities with over 65 inhabitants. This showed that on a scale of 0–1, where 1 is the highest, the average score for the 541 First Nations communities was 0.66, compared with 0.81 for other Canadian communities. Geographical differences emerged as the predominant factor in variation among First Nation communities, with those around Canada's borders generally rating better than those in the Prairie provinces. While this measure does not capture the multiple aspects of indigenous well-being discussed above, it is a useful attempt to measure well-being at a community level (INAC, 2004).

Measuring gender differences in well-being in indigenous communities
Some work on gender differences in well-being has also been undertaken in Canada. Researchers there have developed a Registered Indian Human Development Index drawing on Statistics Canada data, and explored the gender differences which this reveals. This showed a wider gender gap between Registered Indian men and women than the gender differences between other Canadians. This was especially evident among Indians living on reserves and settlements. Interestingly, women's scores were higher than men's in education and life expectancy measures, but lower in the measure of average income (INAC, 2004).

Some similar work is under way in Australia to construct a Gender-Related Index for indigenous Australians. Initial work, like that in Canada, has involved drawing on existing census data to explore gender differences in outcomes among indigenous people (Yap and Biddle, 2009), and was limited to data which is sex-disaggregated by indigenous status. In this work the major variables included related to employment to population ratio, income level, managerial or professional occupational status, and education (for instance, Year 12 completion, degree or equivalent qualification, or no schooling). The analysis was undertaken by the 37 indigenous regions into which Australia is divided for statistical purposes. One finding was that in most indigenous regions of Australia, there are more young men (that is, under 25 years) than women, but more women than men in the 55 years and over age group. As Yap and Biddle indicate, this may have social implications, since research in developing (and developed) countries indicates an association between gender imbalance favouring young men and social problems such as violence and crime (see Alexander, Chapter 41, this volume). As in Canada, the Australian research has also highlighted the higher educational levels of indigenous women compared to indigenous men. While these differences are also true in the non-indigenous population, the extent of the difference is considerably greater within the indigenous population, with more women completing high school and gaining university degrees. Furthermore, despite the higher educational achievements of women, indigenous men are more likely to be participating in the labour force, working full-time, and more likely to be employed as managers (although women are more numerous in professional occupations). One factor contributing to this labour force pattern may be the high fertility rates of indigenous women compared with other Australians (2.12 children versus 1.93 respectively). Young indigenous women (15–24 years) in particular have on average four times as many children as non-indigenous women in that age bracket; non-indigenous women tend to have their children later. However, Yap and Biddle (2009) suggest other factors may also be at work, such as residential location, educational levels, other sources of household income and interaction with the criminal justice system.

Higher educational achievement among indigenous women in Canada and Australia is also reflected in other indigenous communities, but is generating concerns. Arctic indigenous women in Greenland, Samiland (in Norway) and Eastern Siberia are worried about the impact on their communities of the numbers of young women moving away to gain education, leaving behind isolated communities of men living in poverty. Thus gender analysis can highlight issues facing men and communities, as well as women.

While this Australian analysis, like the Canadian research, is a useful start in bringing a gender lens to data on indigenous socio-economic status, clearly more work is required to reflect the issues that matter to indigenous people themselves. Yap and Biddle (2009) recognise that other data, such as on women's leadership, violence, imprisonment, substance abuse and language use among others, would all be important in a more fully developed gender-related index for indigenous Australia.

Capturing gendered indigenous health indicators
Research on a gender-based analysis within an Inuit cultural context[2] illustrates well some of the complexities and knowledge required to construct measures of well-being which are both culturally and gender sensitive in an indigenous context. Canada's 55 000 Inuit people live in extremely remote and small Arctic communities, mostly along the coast, and find that even measures relevant to other Aboriginal people in Canada may not capture the specificities of their situation. The non-governmental organisation (NGO) Pauktuutit Inuit Women of Canada is engaged in research to develop culturally relevant health indicators for Inuit women. Its initial work involved developing a culturally relevant Gender Based Analysis Framework, which would reflect an Inuit perspective. This research noted that while Inuit women remain interested in determinants of health of concern to other Canadian women, such as employment, income, educational attainment and so on, there are important additional aspects of their holistic approach to well-being which need to be factored in to any measurements. Thus, the Inuit Gender Based Analysis Framework proposes four major themes:

1. The Inuk woman, and her family and community.
2. Elders, culture and language.
3. Land, country and food.
4. Euro-Canadian economy, institutions and government (see Guillou and Rasmussen, 2007: 7).

In relation to the first theme, it is noted that Inuit women gain very high levels of support from extended family members in relation to childcare, compared with other Canadian women; often there may be three generations living close by. One measure of an Inuk woman's well-being may be the number of female relatives she has living within 5 kilometres. Decreases in this aspect of social connection could indicate greater isolation or greater dependence on more formal childcare services. Inuit households are also sites of production (for example, crafts, sewing, quilting, weaving and knitting small businesses), so measures of such production, not simply conventional household consumption, would be important to women, as well as measures of adequate household space to carry out such livelihood activities.

In relation to the second theme, learning from elders is as important as formal learning, so another measure of women's well-being may be related to their frequency of interaction with more senior members of the community. Furthermore, Inuit healing practices emphasise the role of people who have traditional ways of helping people heal themselves; so another well-being measure may relate to 'the availability of traditional health support and blended Inuit-European health services' (Guillou and Rasmussen, 2007: 15).

For Inuit women food is a critical aspect of their well-being. Hunting and gathering, and eating 'country' food, rather than shop-purchased foodstuffs, is central to their identity, yet there is a wide variation in the amount of this food that men and women eat. The high cost of hunting equipment appears to be a significant factor constraining women's ability to hunt and fish. Thus one suggested measure of women's well-being may be access to a functioning community freezer in which hunted food is stored and made freely available to those who need it. However, Inuit, particularly pregnant women, are also highly vulnerable to persistent organic pollutants and heavy metals (which are extremely concentrated in the Arctic region) in their food, so measures of these concentrations in different food sources (for example, caribou, polar bear, walrus, blubber) may allow women to make informed choices about the amount of toxins and fat levels in their diets.

Finally, Inuit women often find that regulatory regimes of the Euro-Canadian economy, which restrict Inuit hunting, Inuit midwifery, Inuit childcare and home businesses (for example, because they live in social housing and are not allowed to engage in business from them) can cause them stress. Indicators which could capture these regulatory restrictions which inhibit women's well-being are needed. This research illustrates well how much cultural context matters in relation to defining gender-sensitive measures of well-being.

In conclusion, the emerging research indicated in this chapter illustrates how important it is to foster research into more context-specific, gender-sensitive and culturally appropriate measures of poverty, development and well-being, to support the more culturally relevant development strategies necessary to achieve indigenous well-being in diverse contexts.

Notes

1. This research was conducted by Dr Julie Lahn, of the Centre for Aboriginal Economic Policy Research at The Australian National University (ANU) and was presented at a seminar on 24 September 2008 at ANU, entitled 'Aboriginal Poverty. What's Social Capital Got to Do With It?'. It had not been published at the time of writing.
2. Undertaken for the Paukuutit Inuit Women of Canada and Women's Health Bureau of Canada.

Select bibliography

Durie, Mason (2006) 'Measuring Maori well-being', New Zealand Treasury Guest Lecture Series, The Treasury, 1 The Terrace, Wellington, 1 August.
Guillou, Jessica and Derek Rasmussen (2007) 'Inuit Gender-Based Analysis Framework: excerpts from a report on the health of Pauktuutit Inuit Women of Canada', Ecojustice Review, available at: http://ecojusticeeducation.org/index.php?option=com_content&task=view&id=46&Itemid=4 (accessed 10 June 2009).

Indian and Northern Affairs Canada (INAC) (2004) *Measuring First Nations Well-Being*, Ottawa: Strategic Research and Analysis Directorate, Canada, available at: http://www.ainc-inac.gc.ca/ai/rs/pubs/re/wbp/wbp-eng.pdf (accessed 10 June 2009)

Taylor, John (2006) *Indigenous Peoples and Indicators of Well-Being: An Australian Perspective on UNFPII Global Frameworks*, CAEPR Working Paper No. 33/2006, Canberra: Australian National University.

United Nations Permanent Forum on Indigenous Issues (UNPFII) (2008) *Indicators of Well-being, Poverty and Sustainability Relevant to Indigenous Peoples*, report submitted to the seventh session of the UNPFII, E/C.19/2008/9, New York, 21 April–2 May, available at: http://daccessdds.un.org/doc/UNDOC/GEN/N08/247/04/PDF/N0824704.pdf?OpenElement (accessed 9 June 2009).

Wereta, Whetu and Darin Bishop (2004) 'Towards a Maori statistics framework' (Maori Statistics Unit, Statistics New Zealand), paper presented to Meeting on Indigenous Peoples and Indicators of Well-Being, Aboriginal Policy Research Conference, Ottawa, 22–23 March.

Yap, Mandy and Nicholas Biddle (2009), *Towards a Gender-related Index for Indigenous Australians*, Centre for Aboriginal Economic Policy Research (CAEPR) Working Paper No. 52, Canberra: Australian National University, available at: http://www.anu.edu.au/caper/Publications/WP/2009/WP52.php (accessed 19 October 2009).

37 Gender and ethnicity in the shaping of differentiated outcomes of Mexico's *Progresa-Oportunidades* conditional cash transfer programme
Mercedes González de la Rocha

Social impacts of economic crises, economic liberalisation and other local, regional, national and global changes are gender-differentiated. Women have been found to carry a heavier load of work and responsibilities when transformations in the economy occur (Benería, 1992; González de la Rocha, 1994). Since the 1990s, congruent with trends in Latin American social policy as a whole, programmes and policies related to poverty have enjoyed unparalleled priority throughout the whole region (Abel and Lewis, 2002). Social policy was redefined as a result, amongst other factors, of the post-Washington Consensus, which recognised that the social deficit accumulated during the years of crises and restructuring must be dealt with by social policy, which demanded that reducing poverty be the ultimate and primary objective of social programmes (Fine, 2001; Molyneux, 2006).

During the late 1990s, after prolonged and successive economic turmoil, social policy in Mexico experienced a significant upturn. In 1997, the *Programa de Educación, Salud y Alimentación* (Education, Healthcare and Nutrition Programme) was created. Known by its Spanish acronym, PROGRESA, this programme was the predecessor of the current *Oportunidades* and, since its creation, has focused on the application of conditional disbursals with the aim to influence – through improvements to diet, healthcare and education in the country's poorest families – the formation and strengthening of human capital in order to break the cycle of intergenerational reproduction of poverty. Today, *Oportunidades* has become the most important arm of Mexican social policy.

The poor are not a homogeneous mass and the outcomes of social programmes are as diverse as those of crises. Previous research findings highlighted factors and processes leading to the programme's long-term impact – attaining the objective of improving the life conditions of future generations of adults – and those which lead to short or immediate term impacts only (such as improved consumption). The analysis of data derived from annual external qualitative evaluations between the years 2000 and 2005 showed the programme's heterogeneous impacts in respect of progressive advantage accumulation according to household composition, differences in the amount and type of resources possessed by households, and the possibilities of converting such resources into real – and not only potential – assets (Escobar and González de la Rocha, 2008; González de la Rocha, 2006; see also Moser, Chapter 60, this volume). Among the households which showed a greater and longer term impact of the *Oportunidades* programme, with significant improvements in levels of children's educational attainment, and prospectively better occupational options in the future were: first, those in receipt of the programme's benefits since its creation (long-term exposure) where cash transfers coexist with at least one regular waged income; second, households in which both adult men and women work for a salary, and where the work of more than one adult female reduces tensions coming from women's waged and domestic work, besides the tasks demanded by the programme ('co-responsibilities'); and, third, households in an advanced stage of expansion where all or most of children are eligible for the programme's scholarships. At the other end of the spectrum, among households experiencing the fewest advantages from the programme – except in respect of short-term or minor increases in food consumption – were very young or elderly households with very precarious (low and irregular) participation in the labour market and overburdened breadwinner mothers lacking the help of other female adult members to comply with co-responsibilities and reproductive work, and elderly households with sick members suffering from chronic diseases.

Conditional cash transfer (CCT) programmes rely on women's (mothers') involvement in the programme's activities, overloading them with responsibilities (Escobar and González de la Rocha, 2008; Molyneux, 2006; see also Bradshaw and Linneker, Chapter 79, this volume). Most CCT programmes guide their actions by a household notion that does not resemble real household life (a traditional model where women are thought as only in charge of reproductive work), with tensions arising from the juxtaposition of co-responsibilities (what the programme demands from women) and women's work (both as breadwinners and care providers). Scarce attention has been given to such programmes' gendered long-term impacts on the young generation, and even less to ethnic-differentiated effects of CCTs. The maturity of the *Oportunidades* programme, after ten years of operation, allows us now to assess generational changes in the educational outcomes of beneficiaries (grantholders), comparing parents and children from both beneficiary and non-beneficiary households, as well as inter-ethnic outcomes in school levels amongst beneficiaries and non-beneficiaries, indigenous and *mestizo* (non-indigenous) young males and females who started receiving the programme's support since early childhood, ten years previously.[1] Former grantholders are those who received the grant during a variable period of time, whether they remained at school or not. The analysis presented in this chapter focuses on the differential impact of *Oportunidades* among the population cohort with the longest potential exposure (today) by gender and ethnicity.

The *Oportunidades* programme
Since its inception, households which are to benefit from the programme are selected by the application of technical criteria based on poverty indicators and by establishing, as a condition of entering the scheme, the obligation of each beneficiary to hold co-responsibility. The disbursals are made bi-monthly through bank accounts or directly to the mothers within households, who are the *titulares* or legally entitled beneficiaries under the programme. The support is provided on condition that the beneficiaries fulfil certain requirements: regular school attendance by the children, medical appointments by all family members and punctual and regular attendance at the health chats. Although not formally part of the requirements, many female *titulares* must also participate in collective work organised by the doctors and nurses, with the aim of cleaning up schools, clinics and the town's public areas (the central plaza or the streets, for instance) or get involved in campaigns against dengue fever and other diseases through community sanitation schemes.

The programme offers different types of support. Selected households receive supplemental nutritional in-kind assistance for pregnant women and breastfeeding mothers, for all infants between 6 months and 2 years of age and for young children, aged between 2 and 5, who show signs of malnutrition. In addition, the selected families receive cash disbursals to complement household earnings, to promote a better diet (the nutritional cash support) and educational grants (also in cash) for school-age children from the third year of primary school. Until 2001, education grants were restricted to students from year three of primary school up to the third year of secondary school. In 2001 the scholarships were extended to include children attending high schools. The grants are disbursed according to school level, with greater amounts going to those in higher years and with females receiving more financial support than their male counterparts (this gender differential begins from the first year of secondary education as an affirmative action against observed gendered differences in school attendance, when the programme was created, with girls and young females deserting schools before boys and young males).[2]

The development of the programme has been overwhelming. Operations began in rural areas in 1997, and since then have expanded both in terms of the geographical territory covered and in the number of households now involved. Today, five million rural and urban households are receiving support from the *Oportunidades* programme.

Questions and analysis
Short-term impacts have been found by previous studies, such as the rise in school attendance among children of beneficiary households, the increase in consumption (particularly food), and housing improvements. Three variables are crucial in the present analysis: the long-term exposure to the programme, ethnic ascription and gender. This is the first study, in the entire history of *Progresa-Oportunidades*, that takes ethnicity into consideration in order to assess if the programme produces different outcomes among indigenous and non-indigenous populations. Individuals who started receiving the programme's grants when they were third-year primary schoolchildren in 1998 are now old enough to have finished school and some of them are fully incorporated in the labour market. Ethnographic fieldwork was conducted in four Mexican states – Chiapas, Chihuahua, Oaxaca and Sonora – characterised by ethnic diversity (coexistence of indigenous and *mestizos*). An analytical sample was created in order to collect information on a balanced number of households (case studies) according to: (1) ethnicity (indigenous and non-indigenous) and (2) status within the programme (long-term beneficiary households – since 1998 – and non-beneficiary households). Beneficiary households were selected only if, in 1998, they had at least one child in the third year of primary school and started receiving the programme's grant then. Non-beneficiary households had to be as similar as possible as beneficiary households in 1998 (in terms of access to land and other productive assets, parents' education and occupation, housing characteristics), including the age of children and their levels of education at that year but, since these households were not incorporated (non-beneficiaries), had at least one child in the third year of primary school who did not receive the grant. Today, those children are between 18 and 20 years old and provide us with fertile quasi-experimental analytical possibilities.

Information from all parents and children or other household members aged 15–25 from 183 case studies of households (793 individuals) conformed with the requirements of the database under scrutiny.[3]

Research findings

Gender and ethnic gaps are social facts in Mexico amid the generation of adults, more so among the elderly, particularly in the context of the economically deprived. Women from the parental generation attained lower levels of education than men, and the non-indigenous are favoured – in most social and economic indicators – vis-à-vis members of indigenous groups. The analysis of data collected in four rural ethnically diverse regions (with presence of both indigenous and *mestizo* populations) where the *Oportunidades* programme has been in operation since 1997 shows, first, that the gender gap has reversed among the generation of young men and women who were exposed to *Progresa-Oportunidades* since they were 8 or 9 years old and, second, that the ethnic gap has closed significantly in the case of males and has reversed in the case of females.[4]

Intergenerational mobility in school levels rose by two years with the influence of the *Oportunidades* programme. This means that while non-beneficiary children surpass their parents in terms of educational attainment by three years, children who were exposed to the programme exhibit an increase of five years relative to their parents. The greatest impact in terms of the intergenerational mobility in schooling is found among the indigenous population, mainly because indigenous parents show lower levels of schooling than non-indigenous parents and indigenous beneficiaries are attaining similar or higher levels of schooling than *mestizos*, with indigenous young women heading this new trend: the attained school level of male indigenous beneficiaries is 9.63 (equivalent to almost one year over secondary school, compared with 6.48 – or just primary school – among the non-beneficiary indigenous males), and indigenous female beneficiaries reached 9.73 (6.82 for the non-beneficiaries). Among the non-indigenous beneficiary children, men reach 10.04 (8.74 for non-beneficiary *mestizo* males) while women studied up to year 8.91 (compared to 8.50 for the never exposed to *Oportunidades*). These results underestimate the final school impact of the programme since around one-quarter of former beneficiaries are still at school (many of them, especially women, are currently pursuing a university degree): 22.9 per cent of former male non-indigenous grantholders, 26.6 per cent of indigenous males, 28 per cent of indigenous women and 32.7 of *mestizo* women declare 'study' as their main occupation and are currently engaged in formal studies. It is clear that although the gender gap also decreases among the *mestizo* non-beneficiary children or the never-exposed population, it is not inverted in favour of women as seen among children exposed to the programme, and the ethnic gap is even more evident than the gender gap in the children's generation which never received the programme's grants.

The qualitative analysis of 183 case studies of households shows that the programme's impact in schooling among beneficiaries (children with the longest potential exposure) is shaped by the following factors: (1) the presence of schools of all levels in the community or the micro-region (proximity of schools positively affects educational attainment, especially among women); (2) quality and cultural pertinence of education (the capacity of schools to retain students and to motivate them to continue school trajectories); (3) parents' capabilities to act as breadwinners and to generate incomes (death or incapacity of the father or main provider is a clear factor against children's education); (4) existence of productive assets and monetary income (for example, from migrant older brothers/sisters' remittances) in order to cover school-related expenses such as transport to the towns where high-schools are located, and Internet-computer rental; (5) the individual's position in the reproductive cycle of the household (to be the youngest usually favours long school trajectories and to be the oldest usually implies the need to leave school in order to help the family with a waged income); (6) good health or lack of diseases in the household; and (7) the individual's sex, due to gender-differentiated obligations that males and females have within the household economy and domestic division of labour. Young women are not considered, as young men, as potential income-generators for the household economy, which favours their schooling achievements.

Due to the historical subordination and marginalisation of indigenous populations in Mexico, we expected to find differential outcomes of the programme favouring the non-indigenous population. Findings contradicted the research team's hypothesis. It is precisely the lack of economic options which makes cash transfers so effective, even with conditional responsibilities which mean an extra burden to mothers. Regular and secure income from the programme has become one of the main economic pillars which sustain, today, these indigenous poor households. Mothers and grandmothers are certain that their daughters and granddaughters will have different lives than theirs, with more opportunities and more independence, because, as they say, 'nobody knows what type of husband they are going to get'. Children's regular school attendance has become the best way to obtain income in the present and, at the same time, higher school achievements as a tool for the future. Paradoxically, women's disadvantages – associated with gender-stereotyped views of women as inferior economic providers – are working towards some advantages for young women.

Future research will have to include a comprehensive study of life after *Oportunidades*. Whether former grantholders are finding jobs, in addition to whether their recently awarded academic degrees serve as credentials to enter higher niches in labour markets, are aspects which new research will clarify. The evidence collected shows that former grantholders are located in higher echelons of the occupational hierarchy. Women seem to be, again, the main actors in these new processes while men tend to follow traditional paths (international migration or agricultural activities). But labour markets and the economy as a whole plainly shape employment opportunities with new and deeper crises' threats and constraints acting as barriers to people's social and economic improvement. Economic crises produce social responses of various types. In Mexico, the rural and urban poor have revealed their resistance with strategies that include, among other elements, using children's labour to enhance household income. That short-term survival strategies can undermine the mechanisms which contribute to long-term achievements is something which programes like *Oportunidades* seem to be helping low-income people to avoid.

Notes

1. Impacts on the occupational position of beneficiary and non-beneficiary members of the children's generation, as well as changes in reproductive patterns (age of women former grantholders at first pregnancy/delivery, compared to never beneficiaries) have also been studied. The focus of this chapter is, however, limited to educational attainment.
2. Monthly educational grants for third to sixth grade primary level students were, in 2006, 120, 140, 180 and 240 Mexican pesos a month (ranging from US$8.2 to US$16.3), respectively, for both boys and girls. Grants for first-year secondary school students were 350 pesos (US$23.8) for males and 370 pesos (US$25.2 for females; for second-year secondary students the awards were 370 for males and 410 pesos (US$27.9) for females. Male grantholders in the third year of secondary education received 390 pesos (US$26.6) while females at the same level received 450 pesos (US$30.7). The gender differential in high schools continued: 585 pesos (US$39.9) for boys and females getting 675 pesos (US$46). Males studying

in the second year of these schools received 630 pesos (US$42.9) and females 715 pesos (US$48.7). Finally, third-year male students of high schools had awards of 665 pesos (US$45.3) while females got 760 pesos (US$51.8) (*Oportunidades* programme, available at: http://www.oportunidades.gob.mx/Wn_Inf_General/ Padron_Liq/Mon_Apoyos/index.html (accessed 30 November 2008).
3. The variables included in the database are: state, region, locality, household ID, sex, name, age, kinship (father, mother, son/daughter, others), programme status (beneficiary or non-beneficiary), ethnicity, language, place of residence, civil status, maximum school level attained, main occupation, secondary occupation and, for the case of women, their age at first pregnancy/delivery.
4. The data and the analysis come from a research project in the framework of the External Qualitative Evaluation of the Human Development Programme *Oportunidades*, Long Term Impact, 2008, which I coordinated.

Select bibliography

Abel, Christopher and Colin M. Lewis (2002) 'Exclusion and engagement: a diagnosis of social policy in Latin America in the long run', in Christopher Abel and Colin M. Lewis (eds), *Exclusion and Engagement: Social Policy in Latin America*, London: University of London, Institute of Latin American Studies, pp. 3–53.

Benería, Lourdes (1992) 'The Mexican debt crisis: restructuring the economy and the household', in Lourdes Benería and Shelley Feldman (eds), *Unequal Burden: Economic Crises, Persistent Poverty, and Women's Work*, Boulder, CO: Westview Press, pp. 83–104.

Escobar, Agustín and Mercedes González de la Rocha (2008) 'Girls, mothers and poverty reduction in Mexico: evaluating *Progresa-Oportunidades*', in Shahra Razavi (ed.), *The Gendered Impacts of Liberalisation: Towards 'Embedded Liberalism'?*, London: Routledge, pp. 267–89.

Fine, Ben (2001) *Social Capital and Social Policy*, London: Routledge.

González de la Rocha, Mercedes (1994) *The Resources of Poverty: Women and Survival in a Mexican City*, Oxford: Blackwell.

González de la Rocha, Mercedes (2006) *Procesos Domésticos y Vulnerabilidad: Perspectivas Antropológicas de los Hogares con Oportunidades*, Mexico City: Publicaciones de la Casa Chata.

Molyneux, Maxine (2006) 'Mothers at the service of the new poverty agenda: Progresa/Oportunidades, Mexico's conditional transfer programme', *Social Policy and Administration*, **40** (4), 425–49.

38 Gender, poverty, and national identity in afrodescendent and indigenous movements in Latin America
Helen I. Safa

The emergence of indigenous and afrodescendent movements in Latin America is challenging the framework for national identity. They are questioning the way in which Latin American countries used *mestizaje* and *blanqueamiento* (racial and cultural 'mixing' and 'whitening' respectively) to forge a unified national image (Safa, 2005). The indigenous primarily demand special collective land rights to preserve ethnic identity, while afrodescendents emphasise redistributive rights to redress past injustices like slavery and continual racial discrimination. The emphasis placed on either identity or redistribution depends largely on the way afrodescendent and indigenous groups were incorporated into their respective nation states.

Indigenous groups in Latin America have always stressed ethnic identity as a way of safeguarding their territorial rights to land. Their rights stem largely from their special juridical status in *resguardos* (reservations) in colonial times, which contributed to the development of an 'institutionalised identity' and ability to maintain their own language and traditions (Wade, 1997). By contrast, most afrodescendents were brought in as slaves, denied their right to land and language, and subordinated through *blanqueamiento* to European norms. Some slaves escaped to establish their own remote 'maroon' communities, and did maintain a distinct identity and economy. The Garifuna of Central America claim never to have been enslaved, and maintain both indigenous and afrodescendent traditions resulting from the union of African men with Arawak/Carib women in Saint Vincent in the Caribbean. Former West Indian slaves were brought by the British or the United States (US) into Central America as contract labourers on railroads, plantations, and the Panama Canal. More recently, large diasporas of Caribbean, Central American and other Latin American migrants have begun to form new transnational communities in the US and Europe.

Clearly indigenous peoples are as heterogeneous as their afrodescendent counterparts, but this chapter focuses mainly on the latter. Afrodescendents are far more numerous in the region, and now comprise about one-third of the Latin American and Caribbean population, with the largest number in Brazil, where the black movement is also the most organised. But far more has been written on the indigenous, whom social scientists have treated as a people worthy of study in its own right, whereas afrodescendents were regarded as 'assimilated' or deviant versions of Euro-American culture (Wade, 1997). This has contributed to the indigenous movements becoming stronger and more visible, even to international agencies like the International Labour Organisation (ILO).

These different forms of incorporation help to explain their emphasis on either identity or redistribution. Redistribution has become more important to both groups as neoliberal policies contributed to greater immiseration of the poor and to reduction in basic state services. Women have begun taking leadership in these movements, spurred on by poverty and racial/ethnic discrimination.

The Andean indigenous movement
Indigenous movements are strong in the Andean Latin American countries with large indigenous populations, especially Ecuador and Bolivia, and have translated their focus on ethnic identity into the creation of ethnically based political parties seeking greater representation at all levels. The indigenous movement is aided by regional concentration and a long history of ethnic identity, reinforced by resistance to *mestizo* colonisation on their land. In order to protect their land base, the indigenous people formed regional and then national organisations, which grew into political parties with the assistance of transcommunity networks of unions, churches and non-governmental organisations (NGOs) (Yashar, 2005).

Land is both a productive and a cultural resource for the indigenous people, and collective land ownership enables cultural continuity and autonomy. The 1996 ILO Convention on Indigenous and Tribal Peoples defines beneficiaries in terms of their ancestral or pre-colonial link to land and their maintenance of cultural difference. This explains why land is so linked to the preservation of ethnic identity, though many indigenous people are now migrating to urban areas and even abroad. Their participation in electoral politics also increases the prospects of fragmentation and co-optation, challenging the important unity of the indigenous movement.

Afrodescendent movements in *mestizo* nations
Afrodescendent movements in some Latin American countries with a strong *mestizo* identity like Colombia and Central America tend to follow the path of the more visible indigenous movement in stressing the importance of land and cultural autonomy. Many of these communities developed in relative isolation from colonial domination, like the afrodescendents of the Pacific coast of Ecuador and Colombia, who remained in the region after the collapse of the eighteenth-century mining industry. Afro-Colombians have succeeded in gaining some state recognition of their territorial rights, but far less than the much smaller indigenous communities in the Pacific area. This privileging of the indigenous is reinforced by the heterogeneity and geographic dispersion of afrodescendents from the Pacific region, many of whom have migrated to cities provoked by armed conflict and foreign capital investment. Yet Colombia retains its strong *mestizo* identity and is reluctant to recognise the rights of these urbanised afrodescendents as equal to their rural Pacific counterparts, whose claims look more like that of the indigenous people.

Afrodescendent communities along the Atlantic coast of Central America have faced similar challenges. *Mestizaje* in Nicaragua excluded afrodescendents from the self-image of the nation and legitimates the state's efforts to colonise outlying areas such as the Atlantic coast (Hooker, 2005). Afro-Creoles living along the coast, who speak English and are mostly Protestant, are perceived as inauthentic and not worthy of state protection.

Many West Indians in Central America were brought in as contract labourers in the late nineteenth century to work on plantations and build a railroad. Favoured by the British and speaking English, the Afro-Creoles gained a higher status than the rural

Garifuna, whom they treated with disrespect. This has contributed to enmity between the Afro-Creoles and the less educated Garifuna, who are settled primarily along the north coast of Honduras and in Belize. The Garifuna claimed status as an 'autochthonous' group, but have recently privileged their indigenous rather than afrodescendent roots. Apparently, this serves as a stronger basis for their land claims, which are in danger of tourism development and *mestizo* colonisation along the Honduran coast. It also gives them greater claim to authenticity than Afro-Creoles, with whom they compete for resources and political power.

Both the Garifuna and Creole communities in Central America are heavily dependent on remittances, chiefly from the US. England (2006) argues that what is emerging among the Garifuna is a transnational ethnic identity tied by common language, culture and history, but not bound by any territorial state, a concept which may be applied to other diasporic communities discussed below.

In sum, afrodescendent movements in Central America and other *mestizo* nations face severe challenges, beyond the strong *mestizo* identification of these nation states and their long history of marginalising afrodescendents. By emphasising territorial rights (like the indigenous people), they lose the support of urbanised afrodescendent migrants, whom the *mestizo* state do not equate with their rural counterparts. In Central America, political fragmentation is augmented by mass migration overseas, and by the splits within the afrodescendent movement.

Assimilated afrodescendents in Brazil and Cuba
Most afrodescendents in Latin American and the Caribbean stem from a long history of slavery, which in countries like Brazil and Cuba only ended in the 1880s, resulting in large afrodescendent populations. *Mestizaje* assimilated afrodescendents into the nation and subordinated them through *blanqueamiento* to European norms, except for smaller maroon communities of runaway slaves like the Brazilian '*quilombos*'. Brazil and Cuba did maintain census records of afrodescendents, which has now become a major demand of afrodescendents throughout the region, because it increases their visibility. Census records also enabled Afro-Brazilians to document racial inequalities as a basis for their claims on the state.

These records helped demolish the myth of 'racial democracy' in Brazil, by pointing out the continued racial gaps in socio-economic status, even for the black middle class. Support was solidified with strong Afro-Brazilian participation, especially by women, in the 2001 UN World Conference against Racism held in Durban, South Africa, and the assistance of US African American civil rights activists (Safa, 2005).

The state also backs Afro-Brazilian demands for affirmative action, first in the 1990s under President Fernando Henrique Cardoso and later under President Luiz Inacio Lula da Silva of the Workers Party. Quotas for Afro-Brazilians have been established for admission to federal universities, for employment in some federal and state public agencies, and for candidates for political parties. Affirmative action has been strongly opposed on the grounds that it will enhance racial divisions, but seems to be an appropriate response for an urban, wage-earning population primarily concerned with the redistribution of rights in education, employment and political power. Afro-Brazilians are spread across a large, regionally diverse country at different class levels and many do not identify with the movement, because of a long history of *blanqueamiento* and black stigmatisation.

The afrodescendent movement promotes racial identity through cultural and educational programmes, but the focus is on redistribution through affirmative action.

There is little state support specifically for afrodescendent organisations in Cuba, except for some Afro-Cuban cultural groups in music and dance, which are a major tourist attraction. This stems partly from a long fear of racial division, despite the allegiance displayed by Afro-Cubans in the country's Wars of Independence. The socialist revolution in 1959 aimed to do away with regional and racial divisions and stressed national unity and solidarity, especially in face of the US embargo. The socialist emphasis on overcoming class inequality substantially eliminated racial differences in such basic areas as education, employment, and health (Sawyer, 2006), and is reflected in the erosion of racial and class barriers and in the growth of interracial unions, especially among the working class (Safa, 2009). But the economic crisis starting in Cuba in 1989 following the breakup of the socialist bloc threatens to lead to the resurgence of old racial, class and gender barriers. Afro-Cubans have more difficulty finding jobs in the emerging and more lucrative tourist sectors, and they also receive fewer remittances from abroad.

In Brazil and Cuba, as well as most Latin American countries, national identity supersedes racial identity (Sawyer, 2006), which in Cuba can be partly explained by the need for unity in the long struggle against colonialism. Assimilation demanded a love of *la patria* (fatherland) above all other allegiances, and afrodescendents' attempt to form their own political parties in either Cuba or Brazil was suppressed. Instead most Afro-Brazilians give their support to leftist, class-based political parties, like the Workers Party currently in power in Brazil. This political involvement, and their long history of participation in labour unions, suggests Afro-Brazilians' class consciousness may be stronger then their racial consciousness, which may be heightened through affirmative action.

Diaspora communities of afrodescendents

Diaspora communities are not included in studies of afrodescendent movements, although many have noted their importance in terms of developing transnational ties (see, for example, England, 2006; Sawyer, 2006). Given the growing importance of migration for Latin American and Caribbean countries, its impact on afrodescendent (and indigenous) movements certainly bears further investigation.

The marginalisation faced by West Indian migrants to Central America demonstrates the difficulties faced by these 'foreign' afrodescendents. Many West Indians did not gain citizenship until the late 1940s, as in Costa Rica and Panama, which still distinguishes between '*negros coloniales*', bought in the colonial period as slaves, and West Indians brought in the middle of the nineteenth century as contract labour. Only West Indians are regarded as black, much as Haitians living in the Dominican Republic are distinguished from native '*indios*', suggesting another way in which assimilation whitens and subsumes racial under national identity. The need for national unity is especially strong in countries like Panama, which as a result of the canal, has suffered several US invasions and tight economic and political control (as with Cuba and the Dominican Republic). The Afro-Panamanian diaspora in the US has pressured the Panamanian government for local reform, but their only demand to meet with legislative approval is the absentee ballot for Panamanians living in the US. Other Central American and Caribbean countries, such as the Dominican Republic, have also adopted the absentee ballot and expanded this to include dual citizenship. While this could be seen as a measure of inclusion (not limited to afrodescendents) and gives the diaspora community some political power, it also allows political parties to tap their resources.

Remittances now constitute a major source of national income, especially for labour-exporting countries in Central America and the Caribbean, and have increased dramatically over the past 20 years. This mass migration of Central American and Caribbean afrodescendents weakens their territorial rights in the homeland, but leads to the development of a transnational identity, whose impact on afrodescendent and indigenous movements is just beginning to be explored. Though migration was traditionally male among the Garifuna, women are increasingly participants in the New York City diaspora. More importantly, transnational networks are matrifocal, because remittances are overwhelmingly sent to women (by men as well), who use it to build or furnish a house, or to take care of the migrant's children or other relatives (England, 2006). Migration from other Latin American and Caribbean communities, like the Dominican Republic and Puerto Rico, has often served to enhance the women's role, and to increase racial consciousness, because racial divisions are sharper.

Gender ideology and consciousness among afrodescendent and indigenous women
Afrodescendent and indigenous women maintain different gender ideologies from *mestiza* women, who generally subscribe to the dominance of the male breadwinner, inscribed in the colonial moral codes of *mestizaje*. Their forms of incorporation limit the resources available to men in both communities and oblige women to take on additional economic responsibility. Ethnic identity is protected where possible by confining indigenous women to the local community economically and through endogamy. This restricts socio-economic advances by traditional indigenous women, who subordinate gender consciousness to ethnic consciousness, in order to avoid gender divisions within the indigenous community.

Garifuna women activists, drawing on indigenous roots, have downplayed their loss of land to *mestizo* and Garifuna men, though traditional land use rights passed through matrilineal lines. However, where indigenous women have participated in ethnically based political parties as in Bolivia, they have succeeded in passing legislation granting equal rights to domestic workers, among whom indigenous women predominate. Clearly their concerns are going beyond land rights.

Afrodescendent women generally developed greater gender consciousness and sexual autonomy, reinforced in the Caribbean and Central America by a long history of male emigration. Families are often matrifocal, with a high percentage of female heads of household, often living in extended households, and requiring high levels of female labour force participation (Safa, 2009). The core of their identity rests not in land, but in economic autonomy. Afro-Creole women in Costa Rica work more than *mestiza* women, and have higher educational levels, higher incomes and a higher percentage are professionals (Safa, 2005).

In Brazil, thanks to the strong feminist movement, there has been more reduction in inequality by gender than by race. Overall gender gaps in education have been eliminated, while the racial gap has remained unchanged. To meet these challenges, Afro-Brazilian women formed their own organisations, focusing on health and education as well as racial identity. They now surpass black men in education, and professional and technical occupations, but continue to receive the lowest levels of wages (Safa, 2005). Afro-Brazilian women have also gained in electoral office at both the municipal and federal levels.

The Federation of Cuban Women (FMC/Federación de Mujeres Cubanas) was instrumental in advancing women's socio-economic status after the revolution, with substantial increases in female educational levels and job opportunities, so that today two-thirds of Cuban working women are in professional and technical occupations. The revolution's redistribution programme eroded local gender and racial hierarchies, but national political power remains concentrated in the hands of white (older) men. Female-headed households have increased substantially, even among professional women, aided by the provision of free healthcare and education, which made it easier for women to have children on their own. The inequalities generated by the economic crisis, including a decline in female labour force participation, growing unemployment, and the loss in purchasing power of state wages, threatens these gains (Safa, 2009).

Final reflections
Which strategy has been more effective for ethnic/racial vindication – ethnic identity or redistribution? Both strategies are vital, and often flow into each other. Land rights are also a form of redistribution, but may evolve into wider, class-based rights as politicised groups urbanise and seek broader support. Affirmative action is not only redistribution but also another way of asserting ethnic/racial identity. Redistribution requires the ability to command state resources, which both the Afro-Brazilian movement and the Bolivian indigenous party have been able to achieve. Afro-Brazilians benefit from class-based state redistribution programmes like Bolsa Familia (Family Grants) which has sharply reduced extreme poverty in Brazil, especially in the heavily Afro-Brazilian Northeast (see also Razavi and Staab, Chapter 65, this volume). These class-based programmes may have more public support than race-based affirmative action, which is an important policy consideration.

Despite some gains by afrodescendents, the indigenous people are still privileged in Latin America because of their historic claim to cultural difference and centuries of black marginalisation, especially in *mestizo* countries. Cultural survival is also favoured by international funding agencies. This helps explain why Garifuna women activists in Honduras stress their indigenous heritage in legitimating land claims, even at the expense of traditional matrilineal rights. In spite of its claim to multiculturalism, Honduras, like other Latin American countries, clings to the image of a unitary *mestizaje* as justification for marginalising these afrodescendent and indigenous movements in the region.

Select bibliography
England, Sarah (2006) *Afro Central Americans in New York City: Garifuna Tales of Transnational Movements in Racialised Space*, Gainesville, FL: University Press of Florida.
Hooker, Juliet (2005) '"Beloved enemies": race and official mestizo nationalism in Nicaragua', *Latin American Research Review*, **40** (3), 14–39.
Safa, Helen I. (2005) 'Challenging Mestizaje: a gender perspective on indigenous and afrodescendent movements in Latin America', *Critique of Anthropology*, **25** (3), 307–30.
Safa, Helen I. (2009) 'Hierarchies and household change in postrevolutionary Cuba', *Latin American Perspectives*, **36** (1), 42–52.
Sawyer, Mark (2006) *Racial Politics in Post-Revolutionary Cuba*, New York: Cambridge University Press.
Wade, Peter (1997) *Race and Ethnicity in Latin America*, Chicago, IL: Pluto Press.
Yashar, Deborah J. (2005) *Contesting Citizenship in Latin America: The Rise of Indigenous Movements and the Postliberal Challenge*, New York: Cambridge University Press.

39 The gendered exclusions of international migration: perspectives from Latin American migrants in London
Cathy McIlwaine

This chapter explores the broad relationship between the feminisation of international migration and the feminisation of poverty drawing on the experiences of Latin American migrant women and men living in London, mainly from Colombia, Ecuador and Bolivia.[1] As 'ordinary' migrants living in the most deprived parts of inner city London and working in the lowest echelons of the city's labour market, Latin Americans experience widespread exploitation as a group. Although they were not the poorest in their countries of origin and many still manage to send money to sustain families back home, life in London is characterised by considerable deprivation. Moreover, migrants' experiences of vulnerability are deeply gendered, if not always in ways which conform with stereotypical expectations. Some women do indeed suffer disproportionately to men as a result of their irregular immigration status, which strips them of political rights and can render them powerless in the face of abuse. However, other migrant women make important gains due to preferential labour recruitment over their male counterparts. Although this is often in relatively menial occupations in cleaning and catering, the difficulties migrant men face in attaining the same opportunities as women can lead to their perceived emasculation. In order to capture the types of gendered ambiguities experienced by Latin American migrants, this chapter suggests that it is most appropriate to talk of the gendered exclusions of international migration.

Does the feminisation of international migration overlap with the feminisation of poverty?
With the increasing migration of people across borders in the past few decades, so the feminised nature of these moves has been gradually acknowledged. Although the actual proportion of women moving has not grown significantly, constituting almost a half since the 1960s, the increasing visibility of women as international migrants has been marked. Furthermore, the nature of women's migration has also changed as they are more likely now to move independently of men rather than for family reunification and as labour migrants. The so-called 'feminisation of poverty' has been associated with the 'feminisation of international migration' for two main reasons. First, it has been widely suggested that the neoliberal policies imposed on most countries of the Global South since the 1980s have created increased impoverishment across and within societies with a concomitant 'feminisation of responsibility and/or obligation' (Chant, Chapter 15, this volume). This has prompted some women to try and improve their lives by moving abroad. However, it is important to recognise that the very poor in countries of the Global South are rarely able to migrate, with most international migrants having reasonable access to resources in order to facilitate their movement (with the exception of conflict-induced migration and human trafficking). Yet, even economically better-off migrants migrate to mitigate

the risk of their own or their family's future impoverishment through the sending of remittances for investment back home. In addition, the escape from disadvantage more generally, socially, culturally or politically within households or beyond, underpins why people migrate, with women being more likely than men to be motivated by restrictive conditions back home (Kofman et al., 2000).

The second reason for linking the feminisation of poverty with the feminisation of international migration relates to the concentration of women migrants living in precarious circumstances in destination countries. Although male migrants also face discrimination in host societies, Piper (2005: 2) suggests that women face a 'triple disadvantage' on grounds of their gender, race and occupational status as migrants. This disadvantage arises partly from the increasing global demand for labour in the service sectors of economies of the Global North especially in domestic service, caring and other low-status, low-paid and largely feminised occupations that is increasingly being met by female immigrant labour. This in turn creates exploitative 'global care chains' whereby women from the Global South provide the caring labour for middle-class women in the North to allow them to go out to work, while many leave their own children back home in the care of others. Their disadvantage is compounded by state immigration regimes that regulate migration flows often to the detriment of women migrants who often end up with fewer rights than migrant men (Arya and Roy, 2006). Such regimes also contribute to the process of 'deskilling' whereby many women (and men) migrants from the Global South hold educational or professional qualifications which are not recognised by host governments, forcing them to work in inferior jobs. Although skilled female migrants also move internationally, this is mainly to work in feminised welfare professions where deskilling also occurs.

In reality, however, a clear-cut relationship between income poverty and women's international migration does not exist. Although international migrants in host countries of the North tend to be the poorest and most marginalised members of society, there are wide variations according, *inter alia*, to nationality, immigration status, class and race, as well as gender (see Wills et al., 2010). Furthermore, when focusing on the gendered outcomes of international migration, debates have tended to highlight the ways in which gender ideologies and identities have transformed as women and men migrate rather than on patterns of gendered impoverishment. Following early research that heralded international migration as a largely emancipatory process for women, it is now acknowledged to be a much more contradictory process for both women and men. Pessar (2005) has summarised these into a typology of potential (and intersecting) outcomes that include, first, how migration can lead to a re-negotiation of pre-migration gender ideologies and practices; second, how it can consolidate counter-hegemonic gender regimes from home countries; and, third, how it can intensify gender inequalities prevalent before migration.

This indicates a much more complex set of gendered processes that need to move beyond a simplistic assumption that the feminisation of international migration is underpinned by and creates a feminisation of poverty conceived in narrow income terms. Indeed, wider analyses of the diverse circumstances of international migrants have highlighted the need to recognise the economic, social and political exclusion of migrants rather than their poverty per se (Wills et al., 2010). This emphasis on exclusion rather than poverty has increasingly been recognised from a gender perspective as suggested by

Arya and Roy (2006: 23) who point out how transnational migration has 'unfolded as a continuing process of exclusion and deprivation whereby state policies have promoted migration but withdrawn from assuring protective support' with marked exclusionary outcomes for women.

While the bulk of research on the gendered nature and outcomes of international migration has tended to focus on Latin American or Asian migrants in the United States, this chapter explores how women and men from Latin America negotiate widespread marginalisation and exclusion in London in the United Kingdom.

Experiencing gendered exclusions: reflections from Latin American migrants in London
Echoing research conducted across the world, many migrants from the Global South who end up working in global cities such as London invariably find themselves in marginalised situations. Their exclusion is often exacerbated by precarious immigration status, restricting their access to political, social and cultural rights, and manifested in poor living conditions and limited access to basic welfare services (Wills et al., 2010). In London, Latin American migrants are an increasingly important, although largely invisible, 'new migrant group' with no previous colonial or historical ties with the UK, yet who are contributing to the city's 'super-diversity'. Although very small numbers of 'elite' migrants have moved to London since the days of independence struggles in Latin America, the bulk of migrants in the city today are middle- and working-class people, with slightly more women than men.[2] While many migrants had previously worked in professional, managerial or artisan jobs back home, both women and men have ended up working in the cleaning and catering sector for low wages. Although there are no specific 'Latin American enclaves' in London, there are marked concentrations in several inner-city areas, all of which are characterised by high levels of deprivation. In these areas, many Latin Americans have little option but to live in overcrowded accommodation because of high rents and low wages. There are also differences among nationalities, with the more established Colombians, who are more likely to have refugee status or citizenship, experiencing fewer hardships than Bolivians who have migrated more recently on temporary visas with many residing on an irregular basis and experiencing widespread deprivation as a result. Despite these broad patterns of deprivation, the vast majority also manage to send money back home, averaging £100 (c. US$140) per month (McIlwaine, 2008).

While this picture of impoverishment is broadly accurate, closer examination reveals a more complicated situation from a gender perspective. Both women and men experience a range of exclusions, yet they negotiate these in different ways in relation to their paid employment, the household, and the state, with contradictory outcomes for gender ideologies. Furthermore, and recalling Pessar's (2005) typology, these negotiations are also rooted in the mutability of pre-migration gender regimes. Indeed, while all migrants tended to remember such regimes in reified ways that emphasised deep-seated gender asymmetries associated with *machismo*, many women were keen to stress the transformations in their lives towards greater freedom and equality vis-à-vis men. In contrast, many men were nostalgic for their previous lives of greater power and control, despite a grudging acceptance of changes at a practical level.

More specifically, empirical research reveals a picture of ambiguous gendered exclusions in the labour market. Just as access to paid employment is crucial in transforming gender identities more broadly, it is especially important for destabilising gender norms among migrant men and women (Pessar, 2005). Although labour force participation was nothing new for Latin American women, the ways in which migrants were inserted into London's low-paid labour market tended to favour women. Not only were most jobs available to migrants in feminised service sectors of the labour market, mainly in office cleaning and catering jobs, but women and men worked side by side, earning the same (low) wages and under the same (poor) working conditions usually involving early morning and late night shifts for 4 hours at a time. Although women recognised the broadly exploitative nature of their employment in these elementary jobs, they were accustomed to earning less than men back home and so they accepted their employment as necessary and valuable. As one Bolivian woman stated: 'Here, I feel useful, people value what I do, they say I work well, I clean well, and I feel good when they say this.' Men, in contrast, struggled with working in feminised jobs that they perceived as undermining their masculinity and self-esteem. As one Colombian male respondent pointed out: 'In my life, I had never done cleaning, but to arrive and to have to dust, to wipe, to brush-up, it affects your self-esteem, you feel really, really bad.'

Perhaps not surprisingly in light of this, women were much keener to progress through the employment hierarchy in cleaning companies to become part of the predominantly female rank of supervisors. Further compounding their favoured employment status was that women could obtain domestic service jobs in private homes more easily than men; these were viewed as higher status work than contract cleaning because of higher wages, 'cash in hand', and no immigration paper requirements. It also emerged that women were more likely than men to establish small businesses (usually cafés, restaurants or small shops oriented to the Latin American market). In addition, although balancing reproductive responsibilities in the home remained a problem for most women, the part-time, fragmented and unsocial working hours of many cleaning jobs actually allowed them to negotiate these demands more easily.

These labour market processes had important ramifications for gender ideologies at the household level, although again, the changes were ambiguous. Both women and men agreed that gender divisions of reproductive labour within households had changed quite dramatically post-migration. In practical terms, men had started doing housework, especially childcare that was often viewed as the least threatening to hegemonic masculine norms. Yet, men stressed that these shifts towards more egalitarian divisions of labour were for practical reasons related to women's working patterns. Ideologically, changes were much less apparent. Indeed, it was at the household level where some men sought to empower themselves in violent and damaging ways through physical and verbal violence against their female partners and sometimes their children. With one in four women speaking openly about the physical abuse they had suffered in London at the hands of their partners, this represented a worrying backlash against women's gains in the labour market. It also represented a source of deep insecurity for women, especially if their immigration status was insecure (Pessar, 2005).

Indeed, migrants' relationships with the state in terms of immigration status and access to welfare benefits not only underpinned the extent of their economic and political exclusion, but it was also fundamental to gendered power relations. Although it is now acknowledged that immigration legislation is deeply gendered and tends to represent migrant women in particularly stereotyped ways as dependants and so-called 'purveyors of culture and ethnicity' (Kofman et al., 2000), it can simultaneously work to include them into, and exclude them from, wider society. For those migrants fortunate enough to secure citizenship rights (mainly Colombians and some Ecuadorians), access to state benefits gave women considerable economic freedom to live independent lives. This was especially significant when women were trapped in unhappy and/or abusive relationships.

However, for those without such privileges, including the majority of Bolivians, their exclusion was marked. For migrant women without regular status or with temporary visas, their disempowerment was acute. Not only did they often work in the worst jobs, washing dishes and cleaning toilets, but among women in dependent relationships with partners, it emerged that men manipulated their privileged access to visas in order to maintain control. Several instances emerged whereby women were living with abusive partners simply because their only other choice was deportation or a life of irregularity. For those who were irregular, the threat of reporting their status to the authorities was used as a form of insidious control by men. Thus, while immigration status can be a potential route towards greater autonomy for many women, it can also be a dangerous tool of manipulation leaving them with little room to manoeuvre economically, politically or socially.

The gendered exclusions of international migration
Reflecting on the experiences of Latin American migrants in London highlights how, like many of their counterparts from elsewhere in the Global South, they experience widespread marginalisation on the margins of the city (Wills et al., 2010). Although most manage to send money back home, many live and work in deprivation in order to do so. However, the specific ways in which migrants negotiate their well-being from a gender perspective requires an approach that emphasises the gendered exclusions of migration rather than its inherently impoverishing role. This captures the contradictory ways in which women and men make gains and losses in the labour market, the household and vis-à-vis the state in relation to welfare and immigration status. Although at face value migrant women appear to have made considerable gains from migration, it is also important to stress that any transformations in their lives tend to focus on gender practices rather than gender ideologies (McIlwaine, 2008).

Therefore, on the basis of these ambivalent experiences of exclusion, which is echoed throughout the rest of Europe and North America (Kofman et al., 2000; Pessar, 2005), a simple relationship between the feminisation of international migration and the feminisation of poverty needs to be questioned. Instead, it is suggested that it is most appropriate to talk of the gendered exclusions of international migration. This allows for a historically contingent, dynamic perspective that recognises, first, that migrants are not necessarily the poorest members of the societies where they originate and, second, that although migrants experience impoverishment in destination countries, their wider exclusion socially and politically is gender-differentiated with ambiguous outcomes for both women and men (Arya and Roy, 2006).

Acknowledgements
The research discussed in this chapter was made possible by a fellowship from the Leverhulme Trust (Award no. RF/7/2006/0080) to whom I am extremely grateful. Many

aspects of the research were facilitated by the Carila Latin American Welfare Group and I would like to thank all the staff, especially Alba Arbelaez, for their support. I would also like to thank Carolina Velásquez Correa, Flor Alba Robayo and Emilia Girardo for their research assistance, as well as all the migrants who agreed to be interviewed.

Notes

1. The research on which this chapter is based draws on qualitative interviews with 70 Latin American migrants of Colombian (28), Ecuadorian (22) and Bolivian (20) origin, among whom 44 were women and 26 were men. In addition, focus group discussions were carried out with a further 17 men and women (including Peruvians, Venezuelans, and a Brazilian), together with interviews with ten people working with the community. The fieldwork took place between 2006 and 2007, and I also spent two years serving on the Management Committee of a Latin American migrant organisation in London.
2. Most migration has been 'family migration' or through 'family reunification'. Although the research found several women who had lived for short periods of time as 'transnational mothers', most had endeavoured to bring their children to the UK as quickly as possible after they migrated.

Select bibliography

Arya, Sadhna and Anupama Roy (eds) (2006) *Poverty, Gender and Migration*, New Delhi: Sage.

Kofman, Eleonore, Annie Phizacklea and Parvati Raghuram (eds) (2000) *Gender and International Migration in Europe: Employment, Welfare, and Politics*, London: Routledge.

McIlwaine, Cathy (2008) *Subversion or Subjugation: Transforming Gender Ideologies among Latin American Migrants in London*, London: Working Paper, Department of Geography, Queen Mary, University of London, available at: http://www.geog.qmul.ac.uk/docs/staff/6313.pdf (accessed 27 March 2009).

Pessar, Patricia (2005) *Women, Gender, and International Migration Across and Beyond the Americas: Inequalities and Limited Empowerment*, New York: United Nations Expert Group Meeting on International Migration and Development in Latin America and the Caribbean, available at: http://www.un.org/esa/population/publications/IttMigLAC/P08_PPessar.pdf (accessed 27 March 2009).

Piper, Nicola (2005) *Gender and Migration*, Geneva: Working Paper, Policy Analysis and Research Programme of the Global Commission on International Migration, available at: http://www.gcim.org/attachements/TP10.pdf (accessed 27 March 2009).

Wills, Jane, Kavita Datta, Yara Evans, Joanna Herbert, Jon May and Cathy McIlwaine (2010) *Global Cities at Work: New Migrant Divisions of Labour*, London: Pluto.

40 Latino immigrants, gender and poverty in the United States
Cecilia Menjívar

The foreign-born make up 40 per cent of the Latino population in the United States. Thus, instead of taking a broad look at the intersection of gender and poverty in the entire Latino population, I concentrate on the foreign-born, highlighting the case of Central Americans, among whom the foreign-born comprise 70 per cent of the population. I will underscore the central place of legal status in shaping the lives of these immigrants and what it might mean for their futures in the United States (US).

Latin American-origin immigrants in the US, like contemporary immigrants around the world, face increasingly hostile environments in receiving countries, which affect deeply how they fare economically. Immigrants' prospects for socio-economic advancement are intimately tied to this broader context of reception, and 'making it' economically depends only partially on individual motivations and abilities (Portes and Rumbaut, 2006). Historically, immigrants also encountered unfriendly environments that impinged on their economic advancement, but certain conditions coalesce today to make immigrant contexts of reception qualitatively different from those in the past. Technological improvements in travel have led to increased migrant mobility; migration flows have concentrated highly in regions and countries; economic crises have led to fewer opportunities for advancement for both native and immigrant populations; and publics in immigrant-receiving countries have felt threatened by images linking migrants with terrorists and drug smugglers and therefore their governments have been less inclined to extend rights and protection to foreigners.

A particularly important factor in the context of reception that shapes immigrants' economic chances are the efforts on the part of receiving states to formally exclude immigrants – through immigration laws – or to keep them on the margins of society for much longer. In her research on immigration, Calavita (1998: 530) observes that immigration law 'actively "irregularises" people by making it all but impossible to retain legal status over time. Indeed, it makes little sense to draw distinctions between legal and illegal immigrants . . . because the law ensures that legal status is temporary and subject to continuous disruptions.' Thus, in the US, as in other major receiving countries, contemporary immigration law creates and recreates an excluded population and ensures its vulnerability and precariousness by blurring the boundaries of legality and illegality to create areas of marginalisation. To be sure, immigrants' individual characteristics matter a great deal for their economic prospects, but how immigrants use their personal resources does not depend solely on their own volition but also on political, economic, and historical factors over which individuals have little, if any, control.

The contemporary immigration regime in the United States has created a stratified system of legal categories that shape membership and belonging. In today's context, these legal categories mark immigrants not only as 'non-nationals' but also as deportable and, thus, such categories become marks of exclusion. And not all groups have equal access to permanent statuses, an aspect of immigration law that undermines the assumption of equality of status and belonging in citizenship. Thus immigrant incorporation or assimilation does not occur unilinearly or monolithically, and the multiple categories created by the law generate layered or fragmented forms of belonging. As such, legal status has become an important axis of stratification that can shape immigrants' assimilation in critical ways, particularly in their paths of economic integration.

To capture the effects of legal status on the economic prospects of immigrants and examine any related gender differences, I concentrate on the case of Central American immigrants – mostly Guatemalans, Hondurans and Salvadorans. These Central Americans' legality is complex and has been a paradigmatic case of legal instability (Menjívar, 2006). They have been extended temporary permits with no links to establishing permanent residence, and the relatively few who qualify for legal residence wait for years, often decades, for their cases to be adjudicated. Their legal instability, sometimes referred to as 'permanent temporariness' (Bailey et al., 2002) or 'liminal legality' (Menjívar 2006), brings out vividly the consequences of unstable legal statuses on the lives of immigrants. However, the Central Americans' case is not exceptional in the United States or in other major immigrant-receiving countries today. Their unstable situation, compounded by fear of deportation and immigration raids, as well as by an increased anti-immigrant sentiment (regardless of the health of the economy) finds echoes in other immigrant destinations around the world.

Legal categories
The US contemporary legal framework is shaped by the Illegal Immigration Reform and Immigrant Responsibility Act (IIRIRA) of 1996, which set new grounds for inadmissibility and for removal (deportation) proceedings, new provisions for restricting non-citizens from receiving public benefits, and for the first time, the deportability of permanent legal residents. In addition, local-level governments have passed laws that exacerbate the effects of federal law, such as punishing employers who hire undocumented immigrants by taking away their business licenses (in Arizona), by denying undocumented immigrants drivers' licenses, and by barring undocumented children access to higher education (in several states). All of these laws have direct and indirect effects on the economic prospects of immigrants, as they compound the effects of labour market disadvantages and result in vulnerability to deportation, confinement to low-wage jobs, and the denial of basic rights, such as access to decent housing, education, food and healthcare. As such, an uncertain legal status does not only affect incomes, but it also restricts access to resources and to benefits in society, and impinges on fundamental rights.

Economic participation
Even though some Central Americans with relatively higher levels of education and English language skills are employed in technical and administrative jobs, and those with lower educational levels and English language proficiency are likely to be working in service occupations or as operators and labourers, these are not clear-cut distinctions. Generally, those who lack a permanent legal status tend to labour in low-paying jobs that require few skills. Among these immigrants there are many stories of former teachers working as dishwashers, former accountants taking care of other people's children,

former nurses cleaning houses, former business owners cleaning office buildings at night, and college graduates looking for work as day labourers. Central Americans' concentrations in these jobs do not depend only on their legality, individual characteristics or human capital levels, but also on the jobs available at the time of their migration and place of their US destination. However, given their continued uncertain legality, niches created during harsh economic times have endured and become some of these immigrants' most important avenues for permanent, long-term employment.

Gender and poverty
The relationship between gender differences and legal status is not an easy one to examine in relation to the economic prospects and poverty of Central American immigrants. When poverty comes into the picture, the linkages become even more complex. On the one hand, there are more Central American women who live in the US in legal uncertainty or in undocumented statuses; on the other hand, the jobs that these immigrant women tend to land – caretakers of the elderly, babysitters, domestics, cleaners – are available even in times of economic downturn and considered to be 'recession proof'. Also, these jobs tend to be performed away from the public eye – in a private home – and thus not as exposed to immigration inspections. Furthermore, the jobs men tend to obtain are situated in areas that have been targeted for immigration raids, like in factories, restaurants and construction, and they tend to dwindle during recessionary times because their demand decreases. Importantly, even when women work more hours than do men and hold jobs for longer, men tend to earn more than women. However, in general, the jobs that Central Americans get are unstable, low paid and offer few if any opportunities for real advancement. This leaves both women and men who perform them in situations of vulnerability and precariousness.

The above scenario means that, in general, Central Americans have high labour force participation rates and low incomes in relation to the national population as a whole. According to the American Community Survey or ACS (the US Census Bureau mid-decennial figures), in 2005–2007, the labour force participation rate for Central Americans was 75 per cent, with 64 per cent among women – high rates when compared to the average for the US population of 65 per cent and 58 per cent respectively. Even though most adult Central Americans are in the labour force, their average incomes are low. The per capita income for Guatemalans in 2005–2007 was US$14286, for Hondurans, US$14067, and US$15116 for Salvadorans, whereas their household incomes were close to US$40000, the average for the overall Latino population (but far from the US$50000 for the US population), which is probably a result of their living arrangements. Many unrelated Central Americans share living quarters; close to 50 per cent live in households of four or more, and close to two-thirds live in rented housing. And their poverty rates are high; approximately 20 per cent of Central American households (close to one-fourth among Hondurans) live in poverty (compared to 10 per cent for the US population). This proportion goes up in households headed by women, particularly when children under 5 are present; 44 per cent of these live in poverty.

It is noteworthy that the earnings of many Central Americans do not come from a single job or from working full-time; many stitch together two or three part-time jobs to earn the incomes reported in the statistics above, a pattern that is evident among women and men alike. Many women I have interviewed have mentioned that they clean several houses a week, make food for sale, and sell products out of their home, and if someone needs help with cooking or baby-sitting they are ready to help as well. It is the same for men, among whom it is not uncommon to hear that they work at a factory or a restaurant during the daytime and as parking lot attendants at night, while filling in for an ill co-worker at a third place of employment on weekends whenever necessary.

The unstable legal status of the Central Americans plays a key role in their employment and economic prospects, but education also figures prominently and compounds their predicament. It becomes increasingly more difficult to get out of these initial jobs when the immigrants do not have the educational requirements and job experience required for better-paying jobs. Central Americans in general have low educational levels; according to the American Community Survey, about 47 per cent have less than a high school education and 25 per cent have high school or its equivalent, figures that are roughly equal for women and men. Their English language proficiency tends to be low; almost 60 per cent speak English 'less than very well'. Importantly, however, the Central Americans' educational and English language skills are not independent of their legal status and their poor conditions, as many cannot take time away from their work schedules to enrol in school to improve their economic chances. They have huge pressures to generate incomes – both in the United States and in their countries of origin, a topic to which I turn below.

Poverty beyond income
As may be gleaned from the above discussion, an income is only one indicator of an individual's economic standing. Access to resources – whether educational, like access to language training or college, or social services, such as health care and benefits – impinges vitally on an individual's poverty status and their chances to advance socioeconomically. Legal status is determinant here, as immigrants who find themselves in uncertain legal statuses do not have access to most social benefits in the United States today, except to those mandated federally, such as emergency treatment in hospitals and K-12 education for children. Therefore, they do not have access to regular healthcare, to unemployment benefits, to workers' compensation, and when their immigrant children finish high school, they rarely go on to higher education because they do not have access to student loans or to most scholarships (Abrego, 2008). Moreover, with their uncertain legal status and the threat of deportation, they are unlikely to turn to law enforcement agents in cases of crime, a situation that affects women in domestic violence situations in particular. In addition, foreign-born Latinos become more vulnerable in other areas as well, such as housing. The Pew Hispanic Center just reported that during the 2008–2009 home loan crises in the United States, over one-third of Latino home owners declared fears of going into foreclosure, a figure that goes up to 53 per cent among foreign-born Latinos. A combination of legal status and limited English language skills might have made it especially difficult for them to follow the terms of a contract or to report any inconsistencies in the sale of a home.

The lack of access to social services is particularly damaging for this population because the kinds of jobs Central Americans tend to obtain do not provide benefits, like health insurance; thus, they are left with few, if any, social service resources. There is an important gender angle here. Gender ideologies place women in charge of caring for their families, and when immigrants do not have access to healthcare, particularly for the children, women seek ways to procure it. Central American immigrant women often frequent community organisations to obtain information about free clinics or about food distribution programmes, locales where they have the opportunity to meet other immigrant women or individuals who put them in touch with sources of assistance. Thus, it is the women, irrespective of how many jobs they hold or how many hours per week they work, who take charge in locating medical treatments for their family members (Menjívar, 2002). In the process, they create community and establish important informal networks through which goods and information are exchanged. However, it is also the women who worry about obtaining these benefits for their husbands and their children. A Salvadoran woman I interviewed in Phoenix lived terrified at the possibility of being separated from her children if they are deported and at the near impossibility of trying to make it back into the country. When asked about her health situation, she said:

> I feel fine now. Insurance? Our insurance company, we call it Our Heavenly Father Company [laughing]. You know why? Because we simply pray to God that we don't get sick or else we wouldn't know what to do. So He keeps us healthy. We try not to go to the doctor, as you know, we cannot expose our [undocumented] situation to everyone. So if anyone gets sick we use our medicines that people bring from Mexico or El Salvador, you know a little penicillin here or there. Stuff like that. But mostly I just try to eat well and once in a while I'll have an aspirin. Do you understand me? We take it one day at a time.

Demands beyond the United States

The demands placed on women are not limited to their family members in the United States. Central Americans send some of highest volumes of remittances and their countries' economies have come to depend on these sources of currency; each of the Central American immigrant groups sends approximately US$2.5 billion annually.[1] Indeed, Guatemala, Honduras and El Salvador are some of the highest remittance-receiving countries in Latin America today. Even though some immigrants send large amounts, most send about US$150 monthly and many have been doing so for several years, which indicates that those who send them as well as those who receive them are not wealthy individuals. Thus, the already small incomes these immigrants make are stretched significantly and in different directions. And when the immigrants have left their children in their home countries and send remittances to sustain them, women tend to send more and for longer periods of time than do men. As mothers, women often feel guilty for leaving their children behind and are concerned that they are perceived as 'bad mothers' for having left the children. This situation worsens when their own children reproach them for having been left 'abandoned', even though the women never stop remitting and sending them gifts.

Concluding points

The political-economic context into which immigrants arrive can translate into a favourable reception – relaxed or even friendly immigration laws and a viable economy with abundant jobs – or an adverse one – stiff immigration laws and fewer or low-paying jobs. As such, this broader context, over which the immigrants have no control, shapes their economic prospects. Although other individual characteristics, such as education and English language skills, influence how immigrants fare economically, factors such as legal status are pivotal in determining whether immigrants will access the receiving society's benefits or will become some of its most marginalised members.

There are some important gender angles that affect how women and men experience situations shaped by the confluence of factors in the receiving context. Women and men work in different sectors and jobs, and whereas women have more access to some jobs even during recessionary times, this does not translate into higher incomes than those of men. Legal status restricts access to society's benefits, but women experience this constraint differently than men, as they often are in charge of procuring assistance for others in their families. When social services become unavailable, it is women who feel pressured to seek out other avenues to assist their families. Central American immigrants' often inadequate incomes must be stretched to support families in the origin countries. And owing to gender ideologies that position women as primary caretakers of their children, they often feel obligated to remit more, and more regularly. Thus, as the Central American case demonstrates, whereas both immigrant women and men face similar constraints in the receiving context, gender ideologies shape their experiences differently.

Note

1. Remittance Trends in Central America, Migration Information Resource, available at: http://www.migrationinformation.org/Feature/display.cfm?ID=393 (accessed 23 February 2009).

Select bibliography

Abrego, Leisy (2008) 'Barely subsisting, surviving, or thriving: how parents' legal status and gender shape the economic and emotional well-being of Salvadoran transnational families', unpublished PhD dissertation, Department of Sociology, University of California, Los Angeles.

Bailey, Adrian, Richard Wright, Alison Mountz and Inés Miyares (2002) '(Re)producing Salvadoran transnational geographies', *Annals of the Association of American Geographers*, **92** (1), 125–44.

Calavita, Kitty (1998) 'Immigration, law and marginalisation in a global economy: notes from Spain', *Law and Society Review*, **32** (3), 529–66.

Menjívar, Cecilia (2002) 'The ties that heal: Guatemalan immigrant women's networks and medical treatment', *International Migration Review*, **36** (2), 437–66.

Menjívar, Cecilia (2006) '"Liminal legality": Salvadoran and Guatemalan immigrants' lives in the United States', *American Journal of Sociology*, **111** (4), 999–1037.

Portes, Alejandro and Rubén G. Rumbaut (2006) *Immigrant America: A Portrait*, 3rd edn, Berkeley, CA: University of California Press.

41 Culturing poverty? Ethnicity, religion, gender and social disadvantage among South Asian Muslim communities in the United Kingdom
Claire Alexander

Introduction: Britain in the twenty-first century – from multiculturalism to cohesion
On 22 September 2005, in a speech to the Manchester Council for Community Relations, Trevor Phillips, Chair of the then Commission for Racial Equality (CRE)[1] proclaimed:

> Some districts [in Britain] are on their way to becoming fully fledged ghettos – black holes into which no-one goes without fear and trepidation and from which no-one ever escapes undamaged. The walls are going up around many of our communities, and the bridges . . . are crumbling . . . The aftermath of 7/7 forces us to assess where we are. And this is where I think we are: we are sleepwalking into segregation. We are becoming strangers to each other and we are leaving communities to be marooned outside the mainstream . . . We know what follows then: crime, no-go areas and chronic cultural conflict. (Cited in Finney and Simpson, 2009: 116).

For Phillips, this move towards segregation emerges from the multicultural policies that have defined Britain's response to its Black and Minority Ethnic (BME) communities for the past 20 years, where 'we have allowed tolerance of diversity to harden into the effective isolation of communities' (cited in Finney and Simpson, 2009: 94). Phillips's account, echoed by politicians, policy pundits and the press, reflects a number of important shifts in the way in which issues of ethnicity, cultural diversity and social exclusion have been understood in the past decade. First, there is the assertion of increasing levels of social and spatial segregation defined along racial, cultural and religious lines – what has become captioned as 'parallel lives'. Second, there is the assumption that social and economic disadvantage and exclusion are the direct results of this self-imposed segregation, and that poverty is the result of cultural choice rather than structural constraints. Third, the potent image of the 'ghetto' points strongly to the highly racialised undertones of the debate with the focus of concern very much on BME communities – the ghetto is literally and symbolically a 'black hole'. Fourth, as the reference to the terror attacks of 7 July 2005 makes explicit, the primary source of these isolationist, chronically culturally conflicted communities are Britain's Muslim communities. Phillips's (con)fusion of images of racial, cultural and religious difference with social exclusion and poverty, and of both with the spectre of terrorism, reflects broader transformations in the ways in which Britain's ethnic diversity has been conceptualised and 'managed' in the new millennium, with a move away from multicultural 'Cool Britannia', towards the insistence on community cohesion and a reinvigorated monochrome 'Britishness', bolstered by 'managed migration' at the borders and 'integration' within. At the same time, the commitment to racial justice so lauded by New Labour at their election in 1997, and partially fulfilled by the Race Relations Amendment Act 2000, has given way to the disciplinary spectre of 'home grown terrorism' and 'gang cultures' (Alexander, 2007; McGhee, 2008).

The present chapter focuses on issues of social disadvantage among Britain's BME communities and explores the shift from structural to cultural explanations of poverty, with a focus on Muslim communities. The chapter considers the ways in which these discourses are both gendered and generational, positioning women as the bearers of dysfunctional traditional cultures and (young) men as their marginalised and terrorising heirs. This in turn links to broader political and policy concerns around social cohesion and citizenship, which have targeted young Muslims, male and female, as outside and opposed to the social and cultural boundaries – the 'norms and values' – of the nation. The next section outlines the longstanding links between race, ethnicity and poverty in the United Kingdom (UK) and the increasing diversity between BME communities, particularly characterised along religious lines. The third section explores the 'culturing' of poverty in debates around 'parallel lives' and 'community cohesion', focusing on the construction of 'the Muslim community' within these debates and the gendering of these discourses – most particularly around the emergence of the Asian/Muslim male 'folk devil' (Alexander, 2004).

'Race', ethnicity and poverty: disadvantage and diversity
According to the Office of National Statistics, in December 2005, the population of the UK stood at just under 60 million people, of which 7.9 per cent (around 4.6 million people) were from 'non-white' ethnic minority backgrounds, primarily of South Asian, African and Caribbean descent (ONS, 2009).[2] Although there has been a black presence in Britain since Roman times, the majority of non-white migration from Britain's then and former colonies arrived in the three decades after the end of the Second World War, and today's BME communities are in their second, third or fourth generations, with over half born in the UK (Finney and Simpson, 2009). Despite this length of presence and over 40 years of legislation against racial discrimination, however, BME communities are marked by continued inequality and socio-economic disadvantage. A 2000 Cabinet Office Report noted: 'Overall, people from minority ethnic communities are more likely than others to live in deprived areas and in unpopular and overcrowded housing. They are more likely to be poor and to be unemployed, regardless of their age, sex, qualifications and place of residence' (cited in Finney and Simpson, 2009: 27–8).

In 2005, a strategy document from the Department of Communities and Local Government (DCLG), *Improving Opportunity, Strengthening Society*, with a telling dual focus on tackling race equality and increasing community cohesion, stated similarly: 'Many members of Black and minority ethnic communities are already doing well in Britain today. But the picture is by no means uniform. Many still suffer particularly poor outcomes in education, employment, health and other life chances'.[3]

There are two significant shifts in emphasis between these two documents: first, the DCLG points to the increasing socio-economic divergence within and between BME communities that emerged through the 1990s, with Indian and Chinese groups performing as well or better than white groups in terms of education and employment, while Pakistani and Bangladeshi groups fared less well across a range of indicators.[4] Indeed, the consistent disadvantage of these South Asian Muslim communities has led Tariq Modood et al. (1997: 147) to identify an emerging 'Muslim underclass' defined by 'severe disadvantage', political alienation and potential criminalisation.

Certainly, the picture for Muslim communities is a troubling one: the 2007 DCLG update on *Improving Opportunity, Strengthening Society* noted that, despite some signs of improvement, Pakistani and Bangladeshi families were most likely to live in poor quality, overcrowded housing[5] and were more likely to be unemployed.[6] Pakistani and Bangladeshi young people were three times more likely to live in poverty[7], and Muslim boys, along with Black Caribbean and African groups, were more likely to underperform at GCSE level and in higher education. Asian young men are twice as likely to be stopped and searched than whites, and more likely to be victims of crime; and while Asian groups are underrepresented in the criminal justice system, evidence suggests that the Muslim male population in prison is increasing dramatically.[8]

Second, the DCLG report of two years earlier had signalled a changing emphasis in the *reasons* for continued levels of inequality and disadvantage, stating revealingly that this inequality could be attributed to: 'A complex mixture of reasons, including racial discrimination, lack of opportunities . . . *the neighbourhoods they live in, longstanding lack of skills and cultural factors*' (emphasis added).[9] The conflation of inequality with issues of location/neighbourhood and with cultural disadvantage, which is transmitted across the generations, echoes the broader concerns around cultural difference, segregation and 'parallel lives' which dominate public, policy and political discourses in the wake of the 2001 'riots' and the attacks of 11 September 2001 in New York and 7 July 2005 in London (Alexander 2004, 2007; McGhee 2008). The demand for integration and community cohesion has shifted attention from issues of structural inequality or class which cut across race, ethnicity or religion, and has posited culture and 'self-segregation' by BME communities as the primary faultline and cause of poverty. In 2006, Trevor Phillips stated again: '[S]eparateness in and of itself tends to encourage inequality of treatment . . . living separately means that different groups of people have their life experiences defined by their ethnicity rather than their ambitions . . . polarisation feeds a growing and dangerous tribalisation of our communities' (cited in Finney and Simpson, 2009: 134).

The 'Muslim factor': religion, gender and 'parallel lives'
The increasing diversity between the socio-economic experiences of Britain's BME communities in the 1990s reflects contemporaneous shifts in the formation of cultural identities, from the fracturing of the inclusive political category 'black' to Black and Asian in the mid-1980s and to the proliferation of national, ethnic and, most notably, religious identities from the late 1980s onwards. From 1989, when the furore around the publication of Salman Rushdie's *Satanic Verses* broke, questions were voiced about the 'Britishness' (or not) of Muslim communities, questions that were only deepened with the angry demonstrations by Muslims against the first Gulf War in 1990–1991, as debates around the 'clash of civilisations' between the 'West' and the 'Muslim' world grew louder.

This period saw an emerging concern with gendered and generational difference and conflict, with Muslim young men moving from the earlier obscurity and conformity of 'law-abiding' Asian communities to occupy the spotlight as Britain's 'Public Enemy Number One' (Alexander, 2004). Where previous moral panics had been focused on the internal 'plight' of Asian young women around issues of arranged/forced marriage, domestic violence and self-harm, the 1990s saw the growth of discourses around an externalised masculine aggression and criminality linked to social deprivation and exclusion, on the one hand, and to culture conflict and identity crisis, on the other. These two paradigms underpinned the notion of 'the Muslim underclass' and the focus on Asian/ Muslim 'gangs', in which religio-cultural difference intersected with racial alienation and socio-economic neglect in a potent image of hyper-masculine threat. As with Black young men from the 1970s, Muslim young men were seen as 'in crisis' – caught between an anachronistic parental culture and a hostile wider society, failing in mainstream masculine social roles as breadwinner, and turning to crime and violence to compensate for this. As the 1990s wore on this spectre of threat was compounded by the fear of rising religiosity and fundamentalist ideologies.

This potential threat seemed, to some at least, to be fulfilled five years later with the outbreak of incidents of urban unrest across the former milltowns of northern England in the spring and summer of 2001. Hailed as the first 'race riots' in Britain since the 1980s, British-Muslim young men confronted police and National Front supporters in a series of angry clashes, most notoriously in Bradford, Burnley and Oldham, all towns with large, well-established, and impoverished Muslim (primarily Pakistani) communities. Explanations for the unrest fell into two camps: those focusing on structural issues of socio-economic marginalisation and neglect in a situation of post-industrial decline, and those stressing cultural dysfunction, crime and law and order (Alexander, 2004). However, these two strands were increasingly indistinguishable, with poverty and unemployment being increasingly explained through the lens of 'culture' and 'choice', and with the 'Muslim underclass' standing at the crossroad of religious, cultural and class failure – what McGhee (2008:93) terms the 'cultural-deficit model' of inequality. Perceived religious and cultural norms around gender were seen as of particular significance in perpetuating poverty with commentators pointing to the low rates of participation of Muslim women in the labour market, and low educational achievement and high unemployment and crime rates among (especially young) Muslim men.

The subsequent government reports emphasised the role of religio-cultural difference and self-segregation as the key factors in the disturbances – what became known as 'parallel lives'. The Denham Report on *Building Cohesive Communities* (2001) pointed to: 'The fragmentation and polarisation of communities – on economic, geographical, racial and cultural lines – on a scale which amounts to *segregation, albeit to an extent by choice*' (emphasis added).[10] The government response to these 'problems' of cultural difference and self-segregation[11] was to promote a strategy of integration and community cohesion through an emphasis on what then Home Secretary David Blunkett termed the 'shared norms and values' underlying claims to British citizenship and identity (Alexander, 2004, 2007). McGhee (2009: 88) has argued that this has led to policies aimed at 'civil renewal' in which cultural difference is relegated to the private sphere while 'the public realm represents uniformity'. Accordingly, there has been a retreat from multiculturalist policies and ideologies, which stand accused of promoting divisions and exacerbating inter-communal tensions. At the same time, by privileging issues of culture, community and identity, new policies have tended to reinscribe notions of racial, ethnic and religious difference and underplay issues of cultural commonality and shared socio-economic disadvantage.

If 'the Muslim community' is the primary target of the new integrationism, these policies are also gendered and generational, with Muslim young men as the key focal point of concern. In the wake of the War on Terror, and the attacks on London in July 2005, policies around community cohesion have been inextricable from strategies for dealing with religious extremism, security and terrorism, in which the threat is crucially figured as young and male. McGhee (2008) has argued that fears over the potential links between socio-economic marginalisation and racism, and the emergence of extremist ideologies, has led to a recent rebalancing of 'the economic' and 'the cultural' explanations of ethnic inequality in recent public policy – tackling poverty in Muslim communities has become synonymous with tackling extremism in Muslim youth. Nevertheless, the focus on 'culture' and 'integration' remains paramount, with gender a key element of public discourse and policy formation. Thus, although young men remain the locus of assumed threat, women are positioned as the source of cultural difference and targeted for cultural reform (Alexander, 2007). For example, current policies around immigration have targeted subcontinental 'arranged/forced' marriage practices as a threat to integration and social cohesion, while the growing practice of veiling among British-born Muslim young women has been subject to increased public and political criticism; most notably after then Foreign Secretary Jack Straw's intervention in 2006, in which he described the veil as 'a visible statement of separation and difference' (cited in McGhee, 2008: 96). Young Muslim men, meanwhile, are the objects of counter-terrorist strategies, surveillance, arrests, detentions, interrogations, searches and shootings – all in the name of community cohesion.

Conclusion

The 2005 DCLG *Improving Opportunity, Strengthening Society* strategy stated the government's commitment to: 'Equal life chances for all, within the context of an inclusive British society that helps people come together to thrive economically, socially and culturally'.[12] It is salutary to reflect on the echoes of this commitment with the famous formulation of Labour Home Secretary Roy Jenkins in 1966, of integration as 'equal opportunity, accompanied by cultural diversity in an atmosphere of mutual tolerance'. Over 40 years later, issues of equality for Britain's BME communities remain unresolved, while the 'tolerance' of social, cultural or religious diversity is under attack in the wake of contemporary shifts in global movements and security, and the resurrection of exclusive and particularist national identities.

The current chapter has explored the way in which questions of equality and social justice in Britain have become subsumed by issues of culture and identity – or more accurately, by issues of *cultural/religious difference*. It has considered, too, the ways in which culture is constructed and fragmented by gendered and generational formations – most particularly the way in which Asian-Muslim young men have become emblematic of imagined national, racial and cultural crisis. The challenge for policymakers is to think outside the dominant and convenient narratives of segregation, culture and 'parallel lives', which work to blame the victims of poverty for their social exclusion and ignore broader societal processes and responsibilities. As Finney and Simpson (2009: 173) argue: 'Tensions in society result from inequalities and perceptions of inequalities. Ethnicity per se is not the cause, except where racism is a driving force . . . In many ways, ethnic differences are ordinary and banal. It is the litany that makes them a threat.'

Notes

1. The Commission for Racial Equality was, until recently, the non-governmental organisation concerned with issues of racial justice in the UK. It was replaced by the Commission for Equality and Human Rights in 2007, with Trevor Phillips appointed as its first Chair.

2. Indians were the largest group at 22.7 per cent of the BME population, with Pakistanis making up 16.1 per cent, Black Caribbeans 12.2 per cent, Black Africans 10.5 per cent, Bangladeshis 6.1 per cent and Chinese 5.3 per cent. The fastest growing 'community' is the 'mixed race' population at 14.6 per cent. According to the 2001 Census, there were nearly 1.6 million self-defined Muslims in the UK, constituting around 2.7 per cent of the population (ONS, 2009).
3. This citation is taken verbatim from page 8 of the 2005 DCLG report, available at: http://www.communities.gov.uk/publications/communities/210470 (accessed 16 May 2009).
4. Black Caribbean groups occupied an intermediary position in most of the areas addressed; what Modood et al. (1997) term 'relative disadvantage'.
5. According to DCLG (2007:35), as of 2004 33 per cent of BME households were living in 'non-decent homes' (a drop from 50 per cent in 1996). As many as 27 per cent of Bangladeshi households were overcrowded, compared with 2 per cent of white households, and with the lowest levels of owner-occupation. Muslim households were also more likely to be in areas of multiple deprivation.
6. As per DCLG (2007:29), unemployment for Bangladeshi men stood at 17 per cent, Black Caribbean, Black African and mixed race men at 15 per cent, and Pakistani men at 11 per cent compared to white men at 5 per cent. Muslims had the highest rates of unemployment at 16 per cent, compared to Sikhs and Hindus (8 per cent) and Christians (5 per cent). The rates of economic inactivity for Pakistani and Bangladeshi women was three times the level for Christian women (68 per cent, 72 per cent to 24 per cent respectively).
7. Defined as living at 60 per cent of median household income.
8. The Asian Muslim male prison population grew by 105 per cent between 1985 and 2002.
9. This quote is taken from page 8 of the 2005 DCLG report, available at: http://www.communities.gov.uk/publications/communities/210470 (accessed 16 May 2009).
10. This quote is taken from page 11 of the Denham Report, available at: http://www.cohesioninstitute.org.uk/resources/Publications/BuildingCohesiveCommunities%20Denham.pdf (accessed 17 May 2009).
11. See Finney and Simpson (2009) for an useful statistical analysis and critique of these claims.
12. This quote is taken from page 13 of the 2005 DCLG report, available at: http://www.communities.gov.uk/publications/communities/210470 (accessed 16 May 2009).

Select bibliography

Alexander, Claire (2004) 'Imagining the Asian gang: ethnicity, masculinity and youth after the "riots"', *Critical Social Policy*, **24** (4), 526–49.

Alexander, Claire (2007) 'Cohesive identities: the distance between meaning and understanding', in Margaret Wetherell, Michelynn LaFleche and Robert Berkeley (eds), *Identity, Ethnic Diversity and Community Cohesion*, London: Sage, pp. 115–25.

Department for Communities and Local Government (DCLG) (2007) *Improving Opportunity, Strengthening Society*, London: DCLG.

Finney, Nissa and Ludi Simpson (2009) *Sleepwalking to Segregation? Challenging Myths about Race and Migration*, Bristol: Policy Press.

McGhee, Derek (2008) *The End of Multiculturalism? Terrorism, Integration and Human Rights*, Milton Keynes: Open University Press.

Modood, Tariq, Richard Berthoud, Jane Lakey, James Nazroo, Patten Smith, Satnam Virdee and Sharon Bieshon (1997) *Ethnic Minorities in Britain: Diversity and Disadvantage*, London: Policy Studies Institute.

Office of National Statistics (ONS) (2009) *People and Migration: Ethnicity*, London: ONS, available at: www.statistics.gov.uk (accessed 5 May 2009).

42 Gender, occupation, loss and dislocation: a Latvian perspective
Linda McDowell

One of the typical consequences of transnational migration is downward social mobility, sometimes temporary but often permanent. Moving between countries for work, to escape tyranny or natural disaster, or because of war or occupation, disrupts everyday life and necessitates the reconstruction of social relations in another place: an everyday life often haunted by what might have been and memories of trauma and dislocation. In this chapter, I explore an extreme version of such disruption for a group of adolescent girls and young women born in Latvia, one of the three Baltic States, in the interwar period which was a time of relative prosperity for the then newly independent country. Relative economic prosperity, rising expectations and an expanding educational system were associated with growing independence for middle class girls. This era came to an abrupt end at the start of the Second World War. Latvia was invaded and occupied, first by the Soviet Army, then by the Third Reich and, on Germany's imminent defeat in 1944, again by the Soviet Army. Under the Yalta agreement, Latvia became a Soviet Socialist Republic in 1945.

Here I explore the implications for young women of living under the two foreign occupations, assessing the effects of occupation on the typical transitions experienced by young women as they grow up and move from the dependence of childhood to the independence of adulthood. The case study is based on interviews with by then elderly Latvian women undertaken in 2001–2002. These women left Latvia in 1944 and became in turn refugees, workers for the Third Reich, residents of displaced persons camps and economic migrants. These events resulted in downward social mobility and a lifetime of exile and hardship as members of the British working class.

Growing up under Stalin and Hitler
Is everyday life possible in a situation of total war, foreign occupation and subjection to a Nazi or Fascist ideology? This is a question posed by historian Robert Gildea (2006) and his colleagues, and in its exploration in the present chapter my focus is on adolescent girls, for whom the impact of occupation was perhaps less evident than for adults, who attempted to protect their younger dependants from the most pernicious aspects of life under occupation. It was perhaps less dangerous than for their male peers who had forcible recruitment to fear as they grew older, although for young women, becoming sexually active at a time when the fear of harassment and rape by the occupying forces was a significant issue. Occupation clearly affects not only daily life in the home and in the locality, from food shortages to more significant traumas, when, for example, relatives were arrested or forcibly deported, but also daily life in schools and in higher educational institutions, as national languages were often suppressed and curricula changed. In 1940 and 1941 under Soviet occupation, many people disappeared – killed or transported to

Soviet prison camps, culminating in the removal of 15 000 people, including women and children in June 1941 as the Soviet occupation came to an end. A brutal Nazi regime replaced it that officially lasted until Germany's surrender in May 1945, although Latvia was partially reoccupied by the Red Army from autumn 1944. In 1941, the German occupiers immediately began to implement a plan to turn the Baltic into an area of German settlement, as well as recruiting workers for the Third Reich. Although Latvia was not subjected to such thorough processes of Nazification as areas further west with a higher proportion of ethnic Germans in their population, Latvia experienced economic exploitation, military order and extreme measures of security enforced by the police. The local population was starved to feed the occupying troops; Jews, gypsies and Russian prisoners of war were exterminated and Slavs were deported. Nevertheless, despite these hardships, a version of everyday life in Latvia was maintained, at least until 1944. Many children continued to go to school, some students were able to transfer into higher education institutions, and young people in general managed to enter the labour market as well as to construct forms of social life during the war years. Some of them were also able to leave the relative security of their parental homes and establish a version of adult independence, even under conditions of national emergency.

Adolescent transitions
One of the advantages of focusing on adolescence as a lens through which to address the continuities and discontinuities in everyday life under occupation is that, in more 'normal times' it is a period during which young people expect to mark the passage to adulthood by a series of significant changes in their life. In the modern economies that developed during the twentieth century, the accepted symbols of adulthood became the movement out of the parental home and the achievement of independent living. For men, this was based primarily on labour market participation, whereas for women, especially before the Second World War when female labour force participation, especially for married women, was lower than it became in later decades, the conventional marker of adult status was the re-establishment of a familial home on marriage (Drew et al., 1998; Lewis, 1992). For women born during the inter-war era, in most European countries, marriage during their early twenties was the expectation, perhaps followed by a short period of waged work before withdrawal from the labour force on the birth of children. Women expected to receive financial support from a male breadwinner in exchange for domestic labour, sexual services and the provision of emotional support. For young women in Latvia during the Second World War, the double occupation meant that they had to face the prospect of family destabilisation, broken schooling, reduced opportunities for higher education, and possibly the need to earn their own living. They had to try to establish themselves as independent individuals during conditions which almost inevitably placed either severe restrictions on their prospect of growing independence or demanded a sudden, often brutal, transition into self-sufficiency and independence.

To understand the effects of the two occupations on the daily lives of young women, I collected oral narratives from 25 women born in Latvia between 1916 and 1931. They fled from the country between autumn 1944 and spring 1945 in the face of the advancing Soviet front, all aged between 13 and 28, with the majority between 17 and 21 years old. They were a tiny number among the 200 000 of their compatriots who left Latvia over a period of less than six months, walking to the coast and then escaping by sea to either occupied Poland or to Scandinavia. For many of them a member of their family – a father or uncle, sometimes a brother – had been deported or murdered by the occupying Soviet administration in 1941, just before Latvia was occupied by the forces of the Third Reich. For others, brothers had been recruited into the Latvian Legion, an SS (Schutzstaffel) regiment. Yet other members had become part of the Reich's large-scale labour recruitment schemes, under which over 8 million people from occupied territories were sent to work in Germany (Herbert, 1997).

In late 1944, as German forces were evacuated from Latvia, the families of these girls and young women, all of whom were unmarried, were anxious to escape, fearing retribution by the Soviet Union. Some of the young women left the country in the company of their family, others with friends, one or two alone and as they fled west through German-occupied territory, they were often separated from their travelling companions. Eventually the women whom I interviewed found refuge as the war ended in the displaced persons camps established in the Allied zones. There, many of them were reunited with family members and compatriots and re-established a semblance of 'normal' life, albeit under conditions of considerable hardship.

Everyday life under occupation
Most of the women whom I interviewed were still at school or in post-compulsory education when the war started in Europe in 1939. Eight of them had been born in Riga, Latvia's capital city, and seven had grown up there, nine in small towns and the rest in villages or in the countryside. In terms of class position they ranged from daughters of the middle class (with fathers who were ministry officials or head teachers for example), petit bourgeois (for example, fathers who owned a smallholding or a modest hotel) and craftsmen (electricians, builders). Four fathers were army officials, one of whom was shot by the Germans and another by the Russians during the early 1940s. Their mothers' lives revolved around running the home – almost half had no paid work – and, for the rural dwellers, helping on the farm or in the mill was a regular, although unpaid, part of familial reproduction. Two mothers had professional jobs; another two were book-keepers in commercial organisations. For these families, apart from two where the male head of household had died before the war, the 1930s were a period of relative stability and, for many, growing prosperity as overall standards of living rose. These women reported that they had had, on the whole, happy childhoods in which living in the countryside was a significant summer ritual. The children brought up in Riga and in small towns typically spent several summer weeks with their rural grandparents. All attended school to at least the age of 14, many had attended, or were still attending in 1939, the senior school and one or two had entered higher education.

The younger girls among the 25 were probably least affected by the occupations which, initially, had little outward impact on their lives. They continued to go to school, although the curriculum and the language of instruction had changed. Teaching, first in Russian until 1941 and then in German until the surrender in Europe, was compulsory in most lessons. Other smaller changes, such as which flag was flown and the introduction of new youth movements, overall had relatively minimal material effects on the children. The symbolic meaning of flying the flag of the occupiers was a more serious matter for many adults. Overall, life in the countryside and in villages went on much the same as before. In the cities, food became short although many city dwellers were protected to some extent by their rural contacts from the extremes of shortages.

Here is Jelena, born in 1931, talking about her girlhood:

> My father was a forester ... There was also a little farm attached to the job, about ten hectares, we had about four or five cows and some sheep and a couple of horses. For self sufficiency ... It was pleasant life, we lived quite well ... We didn't go short of anything.
>
> In 1940 the Russians came. I don't remember much of it. They [adults] didn't say anything to children but I can remember people being uneasy. The first year the school was changed. The Pioneers was organised, red scarves and that.
>
> The Germans [who occupied Latvia in 1941] didn't bother us much in the countryside although there were shortages and you had to give a certain part of farm produce to the Germans. You had to register every animal and you couldn't slaughter anything without permission. And soldier and army movement was increased and we had soldiers billeted on us.

Some of the older adolescents were more aware of the political and practical implications of the occupations which had differential impacts on their families depending on their location and their fathers' occupations. Those working for the state – as officials, in the police and army – were particularly at risk during the occupations. Natalija, 14 in 1940 when the Soviet occupation began, explains how her childhood came to an abrupt end: 'My father was a policeman. We left Riga in 1940 because my father would have been one of the first ones shot [by the Soviet occupiers], despite the fact that he was only a policeman directing traffic. We went to my grandfather's house in the country, lying low.' When the Germans took over in 1941, the family's problems intensified as Natalija's brother, then aged 20, was conscripted by the Nazi occupiers: 'My brother was recruited by the Germans and sent in army to Russia. He was killed in July 1944.'

For most of the 25 women, the key change in their lives under occupation was the effects it had on their career plans. As educated, largely middle-class girls, most of them expected to enter the labour market, taking up a suitably feminised occupation before marriage. During the occupation, many of the girls coming up to school-leaving age had to re-evaluate their opportunities and enter forms of work that did not necessitate college-level credentials. Others were caught up in the German war effort as, between 1942 and 1944, there were huge forced labour drives across the occupied territories as well as local schemes of directed labour, as Helena explained: 'During the occupation we were slave labour for next to nothing – directed labour under the Germans. You had to go where you were sent and you were paid only a few marks. On our own farm only three people were allowed to work on the acres we had so I was sent away [to work on another family's farm].'

The most severe disruption to these young women's lives, however, occurred in 1944 as they left their parental homes. What should have been a mark of a successful transition to adulthood instead was a traumatic dislocation, as the Soviet forces reoccupied Latvia from autumn 1944.

Working lives

Escape from Latvia was achieved in the wake of the retreating German armed forces. The women whom I interviewed left alone, with a group of friends, with their mother and occasionally as an entire family, escaping by sea from Latvia's main port, Leipaj, and landing in occupied Danzig, now Gdansk in Poland. At the port, while waiting for onward transport across occupied Europe, most of the then young women were immediately recruited as part of the Third Reich's foreign labour force. Although by late 1944, the large-scale programmes of forced labour were beginning to falter, as the Reich's days were numbered, foreign workers were still numerically significant – a third of the labour force in the armaments industry, for example, about a quarter in the chemical and machinery industries (Herbert, 1997). Men and women also worked on the land and women as domestic servants. Here is Elvira's explanation of what happened to her in 1944 as she landed at Danzig: 'There was a sort of camp there . . . From Danzig we were sent to Colberg, to work in a paper mill. It wasn't all that hard really but we had to walk a long way from the camp which was in a factory. We had to walk and sometimes I did night shifts.' Agnese, initially allocated to domestic service, was moved into the armaments industry: 'I was sent on my own and put in a house, house cleaning. That wasn't too bad. Then we were sent working in a munitions factory with a few other Latvian girls.' Vieda was sent to a German hospital: 'I was allocated to go to a German hospital. I was by then 16 already and I was sent to work in a laundry which was dreadful, with the cold water and so on.' And Lina, only 14 years old, had one of the hardest jobs:

> They just send you on the street to clean, the street. We were living in the camps. In the morning they gave us a coffee, we had cups, half a pint something like that and one piece of bread and I think they gave us a slice of cheese or something to put on that bread. And that was it, finish, you had to wait til the night. You had to go and clean the snow and the ice, like chipped ice, on the streets.

For these young women this introduction to manual labour was the start of a long life of poor work and relative poverty. In 1945 as Germany collapsed they were directed to displaced persons camps run by the Allies (Wyman, 1998). Here, too, employment opportunities were limited: predominantly manual work or, for the more fortunate, office work. The camps provided a relatively secure environment and some of the women whom I interviewed told me that it was here they were able to begin to enjoy leisure opportunities, even to develop personal and intimate relationships. But life was difficult. Overcrowded, short of food and lacking privacy, young women felt restricted, as well as anxious about absent relatives and the fear of being returned to Latvia, now under Soviet control.

Becoming economic migrants
Between 1946 and 1949, another move was made by many displaced persons. Under migrant labour schemes, several West European governments, as well as Canada, the USA and Australia imported displaced people to fill vacancies in shortage sectors as part of the post-war reconstruction programmes, and to replace the labour of women nationals who returned to the home in significant numbers at the end of the war. The first directed labour scheme – the Baltic Cygnet Scheme – was introduced by the UK for young single women aged between 16 and 40 (Tannahill, 1958). Several thousand young women were recruited for employment in the textile industry and for domestic work in hospitals (McDowell, 2005). Here, too, the work was uncongenial, physically hard and poorly paid. A second scheme instituted a year later brought men to the UK into mining, agriculture and the iron and steel industry. Many women married their compatriots and built a life in working-class areas in British towns and cities, predominantly in the

north of England. Life there remained restricted by financial hardship and geographical immobility, although they were ambitious for their children to reclaim their own lost class status.

Conclusions

This is a story of dislocation, downward mobility and a lifetime of relative poverty for women who through their age and nationality found themselves the subjects of a double occupation during the war. Occupation disrupted the typical path that women of their age and class expected as the corollary of the transition to adulthood. The decision to flee from Soviet repression made by them, or more accurately by their parents or other adult relatives, had a radical effect on their life chances.

Geographical movement was associated with disruption, loss and hardship, as their recruitment as economic migrants rather than refugees by the British government necessitated participation in poorly paid female-dominated occupations in post-war Britain. Low incomes and financial hardship meant that most of these women continued in waged employment throughout their lives, often on a full-time basis, unlike most British women of the same age and class background. War, occupation and transnational migration had a lasting impact, marked on the bodies, homes and life chances of young women who were caught up in world events beyond their control.

Select bibliography

Drew, Eileen, Ruth Emerek and Evelyn Mahon (1998) *Women, Work and Family in Europe*, London: Routledge.
Gildea, Robert, Olivier Wieviorka and Anette Warring (eds) (2006) *Surviving Hitler and Mussolini: Daily Life in Occupied Europe*, Oxford: Berg.
Herbert, Ullrich (1997) *Hitler's Foreign Workers: Enforced Labour in Germany under the Third Reich*, Cambridge University Press: Cambridge.
Lewis, Jane (1992) *Women in Britain since 1945*, London: Heinemann.
McDowell, Linda (2005) *Hard Labour: The Forgotten Voices of Latvian Migrant Volunteer Workers*, London: UCL Press.
Tannahill, J.A. (1958) *European Volunteer Workers in Britain*, Manchester: Manchester University Press.
Wyman, Mark (1998) *DPs: Europe's Displaced Persons, 1945–1951*, revd edn, Ithaca, NY and London: Cornell University Press.

43 Gender, poverty and migration in Mexico
Haydea Izazola

Gender and poverty in Mexico

Women in Mexico have been relegated to the domestic sphere for centuries, with the roles of mother and householder's companion constituting the principal sources of their identity and determinants of their behaviour. Women's presence in the extra-domestic sphere has also been linked to roles as educator, teacher, servant and nurse, for example. It is only since the second half of the twentieth century, as a result of macrostructural changes linked to rapid industrialisation and urbanisation, that major changes have been recorded in women's status as a result of their access to higher levels of educational attainment and birth control. From the 1970s onwards, Mexican women increased their participation in the labour force. In some cases, their resulting economic independence enabled them to overcome their subordinate situation, and increasingly assume the headship of their households. The recurrent economic crises of recent decades, however, as well as the adoption of structural adjustment policies that dismantled the nascent Mexican welfare state, has revealed the precarious living conditions of most of the population, particularly poor women.

Poverty in Mexico

Mexico is regarded as one of the countries with the greatest biodiversity worldwide. It has a population of 107 million, the majority of which (65 per cent) are within economically active ages, and it is conveniently located for the international market. These and other factors have made Mexico one of the world's main economies. However, for several centuries it has been characterised by sharp socio-economic inequalities, resulting from authoritarian political regimes that have promoted the concentration of wealth, keeping most of the population in conditions of poverty and destitution. By the early nineteenth century, Alexander von Humboldt had already documented the sharp inequalities that left most of the indigenous population in subsistence conditions, despite the creation of enormous wealth in New Spain that ended up in the hands of the Spanish Crown and colonial elites. This situation has yet to be overcome, unfortunately, and at present, Mexico is one of the most unequal countries in the world, with nearly half its population living in poverty.

There has been considerable debate on the current extent of poverty, particularly since universal social policy was replaced by targeted programmes for alleviating poverty as a result of structural adjustment policies adopted in the 1980s. The lack of conceptual, theoretical and methodological consensus has guided the recent discussion on poverty. It has officially been recognised that over 40 per cent of the population was in this situation in 2006, a proportion that doubles if alternative measures are used.

A similar debate has guided the discussion on the 'feminisation of poverty'. It is assumed that, as a result of both familial and social gender disadvantages, women are the poorest of the poor, particularly female householders. This assumption has determined the majority of programmes designed to combat poverty, although it has also been widely criticised. The diversity of situations experienced by women means that caution must be exercised in characterising women in the debate on poverty. Depending on their social status and their position in the individual and familial life cycle, as well as their own biographies that define the various ways in which they perform their roles, women use multiple strategies to cope with poverty and that of their families. The absence of a male household head often leads to situations of greater gender and generational equity, owing to a better distribution of resources and domestic work in a less violent atmosphere (Chant, 2007). Paradoxically, it is under this assumption that the current targeted programmes have conceived of the joint responsibility of women (as household heads and spouses) with their traditional gender roles as an ideal means of achieving gender equality and overcoming poverty, thereby threatening to reinforce their subordinate position in both intrafamilial relations and society as a whole (Molyneux, 2006). It is currently estimated that the main targeted human development programme, *Oportunidades*, helps nearly 5 million households, with women receiving the benefits of these programmes in 96 per cent of all cases (see González de la Rocha, Chapter 37, this volume).

Poverty and minimum wages
Regardless of the way in which the incidence of poverty is measured, the fact that it is officially recognised that nearly half the population is in this situation is partly due to the extremely low income levels of the working poor. Although the Mexican Constitution enshrines the right to a minimum wage covering the needs of the workers and their families, in practice only a minority have benefited from this right. As a result of structural adjustment policies (SAPs), the minimum wage experienced its most severe decline; between 1982 and early 2009, it lost 82 per cent of its purchasing power. As of 2009, the minimum salary stood at just 54.80 Mexican pesos a day (US$3.6). Mexico's low labour costs have long provided one of its major competitive advantages for the country's insertion in the global market, as manifested in the massive employment of young women in the *maquiladora* (assembly) industry, mainly in the border cities.

Income diversification

Female extra-domestic labour
Given the precariousness of work and wages, households have resorted to a series of strategies for diversifying income. These include the incorporation of their members into economic activity, particularly women and especially married women. The rate of female participation in economic activity has therefore risen from 17 per cent in 1970 to 19.6 per cent in 1990, 31.3 per cent in 2000 and 41.4 per cent in 2008.

There is an ample literature on the diversity of factors that have led to the increase in female extra-domestic labour, such as higher educational achievement, lower fertility and the tertiarisation of the economy. The implications of these trends have also been investigated in terms of autonomy and empowerment, as well as vulnerability and exploitation. In some cases, married women's increased participation has not translated into the ability to overcome subordination. Indeed, it has actually created an extra burden, since women continue to do the same amount of housework,

Table 43.1 Evolution of income by gender in ranks of minimum wages. Mexico, 1990–2008

Income in ranks of minimum wages	Female 1990 (%)	Female 2008 (%)	Male 1990 (%)	Male 2008 (%)
No income	2.8	10.6	8.6	7.7
Up to one minimum wage (MW)	22.4	16.1	18.3	9.1
1–2 MWs	42.7	23.9	34.8	24.9
2–3 MWs	14.6	21.1	15.3	17.7
3–5 MWs	8.3	13.1	10.2	19.2
More than 5 MWs	5.0	8.8	8.4	13.5
Not specified	4.2	6.3	4.4	7.8

Sources: INEGI (1993, 2009).

meaning that they now perform a double shift. In cases where women also engage in community work (particularly when spouses have emigrated or women are involved in programmes such as *Oportunidades*) they work a triple shift. Greater female participation in extra-domestic work has occasionally triggered or exacerbated violent reactions from women's partners. In other cases, extra-domestic work has contributed to women's greater autonomy and control over their resources, and more egalitarian gender relations. Among the factors helping to account for this diversity of outcomes of extra-domestic work are women's work experience and type of occupation, their educational levels, urban versus rural residence, relations with their families of origin, and mothers' participation in the labour force. However, traditional gender roles that give women a key role in everyday, intergenerational reproduction (as mothers and wives) continue to be deeply rooted in Mexican culture and female identity. The majority of married women who take part in the labour market do so more out of necessity than as a means of achieving personal fulfilment (García and Oliveira, 2007). Women's greater participation in economic activity has also been dominated by discriminatory labour relations expressed in low or no income from their work (see Table 43.1).

In 1990, approximately 15 600 women were reported to work for no pay, whereas in 2008, there were over 1.8 million. Nowadays, on average, women only earn 5 per cent less per hour than men and spend only 18 per cent less time a week than them on extra-domestic work (INEGI, 2009). Yet this apparent reduction of inequality is due more to the decline in real salaries for workers of both sexes than to women's achievements in the labour sphere. The outlook changes when one examines the population organised by households. Although the proportion of women-headed households in Mexico rose from 13.5 per cent in 1976 to 24.8 per cent in 2008, this is fairly low in comparison with some other countries in Latin America and the Global South (see Chant, 2007). By the same token, echoing findings from other localities which urge caution about the blanket association between female household headship and poverty (ibid.), only two-thirds of the population in Mexican women-headed households were poor in 2006 as opposed to 72 per cent of members in male-headed units, according to alternative, non-governmental estimates (Damián, forthcoming).

Migration in Mexico

Given the adverse economic conditions of recent decades, households have increasingly engaged in international migration as part of their strategies for diversifying income. Unlike in the past, when internal migration with a greater female presence had dominated the population's mobility, in recent years this has been increasingly replaced by migration to the United States. Between 1995–2000 and 2000–2005, internal migration fell from 3.8 million to 2.6 million, while international migration rose from 1.2 million to nearly 3 million.

Changes in national and international migratory patterns show a greater diversification of flows at both origin and destination and migrants' characteristics have also undergone significant changes. The rural–urban migration directed to the country's major cities has been joined by flows of indigenous people and professionals towards medium-sized cities and abroad. The image of impoverished peasants and/or unemployed persons looking for work has accordingly shifted as men and women with high educational attainment and occupational status have started to move away from large metropolises. A new 'migratory mosaic' has emerged which comprises groups of various demographic, social and economic origins, with equally diverse reasons for changing residence. In turn, in some cases, migration has contributed to more equal gender relations within households, whereas in others, it has exacerbated existing inequalities.

Analysing these processes, however, is hampered by the insufficiency of conventional sources of information. Census and survey data are available for the spatiality of internal migration at the state level and occasionally at the municipal level, as in the case of the 2000 census. The information also distinguishes between long- and short-term migrants, by their place of birth or place of residence five years prior to the time when the survey or census was taken. Where international migration is concerned, Mexican information is drawn, among other sources, from censuses, household surveys and surveys carried out on the border that register crossings by land, all of which underestimate the real scope of emigration. US surveys and censuses are a more reliable source of information on Mexican emigration to that country, as they capture the Mexican population living in the US.

According to census data, Mexican women accounted for 48 and 52 per cent of intranational migration flows in 1900 and 2000 respectively. Mexican surveys and censuses estimated female emigration to the US between 4 and 25 per cent of the total flow during the last decades, compared with 46–44 per cent of the total flow reported by US surveys. This phenomenon is analysed below.

Mexico–US migration

It is estimated that net international migration rose from an annual average of 27 500 in the 1970s to 558 000 persons in 2008, nearly all of whom went to the USA. Indeed, Mexico now loses more of its population annually to emigration than to death, with deaths in 2008 being estimated at 518 000. Thirty out of 32 states in the country show negative international migration rates.

According to the US Current Population Survey, the volume of Mexican-born persons residing in the United States rose from 4 million in 1990 to 11.8 million in 2007, 45 per cent of whom entered the country after 1995. Yet only 21.5 per cent of the total population of Mexican-born immigrants currently possess US citizenship.

The effects of this exodus remain difficult to grasp in all its complexity, since migrants are usually young people with higher educational attainment than the rest of the country's inhabitants, which in itself constitutes a brain drain (although see also Gutmann, Chapter 49, this volume). It is estimated that every year 20 000 Mexicans with high educational attainment emigrate. A total of 552 000 Mexican people with BAs, MAs or PhDs reside in the US, while the figure for the European Union is 23 000.

From an economic perspective, the flow of foreign currency via family remittances rose from approximately US$10 billion in 2002 to over US$23 billion in 2008, second only to the revenue obtained from oil exports. This amount has provided major macro-economic advantages, but above all, despite the existing debate on its actual scope, it has helped many families overcome or prevent poverty.

International female migration

In the past, international female migration was regarded as part of a process of family accompaniment. Women tended to move with and/or follow in the footsteps of their menfolk, and at the latter's behest. In turn, it was often observed that 'traditional' gender roles and relations were reproduced in destination areas. Over time, however, international female emigration has become more independent, as a result of recent social changes, including higher female educational attainment, lower fertility and greater participation in the labour market. Thus, together with economic pull and push factors, the existence of social and family networks and a more favourable institutional context for women, the female presence among the emigrant population is becoming increasingly important.

The proportion of women among migrants to the USA has oscillated between 46 and 44 per cent over the past decade, with the share of female-headed households among international migrants rising to 41.4 per cent in 2007, compared with only 24 per cent in Mexico. Although women migrants report higher educational attainment than men, 26.3 per cent are considered poor, as opposed to 18 per cent of men. Women migrants' participation in economic activity was 47.5 per cent that same year, mainly in the tertiary sector (80 per cent). Their average weekly work shift was 36.8 hours while their average salary totalled US$19 237 annually (approximately US$10 an hour) as opposed to US$26 265 for men (approximately US$12 an hour) (CONAPO, 2008).

Repercussions on gender relations are difficult to generalise, since there is a wide variety of situations into which migrant women are incorporated. Some manage to establish more equal relations both inside and outside the home, yet many of them remain under the domination and control of male relatives.

Women left behind

One aspect that has rarely been studied, although it has increasingly attracted attention in qualitative research, concerns the women and families left behind.

Women who remain in migrant source areas contribute to the maintenance of binational family and social networks, although in the process many are affected by heavier workloads and symbolic obligations that reproduce and even exacerbate their situation of subordination. The control to which they are subjected by the community and above all, their in-laws, show how subordinate gender relations continue to operate, sometimes producing even higher levels of violence. For their part, some women have achieved more equitable gender relations, as a result of the greater autonomy provided by remittances, as well as their greater involvement in the decisions of their families and communities. Many families left behind, however, do not regularly receive remittances and often stop receiving them altogether once they lose track of the relatives who emigrated, which puts them in an even more vulnerable situation.

These social costs and benefits are difficult to document through sample surveys. Qualitative studies have revealed the complex repercussions triggered by migration in generic and intergenerational terms. Further studies are required to understand better the impact of this exodus, both in Mexico and the USA, particularly in view of the current world financial and economic crisis.

Select bibliography

Chant, Sylvia (2007) *Gender, Generation and Poverty: Exploring the 'Feminisation of Poverty' in Africa, Asia and Latin America*, Cheltenham, UK and Northampton, MA, USA: Edward Elgar.

Consejo Nacional de Población (CONAPO) (2008) *Series Sobre Migración Internacional 2008*, México DF: CONAPO, available at: http://www.conapo.gob.mx/mig_int/s2008/pdfs/03.pdf (accessed 18 November 2008).

Damián, Araceli (forthcoming) 'Pobreza y Derechos Socioeconómicos en México. Una Mirada Desde la Perspectiva de Género', in Ana María Tepichin (ed.), *Género, Pobreza y Desarrollo*, México DF: El Colegio de México.

García, Brígida and Orlandina de Oliveira (2007) 'Trabajo Extradoméstico y Relaciones de Género: Una Nueva Mirada', in María Alicia Gutiérrez (ed.), *Género, Familias y Trabajo: Rupturas y Continuidades. Desafíos para la Investigación Política*, Buenos Aires: CLACSO, pp. 49–87.

Instituto Nacional de Estadística, Geografía e Informática (INEGI) (1993) *La Mujer en México*, 2nd edn, Aguascalientes: INEGI.

Instituto Nacional de Estadística, Geografía e Informática (INEGI) (2009) *Encuesta Nacional de Ocupación y Empleo 2008*, Aguascalientes: INEGI, available at: http://www.inegi.org.mx/est/contenidos/espanol/sistemas/enoe/ind_trim/default.asp?s=est&c=11415 (accessed 16 February 2009).

Molyneux, Maxine (2006) 'Mothers at the service of the new poverty agenda: Progresa/Oportunidades, Mexico's conditional transfer programme', *Social Policy and Administration*, **40** (4), 425–49.

44 Migration, gender and sexual economies: young female rural–urban migrants in Nigeria
Daniel Jordan Smith

As in much of sub-Saharan Africa, in Nigeria, a combination of increasing aspirations and opportunities, challenging economic circumstances, and burdensome kinship obligations compel large numbers of single young women to migrate from rural to urban areas. Many young female migrants adapt to the challenges of the city by engaging in sexual relationships with men who can provide them resources, a strategy that can be experienced as both demeaning and empowering. This chapter draws on an ethnographic study of young Igbo-speaking migrants in the northern Nigerian city of Kano. The scope and diversity of the local sexual economy, the spectrum of young women's experiences, and the moral discourses about migration, gender, and sexuality that are produced and circulate in response to this situation reveal the complexity and contradictions inherent in Nigeria's changing structure of gender inequality.

In recent decades, demographers and other social scientists have drawn attention to and begun to analyse the growing proportion of rural–urban migrants in sub-Saharan Africa who are female, young, and unmarried (Gugler and Ludwar-Ene, 1995; Makinwa-Adebusoye, 1990). This trend represents a relatively new pattern, as previous rural–urban migration streams have been predominantly male, and women tended to move in more significant numbers as the married partners of male migrants than as single and independent agents in their own right. In Nigeria, as in much of the continent, the factors that propel this migration are many, and reflect the multifaceted and tangled ways in which this pattern of mobility is indicative of both persistent gender inequality and significant transformations that can legitimately be seen as positive for women.

Young women in Nigeria typically leave their rural communities in search of opportunities, especially further education or employment. The idea that socially acceptable trajectories for success for women include education, employment, and other means of income generation beyond farming and local rural trade has taken hold throughout much of the country. Indeed, these pathways are not only economically valued, they are seen as important for a woman's success in the marriage market, and as measures of her future competence at motherhood (more educated and economically successful women are viewed as able to impart these skills to their children). Even with young single women's growing participation in rural–urban migration, their greater access to education, and their entry and success in the labour and commercial marketplaces, marriage and parenthood remain paramount values and imperative lifecourse aims (Smith, 2001). The fact that young Nigerian women are, almost universally, still required to fulfil the domestic obligations that were expected of their mothers' and grandmothers' generations raises the question of whether these young female migrants are ultimately being asked to shoulder a double burden, an issue that has been examined in the literature (Hollos and Larsen, 1992).

In Nigeria, questions about the consequences for women due to their increasing participation in rural–urban migration are further complicated by the varying ways in which young women are propelled to migrate. In most circumstances, the decision to migrate is viewed in economic terms (whether it is more immediate, as when looking for a job, or longer term, as when seeking higher education as a gateway to future economic success). Further, more often than not, young women undertake migration with family and parental consultation and consent. While most young women make migration decisions in consultation with kin, the spectrum of experiences is broad. Regardless of the relative level and tenor of family support or coercion, nearly all young female migrants are expected to try to help parents and other kin at home through whatever success they achieve as migrants. Indeed, it is imperative not to exaggerate the differences between young men and young women in this regard. For the vast majority of young rural–urban migrants in Nigeria the continued ties and obligations to parents, siblings, and wider networks of kin in their rural places of origin stand out as a paramount factor in how these young migrants experience and try to navigate the opportunities and challenges of city life (Chukwuezi, 2001).

This chapter focuses on understanding how young single female migrants from south-eastern Nigeria traverse and survive urban life in Kano, the largest city in northern Nigeria and a major destination for Igbo rural–urban migrants. Although the ways in which young female migrants participate in urban sexual economies are typically seen as evidence of gender unequal economic and cultural systems and processes, the ethnographic data presented below suggest that the situation is more nuanced. While many forms of young female migrants' participation in Kano's sexual economy can be viewed as exploitive, in lots of circumstances women utilise their sexuality and their sexual relationships with men productively, raising questions about its ultimate effects and meanings vis-à-vis issues of gender inequality. Further, it is difficult to disentangle the moral and material aspects of Kano's sexual economy. The experiences of the young female migrants who are the subject of the study reported here suggest that the moral dimensions of this sexual economy can have equal or greater consequences for the reproduction of gender inequality as the more material aspects.

'My daughter is working in Kano': migration, economic aspirations, and the moral paradoxes of an urban sexual economy

The findings presented here are the result of a two-year study in 2001 and 2002 of unmarried Igbo rural–urban migrants from southeastern Nigeria between 15 and 24 years old who were residing in Kano (Smith, 2003). The study included a survey of 431 male and female migrants, intensive interviews with 20 people from the larger sample, and several months of participant observation. In analysing the strategies that enable young women to adjust and adapt to city life, it became clear that female migrants inevitably navigated the local sexual economy as they strived to survive and succeed in their new environment. For most young women, sexual relationships with men proved to be a major means for garnering economic support, albeit in ways that spanned a wide range of forms with regard to the explicitness of the economic basis for the relationship, the intimacy and duration of ties, and the moral valence for the women, their partners, and the larger community.

For analytical purposes, three positions in the spectrum of relationships in Kano's migrant community's sexual economy are identified and examined with regard to their relationship to and effects on gender inequality. The three forms of relationship described are: (1) commercial sex work, mostly associated with brothels; (2) sexual relationships that originate from connections that are established in the plethora of local bars, taverns, and eateries that serve alcohol in Kano's migrant quarter; and (3) longer-term relationships that are less explicitly economic and often include a notion of romance and commitment. Of course, many kinds of relationships do not fit neatly in one category, some relationships evolve over time from one type to another, and many women experience more than one type of relationship, either over time or concurrently. The conventional view is that the more overtly economic a relationship is the more likely a woman has been compelled to participate because of poverty, and the more pernicious it is for the perpetuation of gender inequality. The picture is somewhat more complicated when the social and moral aspects of gender inequality are figured in with the economic aspects. In-depth interviews and participant observation suggest that, in many ways, the most overtly economic relationships are morally less constraining for women and vice versa. Understanding the relationship between rural–urban migration, gender, and the local sexual economy requires consideration not only of the economic underpinnings of gender inequality, but also its moral dimensions.

Commercial sex workers: economic dependence and moral independence
When the survey team, made up mostly of young Igbos from the major university in Kano, spanned out across the city to interview migrants, one of the supervisors, a middle-aged university lecturer from the Southeast, expressed considerable surprise at the number of young migrant women working as commercial sex workers in brothels. He characterised his palpable dismay in a phrase that was repeated frequently by members of the research team over the study period. He lamented that he would never again react the same when back home in the Southeast the parent of a young female migrant announced proudly: 'My daughter is working in Kano'. Little did their parents suspect, he suggested, what sort of work their daughters were doing.

Interviews with young women working in brothels confirmed that most of them resorted to sex work in response to economic needs in circumstances where they felt they had few, if any, other viable options. Data from the larger survey sample indicated that women who were sex workers had few (and often no) kin in Kano who could help them. In the larger overall migrant population, more than half of the young female migrants had kin in the city, and many of them boarded with a relative. The lack of kinship ties increased young women's economic desperation, but it also freed them somewhat from the moral gaze of extended family who would have considered sex work extremely stigmatising.

Commercial sex work is viewed as morally unacceptable in the larger Igbo migrant community. Indeed, its unacceptability is exacerbated by the fact that many of the migrants sex workers' clients are local men, who differ from Igbo migrants in ethnicity and religion (Igbo migrants are predominantly Christian; the local population in Kano is mostly Hausa-speaking and Muslim). But, ironically, young Igbo migrant women who engaged in professional sex work seemed to escape many of the moral boundaries that constrain the behaviour of most Igbo women. Commercial sex workers in the study drank and smoked much more commonly and openly then other migrant women. More significantly, they talked to men with much greater liberty, arguing with them, laughing at them, and cursing them in ways that most women would find difficult and even dangerous. Sex workers certainly engaged in their trade primarily out of economic desperation. Some of them faced exploitation and mistreatment from clients and from the men who owned and ran the hotels where they worked. But they also had considerable freedom with regard to their mobility when they were not working, and with regard to how to spend their savings. They had freedoms of certain kinds in arenas that were more constrained for women who were more bound to their kin and to particular men.

This does not mean to suggest that female sex work is a path to gender equality. But because sex work puts women 'beyond the pale' morally, their source of economic livelihood offers them considerable liberties that are unavailable to women who are more observant of social and moral norms. The point is not some misguided celebration of sex work, but rather to contrast it to other ways that young migrant women navigate Kano's urban sexual economy. This illuminates how the moral foundations of gender inequality that can be as powerful – and sometimes as pernicious – as the economic foundations.

Bar girls. 'Is she or isn't she?'
While full-fledged commercial sex work is undertaken by a relatively small fraction of young unmarried Igbo migrants, many more young women worked in jobs at bars, taverns, eateries, and a range of other entertainment establishments. At these venues, male clientele commonly banter playfully with female cooks, servers, and other employees. In many cases (but certainly not most), these encounters evolve into sexual relationships. The spectrum of entertainment establishments, the intentions and behaviours of young women, and the kinds of relationships that unfold are highly diverse. In some cases, the line between sex work and tavern work is blurry; in others, young women would only sleep with a man when the relationship could be understood as romantically inclined or emotionally committed. But in almost all instances neither the man nor the woman views these relationships as commercial sex. It is equally the case that in all cases the man is expected to provide some form of economic support to his sexual partner.

In these contexts, young women must be careful not to behave too much like sex workers, as their physical attraction, emotional appeal, and moral authenticity depends on obscuring or euphemising the economic aspect of a sexual relationship. In the evenings when the survey team sometimes assembled at a tavern for a meal or a drink, male members of the team openly speculated about whether some of the bar girls were 'really' commercial sex workers. Most illuminating was the fact that these men – as many do – seemed to find most alluring those young women who appeared least obviously interested in their money. Yet based on in-depth interviews and informal discussions with many men and women, it became apparent that the actual level of economic support that was provided when sexual relations occurred was not smaller when the encounter was perceived in less overtly economic terms. Indeed, there was some evidence to suggest that young women accrued greater economic rewards the more able they were to shroud any economic motivations.

Perhaps not surprisingly, women who behaved more conservatively – exhibiting shyness, a degree of submissiveness to male authority, and a naïveté (whether genuine or feigned) about the sexual undertones of men's overtures – were both more likely not be judged as sex workers and more actively pursued by men who sought a less morally stigmatised sexual union than commercial sex. In certain respects, the decorum required to distinguish oneself from a prostitute required of young migrants behaviour that reinforced gendered stereotypes that kept women subservient to men. Perhaps the most significant and potentially deleterious example of this was with regard to the use of condoms. Many young women reported that it was difficult and awkward for them to suggest using condoms with their lovers, partly because such a suggestion made them appear, as several men and women put it, 'too professional'. This contrasted starkly with the reports of women working in the brothels, who reported the most regular use of condoms of any women in the sample, and who commonly asserted that they demanded their clients use them.

Good girls. 'No finance without romance'
The pressures that bar girls and others in the entertainment sector face in concealing or obfuscating any economic motives they might have for their sexual relationships with men are heightened for the majority of young female migrants who are neither commercial sex workers nor entertainment industry workers. While the survey data suggested that sex workers and entertainment industry service workers tended to be economically and socially more vulnerable than many other migrant women (they generally had less income, poorer housing, and fewer Kano-based kin), many young migrants who fit neither category also had precarious livelihoods and depended on men with whom they had sexual relationships for economic support. For such women, the importance of assuring the perceived morality of the relationship was paramount, as men were much more likely to spend significantly on women who they believed were exclusive and emotionally bound to them.

Throughout Nigeria, young women commonly express self-consciousness about the economic motivations for sexual relationships with men (even as they are socially bound to minimise men's perception of these motives) with the phrase 'no romance without finance'. While this expression reveals women's strategic economic use of their sexuality, it is equally revealing to invert the phrase and note that for women to succeed in securing the most valuable male support – that which is not only the most financially lucrative, but also the most socially acceptable – they must behave in ways that privilege other aspects of the relationship above bald material exchange. In this sense, for most women, 'there is no finance without romance'. Most young migrants interviewed in the study wholeheartedly preferred relationships where they received financial support in the context of emotionally supportive and socially and morally sanctioned relationships. But it was clear that, in this gender-unequal society, in order to please men, women had to behave in ways that reinforced aspects of gender inequality. Men expected significant degrees of acquiescence to male needs and priorities in order to reward women with both money and moral approval.

Conclusion
Young female migrants in Nigeria must steer their way through entrenched forms of gender inequality, navigating a complex sexual economy as they try to survive and succeed in urban environments. The findings from this study, which emphasise the moral as well as the material dimensions of gender unequal social systems, do not lessen the

economic foundations and consequences of gender inequality. But by examining the complex terrain of the Kano migrant community's sexual economy, the intertwining of the material and the moral becomes apparent, producing circumstances, strategies, and consequences that are multifaceted and sometimes contradictory. While an ideal scenario would move women towards both economic and moral equality, a brief survey of the sexual economy that young female migrants in Kano must traverse suggests that young women frequently have to navigate uneven moral and material terrains, trading currencies across domains, risking failure in one realm for success in the other, trying to keep their reputations in tact even as they secure their livelihoods, and reinforcing some aspects of gender inequality even as they challenge others.

Select bibliography

Chukwuezi, Barth (2001) 'Through thick and thin: Igbo rural–urban circularity, identity and investment', *Journal of Contemporary African Studies*, **19** (1), 55–66.

Gugler, Josef and Gudrun Ludwar-Ene (1995) 'Gender and migration in Africa south of the Sahara', in Jonathan Baker and Tade Aina (eds), *Migration Experiences in Africa*, Uppsala: Nordiska Afrikainstitutet, pp. 257–68.

Hollos, Marida and Ulla Larsen (1992) 'Fertility differentials among the Ijo in southern Nigeria: does urban residence make a difference?', *Social Science and Medicine*, **35** (9), 1199–210.

Makinwa-Adebusoye, Paulina (1990) 'Female migration in Africa', in *Conference on the Role of Migration in African Development: Issues and Policies for the '90s, Vol. I Commissioned Papers*, Dakar: Union for African Population Studies, pp. 198–211.

Smith, Daniel Jordan (2001) 'Romance, parenthood and gender in a modern African society', *Ethnology*, **40** (2), 129–51.

Smith, Daniel Jordan (2003) 'Imagining HIV/AIDS: morality and perceptions of personal risk in Nigeria', *Medical Anthropology*, **22** (4), 343–72.

45 Internal mobility, migration and changing gender relations: case study perspectives from Mali, Nigeria, Tanzania and Vietnam
Cecilia Tacoli

Migration plays a key role in reflecting and shaping processes of social, economic, cultural and political change. It is thus not surprising that patterns of mobility have become increasingly complex and dynamic to encompass a wide range of forms and types of movement, a growing number of destinations, and migrant flows with diverse sex, age and ethnic compositions.

Much research on migration focuses on international movement, and it is mainly in this arena that the conceptualisation of the 'feminisation of migration' has emerged, producing important insights on the deeply gendered nature of both migration and globalisation (see Sassen, Chapter 2, this volume). Less attention has been given to internal mobility, despite the fact that this type of movement closely reflects demographic, socio-economic and cultural transformations in low- and middle-income nations. The latter include changes in population distribution, accompanied in many cases by rapid rates of urbanisation, and changes in the economic base, with industry and services accounting for a growing proportion of national Gross Domestic Product (GDP) and of the labour force. Gender relations are key elements that both shape and are shaped by these transformative processes.

Following a brief overview of the diversity of internal population movement, this chapter draws on research conducted in the past decade in Mali, Nigeria, Tanzania and Vietnam to explore the different ways in which mobility and migration intersect with the changing relations between rural and urban areas, people and activities, and in the process transform livelihoods and power inequalities at both intrahousehold and interhousehold levels. It then summarises the main implications for policy, particularly in relation to current and emerging challenges such as the impacts of climate change and global economic downturns.

The diversity of internal migration and mobility
It is often assumed that internal migration consists primarily of rural to urban permanent movement, since this is consistent with economic theories of migration which posit that migrants move from low-wage (rural) to high-wage (urban) areas. It is also often assumed that migrants are primarily male and young. In part, such assumptions are based on data collection systems such as national censuses which tend to underestimate the often large flows of temporary migrants, and in many instances do not include any detailed information on migration. The analysis of demographic and health surveys of recent migrants (defined as having moved during the six years preceding the interview) shows, however, a more varied picture (UNPD, 2008). Rural–rural migration is the most common type of movement among female migrants, and tends to be highest in Africa,

although urban–urban migration predominates in Brazil, Peru, Paraguay, Colombia and Bolivia. Rural–urban migrant women in countries with large afrodescendent populations are the majority only in the Comoros, the Dominican Republic and Haiti (see also Safa, Chapter 17, this volume). With regard to male migrants, urban-urban migration predominates, although rural–rural migration is most common in Africa. Rural–urban migration is predominant only in Kazakhstan, while urban–rural movement is the most common for men in Burundi, Kenya, Mali and Nigeria.

Although data (and especially data disaggregated by sex) is available only for a small number of countries, it certainly contributes to debunking the myth of male-dominated, primarily rural–urban internal migration. Indeed, women tend to outnumber men in all types of movements, although in most cases the difference is small. Sex-selectivity is also more pronounced depending on specific flows: for example, women outnumber men in rural–rural flows in India and Egypt, and in rural–urban flows in Brazil, Honduras, the Philippines and Thailand (UNPD, 2008). Overall, then, macrolevel data suggests that internal migration is highly diverse, and that gender certainly matters.

Mobility, income diversification and livelihoods: why and how gender matters
In general terms, mobility can be described as an adaptation to the unequal spatial distribution of resources, including natural resources, markets and employment opportunities. As such, mobility is increasingly recognised as a key element of livelihood strategies, overlapping with the diversification of income sources. However, livelihood strategies are largely based on access to assets and such access is mediated by economic, sociocultural and political normative systems which reflect evolving power relations between different groups. Hence, an important distinction is that between strategies which lead to the accumulation of assets and more secure livelihoods, and strategies which only ensure the survival of those who undertake them. Gender clearly plays an important role in livelihood strategies, and this is reflected in the diversity of the patterns of internal migration.

Research on livelihood strategies usually takes the household as the unit of analysis. Attention to how gender and, in many cases, generation, determine household members' access to and decision-making power over the use of household resources and assets, brings in a more nuanced understanding of the ways in which livelihood strategies contribute to the wellbeing of individuals within the household unit (see also Quisumbing, Chapter 23, this volume).

At the same time, a gender perspective on mobility and migration does not focus exclusively on intrahousehold relations, but includes attention to place-specific gender relations and social relations, including interhousehold inequalities such as class, caste and ethnicity. It also includes attention to the mesolevels and macrolevels, or the ways in which the globalisation of production, consumption and trade, itself deeply gendered, is enacted in specific locations, and the many ways in which economic and non-economic dimensions overlap and intersect.

In all the case study locations in Mali, Nigeria, Tanzania and Vietnam, the numbers of young people migrating, especially young women moving independently, have increased substantially. Overall, this is due to the combination of increasing employment opportunities away from the home settlements, as well as economic and resource constraints within the settlements. Perhaps more important, however, are the sociocultural transformations that underpin the changing aspirations of both young men and women, as described below.

One of the key assets for households in low- and middle-income countries is land. Access to land is unequally distributed both between and within households, and where local economic activities are based on farming and provide limited opportunities for non-agricultural income-generation, landlessness is closely related to poverty. Poverty does not generally increase out-migration from rural settlements, although it does have an impact on destinations, with more rural–rural movement among lower-income than higher income groups. Access to land does, however, have an impact on intrahousehold gender-selective movement when women do not have the same land inheritance rights as men. In northern Tanzania, where daughters are expected to contribute unpaid labour to the family farm but do not traditionally inherit it, employment opportunities for women in tourist resorts and in urban centres have become increasingly attractive for young women, and one-third of the case study respondents reported that at least one young woman in their household had migrated. While this proportion is significantly lower than that of households with migrant sons (almost two-thirds of respondents), there are substantial gender-based differences in destinations. Young women tend to move further afield that young men, who in contrast are more likely to engage in seasonal and temporary movement (Diyamett et al., 2001).

In southern Vietnam, where access to land is restricted by a relative shortage of agricultural land rather than inequalities in access, the proportion of mobile women and men is broadly similar. There are, however, significant differences in destinations and forms of mobility which to some extent reflect those in northern Tanzania. Men dominate short-distance and short-term migration, often moving within the same districts or to neighbouring ones, whereas women tend to move for longer periods of time to work in export-oriented factories in peri-urban areas, or as maids in urban centres. Compared with women, men's destinations and employment opportunities are more diverse (Hoang et al., 2008). Beyond intrahousehold relations, the gendered nature of labour markets is thus an important explanatory factor of the diversity of internal migration. This is not only related to 'emerging' sectors of employment in manufacturing and domestic service. In Mali, women, for whom access to farm land is traditionally limited, have long had a key role as highly mobile small- and medium-scale traders in ensuring small-scale farmers' access to urban markets. Their important contribution to rural economies and urban food supplies is, however, largely overlooked, and rural development policies generally ignore them. Perhaps an unintended consequence of these deeply gendered labour markets is that in the region surrounding Bamako, Mali's rapidly expanding capital city, women appear to be better equipped to benefit from demographic and economic transformations than men. While the latter resent the loss of agricultural land to residential use, which is not compensated by employment in urban and peri-urban factories, women benefit from the ever-expanding urban demand for horticultural products. Indeed, this has allowed the most successful among them to start purchasing land for residential and commercial use (Tacoli, 2002).

Economic change intersects with sociocultural transformations in all the case study locations. In southeast Nigeria, young men's migration, often temporary, to urban centres is seen as a rite of passage. Those who do not move are often labelled as idle and shying away from hard labour, and may become the object of ridicule. At the same time, the demands for community work on those who stay are a major obstacle to gain economic independence, and migration is therefore perceived as offering a socially acceptable way to escape from obligations to, and control from community elders. For young women, similar constraints operate, albeit at the level of the household rather than that of the community. In this case, too, migration is a way to negotiate power relations and increase personal independence while avoiding conflict over gender and generational norms. Significantly, the sending of remittances to the parental household has greatly contributed to making young women's migration socially acceptable (Tacoli, 2002). Having said this, while in all four countries remittances constitute a crucial, and in many cases the most important, source of family cash, their worth is almost everywhere underestimated if not downright dismissed by parents. This probably reflects ongoing struggles over power and authority in contexts where rapid socio-economic transformations redesign intrahousehold and traditional community relations.

Mobility, poverty and the challenges ahead
While mobility is without doubt an increasingly important component of livelihood strategies, it is more closely linked to accumulation rather than survival. In other words, for the poorest groups and individuals, be they men or women, it is often difficult to muster the resources necessary to move. This is especially the case for movement to locations that offer better paid – and often more skilled – employment, and is reflected in the fact that the poor usually concentrate in rural–rural movements. From a policy perspective, it is important to understand the links between mobility and income diversification. Access to non-agricultural income sources is often crucial for rural residents, as it allows them to spread risk and fund farming innovation and intensification, which, in turn, can improve access to markets. Local non-farm employment opportunities, for example in small towns, can contribute to the reduction of poverty and vulnerability. However, they are unlikely to reduce mobility and migration precisely because of the importance of non-economic factors that underpin decisions to migrate. Negotiations around power inequalities both within and outside households are thus played out in a wider space which enables migrants to pursue individual aspirations while retaining household and community responsibilities, and hence social acceptability.

Having said this, internal migration is intimately linked to global labour markets dynamics. While it is still early to fully understand the implications of the current economic downturn on mobility and on gender-selective employment trends, the slowing down of consumption in wealthy countries is heavily affecting export-manufacturing sectors, where women are a large proportion of the labour force. The issue here is whether, and how, the current situation will result in a radical restructuring of production or only in relatively minor adjustments. The second issue gaining prominence in policy discourses is the impact of climate change on mobility and migration. While the debate is still largely dominated by alarmist predictions of massive flows of refugees, what seems to be overlooked is that mobility and migration will be key adaptive strategies for large numbers of people in the poorest and most affected regions in the world. Most policies related to internal migration aim to control and reduce movement, especially rural–urban flows. Supporting adaptation to the impacts of climate change will require a radical change in current perceptions of mobility and the development of policies that accommodate and support migration (Tacoli, 2009). In this context, a gender perspective can help provide a more nuanced and location-specific understanding of both economic and non-economic dimensions of mobility, of the need for multi-scale approaches and initiatives – from the household to the community to the national and global levels – and of the need to address power inequalities.

Acknowledgements
This chapter draws on collaborative research funded by the Swedish International Development Agency (Sida), the Danish International Development Agency (Danida), the UK Department for International Development (DFID), and the European Union (EU). I am deeply indebted to partners in all four countries, especially Bitrina Diyamett and Richard Mabala in northern Tanzania, David Okali in Nigeria, Idrissa Maiga and Gouro Diallo in Mali, and Hoang Xuan Thanh in Vietnam.

Select bibliography
Diyamett, Bitrina, Mathew Diyamett, Jovita James and Richard Mabala (2001) *The Case of Himo and its Region, Northern Tanzania*, Rural-Urban Working Paper 1, International Institute for Environment and Development, London, available at: http://www.iied.org/pubs/search.php?s=RUWP&x=Y (accessed 25 May 2009).
Hoang, Xuan Thanh, Thi Thu Phuong Dinh and Thu Huong Nguyen with Cecilia Tacoli (2008) *Urbanisation and Rural Development in Vietnam's Mekong Delta: Livelihood Transformations in Three Fruit-Growing Settlements*, Rural–Urban Working Paper 14, International Institute for Environment and Development, London, available at: http://www.iied.org/pubs/search.php?s=RUWP&x=Y (accessed 25 May 2009).
Tacoli, Cecilia (2002) *Changing Rural–Urban Interactions in Sub-Saharan Africa and their Impact on Livelihoods: A Summary*, Rural–Urban Working Paper 7, International Institute for Environment and Development, London, available at: http://www.iied.org/pubs/search.php?s=RUWP&x=Y (accessed 25 May 2009).
Tacoli, Cecilia (2009) 'Crisis or adaptation? Migration and climate change in a context of high mobility', *Environment and Urbanisation*, **21** (2), 513–25.
United Nations Population Division (UNPD) (2008) *An Overview of Urbanisation, Internal Migration, Population Distribution and Development in the World*, New York: UNPD.

46 Picturing gender and poverty: from 'victimhood' to 'agency'?
Kalpana Wilson

This chapter explores the processes through which neoliberal notions of agency and empowerment have shaped representations of poor women by development institutions. Policies promoting the use of 'positive' images of women in developing countries have been adopted partly in response to critiques of earlier constructions of 'Third World women' as 'passive victims', and the process of 'othering' this implies (see, for example, Mohanty, 1991). The chapter examines the specific ways in which these more recent visual productions are both gendered and racialised, exploring parallels and continuities between colonial representations and today's images.[1]

Feminists have challenged development interventions which reproduced a colonial discourse of 'saving' women from their backward social customs and oppressive men, and have highlighted women's agency. However, as I have argued elsewhere, they have increasingly found their ideas being incorporated into discourses promoting neoliberal models of development in which a further intensification of poor women's labour is expected to provide a buffer for their households against the ravages of neoliberal economic restructuring (Wilson, 2007).

The construction of the poor woman as a 'rational economic agent' exercising choice is elaborated within the moral framework of neoliberalism, which ascribes 'responsibilities' to the poor as a condition for the enjoyment of 'rights'. It is emphasised that women work harder, and expend less resources on themselves (in terms of leisure time as well as consumption) than their male counterparts, and women's access to the market and earnings will therefore have a far greater impact on children's well-being. The fact that these differences in behaviour result from patriarchal relations of power, both material and ideological, is rarely acknowledged. Yet when women have engaged in collective struggles with a transformative agenda, it is often precisely those gendered inequalities which make women more 'efficient' neoliberal subjects (such as women's primary responsibility for children, the acute scarcity of time not spent working, and the ubiquitous threat of violence), which are challenged (Wilson, 2007).[2]

While neoliberal economic orthodoxy can no longer be taken for granted by dominant development institutions, there are signs that approaches involving the further 'feminisation of responsibility' for survival will become even more significant in the period of global recession (see Chant, Chapter 15, this volume). The instrumentalisation of poor women is perhaps epitomised by the World Bank's current Gender Action Plan (2007–2010) and its slogan 'Gender Equality as Smart Economics'. But this represents a much wider consensus across development institutions, including the vast majority of non-governmental organisations (NGOs). Central to this consensus has been the remarkable rise of microfinance models, with their emphasis on women as better borrowers as well as better providers, and a claim to be able to simultaneously resolve problems of poverty as well as gender inequality, even as they integrate women more deeply into global circuits of capital (see Maclean, Chapter 87, this volume).

As a result of this consensus, while the concept of agency is regularly mobilised in the construction of poor women in the South as 'enterprising' subjects with limitless capacity to 'cope', movements which run counter to the neoliberal model, demanding the redistribution of resources, challenging the operation of markets, or confronting the violence of the 'democratic' neoliberal state, are rendered invisible.

So how are these processes reflected and reproduced in the images circulated by development institutions? This question can only be addressed through an exploration of the relationships between representation, knowledge, and power. If the subject of a photograph is transformed into an object to be 'known' by virtue of the asymmetry implicit in the relationship between the photographer and the photographed, this process is shaped by material and discursive relations of power such as those of class, 'race' and gender. As Said (1978) argued in *Orientalism*, the work of representation and specifically the construction of the 'other', who is paradoxically both entirely 'knowable' and irreducibly alien, was central to the reproduction of colonial power.

The reading of individual images depends on an accumulation of meanings, where one image implicitly refers to a series of others, or has its meaning altered by being read in the context of others: a process of establishing regimes of representation (Hall, 1997: 232) which has been explored in depth in the context of 'race' and racism. Dominant images are rarely static however – they are (re)shaped by changing configurations of power and by the resistance of those who are represented.

The rise of the 'positive' image

The debate within development institutions (and NGOs in particular) concerning the use of images is often traced back to the period following the Ethiopian famine of 1984–85. The response to the famine was possibly the high water mark of a tide of charity images that objectified and dehumanised people in the 'Third World'. If the scale of this was facilitated by the increasingly symbiotic relationship between NGOs and the media (epitomised by Band Aid and its descendants), the period also saw the beginning of a massive increase in the role of NGOs as a result of a series of interlinked changes associated with neoliberal economic reforms. The privatisation of aid, the substitution of NGOs for the state in social provision, and the reconfiguration, within the framework of the liberal democracy/liberalised economy dyad, of 'civil society' as an arena for donor intervention and direction, all contributed to a new, and expanded, role for development NGOs from the 1990s onwards. It is this incorporation of NGOs into structures of neoliberal governance that has primarily informed the new types of representations produced by them.

In 1989, the 'Code of Conduct on Images and Messages Relating to the Third World' adopted by the General Assembly of European NGOs (since updated to 'Code of Conduct on Images and Messages') stated that:

> The image of our Third World partners as dependent, poor and powerless is most often applied to women who are invariably portrayed as dependent victims, or worse still, simply do not figure in the picture. An improvement in the images used in educational material on the Third World evidently requires a positive change in the images projected of Southern women.[3]

Structural aspects of the relationship between Northern-based international NGOs and people in the South who are portrayed in the images they produce make adherence to these guidelines in many respects a contradiction in terms, so it is perhaps hardly surprising that a number of major NGOs continued to use, for example, photographs of vulnerable children in the South extensively in their publicity. However, my focus here is on a new set of images. What are the implications of the kinds of 'positive' images of women which are produced? How is another recommendation which comes earlier in the guidelines – 'People's ability to *take responsibility for themselves* must be highlighted' – interpreted? In what ways are these images gendered and racialised?

Exoticising the 'deserving' poor
Oxfam's 'Oxfam Unwrapped' campaign encourages people to make purpose-specific donations to Oxfam on behalf of their friends and family as an alternative to gifts. The campaign's Winter 2007 catalogue is divided into several sections, each illustrating the effects of a particular type of 'gift'.

The single largest section, 'working wonders', refers to support for small-scale enterprise: combined with 'gifts that grow' which refers specifically to agricultural production, this section comprises ten pages at the beginning of the 45-page catalogue, which includes shorter sections relating to other Oxfam activities. The people whose photographs appear in this section are overwhelmingly women. Those few images (three out of 19) which do show men are all relatively unobtrusive due to their small size and/or the fact that the men's faces are not clearly visible. By contrast, the photographs of women are larger, clearer, and evidently intended to engage the viewer. Although only a small number of the women are identified or located geographically in the text, all the women are depicted working. They are photographed surrounded by vegetation, agricultural produce, or handicrafts, the natural tones emphasised by their brightly coloured clothing. The most prominent image on the first page shows two Masai women[4] wearing large, elaborate necklaces and earrings pouring seeds into a sack. Most strikingly, these women and a majority of the others (nine out of 15) are looking away from the camera at the task they are doing but at the same time smiling broadly.

The viewer is thus encouraged to consume the image on multiple interlinked levels: as a consumer of the exoticised, racialised bodies and 'natural' surroundings of the women; as a (potential) donor deriving gratification from observing (unobserved) the effects of his/her generosity; and as a consumer in the North enjoying not only the undervalued product of the labour applied by 'poor women in the South' but using their leisure time to vicariously share the pleasure which these women are portrayed as deriving from their own labour.

A browse through these pages creates, through a process of repetition and accumulation of images, an overwhelming sense of 'the South' as a single, though endlessly diverse, place where 'poor women' are constantly, diligently and happily engaged in small-scale but productive labour for the market. Not only does the process of 'othering' continue, but the construction of these women as hyper-industrious 'entrepreneurs' is incorporated in this process.

This is not so much a new development as a rediscovery and reformulation of an earlier narrative: that of late colonial enterprises which were based on the acute exploitation of largely female labour. In her analysis of British advertising in the colonial period, Ramamurthy (2003) has demonstrated how tea advertising in the 1920s worked to provide legitimacy for the continuation of colonial rule in the context of growing demands for independence, using images of the Indian woman tea-picker who was not only represented as 'alluring and sensual, but through her apparent contentment and productivity within an ordered environment symbolically affirmed the need for empire' (ibid.: 126). These images were also read in the context of discourses of the 'work ethic', individual responsibility and the 'deserving' and 'undeserving' poor deployed to extract ever greater surpluses from the working class in Britain and, via missionaries in particular, from its colonial subjects.

In the absence then of any problematisation of the current global order, and the gendered and racialised divisions within it, the 'positivity' of contemporary development images, from which any contradictions appear to have been elided, implicitly confirms neoliberal narratives in which the 'empowerment' of poor women via the market is the 'solution'. In a reworking of colonial representations, relations of oppression and exploitation are thus obscured, or reconfigured as 'obstacles' which can be overcome through hard work and a helping hand from the Northern donor/consumer.

Like the image of the cycling Bangladeshi health worker 'Elizabeth' used in a 1990 Christian Aid campaign discussed by Lidchi (1999: 97), each of the women in the Oxfam catalogue is constituted 'not as the object of development – helpless and despairing', but as 'the image of an empowered "participating . . . hardworking, industrious and self-determined" subject' (ibid.: 99). However whereas, as Lidchi notes, there is an ambiguity in the status of 'Elizabeth', who can be viewed as a 'conscientious worker' mediating between the viewer/donor and the 'poorest of the poor' beneficiaries of her services, in the more recent images it is the beneficiaries themselves, assumed to be working – as rational economic agents – only for themselves and their children, who are represented as 'empowered subjects'. Just as all remaining barriers to global capital have been removed in the interim, similarly it seems any intermediaries who might imply a lingering role for the state have been erased from the picture, allowing direct access for the viewer/consumer/donor to the hardworking 'poor' woman within the framework of neoliberal globalisation.

'Race', gender and guilt
Divine chocolate is a leading Fair Trade brand in the United Kingdom. It promotes an understanding of 'fair trade' to which the notion of 'empowerment' of women small-scale cocoa farmers is central. In 2006 Divine launched a series of full-page magazine advertisements, in each of which a different woman is photographed against a background of lush vegetation, holding up a piece of chocolate between her fingertips.

On one level, these advertisements move away from the contemporary patterns of development images, as well as disrupting some of the conventions of mainstream advertising. This would appear to be in line with Divine's model of cooperative ownership of the company by farmers which involves a critique of the 'unfair' operation of global markets while claiming to be able to engage with them beneficially through 'radical mainstream', 'alternative high street' marketing. In each of these advertisements the woman appears at first glance to be a professional model, but the accompanying text belies our expectations by informing us that she is a member of the Kuapa Kokoo Cooperative in Ghana. While a farmer, however, she is not depicted working. She wears African dress, but the photography and pose emphasise mainstream notions of fashion and 'glamour' rather than, as in the Oxfam images, tradition and authenticity. One reaction that this is intended to generate in the (mainly female and fairly affluent) target audience is clearly of empathy, as co-inhabitants of a post-feminist world where pleasure derives from spending one's own earnings on one's own commodification (see also Richey, Chapter 77, this volume).

But the implications of these images and how they operate can only be fully grasped through a reading which engages with regimes of representation and places them in a historical context.

A feature of contemporary development representations of work and production in the South which is particularly explicit in the Divine advertisements is the conflation of the worker/producer with her product. In her analysis of advertising by fair trade coffee company Cafédirect, Wright (2004: 671) argues that while photographic images of producers 'could . . . be understood as a deliberate attempt to undermine commodity fetishism, to make part of the potential consumer's relationship with the product, coffee, also a relationship with the coffee producer(s)', 'in fact, social relations are but partially revealed, in ways that render them commodities in their own right', and the reader is 'invited to consume (metaphorically) the very body of the coffee producer' (ibid.: 676).

Once again, there are very clear continuities with colonial representations. The Divine advertisements recall a long history of explicitly racist advertising by European cocoa companies in which the African producers were represented as inseparable from their produce and their skin colour was associated with chocolate (Ramamurthy, 2003: 63–91). Unlike these earlier images, however, these advertisements sexualise this association through their focus on the figure of the beautiful African woman, who is pictured languidly casting a sidelong glance at the viewer. Leaving aside the question of whether such objectification can be considered empowering, we need to ask whether a sexualised image of an African woman being used in the context of global trade – to sell a product to consumers in Britain – can ever be de-historicised. In fact a closer look suggests that Divine does not quite wish us to forget the past: while the colours of the image are intense and hyper-real, they are framed by sepia-tinted text in a nineteenth-century style font. The whole history of plunder, slavery, sexual violence and colonialism is in fact very much present, and is underlined by the slogan of one of the advertisements: 'a not-so-guilty pleasure'. This slogan works on several levels, referring to the 'guilty pleasure' of consuming chocolate which undermines the gendered regime of the body; and the 'guilt' of ongoing exploitative trade relations (and by extension, of slavery and colonialism) borne by the white British consumer which is supposedly mitigated by Fair Trade practices. If these two meanings are explicit, implicitly there is also the 'guilty pleasure' of enjoying the image itself: guilt associated with desire for the racialised 'other' in the form of the African woman, which is partially absolved through the viewer's recognition of the image as representing an 'empowered' participant in global markets.

Conclusion
This preliminary exploration suggests a need for further research which would critically analyse contemporary representations in development from the perspective of 'race' as well as gender. Such research would examine the contexts in which these representations

are produced, and those in which they are read, and the contribution they may make to privileging certain voices and ideas and silencing others.

I have suggested that contemporary 'positive' visual representations of women in the South produced by development institutions are rooted in a notion of 'agency' consistent with – and necessary for – neoliberal capitalism. Critiques of the objectification of people in the South – and women in particular – as passively suffering victims have been widely interpreted as an imperative to represent these women as universally enterprising, productive, and happy. These images are consistent with a current consensus among development institutions which portrays an intensification of labour applied by poor women in the South as the 'solution' to poverty as well as gender inequality. In this context, I would argue that these images operate in the same way as did images of 'contented and productive' workers in colonial enterprises: to reassure the viewer of the legitimacy and justice of existing relationships and structures. Suffering has been replaced by its opposite – but anger, protest and the desire for transformation remain out of the picture.

Notes

1. The two case studies discussed here form part of a wider study in which I am currently engaged.
2. These issues have been raised, for example, by Dalit women in agricultural labourers' movements in Bihar in India (Wilson, 2007).
3. See weblink for Code of Conduct on Images and Messages Relating to the Third World, available at: www.dgcd.be/documents/en/topics/european_conference_public_awareness/code_of_conduct.doc (accessed 28 May 2009).
4. This is my own deduction: no information is provided about these women.

Select bibliography

Hall, Stuart (1997) 'The spectacle of the "other"', in Stuart Hall (ed.), *Representation: Cultural Representation: Cultural Representatives and Signifying Practices*, London: Sage, pp. 225–79.

Lidchi, Henrietta (1999) 'Finding the right image: British development NGOs and the regulation of imagery', in Tracy Skelton and Tim Allen (eds), *Culture and Global Change*, London: Routledge, pp. 87–101.

Mohanty, Chandra Talpade (1991) 'Under Western eyes: feminist scholarship and colonial discourse', in Chandra Talpade Mohanty, Ann Russo and Lourdes Torres (eds), *Third World Women and the Politics of Feminism*, Bloomington, IN: Indiana University Press, pp. 51–80.

Ramamurthy, Anandi (2003) *Imperial Persuaders: Images of Africa and Asia in British Advertising*, Manchester: Manchester University Press.

Said, Edward W. (1978) *Orientalism*, Harmondsworth: Penguin.

Wilson, Kalpana (2007) 'Agency', in Georgina Blakeley and Valerie Bryson (eds), *The Impact of Feminism on Political Concepts and Debates*, Manchester: Manchester University Press, pp. 126–45.

Wright, Caroline (2004) 'Consuming lives, consuming landscapes: interpreting advertisements for Cafedirect coffees', *Journal of International Development*, **16** (5), 665–80.

PART V

GENDER, HEALTH AND POVERTY

47 Poverty, gender and the right to health: reflections with particular reference to Chile
Jasmine Gideon

Introduction
There is a general consensus that good health is about more than the absence of infirmity and that, as stated in the 1978 World Health Organisation (WHO) Alma Ata Declaration, it encompasses 'a state of complete mental, physical and social well-being' and is 'a fundamental human right'. The right to health is also enshrined in Article 12 of the International Covenant on Economic, Social and Cultural Rights (ICESCR). A total of 160 states – including Chile – have ratified the ICESCR and therefore have a duty under international law to fulfil the obligations as laid out in the Covenant. Article 12 states that:

1. The States Parties to the present Covenant recognise the right of everyone to the enjoyment of the highest attainable standard of physical and mental health.
2. The steps to be taken by the States Parties to the present Covenant to achieve full realisation of this right shall include those necessary for:
    (a) The provision for the reduction of the still-birth rate and of infant mortality and for the healthy development of the child;
    (b) The improvement of all aspects of environmental and industrial hygiene;
    (c) The prevention, treatment and control of epidemic, endemic, occupational and other diseases;
    (d) The creation of conditions which would assure to all medical service and medical attention in the event of sickness.

The ICESCR is considered to impose three types of obligations on states that are party to it (termed 'states parties'): the obligations to respect, protect and fulfil the rights enumerated in it. The obligations on states parties are qualified in Article 2(i) of the ICESCR. This says that 'Each State Party to the present Covenant undertakes to take steps, individually and through international assistance and co-operation, especially economic and technical, to the maximum of available resources, with a view to achieving progressively the full realisation of the rights recognised in the present Covenant'. Article 2(ii) sets out the principles of equality and non-discrimination in relation to the provision of covenant rights. The implication of the phrases 'to the maximum of available resources' and 'with a view to achieving progressively' is to allow states to realise their obligations over a(n) (indefinite) period of time.

By signing up to international human rights treaties states also commit themselves to the principle of the indivisibility of rights, that is, the necessary integration among different 'generations' of human rights where civil and political rights are seen as first generation rights and economic and social rights are considered as second generation rights. Petchesky (2000) argues that this principle of indivisibility extends to recognising the intersections between human rights, economic justice and women and men's reproductive rights. Yet in reality this rarely happens and, as this chapter argues, it is often low-income women whose rights are most difficult to secure.

While the contradictions between guaranteeing economic and social rights to all citizens and the introduction of capitalist market systems have long been established, it could be argued that recent neoliberal reforms have further exacerbated these tensions with particularly negative impacts on low-income households. Under neoliberalism citizens in Chile have seen a reshaping of social service delivery, particularly in the health sector. The privatisation of many services undertaken as part of reform programmes implemented in the 1980s and 1990s meant that health was no longer a right to which all citizens where entitled but instead a service to which access is determined according to ability to pay. At the same time citizens were encouraged to take responsibility for their own health and welfare, as well as that of their families.

The privatisation of healthcare services has resulted in many activities being transferred back into the household where the gender division of labour generally means that women have had to take responsibility. At the same time changes in production processes that have also been part of neoliberal reform programmes have led to a growing number of women moving into the paid workforce. Many women are therefore subject to competing demands on their time. By the same token, many of the jobs created for women are located in the informal economy and lack stability and benefits such as membership of health insurance and pension schemes. As this chapter argues, this further exposes many low-income households to health risks.

Labour market deregulation and the growth of informal work
The ascendancy of neoliberalism across Latin America has presented important new challenges to governments in guaranteeing social and economic rights to their citizens. While new employment opportunities have developed, facilitating citizens' right to work and increasing individual autonomy for many female workers, there are also new challenges when viewed from a rights perspective. As the discussion here will show, workers are often subject to discrimination and exploitation, thus violating their rights to just and favourable working conditions as laid out in the ICESCR. The current gender division of labour in Chile also means that the majority of workers in these precarious forms of employment are women.

An integral part of neoliberal reforms has been a deregulation of labour markets in order to increase foreign investment, for example through lowering labour costs and introducing more flexible forms of working. This has been a prominent feature of Chilean reforms where new labour codes have facilitated the replacement of indefinite contracts with fixed-term contracts, and have promoted the use of temporary, part-time, seasonal and hourly contracts in hiring, along with restrictions on the right to strike, collective bargaining and worker organisation (see also Barrientos, Chapter 67, this volume). Consequently, there has been an unprecedented expansion of the informal economy in recent years. Furthermore there has been a dramatic restructuring of production and distribution in many key industries, characterised by outsourcing or subcontracting through global commodity chains. The textile and clothing industries in Chile have undergone these kinds of transformations and, following processes of restructuring since the early 1980s, much garment assembly is subcontracted to home-based workers employed on an informal basis. The connection between this growth of informal work and the large numbers of women entering paid employment remains subject to debate, but the majority of informal workers are female.

The marketisation of healthcare
Within the context of the increased marketisation of healthcare the failure of governments to extend the right to fair and equal remuneration to all workers is an important concern, since access to healthcare is no longer equally distributed. Health reforms in Chile are continuing to move towards replacing the system of social insurance, where risks are shared across the population, to a system of individualised private insurance, where users buy a health plan and make additional co-payments for any extra services they require.

Chile has had a mixed insurance system since the mid-1980s. Workers choose between the public (Fondo Nacional de Salud/FONASA) and private (Institutos de Salud Previsional/ISAPRES) sector to contract their mandatory 7 per cent health insurance contributions. Within FONASA, which covers around 60 per cent of the population, entitlements depend upon earnings-related contributions, in contrast to ISAPRES, which covers most of the remaining population, where users can select a health plan of their choice, although more extensive levels of coverage require higher additional payments.

In recognition of the growing inequalities in the health sector, particularly gender-based exclusion from accessing services, recent reforms have concentrated on improving access for the lowest income groups and in 2002 the Plan for Universal Care with Explicit Guarantees (Plan Acceso Universal con Garantías Explicítas en Salud/AUGE) was introduced. This was intended to improve access to, and quality of, services for more complex health conditions, with 56 conditions being included in the proposals. Healthcare for these selected conditions is free to indigents and the lowest income groups, while the remainder of the population has to pay a proportion of the cost, although additional co-payments may be applicable.

While Plan AUGE represents a positive development and should improve access for many users, the guarantees do only apply to a limited number of conditions. Users requiring treatment for other health problems are still dependent on the 'pre-AUGE' model of provision. Moreover AUGE is primarily focused on health access rather than health outcomes and as the discussion below illustrates much of the home-based healthcare that contributes to improving health outcomes is carried out by women and is not sufficiently addressed by the reforms (see also Nakray, Chapter 51, this volume). Feminist critics have pointed to the exclusionary decision-making processes that determined the list of health conditions that would be covered and have argued that the final selection is relatively gender-blind. Furthermore, Plan Auge does not represent a reversal of the process of health marketisation since the system remains guided by logic of market forces to distribute resources and health continues to be treated as a commodity and not a right.

Informal work, access to health and gender divisions of labour
Given the nature of informal employment, the majority of workers are excluded from non-wage benefits such as health insurance, pensions, paid sick leave and maternity

leave. Since women are more likely to be informally employed, these exclusions are gendered and women are less able to access these benefits than men (see also Chen, Chapter 71, this volume; Heintz, Chapter 66, this volume).

The variable nature of subcontracted work and salaries makes it difficult for households working in the informal economy to make regular contributions required by health insurance plans. In some instances women register as dependents of their husbands, but most female informal workers tend to register as indigents (Pearson, 2004). Although the rights of access for indigents have been expanded under Plan AUGE, this still raises issues around questions of exclusion and well-being. Registering as an indigent can impact on people's self-esteem and many women report being badly treated by health staff. While special mention is made in the ICESCR of 'the family' being accorded 'the widest possible protection and assistance', it seems that in reality governments are unable to fulfil this obligation, and many households comprising informal workers face increasing vulnerability and are unable to protect themselves against risks such as poor health. One recent study on the nature of poverty in Chile points to the central importance of health problems in determining whether or not households are able to move out of the poverty cycle (Neilson et al., 2008). In reality many poor households manage the cost of sickness by extending the threshold of seriousness at which they seek treatment.

Households are continuing to absorb the care and management of the sick and prevailing gender divisions of labour mean that it is often female family members who take on the responsibility of acting as primary or secondary caregivers. Research in Greater Santiago has found that the most time-consuming tasks are often those least visible to policymakers, for example, taking patients to appointments and adapting their living space (Medel et al., 2006). At the same time these kinds of activities are critical to the well-being of patients and other research has highlighted the importance of 'tender loving care' in caring for the sick. In many cases women working as primary care providers also have full-time employment outside of the household and spend up to eight hours a day in their place of work, plus additional travel time. This is particularly the case for women in the middle- and lower-income groups who are primary breadwinners. Many of these women opt for informal employment in the belief that its relative flexibility will make it more compatible with their caring responsibilities.

Often women also sleep in the same room as patients – either with them or near them – which has clear implications for their ability to have a full night's sleep (Reca et al., 2002). The toll of this unpaid carework on women's health cannot be underestimated, particularly in relation to stress levels. Yet although many women report stress-related symptoms and suffer from insomnia and depression as a result of their caring roles, few consult doctors about their own health. While some male carers also participate in paid work outside of the household Medel et al. (2006) found that only a small number of men played this role compared to women, and that whereas women took responsibility for unpaid care work throughout their adult lives men often only did so where a close relative needed specific healthcare. Moreover women talked about their caring roles in terms of family responsibilities and obligations whereas men did not.

New occupational health risks
The right of workers to the highest attainable standard of physical and mental health is also challenged by many of the new forms of employment that have developed over

the past few decades. While historically men have been more at risk from occupational health hazards, the changing nature of employment has created new and different risks for women. More importantly, since women are less likely than men to have a contract, they are unlikely to be eligible for sick pay and are not covered by Law 16,744, which legislates against work-related illness and accidents. This also means that any occupational health problems that do arise for this sector of the population are not recorded and this has important policy implications.

Many of the jobs in the informal economy, particularly in the commercial and financial sectors, demand long and extended working hours to dovetail with the demands of the service sector. While many men are also expected to work long hours, given the relatively rigid gender division of labour in Chile they do not have the additional caring responsibilities that many women have. As argued above this 'double burden' means that women often have little time to recuperate after working extended shifts or night shifts.

Many of the women interviewed also reported repetitive strain injuries resulting from the nature of their work, such as data inputting, as, in order to earn a decent salary, they had to reach certain targets and were often unable to take breaks if they wanted to complete their work on time. The expansion of horticultural exports in Chile and other parts of the region has also introduced new health hazards and increased workloads. The high use of pesticides can mean workers face a range of physical and mental health risks, including nausea, birth defects and acute depression. Studies from Chile have shown that there is a high incidence of alcohol and drug consumption (prescription and non-prescription) among temporary fruit-pickers and high rates of mental illness and higher rates of child malformation have been observed in the areas where fruit-growing is concentrated (Barrientos and Barrientos, 2002). Many of these conditions are excluded from the guarantees offered by AUGE and therefore remain a cause for concern. In addition the health sector is marked by severe rural–urban disparities and many rural health services are relatively under-funded. Municipalities in greatest need are often those that receive the lowest levels of funding and have difficulties in attracting doctors and health professionals. These issues raise important concerns regarding the ability of health services to guarantee the rights of rural users.

Reproductive rights
The most significant omission of current reforms has arguably been the failure to address women's reproductive rights fully. Despite the strength of women's demands as expressed in their proposals emerging from the Women's Parliaments, successive governments have maintained an active pro-life policy. Many women's groups have complained about the large gap between the government-defined gender equity agenda and the needs and priorities of women, particularly working-class women. Some limited gains were made when women secured the right to emergency contraception but abortion remains illegal. Although all women are affected by this, lower-income women are more vulnerable, especially as they are more dependent on the public sector where there is more state control. In some instances women can be prescribed an abortion-inducing drug by doctors or midwives in the private sector but this is only available to those who are able to pay, with a further option confined to the latter being to travel outside Chile to secure a safe and legal termination. So, in many cases poorer women undergo unsafe and illegal abortions or obtain drugs on the black market, or over the internet, and/or self-medicate.

While few women now die from abortion-related causes many do suffer long-term consequences – both mental and physical. However, given the clandestine nature of this issue very little data are available (Shepherd and Casas Becarra, 2007).

Conclusions

Drawing on the case of Chile, this chapter has reviewed the inherent tensions faced by states that, on one hand, have tried to guarantee the right to health of their citizens but, on the other, have promoted economic reforms which have included the deregulation of labour markets and privatisation of health services. Following the privatisation of healthcare provision as part of broader neoliberal reforms, the Chilean case reveals that gender inequalities in accessing health worsened and for many women the burden of unpaid care also increased. For those in the informal economy, the situation is bleakest since they are denied access to many of the benefits associated with formal employment, including health insurance.

While the current reform in Chile has taken steps to improve access through the implementation of Plan AUGE the embedded gender inequalities around the division of labour in healthcare remain rigid. More significantly AUGE has also avoided the contentious issue of reproductive rights and the question of abortion, which remains illegal in Chile, and poorly performed illegal abortions remain one of the central causes of maternal mortality. Once this issue is addressed women can begin to be really confident that their right to health will be guaranteed.

Select bibliography

Barrientos, Armando and Stephanie Barrientos (2002) *Social Protection for Workers in the Informal Economy: Case Study on Horticulture*, Social Protection Discussion Paper 0216, Washington, DC: World Bank.

Medel, Julia, Ximena Díaz and Amalia Mauro (2006) *Cuidadoras de la Vida. Visibilización de los Costos de la Producción de Salud en el Hogar. Impacto Sobre el Trabajo total de las Mujeres*, Santiago: Centro de Estudios de la Mujer.

Neilson, Christopher, Dante Contreras, Ryan Cooper and Jorge Hermann (2008) 'The dynamics of poverty in Chile', *Journal of Latin American Studies*, **40**, 251–73.

Pearson, Ruth (2004) 'Organising home-based workers in the global economy: an action-research approach', *Development in Practice*, **14** (1–2), 136–48.

Petchesky, Rosalind (2000) 'Human rights, reproductive rights and economic justice: why they are indivisible', *Reproductive Health Matters*, **8** (15), 12–17.

Reca, Ines, Madelin Alvarez and M. Emilia Tijoux (2002) 'Costos No Visibles del Cuidado de Enfermos en el Hogar. Una Metodologdía para su Estudio. Estudio de Caso, Santiago', mimeo, available at: http://www.generoreforma.org/Documentos.htm (accessed 10 February 2007).

Shepard, Bonnie L. and Lidia Casas Becerra (2007) 'Abortion policies and practices in Chile: ambiguities and dilemmas', *Reproductive Health Matters*, **15** (30), 202–10.

48 Maternal mortality in Latin America: a matter of gender and ethnic equality

Anna Coates

The global maternal mortality ratio (MMR) is around 400 maternal deaths per 100 000 live births but increases to 700 in countries such as Burkina Faso and to as many as 1800 in Niger and Afghanistan (WHO, 2007). At 190 per 100 000 live births the average for Latin America and the Caribbean (LAC) may appear relatively low. However, there are some sharp contrasts between countries: for example, Haiti has an MMR of 670 while Cuba has an MMR of 22. Furthermore, given that the MMR for developed regions of the world is only 11 and that maternal death is almost completely preventable with simple, well-known medical interventions, maternal death is a clear indicator of inequalities in the region as well as of the wider context of social and economic development and women's low status. Indeed, while world attention to maternal mortality issues has neglected LAC because of its relatively low national MMRs, LAC is the most unequal region in the world and the structural inequalities (including those related to poverty, gender and ethnicity) that mark extreme differences in capacities and opportunities between different social groups *within* countries also signify clear differences in vulnerability to maternal death which are not reflected in national figures. For example, while Mexico has a national MMR of 60 (UNICEF, 2008), in some poorer and rural areas, such as the states of Chiapas and Oaxaca, it is estimated that the MMR could reach 270. Similarly, in Ecuador, the national MMR in 2003 was 74.3 maternal deaths per 100 000 live births. However, the Pan-American Health Organisation (PAHO) has noted that the MMR may increase to as much as 250 in remote indigenous communities.

This vulnerability is increasingly being recognised within the region, with initiatives such as Proyecto MesoAmérica including maternal health within its 2008 priorities. However, Goal 5 of the United Nations (UN) Millennium Development Goals (MDGs), established in 2000, is to 'improve maternal health' by reducing the maternal mortality ratio (MMR) by 75 per cent by 2015 from its 1990 figure. The LAC region as a whole reduced its average MMR by only 27.9 per cent between 1990 and 2005 (UNICEF, 2008), with pockets of persistently high maternal mortality which have witnessed little decline. This leaves countries with an uphill struggle if they are to achieve a 75 per cent decrease by 2015.

Skilled attendance at birth

A maternal death is defined as any death occurring during pregnancy or within 42 days of termination of the pregnancy from any cause related to or aggravated by the pregnancy or its management. Indirect medical causes are correlated with poverty and include, for example, malaria, anaemia and malnutrition. Primary causes, which include haemorrhage, obstructed labour and sepsis, are difficult to predict and require immediate referral to emergency obstetric care (EmOC). Thus, MDG5 progress indicators include both the MMR and the proportion of births attended by skilled birth personnel.

316 *The international handbook of gender and poverty*

The existence of the latter indicator (recommended during the UN's 1994 International Conference on Population and Development [ICPD]) is also justified by the difficulties in accurately measuring maternal mortality and determining the MMR, particularly in countries with poor monitoring and data collection. Therefore attendance rates are used as a 'proxy' indicator for determining progress.

The average proportion of births with a skilled attendant in LAC is 88.5 per cent compared with 99.5 per cent for developed regions (WHO, 2006). Coverage of health personnel is also generally high compared with other regions. However, several countries have a critical shortage of doctors, nurses and midwives requiring, on average, a 40 per cent increase to combat the shortage (ibid.). Within LAC countries, there exists significant variation in relation to health service coverage. In many rural (usually indigenous) contexts, skilled attendance is low. For example, in Mexico, more than 85 per cent of births are attended by a skilled attendant, but it is estimated that in some poor rural indigenous areas this drops to as few as 20 per cent. By contrast, there is a generally higher than average overall rate of skilled attendance in urban contexts, notwithstanding that this can sometimes be prejudicial rather than advantageous since Caesarean rates in LAC actually exceed the 10–15 per cent recommended by the World Health Organisation (WHO), with unnecessary Caesareans also linked to high maternal mortality.

Common policies to reduce maternal mortality
Over time there have been notable shifts between attention aimed specifically at 'maternal health' and that aimed at 'maternal, neonatal and child health', with occasionally unbalanced attention towards the woman in function of the viability of the child rather than in the woman's own right. For example, more priority is often accorded to antenatal care which has little proven effect on risk of maternal death but which is important for ensuring neonatal health. However, in recent years, the international maternal health agenda has focused more upon skilled attendance. While this reflects the dominance of medical experts from the fields of health and epidemiology and the fact that '[t]he process of global agenda setting [for safe motherhood] was driven by a relatively small set of international actors with particular ideologies' (Campbell, 2001: 436), one positive outcome has been the formulation of services that focus as much upon women's health needs as those of their children. For example, recommendations and programmes have targeted health services and improved coverage of skilled attendance for delivery, with increasing attention also given to access to EmOC in the case of complications. Indeed EmOC coverage is recommended as an additional MDG5 indicator.

In response to these shifting priorities, policies have reflected the concern that distance to medical services and cost of care represent significant barriers to access to maternal healthcare. Common policies have included for example:

1. Elimination of fees for deliveries in medical institutions (for example, Peru's efforts to eliminate fees for the pregnant women in the poorest populations).
2. Strategies to improve coverage of services for normal deliveries (for example, assigning midwives with basic training to remote areas).
3. Delegating competencies to health professionals (including the training of general surgeons to perform Caesarean sections, use vacuum and forceps, treat ectopic pregnancy and provide post-abortion care).

While maternal health interventions have been characterised as *complex*, such policies focus on specific aspects of the health service and/or related institutions. Wider health sector issues related to the quality of services offered and the harmonisation and functionality of different levels of health services, for example, primary and secondary services involved in referral and access to EmOC, have proved more difficult to tackle and relate to more structurally rooted institutional challenges. It is, however, increasingly recognised that maternal mortality is an issue requiring an intersectoral approach, also implying attention to different sectors of social development beyond the health system, such as social infrastructure including, for example, road and transportation systems. Those interventions which have attempted to broach some of these wider issues of social development have often relied upon community-level systems of preparedness to put into place immediate strategies to deal with problems related to access in remote poor communities. For instance a Guatemalan programme implemented in 100 communities aimed at engaging communities to save mothers through community consultation, media, and development of family and community 'emergency plans'.

The kinds of strategies noted above are arguably appropriate given the context of widespread poverty and the weaknesses of health systems in sub-Saharan Africa and other regions such as Asia where national MMRs are highest. However, the differing realities of LAC suggest the need to promote more specific, complex and expanded strategies related to individual contexts of, and access to, health systems, and linked with the broader context of development, particularly social and gender inequalities and cultural exclusion. The latter factors work together to restrict access to maternal healthcare and operate at both community and institutional levels. Thus, the World Bank has designated maternal mortality as one of the key gender issues in LAC, and the UN and other agencies have proposed objectives related to equity and marginalised groups.

Gender and ethnic inequality: intersecting issues in maternal health
The centrality of women's autonomy to many health and development goals is widely recognised, particularly in relation to reproductive health. Indeed, Cook and Dicken (2002: 64) note that 'women's unjust legal, political, economic and social powerlessness explains much unsafe motherhood and maternal mortality and morbidity'. While often missing in medical discussions of maternal death, gender inequality and the low status of women (including their over-representation among the poorest) can be connected to several indirect causes of maternal mortality, including domestic violence, suicide, and unsafe abortion. For example, investigations in Mexico have shown that induced abortion may contribute to 13.5 per cent of all maternal deaths. Suicide risk is higher among women with unwanted pregnancies, while domestic violence has been found to affect a considerable proportion of women during pregnancy, often resulting in abdominal traumas leading to maternal death.

The British Department for International Development (DFID) also recommends that attention should be given to the underlying social and cultural factors that perpetuate women's inability to access services. The disadvantaged status of women and unequal power relations between men and women can restrict women's autonomy in numerous ways. This translates into barriers to health service access and use including lack of independent decision-making, social restrictions on mobility outside the home (for example, without accompaniment or permission), low levels of education and literacy (and associated limited healthcare knowledge), and lack of access to financial resources in the household to pay for the costs of access including fees, medicines and transport (if available). Any or all of these restrictions, which constitute an obstacle to a woman being fully empowered over her own body and health, can be characterised as harmful and thus as an indirect form of gender violence.

An understanding of cultural beliefs and practices related to birth and reproduction is fundamental and in many cases related to gender equality. Comprehending the complex interrelationships between women's everyday realities and level of autonomy (as related to cultural beliefs and practices), and the acceptability of, and ability to access, health services, is central to unpacking the dynamics of how a maternal health policy affects uptake of services.

In LAC, indigenous groups are often socially, economically, politically, and culturally marginalised, featuring not only among the poorest in terms of household income, but also with the least access to public services. Consequently, indigenous populations are often those with the lowest levels of human development. As Montenegro and Stephens (2006: 1865) note, not only do '[i]ndigenous peoples of Latin America still have inadequate access to mainstream health services, and health prevention and promotion programmes . . . [those] services that do exist are often culturally inappropriate'. In the area of obstetric health services, conceptualisation of reproduction and cultural understandings of the body and reproduction, women's status, and traditional birthing practices may intertwine and affect both the ability of women to access the limited services that do exist as well as the acceptability of such services.

Given that understandings of reproduction are socially constructed through shared cultural knowledge and values, and that women are centrally concerned in reproduction, women themselves can be among the most active in choosing and/or promoting related birthing practices. However, this active decision-making role is not necessarily exercised by women of reproductive age themselves but may be mediated through women's roles as traditional birth attendants (TBAs) or the influence that older female family members have over younger women's maternal health choices. The latter is recognised in the support and promotion of grandmothers' involvement in community programmes around mother and child health and well-being by the United Nations Children's Fund (UNICEF), WHO and the World Bank. It can thus be difficult to judge how far decisions around maternal health are free and informed. However, while women's education is a key indicator of maternal health, maternal health knowledge (from a biomedical perspective) and expanded coverage of services do not necessarily mean that women will wholly abandon traditional cultural beliefs and practices. A gender-empowered strategy implies that women of reproductive age have the ability and knowledge to exercise their own preferences for care. In many indigenous contexts, where these preferences may include traditional practices, integration of such practices with skilled care may be the best option. For example, Ecuador is experimenting with combining services to provide both modern and safe indigenous medicine, with positive results.

Internationally, evidence suggests that attitudes of health professionals towards users can substantially decrease motivation to seek formal care. In LAC there is substantial evidence of institutional racism towards indigenous women in various institutions, including those related to health. The abusive nature, and even negation, of treatment can be characterised as a form of gender violence. The location of care close to the community is important to promote provision that is more respectful of women, their needs and preferences. Not only will reducing travel distance help overcome some of the financial barriers encountered by poor women (often exacerbated by their lack of autonomy and access to household income), it is also likely to enable greater understanding by health professionals of different cultural beliefs and practices.

A rights and equality perspective on maternal mortality policies
Currently MDG5 is helping to generate the essential political priority and will to reduce maternal mortality in LAC. Other international commitments to reduce maternal mortality have been established at UN Conferences, such as the ICPD as mentioned above, the follow-up ICPD +5 conference in 1999, and the World Summit for Social Development of 1995. However, in the longer term, success in achieving and maintaining any reduction will require more general attention to marginalised ethnic populations, to gender equality and to all women, regardless of their identity, as subjects of human rights in their own right, not just as reproductive beings in function of their child. Traditionally, rights associated with maternal mortality have been expressed in relation to the:

1. Right to life – everyone has the right to life, liberty and personal security.
2. Right to health – the enjoyment of the highest attainable standard of health is one of the fundamental rights of every human being.
3. Sexual and reproductive rights – physical, sexual and reproductive health and the right to choice in relation to fertility and sexuality, free of discrimination, coercion and violence.

Most fundamental among these is the right to life, since there are few medical reasons why pregnancy and birth should pose a risk to life. The right to life is linked to a number of other human rights, guaranteed by the conventions of international agencies and ratified in virtually all countries worldwide. In LAC there are several international agreements that should be recognised by their respective countries, as well as the commitments made by each nation to women's health, reproductive rights, and the reduction of maternal mortality. International agreements include the Convention on the Elimination of All Forms of Discrimination Against Women (CEDAW), adopted in 1979, which specifically targets women's health issues, while also advocating for basic human rights. The 1966 International Covenant on Economic, Social and Cultural Rights (ICESCR) and, specifically in relation to LAC, the 2007 Quito Consensus have also established women's right to health (see Gideon, Chapter 47, this volume).

Similarly, and particularly relevant to the context of maternal mortality in LAC, several international instruments also protect and promote the rights of indigenous people, including the 2007 UN Declaration on the Rights of Indigenous People and Convention 169 of the International Labour Organisation adopted in 1989. Such rights include those related to culture and identity and specifically refer to the right to health (among other social benefits) within a framework of the pursuit of indigenous people's own priorities regarding economic, social and cultural development. Also specified is the prohibition of discrimination against indigenous peoples and the promotion of their full and effective participation in all matters that concern them thus necessitating the consideration of the specific rights of indigenous women in the formulation of any maternal health policy.

Successful strategies that have maintained priority for women's health are not unknown to the region. Since 1961, Cuba has considered specialised attention and care regarding both mother and child to be priorities within the national health system and, consequently, reduced the Cuban MMR from 118 to 22 between 1962 and 1997. Similarly rights-based approaches have been formulated, such as Bolivia's Charter of Rights for Pregnant Women, which provides both mutual rights and obligations of the state, community, individual and health professionals. Furthermore, interventions incorporating knowledge of different cultural practices of childbirth are becoming more common, as exemplified in Peru's promotion of respect for traditional practices in outreach and community education to promote safe motherhood.

Nonetheless, there are many challenges still remaining in Latin America. Many common interventions take a more 'practical' stance in relation to short-term obstacles related to gender and ethnicity, rather than more comprehensive and sustainable strategies. Indeed, even those which recognise structural inequalities often seek to work around such obstacles rather than attempt to address them. However, in order to reduce the pockets of persistently high maternal mortality in the long-term, and in the context of extreme inequality in Latin America, intersectoral, multidisciplinary strategies are required. Public health policies aimed at reducing maternal deaths should be designed in conjunction with other policies which seek to reduce and eliminate institutional and structural gender and ethnic inequalities for the promotion of social development more generally. Approaches to maternal health in LAC need to go beyond a health focus and should be based upon all women as citizens and as subjects of human rights, with equality issues at their heart.

Select bibliography

Campbell, Oona (2001) 'What are maternal health policies in developing countries and who drives them? A review of the last half-century', in Vincent De Brouwere and Wim Van Lerberghe (eds), *Safe Motherhood Strategies: A Review of the Evidence (Studies in Heath Services Organisation and Policy 17)*, Antwerp: ITG Press, pp. 415–37.

Cook, Rebecca and Bernard Dickens (2002) 'The injustice of unsafe motherhood', *Developing World Bioethics*, **2** (1), 64–81.

Montenegro, Raul and Carolyn Stephens (2006) 'Indigenous health in Latin America and the Caribbean', *The Lancet*, **367**, 1859–69.

United Nations Children's Fund (UNICEF) (2008) *State of the World's Children 2008: Child Survival*, New York: UNICEF.

World Health Organisation (WHO) (2006) *World Health Report 2006: Working Together for Health*, Geneva: WHO.

World Health Organisation (WHO) (2007) *Maternal Mortality in 2005: Estimates Developed by WHO, UNICEF, UNFPA and the World Bank*, Geneva: WHO.

49 New labyrinths of solitude: lonesome Mexican migrant men and AIDS
Matthew Gutmann

In contemporary Mexico, AIDS is a disease of migration and modernity. Worldwide AIDS is often argued to be a direct product of neoliberal policies that have prompted the decentralisation and privatisation of healthcare. At the same time, structural adjustments related to these changes in healthcare which have been imposed by international agencies like the World Bank have fostered conditions in which populations are forced to flee their homelands in search of better economic prospects in other countries. This is clearly the case in Mexico, where local impoverished circumstances lead millions to try their luck on the other side of the border in the United States (US). In the southern Mexican state of Oaxaca, for instance, where detailed ethnographic fieldwork over several years provides the basis of this chapter, to be a migrant means that you are poor and likely to be from one of the area's many indigenous groups.[1] Extrapolating from notoriously unreliable government statistics, by 2000 there were probably over 100 000 men and women from Oaxaca working as migrants in northern parts of Mexico and the United States. It was also estimated by this time that 60 per cent of Oaxaca's *municipios* (municipalities) had experienced significant emigration.

Leading on from the above, the political economy of AIDS in Oaxaca involves several features which are also global in scope, with transnational migration being key: the largest demographic group in the state who are HIV-positive are poor Indian men who have worked in the United States and returned to Oaxaca infected with the virus. The second largest demographic group who are HIV-positive are women who have had sex with these migrant men. Since the late 1990s, in a process called 'medical profiling', migrant men and their sexual partners have become slotted into the public health category of 'dangerous citizens', capable of infecting the better-off sectors of Oaxacan society.

Another global factor pertains to the international pharmaceutical industry. Unlike in certain other countries in the world such as Brazil, South Africa, and India where antiretrovirals are available for far less than the cost the drug companies would like to charge – either because the medications are produced locally in these countries or because national governments have refused to pay the pharmaceutical firms full royalties on the patents for the drugs – in Mexico the government pays whatever the drug companies demand. Thus, in Mexico, instead of paying a fraction of the cost of antiretrovirals demanded by pharmaceutical firms, only a small number of people who need the drugs are able to receive them. This shortfall is compounded by the fact that few seek out the state clinic for AIDS in Oaxaca, either because they do not know of its existence or because they do not know they are HIV-positive.

Numbers and vectors

Thousands of people in Oaxaca are sick and dying with HIV and AIDS. How these people are identified (and ignored) and treated (and ignored) is grounded in cultural beliefs about men's sexuality and a culturalist resignation that men with dangerous sexual practices may die as a result of AIDS. Although it is true that in a narrow biological sense the AIDS virus knows no class or ethnic boundaries, and that many *mestizos* (mixed race Mexicans) of means have succumbed to the disease, even casual acquaintance with the COESIDA (Consejo Estatal para la Prevención del VIH/SIDA) clinic in Oaxaca City makes evident that the patients there are disproportionately poor and indigenous. Having money and social standing are not in themselves sufficient barriers to prevent infection, but men and women from the upper strata are far more likely than those from the ranks of the dispossessed to know about AIDS, know how to avoid contracting the virus, and know what to do if they become infected.

According to official figures in Oaxaca the number of people diagnosed with AIDS as of 2005 was around 3000 people living and dead (less than 0.1 per cent of the state's population). Off the record, state officials put the number at anywhere from 5000 to 15 000 people with HIV in Oaxaca. Of great significance, despite being tenth largest in population, by 2005 Oaxaca had more new cases of AIDS than all but three other jurisdictions: Mexico City, Mexico State, and Veracruz.

The fact that hundreds or even thousands of Mexican migrant men are now returning to Oaxaca infected with HIV stems largely from the fact that they seek out sexual relations with female prostitutes and fellow male migrants while in the United States. In this way structural factors shape the vulnerability to HIV for millions of Mexican men working in the fields, factories, and construction sites of the United States. This chapter introduces a few of the men with AIDS – migrant and non-migrant, heterosexual and bisexual – who talked with me about the virus, how they thought they had become infected, their sexual relationships with women and men in the past, present, and future, and their experiences with medications they were able to secure from the state-run AIDS clinic known as COESIDA. Most of the men and women I talked with about AIDS depended on the medical care they received from COESIDA, and I met most of them at the government AIDS clinic in Oaxaca City during a period of ethnographic fieldwork from 2001 to 2005.

I talked one day with Jesús Hernández, who worked for some years around Watsonville, near San Jose, California. There are lots of strawberries around there, he told me. He had also worked harvesting cauliflower, celery, and lettuce in the fields of the southwest United States. It was scarier crossing the border now, he told me in late 2001. 'Now there's a lot of fear about biological war.' He came back to Oaxaca sick one year, and they ordered blood tests for him in a clinic in his village. They told him he was seropositive and had HIV. 'What's that?' I ask. 'Have you heard of AIDS?' 'Yes. That's what this is. I felt like dying. I thought I was dying right then. No. There was no way out for me. Not forward, not backward. They told me they were going to send me to the COESIDA clinic where I could get help.'

I asked Jesús how he became infected. He answered at length,

'I was a hard worker. I worked in the fields. I killed myself in the fields! Sometimes I worked by the hour. Sometimes by contract. The bosses always looked at me like a good worker. I have a lot of experience. But I am illegal. My family was here. One day . . .

because I was always responsible about what I did . . . well . . . That's why I never, well, how was I going to get through it? Because I felt so alone, right, and I wanted a little distraction . . .'.

'Loneliness', I murmured sympathetically.

'I went out cruising, and went into a bar.

'I got infected in the United States, in Watsonville. But I won't hold that against my brother country.' Then he laughed. 'I would like to go, to work again. But what I am scared of is my medicine. Because if I leave here they will cut off my medicine. If I get there and fight, they will do other studies and as I am illegal there are fewer resources for me. That's why I say, "Better here".'

What is life like for Mexican migrant labourers in unregistered, temporary, and makeshift encampments who live in California's agricultural regions? The lucky men might have lived in rental housing, six or more farm workers to an apartment. Others were found living on hillsides and in canyons, river beds, and groves where they harvested fruits and vegetables for the US market. Plywood covered with tar paper and corrugated plastic sheets or old mattresses were pulled together to form the walls of the makeshift housing. Some men lived in what they called 'spider holes' dug in the ground under thick bushes that were just large enough to sleep in and remain unseen by immigration agents. A *fayuquero* (dealer in contraband) drove a van from encampment to encampment selling meals, toiletries, other goods. At the time of research in the mid-1990s, few encampments had potable water, gas, electricity, or waste disposal. These conditions no doubt contributed to the chronic stomach aches and diarrhoea that plagued the men, some of whom sought to relieve these symptoms by injecting vitamins and antibiotics on a regular basis, just as they had in their villages in Mexico.

In spite of the increase in the number of Border Patrol agents from 4000 to 11 000 in the period 1995–2005, as many as a million Mexicans each year continue to try their luck in crossing the geopolitical divide to find work and mail back as much money to their families as they can. And if their challenges were not already great enough, the modern plague of AIDS is now an additional threat to the lives of these migrants.

Paths to AIDS

All these factors have for decades contributed to a transnational labyrinth of solitude for millions of Mexican migrant men living and working in the United States. What has also changed in recent years is AIDS, a disease that has had severe consequences for men who are not careful enough about how and with whom they have sexual relations during their sojourns in the United States. And what has changed with AIDS is that it became a disease of migrants and, increasingly, of women. By 2005, of the 102 575 registered cases of AIDS in Mexico the proportion of women had climbed from less than 5 per cent to almost 16 per cent in less than ten years.

One man I interviewed at the AIDS clinic in Oaxaca talked about the two years he had spent as a plumber in Los Angeles. He told me that on weekends he sometimes visited friends who worked near Bakersfield. It was common for prostitutes to visit on Saturday nights. Some men wasted so much money on these *pachanga*-parties they had none to send home to their families in Mexico. He denied ever having sex with a prostitute – in other words, that he had ever paid for sex – but acknowledged that he used to drink a lot and often awoke with '*una mujer desconocida*' (a woman he did not know). He tried to be careful and use a condom, but because of the alcohol he consumed he was not always able to do this, he said. When we talked he was living at home in Oaxaca, suffering badly from diarrhoea and aches. He and his wife had not had sex for years and, he admitted, now she would not even cook for him anymore.

Despite some excellent ethnographic fieldwork and vivid portraits of social suffering among the Mexican farm workers resident in the United States, research in this population is more characterised by ignorance than knowledge. In 1996, Mishra et al. (1996: vii) wrote, 'Little, however, is known about the impact of the HIV/AIDS epidemic on Latino farm workers'. Around the same time, Bronfman and López (1996: 49) concluded, 'Mexico does not have enough information, based on reliable research, on the sexuality of its population and, in the case of migrants, there is no information at all'.[2]

Nonetheless, despite the paucity of reliable information, including well-grounded epidemiological studies, about Mexican migrant men's sexual activities and how some become infected with HIV in the United States, researchers believe that the virus is transmitted among this population by sex with female prostitutes and by sex between the men themselves.

The primary route of transmission for the AIDS virus in Latin America is through sexual relations between men. Reports from epidemiological research in Oaxaca also show that a high percentage of cases of AIDS can be traced back to men who had sex with other men. Nonetheless, although we have broad outlines about male–male sexual transmission, we still lack details on sexual relations among migrant men. In the absence of better ways to verify other possible vectors for the transmission of the AIDS virus, like sex with female prostitutes, we are still too often left with speculation, rumours, and accusations among those who study Mexican male sexuality.

Mexican men are undoubtedly having sex with female prostitutes who originally became infected as a result of intravenous (IV) drug use or male sex partners. Not only are rates of IV drug use higher on the United States side of the international border, but in Mexico, where prostitution is essentially legal if prostitutes go for monthly medical examinations, Mishra et al. (1996) report that if registered sex workers suspect they are infected they move into the underground, unorganised, unregistered sector of sex work, where prostitutes undergo serologic assessments only when they are apprehended for selling sex without legal credentials. This same study reported higher seroprevalence rates among African-American farm workers, and higher rates of IV drug use among this population, and speculated that Mexican migrant farm workers might have become infected with HIV through casual sex with the African-Americans with whom they worked; it is possible, too, that racist stigma influenced the Mexicans not to report such sexual experiences.

Regardless of how HIV is transmitted, loneliness is also an important feature of life for Mexican men who never make it to the United States, but only migrate to other parts of Mexico. Loneliness is associated with the issue of male sexuality because healthcare practitioners, in Oaxaca and elsewhere in the Mexican republic, tend to assume that men everywhere will normally seek sexual pleasures, and that lonely men will seek these any way they can. In other words, even self-identified heterosexual men who would 'normally' seek women will succumb to sex with other men if they have no other options. Unfortunately, we still lack detailed studies of what is happening in migrant camps and apartment complexes where migrant workers live and have sex and, for the unluckiest, become infected with HIV. We know more about sexual regulation and stigma than we do about the sexual scripts written on migrant bodies in furtive and transgressive and, for the luckiest, in loving ways.

In the most candid sense, providing care for Mexican migrant men who have AIDS requires they be viewed as vital citizens whose lives are both worth saving and are able to be saved. As the space of healthcare in Mexico is shifted from public to private, and from clinic to home, the underlying false choice of 'either prevention or treatment' comes into clearer focus. Whereas primary prevention is more cost-effective, the space of healing is both more costly and it requires that there are people and resources to actually tend to the afflicted. The view that only the developed countries can afford adequate AIDS care is short-sighted.

In Mexico in the 2000s, migrants who are HIV-positive and their sexual partners whom they infect with the disease became labelled in a process similar to what Briggs and Mantini-Briggs (2003), in their study of cholera in Venezuela, call 'medical profiling'. In the case of Oaxaca, since the late 1990s, AIDS has come to be ever more associated in the state with migrant men and their female sexual partners. This is more than a simple epidemiological and demographic issue, as the public discourse within the medical community treating AIDS patients is acutely aware of the fact that the individuals who migrate are from very specific socio-economic backgrounds: when one talks of migrant men and their spouses, in Oaxaca this means *indigenous* and *poor* men and women. The professional middle class is never implicated in the label 'migrants' (see also Jassey, Chapter 78, this volume). Thus the population is divided, to again borrow from Briggs and Mantini-Briggs (2003), into 'unsanitary subjects' and 'sanitary citizens', that is, those who are, potentially at least, carriers and transmitters of disease and those about whom the health authorities have little cause for worry. The stigmatising implications of such typologising, even when just implicit, are severe for AIDS care in Oaxaca.

Notes

1. This chapter is drawn from Gutmann (2007), with my study of heterosexual couples being conducted in Oaxaca de Juárez, a metropolitan area of around 500 000 people located in a mountain region 300 miles south of the Mexican capital. Approximately half the population of the state, totalling over 3 million people, self-identifies as belonging to one or another indigenous group. Living standards in the state of Oaxaca are among the lowest in Mexico, especially in the countryside. My fieldwork was supported by the National Endowment for the Humanities and Brown University.
2. Since 1996, this situation has improved with the work of researchers like Carrillo (2002), Hirsch (2003), and González-López (2005), but still far too little is known about the sex lives and transmission of HIV among Mexican migrant men.

Select bibliography

Briggs, Charles and Clara Mantini-Briggs (2003) *Stories in the Time of Cholera: Racial Profiling During a Medical Nightmare*, Berkeley, CA: University of California Press.
Bronfman, Mario and Sergio López (1996) 'Perspectives on HIV/AIDS prevention among immigrants on the U.S.–Mexico Border', in Shiraz Mishra, Ross Conner and J. Raul Magaña (eds), *AIDS Crossing Borders: The Spread of HIV among Migrant Latinos*, Boulder, CO: Westview, pp. 49–76.
Carrillo, Héctor (2002) *The Night is Young: Sexuality in Mexico in the Time of AIDS*, Chicago, IL: University of Chicago Press.
González-López, Gloria (2005) *Erotic Journeys: Mexican Immigrants and their Sex Lives*, Berkeley, CA: University of California Press.
Gutmann, Matthew (2007) *Fixing Men: Sex, Birth Control, and AIDS in Mexico*, Berkeley, CA: University of California Press.

Hirsch, Jennifer (2003) *A Courtship after Marriage: Sexuality and Love in Mexican Transnational Families*, Berkeley, CA: University of California Press.

Mishra, Shiraz; Ross Conner and J. Raul Magaña (1996) 'Preface', in Shiraz Mishra, Ross Conner and J. Raul Magaña (eds), *AIDS Crossing Borders: The Spread of HIV among Migrant Latinos*, Boulder, CO: Westview, p. vii.

50 Gender, poverty and AIDS: perspectives with particular reference to sub-Saharan Africa
Catherine Campbell and Andrew Gibbs

In many contexts, gender and poverty intertwine to undermine women's ability to avoid HIV infection, access appropriate AIDS care and treatment, care for AIDS-affected loved ones, and engage in collective action to challenge the social circumstances placing their health at risk. Globally, equal numbers of men and women are HIV positive. In sub-Saharan Africa (SSA), however, women comprise 60 per cent of those infected (UN AIDS, 2008). Moreover women contract HIV much earlier than men, with girls in their early teens up to five times more likely to be infected than boys of the same age group. SSA, the poorest region in the world, is home to 67 per cent of all people living with HIV/AIDS. Against this background, we will give most of our attention to the heterosexual epidemic in SSA, though many of our arguments will be applicable to other contexts.

Poverty alone cannot be regarded as a driver of the pandemic. AIDS is highest in India's wealthiest states, for example. It is particularly high in Botswana and South Africa, two of Africa's richest countries. Both are characterised by strong urban–rural economic interchange, good transport links and high professional mobility, all translating into higher incomes and higher levels of HIV in specific settings. In many African countries, HIV transmission has historically been concentrated among the affluent, educated and mobile.

This pattern may be changing, with the heaviest burden of AIDS gradually shifting towards socially disadvantaged groups, especially poor young women. Citing evidence linking higher HIV prevalence with greater income inequality in Africa, Asia and Latin America, Kim et al. (2008) argue that rather than being a disease of poverty per se, AIDS is a disease of inequality, often associated with social and economic transition, and neoliberal economic policies that prioritise market competition over investment in supporting and building the capacities of women and the poor. In this chapter we examine how poverty and gender interact to frame the arenas in which peoples' health-related agency is negotiated, and in ways that enable or hinder their abilities to cope with HIV/AIDS.

AIDS: a technical or social challenge?
Billions of dollars have been poured into technical HIV/AIDS management interventions in SSA, often with disappointing results. These include health education, condom distribution, circumcision, voluntary counselling and testing, drug treatments and so on. Interventions are usually imposed on target communities by outside experts, often from northern countries. They generally view HIV/AIDS as a problem best tackled at the individual level, through biomedical or individual behaviour-change interventions, with the latter relying heavily on the provision of information about health risks. Less attention is paid to the interaction of gender, social status and poverty in shaping individuals' sexual choices, and few attempts are made to tackle the social circumstances

that prevent people from making optimal use of prevention, care and treatment where they exist.

Starting from the assumption that women's sexual subordination is a key driver of HIV transmission in SSA, we allude to some of the economic, historical and political dynamics shaping the contexts of sexuality. In pre-colonial times, women had a degree of flexibility and autonomy in their relationships with men (Susser, 2008). This was often undermined by colonial authorities, who privileged men through their interpretation and codification of customary law in ways that excluded women from decision-making and the inheritance of land.

Many countries have seen a significant lack of commitment by politicians to prioritise AIDS in formulating national priorities. In South Africa, for example, the 1990s saw the gradual erosion of progressive post-apartheid AIDS policies in the face of neoliberal economic strategies – together with the mobilisation of 'traditional (patriarchal) African values' by Presidents Thabo Mbeki and Jacob Zuma as tools to further their political ambitions. Economic policies have focused on developing the formal economy at the expense of building the capacity of women and the poor to take better control over their health. They have been increasingly marginalised by the prioritisation of market competition over collective public projects and by the lack of adequate investment in health and welfare services.

In such contexts, relative to men, women tend to be poorly educated, to have limited access to paid work, to engage in informal jobs characterised by income insecurity and poor working conditions, and to experience limited access to property and inheritance rights and credit (see Meagher, Chapter 72, this volume). Each of these factors is implicated in the web of factors driving HIV/AIDS in poor communities (Greig et al., 2008; Kim et al., 2008; Stillwagon, 2005).

Women's vulnerability to AIDS

In circumstances of poverty, women are often forced to trade their sexual and domestic services for economic support by men. They have little power in such relationships – either in marriage or extra-marital liaisons. These economic imperatives are overlaid by the social construction of a masculinity that reinforces male dominance over women, the acceptability of multiple sexual partners for men, and a strong male resistance to condoms. Condom resistance is fuelled by 'macho' representations of insatiable male sexuality, male fearlessness in the face of risks, and the urgency of the male drive to father children.

Within this context, various types of relationships place women at particular risk of AIDS. Poverty and food insufficiency drive teenage girls to embark on sexual liaisons at a young age. They engage in transactional relationships with older men in exchange for money for transport, school fees and other necessities, as well as for more expensive, coveted, 'luxury' goods (see also Evans, Chapter 30, this volume; Jolly and Cornwall, Chapter 103, this volume; Nyanzi, Chapter 31, this volume). Such age-mixing is a key driver of the epidemic. Formal polygamy, and informal polygyny, is quite common in SSA, and even married women, though expected to be monogamous, often resort to multiple male partners.

Each of these relationships provides different contexts in which women's economic dependence on men reduces or removes their power to refuse sex, negotiate condom use, discuss fidelity with their partners, delay the age of first sex, or leave sexually risky or violent relationships – all factors that increase their HIV/AIDS vulnerability (Kim et al., 2008; Stillwagon, 2005).

With the erosion of traditional livelihoods and increasing unemployment associated with neoliberal economic policies, a growing number of men are prevented from fulfilling their socially constructed breadwinner role. To compensate, they often fall back on their 'traditional' power over women as a way to fulfil their masculinity, in contexts where a sense of economic inadequacy may lead to an increased unwillingness to take women seriously, as well as heightened domestic violence (another factor associated with increased HIV risk), particularly when women try to negotiate safe sex.

The ability of poor women to protect their sexual health has been further limited by the regulation of international AIDS funding, particularly from the United States (US) (Susser, 2008). In 2008 the US President's Emergency Plan for AIDS Relief (PEPFAR) contributed the largest proportion of money for global AIDS prevention and treatment. Resonating with the moralistic attitudes of the American religious right, PEPFAR refused to fund the distribution of condoms or sex education to young people. They favoured prevention programmes that promoted sexual abstinence outside marriage as their sole prevention strategy, even though levels of HIV are highest among monogamous married women in many African settings. They also refused to fund programmes that supported commercial sex workers, despite ample evidence that transactional sex is the only route to survival for many women.

In the light of warnings to guard against one-dimensional views of African women as helpless victims of inexorable social forces (see Richey, Chapter 77, this volume), many argue for taking greater account of women's sexual agency (Cornwall and Jolly, Chapter 103, this volume). Some women choose to engage in unprotected sex – experiencing it as more pleasurable than sex with condoms, both physically and in terms of the intimacy associated with 'flesh-to-flesh' contact. Others choose unprotected sex because they believe a child will consolidate their relationship with a valued partner. Some wives refuse condoms because they prefer to turn a blind eye to their husbands' infidelities.

It has been argued that many teenage girls 'choose' transactional sex with older men to attain valued status symbols such as cell phones and designer clothes, rather than solely out of economic need, and are thus sexually empowered rather than oppressed. Given the associated risks of potentially lethal HIV infection, others have questioned the extent to which such behaviours can be said to constitute evidence for their empowered sexual agency.

Women's care for the sick and dying
Structural Adjustment Programmes (SAPs) of the 1970s and 1980s led to cuts in social and health spending in many SSA contexts, leading to a decline in affordable healthcare. The AIDS epidemic has put further strain on overstretched healthcare systems, leading governments and development agencies to promote home-based care – mostly by women – as the most appropriate strategy for nursing the sick and dying. Caring for the sick depletes household resources and reduces the time available to girls and women to engage in other productive activities such as earning money, securing food or going to school (see also Nakray, Chapter 51, this volume).

Multiple studies have demonstrated the devastating physical and psychological impacts of care on women already burdened with multiple responsibilities for domestic and informal subsistence activities. Nursing a series of sick or dying family members, often young people who will leave behind small children, frequently in conditions of tremendous pain and suffering, with no medical supplies or equipment, drains already scarce household resources and may be extremely traumatic for carers. The tendency for governments to invest in highways and bridges rather than affordable public transport has exacerbated the suffering of people with AIDS and their carers in SSA contexts where transport to hospitals constitutes 40 per cent of the costs of caring for someone with AIDS. The growing move towards privatising clean water also makes nursing difficult in cases where people dying of AIDS may have diarrhoea up to 15 times a day.

Women's advantage in treatment access
While the number of people on antiretroviral treatment increased tenfold from 2002 to 2008, treatment is still only available to one-third of those who need it, and the number of new infections outstrips the increase in those accessing treatment by 2.5 to 1 (UN AIDS, 2008). Gender and poverty are key factors shaping treatment access. In the developing world it is men who are disadvantaged in this respect. While men constitute about 43 per cent of those needing treatment in South Africa, they currently only constitute 30 per cent of those who receive it. Men who do access treatment typically do so later than women, often at a stage when their ill-health is more advanced, and their condition is more difficult and costly to treat.

Constructions of masculinity frame illness as 'unmanly weakness', deterring men from approaching health services. Some men in South Africa resist being tested, fearing that a positive diagnosis will limit their opportunities to father children and prevent them from fulfilling their masculine destiny. Conversely, women's roles place them in constant interaction with health services, through antenatal services and taking children to clinics. This has the positive outcome of their higher access to antiretroviral therapy. It serves as a 'double-edged sword' however insofar as they also bear the disproportionate burden of disclosure of HIV-positive status to partners and families, with the associated risks of blame, violence and abandonment.

Poverty is a major obstacle to accessing life-saving treatment. Poverty-related barriers include the cost of transport to hospitals, user-fees for healthcare, and the need to eat well when on medication. When financial barriers have been removed, the uptake of treatment increases dramatically.

Responding to AIDS: a case study
Despite ample evidence for the role of the gender–poverty interaction in fuelling AIDS in many contexts, public health and development agencies persist in favouring technical responses that treat HIV/AIDS as an individual medical problem. More 'social' responses tend to focus on providing information to vulnerable individuals, with little attention to social circumstances that prevent them from acting on it.

Despite much lip service paid to the importance of gender in national and international AIDS policy documents and conferences, in practice those gender interventions that do exist tend to be small in scale, seldom rooted in national AIDS plans, and rarely regarded as 'mainstream' responses. Those who seek to promote gender-sensitive AIDS programming face multiple obstacles: resistance by programmers and managers to acknowledging the centrality of human rights and gender equality to their work, the difficulties of turning gender analysis into actionable strategies, and a lack of technical capacity to develop and deliver strong gender initiatives (Greig et al., 2008). Gender-focused AIDS organisations often struggle to secure funding for policy and advocacy work.

One-off programmes that seek to build women's agency and capacity to avoid AIDS themselves, and providing adequate care for the sick and dying, often face substantial obstacles. In an intervention designed to build the skills of female home-based carers in an impoverished South African rural community, Campbell et al. (2009) found that rural women provided vital unpaid welfare services to local people, and constituted a motivated and talented pool of AIDS workers and potential leaders. Yet their efforts to build a women-led sustainable AIDS committee to spearhead more effective local responses faced multiple challenges.

Like many community health projects in SSA, the project relied heavily on unpaid volunteers. While the government had made frequent ambiguous promises to provide local volunteers with small stipends, these failed to materialise. This resulted in high drop-out rates among carers, especially those supporting children. It also discouraged unemployed youth – a strong pool of potential project participants – from becoming involved.

Men refused to take any interest in the project, dismissing tasks related to health and caring as 'women's work' and sneering at volunteers for being prepared to work so hard for no payment. The project's AIDS prevention messages had little resonance with the identities of local men. The community's traditional leader was committed to AIDS reduction, and supported the intervention. However, his relationship with the project was ambiguous, since he himself had several wives and girlfriends, and frequently expressed his view that polygamy played no role in AIDS transmission as long as women were faithful and virtuous.

Local public sector health and welfare agencies – envisaged as key 'partners' in the project plan – expressed strong support for the project, but failed to action this effectively. Hierarchical work structures undermined the flexibility of civil servants to respond to grassroots community needs. Overworked and under-resourced officials lacked training in community outreach skills. They also lacked confidence that they could make any impact on the overwhelming problems of AIDS and poverty. Most of all, many lacked the motivation to engage with poor people as equals. With no strong national pressure to prioritise engagement with poor communities, the public sector involvement that did take place was motivated by the interest of particular individuals, undermining the project's goal to become formally institutionalised into existing public sector structures over time. Project funding was cut short when the project's American funders appointed a new financial controller. She said the project's goals of empowering poor women to lead an effective grassroots AIDS response did not fit the agency's more technical view of what constituted an appropriate HIV/AIDS management strategy.

Towards the politicisation of AIDS?
Our case study illustrates the multilayered lack of political will to build the agency and capacity of poor women to take control of their sexual health and participate in spearheading effective community AIDS projects. It is increasingly argued that until there is

strong civil society pressure on donor and recipient governments, the historical failure to turn much AIDS-gender rhetoric into action will continue.

In this regard, many are encouraged by the role that global and national AIDS movements have played in challenging unjust practices by international pharmaceutical companies, forcing them to permit lower AIDS drug pricing for poor countries. These are seen as evidence of companies being forced to take needs of the poor into account in unprecedented ways.

The South African Treatment Action Campaign (TAC) is similarly often cited as an exemplar social movement in that it draws most of its membership from poor younger women. Using strategies ranging from legal challenges through the courts, to mass mobilisation, it has successfully pressurised a reluctant South African government to commit to rolling out free antiretroviral drug treatment to all through the public health system; a long-term project which is gradually being implemented.

Susser (2009) highlights many isolated instances in which small groups of poor women have managed to take control over their sexual health, resisting male oppression and calling governments to account in various ways. She refers to these women as Gramscian 'organic intellectuals', arguing that their indigenous critical analyses of poverty and gender inequalities constitute a vital resource for the gradual larger-scale mobilisation of women, leading to empowering social change. In the light of the massive structural violence suffered by poor women, as well as the multilayered lack of political will to implement policies and programmes that support them, many challenges lie ahead in the task of turning this vision of 'poor women rising up to protect their sexual health' into a reality.

Acknowledgements

We have drawn particularly heavily in this chapter on the work of Kim et al. (2008) and Greig et al. (2008) and the references cited therein.

Select bibliography

Campbell, Catherine, Yugi Nair, Sbongile Maimane and Andrew Gibbs (2009) 'Strengthening community responses to AIDS: possibilities and challenges', in Poul Rohleder, Leslie Swartz, Seth Kalichman and Leickness Simbayi (eds), *HIV/AIDS in South Africa 25 Years On: Psychosocial Perspectives*, London: Springer.
Greig, Alan, Dean Peacock, Rachel Jewkes and Sisonke Msimang (2008) 'Gender and AIDS: time to act', *AIDS*, **22** (suppl. 2), pp. S35–43.
Kim, Julia, Paul Pronyk, Tony Barnett and Charlotte Watts (2008) 'Exploring the role of economic empowerment in HIV prevention', *AIDS*, **22** (suppl. 4), pp. S57–71.
Stillwagon, Eileen (2005) *AIDS and the Ecology of Poverty*, Oxford: Oxford University Press.
Susser, Ida (2009) *AIDS, Sex and Culture*, Chichester: Wiley Blackwell.
UN AIDS (2008) *Report on the Global AIDS Epidemic*, Geneva: UN AIDS.

51 Gender, HIV/AIDS and carework in India: a need for gender-sensitive policy
Keerty Nakray

This chapter explores the relevance of gender-sensitive budgeting in the context of gendered experience of Human Immunodeficiency Virus or Acquired Immunological Syndrome (HIV/AIDS). It draws attention to the strenuous nature of the carework women undertake for their intimate partners. Women in India contract the illness owing to their biological, social and economic vulnerability. Furthermore, the onset of this stigmatising condition exacerbates the poverty and privation women suffer on account of their lack of formal and informal support systems and poor entitlements in relation to property, education, nutrition and financial resources. In order to explore how HIV/AIDS is associated with, as well as deepening, women's experience of poverty, this chapter draws upon qualitative in-depth interviews carried out in 2007 with 60 poor women living with HIV/AIDS, and with policy informants, in three Indian cities: Chennai, Mumbai and New Delhi. The narratives of these women draw attention to the need for gender-sensitive policies in relation to HIV/AIDS.

Understanding the feminisation of HIV/AIDS in the Indian context
In the year 2006, it was estimated that 2.5 million (between 2 and 3.1 million) persons in India lived with HIV, which approximates to around 0.36 per cent of the adult population. Of these, 39 per cent are women and 3.8 per cent are children. According to the National AIDS Control Organisation (NACO), India is a low prevalence country, and more men are infected than women; in absolute numbers the prevalence rate for adult females is 0.29 per cent while for males it is 0.43 per cent (NACO, 2007). In India, HIV/AIDS is constructed as a disease of poverty and is associated with sex workers, injecting drug users, men who have sex with men (MSM) and migrant workers. The levels of stigma and discrimination are high, and even where people do not belong to the high-risk category themselves, infection implies association with severe consequences for their social standing and social, economic and emotional well-being.

The concept of the feminisation of HIV/AIDS draws attention to the biological, social and economic factors which make women vulnerable to HIV/AIDS. Biologically, male-to-female HIV transmission has been estimated to be two-to-three times higher than that from female to male although this finding has not been reported consistently. However, there is widespread consensus that young women are particularly at risk of infection compared with older women because the immature cervix has a larger area of cervical ectopy which is rich in HIV target cells, and the immature genital tract is more susceptible to trauma (Barnabas et al., 2008). Socially, women generally contract HIV/AIDS through having limited negotiating power in sexual relationships both within and outside marriage. Intimate partner violence is also found to be strongly associated with risk factors for HIV infection. Economically, poor entitlements to education, remunerated work, and financial autonomy and property rights also render women very vulnerable.

Even though the 'feminisation of HIV' has become a catchphrase in the discourse of many international and government agencies at a world scale, very little effort in practice has been directed towards sensitising policies and programmes to recognise the myriad roles of women in the context of the illness. Booth (2004: 56) contends that 'the "Madonna–Whore" duality, whereby the health and other needs of the majority of women are not regarded as requiring special attention, has underpinned HIV/AIDS policies all across the world'. Interventions to date have largely focused on women whose behaviours are overtly linked with the spread of the epidemic (as in sex work), and/or are oriented to slowing down rates of new infection (as in mother-to-child transmission). The needs for care and support of ordinary women themselves who have already been infected with the virus remain on the backburner.

Treatment and support for people living with HIV/AIDS in India
In India, HIV was first diagnosed in 1986 in the city of Chennai. The year 1987 saw the launch of the National AIDS Control Programme (NACP) of India, which has gone through three phases since its inception, evolving from one of complete denial to a limited acceptance of HIV/AIDS as a problem of 'high risk groups'. The main thrust of more recent NACP interventions has been to focus on 'high risk' groups, such as sex workers, injecting drug users, pregnant women, MSM, and migrants. The third phase of NACP has been operational from 2006 and will continue until 2011.

In terms of care and support the activities of NACO have largely focused on the provision of anti-retroviral medicines (ARV). Successive national HIV programmes have been able to upscale the availability of ARV, and as of 2007 there were 137 centres in 31 federal states of India providing free ARV to 118 052 adults and 8347 children (NACO, 2007). India has also rolled out second-line ARV for those patients experiencing treatment failure.[1] Almost two-thirds of patients on ARV are men, another 30 per cent are women and the remainder are children and transgendered persons.

Transnational development agencies such as United Nations (UN) allied organisations, the Bill and Melinda Gates Foundation, the Clinton Foundation, the Global Fund to fight AIDS, Tuberculosis and Malaria, and the British Department for International Development (DFID) play an important role in providing technical expertise and funding for HIV/AIDS programmes in India. While the government has encouraged the formation of support groups of people living with HIV/AIDS, which share crucial information such as the availability of medicines and social assistance schemes, and also provide emotional support to people living with HIV/AIDS, current HIV/AIDS policies do not address the myriad needs of women which arise due to their role as carers.

Invisible care: forced labour or a 'labour of love?'
Leading on from the above I would like to reflect on narratives of the HIV-positive women interviewed in the course of my research in India and demonstrate the importance of linking HIV/AIDS policies with the needs of these women. Caring is fundamental to all human beings, perhaps particularly with respect to the development of their capabilities. The carework women do in the context of HIV is distinctive as it is undertaken in difficult emotional, social and economic conditions in resource-poor settings like India. Caring

for someone living with HIV/AIDS includes providing emotional or financial support and in many cases women have to provide care to an adult, often an intimate partner or adult son or children infected with HIV/AIDS. Since HIV/AIDS is a chronic illness the health of infected persons usually deteriorates slowly, although they may spend long periods being seriously ill and weak. They may get to a point, for example, where they are completely bedridden and suffer from repeated bouts of diarrhoea, which requires considerable attention from others in matters of personal hygiene.

Most of the care in the context of HIV/AIDS in developing countries like India is informal and is undertaken within the context of the family (see also Campbell and Gibbs, Chapter 50, this volume). Women have traditionally been the primary informal caregivers because of their biological roles as mothers and nurturers of young infants. These are effectively enshrined within the patriarchal institution of marriage which often sees women pushed into arranged unions by parents, and thereafter subjected to the will of their spouses and in-laws. Sociologically, such patterns have been analysed in terms of the politics and power relations of marriage and kinship; economically, they have been linked to the division of labour and the distribution of economic privilege and power (Daly, 2002). Yet in the context of HIV/AIDS, there are new and more disturbing dimensions. For example, sometimes women have been married unwittingly to men who are aware of their HIV-positive status but do not inform the bride and her family. In other cases, men may conduct extra-marital affairs involving unprotected sex with HIV/AIDS-infected partners, and again fail to disclose the information. In whichever case, because most married women cannot refuse to have sex with their husbands or negotiate safe sex, they become infected themselves. Generally speaking they do not find this out until the symptoms start showing in the husband, and it is particularly traumatising where women were virgins on marriage. Neelam (pseudonyms have been used), aged 24, comes from a rural area near the city of Mumbai, and represents a typical example of a young wife in such a situation:

> When they would take my husband to the doctor only my father-in-law and brother-in-law would go with him. They never took me along or told me anything about his illness. They might have known before our marriage. But then too they never informed me that you stay away from him or abstain from having sex with him.

Another young respondent, Lalita, who comes from a rural area in New Delhi, reported a similar fate:

> I was very young when I was married off by my parents. I was barely 18 years old. When I got married I had no information as I had never ventured outside my parents' house. My husband always suffered from fever after marriage. One year passed since my marriage and he suffered a paralysis attack and he was bedridden. I would take care of him in the hospital. I was hungry and I would feel like fainting in that place and I had a very deep shock when I found out that I too had the illness.

Carework for an intimate partner is often of an intense nature, especially for women like Neelam and Lalita who are HIV-positive themselves. It is physically strenuous as women are often the main, if not sole, caregivers for their intimate partners.

There is also an opportunity cost related to this unpaid carework with women having to forgo opportunities such as education or paid employment which might alleviate their financial insecurity (see also Campbell and Gibbs, Chapter 50, this volume). Yet even in these circumstances, not all carework is deemed discursively to be undertaken out of obligation or violence perpetrated by husbands or their families, but instead is experienced and portrayed as a 'labour of love'. Women may focus on forgiving the past deeds of their husband and focus on the better moments of shared happiness and intimacy. Women may also gain satisfaction – and earn more respect from their spouses and in-laws – when they dedicate themselves to improving the life chances and quality of life of their sick husbands by providing round-the-clock care and emotional support. As Vani aged 35, who lives on the periphery of Mumbai, articulates: 'What is the point of getting angry at the husband? I never talk to him about the past; I want him to live – that is of great importance to me.'

Women's plight might be rather less traumatic if their participation in caring for their husbands were actually to enhance their personal entitlements to being looked after as HIV/AIDS patients themselves, and/or to enjoy the peace of mind of having a domestic infrastructure to enable them better to cope with survival on their husbands' demise. However, in situations where husbands pass away, women (and children) may face the prospect of being ousted from the marital home, especially where this involves living with, or alongside, in-laws. In some cases, women may be physically threatened into leaving their husband's property. If they are unable to fend for themselves, the cost of staying with their in-laws, or even their natal families, may be to put up with abusive relationships. Shobha, aged 30, is a widow with two daughters, now living with her birth family in Mumbai. She reports how she and her children are repeatedly verbally abused: 'My mother and sister constantly tell my children that your mother is a sinner because I have HIV. I am so weak I cannot do anything for my children. I continue to stay with my mother.'

Women's options of returning home to their own parents are also held in check by the fact that married women have few property and inheritance rights and that few parents wish to bring infected daughters back home because of the social stigma of HIV/AIDS. Despite this, however, women's natal families are more likely to provide them with support than their in-laws, as is the case with 28 year old Shama from New Delhi: 'My parents live in a village in Uttar Pradesh and are old and they cannot support me because they are in dire poverty. However they are more understanding of my problems.'

Although women are likely to get more emotional support from their birth families, the degree of financial support available clearly depends on the social and economic situation of their parents and other siblings. Moreover, family support is not an option if women ill with HIV/AIDS have migrated from elsewhere (for example, to urban areas), in order to gain access to drugs and medical treatment.

Gender-sensitive policies for HIV/AIDS
The above discussion has highlighted the neglected aspect of the carework women do in the context of their own illness and also their lack of entitlements. The application of gender-budget analysis (GBA) may be useful in the context of HIV/AIDS in so far as it carries the potential to address structures of oppression and ensure that women personally living with, or dealing with, HIV/AIDS, get a better deal. There are frameworks that advocate the application of the gender-sensitive budgeting to all public policies, dating back to the Convention on the Elimination of All Forms of Discrimination Against

Women (CEDAW) of 1979, and the Beijing Platform for Action (BPFA) of 1995. These advocate the allocation of public funds to help achieve equitable development for women and men (see Elson, 2006; also Elson and Sharp, Chapter 80, this volume). India is no exception here in having committed itself to gender-sensitive budgeting by ratifying the Beijing Declaration (1995). Leading on from this, since 2005, the Indian government has included a gender-budgeting statement which presents information on programmes wherein at least 30 per cent of expenditure is 'pro-women'. However, the HIV/AIDS budget has not been disaggregated in a detailed way. Most importantly there is no earmarked funding for income and nutritional support for women living with HIV/AIDS. However, in some federal states like Tamil Nadu support groups such as the Positive Women's Network (PWN) are advocating for a gender-sensitive approach to HIV budgeting, and scored a success in achieving the provision of income support for widows who are HIV-positive. As one of the policy informants in Chennai, Kiran, mentioned:

> We have set up a free legal clinic in Namakkal district of Tamilnadu and it is accessed by men and also a large number of women. Ten more such clinics will be set up. Women's concerns are being mainstreamed in the existing government programmes we have tied up with the district collectors and through the district collector's office we are providing widows with pensions.

As the discussion in this chapter has indicated, gender-sensitive budgeting in the context of HIV/AIDS needs to take into consideration the myriad needs of women. For example, women's vulnerability needs to be exposed and addressed in public education programmes and school education, and should involve parents as far as possible. Support groups have a vital role to play in helping women to gain access to legal aid to assist them in property and inheritance disputes and negotiations. Economically, women living with HIV/AIDS should receive formal income support adequate to the task (at the very minimum) of fulfilling nutritional, shelter and health needs. Since the vital carework which women and children perform in the context HIV/AIDS restricts their opportunities to seek employment and has manifold physiological and psychological implications, the government should recognise women's roles as carers and institute policies to support them economically, psychologically and socially, such as in matters of access to state healthcare (for mental as well as physical conditions), and social security protection. Although women's carework can, in some respects, be regarded as a 'labour of love' and may have great emotional value for them and their care recipients, in the context of additional strains on time, energy and capacity posed by HIV/AIDS there is a major need to promote some form of financial compensation for carework so that women dealing with, and/or afflicted directly by the condition, are not forced into extreme poverty.

Acknowledgements

I am grateful to Queen's University, Belfast for funding this study. I am also indebted to Udhaan Trust, Network in Thane of People Living with HIV/AIDS, and Positive Women's Network, India for their support in gaining access to the women and other policy informants who participated in this study. I would like to thank Dr Pauline Prior for her inputs on the drafts of this chapter and to Professors Sylvia Chant and Mary Daly for the opportunity to contribute to this handbook.

Note

1. The ability of HIV to mutate and reproduce itself in the presence of antiretroviral drugs is called HIV drug resistance and treatment failure is a result of drug resistance. The use of ARV is a combination of three or more drugs and it prevents the HIV virus from multiplying inside a person and enables the body's immune cells (notably CD4 cells) to live. The first combination of drugs taken by a patient is usually called the first line regimen and when it stops working, perhaps after many years, the second regime is introduced. When the latter eventually fails, a third line, comprising a salvage cocktail of medicines is recommended (Bennett et al., 2008).

Select bibliography

Barnabas, Ruanne, Ann Duerr and Judith Wasserheit (2008) 'HIV/AIDS vaccine research', in David Celentano and Chris Beyrer (eds), *Public Health Aspects of HIV/AIDS in Developing Countries: Epidemiology, Prevention and Care*, New York: Springer, pp. 85–114.

Bennett, Diane, Silvia Bertagnolia, Donald Sutherland and Charles Gilts (2008) 'The World Health Organisation's global strategy for prevention and assessment of HIV drug resistance', *Antiviral Therapy*, **13** (suppl. 2), 1–13.

Booth, Karen (2004) *Local Women, Global Science: Fighting AIDS in Kenya*, Bloomington, IN: Indiana University Press.

Daly, Mary (2002) 'Care as a good for social policy', *Journal of Social Policy*, **31** (2), 251–70.

Elson, Diane (2006) *Budgeting for Women's Rights: Monitoring Government Budgets for Compliance with CEDAW*, New York: UNIFEM.

National AIDS Control Organisation (NACO) (2007) *UNGASS Country Progress Report 2008*, New Delhi: Ministry of Health and Family Welfare.

52 Women's smoking and social disadvantage
Hilary Graham

Introduction

A hundred years ago, few people smoked cigarettes and those who did were well-off men from high-income countries like the United States (US) and the United Kingdom (UK). Today, cigarettes are a global commodity, and poor women make up an increasing proportion of the smoking population. Between then and now lies the history of an everyday habit which has become a global killer and a major reason why death rates are higher among poorer groups in a range of countries.

The chapter begins by discussing how the economic and social changes of the last century have exposed populations to new risk factors which, as they enter and take hold of society, typically change their social profile. It then outlines the changing patterns of cigarette smoking over time and across societies before looking in more depth at the links between social disadvantage and cigarette smoking among women. While the primary focus is on high-income societies, a central theme is that the patterns evident in these countries are set to be repeated on a global scale.

Changing societies, new causes of death

The twentieth century saw rapid changes in major causes of death, both in high-income countries and worldwide. In particular, chronic diseases like heart disease and lung cancer emerged as 'the big killers', a trend linked to the disruption of long-established ways of life which accompanied the process of urbanisation. First in high-income countries and now in emerging economies, the transition from an agriculture-based economy to one based on manufacturing and service industries has transformed traditional lifestyles. Workers leave manual work in rural areas for sedentary jobs in densely packed urban centres, they substitute diets based on grains and vegetables for processed foods high in fats and sugars, and they switch from local forms of tobacco use to new tobacco products. It is these lifestyle changes which lie behind the rapid increase in chronic diseases. It is estimated that cigarette smoking, poor diet and physical inactivity explain over 75 per cent of new cases of heart disease, the leading global cause of death, and cigarette smoking is estimated to account for 90 per cent of cases of lung cancer, the leading global cause of cancer.

In early-industrialising countries where these new diseases first took hold, they were initially more prevalent among men and higher socio-economic groups. In the middle decades of the twentieth century, the gender-patterning of chronic disease began to change as rates among women rose; at the same time, heart disease and lung cancer increasingly became diseases of disadvantage. Since then death rates from these diseases have fallen more rapidly among better-off groups, a trend that underlies the widening of socio-economic inequalities in health in high-income countries. Behind these changing social gradients in chronic disease are changes in the social patterning of their major risk factors, like cigarette smoking.

Changing patterns of tobacco use

The first manufactured cigarettes were produced in the US in the late nineteenth century. Until then, tobacco products had been handmade and socially regulated: consumption was low and, in most societies, seen as a male prerogative. Dispensing nicotine more efficiently, manufactured cigarettes were more addictive. Because it was machine-produced, it could also be made more cheaply and on a much larger scale. Tobacco companies were quick to promote their new product. The result was a rapid increase in cigarette smoking, initially in high-income countries and subsequently in middle- and low-income countries.

In places where cigarette smoking was first established, like North America and northern Europe, trends in cigarette smoking have followed a distinctive pattern. Marketed by tobacco companies as a product of choice for the discerning consumer with sophisticated tastes, manufactured cigarettes were taken up by young adults in the advantaged positions in the gender and social class hierarchies. Thus in the UK, male consumption of cigarettes rose rapidly from 1900 and, by 1920, men were consuming more tobacco in this form than as pipe tobacco, cigars and snuff. At this point, tobacco consumption among women was still too low to record. However from the mid-1920s, women started to smoke manufactured cigarettes, and their consumption increased rapidly over the next two decades. Among both men and women, higher socio-economic groups led the way, with cigarette smoking then spreading across the population. By the 1940s, over 65 per cent of men and 40 per cent of women in all socio-economic groups were cigarette smokers (Wald and Nicolaides-Bouman, 1991).

When prevalence started to decline, the trend again emerged first in more advantaged groups. A common pattern in early-industrialising countries (for example, northern Europe and North America) has been for rates to start to fall among men and higher socio-economic groups – and, as a consequence, for gender differences to narrow and socio-economic differences to widen over time. Thus in Britain, there is now no gender gap in most age groups: among young adults for example, one in four men and women smoke cigarettes. Meanwhile the link between poverty and smoking has continued to strengthen: for example, among women, reported rates of cigarette smoking are more than twice as high in the poorest fifth of households (32 per cent) than the richest fifth (13 per cent) (Craig and Skelton, 2008). Similarly in the US, recent decades have seen a narrowing of the gender gap and widening of the socio-economic gap; among women, rates of cigarette smoking are nearly three times higher in poorer groups than in advantaged groups (NCHS, 2007).

Similar trends are emerging in southern Europe. Cigarette smoking – like tobacco use in general – was rare among women in Italy, Spain, Greece and Portugal until the 1970s and 1980s. Again, women followed men into cigarette smoking. Also, the trend among women was led by more affluent groups, with rates then increasingly rapid among poorer groups (Graham, 1996). This pattern is captured in Figure 52.1, which provides a snapshot of cigarette smoking among women in Spain in the late 1980s. Rates of cigarette smoking among women over 45 were low in all socio-economic groups, indicating that the habit first took hold in the cohort aged 25–44 in the late 1980s. In this 'trend-setting' generation, rates increased in line with increasing social advantage: they were three times higher among women in advantaged circumstances (52 per cent) than among those in the most disadvantaged group (17 per cent). In the subsequent cohort (16–24 years),

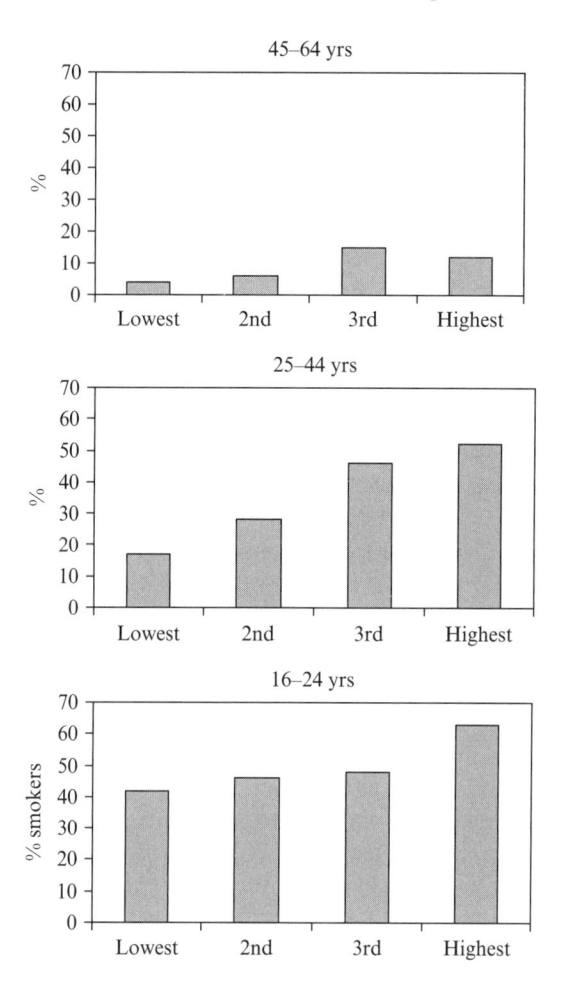

Figure 52.1 Cigarette smoking among women by socio-economic group, Spain, 1987

prevalence was substantially higher among poorer groups and, consequently, the socio-economic gradient was much flatter. In more recent Spanish studies, prevalence among women aged 16–24 is now higher in lower socio-economic groups. As this suggests, the link between social disadvantage and cigarette smoking established in northern Europe and the USA is emerging in southern Europe.

There is evidence to suggest that these patterns are being repeated on a global scale, and at an accelerated pace. In the ten years from 1992, smoking rates doubled among women in Russia, from 7 per cent to 15 per cent. A strong inverse gradient also emerged, with rates twice as high in poorer than richer groups (Perlman et al., 2007). Similar rapid changes have been reported elsewhere (Graham, 2007). This suggests that, while there are important variations within and between countries, women in poorer circumstances are set to become an increasingly significant proportion of the smoking population.

Table 52.1 *Social disadvantage and cigarette smoking among women with young children, UK, 2001–2002 (n = 13 573)*

	Smoker* (%)
All mothers	28
Mothers with childhood disadvantage:[1]	33
+ left education ≤ 16	44
+ a mother < 20	63
+ adult disadvantage[2]	69
+ lone mother	72
Mothers experiencing none of these disadvantages	12

Notes:
* ≥ 1 cigarette a day.
1. Childhood disadvantage measured by father's occupation when the woman was aged 14.
2. Adult disadvantage = annual household income of ≤ £11 000 (*c.*US$16 000).

Source: UK Millennium Cohort Study, 2009.

Studies in high-income countries are shedding important light on how women's smoking habits are influenced by their experiences of inequality as they grow up, negotiate adolescence and move through adulthood.

Cigarette smoking across the lifecourse

Smoking habits are laid down in adolescence. Young people who make the transition to adulthood as non-smokers are unlikely to take up smoking later in life, while most adult smokers started smoking as teenagers and will continue to smoke well into middle age. Smoking habits are, in turn, shaped by the social pathways along which people are travelling. In today's high-income countries, a privileged journey through life is associated with lower rates of cigarette smoking and higher rates of quitting. For both men and women, smoking rates are lower among those from well-off families who did well in the educational system and went on to secure a place in the higher echelons of the occupational structure. For women, domestic pathways also matter. Even in societies where the majority of working age women are in paid employment, partnership status and parenthood histories remain the critical determinants of their lifetime circumstances (Graham, 2007). These major influences on their lives are, in turn, important predictors of their smoking status.

Cigarette smoking in the UK provides an illustration. Table 52.1 is based on a study of mothers whose child was born in 2000/2001, and captures the patterns of maternal smoking nine months after birth. The table focuses on mothers from poorer childhood backgrounds, and looks at how smoking rates increase in line with increasing social disadvantage. One-third (33 per cent) of the mothers from poor backgrounds were smokers; prevalence rises to 44 per cent among those who, additionally, left school at or before the age of 16 (the UK's minimum school leaving age). When the table hones in further on mothers who experienced not only childhood disadvantage and educational disadvantage but also had their first child in their teenage years, the smoking rate climbs to 63 per cent. For women who faced these multiple disadvantages and whose current circumstances were also poor, prevalence was 69 per cent; when being a lone mother is also included, prevalence rises to 72 per cent. In contrast, among those who had had none of these experiences, prevalence stood at 12 per cent.

Conclusion

Gender and poverty are central to understanding a habit which is estimated to kill half of those who take it up. In high-income countries, it was those in privileged positions who introduced cigarette smoking into the population. It was not until cigarette smoking was well established among men and affluent women that poor women took up smoking in large numbers. By this point, cigarette smoking had lost its allure, able to convey neither gender superiority nor class distinction. Rates of smoking started to fall among the groups who had been first to adopt the habit, leaving behind a population which is increasingly female and poor. While not inexorable, it appears that patterns established in early-industrialising countries are being repeated in other high-income countries and, while the evidence is scant, in at least some middle- and low-income countries.

Perspectives which set cigarette smoking in the context of women's lives can illuminate the links between social disadvantage and cigarette smoking. Taking the example of the UK, the chapter has illustrated how gendered pathways of disadvantage – running from childhood through the teenage years and into adulthood – provide the context in which women become and remain smokers. Such analyses suggest that breaking the link between social disadvantage and cigarette smoking requires policies that not only target smoking behaviour but also address the social inequalities which shape it.

Acknowledgements

Analyses of the UK Millennium Cohort Study presented in Table 52.1 were undertaken with Summer Sherburne Hawkins and Catherine Law, UCL Institute of Child Health, London, UK.

Select bibliography

Craig, Rachel and Nicola Skelton (eds) (2008) *Health Survey for England 2007, Volume 1, Healthy Lifestyles: Knowledge, Attitudes and Behaviour*, London: National Statistics, available at: http://www.ic.nhs.uk/pubs/hse07healthylifestyles (accessed 27 January 2009).

De Onis, Mercedes and José Villar (1991) 'La Consommatión de Tabac Chez la Femme Espagnole', *Rapport Trimestriel de Statistiques Sanitaires Mondiales*, **44**, 80–88.

Graham, Hilary (1996) 'Smoking prevalence among women in the European Community 1950–1990', *Social Science and Medicine*, **43**, 243–54.

Graham, Hilary (2007) *Unequal Lives: Health and Socio-economic Inequalities*, Buckingham: Open University Press.

National Center for Health Statistics (NCHS) (2007) *Health, United States 2007*, Hyattsville, MD: National Center for Health Statistics, available at: http://www.cdc.gov/nchs/hus.htm (accessed 27 January 2009).

Perlman, Francesca, Martin Bobak, Anna Gilmore and Martin McKee (2007) 'Trends in the prevalence of smoking in Russia during the transition to a market economy', *Tobacco Control*, **16**, 299–305.

Wald, Nicholas and Ans Nicolaides-Bouman (1991) *UK Tobacco Statistics*, Oxford: Oxford University Press.

PART VI

GENDER, POVERTY AND ASSETS

53 Household wealth and women's poverty: conceptual and methodological issues in assessing gender inequality in asset ownership
Carmen Diana Deere

One of the main criticisms levelled at poverty studies is that they are inevitably based on the household as the unit of analysis. This means that a gender analysis of poverty is usually limited to analysing the differences between male and female household heads or men and women based on per capita indicators (Medeiros and Costa, 2008; also Sen, Chapter 13, this volume). This approach tells us little about the relative poverty of men and women within households and specifically, about the situation of women in male-headed households. This chapter considers the extent to which a focus on asset ownership can shed light on intrahousehold inequality and hence, on women's poverty relative to men's.

A trend in recent poverty studies is that they complement income or consumption measures with broader measures that take into account the multifaceted dimensions of poverty. Among these approaches are those that focus on a household's standard of living as measured by deprivations (in respect of running water, electricity, and so on) and the assets-based approach. Assets-based studies generally give combined attention to human, physical, financial, natural and social capital assets (see Moser, Chapter 60, this volume). To date neither of these approaches has been gendered beyond the usual headship measure.

Deere and Doss (2006) propose a focus on the gender distribution of wealth as a means of examining gender inequality within the household. Economists define wealth as the value of physical and financial assets minus debt (Davies, 2008). The standard components of wealth are housing, land, farm equipment and installations, livestock, non-agricultural business assets, consumer durables, pensions, and savings and other financial instruments such as stocks and bonds. This chapter focuses on the assets which are components of wealth rather than the broader asset-based approach.[1]

Why might a focus on wealth prove useful for the study of poverty and gender inequality? First, ownership of productive assets constitutes one of the main means of generating income and hence, expenditures and consumption. This is evident in the case of land and agricultural production, but equally relevant in the case of the urban informal sector where ownership of consumer durables (such as a sewing machine, stove or refrigerator) may also constitute business assets and support a broad range of income-generating activities. In addition to being means of production, some productive assets may also generate rent (housing and land), interest (savings) and profit (land and business assets), or components of income. They also have current use value or provide services, such as housing. Assets constitute an important buffer during emergencies, since they can be pawned or sold. They are also a potential source of current consumption to the extent that they can be converted to cash and thus are an important indicator of a household's potential vulnerability to shocks. In addition, productive assets may serve as collateral for loans. Finally, they are a store of wealth that can be passed on to future generations and generate status and social advantage (Deere and Doss, 2006).

Asset ownership is important to an individual's fall-back position, or how well-off s/he might be in the case of a household dissolving – whether due to separation, divorce or death. For developed countries it is well established that divorce often drives women into poverty and that divorced mothers fare much worse than divorced fathers. In the literature on developing countries it is often stressed how the welfare of widows is related to whether they own land or their own home. In feminist theory women's bargaining power within the household is also posited to be related to their fall-back position and hence the assets that women own and control. Ownership of assets is thus an important element of women's economic empowerment to the extent that such ownership increases their participation in household decision-making and their range of choices and ability to respond to opportunities, or their capabilities (see Quisumbing, Chapter 23, this volume).

Deere and Doss (2006) reviewed the available literature on women and wealth for both developed and developing countries and, finding it scanty, asked why we do not know more. One of the main reasons is that household surveys have only recently begun to collect data systematically on all of the components of household wealth and many still do not do so. Moreover, when such data are collected this tends to be at the household rather than at the individual level. In other words, it is implicitly assumed that household wealth is pooled and that its benefits accrue to all household members.

Doss et al. (2008) present evidence pertaining to the questionnaires for 72 Living Standard Measurement Surveys (LSMS) recently employed in five world regions. They found that while most ask for information on household assets, few consider the fact that assets may be individually owned. Data were most frequently elicited about individual ownership of housing, followed by land and business assets. Individual level data were rarely collected regarding the ownership of livestock, consumer durables, pensions or savings and other financial assets (ibid.: table 4). They conclude that a number of the questions that are needed to gather data on the gender distribution of wealth are already included in many of the LSMS questionnaires and that it would be relatively easy to vastly enhance the amount of data collected at the individual level, since in most cases this would require only asking an additional question or two.

Deere et al. (2009) reviewed 167 LSMS and other multi-purpose questionnaires for Latin America and the Caribbean and found that 24 surveys (for 11 countries) had individual-level data for one or more assets. The asset ownership data most frequently available (for ten countries) were for housing. They found that housing is the main asset whose ownership appears to be most equitably distributed in Latin America, with women's share of homeowners nationally ranging from a low of 27 per cent in Guatemala (in 2000) to nearly 50 per cent in Nicaragua (in 2005) and Panama (in 2003).[2] There was a marked difference between urban and rural areas, with urban women constituting a much larger share of the total homeowners than rural women in these countries.

Individual-level data on land ownership in these surveys were available for only five countries. The degree of gender inequality in land ownership is considerably greater, with women's share of landowners nationally ranging from a low of 13 per cent in Honduras (in 2004) to 32 per cent in Mexico (in 2002). Individual-level data on ownership of business assets were collected for only two countries, Nicaragua (in 2001) and Guatemala (in 2006), and in both cases, women constitute the majority of the asset owners. Appropriate individual-level data on livestock and consumer durables were available only for Nicaragua (in 2001). What this data demonstrated was how the ownership of particular types of assets is quite gender differentiated. For example, in the case of livestock, men in Nicaraguan households own the majority of the cattle and work animals whereas women own the pigs and poultry. The main gender differentiation in terms of consumer durables was between those that are associated with women's domestic labour and men's income-generating opportunities. In over half of the households women individually own the sewing machines, blenders, stoves, washing machines, and refrigerators. In contrast, in over half of the households men individually own the bicycles, cars, and motorcycles. Overall, the mean and median value of the land, farm equipment and installations, livestock and business assets owned by men exceeds that of women. On the other hand, the mean and median value of the housing, consumer durables and other real estate owned by women exceeds that of men.

One of the main results of the Deere et al. (2009) study is to demonstrate that household headship does not capture very well the gender distribution of asset ownership. For housing, land and businesses, the share of women property owners among total owners is always much higher than the share of female household heads among total heads owning the particular asset. The implication of this finding is that basing poverty studies only on headship potentially underestimates women's wealth and, hence, their relative poverty. This is primarily because women own property individually not only when they are household heads, but also when they are spouses, daughters and mothers or mothers-in-law – household positions that are ignored in a headship analysis of relative poverty. Depending upon the marital regime, joint property rights to assets acquired during the marriage may also significantly increase the asset-owning potential of married women.[3] At the same time, in other contexts, relying on headship alone may overstate the extent of women's property ownership, for example, in the case where the home or land owned by a self-declared female head is actually the property of her son or an absent partner. The point is that to estimate gender inequality we need direct measures of individual asset ownership.

The Nicaragua 2001 LSMS survey is the only one with data on a sufficient number of assets and their valuation to allow estimation of the distribution of household wealth by gender.[4] Deere et al. (2009) found that men owned 55.1 per cent of gross household wealth, and women, 40.5 per cent. Data on individual ownership corresponding to 4.4 per cent of the value of total household assets were missing.[5] In contrast, if the wealth analysis is done according to the gender of the household head, 73.2 per cent of gross household wealth corresponds to male heads, 23.2 per cent to female heads, and 3.3 per cent is unaccounted for.

Improving data collection and analysis of individual asset ownership
Besides the need to ask specifically who in the household owns each asset, there are a number of ways that household surveys and their analyses could be improved to better allow the estimation of gender-differentiated wealth and relative poverty.[6] A major source of underestimation of women's ownership of assets in the Latin American context is lack of attention to joint property. As a minimum, surveys should always allow for

more than one owner of an asset to be reported. Moreover, it is preferable if the owners are always identified by ID codes rather than by codes referring to their relation to the household head. The latter practice often results in the inability to subsequently identify the individual characteristics of each asset owner.[7]

In the analysis of joint property, it is important to distinguish between the joint marital property of spouses (or those in a consensual union) and the situation of co-ownership of assets by different family members, such as father and sons, and in particular, when they are of different sexes and could be confused as a couple (mothers and sons). This differentiation is especially important if one is interested in comparing the impact of different marital regimes on women's ownership of assets.[8]

Another source of potential underestimation of women's ownership of assets is that many of the current household surveys ask about individual ownership only with respect to dwellings or land for which there is a property document. While the question 'in whose name is the title?' may seem a convenient way of eliciting individual ownership information, it results in data not being collected by sex on the owners in households whose assets are not formally titled or who lack an ownership document. A related problem is that considerable information is lost when under the tenancy question it is reported that the home is owner-occupied, but the name on the property document corresponds to someone not residing in the household. This is a common problem in the case of inherited assets, and results in a considerable amount of lost information on the sex of the *de facto* owner.

The valuation of assets presents a number of challenges for researchers. While asking people what they own from a list of assets usually results in fewer problems of recall or measurement errors as compared with income or consumption data (Moser and Felton, 2007), their valuation is not straightforward. In the household surveys reviewed for Latin America and the Caribbean four different measures were used, sometimes in the same questionnaire: the realisation or market value (for how much an asset could be sold); the reservation price (for how much would the owner be willing to sell an asset); the replacement cost; and the average value in the locale or region of assets of similar quality. According to Davies (2008) for businesses ('going concerns') it is usual to value assets according to their replacement value. But it may not be possible to replace all assets with those of similar age and/or quality. It is thus more common to value assets according to their market value. This measure has the advantage of implicitly taking into account the age and quality of the asset. Both procedures, however, assume that markets exist for all physical assets. The problem of 'missing markets', particularly in the context of less developed countries, results in valuation questions often having a large number of missing cases (where the respondent answers – probably quite truthfully – 'don't know') as well as high standard deviations (Deere et al., 2009).

Another problem in estimating household wealth, and one particularly problematic in estimating the gender division of household wealth, is when the value of an asset can only be estimated from data on its rental value. The household surveys reviewed for Latin America, for example, do not ask respondents about the value of their home, but rather (since they were primarily focused on estimating household expenditures) enquired as to the potential rental value of the dwelling.[9] In order to calculate the present value of the home then requires information on the appropriate discount rate. The usual proxy for the discount rate is the average interest rate on mortgages. Yet an important characteristic of many less developed countries is the absence of a long-term credit market, specifically for mortgages. To the extent that homes constitute the most commonly owned major asset as well as the asset that women are most likely to own either individually or jointly with their spouses, estimates of the gender division of wealth are particularly sensitive to the chosen discount rate.[10]

The research agenda

Much remains to be done to develop the full potential of a wealth-based approach to the study of poverty and gender inequality within and among households. Although it is generally accepted that wealth is more concentrated than income, and that wealth is an important determinant of income, little research has been done to date on the specific relationship between physical and financial assets, income and poverty (Davies, 2008). Specifically, more work is needed on how well the ownership of assets predicts household poverty by other measures, including that of female-headed households, and on the extent to which female ownership of assets makes a difference in keeping male-headed households out of poverty. Given the lacunae of rigorous studies on intrahousehold income or consumption inequality, the first order of business on the research agenda is improving the quantity and quality of data on the individual ownership of assets in household surveys.

Notes

1. An important difference between the standard definition of wealth and the assets-based approach, such as in the work of Moser and Fenton (2007: table 1), is that they include migrant remittances and rental income as part of what they term 'financial/productive capital'. In the wealth framework, remittances and rents represent a flow of income rather than a financial asset.
2. The year of the survey is reported in the parentheses.
3. Marital regimes are primarily differentiated according to how property acquired prior to and during the marriage is treated. See Deere and León (2001) on Latin America, and Deere and Doss (2006) for a global overview.
4. Missing in this estimate for Nicaragua are data on the value of pensions, savings and other financial assets; also, data on debt were not available, thus what is presented is an estimate of gross rather than net household wealth.
5. The missing data on the sex of the owner was largely due to situations where the ownership document was in the name of a non-household member.
6. See Doss et al. (2008) for a detailed analysis of how the LSMS questionnaires could be improved as well as a proposal for an asset module conducive to gender analysis.
7. For example, while little information is lost with the code 'head and spouse', the code 'head and other' results in lost information on the sex and other characteristics of the specific child, parent or other family member who is the co-owner of the asset.
8. Rigorous analysis of the impact of marital regimes on women's ownership of assets would also require that information be collected directly on the system under which each marriage took place (civil law versus customary law, for example), and in the case of civil law, on the specific marital regime (Doss et al., 2008).
9. These surveys did not inquire about pension wealth. See Davies (2008) on why the valuation of pensions is also not straightforward.
10. Deere et al. (2009) present a lower and upper bound of the present value of housing, based on different potential discount rates. The estimate presented in the text reflects the upper bound and is based on a discount rate of 8.6 per cent (the Nicaraguan Central Bank's average interest rate on savings during the period of the survey).

Select bibliography

Davies, James B. (2008) 'An overview of personal wealth', in James B. Davies (ed.), *Personal Wealth from a Global Perspective*, Oxford: Oxford University Press, 1–23.

Deere, Carmen Diana and Magdalena León (2001) *Empowering Women: Land and Property in Latin America*, Pittsburgh, PA: University of Pittsburgh Press.

Deere, Carmen Diana and Cheryl R. Doss (2006) 'The gender asset gap: what do we know and why does it matter?', *Feminist Economics*, **12** (1–2), 1–50.

Deere, Carmen Diana, Gina Alvarado and Jennifer Twyman (2009) 'Poverty, headship and gender inequality in asset ownership in Latin America', paper prepared for delivery to the Latin American Studies Association International Congress, Rio de Janeiro, June.

Doss, Cheryl R., Caren Grown and Carmen Diana Deere (2008) *Gender and Asset Ownership: A Guide to Collecting Individual-Level Data*, Policy Research Working Paper WPS 4704, Washington, DC: World Bank, available at: http://econ.worldbank.org/docsearch (accessed 2 January 2009).

Medeiros, Marcelo and Joana Costa (2008) 'Is there a feminisation of poverty in Latin America?', *World Development*, **36** (1), 115–27.

Moser, Caroline and Andrew Felton (2007) *The Construction of an Asset Index Measuring Asset Accumulation in Ecuador*, Chronic Poverty Research Centre Working Paper 87, Washington, DC: The Brookings Institution.

54 Gender, poverty and access to land in cities of the South
Carole Rakodi

What all urban people need for well-being is a secure place to live, in a healthy environment within reach of work opportunities and essential services. In practical terms, security means both affordability and protection against arbitrary eviction, whether by agents of the state, private owners or people's own relatives.[1] In considering whether all groups of urban residents have a secure place to live it is first necessary to understand how they can gain access to land and property. This entails knowledge of the types of land and housing tenure that are available, the delivery channels that are open to people (especially the poor) and how they function, and whether those seeking land have the financial and other resources needed, such as time, literacy and contacts. It is also necessary to consider what happens if households' or individuals' claims to land or residence are contested, the legislative safeguards that are available, and the processes by which such safeguards can be enforced.

Access to land therefore implies that three related sets of issues must be considered: law and regulation, socio-political structures and relationships, and economic context. Both land and property law and family law are critical, since the former defines and distinguishes interests in land and property, provides for registration and regulation of use, and contains mechanisms for the resolution of conflicts, while the latter governs marital relationships and inheritance. Family and kinship relationships are significant, since much access to land is linked to family position, but the arrangements for land governance (including the administrative and political system) are also important. The economic context influences the income-earning opportunities available to people and thus their ability to afford land and property, as well as prices, which vary between urban locations. All are gendered, yet laws and regulations, administrative structures and processes and arrangements for representation and decision-making often do not explicitly consider gender. Even if they do, and particularly if assumptions about gender relationships are implicit, they reflect established social structures and customs rather than contemporary ideas about gender equality, as embodied, for example, in the series of international conventions to which most governments have signed up. The increasing recognition that women are generally disadvantaged compared to men in terms of secure access to land and property has fuelled a growing debate. Gradually, the conceptual frameworks for research and policy have improved, although in much of the published work the issue of gender and access to land, especially in urban areas, remains neglected or is dealt with in an oversimplified way.

Much of the debate is couched in terms of rights, leading to campaigns for tenure reform to provide 'equal access to land for men and women' or for women to 'have the right to land in their own names'.[2] Arguably, many such campaigns, which are often driven by elite groups and civil society organisations (CSOs), are ill-informed and the reforms demanded are inappropriate, while promising initiatives to tackle gender inequality remain small-scale and non-systemic. In addition, framing the demand for reform in terms of rights leads to a strong legal focus, which is important but only part of the story. As noted above, because access to land and secure tenure is gendered, it must also be understood in terms of social relations. Indeed there is an argument that 'tenure' itself is a social construct that reflects the relationships between those with interests in land and not merely a set of defined legal rights. Also, because the gendered social position of men and women is reflected in their access to and ability to retain resources within the family and wider community, it is important to consider family law as well as property law, people's ability to command economic resources as well as the design of government land and housing policies and programmes, and the social and political networks that can potentially empower as well as exclude people. Finally, it is insufficient to focus only on the disadvantaged position of women or their rights. The gender relations that advantage men and differentiation among women, both of which vary with class position and in different cultural and religious contexts, must be part of the analysis.

Poor people's access to land and property, and gender
I started by noting that urban residents need a secure place in which to live, in a healthy environment and within reach of work opportunities and essential services. Governments' basic responsibility to regulate conflict, provide a conducive environment for markets to operate, and to formulate and enforce laws, have typically been extended to regulating or taking over the role of markets and ensuring the welfare of all their citizens by, *inter alia*, managing urban development, facilitating and regulating land and housing markets, and providing plots and dwellings for some or all urban uses and households. The extent and nature of public sector involvement have varied between countries and over time. In practice, the need for affordable plots in urban areas of developing countries is rarely met through formal regulated land subdivision by either the public or private sector. A large proportion of urban residents, especially the poor, have little choice but to seek accommodation through other channels, as discussed below.

Public programmes for land delivery to the poor
Public programmes to meet the housing needs of the urban poor have traditionally focused on the subdivision of publicly owned land into serviced plots for 'self-help' house construction or the construction of complete housing units, usually for rent, especially in the former planned economies. However, efforts to subdivide and service publicly owned land in volumes sufficient to meet demand and at costs affordable to poor residents have met with mixed and generally limited results. Moreover, a combination of state financial and managerial crises and ideological liberalisation in the 1980s led to the sale of most public sector housing. In addition, shortages of relatively cheap residential plots on public land lead to their 'leakage' up the income distribution. As a result, in many cities of the South today, few poor households can access publicly provided land.

Almost without exception, public programmes deal with households. This makes much sense in urban areas, where households most often constitute the basic economic and social units in which people live, and in some cases women can benefit. For example, in Dakar (Senegal) and Ekurhuleni (South Africa), the proportion of female household heads among those allocated plots is roughly equal to their share of all households and they are more likely than their male counterparts to complete the titling process once allocated plots because of the increased personal security this provides (Payne et al., 2008; also Mills, Chapter 57, this volume). However, if an adult male is present, he is assumed by officials in most cities to be the 'household head'. Allocation and registration documents (and credit agreements) are almost always issued in the name of the man, unless a household clearly has a female head (typically a widow, divorcée or never married woman), even when joint tenure is possible. In addition, the time and money costs of completing the cumbersome procedures required to convert initial allocation into title are often a deterrent: widows, divorcées and separated women frequently do not have equal inheritance rights; and fear that joint tenure may indicate a woman's distrust of her husband (and a marriage in trouble) hinders the realisation of this right (Rakodi, 2006). Moreover, adding a wife's name to an already issued title may be obstructed by social, bureaucratic or pecuniary hurdles as in Ahmedabad, India (see Baruah, 2007; Unni, 1999).

While today most formal laws and policies recognise that women should be treated as legal persons and that both male and female household heads should be eligible for serviced plots, social disapprobation of women who remain unmarried coupled with economic disadvantage prevent many women from establishing independent households and, if they do, constrain their ability to afford land and house purchase or construction. In addition, the property rights and security of those living in male-headed households are, in the absence of joint title, determined by family law governing inheritance and divorce, by social custom and, in many countries, by customary law. As a result, although women's financial and labour contributions are vital to land and house purchase and construction, they often lack security following partnership breakdown or bereavement (see Nakray, Chapter 51, this volume).

Formal private sector land delivery
Alternatives to public provision of residential plots range from market supply that complies with the full regulatory framework through informal subdivision to squatting. Those available vary from country to country (and even city to city), depending on such factors as the legal regime, patterns of landholding within a city and in the areas into which it is expanding, topography, price of land and the cost of construction, the socio-cultural context, and the political economy.

The principles on which legal systems are based and the way in which law is formalised vary, especially between civil and common law systems. The legal systems imported into most developing countries by colonising powers (whether civil law or codified common law) were superimposed upon indigenous legal systems, giving rise to considerable difficulties, especially with respect to land, where mutual incomprehension of the principles underlying concepts of tenure and ownership in the different systems lies at the root of many of the difficulties in establishing working land law today. The private market in residential land and property is, in theory, underpinned by state law governing tenure, subdivision, transfer, regulation of use and property taxation. On the surface, contemporary constitutions pose few legal obstacles to women's land and property ownership and inheritance rights, although constitutional provisions have not always been translated into state law and even when they have, state law can in many countries be overruled by customary or religious personal law. Nevertheless, returns from nearly 150 developing world cities in 1998 revealed that in 40 per cent of cases there were some, and often considerable, legal impediments to women owning land. The situation of women was best in Latin American and Caribbean cities, and worst in African cities, with Asian cities in an intermediate position (UN-HABITAT, 2007: 396–8).

To deal with rapid urban growth, implementation of a legal framework requires an administrative and political system with considerable resources, management capacity and wide public backing. In practice, not only is effective control over private land subdivision generally lacking, despite the assumption in most countries that state law will govern urban land, but also, given the cumbersome nature of legal processes, the limited management capacity of the agencies concerned, and the cost of complying with official standards and legal requirements, the volume of officially subdivided residential plots lags far behind demand and the costs exceed the capacity of many urban residents to pay, even if they can access credit. In addition, although for women who can afford to purchase land in this limited market, their ability to do so may increase their economic independence and security, in general, legal, social and economic restrictions disadvantage women relative to men, whether as household heads or individuals.

Alternatives to public land delivery: multiple channels
Leading on from the above, many middle- and low-income households have to obtain land through informal channels or, in many cases, rent accommodation. Indeed, many women's disadvantage in terms of education, income earning capacity and marital position means that when they head households, they are disproportionately represented among renters. The latter are typically even less secure than many 'owner-occupiers'. Their insecurity is exacerbated when they rent accommodation in informal settlements where landlords themselves have only limited security (see Kumar, Chapter 56, this volume). The remainder of this chapter nevertheless focuses on land rather than housing, mainly because access to land and secure tenure is a prerequisite for both the construction of accommodation for an owner's own family and an adequate supply of low-cost rental housing.

The factors that affect the formal private sector supply of residential land outlined above also influence informal supply channels, which can be categorised in terms of the proportion of total demand met, extent of compliance with formal regulations or degree of security provided to their occupants. Probably most common today is informal subdivision of land to which the subdivider has formal or customary rights. Such subdivision complies with formal planning practices and standards to varying degrees, depending on the appropriateness and affordability of standards and the likelihood that subdivisions which comply with them will later be regularised. Location and scale in relation to urban employment centres and services vary, depending on patterns of land ownership, the availability of formal or informal public transport, and the extent to which the public authorities use strategic investment in roads and other infrastructure to guide urban expansion. This is a market operating much like any other: prices are determined by the volume of supply, location and standards, but also by the reliance on social contacts for information and handling transactions, lack of access to credit, threat of public sanctions, substandard services, and informal social rules. Informal settlements provide access to land for those with low and middle income, including those women who can both act independently and afford to purchase land, if not to the poorest.

In Africa in particular, cities are often surrounded by land held under customary tenure, implying traditional norms and practices modified by decades of socio-economic change. Within the relevant group, homestead land is retained by the group and rarely alienated, although plots may be allocated to those with entitlements – generally men upon marriage. Within the group, therefore, while land is available, group members can obtain access to land and, because of customary norms and the need for group agreement to sale, security is high, despite the absence of documented title. Generally, in these systems, women's property rights are linked to their familial relationships, particularly with husbands, fathers and sons. Their use rights and concomitant responsibilities for household maintenance and childcare are secure as long as their marriages are intact, but reliance on secondary rights reduces their bargaining power and makes them vulnerable to dispossession in the event of conjugal dissolution. In some societies, widows officially retain use rights while they remain unmarried and care for minor children, but the increasing value of urban property often tempts husbands' families to claim the property and evict the widow (Rakodi, 2006). Sometimes widows may be entitled to land or property from their natal family; but more often they are forced to move into inferior and more insecure accommodation where they are vulnerable to violence and impoverishment.

Today, the proportion of households which can obtain access to free or low-cost land through incremental squatting or invasion has declined because areas of undeveloped publicly owned land have diminished and those holding land rights can generally either subdivide and sell their land or use the formal court system to evict squatters and those with informal occupancy or rental arrangements. Often, such squatting is restricted to areas considered unsuitable for residential use, in which living environments may be particularly unhealthy and dangerous and residents especially vulnerable to eviction, although their prospects depend on their political influence and whether the government system has enforcement capacity. Although this is a cheap way of obtaining land, limited opportunities, the physical hardships and level of vulnerability rule it out for many women.

After many years of international and national advocacy, governments have increasingly adopted accommodating policies towards informal settlements, varying from neglect through basic service provision to regularisation. Whether these policies redress existing gender inequalities and injustices depends not only on the policies themselves and their practical implementation, but also on social and familial relations.

Gendered evaluations of upgrading and regularisation policies do exist, although more often gender is rather inadequately dealt with because of blindness to the issues on the part of those concerned or their complexity. They demonstrate that when women and men are not involved in decision-making, issues important to poor residents are sidelined, and the design of infrastructure and cost recovery arrangements fail to reflect the situation and needs of all residents, especially women and children. As a result, regularisation and upgrading may result in increased rents and costs that penalise poorer households, the eviction of some residents, and gentrification and pressure to sell to higher income purchasers, in which the preferences of women are often overruled especially if certificates of occupancy or titles are issued in the sole name of the household head (Varley, 2007). Research in Chandigarh, India shows that joint titling increased 'women's participation in decision making, access to knowledge and information about public matters, sense of security, self esteem, and the respect that they receive from their spouses' (Datta, 2006: 271). In addition, women with joint title feared divorce or abandonment less and displayed 'a higher attachment to their houses than men . . . because houses play a valuable role in fulfilling women's practical and gender needs . . . [which] helps reduce turnover in regularised settlements' (ibid.).

Yet not all informal settlements are suitable for upgrading, because the land on which they are located is dangerous, is required for legitimate alternative uses or is merely attractive to private developers or local authorities seeking to 'beautify' the city. Research also shows that forced evictions disproportionately affect the poor and, when they occur, women are particularly vulnerable to physical violence during and after evictions, psychological and emotional stress, disruption to their social support networks, and impoverishment.[3]

Conclusion
The full complexity of women's access to land in urban areas is poorly understood and there is a tendency to generalise on the basis of superficial analysis and relatively few case studies. Despite recent efforts to address the gaps, conceptual frameworks for analysing gendered access to secure tenure and useful data, especially on the gender asset gap, are lacking (see Deere, Chapter 53, this volume; Moser, Chapter 60, this volume). Nonetheless, it is likely that independent assets or joint entitlements to family/household assets provide additional bargaining power for women in households, protecting them from domestic violence and providing them with security, in communities and in public arenas.

Despite gaps in knowledge, with the proviso that approaches need to be carefully tailored to the legal system, political and economic circumstances, social and cultural characteristics, and urban development processes of each country and city, it is possible to identify a few principles for policy and practice, as follows:

1. The right to equality, non-discrimination and secure tenure (and thus to housing) enshrined in international human rights instruments should be reflected in state laws related to land, housing and family or personal laws dealing with inheritance, marriage and marital property, and should be effectively implemented.
2. Bodies and officials dealing with land allocation, inheritance and dispute settlement, including land professionals, government employees, judges and magistrates, should be trained in 'gender-awareness'.
3. Urban residents should be protected from forced eviction and displacement and, where relocation is necessary, internationally recognised good resettlement guidelines should be followed.
4. Forums and processes that provide opportunities for all urban residents, including disadvantaged groups, to participate in decision-making should be institutionalised.
5. Joint tenure, especially of men and women in partnerships, should be mandatory, based on a legal framework that clarifies when property becomes the property of the community, which property is jointly owned, who is responsible for managing the community property, who is entitled to the income from it, whether consensual unions trigger joint tenure rules and protections, and whether joint tenure is presumed or registration is required.

6. Civil society organisations (CSOs) have an important role to play in making disadvantaged groups (especially women) aware of their rights over land, housing and property, and supporting their efforts to claim those rights.
7. Civil society organisations can also play an important role in exploring whether and how customary or religious law, especially alternative interpretations and innovative practices, can be drawn upon to reduce gender inequalities in access to, control over and inheritance of urban land and property.

Notes

1. UN-HABITAT defines secure tenure as the right of all individuals and groups to effective protection against forced evictions. People have secure tenure when there is *evidence of documentation* that can be used as proof of secure tenure status or when there is either *de facto* or *perceived protection against forced evictions*. Its Global Land Tools Network (see www.gltn.net, accessed 14 October 2009) prioritises gender issues.
2. See, for example, the website of the Centre for Housing Rights and Evictions (www.cohre.org, accessed 14 October 2009), which has a Programme on Women and Housing Rights.
3. See www.cohre.org (accessed 14 October 2009).

Select bibliography

Baruah, Bipasha (2007) 'Gendered realities: exploring property ownership and tenancy agreements in urban India', *World Development*, **35** (12), 2096–109.

Datta, Namita (2006) 'Joint titling – a win–win policy? Gender and property rights in urban informal settlements in India', *Feminist Economics*, **12** (1–2), 271–98.

Payne, Geoffrey, Alain Durand-Lasserve and Carole Rakodi (2008) *Social and Economic Impacts of Land Titling Programmes in Urban and Peri-urban Areas: International Experience and Case Studies of Senegal and South Africa*, London: Geoffrey Payne and Associates.

Rakodi, Carole (2006) 'Social agency and state authority in land delivery processes in African cities: compliance, conflict and cooperation', *International Development Planning Review*, **28** (2), 263–85.

UN-HABITAT (2007) *Global Report on Human Settlements 2007: Enhancing Urban Safety and Security*, London: Earthscan.

Unni, Jeemol (1999) 'Property rights for women: case for joint titles to agricultural land and urban housing', *Economic and Political Weekly*, **34** (21), 1281–6.

Varley, Ann (2007) 'Gender and property formalisation: conventional and alternative approaches', *World Development*, **35** (10), 1739–58.

55 Power, patriarchy and land: examining women's land rights in Uganda and Rwanda
Kate Bird and Jessica Espey

Introduction
This chapter seeks to shed light upon the complex structural inequalities that pervade an important aspect of social and economic institutions and practices across much of Africa. It explores land rights and inheritance practices in Rwanda and Uganda and demonstrates that the persistent gender inequality and discrimination found in these norms and practices are both underpinned by deep-seated power asymmetries and serve to reinforce them.

Despite considerable legislative achievements in women's rights and in addressing gendered inequalities across East Africa, taking a closer lens to the household and extended family management of assets (and the way in which *de jure* and *de facto* inheritance rights play out at the local level) reveals the extent to which gendered discrimination remains a potent reality for many women, with major economic, social and political outcomes.

The persistence of intrahousehold inequality relates strongly to women's differential access to and control of productive assets, including land (see Deere, Chapter 53, this volume). The weak articulation of women's rights in this area arguably results in part from what we might term 'fracture points' in the policy process. The first fracture point relates to there being limited relevant evidence for policymakers. This owes to a common tendency among (non-feminist) social scientists to shy away from intrahousehold analysis. Many regard the household as the most basic (and inherently equitable) social unit and neither collect or analyse finer-resolution data. This results in a considerable blindspot in policy formation and in efforts to ensure social equality. Second are the fracture points undermining gendered policy formation, setting and implementation. By way of an example national, local and regional officials often fear to address culturally rooted and 'traditional' social practices, as so doing may compromise their popularity in the polls. Alternatively they may see such issues as ingrained in the social fabric and therefore requiring long-term strategies with few 'quick-fix' results.

In light of the above, this chapter first seeks to highlight the considerable ramifications of socially and culturally embedded gender discrimination, with specific reference to inheritance practices. It then uses two illustrative country examples from East Africa to demonstrate the extent to which the pervasiveness of gender discrimination impacts upon the daily functions and realities of households and to highlight the inadequacies of current legislation. We conclude by suggesting why detailed attention has not been given to the pervasiveness of gender inequalities by policymakers, highlighting the lack of intrahousehold analysis and fracture points in the policy development and implementation process.

Gendered structural inequalities: customary social systems and the household
Societies all around the world are subject to considerable structural inequalities. At national, local, community and household levels human relations are determined by

traditions of social mores and by conceptualisations of authority which are themselves rooted in long histories of social inequality; gender discrimination and hierarchy. In many societies these systems have been and continue to be explicitly patriarchal: men dominate and control women's labour, reproduction and sexuality as well as define women's status, privileges and rights (Kalabamu, 2006). Over the past century, the feminist movement and increasingly gender equitable legislation has done much to rectify gendered inequalities at the national (and to some extent regional) level, and the Millennium Development Goals (MDGs) include specific indicators relating to the number of female parliamentary representatives, the percentage of women in non-agricultural wage employment and the ratio of girls to boys in education enrolment. However, patriarchal norms and practices are still a potent reality in many countries and are played out at all levels of society, economy and polity. Such norms place limits on women's agency and on their negotiating power within political and social space, within markets and in other economic institutions, and within the household, extended family or clan. The household can also be seen as a reflection of the broader social constructs in society, as articulated by Folbre (1997: 263): 'policymakers themselves are often described as if they were benevolent heads of that larger household known as the state'.

A major limitation of social science efforts to conceptualise inequalities and power dynamics within society is that the household has traditionally been viewed as the basic unit of analysis. This ignores the complex web of family relations and economic transactions that take place within it. The household means different things to different people, in different times and places, and by using the household as a unit, researchers and policymakers make implicit assumptions about its internal workings. Households are assumed to be unitary bodies that are inherently equitable and which enable equal access to and control of resources. However, these assumptions have been widely criticised for failing to pay attention to evidence which suggests that important power asymmetries are reflected by differentiated outcomes, such as the balance of leisure and work, consumption, human capital, autonomy and freedom. In patriarchal social systems, women are commonly subordinated by men, who often control household property, resources and income of the household (Ellis, 1988; see also Quisumbing, Chapter 23, this volume). It is also increasingly recognised that intrahousehold resource allocation and decision-making are affected by multiple factors including individual agency, power and information asymmetries, supra-household social relations and non-household institutions (Bolt and Bird, 2003). Our limited knowledge of what happens within the bounds of the household owes both to the difficulty of obtaining accurate and affordable sub-household level data and the methodological challenge of exploring complex familial relations in a robust manner. However understanding the way in which household members inter-relate, the customary practices that govern their familial structures, the traditional mores that affect their methods of managing assets, and the complex of economic, social and emotional calculations made by women and men when making decisions, is vital for equitable social and economic development.

Gendered inequalities in land use, access, control, ownership and inheritance are just one way in which society-wide structures, norms and 'rules of the game' play out in the lives of women and men as they interact in the intersecting spheres of household, community and society/economy/polity. In the East African region customary practices mean that land inheritance and ownership is predominantly patrilineal. This means that land is only transferred to males within the household or clan (see also Rakodi, Chapter 54, this volume). At the moment of marriage women and men enter into 'a conjugal contract', which refers to the terms under which household members make joint or separate decisions around the exchange of goods, allocation of labour, leisure and services, access to and control of productive resources and distribution of income and investment. Such contracts here, as elsewhere in the world, are determined by both society-wide structures and norms and the relative power and agency of the individual parties. These latter characteristics are influenced by the relative backstop (or 'fall-back') positions of individuals, in other words their power in any negotiation or the minimum that they are willing to accept in any situation before they assert their right to break the conjugal contract and exit the relationship. Typically women have less access to or control of productive assets or the returns on those assets (income, produce). They must negotiate such access or control through their fathers, husbands, sons or clansmen. Their limited agency locks together with more limited livelihood options to restrict their capabilities. This gives rural women, in particular, few choices but to accept the default option presented by their societies; which is to take a subjugated role within the conjugal contract and therefore the household. This has significant implications for women's freedom of choice, economic independence, development and wider rights, and is most clearly apparent for widows, unfavoured wives in polygamous households, separated and divorced women, orphaned children; and households affected by HIV/AIDS. Although traditional *de facto* law or clan practice protected such categories of people, market penetration, the increased adoption of the nuclear family model, the increased value given to individualised accumulation and consumption over wealth and risk-spreading within the extended household and clan, and pressure on traditional safety nets, has shifted norms and practices. For example, Ugandan customary inheritance practice suggests that the heir to the land is responsible for supporting the deceased head of household's former dependants, but evidence suggests that this is sometimes disregarded, with women finding themselves forced from their homes and land and stripped of all their assets (see Bird and Pratt, 2004).

Women are, however, not only disadvantaged by the erosion of customary practices in the event of separation or widowhood. Intrahousehold allocation of resources and assets, including land, also has a substantial impact upon the well-being of individual women who continue to reside with men (Deininger, 2003). Equitable access, control and ownership of land has instrumental value in terms of its positive impact upon consumption (increasing spending on food, children's welfare and education) and productivity. This is especially so in countries like Uganda and Rwanda where women are responsible for the bulk of land cultivation. Land ownership also enables women to access other assets and resources, such as credit, which enables investment and diversification (Dolan, 2002) and increases their economic independence and power, which can have a positive influence on other areas of gender equality. The inheritance or non-inheritance of assets on marriage or death of the household head has also been integrally linked to people's poverty trajectories and their likelihood of remaining in or moving out of chronic poverty.[1] The gradual accumulation of assets, which can provide collateral for formal sector borrowing, facilitate investment and reduce vulnerability to the impact of shocks, can boost resilience and limit the need for the adoption of adverse coping strategies. Assets, when held by someone with both the necessary capabilities and agency to use them effectively, can therefore be an important source of social mobility. This suggests that tackling gendered differentiation in power and agency within the household *and* access to and control of resources will help developing countries to achieve the MDGs; both in terms of objectives for gender equality (MDG3), and the improvement of absolute poverty levels (MDG1). Greater equity can also enable greater productivity and economic growth (see Drechsler and Jütting, Chapter 10, this volume)

Inheritance practices and gender equality in Uganda and Rwanda
In Uganda women's access to land depends on the particular kinship and marriage traditions of their ethnic group. Inheritance is usually patrilineal and where women do inherit land, they normally inherit less than their male siblings. Bride price arrangements continue to be widespread – geographically and across social classes – and, while married women are given use rights (usufruct) to parcels of land by their husbands they lack rights to either own or control that land, meaning that they do not control income generated from it or from its sale or transfer. Land markets are fragmented and localised, so women have few options but to access land through their husbands. Not only that, in many parts of Uganda, women who purchase land in their own name, may well see it adopted or sold by their husbands. This acts as a powerful disincentive to female accumulation and combines with the inability of many women to control income derived from agricultural surpluses to dampen women's economic autonomy and more widespread growth in the agricultural sector.

Women's lack of rights over and inheritance of land is, in large part, due to the dominance of patrilocal marriage systems (where women move to their husband's village). Women in Uganda are commonly reminded that they are 'guests' in their husbands' households and the combination of patrilocal marriage and patriarchal inheritance through the male line results in the total dependence of women upon their husband, his family and any community-based network the woman can form post-marriage. This leaves women in an extremely insecure position in the event that husband and wife separate or where they are widowed. As we have mentioned before, the heir to the land (as agreed before death by the clan leaders or the closest male relative) is responsible for supporting the husband's former dependants. However, where this custom is disregarded, women and their dependants can find themselves forced from their homes and land and stripped of all their assets (including livestock, tools, furniture and cooking utensils). This can happen despite national legislation which nominally upholds widows' rights to remain in the matrimonial home until remarriage or death.

Uganda's 1972 Amendment Decree is just one example of the disjuncture between formal legislation and persistent customary practice. The 1998 Land Act also contains a number of measures that seek to rectify women's precarious position in relation to land; however like the Amendment Decree the legal rhetoric is not accompanied by effective strategies for implementation at the local level. There are also inherent contradictions in the Act; for instance the second objective of the Land Act, after formalising customary tenure systems, is to enhance the land security of marginalised groups, including women. However the Act's explicit support for customary systems sits uncomfortably with the stipulation that customary practices should not be implemented when they deny women, children or people with disabilities from ownership, occupation or use of land. Given that patrilineal land transfers and ownership are the bedrock of customary systems in much of Uganda, there seems to be a substantial inconsistency here.

A similar disjuncture between customary and formal land inheritance and ownership systems is found across much of Rwanda. In the Rwandan case, however, inequitable systems of land ownership and access are intensified by high population density, and since the 1994 genocide issues relating to refugee resettlement and a high proportion of female headed households (see Koster, Chapter 19, this volume). There have been a number of achievements in formal legislation regarding equitable land rights and inheritance such as the 1999 Inheritance and Marital Property Law and the Matrimonial Regimes, Liberties and Succession Law of 2000. The latter allows Rwandan women and girls to inherit land and own property. It also allows women to become official heads of household. However, the implementation of this legislation at the local level has been weak. Discrimination and abuse persist, and women and girls are denied their equal rights to land under strongly rooted Rwandan customary laws, which privilege male household heads. There have been more recent efforts to facilitate women's private ownership of land under a series of land reforms. For example, in the 2004 Land Policy the insecurity of women's rights within customary tenure practices – particularly concerning inheritance – is heavily emphasised and reform strongly encouraged. The 2005 Land Law pays specific attention to make each premise 'gender-neutral'. Nonetheless, land registration in Rwanda still uses forms that require the single name of the owner or the 'head' of a household which, in effect, dismisses the rights of women within the household to the land on which they too live and work, but are not the household 'head'. In addition, this law was not accompanied by either implementation or social legitimation strategies, which are of crucial importance if customary conceptions of women's inheritance and ownership rights are to be overcome. This means that very progressive legislation remains 'policy on paper' and has not yet become widespread 'policy in practice'.

Why is women's exclusion in inheritance and land ownership left off the political agenda? Policy fracture points and research recommendations
Although addressing women's exclusion in inheritance and land ownership requires coordinated policy responses, the evidence from Rwanda and Uganda suggests that policy processes have not yet successfully addressed gender imbalances. This is due to an array of fracture points or weaknesses in the entire policy process, from agenda-setting, through policy formation to implementation. In terms of *agenda-setting*, an issue such as access to land or inheritance, which is important to women or other marginalised individuals or groups, may never get onto the policy agenda because the scale, severity and importance of the issue is not recognised by key decision-makers. This is particularly true where the issues are those faced by chronically poor, marginalised and vulnerable people because they tend to have low visibility or low priority to policymakers, and their issues are complex or 'outside the box' of mainstream development thinking. In terms of *policy formation*, even the explicit inclusion of an issue on national, local or international policy agendas does not automatically mean that an appropriate policy will be formed. In respect of *implementation*, there may also be barriers to legitimation, constituency-building, and the like.

Many barriers prevent the representation of poor women's interests in national policy debates. Tackling gender discrimination is often complex and costly, making it unattractive to politicians who wish to appear decisive and effective over the short term. Additionally, the problems of poor women may not be deemed sufficiently severe or large scale to warrant the allocation of time or budgetary resources. This can be because the issues are poorly understood or because other constituencies and interest groups are more effective or more powerful and therefore more able to dominate the attention of policymakers. It may also be that international or national policy narratives are such that there is low demand for information on these issues, and so little research has been undertaken or it has been poorly disseminated. At the heart of the problem of policies relating to women's land and inheritance rights is the need to acknowledge that the promotion of women's rights and gender equality cannot be tackled outside the wider socio-economic structures and power hierarchies that determine women's roles in society. As such government-led reform and changes in *de jure* legislation will have little impact on *de facto* practice unless such changes are accompanied by measures to achieve social legitimation. This requires resources, careful strategising and an abundance of political will.

Another key problem blocking progressive policy responses is a lack of appropriate evidence for decision-making (Bird and Pratt, 2004). Inadequate research funding for gendered microevel studies limits the generation of robust empirical evidence which might challenge the perceived unimportance of intrahousehold and gendered concerns. The framing of research questions and the availability, or otherwise, of empirical evidence has an interactive relationship with both agenda-setting and policy formation. As previously highlighted, there is a need for greater disaggregated household analysis. One method of delivering such analysis would be through the application of gender frameworks such as the Harvard Tool (which measures the economic efficiency and equitability of households) or the Social Relations Approach, which is a method for analysing gender inequalities regarding the distribution of resources, responsibilities and power and incorporates an institutional analysis. . Alternatively Bolt and Bird (2003) have devised an intrahousehold disadvantages framework that examines clusters of disadvantage that affect individuals within the community and household, aggravating their personal levels of poverty and vulnerability.[2] Using such tools can ensure a more systematic and gender-equitable understanding of social inequalities and daily realities from the national to the household level.

A lack of evidence for decision-making can have a considerable impact upon policy priorities, which may, as a consequence, derive largely from the ideology and personal preferences of key decision-makers or the degree of pressure that they have come under from particular lobbies or special interest groups. The poor articulation of the needs of women and marginalised groups is also due to poor mobilisation around social movements, co-opted and low-capacity leadership, weak identification of constituencies by elected leaders, and poor or partial representation by interlocutors. These contribute to weak agenda-setting. Support from international non-governmental organisations (NGOs), the international labour movement, cross-national faith-based networks, members of international epistemic communities (for example, feminist academics and the women's movement) and the international community can all provide support to both social movements and the leaders of civil society. This support may take the form of new empirical evidence, collaborative engagement with policy communities, resources and/or capacity support.

As we have sought to highlight, overcoming gendered inequalities in access to land and inheritance (in Rwanda, Uganda and across the wider world) has much to do with addressing fracture points in processes of policy formation and in a more widespread lack of intrahousehold understanding. Conceptualising the household as a unitary and equitable body is the first blindspot in agenda-setting; this compounds women's lack of political voice and agency, as well as their limited economic opportunities, which results in the low visibility of gendered social inequalities. Effective attempts at rectifying gender inequalities within society must also take into account that legislation has to be accompanied by strategies for the roll-out of policies at the local level. Identifying fracture points in policy formation and allocating time and resources to overcoming these are also vital. Such measures not only constitute obligations for the preservation of fundamental human rights, but will encourage wider socio-economic development by enabling women to contribute more effectively to national economies and to build-up the necessary assets to facilitate their own social mobility.

Notes

1. As such, the management of assets is a core theme for the Chronic Poverty Research Centre, with which both authors are involved. See www.chronicpoverty.org (accessed 14 October 2009).
2. For further information on the intrahousehold disadvantages framework and on tools for analysing intrahousehold inequalities see Bolt and Bird (2003).

Select bibliography

Bird, Kate and Nicola Pratt (2004) *Fracture Points in Social Policies for Chronic Poverty Reduction*, Overseas Development Institute Working Paper 242 and Chronic Poverty Research Centre No. 47, London: Overseas Development Institute.

Bolt, Vincent and Kate Bird (2003) *The Intrahousehold Disadvantages Framework: A Framework for the Analysis of Intrahousehold Difference and Inequality*, Chronic Poverty Research Centre Working Paper No. 32, London: Overseas Development Institute.

Deininger, Klaus (2003) *Land Policies for Growth and Poverty Reduction*, Washington, DC: World Bank, available at: http://www.fig.net/pub/mexico/papers_eng/ts2_deininger_eng.pdf (accessed 9 June 2009).

Dolan, Catherine (2002) *Gender and Diverse Livelihoods in Uganda*, LADDER Working Paper No. 10, Norwich: School of Development Studies, University of East Anglia.

Ellis, Frank (1988) *Peasant Economics: Farm Households and Agrarian Development*, 2nd edn, Cambridge: Cambridge University Press.

Folbre, Nancy (1997) 'Gender coalitions: extrafamily influences on intrafamily inequality', in Lawrence Haddad, John Hoddinot and Harold Alderman (eds), *Intrahousehold Resource Allocation in Developing Countries*, Washington, DC: International Food Policy Research Institute, pp. 263–74.

Kalabamu, Faustin (2006) 'Patriarchy and women's land rights in Botswana', *Land Use Policy*, **23** (3), 237–46.

56 Gender, livelihoods and rental housing markets in the Global South: the urban poor as landlords and tenants

Sunil Kumar

Drawing upon research from cities in India, Mexico and Botswana, this chapter explores the meaning and significance of a gendered perspective on urban rental housing markets. The role of rental housing as a livelihood has been neglected in relation to ownership, despite the evidence that the poor rent rooms to a significant proportion of other urban poor individuals and households in the Global South. Furthermore, gendered perspectives on housing tenure have examined the role of men and women 'separately' rather than exploring the 'relationship' between men and women in rental housing markets. The main emphasis of this chapter is on a gendered treatment of how rental housing is (1) part of a livelihood portfolio in its own right for those who provide it, and (2) as a pathway to other livelihood opportunities for tenants. Specifically in relation to women-headed and women-maintained households it can also play an important psycho-social role. It is argued that such a perspective provides sympathetic policymakers with a stronger case for the implementation of a gendered rental housing policy.

A gendered perspective on urban housing and human settlements

The importance of identifying and incorporating gender into the design of urban housing as well as planning for urban development has been stressed since the mid-1980s (see for example, Chant, 1996; Moser, 1987). However, such explicit attention has, by and large, not been made in relation to rental housing markets (an exception being Datta, 1995).

Moser (1987) was one of the first to stress the connection between the 'triple role of women', and their relationship to housing in general. The triple role of women is conceptualised as comprising of: 'reproductive' tasks (childbearing and child-rearing); 'productive' tasks (as primary or secondary income earners); and 'community managing' tasks (organising and demanding for services such as water and sanitation). Each of these roles are, individually and collectively, linked to housing and human settlements. For instance, the lack of water and sanitation adversely affects the reproductive role primarily undertaken by women. Similarly, poor housing design or the unfavourable location of housing projects can affect the productive role of women in relation to home-based work as well as labour market access respectively. Finally, inadequate housing and basic services not only affect women more but also reinforce the gendered division of labour as they are forced into a community management role.

All these relate to women meeting their practical gender needs, defined as 'those needs which arise from the concrete condition of women's positioning, by virtue of their gender, within the sexual division of labour' (Moser, 1987: 29).[1] Strategic gender needs, however, are correlated with 'the analysis of women's subordination, and, deriving out of this, the formulation of an alternative more satisfactory organisation of society to those which exist at present, in terms of the structure and nature of relationships between men and women' (ibid.: 29).

A second aspect of a gender perspective on housing and urban development relates to understanding how these are played out not only in terms of the relationship between men and women but also by women on their own as either *de jure* (women-headed households) or *de facto* (women-managed households) heads of households – the so called 'feminisation of household headship' (see Chant, 1996, and Chapter 15, this volume).

Gender and urban rental housing markets: key issues
Contrary to popular belief, a significant proportion of the urban poor are not owners (either *de jure* or *de facto*) but tenants. Unfortunately, there are no comparable figures for landlords,[2] who are subsumed under the category of owners. A third group comprise 'sharers' who reside on the same plot as the owners but pay no rent. The practice of sharing seems to be an urban Latin America phenomenon found in Mexican cities such as Mexico City, Guadalajara and Puebla). Varley (1993: 25–26) notes that 'whilst married daughters as well as married sons were recorded sharing with their parents, single parents were . . . counted as part of their parents extended household . . .', leading to the conclusion that '. . . sharing therefore reinforces the patriarchal norm of the nuclear family, insofar as it is a privilege accorded only to those who are married'.

Urban rental housing markets are multilayered. First, unlike ownership, rental housing markets involve a temporary exchange relationship between two parties – those that let rooms (landlords) and those that pay rent for the use of the room (tenants). Women as well as men may be either landlords or tenants. Second, rental housing markets are found in settlements governed by a continuum of property rights ranging from legal, through quasi-legal, to illegal arrangements. In reality, the level of rights seems to have little or no bearing on either the evolution or operation of rental housing markets (Kumar, 2001). Third, landlords may be resident (living on the same property as their tenants) or absentee (living elsewhere, in either the same or different settlement). The degree of proximity of residence has a bearing on landlord–tenant gender relations.

Rental housing markets are not automatically predisposed to being gendered, but become so, directly and indirectly, when two meanings of the concept of gender are invoked. First, gender as 'social construct', akin to strategic gender needs, indirectly generates gender-related questions about the routes into landlordism and tenancy for women as well as men. Secondly, gender as 'social relationship' makes explicit the gender relations between landlords and tenants.

Women face several disadvantages in rental housing markets. These include limited access to land and credit as well as discriminatory practices in relation to property inheritance and exclusion from being named on land title deeds. From a strategic gender needs perspective, it has been argued that joint land titles (in the name of both the man and the woman) can positively alter the relationship between women and men (see Deere, Chapter 53, this volume; Rakodi, Chapter 54, this volume). However, it is important to recognise that a vast proportion of poor urban households reside on land that is officially judged to be illegally or quasi-legally occupied. Furthermore, the prevalence of female and male landlords as well as tenants is also influenced by local contexts (Kumar, 2001).

For example, female landlords were almost unknown in the Indian city of Surat where the sex ratio as per the last reliable statistics (in 1991) record is heavily male-biased (839 women per 1000 men) but more visible in Bangalore (902 women per 1000). Moreover, female labour force participation rates in 1991 in Surat (6.3 per cent) were almost half that in Bangalore (11.5 per cent). Factors such as these explain the variations in how gender relations are played out in rental housing markets. It is worth recalling here that a discussion of gender and rental housing markets must not focus exclusively on women-headed or women-maintained households in order to avoid 'rendering the majority of women, once again, invisible' (Varley, 1993: 13).

Gender and rental housing markets: landlords
As previously indicated, rental housing markets operate on a legal–illegal property rights continuum. Where property rights are legal and women are able to inherit property, such as in the inner-city areas of Guadalajara and Puebla, Mexico, renting is often referred to as a 'widow's business' (Varley, 1997). However, since a majority of the poor live on land that veers towards the illegal end of the spectrum, routes into landlordism often discriminate on the basis of gender. Since access to land (irrespective of legal status) and credit is a prerequisite for the development of landlordism, two observations are appropriate. First, it not uncommon for gender relations to be rendered opaque among landlords in male-headed households[3] since an understanding of how decisions relating to the renting of rooms and the use of rental income were made – the complex working of the 'household blank box' – remain unknown (Kumar, 2001). One exception to this can be found in the city of Gaborone, Botswana (Datta, 1995). In legal self-help housing areas, women outnumbered men as landlords (50 per cent in female-headed households, 34 per cent in male-headed nuclear households). Two main explanations are provided for both types of households: first, that low incomes give rise to the need to find alternative sources of earning; and, second, that those with low incomes as well as a large number of dependants were more inclined to rent out rooms despite the resultant overcrowding. Interestingly, in nuclear households 'there was little evidence that members of households share income . . . rent gives them (married women) money in hand' (Datta, 1995: 6).

Second, although the gendered dimensions in female-headed landlord households are more transparent as decision-making involves only or most women, they tend to be at a disadvantage. For example, women landlords in female-headed households in Gaborone, Botswana, have on average fewer rooms to let (and therefore fewer tenants) than those in male-headed nuclear households due to a combination of lack of access to credit, having to hire skilled labour and not being owners for a long time and thus low levels of housing consolidation. This has affected the number, size and quality of rooms they have been able to construct which has in turn impacted on the level of rental income (Datta, 1995). Furthermore, practices that discriminate against female-headed households accessing land (purchase and inheritance) and credit, in addition to poor labour market opportunities and low earnings, deprives them of the opportunity to rent out rooms and thus generate additional income (see Chant, 1996). Evidence suggests that even the granting of titles in the names of both partners in nuclear households does little to include women in housing-related decisions. Women, thus, tend to be a minority among landlords (Kumar, 2001; Varley, 1997).

Gender and rental housing markets: tenants
It has been argued that some individuals and households 'choose' to become tenants whereas, for others, 'constraints' on becoming owner-occupiers leave them little choice but to rent (Gilbert, 1983). In relation to the 'choice' thesis, gender relations differ for nuclear households compared to women-headed and women-managed households. For the former, discussions and decisions about choosing to rent are played out in the 'household blank box'. In the latter, they are predicated more on female household heads considering issues ranging from labour market proximity to supportive social networks.

The 'constraint' thesis relegates gender relations to the background. Male-headed households have little room for manoeuvre on the gender front since their inability to become owners makes renting the only option. The very same constraints that prevent women-headed or women-managed households from becoming landlords makes renting or sharing the only alternative (see Varley, 1993). Even here, female-headed and female-managed household tenants are likely to be discriminated against due to their household circumstances.

By and large, single male and female migrants choose to rent as they perceive their stay in the city to be temporary. However, single migrant men and women face different sets of constraints. In Surat, India, the migrant majority is made up of single men from the state of Orissa employed in the textile-weaving industry. Up to 14 migrants were found to share a room given the shift-based nature of their work and rented rooms from male-headed nuclear households due to the male migration bias (Kumar, 2001). While working women's hostels can be found in many urban centres in India, these often do not cater to poor women. Access to rental housing for this group is extremely problematic and hinders them from meeting their practical gender needs.

Gender and rental housing markets: landlord–tenant relations
Landlord–tenant relations bring gender issues to the fore due to exchange relationships between men and women. This is especially significant for resident female landlords as they live in constant proximity to their tenants. Such landlords use several strategies to mitigate against landlord–tenant conflicts arising from acts of misbehaviour or non-payment of rent which may eventually lead to the need to evict their tenants. One such strategy (in the cities of Surat and Bangalore, India) was to let rooms to tenants who had been recommended by a local contact. Given a lack of recourse to the law (for all poor landlords in general), recommendations from contacts with a high local social standing were sought wherever possible in order to ensure recourse to fair arbitration and effective action in the event of a conflict (Kumar, 2001).

A second strategy is to let to relatives, a practice not uncommon among poorer households. While this may reduce conflicts, the social obligations and reciprocities involved are not conducive to charging market rents or acting with impunity in relation to rent defaults. This, however, applies to both female and male landlords (Datta, 1995; Kumar, 2001).

A third strategy is to carefully choose tenants. Women landlords from both female and nuclear households in Gaborone paid less attention to whether prospective renters could meet payment terms (as was the case of landlords in male-headed households) but focused instead on whether they were obedient, quiet, clean and/or cared for the property – creating an impression that 'women made harsher landlords in terms of "rules and regulations" than men' (Datta, 1995: 10). The setting out of these conditions is ascribed to the fact that women looked after the dwelling, managed the letting business and spent more time at home, which meant that they interacted more with their tenants. In contrast, landlord–tenant relations can become problematic for those women in male-headed nuclear households who were not involved in the choice of tenants if they become *de facto* women-headed households and landlords at the same time due to the death of a spouse or desertion. In such cases, the presence of older male children or the support of male relatives helps to a certain extent (Kumar, 2001: 92–3)

A fourth option is to let to other women-headed households. For some this may be the preferred option as it enables landlords, particularly from women-headed households, to receive greater psycho-socio support from their tenants. For others, it may be the least preferred outcome as it is likely to produce lower rental returns.

Gender-neutral rental housing markets: plausible or implausible?
Gender-neutral housing markets are plausible. Despite limited evidence, women in male-headed nuclear households as well as female-headed and female-managed households have demonstrated that they can negotiate gender as both 'social relation' as well as 'social construct' by becoming landlords. However, unfavourable conditions and discriminatory practices prevent the vast majority of women accessing land and credit, thus denying them the same opportunities as men to become landlords. Several policy interventions are worth considering. First, the need to equitably treat women and men in relation to property rights (formal and informal) irrespective of household structure. Securing gender-neutral decision-making within the household blank box is a more challenging task. Second, to recognise the role that rental housing markets play in the livelihoods for landlords as well as tenants, women and men alike. Rents are an important source of diversified income for both poor male and female landlords. The availability of rooms for rent provides tenants with improved housing choices, enhances their access to labour markets, and opens up membership to new social networks, all of which contribute to a reduction in individual and household vulnerability. Third, improving access to affordable institutional credit, especially for women-headed or women-managed households, would greatly enhance their ability to invest in housing and let rooms as a means of generating additional income. Fourth and finally, attention needs to be paid to the short-term housing needs of single migrant women who may face discrimination in the rental housing market. The involvement of non-governmental organisations (NGOs) in the provision of affordable rental housing would help plug gaps in market provision for this group.

On the research front there is a huge gap in understanding gender relations in rental housing markets per se. The following are some gender-related questions that need to be pursued. How do women and men in nuclear households decide whether to let rooms and make use of the income from rent? How does sex of headship influence decisions to let or not let rooms, and what additional constraints do female heads face apart from credit and low incomes? How are single, especially young, female households constrained in meeting their housing needs?

Notes
1. The concepts of practical and strategic gender needs were adapted from the seminal work of Maxine Molyneux on practical and strategic gender interests, notwithstanding their lack of theoretical equivalence (see Chant, 1996: xii–xiiin for discussion and references).

2. Unlike the word 'tenant' which is gender-neutral, landlords and landladies are used to denote whether it is men or women who rent out rooms. This, however, only serves to identify the sex of the person letting out rooms and does not refer to gender as 'social relationship' or 'social construct'. However, given the lexical gender revolution of the 1970s and 1980s which has resulted in words like 'actor' now referring to both women and men, I use the term landlord to refer to both men and women by using the word 'lord' to convey control over the letting of rooms.
3. The word household needs clarification as there is little consistency in its use in the literature. When the terms female-managed and male-headed households are used, reference is made in general to both nuclear as well as extended households unless specified. Female-managed households refer to those households where a male partner is present but does not contribute to household income, primarily due to ill health. The use of the term female-headed households refers specifically to lone mother households.

Select bibliography

Chant, Sylvia (1996) *Gender, Urban Development and Housing*, New York: United Nations Development Programme.

Datta, Kavita (1995) 'Strategies for urban survival? Women landlords in Gaborone, Botswana', *Habitat International*, **19** (1), 1–12.

Gilbert, Alan (1983) 'The tenants of self-help housing: choice and constraint in the housing markets of less developed countries', *Development and Change*, **14** (3), 449–77.

Kumar, Sunil (2001) *Social Relations, Rental Housing Markets and the Poor in Urban India*, London: Department of Social Policy, London School of Economics, available at: http://www.worldbank.org/urban/poverty/docs/social-relation-kumar.pdf or http://www.research4development.info/PDF/Outputs/R6856.pdf (accessed 30 April 2009).

Moser, Caroline (1987) 'Women, human settlements and housing: a conceptual framework for analysis and policy-making', in Caroline Moser and Linda Peake (eds), *Women, Human Settlements and Housing*, London: Tavistock, pp. 12–32.

Varley, Ann (1993) 'Gender and housing: the provision of accommodation for young adults in three Mexican cities', *Habitat International*, **17** (4), 13–30.

Varley, Ann (1997) 'Neither victims nor heroines: women, land and housing in Mexican cities', *Third World Planning Review*, **17** (2), 169–82.

57 Renegotiating the household: successfully leveraging women's access to housing microfinance in South Africa
Sophie Mills

Based on research carried out with men and women in male and female-headed households in two townships of Cape Town, South Africa,[1] this chapter explores how effective housing microfinance can be in empowering women to negotiate improved bargaining positions within their households. It begins by exploring the impact at the household level of improved housing due to credit provision and the link which many women and men make between women's access to a housing microloan and wider benefits around women's improved decision-making ability. Subsequently, the potential for intrahousehold conflict is discussed, as women's expectation of greater entitlements as a consequence of their contribution can be blocked or undermined by men seeking to subsume their achievements in order to preserve existing household power relations. The detrimental impact on women's household position of detaching reward from investment exemplifies the caution with which such interventions should be viewed and suggests future policy should be cautious in correlating women's increased input with increased opportunity.

Housing microfinance: a positive intervention for women in households?
Housing has been a key policy area for the South African government, which implemented a housing subsidy programme in 1996 in order to address the spatial inequalities of the apartheid era. The subsidy was targeted at low-income households, financing a complete unit for those earning below ZAR3500 (US$369). A critical component of the original housing strategy was the participation of the country's formal banking sector in lending to this market. However, despite voluntary commitments by the financial sector to increase service provision to the low-income population, those working in the informal economy continue to be excluded from access to affordable finance.

In response to this, a housing microfinance institution (MFI), the Kuyasa Fund, began, as of 2000, to lend to recipients of the housing subsidy in Cape Town. The provision of appropriate microfinance was intended to enable the poor to incrementally improve their housing situation as well as to demonstrate the ability of this perceived high risk market to manage appropriately priced credit. To date, the fund has lent to some 10000 clients, of whom 76 per cent have been women. The MFI initially had no implicit policy of targeting women, but found that uptake was predominantly by women, even within male-headed households. To some extent this is a reflection of the emphasis the organisation placed on recruiting participants from savings groups, which tend to be overwhelmingly women based. This not only ensured clients had a history of managing savings, but also gave clear indication of women's increasing responsibilities even within nominally male-headed households.

Analysis at the intrahousehold level illustrated that resources such as housing or finance do not impact upon the household as a cohesive entity, but rather that inequality within household power relations can be entrenched or reordered by externally derived resources (Folbre and Nelson, 2000). An exploration of the role of housing microfinance and the physical manifestation of women's involvement, in the form of a formal house, increased space or improved living conditions, gives interesting insight into the accepted importance of income as a predicator of bargaining power. An assumption that income/ control over income is the main mechanism by which power is accessed and exercised within the household was often found to be erroneous (Cantillion and Nolan, 2001). In the case of Kuyasa clients, facilitating access to improved housing, rather than income generation, was perceived as a critical factor in improving women's bargaining position within their households, even for those earning incomes (Mills, 2004).

In the majority of cases, women were the primary motivators for housing and managed the housing process, from membership and participation in the savings groups through to overseeing delivery of materials, initial construction and loan repayment. Both men and women gave it as their opinion that housing provision was the prerogative of women, linked to their duties as custodians of the family. This has rather detrimental implications for women, and initially suggests significant constraints in the ability of microfinance to meaningfully empower women with regard to the position they occupy in the housing process. The majority of women interviewed described a housing process in which they devoted a considerable amount of their time to organising and attending meetings and keeping momentum for the housing process going in the wait between subsidy application and materials delivery, as well as ensuring regular savings in order to qualify for microfinance, negotiating a loan and managing loan repayments in the face of male disapproval or disinterest. Men were participants 'on paper' but their direct involvement was rarely maintained throughout the sometimes lengthy housing process, tending to arise at the initial point of loan application and then again with the final stages of the construction process.

However, most women accepted the higher time cost they incurred as inevitable, and once the construction financed by the loan was completed, reported an overwhelmingly positive response around their sense of achievement and perception within the household. Women, and particularly those who were heads of their households, saw the house as proof of their ability to manage finance and construction, a typically male preserve. In instances where ownership meant that families were able to move out of overcrowded accommodation, with the tensions such living arrangements engender, respondents reported much better physical and emotional living conditions, with acknowledgement of the role women had played in enabling the change.

Single women considered that the housing process and access to microfinance had enabled them to validate their decision to live alone, particularly where they had separated from male partners. The house was seen as physical proof of their ability to manage without a husband, often better than women with husbands who were still living in shacks.

One of the most important ways in which women's involvement with housing projects affected their well-being was through improved relationships with their husbands. While many women identified their husbands' non-involvement and attempts to curtail their wives' involvement as constraints to their participation and negative influences on their relationships, almost without exception they said that their husbands' attitudes had changed as the house was being built. While some men may not have gone so far as to actively help their spouses, they at least ceased in their objections to wives' participation. In other cases men became more heavily involved and wives said their relationship had improved. In most instances, taking a loan and financing improvements illustrated to the household a woman's capability with money. Many women thus explained the importance of the project in enabling them to illustrate their capabilities not only to themselves, but also to their husbands. The positive impact on women was recognised by male respondents, who, for the most part, considered the experience to be positive both for the household and their wives. In particular both referred to the increased role women played in decision-making and saw the relationship as more equitable since participation started, although the evidence for this translating into actual authority is limited, as discussed in the next section.

Not going far enough? Conflict, bargaining and obstruction
The experience of the women who accessed microfinance loans was not without problems. Home ownership can be a problematic asset. This is particularly the case where it is exploited by other household members, as in the case of pensioners whose children or grandchildren moved into their new homes without a corresponding contribution to the household budget, or can be used by the owner in a manner that threatens the well-being of other household members, such as threats of eviction for non-compliance. Additionally, the sense of well-being that was reported can be short-lived. The transition from a shack to a brick house is a very positive experience, but feedback from clients who had been in their subsidy house for some time and were on their second or third loan cycle of upgrading suggested that perceptions of improvements lessened with time. Thus respondents referred to the additional costs related to formality (such as municipal service charges), the need for further investment of microloans in housing in order to complete it and the need to 'upgrade' furnishings which had been adequate in shacks but were considered inappropriate for the new house. The visible value of women's input was therefore reduced over time. A final problem experienced was the high cost of building, whereby large building projects or households only able to qualify for minimal loans may require multiple loan cycles before construction is finished. The impact of this delay, with a spate of building followed by a period of inactivity and repayment, is to once again reduce the perception of input by women or even to portray it in a negative light, as repayments become due on incomplete building work. In particular, those households that are not capable of taking on the expenses of housing and housing finance may do so to the detriment of their quality of life and financial status for some time to come, with negative effects on the household member who saddled the household with debt.

The positive outputs secured by women through participation tended to be diminished by men in the household who downplayed the importance of women's achievements, emphasised their own financial contributions above those of women or considered women's achievements as an integral part of their gender obligations to the household when women attempted to leverage these intangibles into concrete rights. Through these mechanisms, the value of women's investment in the house could be separated from the entitlements they might have expected (see Chant, 2008, and Chapter 15, this volume).

This obstruction relied predominantly on men's attempts to enforce traditional understandings of household gender roles and thus block women's attempts to win more decision-making authority as an outcome of their actions. Through this mechanism, expectation of greater bargaining authority could be subtly divorced from women's achievements.

Male respondents expressed a belief that the nature of marriage was changing as relationships between husbands and wives were renegotiated. The model of traditional marriage was already being challenged by shifting employment patterns and the increased financial contributions of women as well as their greater emancipation in society. Thus men spoke of their fathers' or grandfathers' eras, when men exercised much greater control over wives and households, and compared them to their own experiences of marriage, which has come to include a higher degree of negotiation with women. While some men considered these kinds of changes to be for the worse, most men considered them reasonable. They could perceive the benefits of harmonious marital relations, the emotional benefits of shared, negotiated decision-making and the 'right' of women to greater freedoms. Where men did experience problems was where they associated this change with threats to their own well-being. Thus many men would argue that they supported women's right to work, yet were hostile to the notion that they participate more in undertaking domestic labour.

The success or otherwise of the microfinance intervention therefore needs to be understood in the context of the unequal power relations within households, where women in particular struggle to access and control resources and for whom credit may be problematic. Part of this struggle is around the way in which women, despite considering that they had made an important contribution to household welfare which merited increased decision-making power, rarely contradicted their husbands' claims to household headship and the privileges this conferred. They articulated a desire to challenge male cultural prerogatives, such as tolerance of domestic violence and constraints to female labour-force participation, but sought to do this within existing gendered frameworks. The dichotomy between men, who assumed titular household headship, and women, who often carried the burdens of headship, could be problematic in that it constrained the extent to which women could carry out their duties where there was the possibility that doing so might adversely affect male prestige. Thus some women reported that they often operated without their husbands' knowledge or in defiance of their wishes in participating in housing schemes or taking microfinance loans (cf. Mutalima, Chapter 93, this volume).

Household headship was not predicated on income-generation, nor did the head necessarily have financial control over household resources. Indeed, employment in the lower echelons of the South African labour market is characterised by insecurity, with periods of unemployment among household heads being frequent for many of the households interviewed. For most men, headship is not only defined through what a man does for the household – such as providing income and security – but through what his position entitles him to. If headship is regarded in this light, then it is possible to understand how men can agree that women are entitled to equality and yet consider that this should not apply where it infringes on their traditional rights to block women's access to greater decision-making power, particularly where this might diminish their own authority or access to resources.

Ways forward
For the overwhelming majority of participants, the microfinance interventions were successful because they provided access to improved housing. In this way, the overall outcome of participation can be interpreted as positive. Moreover, disempowered members of society were able to access and use the government housing subsidy, plan and implement house construction, manage and administer financial and logistical aspects of the housing process and move into a brick house with secure tenure.

The assumption of a link between housing microfinance and greater decision-making authority needs to be evaluated with caution. It became increasingly evident throughout the research that power as expressed by respondents was not always used to reorder existing gender and decision-making relations, but was more likely to be used to increase performance capacity within these pre-defined roles. This was interesting in displaying the extent to which gender roles were considered to convey advantage as well as disadvantage and so were actively defended. Women were very self-aware that they moved between formal cultural understandings of 'wifehood' and their own personal identities, using their own agency to manipulate culturally prescribed roles to their advantage and choosing to modify existing gender roles rather than reject them outright.

However, it was also clear that for many women the advantages participation brought were not necessarily translated into the long term, and that manipulation within gender roles took place instead of direct challenges to male authority. The predominant focus on income has tended to obscure the ways in which women, as the usual custodians of household welfare, can use non-economic factors to influence and exert power. That this is the case was clearly defined in the research, where women's descriptions of how they exercised power were directly related to their nurturing roles as mothers and wives and rarely set in open conflict with men.

Two key issues became clear from the research – the need to solidify the advantages women gained for themselves in the short term and the need to integrate men's participation into the process. The first issue is critical if the short-term advantages women gained are to be consolidated in a permanently improved bargaining position. The housing intervention generated a *perception* of women's increased bargaining authority by both men and women but this was rarely translated into the ability to directly control household resources. A key factor in the subsidy housing process in South Africa is the conferral of tenure, giving title to the adult applicant and their spouse. Combined with a microfinance intervention, this consolidated women's position, securing their right to the house and protecting their investment in the long term, even if this was not immediately realised. Future policy may do well to leverage women's asset ownership and limited financial decision-making power through financial literacy education or a similar intervention which builds women's autonomy and emphasises the value of their achievements.

Second, increasing the participation of men would contribute not only to reducing the burden of responsibility carried by women but also ensure the inclusion of men's economic resources, increasing the impact of a microfinance intervention. A focus on men as well as women would reduce the difficulties women face in accessing and managing finance and encourage men's resource contribution.

Note

1. Research was carried out over eight months in 2001 with Kuyasa Fund clients across two main sites in Khayelitsha and Philippi townships, Cape Town. This comprised 118 individual qualitative interviews with men and women and three focus groups with women.

Select bibliography

Cantillion, Sara and Brian Nolan (2001) 'Poverty within households: measuring gender differences using non-monetary indicators', *Feminist Economics*, **7** (1), 5–23.

Chant, Sylvia (2008) 'The "feminisation of poverty" and the "feminisation" of anti-poverty programmes: room for revision?', *Journal of Development Studies*, **44** (2), 165–97.

Folbre, Nancy and Joan A. Nelson (2000) 'For love or money – or both?', *Journal of Economic Perspectives*, **14** (4),123–40.

Mills, Sophie (2004) 'Housing the household: gender and empowerment in South Africa' unpublished PhD dissertation, Department of Geography and Environment, London School of Economics.

58 Gender issues and shack/slum dweller federations
Sheela Patel and Diana Mitlin

Introduction

In over 15 countries in the Global South, federations formed by the urban poor (slum and shack dwellers and the homeless) have become important actors in poverty reduction, working not only on community-level initiatives but also at the level of cities and nations. The foundations of these federations are savings groups in local neighbourhoods, initiated and managed by women. Federations form as savings groups from 'slums', and informal settlements come together, first at the city and then at the national level.

These savings groups and the larger federations they create not only manage savings and credit but undertake many initiatives, such as securing land, upgrading homes, and improving community services and infrastructure – for instance community toilets with washing facilities. In many nations, these federations' initiatives reach thousands of households; in some, tens of thousands. All these federations visit each other, learn from and support each other; they have also formed a network organisation, Shack/Slum Dwellers International (SDI), to support their international exchange programmes and their negotiations with international agencies. Most federations also work in partnership with a local non-governmental organisation (NGO)

One of the most notable aspects of these federations is the central role that women have in all of them. This is even so in nations where gender relations are very unequal and grassroots organisations have long been controlled by men. Since women's participation and representation were not easily achieved, it is instructive to consider the vision and practice of this network.

The emergence of a women-centred federation in India

The first women-led slum dweller federation originated in India, based on savings groups formed by pavement dwellers in Mumbai in 1986 (Patel and Mitlin, 2004). It was named Mahila Milan (Women Together). A local NGO, the Society for the Promotion of Area Resource Centres (SPARC),[1] had been formed at that time by people who previously worked in a conventional social welfare NGO and were searching for a more effective, empowering model for slum and pavement dwellers. They began conversations with the women pavement dwellers, one of the lowest-income and most disadvantaged groups and also very much at risk of eviction. What these women said was that they could not seek any change in their own status if it did not mean an improvement in the lives of their families and communities (in part because these were also their safety nets). They also explained how they could not directly confront the gender-based inequalities they lived with. They could not travel out of their neighbourhood to engage in such initiatives as learning exchanges with other savings groups without permission from their husbands and traditional (male) leaders. But this permission was negotiated and they began to explore ways to engage the wider city to address their problems through visiting government departments, police stations, hospitals and ration shops. As groups they developed confidence to ask questions, to investigate who had access to services, and which rules and regulations excluded them. They worked out how to obtain ration cards that allow access to subsidised fuel and basic food (which at that time were off limits to pavement dwellers), how to access healthcare, and how to make complaints to the police. The women found that they could breach their exclusion, and through learning how to do so, they taught other women's groups to do the same. Others in their communities, including husbands and leaders, saw the benefits and began to give space to these women's collective groups to participate more openly in community decision-making.

This process widened to address housing issues when pavement dwellers were threatened with eviction after a court judgement. Although the eviction was avoided, the women asked why they were always excluded from any possibility of getting land or housing from the government. Since no one from the SPARC had experience in this area, this led women to discussions with the National Slum Dwellers Federation (NSDF) that had been set up in 1975 to support slum dwellers in fighting eviction. Women were involved in this federation but the male leadership had tended to see women as passive contributors to mass rallies and protest marches. The SPARC suggested a partnership of the three organisations and the NSDF leadership accepted, recognising that men were good at protest but rarely went beyond this to develop outcomes for the communities. The federations affiliated with NSDF began to nurture women's collectives that became members of Mahila Milan. With support from NSDF leaders, the space for women to embrace leadership opened.

Savings groups that could provide financial services were explored by many groups and these proved to be initiatives that women managed. By saving together, they developed and demonstrated trust, transparency and accountability to each other and showed state or other agencies that they were organised. The loans began modestly, to help members buy food or emergency medicines and grew to include livelihood and housing loans.

These savings groups were not opposed by community leaders, partly because some of their activities were not of much interest to men – for instance, the design, construction and management of community toilets with washing facilities – even if these benefited the whole community. However, when savings groups began to achieve successful outcomes, Mahila Milan women often faced opposition from traditional leaders. Fortunately they were able to call on NSDF's mainly male leaders for support. Moreover, as Mahila Milan groups demonstrated success, so their work and organisation generated greater acceptance.

Initially, loans from savings groups were available only for women but the women from the federations insisted that loans also be available to men. Their logic was that it was important for men to work; if they did not, they created many additional burdens for women – for instance, as they no longer sought work or drank. But the loan was only available to men through their wives (as savings group members) and they had repayment responsibilities to the collective (female) leadership and pressure from the whole group if they failed to pay!

Most of the most powerful women leaders came from among the lowest-income and most socially disadvantaged neighbourhoods, in part because in these areas the men had given up. In better circumstances, male leaders tend to want to retain power and manage links with politicians and government agencies.

Over time, Mahila Milan savings groups came to have central roles in hundreds of community designed and managed toilet programmes, many housing initiatives and the setting-up and running of police stations in slums supported by resident committees in which women are the majority (Burra et al., 2003). The means by which women in India became organisers of credit and of many other initiatives have been applied in all the other federations.

Gendered responses to poverty within the SDI federations
Drawing on the experiences of federations that are members of SDI enables us to understand the multiple ways in which SDI methodologies change social relations, both within and beyond the community. Three activities combine to produce a gendered response to poverty. The first is supportive space for women to become active in local collective organisation and then in larger development issues, the second is leadership experience, and the third, dedicated women's programmes.

On the first of these, savings groups draw in women and provide a space for 'safe' participation as women are in the majority; men are less interested in savings. Generally as savings schemes grow and network with each other, more men are drawn into the process. In most nations, groups recognise the importance of providing a 'safe' space for women, notwithstanding that what such a space actually involves develops differently depending on local circumstance. For example, initially, the Malawi Homeless People's Federation argued that only women should be involved in savings schemes. Then as the federation developed, the women members allowed men to join. One reason was that the leadership felt strong enough to manage the incorporation of men. Another was that many men were keen to join. Also important in maintaining women's leadership has been the federation's ability to negotiate with the state for land that supported a large housing construction programme managed by the savings groups (Manda, 2007). Success encouraged membership to grow but all the national leaders and most of the regional leaders are women.

Another way in which the federations create a supportive space for women is by the kinds of activities that are undertaken and validated. In house construction projects in Zimbabwe, for example, it is common for some of the poorest families to be selected for free houses with the costs being shared by all participants. Even with the acute difficulties facing households, federation members are aware of their need for solidarity and of creating practices that care for the most vulnerable. In validating such needs, SDI practices fit with women's gendered role in many societies which emphasises the importance of a caring response to need.

In all SDI federations, there is a deliberate attempt to build a culture that, in terms of gendered relations, favours women. This develops through dialogue, action, documentation, leadership interventions, and ongoing practice to include:

1. Empathy which the problems of poverty rather than discipline for the failed individual (for instance, exclusion for missing loan repayments).
2. Incremental affordable development rather than maximum material consumption.
3. Collective rather than individual decisions and actions.
4. Flexibility in regard to local need (rather than rule bound and formalistic procedures) and to timing (serving community dynamics rather than externally imposed timetables).

5. Membership through participation (social engagement) rather than fixed financial contributions.
6. Recognition that everyone has a contribution to make rather than leaders who dominate.
7. Experiential learning rather than making recourse to professional 'experts'.

Providing an experience in leadership
Many of the leaders in SDI federations are women who first became active as managers of local savings groups and, in all federations, women have leadership roles. As one Ugandan member commented: 'This Shack Dwellers International is participation 90 per cent women. So it is a challenge to you women whether you want to take it up and make your position or whether you want to give it to your husband.'[2] Ensuring women can become leaders is not easily achieved and federation leaders and the local NGOs that support them seek ways to achieve this. In Kenya at present there are concerns about the dominance of men in leadership positions within the Homeless People's Federation and a number of interventions are planned to shift the space for decision-making towards one that favours greater participation of women.

Many federation women leaders had (and still have) to deal with opposition from their husbands. Moreover, they work within a culture where government agencies, civil servants, politicians and international agencies favour men and encourage behaviours that are more likely to be demonstrated by men. External agencies find it more convenient to work with individual leaders rather than the collective processes that women's savings groups entail. By grounding leadership within savings schemes and ensuring that community to community exchanges are the vector of learning, SDI processes seek to validate an alternative type of leader. Federation meetings frequently begin with members' introductions talking about their savings groups, their members and savings, and their activities. The constant reference back to local activities helps to ensure that leaders (whether male or female) are accountable to a strong women's membership base.

Providing opportunities to address women's disadvantages in SDI federations
Domestic violence is an issue that many savings schemes have to consider. For instance, the Zambian Federation had a particular emphasis on domestic violence because when it was emerging between 2005 and 2007, many men saw their partners' membership as a threat to their own position in the household. The federation developed an informal theatre presentation to show how husbands and wives could work together to address their development needs non-conflictually through the federation. This encouraged much more understanding among federation members and potential members about the need to address domestic violence. In Mumbai, Mahila Milan groups work with the police to set up community police stations in slums and they closed down many illegal drinking places given the commonly drawn link between domestic violence and alcohol abuse.

Women-dominated savings groups also take the lead in federation-led initiatives to acquire and develop land for housing, even if men are often keen to join once the construction phase begins. This includes undertaking the house-by-house enumerations that provide the information and maps that support upgrading (Weru, 2004). For new housing, it includes their engagement in the design and construction of housing, including planning the layout with architects and choice of building materials (see Boonyabancha,

2005). In designing community toilet blocks, it has included design modifications that address women's needs – for instance, separate toilets for women and men and separate queues (when there is only one queue, men often push in). In the development of neighbourhoods, women's safety is explicitly considered in design discussions.

Conclusions

The (re)construction of social relations, and hence activities, within the SDI federations are grounded in a gendered understanding of poverty. In all federations, there is a recognition that only if groups succeed in creating and supporting a local organising space for women will the programme and associated processes address the needs of women. To do this requires changing the culture of social relations, changing the way in which power is distributed within communities, city and national politics, and the way in which power functions, so that it is used to include and validate local members rather than to exclude and dominate.

The SDI methodology brings three particular aspects to its focus on addressing the gendered needs and interests of women: practical, political and empowerment

As far as material interests are concerned, the organising methodology seeks to define and protect a space in which women are comfortable and hence engaged. High levels of women's participation mean that many interventions focus on addressing women's gendered needs, such as secure tenure, housing and access to basic services such as water, sanitation, schools and healthcare. In part this responds to a recognition that shelter and basic services are a women's domain and not a priority for male-led development organisations.

To date, across 16 nations, the SDI federations have secured a total of 108 000 plots, 54 000 houses, services for thousands of additional plots, and over 600 communal washing and toilet blocks serving hundreds of thousands of people. Such achievements mean a lot at the local level, as reported by Mary, from Chilindi, Malawi:

> We came to town for a better life. But it is a troubled life. We are alone. We rent this broken house, without it we are homeless . . . We are prisoners of our poverty. There is no one to talk to, no one to share my troubles with, no one to discuss solutions with. [Then] I joined the Federation and learned to save and loan. The savings group women all know each other. We all help each other in our troubles. We sing and dance! In our group, we share ideas, so many ideas. We are rich with ideas.

In respect of political interests, within societies where men have always dominated leadership positions, the SDI methodology supports the emergence of women leaders through the organising space created by savings groups. As federations are made up of savings schemes, and as these schemes constantly legitimate and validate regional and national leaders, then women's leadership is encouraged and advanced.

Strong women leaders throughout the higher levels of the federations and the international network mean that women's interests are more likely to be identified and met than if there is a single high profile leader. The constant presence of a critical mass of women leaders increases the capacity of the federations to secure gains that are gender sensitive and the presence of women leaders encourages other women to aspire to this role. Collective activities can give individuals the capacity to talk to officials in ways that they could not have imagined previously. As articulated by Noluthando (Mbaliso, South Africa):

> We have started building 56 houses with a loan from uTshani. The federation has been very good for me. I am a happy member as I am respected by politicians, government and officials! I raise the voice of the poor proudly, because ultimately we built our houses through our own hard work and savings.

Last, but least, in terms of empowerment, the SDI methodologies produce a 'culture to aspire' which enables the poor 'to contest and alter the conditions of their own poverty' (Appadurai, 2004: 59). The space provided for women leaders also means a greater capacity to operate in dominant cultures, recognising, protecting and enhancing an alternative way of relating.

There is a deeply rooted belief in federation practices that successful poverty reduction will require a change in operational practices among external agencies towards those that favour the central participation of women. As the collective process engages with the external world, this becomes more difficult and the programme of community exchanges is designed to strengthen women's collective awareness and capacity to maintain their momentum. Local groups have to be strong enough to both challenge this external culture and operate within it, successfully securing benefits and political inclusion. At the same time, women know their future strength requires them to protect their autonomy, integrity and chosen direction. As summed up in the words of Ethelo (Chilindi, Malawi):

> The Federation changed my life. I joined a savings group . . . The group became my friends. We help each other, we share all our troubles. We look after each other's kids. When someone is sick, the group looks after them. I have a family and I have friends. I am happy.[3]

Acknowledgements
The authors would like to thank David Satterthwaite for his assistance in preparing this chapter.

Notes
1. It should be noted that one of us (Patel) is the Director of SPARC, as well as Chair of the Board of SDI.
2. All quotes from Federation members in this chapter are drawn from SDI (2007) (see below).
3. For further details of the work of the Federations see the SDI website at www.sdinet.co.za (accessed 25 June 2009).

Select bibliography
Appadurai, Arjun (2004) 'The capacity to aspire', in Vijayendra Rao and Michael Walton (eds), *Cultural and Public Action*, Stanford, CA: Stanford University Press, pp. 59–84.
Boonyabancha, Somsook (2005) 'Baan Mankong; going to scale with "slum" and squatter upgrading in Thailand', *Environment and Urbanisation*, **17** (1), 21–46.
Burra, Sundar, Sheela Patel and Tom Kerr (2003) 'Community-designed, built and managed toilet blocks in Indian cities', *Environment and Urbanisation*, **15** (2), 11–32.
Manda, Mtafu A. Zeleza (2007) 'Mchenga: urban poor housing fund in Malawi', *Environment and Urbanisation*, **19** (2), 337–59.
Patel, Sheela and Diana Mitlin (2004) 'Grassroots-driven development: the alliance of SPARC, the National Slum Dwellers Federation and Mahila Milan', in Diana Mitlin and David Satterthwaite (eds), *Empowering Squatter Citizen*, London: Earthscan, pp. 216–41.
Shack/Slum Dwellers International (SDI) (2007) *Voices from the Slums*, Cape Town: Shack/Slum Dwellers International.
Weru, Jane (2004) 'Community federations and city upgrading: the work of Pamoja Trust and Muungano in Kenya', *Environment and Urbanisation*, **16** (1), 47–62.

59 Gender, poverty and social capital: the case of Oaxaca City, Mexico
Katie Willis

Introduction: social capital and poverty alleviation
Since the mid-1990s, social capital has been increasingly identified as a tool in poverty-alleviation strategies in the Global South. While there are significant debates about what social capital is (see Bebbington, 2008, for a useful review in relation to development), definitions usually revolve around social ties, the nature of those relations and their use. For Moser (1998: 4) social capital can be defined as 'reciprocity within communities and between households based on trust deriving from social ties'. Social capital can therefore be seen as an asset held by individuals, households or communities to enable them to meet their needs, or to be mobilised as part of development interventions.

In this chapter I focus on social capital as an asset for individuals and households alongside other tangible assets (such as property) and intangible stocks (such as cultural capital). This focus on what households (particularly the poorest) have, rather than what they lack, has been consolidated into the Sustainable Livelihoods Approach (SLA) which has been adopted by international development organisations, most notably the United Kingdom (UK) Department for International Development (DFID).[1]

Despite the widespread adoption of the concept of social capital, gender, as Molyneux (2002) highlights, has often been ignored, or problematic gendered assumptions about social capital have been used in policy design and implementation. These assumptions include the essentialisation of women as good social networkers with well-developed contacts, particularly in the local 'community'. As such, women are viewed as potential channels through which community programmes can be mobilised or as sources of support when times are hard (see also Lind, Chapter 100, this volume; Miraftab, Chapter 99, this volume).

This chapter focuses on the role of social capital by women across the socio-economic spectrum in Oaxaca City, Mexico, with particular attention paid to the support women receive to meet the demands of their paid and unpaid work.[2] It draws out how and why social capital can be an asset for some women, but for others, social isolation means that they are often left to fend for themselves or to rely on the support of other household members. The diversity of women's experiences depends, among other things, on socio-economic status, household structure and employment. Finally, it is important to remember that social networks can bring their own benefits in terms of happiness and friendship which may not help alleviate economic-based poverty, but do contribute to wider concepts of well-being.

Women's social capital in Oaxaca City
Oaxaca City in southern Mexico, is capital of one of the poorest states in the country. In the early 1990s, when the fieldwork for this chapter was carried out, the city's economy

Table 59.1 Women's use of social networks by socio-economic status, Oaxaca City, Mexico

Socio-economic status	Childcare (%)[1]	Housework (%)	Job information (%)[2]	Money (%)	Total (%)[3]
Lower (N = 142)	68.7	4.2	11.5	10.2	76.9
Lower middle (N = 64)	83.3	10.9	24.0	23.1	64.1
Upper middle (N = 94)	75.6	0	22.6	6.0	50.0

Notes:
1. Percentage of women with children aged 12 and under who received help with childcare from social contacts outside household. Does not include paid assistance.
2. Percentage of women in waged work who found out about their current job from friend or relative.
3. This is the total percentage of women who use their social networks for childcare, housework, money and/or job information.

Source: Author's own data.

was dominated by government employment, tourism and services, the latter being predominantly identified as informal sector work. In 2009 this profile remains, but with tourism employment greatly affected by political unrest and global recession.

Of the 300 women interviewed in the household survey, the majority called on their friends and non-resident kin for support for childcare, assistance with domestic chores, financial help and/or job information. However, the use of women's social capital varied by socio-economic group (see Table 59.1). Over three-quarters of women in households of lower socio-economic status[3] used contacts outside the household, while the figures for households of lower-middle and upper-middle levels are lower, with only half the women in the highest status households using their social networks for at least one of the four identified purposes.

These figures could be interpreted in two main ways: first, that social capital assets are inversely proportional to socio-economic status, that is, that social networks decline as socio-economic status increases. There was no evidence of this; in fact, the general trend was for women in higher status groups to have more extensive networks of friends than those in lower socio-economic groups. The second possible interpretation is that women in lower-status households have greater need to call on these resources and social capital can therefore be seen as an important aspect in maintaining households, so supporting the concept of social capital as an asset to be mobilised in times of need or to reduce vulnerability (Moser, 1998). This interpretation will be discussed in the following sections, but other aspects of women's lives will also be examined, most notably household structure and employment.

Reproductive work
In all the surveyed households women were primarily responsible for domestic chores, with husbands, sons and other male household members usually contributing very little. While housework and childcare could sometimes be completed through the use of household labour alone, in many cases women drew on the assistance of others. For all

the women in upper-middle-status households, and a few belonging to the lower-middle-status group, some of that assistance came in the form of paid domestic help, but, as shown in Table 59.1, even among the richer households, kin and friends are key.

For female household heads, being able to maintain an upper-middle-status household without the presence of a male partner was often reliant on external childcare networks which supplemented paid domestic assistance. For Claudia, a state education worker who brought up four children on her own after her husband left her, household maintenance was only possible due to assistance from her family, despite having daily help.

> I took on another job to increase our income. I used to tutor secondary school pupils in the evenings, once I'd got back from the office and at the weekend . . . My family was also a great help, especially my mother. She would come and look after the children when the maid was not around, and would help do the dishes if necessary.

Thus for Claudia and for many other upper-middle-status female household heads, social capital assets were of great importance in ensuring that they did not fall into the stereotypical position of women-headed households living in poverty.

For lower-status women, regardless of household type, use of their social capital for housework and childcare was much lower than would be anticipated given their lack of paid domestic assistance. In many cases this reflected the already heavy burdens placed on female friends, neighbours and kin due to poor living conditions, including lack of water on the plot, the need to save money by shopping around or producing food and clothing in the home. This is similar to Moser's findings in four low-income urban districts of Lusaka, Guayaquil, Metro Manila and Budapest between 1978 and 1992, where forms of solidarity and support between households were often eroded due to economic crisis (Moser, 1998). In addition, some women were unwilling to ask for assistance as their own lack of resources prevented them from reciprocating (see also Chant, 2007: 102).

However, some women did not need to call on external assistance as they had been able to find income-generating activities which allowed them to combine waged work with domestic responsibilities. Alternatively, other household members, including children, were tasked with completing housework or caring for younger siblings. Taking advantage of limited income-generating opportunities, or children's withdrawal from school are likely to have longer-term effects on household poverty, even if these strategies enable households to cope in the short term.

In both lower- and lower-middle-status households there were cases where women refrained from calling on external contacts for support with reproductive work because they lacked appropriate networks. In some cases this was because they were migrants from rural Oaxaca whose main kin networks remained in their natal villages, while in others, household breakdown led to the loss of previous kinship relations and friendships. However, there were also a few cases of women whose husbands refused to let them leave the house without permission or alone, so they had not been able to develop or maintain contacts with neighbours who could have provided assistance.

Social capital as an asset to support women in their reproductive duties was therefore very unequally mobilised, reflecting socio-economic status, household type, migrant status and employment. What is clear is that some of the women most in need of such support were unable to receive it, either because of limited overall social capital, or because friends and relatives were in equally difficult circumstances.

Waged work

Of the 300 women interviewed in 1992, 139 were in waged work, a further 31 worked in family businesses and the remaining 130 were full-time housewives. Participation in waged work differed by socio-economic group, with just over 60 per cent of lower-status women in paid work compared with 53 per cent and 25 per cent of upper-middle and lower-middle-status women respectively. Socio-economic status is both a result and a cause of women's waged labour position. For example, in many lower-status households limited financial resources demanded greater income-generation from all household members, but the paltry amounts members could earn left the household in a poor economic state.

In relation to social capital and waged work the pattern is very different. Social capital as an asset has often been identified as useful in gaining information about employment opportunities, but in the Oaxaca case, women were much more likely to use their contacts for job information among the middle-status groups which had lower labour-force participation. This is a very clear example of how social capital acts in conjunction with other household assets, most notably human capital (skills and education). Most lower-middle and upper-middle-status women worked in formal sector jobs requiring high-level educational qualifications and experience. They were also jobs which were formally advertised or were recruited through recommendations from existing employees. Having contacts more widely dispersed throughout the city and already working in these formal sector jobs meant that women of middle socio-economic status were more likely to find employment through these routes. A similar pattern was described by Madrid and Lovell (2007) in their discussion of recruitment into the Colombian flower industry, where employers usually relied on recommendations from existing employees.

Among lower-status women, informal sector employment, particularly in domestic service or other cleaning jobs, was the norm. In these cases women usually responded to notices posted outside houses or businesses, rather than drawing on existing contacts. For their male counterparts, social capital was much more important in finding employment, especially in informal construction work where most men found waged work.

Not only did social capital affect the ability to find employment, but employment type also affected social capital, so leading in some cases to positive or negative cycles. Domestic service is often a lonely job where women work alone behind the closed doors of their employers' homes. This can lead to increasing feelings of isolation and few opportunities to develop other contacts and build-up social capital assets. For example, Josefina, a 51-year-old domestic servant said:

> I hate my work and would give it up right now if I could, but we're short of money and everybody has to contribute something . . . It's the same thing every day – mopping floors, washing up and washing clothes. Bloody children! [employer's children], they're always getting their clothes dirty and I have to wash them. Look at my hands! They've never been much to look at, but they are terrible now . . . I get so tired sometimes I want to just stay in my bed and never get up. It would be better if I had someone to talk to, but they all ignore me or shout at me.

For Josefina it is not just the hard work, but the loneliness and her treatment which affects her opinions of work. She was planning to give up as soon as her daughter was old enough to get a reasonably paid job.

In contrast, Paulina, a local government secretary aged 35 was very positive about both her work and the opportunities it gave her to make new friends:

> I have lots of friends at work. Everyone is very friendly and I have been happy working there. We always help each other and give each other advice. It makes work much more interesting and stops us getting bored. I play in a basketball team with some of the women from the office. We train two or three times a week and then play a match at the weekend. We're not very good, but at least it's a chance to do something different.

These two examples demonstrate how stocks of social capital can be expanded over time through new contacts and experiences, while in other cases women are left feeling isolated and unsupported.

Gender, social capital and neoliberalism
This chapter has drawn on the concept of social capital as a livelihood asset in the context of women's paid and unpaid work in Oaxaca City, Mexico. The findings clearly demonstrate that for some women, their kin, friendship and neighbourhood networks are vital in providing practical assistance, financial support and job information to help them maintain their households. However, the Oaxaca case also shows very starkly that the assumptions regarding women's inherent abilities to generate and support social networks are unfounded (see also Molyneux, 2002).

While some women's social capital allows them to escape poverty, in other cases, situations of low income, poor levels of education and sub-standard living conditions all combine to limit women's social capital. This highlights the importance of understanding how wider social, economic and political structures can frame and limit women's choices. A focus on individuals' and households' assets has been very useful in moving away from concentrating on what people lack. Within a neoliberal paradigm, however, the danger is that this focus can be viewed as part of a process of individualisation (Beck, 1992), whereby choice and autonomy are prioritised and success or failure is down to individuals, rather than being tied into wider systems of power relations.

Economic reorganisation and reductions in government spending in Oaxaca during the 1980s as part of Mexican national structural adjustment programmes had devastating effects on the vast majority of the city's population. While the economy had begun to improve when this research was conducted, Oaxaca's marginal status in the national economy, combined with massive economic and political inequalities in the city meant that most of the women interviewed were greatly constrained in their choices. Patriarchal norms both within households and in wider society also presented obstacles. Thus, even with high levels of social capital, women's autonomy was limited.

Finally, the role of social capital in providing emotional support should not be underestimated and could be an area of important policy and research attention in the future. Friendship and the support of relatives can bring great happiness. This is key not only because it is usually associated with better health and therefore ability to undertake paid and unpaid work, but also because it contributes to feelings of well-being. While poverty alleviation has focused on income and the provision of services, happiness should also be considered as a key dimension of development.

Acknowledgements

The data in this chapter were collected during fieldwork in Oaxaca in 1992 and 1993 and 1995. The 1992 fieldwork was funded by the Economic and Social Research Council (Award no.R00429124300) and the1993 fieldwork was funded by a Study and Action Fellowship from the International Federation of University Women.

Notes

1. See Livelihoods Connect website at www.eldis.org/go/livelihoods/ (accessed 14 October 2009). This provides information about the Sustainable Livelihoods Approach and the role of social capital within it. See also World Bank social capital website at www.worldbank.org/poverty/scapital (accessed 14 October 2009).
2. The empirical material draws from surveys undertaken in 1992 and 1993 in three *colonias* (neighbourhoods) of Oaxaca City: Colonia Aurora, La Noria and Colonia Reforma. In 1992 I conducted a questionnaire survey of 100 households in each district based on random sampling. The survey interviews were conducted with the female household head, or the wife of the male head. Semi-structured interviews were carried out with a sub-sample of 30 women. For further details of the methodology see Willis (2000).
3. The socio-economic status of households was determined by using information about household income, education levels, employment status, material possessions and housing quality. See Willis (2000) for more details.

Select bibliography

Bebbington, Anthony (2008) 'Social capital and development', in Vandana Desai and Robert Potter (eds), *The Companion to Development Studies*, 2nd edn, London: Hodder Arnold, pp. 132–6.
Beck, Ulrich (1992) *Risk Society: Towards a New Modernity*, London: Sage.
Chant, Sylvia (2007) *Gender, Generation and Poverty: Exploring the 'Feminisation of Poverty' in Africa, Asia and Latin America*, Cheltenham, UK and Northampton, MA, USA: Edward Elgar.
Madrid, Gilma and Terry Lovell (2007) 'Working with flowers in Colombia: the "lucky chance"?', *Women's Studies International Forum*, **30** (3), 217–27.
Molyneux, Maxine (2002) 'Gender and the silences of social capital: lessons from Latin America', *Development and Change*, **33** (2), 167–88.
Moser, Caroline (1998) 'The Asset Vulnerability Framework: reassessing Urban Poverty Reduction strategies', *World Development*, **26** (1), 1–19.
Willis, Katie (2000) '*No es fácil, pero es possible*: the maintenance of middle-class women-headed households in Mexico', *European Review of Latin American and Caribbean Studies*, **69** (2), 29–45.

60 Moving beyond gender and poverty to asset accumulation: evidence from low-income households in Guayaquil, Ecuador
Caroline Moser

Introduction
Feminist development debates have extensively examined the complexity of the gendered nature of poverty. Recent seminal contributions include the gendered impact of neoliberal reforms in which the 'male bias' in macroeconomic structural adjustment processes has forced women to increase their labour both within the market and the household (see Elson, 1991; Moser, 1993). Closely linked has been a second debate, first elaborated by Buvinic and Youssef (1978) that female-headed households are poorer than those headed by males. Since the 1990s this has been popularised as the 'feminisation of poverty' by UNICEF, the World Bank and various bilateral agencies (Jackson, 1998). Despite widespread evidence of the diversity among female-headed households and the fact that the 'feminisation of poverty' tends to victimise women, it remains a contentious debate – useful for donor support but not necessarily empirically accurate (Chant, 2008, and Chapter 15, this volume; Medeiros and Costa, Chapter 12, this volume).

Yet, to date, the lack of adequate data, as well as appropriate methodology, has meant that the gendered nature of asset ownership and accumulation has received far less attention. For instance, research surveys of the ownership of land, housing, livestock and other productive assets tend to collect data at the household rather than the individual level. This chapter seeks to redress this, by comparing the gendered nature of income poverty and asset accumulation, illustrated by data from a longitudinal study of an urban community in Ecuador. It focuses on two dimensions of gendered-asset accumulation; first, household headship, differentiating between male and female-headed units,[1] and second, intrahousehold gender-based ownership of capital assets such as human, productive and physical capital, which contributes to debates about gender empowerment from an asset perspective. In so doing it also contributes a gendered dimension to the widespread critique of consumption and income poverty measurements, and the rolling out of new policy approaches including sustainable livelihoods, social protection, and most recently asset-based approaches and their associated asset accumulation strategies (see Moser, 2007 [see the Acknowledgements at the end of this chapter]; also Deere, Chapter 53, this volume).

The 'Moser' methodology for researching assets
The dearth of data on the gendered nature of capital assets is not surprising, given the complexity of undertaking this type of research. Therefore it is important to describe my methodology in the text – rather than just assigning it to a footnote as is more usual. In examining the gendered nature of asset accumulation over a 26-year period between 1978 and 2004, in Indio Guayas, a low-income community on the periphery of the coastal

> **BOX 60.1 DEFINITION OF THE MOST IMPORTANT CAPITAL ASSETS**
>
> *Physical capital:* the stock of plant, equipment, infrastructure, and other productive resources owned by individuals, the business sector, or the country itself.
> *Financial capital:* the financial resources available to people (such as savings and supplies of credit).
> *Human capital:* investments in education, health, and the nutrition of individuals. Labour is linked to investments in human capital, health status determines people's capacity to work, and skills and education determine the returns from their labour.
> *Social capital:* an intangible asset, defined as the rules, norms, obligations, reciprocity, and trust embedded in social relations, social structures, and societies' institutional arrangements. It is embedded at the microinstitutional level (communities and households) as well as in the rules and regulations governing formalised institutions in the marketplace, political system, and civil society.
> *Natural capital:* the stock of environmentally provided assets such as soil, atmosphere, forests, minerals, water, and wetlands. In rural communities land is a critical productive asset for the poor
>
> *Source:* Moser (2007) [see Acknowledgements].

city of Guayaquil, Ecuador, my methodology combined quantitative and qualitative intrahousehold data, as well as a longitudinal perspective, rather than the more common static 'snapshot' studies undertaken at a single point in time. It uses González de la Rocha's (1994) distinction between expanding, consolidating and contracting households to capture the way in which household lifecourse stage changes occur along with the dynamics of the broader economic and political context of urbanisation. The research was based on anthropological participant observation based fieldwork living in the community, with a longitudinal sociological survey – a panel data set of 51 households that had been visited and interviewed with the same questionnaires in 1978, 1992, and 2004.

The data analysis included 'narrative econometrics', a cross-disciplinary 'qual-quant' methodology (Kanbur, 2002) that combines the econometric measurement of changes in asset accumulation, derived from the sociological panel data surveys, with in-depth anthropological narratives. Finally, the quantitative measurement of different assets required the construction an asset index relating to physical, social, financial and human capital, and their associated asset index categories, each of which contains a number of index components (see Box 60.1; Table 60.1).[2] The empirical panel data-set ultimately identified which assets could be quantitatively measured with composite asset indexes associated with each capital asset then constructed.

Household headship and asset accumulation
Both external factors as well as internal lifecourse issues determined levels of asset accumulation as measured by household headship, with opportunities and constraints

Table 60.1   Asset types by index categories and components

Capital type	Asset index categories	Index components
Physical	Housing	Roof material
		Walls material
		Floor material
		Lighting source
		Toilet type
	Consumer durables	Television (none, black and white, colour, or both)
		Radio
		Washing machine
		Bike
		Motorcycle
		VCR
		DVD player
		Record player
		Computer
Financial-productive	Employment security	State employee
		Private sector permanent worker
		Self-employed
		Contract or temporary worker
	Productive durables	Refrigerator
		Car
		Sewing machine
	Transfer-rental income	Remittances
		Rental income
Human	Education	Level of education:
		Illiterate
		Some primary school
		Completed primary school
		Secondary school or technical degree
		Some tertiary education
Social	Household	Jointly headed household
		Other households on plot
		'Hidden' female-headed households
	Community	Whether someone on the plot:
		Attends church
		Plays in sports groups
		Participates in community groups

Sources: Moser (2007); Moser and Felton (2009b) [see Acknowledgements].

contextualised within an urban community that changed over nearly 30 years from a physically insecure marginalised squatter settlement on a mangrove swamp to a recognised suburb of the city. Thus, in the early 1970s, when the first 'homeowners' acquired plots in the water, the population lacked land and all physical and social services. It was a young, homogeneous population, many just starting families. While men and women averaged 30 years of age, children averaged 7 years. Adults had little education and few assets other than the 'land' provided by the municipality. Almost all households were male-headed nuclear family units; of the 51 households in the panel data set only five were headed by women, of whom two were widows and the other three had never been in a stable relationship.

The 1992 data shows that this was the consolidation period in household lifecourses (see González de la Rocha, 1994), with one-quarter now headed by women due to death, desertion or separation. Important differences in household composition and characteristics had begun to occur. In particular female-headed households were smaller and had a lower dependency ratio than those headed by men. At the same time there were fewer workers within households. By 2004 the number of female heads had grown to one-third of all households and was likely to contain 'hidden' (or 'embedded') female-headed sub-units. These were unmarried female relatives raising their children within the household to share resources and responsibilities with others. In addition more than half the children of the original settlers, although now adults with their own families, still lived on the family plot, either independently or within the primary household.

Were female-headed households poorer in terms of income than male-headed households? In 1978 most households were below the poverty line, while the small number of female-headed households makes conclusions about headship difficult. The vast majority of households regardless of headship were still below the poverty line in 1992, reflecting the severe broader economic context. Female-headed households were slightly less likely to fall below the poverty line than male-headed households, but those that were poor tended to be very poor. This trend continued: by 2004, despite having lower dependency ratios, male-headed households were more likely to fall below the poverty line. While less than one-third of the male-headed households were not poor, more than half the female-headed households had successfully moved out of poverty. Although a few such households were headed by widows, the majority had separated, generally because their male partner had gone off with a younger woman.

While income poverty data is important, understanding household accumulation of assets complements this by providing a more accurate picture of well-being. It helps to identify why some households were more income-mobile than others, how some households successfully pulled themselves out of poverty when others failed, and which types of assets were particularly important for poverty reduction. Above all it showed that the accumulation of assets might ultimately be more important for household wellbeing than pure income measures.

Table 60.2 shows the amounts of different types of assets acquired by the households in the sample. Most households had significantly negative scores in 1978 (a positive or negative score does not mean anything in itself – it is simply relative to the average for the entire data-set). However between 1992 and 2004 most households had positive acquisition of every asset type except for community social capital, which declined.

At the same time there were similarities and significant differences between male- and female-headed households. Between 1992 and 2004 the impact of globalisation was reflected in a city flooded with cheap electrical and technological goods. Hence the rise in consumer durables as households sought to acquire symbols of modernity. Interestingly, in 2004 female-headed households had higher levels of consumer durables than male-headed households. With higher income levels and larger household size, especially more adult income-earning children that had chosen to remain within the fold of the extended

Table 60.2 Asset accumulation by headship in Indio Guayas, 1992–2004 (standard deviations above average)

Headship type	Capital assets					
	Housing	Consumer durables	Human capital	Financial capital	Community social capital	Household social capital
1992						
Male-headed	1.226	0.856	1.124	0.923	1.317	1.132
Female-headed	1.086	0.737	0.906	1.062	0.751	0.082
2004						
Male-headed	1.346	1.590	1.146	1.573	0.877	1.373
Female-headed	1.379	1.784	1.089	1.567	0.681	0.797

Note: See Box 60.1 for explanation of different capital assets.

Source: Moser and Felton (2009a) [see Acknowledgements].

family, there was more demand for consumer goods, especially entertainment and communications devices such as televisions and mobile phones.

The fact that female-headed households had lower levels of household social capital was in large part because male-headed households, with an adult couple or partners, counted positively as one of the index components. This obviously was weighted against women-headed households which by definition were in almost all cases headed by a single individual, and can be considered a limitation of the index. At the same time the fact that male-headed households had higher levels of community social capital reflected a number of different issues; in 1992 female participation in two components of community social capital, church but particularly community organisations, was higher among the spouses of male-headed households than women household heads who frequently were so overstretched managing both productive and reproductive tasks that they had no time for community-managing work (Moser, 1993). By 2004 when most physical and social infrastructure had been acquired and the community-based programmes withdrawn, participation in both activities had declined to levels below those of 1992. Higher levels for male-headed households in 2004 was a reflection of male participation in street-level football leagues, which itself was the outcome of an upgraded paved street, an important municipal improvement in the area.

Unpacking the financial capital variable helps understand why female-headed households tended to be more likely to be above the poverty line in 1992. Women were more likely to be unemployed than men were in every year surveyed. Yet female-headed households had more people employed in good jobs in private industry or the government. Men were much more likely to be self-employed or working with temporary job status. However, male-headed households did as well or better on the other aspects of financial capital, including taking in lodgers and remittance income sent from families abroad, as shown in Table 60.2. Although high dependency ratios were often associated with poverty, in female-headed households a high level of dependants also meant that households often adopted complex intrahousehold divisions of labour that released some adult females into the labour market while others undertook the cooking, childcare and other household chores. Finally, the data showed overall differences in the processes of asset accumulation. Male-headed households accumulated faster than female-headed households, who were slower to acquire most assets, even though male-headed households had less household social capital. In the long run, female-headed households were less likely to be income-poor than male-headed households but on balance still had slightly fewer assets.

Asset accumulation and changing intrahousehold gender roles
While headship is an important starting point for identifying the gendered nature of asset accumulation, assets in this case are aggregated at the household level. A second more detailed aspect within the household relates to the gendered breakdown around specific capital assets at the individual level. As the following description shows, this can give a more comprehensive picture of the gendering of assets.

Human capital, for instance, represents the most dramatic intergenerational changes in asset accumulation. While fathers in Indio Guayas in general were better educated than mothers (seven years of primary education versus five years), daughters were all better educated (seven years of secondary) than sons (five years of secondary). This counter-intuitive finding is reinforced by information on parents' school priorities in terms of the types of schools attended. Parents consistently invested more in the education of their daughters with larger numbers in private schooling than was the case with their sons (see also Sender, Chapter 25, this volume).

Linked to educational levels but also to labour market segmentation are employment-related issues of financial-productive capital. In 1978 only a small percentage of the male active labour force was absorbed into the stable wage sector, and competition between men and women existed in some informal sector activities. Where existing gender divisions of labour were rigid, such as in domestic service, 'women's work' remained protected, while in retail selling, where there was no gender segregation, men and women competed with one other. Employment security data, with its associated level of income stability, was one of the asset index categories. Intergenerational 2004 data shows that women consistently found more stable employment than their male partners and kin. This had significant implications for women's autonomy and control over resources since they were more often family breadwinners, and thus had more control over budget allocations for food and education. Additional data on the type of employer showed the dramatic increase in the numbers of women working in government employment, particularly in terms of intergenerational data, increasing from nil in 1978 for mothers to just over one in five of daughters in 2004. In contrast, few sons are employed in government service, with more than two-thirds engaged in a range of self-employed activities.

A third important area that has been widely cited as contributing to women's empowerment is land ownership (see Bird and Espey, Chapter 55, this volume; Rakodi, Chapter 54, this volume). In Indio Guayas the story of Ana and her daughters illustrates this well. The single mother of 11 children, her plot ownership and land title were linked to the stage of urbanisation when she came to Indio Guayas. The choice as to which of her many children got space to live on the plot, let alone inherit it, was influenced by a number of factors. These included getting on with in-laws, financial resources available to acquire a plot, the necessity of living nearby for assistance with childcare, and number and birth order of offspring. Daughter number three, Maria, for instance, was adamant that as a single mother herself she had rights; she refused to live with the mother-in-law as her ex-husband expected, wanting her independence in her own home. Thus she built her own house at the back of her mother's plot. In contrast, daughter number four, Clemencia, who lived in her in-laws' house had to stay in their house even after her husband became involved with another woman, because she lacked any title to the housing herself and could not return to her mother's overcrowded house.

Conclusion
The Indio Guayas study finding that overall female-headed households do better than male-headed households in terms of income poverty, but worse in terms of asset accumulation, contributes to the debate contesting the generalisation that female-headed households are poorer than male-headed households (see Chant, 2008; Davids and van Driel, Chapter 14, this volume; Safa, Chapter 17, this volume). My longitudinal study made it possible to disaggregate the accumulation of individual assets within households to the next generation. This showed that daughters were doing better than sons in terms of human capital, as well as in the job market, reflecting the lack of stable skilled work opportunities for young men in Guayaquil, despite their levels of education. At the same time access to housing presented the next generation with the greatest challenge, and one which particularly disadvantaged women.

The econometric data on both headship and on asset accumulation was underpinned by anthropological narrative that made it possible to provide causal interpretations around a range of issues. This highlighted the gendered complexity of household structure. For instance, by 2004 with their children grown up, female-headed households benefited more from sons and daughters who had chosen to remain in their mother's home and contribute to household income – thus reducing income poverty – than did male-headed households (see also Aboderin, Chapter 32, this volume). At the same time the increased consumerism of the modern generation assumed an important role in household decision-making around the allocation of resources spending more on consumer durables than was the case in male-headed households. These results point to the limitations of simple generalisations relating to female headship and poverty and to the importance of measurements of the accumulation of assets, particularly longitudinally, so that different lifecourse stages can be reflected.

Acknowledgements
This chapter draws substantially on my two most recent books: *Reducing Global Poverty: The Case for Asset Accumulation* (Washington, DC: Brookings Press, 2007), and *Ordinary Families, Extraordinary Lives: Intergenerational Asset Accumulation and Poverty Reduction in Indio Guayas, Guayaquil, Ecuador* (Washington, DC: Brookings Press, 2009), as well as on two co-authored articles with Andrew Felton: 'The gendered nature of asset accumulation in urban contexts: longitudinal results from Guayaquil, Ecuador', in Jo Beall, Basudeb Guha-Khasnobis and Ravi Kanbur (eds), *Beyond the Tipping Point: The Benefits and Challenges of Urbanisation* (Oxford: Oxford University Press) (Moser and Felton, 2009a), and 'The construction of an asset index: measuring asset accumulation in Ecuador', in Anthony Addison, David Hulme and Ravi Kanbur (eds), *Poverty Dynamics: A Cross-Disciplinary Perspective* (Oxford: Oxford University

Press) (Moser and Felton, 2009b). These more extensive publications provide more detailed information on the empirical data summarised here.

Notes
1. Male-headed households can also be called 'couple-' or 'joint-headed households'. However, this study follows local perceptions of headship in which any household with an adult male partner or husband identified the latter as household head. With one or two exceptions where women were the primary income-earners, in all female-headed household there was no normally co-resident male partner.
2. See Moser and Felton (2009b) [see Acknowledgements above] for an econometric description of the construction of an asset index and details on its different components.

Select bibliography

Buvinic, Mayra and Nadia Youssef (1978) *Women-Headed Households: The Ignored Factor in Development Planning*, Washington, DC: International Center for Research on Women.
Chant, Sylvia (2008) 'The "feminisation of poverty" and the "feminisation" of anti-poverty programmes: room for revision?', *Journal of Development Studies*, **44** (2), 165–97.
Elson, Diane (ed.) (1991) *Male Bias in the Development Process*, Manchester: Manchester University Press.
González de la Rocha, Mercedes (1994) *The Resources of Poverty: Women and Survival in a Mexican City*, Oxford: Blackwell.
Jackson, Cecile (1998) 'Rescuing gender from the poverty trap', in Cecile Jackson and Ruth Pearson (eds), *Feminist Visions of Development: Gender Analysis and Policy*, London: Routledge, pp. 39–64.
Kanbur, Ravi (ed.) (2002) *Qual-Quant: Qualitative and Quantitative Methods of Poverty Appraisal*, Delhi: Permanent Black.
Moser, Caroline (1993) *Gender Planning and Development: Theory, Practice and Training*, New York and London: Routledge.

61 Conceptual and practical issues for gender and social protection: lessons from Lesotho
Rachel Slater, Rebecca Holmes, Nicola Jones and Matšeliso Mphale

There is growing recognition that experiences of poverty and vulnerability are multidimensional and vary widely. Of the five poverty traps identified in the Chronic Poverty Report, four were non-income measures: insecurity, limited citizenship, spatial disadvantage, and social discrimination (CPRC, 2008). Experiences of poverty traps vary depending on gender, age, ethnicity, caste, religion and location, affecting not only the extent and type of poverty experienced, but also shaping the root causes of poverty. Recognising differential experiences of poverty and vulnerability is therefore vital for programmes supporting trajectories out of poverty.

In recent years, social protection has become an important strategy to address chronic poverty and reduce risk and vulnerability among poor households. To date, however, social protection has largely dealt with economic protection, namely, shocks and chronic poverty of an economic nature. Social risks, such as gender inequality, domestic violence and social discrimination at the community, household and intrahousehold level, have largely been absent from the broader social protection debate. In reality economic and social risks are deeply intertwined.

This chapter focuses on why greater attention to the gendered dynamics of both economic and social risks is critical for harnessing the potential of social protection to reduce gender inequalities and promote gender empowerment.

Conceptualising social protection
Conceptually, social protection can be defined as encompassing a subset of interventions for the poor, which seek to address risk, vulnerability and poverty. Social protection can be carried out formally by the state or the private sector but informal mechanisms such as remittances and faith-based institutional support continue to play an important role in supporting the poor (see also C. Brickell, Chapter 102, this volume).

The transformative social protection framework, developed by Devereux and Sabates-Wheeler (2004), introduces an important emphasis on addressing social equity and exclusion. This transformative view extends social protection from targeted income support to areas such as equity, empowerment and economic, social and cultural rights, and highlights the importance of anti-discrimination legislation, awareness-raising initiatives, skills training, provision of access to microcredit, among others.

Recognising the diversity of risks poor households face, Figure 61.1 uses a gender and lifecourse lens to unpack how economic and social risks can be reinforced or mediated at different levels through, for example, policy interventions, discriminatory practices embedded in institutions (for example, social exclusion and discrimination in the labour

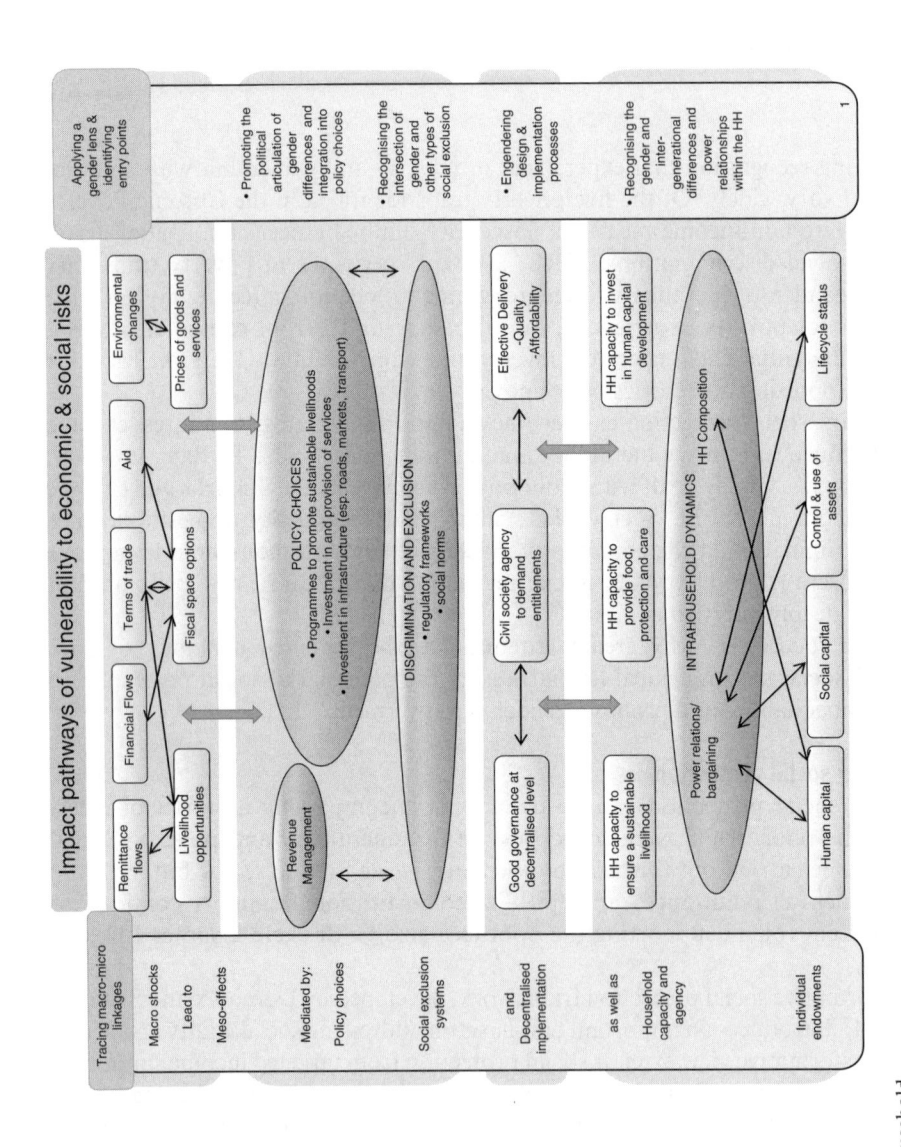

Note: HH = household.

Source: Holmes and Jones (2009).

Figure 61.1 Impact pathways of vulnerability to economic and social risk

market), and community, household and individual capacity and agency (Holmes and Jones, 2009).

Gendered economic risks
Because of the differential distribution of resources (financial, social, human and physical capital) between men and women, as well as differential social roles and responsibilities, the options available to them to respond to *macrolevel* shocks and stresses are likely to vary (Holmes and Jones, 2009). Women, for example, are often the first to lose jobs in the formal sector, such as in Korea during the financial crisis of 1997/1998 (World Bank, 2009). In other parts of East Asia, including Indonesia and the Philippines, however, women gained in overall employment due to their lower wages and lower levels of union organisation (ibid.). Cuts in funding for basic services are also likely to affect women more in many contexts because they typically have greater responsibility for household health and education access (Quisumbing et al., 2008).

At the *meso or community level* the impacts of economic shocks are mediated by, for example, gender segmented labour markets, and institutional discrimination (for example, absence of affirmative action to address historical discrimination of women and marginalised social groups) which leads to poor access and utilisation of services by women. Women have less access to credit, inputs (such as fertiliser), extension services and, therefore, improved technologies (World Bank et al., 2009).

How poor households are able to cope with shocks depends on a number of factors at the *micro and intrahousehold level*. The vulnerability of household members is likely to vary according to the composition of households (for example, dependency ratios, sex of the household head, number of boys and girls in the household), individual and household ownership and control of assets (land, labour, financial capital, livestock, time, and so on), access to labour markets, social networks and social capital and levels of education (see also Moser, Chapter 60, this volume). Women typically have lower levels of education, have less access, ownership and control of productive assets and different social networks to men, leading to lower economic productivity and income generation, and weaker bargaining positions in the household (see also Willis, Chapter 59, this volume). In times of crisis, underlying gender biases may mean that women's or female-headed households' assets are more vulnerable to stripping than those of men, the impact of which may be lengthy if what has been sold cannot be replaced.

Gendered social risks
Social sources of vulnerability are often as or more important barriers to sustainable livelihoods and general well-being than economic shocks and stresses (CPRC, 2008).

At a *macrolevel*, social exclusion and discrimination often inform and/or are perpetuated by formal policies, legislation and institutions (for example, low representation of women or minority groups in senior positions). In many countries, efforts to ensure that national laws and policies are consistent in terms of providing equal treatment and/or opportunities to citizens irrespective of gender, caste, race, ethnicity, religion, class, sexuality and disability are often weak or uneven (see for example, Coates, Chapter 8, this volume; Williams, Chapter 28, this volume). Moreover, although there have been considerable improvements over the last two decades in part due to international movements to address social exclusion, the enforcement of existing anti-discrimination policies and laws is often under-resourced, especially at the sub-national level. Changing entrenched social practices and values often requires a proactive approach (for example, affirmative action measures such as quotas for women for political office) with high-level political commitments and monitoring mechanisms needed to tackle informal practices and resistance.

At the *meso or community level*, absence of voice in community dialogues is a key source of vulnerability. For instance, women are often excluded from decision-making roles in community-level committees, and this gender-based exclusion is exacerbated by caste, class or religion too (see also Beall, Chapter 97, this volume; Madhok, Chapter 98, this volume). Indeed, some excluded groups are reluctant to access programmes or claim rights and entitlements fearing violence or abuse from more dominant community members. Another critical and related variable is social capital. Poverty may be compounded by a lack of access to social networks which provide access to employment opportunities but also support in times of crisis. It can also reinforce marginalisation from policy decision-making processes.

At *micro or intrahousehold level* the patterning of multiple potential sources of social vulnerability depends on household composition (nuclear versus extended; female versus male headed; high versus low dependency ratio), but broad trends can be identified. Social risk is related to limited intrahousehold decision-making and bargaining power based on age and/or gender, and time poverty as a result of unpaid productive work responsibilities (for example, labour in family businesses including agricultural production) and/or familial carework. This may also result in varying degrees of power over the production, sale and use of household assets. In much of sub-Saharan Africa women frequently have responsibility for food crops and petty livestock, but not decision-making power over the use of these assets or access to any profits derived (World Bank et al., 2009).

Time poverty is another important source of vulnerability. It can reinforce economic and social vulnerabilities by reducing time available for wider livelihood or coping strategies, and may contribute to women tolerating discriminatory and insecure employment conditions and/or abusive domestic relationships (see also Gammage, Chapter 9, this volume).

Finally, lifecourse status may also exacerbate intrahousehold social vulnerabilities. Girls are often relatively voiceless within the family, and a source of unpaid domestic/carework labour. The elderly (especially widows) face marginalisation as they come to be seen as non-productive and even a threat to scarce resources (see also Vera-Sanso, Chapter 33, this volume)).

Responses to intersecting economic and social risks
Vulnerabilities to economic and social risks are intertwined. Understanding this intersection is critical for social protection programme design as well as effective monitoring and evaluation processes (Holmes and Jones, 2009). To date, gendered social and economic risks have been addressed to varying degrees in a number of social protection programme initiatives, but often unevenly and informed by narrow understandings of gender relations (Holmes and Jones, 2009). Indeed, social assistance and public works programmes often target women, informed by arguments that the involvement of women in development leads to greater programme effectiveness and investment of additional income in family well-being. However, the role that gender relations play in social protection

effectiveness constitutes more than a narrow focus on women beneficiaries, shaping not only the type of risk that is tackled, but also influencing programme impacts at the community and household levels.

Social transfer programmes often seek to link economic and social empowerment. Conditional cash transfers (CCTs), for instance, have focused on improving household access to cash income, albeit while reinforcing a traditional view of women's caring roles within the household (see also Bali Swain, Chapter 91, this volume; Bradshaw and Linneker, Chapter 79, this volume). Other similar programmes have made participation contingent upon protecting women and girls from violence and abuse (for example, the cessation of domestic violence in Papua New Guinea). Health waivers and/or social health insurance have similarly sought to address social exclusion barriers that women face in accessing and utilising health services. Ghana's social health insurance system, for instance, recently introduced a premium waiver for all pregnant women.

However, a disjuncture remains in linking up the robust body of evidence on the gendered nature of poverty and vulnerability with programme design. In particular there has been a dearth of concerted effort to address gendered labour-market discrimination and limited focus on lifecourse vulnerabilities and limited attention beyond provisions for greater income generation opportunities to enhance women's position in the household (Holmes and Jones, 2009). Innovative mechanisms to support women's empowerment (improved access to reproductive health services and affordable childcare services) and to tackle social risks like gender-based violence, abuse, trafficking, and child marriage are rare (Holmes and Jones, 2009).

The following case study from Lesotho seeks to illustrate some of the design challenges involved in addressing both gendered economic and social risks. It goes beyond a narrow focus on targeting women and instead explores actual impacts of a cash transfer programme on men and women in the context of significant labour market restructuring and related social upheavals. The study explores a Lesotho emergency cash transfer case study (see Box 61.1). Too often policy debates on cash transfers are confined to concerns that 1) cash transfers may be captured by men and used for anti-social expenditures such as alcohol and cigarettes; and 2) that putting cash in the hands of women endangers rather than empowers women because it creates conflicts between men and women within households. Importantly the Lesotho pilot project provided an opportunity to generate more nuanced empirical evidence regarding cash transfers and gender impacts.

Interviews with cash, food and cash/food beneficiaries in the two districts where the project was piloted found that intrahousehold impacts of cash transfers are situated in a broader context where changing gender relations are closely tied to shifting employment opportunities resulting from the retrenchment of men from South Africa's mining industry and the emergence of new employment opportunities for women in Lesotho's textile industry. This suggests that, whatever the country, the impacts of cash transfers on gender will depend, in part, on the influence of wider structural changes in the economy that in turn affect household gender relations. The retrenchment of men from mining jobs results in gender conflicts in many households in Lesotho, particularly where women are the new breadwinners. In times of crisis, for example, when drought leads to food shortages and emergency programmes such as this pilot, existing gender conflicts are magnified.

There was strong evidence that cash transfers can relieve some of the pressure on

404 *The international handbook of gender and poverty*

> ### BOX 61.1 WORLD VISION CASH AND FOOD TRANSFERS PILOT PROJECT, LESOTHO
>
> World Visions Cash and Food Transfers Pilot Project aimed to address food insecurity initially in 6500 and subsequently in 9172 drought-affected households. The project operated between November 2007 and April 2008 in six constituencies in two districts of Lesotho – Maseru and Mohale's Hoek (see table below).
>
> In two constituencies, beneficiary households received a cash transfer to the value of M80 (approximately US$10) per household member. In a further two constituencies households received a food transfer based on the World Food Programme (WFP) ration (60 kg of cereal, 9 kg of pulses and 3 kg of vegetable oil for an average household of five members), while in the final two constituencies, households received a combination of cash and food. No work was required of any of the beneficiary households.
>
> The pilot project also had learning objectives, namely to strengthen World Vision's capacity to deliver cash transfer programmes effectively and to assess where they are appropriate.
>
> | District | Constituency | Beneficiary households | Per cent of programme | Type of transfer |
> |---|---|---|---|---|
> | Maseru | Matsieng | 2079 | 23 | Cash |
> | | Rothe | 1600 | 17 | Cash and food |
> | | Korokoro | 1172 | 13 | Food |
> | Mohale's Hoek | Mekaling | 1745 | 19 | Cash |
> | | Mpharane | 1076 | 12 | Cash and food |
> | | Taung | 1500 | 16 | Food |
> | | Totals | 9172 | 100 | |
>
> *Source:* Slater and Mphale (2008).

resources and, by extension, gender conflicts: when food shortages are reduced, intrahousehold conflict declines. The cash transfers had wider impacts on gender relations. For example, begging and abandonment, both sources of intrahousehold conflict, were both reduced in households receiving transfers.

Although men, and sometimes women, do use their cash income to purchase beer and other 'anti-social' items, there is no evidence that these anti-social expenditures are exacerbated in beneficiary households. The consumption of home-brewed beer is part of the social fabric of village life in Lesotho and many women earn income from its sale.

Evidence from the pilot shows that getting programme design and implementation right is critical if programmes are to result in positive effects on gender relations. In Lesotho, the evidence from interviews at household level suggests that benefits are shared among household members using a 'whole-wage system' where household income is distributed among household members by a woman. Slater and Mphale (2008: 15) argue that 'the equitable whole-wage system of managing cash transfer income that has emerged in Lesotho differs from systems for managing other sources of income (migrant labour income/remittances, pensions, public works, piece work)'. They suggest that the design and implementation of the pilot – in particular the ways in which community orientation/sensitisation meetings were used to explain the objectives of the project and the ways in which benefits are allocated to different households – were important drivers of this equitable system.

Conclusions and future directions
Though gender relations are context-specific, there is much to learn from the Lesotho pilot about the gendered impact pathways between macrolevel economic shocks and stresses and microlevel experiences of gender conflict which have important implications for social protection policy and programming. The Lesotho case highlights ways in which social protection programmes can be designed to support gender equality within households by identifying and addressing the potential sources of gender-based tensions and unequal power relations.

Other areas where social protection can build on supporting empowerment and equity-based poverty and vulnerability reduction include: programme design which facilitates a better balance between caregiving and productive work responsibilities; promoting men's involvement in carework; considering lifecourse vulnerabilities; and addressing the distinct and often unequal experiences of men and women in the labour market. Strengthening staff skills and participatory programme design are also important, for example, supporting gender-awareness and gender-analysis training for programme staff so they are better able to identify gender-specific risks and vulnerabilities and tackle them through programme interventions.

Finally, the effectiveness of any social protection programme depends not just on design and implementation issues, but also on the quality of governance and decentralisation, and on civil society agency in demanding social protection and actively pursuing the recognition and implementation of legal rights and entitlements.

Select bibliography
Chronic Poverty Research Centre (CPRC) (2008) *The Chronic Poverty Report 2008–09: Escaping Poverty Traps*, Manchester: CPRC.
Devereux, Stephen and Rachel Sabates-Wheeler (2004) *Transformative Social Protection*, Institute of Development Studies Working Paper 232, Brighton: University of Sussex.
Holmes, Rebecca and Nicola Jones (2009) *Putting the Social Back into Social Protection: Understanding the Linkages between Economic and Social Risks for Poverty Reduction*, background note, London: Overseas Development Institute.
Quisumbing, Agnes, Ruth Meinzen-Dick and Lucy Bassett (2008) *Helping Women Respond to the Global Food Price Crisis*, IFPRI Policy Brief 7, Washington, DC: International Food Research and Policy Institute.
Slater, Rachel and Matšeliso Mphale (2008) *Cash Transfers, Gender and Generational Relations: Evidence from a Pilot Project in Lesotho*, Report commissioned by World Vision International (WIV), Humanitarian Policy Group, London; Overseas Development Institute.
World Bank (2009) *Technical Briefing: Impact of Financial Crisis on Women and Families*, Poverty Reduction and Economic Management (PREM), Gender and Development, Washington, DC: World Bank.
World Bank, Food and Agriculture Organisation (FAO) and International Fund for Agricultural Development (IFAD) (2009) *Gender in Agriculture Sourcebook*, Washington, DC: World Bank.

PART VII

GENDER, POVERTY AND WORK

62 Gender, work and poverty in high-income countries
Diane Perrons

A defining feature of contemporary high-income neoliberal economies is the feminisation of employment in the context of widening economic inequality, enduring gender inequality and persistent child poverty. This chapter identifies some analytical links between these characteristics, focusing on connections between earnings inequalities, the undervaluation of 'women's' work and their over-representation among the working poor with related implications for child poverty.[1] As the efficacy of the neoliberal model is now in question with the financial crisis and recession, this is an appropriate moment to restate these long standing feminist concerns as societies reconsider their modus operandi.

All states are constrained in their freedom to manage their economies and finance social policy by wider economic considerations, albeit partially self-imposed. Until the end of the first decade of the twenty-first century these constraints were set by the supremacy of neoliberalism, characterised by economic deregulation, privatisation, and fiscal discipline. Nonetheless the processes underlying gender inequality and poverty materialise differently in different locations, especially when moderated by state policy, so while some of the theoretical tendencies are outlined in generic terms the detailed illustrations are more country specific. Empirical references are made to high-income (Organisation for Economic Co-operation and Development (OECD)) countries with a particular focus on the United Kingdom (UK).

Rising inequality, enduring gender inequality and child poverty
Society as a whole has never been more opulent. In the two decades prior to 2007 world income doubled and for an unprecedented number of people, *the economic problem*, defined by Keynes as the provisioning of basic survival needs including food, shelter and clothing has been resolved. Despite this unparalleled wealth, inequality (+2 Gini points) and poverty (+1.5 per cent points) have increased since the mid-1980s in the OECD. The patterns vary across social groups so while the incomes of older workers and pensioners increased, so too did child poverty and the proportion of working poor (OECD, 2008).

Earnings form the largest element of household income in these countries, so play a vital role in shaping overall income inequality and poverty. In recent years, the share of output accruing to labour, especially the low paid has fallen and inequality widened. For 11 OECD[2] countries, earnings dispersion increased by 11 per cent for women and 10 per cent for men between 1985 and 2005. For both women and men the increase was greater at the upper end of the distribution. Thus high-earning women and men now receive a greater share of overall earnings. When full-time workers are taken together the increase in inequality is less marked, owing to a decline in the gender wage gap.

With a small number of exceptions the size of the gender pay gap is wider at the top of the distribution, reflecting a change in the occupational composition of employment.

This widening is associated with increased global integration and expansion of the service sector characterised by a wider earnings distribution. At the upper end of the distribution women have moved into an expanding range of professional and managerial jobs but rarely reach the top; many stereotypically male jobs in the middle of the distribution have disappeared; and male pay in personal services and elementary occupations at the bottom of the distribution more closely approximates women's. The fall in the gender pay gap is therefore a consequence of widening inequalities by social class, which highlights the importance of examining how gender intersects other dimensions of social difference in order to accurately reflect the complexity of lived experiences. Nonetheless the gender pay gap (18 per cent for the OECD) endures and at the current rate of closure will do so for many decades.

States moderate the impact of earnings inequalities through tax and benefit policies in different ways but this cannot be relied upon. Surveys among OECD residents have found that while people are concerned about poverty and inequality, especially when it is shown to be excessive, somewhat contradictorily, they are resistant to redistributive policies (OECD, 2008). Moreover state moderation of incomes often takes place in relation to households which is problematic for two main reasons. First, it cannot be assumed that household income is shared equally and second, households are becoming less stable, thus well-being is likely to depend on individual earnings rather than household incomes. As redistribution cannot be guaranteed and as individuals cannot necessarily rely on the stability of their household setting, it is important to understand the ex ante processes leading to inequality and in-work poverty, while not negating the way that well-being is strongly influenced by differential ex-poste corrective policy. As the OECD (2008: 116) argue: 'relying on taxing more and spending more as a response to inequality can only be a temporary measure. The only sustainable way to reduce inequality is to stop the underlying widening of wages.' Understanding the processes generating inequality, and in particular low wages, is necessary to appreciate how people enter into and exit from poverty, that is, to grasp the dynamics of poverty rather than to focus only on the characteristics of those who are currently poor.

Child poverty, gender and the working poor
Children are generally at greater risk of income poverty than the population as a whole. Within the OECD countries 12 per cent of children were at risk of poverty[3] in the mid-2000s, which is similar to the European Union (EU) average. This is a static figure and reflects the proportion of children who are poor in a particular year. A more dynamic perspective recognises that children and their parents fall in and out of poverty and, if all those who were poor at some time over five years were counted, then for most countries the figure at least doubles (Mickelwright et al., 2001). There are wide variations between states, with higher rates found in countries closely following a neoliberal regime. With some exceptions children with a high risk of income poverty are those living with a sole parent without paid work.

One notable feature of discussions of child poverty is the gender neutrality of the language which serves to overlook the reality that lone parents are overwhelmingly mothers. Further, even when in paid work, they are over-represented among the low paid, that is, policymakers often fail to make connections between child poverty and the low or no pay received by their parents, especially their mothers. This is particularly important in the

European Union where employment is considered to be a key element in fighting poverty and promoting social inclusion, and yet paid employment does not eliminate the risk of poverty for everyone, especially women and low-qualified men (EC, 2006). Indeed a growing proportion of children in poverty now live in households with working parents.[4] In the UK, 44 per cent of these children live in working couple households and 8 per cent in households with a working 'lone parent' (Hirsch, 2009). Here, 25 per cent of women in work, work in low-paid jobs[5] (making up two-thirds of the total) many of which are part-time. This recognition begins to identify the dual determination of women's low pay: first, they are concentrated into a smaller range of comparatively low-paid occupations, where part-time work is available, and second, even when more widely distributed across occupations they occupy lower positions in the hierarchy. But this identification fails to explain why women are concentrated into a limited range of occupations and why these occupations are comparatively low paid.

Undervaluation of care and reproductive work
Damian Grimshaw and Jill Rubery (2007) identify five 'V's that help to account for the undervaluation of jobs done disproportionately by women: *visibility*, relating to the compression of a range of skills into a single group and the correspondingly limited opportunities for career progression; *valuation*, which refers to the low value accorded to the skills involved; *vocation*, the way that complex work is attributed to women's 'natural talents' rather than skills; *value added*, the comparatively low monetary value of the output; and finally, *variance*, which relates more specifically to the UK and the fact that women are over-represented in part-time employment which confines them to a narrower range of sectors and occupations (see also Chen, Chapter 71, this volume).

Relating these dimensions specifically to carework, by which I mean the tasks of social reproduction and include childcare, elder care and some aspects of nursing or teaching, helps to clarify the link between 'women's work' and low pay. With respect to *visibility*, while there are hierarchical career structures within carework, ranging from qualified teachers and nurses to classroom assistants with little formal training, the work itself, involves direct personal encounters and people's needs are often unpredictable and not easily differentiated by task or 'skill', at least not at the moment required. So in practice the work done often involves a range of tasks. As a formally qualified nursery manager referring to work of assistants, commented: 'they have an equal say in planning and in contact with the children, there is no difference in the work they do'.[6] Despite similarity in work done, pay differences vary by qualification. Even so, the highly qualified within these sectors, earn considerably less than equivalently qualified people working in more masculinised sectors, including finance. Their comparatively low pay is often attributed to *vocation*, the idea that they are using their natural talents rather than formal skills, such that they do not require commensurate monetary recompense.

Carework is also characterised by low *value added* in the sense that the output has a low market value owing, in part, to the economic properties of the work. There is very limited potential for productivity increases unless the character of the work is profoundly, and many would consider adversely, changed. Care is also a composite good (Folbre and Nelson, 2000), simultaneously consisting of guarding (protecting against harm), caring for identifiable bodily needs, and nurturing. It involves direct human encounters and so possesses an inherently affective dimension that not only makes carework difficult to measure but also means that the relative costs tend to rise over time. As these properties are rarely acknowledged in social policy, rising costs are often attributed to an assumed inefficiency of the public sector and, as a consequence, services have been increasingly privatised. The private producers often struggle to make a profit and many do so by restricting their services to an elite or subsidised clientele and by employing people with labour-market disadvantage on low wages.

By exploring the character of carework it is possible to account for some of the reasons for low pay, and, given women's over-representation, how this contributes to explaining one dimension of women's disproportionate presence among the working poor. What is less clear is why the social value of this form of work is not recognised and rewarded. Good quality carework creates positive social externalities or social gains in terms of happier, more educated and rounded social citizens irrespective of the gains to the individuals themselves. Recognising the social value of the work provides an economically rational argument for this sector and the workers employed to receive a larger share of social output. It might also be argued that the social value is far higher than that arising from the work of highly paid workers in investment banks, hedge funds and the like, who seem to have contributed to the current crisis in global finance. One stark illustration is that an executive from a failed UK bank was retained to advise on its restructuring at a monthly salary equivalent to three and a half times the annual salary of a childcare worker with 20 years' experience.[7]

With respect to social values, care and finance work both reflect market misrecognition or imperfection: finance is associated with negative social externalities and some very overpaid workers, while carework is associated with positive social externalities and underpaid workers. By drawing on theoretical understandings of different forms of work and their likely returns economists (including feminist economists) can provide a rationale for some of the inequality in earnings. Less well understood, though repeatedly found, are the processes driving the gendering of these activities. I turn very briefly to some ideas from gender theory to help explain the gendering of employment segregation, recognising that this is an area that requires more research.

There are no concrete walls or armed guards barring women's access to the labour market in the Western world (Epstein, 2006) and there is now greater gender balance as women's presence in the workplace has increased overall and in a widening range of occupations leading to greater symmetry between women's and men's lives. However, the convergence has been principally one-sided, with women being partially assimilated into the largely unmodified masculinised model of working to a greater extent than men have been assimilated into the feminised world of domestic reproduction and care.

What exists instead are 'cultural boundaries' (Epstein, 2006) or deeply embedded cultural practices and gendered social norms that uphold and reinforce existing practices and understandings of appropriate roles for women and men, the value of different activities, and understanding of the economy as a whole. These cultural boundaries or understandings of appropriate gendered behaviours are deeply rooted and have become naturalised through repeated practice, and proscribe, or at least limit, boundary crossings despite formally permissive equalities legislation.

These practices become cumulative as some social groups or identities are not considered suitable for certain positions and then become unsuitable by virtue of not having had the necessary practice, experience or social networks. The gender of people holding positions then become identified with those positions, such that leadership and authority 'stick'[8] to and become equated more with men who then shape the notion of leadership as male. Likewise, aptitudes for social carework, perceived to be 'physically but not intellectually challenging', 'dirty, gruelling and low paid', and so on, stick to women, who are believed to have the apposite 'natural predisposition' or 'personality type'. Thus particular economic or social attributes are inextricably identified with particular social beings. In this way occupations become gender stereotyped and, while the boundaries are permeable and divisions vary across cultures and over time, indeed such variations reflecting their social/cultural rather than natural construction, they nonetheless have a certain fixity that shapes expectations and creates difficulty for those who transgress by entering gender incongruent occupations. Similarly reward structures reflect social understandings of what is deserving or undeserving, ideas about what is skilful, economically crucial and worthy of financial recompense, and these notions are gendered yet become sedimented in the social imagination as natural and difficult to challenge.

Conclusion: towards an inclusive regime
Following 30 years of the myth of the ideal and irresistible market economy the present represents an opportunity for challenging market rationality. Such challenges have always been made, but the current context perhaps represents a tipping point, where such challenges might receive a more a more receptive hearing among policymakers. The existing high levels of inequality cannot be sustained economically and, in fact, form one element of the current financial crisis. With this in mind, I documented the extent of rising earnings and enduring gender inequalities in OECD countries. I highlighted how the asymmetric convergence of gender roles, together with continuing gender segregation and uneven gendered monetary returns within paid work, contributes to enduring disadvantages to women in the workplace and in their lifetime earnings. This disadvantage, in turn, helps to explain women's over-representation among the working poor and the higher rate of income poverty among children living in households with absentee fathers. I also considered the productive character of reproductive work, how this is currently misrecognised within market economies and so provided a rationale for widening understandings of 'the economy' to recognise the value of paid caring work, and unpaid reproductive work within households.

In thinking more broadly about alternative models of economic and social regulation there has been renewed interest in Keynesian ideas. Yet there are problems with the application of these ideas in the contemporary context and from a feminist perspective. Modifying Keynesian policies to take account of the increasing openness of economies with globalisation and widening the understanding of the economy to include the productive value of care and reproductive work perhaps represents one way of moving towards a more inclusive and sustainable society with lower overall inequality, greater gender equity and lower poverty.

Notes
1. While not denying the multidimensional character of poverty, this chapter focuses on income poverty. Research suggests that increases in incomes impact positively on the quality of life. For a review of poverty in the European Union see EC (2006).
2. OECD 11 refers to Canada, Finland, France, Germany, Japan, the Netherlands, New Zealand Sweden, the USA, the UK and Korea.

3. The OECD's (2008) definition is the share of all children living in households with an equivalised income of less than 50 per cent of the median. This is a weak measure – the poverty line is frequently drawn at 60 per cent. See www.oecd.org/els/social/family/database (OECD Family Database) (accessed February 2009)
4. UK poverty is defined at 60 per cent of the median equivalised household disposable income.
5. Defined as 60 per cent of the full time median hourly wage for all employees.
6. For empirical and theoretical elaboration of carework see related publications on the author's website: http://www.lse.ac.uk/collections/genderInstitute/whosWho/profiles/dianeperrons.htm
7. Source: own calculation from press reports of salary and ASHE (the national earnings database for the UK) data with respect to childcare earnings.
8. A term used by Sara Ahmed.

Select bibliography

European Commission (EC) (2006) *Gender Inequalities in the Risks of Poverty and Social Exclusion for Disadvantaged Groups in Thirty European Countries*, Brussels: EC, available at: http://ec.europa.eu/employment_social/publications/2006/ke7606201_en.pdf (accessed February 2009).

Epstein, Cynthia (2006) 'Border crossings: the constraints of time norms in transgressions of gender and professional roles', in Cynthia Epstein and Arne Kalleberg (eds), *Fighting for Time*, New York: Russell Sage Foundation, pp. 317–40.

Folbre, Nancy and Julie Nelson (2000) 'For love or money – or both?', *Journal of Economic Perspectives*, **14** (4), 123–40.

Grimshaw, Damian and Jill Rubery (2007) *Undervaluing Women's Work*, EOC Working Paper No. 53, Manchester: Equal Opportunities Commission.

Hirsch, Donald (2009) *Ending Child Poverty in a Changing Economy*, York: Joseph Rowntree Foundation, available at: http://www.jrf.org.uk/publications/ending-child-poverty-changing-economy (accessed February 2009).

Mickelwright, John, Bruce Bradbury and Stephen Jenkins (2001) *The Dynamics of Child Poverty in Industrialised Countries*, Cambridge: Cambridge University Press.

Organisation for Economic Co-operation and Development (OECD) (2008) *Growing Unequal. Income Distribution and Poverty in OECD Countries*, Paris: OECD.

63 The extent and origin of the gender pay gap in Europe
Janneke Plantenga and Eva Fransen

Over the past decades, women's employment rates have increased quite dramatically. Women have taken up most of the new jobs created in the European Union (EU) and have demonstrated an increasing commitment to the labour market, particularly over the core child-rearing years. Several factors have contributed to this development. First, women have become better educated; looking at young age categories, the gap in educational attainment is now even favouring women. In addition, women's labour market attachment has been facilitated by a growing service sector, an increased availability of part-time jobs and the possibility to outsource some traditional household activities. In short, women have been increasingly well-positioned for successful labour force participation because of developments on the supply and demand sides.

However, these developments have not yet led to full economic equality between men and women. The concentration of female employment in specific sectors has not changed and women throughout Europe remain significantly less well paid than men. This chapter provides an overview on the extent of the gender pay gap, the origins and the policy responses. The first part deals with the facts and present data on wage inequality in the EU member states. The second part is more theoretical and concentrates on the factors underpinning the gender pay gap. The final section deals with policy implications.

The extent of the gender pay gap

The gender pay gap refers to the difference between the wages earned by women and by men. In order to take into account differences in working hours and the impact of the income tax system, most estimates are based on differences in gross hourly wages. The gender pay gap is then calculated as the ratio of women's average gross hourly wage to men's average gross hourly wage, or as the difference between men's and women's gross hourly wage as a percentage of men's average gross hourly wage. In the latter case the gender pay gap indicates how many percentage points the earnings of men have to decrease in order to be equal to those of women. Another method is to use the earnings of women as the reference point. Here the gender pay gap indicates how many percentage points the earnings of women have to increase in order to be equal to those of men. From a policy point of view this definition seems to be more correct. Yet, as most research takes the earnings of men as point of reference, the gender pay gap in this chapter is also calculated as the difference between men's and women's average gross hourly wage as a percentage of men's average gross hourly wage.

Quite apart from differences in definition, estimations of the gender pay gap differ widely and depend for a great deal on the data that are available, the definitions that are used, the specific sample that is taken, and so on. However, there are a few

Table 63.1 Gender pay gaps in selected European countries

	Gender pay gap (per cent)	
	2002	2006
Romania	16.1	6.5
Poland	7.4	7.2
Slovenia	6.5	7.5
Bulgaria	17.8	10.8
Latvia	n.a.	13.4
Hungary	n.a.	14.6
Sweden	n.a.	16.4
Lithuania	13.7	16.7
Ireland	14.5	17.6
Denmark	n.a.	17.6
Finland	n.a.	21.2
Cyprus	22.9	22.2
Netherlands	18.7	23.1
Czech Republic	21.0	23.1
United Kingdom	27.2	24.0
Slovakia	27.7	25.2
Estonia	n.a.	28.2
Average	17.6	17.4

Source: EC (2006).

regularities in cross-country estimations of gender pay gaps. For one, the gender pay gap widens with age. The gap among new entrants in the labour market is much smaller than the gap among those aged 55 years or more. Secondly, the gap is smaller in the public sector than in the private sector. This is perhaps due to the fact that public employers are more concerned with equal opportunities policies than private employers, or to the fact that the public sectors employs a larger share of professional female workers. Moreover, the public sectors might have a more compressed wage structure compared to the labour market as a whole (see also Chen, Chapter 71, this volume).

The Structure of Earnings Survey has collected harmonised pay data of several European countries for the years 2002 and 2006. The statistics cover all economic activities defined in sections C to K and M to O of the general industrial classification of economic activities within the European Communities in enterprises with at least ten employees.[1] Although only the metadata are currently available and these do not allow for a detailed analysis of the gender pay gap across different sectors and subgroups, it is possible to draw a reliable comparison of the unadjusted gender pay gap across countries, as shown in Table 63.1.

Table 63.1 demonstrates that women in Europe currently earn approximately 17 per cent less per hour than men. There is great variation across European countries. In 2006, the largest pay gap is found in Estonia, the smallest in Romania. In general, the new member states of the EU show a somewhat smaller gender pay gap than the former member states, but the differences are not very large.

Table 63.1 also provides some information on developments over time; it appears there is no clear trend towards closing the gender pay gap in Europe. While the gender pay gap declined in six countries, it increased in five. This differentiated pattern is in line with findings based on other data sources and/or different periods such as those of Plantenga and Remery (2006) for the period 1994–2004 and of Rubery et al., (2002) for the period 1994–98. Both these studies also found no evidence of a narrowing pay gap. However, when looking over a longer period of time, the data do show the pay gap decreases. The greatest decrease actually took place in the 1980s, with various data sources indicating that this decrease seemed to stagnate in the 1990s.

In line with the observation that women on average earn lower wages than men, women are much more likely to receive low pay than men – low pay being defined as earnings below two-thirds of the median gross hourly wage. In 2001, the incidence of women earning low pay in the 15 original member states of the EU was twice as high as for men. Countries that have a relatively large incidence of women earning low pay are: Germany (29.6 per cent of all working women); the United Kingdom (UK) (26.6 per cent) and the Netherlands (21 per cent) (Van Klaveren et al., 2007). Low-paid workers face a high risk of becoming working poor. Data for the UK have shown that the overlap between receiving low pay and being poor is now much higher than in the 1970s and 1980s (Millar and Gardiner, 2004). Low pay is an important reason why many women are still not economically independent.

Like the gender wage gap, the problem of low pay is persistent. European Union figures make clear that 60 per cent of those that were working poor in the course of the 1990s were still in that situation three years later or had even fallen into the category of 'inactive poor' (Van Klaveren et al., 2007).

Explaining the gender pay gap
The gender pay gap is determined by several factors. Traditionally, differences in pay are explained by differences in individual characteristics. Especially within the context of human capital theory, the gender pay gap is analysed in terms of gender differences in productivity-related qualifications such as age, education, training and experience. Given the gendered division of labour, women are considered less likely to invest in market-oriented formal education because they expect a shorter and more discontinuous working life; an investment in education will therefore not pay off well in the future. More limited experience and less investment in education will reduce productivity and will be reflected in lower wages.

Evidence suggests, however, that human capital differences play a decreasing role in the persistence of the gender pay gap. Although in some countries gender differences in work experience still play a role, the improved educational situation and increased female participation rates have strongly diminished gender-specific differences in individual characteristics. As such, the gender pay gap today seems more related to the level of occupational segregation and the wage structure. Women tend to work in different occupations and industries than men and are penalised for that, because the sectors and occupations that employ mainly women tend to pay lower wages than typical male sectors and occupations (see Perrons, Chapter 62, this volume).

The extent of the wage penalty related to working in a female-dominated sector or occupation may differ by country, though, depending on the wage structure. The wage structure can be regarded as the prices attached to skills and the rents accrued to those working in favoured sectors. All else being equal, a more compressed wage structure is likely to result in a smaller gender pay gap. The logic behind this is quite straightforward. Since women, on average, tend to have less labour market experience than men and work in different occupations, the gender pay gap will be relatively wide if the return to experience is relatively large and/or if occupational wage differences are relatively large. As articulated by Blau and Kahn (2000: 81):

> If, as the human capital model suggests, women have less experience than men, on average, the higher the return to experience received by workers regardless of sex, the larger will be the gender gap in pay. Similarly, if women tend to work in different occupations and industries than men, perhaps due to discrimination or other factors, the higher the premium received by workers, both male and female, for working in the male sector, the larger will be the gender pay gap.

A country's wage structure may be affected by the structure of labour supply and demand, technological change (strongly growing innovative firms might pay higher wages for highly skilled workers) and by its wage-setting institutions. Centralised systems of wage-setting, for example, tend to reduce inter-firm and inter-industry wage variation, thereby potentially lowering the gender pay gap. In addition, because in most (if not in all) countries the female wage distribution lies below the male distribution, centralised systems that raise the minimum pay levels, regardless of gender, may also have a positive impact on the gender pay gap. Studies that have decomposed the gender pay gap into gender-specific factors on the one hand, and the country's wage structure on the other, have consistently found a growing importance of the wage structure (see, for example, Blau and Kahn, 2000; Rubery et al., 2002).

In line with the growing emphasis on the importance of wage-setting institutions, Rubery et al., (2002) argue that the increasing interest in gender pay equality in the EU needs to be translated into an active debate on the gender effect of pay policies. The importance of this gender mainstreaming approach is that it shifts the focus from female deficits or deficiencies to discrimination within policies and practices as embedded in institutional arrangements, social norms, market system and pay policies. Wage structures, according to Rubery et al., (2002: 4), are not simply based on the productivity of workers:

> The reality is much more messy and reflects current and historical influences. Social norms on the one hand and managerial strategies on the other interact with market processes to shape payment systems. This messy reality allows considerable scope for changing pay structures and practices in both public and private sectors.

The role of social norms and collective wage-setting institutions in generating pay discrimination against women also constitutes the core of the argument in feminist literature pointing to the social undervaluation of women's work as a distinct factor explaining the gender pay gap. According to this argument, the gender pay gap cannot only be explained by gender differences in average human capital characteristics, occupational segregation, and direct discrimination by employers, but also by the undervaluation of women's work in female-dominated occupations and industries (Karamessini and Ioakimoglou, 2007).

Policy implications

The persistence of the gender pay gap and the complex factors explaining the wage differential have initiated a range of policy measures. In principle policy responses can be organised along three lines:

1. *Equal pay policy* aiming at tackling direct or indirect gender wage discrimination.
2. *Equal opportunities policy* aiming at encouraging women to have continuous employment patterns, and de-segregating employment by gender.
3. *Wage policies* aiming at reducing wage inequality and improving the remuneration of low paid and/or female-dominated jobs.

The expected positive effect of equal pay legislation on the gender pay gap is reasonably straightforward, although the impact will presumably depend on the effectiveness of the enforcement of the legislation. Some countries, for example, have introduced equal pay legislation which imposes the obligation to justify pay differentials on the employer. Most countries, however, are rather reluctant to interfere in the wage-setting mechanism which is seen as the primary responsibility of social partners. The emphasis on deregulation and voluntary action by employers of course limits the support of an effective equal pay strategy.

Another important subset of policy refers to equal opportunities. Given that an uninterrupted career is still a significant factor in explaining the overall gender pay gap, it is extremely important to enable women to have more continuous employment patterns. Policies targeted towards increasing childcare facilities are therefore important. Another element of equal opportunities policy would be to encourage young girls to consider a wider range of occupational options, and to opt for science and technology, instead of caring, cleaning and catering.

Finally, wage policies should be mentioned as an important policy lever to address the issue of equal pay. Wage policies in this respect may vary from the introduction of a mandatory minimum wage, thereby setting a floor to the wage structure, the centralisation of the system of wage-bargaining, thereby decreasing inter-industry and inter-firm wage differentials, and the revaluing of low paid and/or female-dominated jobs, for example as part of an equality or anti-poverty strategy.

Note

1. To view the complete statistical classification of economic activities (NACE Revision 1.1), please consult http://ec.europa.eu/competition/mergers/cases/index/nace_all.html (accessed 14 october 2009).

Select bibliography

Blau, Francine and Lawrence Kahn (2000) 'Gender differences in pay', *Journal of Economic Perspectives*, **14** (4), 75–99.
European Commission (EC) (2006) *Structure of Earnings Survey 2002/2006*, Luxembourg: EC.
Karamessini, Maria and Elias Ioakimoglou (2007) 'Wage determination and the gender pay gap: a feminist political economy analysis and decomposition', *Feminist Economics*, **13** (1), 31–66.
Millar, Jane and Karen Gardiner (2004) *Low Pay, Household Resources and Poverty*, York: Joseph Rowntree Foundation.

Plantenga, Janneke and Chantal Remery (2006) *The Gender Pay Gap. Origins and Policy Responses. A Comparative Review of Thirty European Countries*, Luxembourg: European Commission.
Rubery, Jill, Damian Grimshaw and Hugo Figueiredo (2002) *The Gender Pay Gap and Gender Mainstreaming Pay Policy in EU Member States*, Manchester: European Work and Employment Research Centre.
Van Klaveren, Maarten, Kea Tijdens and Nuria Ramos Martin (2007) *WIBAR Report No 2: Low Pay*, Amsterdam: Wageindicator Foundation.

64 Women's work, nimble fingers and women's mobility in the global economy
Ruth Pearson

Introduction

Since the 1970s there has been a rapid growth in women's female economic activity all over the world, as women have increasingly entered the paid labour force, seeking to earn income to support themselves and their families. Despite the prevalence of the 'male breadwinner myth' (see Safa, Chapter 17, this volume), globalisation has been in many ways a story of the feminisation of labour. As in previous decades it is important to recognise that women's labour is particularly in demand for certain kinds of work – often work that involves repetitive movements, attention to detail, implies standing still for long periods or time, and utilises manual dexterity – the so called 'nimble fingers' argument (Elson and Pearson, 1981). But the nature and pace of the feminisation of the labour force has been uneven between sectors, countries and regions, and is constantly changing.

There are also new features of the global economy that are necessary to take into account in order to analyse effectively the ways in which women are part of its contemporary phase. First, the way in which global production is organised has changed considerably over the past decades. Rather than transnational corporations (TNCs) investing in cheap-labour countries to capture the advantage of employing low-paid women in order to reduce the costs of goods produced to compete in markets of the Global North, increasingly such supply chains are organised at arm's length through serial subcontracting, creating challenges, especially for those committed to improve the wages and working conditions in such 'world factories'.

Second, the long-held distinction between 'good jobs' – predominantly for men and for educated minorities – and the other and less desirable ways of earning a living in the informal sector has been progressively dismantled, both in theory and in practice. The feminisation of waged labour has been paralleled by the explosion of myriad different ways of organising production of goods and services, in factories, in offices, in small workshops and in people's homes. At the same time, and in spite of the best efforts of agencies such as the International Labour Organisation (ILO), the regulation of employment to protect workers and their rights has been progressively diminished, not least because of prevailing consensus in the 1980s and 1990s that the state was an impediment to global competition, and thus to economic growth and development. However, the precarious nature of much of this employment makes it even more difficult for women workers to organise to protect their jobs and improve their working conditions.

Third, in spite of extensive regulatory frameworks to prevent it, labour has become increasingly mobile in the last decades of global change. This has meant not only that supply chains employing women workers stretch to increasingly dispersed and distant locations, but that women themselves are moving specifically to seek employment as new opportunities arise. For many women the necessity to leave home and travel to another location within or outside their countries constitutes an additional factor contributing to their insecurity and stress.

Finally, the current global financial crisis is likely to impact directly on women's work in a range of export sectors in low-income economies. On top of this, the squeeze on government revenues will threaten already inadequate services such as healthcare, education, housing construction and other essential services which women need in order to juggle their dual responsibilities for paid work and unpaid carework. Echoing the cuts made during the dark days of structural adjustment programmes (SAPs) in the 1980s, the further withdrawal of the state from public provisioning will throw working women back on their own or their family's resources, or on other institutions such as religious organisations and political parties.

Feminisation in the global economy
Since the middle of the twentieth century women workers have played an increasing important role in the global economy. This is particularly visible in the supply chains which export goods and services to Western economies. Many have dubbed this trend of rapid expansion in the number of women working in horticulture, electronics, garments, textiles and footwear to supply the consumer markets of the world as 'global feminisation' (Standing, 1999). There has also been a parallel growth in employment for women in Information and Communications Technology (ICT). Historically this involved data entry work which involved women's fingers converting information to machine-readable form (Freeman, 2000). More recently women have been engaged in call centres which supply customer and technical services worldwide.

Expansion in these sectors has not been even, however, and women's work is far from assured. In the manufacturing of clothes for export, for example, when Mexico and the original 'Asian tigers' became too expensive, sourcing garments moved to lower-wage Central America, such as Nicaragua and El Salvador, and to second-tier newly industrialising countries (NICs) such as Thailand, Vietnam, Bangladesh, and Cambodia. There has also been expansion in North Africa, particularly Morocco and Tunisia, as well as in East European countries, and in recent years the growth in employment and supply from China, and to a lesser extent India, has been exponential.

Notwithstanding frequent geographical shifts in sourcing, women remain the majority of the workforce (between 70 and 90 per cent) in the export-manufacturing of garments. Yet in some sectors, such as electronics, there has been a steady masculinisation of the labour force, often linked with new technology, new product development and the automation of production. Where electronics and other male-employing sectors have replaced the female-intensive garments sector, as in some locations in northern Mexico, women have become disposable and devalued, and in some cases endangered, given that they are not the employees of choice in more technologically sophisticated and capital-intensive sectors (Wright, 2006).

Debates about 'feminisation of labour' are not just about the gender of workers, but about the conditions under which they are employed (Heintz, Chapter 66, this volume). Labour markets have historically been conceptualised on the basis of the regulated markets of advanced economies, hence the heroic efforts of the ILO in setting out Core Labour Standards, which governments are encouraged to honour, in spite of progressive deregulation in recent decades which has led to the erosion of labour rights and entitlements. But the 'emerging' labour markets of the Global South were forged under different circumstances, in which the (male) labour aristocracy was never a norm. Formal (regulated) employment accounts for less than one-third of total non-agricultural employment, and this proportion is falling (see Chen, Chapter 71, this volume). So labour markets are also gendered as the result of supply-side policies have supported deregulation and flexibilisation, characteristics of a female labour force in which it is the workers, rather than capital, who are required to exercise flexibility.

Informalisation
The issue of the informal economy and informalisation cross-cuts any discussion of industrialisation and feminisation in the global economy. Much of the early excitement from scholars such as myself and others about women's participation in what we then called 'world market factories' was generated by the fact that for the first time in history women's contribution to manufactured outputs would be recognised because national governments would (and did eventually) recognise the contribution of women's work to export-led development strategies (Pearson, 1998).

Yet, however welcomed by women who continue to seek employment in factories, fields and other workplaces, jobs for women in new export sectors never approached the secure, regulated and protected employment conditions increasingly confined to the 'labour aristocracy' in developing countries. For many, deregulation and flexibilisation have become synonymous with informalisation, mirroring debates about post-Fordism and core and peripheral labour markets. Women have increased their participation in the labour market in response to the greater demand for cash to meet household survival needs because of a number of factors including structural adjustment programmes, the liberalisation of previously centrally planned economies and/or because of the changing nature of global consumption patterns (Standing, 1999). While women have appreciated the rewards from paid work in the global economy, they have had little success in negotiating an equitable 'reproductive bargain'. This is a term I have used to conceptualise the struggle over how much of the resource cost of daily and generational reproduction has to be met by the individual (through the wage) and how much by the state (through non-wage benefits, entitlements and service provision) (Pearson, 1997).

However the nature of global supply chains has changed: rather than working for subsidiaries of TNCs in so-called Export Processing Zones (EPZs), women workers are increasingly to be found working in nationally owned factories, or in informal workshops as the result of outsourcing and subcontracting. This has had several implications. First, there are many women whose contribution to export production is invisible if not hidden. While the classic image of the female industrial worker is of serried ranks of young women at sewing machines, or on electronic assembly lines, the less dramatic but no less frequent reality is the millions of women in small workshops, in what are called 'house-factories', and/or who are engaged in piece-rate production in or near their own homes . And subcontracting does not just apply to the producers or factories; increasingly the recruitment and employment of workers in global supply chains is in the hands of some form of labour contractor so that even within the same factory or workplace a growing proportion of the workforce is not employed directly but has a formal or informal relationship with an agent or labour supplier.

The poor conditions of women's work have not gone unnoticed. In the past two decades there has been increasing attention paid to the issue of the rights of women workers, both in the context of workplace conditions and rewards, and in terms of basic human rights concerning legal and social protection and entitlements. There have been (more or less) successful 'anti-sweat shop' campaigns to ensure that customers are aware of the working conditions under which garments and sportswear are produced, which have been particularly effective amongst certain demographic groups, especially students and politically-aware young people who are major consumers of global brands. But the complexity of global supply chains makes it very difficult for workers, particularly women, to organise in defence of their own rights, although there are examples of success, such as HomeWorkers Worldwide (HWW), Women Working Worldwide (WWW) and the Central America Women's Network (CAWN).[1] However sector or multi stakeholder initiatives such as the Ethical Trading Initiative (ETI)[2] have been working to promote a system where Northern (United Kingdom/UK) retailers and buyers take responsibility for all parts of their production chain, including informal and home-based workers (see Barrientos, Chapter 67, this volume) and the gendered demands and priorities of women workers are increasingly championed.

Migrant workers and human rights
Increasingly the simple equation of 'cheap labour' with women's nimble fingers has grown more complex, as international capital has had growing access to migrant labour, young workers and ethnic minorities, all of whom offer alternatives to adult women in low-income countries as the principal source of cheap labour. Indeed, a growing number of female migrants are engaged in production for export beyond their national borders, many of whom operate in precarious situations in locations which are largely hidden from international scrutiny. For example, although there are over 1 million Burmese migrants employed in Thailand's export factories (Kusukabe and Pearson, forthcoming) this is not mentioned in accounts of the 'successful' export-led industrialisation of East and Southeast Asia. And there are also millions of migrant workers, mostly women, who migrate to the export factories of southwest China to operate under a *huku* (household registration) system, which in many ways parallels the situation of migrant workers elsewhere (Ngai, 2005). Not only do these workers lack access to a range of non-wage benefits, and other elements of labour protection, but they are also prevented (either *de jure* or *de facto*) from forming organisations to bargain collectively for improvements in their conditions and their rights. In the context of already weakened regulatory systems built on national sovereignty, migrant women workers are among the most vulnerable within the global economy (see also Sassen, Chapter 2, this volume).

At the same time, like other women workers, migrant women have to juggle their productive and reproductive responsibilities, complicated by the transborder and transnational nature of their families and responsibilities. In Thailand, where even registered migrant workers are temporary, exploited and insecure, women have to make very difficult decisions about their caring and other family obligations. Primarily women migrate to earn money to send to their families back home, so maintaining the flow of remittances is their priority. Increasingly, however, they not only have to think about sons and daughters, brothers and sisters left behind, but also the well-being of ageing parents, and that of their own children born while they are working in Thailand. With virtually no support from either their country of origin or their host country, women take on the primary responsibility for deciding where the child should be born, whether it should remain with them or be sent back home to be cared for by family members, whether to send for their parents to help them with childcare, and/or to ensure housing and food for them, as well as issues concerning education, nationality and citizenship.

With the additional pressure of the current global financial crisis, the future does not look positive for migrant workers in terms of meeting their economic or domestic responsibilities. In many countries there are reports of migrants losing their jobs, or being forced to accept cuts in already low wages. Domestic workers and others are being sent back to South and Southeast Asia, having lost their employment in the workshops, hotels and houses of the Gulf states, and Malaysia is deporting tens of thousands of migrant workers back to Indonesia. In theory those who are 'legal' should have the right to remain in the country, but the enthusiasm of states to expel illegal migrants means that all foreign workers are caught up in deportation drives, and these in turn fuel the xenophobic tendencies in many countries – South Africa, Thailand, Malaysia, the UK, and elsewhere – which are generally particularly intensive in times of crisis.

For women caught up in these situations, their fates become bleaker still. Most international women migrants seek work to fulfil their gendered reproductive responsibilities to families in their countries of origin and, in the course of this, they frequently acquire caring responsibilities for dependants in their countries of employment too. Governments in some source countries are already bemoaning the rapid shrinking of remittances from migrant workers which for many years have contributed directly to official foreign exchange flows, as well as to family income, and in some instances local development initiatives. For women migrant workers themselves, and for the households that depend on their income, what has for years become a potential route out of poverty is proving increasingly problematic and precarious.

Conclusion

As has been argued over many years, the wage earned by many workers has never covered the full cost of the reproduction of labour power. Where it is sufficiently high in money terms, wage labour can cover the commodity cost of reproduction, but all commodities require (unpaid) domestic work to convert them into goods and services that people can consume and benefit from. Worker struggles over the past century have not only concentrated on increasing the money value of the wage, but also on '(re)negotiating the reproductive bargain' such that the public provisioning of services such as childcare, education, health, elderly care and so on are extended to assist women – especially those on low incomes – to engage in employment. The situation of migrant workers makes it clear that the responsibility for the well-being of all lies with all, not just the community or country in which workers are born, or the responsibility of the company or individual that is their immediate employer. The global supply chain indicates a complex linkage of different enterprises – and ultimately of consumers – who profit and benefit from production in different parts of the world. Although the immediate prospects for 'unskilled' women workers, particularly for those working beyond national borders, look bleak, there is also, arguably, unprecedented potential for mobilising political and economic support at a transnational level to protect their livelihoods and well-being.

Acknowledgements

This material on Burmese migrant workers in Thailand draws in part on an article jointly written with Kyoko Kusukabe, entitled 'Transborder migration, social reproduction and economic development: a case study of Burmese women workers in Thailand', forthcoming in the *International Migration Journal*.

Notes

1. See their websites at www.homeworkersww.org.uk, www.women-ww.org and www.cawn.org (accessed 14 October 2009).
2. See their website at www.ethicaltrading.org.uk (accessed 14 October 2009).

Select bibliography

Elson, Diane and Ruth Pearson (1981) '"Nimble fingers make cheap workers": an analysis of women's employment in Third World export manufacturing', *Feminist Review*, **7**, 87–107.
Freeman, Carla (2000) *High Tech and High Heels in the Global Economy: Women, Work and Pink-collar Identities in the Caribbean*, Durham, NC: Duke University Press.
Ngai, Pun (2005) *Made in China: Women Factory Workers in a Global Workplace*, Durham, NC: Duke University Press.
Pearson, Ruth (1997) 'Renegotiating the reproductive bargain: gender analysis of economic transition in Cuba in the 1990s', *Development and Change*, **28**, 671–705.
Pearson, Ruth (1998) '"Nimble fingers" revisited: reflections on women and Third World industrialisation in the late twentieth century', in Cecile Jackson and Ruth Pearson (eds), *Feminist Visions of Development: Gender Analysis and Policy*, London, Routledge, pp. 171–88.
Standing, Guy (1999) *Global Labour Flexibility: Seeking Distributive Justice*, Basingstoke: Macmillan.
Wright, Melissa (2006) *Disposable Women and Other Myths of Global Capitalism*, London: Routledge.

65 Gender, poverty and inequality: the role of markets, states and households
Shahra Razavi and Silke Staab

The convergence in women's and men's labour force participation which has taken place across different regions has to be seen alongside the persistence of gender segmentations in labour markets that feed into inequalities in earnings, rights at work and rights to social security. This constitutes an important pillar of unequal gender relations. Gender inequalities overlap with persistent inequalities between a more formalised and regulated workforce, and an expanding pool of workers who are unorganised and denied many of the rights associated with formal employment. These two structural patterns seem to cut across a number of otherwise diverse countries. Does this signify the 'policy convergence' that some observers claim is taking place in the context of liberalisation? And do women's labour market disadvantages signify a 'feminisation of poverty' as it has been widely claimed? The answer to both questions must be a qualified no. Social policies, household structures and income pooling within households interface with labour market inequalities and shape women's and men's poverty risk in different ways (UNRISD, 2010).

Gendering income poverty: the role of markets, states and households
Three social institutions mediate men's and women's access to income and the risk of being poor: labour markets, states and households. Our approach considers individuals poor if they live in households with poverty level income, with per capita income counted at the household level (based on a simple division of aggregate household income) – an approach that inevitably produces relatively small gender gaps among adults who are partnered. We also use the concept of 'working poor' defined as those individuals who are employed and living in households whose income levels fall below a poverty threshold (Heintz, 2008).

As the capabilities framework has made clear, an insufficient level of income is a very narrow conceptualisation of poverty which does not capture its multiple dimensions, including poor health, shortened lives, emotional stress, and social exclusion. There are three primary reasons why we adopt this narrow approach. First, the employment–poverty relationship is most clearly expressed in terms of income poverty. Second, standard measures of income or consumption poverty facilitate the analysis of quantitative data upon which this chapter relies. Third, income poverty is often correlated with other dimensions of poverty.

Labour market institutions play a crucial role in access to income as well as in the commodification and stratification of labour along gender and class lines. Economic development strategies differ in the extent to which they are able to generate employment of sufficient quantity and quality for both women and men, with some policy configurations being more inclusive of female labour and less likely to entrench employment inequalities than others. Women face additional gender-specific constraints both on their ability to commodify their labour and to receive a decent wage. These include restrictive social norms and practices as well as the social allocation to women of the responsibility for the provision of unpaid care which often confines them to more casual jobs and lower wages – factors which can in turn translate into weaker claims to social security. Despite some improvements in the 1990s, women remain more concentrated in occupations with lower pay, poorer working conditions, and limited prospects for advancement than men.

In addition to labour market earnings *state-mediated fiscal policy* can provide resources through tax-and-transfer systems as well as through the use of public revenues for social services and infrastructure (piped water, sanitation), or, typically, through a combination of these approaches. We consider the role played by state welfare policy in mitigating the gendered poverty risks created by labour markets. Clearly, some countries are far more effective than others in addressing inequalities of both class and gender thereby reducing women's poverty risk and their dependence on male incomes.

Finally, states and markets interface with *households* in two fundamental ways. First, labour power itself is a produced means of production. It is not just schools and universities that produce 'human capital'; families and households do so far more extensively, on a daily and generational basis. However, while reproductive labour is essential for societies and economies to grow and flourish, women and girls assume a disproportionate share of such work. Second, as individually earned incomes are mediated through household relations, assessing gender gaps in poverty raises thorny methodological problems (see Lister, Chapter 24, this volume). As gender is fundamentally an individual characteristic whereas poverty is measured at the household level, the poverty status of both women and men is determined, both by their own employment status and the employment status of others in the household (see also Medeiros and Costa, Chapter 12, this volume).

As decades of feminist research on the household has shown, the pooled income approach upon which poverty measurement is based assumes that household income is equitably divided among household members; in reality some women may not escape individual poverty even when they live in non-poor households, due to the unequal distribution of resources. Even where women are able to escape poverty through income pooling at the household level, and especially where entitlements to state transfers do not provide a secure fall-back position, this may leave them in a situation of dependence on male breadwinners, stifling their 'voice' in domestic relations and closing their 'exit' options.

Welfare regimes, gender and access to income: evidence from advanced industrialised countries
While women have increasingly entered the labour markets of advanced industrialised countries, they have done so to a large extent in part-time employment. This indicates important continuities in the gender division of labour, with men still specialising in full-time paid employment, while women do the bulk of unpaid care work and adapt their labour market behaviour to the possibility of combining both. A further feature of men's and women's labour market participation is the wage gap caused by occupational segregation and associated wage penalties for 'women's jobs' as well as discrimination.

Due to their weaker labour market attachment, women are more likely to be poor than their male counterparts in many of these countries. However, significant cross-country differences emerge in the extent to which state policies mitigate women's disadvantages. Social transfers can offset uneven market distribution of income vertically (across social class or income deciles) *and* horizontally (across social groups differentiated by gender or ethnicity). Gender progressive social transfers narrow the poverty gap between women and men – and some countries do better in this respect than others. The poverty-reducing effect of transfers is much stronger, for example, in the social-democratic Northern European countries than in liberal market economies, such as the United States (US), or in Southern European countries. State transfers narrow the gender gap in poverty almost everywhere, but women are still slightly more likely to be poor than men in most countries, except in the Northern and some Eastern European countries whose transfer systems seem most progressive both in terms of social class and gender (Gornick and Jäntti, 2008).

This has important implications for women's dependence on intrahousehold income-pooling and the income of other household members, usually male partners. Here, Northern and Southern European countries represent two opposite scenarios, with women's reliance on a male breadwinner being low in the first and extremely high in the second group. In the Nordic countries, households do not seem to play a major role in providing poor women with income while that role is largely assumed by the tax-and-transfer system. On average, poor women's individual and household income is higher than that of poor men after transfers. This has important implications for single mothers who cannot count on the mitigating effect of a partner's market income (see Ypeij, Chapter 20, this volume).

Some similarities may be discerned between gender arrangements in Southern European countries and the economically dynamic countries of East Asia. A much noted feature of the latter has been their ability to avoid the income inequalities that marked the early history of industrialisation of some of the now developed economies. Yet the low levels of class inequality in these countries have gone hand-in-hand with a significant degree of *gender* inequality in the labour market during the heyday of developmentalism. Indeed women's low wages, roughly half those of men, were a stimulus to growth as they kept the cost of manufacturing exports low while generating the foreign exchange needed for technology imports (Seguino, 2000). The sectoral shift in Korean employment from manufacturing to services has been accompanied by greater labour market 'flexibility' and the increased use of non-standard (temporary and daily) workers, especially since 1997. Non-standard employment accounts for 24.1 per cent of men's employment and 40.3 per cent of women's employment. Weekly hours of work are significantly lower in non-standard employment compared to regular wage employment, as are hourly earnings.

In the Southern European countries the fact that women are not significantly poorer than men despite relatively low labour market earnings, is largely due to income pooling at the household level. Are women's labour market disadvantages and lower earnings in Korea being 'compensated' in a similar manner? The working poor poverty rates for Korea suggest a more complicated story. For temporary and daily women workers income pooling does *not* seem to be sufficient to close the gender poverty gaps. The estimated poverty rates among women working as temporary and daily workers are much higher than those of men in similar employment, while for regular workers the gender gap is closed. This may be related to the fact that a larger proportion of daily and temporary female workers are the only earner, or the primary earner, in their households. Given the large gender gaps in wages, poverty rates for households where women are the only or the main earner are thereby higher than in households where men assume this role.

Do state transfers make a difference to women who are otherwise economically disadvantaged? Vertical income equality in Korea until recently was the outcome of sustained growth rates and the type of institutional arrangement that provided male breadwinners with basic employment security and a 'family wage', with explicit social policies playing a marginal role in income equalisation. The Korean state's response to labour market liberalisation has been to extend the reach of key social welfare programmes. The accent has been placed on the 'universalisation' of key *social insurance* schemes, rather than *social assistance* programmes (the path taken in Brazil and South Africa to which we turn below). By the early 2000s, multiple health insurance funds had been merged into an integrated public scheme, the National Health Insurance, and universal coverage for old-age security was achieved through the National Pension Plan. Yet efforts towards 'universalisation' have not eroded gender inequalities, especially in terms of pension entitlements (see also Budowski, Chapter 34, this volume). At the same time, both political contestation and demographic imperatives have catapulted social care onto the national policy agenda. The state has extended and redesigned parental leave; expanded childcare systems (with subsidies to daycare centres and tax exemptions for families); and introduced Elderly Care Insurance to cover long-term care needs (Peng, 2008). It is too early however to assess the full impact of these policies on women's unpaid care burdens and employment prospects.

In sum, gender inequalities in labour markets remain significant in Korea. Working women's poverty rates are to some extent buffered by income pooling in the case of regular female workers. However, the expansion of precarious forms of work under the current labour market regime does not bode well for women who are also less likely to benefit from state-mediated transfers despite their recent expansion.

Gender, poverty and inequality in highly unequal societies
Brazil and South Africa are two middle-income countries characterised by gender, race and class inequalities. While income distribution is generally skewed, women's employment situation is particularly precarious. Three factors conspire to push women into an unfavourable economic position vis-à-vis men: employment segmentation (women are disproportionately employed in lower-quality employment, including informal employment); the gender earnings gap (generally, women earn less for a given amount and type of work than men), and fewer hours of work (due to the competing demands of unpaid care work and non-market production).

Informal employment is far more important in Brazil than it is in South Africa, but constitutes a much larger share of women's employment than men's in both countries. This reflects in part the large numbers of domestic workers – a phenomenon closely tied up to income inequality. Unemployment, in turn, is much higher in South Africa than in Brazil, but significantly higher for women in both countries. In Brazil, women are almost twice as likely as men to be unemployed.

Yet women's weaker employment status is not always reflected in gender-disaggregated poverty estimates (working poor poverty rates). We find an interesting contrast between Brazil and South Africa in this respect. In Brazil, employed women's average poverty rates are often lower than men's. This seemingly contradictory result emerges because aggregate household income, not an individual's position in the labour market, determines poverty status. Thus, employed women may have lower poverty rates than men in similar employment categories either because their contribution to family income makes the difference as to whether the household is poor or not – even when women's employment is of very low quality – or because their relatively low earnings are pooled with the earnings of other household members.

In South Africa, on the other hand, poverty rates among employed women are almost always higher than those among employed men, suggesting that income-pooling does not play the same role. One possible explanation can be found in the different combinations of employment and household structures, the latter exhibiting notable differences across the two countries. First, dual-earner households are much more common in Brazil than they are in South Africa, meaning that women's lower average earnings are at least theoretically set off through combined household income. Second, households in which women are the single or dominant earner are more common in South Africa than they are in Brazil – because men are either absent, unemployed or economically inactive. This increases women's poverty risk since they have no male partner to 'pool' their income with. The South African phenomenon of 'absent men' has been attributed to the country's historical development trajectory characterised by an extensive male migrant system which has left an indelible imprint on household structures and gender relations to this day (Budlender and Lund, 2007).

What about state policies? How do they influence male and female poverty? Both Brazil and South Africa are middle-income countries that have expanded social assistance programmes considerably over the past decade and means-tested cash transfers (CTs), both conditional and unconditional, now cover a significant proportion of their population. In South Africa social assistance programmes reach around 25 per cent of the population. Grants are non-contributory, unconditional (apart from means-testing) and financed out of tax revenues, which makes them highly redistributive. They are claimed to have reduced poverty by around 2 per cent, with beneficiaries being overwhelmingly women.

In Brazil, CTs targeted to the poor have also been expanded. The programme *Bolsa Familia* (Family Grants Programme), for example, counted 11 million beneficiaries by the end of 2006, and along with other CT programmes has also been estimated to have reduced poverty by 2 per cent. As most conditional CTs, *Bolsa Familia* stipends are channelled through women. Although data on the effects on gendered poverty is lacking, we can assume that CTs have a positive effect on the resources poor women have at their disposal for the management of their households – or the management of household poverty. Whether this leads to net benefits for the women beneficiaries themselves, especially in terms of labour market access and economic security, is debatable.

The challenges of gendered poverty in agrarian contexts
Employment in many low-income countries, including India and Kenya, is largely informalised and dominated by the agricultural sector. While in Kenya both women's and men's labour force participation rates are relatively high and fairly close to each other,

India exhibits a very large gender gap in labour force participation rates. Agriculture accounts for a *larger* share of women's employment than men's in these two countries. Gender differences in terms of average earnings, which are larger in India than in Kenya, are *not* necessarily reflected in women's and men's poverty rates. In India poverty among employed women is almost always higher than among employed men, as women's labour force entry often has a 'distress' character. It is financial exigency which pushes women into the paid workforce, and often in marginal forms of employment with very low pay. The same generalisation cannot be made for Kenya where female participation in the workforce seems to be generally high and evenly spread across income strata.

Development strategies can have very direct effects on the extent and severity of income poverty by creating jobs and incomes. Stimulating productivity and growth in agriculture would be important for both countries' long-term quest for poverty reduction, and especially for women's economic prospects. Yet agricultural growth rates in India in the 1990s were sluggish, especially when compared with the strong growth record of the economy as a whole, and public investment in agriculture has been low.

In addition to macroeconomic strategies, tax-and-transfer systems in a more narrow sense can play a decisive role, as we saw earlier. In low-income agrarian regimes, however, social policies often come in different forms, for example, through redistributive land reform, public support for smallholders, subsidised food distribution, and public employment schemes. The gender implications of such generic programmes, however, cannot be taken for granted. For example, the most disabling feature of the recently introduced National Employment Guarantee Scheme in India has been the guarantee of a hundred days of work per rural *household*. This dilutes adult entitlements in general and, given the rural power equations and inequalities, risks putting women at the end of the queue. Moreover, worksites' facilities are highly inadequate, especially in the provision of childcare – another obstacle from women workers' point of view.

Conclusion
Our analysis underlines the pervasive ways in which gender norms and structures are embedded within labour markets – a form of *social* regulation (Harriss-White 2003) – rather than state regulation of markets on which economic order rests. Yet despite their shared disadvantages within labour markets, the risk of living in poor households does not afflict all women equally, as some are able to pool their income with other household members (often male) and/or rely on state transfers and programmes. In contexts marked by the high incidence of households that are maintained primarily by women, acute questions arise about the viability of income pooling as a way of escaping poverty. However, reliance on male breadwinners can also stifle women's voices and options. Not only can states put in place programmes aimed at creating decent employment for women and/or providing income support that can expand women's options, the state has an essential part to play in countering market-based discrimination through recruitment into its own workforce and by regulating labour markets. The latter role has been downplayed over the past two decades of 'de-regulation'. Now that the financial crisis has re-legitimised the 'regulation' of markets, trade unions and women's movements may be able to seize the opportunity to place the right to work and the rights at work back on the agenda – this time with women as central actors.

Select bibliography

Budlender, Debbie and Francie Lund (2007) *The Political and Social Economy of Care: South Africa Research Report 1 Setting the Context*, Geneva: United Nations Research Institute for Social Development, available at: www.unrisd.org (accessed 21 April 2009).

Gornick, Janet and Markus Jäntti (2008) *Gender, Poverty, and Social Policy Regimes: A Comparative Analysis of Twenty-Four Upper-Income Countries*, background paper for the flagship report on Poverty and Policy Regimes, Geneva: United Nations Research Institute for Social Development, available at: www.unrisd.org (accessed 21 April 2009).

Harriss-White, Barbara (2003) 'Inequality at work in the informal economy: key issues and illustrations', *International Labour Review*, **142** (4), 459–69.

Heintz, James (2008) *Employment, Informality and Poverty: An Empirical Overview of Six Countries with a Focus on Gender and Race*, background paper for the flagship report on Poverty and Policy Regimes, Geneva: United Nations Research Institute for Social Development, available at: www.unrisd.org (accessed 21 April 2009).

Peng, Ito (2008) *The Political and Social Economy of Care: Korea Research Report 3*, Geneva: United Nations Research Institute for Social Development, available at: www.unrisd.org (accessed 21 April 2009).

Seguino, Stephanie (2000) 'Accounting for gender in Asian economic growth', *Feminist Economics*, **6** (3), 22–58.

United Nations Research Institute for Social Development (UNRISD) (2010) *Combating Poverty and Inequality: Structural Change, Social Policy and Politics* (provisional title), Geneva: UNRISD.

66 Women's employment, economic risk and poverty
James Heintz

Introduction

The transformation of women's position in remunerative employment has been far-reaching during the recent era of rapid global integration. Although the situation varies from country to country, currently more women participate in paid employment worldwide than at any other time in history (Heintz, 2006). However, equality of opportunity remains elusive. Gender segmentation of labour markets is endemic, with women concentrated in more precarious forms of employment, including informal employment (Chen et al., 2005). Economic stabilisation programmes and the process of global integration have frequently placed pressure on household incomes, pushing women into the paid labour force. At the same time, economic reforms have intensified demands on women's unpaid work. Increasing the supply of women's labour has been a central strategy by which families cope with economic change.

As women have entered the global labour force in increasing numbers, the overall structure of employment has changed dramatically. Recent decades have witnessed growing pressures for labour market deregulation, episodes of 'jobless growth', growing informalisation and casualisation, improvements in jobs for the highly skilled, and declining opportunities for the less skilled. New opportunities have been created in many countries due to the expansion of production linked into global markets, providing new possibilities for employment. However, much of this new employment is precarious, and the size of the working poor population remains staggering. Against this backdrop, this chapter examines the often complex dynamics of women's paid employment and its impact on standards of living, poverty outcomes, and women's welfare.

Gender dynamics and women's paid employment

Analysis of the relationships among growth, employment, and poverty reduction often focus exclusively on processes and outcomes that take place in the market economy. These market transactions are varied. For instance, in wage labour markets, individuals exchange their labour directly for a salary or wage. The terms of this exchange have a direct impact on the living standards and poverty status of households. However, an exclusive focus on the market relationships that govern employment dynamics ignores non-market activities that have an enormous effect on poverty status, development outcomes, and the production of human potential. Much of this non-market work takes place in households, families, and communities. In addition, intrahousehold dynamics directly influence the distribution of labour and resources in ways that impact access to employment opportunities.

Many have recognised that the most abundant resource the poor have at their disposal is their labour. Therefore, policies that more fully employ labour resources and raise the returns to the labour of the poor will have a direct impact on income poverty. However, it is misleading to state that poor women necessarily command their own labour in relative abundance. The gender dynamics of the household and the division of labour between unpaid/non-market work and remunerative employment constrains women's ability to realise the value of their labour (Benería, 2003). These constraints affect the efficacy with which better employment policies translate into real improvements in poverty and human development outcomes.

Gender relations determine the ways in which market and non-market work are organised. Women often have primary responsibility for non-market (unpaid) housework and caring labour. The allocation of time to non-market as opposed to market work limits the household income that women control directly. Furthermore, with more time allocated to non-market work, women frequently have less paid work experience or interrupt their employment, factors which often translate into lower earnings. The growth of women's labour force participation rates relative to men's is a widely recognised trend in many countries. However, the relationship between greater labour force participation and changes in gender equity is complex.

The quality of employment matters, not just greater labour market participation. Gender segmentation in labour markets is commonplace, with women often concentrated in low-paid, unstable and informal employment. Wage labour markets are not the only, and often not the most important, form of market exchange governing women's employment. For instance, quasi-labour markets exist in which workers sell a product or service, but within a set of dependent relationships that limit their authority over the employment arrangement. Examples include subcontracted production, in which workers produce or assemble goods within a longer supply chain. Distinct market dynamics, apart from those of labour markets, govern various forms of self-employment or quasi wage employment. Often social insurance policies are absent for these types of precarious and informal employment, raising the economic risk that women working in these activities face.

Labour force segmentation reduces women's earning potential. With lower expected earnings, investment in girls' and women's education frequently lags behind that of men. Similarly, women's lower earning potential reinforces the gender division of labour within the household, since the opportunity cost, in terms of foregone income, of specialising in unpaid care work is lower for women than for men. Women who specialise in providing unpaid caring labour face enormous economic risks (Folbre, 1994). Such specialisation lowers their earnings potential and reinforces dependencies on a male 'breadwinner'. Often women do not have the same access to social protection, such as pensions for old age, thereby increasing their risk of falling into poverty (see Budowski, Chapter 34, this volume).

The gender division between market and non-market work, the unequal distribution of employment opportunities, and women's lower earnings potential reinforce established gender dynamics. For example, women's influence over the distribution of resources and labour within the household is weakened when opportunities to earn income through employment are limited. Therefore, increasing women's access to paid employment has the potential to change gender roles, depending on the resilience of gender norms in society and the type of employment to which women have access (Benería, 2003). The relationship between paid market work and prevailing gender relations is not simple or unidirectional. Access to remunerative employment does not always translate into control over a portion of the household's income. Similarly, labour market participation may involve costs as well as benefits (Elson, 1999).

Women's labour force participation is not only determined by prevailing gender norms. Women respond to adverse economic conditions – including rising unemployment – by increasing their rate of labour force participation. For instance, increases in women's labour force participation have corresponded with the implementation of structural adjustment programmes (SAPs). Similarly, women's labour force participation has been shown to increase with economic crises and policies that trigger labour displacement, job instability, and higher rates of unemployment. Women also increase their labour force participation in response to sustained structural unemployment (Heintz, 2006).

The coping strategies adopted at the household level in response to negative economic shocks underscore the importance of taking these dynamics into account when considering the linkages between growth, employment, and income poverty. For countries with well-developed social welfare systems, government policies mitigate these negative consequences. However, for countries without publicly supported systems of social protection, households become a safety net of last resort.

An additional link exists between paid employment, non-market work, and human development. The ability to translate access to paid employment into new capabilities, greater freedom, and improved investments in children depends on the nature of relationships within the household and the process by which decisions are made concerning the allocation of labour time and economic resources (Folbre, 1994; see also Chant, Chapter 15, this volume). Indeed, increased gender inequalities, even in the short-run, can have long-term consequences for economic growth and human development.

Women's employment and income poverty

Given the segmented nature of labour markets and employment opportunities, women are frequently concentrated in types of employment with high risks of income poverty (Chen et al., 2005). Moreover, gender earnings gaps are often observed across different categories of employment – both formal and informal employment, both wage- and self-employment. Given that women are concentrated in lower-quality employment and that women earn less than men within similar categories of employment, we would expect that the poverty rates of employed women should be higher than the poverty rates of employed men in similar types of employment. However, studies that have examined the poverty rates of employed individuals (often called the 'working poor' poverty rate) have found no clear pattern in terms of the poverty risk observed for employed men and employed women within specific employment categories, defined by employment status (employee, own-account worker, employer, and so on) and informality status (informal versus formal) (Chen et al., 2005). That is, in some cases, employed women have lower poverty rates than men; in others, women's poverty rates are higher.

This seemingly contradictory result arises because of the complexities involved when analysing gender dynamics, employment and poverty. These complexities emerge when connecting employment status, which is analysed at the individual level, with poverty status, defined at the household level. For example, the fact that women spend time in paid work can lower the household's risk of income poverty, since the additional employment income determines whether the household is considered poor or not. In households in which women do not engage in market work, the risk of poverty may be higher. Therefore, the poverty rate among working women may be lower on average than that among working men, even if women are engaged in precarious work with low earnings.

Note that the poverty outcomes for employed women depend crucially on the composition of the household. Women who can pool their employment earnings, at least in part, with another earner face a lower risk of poverty than women who maintain households on their incomes alone. Given the lower quality of employment opportunities, single women who must support a family alone face extremely high risks of material poverty. Therefore, two economic institutions fundamentally shape the employment–poverty connection: the labour market and the household. These institutions are highly gendered and closely intertwined. The impact of employment on poverty and human development cannot be understood without incorporating an analysis of the household and the associated gender dynamics.

The twin feminisations: labour and poverty

Two important discourses have emerged in recent years that shape how the relationships between women's paid work, employment and the risk of poverty are understood: the 'feminisation of labour' and the 'feminisation of poverty'. These analyses were developed during the period of global integration and economic liberalisation and therefore they have had a fundamental influence on how the social dimensions of globalisation are analysed – particularly, how globalisation has affected the economic reality facing women. However, both these discourses, at least as originally formulated, have limitations that obscure, rather than clarify, the links between employment and poverty. Therefore, it is important to take some time to interrogate the dual feminisations of labour and poverty.

The term 'feminisation of labour' was first coined by Standing (1989) and initially focused on the increase in women's labour force participation. Women's entry into the paid labour force was seen as a contributory factor in the increase in flexible work arrangements, growing informality, and the deterioration in the average quality of employment. Women provided a new and lower-cost source of labour that could substitute for men's labour. Jobs became 'feminised' as they took on characteristics traditionally associated with women's work: pay was low, drudgery increased, occupational mobility declined, and job tenure became more uncertain.

This conceptualisation of the feminisation of labour has been criticised on a number of fronts. The causal link presumed to exist between women's labour force participation and growing precariousness may be spurious. Other economic forces, including macroeconomic policies and development strategies, have simultaneously influenced the rise of precariousness and the expansion of women's labour force participation. The expansion of women's low-wage employment has resulted from women's entry into paid employment and the concurrent growth of poor quality employment opportunities. Instead of an erosion of labour market segmentation that we would expect to see if there were widespread substitution of women's labour for men's, we would see persistence of segmentation, at least in many categories of employment.

The original feminisation of labour framework also fails to integrate the division of labour between paid (market) and unpaid (non-market) work into its analysis. The constraints under which labour has been supplied differ markedly between men and women. Ongoing responsibilities for childcare and other unpaid activities limit the labour market opportunities available to women. Under these conditions, part-time, own-account, or home-based work might be the best options for remunerative employment available to women.

The 'feminisation of poverty' refers to the assertion that women account for a disproportionate share, and a growing share, of the world's poor. Since women's economic position is almost everywhere inferior to men's – in terms of earnings, opportunities, and assets – it seems reasonable to assume that women should face a higher risk of poverty. Female-headed households were the focus of the original feminisation of poverty proposition. Given the economic disadvantages facing women, female-headed households were expected to have a higher poverty rate on average than male-headed households. However, in reality, the determinants of the poverty risks that women face are more complex (Chant, 2003).

The empirical evidence supporting the argument that female-headed households exhibit higher and growing poverty rates is not strong (see Medeiros and Costa, Chapter 12, this volume). There are numerous reasons why this may be the case. Not all female-headed households are disadvantaged to the same degree or in the same way. It may be more appropriate to talk of particular types of female-headed households in the context of women's poverty risk, for instance, a family unit with children maintained by a woman alone (Folbre, 1994). Also, intrahousehold dynamics must be taken into account. For example, in some cases women in female-headed households may face fewer labour market constraints and exert more direct control over employment income than other households (Chant, 2003). Women may improve their welfare in other ways by leaving male-headed households, for example, by escaping domestic violence (see Chant, Chapter 15, this volume; Davids and van Driel, Chapter 14, this volume).

The types of employment available to women, and to other earners in the household, matter for determining the risk of income poverty. The class position of the household has a sizeable impact on poverty rates, regardless of headship. For example, households that rely on informal employment as their primary source of income face higher poverty rates than households that have access to formal jobs. The interaction between employment dynamics and the nature of the household have a direct impact on women's poverty risk. In this context, female headship is not necessarily a critical factor determining overall poverty risks.

Distributive dynamics within the household have a direct impact on social welfare in ways that total household income fails to capture. This is particularly important for understanding women's risk of poverty, since men may control income and expenditures at home (Chant, 2003). In addition, income represents only one economic resource that affects the risk of poverty. Access to various kinds of assets – physical assets, education and skills, natural assets and financial assets – determine the livelihoods available to the members of the household and influence the distribution of resources within the household.

Intrahousehold dynamics are important to take into account in terms of another link between employment and poverty: the welfare contributions of both market and non-market work. Non-market work is essential for maintaining a household's living standards and for sustaining human development. At the same time, women's paid employment can be essential for keeping household income above the poverty threshold. Women may not be able to maintain the same level of caring labour once they enter the labour force. If men do not fill the gap, some of the gains in terms of market-based income will be lost in terms of non-market labour. Measurements of poverty and well-being should take these factors into account.

Conclusion

Despite this call for a more complex analysis of the connections between gender relations, employment and poverty, one fact remains clear: women's paid employment is an essential factor determining the risk of poverty that all families face. Women's employment contributes to total household income; women's participation in the labour market can affect intrahousehold bargaining outcomes, conditional on decision-making processes and who controls the income; and access to employment has important implications for individual freedoms, capabilities and dignity. Exactly how women's employment affects social and economic well-being will depend on the institutional context and the gender relationships that prevail in a given context. None of this diminishes the importance of understanding the economic factors that determine the quantity and quality of remunerative work.

Select bibliography

Benería, Lourdes (2003) *Gender, Development, and Globalisation: Economics as if All People Mattered*, London: Routledge.

Chant, Sylvia (2003) *New Contributions to the Analysis of Poverty: Methodological and Conceptual Challenges to Understanding Poverty from a Gender Perspective*, Santiago: Economic Commission for Latin America and the Caribbean.

Chen, Martha, Joann Vanek, Francine Lund and James Heintz, in association with Renana Jhabvala and Christine Bonner (2005) *Progress of the World's Women 2005: Women, Work, and Poverty*, New York: UNIFEM.

Elson, Diane (1999) 'Labour markets as gendered institutions: equality, efficiency and empowerment issues', *World Development*, **27** (3), 611–27.

Folbre, Nancy (1994) *Who Pays for the Kids? Gender and the Social Structures of Constraint*, London: Routledge.

Heintz, James (2006) *Globalisation, Economic Policy, and Employment: Poverty and Gender Implications*, Employment Strategy Paper, 2006/3, Geneva: International Labour Office.

Standing, Guy (1989), 'Global feminisation through flexible labour', *World Development*, **17** (7), 1077–95.

67 Gender and ethical trade: can vulnerable women workers benefit?
Stephanie Barrientos

Introduction

Corporate brands and retailers have long been the subject of campaigns by non-governmental organisations (NGOs) and trade unions for poor working conditions in their global supply base. In response, a large number of global buyers have introduced codes of labour practice to ensure that their suppliers observe minimum international labour standards. The more comprehensive codes are based on core International Labour Organisation (ILO) Conventions, including no discrimination.

A significant number of workers in export production are women. They are often concentrated in insecure and vulnerable employment (seasonal, casual, migrant, homework and contract work). It is among these groups of workers that the worst conditions of employment are usually found – low wages, long hours, lack of contracts, no unionisation, poor health and safety, and lack of social protection. But codes of labour practice often fail to reach more vulnerable women workers, with little impact on reducing casualisation or gender discrimination. This chapter asks whether codes of labour practice can help improve conditions for more vulnerable women workers. It argues that gender discrimination is embedded in the commercial practices of global value chains (GVCs). Global buyers need to integrate better the principles of ethical sourcing into their own business practices if more vulnerable women workers are to benefit.

Codes of labour practice in global value chains

Global brands and retailers now outsource much of their production to suppliers across the Global South. They are able to coordinate production, distribution and retailing across countries through GVCs. Global brands and retailers exert important commercial power over suppliers. They rarely own production or are direct employers within their sourcing countries, but their decisions and actions can have direct implications for production operations and working conditions. Global buyers are beyond the reach of government regulation in the countries in which they source. This has weakened the effectiveness of national labour regulation as the channel for ensuring workers' rights.

Corporate codes of labour practice arose as a result of civil society pressure (trade unions and NGOs) on corporate brands and retailers because of poor working conditions in their GVCs. Global trade unions and NGOs now play an increasingly important role in holding corporate buyers to account for labour standards of their suppliers. They are able to link brands and retailers to specific cases of worker abuse, mobilise consumer campaigns and fuel adverse media publicity against brands and retailers who fail to ensure minimum labour standards in their global sourcing base.

Corporate codes of labour practice set minimum standards on working conditions which suppliers have to meet. They are increasingly applied by global brands and

Table 67.1   Comparison of employment in selected sectors linked to Global Value Chains

Country	Level of employment	Gender composition	Type of employment
Kenya flowers	40 000 wage workers (+ 4–5000 smallholders)	75 per cent female	65 per cent temporary
Chile fruit	336 739 wage workers	Female workers: 52 per cent temporary workers and 5 per cent of permanent	85 per cent temporary 15 per cent permanent Waged work
Bangladesh garments	1.5 million wage workers	90 per cent female	Permanent (often without formal contracts)
China garments and textiles	8.39 million wage workers	70 per cent female	Mainly internal migrant labour recruited annually

Sources: Dolan and Sorby (2003); Kabeer and Mahmud (2004); Yusuf et al. (2007).

retailers who have close linkages to the producers from whom they source. Most codes cover issues such as health and safety, child labour and working hours. The more comprehensive codes are based on 'Core Conventions' of the ILO. These include freedom of association and the right to collective bargaining, no discrimination, no child and no forced labour. It is estimated by Neil Kearney of the International Textile, Garment and Leather Workers Federation that there are over 10 000 company codes of labour practice.

Gender and vulnerable workers
Women form a significant portion of the labour force in many countries exporting consumer goods in buyer-led global value chains. It is estimated that there are 40 million workers engaged in garment production globally. Research on just eight countries in Africa and Latin America indicates that over 2 million workers are in high-value agriculture exports (Dolan and Sorby, 2003; Hale and Wills, 2005). Access to paid work in global value chains has provided women with a new source of income and financial independence. But in many sectors, women are clustered in insecure work (usually as seasonal, contract or casual workers), while men are more concentrated in permanent employment. Women are likely to be located in labour-intensive areas of production, and less likely to be found in more skilled or supervisory and managerial positions. Table 67.1 provides examples of different countries where a high level of female employment is found.

Women in non-permanent work face heightened employment vulnerability and an increased risk that codes fail to protect them. Particular problems include unequal wages, lack of freedom of association, discrimination in training and promotion, verbal and sexual abuse by supervisors and difficulties in combining childcare with long hours and compulsory overtime (often at short notice). The NGO Women Working Worldwide, which promotes the rights of women workers in global value chains, has undertaken a number of studies on this.[1]

Underlying the problems faced by many women is embedded discrimination that allocates them to insecure and vulnerable employment, undermining their rights as workers. This is reflected at different levels. At an institutional level, women in insecure work often lack protection in labour law that would allow them legally to claim rights as workers. At an employment level, they often lack access to information that would enlighten them to their rights, either by law and/or through a code of labour practice. Lack of organisation or representation reinforces that position and ensures they lack voice or ability to influence change. At a personal level, women's employment conditions are often embedded in gendered norms and practices which they have been conditioned to accept. Hence they are less likely to challenge a situation, even where it is in violation of the law and/or a code of labour practice.

The Ethical Trading Initiative (ETI) Impact Assessment
Multi-stakeholder initiatives (MSIs) promote alliances between suppliers, independent trade unions, NGOs and government to provide a more collaborative approach to improving labour standards. They promote greater accountability than companies operating alone. One example of an MSI is the UK Ethical Trading Initiative (ETI). By the end of 2008 it had a membership of over 50 companies, 15 NGOs, the UK Trades Union Congress (TUC), the International Trade Union Confederation (ITUC), and the Council of Global Unions. All ETI companies agree to adopt a code of labour practice based on the ETI base code in their global value chains.

In 2003 the ETI set out to examine how effective company codes of labour practice are for improving employment conditions and the lives of workers by commissioning an independent impact assessment. The ETI Impact Assessment involved in-depth case studies in manufacturing and agriculture in Costa Rica, India, South Africa, the UK and Vietnam (plus a scoping study in China). The value chains of 11 ETI member countries were mapped to these countries, where a total of 25 supplier sites were selected for more in-depth research. In total 418 workers were interviewed, 46 per cent women and 54 per cent men, reflecting the gender profile of employment across the supplier sites.[2] Interview methods included a short worker-survey and focus group discussions on each site (single and mixed sex). Interviews were also carried out with over 80 trade professionals, NGOs and trade unions across the five countries.

The ETI Impact Assessment found that codes of labour practice were exerting a positive effect on improving certain 'visual issues'. The biggest impact was on health and safety, with positive changes found in 20 out of 25 sites. This led to improvements in the lives of workers' families through greater observance of health and safety at home, for example, banana workers no longer hugging their children in overalls used for pesticide spraying. Other changes were in better adherence to minimum wage legislation and documented employment benefits for regular workers. For example, workers in one focus group recounted the situation of a female worker who was covered by Employees' State Insurance (ESI) as a result of codes. Her partner had come to the unit to distribute sweets because the expenses of delivering their baby were covered by ESI, and they did not realise that the monthly deductions would pay off so well. Codes are also helping to raise awareness of the need to comply with national regulation.

But codes have had little impact on the improvement of 'less visual issues' such as the freedom of association and no discrimination. On no site did workers feel able to join a trade union as a result of codes (although unions had already existed prior to

Gender and ethical trade: can vulnerable women workers benefit? 443

codes on some sites in the study). Codes had also had little effect on the hiring, training and promotion of women workers, with the persistence of deeply embedded forms of discrimination.

An important finding in the study was that regular and permanent workers were most likely to have benefited from changes resulting from codes. Casual and migrant workers (international or internal) were found in all case study countries, with Vietnam being the only one in which third-party labour contractors were not utilised in their hire. Internal migrant workers are also predominantly female, particularly in Vietnam and China. Migrant workers were least likely to have benefited from the implementation of codes of labour practice, and on many sites they faced significant difficulties. Workers hired through third-party labour contractors faced the greatest problems of code violation. They normally have no security, they can face illicit wage deductions by contractors and can be subject to harassment or abuse by contractors. Many such workers receive no employer or state protection. They are most vulnerable in the event of illness, injury, lack of mobility, old age, childbirth and carer responsibilities.

Casual and migrant female workers are very vulnerable to discrimination, abuse and poverty. Their wages are often lowest, their employment is insecure and they can regularly face periods without paid work. As workers in one focus group discussion (FGD) commented:

> Contractors only pay workers total wages at the end of the month; only a part of the wages are paid to workers. The remaining money is paid to workers in instalments. Our workday ends at 6pm and we usually put in 3 hours overtime. Overtime is not voluntary; if a worker refuses to do overtime hours the same day, they risk losing their job.

Overtime is a particular issue for women workers with children. They are often required to work with very little notice, and are unable to arrange childcare. But if they fail to comply they risk losing future work. Women are also vulnerable to abuse by male supervisors and labour contractors, who can exploit their position of authority over them.

Corporate buyers and their suppliers now devote large resources to the monitoring of codes of labour practice. This has spawned an industry engaged in social compliance and independent social auditing. All the sites in the ETI impact Assessment had fulfilled either a self-assessment or been monitored through social audits in relation to their buyers' codes. Yet the research still found issues of non-compliance on many of the sites in the study. While snapshot social auditing has been fairly successful at identifying visual issues such as health and safety, it is failing to pick up more embedded issues such as discrimination and freedom of association which are central to workers' rights. Casual, migrant and contract workers are often overlooked in audits. Some suppliers send such workers away during buyer or audit visits, or use 'double book keeping' to mask code violation. Workers said in a FGD:

> When buyers come for inspections to the unit, we are told to leave the premises for some time and take a break and have tea or that there is no more work on that day. We are made to exit from the back gate of the unit and not paid on these days. Since we work on a separate floor we usually have no access to other workers in the factory.

Women workers, particularly where their work is insecure, often lack awareness of their rights and lack the confidence or are fearful of voicing complaints to outsiders. Social auditors often lack sensitivity to gender issues, and fail to reveal non-compliances in this situation. Capturing the specific issues faced by women workers necessitates careful planning to ensure their inclusion in a social audit. In this context, maximum involvement of women must be facilitated throughout the entire social auditing process, and the gender-awareness of auditors raised.

Vulnerable women workers often have little information about their rights and are often denied their legal entitlements. They fear raising issues with employers, in case it could affect their re-employment. They are rarely represented on workers' committees, and are least likely to be organised in trade unions. Codes of labour practice are playing a positive role in helping to improve the conditions for regular workers but they often fail to reach more insecure and vulnerable workers. Yet this is where the poorest labour conditions are likely to be found.

Vulnerable women workers in global value chains
Reasons why codes of labour practice are failing to reach more vulnerable women workers are complex, and are tied up with commercial dynamics of global value chains. A few of the largest brands and retailers source from highly integrated value chains and have close relationships with their suppliers. These firms are in a better position to influence adherence to their codes of labour practice and reduce workers' vulnerability. But many companies operate in complex value chains, where suppliers deal with multiple buyers and agents. Embedded gender discrimination in employment practices within global value chains affects the way codes relate to women and men workers. Suppliers can be faced by a multitude of company codes, which they have to juggle with increasing commercial pressures to meet more stringent commercial demands.

A gender value chain analysis provides a framework for examining the subordinate position of many women within export production (Barrientos et al., 2003). The gender division of labour in most societies attributes to men primary responsibility for productive paid work, and to women primary responsibility for unpaid reproductive work such as household and childcare. Where women are in paid employment, the gender division of labour is reflected in the types of work allocated to women and men. Women are often allocated to jobs that require manual dexterity and attention to quality (such as sewing garments and packing fruit). They have acquired skills to undertake these jobs through social conditioning in the home, yet those skills are not sufficiently recompensed. The fact that women normally combine paid work with their unpaid reproductive role helps to socially 'legitimise' their role in casualised employment, where they are mobile between paid employment and home. Lack of formal employment benefits are supposedly compensated by women's unremunerated family and community support networks.

A complaint made vocally by many suppliers in the ETI study was the pressure they are under from buyers to reduce prices, carry more of the costs and meet tighter delivery deadlines. Some complained of the double standards of many global brands and retailers. Buyers often make commercial demands that undermine observance of their own company code of labour practice. A prime example is with orders placed at short notice that necessitate extra overtime in direct contravention of their own code. Many suppliers use casual workers and labour contractors to cope with volatile orders, meet sudden production surges and keep labour costs down. Women workers are drawn in as a low cost, compliant and mobile workforce that helps to meet these commercial pressures.

The commercial practices of many buyers thus reinforce an embedded gender discrimination that appropriates female labour at low cost, with little security or protection. Given a choice between meeting the code of labour practice or the specification of a commercial order from a global brand or retailer, suppliers will prioritise the latter. Codes may benefit regular women workers, and at the margins improve some of the visible issues facing vulnerable workers (such as health and safety). But alone these are unable to turn the tide of embedded discrimination reinforced by commercial buying practices. Hence, the campaigns of NGOs are increasingly targeted at the purchasing practices of the large brands and buyers as an essential way forward in improving the benefits of codes of labour practice to workers.

Concluding remarks

There are significant challenges in addressing the poor employment conditions and rights of casual, contract, female and migrant workers in global production. Codes have resulted from civil society pressure on corporate brands and retailers to ensure minimum labour standards are observed by suppliers. They are leading to some positive benefits for regular workers but codes operated through commercial GVCs have failed to reach the most vulnerable women workers. The commercial dynamics of global value chains are gendered. Women workers provide essential skills to meet quality production, but often these are poorly remunerated and provide a buffer against the risks of commercial volatility. The use and abuse of female casual, migrant and contract labour cannot be addressed without the more sustained integration of the principles of ethical sourcing throughout the value chains of global brands and retailers.

Notes
1. See Working Women Worldwide's website at: http://www.poptel.org.uk/women-ww/ (accessed 24 June 2009).
2. For the full findings and country reports go to www.ethicaltrade.org/d/impactreport (accessed 24 June 2009), and search for Barrientos, Stephanie and Smith, Sally (2006) *Ethical Trading Initiative Impact Assessment Report, Phases 1 and 2*, London: ETI. This includes ten reports comprising overviews, country studies and methodology.

Select bibliography

Barrientos, Stephanie, Catherine Dolan and Anne Tallontire (2003) 'A gendered value chain approach to codes of conduct in African horticulture', *World Development*, 31 (9), 1511–26.
Barrientos, Stephanie and Catherine Dolan (eds) (2006) *Ethical Sourcing in the Global Food System*, London: Earthscan.
Dolan, Catherine and Kristina Sorby (2003) *Gender and Employment in High-Value Agriculture Industries*, Washington DC: World Bank.
Hale, Angela and Jane Wills (eds) (2005) *Threads of Labour: Garment Industry Supply Chains from the Workers' Perspective*, Oxford: Blackwell.
Kabeer, Naila and Simeen Mahmud (2004) 'Globalization, gender and poverty: Bangladeshi women workers in export and local markets', *Journal of International Development*, 16, 93–109.
Oxfam (2004) *Trading Away Our Rights. Women Working in Global Supply Chains*, Oxford: Oxfam International.
Yusuf, Shahid, Kaoru Nabeshima and Dwight Perkins (2007) 'China and India reshape global industrial geography', in Alan Winters and Shaid Yusuf (eds), *Dancing with Giants: China, India and the Global Economy*, Washington, DC: World Bank, pp. 35–66.

68 Fraternal capital and the feminisation of labour in South India
Sharad Chari

This chapter reflects on processes of industrialisation and global production in the town of Tiruppur, South India, in the late twentieth century, to draw implications for a gendered critique of capitalist hegemony (Chari, 2004). The first section recounts Tiruppur's transformation into India's centre for the global production of knitted fashion garments. Work in Tiruppur is organised in networks of small firms, not unlike the much vaunted 'industrial districts' of Silicon Valley or the Third Italy (Terza Italia) (Piore and Sable, 1984). My research[1] critiques these metropolitan expectations by turning to the fraternity of capitalists of modest worker-peasant origins who made Tiruppur a powerhouse of global production.

In the second part of the chapter I reflect upon why gender enters debates about Tiruppur when a male-dominated work regime admits women workers. The equation of gender with women's problems does have a basis in the exploitation of women workers, but the changes and challenges run deeper. I ask how the 'feminisation of labour' has taken specific form through gendered discourses that accompanied Tiruppur's shifts to global production through a diverse and unequal workforce. I conclude that Tiruppur's social formation can be seen as one instance of global production in which gender articulates sexed bodies to processes of capitalist accumulation in diverse ways (Salzinger, 2003). As Marx (1967) reminds us, accumulation is not just 'economic growth', or the amassing of wealth through increased productivity, but also the amassing of working-class poverty and insecurity. Tiruppur shows how both processes of accumulation are linked through gendered hegemonies forged, and perhaps resisted, in specific historical conjunctures.

Agrarian transition and industrialisation in Tiruppur
Fraternal Capital (Chari, 2004) centres on transformations in the town of Tiruppur, in Tamilnad state of India, in a semi-arid region that was once a cotton farming, ginning and textile mill economy. Since the late 1980s, Tiruppur reached fame and fortune as a production and export centre for cotton knitwear: T-shirts, fleece and other garments made of knitted cloth. By 1997, Tiruppur had captured 75 to 90 per cent of the Indian market and its export earnings had expanded from US$25 million in 1986 to US$636 million in 1997. The number of garments exported from Tiruppur increased more than ninefold over the same decade, and the product shifted from basic T-shirts to fashion garments. What is key is that the industry is organised through networks of small firms integrated through intricate subcontracting arrangements controlled by capital of the Gounder caste. In effect the whole town works like a decentralised factory for the global economy, but with local capital of peasant-worker origins at the helm. What is more, these self-made men hinge their retrospective narratives of class mobility and industrial success on what they call their 'toil'. The central question I ask is, how did Gounder

peasant-workers remake themselves through what they call their 'toil', to make Tiruppur a powerhouse of global production?

I explain Tiruppur's industrial dynamics as a consequence of regional forces that took formative shape in the late 1970s, before Tiruppur turned to global production, when the town was known for *banians* (men's cotton knitted undershirts). Tiruppur's rise in the national market through this quintessentially working man's garment mirrors the rise to dominance of a class of fraternal capitalists who created the conditions for Tiruppur's subsequent turn to the export market. Abstract models about 'industrial districts' cannot explain how this form of capital has emerged, as they rely on the mythology of capitalism as universal, ungendered 'economic growth'.

Through a combination of life history, survey, ethnographic and archival research, I sought to identify, to put it crudely, how the histories and affiliations of owners made a difference to their class practice as capitalists. This evidence allowed me to then explore how a process of decentralisation, which began in the 1970s, was crucially linked to the ways in which Gounders of worker-peasant origins consolidated their hold over industrial work. When Gounders first came to Tiruppur as workers between the 1940s and early 1960s, knitwear was organised in integrated firms with all work under one roof, an entirely male workforce and militant labour unions which secured a period of expanding workers' entitlements. Early owners were from traditional 'business communities': Muslims, Chettiars, Mudaliars and Iyers. By the 1970s these owners were largely outcompeted by their former workers, mainly Gounders, who had taken over the industrial form from within, changing the spatial organisation of work into an elaborate decentralised structure that makes the whole town work like a factory.

There is something specific about the labour process in stitching which highlights the centrality of manual labour and the persisting challenge of labour control in knitwear production, particularly in the extremely differentiated world of fashion garments. Stitching is done on six to eight machines fitted to a common motor on a 'power table', an arrangement particularly suited to contracting out batches of garments of particular qualities. The contractor is responsible for securing and managing a group of workers who work at the power table on a specific batch. This form of batch production has proven to work particularly well with the incredibly differentiated export orders for fashion garments that pose strong challenges for labour supervision and control.

Overwhelmingly, Gounders of working-class origins became owners through these stitching sections at the heart of the blizzard of firms where labour control remains central, yet tenuous. Moreover, these Gounder men continued to draw in others like them, their fictive 'brothers', as partners in similar 'sister concerns' that linked control of labour in the detail division of labour to control of social labour in the delicate work of coordinating work across networked worksites in order to make a cheap garment of the right qualities at the right time.

Turning to their social origins, what is surprising is that Tiruppur's Gounder entrepreneurs did not emerge from a prosperous capitalist farming class, but from the poor end of a differentiating peasantry; that is, from poor peasant households stretched across agriculture, petty trade and waged work. In other words, they were disadvantaged in material terms, but what do they mean when they say that they made it through nothing but their 'toil'? To explain the sociocultural basis of Gonder toil, I turn to their specific regional agrarian past.

I argue that rather than a caste attribute, Gounder toil revives elements of an agrarian labour regime of the 1930s to forge an agrarian transition that relies on the transfer not so much of things but of social and cultural relations. In brief, I trace Gounder toil to a farming system of the 1930s, where Gounder farmers in this semi-arid region developed a form of intensive well-irrigated smallholder agriculture which was extremely flexible in responding to market fluctuations, and which utilised a range of labour arrangements differentiated by gender and caste. What was most important was that the Gounder farmer was not an overseer; he worked alongside his differentiated workforce while appropriating the fruit of their shared work. This work regime provided a practical history for Gounder peasants to draw on in a very different context.

While Gounders came to Tiruppur in a range of ways, they often spoke of their difference as peasant-workers and as owner-operators of stitching sections with reference to their toil. More importantly, Gounder men began to embody and enact the sign as if intrinsic to their dispositions, reinforcing their intertwined gender, caste and class affiliations as Gounder 'self-made men'. They also harnessed petty agrarian savings, and pledged agricultural land as collateral for institutional credit, particularly after the nationalised State Bank of India actively supported small industry after 1970. Part of my research was an ethnography of the bank, and of the ways in which it extended loans liberally to what it saw as the creditworthy peasant. In the context of regional agrarian decline, family savings were the site of conflict between male kin or *pankalis*, literally shareholders, or what I call fictive 'brothers'. When 'brothers' could not be convinced to divide assets or pledge family land in the bank, marriages provided alternate resources to enable the construction of 'self-made men'. In various ways, Tiruppur provided rural families opportunities to divert small savings into partnerships in knitting companies to thereby mitigate some of the increasing risks associated with agricultural decline.

Slowly, 'brothers' or ex-worker castefellows with different skills would pool resources and talents to start a small unit in which they would do the major work. Capital requirements were low, and often a Gounder boss would support his kin, castefellow or ex-worker to start dependent units to work for him when necessary. As I suggested, the knitwear industry rests centrally on manual labour and on close supervision and labour control in stitching sections. Overwhelmingly peasant-workers started out as owners by starting small stitching sections.

While working alongside their workers in stitching sections, Gounder owners enacted what they saw as their propensity to toil. Not everyone could enact toil with a similar authority that these Gounder simply assumed to be part of who they were. By disintegrating stitching sections as separate units of production, these Gounders made space to draw in and make 'toiling owners' of their male kin and castefellows. An exercise of class, Gounder masculinity, and toil allowed Gounder men to link power over stitching workers to power across networks of firms. Consequently, they remade the industrial form while remaking themselves as a new class faction, which I call Tiruppur's fraternal capital. In effect, these toiling capitalists were turning the entire town into a decentralised factory. They institutionalised their power by taking over the main owners' association, securing a long period of class conciliation with Tiruppur's communist labour unions. It seemed until the 1980s that the Gounder fraternity had forged its hegemony over industrial work.

Shifting hegemonies, and 'the feminisation of labour'

Fissures in what Buraway (1985) calls 'the politics of production' became clear in the mid-1980s, when the hegemony of fraternal capital would make way for a deepening of capitalist control through new gendered meanings and practices of work. As Tiruppur drew in more working daughters, fraternal capital became a stepping-stone for new forms of gendered class power and powerlessness, as the allegedly global process of 'the feminisation of labour' took particular form in Tiruppur's order of work.

As Tiruppur shifted to exports in the 1980s, women were employed for the first time in the knitwear industry. Rather than replacing male jobs, women worked in new sections of manual work for export production. While gender appeared in discussions in and about Tiruppur in the late 1980s to specifically address the problems of working women, these problems have to be seen as part of a transition from fraternal discipline of an entirely male workforce to a new mode of regulation of an increasing diversity of workers, wage levels, skill classifications, types of security, exposures to violence, and forms of sexualisation. This was a moment of shifting hegemonies, from a fraternal hegemony with some, albeit exclusionary, class mobility through Gounder toil, to a new gendered hegemony that deploys concern for women workers while routinising work and deepening class antagonisms.

While I explain the origins of fraternal capital as a product of regional forces, the new form of gendered hegemony resonates with much wider circuits of power and knowledge. Late twentieth-century notions of the 'feminisation of labour' operating through transnational media, scholarship, advocacy, production and other networks, assumed a natural connection between dexterous, docile, Asian/Latin American female bodies, on the one hand, and cheap labour for footloose global capital, on the other. The groundbreaking feminist critiques of Third World industrialisation fought this link as unjust, rather than asking how such fictitious articulations were maintained in practice (see, for instance, Elson and Pearson, 1981). More recent research asks how the discourse of feminisation works as a powerful, productive fiction in actual labour regimes, to produce a diversity of local gender politics at work (Lee, 1998; Salzinger, 2003). From the perspective of labour unions, gender struggles at work undermine the phenomenal grounds for labour solidarity based on romantic, masculinist conceptions of male breadwinners with sound family values as the militant vanguard of progressive change.

I explore this point in its particular form in Tiruppur through the 127-Day Strike of 1984, the key strike in Tiruppur's labour history after a decade of decline in union activity. Labour unions won an unprecedented demand for piece-rated workers in an unregulated industry in the South in 1984, 'dearness allowance': in effect, a living wage. The Gounder fraternity refused to abide by the legal victory. They took to the streets and tried physically to obstruct companies that paid dearness allowances. A few were arrested overnight by the embarrassed police, and garlanded as martyrs on their release. Owners' frustrated recourse to obstructing production called into question their ability to exercise hegemony in the context of an increasingly diverse workforce and an unexpected rise in union militancy. However, the strike also points to the ways in which union militancy would be undermined.

For this reason, I explore the way in which communist unions sought support through the long and arduous strike. Unions performed street theatre to spread news about the strike, through a class morality play expressing timeless differences between worker and owner *families*. This narrative is particularly telling of an emerging gendered hegemony. The main contrast is between owner and worker families and, as it progresses, the story zooms in on their daughters. The owner uses the opportunity of the strike to marry off his daughter, while the worker cannot pull together his daughter's dowry, so she commits suicide. What is striking about the play is the contrast with narratives of self-made men, in which the unit of value is the masculine individual. Now, fathers measure their worth in their ability to marry off their daughters, and the working-daughter cannot be the breadwinner fighting for her rights. There are important didactic implications to this gendered lexicon, as dedicated communist organisers are instructed to be impervious to deepening sexual divisions of labour and charged sexual politics. In the context of its audience, a workforce in the process of becoming increasingly differentiated and insecure, these ideas signal the incorporation of trade unionism into a new gendered hegemony that no longer required the visible authority of owners on the street.

There has, as of early 2006, never since been a strike on the scale of that of 1984. Instead the rights of workers have been systematically eroded in the transition to export production. The same period has seen the consolidation of a class of exporters unwilling to risk strikes of the same magnitude when time is of the essence in producing for seasonal export markets. Instead, union and owners' association leaders have sat down every three years since 1984 to chalk out elaborate General Agreements fixing all wage increases and benefits. While these agreements are remarkable on paper, the gap between institutionalised rights and workplace realities was widening in the late 1990s, and this appeared not to have changed in early 2006.

On the one hand, a class of exporters has risen out of the overt hegemony of fraternal capital to govern the industrial town as a whole. On the other hand, 'the feminisation of labour' has meant the domination of the working class through the differentiation of all labour contracts and the deployment of sexual violence and fear to keep workers divided. Tiruppur reveals the accumulation of capital and of working-class poverty and insecurity as gendered processes.

Gender, hegemony, resistance
There are the several implications of this study for a gendered analysis of industrialisation, hegemony and resistance. First, mainstream scholarly and policy analysis has retained an expectation that Tiruppur's dramatic late-twentieth-century growth might be reduced to a model that might be reproduced elsewhere. Attempts to reproduce Tiruppur through buildings and fiscal subsidies in the neighbouring state of Kerala fell flat in late 1998, without any attention to the conditions in Tiruppur that allowed certain 'self-made men' to accumulate capital and control labour.

Second, dominant explanations have it that Tiruppur's growth is a consequence of unleashed entrepreneurial energies that might still be bound by the chains of traditions of caste and sexism. This view neglects the fact that capitalism in Tiruppur, as elsewhere, has been radically transformative, and that it has made use of liberal individualism through, rather than despite, gender and caste exclusion. Finally, effective working-class resistance has to be understood in relation to capitalist hegemony, and to specific ways in which gender, class and caste articulate, and might be undone.

Acknowledgements

Research for this chapter was funded by the Social Science Research Foundation, the Fulbright Foundation, the University of California Chancellor's Dissertation Award, and the Michigan Society of Fellows. I remain indebted to Gillian Hart and Michael Watts, and to countless people who offered their time and thoughts in Tiruppur, 1996–98. Not least, thanks to Sylvia Chant and Lee Mager.

Note

1. The field and archival research for this project was conducted over two years, between 1996 and 1998, through an initial period of open-ended interviews and the collection of 201 life histories, which provided the basis for constructing a survey instrument to address the incidence of practices, norms and institutions surrounding agrarian transition, work histories, mechanisms of class mobility and industrial work practices. Survey research involved the random selection of 218 firm owners across the industrial cluster to determine 'routes of entry and affiliation'.

Select bibliography

Chari, Sharad (2004) *Fraternal Capital: Peasant-Workers, Self-Made Men and Globalization in Provincial India*, Palo Alto, CA: Stanford University Press.

Burawoy, Michael (1985) *The Politics of Production: Factory Regimes under Capitalism and Socialism*, London: Verso.

Elson, Diane and Ruth Pearson (1981) 'Nimble fingers make cheap workers', *Feminist Review*, 7, 87–107.

Lee, Ching-Kwan (1998) *Gender and the South China Miracle: Two Worlds of Factory Women*, Berkeley and Los Angeles, CA: University of California Press.

Marx, Karl (1967) *Capital: A Critique of Political Economy*, vol.1, New York: International Publishers.

Piore, Michael and Charles Sable (1984) *The Second Indus Divide: Possibilities for Prosperity*, New York: Baric Books.

Salzinger, Leslie (2003) *Genders in Production: Making Workers in Mexico's Global Factories*, Berkeley and Los Angeles, CA: University of California Press.

69 Economic transition and the gender wage gap in Vietnam: 1992–2002
Amy Y.C. Liu

Introduction

This chapter examines changes in the gender wage gap from 1992 to 2002 during which period an increase in economic openness has come to be part of Vietnam's reform process. While economic openness is associated with high growth, the benefits of such growth may not be gender-neutral as is sometimes assumed. Some studies find a decrease in the prices of agricultural goods produced by women, a 'masculinisation' of typically female employment such as in the textile industry, and a widening of the gender wage gap (for instance, Nicita and Razzar, 2003). Yet, other studies have shown that openness is beneficial to women, since it leads to less employer discrimination and a feminisation of the comparatively high-paid manufacturing sector. For instance, Oostendorp (2002) finds (trade) openness reduces gender wage gaps. These mixed results indicate that the effect of openness on women's relative economic position could depend on factors that are not traditionally considered as gender related, such as the industrial composition of the liberalisation process, and the initial conditions of the economy (see Fontana, 2003).

My chapter uses Vietnam as a case study to apply the inter-temporal decomposition method of Juhn et al. (1991) to examine explicitly the relationship between the degree of market reform (openness) and the gender pay gap by constructing a variable of the share of foreign-invested firms (joint ventures and 100 per cent foreign-owned companies) at the provincial level as a measure of openness. It addresses an important policy question, namely do women benefit as a result of economic liberalisation and subsequent economic growth? More specifically, does economic liberalisation change the industrial mix in such a way that it affects the extent to which females can reap the benefits of reform? Moreover, does the changing pace of reform in labour markets, along with economic growth rates, impact upon wage dispersion that affects men and women differently?

Having outlined the broad parameters of the study, the next section of this chapter presents background material on Vietnam's transition and the impacts on gender inequality. The third section describes the data and provides an overview of the level and distribution of wages of men and women in 1992, 1997 and 2002, and briefly describes the methodology. The fourth section presents the empirical findings, and the final section concludes with some reflections for policy.

Vietnam in transition and gender inequality

Economy in transition

The collapse of many state-owned enterprises (SOEs) in Vietnam led to the introduction of the market reform, *Doi Moi* (renovation), in 1986. This represented a significant step in Vietnam's transformation into a market-oriented economy, which grew at an unprecedented average rate of 9 per cent during the 1990s. Foreign investment during the earlier part of the 1990s seemed to play a particularly crucial role in Vietnam's economic expansion, providing capital, expertise and ideas for domestic firms to emulate.

In 1998 economic growth slowed sharply, with the growth rate falling to only 4.3 per cent in early 1999. The labour market weakened and unemployment began to rise. Foreign investment declined sharply. The most obvious cause was the economic crisis in the Asian region. The slowdown also had a domestic component: economic reform was incomplete. After the mid-1990s, the pace of reform slowed and, critically, priority was still given to the state sector, with ad hoc preferential measures routinely used to bail out SOEs in financial difficulty. As a result the private sector remained relatively small. For example, between 1995 and 1998 the domestic private sector contributed only 16 per cent of Vietnam's total industrial growth while the state sector accounted for 37 per cent.

The sharp appreciation of the real exchange rate against Vietnam's major trading partners from 1995 to 1998 changed the relative price of tradables to non-tradables. According to Le (2006), this brought about faster growth in non-tradables and in the import substitution industries (ISIs) where the share of women workers is lower than in the export-oriented industries (EOIs). For instance, between 1992 and 1998 employment shares in traditionally male-dominated industries such as construction, mining and utilities increased faster than women's employment. Le also finds that, in general, average wages in non-tradable and import substitution sectors tend to be higher than in the export sector (ibid.). The extent to which these shifts may have forced a widening of the gender pay gap needs to be evaluated in light of institutions to protect women workers put in place by the pre-reform Vietnamese state, and the changes which occurred during economic liberalisation.

Gender equality in transition
Vietnam experienced a long period of war. This provided opportunities for women to play prominent roles in the economy. Prior to economic liberalisation, the Vietnamese state had introduced a variety of regulations to protect women's rights in different spheres. For example, it placed high priority on increasing women's education and literacy, and sought to educate people about equity in marriage (including sharing housework between spouses), as well as introducing a number of measures to enhance women's position in the labour market. In addition to this, the Vietnamese government had provided extensive public services such as subsidised housing, health services, and childcare. These services had affected women indirectly by arguably lowering their cost of labour participation.

Although state regulations in favour of women continued into the early stages of liberalisation, most notably with the Labour Code of 1993 which, *inter alia*, provided for women to take paid maternity leave and which could have potentially worked against the recruitment of female workers, impressive economic growth in Vietnam before the Asian financial crisis brought about significant growth in export manufacturing, which generated significant employment opportunities for women. By the same token, economic liberalisation also carried some negative impacts. First, it led to the progressive withdrawal of public services. The withdrawal of these services increased the costs of labour participation for women, especially those with young children, and could have provided them a strong incentive to leave the workforce altogether. Second, notwithstanding increases in women's wages and employment during the early 1990s, the economic downturn and its aftermath could have adversely affected women if employed predominantly in hard-hit industries. Third, economic liberalisation led to increased autonomy with regard to hiring and firing decisions among employers, whose 'taste' was potentially influenced by a resurgence of 'Confucian values' (see Haughton and Haugton, 1995, and other studies on son preference in Vietnam and on the influence of the Confucian tradition in the post-reform era). The strong association of these with bias against women might have encouraged some employers to discriminate in favour of men in respect of recruitment and wage rates. In addition, this might have led to divergent educational tracks for women and men, thereby also affecting labour force divisions within industries.

Data
In order to explore the effects of openness of the Vietnamese economy on the gender pay gap, I use official data from the Vietnam Living Standards Surveys 1992–93, 1997–98 and the Vietnam Households Living Standards Survey 2001–02 to form a panel to derive a measure for openness at the provincial level. The sample includes wage-earners between 18 and 60 years old who worked in the preceding 12 months and who supplied earnings data. In 1992, this amounted to 1890 wage-earners (of whom 1094 were male), in 1997, 1596 wage-earners (958 of whom were male), and in 2002, 14 962 wage-earners (9184 of whom were male). Wage-earners in this age-group increased from 18 to 28 per cent of all survey respondents between 1992 and 2002, with the ratio of female to male workers staying relatively constant, at around the 40 per cent mark.

The main findings of the analysis are that in the period 1992–2002, the female-to-male wage ratio increased from 0.78 in 1993 to 0.80 in 1998 and 0.86 in 2002 and hence, the gender pay gap declined marginally.[1] This decline in the gender pay gap does not seem to owe to the fact that more females, especially the low skilled, left the labour force as unemployment among men is consistently higher than that of women. Instead, the narrowing of the gender pay gap appears to result from the following factors. First, in the period post-1992, women had consistently higher representation than men in upper secondary, vocational and tertiary education. Since women are on average better educated, they may more readily reap higher returns to their endowment. Second, local labour market openness measured by the employment share of foreign-invested firms, as occurred during the early stages of liberalisation, would raise the wages of female workers, thereby helping to close the gender pay gap. Third, market reforms may bring about increases in competition and hence raise the costs to employers if they discriminate against workers based on their sex rather than their productivity.

That the wage gap between women and men did not decline by a bigger margin over the entire period of the study probably owes to the following processes. First, despite the opening-up of opportunities for women in export-manufacturing in the early stages of liberalisation, women have remained under-represented in most economic sectors, and particularly those which are fast-growing. The exceptions are trade in 1992; manufacturing, trade and finance in 1998; and finance in 2002. Second, and in terms of pay, men generally receive higher wages than women in most branches of employment. Only in very few industries such as transportation, do women have higher average pay.

Finally, the increased autonomy of employers in hiring and firing has often been associated with the re-emergence of the traditional Confucian values. As mentioned earlier, this may increase discrimination against women.

Earning differences between women and men
In order to examine the dynamics of the gender earnings gap in more detail, in this section I estimate an earnings equation, including years of schooling, potential experience and its square, along with a set of industrial, sectoral and control variables, for each gender and year. These control variables include an individual's marital status, urban–rural and regional locations, and majority–minority status.[2] I then construct at a province-level the proportion of wage earners employed in foreign-invested firms, to examine the direct relationship between the pace of market reform (the competitiveness of the local labour market) and the gender wage gap.[3] As argued by Yang (2005), a measure such as the employment share of foreign-invested firms could proxy the openness in the labour market that could be driving local market competitiveness during transition. In addition, it could act as a control variable, as the distribution of foreign-invested enterprises is quite uneven. The provincial employment share in foreign-invested firms rose quite rapidly between 1992 and 1998 before declining. This may suggest that market competitiveness has slowed (either due to the appreciation of the *dong* [the Vietnamese unit of currency] relative to Vietnam's major trading partners, or to incomplete market reforms), or that provincial differences may have narrowed due to a widespread increase in the demand for skilled labour, with more women working for these firms than men.

The small change in the gender earnings gap could simply reflect the limited impact of the labour market reform process. Alternatively, this may be the combined result of other forces. Based on the earnings equations, and applying the decomposition method of Juhn et al. (1991), the principal changes in the gender wage gap could be due to four factors: (1) changes in gender differences in observed labour market characteristics, for example education and experience (observed skill effect); (2) changing prices of men's observed labour market characteristics (observed price effect); (3) discrimination (gap effect);[4] and (4) changing residual inequality (unobserved price effect).[5]

Table 69.1 shows that in the first sub-period, the observed skill effect (543 per cent), and observed and unobserved price effects (451 per cent and 908 per cent respectively), all work together to close the gap. The gap effect is the largest single factor slowing the convergence (1802 per cent). But in the second sub-period, the unobserved price effect (49 per cent) and the gap effect (102 per cent) are the only two converging factors. This more than offsets the disequalising impact of the observed skill, and observed price on equality (20 and 31 per cent respectively).

Factors such as openness and changes in the employment and wage distributions across regions and sectors hindered the closing of the overall gap from 1998 to 2002, despite the fact that these same variables had helped to narrow the gender gap five years earlier. Of the 20 per cent observed skill effect, 10, 10 and 3 per cent are (respectively) attributed to changes in openness and industrial and regional employment. Together they hindered the convergence of the overall pay gap. All other variables, except education, also worked to slow the closing of the gap.

The breakdown of the observed price effect indicates that changes in returns to different sectors increased gender inequality between 1998 and 2002 instead of closing it, as observed in the first sub-period. Notably, gender differences in the returns to

Table 69.1 Decomposition of the gender wage gap in Vietnam, 1992–2002

Inter-temporal decomposition	$D_{98}{}^1$–D_{93}	Percentage change	D_{02}–D_{98}	Percentage change	D_{02}–D_{93}	Percentage change
Change in wage gap in log	−0.005	100.00	−0.067	100.00	−0.072	100.00
Juhn et al (1991)						
Observed skill effect	−0.026	542.50	0.013	−19.80	0.091	−12.72
Observed price effect	−0.022	451.25	0.021	−30.55	−0.023	32.12
Gap effect	0.087	−1802.08	−0.068	−101.61	0.007	−9.48
Unobserved price effect	−0.044	908.33	−0.033	48.74	−0.065	90.07
Of which						
Gender-specific	0.060	−1258.33	−0.055	81.81	0.016	−22.20
Wage structure	−0.065	1360.42	−0.012	18.19	−0.085	122.20

Note: 1. D_t denotes the earnings differentials between men and women in year t. For instance, D_{98} represents the earnings differentials between men and women in 1998.

Source: Author's own calculations.

manufacturing jobs are the main culprits. In addition, openness increases the gender pay gap consistently throughout the ten-year period. The gap effect is positive initially but becomes negative after 1998.

The sum of the observed skill effect and the gap effect is known as the 'gender-specific effect'. Between 1992 and 1998, the relatively large gap effect offsets the observed skill effect, so that the gender-specific effect hinders the convergence of the gender wage gap. After 1998, the gap effect works against the observed skill effect to bring about the narrowing gender gap. If we look at the whole ten-year period, discrimination against women remains an obstacle.

The negative unobserved price effect over the ten-year period suggests that the male residual wage fell, contributing to a narrowing wage gap. Changes in the wage structure captured by the sum of unobserved price and observed price effects persistently contributed to the convergence of the gap. With the converging unobserved price effect offsetting the diverging observed price effect between 1998 and 2002, the gender gap continues to narrow.

Conclusions

During the period of economic liberalisation in Vietnam between 1992 and 2002, the overall gender wage gap decreased. However, this was not by a big margin, and greater narrowing of the gender gap appears to have been offset by two factors. First, men have caught up with women who previously benefited from their higher share of the labour force in foreign-invested firms, resulting in a disequalising impact on the gender gap. Second, the composition and wage structure of industry have worked against women.

Like most economic policies, economic liberalisation is not gender-neutral. It may magnify initial conditions such as gender differences in industry distribution and wage disparities. It is accordingly important to be aware of industries that predominantly employ women and to devise measures which might help women to benefit from the opportunities that economic liberalisation can potentially bring about.

This chapter has only focused on the wage sector and monetary rewards. However, economic liberalisation can clearly affect women in other ways, for example through working conditions, decision-making power, time allocation within households, and labour allocation between wage employment and self-employment (see Razavi and Staab, Chapter 65, this volume). Further research in these areas will improve our understanding of how gender inequality evolves – and how it might best be addressed.

Notes

1. The change in gender earnings gaps (in logarithms) are −0.005, −0.067 and −0.072 for the periods 1993–98, 1998–2002 and 1993–2002 respectively.
2. Seven regions are included: Red River Delta, North Central, Central Coast, Central Highland, South East, Mekong Delta and Northern Upland.
3. The hourly earnings of the main job over a 12-month period include cash and in-kind payment.
4. This component measures the change in the mean female position, for example, between 1992 and 1998 as compared to the residual distribution of Vietnamese males in 1998. It should be noted that the term 'discrimination' refers also to the impact of unobserved and omitted variables.
5. Unless otherwise stated, the shares accounted for by each effect in the overall change in gender earnings gap are reported.

Select bibliography

Fontana, Marzia (2003) *The Gender Effects of Trade Liberalisation in Developing Countries: A Review of Literature*, Discussion Papers in Economics, Brighton: University of Sussex.

Haughton, Jonathan and Dominique Haughton (1995) 'Son preference in Vietnam', *Studies in Family Planning*, **26** (6), 325–37.

Juhn, Chinhui, Kelvin M. Murphy and Brooks Pierce (1991) 'Accounting for the slowdown in black–white wage convergence', in Marvin H. Kosters (ed.), *Workers and Their Wages*, Washington DC: American Enterprise Institute Press, pp. 107–43.

Le, Anh Tu Packard (2006) *Gender Dimensions of Viet Nam's Comprehensive Macroeconomic and Structural Reform Policies*, Occasional Paper 14, Geneva: United Nations Research Institute for Social Development.

Nicita, Alessandro and Susan Razzaz (2003) *Who Benefits and How Much? How Gender Affects Welfare Impacts of a Booming Textile Industry in Madagascar*, Policy Research Working Paper No. 3029, Washington, DC: World Bank.

Oostendorp, Remco (2002) 'Does globalisation reduce the gender wage gap?', paper presented at the World Bank workshop on 'Gender, Growth and Poverty', Washington, DC, 20 June.

Yang, Dennis Tao (2005) 'Determinants of schooling returns during transition: evidence from Chinese cities', *Journal of Comparative Economics*, **33** (2), 244–62.

70 Gender, poverty and work in Cambodia
Katherine Brickell

This chapter focuses on the multidimensional relationships which exist between gender and poverty in contemporary Cambodian society. Within this remit, the chapter examines poverty trends and levels in the country, their gendered dimensions, and some of the everyday challenges that women face in different poverty-affected households, especially in relation to work. Drawing on research from low-income communities in Siem Reap (home to the global tourist site of Angkor)[1] it argues that unless the gendered politics of alleviating poverty both within and beyond the household are addressed, then women will continue to bear a disproportionate share of its burdens.

Poverty levels and trends: a brief overview
While in 1990, the first year of the United Nations Human Development Report, Cambodia's Human Development Index (HDI) placed it in the 'low human development' category, the country has now moved up to the 'medium human development' grouping. Poverty in Cambodia, however, remains a critical issue with the latest 2004 household survey finding that 35 per cent of Cambodians live below the national poverty line (World Bank, 2006). Further selected indicators are illustrated in Table 70.1.

Cambodia's poverty profile reflects the legacy of a political and economic evolution which according to the Asian Development Bank (2001: 2) 'sets it apart from most of its neighbouring countries'. Subjected to aerial bombardments during the US–Vietnam war, the country and its people then endured three decades of conflict, upheaval and displacement. The political and social policies of the Khmer Rouge regime (1975–79) left an estimated 1.7 million Cambodians (almost one-quarter of the population) dead and the populace at large suffering from exhaustion, starvation and/or disease. This decimation of human capital combined with the annihilation of both physical and social infrastructure has had – and continues to have – devastating effects.

Yet since the late 1990s and early 2000s there has been considerable evidence of rehabilitation, reconstruction, and development activity as evidenced by the growth in garment exports, tourism and construction. Progress in the agricultural sector, by contrast, has been slow, with 90 per cent of Cambodia's poor living in rural areas with limited access to roads, markets and basic services (Royal Government of Cambodia (RGC), 2006). This has been accompanied by the broader problem of increasing rural and urban social differentiation as Cambodia's development continues to be marked by urban bias, particularly in regard to enclaves of garment factories. Even in Siem Reap – a key driver of Cambodia's rapid increase in tourist numbers – the impact of tourism has yet to meet its full potential and it is notable that in 2004 Siem Reap was the third poorest province in the whole country (World Bank, 2006). Overall then, there remains an acute need for other sources of growth 'that are more rural, more broad-based and more pro-poor' (World Bank, 2006: ii).

Table 70.1 Selected information on human development, poverty and gender in Cambodia

Human Development Index (HDI) Rank/177 (and value)[1]	131 (0.598)
Human Poverty Index (HPI-1) Rank/108 (and value)[2]	85 (38.6)
Life expectancy at birth (years) 2005	58
Gender-related Development Index (GDI) rank/157 (and value) 2005	114 (0.594)
Gender Empowerment Measure (GEM) rank/93 (and value) 2005	83 (0.377)
Adult literacy rate % (aged 15+ older) 1995–2005 Female/Male	64.1/84.7
Combined gross enrolment ratio for primary, secondary and tertiary education (%), 2005 Female/Male	56/64
Economic activity rate (female rate as % of male rate, aged 15 and older), 2005	93

Notes:
1. The HDI is an aggregate index comprising information on life expectancy at birth, adult literacy among the population aged 15 years or more, the combined primary, second and tertiary gross enrolment ratio, and GDP per capita (expressed in US$ Purchasing Power Parity [PPP]).
2. The Human Poverty Index comprises four indicators: probability at birth of not surviving to the age of 40 years; adult literacy rate; population without sustainable access to an improved water source, and children under weight for age. The lower the value, the lower the incidence of poverty. As expected, given the high rate of infant and child mortality and malnutrition and the lack of public services (indicators used in construction of the HPI in table 1), Cambodia has a high HPI in relation to other Asian countries, except Bangladesh and Pakistan (UNIFEM et al., 2004).

Source: UNDP, *Human Development Report 2007/2008*, tables 1, 3, 28, 29 and 31.

Gender dimensions of poverty in Cambodia

In Cambodia, as elsewhere, poverty and gender are inextricably linked, and it is recognised that poverty cannot be reduced unless policies and programmes address the situation of women. To date however, the Cambodian government has mainly concentrated on the promotion of women as 'Precious Gems', which casts them as instrumental forces for economic development, often to the detriment of their educational opportunities, and with little regard for familial workloads (Brickell, 2008a). This has some resonance with Molyneux's (2006) wider concern about women's frequent use as a 'conduit of policy' in poverty reduction programmes. Indeed, further to this, the RGC (2006) promotes its apparent steady advances in gender equity almost solely in relation to women's increasing share of the total labour force. But while women's economic activity rate (as a percentage of the male rate, aged 15+) is the highest in the Southeast Asian region at 93 per cent, Cambodia has among the *lowest* levels of gender equality in Asia as measured by the GDI and GEM (see Table 70.1). Furthermore, there not only remains a large gulf between women's adult literacy in comparison with men's (64.1 per cent against 84.7 per cent), but gender-based violence is considered to represent the single most important challenge for Cambodia to reach the gender equality targets enshrined in the Millennium Development Goals (see Brickell, 2008b). This national picture is reflected in Cambodia's Participatory Poverty Assessment (PPA) which revealed consistent perceptions on the part of poor women that the time they spent each day meeting basic subsistence needs had increased in comparison with the past (ADB, 2001: 39).

This is well illustrated by the experiences of female construction workers from different types of household who migrated to Siem Reap, because of the aforementioned lack of opportunities for waged work in their rural homelands.[2] Like many other women across the world, the labourers I met were not only responsible for income-generation outside the home, but also for performing the bulk of unpaid reproductive tasks for their menfolk (see also Chant, Chapter 15, this volume). Spurred on variously by the need to pay school fees, to cope financially after divorce, desertion or the death of a family member, to compensate for declining agricultural conditions and, related to this, to counterbalance the perceived precariousness of male employment, female labourers represent an important constituency among Cambodian women who are doing more 'non-traditional' work than in the past (ADB, 2001).

After a day's labouring under the heat of the sun, 29-year-old Phoung still has to cycle over an hour back to her village to cook and clean for her family. Deserted by her husband, she has two sons aged 3 and 8 and told me more about her first job outside the home:

> I have been working in construction for two years and finished two hotels. I saw the construction site and asked for work. I do this because of family difficulties, working more and more. But everyday, I continue to have to cook for my sons before and after work. Luckily my aunt looks after my sons. I do not pay her. I have a pushbike to cycle to work and back – it takes over an hour one way. I get up at 4am and go to sleep at 10pm working 6 days a week. When I am away from home, my eight-year old son cooks and looks after his brother. Sometimes his cooking is raw or sometimes burnt. They often ask me for money and I am broke. I can't give it to them and they cry. I feel so pitiful.

As Phoung intimated in her interview, desertion is a major issue in Cambodia with no legal requisite for men to provide child support on divorce or separation. Phoung's response has been to work on Siem Reap's construction sites for the past two years and to rely on the heightened care responsibilities taken on by her aunt and oldest son. As a daily challenge that confronts all generations within female-headed households, then, material as well as time poverty is a serious problem. Furthermore, while analysis of consumption poverty data does not show female-headed households to be any poorer than those headed by men in Cambodia, locality-studies do show that certain types of female-headed households suffer particular economic disadvantages (UNIFEM et al., 2004). These economic difficulties are compounded, in Phoung's case, by anguish over her inability to provide for her children, thereby highlighting the role of poverty in undermining emotional well-being.

For older women living in male-headed households who are present in smaller numbers on the construction sites, motives for working are, again, primarily economic, and often driven by financial shortfalls on the part of their spouses. Leakthina, for instance, explains how her husband's attempts at growing and selling vegetables profitably are failing and thereby forcing the family into greater poverty. For Leakthina, the decision to migrate and to take on the physically demanding job was from her point of view at least, ever more necessary:

> My husband does not have any creative ideas about earning money for the family and although he didn't agree, I came anyhow! He asks people to tell me to come home soon. He doesn't have enough characteristics to be a man! . . . I work as a labourer because my family are poor and I cannot find an alternative job. My husband had a job beforehand. My husband did not suggest

I work. I decided by myself. I said to him, 'I feel real pity for you, but how can we deal with the difficulties?' Working here is harder than at home. My husband is hopeless now and refuses to work. Nowadays women can make more money than men. Men cannot do all the things like women. That's why men need women! Without women it is a deplorable situation!

As Leakthina suggests, women have little choice but to respond to household needs where men's commitment to work and/or family life is far from guaranteed. Indeed, her husband's refusal to work is compounded by the problem of supporting their five children. Due to high fertility and population boom in the 1980s, Cambodia has a very youthful demographic profile, with 43 per cent of the populace being younger than 15 years in 1998. This results in a high dependency ratio that also increases women's work burden (UNIFEM et al., 2004). Since Leakthina left to work in construction, her eldest daughter has had to drop out of school to look after the other children and do the housework. This endorses the point made by Chant (Chapter 15, this volume) that 'poverty is not just about the privation of minimum basic needs, but of opportunities and choices'.

A further issue of note is the disparity in wages between men and women and the potential impact this has on their relative capabilities to reduce household material poverty. On the building site for example, men can earn up to 5000 riels (US$1.25) per day working as casual laborers, while women commonly receive only 2500 riels for the same work (UNIFEM et al., 2004: 46). Mirroring circumstances such as Leakthina's, the ADB (2001: 40) found nationally that the burden of responsibility is particularly marked for older women living in poverty-affected households who control what little money the household may have. In fact, women are often deemed by men as essential for saving, as Seang, a 24-year-old motorbike driver explains: 'A man without a wife is a man that cannot save money for the future.' Referring to men's propensity to spend excessive amounts of money on alcohol and gambling, Seang's sentiment that men *need* women is also one that Leakthina remarks upon. While on the surface this may appear a potentially progressive assertion, it should not detract from the fact that in practice many women have to deal with the added pressure from their husbands to be thrifty as well as to somehow manage and/or curtail their husbands' household budget-decimating activities.

An additional common tension derives from men's concerns to limit the degree to which women ascend in the ranks of income provision. As Seang continued: 'I would not mind if my wife got a job as a civil servant or teacher but I would not allow her to earn more than me because I must earn the money . . . also she would have to work locally and not in another province. If I allowed her to support the family then I would not be a man!' Again highlighting the perceived centrality of men's provider role (but unlike Leakthina's husband, trying to uphold it), Seang places conditions – in respect of type of work, location and pay – on his wife's employment to ensure the primacy of his own. In a hierarchical culture, which emphasises female deference and respect to men as key values, wives such as Seang's must negotiate their partners' egos and sensitivities at the same time as trying to ensure that household needs are met.

Concluding thoughts

This chapter has highlighted some of the main issues that women negotiate as they try to secure their households' survival. Key issues identified include, *inter alia*, the overarching onus on women to come up with solutions to deal with household poverty and, in male-headed households specifically, to compensate for the gender asymmetry of contributions at the same time as navigating male sensitivities towards women's waged work. In these respects, Cambodian women are left not only to respond to household poverty but also to micro-manage the gendered politics of household poverty alleviation itself. Consonant with this, important avenues for further investigation are men's experiences and perceptions of poverty. This agenda encompasses men's reactions to poverty and/or the strategies that they adopt and, importantly, a deeper comprehension of the ways in which any such responses are influenced by men's understanding of the gendered power dynamics within their own households. Last, but not least, it is clear that many existing policy initiatives in Cambodia, as elsewhere, must move beyond an instrumental focus on women for the promotion of economic growth, to one that pays greater attention to the attainment of gender equity in all spheres of life.

Acknowledgements

The author wishes to thank the Economic and Social Research Council (Award No. PTA-030-2002-00869) for funding the fieldwork on which this chapter is based.

Notes

1. The fieldwork for this chapter was conducted between 2004 and 2005 and forms part of a wider project that charted the changing contours of gender relations in Cambodia's 'post-conflict' period. The research consisted of a total of 165 oral histories, discussion groups and semi-structured interviews. To obtain wider understanding, additional consultations with representatives from the Ministry of Women's Affairs (MOWA), Project Against Domestic Violence (PADV) and Cambodian Men's Network (CMN) were held in Phnom Penh.
2. According to the World Bank (2006: 70), construction is now showing signs of slowing down in the country and may arguably result in the re-entrenchment of livelihood related difficulties for uneducated young men and women who work in the sector.

Select bibliography

Asian Development Bank (ADB) (2001) *Participatory Poverty Assessment in Cambodia*, Manila: ADB.
Brickell, Katherine (2008a) 'Tourism-generated employment and intra-household inequality in Cambodia', in Janet Cochrane (ed.), *Asian Tourism: Growth and Change*, London: Elsevier, pp. 299–310.
Brickell, Katherine (2008b) '"Fire in the house": gendered experiences of drunkenness and violence in Siem Reap, Cambodia', *Geoforum*, 39 (5), 1667–75.
Molyneux, Maxine (2006) 'Mothers at the service of the new poverty agenda: Progresa/Oportunidades, Mexico's conditional transfer programme', *Journal of Social Policy and Administration*, 40 (4), 425–49.
Royal Government of Cambodia (RGC) (2006) *National Strategic Development Plan 2006–2010: For Growth, Employment, Equity and Efficiency to Reach Cambodia Millennium Development Goals*, Phnom Penh: RGC.
United Nations Fund for Women (UNIFEM), World Bank, Asian Development Bank (ADB), United Nations Development Programme (UNDP) and Department for International Development (DFID/UK) with the Ministry of Women's Affairs (2004) *A Fair Share for Women: Cambodia Gender Assessment*, Phnom Penh: UNIFEM, WB, ADB, UNDP and DFID/UK.
World Bank (2006) *Cambodia: Halving Poverty by 2015? Poverty Assessment 2006*, Report no. 35213-KH, 7 February, East Asia and Pacific Region, Washington, DC: World Bank.

# 71 Informality, poverty and gender: evidence from the Global South
Marty Chen

Persistent poverty and gender inequality are major challenges of the twenty-first century. More than 1 billion people struggle to survive on less than US$1 a day (UN, 2005). Of these, roughly half are working (ILO, 2005). By definition, these working poor cannot work their way out of extreme poverty. They simply do not earn enough to feed themselves and their families, much less to deal with the economic risks and uncertainty they face. Most of the working poor are engaged in the informal economy where, on average, earnings are low and risks are high. Women are more likely than men to be engaged in the informal economy, particularly in the lower echelons. This makes it particularly hard for female-headed households, especially those in which there is no adult male earner, to work their way out of poverty. Yet employment is not high on the international agenda for poverty reduction, and the links between informality, poverty and gender are not well understood. This chapter makes the case for an increased focus on employment, particularly informal employment, in efforts to reduce poverty and gender inequality.

The first section of this chapter discusses the definition and concept of informal employment. The second section outlines key links between informality, poverty, and gender. These are then explored in the third section with reference to recent research findings from a cross-section of developing countries. The concluding section calls for a reorientation of economic policies to focus on creating more and better work; and, more specifically, for increased 'Visibility, Voice and Validity' ('3-V') of the working poor, especially women, in the informal economy.

The informal economy

Historical debates
Although its role in economic development has been hotly debated since its 'discovery' in Africa in the early 1970s, the informal economy has continued to prove a useful concept to many policymakers, activists and researchers. This is because the reality it seeks to capture – the large share of the global workforce that remains outside the world of full-time, stable and protected employment – is so significant. At present, there is renewed interest in the informal economy worldwide. This largely stems from the fact that, contrary to the predictions of many economists, the informal sector has not only grown, but has also emerged in new guises and in unexpected places. It now represents a quite significant but largely overlooked share of the world economy and workforce. Moreover, informal employment is likely to expand significantly during the current global economic crisis.

New term and expanded definition
To capture all dimensions of informality, the Statistics Bureau of the International Labour Office (ILO), the International Expert Group on Informal Sector Statistics ('Delhi Group'), and the global research policy network Women in Informal Employment: Globalising and Organising (WIEGO), have worked together to develop an expanded concept and statistical definition of 'informal employment' that includes informal employment both inside and outside informal enterprises. This expanded definition was endorsed at the International Labour Conference (ILC) in 2002 and the International Conference of Labour Statisticians (ICLS) in 2003.[1]

So defined, informal employment is a large and heterogeneous category. For purposes of analysis and policy-making it is useful to divide formal and informal employment into more homogeneous sub-sectors according to status of employment,[2] as follows:

Informal self-employment including:

- employers in informal enterprises
- own-account workers in informal enterprises
- unpaid family workers (in informal and formal enterprises)
- members of informal producers' cooperatives.

Informal wage employment: employees without formal contracts, worker benefits or social protection employed by formal or informal enterprises/employers or by households. Depending on the scope of labour regulations and the extent to which they are enforced and complied with, informal employment relations can exist in almost any type of wage employment. However, certain types of wage work are more likely than others to be informal. These include:

- employees of informal enterprises
- casual or day labourers
- temporary or part-time workers
- paid domestic workers
- unregistered or undeclared workers
- industrial outworkers (also called homeworkers).

Informality, poverty and gender

Size and significance
Informal employment is particularly important in developing countries, where it occupies one-half to three-quarters of the non-agricultural workforce. More specifically, 48 per cent of non-agricultural employment in Northern Africa is informal, 51 per cent in Latin America, 65 per cent in Asia, and 72 per cent in sub-Saharan Africa (or 78 per cent if South Africa is excluded) (ILO, 2002). If informal employment in agriculture is included, as some countries have done, the proportion of informal employment increases substantially: from 83 per cent of non-agricultural employment to 93 per cent of total employment in India; from 55 to 62 per cent in Mexico; and from 28 to 34 per cent in South Africa (ibid.).

Throughout the developing world, informal employment is generally a more significant source of employment for women than formal employment, and also a larger source of employment for women than men. Other than in Northern Africa, where 43 per cent of women workers are in informal employment, 60 per cent or more of women workers in the developing world are in informal employment (outside agriculture). In sub-Saharan Africa, 84 per cent of women non-agricultural workers are informally employed compared with 63 per cent of men, and in Latin America the respective figures are 58 per cent versus 48 per cent. In Asia, the proportion is 65 per cent for both women and men.

Composition and segmentation
In the developing world, self-employment comprises a greater share of informal employment (outside of agriculture) than does wage employment, ranging from 60 to 70 per cent of informal employment, depending on the region. In most countries for which data are available, women (as well as men) in informal employment are more likely to be in self-employment than in wage employment. In Northern Africa and Asia and at least half of the countries of sub-Saharan Africa and Latin America, more women in informal employment (outside agriculture) are in self-employment than in wage employment. By contrast informal wage employment is more important for women in Kenya, South Africa and four countries in South America – Brazil, Chile, Colombia and Costa Rica. In these countries more than half of women in informal employment are wage workers. Moreover, in all but one of these countries – South Africa – women are more likely to be informal wage workers than men. In explaining these patterns, it is important to recognise that paid domestic work is an important category of informal employment for women in all Latin American countries as well as in South Africa.

But the informal economy, especially in developing countries, is more highly segmented than the simple wage employment versus self-employment dichotomy would suggest. The main segments of informal employment, classified by employment status, are as follows:

1. Employers: owner operators of informal enterprises who hire others.
2. Employees: unprotected employees with a known employer: either an informal enterprise, a formal enterprise, a contracting agency or a household.
3. Own-account workers: owner-operators of single-person units or family businesses or farms who do not hire others.
4. Casual labourers: wage workers with no fixed employer who sell their labour on a daily or seasonal basis.
5. Industrial outworkers: subcontracted workers who produce from their homes or a small workshop.
6. Paid contributing members of cooperatives or producer groups.
7. Unpaid contributing family workers: family workers who work in family businesses or farms without remuneration.

With respect to non-agricultural informal employment, women are more likely than men to work as own-account workers, domestic workers, and unpaid contributing workers in family enterprises (Chen et al., 2005). In contrast, men are more likely to work as employers and wage workers (ibid.), and generally comprise the majority of informal agricultural workers. However, in many countries women still account for a large share of own-account agricultural workers and a majority of unpaid workers on family farms. Typically, few women are employed as informal agricultural wage workers. Informal agricultural employment tends to be more precarious than non-agricultural informal work, and it is characterised by very low earnings, uncertain incomes and high risks of poverty.

To understand labour markets in developing countries, it is important to recognise the multi-segmented nature of the informal economy. To address poverty and gender inequality, it is also important to take into account the work arrangements, and associated costs and benefits, of different segments of the informal economy for women and men.

Links among informality, gender and poverty: key findings from recent research
Making the links among informality, gender, and poverty means assessing the costs and benefits associated with different segments of informal employment against the location of the working poor, both women and men, within them. Statistical data on associated costs and benefits are limited, so testing these linkages statistically is very difficult. What follows is a summary of findings on the *average earnings* and/or the *poverty risk* of different segments of the labour force, both formal and informal, from an analysis of national data in five countries – Costa Rica, Egypt, El Salvador, Ghana, and South Africa. This research was commissioned by the United Nations Fund for Women (UNIFEM) for its 2005 issue of *Progress of the World's Women* from the WIEGO network. Findings from analyses of recent national data from Tunisia and India are also presented.

Employment and earnings
The links between employment, gender, and poverty can be seen by comparing first, average earnings in formal and informal employment, and second, average earnings in different categories of informal employment. In respect of the former, in all five countries studied for the UNIFEM publication, average earnings in most forms of informal employment, particularly in agriculture, are well below those in formal employment. In Costa Rica and El Salvador, however, average earnings for *informal employers* are equal to, or higher than, earnings in formal employment, and in Ghana and South Africa, average earnings of *informal public wage workers* are higher than those of *formal private sector employees*. In general, earnings in wage employment in the public sector, both formal and informal, are higher than in wage employment in the private sector (see Chen et al., 2005: ch. 3 for further details).

In terms of differences in average earnings *within* informal employment, these are quite substantial in line with the diverse and segmented nature of the informal economy. For instance, an analysis of 1997 data on employment in the informal sector (small unregistered enterprises) in Tunisia found that the employers who hired others – the microentrepreneurs – were not poor. Indeed, the average income of microentrepreneurs was found to be four times as high as the legal minimum salary and 2.2 times the average salary in the formal sector.

Although microentrepreneurs may have relatively high earnings in Tunisia – and elsewhere – most workers in informal employment do not fare so well. For example, the Tunisian study included information on homeworkers, who are paid by the piece. These earned a monthly average of 60 dinars (approximately US$57 in 1997), which was only 30 per cent of the minimum wage (Charmes and Lakehal, forthcoming).

In all five countries studied for the UNIFEM publication, a similar hierarchy of average earnings across the different segments of the informal economy was found. To begin with, average earnings in agricultural informal employment are lower than average earnings in non-agricultural informal employment. In respect of the latter, informal employers in all five countries have the highest average earnings followed by own-account workers, and then casual wage workers and domestic workers (Charmes and Lakehal, forthcoming; also Chen et al., 2005).

Within informal employment, women's hourly earnings in the UNIFEM country studies uniformly fall below those of men in identical employment statuses. The gender gap in earnings is particularly pronounced among own-account workers – both agricultural and non-agricultural. This gender gap in earnings is compounded by the gendered segmentation of informal employment, as women are more likely to be own-account workers than regular wage workers.

Employment and poverty
Poverty is usually measured at the household level. In order to measure the poverty risk among employed persons, an innovative technique was used for the UNIFEM publication. According to this technique, the 'poverty risk' associated with different employment statuses is defined as the share of all persons employed in a given status residing in households whose incomes place them below the national poverty line. This technique connects the type of employment, measured at the *individual* level, to the risk of poverty, measured at the *household* level. The hierarchy of poverty risk so defined is the reverse of the hierarchy of earnings detailed above: informal agricultural workers have the highest risk of poverty and, among the non-agricultural informally employed, informal employers have the lowest risk of poverty, own-account workers have a higher risk of poverty, while casual wage workers and domestic workers have the highest risk (Chen et al., 2005).

In the UNIFEM study countries, gender-based differences in poverty risk are associated with the multi-segmented character of the labour force, as women are concentrated in forms of employment with low earnings and higher poverty rates. However, no systematic pattern emerged in the country case studies in terms of differences between men's and women's poverty rates *within* a particular employment status. One possible explanation is that households in which women are engaged in remunerative work might have lower poverty rates relative to households in which women do not allocate time to income-generating activities. If this is the case, a household's poverty status can be determined by women's access to paid employment, no matter how low their earnings.

Hierarchies of earnings and poverty risk
The statistical evidence presented above suggests a hierarchy of earnings and poverty risk across the various segments of the labour force. While average earnings are higher in formal employment than in informal, there is also a hierarchy of earnings within the informal economy. Employers have the highest average earnings followed by their employees and other 'regular' informal employees, then own-account workers, followed by casual wage workers and domestic workers, and finally industrial outworkers. Within this hierarchy, women are disproportionately represented in segments of the informal labour force with low earnings (see Figure 71.1). The fact that women tend to be

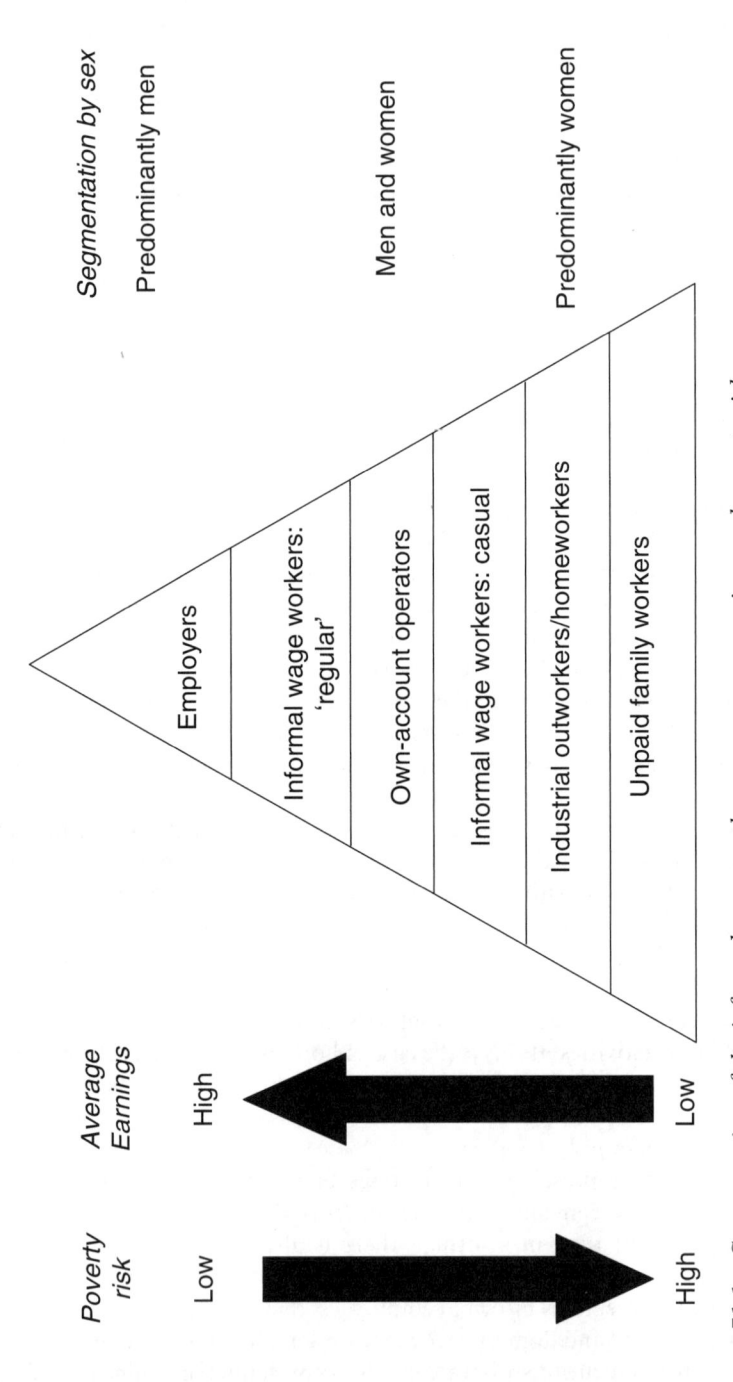

Figure 71.1 Segmentation of the informal economy by sex, average earnings and poverty risk

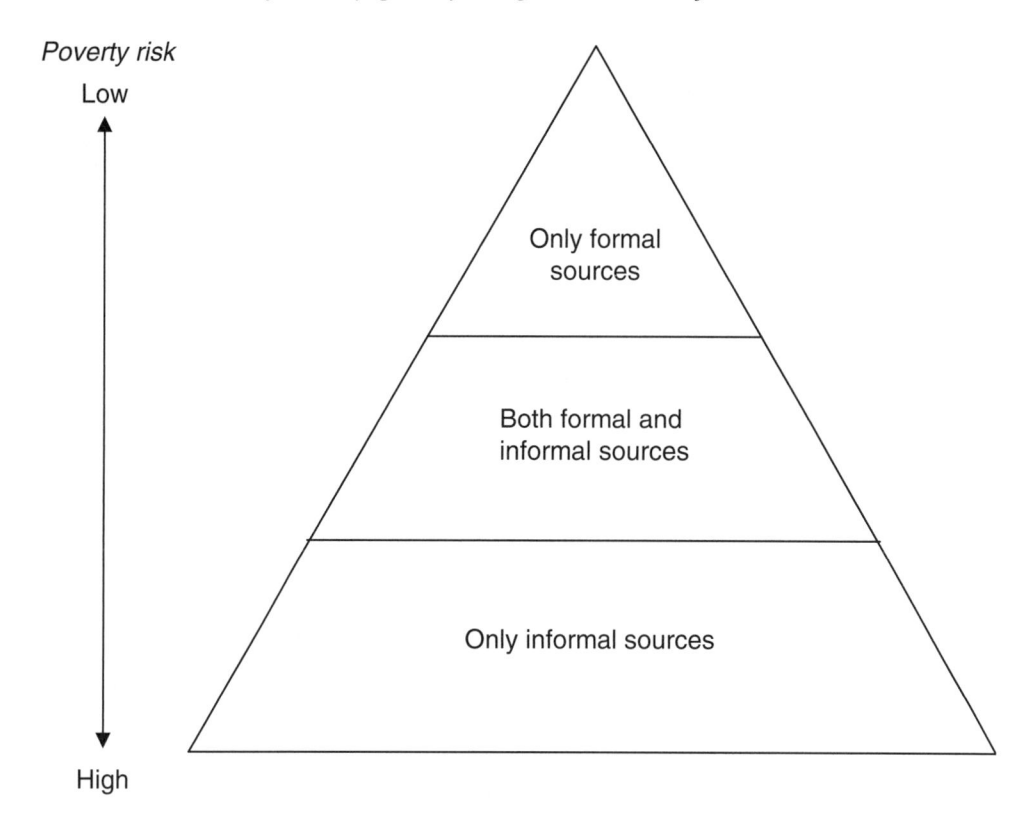

```
Poverty risk
   Low
    ▲
    │
    │           ╱╲
    │          ╱  ╲
    │         ╱    ╲
    │        ╱ Only  ╲
    │       ╱ formal  ╲
    │      ╱  sources   ╲
    │     ╱──────────────╲
    │    ╱                ╲
    │   ╱  Both formal and ╲
    │  ╱   informal sources ╲
    │ ╱──────────────────────╲
    │╱                        ╲
    │                          ╲
    │    Only informal sources
    │
    ▼
   High
```

Figure 71.2   Poverty risk of households by sources of income

under-represented among informal employers and 'regular' informal wage workers and over-represented among industrial outworkers leads to a *gender gap in average earnings and in poverty risk* within the informal economy: average earnings are lower and the risk of poverty is higher among all women workers in the informal economy compared with their male counterparts.

Available evidence from the five UNIFEM study countries suggests a hierarchy of poverty risk among households that depend on different sources of income. Households that rely primarily on income from informal employment face higher poverty rates than those which rely on income from formal employment, as depicted in Figure 71.2. The fact that women are less likely than men to be engaged in formal employment means that female-headed households without an adult male earner are at greater risk of poverty than male-headed households (see also Brydon, Chapter 16, this volume).

Addressing informality, reducing poverty and gender: introducing the '3-V' framework
Since earnings from employment are people's main source of income, the quantity and quality of employment available to women, men and households matter a great deal in determining who is poor and who is not – not only in terms of income poverty but also in terms of other dimensions of poverty. As this chapter has illustrated, most of the working poor are engaged in informal employment. Efforts to combat poverty must,

therefore, pay greater attention to needs and constraints faced by the working poor in the informal economy. This requires creating more and better formal jobs as well as increasing the earnings of those who continue to work in the informal economy. As such, a major reorientation of economic thinking, planning and policy is in order. The global community needs to recognise that there are no shortcuts to reducing poverty and gender inequality, and that economic growth alone – even if supplemented by social policies to compensate the losers – cannot eliminate poverty and inequality. Rather, increasing and improving employment opportunities – especially for working poor women and men – must be a core priority and target of all economic policies.

To ensure that economic policies are (re)oriented towards creating more and better employment, the working poor, especially women, need to be empowered to hold policymakers accountable. This, in turn, requires three enabling conditions: namely, increased 'Voice, Visibility and Validity' ('3-V') (see also Perrons, Chapter 62, this volume).

The condition of 'Visibility' requires that the working poor, especially women in the informal economy are visible in labour force statistics. More countries need to collect statistics on informal employment, broadly defined, and countries that already do so need to improve the quality of the statistics that they collect. Also, all forms of informal employment need to be integrated into economic models of labour markets. Since existing models focus on the supply and demand of wage labour, the self-employed tend to be excluded. A second area of neglect pertains to insufficient delineation between different types of waged workers. A third problem is that the extent of *underemployment* is not taken into account, despite its role in providing a more accurate measure of the 'employment problem' in developing countries than open unemployment.

In respect of the condition of 'Voice', the working poor, especially women, in the informal economy, need a representative – and stronger – voice in the processes and institutions that determine economic policies and formulate the 'rules of the (economic) game'. This requires building and supporting organisations of informal workers and extending the coverage of existing trade unions, cooperatives, and other worker organisations to include informal workers. This also requires making rule-setting and policy-making institutions more inclusive and helping representatives of the working poor gain 'a seat at the (policy) table'.

The condition of 'Validity' refers to recognition and validation. The working poor, especially women, in the informal economy need legal identity and validity as workers and economic agents, and also need to be recognised as legitimate targets of policy.

In conclusion, poverty cannot be reduced by expecting economic policies to generate employment and social policies to compensate the losers. Economic growth often fails to generate sufficient employment or decent employment, and compensation through social policies is seldom sufficient and often neglected altogether. Reducing poverty and gender inequality requires a major reorientation in economic priorities to focus on employment, not just growth and inflation. To be effective, strategies to reduce poverty and promote equality should be *worker centred*: that is, they must focus on the needs and constraints of the working poor, especially women, *as workers*, not only as citizens, as members of a vulnerable group, or as members of poor households. This requires pursuing an inclusive development policy process that includes the voices of the working poor and validates their contribution to the economy.

Notes

1. In 1993 the ICLS adopted an international statistical definition of the 'informal sector' to refer to employment and production in small and/or unregistered enterprises. In 2003 the ICLS endorsed guidelines for measuring certain types of informal wage employment outside informal enterprises. Statisticians refer to this larger concept as 'informal employment'.
2. 'Employment status' is a conceptual framework used by labour statisticians to delineate two key aspects of labour contractual arrangements: the *allocation of authority* over the work process and the outcomes of the work done, and the *allocation of economic risks* involved (ILO, 2002).

Select bibliography

Charmes, Jacques and Lakehal, Mustapha (forthcoming) 'Industrialisation and new forms of employment in Tunisia', in Martha Chen, Renana Jhabvala and Guy Standing (eds), *Rethinking Informality and Work*, Cambridge: Women in Informal Employment: Globalising and Organising/WIEGO.

Chen, Martha, Joann Vanek, Francie Lund and James Heintz, with Renana Jhabvala and Christine Bonner (2005) *Progress of the World's Women 2005: Women, Work and Poverty*, New York: UNIFEM.

International Labour Office (ILO) (2002) *Women and Men in the Informal Economy: A Statistical Picture*, Geneva: ILO.

International Labour Office (ILO) (2005) *World Employment Report 2004–05: Employment, Productivity and Poverty Reduction*, Geneva: ILO.

Sastry, Nittala Subrahmanya (2004) *Estimating Informal Employment and Poverty in India*, Discussion Paper Series No. 7, Delhi: United Nations Development Programme, India.

United Nations (UN) (2005) *The Millennium Development Goals Report*, New York: UN.

72 The empowerment trap: gender, poverty and the informal economy in sub-Saharan Africa
Kate Meagher

The ongoing expansion of the informal economy in the face of liberalisation and globalisation has fuelled debates about whether women's increased participation in informal economic activity contributes to their empowerment or to their impoverishment. Economists and economic anthropologists have tended to see the informal economy as a source of economic opportunity for women in a sphere free of the gender-biased regulations of the formal economy (USAID, 2005). By contrast, more critical feminist and political-economy analyses have argued that the informal economy represents a poverty trap for women, concentrating them in low-skill, low-income activities with little prospect of advancement (see Chant and Pedwell, 2008; Chen et al., 2006; Sassen, Chapter 2, this volume, for discussions and references).

In the past decade, statistical surveys confirm a significant increase in women's informal sector participation, leading to what has been called the 'feminisation of informal labour' (Chant and Pedwell, 2008: 13). Across Africa, Asia and Latin America, 70 per cent of women in the non-agricultural labour force are informally employed, compared with less than 60 per cent of men (USAID, 2005: 18). This feminisation of informality is particularly pronounced in sub-Saharan Africa, where 84 per cent of women are in informal employment, as against 63 per cent of men. However, rising informal economic participation has been accompanied by an intensification rather than a reversal of gender disparities in income, economic opportunity and burdens of reproductive labour. Studies have shown that the gender disparity in income is higher in the informal economy than in the formal economy, for the self-employed as well as for wage workers, owing to differential access to capital and skills, and gender segregation of informal labour markets. A recent review of studies on gender and informality by the International Labour Organisation (ILO) reveals that in Latin America, women earn 64 per cent of men's wages in the *formal* economy, but only 52 per cent of men's wages in the *informal* economy (Chant and Pedwell, 2008: 6).

Attempts to address the link between gender, informality and poverty reflect the diversity of ideological perspectives on the role of the informal economy in development. Free market perspectives continue to represent the informal economy as a sphere of women's empowerment, and advocate the removal of cultural, legal and economic barriers that impede women's access to the full benefits of informal market opportunities. More critical perspectives argue that alleviating women's poverty requires reducing rather than promoting women's participation in informal activities. Indeed, reducing women's reliance on informal work was identified as a strategic priority for the realisation of the third Millennium Development Goal (MDG) of 'promoting gender equality and empowering women' (Chant and Pedwell, 2008: 13).

Debates about the impact of informality on women must begin with a clear understanding of what the informal economy is. While the concept has been much debated, significant consensus has emerged among contemporary scholars and activists. During the 1990s, definitions focused on unregistered firms and their employees, but an extended definition was adopted by the ILO in 2002 which includes all workers, in formal or informal firms, who operate outside the framework of state regulations (Chen et al., 2006: 2132). This includes employers, workers and own-account workers in unregistered enterprises, as well as industrial outworkers and employees in registered firms who are excluded from statutory labour protection (see also Chen, Chapter 71, this volume).

This chapter explores gaps and new directions in the theorisation of the link between gender, informality and poverty, with a particular focus on sub-Saharan Africa, where women have the highest levels of informal sector participation (see Chen, Chapter 71, this volume). It will advocate a more dynamic perspective, which moves away from a focus on removing gender-based obstacles to women's economic advancement, towards an analysis of how the dynamics of gender and informality are shaped by wider macro-economic processes and power structures in ways that systematically disadvantage women. The exploration of more effective theoretical directions will be accompanied by reflections on implications for research and policy.

Informality and gender-based obstacles to empowerment
Conventional interpretations tend to regard gender-based disadvantage within the informal economy as a product of obstacles to full economic participation in informal economic opportunities. Despite mounting evidence of gender inequalities in the informal realm, economists maintain that informal economic participation offers women a sphere of economic and social empowerment as well as contributing to greater poverty alleviation at the household level (USAID, 2005). Informal employment is seen as an ideal solution to the 'double burden' of economic and domestic responsibilities, providing women with more flexible forms of employment that can be adapted to household and childcare demands. The source of inequality is not seen to lie in informal market dynamics, but in market failures caused by discriminatory legal regulations and cultural norms. Economic explanations argue for the need to remove legal and cultural obstacles to women's access to assets, credit, skills and lucrative informal activities in order to unleash the empowering effects of the informal economy. In short, what is needed is to free-up markets in order to maximise women's ability to benefit from informal economic opportunities, supplemented by targeted microfinance, education and social services to rectify gendered inequalities in access to skills and credit.

While identifying genuine constraints to women's economic empowerment within the informal economy, market liberal interpretations tend to ignore the deeper economic and social dynamics governing how these constraints operate. Their rather tautological assumption that women's empowerment in the informal economy only requires stripping away obstacles to fuller participation glosses over mounting evidence that women's increased informal participation is concentrating them in 'survivalist' rather than 'growth' activities owing to the constraints of women's reproductive responsibilities and the gendered structure of informal labour markets (Chant and Pedwell, 2008; Chen et al., 2006; see also Casier, Chapter 94, this volume).

In contrast to market liberal perspectives, feminist economics contends that freer access to informal labour markets will not eliminate the disadvantages arising from male-biased institutions. As Elson (1999) explains, labour markets are 'bearers of gender', embodying and transmitting gender inequalities in ways that systematically disadvantage women, even when constraints on market participation are removed. Feminist analyses were quick to highlight how neoliberal economic reforms increased rather than alleviated women's economic disadvantage by intensifying demands on women's unpaid labour as states withdrew from social service provision, turning the 'double burden' into a 'triple burden' of domestic labour, income generation and voluntary provision of social welfare services (Elson, 1999). The disadvantaging effects of informal employment on women require attention to deeper social and legal constraints that structure markets and patterns of resource control. Recent research on the gendered operation of labour markets highlights the tendency of informal employment to concentrate women in a narrow range of increasingly saturated, low-income activities, owing to women's domestic responsibilities, unequal access to skills and resources, and the gender division of labour within the informal economy (Chant and Pedwell,2008; Chen et al., 2006). It is also noted that women often lack control of the incomes they earn owing to pre-emptive claims of male household members and increasing responsibilities for household maintenance, raising questions about the empowering effects of informal employment and microcredit (Elson, 1999; see also Mohamed, Chapter 86, this volume; Mutalima, Chapter 93, this volume). Despite their deeper focus on the gendered institutional dynamics of markets, feminist perspectives tend to understand empowering women in terms of freeing them from the constraints of male power as well as from barriers to market entry.

Increasing access to informality: empowerment or exposure?
The big question is whether prying women free of male-dominated institutions empowers women or exposes them. Leveraging women's access to income, credit, land and other assets free of male intermediation at the household and community level strips away institutional protection as well as constraints, subjecting women directly to the discipline of the free market. The intensive focus on the constraints of gendered institutions tends to ignore their risk-reducing role, particularly within the informal economy. In most African societies, gendered informal institutions regulate complex use and inheritance rights over landed as well as non-landed property which embed economic rights for women within the household and lineage (see Rakodi, Chapter 54, this volume). While not granting women the same rights as men, the differences are as much risk-minimising as discriminatory – a reality substantiated by the greater vulnerability of most female-headed households. The contemporary disadvantages faced by African women have more to do with the gendered effects of wider economic and political pressures on local institutions than with the inherently oppressive character of those institutions.

Indeed, the effect of stripping away gendered 'constraints' to informal employment and economic decision-making within the household has been more disempowering than liberating, particularly for poor women. Research has shown that informal employment and targeted microcredit have produced an increasing transfer onto women of the burdens of social reproduction abdicated by the state and by poor men, leading to what Saskia Sassen (2002) has called 'the feminisation of survival' (see also Sassen, Chapter 2, this volume). Amid the depredations of economic restructuring, the growing role of women as 'breadwinners' through increased informal income-generation and more direct access to credit have tended to increase women's share of reproductive responsibilities, diminish their control over income, and intensify rather than alleviate women's economic vulnerability in the face of diminishing male household contributions (see Chant, Chapter 15, this volume; also Sassen, Chapter 2, this volume). Elson (1999: 618) refers to this as one of the 'gender paradoxes of restructuring' in which economic empowerment through the informal economy has placed women increasingly at the mercy of global market forces, deepening their vulnerability to poverty. She highlights the need to direct attention beyond the household and national regulatory systems, to the 'command and control structures of the economy' at the global level.

Gender, informality and macroeconomic process
The counter-intuitive effects of increased informal economic participation on women's poverty and vulnerability have shifted analytical attention from 'constraints' at the level of the household and the state, to a consideration of the gendered effect of wider macroeconomic processes. New research on gender and informality emanating from the ILO and from gendered research on global value chains focuses on the gender dynamics of wider processes of global economic change, with specific attention to informal labour markets, global commodity chains and transnational livelihood networks (Barrientos et al., 2003; Pearson, Chapter 64, this volume; Sassen, 2002). Detailed empirical studies explore the impact of new pressures and opportunities on the gendered structure of informal labour markets, as well as tracing the gendered effects of regulatory practices within global commodity chains. These studies show that the effects of global and national economic change have not been to limit women's entry into labour markets, but to incorporate them on worse terms, pushing them into more temporary and vulnerable employment within the informal economy, while excluding them from some of the more lucrative opportunities opened up by globalisation and liberalisation.

These gendered processes of global economic change have played themselves out in distinctive ways in different regions. In African societies, where women's informal economic participation is the highest of any region, many of the most lucrative informal economic opportunities are absent (USAID, 2005). Africa is largely marginalised from global commodity chains involved in manufacturing or data processing, which offer the most advantageous informal employment opportunities for women, but has experienced a significant feminisation of labour in high value agricultural commodity chains for such commodities as fresh flowers, and fresh fruit and vegetables. In Kenya, South Africa and Zambia, which have the most rapidly growing high value agricultural export industries, women make up 50–75 per cent of the agricultural labour force, but are concentrated in the most vulnerable and temporary segments of the chain (Barrientos et al., 2003: 1514).

Outside of agriculture, informal employment opportunities for African women are heavily concentrated in domestic labour, petty trade, and local crafts. Contrary to prevailing assumptions, economic restructuring has precipitated changes in the gender division of labour within informal labour markets across Africa, but these have also tended to increase rather than alleviate women's disadvantage. In the face of high unemployment and intense competition within the informal economy, men have begun to shift into more lucrative women's informal opportunities, such as women's tailoring and informal cosmetics manufacturing in West Africa, and beer-brewing in East Africa (Chant and Pedwell, 2008). Conversely, women are shifting into men's informal activities at the lower end, appearing as employees in the male preserves such as informal auto mechanics. While this represents an erosion of gender segregation within informal labour markets, it is occurring in a way that depresses women's income-generating possibilities, while improving those of men.

In many parts of Africa, informal livelihoods have gone global, triggering a proliferation of transnational informal economic networks, but once again women have been largely concentrated at the most vulnerable, low-income end of these activities. Celebratory references to the 'Mama Benz' trading networks in West Africa gloss over the fact that most of Africa's dynamic global trading networks, such as the Hausa networks of Nigeria, the Mouride networks of Senegal, and the Somali *hawala* (informal money broker) networks, are exclusively male. By contrast, the most rapidly expanding sources of transnational informal employment for African women have revolved largely around 'global care chains' for unregistered domestic labour or care of the elderly, and global prostitution networks associated with rising levels of female trafficking (Meagher, 2001; Pearson, Chapter 64, this volume; Sassen, 2002, and Chapter 2, this volume).

What is clear from the African case is that the dynamics of informality and gender are not just about access to informal employment, but about the wider power structures and institutions that govern how various groups are incorporated into the labour market. As many have argued, the rules of the game within the informal economy are increasingly being set by international financial institutions and multinational corporations at the head of global commodity chains rather than by local norms and legal systems (see for example, Barrientos, Chapter 67, this volume).

Implications for research and policy
Moving from a focus on constraints to informal economic participation, to a concern with the gendered dynamics of power and process, has important implications for research and policy. A reorientation of both quantitative and qualitative research on informality and gender is needed in order to bring to light the invisible workers and hidden processes that are turning the informal economy from an opportunity into a poverty trap for women. Through a clear focus on issues of power and process, research can inform new policy directions that avoid the limitations and unintended consequences of current efforts.

Three areas of research on gender and informality have been singled out as requiring particular attention. In order to increase the visibility of informal workers to policymakers, there has been a vociferous demand for improved statistical research on informal employment (Chant and Pedwell, 2008; Chen et al., 2006). Great strides in statistical data collection on gender and informality have been made, particularly within the ILO and Women in Informal Employment: Globalising and Organising (WIEGO). However, activist researchers emphasise that more and better quantitative information is needed, particularly in the developing world, disaggregated by sex, and accompanied by greater effort to include women's particularly invisible activities such as industrial homework and other informal activities concealed within the home.

In addition to improved quantitative research, Chant and Pedwell (2008: 11) have called for greater qualitative research that traces the processes shaping gendered inequalities within the informal economy. While quantitative indicators can reveal correlations, qualitative tools are needed to assess the interplay of root causes and cross-cutting factors such as class, race, ethnicity or generation within particular contexts. A more fine-grained focus on process is essential to understanding the complexities of social divisions and power relations through which gendered inequalities are produced within the informal economy.

Finally, research on informal labour markets and global commodity chains has indicated the importance of a more concerted focus on the role of macroeconomic institutions in understanding the links between gender, informality and poverty. There is a need for research that traces the gendered effects of macroeconomic structures and macro-regulatory systems linking informally employed women in Third World countries with the international financial institutions (IFIs), global corporations and national economic reforms that ultimately govern informal employment dynamics. Uncovering these invisible linkages between global economic governance and informal outcomes is as important to tackling gender inequalities as reducing the invisibility of vulnerable women workers.

By bringing the complexities of global regulatory structures and power relations into view, it is possible to move beyond the current situation in which well-intentioned policy efforts often reinforce rather than reduce women's disadvantage within the informal economy. As Chen et al. (2006: 2137) make plain, a 'technical fix' based on microcredit and targeted social policy may address immediate obstacles to women's informal economic participation, but they do nothing about the wider economic processes that put vulnerable women workers increasingly at the mercy of global market forces beyond their control. More promising policy directions lie in the 'rights-based' approach advocated by the ILO and WIEGO, which emphasises the importance of enhancing the political voice of informally-employed women through support for collective organisation and greater representation in policy-making.

Select bibliography

Barrientos, Stephanie, Catherine Dolan and Anne Tallontire (2003) 'A gendered value chain approach to codes of conduct in African horticulture', *World Development*, 31 (9), 1511–26.

Chant, Sylvia and Caroline Pedwell (2008) *Women, Gender and the Informal Economy: An Assessment of ILO Research and Suggested Ways Forward*, International Labour Organisation (ILO) Discussion Paper, Geneva: ILO.

Chen, Martha, Joann Vanek and James Heintz (2006) 'Informality, gender and poverty: a global picture', *Economic and Political Weekly*, 27 May, 2131–9.

Elson, Diane (1999) 'Labour markets as gendered institutions: equality, efficiency and empowerment issues', *World Development*, 27 (3), 611–27.

Meagher, Kate (2001) 'Throwing out the baby to keep the bathwater: informal cross-border trade and regional integration in West Africa', in *Regionalism and Regional Integration in Africa. A Debate of Current Aspects and Issues*, Discussion Paper 11, Uppsala: Nordiska Afrikainstitutet.

Sassen, Saskia (2002) 'Women's burden: counter-geographies of globalisation and the feminisation of survival', *Nordic Journal of International Law*, 71, 255–74.

United States Agency for International Development (USAID) (2005) *Gender and Pro-Poor Growth*, Tools and Key Issues for Development Studies, Washington, DC: USAID.

73 A gendered analysis of decent work deficits in India's urban informal economy: case study perspectives from Surat
Paula Kantor

Through case study material from a 2004 study of urban informal employment in Surat, India, this chapter emphasises the importance of improving employment quality in order to reduce poverty, and the need to assess employment quality by gender and employment status to ensure resulting poverty reduction strategies address sources of structural inequality in labour markets. Key development frameworks for poverty reduction, including the Millennium Development Goals (MDGs), pay little attention to employment generation and employment quality as means of achieving their ends. The International Labour Organisation (ILO), through its concept of 'decent work', puts employment and employment quality centre stage, though could give greater attention to the social and economic structures influencing how men and women differently access work, leading to differences in outcomes. This chapter starts with a discussion of the dimensions of decent work and briefly describes the challenges in extending the concept to the informal economy. It then discusses the role of employment in poverty reduction, with specific attention to the gendered nature of opportunities and outcomes within the informal economy. Using case study data, it analyses decent work deficits among workers in Surat's urban informal economy, exploring the influence of the intertwined structural inequalities of gender and employment status on employment quality outcomes. It closes with a discussion of ways forward to address gendered deficits in employment quality.

Decent work for all
In 1999 the ILO set itself the challenge to achieve decent work for all, meaning opportunities for men and women to find productive work in conditions of freedom, equity, security and dignity. Commitment to achieving this outcome 'for all' implicitly extended the ILO's reach from its traditional base of formal sector wage workers to include the informal economy. In 2002 it made this expansion explicit through the International Labour Conference's focus on decent work and the informal economy (ILO, 2002).

The ILO operationalises the concept of decent work at the level of workers through seven indicators representing work-based securities (Anker, 2002). Overall the indicators capture relevant dimensions of work quality and have the potential to be adequately applied to both formal and informal workers. The seven dimensions are as follows:

1. Labour market security: the ability to find and have work.
2. Employment security: security against loss of current work.
3. Job security: have an occupational niche and career prospects.
4. Work security: health and safety at work.
5. Skill reproduction security: opportunities to obtain and retain skills.

6. Income security: adequate income from work and social security benefits.
7. Representation security: protection of collective voice to represent rights at work (ibid.).

In order to apply these securities to the informal economy it is necessary to define the latter. Early definitions focused on enterprises and their characteristics, defining the informal sector as including enterprises small in size, using both family labour and basic technologies. The informal economy is now also understood in terms of employment relations, and includes enterprises outside of the regulatory framework as well as employment relations which are not legally protected (Chen et al., 2004; ILO, 2002). The informal economy is therefore heterogeneous and this must be accounted for in considering work-based securities and decent work.

One key dimension of difference within the informal economy is employment status, which is often gendered. Employment status captures how one is employed – through what employment relations. Distinctions include being self-employed, salaried or a casual worker, with the latter including subcontracted homework. Measures of decent work must accommodate differences in employment status by gender to capture appropriately the breadth of experiences of work quality in the informal economy (Anker, 2002; Unni and Rani, 2003). For example, under employment security, asking if one needs a licence is relevant for self-employed workers while asking if the worker does subcontracting work or works for a labour contractor is relevant for homeworkers and casual workers. Similarly, questions about labour market security would differ by employment status, with the self-employed concerned with demand for products or services, and labourers concerned with competition in labour markets and days of work available.

Employment, poverty and gender
Achieving decent work for informal workers is a complicated and challenging task in an environment characterised by global competition. However, it needs to be a central component of poverty reduction strategies because paid work, whether through self-employment, dependent piece-rate production or casual wage work, is the basis of most livelihoods in the developing world and the informal economy is the source of most of these opportunities (Chen et al., 2004). This is true in India where 83 per cent of non-agricultural employment is informal (see Chen, Chapter 71, this volume; also Heintz, Chapter 66, this volume).

The relative lack of attention to the connection between the quality of work opportunities and poverty reduction in current development thinking is notable (Chen et al., 2004). The MDGs largely ignore employment issues, except for promoting reduced youth unemployment, and there is no mention of employment in the MDGs' poverty reduction goal (Chen et al., 2005). Scholars interested in income poverty also infrequently focus on employment policy as a means to combat it and the World Bank does not list employment as a separate development topic on its website. If India and other countries are to succeed in reducing poverty and inequality they must improve both the number and quality of work opportunities available, with particular focus on improving the quality and conditions of work for both women and men in the informal economy (Chen et al., 2004; ILO, 2002).

The poor quality of work opportunities in the informal economy and high probability that informal workers will be poor are linked to the irregularity and variability of earnings from informal work. The prevalence of income irregularity and instability is associated with the extent of dependence embedded within employment and production relations. The extent of dependence is then associated with gender and employment status (Unni and Rani, 2003). Efforts to eliminate decent work deficits in the informal economy must unravel these associations, particularly focusing on improving the conditions under which different individuals are integrated into the informal economy. As articulated by Chen et al., (2004: 12–13): 'The evidence suggests that the terms on which women and men engage in the labour market have a direct bearing on their level of income, human development and social inclusion, and on whether or not they enjoy decent work.'

In the informal economy it is the nature of the work itself, particularly the hierarchical relations often associated with particular employment status categories, and the ascribed characteristics of the workers, which forms the basis of the insecurities informal workers face (Unni and Rani, 2003). To understand and ameliorate decent work deficits one must examine the conditions and quality of informal work by employment status and ascribed characteristics to capture the non-random insecurities workers face. Assessments of conditions and quality of work must include evaluations of autonomy and control within production processes and employment relations to understand how decent work deficits are linked to compromises made between autonomy and security (ILO, 2002; Sachs, 2004). Decent work deficits will not be eliminated until asymmetrical relations, such as those with suppliers who both provide raw materials to outworkers and buy the finished product, are transformed.

The work-based securities discussed above and some of their empirical applications (Anker, 2002; Unni and Rani, 2003) do not tend to give attention to how workers are incorporated into work, and particularly to the issue of dependence among self-employed and home-based workers. To assess decent work outcomes, questions need to be asked about the number of sources from which these employment status groups purchase/obtain raw materials and the number of outlets/intermediaries to whom they sell their final products. These provide evidence of monopoly and/or monopsony conditions, which place the producer in highly dependent relations of production, increasing insecurity. Limits on autonomy in employment terms are gendered, particularly in contexts like South Asia where women experience more constrained mobility and tend to be concentrated in home-based work. The case study presented next incorporates questions on how workers are included into work to assess issues of autonomy and dependence as part of decent work.

Decent work deficits in Surat's informal economy
Surat is a city of about 2.4 million residents, located in India's Gujarat state. It is known for its diamond-cutting, synthetic silk textile and *jari* (gold thread) industries, all of which serve both domestic and international markets. This economic vibrancy supports strong service and petty trade activities, drawing workers from throughout the country.

The fieldwork for the study was conducted from March to May 2004.[1] Respondents were selected from all wards within Surat's municipal corporation area based on purposive selection of settlements within wards or groups of wards, and random selection of lanes and households within lanes in the selected settlements. A target sample size of 800 total respondents was set, and based on this ceiling and available population data,

A gendered analysis of decent work deficits in India's urban informal economy 481

Table 73.1 *Distribution of sample workers by sex and employment status, Surat, India*

	Salaried	Casual	Self employed	Home-based piece-rate	Total (n)
Percentage of female sample	26.5	21.1	21.9	30.5	407
Percentage of male sample	18.2	47.4	25.3	9.1	407

respondents were distributed across wards by relative ward population size. In the end a total of 814 workers were interviewed, half male (407) and half female (407). The field team over-sampled females due to interest in developing an understanding of gendered experiences of work-based insecurities. Based on lane-level enumerations documenting employment status by sex of all workers located, the team endeavoured to represent proportionately salaried, casual wage, home-based piece-rate and self-employed male and female workers in the sample (see Table 73.1).

Male salaried and casual workers primarily worked in different manufacturing units (textiles, diamond) and female salary workers were mainly domestic workers, who received a fixed monthly salary but few other benefits. Female casual workers often did thread-spinning work and some were cleaners in manufacturing units. Female self-employed workers were tailors and vendors and the men primarily vendors with some being owners of small manufacturing units. Home-based workers were concentrated in the *jari* industry.

Among this sample of residents of low income settlements in Surat, male salaried workers come out as having the lowest decent work deficits. This does not mean they have necessarily achieved decent work – the numbers reporting working excessive hours and the low incidence of non-wage benefits support this – but relative to others they are closer to this end. The worst-off groups are male and female casual and piece-rate workers and female salaried workers. Self-employed workers have more mixed work quality results and often fewer gender differences in outcomes.

Key measures indicating the presence of decent work deficits across all employment status groups include pay levels, amount and regularity of days of work, excess hours of work, access to training and representation. Women's pay levels require particular attention as most earned far less than published minimum wages in the state, making them highly income insecure. Two subgroups of women workers on which to focus are domestic workers and home-based piece-rate workers. For the latter, the 1996 ILO Convention on Homework is in place but clearly needs to be enforced. Enforcing minimum wages for domestic workers is challenging due to the dispersion of workers and employers within private homes.

Underemployment is another problem crossing employment status though not affecting salary workers in the sample. Male and female piece-rate workers reported irregular work the most frequently, followed by male casual workers, female casual workers and similarly lower shares of male and female self-employed. Interestingly, even though high shares of workers reported working excessive hours (86 per cent of all men and 44 per cent of all women), 24 per cent of these said they were willing to work more hours, with the highest share being found among piece-rate workers (see also Chen, Chapter 71, this volume). This is a key indication of poor work quality. How to address underemployment varies across activities; for piece-rate and self-employed workers addressing underemployment requires more numerous and autonomous links with suppliers and contractors. This is a clear need as over half of the self-employed and over 90 per cent of piece-rate workers depend on one input supplier, and 83 per cent of piece-rate workers have one source of work orders. There is no gender difference in this dependence.

For casual workers and female salaried workers improved work quality is linked to obtaining contracted work for specified periods, with clearly stated dismissal criteria. Male salary workers were best off along these decent work dimensions, with 78 per cent having a written or verbal contract and 59 per cent reporting a guarantee of one to three months' dismissal notice. These frequencies far exceed those available to all casual workers and female salaried workers.

Access to informal training was quite high among both female and male respondents and all employment status groups. Similarly respondents reported physical work conditions to be generally acceptable, though casual workers were more likely to report working with dangerous substances, in line with their work in Surat's manufacturing industries. Men were more likely to report this than women.

Access to basic non-wage benefits was negligible among casual workers though both male and female salary workers had some access to these. For females, the more common benefits received were paid holidays, medical care and medical leave and free food. For salaried males, fewer reported free food but many more reported access to pension and redundancy benefits. Men across employment status also had greater representational security than women, with male salary workers reporting the greatest membership in worker organisations (24 per cent). Only 1.5 per cent of women reported such association.

Improving employment quality: ways forward
Considerable gaps in decent work were identified among the sample informal workers, including some clear differences by employment status and gender. To decrease the size of these deficits, action at both the policy and programme levels is required. At the policy level, India has taken the initiative to form a National Commission for Enterprises in the Unorganised Sector, reflecting the strength of advocacy around informal workers' interests in the country. This commission drafted two bills in 2005 to improve work conditions and address social security needs of informal workers, both of which recognised the different needs of workers by employment status. It has more recently made recommendations around the interests of informal workers, such as for skill formation and better statistics to improve monitoring of work conditions, and proposed four packages to increase social protection and to improve credit access for informal workers.[2]

In the end, any changes at policy level, such as adoption of the ILO Homeworker Convention or passage of the proposed bills, are only as good as their enforcement. For these reforms to matter and to be gender-sensitive, considerable attention is required on how to operationalise and enforce them for both women and men within the informal economy.

At the programme level there are a range of interventions that can contribute to improving work quality in the informal economy, in conjunction with efforts to improve the policy and regulatory environment. Continued support to build and sustain organisations of informal workers across gender and employment status is needed to increase their voice and bargaining position. It is one way to enhance these workers' autonomy and power. For self-employed and piece-rate workers, more autonomous links to markets would reduce the potential for exploitation at the hands of suppliers and/or contractors; this requires improved access to information about markets and market linkages and creative manoeuvring around existing constraints on women's mobility. State-sponsored licensing procedures can also improve the legal status of these workers and qualify them for state-based benefit schemes. Training can also improve pay levels and access to more and regular work as higher skills can help workers be more competitive in the labour market. Workers perceived a clear pay-off to skill training as many connected better skills to more work, more regular work and better pay. The challenge is in ensuring the quality and demand responsiveness of the training offered and its accessibility to all.

In the end, a holistic approach which links gender-sensitive, progressive legislation and regulations with microlevel programmes is required to address employment quality deficits coherently. With its National Commission and strong activism in support of workers' rights, India can be a leader in establishing ways forward to address decent work deficits in the informal economy.

Acknowledgements
Research for this chapter was funded by a grant from the National Science Foundation International Research Fellow Award Programme (Grant number 0301856). In conducting the study the author worked with Drs Jeemol Unni and Uma Rani at the Gujarat Institute of Development Research. The views expressed in the chapter are solely those of the author.

Notes
1. See Kantor et al. (2006) for more details on the study methods and findings.
2. See website of National Commission for Enterprises in the Unorganised Sector (NCEUIS): www.nceuis.nic.in (accessed 22 April 2009).

Select bibliography
Anker, Richard (2002) 'People's security surveys: an outline of methodology and concepts', *International Labour Review*, **141** (4), 309–29.
Chen, Martha, Joann Vanek, Francie Lund and James Heintz (2005) *Progress of the World's Women 2005: Women, Work and Poverty*, New York: UNIFEM.
Chen, Martha, Joann Vanek and Marilyn Carr (2004) *Mainstreaming Informal Employment and Gender in Poverty Reduction*, London: Commonwealth Secretariat.
International Labour Organisation (ILO) (2002) *Decent Work and the Informal Economy*, Report VI, International Labour Conference, 90th Session, Geneva: ILO.
Kantor, Paula, Uma Rani and Jeemol Unni (2006) 'Decent work deficits in the informal economy: case of Surat', *Economic and Political Weekly*, **41** (21), 2089–97.
Sachs, Ignacy (2004) 'Inclusive development and decent work for all', *International Labour Review*, **143** (1–2), 161–84.
Unni, Jeemol and Uma Rani (2003) 'Social protection for informal workers in India: insecurities, instruments and institutional mechanisms', *Development and Change*, **34** (1), 127–61.

74 Gender and quality of work in Latin America
Javier Pineda

'Quality of work' in Latin America, as well as in the world more generally, has recently become the focus of considerable attention due to changes introduced by new types of productive organisation, labour reforms, commercial integration dynamics and globalisation. These processes have brought about significant and important shifts in forms of labour integration, job stability, working hours and intensity of work, contractual status and related basic rights. Interest regarding the quality of work has been particularly associated with trends towards increased labour market flexibility (see Infante, 1999; Valenzuela and Reinecke, 2000; also Heintz, Chapter 66, this volume; Perrons, Chapter 62, this volume).

Interest in the quality of work has advanced understanding but has also lacked a general theoretical approach which positions this in relation to poverty. There has also been neglect of the way in which 'quality of work' is different from constructs such as 'informality' and 'decent work', and which tackles the issue of its more accurate measurement.

The present synthesis addresses quality of work from a gender perspective, and is organised into four main sections. First, I outline the multidimensional nature of quality of work, pinpointing its relations with quality of life analysis drawing on capabilities and human development approaches, as well as from feminist contributions to this literature. Second, in light of the growth of 'atypical' work, I present a brief overview of the contemporary Latin American urban labour market based on considerations that incorporate issues of safety and protection, freedom of choice, and compatibility of work and lifestyles. Third, I consider the conceptual and empirical differences between quality of work, 'informality' and 'decent work'. Finally, obstacles and advances in the measurement of quality of work are discussed.

In general terms I conclude that emphasis on the quality of work calls into question the ideal of progress towards equal opportunities between women and men in the workplace. As it currently stands, work quality indicators show highly differentiated tendencies between men and women

Quality of work and quality of life: objective and subjective dimensions

The question of quality of work in a broad sense implies reflecting upon the quality of life that derives from the latter's relation to work. This consideration entails understanding quality of work as a multidimensional phenomenon that goes far beyond a simple wage or income. Although income is associated with choice and freedom, work itself also constitutes a scenario for the construction of identity and a sense of belonging, and brings about the possibility of social recognition and psychological satisfaction.

The conceptual basis of quality of work is found, therefore, in theoretical discussions about quality of life and well-being. This brings us to question the extent to which quality arises from subjective enjoyment, the fulfilment of preferences, and/or the development of capabilities.

From the perspective of the capability approach there is no direct importance bestowed upon the goods and services or the real income derived from labour, which are central premises in the utilitarian mindset. In this particular case the focus is on the importance of these elements in an individual's capacity to opt for a better life. In this sense, work provides an individual with various capacities (for example, professional skills and experience, health benefits, personal relations, status, and so on), and, along with that, the possibility of choosing diverse lifestyles, in other words, different degrees of freedom. These capabilities do not depend exclusively on particular aspects of the work executed, but relate also with a series of formal and informal social regulations and arrangements, such as social protection and work discrimination practice.

One strategy to determine quality of work has consisted of examining individual workers' satisfaction in respect of diverse dimensions of the job in hand. A major difficulty here is that 'subjective' as well as 'objective' elements clearly come into play in the determination of 'job quality'. Leading on from this, 'satisfaction' is a deeply socially embedded construct, such that low expectations may lead to satisfaction in suboptimal conditions. The fact that several studies have reported that women express a higher level of job satisfaction may not correspond with an improvement in objective elements or an improvement in their position in relation to men, but to an enhancement corresponding with situations of extreme oppression, or of a scenario in which they previously had little access to any form of remunerated employment.

The fact that a working woman has learned to contend with adverse labour scenarios and maintain a positive attitude, partly due to the perception that she is in a better situation than her mother probably was, does not signify that this work is of good quality. From the perspective of the capabilities approach a job's enjoyment, its possibilities for enhancing an individual's skills-set, the social status it confers on a worker, and so on, although important, are not the only elements that matter. It is in the manner in which individuals have the freedom to pursue these elements that their true value lies. Facing conceptual difficulties in the assessment of subjective and objective elements, the capabilities approach proposes not to centre discussions on psychological reactions to work but on the capabilities at an individual's disposal, capabilities that include a broader option of possible psychological reactions. According to this, a higher level of job satisfaction cannot be read as an indicator of better employment when lack of protest may be the only option in a scenario of inequality and internalised disadvantage.

Summarising this section, from a capabilities viewpoint it is possible to define the quality of work as *every dimension related to a person's work which allows for the development of their capabilities, the broadening of their options in life and the possibility of having a greater degree of freedom.* This definition, with its central emphasis on capability development, allows us to value aspects rarely explored in the realm of work relations that go beyond the simple duality between objective and subjective factors. Just as with gender-sensitive poverty analyses, quality of work assessments must consider the subjectivities of women and men, but in a way which recognises how these are socially conditioned, as well as how job quality impacts upon people's lives.

As an example of the above, a study undertaken by the author with informal self-employed women workers in Colombia confirmed, as do other investigations, that their work experience broadened their capabilities at a personal level. This took the form of overcoming fears of publicly expressing their thoughts, having more personal time and space, making decisions relating to health and well-being, exerting more power over labour allocation in the household such as the redistribution of domestic chores, and gaining more recognition and respect from other family members for their work in the home as well as in their business ventures (Pineda, 2008; although see also Brydon, Chapter 16, this volume; Chant, Chapter 15, this volume). Not only are a broader range of psychological reactions demonstrated, but these also prove to be decisive in the personal empowerment and quality of life.

Quality of work and labour flexibility
An important element in the literature regarding work quality is its relationship with 'atypical work', notably work which departs from the 'typical' or salaried work that emerges from a hegemonic model historically based on the Taylorist–Fordist regime of production that served as a basis for the construction of work institutions and relations among the state, workers and enterprises in the earlier part of the twentieth century. From a gender perspective, this model has been characterised as an androcentric system whereby families were supported by a male breadwinner, paid a 'family wage', while women took primary responsibility for domestic labour and unpaid carework. Due to processes of flexibilisation, organisational decentralisation and globalisation, this model entered a crisis and a new paradigm has emerged in which the increased labour force participation of women has been an integral part.

Research on the quality of work in this new scenario points to a complex and contradictory transition. On one hand, the weakening of rigid traditional work structures gives rise to possibilities of new lifestyles, new household arrangements, greater personal autonomy and creativity, and more flexible accommodations between work and other activities (for example, family life). On the other hand, flexibility has also been associated with insecurity and lack of protection, an increase in instability and vulnerability, lack of negotiating power, and reductions in non-labour time (for example, time for rest and recreation). Flexibility therefore poses a challenge concerning how to reconcile two intrinsic aspects in the equation: freedom and protection.

From a gender perspective, this presents a major political quandary given that work flexibility has largely been driven by the competitive needs of businesses in a liberalising and globalising economic context, which has privileged freedom over protection (Todaro and Yáñez, 2004). The rising participation of women in the workforce has been taking place in this context of declining protection, with great costs to their quality of life. The tension between these two aspects of the new business and organisational model in which work is inserted calls for the search for, and implementation of, a different paradigm of flexibility, one that goes beyond the neoliberal deregulation framework that has dominated public policies, and whose results have not fulfilled promises for more and better jobs (see Kantor, Chapter 73, this volume). The search for this new paradigm must adopt measures to obtain a goal of a greater social equity as well as the articulation of new family models and equal gender relations.

Decent work, quality of work and informality: interconnections and tensions

Informality
The concept of informality has existed for over four decades and has been tackled from various theoretical approaches. The 1980s and 1990s witnessed the emergence of several

studies which drew attention to the often exploitative relations among the formal and informal sectors. Restructuration processes and productive decentralisation in the context of globalisation, such as in the case of 'outsourcing', highlighted the asymmetry of value being generated by 'delayed developing sectors', and then being appropriated in the interests of accumulation in the 'modern' sector. Within this, gender was a crucial dimension in that low-paid women formed a significant part of the labour force. This 'productive heterogeneity' becomes central in the gender analysis of quality of work since it structures hierarchy and job status, supported by the transference of value from the domestic realm to the productive realm, involving a complex interplay of elements such as gender, class, 'race' and nationality. In this way, the differentiated insertion of men and women into particular activities and businesses inevitably conditions the general framework of their quality of work.

Latin America has historically endured elevated levels of informality, a phenomenon that has increased during the past three decades, with unequal and frequently negative consequences from a gender perspective. In 2003 half of all women engaged in non-agricultural employment in Latin America were in the informal sector, compared with only 44 per cent of men (see also Chen, Chapter 71, this volume for later figures). In the majority of countries in the region with *maquila* (assembly) operations, for example, women constitute a disproportionate share of workers (70 per cent in the Honduran case). This pattern is aggravated by ethnicity in so far as the bulk of women of African or indigenous descent are informally employed (for example, 71 per cent in Brazil). In my own longitudinal research in Colombia, I found that gender divisions in employment have significantly widened in the past decade. For example, in the service sector women have massively increased in their recruitment as part-time workers with the result that the gender gap in weekly working hours has risen dramatically. In 1997 the gap between average hours worked between women and men in services was only four hours, whereas by 2006 this amounted to 16 hours (Pineda, 2008).

Decent work
The concept of decent work was introduced by the International Labour Organisation (ILO) during its 1999 International Work Conference. The definition includes four major components: work, social security, work rights and social dialogue. The first component, work, refers to job opportunities, pay in kind as well as in cash, work safety, security and health conditions. This component is clearly pertinent to quality of work. The second component, social security, not only relates to guarantees of coverage in terms of health services, pension plans, accident and injury and so on, but also comprises stable income. The third component, work rights, entails liberty of association, non-discrimination in the workplace and the absence of obligatory labour or conditions of servitude, as well as child labour. The fourth element, social dialogue, pertains to workers' ability to voice their points of view, defend their interests and negotiate workplace issues with their employers and other bodies (Chant and Pedwell, 2008; Ghai, 2003; Kantor, Chapter 73, this volume).

Both 'decent work' and 'quality of work' are broad, multidimensional terms, and there is some overlap between them. However, there are also key differences. Decent work refers to the overall opportunities of work in a given country, taking into account unemployment. In large measure the concept of decent work is framed by rights enshrined in Fundamental Work Agreements and Conventions approved by the ILO. Quality of work, on the other hand, is associated with the particular situations of employed individuals, with a key element being informality. Sometimes labour informality and quality of work are used interchangeably. Indeed, in most cases, quality of work has been measured by informality indices.

In Latin America, a structuralist approach has dominated official definitions and measurement of informality, basing these on a technological hypothesis of higher productivity dependent on business size and human capital. Given the progressive blurring of the division between formal and informal sector work, particularly in respect of the diminishing degree of formality in labour arrangements across enterprises, these definitions now present great difficulties, and have tended to give way to more of an emphasis on social protection (Perry et al., 2007; Pineda, 2008). As it is, I contend that the quality of employment cannot be taken as synonymous with informality.

Dimensions and measurements of work quality: key challenges
The multidimensional character of work quality calls for a definition and systematisation of its key components. One model, developed in 2002 by the European Foundation for the Improvement of Living and Working Conditions, posits four main criteria for the promotion of quality work: securing stability and employment security; maintaining and promoting health and well-being for workers; developing skills and competence; and reconciling work and home life.[1] Each one of these elements contains diverse dimensions of its own. In an alternative model, developed in the context of Latin America, Valenzuela and Reinecke (2000) identify 30 dimensions of quality of work.

Despite such efforts, there are several obstacles to the comprehensive measurement and evaluation of work quality. One is the dearth of relevant variables recorded in many national household surveys. For example, rarely is information collected on the manner in which individuals value diverse dimensions of work. This tends to leave rather basic proxies for work quality such as earnings, type of contract, affiliation to social security in health and pension plans, length of working day and underemployment. Even then, another difficulty arises in respect of how to weight the different variables that do exist.

Notwithstanding measurement problems that derive from subjective views on quality of work, effective assessment must incorporate qualitative methodologies that capture the voices of both men and women, and which more fully represent the complexity of the phenomenon. Some steps in this direction have recently been taken in Colombia, where new perception variables have been introduced in the national household survey such as compatibility of work hours and family responsibilities, stability of employment, trade union membership and levels of satisfaction. These measures are to be welcomed, not least because they will better assist in comprehending how different groups of male and female workers value different dimensions of work quality. This, in turn, will be central to the design of policies to address gender inequalities in the labour market, and more broadly, gender-differentiated reasons for, and experiences of, poverty.

Note
1. See http://www.eurofound.europa.eu/pubdocs/2002/12/en/1/ef0212en.pdf (accessed 15 May 2009).

Select bibliography

Chant, Sylvia and Carolyn Pedwell (2008) *Women, Gender and the Informal Economy: An Assessment of ILO Research and Suggested Ways Forward*, Geneva: ILO, available at: http://www.ilo.org/wcmsp5/groups/public/---dgreports/---dcomm/documents/publication/wcms_091228.pdf (accessed May 2009).

Ghai, Dharam (2003) 'Decent work: concept and indicators', *International Labour Review*, **142** (2), 113–45.

Infante, Ricardo (ed.) (1999) *La Calidad del Empleo: La Experiencia de los Países Latinoamericanos y de los Estados Unidos*, Lima: Oficina Internacional del Trabajo.

Perry, Guillermo, Omar Arias, Pablo Fajnzylber, William Maloney, Andrew Mason and Jaime Saavedra-Chanduvi (2007) *Informality: Exit and Exclusion*, Washington, DC: The World Bank.

Pineda, Javier (2008) 'Informalidad y Calidad de Empleo', in Carmen Lópes (ed.), *Vías y Escenarios de la Transformación Laboral: Aproximaciones Teóricas y Nuevos Problemas*, Bogotá: Universidad del Rosario, pp. 281–306.

Todaro, Rosalba and Sonia Yáñez (eds) (2004) *El Trabajo se Transforma. Relaciones de Producción y Relaciones de Género*, Santiago: Centro Estudios de la Mujer/CEM, available at: http://www.cem.cl/pdf/trabajo_interior.pdf (accessed 20 June 2008).

Valenzuela, María Elena and Gerhard Reinecke (eds) (2000) *¿Más y Mejores Empleos Para las Mujeres? La Experiencia de los Países del Mercosur y Chile*, Santiago: Oficina Internacional del Trabajo, available at: http://www.oitchile.cl/pdf/publicaciones/igu/igu021.pdf (accessed 20 June 2008).

75 Gender inequalities and poverty: a simulation of the likely impacts of reducing labour market inequalities on poverty incidence in Latin America
Joana Costa and Elydia Silva

A predictable critique to be heard in any conference about gender and poverty is that income poverty indicators are 'gender blind'. This is certainly a legitimate observation, and it is difficult to understand how gender inequalities are not reflected in different poverty indicators among women and men. Yet there are two critical factors which are important in accounting for this. One is the persistent concept of poverty as a household phenomenon. The other is the lack of empirical information about the unequal intra-household distribution of income. One step towards overcoming the problem of deriving indicators about income poverty and gender is to differentiate poverty indicators among households according to the sex of the household head, but this is not adequate to get to the individual women and men in households and, in fact, is not the only possibility despite the limitations of existing data.

The importance of producing more poverty indicators which reveal gender differences in income at an individual level is not only critical for analysis, but policy. It is well known that eliminating gender inequalities would bring many benefits to women's lives, and to their households. Even if policymakers might be more interested in the consequences of reducing gender inequalities for the whole of society, gender inequalities, like any other inequalities caused by discrimination, are intrinsically unfair and they should be fought against even if this implies negative outcomes in other socio-economic indicators. Our position is that policymakers should be aware of all possible consequences of gender-related policies so that they may combine and/or harmonise these with other policies to offset their negative impacts or to enhance their positive effects. With this in mind, in the present chapter we investigate how reducing gender inequalities in the labour market could potentially contribute to reducing poverty levels, presenting empirical evidence from eight Latin American countries: Argentina, Brazil, Chile, the Dominican Republic, El Salvador, Mexico, Paraguay and Uruguay.

Gender inequalities in the labour market
Labour market indicators allow us to recognise the presence of gender inequalities in the labour market (see Costa et al., 2009). Three relevant aspects of the gender gap in the labour market can be generalised for the eight countries analysed. The first is a lower economic activity rate among women compared with men. The second comprises higher rates of both employment informality and unemployment among women in comparison with men. The third aspect is the lower female hourly wage. These indicators reflect the fact that many women are still out of the labour force, that those who are economically active face difficulties finding a job, especially a formal one, and that those who are in work have lower earnings than men.[1]

These gender gaps remain almost unaffected even after controlling for different characteristics and endowments, such as age and education. In other words, we still observe a gap in the probabilities of being economically active among women and men with the same characteristics, as well as with a wage gap and differences in the probability of being unemployed, formally or informally.

One relevant discussion underlying the present analysis is to identify the reasons for women and men with similar characteristics having different probabilities of being economically active, or having different hourly wages, or having distinct probabilities of being informally employed and/or unemployed. At one level, one might argue that these gender differences are the result of women's choice. For instance, women may opt to be economically inactive so that they can dedicate themselves to home production or unpaid carework (UCW), or they may prefer a job with a lower salary or in the informal sector because these types of occupations offer more flexible working hours. On the other hand, it is impossible not to recognise the existence of barriers that act to limit women's options. For example, women may be prevented from entering the labour market or from more formal occupations because they are responsible for domestic duties, and lack support, such as subsidised childcare facilities. It is also plausible that formal employers avoid contracting women of reproductive age or, even if they do, they might offer a lower wage in comparison to men with exactly the same characteristics. Therefore, there are many ways through which gender roles and gender discrimination in society might produce the gender inequalities commonly observed in the Latin American labour market and beyond.

Nonetheless, the objective of this study is not to determine how much of the observed gender differences in labour market indicators are a consequence of women's choice or gender discrimination. Instead, our purpose is to understand how a reduction of different types of gender inequalities might affect poverty indices. To achieve a reduction of gender inequalities in the labour market, we simulate three different and independent scenarios. In the first, women and men with similar characteristics have the same probabilities of being economically active. In the second, the probabilities of being informally employed or unemployed are equal among men and women with equivalent characteristics. In the third, women and men with similar characteristics receive the same hourly wage. In the following section, we explain how we evaluate poverty in each of these hypothetical scenarios.

An approach to understanding how gender inequalities explain poverty
We take advantage of the methodology developed by Bourguignon et al. (2001), which uses a decomposition technique that helps to disentangle the various factors underpinning the dynamics of per capita household income distribution. The use of this kind of method, known as 'micro-simulations', has been helpful in explaining poverty and inequality trajectories. This methodology builds on the fact that household income is the sum of individual members' labour income and non-labour income and, in light of this, proposes an investigation of the determinants of all of these. For instance, if we know how a change in the labour market structure affects individual labour income, we are also able to understand how this event influences household incomes and, in turn, poverty levels overall.

In order to verify the determinants of labour income, labour market participation structures and remuneration structures must be examined empirically. To analyse participation structures, two estimation models are necessary: one to examine the determinants of the probability of being economically active, and another to investigate the determinants of the probabilities of being unemployed, or being formally or informally employed. To study remuneration structures requires an estimation model for examining the determinants of hourly wage levels. In our analysis, each one of these models was estimated separately for women and men so that we were able to distinguish the different ways that the determinants act for women and men.

The following step was to simulate a reduction of gender inequalities in the labour market. With the aim of equalising women's and men's conditions in the labour market, our simulations consisted of equalising the way the determinants act for women and men. Consequently, in the first simulation, the effects of the determinants of labour market participation for women were replaced by those for men, that is, women and men with similar characteristics would have the same probability of being economically active. The second simulation substituted women's effects of the determinants of the occupational status by men's, that is, women and men with comparable characteristics would have the same probabilities of being unemployed, or formally or informally employed. The third simulation changed the female effects of the determinants of hourly wage by the male ones with the result that women and men with equal characteristics would receive the same remuneration. These simulations were done independently and in a ceteris paribus context, so that each one corresponds to the reduction of certain aspects of gender inequalities in the labour market, keeping other circumstances constant. A formal presentation of the methodology used is described in Costa et al. (2009).

For each of these simulations, a counterfactual wage distribution was constructed and also a counterfactual household income distribution. These counterfactuals of income distribution represent how income distribution would look if certain aspects of gender inequalities were eliminated from the labour market. Based on these counterfactuals, we were able to estimate poverty levels and to investigate not only how gender inequalities affect poverty but also which aspect of gender inequality has the highest impacts on poverty.

The results of this simulation must be considered with the caveat that they are products of partial equilibrium exercises. As a consequence, effects of a general equilibrium in the economy are not considered; hence, our results do not represent the final equilibrium outcome. Nonetheless, they do correspond to a rough estimate of the effect of gender inequalities on poverty. In addition, this analysis allows an assessment of the relative importance of each aspect of gender inequalities for poverty levels.

Empirical evidence from Latin America
Figure 75.1 presents rough estimates of how poverty levels might be affected by a reduction of gender inequalities in the labour market. The poverty measure used is poverty incidence, which is the proportion of poor among a specific group. The poverty lines used are chosen in a way that originally 20 per cent of the population is poor in each country. This means that the poverty line is set at the value of the twentieth percentile of the household per capita income distribution in each country. Other poverty measures and poverty lines are considered in Costa et al., (2009).

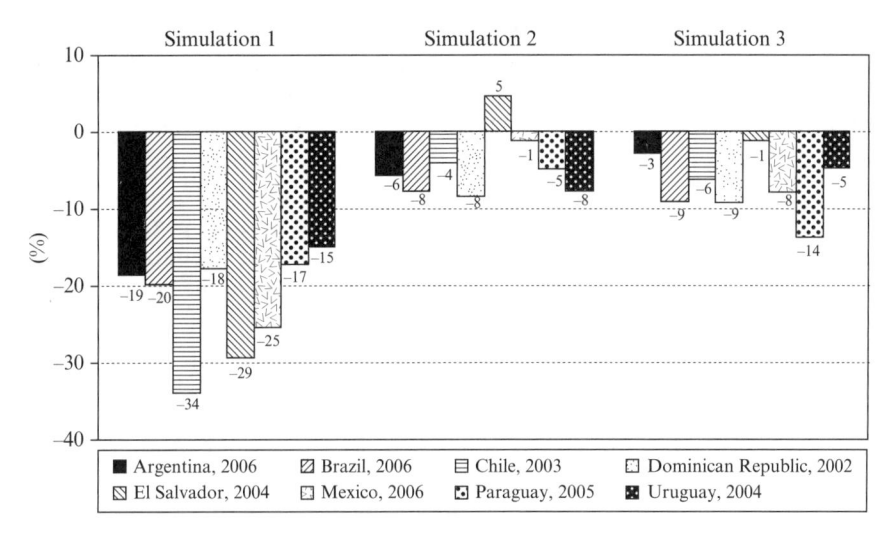

Figure 75.1 The contribution of reducing gender inequalities in the labour market to poverty reduction: selected Latin American countries

If similar women and men had the same probabilities of being economically active (simulation 1), female labour force participation would increase in all countries in the study, even if it would still not achieve male levels. Consequently, there would be a decrease in poverty incidence in all countries studied. In Chile, one would find the highest potential poverty decrease (34 per cent), and in Uruguay the lowest (15 per cent).

In the second simulation, women and men with equal characteristics have the same probabilities of equality in each occupational segment. This would imply an increase in the female formality rate and a decrease in the female informality and unemployment rates for most countries analysed. Therefore, women would either improve their wage or actually receive a wage, and this would correspondingly lead to a decline in poverty incidence. The highest potential reduction of poverty incidence, 8 per cent, would be observed in Brazil and the Dominican Republic. In El Salvador, this simulation results in a rise of the female unemployment rate because men here have a higher probability of being unemployed than women. Correspondingly, in El Salvador, poverty incidence would increase.

The third simulation assumes that women receive the same remuneration as men in accordance with their characteristics, which implies an increase in the female wage (in some countries, this would be even higher than the male one). As a result, poverty levels would fall in all countries. The decline in poverty incidence in some countries, notably Paraguay, would be up to 14 per cent.

Our results show that the reduction of gender inequalities has the potential to decrease poverty levels. The most noticeable fall in poverty incidence is observed when women's probabilities of being economically active are equalised with men's, and the female labour force participation rate increases. Therefore, promoting women's participation in the labour force is an aspect of gender inequality analysed here with enormous potential to contribute to poverty reduction.

How feasible is the decline of poverty through reducing gender inequalities?
Even though the results presented in this chapter correspond to partial equilibrium exercises, they provide an important statistical endorsement of the fact that gender inequalities act as barriers to poverty reduction. The outcomes represent rough estimates of how much poverty could decline if gender inequalities were eradicated from the labour market.

Despite the fact that each country has its specificities, we may generalise the result that the three aspects of gender inequalities investigated proved to contribute to poverty levels. Therefore, policies that fight against gender inequalities in the labour market also have the potential to be pro-poor policies.

In addition, our findings highlight the relevance of reducing the gender gap in labour force participation as a key policy to achieve both gender equality and poverty reduction. The magnitude of the decrease in poverty levels depends especially on improving poor women's access to the labour market. The best policies to promote women's participation in the labour market constitute a relevant and open discussion. Based on our results that children negatively affect the probability of women entering the labour market, one important way to increase the female labour force might be the greater provision of childcare facilities, especially for poor women.

Acknowledgements
This chapter has benefited from the valuable suggestions of Sergei Soares, Andrew Morrison and Fábio Veras. We are also indebted to Guilherme Hirata, Rafael Ribas, Marcelo Medeiros and Rafael Osório for their comments, and Célio Silva Jr for research assistance.

Note
1. In this study, the term 'economically active' refers to people who either work for a wage at least one hour per week (on a formal or informal basis), or who are searching for a job (unemployed). The umbrella category of informally employed comprises paid domestic servants, non-professional self-employed persons and employees or employers in industrial or service enterprises with five or less workers. Agriculture, public and unpaid occupations were not included in our analysis. Further details about the definitions used can be found in Costa et al., (2009)

Select bibliography
Bourguignon, François, Martin Fournier and Marc Gurgand (2001) 'Fast development with a stable income distribution: Taiwan, 1979–1994', *Review of Income and Wealth*, **47** (2), 1–25.

Costa, Joana, Elydia Silva and Fábio Vaz (2009) *The Role of Gender Inequalities in Explaining Income Growth, Poverty and Inequality: Evidence from Latin American Countries*, Working Paper No. 52, Brasilia: International Policy Centre for Inclusive Growth.

PART VIII

GENDERED POVERTY AND POLICY INTERVENTIONS

76 Gender, poverty and aid architecture
Gwendolyn Beetham

In recent years, gender advocates have been concerned with the gendered effects of changes to the 'aid architecture', or the different modalities through which international development aid is financed and channelled to recipient countries and organisations. These changes, primarily reflected in the Paris Declaration on Aid Effectiveness (PD), have grown out of the contemporary focus on achieving the Millennium Development Goals (MDGs) on the one hand, and feminist and postcolonial critiques of donor-driven (top-down) agendas on the other. This chapter provides an overview of concerns with different aid frameworks from a gender perspective, highlighting recent studies that seek to document existing funding for gender and development programmes and organisations, as well as work that provides information on ways through which donor and recipient organisations can ensure that gender equality and women's rights remain a priority in the shifting aid climate. Questions emerging from the debates, such as whether gender is being written out of the picture under the focus on 'aid effectiveness' for poverty alleviation and whether certain aid modalities (like direct budget support and alignment strategies) take into consideration gender equality and women's rights goals, are highlighted. The chapter closes with a synthesis of key recommendations for donor and recipient organisations that are emerging from the research, as well as suggested areas for future study.

'New' aid modalities: new or more of the same?

Often referred to as the 'new aid modalities', the frameworks that currently structure the giving and getting of development aid are outlined in the Paris Declaration for Aid Effectiveness of 2005. The Paris Declaration has been endorsed by 35 countries, 26 multilateral agencies, 56 aid-recipient countries, and 14 Civil Society Organisations (CSOs), who have pledged to 'continue to increase efforts in harmonisation, alignment and managing aid for results with a set of monitorable actions and indicators'.[1] The goals set out in the PD are grouped into five categories, or 'principles': ownership, alignment, harmonisation, mutual accountability and managing for results (see Table 76.1). While these goals certainly embody the buzzwords (ownership, accountability) of the contemporary trend of 'inclusive' development popular in activist, academic and policy circles, the phrase 'continue to' is also key here, because the new aid modalities must be seen as a *continuation* of previously agreed documents on financing for development, such as the Monterrey Consensus, which have as their stated goal the reformulation of aid processes in order to help aid become more effective in achieving the MDGs.

The Monterrey Consensus was the final document agreed to at the four-day International Conference on Financing for Development (ICFFD), held in Monterrey, Mexico, March 2002. The Consensus was the third major agreement on financing for development reached between 2000 and 2002. Its predecessors include the Millennium Conference in 2000 and the Fourth Ministerial Conference of the World Trade

Organization (WTO), held in 2001 (known as the Doha Round). These three agreements are not only closely related themselves, but their recommendations and commitments are, to some degree, reflected in the Monterrey Consensus (which is itself sorely lacking in its attention to the gendered effects of the aid modalities championed therein). Further, since the PD's 2005 endorsement, there have been two follow-up forums, the Third High Level Forum on Aid Effectiveness (HLF3) and Follow-up International Conference on Financing for Development to Review the Monterrey Consensus, held in 2008 in Accra and Qatar, respectively. However, despite the relatively larger presence of women's rights organisations and gender experts within donor country agencies at these follow-up meetings, gender remained marginalised in both reviews' outcome documents. The principles championed in the Paris Declaration on Aid Effectiveness, then, are highly influenced by previous frameworks and agreements that marginalise gender equality and women's rights goals.

The historic – and continued – disregard for gender in this instance is important not only because the MDGs themselves have been critiqued for not paying enough attention to gender (particularly when seen next to the more comprehensive Beijing Platform for Action [BPFA]), but because the principles and modalities championed through these approaches are not particularly gender sensitive in themselves, but rely on gender being integrated (or mainstreamed) throughout the development process (Collinson et al., 2008). In addition, 'the indicators of progress' which aim to monitor the success of the implementation of the PD are not gender sensitive (see Table 76.1).

Gendering the new modalities
Collinson et al. (2008: 6) refer to the changing patterns in aid delivery as 'the depoliticisation of aid', whereby a focus on administration and 'results' is emphasised over 'transformation and change on the ground' (the technical term for which is 'Results-Based Management'). A key concern for those working on gender and development in this area has been attention to 'alignment' and 'harmonisation' between donors and recipient countries. Alignment in this sense is defined as donor countries' alignment of their development strategies for any particular country with the country's own national development plan. Such a strategy is usually accompanied by an increase in modalities like Direct Budget Support (aid contributed to the overall budget), rather than programme-based funding. In theory, this is a positive development, as it indicates a move toward country ownership ('ownership' being another priority of the Paris Declaration) and away from top-down agendas, 'tied' aid, and the like. However, in practice national priorities may be problematic in terms of addressing gender concerns, as the attention to internationally recognised gender equality goals varies widely by national government. Further, even when national governments recognise gender equality goals rhetorically, these policy statements often are not backed up with sufficient funding or allocation of responsibility.

This danger is the greatest when national development plans do not fully integrate gender from the outset. Unfortunately, numerous studies that have documented the failure to integrate gender into Poverty Reduction Strategy Papers (PRSPs) do not offer a particularly positive outlook. Importantly, since many national development strategies in Heavily Indebted Poor Countries (HIPCs) draw directly on their PRSPs (in order to secure debt-relief agreements with the World Bank and International Monetary Fund),

Table 76.1 The Paris Declaration's five principles, twelve indicators of progress and examples of gender-sensitive indicators

Principle	Official indicator	Suggestions for including gender-sensitive elements
Ownership	• Recipient countries have operational development strategies, measured by number of countries with national development strategies with priorities for middle-term expenditure reflected in annual budgets	• National governments' involvement of 'key stakeholders' in shaping operational development strategies must include organisations representing poor women and other marginalised groups
Alignment	• Reliable country systems, measured by number of countries with procurement and financial management systems that aim for good practices • Aid flows are aligned on national priorities, measured by percentage of aid flows to public sectors • Strengthen capacity by coordinated support, measured by percentage of donor capacity development support • Use of country public financial management systems, measured by percentage of donors and aid flows that use systems in partner countries which adhere to good practices or have reforms to achieve these • Use of country procurement systems, measured by percentage of donor countries and aid flows that use systems in recipient countries which adhere to good practices or have reforms to achieve these • Strengthen capacity by avoiding parallel implementation structures, measured by number of parallel project implementation units per country • Aid is more predictable, measured by percentage of aid disbursements released in agreed schedules • Aid is untied, measured by percentage of bilateral aid that is untied	• Gender Responsive Budgeting should be put in place on the national level • Gender policies should include adherence to international commitments such as CEDAW and BPFA
Harmonisation	• Use of common arrangements or procedures, measured by percentage of aid provided as programme-based approaches	• Donor agencies' approaches to gender quality and empowerment of women should be both coordinated and comprehensive

Table 76.1 (continued)

Principle	Official indicator	Suggestions for including gender-sensitive elements
	● Encourage shared analysis, measured by percentage of field missions and/or country analytic work	● Division of labour mechanisms should ensure that responsibility for gender equality dimensions is explicit
Managing for results	● Results-oriented framework, measured by number of countries with transparent and monitorable frameworks to assess progress against national development strategies and sector programmes	● Data analysis should be gender sensitive, including qualitative analysis, tracking sex-disaggregated data, development of gender-responsive indicators, and performance of gender audits at regular intervals
Mutual accountability	● Mutual accountability/mutual assessments, measured by number of partner countries that undertake mutual assessments of progress in implementing agreed commitments	● Utilise gender-sensitive accountability tools such as gender analysis, gender auditing, sex-disaggregated data collection, and gender-responsive indicators

Sources: Adapted from AWID (2007) and Gaynor (2007).

the initial failure to mainstream gender becomes carried over into the national development strategy, and further into the alignment and aid allocation process. In the sub-Saharan African context, for example, recent research on gender equality in the context of new aid modalities found:

> (t)o date, few national development plans have strong gender equality elements, while national gender equality action plans have little or no connection to national development strategies . . . [t]hese weaknesses have become particularly evident in the new aid environment, as national development plans are increasingly defining priorities for government expenditure allocation. (UNIFEM, 2007: 2)

These weaknesses are deepened in the context of 'fragile' (post-conflict or transitional) states, when gender inclusiveness is often further marginalised as more 'pressing' issues such as infrastructure, state-building, and economic stability-measures take precedence during reconstructive national development planning.[2]

Along the same lines, the seemingly positive move of 'harmonisation' – directing that donors better coordinate their aid efforts in order to make the complex aid system more cohesive – should in theory alleviate much of the burden on recipient countries and organisations in terms of implementation costs, as well as streamlining time and labour-intensive reporting and assessment procedures. Interestingly, the discussion on 'harmonisation' also marks the only point in the Paris Declaration where gender equality is mentioned (in paragraph 42): 'harmonisation efforts . . . are also needed on other cross-cutting issues, such as gender equality and other thematic issues including those financed by dedicated funds'. However, the concern from a gender perspective is that different donors treat gender equality and women's empowerment differently, with some addressing gender equality in a less comprehensive way – or not at all. Under such a framework, if increased 'harmonisation' in donor agencies does not include coordinated approaches to support gender equality then, it is argued, gender equality goals will fall by the wayside (Gaynor, 2007: 4; see also Table 76.1 for examples of how some gender experts have suggested that gender can be incorporated throughout the PD).

The way forward?
Despite its shortcomings, the new aid climate offers opportunities for women's empowerment and gender equality. For example, the focus on accountability under the new aid architecture can be capitalised upon, as it is something that gender advocates have demanded for many years. This section briefly outlines some key recommendations, as well as topics for future study, to help ensure that gender equality remains on the international aid agenda.

In synthesising the main recommendations, the following are highlighted. First, the international community should renew its commitment to key gender equality agreements such as the Convention on the Elimination of All Forms of Discrimination Against Women (CEDAW) and the BPFA in light of the new aid frameworks. The PD should be aligned with these internationally agreed development goals, as well as those on human rights, decent work and environmental sustainability.

Second, the new aid environment should be monitored with gender equality and women's rights in mind, including the development of gender-sensitive indicators to measure progress and to hold national governments, and donors, accountable to gender equality goals.

Third, aid should be as diverse as possible, both in terms of the type of activities and organisations funded, and fourth, gender equality – and environmental sustainability and respect for human rights – should be treated as a sector (rather than a cross-cutting issue) with explicitly allocated resources in national budgets.

Finally, women's rights organisations and other CSOs should have access to resources to enable them to play an effective role in the aid process.

In terms of future study, among three of the most pertinent questions are first, what are the best practices from the PD implementation to date? A few small- and large-scale reviews of the process and its effects on gender equality are currently under way. These include projects coordinated by the member countries of the Organisation for Economic Co-operation and Development (OECD), as well as a three-year project (2007–2010) led by the United Nations Fund for Women (UNIFEM), the European Union (EU) and International Training Centre of the International Labour Organisation (ILO) to map the efforts in 12 countries to integrate gender equality and women's human rights into new aid modalities.[3] More studies of this nature should be undertaken, and their findings integrated into future financing for development strategies and agreements.

A second major question is how funding for women's rights is being affected by shifts in resource allocation and new funding structures. The project undertaken by the

Association for Women's Rights in Development (AWID) 'Where is the Money for Women's Rights?' has developed three cutting-edge reports on funding for women's rights organisations that should be part of any organisation's or agency's attempts to understand how women's rights organisations are faring in today's aid climate.[4] Studies on resource allocation for women's rights organisations that specifically focus on the effects of the MDGs and the PD from the NGO community are beginning to shed light on the issues and concerns of women's rights organisations in the new aid environment. For example, in addition to the report from the UK Gender and Development Network cited in this chapter (Collinson et al., 2008), a recent report by the Central American Women's Network (CAWN, 2008) found that 'despite international commitments to eliminate VAW (Violence Against Women), accessing resources for this work has becoming increasingly difficult, as the donor agenda has been influenced by thematic areas and geographical priorities under the Millennium Development Goals (MDGs) and the Paris Declaration on Aid Effectiveness' framework'. More studies of this kind need to be undertaken in order to gauge the extent of the problem and to offer solutions.

A third major question pertains to how the PD can be used in fragile countries. While growing numbers of studies on the gendered effects of the PD are being embarked on in relatively stable developing countries, the effects of the new aid modalities on 'fragile' states are less known. A recently published report titled 'The applicability of the Paris Declaration in fragile and conflict-affected situations' (OPM/IDL, 2008) highlights the unique challenges faced when attempting to implement the PD's goals in such contexts. The emphasis on political stability and state and institution building in these cases means that gender inclusiveness is often not taken as a primary objective.[5] However, a large body of literature by experts in gender and conflict and reconciliation is available and should be used (and continued to be expanded upon) to ensure that gender is taken into consideration even in these special cases. More case studies in these country contexts are also needed, with the acknowledgement that each situation is unique, and that 'one-size-fits-all' policy approaches in such situations may not only be unsuccessful, but dangerous to the lives of women and men alike.

Acknowledgements
The data for this chapter was gathered during the course of my PhD research, funding for which has been generously provided through Gender Institute LSE Research Studentship awards, an LSE Overseas Research Studentship award, a Metcalfe Studentship for Women award, and the University of London Central Research Fund.

Notes
1. http://www.oecd.org/document/18/0,2340,en_2649_3236398_35401554_1_1_1_1,00.html (accessed 20 January 2009). This section of the OECD website provides information on the main tenets of the PD, along with other useful information, such as country-level action plans and reports which monitor PD implementation.
2. The argument here echoes those made by gender experts focusing on gender and conflict situations. Due to the advocacy of such experts, and many women's rights activists, the United Nations Security Council passed Resolution 1325 (SCR 1325) in 2000. SCR 1325 seeks to mainstream gender throughout the conflict and resolution process, urging UN member states to ensure that women are equally present in peace negotiations, that war crimes against women are fully prosecuted, and that the number of women in conflict prevention, management and resolution should be increased at all decision-making levels (including in the UN itself).

3. See the website of the EC/UN Partnership on Gender Equality for Development and Peace for more information at: http://www.gendermatters.eu/ (accessed 21 January 2009).
4. See http://www.awid.org (accessed 20 January 2009). The website also includes information on another project, Influencing Development Actors & Practice for Women's Rights, which focuses on aid effectiveness and financing for development.
5. Multilateral and bilateral efforts have begun to be made in this area. In 2007, the 'Principles for Good International Engagement in Fragile States and Situations,' or Fragile States principles, were approved at the OECD's Development Assistant Committee (OECD/DAC) High Level Meeting, including 'a commitment to consider the promotion of gender equity, social inclusion, and human rights' (OPM/IDL, 2008: 36).

Select bibliography

Association for Women's Rights in Development (AWID) (2007) 'Monitoring and evaluation of the Paris Declaration implementation', Aid Effectiveness and Women's Rights Series, Primer No. 4, available at: http://www.awid.org (accessed 20 January 2009).

Central America Women's Network (CAWN) (2008) 'The response of international aid agencies to violence against women in Central America – the case of Honduras', report prepared by the London Central America Women's Network, available at: www.cawn.org/html/publications.htm (accessed 23 January 2009).

Collinson, Helen, Helen Derbyshire, Brita Fernandez Schmidt and Tina Wallace, (2008) 'Women's rights and gender equality, the new aid environment and civil society organisations', report prepared for the UK Gender and Development Network, available at: www.gadnetwork.org.uk/pdfs/Jan08/GAD-Network-Report.pdf (accessed 20 January 2009).

Gaynor, Cathy (2007) 'The Paris Declaration on Aid Effectiveness and Gender Equality', paper prepared for the United Nations, Division for the Advancement of Women, Expert Group Meeting on financing for gender equality and the empowerment of women, Oslo, Norway, 4–7 September.

Oxford Policy Management (OPM)/IDL (2008) 'Evaluation of the implementation of the Paris Declaration: thematic study – the applicability of the Paris Declaration in fragile and conflict-affected situations', report prepared by Oxford Policy Management, the IDL Group, available at: www.dfid.gov.uk/pubs/files/gender-rights-inclusion.pdf (accessed 20 January 2009).

United Nations Development Fund for Women (UNIFEM) (2007) *Capacity Development for Promoting Gender Equality in the Aid Effectiveness Agenda: Lessons from Sub-Regional Consultations in Africa*, UNIFEM Discussion Paper, September, New York: United Nations Development Fund for Women.

77 Brand Aid? How shopping has become 'Saving African Women and Children with AIDS'
Lisa Ann Richey

Introduction

Product RED™ was launched by Bono at the World Economic Forum in 2006 to raise awareness and money for the Global Fund to Fight AIDS, Tuberculosis and Malaria. Under this initiative, iconic brands such as American Express, Apple, Converse, Gap, Emporio Armani, Hallmark, Motorola, and now Dell, Microsoft and Starbucks have teamed up to produce RED-branded products and encourage customers to 'do good by dressing well'. The advent of 'Brand Aid' explicitly links international development assistance to commerce and not philanthropy. The RED initiative is an example of a cause-related marketing strategy to finance international development aid.[1] RED relies on stereotypically gendered representations to sell products and 'save lives'. Brand Aid brings modernisation theory into postmodern times as consumption becomes a mechanism for compassion.

RED has both material and symbolic consequences for its target group, 'women and children with AIDS in Africa'. In previous work, we have demonstrated that RED both corporatises aid relations and limits the scope of corporate social responsibility. In RED, Bono is the totem of 'compassionate consumption', steering away attention from the gendered causes of poverty, such as the inequities of systems of production and trade, by focusing on one of the outcomes, HIV and AIDS.

Reputable 'aid celebrities' like Bono negotiate the interface between shopping and helping, yet it is the pivotal role of the consumer that distinguishes 'Brand Aid' from previous modalities of financing development assistance. A 'rock man's burden' – imagined in terms of familiar constructs of sex, gender, race and place – frames Africans as the 'distant others' to be saved. At the same time, RED depicts consumer-citizens as fashion-conscious yet actively engaged and ethically reflective. Brand Aid creates the image of a world in which it is possible to buy as much as you want, while at the same time helping others.

This chapter analyses the RED initiative not only as an example of cause-related marketing, or consumer-driven philanthropy, but also as a meaningful player in representing HIV and AIDS and Africa to external audiences. The United Nations recently pointed to 'the unequal relationships between men and women, as well as gender stereotypes, [that] fuel the spread of HIV'.[2] These stereotypes are, of course, not simply a gender problem for societies that receive development assistance and philanthropy, but are also part of the constitution and representations of aid and giving. Through its selective focus on glamour and consumerism, RED provides highly gendered representations of the epidemic.

Product RED

In the mass media, RED is depicted as the brainchild of the aid celebrity extraordinaire, Bono. RED is described as the outcome of Bono's conviction that a less 'misty-eyed, bleeding-heart' approach needed to be adopted to help the poor. According to Bono, worthy causes should be marketed in the same way as 'a sports-shoe company does, or dare I say it, a cigarette company does'.[3] At the RED launch, Bono declared that: 'Philanthropy is like hippy music, holding hands. Red is more like punk rock, hip hop, this should feel like hard commerce.'[4]

Giorgio Armani was most explicit in his recognition of the capitalist bottom-line with his speech launching the RED Armani sunglasses at Davos: 'One of the main reasons why I like this formula that Bono and Bobby have thought of is the fact that the word "trade" does no longer have a negative connotation.'[5] Bono explicitly rejected the suggestion that he was being used by companies to restore their reputations,[6] and refuted the idea that the Global Fund was endorsing products. On the contrary, Bono claimed that 'We are not endorsing their products, these products endorse us'.[7]

HIV and AIDS provides the quintessential cause as the focus of Brand Aid's 'hard commerce' approach to doing good, because, like fashion, rock music or celebrity, it is about money, power and sex. Furthermore, the distance between RED and its recipients obscures the contradictions between an initiative embedded in privileged, heterosexist frameworks and the actual gendered struggles of preventing and living with AIDS in Africa. Western consumers are encouraged to express their sexuality, their attractiveness and their desire through consumer choices. RED never connects this to the exchange of sexual services for consumer goods within its recipient societies most affected by AIDS (see for example, Campbell and Gibbs, Chapter 50, this volume).

As described in the UK's *Sunday Times*, 'the sex appeal of RED' comes also from stars such as Scarlett Johansson, 'the sizzling face of Bono's new ethical brand': 'Johansson is peeling off her clothes in a photographic studio in LA, in preparation for becoming the pin-up for Bono's new plan.' Johansson's interpretation of why the new product is called RED is that 'It's a sexy, hot colour that's vibrant and attention-grabbing. It has been since the 1940s, such a time of high glamour and red lipstick and red nails. That's probably why they chose it for this campaign – glamour!'[8] The use of stereotypical imagery of sexy, scantily clad women to sell products to consumers is perhaps too commonplace to merit mention; however, using these images to raise funds for international development efforts to respond to AIDS in Africa is distinctive. Ironically, at the same time that many AIDS campaigns seek to dismantle gendered stereotypes that potentially disempower women, RED seems to reinforce the very stereotypes that other campaigns fight against.

The Global Fund

Product RED's beneficiary, the Global Fund, is an independent, private foundation governed by an international board that works in partnership with governments, non-governmental organisations (NGOs), civil society organisations and the private sector. It limits its activities to funding projects rather than implementing them. In its first two years of operation, RED donated US$100 million to the Global Fund's best-performing programmes for AIDS in Africa. So far, funds have gone to Rwanda, Swaziland, Lesotho and Ghana.

The Global Fund has been criticised for its inadequate attention to gender issues, as revealed in the lack of sex-disaggregated data used for monitoring and reporting, and an absence of programmes addressing women's vulnerability to HIV infection, gender inequality and/or violence. Also, despite the fact the innovative country coordinating mechanisms (CCMs) could potentially provide spaces for women's political empowerment and recognition of the political process of AIDS governance, so far participation in these has been gender-biased in all regions, with only 32 per cent or fewer of CCM members in Sub-Saharan Africa being female.[9] Furthermore, the lack of integration between the Global Fund's projects and sexual and reproductive health services has been documented as draining staff and worsening a human resource crisis in some African contexts. If RED is so concerned with women and children, it should advocate better gender monitoring, representation and integration of programmes within the Global Fund.

Africa and fair vanity
As described above, this is the first time that a contributor has been allowed to 'handpick' successes from the Global Fund's repertoire of programmes. RED chooses recipients that are both 'successful' and 'African'. That Product RED's beneficiaries are African is not coincidental, as re-imagining Africa is part of the effect produced by RED. Ferguson (2006) analyses the intertwining of real and imagined ideas of 'Africa' by suggesting that 'Africa' has a particular place in 'globalisation', a 'place' understood as both a location in space and a rank in a system of social categories. The 'forcefully imposed position in the contemporary world – is easily visible if we notice how fantasies of a categorical "Africa" (normally "sub-Saharan" Africa) and "real" political-economic processes on the continent are interrelated' (ibid.: 6). Africa seems the obvious 'place' where RED money could buy pills to save women and children living with HIV and AIDS, and where the constructions of donor and recipient would not be challenged, as Africa's 'place' in the hierarchy of development is well established.

Global AIDS has been described as an 'epidemic of signification' (Treichler, 1999) in which the representations of the infection are intrinsically related to the ways in which the infection is perceived and managed at all levels. Within global AIDS, Africa has been depicted as a dark zone, 'a dark, untamed continent from which devastating viruses emerge to threaten the West' (see Bancroft, 2001: 96 for discussion and references). From the Live Aid concerts onwards, the dominant images of the AIDS pandemic in Africa have been of suffering, and aimed at generating pity more than compassion; these images have portrayed Africans as victims with no agency, and living in circumstances that are far removed from those in developed countries. Yet RED's Africa is not full of suffering, in fact, the only images that could give cause for concern are clearly staged as 'before' pictures, in a 'before and after' scenario.

Product RED seeks to bring 'Africa' to the minds of the idle rich, thus providing an opportunity for them to 'help'. This was epitomised by its recent engagement with *Vanity Fair*, a monthly culture, fashion and 'politics' magazine. In July 2007, Bono was the Guest Editor of a special issue of *Vanity Fair*, which aimed to 'rebrand Africa'.[10] Given the legacy of slavery and colonialism and the extraction of resources and supply of armaments to the continent, it is difficult to imagine a time when the rich have not been interested in Africa. Bono, however, tried to encapsulate a special appeal of the Product RED intervention in his promotional video for the issue: 'That's what this issue of *Vanity Fair* is all about . . . trying to bring some sex appeal to the idea of wanting to change the world.' Assuming that Africa is far from the minds, lives and income-sources of its (comparatively wealthy) readers, *Vanity Fair* contributes to the myth that there is no real linkage between rich and poor, between entrepreneurs and Africa, or between capitalism and disease. With no indications that this was intentional irony, the UK version of the Africa Issue came bundled with a 78-page insert advertising, of all things, diamonds.[11]

RED relies on coexisting notions of familiarity and distance between the shoppers it tries to engage and the beneficiaries it tries to help. Between stereotypical gendered notions of bourgeois feminine beauty and wild adventure-seeking masculinity (an article profiling the first 'woman of colour' to be named as 'The Face of Estée Lauder' and one entitled 'Congo from the Cockpit'), *Vanity Fair* published a story entitled 'The Lazarus Effect'.[12] Two African women and two men, aged between 24 and 34, were shown in paired 'before' and 'after' photographs 'showing how ARV [anti-retroviral] treatment has allowed them to resume their lives'. The article begins with the heading 'A population on the mend', but the text refers not to urban Zambia, as one might expect from photographs taken in Lusaka, but to a health centre in Kigali, Rwanda. We see the effacement of Africans with AIDS into one smooth, global subjectivity in which there is no great difference between being a Rwandan or a Zambian. Of the two, only Rwandans have so far received any money from the RED contributions to the Global Fund.

When the Lazarus Effect images are compared with other RED photographs, their claims to authenticity are even more marked. One could argue that the image that most closely resembles the bodily emaciation, the shadow-like framing, and the claims of urgency of the 'before' photos of AIDS victims is in fact the cover of the RED edition of the *Independent* which shows not an African living with AIDS, but supermodel Kate Moss in black and white titled 'Not a Fashion Statement'.[13]

In this 'blackface' cover of the RED *Independent*, 'skin is used as a means of invoking the experience of an African woman by performing a surface-level transformation of an iconic British supermodel' (Sarna-Wojcicki, 2008: 19). In a rival British newspaper, the *Guardian*, Hannah Pool writes of the Moss cover:

> I suppose it is meant to be subversive, but what does it say about race today when a quality newspaper decides that its readers will only relate to Africa through a blacked-up white model rather than a real-life black woman? What does it say about the fight against HIV/Aids if that is the only way to make us care?[14]

RED is about redeeming sex and stylising gender relations. Percy Hintzen's (2008) detailed critique of the text in the *Vanity Fair* Africa Issue from both its features and its product advertisements draws out the appeal of racialised 'African sexuality'. Of course, the racialisation of sexuality long pre-dates contemporary Brand Aid, but RED puts a new spin to allow the West to reclaim sex as healthy. The sexy blacked-up body of a supermodel is able to stand in for the African woman dying from AIDS. We, as viewers, do not need to actually confront literal images or experiences of suffering, we can have the virtual mediation of a familiar translator. As other critical scholars have also noted, RED has not taken on board any of the central messages of feminist scholars of development, and 'a Hollywood standard of heterosexual sexiness prevails, which may be good marketing but fails to provoke deeper analysis of broadly viable models of sexuality' (Cameron and Haanstra, 2008: 1485). RED actively reinforces, rather than destabilises notions of sexualised distant others.

Conclusion

RED must be understood within the existing history of selling images of AIDS in Africa. Western shoppers are able to 'save African women and children' through the power of their purchase. The beauty of this celebrity simplification is that it provides the possibility that everyday people can engage in low-cost heroism. As an American Express RED advertisement states, it provides 'the union of consumerism and conscience, demonstrating how something as simple as everyday shopping can now help to eliminate AIDS in Africa'.

Branded philanthropy is taking on an increasingly important role in the responses to HIV and AIDS by 'concerned strangers'. According to Fadlalla (2008: 227), '[i]nstituting humanitarianism as the only strategy for eliminating poverty and suffering also reproduces a colonialist narrative of modernity and progress within which the privileged/West is compassionate and agentive and the "third world" is only helpless'. Bono states, 'I represent a lot of [African] people who have no voice at all . . . They haven't asked me to represent them. It's clearly cheeky but I hope they're glad I do.'[15] The rock star's burden shows how aid celebrities like Bono are shaping the AIDS agenda in ways to suggest how wealthy Western consumers should shop to the aid of their less fortunate global citizens.

While Product RED explicitly claims to link development goals with capitalist methods, to constitute shopping 'at home' as an effective means of combatting AIDS in Africa, the gendered and racial tensions that underpin such an approach tap into traditional discourses of power. In an interview with the *New York Times*, Bono said that 'Africa is sexy and people need to know that'.[16] While Product RED's aid celebrities redeem sex in 'sexy' Africa, they never challenge the global inequities of masculinity, the racialisation of sexuality, or the social hierarchy where cool, rich, white men save poor African women and children.

Acknowledgements

This chapter draws heavily on my forthcoming book written with Stefano Ponte, *Brand Aid: Celebrities, Consumption and Development* (Minneapolis and London: University of Minnesota/Zed), as well as two articles, entitled 'Bono's Product (RED) initiative: corporate social responsibility that solves the problems of "distant others"' (co-authored with Stefano Ponte and Mike Baab) in *Third World Quarterly*, **30** (2), 301–17 (2009) and 'Better RED Than Dead? From "Band Aid" to "Brand Aid"' (co-authored with Stefano Ponte) in *Third World Quarterly*, **29** (4), 711–29 (2008).

Notes

1. Cause-related marketing links the promotion of a brand, company, product or service directly to a social cause, most often with a portion of sales revenue going to support the cause.
2. United Nations (UN) (2008) *Declaration of Commitment on HIV/AIDS and Political Declaration on HIV/AIDS: Midway to the Millennium Development Goals*, report of the Secretary-General. A/62/780, 1 April, New York: UN, available at: http://data.unaids.org/pub/Report/2008/20080429_sg_progress_report_en.pdf (accessed 15 October 2008).
3. 'View from Davos: Bono marketing his red badge of virtue' by Matthew Bishop, *Daily Telegraph*, 27 January 2006, available at: http://www.telegraph.co.uk/finance/2930938/View-from-Davos-Bono-marketing-his-red-badge-of-virtue.html (accessed 15 October 2008).
4. 'Bono bets on Red to battle AIDS', by Tim Weber, *BBC News*, 26 January 2006, available at: http://news.bbc.co.uk/2/hi/business/4650024.stm (accessed 15 October 2008).

5. I use the English version spoken by the translator in the audio of spoken words in Italian. Initially shown in the RED product launch at Davos video, and viewed on www.joinred.com, this can now only be accessed in audio form, available at: http://streamstudio.world-television.com/gaia/wef/worldeconomic-forum_annualmeeting2006/podcast/press1.mp3 (accessed 13 March 2009).
6. For example, Converse is owned by Nike, a company accused in the past of using sweatshop labour.
7. 'Bono bets on Red to battle AIDS', by Tim Weber, *BBC News*, 26 January, 2006, available at: http://news.bbc.co.uk/2/hi/business/4650024.stm (accessed 15 October 2008).
8. 'The sex appeal of red', by Tiffanie Darke, *The Sunday Times*, 26 February 2006, available at: http://women.timesonline.co.uk/tol/life_and_style/women/beauty/article732241.ece (accessed 15 October 2008).
9. Hanefeld, Johanna, Neil Spicer, Ruairi Brugha and Gill Walt (2007) *How Have Global Health Initiatives Impacted on Health Equity?* Geneva: World Health Organisation System Network, available at: http://www.who.int/social_determinants/resources/csdh_media/global_health_initiative2007_en.pdf (accessed 1 April 2009).
10. 'Citizen Bono brings Africa to idle rich', by David Carr, *New York Times*, 5 March 2007, available at: http://www.nytimes.com/2007/03/05/business/media/05carr.html?ex=1330750800&en=a49746a2935ab3e9&ei=5088&partner=rssnyt&emc=rss (accessed 15 October 2008).
11. See http://gawker.com/news/ (accessed 20 October 2009). There were no articles on the diamond trade in Africa, which might have been expected given Leonardo DiCaprio's awareness-raising of the topic of 'blood diamonds' and its prevalence in popular media.
12. See article 'The Lazarus Effect', by Alex Shoumatoff, *Vanity Fair*, 1 July 2007, 156–61, available at: http://www.vanityfair.com/features/2007/07/lazarus200707 (accessed 1 April 2009).
13. On 21 September 2007 the *Independent* published its second RED edition, this one edited by Giorgio Armani, including articles by Leonardo DiCaprio, George Clooney, Bill Gates and Beyoncé.
14. 'Return to the Dark Ages' by Hannah Pool, the *Guardian* (UK), 22 September 2006, available at: http://www.guardian.co.uk/ (accessed 1 May 2009).
15. See 'Africa: A stage for political poseurs', by MXXX Hume, *spiked*, 10 June 2005, available at: (http://www.spiked-online.com/index.php?/site/printable/329) (accessed 15 October 2008).
16. 'Citizen Bono brings Africa to idle rich', by David Carr, *New York Times*, 5 March 2007, available at: http://www.nytimes.com/2007/03/05/business/media/05carr.html?ex=1330750800&en=a49746a2935ab3e9&ei=5088&partner=rssnyt&emc=rss (accessed 15 October 2008).

Select bibliography

Bancroft, Angus (2001) 'Globalisation and HIV/AIDS: inequality and the boundaries of a symbolic epidemic', *Health, Risk and Society*, **3** (1), 89–98.

Cameron, John and Anna Haanstra (2008) 'Development made sexy: how it happened and what it means', *Third World Quarterly*, **29** (8), 1475–89.

Fadlalla, Amal Hassan (2008) 'The neoliberalisation of compassion: Darfur and the mediation of American faith, fear and terror', in Jane L. Collins, Micaela di Leonardo and Brett Williams (eds), *New Landscapes of Inequality: Neoliberalism and the Erosion of Democracy in America*, Santa Fe, NM: School for Advanced Research Press, pp. 209–28.

Ferguson, James (2006) *Global Shadows: Africa in the Neoliberal World Order*, Durham, NC: Duke University Press.

Hintzen, Percy C. (2008) 'Desire and the enrapture of capitalist consumption: Product Red, Africa, and the crisis of sustainability', *The Journal of Pan African Studies*, **2** (6), 77–91.

Sarna-Wojcicki, Margaret (2008) 'Refigu(red): talking Africa and Aids in "causumer" culture', *The Journal of Pan African Studies*, **2** (6), 14–31.

Treichler, Paula (1999) *How to Have Theory in an Epidemic: Cultural Chronicles of AIDS*, Durham, NC: Duke University Press.

78 Sweden to the rescue? Fitting brown women into a poverty framework
Katja Jassey

Introduction
For anyone working inside, outside or alongside Swedish development it soon becomes apparent that the Swedes take a pride in being gender-aware and international promoters of gender equality. Swedish development organisations at all levels are dominated by a very specific homogenous group, comprising persons with middle-class, liberal-leftist values, of Swedish ethnic origin, and often members of a so-called nuclear family. Hence, the only structural form of oppression and inequality that most of these people can personally relate to is gender, or sex. This is by no means unique in Europe.

It is these people who get to frame some of the more dominant development discourses, who get to say who is deserving of aid and who is not. And in Sweden 'women' have held a frontrunner position for ages in terms of being deserving of aid. I have also taken part in these processes, shaped and carefully crafted out the words that would guide the Swedish International Development Agency (Sida) in its efforts to reduce poverty. As a bureaucrat working for the Swedish government's aid agency I had at that time not yet fully grasped what makes up the fuel of a policy – the ingredients we need in order to motivate people into action. Together with my close colleagues, I somewhat naively thought that if we got the 'facts' right the policy would be able to lend some support and direction in terms of choices in the future, be it regarding approaches or what and whom to fund. This chapter is an exploration and reflection on my experiences of trying to deal with the gender and poverty nexus.

Brown women[1] – dreadfully poor, nurturing mothers and hardworking victims
The policy in question was dealing with poverty. We had decided once and for all to move beyond the idea of 'women' as one particularly deserving category of poor that held its position in all places and at all times. We wanted to shed some light on the whole 'feminisation of poverty' package. Armed with research which clearly showed that one can never make blanket statements about all women being poor, or all poor being women, we made it our mission to pay extra attention to the formulations on gender and poverty. We clearly stated that while gender was an important variable in poverty analyses, other factors such as age, class, marital status and ethnicity mediate gender roles, and that different combinations of these could reinforce one another negatively or positively.[2] There was some resistance coming from the gender equality advisers, but with no real evidence to back up their claims of 'women' being a category of poor in its own right, we turned a deaf ear.

What is interesting here is to note that we were not the first to do so. In fact Sida's previous Action Programme for Poverty Reduction of 1996 was also preceded by careful research. This included a report from the Taskforce on Poverty Reduction called 'Promoting

Sustainable Livelihoods' which explicitly stated that 'just as it is difficult to generalise about the impact of economic recessions and structural adjustment on women, it is also hazardous to draw wide and categorical conclusions about the incidence and impact of female-headed households without supporting data'. The report also cautioned that '[t]he overemphasised focus on female-headed households leads to a neglect of a gender perspective on poverty in other kinds of households', and that 'Gender subordination can be exacerbated by, but does not arise out of poverty'.[3] These statements were subsequently followed by an action programme that boldly identified 'female-headed households' and 'mothers and children' as specific target groups for all areas of work. So, despite all the studies and research it was back to 'gender business' as usual. Women *are* vulnerable, and that makes children vulnerable too as it is only really women who are mothers who count. The sustainable livelihoods document was also followed by a government report[4] which in its opening statement following the 1995 *Human Development Report* of the United Nations Development Programme (UNDP), and the Beijing Platform for Action (BPFA), argues that among 1.3 billion people living in acute poverty, women and children suffer most. Of course, there is no data to back up the UNDP statement, the methods for collecting poverty data at national level are rarely sex-disaggregated (which is commonly critiqued by those concerned with gender), and yet, the self-same people may quickly spin around and happily accept generalised speculations as this one (see Chant, Chapter 15, this volume). Similar criticisms have been made by Eyben (2007) in relation to the policy documents of the United Kingdom's (UK) Department for International Development (DFID). As the focus shifted in the UK from women in general to women and poverty a whole range of what she calls mythical numbers saw the light of the day. In the DFID's material for the public Eyben (2007: 74–5) found that:

> It is *70 per cent* of women who are poor and women in Africa typically spend more than *five hours a day* travelling mostly on foot to meet the basic needs of their families. Investment in education for girls is the single most effective ways to reduce poverty. Women also protect the environment, maintain peace and keep societies together, make up most of the labour force and pass on knowledge to the next generation. They also have a better track record than men in paying back loans. (Original emphasis)

And today, in 2009, Sida's general director warns the public of a dramatic backlash for gender equality in the world in Sweden's largest daily newspaper.[5] He calls upon Swedish companies to help save the world's poor women as these poor women will be the hardest hit by the financial crisis. Referring to, at the time unpublished, reports by researchers at Stockholm University, he goes on to state that the unemployment within industries such as manufacturing and agricultural production of flowers, vegetable and fruit will strike these women. Among the expected consequences of this unemployment we learn that more unpaid household work will be undertaken by these women, fewer girls will go to school, prostitution and trafficking will increase as being forced to sell your daughter to a brothel can become the last resort for families, and violence against women will increase. Women lack choices, power and material resources as traditional norms and values block their way to development. Despite the headline's reference to gender equality there is only one reference to men, mentioning rather cursorily that they too can become the victims of these traditional values as an unemployed man is considered less of a man if he takes on the tasks usually undertaken by women in the household.

Why is it that these 'poor women' keep bouncing back onto the tables of development makers with such perseverance? Why is it that Sida calls upon Swedish companies to help save poor women and not poor men, or that Swedish Action Aid offers sponsors the chance to support a girl, but not a boy?[6] Why is there such an abundance of statements, reports and policies that disregards evidence and advances these simplistic and essentialist narratives about (brown) women being the victims and (brown) men the problem? Why is it that as the development machinery hurtles forward with the latest fashionable solution, it never stops to consider the complexities beyond these magic bullets?

How to read a policy – the light version
Since the late 1990s a number of anthropologists have tried to make sense of policy processes. Shore and Wright (1997: 7) suggest that policies should be read as 'cultural texts, as classificatory devices with various meanings, as narratives that serve to *justify or condemn the present*, or as rhetorical devices and discursive formations that function to empower some people and silence others' (emphasis added). Mosse (2002) echoes their sentiments and points out that several ideas can be found to exist simultaneously in the policy arena but the idea that is most likely to catch on is the one that is ambiguous enough to allow for multiple interpretations, and that can be used for different purposes and sets of interests. Now there is nothing vague about statements that such as women will be the hardest hit by the global financial crisis or that they make up 70 per cent of the world's poor, but they can serve different purposes. They lend a voice of benevolent morals to Sida's director general as he calls upon Swedish companies to become more pro-development and they serve the purposes of women's activists whose mission it is to lobby for increased gender equality and women's rights. That policies are also full of ideas which are far from vague is explained by Cornwall and Brock (2005) who discuss what they call 'buzzwords' such as 'empowerment' and 'participation' which are used by all actors in development today ranging from international non-governmental organisations (NGOs) to the World Bank. According to them these 'buzzwords' should be understood as myths. We need our myths, not to describe or make sense of reality, but to express a determination to act, to tell ourselves and the world what is right and what is wrong. These myths do not only inform, they also evoke emotions which help summon up the conviction and motivation to act. They give people a sense of a right to intervene on behalf of the poor, and in this case, poor women.

Much of today's policy-making or development discourse creation takes place at a global level, or more accurately in global spaces such as conferences, workshops and seminars which are inhabited by a particular group of people. This may mean that the ingredients for the formulation of new myths, new stories and new policies are to be found further and further away from the context in which those whose lives they intend to change and develop live, work, love, fight and die.

Social agents and the 'rescue industry'
At the beginning of this chapter I suggested that we need to look at the people who shape these policies, namely, the white, middle-class Europeans and North Americans who have dominated most development organisations for decades.

Agustín (2007) has aptly named this sphere of work as well as other social sectors the 'rescue industry'. In her study on sex and migration she notes how when a person from a poor country moves to a new country he or she is labelled 'migrant', while Europeans who live and work abroad are referred to as 'expatriates' (see also Gutmann, Chapter 49, this volume). This use of language does not only label people from poorer countries but also robs them of all power to define themselves in certain settings. Women who have moved from one country to another and taken the decision to sell sex immediately become 'victims of trafficking' in the official discourse and statistics. However, as Agustín shows, there is with very little evidence backing up their victim status and equally little knowledge as to why and how they have embarked on this journey. 'Migrant' and 'victim of trafficking' are two expressions with the ability to disempower those who fit the label. She traces this back to a phenomenon which she calls the 'Rise of the Social' when the educated and newly empowered women of the bourgeoisie created a space and career for themselves as those who can save the less fortunate. This is where we see the beginning of assistentialist discourses which name and describe those who need help in various terms. Social agents, often from middle- and upper-class segments of society, have for a long time been on a mission to save, rescue, support or empower those whom they have defined as needy. Agustín's main criticism of the rescue project is that it relies almost exclusively on identities, desires, needs and agendas defined by the 'rescuer' rather than those who they set out to rescue. When trying to understand the myths behind the development discourses adding the concept of 'help' makes it easier to comprehend how they work.

Mindry (2001) also talks of a transnational 'politics of virtue' where some women are the benevolent providers and others the deserving recipients of their help, be it microcredit, education or empowerment. She notes that Victorian ideas about the good woman being a caring and selfless mother still resonates in today's self-portrayals of people involved in some development organisations as well as the construction of worthy 'beneficiaries' of this aid. According to Mindry identifying 'the grassroots' became an important project for NGOs in the new South Africa (and this rings true for the rest of the world too) and the category of people who were the most deserving of development were poor, black, rural women. These women, says Mindry, can easily be, and often are, portrayed as innocent victims of oppression, poverty and ignorance. The image does little to challenge any stereotypical notions of a 'brown woman' that donors, sponsors and development workers in the West may hold. And those women who do challenge the notions of what a worthy recipient should look like, who shake the foundations of a 'politics of virtue', are not as readily picked up in either development projects or development stories. Mindry refers to other studies in South Africa where it has been noted that the young urban women who had relationships with gangsters were completely forgotten in gender equity efforts in the new South Africa. Elsewhere, I have also made similar observations (Jassey and Nyanzi, 2007) on how in the discourses around HIV and AIDS men are often portrayed as sexual aggressors and women as victims of these men and tradition. We proposed that this could be traced back to the intentions of colonial administrations where they constructed African sexuality as a problem which could be solved by targeting the women to become 'good' mothers. It becomes apparent when looking at HIV and AIDS development discourses that studies on women who willingly and knowingly engage in sexual activities, take on various partners for different reasons, are either very rarely quoted or discussed (see Campbell and Gibbs, Chapter 50, this volume). What we see is an erasure of certain kinds of people from the narratives of development: of men who are in trouble, of women who get themselves into trouble, of men with needs and women who transgress.

Conclusions
The Sida that I left is no longer the same, a major reorganisation has taken place and when I listen to my former colleagues I notice that there is a shift in where they now need to focus their energies. From the early years of the twenty-first century when a multidimensional understanding of poverty was embraced they have now moved towards 'results based management' and 'evidence-based decision-making'. This is not entirely new to public administrations of the West; a certain amount of need to measure the results of policies and programmes has always been part of the mandate. This is probably why there is a long tradition within development to identify 'target groups' where for example, 'female-headed households' as being the poorest of the poor has held a prominent place over decades (see Chant, Chapter 15, this volume; Davids and van Driel, Chapter 14, this volume).

At the time I worked as a policy adviser at Sida we talked more about 'management by objectives', which is probably why so much energy was dedicated to the formulation of goals. Now there is less emphasis on goals, and more on results. Seemingly the two are of similar character although possibly results are closer to a positivistic tradition, where we can establish objective facts about societies and use statistics for measuring progress and change. Hence indicators have become more important, and not the qualitative indicators that were fashionable a decade back or more. Today indicators have to be 'SMART', that is, specific, measurable, achievable, realistic and timely. For anyone with a background in anthropology it goes without saying that this person will be uncomfortable with the assumption that we can quantify social relations, predict social processes as if they were bound by laws of physics or even talk about social 'facts' as our language is not objective to begin with but a social construction. Will we measure what really matters or only measure what can be measured? And if poverty and gender turn out to be too messy to transform into SMART indicators of results is there not a risk that we will fabricate, or at least not question, even more 'mythical numbers' such as those that Eyben (2007) identified in the DFID policy documents?

I have in this chapter tried to show that the development industry needs simple narratives that will justify its own role as saviour. The very basis of development is intervention, and these interventions must be continuously sanctioned and justified. In my mind we face the risk of entrenching the often racist images of brown women being downtrodden helpless victims of their brown men and tradition as there is no room to highlight the complexities of poverty. And by so doing, development organisations are also more at more risk of engaging in support that may very well not serve the ultimate purpose of bringing about equitable change for all.

Acknowledgements
While I take full responsibility for flaws in the arguments made here I am very grateful, as always, for the comments made by Andrea Cornwall and Seema Arora Jonsson on draft versions.

Notes

1. I use the word 'brown' here to signal that the development machinery is concerned with women from poorer countries, and as the Swedish saying goes, 'in the dark all cats are grey', so do all reports, projects, speeches and so on tend to homogenise 'non-white' women.
2. See the report by Sida (2002) *Perspectives on Poverty*, available at: http://www.sida.se/sida/jsp/sida.jsp?d=118&a=1490&language=en_US (accessed 24 May 2009).
3. All these citations are taken from page 53 of Sida (1996) *Promoting Sustainable Livelihoods: A Report from the Taskforce on Poverty Reduction*, available at: http://www.sida.org/?d=118&a=2107&language=en_US (accessed 25 May 2009).
4. The report in question was published by the Swedish Ministry for Foreign Affairs in Stockholm in 1997, and was entitled *The Rights of the Poor – Our Common Responsibility – Combatting Poverty in Sweden's Development Co-operation*, available at: http://www.regeringen.se/sb/d/574/a/20408 (accessed 25 May 2009).
5. See article 'Dramatiskt bakslag för jämställdhet i världen', by Dagens Nyheter, in *DN.se*, 6 March 2009, available at: http://www.dn.se/opinion/dramatiskt-bakslag-for-jamstalldeheten-i-varlden-1.814356 (accessed 28 April 2009).
6. See http://www.actionaid.se/engagera_dig/bli_fadder_nu/index/xml?country=Default (accessed 22 April 2009).

Select bibliography

Agustín, Laura (2007) *Sex at the Margins. Migration, Labour Markets and the Rescue Industry*, London: Zed.

Cornwall, Andrea and Karen Brock (2005) *Beyond Buzzwords. 'Poverty Reduction', 'Participation' and 'Empowerment' in Development Policy*, Overarching Concerns, Programme Paper Number 10, Geneva: United Nations Research Institute for Social Development.

Eyben, Rosalind (2007) 'Battles over booklets: gender myths in the British aid programme', in Andrea Cornwall, Elizabeth Harrison and Ann Whitehead (eds), *Feminisms in Development. Contradictions, Contestations and Challenges*, London: Zed, pp. 56–78.

Jassey, Katja and Stella Nyanzi (2007) *How to Be a 'Proper' Woman in the Time of AIDS*, Uppsala: Nordiska Afrikainstitutet.

Mindry, Deborah (2001) 'Nongovernmental organisations, grassroots, and the politics of virtue', *Signs*, **26** (4), 1187–211.

Mosse, David (2002) 'The making and marketing of participatory development', paper presented at seminar on Participatory Action Research and Participation in Development, 11 April, Uppsala University, Sweden.

Shore, Cris and Susan Wright (1997) 'Policy: a new field of anthropology', in Cris Shore and Susan Wright (eds), *Anthropology of Policy: Critical Perspectives on Governance and Power*, London: Routledge, pp. 3–42.

79 Poverty alleviation in a changing policy and political context: the case of PRSPs with particular reference to Nicaragua
Sarah Bradshaw and Brian Linneker

Since the end of the 1990s there has been a new interest in poverty shown by the International Financial Institutions (IFIs) as witnessed by the enhanced Heavily Indebted Poor Countries (HIPC II) initiative. To obtain further debt relief and concessional lending governments are required to produce a Poverty Reduction Strategy Paper (PRSP) based on both a poverty analysis of the country and a participatory design process. This is to promote 'ownership' of the strategy by governments and civil society, and the IFIs stress their role is only to advise and provide technical support. Although not prescriptive, guidelines are provided by the World Bank in a 'Sourcebook' and the suggested policy bundle does promote a more holistic approach than previous initiatives, including a focus on social policy elements such as health and education, as well as social safety nets for the most vulnerable. A number of issues are suggested as cross-cutting themes, including gender. The PRSP process has been said to mark a new era for the IFIs on a number of counts, not least the new focus on poverty rather than economic growth. However, critics of PRSPs have questioned the extent to which both the process and the focus on poverty is new (Booth, 2003; Bradshaw and Linneker, 2003; Cammack, 2002; Whitehead, 2003).

Guidelines contained in the Sourcebook highlight that economic growth remains the 'single most important factor influencing poverty' and all the new social elements promoted within PRSPs are presented as important to promote economic growth as well as for their intrinsic value. Gender is a good case in point and highlights the World Bank's continued 'efficiency' rather than 'equity' focus. Recent World Bank literature promotes 'Gender Equality as Smart Economics' given that gender disparities lead to 'economically inefficient outcomes'. Based on research around how households function, they also highlight the efficiency of channelling resources through women rather than men, suggesting that women are more likely to use resources for the benefit of the whole family. A good example of how this translates into policy are the increasingly popular Conditional Cash Transfer (CCT) programmes, currently promoted by the World Bank in 13 countries across the globe. They transfer cash to women in an aim to alleviate both short-term poverty and to reduce longer-term poverty through conditioning these transfers through targets around children's healthy development and education. In this way it has been suggested that women are at the service of the new poverty agenda rather than served by it (Molyneux, 2007) in that it reflects a 'feminisation of responsibility' where women are assuming greater liability for dealing with poverty and have progressively less choice other than to do so (Chant, Chapter 15, this volume).

One question that processes of policy feminisation raise is around who is promoting the trend. It is perhaps too easy to assume that it is World Bank efficiency logic alone.

Given that PRSPs are said to be as much country owned as IFI influenced, it should suggest there is room for differences over time and space. A review of early PRSPs showed striking similarities, perhaps not surprisingly given that countries were keen to design a PRSP that would be acceptable to the IFIs in order to receive economic resources as quickly as possible. As those countries who were among the first to be accepted onto HIPC II are now on their second or third PRSP, there is room to examine if policies have evolved over time to reflect the potentially different thinking of the IFIs and of national governments, which, in turn, is influenced by national actors such as civil society and the Church. One possible contentious area lies in understandings of gendered identities, roles and relations.

While across the globe the countries that are included in the initiative now number over 40, only three countries in Latin America qualify for inclusion – Honduras, Nicaragua and Bolivia. Not only do they offer a distinct geographical context but the recent wave of more progressive governments coming to power across the region make them interesting for study. In recent years Nicaragua has been described as a 'veritable laboratory' for projects to reduce poverty and, as such, provides a good case study to explore the intersection of IFI thinking with changing national policy discourse around gender as it relates to anti-poverty strategies.

The evolution of PRSPS: the case of Nicaragua
The first Nicaraguan PRSP was completed in 2000 and civil society organisations (CSOs) suggested the document was more influenced by IFI advisors than by the 'participatory' design process. An IFI evaluation supports this claim suggesting the then Liberal government (Constitutionalist Liberal Party/Partido Liberal Constitucionalista [PLC]) gave the team responsible for producing the PRSP the mandate to prepare as quickly as possible a PRSP which would be acceptable to the IFIs, facilitated by an IMF staff member being located within the team's offices.[1] The final document – The Strengthened Strategy for Economic Growth and Poverty Reduction (Estrategia Reforzada de Crecimiento Económico y Reducción de Pobreza/ECERP) – notes that 'virtually all' of the document will encourage increased social equity, yet there are no specific gender-equality projects and very little mention of women. Where mentioned, the discourse presents women as victims of male abandonment and violence. There is no discussion of women's productive role and very little of their wider reproductive role. Instead, the focus is on reproduction and women's access to family planning in particular. This may reflect IFI macroeconomic concerns around high fertility rates and their purportedly negative impact on economic growth gains.

The second PRSP – the National Development Plan (Plan Nacional de Desarrollo PND) – reflects a change in president, although not party, in power. The PND is more of a 'home grown' strategy. It demonstrates that care needs to be taken when assuming that countries are always forced by the IFIs into adopting policies that go against their own beliefs. While in the ECERP, as per IFI rhetoric, the focus on poverty was explicit and the need for economic growth implicit, in the PND these positions are reversed and the key focus is on economic growth and how to promote this. Despite the fact two of the key areas prioritised for growth – tourism and free trade zones – demand a highly feminised labour force, women's productive roles are still not recognised. More generally, women's roles are not explicitly discussed, however, the construction of women as mothers and the idea that their place is in the home is more strongly implied within the government discourse, and the PND states its aim is to 'promote, strengthen and protect' the family unit and family unity, re-establishing the 'values and morals of families'. The strengthening of this family-centred rhetoric demonstrates the influence of national rather than international actors on the PND and in particular the increasing power of the Church to influence policy at this time (Bradshaw, 2008a).[2]

With the change of government in 2007, so too a new era of poverty reduction began as the 'revolutionary' FSLN government (Sandinista National Liberation Front/Frente Sandinista de Liberación Nacional [FSLN]) regained power and stated its intention to re-focus priorities and direct resources to the poor promoting human development from the bottom up, through citizen power. While accepting many of the international development objectives such as the Millennium Development Goals (MDGs), the government suggests it will change the policy means of approaching these. Although the government rhetoric highlights that the magnitude and depth of poverty in Nicaragua means it cannot be combatted within the neoliberal model of global development, they are still engaged with the IFIs and the PRSP process.

The third PRSP is based on the National Plan for Human Development (PNDH) and is made up of a suite of policies relating to needs, incomes, power and support. Economic growth remains the central objective to make poverty reduction viable and sustainable but the focus is on economic 'reactivation' and, for example, shifts the emphasis to small and medium-sized producers. Another shift in emphasis is toward a greater focus on social policy initiatives and, within this, more overt attention to women. At the time of writing there is very little documentation freely available on the projects associated with the PNDH other than that contained in the speeches of the president, Daniel Ortega, and his wife, Rosario Murillo (the Coordinator of Communication and Citizenship). Of the range of programmes proposed the most central, and most controversial, is the 'Hambre Cero' (Zero Hunger) programme.

The architect of Zero Hunger sees it as directly replacing the CCT promoted by the World Bank – the Social Protection Network (Red de Protección Social/RPS). As with the RPS a proportion of Zero Hunger's funding comes from the World Bank. Unlike the RPS the main source of funds come from loans from Venezuela. As both the RPS and Zero Hunger promote a key role for women they provide an opportunity to explore in more depth any changes these more 'progressive' influences might bring to anti-poverty rhetoric.

Changing anti-poverty discourse
The Red de Protección Social was perhaps the most obvious anti-poverty component of the first two PRSPs. Modelled on Mexico's PROGRESA programme (see González de la Rocha, Chapter 37, this volume), its cash transfers to women were designed to be used to buy food and also to provide 'grants' for the purchase of school supplies and health services for children. The resources were contingent on children meeting health and education targets and on women's participation in classes on health, hygiene and family planning. It differs from other CCT programmes in a number of aspects (Bradshaw, 2008b), perhaps most importantly in the policy discourse that provides the context for the programme. The documentation around the RPS demonstrates two discourses. The first is a World Bank-style focus on efficiency where the targeting of women is justified

through drawing on models of household functioning and evidence that resources controlled by women translate into greater improvements in the well-being of children. The second evokes notions of the family and family values, with a stated aim to promote the 'development of women' in order to 'consolidate the family unit'. Government documentation talks explicitly about the need to change the behaviour of families to promote a 'responsible attitude', building women's knowledge and skills so they become 'proactive' in improving their families' health, nutrition and education. To this end attendance at classes is compulsory, and this, on top of the need to attend health clinics and to ensure children attend school, represents a substantial time commitment for the women involved. It may mean women are forced to forgo income-generating activities and/or take on more reproductive tasks in order to comply with the conditions and ensure children continue to have access to services.

The potentially high opportunity cost to women through being involved in the programme is not recognised, suggesting the programme understands women to have 'free time' to attend classes, to be engaged only in reproductive activities, or to be prepared to sacrifice their productive activities for the benefit of their children. That is, the RPS very explicitly constructs women as mothers, implicitly suggests that they need to learn to be better mothers, and in this way constructs what it means to be a 'good' mother and how a good mother behaves, especially in relation to children. The programme through its lack of engagement with men suggests women to have sole responsibility for their children's well-being, including economic responsibility. A contradiction transpires in so far as when the programme ends after three years, women will not have been provided with the necessary tools to generate economic resources and continue to fulfil this responsibility.

In contrast to the RPS, at first glance the focus of the Zero Hunger programme appears to be firmly on women's productive activities and the creation of sustainable livelihoods. The programme prioritises producing food rather than providing money to buy food, and women's key role within this. Poor families are organised in collectives to receive 'productive grants' which consist of in-kind resources, given in the women's name, including a pregnant cow and pig, chickens, animal feed, construction materials for housing the animals, plus seeds to produce food for animals and the family. Once chosen for the programme there are no conditions, but beneficiaries do have to start to pay back the grants within one year, in the form of making monetary contributions to a collective rotating credit fund.[3] That food is provided for the cow but not for people highlights the aim of the programme, which is to provide families with a sustainable supply of meat, milk, eggs and fruit and in this way eradicate hunger and malnutrition, reduce poverty as well as overseas food dependency, and promote self-sufficiency.

Much is made in the discourse of the presidential couple of the number of women who have benefited from the programme. However, the reason for focusing on women is not as clearly articulated as in the RPS. The rhetoric does not explicitly draw on women as more efficient users of resources in the home as in the RPS, nor on understandings of women as more efficient at paying back loans. The involvement of the World Bank then appears to be limited to providing some funding, rather than influencing the policy discourse. It does to some extent draw on 'equality' arguments inasmuch as it suggests the focus on women is important because of the existence of a 'feminisation of poverty', which is understood to mean that women are poorer and the poorest households are headed by women. However, it only tackles women's economic disadvantage since, apart from giving material resources to women, the only other activities to promote gender equality are training schemes in animal husbandry and farming techniques, and there is no consciousness-raising element to the programme for women or men. The most explicit reasoning for a focus on women draws, once again, on notions of the family and women's role in the family.

Although the focus in the Zero Hunger project is on providing potentially productive assets, the discourse centres on the role of these resources for maintaining the family. The importance and priority of maintaining the nuclear family is a key theme in presidential speeches that are also peppered with references to God and Jesus Christ, demonstrating the continued importance of religious rhetoric in political and policy discourse. The idea of the self-sacrificing mother is also a recurrent theme in the presidential discourse. Even as women's multiple roles are recognised, rather than normalised, they are idolised. Women are described as 'heroic' and, drawing on revolutionary rhetoric of struggle and solidarity, the president's wife, for example, calls on her 'sisters' to help her manage the social programmes and stresses the need to work 'without rest'. The discourse, then, does not focus on women as income-generators but, rather, reinforces ideals of women as selfless mothers working tirelessly to provide resources to improve the well-being of their children and communities, and at the same time, makes poverty alleviation part of this struggle or part of what 'good' mothers do.

Conclusion
Despite the fact that IFI rhetoric might be assumed to clash with that of the progressive governments recently brought to power across Latin America around both gender and measures to reduce poverty alleviation, the case of Nicaragua highlights how seemingly contradictory discourses have a common basis. While the World Bank promotes its arguments as being just 'smart economics', at their basis are notions of how households operate and World Bank-backed anti-poverty programmes exploit women's assumed altruism for economic gain. Competing to influence governments are national actors that have their own agendas and ideologies. An increasingly important actor in the policy context is the Catholic Church, and the discourse here centres not on the household, but the family, and idealised family values. Such ideas justify the focus on women by prioritising women's role as mothers and the need to promote better and more 'responsible' mothering for poverty reduction. Similarly, government rhetoric draws on notions of mothering, evoking revolutionary rhetoric of struggle and, perhaps surprisingly, it is this discourse that most overtly constructs the self-sacrificing mother as the ideal. While the three have a different logic – the IFIs concerned with economic efficiency, the Church with the morals of the country, and progressive governments with promoting alternative political models – all three utilise a similar discourse focused on mothering. Within this discourse notions of what constitutes a good mother are produced and reproduced, and increasingly actions to alleviate poverty are constructed not so much as something for policymakers but as a natural part of mothering. The long-term consequences for women remain to be seen.

Notes
1. 'Issue Notes' prepared for the Independent Evaluation Office/Operations Evaluation Department workshop on PRSPs and the PRGF, Addis Ababa, Ethiopia, January 2004.

2. For example, a government-sponsored sex education manual was withdrawn from schools after the Catholic Church objected to the term 'sexual rights', and in the run-up to the national elections a bill promoted by the Church was passed through Parliament, supported by both the PLC and FSLN, outlawing therapeutic abortion.
3. It is not clear how women are to pay back grants other than through the sale of any surplus produce. There has been little evidence concerning group repayments raising concerns about costs and sustainability.

Select bibliography

Booth, David (2003) 'PRSPs – introduction and overview', *Development Policy Review*, **21** (2), 31–159.

Bradshaw, Sarah (2008a) 'From structural adjustment to social adjustment: a gendered analysis of conditional cash transfer programmes in Mexico and Nicaragua', *Global Social Policy*, **8** (1), 188–207.

Bradshaw Sarah (2008b) 'An unholy trinity: the Church, the State, the banks and the challenges for women mobilising for change in Nicaragua', *IDS Bulletin*, **39** (6), 67–74.

Bradshaw, Sarah and Brian Linneker (2003) *Challenging Women's Poverty: Perspectives on Gender and Poverty Reduction Strategies from Nicaragua and Honduras*, London: Catholic Institute for International Relations/ International Cooperation for Development Briefing.

Cammack, Paul (2002) 'What the World Bank means by poverty reduction and why it matters', *New Political Economy*, **9** (2), 189–211.

Molyneux, Maxine (2007) *Change and Continuity in Social Protection in Latin America: Mothers at the Service of the State*, Gender and Development Paper 1, Geneva: UNRISD, available at: www.unrisd.org (accessed 30 April 2009).

Whitehead, Ann (2003) *Failing Women, Sustaining Poverty: Gender in Poverty Reduction Strategy Papers*, London: Gender and Development Network.

80 Gender-responsive budgeting and women's poverty
Diane Elson and Rhonda Sharp

Government budgets impact on poor people though a variety of channels, both direct and indirect. The direct channels are provision of services, infrastructure, income transfers, public sector jobs, taxation, user charges and budget decision-making processes. The indirect channels operate via the impact of the budget on the private sector through contracts to supply the public sector, and the macroeconomic impacts of the budget on aggregate demand in the economy, and thus on job creation and economic growth. The gender-differentiated character of these impacts can be revealed by gender budget analysis (GBA), and gender-responsive budgeting (GRB) can bring about changes in policies, priorities and budgetary processes.

Gender-responsive budgeting uses a variety of tools to 'follow the money' from government budgets to its impacts and outcomes for different groups of men and women, boys and girls. It also involves strategies for changing budgetary processes and policies so that expenditures and revenues reduce the inequalities between women and men. Over the past 20 years, governments, non-government organisations (NGOs), international organisations, aid agencies, researchers and grassroots activists worldwide have undertaken a variety of initiatives, adapting tools and strategies to local circumstances (Budlender, 2007; Cooper and Sharp, 2007; Elson, 2006).

Gender-responsive budgeting brings into focus issues that are frequently overlooked or obscured in conventional budget analysis and decision-making. These issues include the role of unpaid work in economic and social outcomes, particularly women's disproportionate responsibility for unpaid work; the distribution of resources within as well as between families; and the extent to which women and men participate in budget decision-making.

Gender-responsive budgeting frequently has a focus on poverty as well as on gender equality. An example is Tanzania, where the Tanzania Gender Networking Programme (TGNP) has been active since 1997 in analysing the government budget from gender and poverty perspectives.[1] The TGNP has influenced the government of Tanzania to introduce gender analysis into its budget planning process, and to improve availability of poverty-related sex-disaggregated data. The TGNP persuaded the National Bureau of Statistics to include a time-use survey as part of the Integrated Labour Force Survey in 2005, so as to make women's unpaid work more visible.

In this chapter we focus on three dimensions of budgets: decision-making, expenditure and revenue. We provide examples of how GRB has benefited poor women in a number of countries.

Budget decision-making processes
The interests of powerful groups can converge to reduce public services, reduce taxation for high-income groups and further shift the burden of unpaid work to poor women.

Gender-responsive budgeting can help elected representatives look at the budget from a gender equality perspective; increase the capacity of poor women elected representatives to play an active role in formulating the budget; and facilitate the participation of grassroots women in planning processes.

Parliamentarians in Uganda have been assisted to look at the budget from the perspective of poor women by briefings produced by the Ugandan women's budget group, Forum for Women in Democracy. In the view of a former leading woman member of the Ugandan Parliament these briefings gave gender issues 'credibility and respect'.[2]

In some countries increasing numbers of poor women are being elected to city and village councils because special measures have been introduced to increase women's political representation. A good example is India, where a constitutional amendment was introduced in 1992 that reserved one-third of all seats in local councils for women. The Karnataka Women's Information and Resource Centre, with support from the United Nations Development Fund for Women (UNIFEM), worked with poor women councillors (many of whom were illiterate) to 'build budgets from below'.[3] With some training the women gained the confidence to develop their own priorities for village-level expenditure. Where women councillors have been able to play an effective role in budget decisions in West Bengal and Rajasthan, they have altered local spending patterns to meet women's priorities (Chattopadhyay and Duflo, 2004; see also Beall, Chapter 97, this volume).

Another way in which poor women can participate in budget decision-making is through participatory budgeting, pioneered in the city of Porto Alegre, Brazil, and adopted in many other cities in Latin America and Europe. At its best, participatory budgeting gives poor people a direct say in how local funds for new investment are used to improve local facilities (such as water and sanitation, drainage, paved roads, schools and clinics). In Porto Alegre women have always been present in large numbers in the neighbourhood participatory assemblies, typically constituting over half the participants. However, they were initially in a minority among representatives elected to the Area Forums and the city-wide Participatory Budget Council. Over time their share rose, and in 2000 half of the members of the Budget Council were women (Sugiyama, 2002: 14). Some cities that have adopted participatory budgeting have also examined how budgets can be linked to the gender equality policies of the city. In Cuenca, in Ecuador, this led to earmarking of resources in the city budget for its Equal Opportunity Plan and guidelines to promote the hiring of more women on city investment projects.

Outcomes for poor women can be improved by increasing the participation of grassroots women at the development planning stage and facilitating a closer nexus between planning and budgeting. In Indonesia efforts have been made to make the local development planning process (Musrenbang) a forum for building the capacities of poor women to influence budgeting. Gender-responsive budgeting initiatives supported by the Asia Foundation and partners enable grassroots women to assess the level of poverty in their community, to identify women's development needs in health and education, to understand the budget process, and to make demands for the allocation of resources to meet these needs.[4]

Gender-responsive budgeting can introduce mechanisms into budgeting processes that require decision-makers to take into account the needs of poor women. In response to GRB in Bangladesh, the Ministry of Finance's budget call circular which guides the budget submissions of ministries was amended to require ministries to evaluate their performance against the poverty and gender objectives outlined in the Bangladesh poverty reduction strategy. Budlender (2007) argues that the use of gender-sensitive budget call circulars strengthens the relationship between policies, strategies and the budget cycle. As a result, there is an increased likelihood that poverty reduction policies for poor women are resourced and implemented.

Expenditure
Gender-responsive budgeting has the potential to alleviate poverty for women and girls by improving the quantity and effectiveness of government expenditures in areas including infrastructure (water, energy, roads), services (such as education and training, health, access to credit, support for small business), income transfers (child payments, maternity leave, unemployment benefits, age pensions) and employment generation, including the public service.

Investment in infrastructure, such as water, sanitation and energy, has the potential to reduce the unpaid work of poor people in poor countries. This is particularly beneficial to poor women and girls, who bear most of the burden of fetching water and collecting fuel. In Tanzania, the Ministry of Water was one of six ministries included in the first phase of institutionalising gender analysis in budget processes, in collaboration with TGNP. As a result, poverty and gender issues were included in the guidelines for the water sector budget. The TGNP advocated for more resources for water and can claim some credit for the expansion of the resources going to the Ministry of Water from 3 per cent to 6 per cent of the budget.[5] The TGNP has subsequently campaigned against the privatisation of water and to improve the access of poor women to water.

In some countries GRB initiatives have improved the delivery and funding of services. The Indonesian NGO, the Women's Research Institute (WRI) has promoted the application of GRB to maternal health services at the provincial and district levels. For example, in South Lombok they concluded that maternal health services could be improved if more resources were allocated to the salaries of midwives (as opposed to doctors) and the purchase of motorbikes and sterile equipment for midwives (instead of ambulances and buildings). This led to an increased budget allocation to maternal services in South Lombok over a period of three to four years.[6]

Expenditure cutbacks may jeopardise services of importance to poor women. In Australia, a pioneer in GRB, efforts have at various times focused on ways to prevent declines in the funding of existing services.[7] This was the case for Partnerships Against Domestic Violence (PADV), a government programme, which was allocated AUD$50 million (US$40 million) during the period 1998–2003. However it was disclosed publically in 2002 by a woman Member of Parliament that unspent funds of around AUD$10 million had been reallocated to fund the provision of an anti-terrorism kit to households. In response, the Federal Office for Women commissioned research which estimated the costs of domestic violence at AUD$8 billion (US$6.5 billion) per year.[8] The study was used to advocate maintaining funding for domestic violence programmes.

Income transfers paid directly to women can alleviate poverty for them and their dependent children. In South Africa, GRB can claim some credit for the introduction of the child support grant, which is given to the primary caregivers of young children from poor households. This grant replaced an earlier grant that reached very few of the poor, black and rural women who needed it most.[9] In Australia GRB was given renewed emphasis in 2009. Low-income working women and their children are major beneficiaries of the federal government's 2009/10 budgetary commitment to introduce a national parental leave scheme in January 2011. This scheme provides a means-tested 18 weeks' parental leave at the level of the federal minimum wage and according to the official 2009 Budget Overview is included in the forward budget estimates at a cost of AUD$731 million (US$595 million) over five years.

Government expenditure can create jobs for poor women and men through public employment programmes targeted at poor people, but women do not necessarily benefit equally. In response to calls for budgeting that promoted gender equality and improved the situation of poor women, the South Africa government reviewed the Community Based Public Works Programme, to which 250 million Rand (US$32 million) had been allocated between 1994 and 1998. The Ministry of Finance reported in its 1998 Budget Review that 41 per cent of those employed on the 599 projects were women. While this figure is lower than the female proportion of the population in the rural areas in which the projects operate, it would have been even lower without explicit targeting. Less positive findings were that women were more likely to hold the more menial jobs, had lower average wages, were employed for shorter periods and were less likely to receive training. According to the 1998 Budget Review of the South African Ministry of Finance, the evaluation results formed the basis of the department's strategy to fine-tune the programme and further improve targeting.[10]

Taxation and user fees

Taxation has an impact on poor people, both in terms of tax rates and the exemptions and allowances that are built into tax systems. The poorest people do not come into the income tax net, but they pay broad-based indirect taxes, such as sales tax and value-added tax (VAT). Indirect taxes are often regressive, with the poorest households paying a higher proportion of their income in taxes than the richest households because they have to spend almost all of their income in order to survive. The regressive incidence of VAT on poor people can be mitigated by zero-rating basic items, especially food (see also Trotz, Chapter 101, this volume). This is particularly important for poor women who are typically responsible for purchasing the day-to-day needs of the household. In South Africa a selection of basic foodstuffs has always been zero rated, but some basic necessities were subject to VAT, including paraffin, which is bought by poor women for cooking, lighting and heating. The South African Women's Budget Initiative, a collaboration of parliamentarians and researchers, successfully argued for paraffin to be zero rated, on the grounds that the annual revenue loss to the government would be small and the benefits would be a very well-targeted form of assistance to poor households, as better-off households do not make much use of paraffin (Smith, 2000).

In countries with a welfare state, welfare benefits have been increasingly delivered through the tax system, using tax credits of various kinds. The design of the tax credit system has been the focus of attention of the Women's Budget Group of the United Kingdom (UK), a network of women researchers and policy analysts based in universities, trade unions and NGOs. In 1999 the UK government planned to abolish Income Support, a welfare payment to low-income families with children, which was paid to the main carer of the children, almost always the mother, and to introduce a Working

Families Tax Credit, which would add money to the take-home pay of the main earner in low-income families with children. The UK Women's Budget Group pointed out that, since the main earner in two-parent low-income families was likely to be the father, this would take money away from poor women and give it to poor men, and would be likely to reduce the amount of family income spent on the welfare of children, since the evidence showed that poor men were likely to spend less of any extra money on children than were poor women. The UK Women's Budget Group successfully lobbied for the Working Families Tax Credit to be changed, so that parents could choose whether it would be paid to the main earner or the main carer (St Hill, 2002; see also Lister, Chapter 24, this volume).

In countries which charge user fees for public services, poor people often cannot afford to use these services. In Mexico a gender budget analysis by academics involving a survey of the impact of user-pays policies on women found that the poorest and the richest women were accessing services less, with middle-income women using them the most. For example, the better-off women paid for private childcare services. The poorest women could not afford either private or public childcare services and could not comply with requirements of the latter, such as providing disposable diapers (Cooper and Sharp, 2007: 219). In the context of the Mexican GRB efforts, Cooper and Sharp (2007) argue that such research projects have enabled women and their organisations to give voice to their concerns, and make government more accountable.

Conclusion

While GRB can benefit poor women, it is not a panacea for poverty alleviation. In some countries GRB has been limited to training exercises funded by international aid with little lasting effect. In other countries there has been an overemphasis on identifying expenditures targeted to women and girls who are only a small proportion of the total expenditure (5 per cent or less). In all countries, GRB faces globalisation-driven pressures to keep taxation and expenditure low. Nevertheless, GRB is unique in its ability to go beyond new laws and policies to focus on resources necessary for their implementation. Gender-responsive budgeting has the potential to be a key element of a package of strategies to end women's poverty.

Notes
1. See UNIFEM webpage on gender responsive budgeting at http://www.gender-budgets.org/content/view/81/151/ and follow links to the 2003 working paper of the Tanzania Gender Networking Programme entitled 'A pro-poor and gender analysis of Tanzania's national budget' (accessed 16 June 2009).
2. Visit www.gender-budgets.org/content/view/155/153 and follow links to the UNIFEM publication edited by Karen Judd entitled *Gender Budget Initiatives: Strategies, Concepts and Experiences*. Citation taken from p.131 of chapter by Winnie Byanyima on 'Parliamentary governance and gender budgeting: the ugandan experience' (accessed 16 June 2009).
3. See 2003 report *Building Budgets from Below* at: www.gender-budgets.org/content/view/112/153/ (accessed 16 June 2009).
4. See, for example, http://asiafoundation.org/resources/pdfs/IndonesiaOverview2007.pdf (accessed 15 June 2009).
5. See http://www.gender-budgets.org/content/view/471/151/ and follow links to the paper by Edward Hiza Mhina on 'Financing for gender equality and the empowerment of women: experiences from Tanzania' (accessed 15 June 2009).
6. This observation draws from recent research by one of us (Sharp) in conjunction with Monica Costa, on the Health Budget and maternal services in South Lombok, Indonesia.
7. See paper presented to the Expert Group Meeting on Financing for Gender Equality and Women's

Empowerment, UN Division for the Advancement of Women, Oslo, Norway, 7 September 2002, by Rhonda Sharp entitled 'Gender-responsive budgets have a place in financing gender equality and women's empowerment', available at: http://www.un.org/womenwatch/daw/egm/financing_gender_equality/ExpertPapers/EP.4%20Sharp.pdf (accessed 11 June 2009).

8. This information is drawn from a 2004 report on the cost of domestic violence to the Australian economy at: http://www.accesseconomics.com.au/publicationsreports/showreport.php?id=23&searchfor=2004&searchby=year (accessed 1 June 2009).
9. This is reported in a 2004 paper by Debbie Budlender entitled 'Expectations versus realities in gender responsive budgeting initiatives', available at: http://www.unrisd.org/80256B3C005BCCF9/httpPublications?OpenForm&view=author&count=1000&expand=86 (accessed 16 June 2009).
10. www.finance.gov.za/search.aspx?cx=018115738860957273853%3Aj5zowsrmpli&cof=FORID%3A11&q=1998#1037) (accessed 16 June 2009).

Select bibliography

Budlender, Debbie, in collaboration with the Commonwealth Secretariat (2007) *Gender-Responsive Budgets in the Commonwealth Progress Report 2005–2007 Commonwealth Finance Ministers' Meeting (Georgetown Guyana 15th –17th October 2007)*, London: Commonwealth Secretariat [FMM{07}17], available at: http://www.gender-budgets.org/content/view/472/153/ (accessed 1 June 2009).

Chattopadhyay, Raghabendra and Esther Duflo (2004) 'Impact of reservations in Panchayati Raj: evidence from a nationwide randomised experiment', *Economic and Political Weekly*, **39** (9), 979–86.

Cooper, Jennifer and Rhonda Sharp (2007) 'Contesting government budgets: gender-responsive budgets and neoliberal globalism in Mexico', in Marjorie Griffin-Cohen and Janine Brodie (eds), *Globalisation and Remapping Gender in Semi-Peripheral Countries*, London: Routledge, pp. 205–22.

Elson, Diane (2006) *Budgeting for Women's Rights: Monitoring Government Budgets for Compliance with CEDAW*, New York: United Nations Development Fund for Women.

Smith, Terence (2000) 'Women and tax in South Africa', in Institute for Democracy in South Africa (IDASA), Community Agency for Social Enquiry (CASE) and Parliamentary Committee on the Quality of Life and Status of Women, *The Women's Budget Series*, Cape Town: IDASA, pp. 1–31.

St Hill, Donna (2002) 'The United Kingdom: a focus on taxes and benefits', in Debbie Budlender and Guy Hewitt (eds), *Gender Budgets Make More Cents: Country Studies and Good Practice*, London: Commonwealth Secretariat, pp. 171–92.

Sugiyama, Natasha (2002) *Gendered Budget Work in the Americas: Selected Country Experiences*, Austin, TX: Department of Government, University of Texas.

81 Reducing gender inequalities in poverty: considering gender-sensitive social programmes in Costa Rica
Monica Budowski and Laura Guzmán Stein

Costa Rica is considered a rather universalistic egalitarian social state due to its positive indicators in gender equality, health and other areas (Budowski and Suter, 2009). Despite trends towards a more liberal model in economics, state organisations have not been dismantled and gender equality has remained on the agenda since 1994. However, women's poverty rate is still higher than men's (for example, 20.6 per cent in 2007 as compared to 15.1 per cent), and there is also evidence for some persistence in this gap. Whereas poverty rates for female-headed households decreased by 6 per cent from 1995 to 2003 (from 30.6 to 24.0 per cent), the corresponding decline for male-headed households was almost 10 per cent (from 26.3 to 16.7 per cent) (Gindling and Oviedo, 2008; see also Chant, 2007: ch. 6).

Although well-educated, women have not been able to capitalise on their higher education, and the gender wage gap has increased. Women's net participation rate in paid work rose from 32 per cent in 1995 to 37 per cent in 2004; in particular (low-income) women-headed households with young children have increasingly entered the labour force. Women's work opportunities (more non-standard work and work in the informal sector) vary in quality when compared with men's. Elements contributing to stagnating poverty rates are identified in the gendered division of labour, structural changes in the labour market and demographic changes (González et al., 2009).

In light of the above, we review the innovative programmes aimed at reducing gender inequalities in poverty in Costa Rica. We present a brief history of social policies oriented to improving women's position and continue by describing the basic ideas, conflicts and actors of the first programme for low-income women-heads of households. We then look at the practical implementation of the programme during three different administrations (1994–2006) and conclude by discussing positive points and problems.

History of policies favouring gender equality
In Costa Rica, the state and elites have played a crucial role in reducing poverty, enhancing quality of life (health) and in providing options for women (Budowski and Suter, 2009).

The main organisation in charge of poverty policies is the 'Mixed Institute for Social Welfare' (Instituto Mixto de Ayuda Social/IMAS)[1] founded in 1971 by Law 4760. Its mandate was progressive from the start, as it was to promote social and human development beyond 'only' providing aid and reducing the effects of hardship. The Social Development and Family Assignation Fund (Fondo de Desarrollo Social y Asignaciones Familiares/FODESAF) was founded in 1974 to finance the IMAS's programmes (see Chant, 2007: 288)

Costa Rica's record on policies for improving women's status is good, although these were implemented eclectically until 1994. Some of the historically most significant interventions include the first Latin American legislation supporting a secular interpretation of marriage in 1888, mandatory education at the turn of the twentieth century, the foundation of the University of Costa Rica in 1940 open to men and women, and the establishment of equal political rights for women with men and for minorities in the late 1940s. In this context, a generation of well-educated women emerged that has actively engaged in improving women's position in society. Today Costa Rica features high on various international indicators regarding gender equality.

A crucial step towards institutionalising gender issues on the political agenda was the foundation of the semi-autonomous Centre for Women and the Family (Centro Nacional del Desarrollo de la Mujer y la Familia/CMF) in 1986. It was transformed in 2001 into the National Institute for Women (Instituto Nacional de las Mujeres/INAMU) with full legal status (Law 7801). It improved women's status by promoting laws that reduce discrimination and designing programmes to overcome identified gender inequalities. Examples include the ratification of the Convention on the Elimination of All Forms of Discrimination Against Women (CEDAW) in 1996, and the introduction of legislation in the spheres of domestic violence (Laws 7476, 7586), the protection of adolescent mothers (Law 7739) and responsible paternity (Law 8101) (see Chant, 2007: 289–92).

The first major programme targeting women heads of households in poverty with a gender focus was launched in 1995. The Comprehensive Training Programme for Women Heads of Households with Scant Resources (Programa de Formación Integral para Mujeres Jefas de Hogar 'Asignación Familiar Temporal') was part of the National Plan to Combat Poverty (Plan Nacional de Combate a la Pobreza/PNCP), 1994–98). This served as the model for Law 7769, Attending Women in Conditions of Poverty (Atención de las Mujeres en Condiciones de Pobreza) that upgraded this programme to a state policy in April 1998. The latter commits the state to help women, especially those who head their own households, to overcome poverty by means of inter-institutional cooperation in 'comprehensive training' comprising human development, empowerment and organisation (information, self-esteem, gender role sensitivity), coupled with economic incentives (30 per cent of the minimum wage), access to academic or vocational education, support in accessing the labour market or generating self-employment and access to decent housing.

The subsequent two programmes were subject to this legal framework: the programme Growing Together (Creciendo Juntas) within the National Solidarity Plan (Plan Nacional de la Solidaridad/PNS, 1998–2002) designed by the United Social Christian Party (Partido Unidad Social Cristiano/PUSC) administration of Rodríguez Echeverría and the programme with the same name in the New Life Plan (Plan Vida Nueva, 2002–2006) of the same party of the Pacheco de la Espriella administration.

The next two sections address the basic ideas, development, actors and implementation of these three programmes for low-income women and female heads of household, novel in Latin America and with regard to gender policies.

Basic ideas, actors and aims of Costa Rica's programmes for low-income women[2]

The idea of the first programme for low-income women emerged during the Figueres Olsen administration (1994–98). The context and the particular structural features of this programme's origins and design are perhaps best understood against the background of the previous administration (1990–94) of Calderón Fournier, which had carried out structural adjustment programmes (SAPs) and downsized the state and services. Poverty had increased and was buffered with targeted programmes of social assistance. The population was disillusioned with prevailing assistentialism, clientelism and social welfare from state institutions (in the context of pressures to trim down the state). This encouraged the Figueres Olsen administration to pursue more democratic and participatory strategies of development, to reassess the state's role, to create opportunities for disadvantaged groups, and to promote the (at the time contradictory) idea that economic and social development enhanced one other. For this purpose there was a reinstatement of the Social Council (Consejo Social) (an idea born under the 1982–86 presidency of Monge Alvarez of the National Liberation Party [Partido Liberación Nacional/PLN]), as a means of best managing the crisis and SAPs. Its members were governmental and non-governmental actors (for example, the University, the Catholic Church, and feminist, labour and employer organisations). This Council fits well both with Costa Rica's non-formalised practice of consensual policy-making *and* with new public management (NPM). It enabled a systematic and integrative approach to combat poverty and to legitimise the country's development.

Factors related to women's position in society and their rights triggered new ventures in social policy. Among them were the positive political conjuncture created by the First Lady, Josette Altman, and the Second Vice President, Rebecca Grynspan; pressure from the women's and feminist movements, and the CMF (the Fourth World Conference on Women, Beijing of 1995 came at the right moment to legitimise these claims); the attractiveness of women for social policy due to the large number of women found among the poor, and the growing awareness of the interrelatedness of women's and national development, as at the 1995 World Summit for Social Development in Copenhagen.

The social policy paradigm changed by considering people, women or communities in poverty as active citizens, who decide how they would like to change their situations, redefine their roles or shape their communities and also take responsibility (Budowski, 2005). Interestingly, the Figueres Olsen administration's overarching programme to combat poverty (PNCP) had not originally planned a women's axis; it was only included later due to the perseverance of the CMF, and the women's and feminist movements.

The original idea for the human and social development programme for low-income women was to promote change in the prevalent (hegemonic national) gender relationships. Therefore it was named Resocialisation of Roles (Resocialización de Roles). Conditions of poverty were considered related to everyday practice in men and women's relationships dominated by *machismo* that reduced quality of life and produced gender inequalities in various domains. One step in overcoming poverty, therefore, was to change gender roles and relations. Public debate about gender roles, their interdependence, advantages and disadvantages were to make visible the taken-for-granted circumstances of men and women, and allow space for new meanings of rights and obligations. Such debates may also have contributed to diminishing men's fear to changing gender roles, changing male identities, obligations, rights or behaviour (although see Chant, 2007: ch. 6 for some contradictory findings in this regard). Nonetheless, in principle the notion of resocialisation followed strategic gender interests as it targeted existing (often tacit and interiorised) inequalities between women and men.

Although there was limited support from some stakeholders, which led to some watering down of aims, the basic ideas were established in the Comprehensive Training Programme for Women Heads of Households with Scant Resources. Beyond addressing basic necessities by investing in human and social development and organisation, there was some provision to change daily practice through gender-sensitisation (Budowski, 2005). Because non-governmental organisations (NGOs) and other institutions implementing the programme had to discuss how to put into practice the idea of 'sensitising for gender', a public debate on roles and identities turned out to be one of the unintended effects. Three administrations with different political priorities transformed these ideas into practice, with significant consequences for programme implementation, as discussed below.

Implementation of Costa Rica's programmes for low-income women during three administrations

The Figueres Olsen administration (1994–98) was the first administration to implement the programme. It was based on a holistic and strategic gender interest approach. It was sensitive to the individual, group, organisational, and political level. It contained two components: (1) inter-institutional participation and cooperation of key government agencies, non-governmental actors, and women's and feminist organisations, and (2) a sequential organisation of programme elements, beginning with human and social development, empowerment and organisation coupled with financial incentives, followed by access to school and vocational education, assistance in finding employment or establishing a business, and access to housing.

Although targeting a specific population group, the programme was universal as it aimed at reaching all 45 000 low-income women heads of households (defined by a certain number of criteria). Women applied to participate, local committees (pre-)selected potential participants and the IMAS confirmed their access. Non-governmental organisations and the University of Costa Rica were contracted to provide the courses. Around 25 000 female household heads participated in the programme. Positive experiences and evaluations led to introducing the principles of this programme in Law 7769. The Law transformed the service from social aid in the first programme to the status of a (claimable) right, emphasising rights and duties (such as participation in programmes for capacity-building, vocational or formal education or entry into the labour markets) compensated by a financial incentive set at 30 per cent of the minimum wage.

Further programmes under the auspices of Growing Together (Creciendo Juntas) implemented by the subsequent PUSC administrations of 1998–2002 and 2002–06 were subject to Law 7769; modification was possible only by changing the modalities of its implementation.

A major focus of the second administration implementing the programme – the Rodríguez Echeverría administration (1998–2002) – was to link achievements in the social domain (notably, reduction of poverty) with achievements in the economic domain (reduction of inflation, increase in growth rates, and so on). It established the National Commission of Solidarity and Human Development (Comisión Nacional de Solidaridad y Desarrollo Humano/CONASOL) that included a majority of social organisations and was put in charge of elaborating plans to address poverty. On the basis of FODESAF financing, IMAS and the Institute for Agrarian Development

(Instituto de Desarrollo Agrario/IDA) became responsible for the coordination of interinstitutional cooperation.

Yet despite Law 7769, gender was not a major objective of the Rodríguez Echeverría administration. When implementing this second programme for low-income women, the emphasis was more on regular monitoring, evaluation and professionalisation. Evaluations shed light on various problems during this administration: the interinstitutional coordination and the participation of actors of NGOs did not work as expected; organisations emphasised the gender component differently and the IMAS – not specialised in gender – could not intervene. The programme suffered considerably due to neglect of the gender component; many women participated only in the human and social development programme (six months). Nonetheless, this programme reached 22 274 women in the course of four years (Montero and Barahona, 2003; see also Chant, 2007: 301).

Gender was not a focus of the following Pacheco de la Espriella administration (2002–06) either. This administration concentrated on regions affected by poverty most and targeted marginal groups, such as the indigenous population. Again, economic growth was considered crucial to produce employment. Regional Social Councils (Consejos Sociales Regionales/COSORE) encompassing public and private organisations were established in the target regions to implement the 'New Life Plan' to combat poverty. However, no clear structures were established to assuring participation of NGOs.

The third programme for low-income women continued with the same name the previous administration had used, but with an important institutional change: the IMAS was charged not only to coordinate but also to implement the programme, Growing Together, thereby excluding the participation of other organisations. This led to loss of know-how, an increase in bureaucracy and a loss of easy access both in terms of the specific population groups and by low-income women themselves. The programme was put into practice slowly; the target population was continuously reduced from almost 5000 women in 2002, to 3991 in 2003 and to 2542 in 2004, totalling only 11 542 in the fourth year of administration (INAMU, n.d.: 59). Commitment to social spending was low in general; in 2002, 14 per cent of the funds available were not spent, despite the IMAS clearly stating its lack of finances to carry out its programmes (Montero and Barahona, 2003: 51).

From the past to present: recent developments in Costa Rican policy
Summing up, the first programme to improve the situation of low-income women heads of households with a gender component was launched in 1995. The Figueres Olsen administration legislated the change in type of support for low-income women from social aid to a right. As the review shows, legislation is not enough: the Rodíguez Echeverría administration of 1998–2002 was not sufficiently committed to the gender component and anchored programme coordination in the IMAS, which is not specialised in gender issues. The subsequent administration of Pacheco de Espriella did not invest the money available for its gender programmes yet still charged the IMAS to implement them. Various evaluations reveal that these two programmes lack continuity; many women participate in one part of the programme only (INAMU, n.d.).

In order to overcome these problems, the present administration of Arías Sánchez (2006–10) modified the IMAS Law to replace the Growing Together programme by one called Attending the Needs of Women in Conditions of Poverty (Atención para Mujeres en Condiciones de Pobreza), and institutionalise the responsibility for design, strategy and financing at the INAMU. The IMAS (in charge of the programme in the former administration) initially opposed this modification due to the inclusion of certain 'undeserving' groups of women in poverty (for example, women in sex work, women deprived of liberty, or indigenous women, who felt they were not addressed by the programme for various reasons). This modification – as modifications in the previous programmes from a charity to a right – again constitutes a paradigm change: selection criteria now take into account the diversity of women's situations in poverty and overcome the distinction between 'deserving' and 'non-deserving' population groups implicit in many policies.

Conclusion

Costa Rica ranks high on gender indices, has a good record in reducing poverty and has long enjoyed broadly balanced economic and social development. The state is committed by Law 7966 to tackle gender inequalities (among others). Demographic changes (longevity, increase in one-person and women-headed households), changes in rights protecting against violence and discrimination, and increased labour market participation of women have changed gender relations in many ways for the better. Costa Rica has also been quite successful in reducing even extreme poverty since 1995, although paradoxically perhaps, women-headed households still feature disproportionately among the poor (Chant, 2007: ch. 6). Part of the failure to close gendered poverty gaps might lie in the fluctuating nature of gender-sensitive social programmes.

As discussed in this chapter, the application of rights (for example, Law 7769) varies by the political orientation of different administrations. The direct impact on poverty reduction of these programmes remains unclear, even if Costa Rica has done well regarding gender equality indicators and reduction of (extreme) poverty. Empowerment and bottom-up designs – as applied in the programmes reviewed – may enhance individual and/or group well-being, yet they need not necessarily lead to changing inequality-(re)producing structures at home, in organisations, the labour markets and/or the state. Changes at the structural level require political will and stakeholder organisation, mobilisation and political action. Besides altering daily routines and attitudes, structural barriers such as gender-differentiated access to the labour market, unequal pay for equal work and lack of affordable and accessible childcare, need to be addressed. Despite their novel approach, the designs of these programmes therefore still have certain limitations. Targeted strategies help overcome inequalities, yet Costa Rica's history shows that universal policies for men and women are also needed as the basis for social development in general.

Notes

1. 'Mixed' refers to the combined contribution of the private business sector (tax) and the state (national budget).
2. In all three plans to combat poverty, there were particular programmes targeting teenage mothers (Madres Adolescentes, Construyendo Oportunidades and Amor Jóven) (see Chant, 2007: ch. 6).

Select bibliography

Budowski, Monica (2005) *Dignity and Daily Practice: The Case of Lone Mothers in Costa Rica*, Berlin: LIT Verlag.

Budowski, Monica and Christian Suter (2009) 'Lateinamerika als Modernisierungsvorbild? Vom korporatistisch-klientelistischen zum neoliberalen Sozialpolitikmodell', in Peter Fleer and Stephan Scheuzger (eds), *Die Moderne in Lateinamerika. Zentren und Peripherien des Wandels*, Berlin: Vervuert Verlag, pp. 377–404.

Chant, Sylvia (2007) *Gender, Generation and Poverty: Exploring the 'Feminisation of Poverty' in Africa, Asia and Latin America*, Cheltenham UK and Northampton, MA, USA: Edward Elgar.

Gindling, Thomas H. and Luis Oviedo (2008) *Single Mothers and Poverty in Costa Rica*, Institute for the Study of Labour (IZA) Discussion Paper No. 3286, Bonn: IZA.

González, Lidia, Laura Guzmán and Irma Sandoval (2009) *¿2 + 2 = 6? El Trabajo que Hacen Hombres y Mujeres en Costa Rica no se Cuenta Igual. Principales Resultados del Módulo de Uso del Tiempo*, San José: Instituto Nacional de Estadísticas y Censos/Instituto Nacional de las Mujeres.

Instituto Nacional de Las Mujeres (INAMU) (n.d.) *Un Estudio Social sobre Percepción de las Mujeres Participantes y el Personal Técnico de las Respuestas Institucionales en Materia de Mujeres y Pobreza*, San José: INAMU.

Montero, Sonia and Manuel Barahona (2003) *La Estrategia de Lucha Contra la Pobreza en Costa Rica. Institucionalidad – Financiamiento – Políticas – Programas*, Serie Policas Sociales 77, Santiago de Chile: Comisión Económica Para América Latina.

82 Is gender inequality a form of poverty? Shifting semantics in Oxfam GB's thinking and practice
Nicholas Piálek

This chapter is not an attempt to examine the struggles, crises or torments of institutionalising gender equality and women's rights thinking and practice within development organisations – these struggles are well known and well documented both by practitioners and academics from an Oxfam GB perspective and beyond. Instead, this chapter seeks to reflect upon the generally positive shifting semantic relationship between gender inequality and poverty in Oxfam GB which has resulted from the aforementioned struggles. In doing so, this chapter discusses how this shift has opened up exciting opportunities for developing a much broader and more explicit women's rights agenda in the organisation's public policy and programme work. At the same time, I urge a note of caution on the potential dangers masked by organisational shifts towards an increasingly progressive language on gender equality and poverty.

Shifting semantics on gender and poverty in Oxfam GB

Oxfam GB (henceforth referred to as Oxfam) is a large international non-governmental development organisation (NGDO) that has an explicit mandate to 'overcome poverty and suffering'. It is not a women's rights organisation, nor does it support a feminist ambition of promoting women's rights and challenging gender inequality for its own sake. As a consequence, work around gender inequality and women's rights issues for much of Oxfam's nearly 70-year history has neither been specifically developed nor an explicitly recognised aspect of the organisation's work. However, building on the sustained endeavours of feminists and gender advocates in the organisation, in 1984 the Oxfam Gender and Development Unit (GADU) was established, formalising a link between Oxfam and the growing body of 'Gender and Development' (GAD) thinking and praxis that had been evolving in the preceding years.

Subsequently, the close association of Oxfam with the development of GAD thinking, brought about through the work of GADU staff (and its later reincarnations) along with the organisation's publications on gender and development, has had a profound impact upon Oxfam's framing of gender equality and women rights language within its organisational discourse around poverty and poverty reduction. This influence has been critical to the realisation of a much stronger articulation of feminist ambitions in the organisation's anti-poverty work.

The bringing together of poverty and gender inequality
In May 1993 the Oxfam Council agreed upon and put into force a 'Gender Policy' for its programme work. This policy was a milestone for the organisation, openly and explicitly drawing the links between the issue of gender inequality and its mandate for tackling 'poverty and suffering' for the first time. In the principles of the policy it states that:

> Women are poor because their lack of material wealth is compounded by a lack of access to power, skills, and resources. Fully integrating gender into Oxfam's programmes should tackle the causes of women's poverty and promote justice to the advantage of women as well as men. Because women are in a subordinate position, special efforts and resources are required to promote their full and active participation in Oxfam's work and to make them equal partners in the fulfilment of Oxfam's mandate. (Porter et al., 1999: 337)

Within this policy, gender inequality is construed as an underlying factor that exacerbates poverty and undermines measures to tackle poverty, especially for women. As such, the policy's rationale is that tackling poverty (or perhaps more accurately, economic poverty) effectively, particularly for poor women, entails addressing and transforming underlying issues of gender inequality. The relationship between gender equality and poverty was argued and illustrated as a causal one, and, as a consequence, the understanding of Oxfam's mandate was stretched to encompass, albeit indirectly, a much broader range of issues than when it was originally conceived.

Since this key moment, the relationship between gender inequality and poverty in Oxfam's discourse has continued to advance. By 1999, through adopting a rights-based approach to its work, an opportunity to 're-vision' and re-establish the relationship between gender inequality and poverty in the organisation arose. For Oxfam, the denial of certain key rights comes to be seen as a critical factor in explaining how and why people enter and stay in poverty. In developing this new approach, Oxfam identified five fundamental rights, the denial of which leads to and/or sustain poverty. Oxfam argued that these rights were so important that they 'individually' deserved promoting and defending in order to achieve its mandate effectively. The first four rights (or so-called 'Strategic Aims') focused on rights relating to livelihoods, basic social services, life and security (particularly in the context of conflict and disasters) and political voice. However, through the tireless efforts of gender advocates in Oxfam, the fifth Strategic Aim under this new rights based framework was established as 'The Right to Equity – Gender and Diversity' and aspired to a situation where 'women and men will enjoy equal rights'.

The establishment of this fifth Strategic Aim created a clear change in the organisation's language. As a result of the rights-based framework and the centrality of gender therein, discourse in the organisation could progress beyond linking gender inequality to poverty as a mere underlying factor that compounds the experience of poverty among women, and instead assert that gender inequality is intrinsically linked to the existence of poverty per se.

More recently, a less clearly stated, but perhaps even more fundamental, shift in discourse around gender inequality and poverty has begun to permeate the organisation. For instance, in a 2008 summary analysis of Oxfam's 64 in-country plans it is stated that:

> Attention to gender inequality does not itself represent a 'change' for Oxfam, but what is perhaps new is that every single National Change Strategy refers to it as central, and that gender inequality is seen not only as a *cause* of poverty . . . but as a *type* of poverty. . . . One way in which countries and regions are planning to address issues of gender inequality more effectively is to address them more directly. . . . The Nigerian National Change Strategy, for example, includes as a key programme pillar, 'increasing women's political representation and participation in decision making at all levels of Nigerian governance'. (Phillips, 2008: 7)

Similarly, in developing a list of strategic focus activities in 2006 that would guide Oxfam country programmes on what issues to engage in under its fifth aim – The Right to Equity – it was agreed that the 'Aim 5 Framework' would commit Oxfam to a 'programme of work that will directly attempt to transform unequal power relations between men and women, challenge and change existing social attitudes that believe that women are of less value, and address social norms, structures and conduct that accept such inequality as "normal"'. In committing Oxfam to such a programme of work, it hopes to achieve a vision whereby 'millions more women will gain power over their lives and overcome the barriers that keep them in poverty' (Oxfam GB, 2006: 6).

Gone from such analyses and policy are the often fundamentally crude and instrumentalist justifications that working on gender equality and women's rights is a critical but secondary and indirect aspect of working on relieving 'poverty and suffering'. Instead, such statements express a more direct relationship between working on gender equality and Oxfam's mandate. The language and tone of such discourse expresses a much greater intrinsic value attached to working on women's rights, based on a growing assertion that gender inequality is more than a mere cause or base factor related to poverty, but that the manifestation of gender inequality, predominantly in the form of female subordination, is in itself a form of poverty requiring direct action.

If one is to take the discourse of organisations at face value, then a fundamental transformation has occurred within Oxfam. Though its mandate to tackle 'poverty and suffering' has remained a constant during the organisation's history, what the organisation includes under this mandate, particularly in relation to women's rights, is now significantly broader. The conceptual validity (or implications) of defining gender inequality as a 'form' of poverty is uncertain, however, analytically valid or not, such a shift has opened up exciting opportunities in Oxfam for gender advocates to promote programmes and projects with an explicit and direct women's rights or even 'feminist agenda' which extend far beyond the realms of working with poor women on income-earning opportunities.

Nevertheless, it is also important to recognise that a shift in discourse in an organisation is only one step on a ladder. Though the reconfigured semantic relationship between gender inequality and poverty in such discourse has been well argued and well grounded by gender advocates in Oxfam, thus visibly shifting the agenda of the organisation, it does not mean that the conceptual understanding and emotional commitment needed to grasp and build on this semantic reconfiguration is equally shared by all in the organisation. Within this new semantic reality, serious challenges to achieving feminist ambitions within the organisations work can become masked.

A new era of action on women's rights in Oxfam GB?
What opportunities have these shifts in organisational discourse created for gender advocates and feminists in the organisation? From my own perspective, as a Global Gender Advisor in the organisation, I would draw attention to three realities in Oxfam that I believe this shift in discourse has made possible. These realities concern: what we work on, how we work and who is working on it.

First, and perhaps most importantly, what we work on has changed considerably. The shifts in discourse have provided significantly greater latitude for gender advocates to argue for a much broader range of issues that Oxfam could directly support and work on under its mandate. As a consequence, there is now a more widespread realisation and appetite in the organisation to engage on gender equality issues that surpass past approaches, centred around including women in poverty (economically conceived) reduction measures. Oxfam's fifth aim now directly commits the organisation to a programme of work on gender and women's rights that includes:

- *Gender mainstreaming* – integrating gender into all work undertaken under Oxfam's other aims (livelihoods, basic social services, humanitarian and political voice work).
- *Ending violence against women* – tackling the issue of domestic violence, violence against women as it relates to HIV/AIDS and violence against women in conflict/post-conflict situations.
- *Strengthening women's leadership and participation* – ensuring more women will achieve and hold effective leadership positions at all levels and in all sectors; and that both men and women will work towards greater gender equality.
- *Upholding women's rights* – ensuring governments and other development actors are held to account on their commitments to uphold women's human rights.
- *Innovation* – exploring new issues and possible areas of work. Such new areas include 'Identity Politics and Gender' (particularly, issues concerning working on gender in Muslim contexts) and 'Climate Change and Gender'.

As a result of this broadly conceived framework of activities, programme work that intentionally focuses on promoting women's rights in a context of poverty, rather than on narrowly conceived actions concerning women in poverty per se, has blossomed over the past few years. A good example of this is the work on women's political leadership undertaken by Oxfam in Sierra Leone with its partner PACER.

The '50:50 project' in Sierra Leone set out to increase both the quality and quantity of women in local council positions as well as to ensure that as leaders they will promote women's rights. The project supported more than 280 women aspirants and 31 candidates by equipping them with the basic knowledge and skills required to aspire to and contest positions of political leadership and decision-making. In addition, the project worked with existing powerbrokers at both the local and national level, such as religious leaders, to overcome barriers to women participating in decision-making processes. Before the project, the Koinadugu district had not fielded a single female candidate. At the 2008 local elections it was a historic first for the district that 14 female candidates ran for local council elections, six of whom were elected (one occupying the deputy chairperson position). Furthermore, 90 per cent of the 53 wards supported by the project now have at least five women members out of ten in the ward committees (Oxfam, 2008a).

Beyond *what* we work on, a shift in discourse has also allowed gender advocates to argue for a substantially revised approach to *how* we tackle gender inequality and women's rights. Having a discourse within Oxfam that focuses more directly on the issues which concern poor women, rather than on decontextualised links between gender equality and poverty, allows gender advocates to highlight issues such as domestic violence or political participation which are relevant to women across a broader socio-economic spectrum. With this established, a much more holistic and effective broader social-change approach (one that responds to both attitudes and beliefs as well as political and legal reforms) can be proposed. This involves developing approaches that involve working at multiple levels in societies, including supporting a range of groups and actors who are perhaps not traditionally associated with development projects, especially ones concerned with 'poor women' (for example, middle-class or elite women and men).

Such an argument was used by Oxfam in its intervention to support a number of women's rights organisations in Africa to advocate for the ratification, domestication and implementation of the African Women's Protocol. In Zambia, for instance, Oxfam has supported WILSA (Women and Law in South Africa). Women and Law in South Africa was one of the organisations that drafted the Protocol in the early 1990s, and with the support of Oxfam has now effectively lobbied their government to incorporate most of the provisions in their draft Constitution. Furthermore, through WILSA's engagement with traditional leaders at the community level, injurious practices such as child marriages and sexual 'cleansing' have been banned (Oxfam GB, 2008b).

A second key change on *how* we work has been the growing practice of, or at least recognition around, supporting women's organisations not just because such partnerships are necessary to achieve the goals of a particular GAD project, but also because working with women's organisations magnifies our investments in gender equality and women's rights work by strengthening the capacity of the women's movements more generally to demand and achieve gains for women. This has clearly been a key element of our work around the African Women's Protocol, as highlighted above.

Finally, *who* is working on gender equality and women's rights issues has also clearly changed with Oxfam's adoption of a discourse which places gender and women's rights as an essential component of its mandate. In 1999, Chris Roche (1999: 203–10) reflected upon being a man and working on gender issues in Oxfam in his article 'Middle-aged man seeks gender team'. In this Roche highlights the 'gendered' nature of working on gender equality issues: male (and female) staff and managers supportive of, or proactive on, gender equality issues were in short supply, male gender advisers an unknown, and there existed an organisational 'identity' that was predominantly 'male' in its outlook and composition (at a senior level).

However, ten years on the picture is considerably different. First, as a male gender adviser myself I represent a challenge to those staff who see the issue of gender equality and women's rights as the preserve of women concerned with 'women's issues'. Second, a new generation of personnel (both male and female) have entered Oxfam with exposure to a more general academic and policy discourse that is much more explicit and open about the relevance of women's rights and gender equality in development work. This new generation seems to have much more open-mindedness towards (and commitment to) working on gender equality and women's rights in its work. Finally, the identity of the organisation as 'male' in its outlook and composition no longer rings true. Senior positions in the organisation are now, if anything, more populated by women rather than men.

Overall, an increasingly progressive semantic relationship between gender inequality and poverty in the organisation's discourse, one that constructs gender inequality as a 'form' of poverty as much as a 'cause', has in many ways been extremely positive for those in Oxfam trying to move forward a gender equality and women's rights agenda in the organisation.

The dangers that lie beneath the words

Despite the considerable benefits brought about by changes in discourse these changes have (at the same time) given rise to potential dangers which those of us working in such contexts need to maintain a watchful eye upon. I wish here to draw attention to two potential dangers in particular.

First, having an extremely progressive discourse on the relationship between gender equality and poverty in an organisation, backed up by clear (showcase) examples of this discourse being put into action, tends to create a belief, both internally and externally, that gender is a 'job done'. With such a belief there is a tendency for downward shifts in resources and political will to deliver further progress. However, as Green (2008: 8) has noted in his recent book on poverty from an Oxfam perspective, 'although [the] multidimensional view of poverty is widely accepted in theory, in practice, attention centres on income poverty'. Oxfam is no exception here having spent only 2 per cent of its annual programme expenditure on initiatives directly addressing gender equality and women's rights over the past seven years. Gender advocates should be strongly concerned about any organisational dips in resources or political will to further this work, even if discourse on gender in organisations becomes increasingly progressive.

Second, although having a progressive discourse on gender equality, and more women in senior and managerial roles, are clearly important (as well as being matters of social justice), this intrinsic good should not be mistaken for representing a greater level of concern with, or activity on, gender equality and women's rights in an organisation's work. The political playing field for gender advocates in organisations such as Oxfam has, in recent years, become increasingly complex. It is no longer the case, if it ever was, that women are the 'natural' allies of a gender-equality agenda and men are the 'natural' blockers. 'Supporters' and 'blockers' of a gender equality and women's rights agenda now come in all guises. Gender advocates need to have a much more acute sense of who these people are and how 'blockers' can be persuaded to come on board.

No matter how discourse evolves in organisations, the fundamental challenge remains the same: how do a handful of gender advocates get large numbers of staff (from top to bottom) to take responsibility for the (often personally challenging) issue of gender inequality in their daily work? Progressive changes in discourse allow gender advocates to push development organisations to do more interesting things in more interesting ways, but fundamentally, the concerns and battles that have plagued those mainstreaming gender in such organisations continue unabated, even if somewhat altered in appearance.

Select bibliography

Green, Duncan (2008) *From Poverty to Power: How Active Citizens and Effective States can Change the World*, Oxford: Oxfam International.
Oxfam GB (2008a) *Supporting Women to Aspire to Election to Political Office in Sierra Leone: The Experience of the PACER Project*, Oxford: Oxfam GB.
Oxfam GB (2008b) 'The Africa Women's Protocol: a tool to mobilise resources for financing gender equality and women's empowerment', in *Programme Insights Series*, Oxford: Oxfam GB.
Oxfam GB (2006) *Oxfam GB Aim 5 Strategic Framework 07/08–09/10*, Oxford: Oxfam GB.
Phillips, Ben (2008) 'Key issues arising for Oxfam globally from the National Change Strategies and related regional strategies', mimeo (internal document), Oxford: Oxfam GB.
Porter, Fenella, Ines Smyth and Caroline Sweetman (eds) (1999) *Gender Works: Oxfam Experience in Policy and Practice*, Oxford: Oxfam GB.
Roche, Chris (1999) 'Middle-aged man seeks gender team', in Fenella Porter, Ines Smyth and Caroline Sweetman (eds), *Gender Works: Oxfam Experience in Policy and Practice*, Oxford: Oxfam GB, pp. 203–10.

83 Tackling poverty: learning together to improve women's rights through partnership – the case of WOMANKIND Worldwide

Tina Wallace and Ceri Hayes

'An almost universal weakness of NGOs working in development is the "limited capacity" to learn, adapt and continuously improve the quality of what they do' (Fowler, 1997: 64). There are good reasons for this, including concern about public image, a focus on 'doing' rather than reflecting, and the pressure to provide good results in a competitive environment. Yet learning is essential for improving work in addressing the complexities of poverty (Kaplan, 2003).

The task is challenging, the contexts varied and the necessary skills diverse, especially when women's rights and working with women lie at the heart of the work. In this chapter we reflect on the successes, challenges and ways forward for international women's human rights and development organisation WOMANKIND Worldwide based on their learning over the last two decades. We use recent case studies to illustrate what is possible, and why improving partnerships with women to address their rights lies at the heart of development and addressing women's poverty.

WOMANKIND Worldwide and its founding principles

WOMANKIND, established 1989, was founded on clear core principles: a commitment to partnership and building the capacity of women's organisations, and an emphasis on the implementation of women's human rights as an end in itself – not only as the means to achieve more efficient development outcomes. WOMANKIND grew out of a belief that women and women's organisations are central to the economic and social development of their communities and countries, as the key actors in health, family and well-being, and local economies – and as activists identifying creative solutions to the problems they and their communities face. Since women's organisations tend to be rooted in local realities, they are well placed to identify the social and cultural barriers to gender equality and women's rights as well as the approaches that will be most culturally relevant and sustainable.

WOMANKIND was also concerned that the dominant arguments for involving women in poverty reduction were instrumentalist and failed to address the root causes of their discrimination and poverty, assuming that targeting women and women's participation would lead to their empowerment. The organisation saw that the lack of women's rights underpinned their marginalisation and poverty and so placed these at the centre of the work using, for example, the UN Convention for the Elimination of all forms of Discrimination against Women (CEDAW) and the Beijing Platform for Action (BPFA). Poverty could not be addressed without tackling women's lack of entitlements and strengthening their capabilities: the work had to be done. As stated by Facio (1995, cited in Watson, 2003: 27n):

Within a broader agenda of social transformation and gender justice, foregrounding issues such as women's rights to bodily integrity, freedom from violence and fear, control over economic and political resources etc. In the development context, it signals a shift from women as passive beneficiaries marginalised from the development process to a focus on women's entitlements . . .

Twenty years later the organisation has grown and evolved while staying true to the founding ideology of partnership to 'strengthen the voices of women to be able to challenge and transform their own positions and that of their wider community' (Watson, 2003: 26n).

Learning in the early years
WOMANKIND initially took a broad approach, supporting a range of partners with whom they shared a vision. Over time this was seen to be too fragmented and, in the 1990s, a conceptually coherent, multi-dimensional approach was developed, known as the 'Four Literacies', comprising Word, Body, Money and Civil literacies. This took an approach that shifted attention away from focusing on the resources provided to an individual or group – for example, providing credit – to a holistic understanding of poverty (beyond income poverty) (Pankhurst, 2002: 13).

Developed in consultation with WOMANKIND's partners, this framework highlighted the interlinkages between different needs and rights, and focused on addressing the barriers that prevented women from attaining them. This approach was implemented through awareness-raising, individual and community support, capacity-building local organisations and policy work.

While it proved extremely useful for communicating the interconnectedness of the constraints facing women and the importance of a 'joined-up' approach to alleviating women's poverty and addressing women's rights, it became clear over time that some partners saw it as a 'manual' to be followed rather than as a framework within which to locate their work. The broad scope of the different literacies proved to be overly ambitious for a small international development organisation, with limited resources and capacity.

WOMANKIND learned that working primarily with small women's organisations to tackle deep-rooted problems of inequality and discrimination is time-consuming; requiring targeted and long-term interventions. A major evaluation of the approach led to an organisational shift to focus on two issues that WOMANKIND and its partners identified as most critical to women's enjoyment of their rights: tackling violence against women and promoting women's civil and political participation.

The continuation of learning: the learning review
WOMANKIND was able to make some major shifts as a result of understanding the challenges of each approach and it continued to ask itself difficult and demanding questions during a learning review (2007–08), involving all policy and programme staff, working with an outside facilitator. The review explored changes in the external funding and aid context, how well WOMANKIND's support was working across a wide range of partners, how to mediate and balance the needs of both donors and partners, and how to enable women's organisations – often small or quite weak organisationally, relying on volunteers and focused on activism – to improve their monitoring and learn more systematically from the women and communities with whom they worked.

The review explored the different methodologies WOMANKIND used to see how and when it was (or was not) contributing to building stronger, sustainable women's organisations capable of enabling women to live a life free from violence, able to participate in decision-making and access opportunities and resources.

The answers, developed through working closely with partners and trustees, were mixed. Although there were many examples of real success and strong evidence of positive change to women's organisations and the lives of poor women, a number of challenges also emerged.

Key findings: the issue of funding
The current funding context is one in which, while there is growing commitment to increasing local ownership – recognising that locally driven work is more sustainable – there is real pressure to show demonstrable results, short-term gains and working 'to scale'. This can be problematic for women's organisations because tackling gender inequality and discrimination is usually a long-term exercise, involving extensive work on attitudes and behaviour.

The gradual shift among UK funders from giving small grants for UK NGOs to larger consolidated, strategic grants has proved a double-edged sword. Many of WOMANKIND's partners are relatively small, supported by volunteers and activists, who are hugely committed, but subject to 'burnout'. While they deliver essential services to whole communities on issues such as legal rights and HIV and AIDS prevention, because they are the *only* NGO in remote areas ill-served by government (as, for example, three small community-based NGOs supported in the Eastern Cape), they usually have limited skills in proposal writing, budget development and reporting. These groups can only access small, sporadic funding and lack the organisational sophistication to become eligible for the larger grants now available. Some other more established agencies that WOMANKIND works with have also found it hard to meet the requirements of substantial external funding because they have, until recently, focused on project work to the detriment of building stronger organisations.

One example is an organisation doing excellent work with women and men in villages in Ghana on violence against women. Over many years, following research on the causes of violence, this organisation built up, through a series of locally based partners and 'COMBATS' (Community Based Action Teams). These COMBATS were local volunteers, men and women, selected, trained and supported to identify women experiencing violence and to find appropriate ways of addressing their condition, usually through counselling and traditional mediation. They also helped their neighbours understand the deleterious effects of violence and its impact on the family and wider community – and that women have a right to be treated equitably.

There was real, positive change over a period of several years as women spoke out and reported incidents, and men recognised their right to live without violence. New ways of working together emerged, around agriculture and trade, and neighbouring villagers saw tangible shifts in attitudes – several asked to join in the programme. However, resistance to change was evident in some contexts, especially in more remote villages.

This work took place in an area where violence against women is culturally acceptable. Inevitably the work is slow and demanding, with some successes and set-backs; change is not linear. It took a long time to put the project in place, train community partners, raise awareness, support the COMBATS, learn and adapt. Simultaneously the organisation was lobbying for a new Act against Domestic Violence and was part of a network of women's organisations that eventually saw the Act passed in 2007.

Visiting WOMANKIND staff focused on learning about the work at village level, auditing the accounts and encouraging better, timelier donor reporting. There was limited funding to do organisational-development work, although this was critical if the organisation was to grow more robust.

WOMANKIND's support and solidarity, its shared understanding of the role of violence against women as a block to development and a denial of rights – and the warmth and interest of the staff – was much appreciated, in contrast to the many problematic relationships now evident in development caused by power differentials and a lack of shared values and trust (Wallace et al., 2006).

However, the lack of time and some of the skills needed to develop good methodologies, organisational policies and promote publications and the dissemination of learning, so needed in Ghana, were a problem. These challenges – and the pressure for achieving results on the ground – made it hard for both WOMANKIND and the partner to develop the organisation. Now there is a greater focus on building the capacities and skills of both the staff and the partner in strategic planning, human resource management, reflection and dissemination of learning. To date this has been supported by WOMANKIND's own funds.

In contrast, new long-term work with a partner in Ethiopia has illustrated clearly the value of a strategic grant, which includes funding for more regular meetings and organisational development. WOMANKIND and the partner have been able to introduce participatory learning techniques, better and simpler documentation of change, increased collaboration with other agencies, and to make real improvements in organisational procedures. This enables an organisation already strong on direct work with the poor to identify and work with allies, to learn and disseminate learning and to become more accountable to staff and communities as well as to donors.

The strengths and challenges of existing partnerships
The learning that emerged around partnership showed the almost universal regard in which WOMANKIND is held, because of its commitment to women's rights and the shared determination with partners to address women's exclusion and inequality that is the root of much global poverty. No one in WOMANKIND is reluctant to do gender training, or argues about whether a focus on women makes sense. This matters to the women's organisations it works with, as does the fact that WOMANKIND is not based in their country and does not attempt to take the space in local policy arenas. Indeed WOMANKIND works hard to promote local voices and their involvement in policy and strengthens this work through partner workshops, taking partners to the UN Commission on the Status of Women (CSW) each year, and doing joint policy work at national and international level.

Some issues need addressing to deepen these relationships. Partners felt a lack of mutuality in accountability and wanted to understand more about WOMANKIND, their funding, staffing and ways of working. They asked for more clarity around roles and responsibilities, and they wanted WOMANKIND to be accountable to partners for their performance as donors and capacity-builders. Increased openness was needed to enable trust to deepen and more honest interactions to grow – both essential to monitoring and learning. Partners also needed to be more transparent, developing and sharing organisational budgets and giving a fuller picture of their donors and the diverse demands on them, in order for WOMANKIND to support them better in good financial and reporting management (without duplication or contradictions) as well as learning.

The reality of the short-term project funding that dominates much of WOMANKIND's work, coupled with the pressure to demonstrate relatively quick results has meant there has not been the time or the funding for WOMANKIND to work systematically with partners in Africa, Asia and Latin America on developing learning, good participatory monitoring and evaluation, or organisational plans and budgets. Strengthening organisations has often been ad hoc; visits may be dominated by the need to ensure data is collected and in place to meet legitimate donor requirements, leaving too little time for the work needed, for example, ensuring partners are properly accountable to communities and women in the slums or villages. There are evident tensions between formal project-cycle management and generating the relationships of openness and downward accountability and building skills for more participatory ways of working, strategic thinking and reflection.

The lack of support for learning was evident in the immense amount of time many partners spent collecting and monitoring data and drawing out lessons, yet the results were pretty unusable, either for donors or for the organisations themselves. Partners' lack of understanding about what to monitor, what methodologies to use and how to collect and analyse manageable and relevant data was obvious; in Ethiopia and Peru the mountains of data proved, on closer inspection, of limited value. Much research endorses this reality that 'when dealing with complex rural-development issues that involve collaborative action by a changing configuration of stakeholders, monitoring practice often falls short' (Guijit, 2008: 34).

Some recommendations will help WOMANKIND to address these challenges. These include spending more time on visits, building carefully on previous visits, and ensuring more staff continuity (high staff turnover makes trust-building difficult). Another is to invest more time and money in understanding appropriate ways of monitoring complexity. A third is to explain the aid context and build local capacities to enable partners to understand the global realities and take control of their own destinies through, for example, undertaking more focused, reflective monitoring; publicising and sharing their challenges and achievements more widely; and seeking funding that can support their work *and* values.

To do this effectively, programme and policy staff need to be multi-skilled especially in a medium-sized organisation where specialisation is not possible. This needs investment if WOMANKIND is to build partnerships and strong partner organisations able to address women's rights and needs. Finding the funding for staff and partner development is a challenge, and efforts are continuing to diversify the funding base so that this work can take place.

There are several examples of the power of WOMANKIND's approach in supporting partners: in advocacy work (for example, in Afghanistan), in encouraging partners to connect more strongly with rural women and engage them in their policy-driven work (in Peru), and in supporting feminist and radical approaches to women's rights (in Peru and South Africa). The work is multifaceted and includes international and local policy work, legal work, promoting political participation at all levels and direct work with women who are marginalised, poor and experience violence, building their confidence to enable them to take part in both political and economic processes.

Advocacy in partnership: Afghanistan
Advocacy – action to inform and influence decision-making processes and attitudes at all levels – is integral to the work of WOMANKIND and its partners. The work is rooted in the priorities of partner organisations and WOMANKIND has a commitment to represent these concerns to policymakers, both with and on behalf of partners and guided by the principles and values set out in CEDAW and the BPFA.

The rise of conservative and fundamentalist forces and a widening gap between rich and poor in Afghanistan has made it essential to voice concern about the impact on the most marginalised women. WOMANKIND has increased investment in policy and advocacy work, building the capacity of partners, facilitating the exchange of information and learning, and communicating the challenges and outcomes of its partners' work to UK policymakers and the wider public.

This work has experienced challenges. For example, the two-way flow of information that is vital for effective advocacy work is sometimes hindered by weak infrastructure and at times deteriorating political situations (partners may be in danger if they speak out).

However, several elements have contributed to the power of the advocacy work. WOMANKIND and the partner spent time assessing needs; providing training on advocacy tools, risk analysis and managing security threats; undertaking sound research into women's rights in Afghanistan, using international and national laws for women's rights as benchmarks, translated into local languages; mapping the advocacy targets in Afghanistan and internationally; drawing up a joint strategy with clearly delineated roles and responsibilities; and raising additional funding for the work.

Perhaps the best example of integrated policy and advocacy work was the joint response by WOMANKIND staff and partners to the Afghan government's proposed re-establishment of the Department for the Promulgation of Vice and Virtue in 2006. Under the Taliban, this Ministry had been responsible for stoning women for 'adultery', arbitrary beatings of women for showing their wrists and ankles, and prohibiting female education. WOMANKIND's partners joined forces with other Afghan women's and human rights organisations to denounce this proposal as a contravention of the Afghan Constitution, and the Afghan government's ratification of CEDAW. WOMANKIND mobilised European agencies and women's rights advocates to petition the UK government and the European Union (EU) – major donors to the Afghan government – to apply pressure externally. The Afghan government subsequently backed down, completely taken aback by the voracity and swiftness of the response, particularly from Afghan civil society organisations.

Conclusion
In the current world where development is often understood as something that can be created or engineered, brought to others by outsiders, and delivered through short-term projects, where change is understood as predictable and proof of change is required, it is critical to have agencies that understand development as a shared commitment to

a set of beliefs and rights that put women and their organisations as the subjects and not the objects of development, and where development is understood as a long-term, locally evolving process. The complexity of causes underlying women's poverty and lack of rights require action that is responsive. As stated by Gujit (2008: 28): 'adaptiveness hinges on the confidence to act, constant seeking of improvement through learning, and the humility to understand the limits of our understanding'.

WOMANKIND has dared to challenge itself and ask difficult questions with its partners. Some of the answers have been affirmative and show the value of building a women's rights approach on partnership and solidarity, while some have highlighted where the practice falls short of the ideal and where WOMANKIND and its partners lack the time, funding, and sometimes the skills to meet all the multiple demands on them. The conditions for doing good work have become a little clearer, including the importance of shared values and commitment; organisational development for often weak women's organisations; mutuality in relationships; balancing both upward and downward accountability; a willingness to question and learn; and working with a range of creative methodologies – with the appropriate skills. Staff and partners need good support to work with complexity and manage some of the inherent contradictions of facilitating locally owned change from an external position.

Acknowledgements

In 2006, the trustees and then Director of WOMANKIND, Maggie Baxter, agreed to fund a participatory learning review to enable the organisation to deepen its understanding of its work and identify strengths to build on and challenges that needed to be addressed to 'make the work work better'. The process was led by Brita Fernandez Schmidt (senior staff), and facilitated by Tina Wallace (external consultant). The new Director, Sue Turrell, continued the process and WOMANKIND is building on the findings.

Select bibliography

Fowler, Alan (1997) *Striking a Balance: A Guide to Enhancing the Effectiveness of Non-governmental Organisations in International Development*, London: Earthscan.
Guijt, Irene (2008) 'Seeking surprise: rethinking monitoring for collective learning in rural resource management', unpublished PhD dissertation, Department of Innovation and Communication Studies, Wageningen University Wageningen, the Netherlands.
Kaplan, Allan (2003) 'Understanding development as a living process', in David Lewis and Tina Wallace (eds), *New Roles and Relevance: Development NGOs and the Challenge of Change*, Hartford, CT: Kumarian, pp. 29–38.
Pankhurst, Helen (2002) 'Passing the buck? Money literacy and alternatives to credit and savings schemes', in Caroline Sweetman (ed.), *Gender, Poverty and Development*, Oxford: Oxfam, pp. 10–21.
Wallace, Tina, Helen Chapman and Lisa Bornstein (eds) (2006) *The Aid Chain: Coercion and Commitment in Development NGOs*, Rugby: Practical Action Publishing.
Watson, Cathy (2003) 'Review of the conceptual approaches and practice of the International Programmes Department', mimeo, London: WOMANKIND Worldwide.

84 Millennial woman: the gender order of development
Ananya Roy

Millennial development

The end of the twentieth century and the start of the new millennium have been marked by the emergence of a new global order of development. Neoliberal ideologies and austerity policies have given way to a concern with poverty and human development. From the remaking of the World Bank as a 'kinder and gentler' institution to the launch of global campaigns that seek to 'make poverty history', a remarkable mobilisation of conscience and effort is afoot. As an ensemble of discourses and practices, 'millennial development' is both global and intimate. The stark fact that of a world population of nearly 7 billion people, 2 billion live presently under conditions of poverty, 1.4 billion of whom live under the unimaginable conditions of earning less than US$1.25 a day, is now common knowledge. Yet, this extraordinary statistic has also become an everyday reality, anchoring a myriad of everyday efforts by everyday citizens to act on poverty. This is the liberal self of the new millennium, one that can both see poverty and seek to alleviate it.

Millennial development is also a gender order. Central to the new poverty agenda is the 'Third World woman'. From health and population programmes to environmental management initiatives, she has emerged as the key agent or, rather, in Jackson's (1996: 489) phrase, an 'instrument' of development. If, in previous phases of development, the Third World woman was constructed as a victim who must be rescued and liberated, then today she is framed as a heroic entrepreneur and selfless altruist. As Molyneux (2006: 432) argues, it is 'global feminism' that made women's poverty a visible and urgent part of the new poverty agenda. Two of the eight Millennium Development Goals (MDGs) are explicitly concerned with gender inequalities. Goal 5 features maternal health as a key indicator of human development. In ambitious fashion, Goal 3 seeks to 'promote gender equality and empower women', operationalising the mandate in targets such as gender disparities in primary school education and women's political participation. It is tricky business. For, on the one hand, millennial development draws attention to systematic and structural patterns of gender inequalities. But, on the other hand, millennial development yokes gender to poverty, seeking to integrate poor women into development programmes. Such instrumental practices of integration reinforce rather than dismantle gender inequalities. It is thus that various poverty programmes, such as *Oportunidades*, Mexico's highly praised cash transfer programme, position motherhood as key to their success (Molyneux, 2006: 432). The programme pivots on the idea of 'co-responsibility', making mothers 'primarily responsible for securing the programme's outcomes' (ibid.: 434). Molyneux (2006: 437) rightly asks if this is 'female altruism at the service of the state'. I have termed such instrumentality a 'feminisation of policy', indicating the ways in which development operates through women-oriented policies that serve to maintain traditional gender roles of social reproduction. Such policies only deepen what Chant (Chapter 15, this volume) has identified as a 'feminisation of responsibility and obligation'. It is thus that the Nike Foundation has proudly proclaimed the 'Girl Effect', celebrating 'the ability of adolescent girls in developing countries to bring unprecedented economic and social change to their families, communities, and countries' (Zamora Moeller, 2009). But key to the gender order is that this global imagination is mediated by the intimate transactions of millennial development. The Third World woman is no longer a figure at a distance. She is now both visible and accessible. The portals of millennial development, such as Kiva.org or Heifer International, make it possible to touch her life, give her a microfinance loan, gift a cow and make a difference. Indeed, the liberal self of the new millennium is made and remade through such a gendered and racialised interface. It is the Third World woman, Millennial Woman, who animates this millennial ethics, anchors a global conscience and transforms the distance of gender and race into a liberal intimacy with the world's poor.

The 'gender order' of microfinance
One of the most prominent and popular ideas of millennial development is microfinance. While the bulk of development budgets remain focused on infrastructure and while most international and local non-governmental organisations (NGOs) focus on sectors such as health and human rights, microfinance seems to be a chip or microprocessor of millennial development. It is everywhere. The United Nations (UN) celebrated 2005 as the International Year of Microcredit. In 2006, Muhammad Yunus and the Grameen Bank, credited with being the pioneers in the field of microcredit, won the 2006 Nobel Peace Prize. From the reconstruction of Afghanistan, to the fight against 'terror' in the Middle East, to the development of capital markets in Latin America, to the alleviation of poverty in the United States, microfinance is the panacea of choice, the instrument that promises to reach the 'bottom billion'. Millennial Woman is central to this millennial idea of microfinance. Microfinance is undertaken in her name (see also Bibars, Chapter 89, this volume; Maclean, Chapter 87, this volume).

The gender order of microfinance is apparent in what is understood to be an original model of microfinance, that pioneered by the Grameen Bank of Bangladesh (see also Casier, Chapter 94, this volume). In almost every account, Muhammad Yunus, founder of the Grameen Bank, tells the origins story as a story of the women in the village of Jobra just outside the university at which he taught economics in the late 1970s. He describes watching these women weave stubborn strands of bamboo to make stools and baskets, icons of hope in these dilapidated villages of poverty, feminine brown hands making beautiful, luminiscent objects. These objects, and these women, were bound in a system of exploitative moneylending, a system that Yunus set out to end. The liberation of rural, poor women came through the transformative power of money:

> The day finally comes when she asks for a first loan, usually about 25 dollars. How does she feel? Terrified. She cannot sleep at night.... When she finally receives the 25 dollars she is trembling. The money burns her fingers. Tears roll down her face. She has never seen so much money in her life.... All her life she has been told that she is no good, that she brings only misery to her family... that she should have been killed at birth.... But today, for the first time in her life, an institution has trusted her with a great sum of money. She promises that she will never let down the institution or herself. She will struggle to make sure that every penny is paid back.[1]

The Grameen Bank's Nobel Prize winning assertion that 'credit is a human right' is thus predicated on this humanistic rendering of the Third World woman.

Today the Grameen Bank model of microfinance is challenged by other models, especially those promoted by the World Bank. Such models seek to transform microfinance into a global 'asset class'. Microfinance then is a particularly important example of the financialisation of the poverty agenda (see Mutalima, Chapter 93, this volume). It bears the promise that the poor are entrepreneurial, can be best served by access to finance, and that such financial services are best provided by finance capital rather than by clumsy donors and bureaucratic governments. But it bears the additional promise that the 'bottom billion' will serve as a 'frontier market,' opening up new horizons of capital accumulation. These frontiers of finance are concerned not only with women but also with poor men, formerly the 'bad' subjects of development, seeking to integrate them into development through the use of new technologies of risk scoring and credit ratings. Indeed, the financialisation of development can be partly interpreted as the demise of the feminisation of policy. This is yet another gendered and racialised encounter, one that hopes to transform male unemployment and masculinist rage into a millennial utopia of small enterprises and vibrant entrepreneurship. Such is the case particularly in the Middle East where, after 9-11, the 'war on terror' has merged with a 'war on poverty'. Here it is the angry young Muslim man on the Arab street who is the new subject of development. Microfinance, a technology perfected by lending to rural, married women in the dense villages of Bangladesh, must now reach him as well. The trope of the terrorist thus comes to overshadow that of Millennial Woman.

And yet, the Third World woman persists; she haunts. The language of financialised development is about information technology and portfolios and equity funds, but the Third World woman is there in the accompanying images. In World Bank reports, she is the indigenous peasant woman, photographed with both 'primitive' abacus and 'modern' calculator, a figure that transcends primitivism to adopt modern, calculative technologies. In the reports of Wall Street banks, she proudly stands behind the counter in her tiny store; she smiles as she sells vegetables at the market; she is at once mother and entrepreneur. As Rankin (2001) notes, she is 'rational economic woman', a free-willed and self-governing subject. Above all, she is a fetish, a magical object. She guarantees the profitability of microfinance markets, thus opening up a new subprime frontier of capital accumulation. After all, poor women always pay back their loans. But she also guarantees a more compassionate rendering of capitalism, one that must demonstrate the 'double bottom line' of financial and social performance. The financialisation of development thus also takes place in her name. It is thus that Spivak (1999: 361 and 386) makes note of how 'this phase of capitalism/feminism' is an instance of the 'gendered postcolonial,' a 'complicitous relationship between UN-style universalist feminism and postcolonial capitalism'.

But the construction of such frontier markets requires work. The original model of microfinance, epitomised by the Grameen Bank, was predicated on the careful management of risk through peer groups, gendered discipline and the presence of a massive NGO in village life. The images of Grameen women at weekly meetings, saluting, being ordered and orderly, chanting the Grameen Bank slogan 'Discipline, Unity, Courage', are well known. As millennial development wrests itself free of such institutional forms, so it must invent new technologies of risk management, those that will create transparent financial markets by rendering transparent financial subjects. Thus, a showcase project of the United States Agency for International Development (USAID), the Global Development

Alliance, is a partnership between credit card giant VISA and village banking pioneer, FINCA International. In this alliance, VISA will provide electronic payment solutions and product platforms, while FINCA will provide access to clients through its network of village banks. But the alliance is ultimately anchored by Millennial Woman. The idea is that a poor woman in Bolivia can stop at a branch office of a microfinance institution, now reconfigured as a private financial fund. At an optical scanning device – similar to an automatic teller machine – she swipes her smart card and verifies her identity by placing her thumb in an electronic fingerprint authenticator attached to the card scanner. The smart card encapsulates her credit history, authorising or deauthorising a loan, and doing away with the need for loan officers or NGO workers. Such technologies integrate poor women, hitherto invisible, into the technofinancial infrastructures of the new millennium. They are now included. Indeed, such new models of microfinance are inaugurated through the language of the 'democratisation of capital'. In the interviews that I conducted with World Bank staffers and Wall Street bankers, a recurring theme was that of financial inclusion. Such a theme has a gendered undercurrent. Rejecting the Grameen Bank model of microfinance, a USAID consultant asked me: 'Do you and I, as women borrowing from a bank, have to do this song and dance when we take out a loan from Bank of America? Why do poor women? True empowerment is to have choice; to be able to purchase a service without all these conditions and rituals.'

The Bangladesh paradox
Bangladesh is one of the poorest countries in the world. It is plagued by political instability and recurring political violence. Yet, in recent years, Bangladesh has witnessed significant improvements in human development. A 2008 World Bank report entitled *Whispers to Voices: Gender and Social Transformation in Bangladesh* notes the halving of fertility rates, the closing of the gender gap in infant mortality, and more girls enrolled in secondary schools than boys. Such trends stand in sharp contrast to its giant neighbour, India, which has enjoyed brisk rates of economic growth but has also seen increases in poverty and inequality. This so-called Bangladesh paradox – strides in human development in a 'cultural context widely believed to be repressive to women'[2] – needs explanation. The report draws attention to a variety of unique global and national forces and conjunctures, including Bangladesh's insertion into a global garment industry fuelled by female labour as well as the formation of a powerful women's movement with NGOs fighting for gender equality. But the report also credits two programmes or policies that were 'expressly intended to improve women's status' – the state's education policy and the 'NGO driven microcredit programme':

> Not only did women learn to save and get access to credit but the credit groups created a sense of solidarity that allowed for other services, such as family planning, to be delivered through them. Women's awareness in many other spheres was enhanced through these collectives as they began to access other opportunities, including training and self-employment (Das, 2008: 5).

Such conclusions are in keeping with the claims of poverty alleviation and gender empowerment put forward by Bangladesh's microfinance institutions (MFIs). While the Grameen Bank is the most well known of such institutions, also significant is the role of BRAC. The sheer scale of these operations requires attention. Originally known as the Bangladesh Rural Advancement Committee, BRAC is perhaps one of the world's largest non-governmental organisations with over 40 000 full-time staff and over 160 000 paraprofessionals, 72 per cent of whom are women. BRAC serves 6 million borrowers through its microfinance programmes and many millions more through its network of primary schools and healthcare centres. In other words, this is a quite extensive development apparatus, one that may be effectively understood to be the state in Bangladesh.

But the conclusions of the report run counter to a large body of academic research that faults microfinance for its oppressive and exploitative patriarchal practices. These critiques argue that microfinance transforms women into 'instruments' of development, using peer groups of women to serve as collateral and joint liability for loans. They also argue that microfinance fails to transform structures of patriarchy, often vesting the control and management of loans in men. Poor women, such studies indicate, simply serve as conduits for a new set of household resources as well as for a new development ideology (see also Molyneux, 2006). Neither their poverty nor their gendered burden of responsibilities and obligations is alleviated by microfinance.

Such debates raise important questions about the conceptualisations of gender and poverty in the context of millennial development. Why, it can be asked, do critiques of microfinance focus on the managerial control of loans? Why, it can be asked, do critiques of microfinance assume the passive acceptance by poor women of the seemingly patriarchal norms of microfinance programmes? Surely such critiques flatten the complexity of women's agency and subjectivity. For example, in her study of microfinance programmes in Nepal, Rankin (2008: 1971) shows how poor women engaged in 'loan swapping', sustained long-term debt financing by taking loans from multiple lenders. While such practices can be critiqued as 'repaying credit with debt', as Rankin notes 'in more elite, urbanised contexts' they would be framed as 'refinancing'. She thus positions such practices as the 'skillful manipulation of a development technology' by poor women in order to support 'subsistence and social investment activities'. Similarly, in the context of Bangladesh, Kabeer (2000) provides a perceptive analysis of the meanings and effects of microfinance programmes on the lives of poor women. She argues that while women may not retain managerial control of loans, their participation in such programmes greatly enhances their decision-making powers within the household. In particular, she makes notes of the contradictions associated with empowerment:

> If empowerment entails the expanded capacity for making choices, for taking actions which express own values and priorities, then it has to be recognised that these values and priorities are likely to be shaped by the values and priorities of the wider community . . . The paradox is that in many cases, this leads women to opt for some form of purdah if they can afford to, both to signal their social standing within the community and to differentiate themselves from those women who do not have this choice. (Kabeer, 2000: 70–1)

This too is the Bangladesh paradox, the ensemble of contradictory meanings and practices that constitute gender empowerment and human development. It belies any simple interpretation of the instrumentalism of millennial development, instead reconfiguring this gender order as a terrain of negotiations and paradoxes.

Acknowledgements
This chapter draws in part on my forthcoming book, *Poverty Capital: Microfinance and the Frontiers of Millennial Development* (Routledge, 2010), as well as on a Comparative

Urban Studies Project brief published in 2002 by the Woodrow Wilson International Center for Scholars, Washington, DC, entitled *Against the Feminisation of Policy*.

Notes

1. This citation is taken directly from pages 64–5 of Muhammad Yunus's (1999) book *Banker to the Poor: Micro-Lending and the Battle Against World Poverty*, published by Public Affairs, New York.
2. This quote is taken from page 3 of the World Bank's *Whispers to Voices: Gender and Social Transformation in Bangladesh* (2008), available at: http://web.worldbank.org/WBSITE/EXTERNAL/COUNTRIES/SOUTHASIAEXT/0,,contentMDK:21685309~pagePK:146736~piPK:146830~theSitePK:223547,00.html (accessed 2 May 2009).

Select bibliography

Jackson, Cecile (1996) 'Rescuing gender from the poverty trap', *World Development*, **24** (3), 489–504.
Kabeer, Naila (2000) 'Conflicts over credit: re-evaluating the empowerment potential of loans to women in rural Bangladesh', *World Development*, **29** (1), 63–84.
Molyneux, Maxine (2006) 'Mothers at the service of the new poverty agenda: Progresa/Oportunidades, Mexico's conditional transfer programme', *Social Policy and Administration*, **40** (4), 425–49.
Rankin, Katharine (2001) 'Governing development: neoliberalism, microcredit, and rational economic woman', *Economy and Society*, **30** (1), 18–37.
Rankin, Katharine (2008) 'Manufacturing rural finance in Asia: institutional assemblages, market societies, entrepreneurial subjects', *Geoforum*, **39**, 1965–77.
Spivak, Gayatri C. (1999) *A Critique of Postcolonial Reason: Toward a History of the Vanishing Present*, Cambridge, MA: Harvard University Press.
Zamora Moeller, Kathryn (2009) 'Deconstructing her production: "girl" as new trope of global capitalism', PhD thesis in preparation, Graduate School of Education, University of California, Berkeley.

PART IX

MICROFINANCE AND WOMEN'S EMPOWERMENT

85 The housewife and the marketplace: practices of credit and savings from the early modern to modern era
Beverly Lemire

The term 'thrifty housewife' conjures up images of an aproned woman making bread pudding from stale bread, or mending the heel of a worn sock – and that is certainly an element of women's traditional resource management. But there is much more. In the long transition to an industrial society, women mediated between household and market, developing key strategies in the administration of credit and savings. Until recent years, these gendered talents escaped the notice of economists and economic historians who rather focused on the large prominent businesses whose activities were deemed to signal the *zeitgeist* of an age. The term 'economy' originates with the Greek word for 'household management' and we can better understand women's roles within the evolving economy by recognising women's liminal functions through their management of credit and savings. The emphasis here is on Western regions during the rise of commercial and industrial capitalism (c. 1600–1900), although timely examples of similar practices will be offered from other societies and contexts.

Generations of women managed in a 'material economy', where monetisation was partial and imperfect and their ordering of physical resources was of critical importance. The gradual spread of monetised economies and monetised thinking represented a fundamental transformation of process and practice that also reordered domestic priorities. But before this epochal shift, however, the commonest feature of life was scarcity. Thus the careful husbandry of resources, through recycling and reuse, was a necessary and commonplace exercise. Scarcity and the threat of scarcity defined Europe's material environment, framing the backdrop of everyday life, a force rarely in abeyance and then only with seasonal or windfall surpluses. This reality remained true for much of Europe leading into and, in some regions, even after industrialisation.

In the pre-industrial period coinage was costly for local authorities to produce and there were insufficient quantities for day-to-day transactions, particularly in low denominations. So alternative currencies were deployed. Tokens have been widely recognised in this role; but textiles and clothing were equally important as commodities readily exchanged for cash or credit. In this context, investments in household and personal accoutrements, things like bedding and clothing, while major outlays, also constituted vital liquid assets for the working poor. In England c. 1700 the purchase of textiles and clothing represented approximately one-quarter of national expenditure (Harte, 1991: 278). The management and manipulation of these textile resources were among the commonest and most important means of arranging credit and savings, an approach that persisted into the twentieth and even twenty-first centuries in rural areas and developing regions. The transition between scarcity and the relatively greater plenty of a developed economy involved critical shifts in gendered practices of credit and savings. But for generations, survival strategies included the management of textiles and were common in many cultures.

Gendered markets and the manipulation of textiles
Textiles were valued for their utility, but also for their mutability. Patterns of exchange familiar in early modern European cities had their precursors in medieval locales, like Cairo, where rare surviving records reveal this general practice. In this instance, a wife waiting for her trader husband to return from India carried household textiles to a pawnbroker to eke out a living until his arrival (Goitein, 1983: 332–3). Throughout the medieval and early modern eras textiles and clothing were the commonest pawned items, goods that could be exchanged for cash or credit, accepted by shopkeepers and pawnbrokers, formal and informal alike. Textiles are so cheaply available today in most markets that it requires an imaginative leap to conceive of a time and place when cloth was so valuable and its purchase was a major part of domestic budgets. But such was the case in early modern Europe, where, as in many other pre-industrial societies, goods served multiple functions. A warm cloak might also cover a bed or a worn shirt be cut down into a child's shift. But aside from this type of utility, these goods were investments whose value could be released as needed.

Women were uniquely positioned as the administrators of household goods, knowledgeable about the care, quality and value of textiles and clothing. Their training in housewifery as well as their work in textile and sewing trades produced a distinct expertise. Men, too, worked in textile trades and as tailors in great numbers. But women's cultural and functional domestic apprenticeship brought unique skills and duties. Thus, it was women who formed the majority of customers at pawnbrokers, handling the business of pawning to balance personal or household budgets. Small enterprises were often embedded in domestic settings or arose directly out of domestic skills. Blending household and income-earning tasks was commonplace and the assigning of cloth a part of balancing budgets. In one 1633 example of thrift, Elizabeth Busby reassigned the goods she inherited by pawning a Christening sheet, selling a waistcoat to a neighbour, remaking a facecloth into an apron and selling off part of a tablecloth to another neighbour (Lemire, 2005: 93). For the poor, there was little division between domestic and income-generating activities. The trek to the pawnbroker became another of the gendered female tasks in many communities, and haggling with the pawnbroker at the doorstep or shop counter became another measure of a housewife's skill.

Pawnbroker networks
From the sixteenth through to the eighteenth centuries, urban communities and even modest towns boasted a growing number of dealers willing to offer credit or accept in pawn all manner of things including coats, blankets, gowns, hats and shoes. Any and every sort of cloth or piece of clothing could find someone willing to take it as collateral for a loan. The credit secured through pawning was vital for the day-to-day functioning of small enterprises, and these ventures in turn were the lifeblood of communities, providing inexpensive goods as well as a way to make a living for generations of street vendor, small artisan and service providers. Pawnbrokers proliferated with growing urban populations, despite the objections of commentators and legislators who disliked the trade on moral and legal grounds. The poor might pay high interest rates to

pawnbrokers, dismaying many commentators; at the same time stolen goods flowed in and out of pawnshops with legal wares, providing another source of anxiety to legislators. But with or without the sanction of moralists, governments were obliged to accept the necessity of pawnbrokers and attempted to regulate the operations through the centuries. One witness before the English Parliament listed those who needed this form of credit:

> the very poor Sort of People, such as Persons who cry Fish, Fruit or other Wares, about the Street, and other People who may be reckoned in the lowest Class of Life, who not having any personal Credit, are obliged to have Recourse to the Pawnbrokers . . . it was likewise a great Benefit to these Journeymen, who, having nothing but their Wages to depend on, must perish when sick, or out of Employment . . . And lastly, To Artificers and Handycraftsmen, who, by the Money borrowed of the Pawnbrokers, were enabled to buy Materials to carry on their Businesses . . . (Lemire, 2005: 31).

Women, as well as men, pawned to make ends meet. Whether in London, Paris, Amsterdam, Brussels, Barcelona and Florence, or in smaller towns and villages, women took the lead in brokering what clothes or bedding they could spare to secure necessary short-term credit.

The structure of pawning was more complex than might be supposed. Large enterprises sometimes had an international reach, selling off unclaimed goods through regional and overseas markets. Few women could amass the capital to underwrite large pawnbroking businesses. The poorest worked as informal pawnbrokers, unlisted in trade directories, known only to their neighbours, while others worked as agents for wealthier pawnbrokers; some combined a modest pawnbroking trade with the sale of food or drink or second-hand wares. The most successful might manage their own shop, but the majority of women were found in the lower levels of trade, trawling neighbourhood streets taking goods in pawn and sometimes passing the items to larger dealers. A few women might also serve in other capacities, such as a guarantor of small loans for the working poor, if that option was available. John Pope was a South London tradesman, who acted as an informal pawnbroker and moneylender in the 1660s and 1670s, in addition to his formal haberdashery trade. Several women appear regularly in his records as guarantors for their neighbours' loans, although one guarantor was married and by law was ineligible to sign a contract. The other worked as a laundress and may have had few resources to repay a defaulted loan. But in these cases, as in many others, personal reputation enabled financial exchanges, regardless of apparent prohibitions. Pope accepted the loan guarantee by washerwoman Roberta Jones, noting that she 'douth pase her word to se it payd' (Lemire, 2005: 300).

Authorities gradually acknowledged how necessary credit was for the poor. In the fifteenth century a Franciscan order addressed the issue of high interest rates on pawns by launching a type of non-profit pawnbroking initiative, beginning first in Italy and spreading through Catholic Europe (Fontaine, 2001). Municipalities in many regions organised similar ventures, providing essential credit to a population living with few resources and many risks. The pawnbroking trade in its totality was a complex network linking kitchen door trade to high street shops, spreading nationally and internationally, transplanted as well to colonial regions such as Mexico where new populations were there to be served.

Institutional change

Poor women and men continued to rely on pawning through the eighteenth and nineteenth centuries. Long lines of housewives stood at pawnbrokers' doors on a Monday morning, remaining as a feature in poorer working-class communities well past 1900. But the broader financial environment was changing over that time. Monetised wages and borrowing became increasingly common from the 1700s onwards and were the norm among the growing middle classes by the nineteenth century. At the same time legislation was enacted over the eighteenth and nineteenth centuries to try to limit payments in kind in many trades (goods which typically flowed through pawnshops). Workers wanted cash wages that could be more readily negotiated for goods and services. Domestic servants, a group that was largely female from the nineteenth century, continued to receive at least part of their wages in kind into the twentieth century, as did agricultural workers. However, along with the spread of monetisation came the growth of more formalised lending institutions, particularly for small loans. Guilds had traditionally provided their members with loans for business purposes; but as guild membership became increasingly male over the early modern period, women in trade or in need of loans had limited options aside from the pawnbroker. Some women who were members of friendly societies practiced rotating savings and lending strategies, a practice that persisted in other forms into the modern era. But female friendly societies were too few in number to meet the needs of the untold legion of enterprising women whose small trades sustained them and their families.[1]

Loan societies became common in the nineteenth century, sources of small-scale credit often run on a for-profit basis. However women represented a small and declining percentage of customers at these loan societies, although in Ireland their numbers were consistent with the percentage of unmarried women in the pre-famine era before 1845 (Hollis, 2001). Working women in an earlier era benefited from an informal reputational authority, which had won them access to small loans in at least some instances whether married or not. But this option had all but disappeared by the Victorian era as credit institutions became increasingly formalised. Only through other institutional innovations were women able to gain access to resources and those they secured were personal savings augmented through interest.

The dawn of the 1800s was also the dawn of the savings bank era. Savings banks were introduced as a social experiment by reformers[2] who wanted to provide security for the small, precious savings of the working classes. With cash wages came the risks of theft, as well as the risk of untimely expenditures. Prudence and foresight were virtues traditionally preached to the poor. But with savings banks, prudence and foresight took a new form with added incentives. For the first time, the working poor were offered the benefits of interest earned on deposits. This new kind of monetised thrift promised to keep savers out of the hands of rapacious lenders. Ideally, rather than pay interest to pawnbrokers, savers could earn interest on their small mite and slowly see it grow. Carters, milk-women, domestic servants, laundresses, nurses, clerks, glove-makers and a variety of artisans were among the first to turn to savings banks. The numbers of these banks grew and governments began to recognise and legislate these financial institutions over the nineteenth century. As state-sponsored elementary education spread through Europe and beyond, penny savings banks were introduced as part of the curriculum, offering savings training at an early age. Children might save for new clothes; young women typically used their accounts to save for marriage or for small enterprises; older men might save to buy pigs to raise up and augment their family's diet; and, in some cases, wives of drunken or abusive husbands secured their means of escape with the connivance of savings bank managers who flouted the law by denying the existence of these savings accounts to predatory husbands.

Clerics and other volunteers engaged in missionary endeavours, carrying the message of saving to slum dwellers and the labouring poor, seeking conversions to new forms of thrift. The poorest of the poor could rarely squeeze their resources to become regular savers. Thus those with slightly higher or more regular incomes became the bulk of account holders and began to take pride in their new patterns of budgeting. Domestic servants were especially numerous as savers, storing away small sums to mitigate the risks of unemployment, ill-health or old age; or if they married they used these new habits to balance resources in family life. Respectability among the working class began to be equated with savings and purchases paid for in cash, with a new fiscal culture that could be described as provident consumerism. With the spread of savings banks and savings accounts among the working poor, they were urged to take pride in their savings and despised the pawnbroker's counter. Successful savers liberated themselves from expensive cycles of credit, further differentiating the social hierarchies within the working class.

Savings banks became part of government policy in many regions through the nineteenth and twentieth centuries. For example, the US government inaugurated the Freedmen's Saving Bank (1865–74) as a safe repository for the newly emancipated African-American population and though short-lived, it indicates how central these institutions had become to contemporary development policies. Maggie Walker, an African-American woman in Richmond, Virginia, launched the Saint Luke Penny Savings Bank in 1903; as an antidote to the failed government initiative, this small bank sought to provide a secure repository for local African-Americans, however small their deposit. The savings bank continues to be a critical ingredient in modern development initiatives, providing a measure of opportunity for savers through their hard-won deposits (De Swaan and Van Der Linden, 2006; Vyas, 2001). The advent of savings banks represents a watershed in the gendered culture of thrift. While sometimes imperfect in their operation, they constitute a vital development strategy in many parts of the world to this day, of particular importance to poor and working women. Indeed, this type of gendered savings culture was, and remains, one of the hallmarks of modern financial discourse and practice

Notes

1. Recent research into women's entrepreneurship has revealed their considerable numbers, typically (though not exclusively) in occupations gendered female. More documentation survives for women's enterprise from the middle ranks of society. But there is no doubt that women in great numbers managed small and medium-sized businesses throughout the era of industrialisation, even as Victorian commentators advised women to restrict themselves to domestic arenas only.
2. Priscilla Wakefield was a Quaker activist who was particularly concerned about the condition of women, including poor working women. She initiated a Female Benefit Club in 1798 in London and followed this with a Children's Bank and then the Tottenham Benefit Bank in the early 1800s.

Select bibliography

De Swaan, Abram and Marcel Van Der Linden (eds) (2006) *Mutualist Microfinance: Informal Savings Funds from the Global Periphery to the Core?*, Amsterdam: Aksant.

Fontaine, Laurence (2001) 'Women's economic sphere and credit in pre-industrial Europe', in Beverly Lemire, Ruth Pearson and Gail Campbell (eds), *Women and Credit: Researching the Past, Refiguring the Future*, Oxford and New York: Berg, pp. 15–32.

Goitein, S.D. (1983) *A Mediterranean Society: The Jewish Communities of the Arab World as Portrayed in the Documents of the Cairo Geniza; Vol. IV. Daily Life*, Berkeley, CA: University of California Press.

Harte, N.B. (1991) 'The economics of clothing in the late seventeenth century', *Textile History*, **22** (2), 277–96.

Hollis, Aiden (2001) 'Women and micro-credit in history: the Irish loan funds', in Beverly Lemire, Ruth Pearson and Gail Campbell (eds), *Women and Credit: Researching the Past, Refiguring the Future*, Oxford and New York: Berg, pp. 73–89.

Lemire, Beverly (2005) *The Business of Everyday Life: Gender, Practice and Social Politics in England, c. 1600–1900*, Manchester: Manchester University Press.

Vyas, Jayshree (2001) 'Banking with poor self-employed women', in Beverly Lemire, Ruth Pearson and Gail Campbell (eds), *Women and Credit: Researching the Past, Refiguring the Future*, Oxford and New York: Berg, pp. 145–65.

86 Money as means or money as end? Gendered poverty, microcredit and women's empowerment in Tanzania
Fauzia Mohamed

Microcredit is deemed to provide the poor with the tools and resources they need to lift themselves and their families out of poverty. Microcredit's global concern is reducing poverty by providing small amounts of credit to generate self-employment in income-generating activities. But there is an urgent need to assess these services as microcredit is currently reaching only a fraction of the poor and does not address gendered poverty. Between 28 January and 1 February 2009, the world's economic leaders gathered in Davos, Switzerland, for the Annual Meeting of the World Economic Forum (WEF). This meeting discussed the global financial crisis and served as an opportunity to campaign for billions of poor people around the world who are hardest hit by the crisis. The Boston-based non-profit organisation, ACCION International, through its newest campaign slogan of 'lend to end poverty' asked people to sign a petition asking the world leaders to make microfinance a priority for ending poverty (Zimmerman, 2009). This campaign focuses on poverty reduction through credit, as the only thing the poor need to permanently lift themselves and their families out of poverty. This chapter argues that this is a narrow and unrealistic perception of poverty. Based on field research conducted in Dar es Salaam among agency personnel and poor women clients of two microcredit agencies – Promotion of Rural Initiatives and Development Enterprises (PRIDE) and Sero Lease and Finance Company Limited (SELFINA) – this chapter argues that although money is an important means in poverty reduction, it cannot serve as an end to gendered poverty.[1]

I further contend that microcredit's focus on money alone as the single most important deprivation facing poor women is an oversight on the part of credit-providing organisations and development partners alike, which tend to offer unrealistic solutions to the diverse and complex problem of poverty. The analysis will also dwell on the meaning and role of money in reducing poverty and empowering women clients of these two microcredit agencies.

Microcredit agencies' perceptions of money and poverty
Microcredit agencies put great emphasis on money since they view it as vital capital investment for client businesses. This categorisation of money as capital provides an interesting perspective on microcredit as a whole, and more so given that the women clients of these microcredit schemes do not necessarily share this perception nor do they use the money they get specifically for their businesses. Echoing the views of many microcredit agency employees, one SELFINA official lamented that 'women use the money for purposes other than economic investment'. Indeed, these women do not see money so much as an end, but rather as a means to wrest themselves from their destitute living

standards. Operating a small-scale enterprise is one means by which poor women reduce their destitute situation, but it is not the only one, and it does not end their poverty.

The understanding of credit as capital raises concerns not only for microcredit but also for poverty reduction as a whole. Microcredit seeks to address poverty reduction as do poor women, but they are addressing this fundamental issue from different perspectives. Microcredit agencies see poverty reduction mainly from the angle of income, while poverty reduction for their clients involves more than income alone. Among the latter stakeholders poverty reduction encompasses the entire conditions of their lives. The agencies' keen interest in income stems from the fact that the agencies are themselves increasingly run as businesses. For this reason, the more money they make from client repayments, the better their business, and they apply the same logic to their clients' businesses. They tend to categorise clients as 'good' when they maintain a high level of repayments, and as such are able to 'repay their loan in ample time'. This perception was challenged during the interviews by some of their clients who claimed that there are ways of maintaining a credible credit record without necessarily having a good business, which does not reflect on the income-generating activities, or improved poverty status. Such clients merely get money from other sources. The officials' concentration on money for business profits is far removed from their clients' survival realities.

Microcredit agencies view money as a business tool that can increase poor women's net wealth, their status within the household, their potential to escape from poverty, and generally improve income and capital accumulation for their members. However, reducing poverty depends on local circumstances. By the same token, money is not a homogeneous entity. Zelizer (1998) argues that like all other social objects, money has meanings that depend on use and context, which are socially structured. Thus, it is misguided to try to 'identify universally representational properties of money and to link these to its meaning' (Carruthers and Espelland, 2002: 294). It is for this reason that women in Dar es Salaam often use the money they get from microcredit agencies for reasons other than that stipulated by microcredit agencies.

Poor women have been known to use loans for medical attention, jewellery, furniture, food and personal effects, prompting credit officials to state that 'credit is designed to help women fight poverty by involving themselves in income-generating activities and is not for purposes of buying clothes or cosmetics to improve their appearance'. Microcredit officials here seem to be making a moral judgement as well as an economic one. Cosmetics and clothes seem to be regarded as frivolous and bad, simply a vanity. However since most female clients interact and deal with people, they are required to have a certain standard of dress and appearance, which the general public expects to be smart, clean and presentable. For this reason clothes and cosmetics become an important part of the way the women conduct their everyday businesses. Moreover such statements ignore the fact that poverty is made up of interrelated and multiple deprivations. Although it may be legitimately argued that buying cosmetics may not be the ideal way of utilising credit, poor women also use the loans for basic essentials, even though microcredit officials may deem these unnecessary. Yet again this is an indication of the disparity between what poverty reduction entails for the two sets of parties concerned. The meaning of money for poor women seems to have transcended 'economic investment' to become 'personal investment', although the line between the two is not easily drawn

Microcredit's persistent emphasis on money has led agency personnel to associate hard work with the ability to make more money. Microcredit officials do not seem to appreciate that their clients do work hard already, juggling income-generating activities with domestic chores and caring for and maintaining their families. This was reflected in one PRIDE official's statement that:

> We try to enlighten our clients that those who are serious in their businesses are the ones who escape the vicious cycle of poverty, since the harder they work, the faster they make their repayments. This gives them more money to invest in their businesses causing these businesses to expand faster, giving these women more money which will eventually reduce their poverty.

Such interpretations seem to imply a stereotype of what is regarded as work, whereby only work which is remunerated is recognised and appreciated. For instance, housewives do not regard their domestic chores as 'work' because these are unpaid. It is possible that credit officers also only see their clients' income-generating activities as 'work' because these activities bring in money, which consequently perpetuates an injurious stereotypical labelling of work which undermines women's vital reproductive labour, unpaid carework, and roles in social networks.

By prioritising the material and business aspects of poverty microcredit agencies fail to understand the multidimensional nature of the gendered poverty that their clients experience. Likewise, only promoting income as the answer to poverty reduction overlooks some important concerns, especially the social and psychological issues that their clients deal with on a daily basis. Microcredit agencies need to listen to their clients so as to come up with more holistic responses to poverty reduction. Microcredit agencies will not solve their clients' material poverty through money targeted solely to business investment because this does not address the reality of women's lack of power to challenge discrimination against them in both the household and the marketplace.

Poor women's perceptions and lived realities of money
Most of the women interviewed in my case study worked in the informal sector. Women enter the informal sector already vulnerable as a result of gender discrimination in the household, which results in unequal resource distribution. The informal sector itself is unregulated and regarded in a negative light. BRIDGE (2001) observes that any poverty-reducing programme may not reach women directly, owing to their lack of command over productive resources and control over output. Some interventions can be problematic where resources are targeted at women (in particular microcredit interventions) without attempting to change the 'rules of the game', where women are targeted with resources and it is assumed that benefits accrue directly to them and their children to a greater extent than resources targeted at men. Microcredit agencies promote poor women's small-scale enterprises without looking at how the informal sector helps them or how they perceive the role of money in their lives. It seems that poor women do not fully benefit from their engagement in informal businesses. Any money that the women obtain is shared with their children and households at large; this reality is missed by microcredit agencies' promotion of money for business investment only. Money and credit for these women mean that they can continue to participate in trade because money can buy small favours with the local authorities and business partners alike as was observed in Dar es Salaam. This money cannot significantly transform their businesses; rather, it enables them to get by on a day-to-day basis while leaving untouched the structures that greatly

contribute to their poverty, such as discriminatory gender practices in the household and marketplace. Hence, focusing only on money to end women's poverty not only overlooks their lived realities but can reinforce the gendered poverty status quo.

Patriarchy plays a big role in the way poor women identify their money. Cultural and gender underpinnings reinforce the idea that the home is a place for unpaid labour and therefore of no economic significance. This became clear in the interviews. Women saw their economic role as secondary to men's role. One woman reported that 'my business money goes to cater for small issues in the household, say food, household utensils, my daughter's tuition fees and other small things in the house instead of giving a heavy burden to my husband. His money goes to the site, for construction of the house.' It can be argued that the inability to see their money as capital is associated with women's economic role being regarded as inferior. Since their economic role is perceived as secondary, it follows that they cannot regard the money they get towards it as important. Capital is associated with money that goes to create big/important things such as a house. As long as women continue to perform their businesses within patriarchal social relations, and microcredit schemes continue to emphasise money as capital for economic investment, women cannot treat money fully as capital unless gender relations change.

For microcredit officials, money given to clients also signifies trust. Money is often used as a symbol of trust since a person who has money is trusted over one who has none. They expect the women to exhibit trustworthiness by being responsible for the money they borrow. The PRIDE branch manager was of the opinion that: 'We entrust women with our money when others cannot, we expect them to do the same and pay it back.' Meanwhile the SELFINA manager pointed out that, being poor, 'women are not creditworthy; hence no one trusts them with their money apart from the few microcredit agencies'. It is therefore crucial for the women to make repayments on time so as to maintain the upkeep of trust and integrity. Failure to do so would earn them a bad reputation, which is extremely negative because 'if nobody can trust you with their money, no one will be able to help you no matter how deeply in trouble you may be'.

A number of the women I interviewed understand and appreciate the issue of trust more than is usually imagined. One interviewee, expressing her views on trust, stated 'I think it is more risky to make enemies with my neighbours. I would rather make enemies with credit officers than with my neighbours because if I mess up in my neighbourhood who will help me in time of need?' The issue of trust is thus an important factor both for microcredit agencies and their clients, even if they approach this from different angles. Women interviewees prefer to put more trust in their neighbours (social relations/network) whereas microcredit officials emphasise repayments (money). This may imply that clients put more value on their social capital than on economic capital, which in turn has far-reaching effects for the meaning and role of money and poverty reduction. This could explain why some interviewees choose to help or visit a sick neighbour (earning them no money, but respect and perhaps the promise of future reciprocity), rather than conduct their business which helps with debt repayment. It can be argued that this is a situation that has not been adequately assessed by microcredit agencies, hence the tendency to emphasise economic investment rather than other aspects of poverty. Such a scenario further exposes the opposing perceptions of money between microcredit organisations and their clients, and hence the notion of money as an end to poverty.

As noted earlier, the ability to contribute economically towards household expenditure and also to influence decisions within the household is regarded as a form of empowerment by microcredit agencies. With the rising level of gender violence, microcredit officials were of the view that 'women are in a better position at the household level if they can contribute economically, or even be in a position to support themselves and their families'. This was deemed possible through investing in income-generating projects. The agencies suppose that women will get money and 'determine its use, as it is their own and not to be given to their husbands or other persons instead'. At some level it is certainly possible to discern some positive advances among women deriving from microcredit. For example, women who have experienced and endured intolerable suffering in their marriages claim to have been empowered by the money that enabled them to leave and start a new life and participate in business. Yet if microcredit aims to empower women and consequently improve the living standards of the whole household, there need to be other mechanisms in place for identifying how empowerment might be achieved, other than by giving money.

Empowerment is a complex and multidimensional process. A comprehensive intervention which embodies different domains of this process is essential for empowering women on a substantial scale (Mayoux, 2006). Finally, if empowerment has to extend beyond the household, there is a greater need for participation, education and awareness-generation among all members of the society. Understandably this might be an expensive undertaking, but ultimately it may create more solid foundations for poor women to respond to gender discrimination. Other mechanisms that might guarantee women's empowerment include reforms in the educational and legal systems. These reforms should do away with mechanisms that justify women's discrimination. Furthermore technological advancement should reduce women's heavy workload in their homes and marketplace. Women should foster wider social networks that improve access to information that boosts their empowerment process.

Concluding thoughts
This chapter has looked at the differing understanding and role of money between microcredit agencies and their clients. It used the case study of Dar es Salaam to show that money is a social entity with various meanings and roles and should not be treated as a universal solution to poverty for all sectors of the population. By focusing on income poverty alone, microcredit is missing the complexities of poverty which their clients experience and respond to in their daily lives. As argued by authors such as Kabeer (1999), Sweetman (2005), Bali Swain (Chapter 91, this volume), and Mutalima (Chapter 93, this volume), poverty cannot simply be resolved by providing access to credit as an isolated strategy since access to material resources does not automatically empower or reduce these women's poverty status. As demonstrated in this case study of Tanzania, access to credit does not address a range of poor women's realities such as gender disparities in allocation and distribution of resources and responsibilities within the household, local traditions and customs, social relations, low technology and skills, and gender-discriminatory legal frameworks and economies. To achieve its potential, microcredit must move beyond credit/money as an end to poverty and listen to their clients' needs so as to find a holistic and sustainable solution for alleviating privation. This chapter concludes that microcredit is a necessary means but not a sufficient end to poverty reduction. It urges future research and policy to reflect on the local reality of the people it aims to

assist and incorporate their concerns from the initial stage of programme formulation in order to achieve better outcomes, particularly in today's global situation where monetary transactions are highly turbulent.

Note

1. The fieldwork was conducted in 2004 as part of my doctoral research. It entailed interviews with six officials in two Tanzanian microfinance agencies (PRIDE and SELFINA), and a total of 40 interviews with their female clients.

Select bibliography

BRIDGE (2001) *Briefing paper on the Feminisation of Poverty*, prepared by BRIDGE for the Swedish International Development Agency (Sida), available at: www.ids.ac.uk/bridge/ (accessed 16 December 2008).

Carruthers, Bruce and Wendy Nelson Espeland (2002) 'Money, meaning and morality', in Nicole Woolsey Biggart (ed.), *Readings in Economic Sociology*, Oxford: Blackwell, pp. 292–314.

Kabeer, Naila (1999) 'Resources, agency, achievements: reflections on the measurement of women's empowerment', *Development and Change*, **30**, 435–64.

Mayoux Linda (2006) *Women's Empowerment Through Sustainable Micro-Finance: Rethinking 'Best Practice'*, discussion paper, Gender and Micro-finance website, available at: http://www.genfinance.net (accessed 27 January 2009).

Sweetman, Caroline (2005) 'Editorial', in Caroline Sweetman (ed.), *Gender and the Millennium Development Goals*, Oxford: Oxfam, pp. 2–8.

Zelizer, Viviana (1998) 'The proliferation of social currencies', in Michael Callon (ed.), *The Law of Markets*, Oxford: Blackwell, pp. 58–68.

Zimmerman, Jamie (2009) *Lend to End Poverty: Selling Microcredit During a Debt-led Recession?* (Washington, DC: New America Foundation), available at: www.microfinancegateway.org (accessed 3 February 2009).

87 Capitalising on women's social capital: gender and microfinance in Bolivia
Kate Maclean

Microfinance is the provision of small loans and savings facilities to people otherwise excluded from formal financial systems. From its beginnings in the 1970s, microfinance has become one of the most lauded development interventions. In 2005 the United Nations celebrated its first International Year for Microfinance, and in 2006 the Grameen Bank and its founder, Muhammad Yunus were awarded the Nobel Peace Prize for 'their efforts to create economic and social development from below'.[1] Microfinance Institutions (MFIs) worldwide have extended their services by targeting women on the basis of their 'social capital', summarised by Rankin (2002: 1) as 'local forms of association that express trust and norms of reciprocity'. Women's social capital is harnessed by MFIs in the form of group guarantees. The value of relationships within groups functions as collateral, and peer pressure ensures repayment. This technique achieves very high repayment rates, often over 95 per cent.[2]

In this chapter, I first explore the use of women's social capital by MFIs and critiques from a gender perspective. Then, on the basis of qualitative research from the valley of Luribay, Bolivia,[3] I examine how women negotiate microfinance's dual approach of group formation and credit. I specifically look at CreCER (Credit with Rural Education), a Bolivian MFI that targets women in rural areas.[4]

Women's social capital and microfinance
One of the main reasons that MFIs target women is the strength of their social capital. Although poor women often lack formal collateral, in part because property tends not to be in their name, they do have social capital. Women's networking and community labour has been shown to be vitally important to survival in the development context. As Molyneux (2002: 177) describes: 'The evidence shows across a range of countries that women among low-income groups are frequently those with the strongest community and kin ties; many such women do network, they do engage in reciprocal supportive relations . . . and participate in local forms of associational life.' By using a group guarantee, MFIs are able to harness this social capital and use it as collateral. Loans are repaid at such a high rate because group members do not want to jeopardise trust within the group or their reputation within the community (see also Casier, Chapter 94, this volume). As well as being excellent collateral, the group collects repayments from individual members, hence reducing administration costs for the MFI.

There are other reasons that MFIs target women. Since its beginnings, microfinance has been associated with women's empowerment. The provision of loans directly to women arguably supports their financial independence, increasing their bargaining power within the household and making their contribution more visible. Women have proved to be the best 'poverty fighters'[5] and are likely to invest profits from their loans in their children's education, healthcare and improvements to the household's standard of living. Group meetings may provide a forum for discussion of women's situation in which members can exchange experiences and offer mutual support (Rankin, 2002). Increasingly, women's empowerment is seen as a result of the credit alone, but critics argue that other elements of microfinance interventions, including group meetings and training, are equally if not more important (Mayoux, 2006).

Microfinance has achieved such high levels of popularity in the development industry in part because it is potentially financially self-sustainable (Mayoux, 2006; but see also Mutalima, Chapter 93, this volume). While other development interventions depend on aid, microfinance could ultimately pay for itself: if interest rates cover administration costs and enough savings are collected, then there is no further need for subsidy. In this context, women's social capital is used predominantly for its potential to support income-generation and the growth of microfinance institutions.

This use reflects the prominent understanding of social capital in mainstream development institutions, based on Putnam's communitarian definition: 'social capital . . . refers to features of social organisation, such as trust, norms, and networks, that can improve the efficiency of society by facilitating co-ordinated actions' (Putnam 1993: 167, quoted in Woolcock, 1998: 189). This defines social capital as a public good, the increase of which is necessarily positive for development. However, traditions and norms underpinning social capital can be the source of gendered inequalities, and relationships can be hierarchical as well as reciprocal and cooperative. Women tend to bear the responsibility for maintaining these traditions and community relationships, but the labour involved in this maintenance, although vital to survival, tends to be naturalised and, so, undervalorised (Molyneux, 2002).

Furthermore, although social capital is assumed to support development and income-generation, the precise dynamics involved in this process are rarely explored. Understanding social capital as a public good overlooks the downside of relationships, traditions and norms, and the restrictions that they impose. Intra-community relationships can involve downward levelling norms as well as mutual support. For instance jealousy and sanctioning of individual achievement can help maintain group cohesion, but is not necessarily beneficial for development at either the social or individual level. It has been argued that while close intra-community ties offer support and safety nets, in order to achieve entrepreneurially one must establish links outside the immediate community (Woolcock, 1998). The following case study of CreCER's programme in rural Bolivia illustrates the complications and trade-offs that the use of women's social capital to promote capitalisation and financial self-sustainability can entail.

Social capital and microfinance in rural Bolivia
Credit with Rural Education targets women in rural and peri-urban areas and aims to promote development by 'capitalising' rural female beneficiaries and 'shoring up' small business'.[6] It achieves these aims by providing loans of between 500bs (bolivianos) (US$62.5) and 8000bs (US$1000)[7] over six months, and holding training sessions on health and women's rights during regular group meetings. It is unique among Bolivian MFIs to adopt this 'double bottom line' approach of social and financial impact.

Credit with Rural Education lends to groups of at least ten women. Groups are self-selecting and promoters encourage potential members to allow only responsible women to participate. Once groups are formed, CreCER lends the sum of money to the whole group over six months. The group is responsible for collecting repayments from individual members and can determine some aspects of the loan, for example initial membership fees. There are nevertheless centralised policies which group members cannot determine, predicated on the long-term aim of financial self-sustainability. The interest rates, 24 per cent at the time of my research, and fortnightly repayment schedule are set centrally.

Credit with Rural Education has been active in the municipality of Luribay since 2000. Luribay is a fruit-producing valley about seven hours by road from La Paz. Aymara, one of Bolivia's official, indigenous languages, and Spanish are spoken. In the centre of the valley is Luribay Town (population 230), the capital of the municipality, where the local government and non-governmental organisations (NGOs) working in the valley have their offices. The town is surrounded by 78 hamlets lying along the river. The road from Luribay to La Paz starts in the town. There is a market fair in the town every Tuesday, and people come from La Paz to sell items such as clothes and kitchen equipment. The distinction between the town and the hamlets has its roots in the colonial period. People who live in Luribay Town tend to speak Spanish rather than Aymara and see themselves as more urban, which is reflected in the way they dress. Although land ownership is still priority in the town, there is more commerce, mainly due to more circulation from outside. As well as seven shops, all selling the basics: soft drinks, biscuits, beer, matches and batteries, there are two restaurants and four hostels, mainly catering to the NGO and local government staff from La Paz who stay in Luribay from Monday to Thursday.

In the hamlets surrounding Luribay Town, people generally speak Aymara (although the majority can also speak Spanish) and focus on land-based production rather than commerce. This distinction between people in commerce (*comerciantes*), and people who work on the land (*productores*), is often evoked to describe the historical, ethnic and cultural difference between the urban/*mestizo* town and the rural/indigenous hamlets. Nevertheless, throughout the valley, land ownership and land-based production are the principal goals and the main activities. Working on the land is made possible by cooperation and reciprocity between kin and friends. This is typical of the Andes, and there is a rich lexicon to describe the norms and the traditions framing social capital. Family and friends work on each others' fields, and by the Aymaran principles of *ayni* and *minkha*, meaning the reliable, direct and commensurate return of gifts, favours and labour, this work is repaid in kind. *Faena* describes public cooperation: communities working together to maintain infrastructure, for example, repairing the town's main road and clearing the irrigation ditch.

The Aymaran term *chachawarmi*, (literally man-woman) encompasses the gender ideology of complementary yet equal roles for men and women. This principle is apparent in political and community events and institutions, but Aymaran feminists argue that it overlooks inequalities in the gender division of labour. Women are entirely responsible for household and reproductive labour, and it is women's responsibility to arrange work on the land. Women organise family and friends to work on a certain day and prepare a 'work party' afterwards. They prepare the lunch to be eaten altogether, which consists of soup, meat and various kinds of potatoes, and on exceptional days, for example, digging the field, harvesting crops or cleaning the irrigation ditch, there is a roast.

Women are also responsible for sales and commercial activity. While work on the land is often referred to by women as 'helping our husbands', shops are known by the women's names. The stereotype commonly evoked in La Paz of a rural Aymaran woman is of a savvy businesswoman who drives a hard bargain. Women in Luribay are very proud of this reputation. Given this, it is striking that there is next to no commercial activity in the hamlets, and goods in the town are mainly sold to outsiders. To profit from family and friends is considered selfish and is sanctioned by gossip. To attempt to make a profit locally is to risk losing the reciprocal, cooperative relationships which constitute the trust and provide the infrastructure that make land-based production possible.

There is hence potential tension between the trust, norms and traditions which underpin the relationships constituting CreCER's group guarantee, and the income-generating activity it promotes. The ability to negotiate this tension depends on the opportunities and time available to invest in income-generating activities that do not threaten the norms and traditions of reciprocity underpinning social capital. The majority of CreCER's group members in the town invest their loan in commerce, but they sell to outsiders and are careful to respect the boundaries of cooperation. Women who own shops take out large loans, over 4000bs (US$500) over six months, and buy in bulk in La Paz to sell retail in Luribay. Other women have smaller commercial activities, and take advantage of the weekly market fair. Group members in the town stress that they manage their loan responsibly, keeping the money from the loan separate and using the profits from commerce to repay the loan in the bi-monthly meetings.

Commerce in the town still has to respect the limits of cooperation. To illustrate, there is a story circulating about one of the shop owners who had tried to undercut everybody else's prices, and sell goods which were seen as other people's speciality, for example, cheese, bread or motor oil. This would seem to make good entrepreneurial sense, but people in Luribay see this behaviour as extremely selfish: 'she was forgetting that we all have to make a living here', as one woman describes, and as a result she lost custom. This illustrates that although social capital supports income-generation, the rational entrepreneur has to respect the norms governing community cohesion.

Women in the hamlets invest their loan almost exclusively in land-based production. The most usual loan amount is 1000bs (US$125) which is used to buy seed, fertiliser and pesticide. Many women, particularly those with smaller plots of land, complain that making the bi-monthly repayments is very difficult, especially in winter because they have to wait several months before seeing any profit from their investment – and even then the harvest is never certain. To meet the repayment schedule they have to borrow from family and friends, straining the relationships on which the solidarity groups are based. Some take on extra work as day labourers in different communities, adding to their already substantial burden of labour. They know that the credit would be better invested in commerce, but would be unwise to risk reciprocal community relationships by engaging in profit-making activity locally. The opportunities that they do have to access cash and meet the repayment schedule strain their vital social capital and place extra burdens on their scarce time.

Capitalising on women's social capital?
This case study of women's use of microfinance in Luribay illustrates the importance of social capital to development, but also the complications involved in using social capital in microfinance. The Andes is an area where traditions of reciprocity and cooperation are strong and enable land-based production to take place. However, the nature of the

various traditions and norms and the way in which they support income-generation need to be understood for microfinance to have an equitable impact. The present exploration reveals that the strength of women's social capital does not necessarily sit well with the income-generating activity that MFIs seek to promote, and highlights the need for research on the gendered construction of social capital and the dynamics between social and economic capital.

Credit with Rural Education recognises the importance of social impact to long-term sustainability, emphasising its 'double bottom line' approach despite industry pressure to reduce subsidies. However, the elements of the loan which are set centrally, in particular the repayment schedule, do not always reflect the configuration of social capital and income-generation. In Luribay the loan terms favour those involved in commerce in the town, which in Bolivia implies an ethnic/urban bias. Women are participating in the intervention in that they are administrating the loan, but they are not given the ability to set loan terms. If they were allowed to determine the repayment schedule, the intervention might better reflect the local balance of social capital and income-generation.

An analysis of the gendered nature of social capital reveals that the strength of women's social capital needs to be viewed critically rather than institutionalised. In Luribay, as in many areas of the developing world, women take on much of the responsibility for maintaining reciprocal family and community relationships. In areas where these relationships are vital to survival women do not have the time or the opportunity to form linkages with outsiders in order to engage in competitive profit-making. Their willingness to undertake further work and debt in order to meet the repayment schedule suggests that certain microfinance techniques take advantage of the importance of these relationships.

This case study suggests that using women's social capital as collateral is capitalising on relationships which are worth far more than the loan. The high repayment rate achieved by women-targeted MFIs reflects the importance of women's social capital to survival. Women cannot risk this social capital, and hence go to onerous lengths to repay. In this context, the current focus in the microfinance industry on financial self-sustainability needs to be reviewed to reflect the complexity of the relationship between social capital and income-generation. While social capital offers a way to valorise norms, traditions and social relationships in development discourse, a more nuanced and specific understanding of the gendered downside of social capital is necessary.

Acknowledgements

Research for this chapter was sponsored by a doctoral grant from the Economic and Social Research Council (PTA 030 2004 00186). I am indebted to Florinda Apaza Henderson, Maria Apaza Mamani, Pastor Apaza Arroyo and staff at CreCER's offices in La Paz and El Alto for their support during fieldwork. Many thanks also to Haleh Afshar, Anne Akeroyd, Sylvia Chant and David Green for their support and comments.

Notes
1. Direct quote from Grameen Foundation website: http://www.grameenfoundation.org/ (accessed 1 April 2009).
2. http://www.grameenfoundation.org/ (accessed 1 April 2009).

3. My fieldwork took place in the Aymaran-speaking municipality of Luribay, Bolivia, from February to September 2006. I lived and worked with women participating in CreCER's intervention and visited 43 credit groups in 11 different localities in the municipality. I focused on six groups in four different locations. I held two focus groups of nine women in two locations and interviews with 25 women, 12 of whom had also participated in focus group discussions.
4. Credit with Rural Education is a national institution operating in eight of Bolivia's nine provinces and reaching 80 000 beneficiaries (or 'members'), 99 per cent of whom are women. It is funded by International Financial Institutions, development organisations and private banks. There are further aspects to CreCER's intervention, including savings and 'internal loans', which are not explored here. The intention in using CreCER as a case study is to illustrate the tensions caused by provision of credit against a group guarantee, rather than to offer an impact assessment of CreCER's programme as a whole.
5. http://www.grameenfoundation.org/ (accessed 1 April 2009).
6. Quote taken from the article 'Nuestro Producto' on CreCER's website: http://www.crecer.org.bo/nuestro-producto.htm (accessed 28 February 2008)
7. At the time of this research the exchange rate was 8 bolivianos to US$1.

Select bibliography

Mayoux, Linda (2006) *Women's Empowerment through Sustainable Micro-finance: Rethinking 'Best Practice'*, discussion paper, available at: http://www.genfinance.info/Documents/Mayoux_Backgroundpaper.pdf (accessed 28 February 2008).
Molyneux, Maxine (2002) 'Gender and the silences of social capital: lessons from Latin America', *Development and Change*, **33** (2), 167–88.
Putnam, Robert (1993) *Making Democracy Work: Civic Traditions in Modern Italy*, Princeton, NJ: Princeton University Press.
Rankin, Katharine (2002) 'Social capital, microfinance, and the politics of development', *Feminist Economics*, **8** (1), 1–24.
Woolcock, Michael (1998) 'Social capital and economic development: toward a theoretical synthesis and policy framework', *Theory and Society*, **27**, 151–208.

88 'A woman and an empty house are never alone for long': autonomy, control, marriage and microfinance in women's livelihoods in Addis Ababa, Ethiopia
Caroline Sweetman

Introduction
Feminist thought on the empowerment of women emphasises the importance of women being able to perceive their interests as individuals. Some see the attainment of autonomy from relatives and the household as virtually synonymous with empowerment (see, for example, Jejeebhoy, 1996). Feminist debates about awareness of oneself as an individual possessing distinct interests are matched by debates about the importance of women independently controlling resources, enabling them to put choices into action (Kabeer, 1999).

Development from a feminist perspective typically tries to expand women's awareness of the potential choices open to them, often through dialogue with outsiders and with each other. It also typically boosts women's livelihoods activities by channelling material resources to them. It is important from the point of view of fostering female autonomy that women invest in their own independent activities, in order to attain economic independence from men in their families and communities.

This chapter draws on research into the impact on women's livelihoods, poverty and empowerment of a microfinance project in Kechene, Addis Ababa, Ethiopia, implemented by the international religious charity the Daughters of Charity, and funded by Oxfam GB. The research took place in 2002 and 2003, with a follow-up visit in 2006.

Craftswork and its importance in Kechene
Kechene is a hilly location on the northern outskirts of Addis Ababa. Its inhabitants are first- and second-generation rural-to-urban migrants: Amhara people from Northern Shoa, and Dorzae from the south. These are craftsworkers, whose skills offer them an economic comparative advantage in the city. Historically marginalised and stigmatised, craftsworkers have been described as an Ethiopian 'caste'. In the city, traditional clothes production provides a relatively decent living as compared to most other informal activities.

Women's considerable contribution to traditional clothes production is undervalued, as witnessed from the activity being referred to as 'weaving', by both craftsworkers and the anthropologists who have studied them. Traditional clothes production requires both men and women as there is a distinct division of labour: men are required to weave, and women to prepare the yarn and do the embroidery which adds great value to the product, balancing this with childcare and household work.

Marriage, independence and autonomy

Women migrate to Addis Ababa for two overlapping reasons: social and economic problems resulting from divorce and marital breakdown, and economic necessity as a result of lack of land, or lack of male labour to work the land. Economic realities dictate that while many women are alone when they arrive, a new man must be found in the city if possible, and women from craftsworker families commonly seek someone within this community. Fourteen of the 31 women participants in my research live as mothers and wives in nuclear households; 16 of the others are in extended family households (of up to four generations).

Marital relations among respondents varied from strongly unequal – with conflict showing either as violence on men's part, or subterfuge and other strategies on women's part – to highly cooperative. The only time at which it was clear that women saw their interests as distinct from those of their families were in relatively rare instances of severe violence, when preserving life and security depended on women behaving autonomously. For all others, life in the marital household was preferable. Even in households where the adult male breadwinner was not providing women with an economic reason to maintain good marital relations, the social difficulties of women living alone in Kechene led them to see poor marriage as better than no marriage.

Thirty-seven-year-old Askale [1] is a widow, whose husband had had a lengthy period of sickness before his death. She now brews *talla* (beer):

> I had no idea what it would be like to live in this community as a widow. If you are a *talla* seller, you get no respect from anyone, old or young. People insult you and beat you. My husband was not able to object to my *talla* brewing and selling, because he was not in a position to. We had so little income it was obvious I had to do what I could. But now that I am a widow, I know that when you do not have a man around, there is harassment and violence whatever you do for a living. Pray to God for me.

Dimimwa, aged 52, had a violent marriage. Her husband had married her because she had a house, and he was a homeless recent migrant: 'My neighbour told me about him, because he was her friend. He needed a place to live, and I needed a husband, because you cannot live alone as a woman in Kechene.' As another respondent, Thiopia, 32, commented: 'A woman and an empty house are never alone for long.'

Understanding the centrality of marriage to women's livelihoods in Kechene is critical if we are to assess the extent to which the Kechene Savings and Credit Assocation (SAC) could offer women a route to empowerment-as-autonomy.

Downward pressures on survival in Kechene

Formerly relatively stable livelihoods in Kechene are currently spiralling downwards. All the households in my research are chronically poor – 'trapped in poverty from some mix of poverty causes, such as absence of political influence, few assets, and lack of market access' (World Bank, 2001: 15). In 2001 the median per capita monthly household income was only 35 birr (around US$4.37). In a participatory exercise, women said they judged the minimum income needed for a family of three adults and three children to survive was 315 birr (US$39.39) – 52.5 birr (US$6.5) per person – to provide the absolute basics of food, fuel, clothing and coffee (to ward off hunger). They did not budget for medical care or other contingencies.

A significant factor in rendering livelihoods more precarious is increased AIDS-related illness and death among adults of productive age. There is also the impact of distress migration of rural people to Addis Ababa, as land degradation and repeated drought signal an end to hopes of making a living from agriculture. Mutual support and help among craftsworkers is straining under the influx into Kechene. The local population was demanding that the city administration send new migrants home.

Individuals were becoming ever more focused on social relations within their households. Research from a variety of contexts suggests that ties and networks beyond the household break under prolonged economic pressures. Here, *yilynta* (reciprocity) is under strain; people are no longer confident to invest in the relationships which traditionally sustain them during crisis. They were even cutting back on the traditional coffee ceremonies with neighbours – a foundation of life for northern Ethiopians. Coffee for neighbours, and time, cannot be afforded. In 2002, some had started to withdraw their savings from *idirs* (burial societies), to pay for Easter celebrations, the climax of the Ethiopian Orthodox Christian year.

The strains on socialising in Kechene are significant: feminist theory stresses the need for women to forge strong relationships with each other, and to draw on these if they suffer from conflict in marriage and the family.

The SAC project: what did it offer women?

In this context of increasing poverty and eroding social capital beyond the immediate family, what were the strengths and limitations of the SAC Association in supporting women's empowerment? Could it help women become more aware of their interests as individuals capable of autonomous activity, support them to gain independent control over resources, or offer opportunities to invest in social relationships with other women?

Unsurprisingly, all but one of the 29 association members reported their rationale for joining and taking a loan as economic need. Decisions about ways women used loans – which averaged 523 birr (US$65) – were based on the need to minimise risk and maximise household income. Since traditional clothes production offered a better return on investment than other activities open to women, they invested money there. Nine women spent all or part of their loans in this way.

Some women's rationales for investment reflected the reason for opting to continue clothes production in Addis Ababa in the first place: this was the best option for people who could not obtain formal employment. In contrast, others had invested their loans in clothes production less as a positive choice as regards the potential of the activity, than because they themselves lacked time to run own-account businesses alongside existing reproductive responsibilities. They did not want to turn down the possibility of an injection of capital into the household. Goetz and Sen Gupta (1996) discuss the vulnerability of women who pass loans to men to use, and others point out the stress of 'credit as debt' (Ahmed and Chowdhury, 2001). Yet despite investing money in joint business with their husbands in a context of unequal power relations, and the risks of not being able to repay, women in Kechene clearly judged *not* doing this to be the more stressful option.

On the upside, 24 women had used some loan money in their own independent informal sector activities. Yet this had not resulted in business success. Nine women – mainly elderly and desperate – had invested small to medium amounts ranging between 100 to

300 birr (US$12.5–37.5). They lacked both access to a male formal wage, or an income from traditional clothes production. Low investment in typically female informal sector activities represented not the intent to build a business, but a hope that a loan would allow them to continue eating.

Eight others had invested relatively higher sums in own-account enterprises, ranging from 400 to 800 birr (US$50–100). But autonomy here, as well, was a chimera: the reason for this investment choice was that it made sense since they were backed by a male wage from the formal economy. For example, Emebet, married to a policeman, invested three loans totalling 3500 birr (US$437.50) on *dube* (trading in traditional clothes). *Dube* was a smart choice, using existing knowledge of the traditional clothing trade.

Women tried to use loans in ways which maintained marital harmony. Conjit, aged 33, had seven children and a husband sitting idle after their clothes business had failed. She initially invested in an *injera* (traditional bread) business, but eventually wound-up the enterprise, giving what remained of the loan to her husband. Ideologies of mutuality and affection, while not necessarily supported by actual emotions, must be respected if one pragmatically wishes to maintain good marital relations. Visions of feminist autonomy can have little practical resonance here.

No one reported going into business jointly with other women, or suggested that other women, neighbours or friends could be helpful. I was routinely told, 'there is no *yilynta* in business'. This finding recalls gender analyses of societies in transition; specifically, Molyneux's (1994) finding that women were, post-Communism, reluctant to work cooperatively.[2] An exception was Almaz, a 23-year-old widow 'I would like to join other women . . . and do a large-scale activity. If we were organised, got some training, and supported each other, that would be the way to be successful.'

Women need money for any of the patchwork of activities they employ to survive. Three women had used money to construct kitchens, to cook food for sale as well as home consumption, and to dry out *jebenas* (clay coffee pots) – another traditional craft made by women. Others had spread money across different livelihoods activities, including consumption. Some had used part of their loan to invest in building social relationships: two women had used part of their money to maintain and strengthen their relationships with rural relatives, which suffer when city-dwellers are unable to meet expectations of sending money home. Two older women had used part of their loans to enable them to join the *idir* and *equub* (rotating loan scheme).

The SAC Association offered some – limited – opportunity for women to build skills and confidence. Being invited onto the management committee and given leadership training (only offered at the start of the project) had enabled one woman, Emebet, aged 'about 40',[3] to challenge her own and her husband's view of her as a dependent woman:

> I was amazed when they selected me, as I was illiterate. I was so happy and proud of making decisions by myself as a woman. However, my husband said, 'why do they want you?' I told him, 'it is not your concern'. He was not happy, he has a superiority complex based on being a man.

Conjit had also found the entrepreneurship training empowering, at least initially: 'The training gave me confidence . . . I wanted to open a restaurant, so I planned to buy raw materials, fuel, and *akimbalos*' (straw covers for *injera*). But her sense of power was dashed by the small size of the loan she received: 'They gave me 150 birr (US$18.75), and all my dreams were lost.'

Discussion: the empowerment of women as an aim in Kechene

Microfinance has been touted across sub-Saharan Africa as the means to empower women to be autonomous entrepreneurs in a market redolent with possibilities, simultaneously swelling national coffers and making selfless decisions in family budgeting, while challenging gender inequality in their spare time. Yet women members of the SAC Association in Kechene were unable to identify a single livelihood opportunity which would enable them to become so. The sums offered by the SAC Association were sufficient to support women's agency in terms of the conservative – yet obviously all-critical – goal of enabling household survival, but they could not offer transformation, either for livelihoods or gender relations (see also Mohamed, Chapter 86, this volume). Economic realities pushed women to invest in joint activities. When women did invest in independent activities, this was in the absence of any other possibility, and hence no woman earned enough to challenge gender norms seriously. The impact of women's borrowing on their relations with men in their households was seen by women as negligible in most cases. Neither did the project offer women real opportunities to forge and invest in social relationships with each other, as a basis for consciousness-raising, shared livelihood activities and/or political action.

The project was, in fact, actively disempowering for some particularly desperate participants. Resourceful participants can subvert the original aims of development interventions, and some women had effectively treated the funds as a gift from wealthy international donors. Women whose loans had been consumed were never likely to pay it back, and the policing and prosecution of defaulters, while underway, did not seem to have yielded results. Yet for some less brave or more socially conformist borrowers, the result of being forced to misuse the loan was trauma. Wagae, aged 'around 45', told me 'my profit is stress', and, very poignantly, cried when she saw me first, assuming I was there to take her to court.

Lessons from Kechene

Donors need to be more sanguine about supporting women whose contexts do not enable them to act autonomously. From women's own perspective, survival in itself is at stake; and without basic resources, empowerment-as-autonomy is obscenely unrealistic as a project aim. Microfinance from a poverty alleviation perspective is arguably less prescriptive than that informed by feminist empowerment perspectives, because it countenances the idea that empowerment starts through commanding resources, extending the chance that women can make choices that make sense to them.

But microfinance is not the answer for many women in contexts like Kechene. If donors are only capable of swapping one globalised big idea for another, then consideration should be given to cash transfers as a more appropriate response. An idea based on entitlements theory, and developed in contexts of famine, is cash interventions as payment for public works, to buy people time at times of crisis, ensuring they do not further erode their resource basis through unsustainable coping strategies. Kechene is facing such a crisis.

In Kechene, a crucial factor in women's survival is the craftsworker identity and economy they share with men. A supportive development intervention would have channelled resources to women for survival, and fostered opportunities to work with women in groups, and with men, to challenge norms about gender roles and power relations, aiming to improve women's bargaining power with husbands and families. It would be based on an understanding that marriage and mixed households are, as Whitehead and Lockwood (1999) have it, complex and shifting arenas, characterised by both separations and interdependencies. Notions of female independence and autonomy from the marital household could not resonate with women's realities in Kechene.

In the absence of such insights, microfinance projects risk forcing women to use time which they do not possess to pursue activities which at best are a waste of that time, and at worst place them at risk by threatening the marital stability which is so critical to their economic survival.

Acknowledgements
This chapter draws on my PhD thesis 'Livelihoods, poverty and the empowerment of women: an Ethiopian case study', which was awarded at the University of Leeds in 2005. This may be consulted for fuller discussion and references.

Notes
1. I refer to the women's first names because they gave me permission to do so.
2. Ethiopia was under the rule of the Communist Derg regime from 1974 to 1991.
3. Some women only had an approximate idea of their age.

Select bibliography
Ahmed, Syed Masud and Mushtaque Chowdhury (2001) 'Micro-credit and emotional well-being: experience of poor rural women from Matlab, Bangladesh', *World Development*, **29** (11), 1957–66.
Goetz, Anne-Marie and Rina Sen Gupta (1996) 'Who takes the credit? Gender, power and control over loan use in rural credit programmes in Bangladesh', *World Development*, **24** (1), 45–63.
Jejeebhoy, Shireen (1996) *Women's Education, Autonomy, and Reproductive Behaviour: Experience from Developing Countries*, Oxford: Clarendon Press.
Kabeer, Naila (1999) 'Resources, agency, achievements: reflections on the measurement of women's empowerment', *Development and Change*, **30** (3), 435–64.
Molyneux, Maxine (1994) 'Women's rights and the international context: some reflections on the post-Communist states', *Millennium*, **23** (2), 287–313.
Whitehead, Ann and Matthew Lockwood (1999) 'Gendering poverty: a review of six World Bank African poverty assessments', *Development and Change*, **30** (3), 525–55.
World Bank (2001) *World Development Report 2000/1*, Washington, DC: World Bank.

89 Gender and poverty in Egypt: do credit projects empower the marginalised and the destitute?
Iman Bibars

Introduction

Unlike the 1980s when poverty considerations were neglected in favour of structural adjustment priorities, the reduction of poverty has reappeared as an overriding development goal. The World Bank and International Labour Organisation (ILO), as well as bilateral donors, have recurrently confirmed their commitment to poverty alleviation. There has also been an international movement in place since the microcredit summit of 1997 to encourage governments, donors and non-governmental organisations (NGOs) to provide 100 million poor people with credit. Since this date the government, the private sector and banks in Egypt decided that this is also a very viable programme. Such global and local commitment and enthusiasm to credit as the new and most appropriate mechanism for poverty reduction has also been influenced by the international success of credit programmes such as the cases of the Grameen Bank and Bangladesh Rural Advancement Committee (BRAC) (see also Roy, Chapter 84, this volume).

It is argued that expanding credit programmes to the poor will improve their economic situation and prospects (Greeley, 1996: 90). Credit to marginalised groups and especially women is promoted as the most appropriate strategy to improve their bargaining powers within their households and communities. In brief, microcredit for women and the destitute is promoted not only as a poverty alleviation strategy but also as a strategy for community and especially women's empowerment (RESULTS, 1996).

However research carried out in different parts of the world and especially in developing countries has recognised that not all the poor are reached by credit projects and from those reached not all achieve the economic standards to which they aspired (see, for example, Greeley, 1996: 90 on Bangladesh). It is also argued that not all those who do get access to credit projects are empowered; on the contrary many women find themselves playing double roles and are overloaded with income-generating work in addition to housework and unpaid carework.

The new trend in social policy, adopted by the Egyptian government during the last two decades, has not been to redefine the poor or to modify the welfare system, but has been directed towards 'empowering' the poor through the provision of income-generating activities, and mainly via the implementation of revolving funds and credit schemes.

In this chapter I argue that in spite of the many successful examples of credit programmes, credit is not always the most appropriate mechanism for reaching the poorest of the poor, especially female-headed households (FHHs). Moreover, it does not always 'empower' the target group. A large number of the vulnerable and the destitute are not thought to be suitable clients for credit programmes. Moreover, in many cases, these people themselves do not have the skills or inclination to become small entrepreneurs. The main argument is that not all the poor are willing or able to manage credit. Not all the poor gain more bargaining power or are empowered by credit projects; on the contrary many marginalised groups are harmed once they join such programmes. I also want to argue that credit, especially when granted to women, may well help them to survive and to protect them against further abuse, but it does not necessarily get them out of poverty.

Four points must be raised at this juncture. First, recognising the limitation of credit as a universal tool for poverty alleviation is not a criticism of what it can do, nor is it undermining many current programmes which help to alleviate the poverty of some groups. Second, differences in the organisational and ideological orientation between various credit programmes also affect the outcome, the targeting system and who is reached and not reached by these programmes. Thus each credit programme must be viewed and assessed on its own merits. Third, several NGOs in Egypt have recognised the reasons behind the exclusion of specific groups and have explored new approaches. The Association for the Development and Enhancement of Women (ADEW) is the first women's NGO in Egypt to address the reasons behind excluding FHHs from credit programmes and to target FHHs exclusively and include them in the development process. Fourth, looking for alternatives to target the poorest of the poor in addition to credit and recognising that this might not be the only solution, does not and should not undermine the impact or importance of credit programmes in improving living standards among a number of groups in our society.

In this chapter I describe the situation of poor women with a focus on FHHs and then I will address two main questions. First, does credit actually alleviate poverty? Second, does credit alone lead to the empowerment of women?

In the conclusion I reiterate that there are many successful microcredit programmes for FHHs, however their success depends on the NGO implementing it and on what is expected from the programme. My last contention is that credit does not lead to economic growth, even if it aids the protection of these families from ruin and violence.

The situation of poor women and female heads of household
The 'feminisation of poverty' has traditionally been linked to the rise of female-headed households in the poorest segments of Western society. Whether this is the case in developing countries has not been accurately documented (see Chant, Chapter 15, this volume; Davids and van Driel, Chapter 14, this volume). However, there is certainly agreement – and empirical substantiation – that there has been a worldwide increase in the proportion of households headed or maintained by women in recent decades. In some cases too, links between poverty and being female or a female head of household are evident. For example, in India, Shanthi (1996: 312) reveals that studies show that the majority of FHHs are either close to the poverty line or even below it, and compared with their male-headed counterparts are in much worse economic conditions. In the mid-1990s, for instance, 44.7 per cent of FHHs with children under 18 years old lived in poverty compared with 7.7 per cent of male-headed households with children (ibid.: 309–26).

Other studies point out that the number of poor people in the Middle East and North Africa has increased significantly, from an estimated 225 million in 1990 to 305 million in 2005.[1] Case studies and surveys have also indicated that poverty in the region has been growing among women in particular, suggesting an association with a significant increase in the number of female heads of households.

A study carried out in 1993 in the Bulaq district of Cairo and which covered 600 households found that the average income of female-headed households is less than that of male-headed households (MHHs), with the monthly income of FHHs being only 48 per cent of that of their male counterparts. In addition, income was less than expenditure in about half of the FHHs studied while this was the case for only 16 per cent of MHHs. FHHs also lived in worse and poorer housing units than MHHs (Farah, 1997: 12).

The cause for concern about female headship is understandable. Low-income illiterate women often get menial and low-paid jobs. Most of these women have no marketable skills because of their limited education and lack of experience. As they cannot be selective in their employment this makes them vulnerable and easily exploited by their employers. Thus women who head their households suffer double the discrimination of other women for they also suffer: (1) mobility constraints as they combine (solely) productive and reproductive tasks, (2) discrimination in access to jobs and (3) discrimination in welfare payments due to the stigmatisation of female headship.

Does credit alleviate poverty?

To answer this question I looked at the impact of two Microcredit Programmes; one that was run by the Egyptian Ministry of Social Affairs (MOSA) known as the Productive Family Programme (PFP), and ADEW's Microcredit Programme targeting FHHs.

The PFP is one of the main programmes of the MOSA targeting the poor. Although the target group is not limited to women, it is believed that women are 60 per cent of the beneficiaries. The PFP started in 1964 to assist poor families in increasing their income. It includes vocational training, technical advice and loans. Loans are the major activity of the programme. The criteria and procedures for application are cumbersome; the required collateral excludes the poor in general and FHHs in particular. Although the loans are given to income-generating projects chosen by the recipients, there are however a number of safe and acceptable projects for women which are the only ones approved by the bureaucrats. These are traditional projects that are a continuation of women's domestic roles (Farah, 1997: 14).

To answer the question about whether the PFP programme itself improved the living standards of those it reached, I met with 38 women in 2000 who had been beneficiaries of this intervention. Among the 38 women interviewed, 17 stated that it definitely improved their living standards but also declared that it had not moved them beyond their economic level. They were able to get by and meet increasing economic pressures but had not reached the economic standard they aspired to.

> After the loan, I was able to repay it and feed my children better food and keep them in schools, however I was not able to expand. I took another loan to maintain the same level and sometimes I go to the mosque for their monthly aid to keep things going.

Seven of the women interviewed admitted that in spite of the loan, they had to send their male children out to work. They stated that the cost of education and of living is continually increasing and the loans' returns were not enough.

The Egyptianised Grameen Bank model implemented by ADEW since 1987 is arguably a more appropriate programme for poor FHHs. It addresses the problems that excluded the destitute, such as the enforcement of a down payment, the presence of a guarantor or collateral and, finally, the insistence on the applicants having identity cards.

However, both ADEW management and the beneficiaries that I spoke with argued that although the Microcredit Programme saves them from extreme need and the ruin of their families, as with the PFP, this did not lead to upward economic mobility. As ADEW management described it, 'microcredit is a protection and survival mechanism, but does not lead to economic growth', and as echoed by one of the female clients of the programme:

> I was divorced and I had 5 children. I am not educated and had never worked before. When I applied to ADEW, they trained me and gave me a loan to start a small grocery shop. It is true that my three older children did not go to school but at least I was able to keep my youngest children in school. I rely also on my children's income to sustain the household, but without the loan I would have abandoned my children and married another man.

Does credit empower marginalised groups such as women and FHHs?

By the term 'empowerment' in this chapter, I refer to whether a particular group has gained more bargaining power within the immediate family (including consanguineal, as well as conjugal and other affinal relationships) and their communities. More specifically, the empowerment of women as a result of joining a credit project could nominally include: an increased income and an increased control over this income. It could include improved status within the household as women become contributors to livelihoods and have a platform from which to negotiate greater decision-making power. It could also include access to wider markets, which would expand women's networks and links to other circles outside the home. All such dimensions are complementary and reinforcing and could potentially provide women with more autonomy and higher self-esteem.

Impact evaluations in other countries such as Bangladesh have concluded that after taking a loan, women's control over their incomes increases, and that their status within their families improves (Goetz and Gupta, 1996). Other positive effects include improved welfare and rising female access to political institutions (ibid.). However it remains rare that such advances can be directly attributed to credit programmes or women's access to credit (see Bali Swain, Chapter 91, this volume).

In the Egyptian case, and drawing on interviews I carried out with 444 women in seven low-income urban areas as part of my doctoral fieldwork in 1997–99, mixed results are also in evidence. For example, while 60 per cent of the women interviewed stated that they had full control over their income, the rest complained that they worked mainly for their father, mother-in-law or son.

> My husband left me for another woman. So I heard about the PFP and I applied . . . I started a small business where I get clothes and sell it on credit. Once my husband realised I was making good money; he came back to me . . . He takes all my revenues and gives me pocket money and what I need to run the business. When I complained he beat me so hard and threatened to take the children away from me. (Hayam, 40 years old)

In many cases I did not find any direct correlation between credit and more bargaining power of the beneficiaries of these programmes.

> I joined the NGO's credit programme four years ago. I started pickling vegetables and sold them to the shops in our area. However my husband told me that we can sell it to merchants in the bigger market. He pretended he will help; now he is in control of the whole business and I

work for him. So not only do I serve him and his children, I am now a worker in his little pickle factory. (Hend, 36 years old)

The situation of Hend is not unique. In NGOs like ADEW, management and staff insist on monitoring who controls resources of the Microcredit Project and this ensures that women manage to decide on how the money is spent. One of the tools used to verify this is to see what type of electronic goods are purchased for the household after the woman gets the loan. If there is a washing machine, stove and refrigerator then women are deemed to be in control of expenditure. However, if the first thing they buy is a fan, TV or receiver, then this is more suggestive that the man is in control even if the woman earns the income. As such, for microcredit programmes to ensure women's empowerment in any meaningful way, strict monitoring mechanisms must be adopted.

Concluding remarks

My chapter is not calling for the abolition of all new models of providing credit to the poor, but it is calling on policymakers to reconsider credit as the only and most appropriate mechanism for poverty alleviation and for reaching the poorest of the poor. The poor do not constitute a homogeneous group. According to the Egyptian Ministry of Social Affairs, they can be classified broadly into two types: those who can work and those who cannot. The first group of persons can be helped with developmental projects such as PFP or other credit programmes. The second group, on the other hand, may not be helped except through direct financial aid (Mansi, 1995: 1).

Since 1952, the Egyptian government has adopted a welfare approach in order to address the needs of the poor. The main problems with the social aid programmes were the size of the benefits and the coverage. Therefore a more equitable and adequate targeting system is needed. The poorest of the poor must be identified and more realistic and accurate criteria for their eligibility for social aid programmes must be established.

I have mentioned negative examples of credit's impacts on women, but I am sure there were many instances when taking a loan was very helpful for the woman's status and that of her family. Therefore I am not contending that none of the beneficiaries are empowered by credit, but rather highlighting the fact that we should not assume that credit projects directly and automatically alleviate poverty or empower its beneficiaries.

Note

1. The poverty line is measured as living on less than U$1.25 per day. Data obtained from PovCalNet, the World Bank Group, available at: http://iresearch.worldbank.org (accessed 18 March 2009).

Select bibliography

Farah, Nadia Ramsis (1997) *Poverty Alleviation with a Focus on Women Headed Households and Micro-credit Programmes in Egypt*, New York: UNICEF.
Goetz, Anne Marie and Rina Sen Gupta (1996) 'Who takes the credit? Gender, power and control over loan use in rural credit programmes in Bangladesh', *World Development*, **24** (1), 45–63.
Greeley, Martin (1996) 'Poverty and well-being: policies for poverty reduction and the role of credit', in Geoffrey D. Wood and Iffath A. Sharif (eds), *Who Needs Credit? Poverty and Finance in Bangladesh*, London: The University Press, pp. 83–96.
Mansi, Ragaa Khalil (1995) 'Child labour from the insurance and social security perspective', paper presented

in workshop on 'Reducing Child Labour in Egypt', organised by Ministry of Labour, Sheraton Hotel, Cairo, March.

RESULTS (1996) *The Microcredit Summit: Draft Declaration*, Washington, DC: RESULTS Educational Fund.

Shanthi, K. (1996) 'Economic and social status of female heads of households – need for intervention under new economic policy', *The Indian Journal of Social Work*, **57** (2), 309–26.

90 Women's empowerment: a critical re-evaluation of a GAD poverty-alleviation project in Egypt
Joanne Sharp, John Briggs, Hoda Yacoub and Nabila Hamed

Introduction
It has now become an expectation that development at all scales adopts the language of gender empowerment, assuming that women's empowerment is a central facet of poverty alleviation, and is something that can be straightforwardly and measurably delivered. This can lead to uncritical outcomes which may reinforce the status quo or enforce inappropriate external ideas. After a brief examination of dominant approaches to women's empowerment in development praxis, this chapter presents the example of a gender and development project established with the Bedouin desert inhabitants of Egypt's Eastern Desert which worked with women on poverty alleviation and, as a consequence of this process, their empowerment. Reflecting on this example, the chapter concludes with a discussion of the complex and entangled networks of power to which development efforts must be sensitive.

Empowerment, women and poverty alleviation
With the recent recognition that standardised top-down approaches to development have generally resulted in failure, increasing numbers of academics and development practitioners have sought alternative approaches that work from the bottom-up, involving the target populations of development in their own programmes. For instance, the United Kingdom's (UK) Department for International Development (DFID) published a gender manual in 2002 which insisted that women's empowerment be a precondition for poverty alleviation. As echoed more widely by Parpart (2002: 338), it appears that empowerment 'has become a popular, largely unquestioned "goal"'.

For many development organisations, power is defined as 'power over'. This is a zero-sum approach which assumes that there is a fixed amount of power to go around – men have it, thus, to empower women, some of men's power much be relinquished. This position accepts gender relations as they are, seeking to reallocate power without challenging the relationships which apparently pit men and women against one another.

Others look at 'power to', which has empowerment as the ability to act in particular ways. What is important about this approach is that it does not produce a zero-sum game where women's advantage is men's disadvantage, but instead recognises that the increased empowerment of women (whether in terms of access to education, markets, land or other resources) will improve the community as a whole. However, there is a danger inherent within such approaches of overburdening women. What might appear as empowerment to Western development perspectives might simply add extra burdens to a woman's work day (see Chant, Chapter 15, this volume; Nakray, Chapter 51, this volume).

Rowlands (1997) points out that there are other forms of empowerment based upon more subtle Foucauldian-inspired understandings of power, including those which prevent people from even thinking about how the world might operate otherwise. Thus, for many involved in empowering women, the most important form of empowerment involves 'power from within' (ibid.: 111), where self-perceptions and understandings are challenged in such a way as to enable women to think of alternative ways of existing, a process which empowers women through the generation of a sense of effective agency. For this understanding of power then, the process of gaining empowerment, of considering oneself a capable agent, is as much an aim of the process and the material end result (women's credit schemes, education, market involvement, and so on) of any particular project.

Thus, more recent formulations of the role of men and women in the development process, especially Gender and Development (GAD), realise that it is not just the formal mechanisms of decision-making that can hinder improvements in the standard of living of women. The internalisation of the status quo is the result of processes of socialisation that reinforce the way things should be. Here, '(e)mpowerment is thus more than participation in decision-making; *it must also include the processes that lead people to perceive themselves as able and entitled to make decisions*' (Rowlands, 1997: 14, emphasis in original).

The role of GAD is accordingly to devise a methodology which will 'help women to perceive the limitations that they place on themselves' (Rowlands, 1997: 134). Only when the critique of current conditions comes from the women themselves can development processes effectively challenge the relations of patriarchal domination and achieve empowerment (in whichever form).

Such an approach cannot ignore men. Although the vast majority of positions of power are occupied by men, this does not mean that all men occupy positions of power. Indeed, many are marginalised by male–male power relations. It is important, therefore, not to assume that all men are direct beneficiaries of current social arrangements, nor that they would be naturally hostile to any changes in the status quo, challenges to which could end up being empowering, regardless of gender. Moreover, women's relationships with men are complex, even in situations where it seems clear that gender relations are exploitative of women. That women may not view men as exploitative is articulated by Cornwall (2000: 20) as follows:

> Those relationships, experiences and identities that fall outside the narrow frame set by oppressive heterosexual 'gender relations' tend to be disregarded. In the midst of all this, there is no space at all for men's experiences of powerlessness, love or dependency in their relationships with women, nor for relations between men that are equally inflected with gender.

Finally, Western-centred development thought tends to assume that women act as autonomous individuals, rather than conceptualising identity as collective or connected, emerging primarily from the household or community.

Empowering Bedouin women
These issues are well illustrated through the example of a GAD project which aimed to investigate the role of Bedouin women in the production of small livestock in Wadi Allaqi in Egypt's Eastern Desert (see Figure 90.1). Previous research in the area has noted the primary economic significance of small livestock rearing and male domination of this sector

Figure 90.1 Location of Wadi Allaqi

(Briggs, 1995). This project, conducted between 2000 and 2004, sought to build on these earlier results to understand the actual and potential roles that women fulfil in this sector. The fieldwork was funded by a DFID Gender and Development grant. Although predominantly a research project, it had the additional aim of poverty alleviation through the development of small-scale agriculture, producing small amounts of livestock feed supplements. Thus, it was hoped that a longer-term aim of the project could be empowerment of the women involved through an increased confidence in their own abilities and respect from others for their enhanced contribution to the household budget (see Sharp et al., 2003).

The research team comprised male and female (non-Bedouin) Egyptian and British researchers, including postgraduate students and staff members. The Egyptian department, the Unit for Environmental Studies and Development at the University of the South Valley in Aswan, has a field centre and agricultural research centre in Wadi Allaqi and has worked in the area (with and without the involvement of the Bedouin) for more than 20 years. The current research project is the first where women were consulted about their own perspectives. Nevertheless, visits were not considered unusual due to this history of contact. Moreover, the visits were not only concerned with the research topics but involved news of relatives and the delivery of produce from Aswan by the research team. Research was carried out in the form of regular discussions with the Bedouin. As is conventional for non-family guests, the male researchers were met by Bedouin men in the designated guest areas, which are at some distance from the private spaces of the household. The female researchers were taken into this domestic space where they could talk with the Bedouin women without the presence of men.

The study area in the downstream part of Wadi Allaqi (the main *wadi* [dry valley] of the southern part of Egypt's Eastern Desert), is located about 180 kilometres to the south of Aswan (Figure 90.1). In this hyper-arid environment, the downstream part of the *wadi* receives virtually no rain, although rainfall events upstream in the Red Sea Hills can result in occasional surface flows along the *wadi* floor downstream (there have been two such events in the last 20 years). This is nevertheless a dynamic environment which changed markedly with the construction of the Aswan High Dam during the 1960s, and the subsequent inundation by the High Dam Lake (Lake Nasser). The resources available to Bedouin groups have changed, as has the social environment as fishermen and farmers have come to the area to seek a living. Superimposed on longer-term lake-level changes, there is also a well-defined pattern of seasonal change, with the lake level peaking in November or December before dropping typically by up to 6–8 metres to its lowest level in July. During these annual lake retreats, grazing opportunities along the emergent lakeshore present themselves for livestock.

The Bedouin have traditionally been a highly mobile group, moving all their belongings to follow seasonal pastures in the hyper-arid environment of the Nubian Desert. With the establishment of Lake Nasser, women no longer migrate with the men but have settled near to the water supply of the lake, moving only to follow shore as it moves with lake level fluctuation.[1]

Wadi Allaqi Bedouin practice Islam, as well as a strict regime of seclusion whereby women are prevented from meeting men who are not from their immediate family. The spatial arrangement of households provides a women's area away from the place where guests are met. The *beit bersh*, the traditional tents used by Bedouin in this area, of extended family groups are arranged between a few metres and a few hundred metres from one another. Each extended household is dominated by a senior patriarch who makes major decisions, while day-to-day decision-making over more minor matters is left to the individual households.

The attractions of downstream Wadi Allaqi for the Bedouin communities inhabiting the area are both the reliable supply of water from the lake and the availability of vegetation resources for livestock grazing that follow after the annual inundation. However, the latter are not quite as productive as they might at first appear. Each year, as the annual lake level recedes (from December until about July–August), grasses and herbs grow on the emergent lakeshore, but they are not always particularly abundant. Hence, although in many ways an attractive area for Bedouin settlement, many of the families still retain an important nomadic component to their economic activities. This entails men taking sheep into upstream Wadi Allaqi or, rather less frequently, the Red Sea Hills, for winter grazing (thus providing some relief for grazing resources in the lakeshore area itself). Other strategies include producing charcoal in the same upstream and hill areas, grazing camels in areas outside Wadi Allaqi, and collecting medicinal plants from a number of locations in the Eastern Desert (Briggs, 1995).

Key research findings
The context of animal production – including the economic and cultural importance of sheep and goats, and the limitations on production – was discussed with various groups

of Bedouin women, particularly in relation to the importance of sheep and goats for households and women's daily workloads, as well as views on what would improve the quality of their animals. What emerged was the view that a more constant and reliable supply of livestock feed could be obtained from growing fodder crops on small plots around the settlements. As a result, some women decided to commence small-scale cultivation.

This approach seemed to follow a non-conflictual sense of empowerment in the sense of 'power to' rather than 'power over' (see Rowlands, 1997). There was no direct challenge to the role of Bedouin men and, indeed, the male members of the research team faced no obvious hostility in their parallel discussions with the men at the time of this project. In Wadi Allaqi, finding and developing ways by which women could improve the quality of the sheep and goats around the household with the use of better quality feed would potentially contribute to a number of other improvements. These included producing higher quality milk, especially from goats, resulting in improvements in children's health in particular; improving animal health generally, and creating greater stability of flock size by reducing stock losses. The overall result would be greater household security, in terms of a more secure and reliable food supply for both the Bedouin women involved and for their children. It might also provide better quality animals for sale in the market.

However, many women chose not to embrace this opportunity for economic empowerment. There was some reluctance to spend additional time supporting sheep and goat production. It seems that there are a number of issues tied up with this reluctance, all of which offer an important reflection upon how 'empowerment' is to be understood in this particular context. Although sheep and goats are seen as important to the household economy, many women were unenthusiastic about trying to develop their role in their production any further. In large part, this appears to be the result of the many other tasks that women have to undertake each day in maintaining the household in this challenging environment. Many Bedouin women told us that they already had a great deal to do, that they were simply too busy to spend time with the animals as men did, and so did not have time to look after sheep specifically. Women clearly felt that their share of household reproduction and subsistence activities was high enough already. For those women in households with existing sources of income – for example, comprising men who had transport to take animals to market – there were clearly more pressing demands on time, or at least any additional time was more valued than any possible improvement to livestock quality.

There was, however, interest among poorer women, and especially widows. Perhaps more than any others, these individuals are acutely aware of the limitations of their immediate environment. In the case of poorer families, lack of camel ownership – necessary to access distant parts of the desert and market – meant that men's mobility was nearly as constrained as that of Bedouin women, and thus their access to resources was similarly constrained to their immediate environment. Within these poor households, both men and women were more enthusiastic about the possibilities for small-scale agricultural production.

Moreover, the problem is compounded for widows within the community as those we consulted did not have menfolk to take their share of managing the livestock.[2] Consequently, their flocks are not only smaller in size, but cannot be grazed and managed over wider geographic areas as there are no male relatives to take the animals. Hence, it was one out of two widows in the sample who showed the greatest interest in improving local conditions and providing more immediately available feed resources for livestock.

Other women who chose to adopt the agricultural practices also featured among the poorer and most marginal members of the community. Thus, while the GAD project seemed partially successful, given the production of operational farms by some women, this was not interpreted by the Bedouin as an empowering move. While the farms may have increased economic security, they did not necessarily enhance a sense of empowerment, as this was an activity which was perceived to have been forced on marginal women by adverse circumstances, which resonates with Kabeer's (1999: 436) definition of 'disempowerment' as the denial of choice. Conversely, to be empowered means to be able to make a choice in a situation where there is the possibility of choosing otherwise (ibid.). The poverty of widows and more marginal households leaves these individuals and units with little choice in economic decision-making. Others in the community did not regard these women as empowered – thus neither the individual nor collective sense of women's activities and potentials is likely to be challenged by this process, at least in the short run.

In the long run, however, farms were more widely adopted. After the farms had been in place for a couple of years and their success had been demonstrated, other households began to adopt them. Once Bedouin women had seen the outcomes of the pioneers' initial experiments in agriculture, discursive knowledge became practical – quite literally. Bedouin women and men had seen the knowledge practised, had seen its outcomes and therefore could form their own understanding of it. At first, the women who had gone ahead with the agricultural experiments had been pitied by the other women, because they had been forced to take this action. However, for women who did have the choice, once the scheme had been demonstrated to be successful, they could choose whether to start farming, but it could be framed as something for the household rather than simply a woman's task. Although it is women who are recognised as being the farmers, the farms are regarded as household assets. Thus over time other women enhanced their contribution to household budgets without contravening their 'proper' role, highlighting subtle understandings and manipulation of power relations, and making it clear that women do have the 'power from within' to enact change, but that this has to operate within the terms of the 'patriarchal bargain' (Kandiyoti, 1988) which normalises gender relations.

Conclusion
The case study in this chapter emphasises the need to understand the motivations, priorities and social relations behind action to be able to enact development work which has the desired outcomes. The confidence that sprang from the concrete and demonstrable success of the farms was the force driving increased empowerment. Yet ultimately it was the Bedouin valuation of practical knowledge which led to the acceptance of the project, rather than a concept of women's empowerment. What this case study highlights, therefore, is the need for longer-term engagement with communities so as to arrive at more meaningful understandings of how development praxis can contribute to sustainable and transformational interventions.

Notes

1. Due to the shallow incline of Wadi Allaqi, on average fluctuations in water height in metres alters the shoreline by approximately the equivalent number of kilometres.
2. In Islamic societies such as the Bedouin, widows are generally looked after by extended family members. However, those widows with whom we did speak had no relatives in the desert to whom they could turn.

Select bibliography

Briggs, John (1995) 'Environmental resources: their use and management by the Bedouin of the Nubian Desert of southern Egypt', in Tony Binns (ed.), *People and Environment in Africa*, Chichester: John Wiley, pp. 61–7.

Cornwall, Andrea (2000) 'Missing men? Reflections on men, masculinities and gender in GAD', *IDS Bulletin* **31** (2), 18–27.

Kabeer, Naila (1999) 'Resources, agency, achievements: reflections on the measurement of women's empowerment', *Development and Change*, **30**, 435–64.

Kandiyoti, Deniz (1988) 'Bargaining with patriarchy', *Gender and Society*, **2** (3), 274–90.

Parpart, Jane (2002) 'Gender and empowerment: new thoughts, new approaches', in Vandana Desai and Robert Potter (eds), *The Companion to Development Studies*, London: Arnold, pp. 338–42.

Rowlands, Jo (1997) *Questioning Empowerment: Working with Women in Honduras*, Oxford: Oxfam.

Sharp, Joanne, John Briggs, Hoda Yacoub and Nabila Hamed (2003) 'Doing gender and development: understanding empowerment and local gender relations', *Transactions, Institute of British Geographers*, **28** (3), 281–95.

91 Impacting women through financial services: the Self Help Group Bank Linkage Programme in India and its effects on women's empowerment
Ranjula Bali Swain

Microfinance programmes such as the Self Help Group (SHG) Bank Linkage Programme in India have been increasingly promoted for their positive economic impacts and the belief that they empower women. This chapter starts by examining the existing literature on microfinance's impact on empowering women and presents a brief critique of some of these studies. Within the South Asian context, the next section discusses women's empowerment, defining it as a process in which women challenge existing cultural norms within the societies in which they live to improve their wellbeing effectively (Bali Swain, 2007). This is followed by discussion on evidence for the empowerment of women using household data on members and non-members of SHG Bank Linkage Programme in India. The results from a household survey analysed with a 'general structural model', comprising indicators pertinent to economic, behavioural, social and political aspects of women's lives demonstrate that there is a significant increase in women's empowerment of the Self Help Group members, especially when compared with a non-member control group (see Bali Swain and Wallentin, 2007; although see also Garikipati, Chapter 92, this volume).

Empowering women through microfinance
Microfinance is the provision of a broad range of financial services such as deposits, loans, payment services, money transfers, and insurance to poor and low-income households. A majority of the microfinance programmes target women with the explicit goal of reducing poverty and empowering them. Some argue that women are among the poorest and the most vulnerable of the underprivileged and, thus, helping them should be a priority. Others believe that investing in women's capabilities empowers them to make choices and further contributes to greater economic growth and development. Moreover, an increasing number of microfinance institutions (MFIs) prefer women members as they believe that they are more trustworthy and reliable (see Maclean, Chapter 87, this volume).

Microfinance is usually administered through microfinance institutions which use various delivery methods, such as group lending and liability, pre-loan savings requirements, gradually increasing loan sizes and an implicit guarantee of ready access to future loans if present loans are repaid fully and promptly. Indeed, the SHG Programme in India uses group lending and liability as a way of delivering microfinance to its predominantly female members (about 90 per cent).

Most microfinance programmes empower their clients through direct and indirect strategies. Direct empowerment through microfinance takes place when women become members of a group and/or when they are exposed to training or workshops intended to foment greater awareness and self-esteem. Belonging to a group leads to the creation of further social capital and a support structure (of other group members) that empowers women to improve their overall (not just economic) well-being. Furthermore, most microfinance programmes encourage frequent group meetings, interactions with loan officers or bank officials, and the keeping of financial records, all of which tend to encourage discussions on issues related to economic activities and other household and village matters, not to mention stimulating greater mobility, literacy and personal confidence. Coupled with training and workshops designed to promote greater 'awareness' among women of their political, social and economic circumstances, it is anticipated that women will acquire the motivation and capacity to improve their personal situations within their households, communities and societies.

Microfinance also leads to an increase in women's empowerment through indirect channels. Access to microfinance nominally encourages and enables members to create income-generating possibilities for themselves. By increasing the relative value of female time and money income, microfinance can enhance women's bargaining and decision-making power within the household.

Several empirical studies have documented that women's access to credit contributes significantly to an increase in women's income, their likelihood of increasing asset holdings in their own names, better nutrition, health and education among their children, lower fertility, higher mobility and increased political and social participation (see Armendariz de Aghion and Morduch, 2005, for a useful review).

Others argue that the impact of microfinance programmes is limited for women as they undertake heavier workloads and repayment pressures for only small gains in income. Researchers have also suggested that loans taken by female borrowers are sometimes used by men in the family to establish enterprises. In such cases the women end up being employed as unpaid family workers with little benefit and greater debt burdens. For example, Goetz and Sen Gupta's (1996) investigation of loan use from credit institutions in Bangladesh found that a significant proportion of women's loans were controlled by male relatives (see also Garikipati, Chapter 92, this volume).

Some researchers further contend that microfinance can reinforce women's traditional roles instead of promoting gender equality. Women's practical needs are closely linked to unequal gender roles, responsibilities and social structures. As such, any improvement in their economic situation may simply enable them to perform their normative gendered duties more efficiently (see, for example, Maclean, Chapter 87, this volume).

Interpreting women's empowerment
Empowerment has become so inclusive a concept that it has arguably lost its meaning. Parpart et al. (2002) explain that empowerment is based on an understanding of social change that is transformational rather than transactional in nature. Thus reductionist, essentialist and economistic explanations are inadequate and a more integrated approach is required.

Kabeer (1999) emphasises that women's empowerment is a multidimensional process of change by which those who have been denied the ability to make strategic life choices acquire such ability. This ability to exercise choice incorporates three interrelated dimensions: *resources*, which include access to and future claims to both material and social resources; *agency*, which includes the process of decision-making, negotiation, deception and manipulation; and *achievements*, that equate to well-being outcomes. Thus, critiques which highlight the limitations of the transformative capacities of microfinance by using single-dimensional empowerment indicators, such as 'managerial control' (Goetz and Sen Gupta, 1996), provide incomplete evidence.

On top of this, not all activities that lead to an increase in well-being among women are necessarily empowering in themselves, let alone challenging to gender inequalities (see Bali Swain, 2007). For instance, project interventions geared to improving children's nutrition may lead to greater efficiency in women's mothering, and, as a by-product, increase their personal confidence and sense of well-being. However, the extent to which this may lead to more radical transformations in gender remains questionable. In a similar vein, community-driven development (CDD) activities promoted through the SHGs, such as solving drinking water problems at the village level, may reduce some demands on women's time, as well as leading to better health of all household members, particularly children. However, their empowering effects may be constrained through the reinforcement of existing gender roles. I would argue that truly empowering activities are those which reflect the changes that women make to better their lives by negotiating new, and more equal, gender roles and relations. Thus, for instance, in a South Asian context, if a woman offers greater resistance to any form of abuse from her husband or family, she could be considered more empowered as she is asserting herself, trying to improve her own well-being and attempting to resist oppressive social and cultural norms (see Bali Swain, 2007).

Most of the empirical research on microfinance's effect on women's empowerment has been empirically and conceptually ungrounded and tends to work with incomplete definitions of empowerment. A number of these studies also suffer from methodological biases and flaws. Only a few studies have successfully investigated the impacts of financial services on women's empowerment in a rigorous manner.

Some empirical studies construct indices and/or indicators of women's empowerment (see Fujikake, Chapter 95, this volume). However, these are often deeply problematic, especially where, for example, different types of decision are given equal weight – a woman's decision to buy cooking oil for the family is different in nature from her participation in a decision to buy a piece of land. By the same token, suggesting an arbitrary weight for these decisions can also be inappropriate, as it is arguably not for researchers or programme implementers themselves to decide the criteria which contribute most to women's empowerment at the grassroots.

Some studies have used factor analysis which establishes a whole set of binary indicators that proxy for women's autonomy, decision-making power, and participation at the household and society level. However, one problem with this technique for measuring women's empowerment is that ordinal latent variables cannot be treated as continuous observed variables (see Bali Swain and Wallentin, 2007).

Correcting for these biases and problems, a 'general structural model' is arguably a more appropriate scientific methodology to estimate the impact of microfinance on women's empowerment. Bali Swain and Wallentin (2007) estimate a general structural model that consists of two parts: a measurement model and a structural model. The measurement model measures the latent 'women empowerment' variable using indicators based on the definition of women's empowerment (Bali Swain, 2007). Using Robust Maximum Likelihood technique, the structural model analyses if women's empowerment takes place over time.

Measuring women's empowerment is operationalised through a series of economic, behavioural, social and political indicators. Literature on intrahousehold bargaining suggests that exogenous increases in female share of income may be interpreted as providing women with more power within the household. Hence participation in the labour market and greater economic independence may be expected to lead to a rise in bargaining power and greater empowerment. This is proxied by respondents' participation in economic activity and their own independent savings.

Behavioural changes among women oriented to improving personal well-being are also crucial indicators of empowerment. In our household survey (see below), respondents were asked questions on what they would do if they were (1) verbally abused, (2) physically battered, and (3) psychologically/emotionally abused, within their family. In response to these questions women make any one of a number of ordinal choices to reflect their degree of resistance or submission, which, in turn, proxies for empowerment status.

Over and above labour force engagement, for example, we regarded women's participation in the political sphere as an important indicator of empowerment. Here we relied upon involvement in the village level politics in the shape of standing for local elections as a candidate, or simply just voting. Other selected aspects of empowerment were women's decision-making regarding their work and household matters, as well as their mobility and participation in social networks. However, due to lack of survey information on some of these indicators for the year 2000, our analysis inevitably underestimates the empowerment impact on women.

The Self Help Group Bank Linkage Programme and women's empowerment
The SHG Programme is one of the largest and fastest-growing microfinance programmes in the developing world. The SHG's main objective is poverty reduction and women's empowerment through financial inclusion. Implemented since 1996 on a national scale in India, by March 2005 it had reached an estimated 121.5 million people, mainly women, who were a priority target group. The SHG had disbursed more than 68 billion Indian rupees (US$1.4 billion) in cumulative bank loans up to March 2005, using a network of 1082 bank branches and 4323 non-governmental organisations (NGOs).

There are three main types of group formation. In the first model, banks act as a self-help group-promoting institution. In the most common, second, model, NGOs form groups. In the third model, NGOs form groups as well as provide lending to SHGs from banks. Rather than follow strict eligibility criteria, SHGs attract poor women through self help promotion agents (SHPAs) which include NGOs, banks and government officials. It should be noted here that the programme's characteristic features of small loan size and frequent meetings tend, by default, to dissuade the non-poor from joining.

Self Help Groups fall under the category of village banking which expands the solidarity (Grameen)-type model to between 10 and 20 (primarily female) members. Credit is not immediately extended to members. Once the groups are formed they first have to build credit discipline by saving a certain amount. After the savings pass a threshold level, the groups receive a loan which is a multiple of the savings amount. The bank then disburses the loan and the group decides how to manage it. As savings increase through the group's life, the group can access more and bigger loans.

The empirical analysis on the SHG Programme in India in this chapter is based on data collected in 2003 from five different states.[1] Around 1000 households were surveyed and their responses were recorded for the years 2003 and 2000 (by recall). The respondents consisted of a sample of women who participated in the SHG Programme, along with a similar number of non-members, with the purpose of attempting to discern the impacts of microcredit.

The household survey provides us with a longitudinal data on various indicators of women's empowerment for 2000 and 2003. The women were usually interviewed in the absence of husbands and other family members. As proposed earlier in this chapter, women's empowerment is interpreted as a process by which women progressively act to challenge existing gender unequal norms in the interests improving their personal wellbeing. To capture the multiple facets of women's empowerment the indicators comprised in the general structural model extend to economic, behavioural, social and political spheres of a woman's life, as previously indicated.

The results from Bali Swain and Wallentin (2007) derived from the application of the general structural model indicate that on average there is a significant increase in the women's empowerment of the SHG members' group. No comparable change is observable for the members of the control group.

Yet while the analysis clearly shows the evidence for a general increase in women's empowerment for SHG members over time, the general structural model is only able to detect overall changes between the two groups. As such, this does not imply that each and every woman who joined the SHG Programme was empowered to the same degree or that they all progressed at the same pace.

Variations in the pace and degree of women's empowerment are likely due to such factors such as household and village characteristics, cultural and religious norms, behavioural differences among the respondents and their family members, and the kinds of training and awareness initiatives to which women have been exposed. Future – and wider – research is necessary to reveal the relative importance of different microfinance interventions in relation to other social, economic and political processes.

Acknowledgements
Funding from the Research Council of the Swedish International Development Cooperation Agency (Sida/Sarec) (2002–05) is gratefully acknowledged.

Note
1. These states (districts in parentheses) are Orissa (Koraput and Rayagada), Andhra Pradesh (Medak and Warangal), Tamil Nadu (Dharamapuri and Villupuram), Uttar Pradesh (Allahabad and Rae Bareli), and Maharashtra (Gadchiroli and Chandrapur).

Select bibliography
Armendariz de Aghion, Beatriz and Jonathan Morduch (2005) *The Economics of Microfinance*, Cambridge, MA: Massachusetts Institute of Technology Press.
Bali Swain, Ranjula (2007) 'Can microfinance empower women? Self-help groups in India', *Dialogue*, **37**, 61–82.
Bali Swain, Ranjula and Fan Yang Wallentin (2007) *Does Microfinance Empower Women? Evidence from Self Help Groups in India*, Working Paper 24, Department of Economics, Uppsala University.
Goetz, Anne Marie and Rina Sen Gupta (1996) 'Who takes the credit? Gender, power, and control over loan use in rural credit programmes in Bangladesh', *World Development*, **24** (1), 45–63.
Kabeer, Naila (1999) 'Resources, agency, achievements: reflections on the measurement of women's empowerment', *Development and Change*, **30**, 435–64.
Parpart, Jane, Shirin Rai and Kathleen Staudt (2002) 'Rethinking em(power)ment, gender and development: an introduction', in Jane Parpart, Shirin Rai and Kathleen Staudt (eds), *Rethinking Empowerment: Gender and Development in a Global/Local World*, London: Routledge, pp. 3–21.

92 Microcredit and women's empowerment: understanding the 'impact paradox' with particular reference to South India
Supriya Garikipati

Microcredit has come to occupy a central place in poverty alleviation strategies all over the developing world. It is mainly targeted at women from the poorer sections of the population. A recent estimate suggests that 84 per cent of microcredit clients worldwide are women (Daley-Harris, 2006). The rationale for lending primarily to women is that they are good credit risks, less likely to misuse loans, more likely to respond to peer-pressure and more inclined to share benefits with others in their households, especially their children. In addition to these economic benefits, it is argued that women's increased role in the household economy will lead to their empowerment. The metaphorical trajectory that took women from the simple act of borrowing money to their emancipation was so fundamental to the early credit interventions that the possibility that this may not happen was not considered. But when the relationship between microcredit and empowerment began to be studied earnestly in the mid-1990s, it spawned an intense debate.

Some of the evaluations claim an extremely positive result while others suggest that microcredit in fact leaves women worse off than before (see also Sweetman, Chapter 88, this volume). The positive evaluations argue that microcredit has helped women increase their incomes, leading to greater confidence and ability to overcome cultural asymmetries, while the negative evaluations assert that the loans made to women are usually controlled by their husbands, leading to women's dependence on them for loan instalments and at times in a context of domestic dissent and violence (for a review, see Garikipati, 2008; see also Mohamed, Chapter 86, this volume). While studies make diametrically opposite claims with respect to the empowering potential of microcredit, paradoxically, researchers almost unanimously accept that microcredit benefits the women clients' households. Studies claim that microcredit improves household incomes, helps diversify livelihoods and improves health and education outcomes (for a review, see Armendáriz de Aghion and Morduch, 2005).

The reasons behind the asymmetric impact that microcredit can have on women clients and their households – the 'impact paradox' – are not well understood. This is at least partly because studies that examine the impact of credit programme participation on women's empowerment are obsessively concerned with empowerment as an *outcome* and there is little attempt to study the *processes* that lead to it. These studies commonly choose to measure empowerment by using proxy indicators that detail women's *outcomes* in certain aspects of their lives, like the ability to contribute to the household economy, share domestic chores, make minor and major financial decisions and access personal spending money (see, for example, Hashemi et al., 1996; also Bali Swain, Chapter 91, this volume; Fujikake, Chapter 95, this volume). The *processes* leading to these *outcomes*, however, are largely ignored, including what is done with women's loans, changes in the use of women's work time, and the circumstances surrounding loan repayment.

This obsession with *outcomes* is despite the fact that feminist discourses have given us a fairly robust conceptual understanding of women's empowerment. Broadly speaking, women's empowerment is understood to comprise *processes* that result in expansion of women's agency, that is, their ability to make choices affecting their lives and situations. Certain conditions that characterise a woman's past and current environment, like parental education, asset ownership and access to credit are expected to facilitate an increase in agency. Expanding women's agency is further expected to affect their *outcomes* such as the ability to participate in household decision-making and to assert and fulfil preferences. Hence, empowerment is conceptualised as comprising both the *processes* that lead to expansion of women's agency and the *outcomes* that epitomise women's empowerment (Kabeer, 1999). The critical feature is that *processes* precede *outcomes*. Ignoring *processes* means that the dynamics of empowerment are understood only in a limited sense.

In this study, I attempt to understand the reasons behind the 'impact paradox' by focusing on the *processes* that invariably occur after women access microcredit. Specifically, I examine the *processes* surrounding the decision to use loans in a particular way and those surrounding repayment of the loan. I use women's testimonies to substantiate the findings. The chapter uses primary data from villages in Andhra Pradesh that participated in the Self Help Group (SHG) programme – India's pivotal state-run group-lending scheme that targets rural women (see also Bali Swain, Chapter 91, this volume).

The remainder of the chapter is organised as follows. The next section briefly describes India's main microcredit scheme. The third section introduces the data used in this study. The fourth section discusses the relationship between loan-use, repayment and women's empowerment. The fifth section closes with concluding comments and brief suggestions for future interventions.

Microcredit in India
In response to the sustainability crisis facing its rural financial sector and inspired by the global success of the microcredit movement, the Indian state launched its own version of a microcredit scheme in 1992 – the SHG programme. An SHG typically consists of around 10–15 women from poor communities who come together to save and access credit. While group formation is facilitated by non-governmental organisations or government agencies, the primary focus is on credit, with little attempt at capacity-building. A group begins its credit activity with each member saving 1 rupee (US$0.02) per day. These savings are collectively used as a revolving fund to provide loans to individual members. After six months of regular saving, the SHG is eligible to enhance its revolving fund by obtaining loans from private and public financial institutions. These institutions are in turn 100 per cent re-financed by the National Bank for Agricultural and Rural Development, India's apex rural bank.

The existing institutional structure is thus linked to individual SHGs and is referred to as the SHG Bank Linkage Programme. It uses the extensive state banking apparatus to provide credit to the rural poor, alongside innovations such as joint liability and peer monitoring to cultivate borrower discipline. With around 40 million clients and an average annual growth rate of 112.2 per cent between 1999 and 2007, it is the biggest and the fastest growing microcredit scheme in the world (Garikipati, 2008).

Data

During 2002–03, I directed and participated in a team survey of 397 women belonging to 27 SHGs from two villages, Gudimalakapura and Vepur in Mahabubnagar District in the southern state of Andhra Pradesh, India (see Garikipati, 2008). The survey included questions on the details of women's most recent loan, who controlled it, how it was used and the processes surrounding its repayment. On average groups comprised 14.7 members and had completed an average of 3.8 loan cycles, ranging from a minimum of one to a maximum of six. Loan terms varied from 6 to 24 months and the average loan amount received by a group was 26138 rupees (US$545) and ranged from 18000 rupees (US$375.3) to 91500 rupees (US$1907.87). Only occasionally did loan amounts vary from cycle to cycle. Self Help Groups generally divided the loan equally among its members and only in two cases did members pool their loans to invest in a joint project. Individual loans were mainly used to meet households' productive and consumption requirements and in some cases to finance self-managed enterprises. Repayment rates were reported to be 100 per cent.

During 2002–03 several individual and focus group interviews were also carried out with some of the SHG women interviewed in the above survey. These interviews were typically unstructured and were designed to capture the nuances behind several distinguishable experiences within the borrower groups. These interviews were used to contextualise the survey data.

Processes surrounding loan-use: implications for empowerment

The 397 SHG women surveyed used their loans in broadly four different ways: in enterprises that they manage or help manage (20.7 per cent), as working capital for family farms or businesses (57.2 per cent), to purchase or improve family land (10.1 per cent), and towards household maintenance (12.1 per cent). This suggests that nearly 80 per cent of women had their loans diverted into household requirements. This, in turn, implies that the demand for credit within the household, both for production and consumption, is high (see also Mohamed, Chapter 86, this volume). It is also the case that the loans received by women are mainly used to enhance or procure assets controlled primarily by their husbands, indicating that lending to women may actually amplify the existing resource divide between men and women.

In this section, I examine the processes surrounding these different loan-uses in order to understand the linkages between loan-use and empowerment. There are two steps to this enquiry. First, I examine whether there is a relationship between control over loan and loan-use. Second, I ask whether the way women's loans are used has any bearing on their repayment.

Control over loan is defined as a continuous variable. The degree or extent of a woman's control over loan is measured by how she relates to five distinct processes surrounding loan-use. These are: whether she had a say in the decision to join the SHG, in the use of the loan, in book-keeping, in marketing the product and in keeping the profit from the sale. If a woman did not participate in any of these processes, she is assumed to have lost control over her loan and is given a score of 0. A woman who participated in one of the processes is given a score of 1, and so on. The maximum score is 5, which is given if the woman participates in all the processes and is therefore assumed to be in full control over her loan.

Table 92.1 Loan-use by control over loan and source of repayment (N = 397), Andhra Pradesh, India

Control over loan	Loan-use				
	Self-managed enterprise	Family farm/ enterprise	Buy or improve land	Consume	No. of cases
Control = 0	0	19	8	0	27
Control = 1	6	89	18	20	133
Control = 2	25	62	7	15	109
Control = 3	32	55	7	13	107
Control = 4	14	2	0	0	16
Control = 5	5	0	0	0	5
No. of cases	82	227	40	48	397
Repayment source[1]					
Self-managed enterprise	70	0	0	0	70
Family farm/enterprise	11	21	7	2	41
Own wages	1	199	33	42	275
Sale of assets	0	7	0	4	11
No. of cases	82	227	40	48	397

Note: 1. In the case of multiple sources (8.3 per cent), the primary source was used.

Source: Author's own data.

The first panel of Table 92.1 presents women's loan-use by the extent of control they exert over their loans. Note that very few women are seen to be in full or near full control of their loans (5.3 per cent, N = 397). The table also shows that women who invest in their own businesses are likely to be ones who are in significant control over their loans (scoring between 3 and 5) (62.2 per cent, N = 82). The majority of the others see their loans used on household production or consumption (75.6 per cent, N = 315). This means that from the viewpoint of the women concerned, investing in self-managed businesses is the best outcome. Indeed, as women lose control over their loans, they are less likely to be able to do this. Women may not prefer using their loans on household requirements as this may mean further erosion of their control over loans. It may also leave them in a weaker position with respect to repayments and jeopardise access to future credit. Indeed, my repayment data suggests this as a possible reason.

The second panel of Table 92.1 presents women's loan-use by the source of repayment. As mentioned earlier, repayment rates in our sample are 100 per cent but, as seen here, this single figure may camouflage the various problems women encounter in repaying loans (see also Mayoux, 2005). In particular, the table shows that where loans were used on household requirements, women mainly relied on their own wages to repay loans (87 per cent, N = 315). Significantly, the majority of the women who use loans for own-enterprise repay from this source (85.4 per cent, N = 82). This suggests that even though a high proportion of women's loans are used to enhance household productive assets (67.3 per cent, N = 397), most are unable to rely on these for repayments.

In order to investigate these experiences further, I used unstructured interviews to gather testimonial evidence from the SHG women. Here I report only on the experiences of those women whose loans had been diverted into household requirements. Many of those who had used their loans for self-managed enterprises did relate positive experiences, as discussed in Garikipati (2008).

The experiences of women who have their loans diverted into family farms or businesses suggest that credit can have a detrimental effect on the women concerned in terms of constraining their livelihood options and their influence over household decisions. Chittamma, Narsamma, Kausalya and Devamma are women whose loans were used as working capital in family farms.[1] Before obtaining SHG loans, these women worked on family farms or within their households, but now they work as wage labourers mainly to meet repayments. In fact Chittamma and Devamma were explicitly told by their husbands to take up agriculture wage labouring to repay their loans. Agricultural wage work in rural India is considered socially inferior to work on own assets. In addition, these women, compelled by their need to make repayments, had pledged their labour for very low wages. In fact, Narsamma expressed the desire to discontinue SHG membership so that she could stop working as a wage labourer. In addition, Devamma finds that her husband, who used to discuss household finances with her, is now secretive about income from crop sales and remittances for fear that she may ask him to make repayments. These interviews revealed a deep resentment among women at having to withdraw their labour from work on their own assets and work for wages instead. Their experiences at least partly explain why women who exert significant control over their loans would prefer not to use them in family farms or businesses.

Among the women whose loans were used to meet the consumption needs of the household, Chandramma, Bheemamma and Laxmamma had voluntarily used their loans to avert a household crisis. Chandramma and Laxmamma also exerted significant control over their loans. All three women were involved in wage labouring prior to joining the SHG but now had to divert their wages into repayments. In addition, as a result of peer pressure, hostile at times, Chandramma had to sell her copper vessels and Laxmamma her goat. Their families did not consent to these sales and both women are suffering the consequences. For instance, Chandramma is not allowed to keep money from sales of crops or her husband's wages, both of which she controlled prior to the incident. She has even lost control over her own wages, which her husband now collects directly from her employer to stop her from using her wages to repay the loan. This was also the experience of several other women I interviewed, like Laxmamma, Hussainabebi and Kalamma. Although not common, women were also actively punished for what were seen as acts of defiance. For instance, Bheemamma and Laxmamma experienced deliberate negligence from their families with respect to their food consumption during particularly lean periods. Some of the women also reported suffering verbal and physical abuse as a result of repayment-related arguments. Testimonies suggest that, prior to procuring loans, these women had a greater say over household decisions and incomes, which has now diminished in case they try to divert resources away from the household. Some women also experienced abuse and coercion in their struggle to repay loans.

Loans procured by women may help their households improve incomes and enhance assets, but women's lack of co-ownership of family assets means they are unable to divert income from these sources towards repayments. In such cases, they may lose control over the allocation of their work time and may even find their relative powers in domestic relations depreciate. Where loans are used to avert a family crisis, using their own wages or selling assets for repayment can result in loss of authority over household resources and, in some instances, even results in hostility towards women. These experiences reveal some of the difficulties women face in repaying loans which are misleadingly obscured by high repayment rates. High repayment rates may in fact be a sign of social pressure that compels women to access credit for others in the household.

Concluding comments
With respect to the 'impact paradox' mentioned in the introduction we can identify three broad points. First, the credit needs of poor households are high and families are by and large able to divert loans procured by women into these activities. If the loan was not available, many households would be worse off in terms of their incomes, while substantial numbers could have plunged into consumption crises. Second, women's lack of co-ownership of their household's productive assets means that they are unable to divert any income from such sources into repayments and have to rely on the limited means available to them – wage labouring and sale of smaller belongings. This has an adverse impact on both the allocation of women's work time and on their say over family resources. Finally, if loans given to women continue to be diverted into household needs without any change in their asset positions then this can widen the existing resource divide between men as owners and women as labourers and prove to be a disempowering experience for the women concerned.

These findings have two main policy implications. First, they indicate that microcredit may not be the right intervention for very poor women. Instead, a social security programme like the IGVGD (Income Generating Vulnerable Group Development) intervention offered by BRAC, which provides monthly food rations to the very poor, may be more suitable (for details, see Ahmed et al., 2007). This may not only mitigate their repayment burdens but also give them the opportunity to be better prepared for future credit interventions. Second, where loan diversion by households cannot be monitored, women's joint ownership of household assets is integral to their empowerment (see also Deere, Chapter 53, this volume). One way to challenge the patriarchal hold on families' productive assets is to make credit conditional on asset transfers in favour of the women concerned. This is likely to be most effectively achieved where assets are acquired using women's loan money.

Acknowledgements
Financial support for this research was received from Department for International Development (Award no. R7617) and Newton Trust (Award no. INT 2.05[d]). I am indebted to my research team for field assistance. Please send comments to S.Garikipati@liv.ac.uk.

Note
1. Pseudonyms are used to protect the identities of women informants.

Select bibliography
Ahmed, Akhter U., Agnes R. Quisumbing and John F. Hoddinott (2007) *Relative Efficacy of Food and Cash Transfers in Improving Food Security and Livelihood of the Ultra-Poor in Bangladesh*, report submitted to

the World Food Programme, Bangladesh, Washington, DC: International Food Policy Research Institute, available at: http://documents.wfp.org/stellent/groups/public/documents/liaison_offices/wfp144615.pdf (accessed 17 June 2009).

Armendáriz de Aghion, Beatrize and Jonathan Morduch (2005) *The Economics of Microfinance*, Cambridge, MA: Massachusetts Institute of Technology Press.

Daley-Harris, Sam (2006) *State of the Microcredit Summit Campaign Report 2006*, Washington, DC: Microcredit Summit Campaign, available at: http://www.microcreditsummit.org/pubs/reports/socr/2006/SOCR06.pdf (accessed 17 June 2009).

Garikipati, Supriya (2008) 'The impact of lending to women on household vulnerability and women's empowerment: evidence from India', *World Development*, **36** (12), 2620–42.

Hashemi, Syed M., Ruth Sidney Schuler and Ann P. Riley (1996) 'Rural credit programs and women's empowerment in Bangladesh', *World Development*, **24** (4), 635–53.

Kabeer, Naila (1999) 'Resources, agency, achievements: reflections on the measurement of women's empowerment', *Development and Change*, **30** (3), 435–64.

Mayoux, Linda (2005) *Women's Empowerment through Sustainable Micro-Finance: Rethinking 'Best Practice'*, Enterprise Development Impact Assessment Information Service (EDIAIS), discussion draft, Manchester: EDIAIS.

93 Gender and poverty in microfinance: illustrations from Zambia
Irene Banda Mutalima

Microfinance is a useful intervention for poverty reduction because it enables poor people to participate in their own development through the establishment or enhancement of enterprises which, in increasing incomes, nominally offer the prospect of improved livelihoods. In recognition of the importance of microcredit, the United Nations (UN) declared 2005 as the year of microfinance, and the 2006 Nobel Peace prize was shared between Dr Muhammad Yunus, a microfinance pioneer, and his microfinance institution (MFI), the Grameen Bank.

In 2007 the Microcredit Summit Campaign reported that as at the end of December 2006, 3316 microfinance institutions had reached 133 million clients, 93 million of whom were among the poorest when they took their first loan. It is assumed that 465 million members of poorest families were positively impacted. This profile of microfinance has triggered change in its perception from a poverty or development programme to a financial sector component.

Traditional banks which previously would not have served this market, are now embracing microentrepreneurs. The industry has accordingly seen tremendous growth in the amounts of money being invested. The Consultative Group for Assisting the Poor (CGAP), the World Bank microfinance body, indicates that between 2004 and 2006, the stock of foreign capital investment into microfinance globally more than tripled to US$4 billion (Reille and Forster, 2008). The report further acknowledges that microfinance

> is a very attractive proposition for a growing segment of socially responsible investors. The socially responsible investment (SRI) market is huge, with over US$4 trillion in assets. The emerging markets share accounts for a meagre US$5 billion, but this is growing fast. The SRI world comprises a wide spectrum of investors with differing expectations, from those willing to receive below-market returns to those seeking competitive returns within the context of a social mandate. SRIs are attracted to microfinance institutions because they are 'double bottom-line' institutions that seek to have a positive social impact alongside financial returns. (Ibid.: 1)

This support was initially driven by the donor community who worked through non-governmental organisations (NGOs), as they were perceived to be appropriately positioned within the poor communities to provide this service. They helped to develop important innovative approaches to provide credit to affected families for immediate poverty relief. Various studies endorsed the understanding that the biggest burden of visible poverty on families is carried by women: it is most likely to be women who worry about putting food on the table and ensuring continued sustenance for the family (see also Chant, Chapter 15, this volume). Gender dimensions drew from this understanding to call for interventions targeted at women. In microfinance, the group methodology was accepted as a way of providing not only credit to women, but additional community support (see also Casier, Chapter 94, this volume).

The focus on women triggered diametrically opposed views that targeting women especially in groups was largely a strategy for institutional advantage given the belief that women tended to be better payers and were more willing to work in groups (see Maclean, Chapter 87, this volume). Another perspective on this issue is that providing services to groups reduces costs for MFIs, even if some surveys show that women are not always keen to work in groups but simply have this methodology imposed upon them (ibid.; see also Musonda, 2006)

The motive for benefits to the MFI is extrapolated to social investors in microfinance. The Reille and Forster report cited above, while acknowledging that social investors commit microfinance institutions to high transparency on their social mission, also cautions that there are other investors who are motivated purely by the returns on their investment. It questions whether a profit-maximising investor will allow an MFI to uphold its social mission to poverty reduction at the expense of potential profits.

While this chapter does not dwell on this debate, it recognises that microfinance does in fact impact both the MFI and its clients, and that there is a lack of clarity on whether the original intention to reduce poverty is being compromised by the evolution of the industry. Working on the premise that gender-sensitive approaches to microfinance are a critical component of poverty reduction, this chapter aims to examine some of the issues that cannot afford to be ignored in future policy.

The need to survive as organisations

Older MFIs that were started with donor funds and with a development focus have had to take stock of the encroaching commercialisation and regulation in microfinance. Donor funds are on the wane and donors are calling for institutional sustainability. Microfinance institutions are under pressure to deliver primarily to the latter goal such that gender priorities are threatened with having to take more of a backseat (see Figure 93.1).

Enhancing a culture of sustainability
Where previously practitioners would have been more concerned with impacts on clients, they now have to worry about keeping their organisations afloat. Quick remedies have been sought such as identifying profitable products that are less risky, and bigger loans to individuals, especially the more creative entrepreneurs. Inadvertently, these products have tended to exclude women clients and smaller loans because they pose the highest risk of default and lack collateral. Some institutions have had to make the painful choice of avoiding risk altogether by shifting their focus to giving credit to employed people so that loan repayments are easier tracked through payrolls. While this has the desired effect in enhancing institutional sustainability, it begins to negate the purpose of microfinance in poverty reduction.

Embracing professionalism
The microfinance employment market is not yet as vibrant as it might be, and securing professional staff continues to be a challenge. This impacts negatively on sustainability as the quality of service fails to meet expectations. These institutions then grapple with staff turnover while gender discussions tend to fall by the wayside.

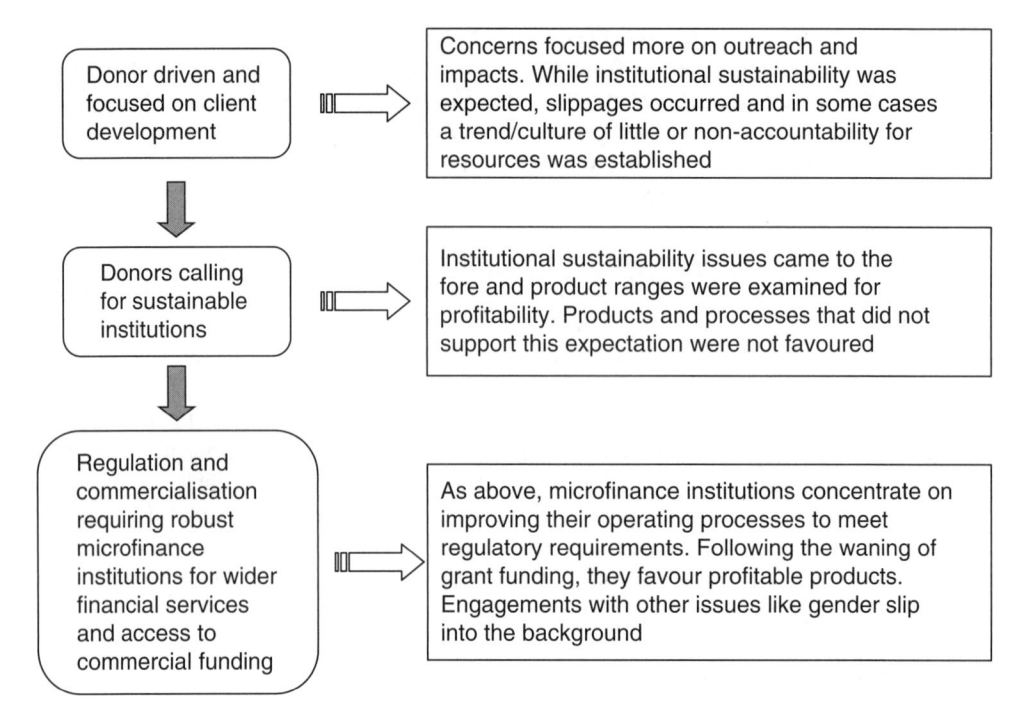

Figure 93.1 Development paths of microfinance institutions (1980s–2000s)

Donor driven and focused on client development	Concerns focused more on outreach and impacts. While institutional sustainability was expected, slippages occurred and in some cases a trend/culture of little or non-accountability for resources was established
Donors calling for sustainable institutions	Institutional sustainability issues came to the fore and product ranges were examined for profitability. Products and processes that did not support this expectation were not favoured
Regulation and commercialisation requiring robust microfinance institutions for wider financial services and access to commercial funding	As above, microfinance institutions concentrate on improving their operating processes to meet regulatory requirements. Following the waning of grant funding, they favour profitable products. Engagements with other issues like gender slip into the background

Figure 93.1 Development paths of microfinance institutions (1980s–2000s)

Securing funding for continued business

With the waning of donor support, MFI funding is mostly available through loans or equity. Both of these require closer inspection of the operations of MFIs, and the need to make them more robust. Of necessity therefore, these institutions opt for minimum risk exposure and assured profit margins. Product design has been tailored to meet these outcomes and not to identify purposefully with poverty reduction.

The situation of women clients

Women often find themselves in the marketplace because of immediate needs to provide a livelihood for their families in times of poverty. Usually they position themselves in the informal sector with scanty preparation, and their businesses frequently perform poorly. With reference to Zambia, JC Parker Development Alternatives Inc. (1996) argue that only entrepreneurs who have had the necessary training and business know-how actually grow their business. The fact that women-run enterprises in Zambia show the shortest life cycle, averaging four years, testifies to weak business performance. This is attributed largely to lack of education and experience among female microentrepreneurs (ibid.; see also Casier, Chapter 94, this volume).

With a lack of key skills to grow businesses, credit may not necessarily produce growth. Indeed, some cases studies have shown that these businesses de-capitalise and hence have difficulties paying the last instalments of the loan (Musonda, 2006: 27). This whole process makes this target market a risky one for the MFI.

Levels of entrepreneurship and ambition
In Zambia, as in many other parts of the world, husbands are expected to provide economically for the family, with wives' contributions regarded merely as supplementing that effort. Even where a husband is no longer in gainful employment, women's incomes may still not be viewed as a long-term means of sustaining the family. The low level of 'ambition' attached to stereotypical gender roles tends to inhibit growth (see also Casier, Chapter 94, this volume; Mohamed, Chapter 86, this volume).

Another factor inhibiting growth is inadequate business planning, with a survey sample in Zambia showing that this was the cause attributed by 57 per cent of respondents to default on loan repayments (Musonda, 2006). The clients confessed to having had little time to reflect on how best to utilise borrowed funds. On top of this, MFIs which focus on survival may not integrate business development services for their clients. Whatever the case, once women become 'bad credit risks', the chances of them getting another loan become slimmer.

Market conditions
Clearly market conditions also determine enterprise survival and growth (see also Casier, Chapter 94, this volume). Where the general macroeconomic outlook is that of minimal growth, market vibrancy is lacking and microenterprises are affected. Where there is strong seasonality in the market, clients often lead a hand-to-mouth existence during lean periods with no business expansion. In such cases MFIs tend to reduce lending to such clients in order to contain risk. Given a lack of business preparation, and low ambitions, it is not surprising that it is often female clients who are most affected by instability in the market and are therefore the ones left out in MFI lending slow-downs.

Mutual compatibility
Although it is nominally intended that poverty reduction and the survival of MFIs should be mutually compatible, these goals are often at odds with one another, with prejudicial effects on the scope for gender-sensitivity. For example, as long as institutions are dealing with issues of their own sustainability, other issues tend to remain overshadowed. Approaches to mainstream gender will not be taken seriously if there is no clear indication of how these will add to MFIs' sustainability. This arguably points to the need to build a sounder business case around gender dimensions in MFI operations.

Learning from gender audits in Zambia
In 2004, the Humanist Institute for Development Co-operation (HIVOS), a Dutch aid organisation, commissioned gender audits with two microfinance institutions in Zambia: the Christian Enterprise Trust of Zambia Limited (CETZAM) and Promotion of Rural Initiatives and Development Enterprises (PRIDE). Both audits were conducted on the basis of interviews with the MFIs' clients and personnel with a view to contributing to the 'improvement of the MFIs' performance, by ensuring that services are equally attractive for men and women, considering the different needs, priorities and characteristics that women and men have' (Athmer, 2004a: 4; also Athmer, 2004b).

The gender discussion in this regard has major importance in the Zambian context. The Zambian Central Statistical Office conducted a Living Conditions Survey in 1998 and found that the members of female-headed households were more likely to be poor than their counterparts in male-headed units. In terms of food poverty, 61 per cent of female-headed households faced food shortages compared with 52 per cent of male-headed households. Furthermore, female-headed households had longer spells of food insecurity, as evidenced by child malnutrition being higher in terms of stunting and being underweight. This information provides a compelling case for MFIs to design products that allow them to address a sex-disaggregated constituency and still be sustainable, as evidenced to some degree by the findings of the gender audits of the two MFIs targeted in Zambia.

The gender audits conducted with the MFIs yielded a mixture of findings. On the positive side, women clients felt that their decision-making power within the household increased after having received loans. By the same token, women's limited levels of personal control over their loans, their limited assets and power within the family, and their triple roles of mother, spouse and entrepreneur posed serious obstacles for business growth – and even creation. For example married women, who generally lacked control over collateral, had to obtain their husbands' permission to take loans in the first place. On top of this, the hours required from clients to spend in meetings diverted precious time from their business ventures, and hit women particularly hard given their already heavy load of multiple responsibilities. Aside from the fact that MFIs had no means of supporting women clients to overcome these obstacles, it was also felt by both female and male clients that MFIs might have provided them with more flexible and diverse services in smaller groups or on an individual basis, faster and more timely disbursements, and a reduction of the risk that clients would lose their own savings when businesses failed to cope with loan repayments. At the level of organisations, it was also noted in the audits that there was little common understanding of gender-sensitivity, that gender was not a sufficient priority in mission statements, and that not enough was being done to monitor numbers of female clients included in outreach services.

Although this feedback potentially benefited both organisations, it should be noted that audits of this nature, while providing useful information, tend to focus more on improving outcomes for clients, without making the link as to how this will help MFIs attain sustainability (although see also Maclean, Chapter 87, this volume). The question remains, therefore, whether it is possible to create a framework that allows development of a 'business case' around the incorporation of gender into microfinance in different contexts.

Issues to consider in a 'business case' framework
It is now increasingly widely recognised that microfinance institutions have to be run as businesses even if there is still a social mission to microfinance. The fact is that most studies also show that gender dimensions are critical in poverty reduction, and these disparate elements have to be brought together in a way that will not only enhance women's position at the grassroots, but also allow MFIs to flourish sufficiently well that they create the desired impact. This chapter proposes that unless this discussion comes together in a business case framework, an opportunity for significant poverty reduction efforts will be lost.

Sahlman (1997) suggests that the business model has to think through the key drivers of success or failure. He proposes, first, that the organisation has the right team with the necessary experience. Second, he draws attention to the importance of targeted markets and growth areas: MFIs need to define their specific niches and how gender issues can be integrated to yield optimum benefit. Third, institutions have to define issues in the external environment and how these will impact on business. Finally, risks and rewards need to be assessed and weighted towards achieving the intended goals of the organisation and all its constituencies. This is the place where gender considerations run the most risk of being filtered out, but by the same token remain even more crucial to take into account.

Conclusion

There is a substantial body of evidence that microfinance can make significant gains in poverty reduction. It is also evident that gender dimensions cannot be ignored in the fight against poverty, just as it is the case that MFIs need to be sustainable. The dilemma is that current popular models of microfinance create a divide that largely promotes one ideal to the detriment of the other. This chapter suggests that acceptable levels of compatibility need to be established in order to strengthen the gender-sensitivity of institutions working towards poverty reduction. One strategy, over and above those highlighted by Sahlman (1997) is that 'champions' within the industry – namely, MFIs which are successfully attaining sustainability as well as fully engaging gender issues – are encouraged to share best practices. Additional steps are for MFIs to incorporate gender properly into their mission statements and commit to regular monitoring and evaluation, for MFIs to explore the profitability of incorporating gender dimensions in product design, and for the lobbying of donors to assist in harmonising gender equality goals with institutional sustainability.

Acknowledgements

This chapter draws substantially on a paper I presented at the Global Microcredit Summit, Trade and Convention Centre, Halifax, Nova Scotia, 12–15 November 2006, on the subject of 'Microfinance and Gender Equality: Are We Getting There?'.

Select bibliography

Athmer, Gabrielle (2004a) 'Gender audit CETZAM Zambia', unpublished report commissioned by Humanist Institute for Development Co-operation (HIVOS), Harare.
Athmer, Gabrielle (2004b) 'Gender audit PRIDE Zambia', unpublished report commissioned by Humanist Institute for Development Co-operation (HIVOS), Harare.
JC Parker Development Alternatives Inc. (JCPDAI) (1996) *Micro and Small-Scale Enterprises in Zambia: Results of the Nationwide Survey*, London: Graham Bannock and Partners Ltd.
Musonda, Clive (2006) 'Suggested solutions and recommendations for managing delinquency in CETZAM', unpublished survey, Christian Enterprise Trust of Zambia Limited, Lusaka.
Reille, Xavier and Sarah Forster (2008) 'Foreign capital investment in microfinance balancing social and financial returns', *CGAP Focus Note*, **44**, 1.
Sahlman, William (1997) 'How to write a great business plan', *Harvard Business Review*, July–August, 97–108, available at: http://web.mit.edu/peso/Pes1/HBS (accessed 8 June 2009).

// 94 The impact of microcredit programmes on survivalist women entrepreneurs in The Gambia and Senegal
Bart Casier

Introduction

The concept of entrepreneurship has become increasingly popular in recent times, as was highlighted in a special report about entrepreneurship by *The Economist* entitled 'Global heroes' in March 2009:

> The entrepreneurial idea has gone mainstream, supported by political leaders on the left as well as on the right, championed by powerful pressure groups, reinforced by a growing infrastructure of universities and venture capitalists and embodied by widely popular business heroes such as Oprah Winfrey, Richard Branson and India's software kings.[1]

This idea is not only confined to the wealthy economies, but has also been exported to poorer nations, where more and more programmes focus on entrepreneurship as a tool for economic development. The most popular approach to stimulate entrepreneurship has been microcredit, as invented by Nobel prizewinner Muhammad Yunus, founder of the Grameen Bank. This has led to what Ananya Roy (Chapter 84, this volume) calls 'the financialisation of development', and has been particularly relevant to women who are often the bulk of clients in microfinance programmes (see Maclean, Chapter 87, this volume; Mohamed, Chapter 86, this volume).

With this in mind, my chapter focuses on the impact of two microcredit programmes on business growth among low-income women in two West African countries: The Gambia and Senegal, former British and French colonies respectively. It considers women's main motivations to start a business, the capacity of microcredit to generate growth at individual and group levels, and the role of gender in business.

Background to the study

My case study focuses on two localities: Cissay Marjow, in The Gambia, and Pikine, in Senegal.

Cissay Marjow is a typical rural village situated in the North Bank region, one of the poorest areas of The Gambia. It is located only 60 kilometres from the capital, Banjul, but it takes about two-and-a-half hours to get there. The village is not connected to a water network and there is no electricity. The majority of the villagers are subsistence farmers. The beneficiaries of the microcredit programme, which is organised by the Gambian non-governmental organisation (NGO), ADWAC (Agency for the Development of Women and Children), are the 50 members of the Cissay Marjow women's group.

In Pikine the setting is quite different. Pikine is located on the outskirts of Dakar, the capital of Senegal, and a bustling city which is home to over 2 million inhabitants. Although Pikine is a poor community, receiving many migrants from the interior of the country, geographically it has huge advantages compared to Cissay Marjow. For example it is located in the centre of a big market and close to many service-providing agencies. There is access to the Internet and transport is not an issue. In Pikine the study focuses on L'Espace de Concertation et d'Orientation de Pikine Nord (ECO/PN), a well-established Senegalese organisation supported by the Belgian NGO Terre Nouvelle, which deals with around ninety women's groups.

The fieldwork on the impacts of the Gambian and Senegalese microcredit programmes was conducted during 2008–09, and entailed on-site standardised open-ended interviews with beneficiaries as well as with administrative staff.

Findings

Business motivation
For the women of Cissay Marjow, the motivation to start a business was very clear: they had no choice. Poverty forced the women to engage in petty trade in order to sustain their families. Agricultural production went down because of a continuing decrease in rainfall during the rainy season. As articulated by one group of women in Cissay Marjow: 'The agricultural income has become very weak because there is not enough water during the rainy season; that's why we are forced more and more to do business to sustain our families. It is because of that we cannot save anything; it is that that makes us tired.'[2]

From the interviews it was clear that the women's motivation to start a business was not a positive choice, but a negative one, a choice made because there were no other options. They have little or no knowledge about what they are doing, how the market is structured and how they could improve the business. Apart from one woman who had a small sewing business, most other women were involved in petty trading and were selling the same kind of merchandise: Omo,[3] vegetable oil, palm oil, dried fish and vegetables.

The idea to start a business came not from the women themselves but was an initiative of ADWAC, who helped them to identify possible enterprises, gave them access to credit, and trained them in basic business practices such as record-keeping, cost–benefit analysis and so on. One woman explains how she got the idea to start a retail business: 'We were all together busy learning and then the people of ADWAC introduced the system. I was thinking about it and then I thought that this could give me some income and could improve the situation of my family.'

In The Gambia, many NGOs and government programmes are involved in the creation of income-generating activities. However, few organisations specialise in this. Instead, most of the organisations treat entrepreneurship as part of a general development package. This means that the knowledge of many NGOs about entrepreneurship is limited and that most offer the same packages of income-generating activities such as poultry, soap-making, tie and dye, and batik.

In Pikine the motivation to engage in business appears more positive. Although poverty remains the main driver, women were also motivated by the success stories of other businesswomen. One member of the women's group succeeded in exporting couscous to Italy and another woman started her own restaurant, employing three people. Although unemployment is very high in Pikine, there are more job opportunities than, for example, in Cissay Marjow, so the chances that women make a positive rational choice in light of opportunity costs are higher. The women started their credit union on their own initiative by seeing other women doing the same thing, so there is proof of collective learning. Non-governmental organisations are supporting them, but the women are the main initiators.

Growth potential
Many evaluations of microcredit programmes focus only on indicators such as repayment rates and the ability of the microcredit programmes to be cost-effective (see for example, Maclean, Chapter 87, this volume; Mohamed, Chapter 86, this volume). Very few studies focus on what the beneficiaries actually do with the money they are lent. Even at the grassroots the people managing microcredit programmes have little knowledge about how money is used by the beneficiaries. This said, there is a growing awareness of the importance of monitoring not only the financial flows but also the impact of the microcredit funds on the lives of the women they aim to help.

Recalling that one aim of my study is to look at whether microcredit programmes are able to create growth and at what level, a review of the two microcredit programmes in The Gambia and Senegal revealed that both experienced significant growth on two counts. First, in respect of capital in the microcredit fund, this grew by 15 per cent per annum for Cissay Marjow between 2002 and 2009, and at 32 per cent per annum in Pikine between 2004 and 2009. Growth was also observed at the level of the number of people having access to microcredit. This doubled in Cissay Marjow from 25 to 50 people, and increased in Pikine from 12 to 90 women's groups.

Annual growth rates at 15 per cent to 32 per cent are results which most modern-managed hedge funds can only dream of, even before the current global financial crisis! We see also that in the village of Cissay Marjow the interest rates are almost double those paid by women in Pikine. In Cissay Marjow the women pay 10 per cent for three months, in Pikine they pay 5 per cent for four months. Nonetheless, capital in Pikine is growing faster than the capital in Cissay Marjow (at 32 per cent per annum). This is because in Pikine the women can benefit from economies of scale and a better market. Every group that joins the credit scheme has to pay an initial join-up fee and at every meeting they have to contribute an amount. They also organise activities at the inter-group level which makes the capital grow faster. The coordinator of Terre Nouvelle West-Africa gives an example of such inter-group reinvestment:

> last year, the women identified an activity; they bought materials for big events, big pots, cooking stoves and the like. And really this activity worked very well, they rented the materials to the members at half price. To have access to that service, the members had to buy a member card at 1000 CFA[4] (US$2.1) for each member, so you can imagine if you have 3000 members you have already three million CFA (US$6366)!

Here the women are exploiting the possibilities of economies of scale, something that is not possible in Cissay Marjow because of the small size and relative isolation of the village. The Pikine women used the proceeds of the capital to invest in collectively oriented and managed goods such as the construction of a maternity centre.

Nonetheless, the data collected in Cissay Marjow shows that the microcredit programme has still had an important impact in the village. Before the microcredit programme there were only seven women who had a business. Now there are 12 women who 'have a table at the market'. However, most women were involved in retail trade, selling virtually identical items at the market. Asked if this increase in women doing the same business in the villages did not increase competition, they said that this was not the case. As explained by one pioneer businesswoman:

> No, my income did not go down. If I make my calculations, in the beginning, I had just one kilo of dried fish to sell and I was just looking for a small profit to be able to cook something. Now I can manage also problems concerning the children's health, education and all that. In the beginning, we were selling in a small place but now with these twelve tables it starts to look like a real market.

It seems that the benefits of the programme are not only evaluated at the individual level, with the fact that the village has now a 'real market' being equally important.

Common to both localities, however, is that women have a tendency to increase the number of people/groups that have access to microfinance instead of increasing the finance available per person or group. This could be socially motivated but could also be a strategy to spread the risk.

Limits to growth
Is microcredit generating growth at the level of small and microenterprises managed by women? Does microfinance kickstart growth? Can it bring about autonomous growth creation?

The conclusion that arises when talking to the women and the people managing the programmes is that microcredit has an important impact at the level of basic poverty alleviation but that it is not sufficient to generate growth. It can lift a woman from level A to level B, but fails to bring them to C or D. Very little of the profit they make is reinvested to improve their business. Although the margins they earn on their businesses are quite high (up to 50 per cent, discounting labour and transport costs), the little profit they have in real terms evaporates once they pay back the loan and take care of family expenditures. Therefore, the growth rate is very low or almost non-existent as articulated by the coordinator of ADWAC:

> Well, the reality is that the woman is mostly the only one acquiring some money for the family, that means that the little that is earned is immediately consumed by the family for food, health and so on. The growth rate is very slow; it will take her more than ten years to reach where you want them to reach. Almost 80 per cent of the profit goes to feeding the family, if she does not have any support, any injection from outside, really it will take this women more than six years before she can ladder up. It is a problem.

The women as well as NGO staff whom I interviewed considered that the credit available to each woman was too low (about US$20 for three months). This was seen as the biggest constraint to growth creation. Apart from the microcredit programme, the women have no access to finance. When asked if they would consider approaching a bank, they answer that they are afraid of banks, and 'normal' banks would probably not lend to illiterate women with little or no collateral to offer. The interviewees also gave some examples of private investors exploiting this vacuum, charging up to 100 per cent interest. Some women, however, are able to access different credit schemes. In Pikine one woman was able to obtain 500 000 CFA (US$1059) through different credit schemes and used that money to have access to a bigger loan at a bank and eventually started her own restaurant. In a place like Cissay Marjow, by contrast, this is not possible. Yet access to credit is not the only barrier to business growth.

Cultural concepts of entrepreneurship and gender
The work of Della-Giusta and Phillips (2006) on female entrepreneurs in The Gambia suggests that gender-differentiated cultural concepts of entrepreneurship constitute one of women's major burdens in the business arena. According to these authors, women are brought up associating the pursuit of money with immorality, and thus value conflict prevention, fairness and equity, alongside distancing themselves from what men see as the virtues that are most needed in business: assertiveness, acquisitiveness and even ruthlessness. The pressures to conform with 'feminine' behavioural norms seem to be stronger than considerations about what might be 'best for business', and this accordingly helps to explain why most women's businesses remain small (ibid.).

Sidy Guèye Ngiang,[5] who manages the Pikine programme noticed similar perceptions of entrepreneurship in the Senegalese context:

> They have a certain value system that makes the social to be more important than financial resources. Everything the women gain is reinvested at the group level. They prefer the accumulation of social capital more then the accumulation of capital that cannot be of use for the whole community. This value system is particularly important in subsistence economies (of women), and makes it difficult for (the women) to succeed. Maybe the entrepreneurial spirit is just not there? Maybe they just want to survive?

Interviews revealed that in general there exists quite a negative perception of entrepreneurship, described by one interviewee as 'making money on the back of others'. This could explain why most individual profit is eventually transferred to the collective level.

In many cases women are the sole breadwinners in the households, as their men are unemployed or have to leave the compound to look for a job elsewhere. The danger is that microcredit programmes that focus only on women might strengthen this tendency, thus increasing the burden on women in poor communities still further. Before women were responsible for the food crops, men provided the cash. This has changed now, as pronounced by the coordinator of the Cissay Marjow programme: 'The woman has now some money, can buy fish for the family, buy candles, even cigarettes for the husband.' Chant (2007), with reference to The Gambia and beyond, refers to such tendencies as the 'feminisation of responsibility and/or obligation' (see also Chant, Chapter 15, this volume). Women tend to take over many responsibilities that were traditionally men's, such as providing income for the family (see also Brydon, Chapter 16, this volume). At the same time men are not generally increasing their participation in reproductive labour, despite their diminishing role as sole or chief earners in households (ibid.: 233; see also Budlender, 2008). This represents something of a paradox for development agencies who focus on women because they feel that by helping them they have the biggest impact on the household. They also claim to strengthen the woman's bargaining power in the household. The question remains as to whether this latter objective is reached (see also Mohamed, Chapter 86, this volume; Sweetman, Chapter 88, this volume).

Conclusion
The aim of this case study was to identify whether microcredit programmes could generate growth and at what level. A clear sign of growth of communal organised capital was noted. This growth was generated through rather high interest rates, admission fees and the organising of income-generating activities at the communal level. Contrary to growth at the group level, however, there was little evidence of growth at the level of individual businesses. This was explained by different potential causes, the first being the motivation to start a business. Although some women showed genuine entrepreneurial behaviour, most women were engaging in income-generating activities out of pure necessity; especially in the case of Cissay Marjow. Second was the fact that the amount of individual credit was very low, the interest rates high, and that, relative to their income, the cost of women's expenditures at the household level made it very difficult for any to reinvest part of their profit in their businesses. Third, the latter was exacerbated by the fact that many women were the only breadwinners in their households. A fourth important element is the perception of entrepreneurship, which is generally regarded as a 'male thing'. Women are allowed to make some money to sustain their family, but social acceptance of real business creation by women is still very low. If microcredit has the ambition to create and support businesses it is important for policymakers to realise these limiting factors and to critically examine the idea that microcredit alone can transform pure survivalist enterprises into thriving growth-generating businesses. More research is needed on the impact of microcredit programmes on individual business growth, since most data focuses too much on indicators such as reimbursement and capital growth, which hides the real impacts on the lives of the beneficiaries.

Acknowledgements
This study would not have been possible without the support of ADWAC and Terre Nouvelle. I would like to thank both organisations for the good work they are doing, their courage, and their intellectual openness.

Notes
1. *The Economist*, 14–20 March 2009, p. 3.
2. All quotes from Gambian informants are presented verbatim. In the case of Senegalese informant quotes, these are translated from French into English by the author.
3. A trade name which in The Gambia is used generically to refer to 'soap'.
4. 'CFA' stands for the African franc, the currency used in former French colonies in Africa, which had a fixed exchange rate with the Euro of around 656 CFA in 2009.
5. I have used informants' real names in cases where I was given explicit consent to do so.

Select bibliography
Budlender, Debbie (2008) *The Statistical Evidence on Care and Non-Care Work Across Six Countries*, Gender and Development Programme Paper Number 4, Geneva: United Nations Research Institute for Social Development.

Chant, Sylvia (2007) *Gender, Generation and Poverty: Exploring the 'Feminisation of Poverty' in Africa, Asia and Latin America*, Cheltenham, UK and Northampton, MA, USA: Edward Elgar.

Della Giusta, Marina and Christine Phillips (2006) 'Small enterprises and development: women entrepreneurs in The Gambia', *Journal of International Development*, **18** (8), 1–15.

95 Methodologies for evaluating women's empowerment in poverty alleviation programmes: illustrations from Paraguay and Honduras
Yoko Fujikake

It is frequently emphasised that the key to women's empowerment is to increase their self-reliance by bolstering their capacity to make choices, to gain confidence through self-determination, and to exercise control over both material and non-material resources. It is also generally stressed that empowerment is a process rather than an 'end state' (see for example, Fujikake, 2008; Kabeer, 1999; Rowlands, 1997; also Bali Swain, Chapter 91, this volume; Bibars, Chapter 89, this volume). The recent focus on empowerment is an important part of the neoliberal transformation taking place around the world as nations attempt to downsize their welfare bureaucracies and reinvent themselves as streamlined and efficient. Along with economic liberalisation, austerity programmes, privatisation and participatory governance, empowerment is now an accepted part of development orthodoxy (Sharma, 2008: xvi).

However, the term 'empowerment' was not coined by international financial institutions (IFIs) such as the World Bank. The term actually emerged from the Non-Governmental Organisation (NGO) Forum of the Second World Conference on Women at Copenhagen in 1980. Yet while in the early stages 'empowerment' was used mainly by feminist NGOs, within a decade it had become common parlance in international institutions and national government organisations. In 1995 the Beijing Platform For Action (BPFA), adopted at the Fourth World Conference on Women, was cast as an 'agenda for women's empowerment'. In light of elevated interest in empowerment issues today, the term empowerment is widely used by a range of different bodies from women's organisations and NGOs, to governments, and bilateral and multilateral agencies. Indeed, arguably the biggest contemporary international platform – the Millennium Development Goals (MDGs) – includes the empowerment of women alongside the promotion of gender equality as a specific goal (MDG3), with frequent proclamations that this third goal is essential for achieving all the others. In short, empowerment has become a means as well as an end of development for many governments and powerful institutions such as the United Nations (UN) (Sharma, 2008: 2).

The demand that women's empowerment be the goal or ultimate objective of many development policies and programmes, especially in relation to poverty reduction, leads, naturally enough, to the necessity for empowerment indicators to reveal the extent to which women have actually benefited in personal terms from specific interventions. However, the monitoring and evaluation of empowerment outcomes (and processes) remain in a liminal state, and project teams in international agencies and national governments alike still lack tools which are sufficiently robust to determine whether and how projects and policies aimed at empowering stakeholders reach their intended goals (Alsop and Heinsohn, 2005).

Part of the reason why evaluating empowerment remains limited is not only because there are a plethora of views on what empowerment is, but because even when defined, empowerment is multifaceted, and is usually rather intangible and uncountable on the ground. It is a considerable challenge to generate quantitative measures of women's empowerment since the criteria for 'richness' and 'happiness' of people in the area where development practice is undertaken (or not) is highly subjective and can differ between individuals and groups, as well as from the criteria of the evaluators (Fujikake, 2008). It also remains questionable as to whether outsiders can ever effectively evaluate whether gender relationships have or have not changed for women in a given society as a result of development interventions (ibid.). This said, there are a variety of methods available, as discussed below.

Measuring women's empowerment

The three most commonly used models or methodologies to measure women's empowerment to date are the World Bank's (WB) model, the Canadian International Development Association (CIDA) model, and the Socio-Economic and Gender Analysis (SEAGA) model developed by the Food and Agriculture Organisation (FAO), International Labour Organisation (ILO) and Clark University. These models entail different types of research method and evaluation frameworks, which are briefly reviewed prior to introducing an alternative model developed by the present author in the context of Japanese-funded development projects in Paraguay and Honduras.

The World Bank model

The WB model is based on a framework comprising three domains (state, market, and society) and three levels (macro, intermediate and local). At the intersection of domains and levels a person can experience varying 'degrees of empowerment' (DOE). Two clusters of interdependent factors are associated with varying DOE in individual or group experiences: the agency of an actor and the opportunity structure within which that actor operates. Simultaneous analysis of agency and opportunity helps explain why an actor is empowered, or not, and to what degree. However, evaluation methods have to be drawn on the basis of individual projects and so are difficult to compare across countries or use in any general sense. Moreover, although factors associated with empowerment such as legal and economic phenomena are taken into consideration, qualitative issues such as power, and the actual processes of change remain out of the picture, even if it is acknowledged that these are important.

The CIDA model

The CIDA adopted the 'Five-Step Women's Empowerment Framework' developed by Sara Longwe in 1988 to evaluate gender equality and women's empowerment. The five steps in question are welfare, access, consciousness transformation, participation and control. Each step is considered an element of empowerment and does not necessarily occur in any specific order. Indeed, it is held that each element circulates and is circularly or spirally bound to the other, in other words, when a power balance between men and women is established at the control level (the last step), it is assumed that welfare (the first step) will also be equal for both sexes, and thus be accompanied by changes in gender relations.

Indicators of empowerment in the CIDA model are classified into two main types:

Type 1 is relatively straightforward and easily quantifiable and Type 2 is less easily quantifiable, concerns social processes and requires qualitative analysis. However, CIDA does not define or suggest any qualitative or subjective indicators to assess people's changes in consciousness. In practical terms the model only deals with more quantitative and 'objective' indicators.

The SEAGA model
Socio-Economic and Gender Analysis is more a social and gender investigation method than an evaluation model. It emphasises the sociocultural, economic, demographic, political, institutional and environmental factors affecting the outcome of development initiatives and the links between them from a gender perspective. Furthermore, SEAGA examines the links among these factors at three levels: macro (programmes and policies), intermediate (institutions) and field (communities, households and individuals).

Socio-Economic and Gender Analysis presents a detailed methodological manual for the collection of data classified by target stratum and thus has merits in that anyone, even those who are not gender specialists, can collect data from a gender viewpoint and utilise the data for empowerment evaluation according to the situation. Clearly, however, a separate gender-sensitive empowerment framework is necessary to evaluate and analyse collected data.

Summing-up this very brief introduction to different models, all have their strengths and weaknesses. In the case of both the WB and CIDA models, for example, the heavy reliance on 'objective' indicators, which generally only refer to such issues as economic or legal factors, makes it very difficult to discern the processual aspects of empowerment. Although SEAGA offers promise through its potential to gather a rich body of gender-relevant data, the lack of an empowerment evaluation framework renders this somewhat limited to gender specialists only.

In light of these shortcomings I developed an 'Empowerment Evaluation Model' (EEM) while working on a development project in Paraguay, that was subsequently used there as well as in Honduras, as discussed below.

Empowerment indicators and evaluation models in life improvement programmes: developing a model from a Japanese-funded development project in Paraguay
The EEM was developed in the context of longitudinal fieldwork I carried out in a rural area of Paraguay during 1993–2004. I was sent to the Agricultural Extension Services of the Ministerio de Agricultura y Ganadería (MAG) as a volunteer from the Japan Overseas Cooperation Volunteer (JOCV) programme under the Japan International Cooperation Agency (JICA) in 1993–95. My brief was to support the Increasing Consumption of Vegetables Project (ICVP) with the goal of improving the lives of rural women and children.

Although Village S was originally not the subject of the project, the women from the village approached the author to organise a community meeting in which the implementation of ICVP was agreed upon. Consultations with the women of Village S indicated that their foremost priorities were to acquire more knowledge of vegetable cultivation and nutrition, training for enhanced skills in cooking, sewing and knitting, better educational opportunities for their children and schemes to generate income through the production and sale of processed foods. On the basis of the 'practical gender interests'

> **BOX 95.1 SUB-PROJECTS OF THE ILSP, PARAGUAY**
>
> 1. *Hygiene and nutrition*
> a. To increase knowledge of hygiene and nutrition.
> b. To diversify nutrition.
> c. To increase cultivated vegetable varieties.
> d. To generate income.
>
> 2. *'Mitai Roga' (A Place for Children) Establishment and Management Project*
> a. To construct and manage an area in which to offer village children the same opportunity to learn Spanish as urban children.
> b. To use the same area as a multipurpose hall
>
> 3. *Jam Factory Management and Marketing Project*
> a. To manage a jam factory.
> b. To generate income by selling processed foods
>
> *Source:* Fujikake (2008).

articulated by the women of Village S became beneficiaries of the Improving Living Standards Project (ILSP) (see Box 95.1).[1]

From 1994 onwards, the women started taking the ILSP into their own hands, driving a new and expanded agenda by diversifying into areas not covered by the initial project. On the basis of courses and the experience of working together, women started challenging conventional wisdoms and practices pertaining to gender. One notable change was in the area of family planning. Women began questioning religious discourses around fertility control, and particularly ideas such as 'family planning is contrary to God's will' and 'Hasta que Diós diga basta' ('Until God says that's enough'). Within a few years after the project a number of women had started to use contraceptive methods beyond the rhythm method and *yuyo* (a medicinal herb), such as the pill and even male condoms. Another change was for women to be more open to the idea in principle and in practice of working outside the home, which flouted the traditional belief that women who did so were not 'decent' or 'respectable'. This seemed mainly to be due to the courses and experience of the jam-making project. One aspect of this new pattern was that women started to work in areas that had previously been considered for men only, like the selling of vegetables. About this activity, women said that 'work is fun', or ' I want to work more'. Another very interesting, and possibly surprising change, was an increase in men's participation in reproductive labour. With more women working in the open-air market, a number of men began preparing breakfast and taking a larger role in the care of children. Previously, men had never prepared breakfast.

It was obvious to me that the women of Village S had started to gain more self-esteem, self-respect and self-reliance through their accumulation of small successes and achievements in cooking skills, retail and so on, as well as with what the project, and its

> **BOX 95.2   CRITERIA FOR THE EVALUATION OF EMPOWERMENT**
>
> 1. Participation
> 2. Voicing opinions
> 3. Change of consciousness
> 4. Taking action
> 5. Solidarity
> 6. Creativity
> 7. Setting new goals
> 8. Negotiation
> 9. Satisfaction
> 10. Self confidence
> 11. Administrative and economic management
> 12. Decision-making
>
> *Source:*   Fujikake (2008).

aftermath, entailed in terms of coming into contact with women in other towns, and with personnel such as development assistants and aid fieldworkers.

In the wake of this diverse array of changes and evolution from practical to strategic gender interests (see note 1), I analysed narratives of ILSP members from 1993 to 1999 (Fujikake, 2008). The rural women personally and mutually evaluated their changes as 'very good', 'I have changed' and 'I am not like I was before'. In the interests of corroboration and 'triangulation', opinions of changes witnessed in women participants were also sought from people close to them, such as partners, mothers-in-law, fathers-in-law, daughters, sons and people from outside the village. These narratives were all converted to text, classified according to person and research period, and compiled to compare the frequency with which the same word or expression appeared so as to pull out the most commonly-identified changes. From this extended research and analysis, twelve different criteria relating to empowerment were derived (see Box 95.2).

To share the results of the research with collaborators in a user-friendly manner, each indicator of the women's narratives was assigned a value of 1 point. These points were then totalled for an overall empowerment indicator although it should be noted that the purpose of the exercise was not to impose a value judgement as to whether a low level of empowerment in the terms specified was, or was not, 'good' (see Fujikake, 2008 for full details).

Perceived changes were classified as 'Three Types of Results' (TTR), subdivided as follows: Type 1 (results of objective; satisfaction of practical gender interests), Type 2 (unexpected by-products additional to objectives), or Type 3 (recognition and satisfaction of strategic gender interests) (see Figure 95.1).

Application of the EEM to the microbusiness promotion project for rural women in Honduras
An experiment with the EEM was conducted for another Japanese development project a few years later.

Methodologies for evaluating women's empowerment: Paraguay and Honduras 623

```
                    ┌─────────────────────────────────────────┐
                    │ • RESULTS OF OBJECTIVE                  │
                    │ • SATISFACTION OF PRACTICAL GENDER      │  'TYPE 1'
                    │   INTERESTS                             │
                    │ • MAINLY QUANTITATIVE CHANGE            │
                    └─────────────────────────────────────────┘
                                        ↓
                    ┌─────────────────────────────────────────┐
P                   │ • UNEXPECTED SUB-PRODUCTS OUTSIDE OF    │
R                   │   OBJECTIVE (INCLUDES 'HAPPINESS' AND   │
O                   │   'SATISFACTION')                       │
C                   │ • RECOGNITION AND SATISFACTION OF       │  'TYPE 2'
E                   │   UNEXPECTED PRACTICAL GENDER INTERESTS │
S                   │ • QUANTITATIVE AND QUALITATIVE CHANGE   │
S                   └─────────────────────────────────────────┘
                                        ↓
O                   ┌─────────────────────────────────────────┐
F                   │ • RECOGNITION AND SATISFACTION OF       │
                    │   STRATEGIC GENDER INTERESTS (AND       │
E                   │   ACTIONS TAKEN FOR THESE ENDS)         │  'TYPE 3'
M                   │ • QUANTITATIVE AND QUALITATIVE CHANGE   │
P                   └─────────────────────────────────────────┘
```

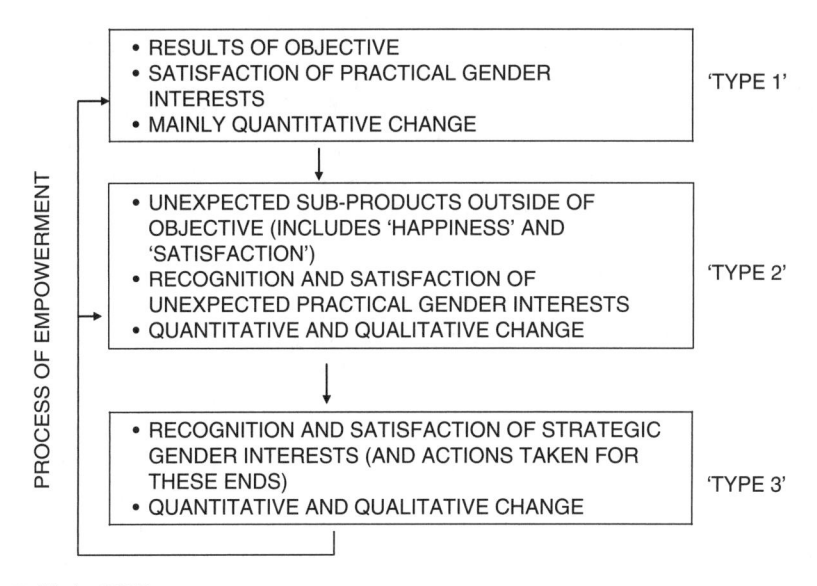

Source: Fujikake (2008).

Figure 95.1 Schematic matrix of 'empowerment' outcomes for women of the Improving Living Standards Project (ILSP), Paraguay

The Promotion of Self-managed Enterprises project of Women in Rural Areas of Honduras (PEWH) was conducted by JICA between 2003 and 2008 in the provinces of Lempira and Copán. The purpose of PEWH was for 'women beneficiaries of the project to establish and manage micro-businesses appropriate to local resources', and the overall goal was 'to achieve empowerment of the people in the target group' (JICA, 2006: 2–4). With the aim of assessing women's empowerment in the target group, expert teams utilised the EEM for mid-term and final evaluations of the project.

There were 76 women organised into 12 groups who were interviewed and individually evaluated, with some degree of 'empowerment' observed across all participants. Through participation in the training courses of the project, many women were able to earn income to contribute to family finances and thus buy food and medicine for their families. As in Paraguay, further to satisfying their practical gender interests, more strategic gender interests emerged. Before participating in the PEWH, few women in the rural localities covered by the project were practising family planning. However, as awareness dawned that women in urban areas were using contraception, the rural women started thinking about reproductive rights, and to negotiate fertility control with their partners. Some women also began protesting about domestic violence.

On the other hand, women with little or no schooling showed scant evidence of change in some of the specific arenas of empowerment, especially administrative and economic management, and decision-making, a tendency which had also been observed in rural Paraguay (Fujikake, 2008).

Taking into account these results, it is possible to map a course for future follow-ups to the project which would direct more effort into the areas in which particular empowerment outcomes tend to be lacking. The model also has potential to inform poverty alleviation policies and gender-responsive budgeting (see Elson and Sharp, Chapter 80, this volume).

With ever-heightening interest in the increasing prominence of the empowerment phenomenon, not only at the grassroots level but also in international society, it would be helpful to introduce the EEM to other projects, whether on its own, or in conjunction with other methods such as the WB model.

Conclusion

This chapter has talked about the need to measure empowerment, and discussed an Empowerment Evaluation Model (EEM) which recognises the importance of qualitative data to which other models to date have referred but inadequately incorporated. By evaluating the discourses of project clients in a 'bottom-up' way, it is possible to derive indicators which are meaningful to women themselves and which document something of the process of empowerment. Although the formation of a close rapport between researchers and research collaborators is necessary in order to distil key criteria of empowerment, and the collection and analysis of narrative data from women themselves and those close to them is very time-consuming, further development and applications of the EEM would be a desirable component of the design and implementation of poverty alleviation and women's empowerment programmes in the future.

Note

1. See Molyneux (2001) on the definition of practical and strategic gender interests.

Select bibliography

Alsop, Ruth and Nina Heinsohn (2005) *Measuring Empowerment in Practice: Structuring Analysis and Framing Indicators*, Policy Research Working Paper 3510, Washington, DC: World Bank.

Fujikake, Yoko (2008) 'Qualitative evaluation: evaluating people's empowerment', *Japan Evaluation Society*, **8** (2), 25–37.

Japan International Cooperation Agency (JICA) (2006) *Honduras Kyowakoku Chiho Josei no Tameno Shokibo Kigyo Shien Project Unei Shido Chosa Houkokusho* (*Investigative Report on the Project of Promotion of Women's Self-Management Enterprises in Rural Honduras*), Tokyo: JICA.

Kabeer, Naila (1999) 'Resources, agency, achievements: reflections on the measurement of women's empowerment', *Development and Change*, **30**, 435–64.

Molyneux, Maxine (2001) *Women's Movement in International Perspective; Latin America and Beyond*, Basingstoke: Palgrave Macmillan.

Rowlands, Jo (1997) *Questioning Empowerment: Working with Women in Honduras*, Oxford: Oxfam.

Sharma, Aradhana (2008) *Logics of Empowerment: Development, Gender, and Governance in Neoliberal India*, Minneapolis, MN: University of Minnesota Press.

PART X

NEW FRONTIERS IN GENDERED POVERTY RESEARCH AND ANALYSIS

96 Women, poverty and disasters: exploring the links through Hurricane Mitch in Nicaragua
Sarah Bradshaw

What is interesting about disaster writing in the developing world context is that while 'natural disasters' are such a common occurrence for so many Third World countries, the topic is generally not discussed within mainstream development literature, and disasters are noticeable by their absence from development textbooks and courses. Despite the regularity with which they occur, disasters are conceptualised as extraordinary events that break the 'normal' routine of everyday life, including the established process of development. For example, immediately after an event it is not unusual to hear commentators talking of how the disaster has 'set back' development by five or more years. Nor is it unusual to still hear the expression 'natural disaster'. Disaster academics have long pointed out that the natural hazards that may potentially produce a disaster are not unusual or even surprise events.[1] They have also pointed out that a hazard does not automatically lead to a disaster, and a disaster only occurs when there is an inability to respond to, cope with, or recover from the event resulting in significant loss of life and/or property. That is, disasters are a product of both the natural hazard and the relative vulnerability to the hazard, where the latter is determined by socio-economic factors. As such, disasters should be better understood, not as interrupting development but as the outcome of historical processes that create vulnerability (Bankoff, 2001). An outcome of the 'development' to date that has not improved the ability of the population to respond to the natural hazard and thus avoid the associated potential 'disaster' (Wisner et al., 2005). This suggests a need to mainstream disaster prevention initiatives into development practice.

While the need to integrate development and disasters has become more widely accepted there have been few concrete initiatives to advance this aim. For example, the Millennium Declaration recognised the risks to development of disasters but this did not translate into an associated Goal. The disaster equivalent of the Millennium Declaration – the Hyogo Framework for Action – likewise suggests disaster risk reduction is an important element for the achievement of internationally agreed development goals 'including those contained in the Millennium Declaration', but makes few concrete suggestions as to how to link the two. The new integrated focus is still more rhetoric than reality. Within this rhetoric the tendency has been to focus on how disasters damage development, rather than how processes of development can provide conditions conducive to disasters. There has also been an increasing focus on the link between poverty and disasters. The Global Facility for Disaster Reduction and Recovery, a partnership between the United Nation's International Strategy for Disaster Reduction (ISDR) and the World Bank, justifies its aim to mainstream disaster resilience into poverty reduction through noting that poverty-related policy objectives cannot be met if disaster risks are not taken into account, suggesting there is 'ample evidence' that poverty is the most important trigger which turns hazards into disasters. The United Kingdom's Department for International Development (DFID), in its call to 'disaster proof' development, similarly notes how poorer people tend to be more susceptible to hazards and how disasters can induce poverty making the poor destitute. They go one step further in their analysis, adding gender to the mix, noting, for example, that female-headed households are among the most asset-poor and have been found to be among the most affected by natural disasters. As they do not cite any study to back up this claim around impact it appears to be based on three assumptions: that the poor are more at risk from disaster, that women are more poor, and that female heads are the poorest of the poor. That is, it is based on popular notions of gendered poverty contained within the 'feminisation of poverty' thesis (see also Chant, Chapter 15, this volume).

The idea of being able to say with certainty who is the most affected by disasters is interesting given that the impact of any event will be time, place and person specific or depend on a mix of location, event and vulnerability. While poverty is a key component of vulnerability, it is not the only, nor necessarily the best, component in terms of predicting impact. Ideas around relative poverty are themselves contested, particularly the notion of feminised poverty. Using poverty as a proxy for vulnerability ignores factors such as social norms and relations which inform individual response. Responses are subjective and will be framed by individual understandings of appropriate behaviour which, in turn, are shaped by cultural norms, including gender norms. Within Latino cultures, for example, the cult of '*machismo*' may make men not women more likely to suffer loss of life during an event, whatever their relative poverty, due to their socially constructed roles and associated riskier behaviour patterns in the face of danger. On the other hand, women's social conditioning may make them so risk-averse that this becomes a risk in itself as they remain in their homes despite rising water levels, waiting for a male authority figure to arrive to grant them permission and/or assist them in leaving. Such behaviour will affect middle-income women who are 'housewives' as much, if not more so, than low-income women workers. It is also difficult to argue that women suffer more material damage than men, not least since very little reliable data exist. Post-disaster measures tend not to look inside households and measure relative individual loss, and this means, as noted similarly for measures of poverty, reported differences between the sexes are actually differences between households or by sex of head.

Just as women's greater risk of being impacted by an event has been assumed, so too has the opportunity to change their situation through post-disaster interventions become received wisdom. Despite the efforts of a small but dedicated group of scholars working in the field (Enarson and Morrow, 1998; GDN, 2005) little research exists on which to base such ideas. Despite this, much of the literature no longer only talks of reconstruction but also of a 'window of opportunity' for transformation, and one key area highlighted as being open for such transformative change is in gender roles and relations. The widespread destruction of all that is 'normal' and the resultant need to adapt to new circumstances is said to promote changes in gender roles and bring associated changes in gender relations that can be built upon through planned reconstruction initiatives. Increasingly post-disaster projects do have developmental aims and seek not only to restore normalcy, and 'to build back', but also seek to change the position and situation of women, including their economic situation, or to 'build back better'.

In recent years a 'feminisation of disaster response' has been noted in that women have become a key target of post-disaster reconstruction initiatives. This focus may be linked to assumed relationships around women-poverty-disaster, that has led to a perception of a 'feminised risk' of impact informed by the 'feminisation of poverty' thesis (Bradshaw, 2009). However, it may also be informed by, and part of, wider processes of 'feminisation of responsibility' especially responsibility for poverty alleviation (Chant, Chapter 15, this volume). The next section will use case study evidence from a number of studies of post-Hurricane Mitch households in Nicaragua to explore these notions further.[2]

Disasters and their impact on women's experiences of poverty: a case study of Nicaragua
Mitch was a 'Category 5' hurricane which swept through Central America in late October of 1998 leaving almost 3.5 million people affected, mainly in Honduras and Nicaragua. An estimated 18 000 people died or disappeared, and financial losses amounted to over US$6 billion. Interestingly Nicaragua was not in the direct path of the Hurricane but suffered from the incessant and heavy rainfall that followed. Damage was due not only to flooding but also to mudslides that caused extensive loss of life, with one single event on the slopes of Volcano Casitas wiping out two villages and killing the majority of the nearly 2000 inhabitants in the space of minutes.

There were no reliable data to suggest that women more than men suffered physical damage or injury from the hurricane, nor that more men, or women, were killed. This may in part be due to the fact that post-event the 'tyranny of the urgent' often means that basic information like the sex of the injured or even deceased is not recorded, especially when bodies are burnt where they lie to stop the spread of disease. There was also little sex-disaggregated data on material loss in the initial stages that would allow analysis of the wider relative gendered impact. However, there is evidence to suggest that it was assumed that women heads at least were equally hit, if not more so than men. For example, similar proportions of female heads as male heads received help in order to sow their land after Mitch, while a higher proportion of female- than male-headed households received help with housing. Two issues are raised by these examples, first, in terms of the quantity of aid received and, second, its quality. While female heads benefited on a par with men within reconstruction, within the population they represent a smaller group (around one-third of all households) and, given cultural norms, represent an even smaller proportion of farmers. This might suggest that assumptions about their relative poverty and assumed related need informed targeting as much as losses sustained. However, while they were more likely to receive resources, in terms of housing projects, fewer female than male heads felt that their opinions had been taken into account about where to build the new housing, and even fewer in terms of how to construct new housing. Similarly, although women farmers received help with rehabilitating their land post-Mitch they were less likely than men to receive cash or agricultural training, and more likely to receive inputs such as seeds. Women often have to rely on male labour to complete crucial agricultural tasks and this lack of cash to pay day labourers and lack of training in order to do it themselves may help explain why, despite receiving help in equal numbers, fewer female heads than male heads actually did sow crops one year after Mitch and remained instead living from donations.

While assumptions about women heads' relative poverty may have informed distribution of resources, lack of understanding of what informs their gendered experience of poverty meant the resources provided did not tackle the causes of that poverty, merely compensated for it. What may occur post-disaster is not necessarily an increase in poverty per se, but rather changes in how poverty is experienced, especially within households. For example, the perception among female heads of the value of their own contribution to the household declined post-Mitch and they were also less likely to name themselves as the key decision-maker post-Mitch compared with pre-Mitch. This is despite the fact that they continued to bring resources into the household either via productive work or through participation in reconstruction projects, or both.

In general the proportion of women in productive activities did decline post-Mitch, both in absolute terms and relative to men's reported employment in income-generating activities. However, care must be taken as men tend to continue to define themselves as farmers even when they cannot farm – 'farmer' being more about male identity than physical activity. In contrast women will label themselves as 'housewives' when not actively engaged in productive activities or at times even when they are engaged in productive activities if these are seen to be an extension of their reproductive work. Such labelling helps to inform ideas of the organisations initiating reconstruction projects, as well as women and men, around who has 'free time' to engage in activities such as those associated with reconstruction. In contrast to declines in income-generating activities, participation in community-based projects and programmes increased among all women after Hurricane Mitch, rising from under one-quarter to over one-half of the women interviewed. While female heads appeared to have juggled productive work with reconstruction activities and the added burdens this entailed, women with male partners were less likely to return to income generating activities after Mitch. It is not clear whether they were able to become more involved in reconstruction projects because they were no longer engaged in income-generating activities, or whether their inclusion in projects effectively negated their ability to undertake productive work.

The resources provided via women post-reconstruction tend to seek to fulfil their 'practical needs' associated with caring for the family and children. For example, one project sponsored by a well-known international NGO gave shared ownership of cows to women in the community. This focus on women promoted a potential backlash from men who felt excluded. At the end of the day this came to nothing, and the project representative explained that men did not cause trouble since, while the women had their cows, the men were drinking the milk. This notion that all the family, including men, should benefit directly from the resources provided by a project is not unusual. While over half the women in the study felt it was women who were participating most in reconstruction, only one-quarter felt women benefited most and few saw any personal benefits, practical or strategic, from their involvement.

Although to receive resources demands women's involvement in reconstruction activities this is very seldom conceptualised as 'work', especially by men who may see it as an extension of women's reproductive role or 'women's work' (see also Mohamed, Chapter 86, this volume). Men also often do not value women's work that does not bring an income into the home, and the study suggested this appeared to include project work where the benefit is 'in kind', non-monetary or longer-term. The resources gained, however potentially valuable, may be little valued within the household compared with monetary resources earned through 'work' even when the latter have a lesser economic value. This may help to explain why, while women with male partners had an improved perception of themselves as having a greater voice in decision making in the home post-Mitch, when asked, over one-third of their male partners said they alone made decisions in the home. Divergences of opinion, at the very least, may also help to explain the perception that arguments in the home increased post-Mitch and suggests there are costs, not just financial but emotional, to reconstruction that focuses on women. Once again, while income poverty may not increase, how poverty is lived and understood may change. In this case valuable economic resources did not necessarily translate into improved perceptions of the 'value' of the recipient with subsequent consequences for decision-making over these and other household resources.

Conclusions

The notion of the need to 'disaster proof' development is increasingly being recognised. This draws on understandings of the relationship between disasters and poverty that presents the relationship between the two as clear and direct. Within this new discourse other assumptions related to understandings of poverty are also seemingly translating into understandings of disasters, not least the assumed link between female heads and poverty. This has translated into the perceived need to include this group in reconstruction efforts, often in numbers disproportionate to their share of the population and the impact of the event. While their inclusion is informed by assumptions around poverty the nature of their inclusion is not informed by understandings of how they experience poverty and as such may not improve their well-being and at the very best may leave them financially non-poor but poorer emotionally and in terms of self-perceptions of their own worth.

Women with male partners are also increasingly being targeted within reconstruction. This is not informed by any notion of a greater impact since there is very little information on how men and women in the same household are impacted. So, too, are projects that target women in reconstruction focused on the household as a whole and should be understood as seeking to provide resources to the household *via* women rather than providing resources *to* women. This suggests that rather than the 'feminisation of poverty' thesis as informing targeting, women's inclusion is another example of the 'feminisation of responsibility' for poverty alleviation. Women appear to gain very little in the process, not least because their male partners may not value resources not gained through 'work' and which are in kind rather than cash. As such, while projects may ensure that resources are available to women and that the poverty of the household does not increase post-disaster, how women experience poverty and well-being may be changed, and this may not be a change for the better. Lack of research in the field makes it difficult to make a definitive case for this argument, so until more studies exist, assumptions around women-poverty-disaster will continue to be the basis for policy choices that may ultimately reinforce women's relative poverty.

Notes

1. Consult 'Radical interpretations of disasters', available at: http://www.radixonline.org/ (accessed 18 October 2009).
2. This case study evidence draws on an in-depth study of four communities undertaken by the author with the Nicaraguan feminist NGO, Puntos de Encuentro, and a large-scale national survey commissioned by the Civil Coordinator (CCER) of which the author was part of the design and analysis team. See in particular Bradshaw (2001, 2002).

Select bibliography

Bankoff, Greg (2001) 'Rendering the world unsafe: "vulnerability" as Western discourse', *Disasters*, **25** (1), 19–35.
Bradshaw, Sarah (2001) *Dangerous Liaisons: Women, Men and Hurricane Mitch*, Managua: Puntos de Encuentro.
Bradshaw, Sarah (2002) 'Exploring the gender dimensions of reconstruction processes post-Hurricane Mitch', *Journal of International Development*, **14**, 871–9.
Bradshaw, Sarah (2009) 'Engendering disasters: feminisation of response or a feminisation of responsibility?', *Regional Development Dialogue*, Hyogo: United Nations Centre for Regional Development, special edn, 'Engendering disaster risk reduction: global and regional contexts', **30** (1), 123–31.
Enarson, Elaine and Betty Morrow (eds) (1998) *The Gendered Terrain of Disaster: Through Women's Eyes*, Westport, CT: Praeger.
Gender and Disasters Network (GDN) (2005) *The Gender and Disaster Sourcebook*, London: GDN, available at: http://www.gdnonline.org/sourcebook/ (accessed April 2009).
Wisner, Ben, Piers Blaikie, Terry Cannon and Ian Davis (2005) *At Risk: Natural Hazards, People's Vulnerability and Disasters*, London and New York: Routledge.

97 Decentralisation, women's rights and poverty: learning from India and South Africa
Jo Beall

Introduction

From the early 1980s decentralisation became integral to international development and by the mid-1990s 80 per cent of countries were engaged in some form of decentralisation. Much of the enthusiasm for devolved governance and for enhancing the powers and responsibilities of local units of government is based on the idea that they are closer to the people that the state is supposed to serve. It is also often assumed that the global trend towards the decentralisation of public roles, responsibilities and resources is also good for women, as a vehicle for increasing women's participation in local government and because women are concerned with things homebound and local, such as basic infrastructure and services. Yet in reality localisation has its limits and even when the benefits of decentralisation can be demonstrated it is not guaranteed that these are extended to all women.

Localisation is often associated with notions of democratic decentralisation and rights-based approaches (RBAs) to development. Rights-based approaches attempt to integrate the norms, standards and principles of the international human rights system into development and constitute an advance on a strictly legal approach to rights by including a focus on the socio-economic and political rights of poor and marginal social groups. This is especially important for poor women who have little access to lawyers and courts and who depend on the meeting of socio-economic rights for exercising their gendered responsibilities. The value of RBAs is that they have extended the analysis of women in development analysis from a primary concern with women's legal and to a degree, political rights, to a focus on socio-economic or 'third generation rights'.

Despite the prevalence of the discourse of decentralisation and RBAs in development, they have come under significant criticism in terms of their impact on women and, especially, poor women. Nevertheless, they have continued salience and influence on development policy agendas in critical ways and so we need to understand why they hold such appeal and if they benefit poor women. The chapter explores these issues in the context of India and South Africa, chosen because they have both gone further than many other countries in attempting to implement democratic decentralisation and gender equity in local governance. While their experience points to many positive processes and outcomes it is also the case that decentralisation and local politics have impacted on women in paradoxical ways, particularly with regard to advancing the rights of poor women.

Democratic decentralisation and women's rights

Decentralisation takes various forms. At one end of the spectrum is the geographical dispersement of government without transfer of authority from the centre, known as deconcentration. At the other end, strong decentralisation involves the delegation or devolution of responsibility to semi-independent authorities or lower tiers of government. From the 1980s, in relation to development policy, decentralisation was often used to put in place privatisation and deregulation of the provision of public services. In the 1990s it was associated with reversing this 'over-withdrawal of the state' by breaking government into smaller units that could enter into multi-sector partnerships with the private and social sectors. It became an article of faith that decentralised states engaged in public–private partnerships would become more efficient and lead to effective delivery. A broader consensus developed around the view that decentralisation had an explicitly democratising function, which spanned a wide ideological terrain. While the World Bank articulated a liberal discourse on decentralisation, others saw the vitalisation of democracy as being predicated on popular participation in local public spheres. Critics of notions of democratic decentralisation point out that there are no a priori reasons why more localised forms of governance are more accountable and that localism can also serve powerful and global interests by distracting attention from supra-local issues and processes.

Studies of gendered citizenship have added to this scepticism through their critical analyses of women's relationship with the state. This impinges on physical and social reproduction, power dynamics within households and communities, and the complicity of the state in the construction of gendered and other identities. Less attention has been paid to local-level citizenship but the development literature, at least, tends to support the idea that women are more politically active and influential in this domain.[1] It is also argued that women's interests are linked to their gendered responsibilities in households and communities, which often relate to the provision of local infrastructure and services that in turn become policy priorities for women (Lind, Chapter 100, this volume; Miraftab, Chapter 99, this volume). Yet evidence from India and South Africa suggests that the purported ease of entry into local political processes for women is exaggerated and once in office they face tremendous difficulties. Furthermore, greater efficiency in service delivery at the local level does not necessarily guarantee sensitivity to women's gendered interests and socio-economic rights.

Localisation and women's rights in India and South Africa
India and South Africa are chosen as a focus for this exploration in that they have done better than most in advancing poor women's rights in and through local government. The Indian Constitution provides for local government institutions in rural and urban areas of India and following a recommendation in 1988 on reservations for women by the National Perspective Plan for Women, the 73rd and 74th Amendments to the Indian Constitution were enacted in 1992. They reserved one-third of seats for women in the three-tier *Panchayati Raj* system – local councils in rural areas and urban ward councils in towns and cities – constituting a bold step towards increasing women's political participation and empowerment. South Africa's experience is more recent but following the poor showing of women in the first democratic local government elections in 1995, campaigns were launched to increase the representation of women (van Donk, 2000). This led to a rise from 19 per cent women local councillors to 28 per cent in the 2000 local government elections.

Despite their relative success in including women in local government when compared to many other contexts in low- and middle-income countries, local governance in

India and South Africa is disappointing in respect of women. Political power and social authority is often more deeply embedded at the local level. One of the reasons why local governance is a disappointing arena for women is that it is often responsive to informal networks of power and influence, which undermine or bypass formal rules and procedures. Women rarely have access to the informal networks that often sustain and reproduce the institutions and social practices that make up local governance, institutions and practices that in any case are hostile to or exclusionary of women.

In India, for example, despite a 33 per cent reservation for women in India, the seats reserved for them rotate in every election. Hence after a ward has been reserved for all female competition in one election, it becomes a general ward in the next, in which both women and men can compete: 'As a result political parties simply do not take women's candidacy seriously nor do they invest in the elected woman candidate knowing very well that in the next round of elections these women are of no use to their electoral prospects' (Mukhopadhyay, 2005: 14). Customary *panchayats* have played a vital gatekeeping role in relation to local elections in India, controlling nominations and the selection of women, and actively discouraging certain women from contesting or re-contesting elections, thereby reducing their chances of continuity. In South Africa 'traditional' authorities and customary institutions exercise a strong influence on local governance. Based on male hereditary principles, chieftaincy is antithetical to a local democracy that is inclusive of women and respectful of their rights (Beall, 2005). Customary law discriminates against women who cannot own land or property in their own right and who lose any access rights on the death of their husbands unless arbitrated otherwise by the chief, a principle of primogeniture upheld by the Supreme Court as recently as 2000 even though under the South African Constitution principles of gender equity are supposed to prevail over the exercise of customary law (Hassim, 2006; see also Rakodi, Chapter 54, this volume). While local government might be the sphere of governance closest to women's life concerns, it is also the tier of governance most proximate to peoples' prejudices and networks of power and influence that are exclusive of women and sometimes abusive of them. Indeed, the backlash against women who raise their heads above the political parapet has sometimes been extreme, ranging from censure to ostracism and witchcraft accusations for stepping outside conventional gender roles (Mbatha, 2003; see also Madhok, Chapter 98, this volume).

In India, some state governments have been slow to implement the necessary provisions to enable governance of local *panchayats* to operate effectively, for example, by not transferring the necessary revenue, or leaving local politics in the control of village and urban elites.[2] The media has focused on so-called 'proxy women' who are in decision-making positions as the relatives of influential men, only called upon for their presence or signatures rather than exercising real influence on behalf of women (Everett, 2008). However, there are some really positive outcomes from the Indian experience as well. It has been demonstrated that women are more likely than men to raise issues related to basic services such as drinking water, and where women are *panchayati* chairs more investment for basic services is likely to be forthcoming (see Elson and Sharp, Chapter 80, this volume).

In South Africa decentralisation and neoliberal policies have gone hand in hand, including the requirement that all but the poorest local authorities raise a large proportion of their own revenue. The demand for cost recovery has given rise to growing user charges for local services, with a devastating impact on low-income households and communities, in which women bear the burden of cost recovery and the consequences of failure to pay. This can take the form of service cut-offs which prevent women undertaking their domestic roles; escalating household debts or reducing consumption in order to meet utility bills, both often the responsibility of women (Beall, 2005). Social movements that mobilise poor people around these issues, such as the Anti-Privatisation Forum in South Africa, tend to include women among their rank and file but do not always take up their gendered interests in campaigns (Hassim, 2006).

In both countries there are limits to women's local political effectiveness but also considerable evidence, especially from India, of women successfully engaging in local governance and of women leaders articulating priorities in local planning and impacting upon decision-making and spending patterns (Elson and Sharp, Chapter 80, this volume). In both countries, scholarship shows that presence matters. As women spend longer in local politics they gain greater confidence and face declining resistance from men, and when their numbers in local councils reach a critical mass they gain more influence.

Conclusion

In both India and South Africa women have not always been able to take effective advantage of the opportunities offered by decentralised governance and policies focusing on rights and gender equity. On the contrary they have sometimes been impacted negatively by decentralisation and localisation, especially when accompanied by neoliberal policies such as cost recovery. Yet for all its deficiencies, at the present time the focus on democratic decentralisation and rights currently provides 'the only effective means to challenge inequality and to advance programmes that would promote greater social justice and more equitable development' (Molyneux and Razavi, 2002: 4).

To be blindly critical of democratic decentralisation and RBAs is to miss the opportunities they offer for widening the room for manoeuvre at the local level in terms of enhanced participation of women in local politics and increased accountability for effective and gender-sensitive service delivery. There is a compelling argument for supporting women's participation in an embedded local politics that coordinates with state policy at all levels. Nevertheless, the way in which social, economic and political forces intermesh at the local level makes this a particularly difficult arena for women's political engagement, rather than a site of easy entrance into public life as is so often assumed.

If local democracy is to be engendered and women's political and socio-economic rights advanced at the local level, then some of the sub-texts and dangers of decentralisation processes and how these might undermine RBA agendas must be acknowledged, especially in the context of a dominant neoliberal development agenda. Put another way, it is important that the pursuit of decentralisation and women's rights does not become a vehicle for putting a human face on neoliberal preoccupations with privatisation, deregulation and cost recovery at the expense of poor women. For decentralisation and women's rights to be positively correlated they both need to be part of wider democratic processes in which women are represented politically at all levels of governance. Rather women's political gains through participation in local governance need to permeate upwards and articulate with national-level politics and policy.

The experience of India and South Africa suggest that there are two key prerequisites for decentralisation to be positively associated with women's rights. First, women need to be organised and represented locally, otherwise decentralisation remains nothing more than an administrative exercise, and one that invariably ignores the interests and priorities of poor women. Second, decentralisation is best pursued in the context of a strong state that is willing and able to engage with organised women across all spheres and tiers of government, and not simply at the local level.

The experiences of democratic decentralisation in India and South Africa show many positive results both in terms of process and outcome. However, advancing the rights and especially the socio-economic rights of poor women cannot be left to the local level alone, especially where local government is resource-constrained. By the same token, holding right-bearers to account at supra-local levels is often difficult for poor women, whose interests need to be represented first in locally embedded democratic institutions that are connected into national accountability mechanisms. With these dimensions in place, rights-based approaches can serve to cancel out some of the limitations of decentralisation, while a focus on decentralisation can help advance the rights agenda to a greater concern with socio-economic rights.

Notes

1. http://www.kit.nl/gcg/assets/images/Gender_and_Local_Governance.doc. (accessed 15 July 2009).
2. See also article on 'Panchayati Raj and rural governance: experiences of a decade', in *Economic and Political Weekly*, 10 January 2004, 137–43, by Mahi Pal, available at: http://www.epw.org.in (accessed 15 July 2009).

Select bibliography

Beall, Jo (2005) 'Decentralising government and de-centering gender: lessons from local government reform in South Africa', *Politics and Society*, **33** (2), 253–76.

Everett, Jana (2008) 'Women in local government in India', in Anne-Marie Goetz (ed.), *Governing Women, Women's Political Effectiveness in Contexts of Democratisation and Governance Reform*, New York and London: Routledge, pp. 196–215.

Hassim, Shireen (2006) *Women's Organisations and Democracy in South Africa, Contesting Authority*, Madison, WI: University of Wisconsin Press.

Mbatha, Likhapa (2003) 'Democratising local government: problems and opportunities in the advancement of gender equality in South Africa', in Anne-Marie Goetz and Shireen Hassim (eds), *No Shortcuts to Power: African Women in Politics and Policy Making*, London: Zed, pp. 188–212.

Molyneux, Maxine and Shahra Razavi (2002) 'Introduction', in Maxine Molyneux and Shahra Razavi (eds), *Gender Justice, Development and Rights*, Oxford: Oxford University Press, pp. 1–42.

Mukhopadhyay, Maitrayee (2005) 'Decentralisation and gender equity in South Asia: an issues paper', paper prepared for the Women's Rights and Citizenship Programme of the International Development Research Centre (IDRC).

Van Donk, Mirjam (2000) 'Local government: a strategic site of struggle for gender equity', *Agenda – Empowering Women for Gender Equity*, **45**, 4–12.

98 Poverty, entitlement and citizenship: vernacular rights cultures in Southern Asia
Sumi Madhok

Introduction

Some parts of rural Southern Asia are witnessing the appearance of 'rights-scapes' or newly emerging forms of political cultures underpinned by an unambiguous language of rights. These 'rights-scapes' are constitutive elements of what I have elaborated elsewhere as 'vernacular rights cultures' (Madhok, 2009 [see Acknowledgements at the end of this chapter]). The new forms of political cultures produced are predominantly non-party political, they articulate political claims in a language of rights, they mobilise in support of public policy legislation, and they justify rights on philosophical premises that are in large part independent of the state. By vernacular rights cultures, I do not mean that rights govern interpersonal relations or indeed that they command consensus and recognition within everyday discourse; on the contrary, they open up new arenas of conflict particularly in the realm of gender and caste relations. While being mindful of these, however, I do intend to draw attention to a certain unhesitant use of a rights language to define entitlements and to make very specific claims in relation to the state.

Political mobilisations centred on citizenship rights have not only contributed to fashioning innovative rights thinking, rights politics and citizenship claims, but have also resulted in the passage of several significant anti-poverty legislative measures, particularly in India. It is important to note that these rights articulations are expressed not through neologisms but within the vernacular, and that they do not occur as singular or even odd prototypes but draw upon, and are accommodated within, existing vocabularies and norms governing entitlements, roles and identities. In this chapter I focus particularly on the use of the Urdu/Arabic term '*haq*' which is predominantly invoked in contemporary rights mobilisations in South Asia.

Conceptualising and contextualising *haq*

The term '*haq*' is remarkably cosmopolitan and has an interesting intellectual history. As the principal Arabic word used to denote a 'right', it enjoys an intellectual recognition across Arabic-speaking peoples in the Middle East and North Africa and among several communities in South Asia too. Yet *haq* is also a pre-Islamic Arabic word, as well as being found in Hebrew, Persian (Farsi) and in some of the older Semitic languages such as Aramaic and Mendian. *Haq* or *Hukk* appears in the Hindustani/Urdu language through the historic influence of Persian in the Indian subcontinent. In Southern Asia, the literal term *haq* is uniquely placed as a case study to examine the historical and the modern meaning of rights as it easily transcends geographical and religious boundaries and is used to invoke a 'right' by different religious and linguistic communities in northern India as well as in Pakistan.

As a conceptual intervention, the lens of vernacular rights cultures helps steer clear from the theoretical foreclosures and deadlock of mainstream discussions on rights in the non-Western world. As an alternative to these explanations, I argue instead, that vernacular rights cultures are not wholly derivative from the three major revolutions of the modern West – the English (1680), the American (1776) and the French (1789) – or entirely oppositional to Western notions and conventions of human rights. Nor are they discrete in form. Indeed, one would be hard-pressed to find hermetically sealed or 'pure' indigenous rights traditions in place of those which are interlocked into relations that are historically, productively, intimately, and coercively produced and experienced.

I use the conceptual language of 'vernacular rights cultures' for three reasons. The first is as a rhetorical strategy to demarcate boundaries and convey specificity, in other words, to draw attention to these not being mere local variants of 'global human rights cultures'. A second reason for using the term 'vernacular rights cultures' is to highlight their specificity in terms of the nature of rights that are articulated. The third reason relates to their sociology – the fact that the exercise of ethical political agency accompanying such demands for entitlements within this region is predominantly couched within religious, caste and regional terms. So, while the language of entitlement articulated in the vernacular arises out of the failure of democratic representative politics and state developmentalism, it does not preclude or diminish the inclusion of identity as a chief marker.

But it is not enough only to speak of, and point to, discrete sightings of the existence of 'rights-scapes' in different parts of southern Asia. One also needs to actively investigate the specific linguistic, sociological, political histories and practices that underpin and make possible these rights cultures and to examine the forms of political cultures, subjectivities, administering practices and subjections produced by them. While these questions are beyond the scope of this submission, I shall here draw upon my ethnographic fieldwork documenting the use of rights language by mainly rural women participants within various citizen mobilisations in India and in Pakistan in order to highlight the various rights meanings sustaining the articulation of *haq*.

During the course of my fieldwork, I documented five different justificatory premises underpinning the use of the word *haq*. The justificatory premise of rights within Western canonical philosophy and its contemporary theoretical articulations resides principally in the autonomy of persons and their capacities for self-governance. In the twentieth century, influential texts on rights regarded rights to be liberties, immunities, claims and powers to be exercised in relation to others, and designated rights as crucial for dignity and self-respect (see Feinberg, 1970; Hohfield, 2001). The different justificatory premises of *haq* do not defend rights upon securing the autonomy of the self-governing individual but they present an intellectual defence of rights in a language in the following way. The two most common justificatory theses historically advanced in relation to *haq* are that it was legal or state-derived and/or that it obtained its efficacy from established constitutional freedoms outlining rights of citizens. In both cases, however, it was always clarified that although law/constitution justified and upheld these rights, *haq* had an independent justificatory premise separate from the prevailing legal regime. In other words, while the law regulates and upholds rights, these rights are not limited by law and the latter cannot extirpate these. In addition to the above justifications, *haq* was also invoked in moral/ normative terms, as an ancestral or a cosmological claim. Finally, its use was also linked to specific invocations and meanings within Islamic texts and law (Madhok, 2009 [see Acknowledgement]). It is noteworthy to mention here, that according to my female field respondents, *haq* was predominantly a masculine term belonging to a male vocabulary and that women almost never used the term among themselves. Consequently, they were only too aware of the conflictual nature of rights-based assertions and thus spoke of using *haq* mostly to demand entitlements from the state and very rarely to regulate intimate relations.

Rights mobilisations in Rajasthan

To elaborate upon one of *haq*'s justificatory premises I draw on my ethnographic study of women participants in anti-corruption and anti-poverty citizen mobilisations in Rajasthan, northwest India.

Rajasthan has established itself at the forefront of several citizen rights mobilisations, many of which have had a spectacular impact on federal policy resulting in the formulation of several national and internationally recognised innovations to public policy which include legislative passage of the 'Right To Information Act India' (2005),[1] the 'National Rural Employment Guarantee Act' (NREGA) (2005) and the 'Midday Meal Scheme' (2002) which laid down the mandatory provision of a cooked meal to all children attending government-aided schools across the country.[2] In 1997, responding to a Public Interest Litigation filed at India's Supreme Court by Vishakha, a non-governmental organisation (NGO) based in the state capital of Rajasthan, Jaipur, legal guidelines were framed to prevent sexual harassment of women in the workplace.[3]

The reasons for Rajasthan's pre-eminent position in matters of citizenship struggles are not altogether clear. Going by cold statistical print alone, its social and economic indicators, especially in respect of gender, are nowhere near satisfactory. In terms of the Millennium Development Goals (MDGs), Rajasthan is among the poorer performing states in India: the sex ratio is heavily masculinised (1000 males for every 922 females), 31 per cent of 6–14-year-old girls do not go to school, and 9673 women died in childbirth in 1999 (India-wide figures were 87 574 for that year).[4] Despite the plurality of social contexts inside rural Rajasthan, this statistical evidence bears out the fairly common social practices, experiences and conditions one witnesses at first hand in the hamlets and the villages: that girls are very seldom in secondary education let alone in primary schools, that iniquitous caste practices still determine interpersonal social relations, that access to public amenities is strictly regulated according to one's position in the caste hierarchy, that child marriages abound and are celebrated in annual religious festivals, and that female infanticide occurs in several communities, helping to account for the state's skewed sex ratio (see also Jackson, Chapter 5, this volume). On top of this, there is acute and widespread poverty.

By the same token, and somewhat paradoxically, Rajasthan has a vibrant women's movement, boasts of high female visibility in the public sphere, has substantial voting turnouts among women, and a high proportion of Scheduled Caste/Scheduled Tribe (SC/ST) women contest and are elected to local government bodies. Possibly because of the gender inequalities outlined in the previous paragraph, however, women's political manoeuvrings are often far from straightforward (see also Beall, Chapter 97, this volume). Consider for instance, the case of Manohari Bai, a *dalit* woman and one of my interviewees, who stood up during a meeting of her village council in order to exercise her 'right to know'. She was mercilessly beaten by the head of the village council (Sarpanch) and his supporters, all of whom belonged to higher castes. Manohari Bai describes the incident in the following interview:

It was in 2002, sometime in August–September that I went to the *gram sabha* meeting and queried after an approved proposal to build a girl's school. The *Sarpanch* responded by saying '*chup ho ja, tu kaun hain bolni* wali' (shut up for who are you to pose these questions')? Then suddenly all violence broke loose. I was beaten up and my *dupatta* (veil) and other clothes were torn off me whilst all the time, the people kept shouting '*randi baith ja*' (sit down you whore). My attackers were mainly upper caste men but there was also a *Patwari* – a state official – who joined in. The Police refused to register a complaint against my attackers.[5]

Conducted between 2004 and 2006, my fieldwork recorded the narratives of women development workers, grassroots political activists and participants within various citizen movements demanding rights to food, employment and public information, as well as the rights of *dalits* (those belonging to the formerly untouchable castes) and indigenous peoples. While the spectrum of rights covered by these movements is quite broad, they are often interconnected. For example, demanding the right to information about public work programmes of health, education or drought relief can, in many cases, involve a simultaneous claim for gender and caste equality while in the same breath drawing attention to corruption within the local and state bureaucracies and the judiciary, and to the flouting of procedural norms within the administrative, executive and legislative system itself.

Although my fieldwork focused on the articulations of *haq* among rural participants within these rights mobilisations, it is important to keep in mind that these were not spontaneous but a result of an intricately organised and coordinated rights initiatives by NGOs with a long-standing presence in the area. From the mid-1980s onwards, the streets of Jaipur began witnessing large popular mobilisations voicing protest over a diverse array of issues, many related to gender. These included demonstrations against official inaction over the *sati* (widow immolation) of a young woman, Roop Kanwar, at Deorala in 1987, calls for stringent laws on sexual harassment and violence in the workplace in the wake of the gang rape of a village development worker in 1992, demands for state legislation in favour of minimum employment guarantees and citizens' 'right to know', with the latter seen both as a tool against corrupt bureaucratic practices and as a means of enforcing accountability and transparency within governmental mechanisms (Madhok, 2009 [see Acknowledgement]; see also Goetz and Jenkins, 1999).

Before we can begin to understand the nature of the meaning-making exercises that people were engaged in within these citizen movements, two questions need to be asked, namely, why are these rights movements such a public draw in the first place, and why are political rights seen as monumentally important? After all, is it not conventional political theoretical thinking that political rights can only be meaningful in the context of certain economic baselines? Rajeev Bhargava (2006: 448) writes that it is not a case of economic rights simply predicating political ones and that 'causal arrows do not fly only in one direction . . . democratic freedoms are crucial for enhancing socio-economic well-being'. This loosening of the distinctions between civil, political and economic in order to accommodate new forms of political thinking on poverty is borne out by my research findings where political rights were said to matter precisely because they provided people with tools to make sense of and scrutinise the reasons for their poverty. So, for instance, why was it that the money earmarked for poverty alleviation, development projects, drought relief and other welfare assistance failed to find its way into the pockets of its intended beneficiaries, that is, the poor? Why was there a gross failure on the part of the state to uphold minimum wage legislation? Why did the state condone rampant caste and gender bias within drought relief programmes established to provide employment to people in drought-affected districts, and why was the Public Distribution System (PDS) with its network of fair price ration shops beset by flagrant procedural inefficiencies and corrosive corruption ostensibly under the benign gaze of the state? All of these issues, according to my field subjects, were responsible for an institutionalisation of endemic poverty which itself resulted from a triadic and mutually reinforcing relationship between a lack of transparency in procedural rules of government, the general failure of democratic accountability in political life, and routinised official corruption.

The most ubiquitous use of *haq* I encountered during the course of my fieldwork in Rajasthan was in relation to claiming what were seen as legitimate entitlements from the state. As a consequence, *haq* is often used as a right that is owed by the state to its citizens. This was patently the case in respect of the 'Right to Food' campaign, in which a number of my informants were involved. The 'Right to Food' network was formed as an umbrella group by several NGOs predominantly based in Rajasthan in order to frame a people's response in the wake of the state government's apathy to growing hunger and destitution resulting from successive droughts. These strategies included the formation of village-level *Akal Sangharsh Samiti* (ASS) or 'drought action committees' which scrutinised aspects of drought relief governance procedures and processes set in motion by the state, lobbying the state administration for increased development relief and assistance in villages and mobilising popular support in favour of a social rights legislation guaranteeing the 'right to work'. These village-level committees did not, however, always function democratically and in an open manner. Many of my women respondents, for instance, spoke of the struggle to be included within these committees or secure any state relief for drought-hit female-headed low-caste households. But amid the many difficulties outlined by these women, what remained remarkably undiminished was their resolute demand for more expansive social rights legislation.

> On 5 June 2003, we attended a public rally at Jaipur where we demanded our *haq*. We said we wanted *'kam ka adhikaar'* (right to employment/work or employment guarantee). This right to work or employment guarantee is very important to us for in face of severe drought, successive crop failures, disappearance of water, food and livestock feed, how are we meant to live? . . . The people are the wealth creators . . . and the government in guaranteeing a right to employment would only be giving us what is rightfully our due.[6]

Concluding remarks
The above citations come from interviews recorded before the successful passage of NREGA in 2005. Under the provisions of the Act, the federal state is legally bound to provide 100 days of employment to earmarked rural districts identified as the most vulnerable, thereby ensuring a basic subsistence for the poorest households. This public policy legislation is unique on at least three counts. One, it is an outcome of a democratic impulse evidenced in a widespread grassroots mobilisation in support of a legislation securing social provisioning for the most vulnerable households in India. Two, through its legislative enactment, it brings together social rights with citizenship rights (Bhargava, 2006), and thereby establishes horizontal linkages across the spectrum on rights thinking, albeit in an institutional rather than a theoretical sense. Three, in the light of the hegemonic ascendance of neoliberal political projects prescribing 'one size fits all' models

of self-sufficiency, autonomy and entrepreneurial citizenship, it is indeed remarkable that the state should resist prevailing economic orthodoxies in order to legislate on what is by all accounts 'old-fashioned' social welfarist legislation. But legislative achievement and democratic victory notwithstanding, it is also the case that the formal promise of rights generates new forms of despair brought on by the contradictory effects rights engender including heightened conflict and injuries (Brown, 1995; Crenshaw, 2000; Menon, 2004). The empirical workings of NREGA have not been without its share of these, and as such it would be interesting to view the actual working of this Act as an opportunity for investigation into how rights actually operate, and the new forms of subjectivities they produce especially, when coupled alongside strong claims for social justice, many of which are driven by women.

Acknowledgements
I thank Sylvia Chant for her thoughtful reading of the text, and the British Academy, Mellon Research Foundation and Ford Foundation for funding ongoing research on which this chapter is based. The chapter draws particularly from my 2009 working paper, *Five Notions of Haq: Exploring Vernacular Rights Cultures in Southern Asia*, published by the Gender Institute, London School of Economics and Political Science.

Notes
1. The Act extends to the whole of India except the State of Jammu and Kashmir.
2. See www.righttofoodindia.org (accessed 20 March 2009).
3. Information from *All India Reporter of the Supreme Court* (1997: 3011), available at: (http://www.allindiareporter.in) (accessed 28 June 2009).
4. See the 2004 *Country Strategy For India* by the International Bank for Reconstruction and Development, International Development Association and International Finance Corporation, available at: www.wds.worldbank.org/external/default/WDSContentServer/WDSP/IB/2004/09/20/000160016_20040920102445/Rendered/PDF/293740REV.pdf (accessed 20 March 2009).
5. Interview with Maohari Devi, Baodi Village, Panchayat Samiti Osian, Jodhpur District, 2005.
6. Field interview, Jhadla Village (Phagi Block), Jaipur District, Rajasthan 2004.

Select bibliography
Bhargava, Rajeev (2006) 'Indian democracy and well being: employment as a right', *Public Culture*, **18** (3), 445–51.
Brown, Wendy (1995) *States of Injury*, Princeton, NJ: Princeton University Press.
Crenshaw, Kimberley (2000) 'Were the critics right about rights? Reassessing the American debate about rights in post-reform era', in Mahmood Madani (ed.), *Beyond Rights Talk and Culture Talk*, Cape Town: David Phillip, pp. 61–74.
Feinberg, Joel (1970) 'The nature and value of rights', *Journal of Value Enquiry*, **4** (4), 243–60.
Goetz, Anne Marie and Rob Jenkins (1999) 'Accounts and accountability: theoretical implications of the Right to Information Movement in India', *Third World Quarterly*, **20** (3), 603–22.
Hohfield, Wesley (2001) *Fundamental Legal Conceptions as Applied in Judicial Reasoning*, new edn, Aldershot: Ashgate.
Menon, Nivedita (2004) *Recovering Subversion: Feminist Politics Beyond the Law*, Urbana, IL: University of Illinois Press.

99 Contradictions in the gender–poverty nexus: reflections on the privatisation of social reproduction and urban informality in South African townships
Faranak Miraftab

This chapter stresses the importance of two analytical considerations in understanding the relationship between gender and poverty in the Global South: first, the deep informality of the cities in spatial and economic terms, and second, the re-articulation of production–social reproduction relations for the development of cities in the context of global neoliberal capitalism. These two conditions, I argue, simultaneously intensify the burdens that urban development places on women and hence their greater poverty and increase opportunities for active citizenship and collective action by poor women. Combined they place women's grassroots activism at the centre of a gendered urban poverty analysis. To substantiate this argument I reflect on the experience of poor women in townships of post-apartheid South Africa, whose burden and responsibilities for social reproduction both at home for family and in the neighbourhood for municipal services has expanded. But at the same time, and most importantly, through their community activism for shelter and against evictions and service cut-offs their arena of citizenship practice and collective action has expanded to achieve a more just city.

Before I delve further into this discussion I need to make two clarifications: first, to what extent can we assume categories such as 'women' or 'Third World' in order to present a perspective based on experience of women in cities in the Global South? Of course, women's experiences internationally are structured by class, ethnicity and race, and locally specific social hierarchies. But in the urban formations of the Global South certain commonalities persist which set the structural bearings for common gendered experiences of urban development. The shared history of colonialism and the process of urbanisation decoupled from industrialisation have had important implications for the development of cities in former colonies, and for the experience of their urban inhabitants and, specifically, of women.

Second, to what extent could the urban experience of disadvantaged women in post-apartheid neoliberal South Africa be relevant to other societies in the South? The struggle for urban citizenship and against urban exclusion has been at the centre of people's, in particular women's, struggle in South Africa. While during the apartheid cities belonged to white settlers and blacks were excluded from urban citizenship, women were in particular excluded as their permission to visit the cities was also tied to their relationship with their migrant male partners with temporary urban work permits. This history of overt exclusion now being subject to a global neoliberal turn offers a lucid perspective to observe the workings of neoliberalism in relation to women and cities. The post-apartheid neoliberal city is a microcosm of the processes observed elsewhere in the cities of the Global South.

Bearing in mind these preliminary clarifications, I now turn to the two interconnected conditions of informality and the (re)privatisation of social reproduction previously highlighted.

Deep informality

More than two-thirds of cities in the Global South are developed through spontaneous, unplanned activities. As many as 85 per cent of Third World urban residents have tenuous claims to land, and 78 per cent live in slums (see Rakodi, Chapter 54, this volume). In urban Africa, an estimated 57 per cent of people lack access to basic sanitation, and only 11 per cent in poor neighbourhoods in Manila and 18 per cent in Dhaka have formal means for disposing of sewage.

In terms of labour market activities, formal employment channels or formal employer–employee relationships play only a minor role in many Third World economies. Worldwide the informal economy has increased its share as a percentage of non-agricultural employment, by the 1990s reaching 43.4 per cent in North Africa; 74.8 per cent in sub-Saharan Africa; 56.9 per cent in Latin America and 63 per cent in Asia (Benería, 2003: 111, table 4.2; see also Chen, Chapter 71, this volume). Further, women increasingly find employment in the informal sector; worldwide, with 27.6 per cent of the female non-agricultural labour force being self-employed (Benería, 2003: 117).

These figures suggest that only a small share of cities in the Global South are spatially and economically developed through formal processes and the structures of state decision-making and planning. Having had to seek shelter and earn a livelihood through the informal sector, the majority of poor women in the Global South have taken into their own hands the challenge of combining the multiple responsibilities of caring for their families and generating income. Hence, in the developing world context, feminists' focal concern with the urban experience of poor women centres on community-based processes and practices that are outside the control and regulatory machinery of the state and its planning authorities.

This has important implications for women's urban citizenship. Many feminist scholars who study women's community-based activism for housing, neighbourhood services or other livelihood needs have emphasised the significance of informal politics as the arena of grassroots women's collective action. Where formal channels of citizen participation and the invited spaces for asserting citizenship rights are ineffective, grassroots women often bypass the male-dominated formal politics of the elite, asserting their right to the city through informal politics of community-based activism and invented spaces of citizenship (Miraftab, 2006). Grassroots efforts and, in particular, grassroots women's efforts, have invented spaces of active urban citizenship, and have done so despite, not because of, formal planning and policy structures and processes. The deep urban informality of the Global South therefore places grassroots women's activism at the centre of urban poverty research.

Global neoliberal capitalism and production: social reproduction relations

Global neoliberal capitalism has altered relations of production and social reproduction and accordingly affected women's roles particularly with respect to their communities. Whether called restructuring and liberalisation in the Global North, or structural adjustment and debt management in the Global South, neoliberal policies withdraw public support for basic and social services and thus have intensified gender-specific responsibilities, with the burden of compensating for the service shortfall accruing disproportionately to poor women. Based on an assumption of women's infinite and elastic labour supply, capitalism relies on women's free and underpaid work to compensate for neoliberalism's erosion of the public realm and abandonment of civic responsibilities (see Roy, Chapter 84, this volume; Tonkiss, Chapter 22, this volume).

Socialist feminist scholarship of the 1970s and 1980s connected housework and waged work to capitalist processes of accumulation and, in so doing, demonstrated that domestic work is as much a part of the productive process as is manufacturing. Such scholarship traces the relationships among patriarchy, capitalism, and the spatial structure and organisation of production and reproduction. Emerging scholarship on global economic restructuring pushes this revelation further, arguing that the ontology of neoliberalism entails 'new patterns of exploitation and control of labour in the production–reproduction relationship' (Bakker and Gill, 2003: 18). These researchers assert that accumulation of capital, in its current crisis, has had to (re)privatise social reproduction, moving it to the family, where it 'naturally belongs'.

Feminist empirical scholarship in cities of the Global South carries these new insights further by arguing that the (re)privatisation of social reproduction in these cities is 'naturalised' not only within the family, but also at the community level through women's informal labour in providing neighbourhood care and municipal services (see Kumar, Chapter 56, this volume). Such scholarship opens the category of labour not only by rearticulating formal–informal linkages but also by expanding the scale of the analysis of providing social reproduction, *from family to community*.

As in post-welfare societies, the household is the primary site of privatising social risk and social reproduction, so in the Global South, neighbourhood and community are the prominent sites. The historical account of women asserting their public responsibility through the notion of municipal housekeeping in turn-of-the-century United States could stand as a contemporary account of women's burden in many low-income communities of the contemporary Global South, where in the absence of municipal public services women have to perform such tasks for free as an extension of their domestic responsibilities. In the Global South, neoliberal budget cuts and cash-strapped local governments privatise the provision of basic municipal services, not only by contracting them to private firms, but also by moving the public responsibilities for urban and neighbourhood development to the private sphere of women's free work (Miraftab, 2006; Samson, 2008). Therefore, there has been a feminisation of informal urban development, whereby in many cities of the Global South women act as 'unpaid urban developers and urbanisers' (Miraftab, 1998: 291).

The case of gender in South African townships
To illuminate the above point I share an example that I have developed in detail elsewhere (Miraftab, 2004). After the 1994 political transition in South Africa, the post-apartheid state assumed the responsibility for provision of municipal services to an expanded constituency including the populations categorised by apartheid as 'Blacks' and 'Coloureds'. This expanded responsibility in the context of state neoliberal restructuring led to municipal adoption of entrepreneurial strategies that promote citizens as fee-paying customers (Miraft, 2008). Within this wider policy framework in the early 2000s Cape

Town municipality launched a multi-tiered programme for collection of solid waste in its jurisdiction that nominally offered tailored services to socio-economically differentiated neighbourhoods and suburbs. While garbage collection in the affluent suburbs continued to be through paid unionised public sector employees or municipal workers, in the largest townships of the city this involved women residents in collection of solid waste without any pay. Relying on unpaid labour by women residents for collection of waste in poor townships was, however, justified to participating women and to the public at large through the rhetoric of 'women's empowerment' and 'good motherhood'.

Although major resistance from citizens and public officials on account of its neglect of labour laws and regulations led to discontinuation of the programme, the example is illuminating in how neoliberal governance privatises the responsibility of neighbourhood clean-up as an extension of women's realm of responsibility towards home and family and in doing so re-articulates the relationship between social reproduction and production that earlier feminist scholarship illuminated as a way of subsidising capital. In the neoliberal era, accumulation of capital relies on reprivatising some of the basic services that were formerly assumed by municipal authorities. (Re)privatising these social reproduction responsibilities expands the burden of poor women who not only have to undertake additional unpaid work at home for their families, but also for the community at neighbourhood and municipal levels (see also Lind, Chapter 100, this volume).

The complexity of the situation is, however, that the entrepreneurial strategies in governance that intensify women's burden by relying on their free labour for municipal services provision also increases their political participation in the public arena for collective action at neighbourhood and municipal levels. Their participation in so-called 'invited spaces of citizenship', such as municipal led and designed community-based waste collection schemes, offers the opportunity for greater presence and action by grassroots women in community and municipal levels decision-making arenas that might fall outside the control of the establishment and status quo (what I call 'invented spaces of citizenship') (for further details see Miraftab, 2006).

Grassroots women of the Western Cape Anti-Eviction Campaign (AEC), for example, take advantage of similar combined and contradictory processes. On the one hand, they experience intensified responsibility to feed not only their own children but a growing number of impoverished children in the neighbourhood. They ask for leftover vegetables from stores, mosques, churches and benevolent citizens and offer free meals to township children once a week. On the other hand, through their grassroots campaign AEC women directly mobilise against evictions and against service cut-offs in poor townships. They launch oppositional practices that have limited, slowed and, in many instances, stopped evictions and service suspension.[1] Here we see that while the South African state's inability and unwillingness to deal with poor populations have intensified reliance on poor women's free labour for performance of gendered social reproduction at home and in the community, grassroots women's activism, like that of the AEC, has been able to exert power to affect the processes and outcomes of policy decisions and hence challenge the silent but brutal violence of capitalism through poverty.

In short, this chapter has highlighted that notions of inclusive citizenship and entrepreneurial governance in the context of deep urban informality have worked as complex processes that both intensify women's social burden and increase their political possibilities for pubic action. The deep informality of cities where grassroots efforts afford economic livelihoods for poor populations, combined with entrepreneurial governing strategies that extend women's social reproduction responsibilities from home to neighbourhood and municipality, inevitably place women more than ever at the centre of urban processes (see also Beall, Chapter 97, this volume).

To understand the gender and urban poverty nexus in the Global South, not only women's burdens but also their grassroots activism and transformative collective actions need to shape the analytical centre of this debate.

Note

1. A summary of the achievements of the Western Cape AEC can be found on their website at: http://antieviction.org.za/ (accessed 18 October 2009). Achievements include moratoria on evictions and service cut-offs, and implementation of basic lifeline free water.

Select bibliography

Bakker, Isabella and Stephen Gill (eds) (2003) *Power, Production and Social Reproduction*, New York: Palgrave Macmillan.

Benería, Lourdes (2003) *Gender, Development and Globalisation: Economics As If People Mattered*, New York: Routledge.

Miraftab, Faranak (1998) 'Complexities of the margin: housing decisions of female householders in Mexico', *Society and Space: Environment and Design D*, **16**, 289–310.

Miraftab, Faranak (2004) 'Neoliberalism and casualisation of public sector services: the case of waste collection services in Cape Town, South Africa', *International Journal of Urban and Regional Research*, **28** (4), 874–92.

Miraftab, Faranak (2006) 'Feminist praxis, citizenship and informal politics: reflections on South Africa's Anti-Eviction Campaign', *International Feminist Journal of Politics*, **8** (2), 194–218.

Miraftab, Faranak (2008) 'Decentralisation and entrepreneurial planning', in Victoria Beard, Faranak Miraftab and Chris Silver (eds), *Planning and Decentralisation: Contested Spaces for Public Action in the Global South*, New York: Routledge, pp. 21–35.

Samson, Melanie (2008) 'Rescaling the state, restructuring social relations. Preview', *International Feminist Journal of Politics*, **10** (1), 19–39.

100 Gender, neoliberalism and post-neoliberalism: re-assessing the institutionalisation of women's struggles for survival in Ecuador and Venezuela
Amy Lind

Based on fieldwork in Ecuador and Venezuela, this chapter addresses the effects of neoliberal and 'post-neoliberal' development models on poor sectors, drawing out the implications for women's household, community, and market labour.[1] It starts out by addressing the general conclusions put forward by feminist scholars about the effects of global neoliberal restructuring on sectors of poor women in Latin America and the Global South. It then addresses the shift to the 'new Left' in Latin America; a shift characterised largely as a political and economic response to the failure of neoliberal development models in alleviating poverty in the region. Given the centrality of economic redistribution in socialist-oriented, post-neoliberal forms of governance, I discuss the potential of the Ecuadorian and Venezuelan models for alleviating poverty, redistributing wealth, and addressing longstanding structural (gendered) inequalities in the two countries, drawing out the broader implications for scholarship on neoliberalism and post-neoliberalism. I argue that in both neoliberal and post-neoliberal contexts, a critique of heteronormativity is needed in order to truly transform long-standing gender inequalities.[2]

Gender, neoliberalism and post-neoliberalism
Although since the 2000s we have witnessed a shift to 'post-neoliberal' development and governance in Latin America, there is no clear or abrupt rupture with the neoliberal policies that were central to national governments' development agendas during the 1980s and 1990s. Depending upon the country, the term 'post-neoliberal' arguably connotes more of a political shift than an economic one, although there is evidence to suggest that the new, socialist-inspired emphasis on redistribution, particularly in oil-rich Venezuela, has benefited poor sectors to some extent. Yet to understand post-neoliberal development, which in the cases of Ecuador and Venezuela is based on a conception of a stronger state presence in economic regulation and social service delivery with the ultimate goal of redistributing wealth to poor sectors, one necessarily needs to understand how neoliberal development policies continue to influence state and non-governmental sector agendas, particularly in countries beholden to foreign debt and aid.

The now vast scholarship on gender and neoliberalism has focused largely on three general themes: first, the effects of neoliberal reforms on women's work and daily lives, including their volunteer labour; second, the 'engendering' of macroeconomic development models, and third, the political and material consequences of women's participation in processes of neoliberal development. The large bulk of the literature focuses on linking macrolevel analyses of global economic restructuring with the microlevel and mesolevel effects on households and communities or nations, respectively. In particular, the literature has addressed how sectors of poor women have been disproportionately and negatively affected by neoliberal reforms including structural adjustment, economic liberalisation, free trade initiatives, state retrenchment, privatisation, cuts in social spending, and the general move toward inserting national economies into the global market (Benería and Feldman, 1992; Elson, 1991; Lind, 2005). In addition, some researchers have addressed the symbolic, as well as the material effects, in terms of how women are culturally (mis-)represented in Western gender and development discourse, and in terms of how cultural representations can lead to material inequalities among neoliberal-development policy recipients: 'poor women'. Part of the assumption behind this general approach has been that women, in their socially ascribed roles as mothers, wives and/or caretakers, perform uniquely gendered, often altruistic roles in caring for their families, communities and nations in times of crisis; this observation has been framed more recently in terms of how heteronormativity is central both to women's (and men's) lives and to the development policies that structure their material conditions and opportunities (see Lind, 2010, for discussion and references).

One important theme that has emerged from this literature is the question of whether development policies that 'target' poor women and aim to 'empower' them (a term widely adopted by development practitioners) are actually working. For example, in Latin America thousands of community-based women's organisations emerged in the 1980s as a collective response to the foreign debt crisis. Development policymakers and practitioners utilised this opportunity to incorporate previously unorganised women into local political processes, thereby politically empowering some participants but also relying on their volunteer and/or underpaid labour to manage community efforts aimed at alleviating poverty. Their economic burdens therefore increased rather than decreased, despite the general goal of the Women in Development (WID) field to 'integrate them into development'. Furthermore, in the context of state cuts in social spending and privatisation, women's participation in community-based initiatives such as communal kitchens, daycare centres and community centres became a permanent solution to poverty alleviation rather than a temporary survival strategy, an observation made by many women participants and documented in the research (Lind, 2005). In this sense, neoliberal development (and capitalist development in general) relies on women's 'elastic' or volunteer labour to 'absorb' the costs of broader economic changes; their struggles for survival have become institutionalised and serve as replacements for state support. This question remains of concern in post-neoliberal contexts.

Gender and post-neoliberal development in Ecuador and Venezuela
Both Ecuador and Venezuela have undergone shifts to the 'new Left'. Ecuador's shift evolved through a series of political and financial crises in the late 1990s, ultimately leading the way to the election of socialist economist Rafael Correa in 2006, whose 'citizen revolution' frames his redistribution agenda. In Venezuela, President Hugo Chávez, who has been in power since 1999, has undertaken perhaps the most intensive redistribution process in the region, largely through his 'Bolivarian revolution' which has aimed to re-centralise oil production and other industries and to make education, employment, and healthcare accessible to all Venezuelans. A key strategy of these new Left governments has been to revise and adopt new constitutions as a way to legislate new laws concerning the regulation of the economy. A second but nonetheless important

aspect of these constitutional reforms has involved introducing new language to address the rights of legally-defined 'vulnerable' groups such as women (especially poor women and single mothers), indigenous, and Afro-Venezuelan/Ecuadorian sectors and introduce new labour and environmental legislation. Through a constitutional assembly and national referendum, Ecuador adopted a new constitution in 2008 (only ten years after adopting a neoliberal-oriented constitution in 1998), while Venezuela adopted a new constitution in 1999, which remains in effect as of 2009, despite attempts by the Chávez administration to revise it through national referendum.

Ecuador
Ecuador's neoliberal period (1980–2005) has been characterised as 'mild' by some regional observers yet clearly the effects of structural adjustment and austerity measures have affected millions of people. Following dollarisation in 2000, over 2 million of Ecuador's total population of around 13 million have migrated to Spain as a result of the economic crisis. When President Correa entered office in early 2007, he launched his plan to re-centralise key industries and provide for 'vulnerable' sectors by recognising specific sets of rights (for example, employment, social security, access to healthcare, antidiscrimination) in the 2008 Constitution. Yet Correa has been largely unsuccessful at reclaiming state majority control over Ecuador's largest source of national income, its oil industry. And, given Ecuador's reliance on the value of the US dollar, which has shrunk in recent years, his administration is in a weak position to redistribute wealth to poor sectors. Thus while the new constitution is very promising and 'progressive' on paper, it remains to be seen whether the state's recognition of vulnerable groups will translate into redistributive schemes that directly advantage them. What is innovative about the new Constitution, however, in contrast to the 1998 Constitution, is that it includes language that links the recognition of vulnerable groups to redistribution; that is, unlike during the neoliberal period, when vulnerable groups were recognised but not given access to state benefits, the new Constitution aims to provide these groups with access to material resources such as social security benefits, reproductive healthcare, and hereditary rights, to name only a few.

Venezuela
Venezuela's neoliberal period (mid-1980s–1990s) involved a range of policy approaches, including relatively strict adherence to World Bank and International Monetary Fund (IMF) austerity measures, often imposed from above, and 'milder' approaches that were combined with stronger social policy. Like earlier forms of capitalist development policy, these neoliberal policies tended to benefit already wealthy elites and exacerbated longstanding inequalities between rich and poor. While many believe that Venezuela is a 'rich' country due to its oil reserves, it is poverty, not wealth, that defines the majority. Between 1980 and 2001, poverty increased threefold in the country, while also concentrating wealth in the hands of a few. As a country governed by two parties for almost five decades, the election of President Hugo Chávez represented a break from this past; a past perceived by many Venezuelans as excessive, corrupt and unequal.

President Hugo Chávez's 'Bolivarian Revolution' is distinct in that it is backed by oil development; in this regard, Chávez's socialist-inspired redistributive scheme would not be successful without capitalist profit. Regardless, his social agenda is extensive and reaches poor sectors throughout the country, most notably in the areas of healthcare and education. Through his Cuban-style 'missions', Chávez has been able to guarantee universal healthcare and public education, including vocational training and/or college level education in some instances. His 'Twenty-first-century socialism' agenda has gained widespread support in poor sectors yet has also faced serious opposition at all social-class levels due to his authoritarianism. According to one study, during the first ten years of the Chávez administration (1999–2009), the percentage of households living in poverty decreased by 39 per cent, and extreme poverty decreased by more than 50 per cent. Inequality, as measured by the Gini index, also fell substantially: whereas in 1999 the index measured 47, it fell to 41 in 2008, marking a potentially significant reduction in income inequality (Weisbrot et al., 2009). This does not account for additional access to resources such as healthcare. Thus despite Venezuela's continued inequalities between rich and poor and its comparatively high concentration of wealth, some alleviation has been brought to poor sectors through these state-subsidised forms of support.

From the start, President Chávez has utilised a maternalist discourse to gain popular support for his missions (Espina and Rakowski, 2010). His missions, which number more than 20, address a range of issues including access to employment, illiteracy, combatting disease, poverty, malnutrition, and other social inequalities. Mass numbers of poor and working-class women have been mobilised to participate in these missions, as volunteers or paid employees, including in his Alimentation Mission (Misión Alimentación), which focuses on food security, and Barrio Mothers' Mission (Misión Madres de Barrio), which trains poor women in trades. The Community Councils, another mechanism to organise support for Chávez at the community level, also include high participation rates by women. And in 2001, Chávez established the 'Women's Bank' (Banmujer), which provides small loans to poor women, with the aim of 'empowering' them through microenterprise development. Toward the beginning of his presidency, organised sectors of women, including femocrats (state-based feminists) and other activists, had hoped that poor women would benefit from Chávez's alternative development path through their participation in his populist revolution, including in the missions. However, as observers have pointed out, the outcome of Chávez's 'targeting' of women in their maternal roles has had mixed results at best (Espina and Rakowski, 2010; Fernandes, 2007). While Chávez supports women's rights to some degree, his agenda, like that of neoliberal governments, reinforces the logic that women's labour is elastic and ultimately makes their labour indispensable to 'Twenty-first-century socialism', this finding suggests that scholars pay further attention to how heteronormative notions of femininity (and masculinity) are central to both neoliberal and post-neoliberal development agendas and contribute to reproducing gender inequalities and disempower women economically despite political gains.

From neoliberalism to post-neoliberalism: gendered paradoxes, future considerations
As has been argued in the case of neoliberal development in Ecuador, Venezuela and elsewhere, through the institutionalisation of women's struggles for survival, poor women increasingly have been viewed as the 'answer' to a weak welfare state and as a source of cheap labour in the context of state and global anti-poverty initiatives (see Roy, Chapter 84, this volume). This has led to their disempowerment rather than empowerment or

'integration into the development process', as earlier Women in Development scholars and contemporary proponents have claimed.

Like neoliberal development policies, post-neoliberal development policies such as those implemented by the Chávez administration and proposed by the Correa administration differentially affect specific sectors of women. Clearly the progressive constitutions and participatory initiatives in both countries have elicited larger levels of support by sectors of poor and middle class women, and through this process many have gained a combination of skills, knowledge and experience that is perhaps invaluable for those who feel empowered and/or for those who gain access to additional economic opportunities as a result of their participation. This cannot be denied. Particularly in the case of Venezuela, where massive numbers of women have been professionally trained in historically unprecedented ways, this can be seen as a victory for poverty alleviation. And poverty and inequality data suggest that Chávez's redistribution agenda is working to some extent. Yet many questions remain and long-standing structural inequalities persist.

For one, the Chávez administration continues to rely on a maternalist logic to construct its anti-poverty policies. While clearly women who fulfil normative gender roles and expectations may benefit from these policies, these policies also reinforce and reproduce gender inequalities insofar as they privilege traditional heterosexual coupling over other possible household arrangements, thereby leaving the questions of sexism and patriarchal relations untouched. Just as sectors of poor women have been asked, and even expected, to pick up where the neoliberal state left off, so too does the Boliviarian state expect poor women to (in this case) support the revolution through their seemingly elastic, often volunteer labour. This ultimately has the effect of increasing rather than decreasing women's unequal burdens in household, community and market labour. Thus while clearly sectors of poor women are benefiting from Chávez's redistributive agenda to some extent, far more so than they benefited from neoliberal development policies, there is much more that needs to be done in order to subvert long-standing patriarchal gender inequalities.

Addressing heteronormativity in both neoliberal and post-neoliberal development policy, including in anti-poverty policy, is one way to begin. Scholars, policymakers and practitioners could better assess how households are constructed, who benefits in both two-headed and single-headed household arrangements, how constructions of masculinity and femininity play into household bargaining power, and how these same constructions shape and influence the opportunities (or lack thereof) of specific sectors of women and men in community and national development initiatives. Utilising the lens of heteronormativity, researchers could also assess how state policies, including feminist-inspired policies, may serve to reinforce rather than challenge or subvert patriarchal traditions in families, households and communities. Initial research has begun on these topics but additional empirical work is needed to document and reassess the rich tradition of feminist scholarship on gender, the family, and poverty in the Global South, as a way to better understand both how capitalist and socialist development models reinforce the institutionalisation of women's struggles for survival (albeit to different degrees). In this regard, Ecuador's constitution is much more promising than Venezuela's: not only does it provide protection to vulnerable groups including single mothers but it links their recognition to material benefits. Furthermore, it includes language that recognises 'alternative families', with the goal of including transnational migrant households, non-married couples (which could potentially include same-sex couples), and extended families not previously recognised by law. What the Ecuadorian state lacks is financial support for its redistributive agenda; something which Venezuela does not. Regardless, other countries could learn from the Ecuadorian example as a way to create redistributive schemes that address alternative family models and aim to take the burden of poverty off the shoulders of poor women.[3] This can only be achieved through rethinking heteronormative constructions of gender and 'the family' as they shape state and global development policy as well as societal understandings of survival and poverty.

Acknowledgements
Research for this chapter was funded by a University of Cincinnati (UC) University Research Council Summer Research Grant, a UC Friends of Women's Studies Summer Mini-Research Grant, and a Fulbright Senior Specialists Grant. Special thanks to Gioconda Espina for her warm welcome and intellectual support in Venezuela. Thanks also to Cathy Rakowski for her feedback on my research proposal and for putting me in touch with Venezuelan scholars during my summer 2008 research trip. Additional gratitude is owed to Leticia Rojas for her research assistance in Venezuela and Ecuador.

Notes
1. I place the term 'post-neoliberal' in quotation marks to highlight its conceptual ambiguity with regard to neoliberalism, a point I develop throughout the chapter.
2. By 'heteronormativity', I am referring to the understanding of heterosexuality as a 'normal' and 'natural' institution, form of identity and/or expression, whereas all other sexual practices, identities and relationship arrangements are viewed as deviant and/or abnormal. An analysis of heteronormativity also involves understanding how particular forms of heterosexuality become hegemonic whereas other expressions of sexuality, be they heterosexual or otherwise, are deemed inferior or made invisible.
3. Here I am not implying that the Ecuadorian constitutional assembly explicitly provided a heteronormative critique of 'the family' in its redrafting of the Constitution but rather that, through a long negotiation process, this language was agreed upon and included in the new Constitution. It remains to be seen how this will be put into practice.

Select bibliography
Benería, Lourdes and Shelley Feldman (eds) (1992) *Unequal Burdens: Economic Crisis, Persistent Poverty and Women's Work*, Boulder, CO: Westview Press.
Elson, Diane (ed.) (1991) *Male Bias in the Development Process*, Manchester: Manchester University Press.
Espina, Gioconda and Cathy Rakowski (2010) 'Waking women Up? Hugo Chávez, populism, and Venezuela's "popular" women,' in Karen Kampwirth (ed.), *Women and Populism in Latin America: Passionate Politics*, University Park, PA: Penn State University Press.
Fernandes, Sujatha (2007) 'Barrio women and popular politics in Chávez's Venezuela', *Latin American Politics and Society*, **49** (3), 97–127.
Lind, Amy (2005) *Gendered Paradoxes: Women's Movements, State Restructuring and Global Development in Ecuador*, University Park, PA: Penn State University Press.
Lind, Amy (2010) 'Querying globalisation: sexual subjectivities, development, and the governance of intimacy', in Marianne Marchand and Anne Sisson Runyan (eds), *Gender and Global Restructuring: Sightings, Sites and Resistances*, 2nd edn, London: Routledge.
Weisbrot, Mark, Rebecca Ray and Luis Sandoval (2009) *The Chávez Administration at Ten Years: The Economy and Social Indicators*, Washington, DC: Centre for Economic and Policy Research.

101 Who does the counting? Gender mainstreaming, grassroots initiatives and linking women across space and 'race' in Guyana

D. Alissa Trotz

Over the past two and a half decades, there has been a virtual explosion of women's visibility in the global public arena, in large part the result of lobbying and mobilisation of transnational feminist networks. Gender mainstreaming is everywhere, from national governments collecting data and creating women's bureaux and gender focal points in ministries, to the various international legislative instruments and protocols that give gender institutional recognition and legitimacy on the world stage.

For many the paradox is the way in which gender mainstreaming is invoked at supranational and national levels by the very same institutions that have been the architects of neoliberal economic policies. This is apparent in the Caribbean, more than a decade after the Beijing Platform for Action (BPFA) named women and poverty and women and the economy as two of its strategic objectives and priority areas for action. Notwithstanding the distance between official commitments to gender equality and mainstreaming and on the ground realities, the uneven incorporation of gender within countries and institutions across various poverty assessments and living standards surveys, and the tendency to incorporate gender regularly only in studies that are specifically or stereotypically about women like domestic violence and reproductive health, the limited data that do exist points to a deepening of poverty and an entrenchment of gendered inequalities in a region that has adopted market reforms and structural adjustment programmes (SAPs) since the 1980s (Andaiye, 2003).

While gender is on the Caribbean agenda (albeit unevenly), there appears to have been little progress in disaggregating statistics that relate to women. Although there is some recognition of the need to complicate our understanding of gender – the attention paid to distinguishing between women living with men and female household heads in particular, but also some work on rural–urban divisions – what is clearly lacking is a systematic approach to data collection that offers insights into women's differentiated relationships to the economy, and which might help inform policies that address not just gendered inequalities, but other social relations that result in specific and different experiences of disadvantage. Moreover, if differentiation among women is not addressed from the outset, might policies aimed at tackling gendered inequalities not run the risk of themselves being exclusionary of some constituencies of women?

This is not an oversight that is confined to the Caribbean. Indeed, one could say that gender mainstreaming for the most part continues to define gender as relating to women qua women, an emphasis that is unable to account for interlocking social relations that differentiate women not just from men, but also from each other. That this flattened focus is at odds with the move away from a singular understanding of 'woman' among feminists in North America and Europe, the issues raised by women in the Global South at the various meetings convened in the wake of the declaration of the United Nations (UN) Decade for women, and the realities of difference as a foundational feature of women's activism in places like the Caribbean (Reddock, 2007), raises the question of what happens to more deeply complicated understandings of gender in the process of translation from activism to institutionalisation.

There is now an extensive body of work that explores the difficult relationship between policy institutionalisation at local, state and supra-state levels and transformative feminist agendas. Some researchers posit that gender mainstreaming puts women on the radar of developmentalist protocols seeking to extend the reach of the market to everyone, suggesting that gender gets deployed in ways that enable it to coexist with neoliberal projects (Bergeron, 2006). Others argue that gender mainstreaming instrumentalises and technologises gender as a target of improvement via specific modes of intervention (Manicom, 2001). In the Caribbean, there have been calls for regional feminists to consider the role they play as gatekeepers for the development industry, and to examine closely how this new dispensation runs the risk of disarming the emancipatory potential of the women's movement and turning poor women into clients (Andaiye, (2002).

To be sure, there have been recent and important efforts to extend the narrow remit of gender as pertaining to a relatively undifferentiated category of woman, such as Kimberle Crenshaw's submission, based on her pathbreaking and earlier work on intersectionality, to the sessions leading up to the World Conference Against Racism, Racial Discrimination, Xenophobia and Related Forms of Intolerance (Crenshaw, 2000). At the same time, and taking the feminist critiques of gender mainstreaming into account, one might well ask, what happens when intersectionality – deployed as a more accurate or sensitive diagnostic tool to help practitioners and policymakers count or measure the complex ways in which women's lives are shaped by vulnerability – becomes part of the mainstream itself?

Intersectionality from below? The Red Thread women's organisation in Guyana
A different kind of lesson is offered by the Red Thread women's organisation that is based in Guyana, a Caribbean country located on the north-eastern shoulder of South America that since the mid-1980s has been locked into an unending succession of SAPs. It is important to note that these policies (initially called the Economic Recovery Programme, and dubbed the 'Empty Rice Pot' by Guyanese) have continued and deepened with the return to electoral democracy in 1992 after 28 years of dictatorship. Articulating a coherent challenge to the exclusions accompanying these economic reforms is complicated by a deeply racialised political structure, a legacy of colonial policies of divide and rule that manifests itself today in the competition for state power being monopolised by two political parties that are largely seen as representing African and Indian Guyanese interests. Given this highly polarised environment, the difficulties of comprehensively integrating an intersectional approach to analyses of poverty assume another dimension. The paucity of disaggregated data combine with political sensitivities to elide women's racialised experiences of poverty. Attempting to count in this context runs the risk of reproducing rather than shifting the dominant frame through which 'race' as a meaningful category of experience materialises in Guyana, and can easily lead to accusations of racial discrimination and denial and defensiveness. The political stakes are very high indeed.

Keenly aware of the susceptibility of women's organising to the imperatives of the two major political parties, a weakness that has historically acted to instantiate further racialised divisions while completely obscuring key constituencies like indigenous women, Red Thread's commitment to operate outside any political party structure and thus to include women right across the political spectrum has always been non-negotiable. Red Thread, which was formed in 1986, defines its principal mandate as 'to organise with other women, beginning at the grassroots, in a way which crosses race and other divides and enables us all to transform our conditions'. This marks a shift away from simply naming difference as a category that can be measured or as a detached way of refining our understanding of differential experiences of disadvantage among women. Recognising the damaging uses to which difference can be put – whether as a form of identification that generates divisions among women, or as a guide to policy interventions from above that produce women as clients or dependents – Red Thread aims instead to engage deeply the processes through which such categories come to be infused with meaning in relation to each other (Trotz, 2007).

Especially in the past decade, and in the context of individual and later collective relationships with the global Wages for Housework Campaign, Red Thread has distilled its approach as one that always begins with the unwaged caring labour that underpins the organisation of human life, and that is disproportionately shouldered by grassroots women. It became the national coordinator for the Global Women's Strike which formed in 2000, a transnational anti-racist and anti-imperialist feminist network that is deeply influenced by the efforts of Marxist feminists to foreground unwaged labour as central to capital and to insist on seeing those who perform 'housework' as a section of the working class.

Counting work becomes an analytical and political entry point to understand and challenge the logic of contemporary developmental strategies and their differentiated impact on women, but it does not stop there. In 2004, Red Thread undertook an extensive anti-racist time-use survey with over 100 grassroots women across four racialised categories recognised in the Guyana Census (Indian, African, Indigenous/Amerindian and Mixed). The survey was unprecedented in that it was conducted by grassroots women across rural, urban and hinterland communities across the country. By participating in the exercise as both subject and researcher, grassroots women were reframed from being simply sources of raw data for outside 'experts', whose lives would be converted into statistics or documents far removed from their experiences, into knowledge producers themselves who determined the process and outcome of the information-gathering exercises and who were able to use the material to make connections with each other and to advocate for meaningful change in their lives. Why is this being done, for whom and to what purposes will this information be put, are three questions that take on particular meaning in this instance in relation to feminist praxis. Knowledge production is eminently political, and here that is not just acknowledged, but embraced in the service of a radical liberatory agenda. The survey thus becomes not just a means of accessing information, but an indispensable element of the process of organising with women. In the first instance, it was a way of making women visible to each other. It established the centrality of grassroots women's labour to the sustenance and organisation of households and communities. Through interviews and discussions – women were asked to keep their own diaries as well – participants were able to see the extensive hours they worked (between 14 and

18 hours a day). Interviewers often contributed to sharing and taking on necessary tasks in individual households in order to 'free up' some time for the discussion and diaries to be completed. Communities also took note of the similarities among grassroots women, and the ways in which work differed or intensified for some women (for instance, in interior parts of Guyana, indigenous women walked long distances for water and also tried to double up their efforts during the day in areas where there was little or no electricity). We might, then, characterise the survey as process itself, a way of coming to see oneself in relation to others.

In addition to recognising the centrality of grassroots women's contribution, the act of counting work also revealed to women how little of what they do is recognised as it involves predominantly unwaged forms of social reproduction that subsidise the economy without being acknowledged. The extent to which grassroots women's needs are never seen as a priority by politicians and policymakers became clear. The knowledge gathered through the time-use survey and several other activities has informed numerous interventions, all led by women, to recalibrate the discussion at various levels to reflect the challenges they face better. Two short examples are offered below.

In January 2005 Guyana experienced the worst floods in the country's recorded history, affecting more than 40 per cent of the population (over 90 per cent of whom live along a narrow strip of coastal land that lies 6 feet below sea level). Initially involved in flood relief, Red Thread soon shifted to organising with women in and across their communities. Meetings with women demonstrated acutely the shared vulnerability of those who lived on the coast, underlined how poverty was key in mediating who was most affected by the floods, and revealed specific kinds of vulnerability among the poor – especially female household heads and the disabled. As with the time-use survey, it was obvious that the kinds of issues that faced women from affected communities were not visible in wider discussions of the disaster. For instance, official definitions of flood-related compensation largely based their calculations on earned income. Grassroots women could not see their experiences reflected in the forms generated for such purposes, insisting instead that unwaged work and household items were also essential elements of the organisation of human life for which they too were entitled to compensation. The organising resulted in a national speakout held in the capital city, Georgetown. While government, trade unions, donor agencies, non-governmental organisations (NGOs) and other civil society representatives were invited and present, the speakout was organised by grassroots women, and it was they who presented a list of wide-ranging demands, calling among other things for a cancellation of household as well as Guyana's national debt (a recognition of the implications of economic globalisation for the country's predicament), compensation, the cleaning of schools, a complete audit not only of government but of agencies that had received flood relief monies, and inclusion in future discussions on disaster preparedness programmes (Red Thread, 2005). Out of the flood organising, as well as in response to other initiatives, a network associated with Red Thread was formed, Guyanese Women Across Race (GWAR).

The second example pertains to the government of Guyana's introduction, in 2007, of a punitive value-added tax (VAT) that initially included exemptions for certain non-essential and imported foods that middle-class households could afford, while penalising some basic food items and other household goods. Red Thread began a letter-writing campaign to the local media, detailing typical daily domestic budgets for grassroots families and how they would be affected by the proposed VAT changes. It was a strategy that asked the general public to imagine who was sitting at the table when VAT came up for discussion. Providing information on the food baskets of most Guyanese made clear that grassroots women were neither involved nor considered in these deliberations, an absence that meant that those who could least afford it were being asked to bear the highest burden of the proposed tax. Significantly, the government backed down and zero-rated most of the basic food items, schoolbooks and medicines when the tax was implemented in January 2008. Worried that shopkeepers would pass on the cost of the VAT in the form of increased prices, some women also began keeping regular diaries of their purchases, to share with each other and to provide a longitudinal assessment of VAT-related effects.

These are two instances of innumerable ongoing initiatives: picketing against the budget outside Parliament and appearing on television to discuss the cost of living; presenting household budgets of women to make the case to increase pensions and public assistance; intervening in the unending racialisation of the political process by embarking on a report card project through which grassroots women would keep a continual score of the extent to which political parties kept to their campaign promises; tracking media reports of domestic violence and opening a drop in service at Red Thread's headquarters; opening a library and after-school feeding and education programme for children in the surrounding low-income community; demonstrating on the streets of Guyana in solidarity with Haitian and Venezuelan women. Through these interventions, grassroots women reposition themselves as agentive knowledge producers, capable of organising and self-activity based on their own assessments of their realities. They work to dismantle enduring divisions between rural and urban, coast and hinterland, Amerindian, African and Indian women, while never losing sight of *who* continues to bear the brunt of neoliberal policies. At the same time, this is no model of self-help that dovetails neatly with the incorporation of gender-mainstreaming into agendas ruled by the language of markets, microenterprise and downsizing of the state. Beginning with caring work to develop a language of entitlement and to demand accountability, enables a critique of the devastating consequences of two decades of structural adjustment policies for Guyanese. Moreover, through their connections with the transnational network of the Global Women's Strike (through regularised communication while in Guyana as well as through Red Thread's participation in various Global Strike activities and meetings in Mexico, Venezuela and the United Kingdom [UK]), Red Thread is able to situate the Guyanese reality in a wider context that includes both global neoliberalism as well as learning from other resistant responses that offer inspiration and example on the local terrain. This is intersectionality and gender-mainstreaming at work from below, where what is counted and what counts are inseparable from the question of who does the counting.

Select bibliography

Andaiye (2002) 'The angle you look from determines what you see: toward a critique of feminist politics in the Caribbean', Lucille Mathurin-Mair Lecture, University of the West Indies, Kingston, Jamaica, 2 March.

Andaiye (2003) 'Smoke and mirrors: the illusion of CARICOM women's growing economic empowerment, post-Beijing', in Gemma Tang Nain and Barbara Bailey (eds), *Gender Equality in the Caribbean*, Kingston, Jamaica: Ian Randle, pp. 73–105.

Bergeron, Suzanne (2006) *Fragments of Development: Nation, Gender, and the Space of Modernity*, Ann Arbor, MI: University of Michigan Press.

Crenshaw, Kimberle (2000) Background paper for expert meeting on the Gender Related Aspects of Race Discrimination, 21–24 November, Zagreb, Croatia, available at: http://www.wicej.addr.com/wcar_docs/crenshaw.html (accessed 25 May 2009).
Manicom, Linzi (2001) 'Globalising "gender" in – or as – governance? Questioning the terms of local translations', *Agenda*, **48**, 6–21.
Red Thread (2005) *Organising for Survival: Grassroots Women of the Flood*, DVD and transcript produced by Red Thread, Georgetown.
Reddock, Rhoda (2007) 'Diversity, difference and Caribbean feminism: the challenge of anti-racism', *Caribbean Review of Gender Studies*, **1**, 1–24, available at: http://sta.uwi.edu/crgs/april2007/journals/Diversity-Feb_2007.pdf (accessed 20 May 2009).

102 Poverty, religion and gender: perspectives from Albania
Claire Brickell

Introduction
This chapter examines the ways in which poverty, religion and gender intersect at the local level in Albania. More specifically, it begins by introducing some debate around the rise of religion within development discourse, and highlights the emerging role of faith-based development organisations (FBDOs) as service providers. This is followed by an overview of poverty trends and levels in Albania, with a brief focus on gender. Finally, these three themes are drawn together in field research with women from different age groups in Bathore, a peri-urban settlement in the Kamza municipality, who are engaged in a 'women's empowerment' project run by an Evangelical Christian FBDO.[1] The chapter suggests that despite the potential dangers of engaging with religious discourse, failing to do so will only contribute to a lacuna in understanding that will ultimately be damaging to poverty alleviation goals.

Religion and the development pantheon
From missionary organisations that have been heralded as 'the forerunners of modern-day development NGOs' (Clarke, 2005: 18), to contemporary groups of believers committed to the provision of social services supporting the local poor, religion has always contributed to alleviating poverty. Yet, it is only in recent years that it has been identified as an important area for consideration by development professionals and scholars alike. Moreover, following the events of 11 September 2001 and an intensified focus on terrorist activity, this has often been motivated by a 'know your enemy' mantra. Despite this however, a stream of research is now emerging that seeks to interrogate the dynamics of organised religion, faith and spirituality as both a potential barrier, and a *resource*, in the development process.

This movement contends that development has been mistakenly understood as a wholly secular process. Instead it argues that it cannot be separated from the culture of which it is a product, or of that in which it operates. This perspective recognises for example, that religious sentiment is often found at both an organisational and local level, from the international FBDO whose staff are motivated by faith, to the ways in which a religious worldview shapes the everyday lived experiences of many people in the Global South. This argument is supported by the World Bank's Voices of the Poor: Crying Out For Change project (Narayan et al., 1999), which collected the views of more than 20 000 poor women and men from 23 countries around the world on what 'poverty' meant to them. The research revealed that harmony with transcendent matters is regularly considered to be an essential part of people's day-to-day welfare, and that faith is also perceived to be an important source of hope.

Studies examining the ways in which religion, spirituality and faith intersect with experiences of poverty have been invaluable in underscoring the argument that religion can be an important resource in the development process. Yet, in an Albanian context this petition for religion's inclusion in the development pantheon seems to find less support, given the common perception that Albanians are irreligious. For those that uphold this view the vilification of religion under the country's former communist president, Enver Hoxha (1944–85), is an important factor. Beginning in 1967 a succession of laws forbade religious rites, and at the same time forced the closure of all 2169 religious institutions, which were then either destroyed or converted for other uses. This came to a peak in 1977 when religious activity was announced as punishable by the death sentence, in arguably one of the most intense and prolonged attacks on faith that the world has witnessed.

Following the collapse of Hoxha's isolationist regime, debate around the resurfacing of Albania's traditional religions (Islam, Orthodoxy and Catholicism) is heated. Yet, none is more controversial than emerging literature discussing the influx of Evangelical Christian missionaries and FBDOs which represent a definitively foreign intrusion rather than a home-grown religious movement which might be more appropriate to facilitating and enhancing existing sociocultural structures. In this context, I argue that salient questions have to be tackled concerning both the potential mixing of mission and development, and the efficacy of FBDOs in this environment.

Just as in Albania, FBDOs are becoming a focal point for discussion in wider professional and academic circles, and in turn research funds are being invested in to this area by organisations such as the World Faiths Development Dialogue (WFDD). In the United Kingdom (UK), Birmingham University has also established a Religions and Development Research Programme. As Bradley (2009) argues, such work is essential if we are to grasp the diversity of FBDOs, and to examine their contribution to the development process. For while it is necessary to identify those organisations that hijack development as a medium for proselytisation, research must also be prepared to move beyond negative preconceptions to examine the potential for positive transformation inherent in some FBDOs. Such research could, for example, consider the way in which FBDOs often appear to possess an innate moral authority; question the importance of the large number of well-connected followers they attract; or examine to what extent FBDOs' religious foundations tap in to and shape cosmologies, changing not only the way that people think about the their lives, but also how they live them out in situations of poverty.

Poverty and gender in Albania: a brief overview
In 1993 Albania was languishing on the United Nations (UN) Least Developed Countries List, but today it is ranked at number 68 in human development by the United Nations Development Programme (UNDP), which places it just inside the 'high human development' category (see UNDP, 2007/08). Despite this impressive leap, poverty remains a significant problem within Albania, particularly among the mountain villages of the North. A study conducted jointly by a team of the National Institute of Statistics (INSTAT), UNDP and the World Bank found, for example, that while Albania has witnessed significant reduction in poverty between 2005 and 2008, 12.4 per cent of the population are still considered poor, having a per capita monthly income of less than 5722 lek (*c.* US$62.50) (UNDP, 2009).

Albania's poverty profile reflects the legacy of its recent social, political and economic past, having only just emerged from what Janz (1998: 97) has described as 'one of the boldest social experiments in modern history'. As the last communist domino to fall in the region, Albania continues to undergo a threefold transition: from an officially atheistic state to one that acknowledges religious freedoms, from political authoritarianism to multi-party democracy, and from a communist economic system to one based on open-market capitalist growth. Within this context the neoliberal policies of the World Bank and the International Monetary Fund (IMF) have been adopted in the belief that a 'short, sharp shock' was necessary to kickstart transition. This is often seen to have been responsible for entrenching poverty given the synchronised liberalisation, privatisation, and dismantling of social service delivery and social security mechanisms, which were at the core of the communist welfare state (Townsend, 2002).

As in other post-communist states, and perhaps even to a greater degree, poverty is tightly bound to gender disparities (see Ashwin, Chapter this volume; Falkingham and Baschier, Chapter this volume). This has been recognised by the Albanian government, which has made headway in developing national legislation to promote the protection of women's rights, and to foster equality between men and women in economic, public, and social spheres. In 2007/08 however, Albania was ranked sixty-first in the world on the UNDP's Gender-related Development Index (GDI), with a score of 0.797. While this does reflect progress, given that in 2002 the first ever calculations using the Human Development Indexes ranked Albania ninety-second, there is still clearly room for improvement.

Religion, poverty and gender: a case study from Bathore
Bathore is an informal settlement in the Kamza municipality of Albania, which fans out from both sides of the main northern road out of Tirana, the national capital. Often referred to as the 'City of Cowsheds', it is home to economic migrants from the northern mountains of Albania. Rural exodus began when communist migratory restrictions were removed, allowing those people displaced by the building of a power station on the River Drin, and the closure of state mines, to seek out alternative sources of income near the city. Arriving in the region around Tirana in 1991 the people settled on the land of the former communist cooperatives and sheltered in old cowsheds without access to running water, electricity, schooling or adequate healthcare. Since then some steps have been taken towards improving Bathore's basic infrastructure and alleviating the impoverished conditions of its inhabitants. This process has involved the work of numerous non-governmental organisations (NGOs) and FBDOs, one of which is the UK-based Evangelical Christian charity, Worldwide Action for Children.[2]

Worldwide Action is predominantly a children's charity, although in 2004 a weekly women's group was established to encourage 'women's empowerment'. As the Chief Executive Officer (CEO) of the charity explains, the group is 'trying to integrate women back into society, and to empower women to actually take a role in the community'. Presently in Bathore many women are confined to their homes under a patriarchal system influenced by both a long history of male domination in the Balkans, and the influence of the Kanun of Lek Dukagjini. Originating from the north of Albania, the Kanun is an orally transmitted customary law consisting of 1263 articles, many of which refer to women's conduct. For example, the Kanun stipulates that it is a woman's duty to serve her husband and to be subordinate to him in all matters. In one of the more infamous articles the Kanun states 'a woman is known as a sack, made to endure as long as she lives in her husband's house'. While only a handful of women I interviewed knew the Kanun by name, each participant referred to the proliferation of northern customs that governed their lives, and which ultimately fitted within the Kanun framework. Within this context, Lule,[3] the leader of the women's group explained:

> I think that women in Bathore are not true to themselves. They came from the North and violence still exists within the family. They don't have the freedom to decide anything, to act, or freedom of expression. It is true that we are near Tirana and that in Bathore there are now some very beautiful houses, but if you look deeper there are a lot of social problems too.

Lule goes on to elaborate that the women's groups are a valuable opportunity to 'discuss themes from reality, daily life, their free expression, their problems. In fact when they meet in these groups they talk about all of their problems. It's a compact group so that they can feel free . . . We also often cook and have lunch together, have parties . . .'.

Thirty-one-year-old Rozafa attends these Friday afternoon women's meetings and lives with her husband in a single room in one of Bathore's many cowsheds. Without access to running water or electricity, she is married to an alcoholic husband who is often without work. Ordered to stay home within the confines of the cowshed, she is only able to attend the meetings when her husband has left the house in search of work, and runs the risk of being punished should he discover her disobedience. Despite this, however, Rozafa explained to me that not only was it important for her to have this 'safe space' but that she also valued the opportunity to talk about God. Rozafa first heard about Jesus at one of the women's group meetings and she explains that becoming a Christian has had a significant impact on her way of life. In particular she described how she uses prayer as a coping strategy to endure her husband's violence and the poverty in which they live: 'I pray for us to have a better life and to be equal . . . I pray for my husband not to drink anymore, and for raki[4] not to exist anymore. This and the meetings helps me to overcome my stresses.' She also attributes some of the positive changes in her life to having found faith:

> My husband used to come home drunk and he attacked me. He used to hit me. I had many quarrels with him. But after I started to pray, and read the Bible, he is somehow better now. He is becoming calmer, and not like he used to be. That's why I believe, I think my prayers have changed something in him.

As a lens through which to discuss the interconnections between poverty and religion at the local level in Bathore, Rozafa's narrative is important because it provides an example of the way in which faith can help people to deal with difficult situations. Beyond this, however, Rozafa's experiences also point towards a more nuanced discussion of not only poverty and religion, but gender. Rozafa has thus far been unable to have a child, living in a society where a woman's main role is perceived to be motherhood, and their sphere of influence to be within the home. This was clearly difficult for her, as Elona, a 45-year-old mother of three elucidated: 'It is not in a man's blood to stay home and cook and clean as it is in the woman's . . . they say "that's why I married you, to do the housework, stay at home, and to have my children".' Thus on one level the creation of the women's group is challenging this patriarchal structure by publicly creating a space in which women's voices are valued and respected outside of the home. As Adelina, a 36-year-old mother of seven told me through her laughter:

> Things are changing here since Worldwide Action came and started these groups. I remember when I went to meet Ariana [the project manager] once and I was with my husband. She greeted me first and then my husband. He later asked me 'Why did she greet you first? I am the man, she should have greeted me first'. And I told him that is how things are changing here, women are more respected.

At the same time however the main message of the women's groups is also focused on the importance of motherhood, and the ways in which women can be 'agents of change' within their families, and Bathore more widely. The project manager explained to me,

> We want to work with mums in helping them to understand . . . how important it is to be a mum, and although it is not paid in cash it is paid in other moral values that they have and they bring up with their kids, so that they can bring a change to their families, and also to their husbands . . . we talk with mums a lot about their role in the family and so we believe there is a large effect that they can have on their husbands if they are different.

Recalling that the group's professed aim is to 'integrate women back into society', I question whether this unswerving focus on women as mothers and wives leaves much room for understanding 'empowerment' outside of these categories. Furthermore, while it is difficult to disagree that being a mother is a worthwhile role, this strategy also seems to overlook those women, such as Rozafa, who attend the women's groups and do not have children, or who are able to work outside of the home, either out of necessity or choice. Thus by maintaining this focus I argue that the organisation's religious value, 'we are Christian and I believe that God created man to be head of the household and to provide for his family', leaves little scope to imagine 'woman', other than in the role of mother, wife and homemaker. As such, a situation obtains in which the patriarchal norms which Worldwide Action are trying to challenge are actually being inadvertently upheld, and with it women's poverty of opportunity.

Concluding thoughts

The religious sentiments underpinning FBDOs often permeate the development and 'gender' policies that they promote, as in the women's group presented here. In some cases this is potentially damaging to those living in poverty, and in its most extreme form, exploitative, particularly when an organisation follows what one staff member of this FBDO called the 'I will give you food if you come to my Bible study' philosophy. By the same token, the fieldwork conducted in Bathore also provides a glimpse of how and why the power of faith in everyday people's lives can be a valuable tool in alleviating poverty. From the tireless energy of the staff to the optimism and hopefulness of the participants, Jesus' message did indeed seem to be 'good news' in the midst of poverty. Moreover, of all the development organisations working in Bathore, it is the FBDOs that have stayed the longest. Perhaps, as the CEO of Worldwide Action explained, this is because they have,

> a vision that God can do something here and is interested in liberation, you know . . . He wants to make a difference, God is calling people to make a difference by saying this is unacceptable,

it's wrong, it's unjust and justice must prevail. And unless you have that sort of driving vision you can't take the rough with the smooth.

In bringing this chapter to a close I suggest that future research should remain critical of the relationship between poverty, religion and gender, while also opening itself to the possibility that religion may have a place in the development pantheon, or indeed, that it always has done.

Acknowledgements
The author wishes to thank Belina Kodra for her excellent work as research assistant and translator for the fieldwork on which this chapter is based.

Notes
1. The fieldwork for this chapter was conducted during a two-week period in July 2009 and signals the start of a wider project that will question the inclusion of faith within service provision in an Albanian context. The research consisted of 22 semi-structured interviews, one focus group session and three group discussions, with 30 respondents in total. To obtain further understanding, Co-PLAN, a non-governmental institute for habitat development that has worked in Bathore, was also consulted.
2. Please note that I am using a fictitious name to describe the FBDO I studied.
3. All names of informants in this chapter have been changed to preserve anonymity.
4. Raki is a traditional alcoholic drink in the Balkans.

Select bibliography
Bradley, Tamsin (2009) 'A call for clarification and critical analysis of the work of faith-based development organisations (FBDOs)', *Progress in Development Studies*, **9** (2), 101–14

Clarke, Gerrard (2005) 'Development and the complex world of faith-based organisations', available at: http://www.devstud.org.uk/Conference05/papers/clarke.docwww.devstud.org.uk/Conference05/papers/clarke.doc (accessed 20 July 2008).

Janz, Denis (1998) *World Christianity and Marxism*, New York: Oxford University Press.

Narayan, Deepal, Robert Chambers, Meera Shah and Patti Petesch (2000) *Voices of the Poor: Crying Out for Change*, New York: Oxford University Press for the World Bank.

Townsend, Peter (2002) 'Poverty, social exclusion and social polarisation: the need to construct an international welfare state', in Peter Townsend and David Gordon (eds), *World Poverty: New Policies to Defeat an Old Enemy*, Bristol: Policy Press, pp. 3–25.

United Nations Development Programme (UNDP) (2007/08) *Human Development Report 2007/8: Fighting Climate Change: Human Solidarity in A Divided World*, Oxford: Oxford University Press, available at: http://hdr.undp.org/en/reports/global/hdr2007-2008/ (accessed 7 June 2009).

United Nations Development Programme (UNDP) (2009) 'Albania continues to witness significant poverty reduction', press report, UNDP, New York, available at: http://www.undp.org.al/index.php?page=detail&id=123 (accessed 27 June 2009).

103 Sexuality, gender and poverty
Susie Jolly and Andrea Cornwall

Gender may have gained greater visibility in mainstream development over the last decade, but it is only very recently that the interactions between gender, sexuality and poverty have become more apparent. Development's approach to sexuality has tended to be to reduce it to sex, and to treat it as a problem. We tend to hear about sexuality usually only in relation to disease and violence, and rarely in relation to the more positive sides of life (Cornwall, 2006 [see Acknowledgements at the end of the chapter]; Gosine, 1998; Jolly, 2007 [see Acknowledgements]). Pleasure and love are not presumed important to the 'subjects' of development – poor people in the Global South. Gosine (1998: 5) contrasts representations of sex between white people, as 'about desire, love, romance and pleasure', and between non-white people as 'about reproduction, fertility control, stupidity and misery'. While development has become much less explicitly gender-blind, it is frequently sexuality-blind: much of what we see in development policies and programmes is framed in ways that are generally negative and implicitly or explicitly heteronormative – that is, making the assumption that particular forms of heterosexuality, notably marriage, are everyone's norm (see also Lind, Chapter 100, this volume; Moore, Chapter 3, this volume).

The silences, absences and assumptions that permeate mainstream development policy speak as much about how sexuality, gender and poverty interact, as the little that is explicitly said about these interactions. Take population, for example. It is common to find a focus only on demographic and macroeconomic aspects, with no mention of sexuality at all, although the reality is most people still do not have babies without having sex. Another example is one of the privileged objects of anti-poverty policies: the household. Household models based on the heterosexual nuclear family with a man as household head still form the basic unit for much development programming such as national Poverty Reduction Strategy Programmes (PRSPs). The assumption is made that only if men are absent could the household be female-headed, and a female-headed household must be poorer and more miserable than a male-headed household – leaving out the possibility of households run by lesbian couples or by women who would rather live without a husband than deal with an unsatisfactory relationship (Chant, 2007, and Chapter 15, this volume; Williams, Chapter 28, this volume). A further example is debates on transactional sex and sex work that remain more about morality and health than about economics.

The links between sexuality, social marginalisation and poverty have not been much explored. The fact that sexuality and poverty are themselves intimately connected is not seen, which stems in part from a lack of understanding of sexuality. The World Health Organisation (WHO) convened an international panel of experts, who arrived at the following definition of sexuality in 2004:

> Sexuality is a central aspect of being human throughout life and encompasses sex, gender identities and roles, sexual orientation, eroticism, pleasure, intimacy and reproduction. Sexuality is

experienced and expressed in thoughts, fantasies, desires, beliefs, attitudes, values, behaviours, practices, roles and relationships. While sexuality can include all of these dimensions, not all of them are always experienced or expressed. Sexuality is influenced by the interaction of biological, psychological, social, economic, political, cultural, ethical, legal, historical, religious and spiritual factors.[1]

This definition makes clear that sexuality is not just about sexual relations but is influenced by a whole host of broader factors. As we have suggested previously:

sexuality is about a lot more than having sex. It is also about the social rules, economic structures, political battles and religious ideologies that surround physical expressions of sexuality. It has as much to do with being able to move freely outside the home and walk the streets without fear of sexual harassment or abuse as it has to do with who people have sex with. It is as much concerned with how the body is clothed, from women feeling forced to cover their bodies to avoid unwanted sexual attention to the use of particular colours to mark the gender of infants and begin the process of socialisation of boys and girls as different, as what people do when their clothes are off. And, where society and the state collude in policing gender and sex orders, it can be about the very right to exist, let alone to enjoy sexual relations. (Cornwall et al., 2008: 5–6) [see Acknowledgements]

Once the broader implications of sexuality are understood, the connections with the core business of development – rights, justice, survival, the economy and so on – become more visible.

Making the connections

There is now widespread recognition of the threat that sexual ill-health poses to the economy, security and human well-being more generally. For example, The Maputo Plan of Action, unanimously adopted by Ministers of Health and delegates from 48 African countries in September 2006, states that the Millennium Development Goals (MDGs) cannot be achieved without more work on sexual and reproductive health and rights (SRHH), and that '[a]ddressing poverty and addressing SRHR are mutually reinforcing'.[2]

But there is less acknowledgement of the role that pressure to conform to norms around sexuality plays in influencing well-being, including in contributing to ill-health, but also in other ways. The Lesbian, Gay, Bisexual and Transgender (LGBT) Action Plan of the Swedish International Development Agency (Sida) highlights the impact on LGBT people:

As a result of being marginalised and socially excluded, and as a consequence of the stigma that is culturally imposed, LGBT persons are prevented from participating in society on equal terms, for example by having limited opportunities for earning a livelihood and providing for themselves. This has led to a situation of widespread poverty among LGBT persons in many countries.[3]

Others who are marginalised from dominant norms around sexuality, which include sex workers, single women, women who have sex outside of marriage and non-macho men, may face pressure to conform, and stigma, discrimination and violence if they do not. Those who subscribe to dominant norms of sexuality may also pay a price, for example, if they undergo genital mutilation, early marriage, or engage in unequal and unsatisfying heterosexual relationships. At the same time, conforming to certain norms can secure social inclusion and economic opportunities (for example, marrying a rich man, or simply playing by the rules meaning people will consider you a good family or community member and help you out).

Breakthroughs in thinking about poverty that occurred in the 1990s have opened up new opportunities to draw the connections between sexuality, gender and poverty. Some of the most inspiring contributions have been those of Robert Chambers whose numerous accounts of the multiple dimensions of poverty help to highlight the significance of aspects of poverty that otherwise fell outside the narrowly economistic frames of mainstream development policy. Exploring some of these dimensions shows how norms around sexuality and gender affect well-being, and in return, poverty and disadvantage have an impact on possibilities to seek the relationships or pursue the desires of one's choosing.

Work and livelihoods
Economic empowerment has risen up the development agenda in recent years to become an imperative hailed by the World Bank as 'Smart Economics'. Greater economic independence can expand possibilities for sexual and romantic relationships, and enable women to exercise greater choice over partners as well as exercise greater agency within partnerships. Naila Kabeer's (2007) research provides one example of this happening among women working in export industries in Bangladesh. While not disputing the sometimes terrible conditions and sexual harassment faced by these women, Kabeer shows that such opportunities can also increase their life choices, including about if, when and whom to marry.

Yet while women may have gained greater access to the labour market in many countries, gender-stereotyping remains rampant. A Human Rights Watch and International Gay and Lesbian Human Rights Commission (IGLHRC) report attests to the extent of workplace discrimination and exclusion from employment experienced by those who do not conform to sexual and gender norms. Pat, a coloured lesbian in South Africa, told of how gender conformity affected her ex-girlfriend's worklife: 'Employers would hire her [thinking she was] a man [Even though she could do the jobs fine] . . . as soon as they found out she had a pair of breasts, they would say "no we want a man, we thought you were a man".'[4] This is echoed in work on Latin America where it has been found that it is not simply sexual orientation but gender expression that can be the basis for stigma, prejudice and discrimination in the workplace, making the working lives of women and men who do not conform with gender and sexual norms insecure and difficult. As pointed up by Marcela, an outreach worker for a charity in Bolivia: 'The first thing he [her new boss] did was try to force me to either change my dress style or quit my job. Since I didn't agree to his request, I had to resign. Because of how I dress I often have trouble getting a job, since I'm not exactly the most feminine woman.'[5]

Voice
In many countries, sexual minorities are more marginalised than women from engagement in formal politics or in the many 'new democratic spaces' that have opened up in recent years. Lacking the means of representation, in contexts where there is active repression, and amid fears of repercussions for visibility and voice, LGBT people

may find themselves with few avenues for engagement. Participation may carry high costs. The introduction of the epidemiological category MSM (men who have sex with men) has created possibilities for organising and representation, but not without violently repressive repercussions in some contexts. Lesbians remain largely invisible in many countries. While this may have some advantages, there are longer-term consequences in terms of equitable public policy and addressing the implications of social exclusion.

Education
Sexual harassment and bullying at school blights the lives of transgender and same-sex desiring children, and threatens the educational opportunities of young women whatever their sexuality. Participatory research with men who have sex with men in Bangladesh by the non-governmental organisation (NGO) Naz Foundation International found that almost half said they were bullied in school because they were effeminate.[6] Norms around sexuality may also lead to girls losing educational opportunities. As the coordinator of the Turkish organisation Women for Women's Human Rights and the Coalition for Sexual and Bodily Rights in Muslim Societies, Pinar Ilkkaracan, comments:

> Oppression of women's and girls' sexuality lies at the core of several women's human rights violations related to development. Aside from the blatant violations such as honour crimes or female genital mutilation there are less obvious practices that are directly related to development targets. For example, look at girl children in Turkey. There are still hundreds and thousands of girls who are not sent to school because there is a fear that they will choose their own husbands, and not accept marriages arranged by their parents – thus costing the family both honour and the bride price. Sexuality is a crosscutting issue that lies at the heart of disempowerment of women. So if women are to be empowered, work on sexuality is essential.[7]

Health
Health services often discriminate both against people without money and against people who do not fit gender or sexuality norms. Non-governmental organisations and rights organisations working with sexual minorities report widespread discrimination against those whose gender transgression is visible. Those whose difference may not be observed still face barriers. A lesbian organisation in Delhi reports that enlightened doctors might realise that unmarried women might still be sexually active and require sexual and reproductive health services, but even these more progressive doctors have only thought as far as that the woman might have a boyfriend not a girlfriend. Sex workers face serious barriers. Access to healthcare is far easier for those who reproduce than those who do not, especially in an age where the (vitally important) imperative of saving mothers' lives has eclipsed the need for decent healthcare provision for all genders. However, where family planning is regulated, as in China, for example, insistence on having more babies than allowed can mean the mother will lose her job, and the child will be denied access to state schooling, as well as other penalties.

Housing and home
Women's lack of resources may prevent them from leaving violent or unwanted relationships, and other family members may also be interdependent. The organisation Gays and Lesbians of Zimbabwe (GALZ) reports young men and women with same-sex

sexual orientations not daring to seek relationships or be open for fear of being thrown out by their families. Some development programming based on strengthening family resilience as a poverty reduction strategy can create more pressure on people to marry and/or stay within heterosexual family set-ups – something which might make life more difficult for women facing domestic violence, or LGBT persons who already face pressure to suppress their sexual desires and gender identities, and conform to heterosexual relationship norms (Bedford, 2008).

Law
Having money or status can in some cases protect people from violations of their rights. In the Zamfara state in northern Nigeria, Sharia legal codes were passed in 1999 instating the crime of *zina*, or illicit sexual intercourse, as well as criminalising alcohol consumption and sodomy. Sex outside of marriage is treated as *zina*, and even if a woman is raped, she can be charged with *zina*. BAOBAB, a non-governmental women's human rights organisation in Nigeria, documented the implementation of these laws, and supported people charged under its provisions. Most of those charged under these laws are poor, usually rural, but also urban poor, illiterate women, men and children, with women more often convicted of fornication and adultery, and men more often convicted of alcohol consumption, theft and sodomy. The middle class or elites usually had the social status and connections to avoid charges, and the means to hire a lawyer to protect themselves in the rare cases they were accused.[8]

Violence
Sexual and domestic violence, and power relations within the family, affect access to and control of resources, and what sexual or relationship choices people dare to make. Sexual violence is also a potent weapon of war. As stressed by UNICEF in the 1996 *State of the World's Children* report, the value placed on women's chastity makes sexual violence against women powerful as a weapon of war (see also Parpart, Chapter 104, this volume). Sexual violence not only physically harms and traumatises women, it also shames them and their men precisely because women's chastity is valued, and women's bodies are seen as belonging not to themselves, but are instead repositories of honour for men and the community or nation. Men are also targets of sexual violence, in peace as well as war. Sexual violence against men and boys not only traumatises them, but also leaves them vulnerable to stigmatisation; it may be understood as undermining their masculinity, discrediting themselves, their community or nation (Petchesky, 2005). For this reason sexual violence against men often goes unreported. Transgender people and sex workers worldwide report facing exceptionally high levels of violence, particularly sexual violence from police.

Sex and exchange
Many people use their sexual assets as a commodity of exchange, a source of income, and a livelihood, whether through marrying into a richer family, or selling sex. One example is 'fish for sex and sex for fish', a well reported phenomenon in Kisumu, Kenya, where women are expected to sleep with fishermen as part of the payment for fish which they then take to market to sell. Sometimes a woman fish-trader will hook-up with a fisherman for a season, becoming his lover and buying his fish. The exchange could also be

more short term, with women offering one session of sex in exchange for the opportunity to make one purchase of fish.[9]

Sometimes the role of sex in economic exchange is clear-cut. In other instances, love and money are so entwined that to talk in terms of 'transactional sex' is to deny the other dimensions of those relationships (see Campbell and Gibbs, Chapter 50, this volume; Moore, Chapter 3, this volume; Nyanzi et al., 2005). Many people targeted by HIV/AIDS programmes as engaged in transactional sex do not see themselves as sex workers. Care must be taken about transposing judgements from one cultural context onto another – such as labelling as 'prostitutes' women whose lovers may give them gifts of money or who may take lovers in order to get some help with household expenses. What is clear although not quantified is the importance of such exchanges to many people's livelihoods (see Evans, Chapter 30, this volume).

Where wealth constrains sexual rights
While poverty can make people more vulnerable to abuses of sexual rights, higher economic status may present its own constraints. The Coalition on Violence Against Women in Nairobi reports that about 80 per cent of women seeking support in the face of violence come from the slums, because they are more willing to speak out. Only 20 per cent come from the more middle- or upper-class areas, and these women come only in cases of more extreme violence, or abuse involving their children, indicating that they are more reticent about coming forward, perhaps feeling they have more to lose in terms of reputation.[10] In South Africa, the middle-class white LGBT movement mobilised earlier than more racially and class-representative organisations. However, in parts of East Africa the opposite seems to be true. More open LGBT activists and organisations are often led by those facing economic exclusion as well as other challenges, perhaps again due to fears by better off LGBT of jeopardising reputation and inheritance.[11]

Ways forward
All too often the charge is made that efforts to change sex and gender orders are not the bread and butter concerns of those whose everyday lives revolve around the hard materiality of survival. Feminist, sexual rights and women's movements are regarded in some contexts as failing to engage adequately with these materialities, and pushing for issues that lack resonance with people living in poverty. Some sexual rights and feminist initiatives remain elitist, excluding people living in poverty or failing to address economic barriers. At the same time, there is a need for mainstream development to go beyond the often essentialising view of women and men that has driven recent efforts to push gender equality and women's empowerment up the development agenda. All too often, there is little or no recognition that the women and men who are the subject of gender discourse might not be heterosexual, and might prefer to have non-normative sexual and romantic relationships. They might have powerfully negative and limiting experiences of deprivation and exclusion as a result of their sexuality and gender expression. What is needed is greater recognition of the importance of bringing sexuality into the frame, complicating conventional gender analysis with closer attention to the interactions between sexuality and gender, and exploring the poverty-producing effects of heteronormative poverty-reduction programmes. Without this, it is hard to envisage just and equitable development.

Acknowledgements

This chapter draws on four of our recent publications. These are the book we edited together with Sonia Côrrea *Development with a Body: Perspectives on Sexuality, Rights and Development* (Zed, 2008), a paper by Cornwall in *Gender and Development*, **14** (2) (2006) entitled 'Development's marginalisation of sexuality: report of an IDS workshop', a paper by Jolly (2006) in *Development*, **49** entitled 'Not so strange bedfellows: sexuality and international development', and an IDS working paper (No. 283) by Jolly published in 2007 entitled *Why the Development Industry Should Get Over its Obsession with Bad Sex and Start to Think about Pleasure*. The latter is available online at http://www.ids.ac.uk/go/sexualityanddevelopment (accessed 14 October 2009).

Notes

1. World Health Organisation Working Definitions, available at: http://www.who.int/reproductive-health/gender/sexual_health.html#2 (accessed 27 June 2009).
2. http://www.unfpa.org/publications/docs/maputo.pdf (accessed 14 October 2009), p. 3.
3. Quote taken from page 2 of Sida's LGBT Action Plan 2007–2009.
4. Citation taken from page 211 of report by Human Rights Watch/IGLHRC (2003) *More Than a Name: State-sponsored Homophobia and its Consequences in Southern Africa*, New York: IGLHRC.
5. This quotation is taken from page 115 of the chapter by Alejandra Sarda entitled 'Discrimination against lesbians in the workplace', in Cornwall et al. (2008) [see Acknowledgements above].
6. Visit the website http://www.nfi.net/NFI%Publications/NFI%20Briefing%20Papers/social%20justice.doc (accessed 14 October 2009) to read the Briefing Paper No. 67 (2003), entitled 'Social justice, human rights, and MSM'.
7. This quote is taken from page 78 of Jolly (2006) [see Acknowledgements above].
8. http://www.baobabwomen.org/Sharia%20&%20BAOBAB%20publication.pdf (accessed 27 June 2009).
9. Go to http://www.siyanda.org/search/summary.cfm?nn=3506&ST=SS&Keywords=jolly&SUBJECT=0&Donor=&StartRow=1&Ref=Sim, and follow links to 'Looking at Sida work in Kenya from a sexuality angle, trip report September 26–October 11 2007', by Susie Jolly (accessed 27 June 2009).
10. See Coalition on Violence Against Women – Kenya (COVAW) at http://www.siyanda.org/search/summary.cfm?nn=3506&ST=SS&Keywords=jolly&SUBJECT=0&Donor=&StartRow=1&Ref=Sim (accessed 27 June 2009).
11. As discussed at the conference 'Changing Faces, Changing Spaces: Speaking out for Sexual Minorities in East Africa', hosted by the Kenya Human Rights Commission and Gay and Lesbian Coalition of Kenya (GALCK), Nairobi, 26–28 September 2007.

Select bibliography

Bedford, Kate (2008) 'Embedding neoliberalism: crisis, gender, and sexuality in the post-Washington consensus', paper presented at conference on Sexuality and the Development Industry, Institute of Development Studies, University of Sussex, 3–5 April.

Chant, Sylvia (2007) 'Dangerous equations? How female-headed households became the poorest of the poor: causes, consequences and cautions', in Andrea Cornwall, Elizabeth Harrison and Ann Whitehead (eds), *Feminisms in Development*, London: Zed, pp. 35–47.

Gosine, Andil (1998) 'All the wrong places: looking for love in Third World poverty (notes on the racialisation of sex)', unpublished MPhil thesis, Institute of Development Studies, University of Sussex, Brighton.

Kabeer, Naila (2007) 'Marriage, motherhood and masculinity in the global economy: reconfiguration of personal and economic life', IDS Working Paper 290, Institute of Development Studies, University of Sussex.

Nyanzi, Stella, Ousman Rosenberg-Jallow, Ousman Bah and Susan Nyanzi (2005), 'Bumsters, big black organs and old white gold: embodied racial myths in sexual relationships of Gambian beach boys', *Culture, Health and Sexuality*, 7 (6), 557–69.

Petchesky, Ros (2005) 'Rights of the body and perversions of war: sexual rights and wrongs ten years past Beijing', *UNESCO's International Social Science Journal*, **57** (special issue on Beijing +10), 301–18.

104 Masculinity, poverty and the 'new wars'
Jane L. Parpart

Introduction

The spike in violent conflicts in the early 1990s inspired a body of scholarship seeking to explain this post-Cold War violence. Numerous labels emerged – internal, privatised or informal wars, postmodern wars, low-intensity conflicts, degenerate wars as well as the 'new wars' (Kaldor, 2006: 2). While varying in details, this literature generally argues that there has been a shift in the nature and style of conflict, fuelled by state failure in a world of economic neoliberalism, globalisation and growing inequality (Newman, 2004). While compelling in many ways, this literature has been roundly criticised, particularly for its assertion that these wars are fundamentally different in their methods, strategies, tactics and level of brutality. However, even its critics applaud the efforts to link contemporary conflicts with global economic forces. Moreover, the emergence of a development-security complex closely linked to peacekeeping and 'the war on terror' draws heavily on this literature to rationalise its assertion that poverty and inequality are at the centre of contemporary conflicts (Berdal, 2003; Duffield, 2001). To highlight poverty's central role in war, the literature on the 'new wars' is strewn with pictures of impoverished, unemployed young men in 'guerrilla chic' clothing, with Ray-Ban sunglasses, waving AK47s menacingly in the back of pick-up trucks, suggesting a link between poverty, young males, masculinity and contemporary conflicts. Yet little is written or said about this intersection. The chapter proposes to explore this still rather uncharted arena with the aim of laying out an agenda for research.

The 'new wars' debate

The 'new wars' literature emerged out of the need to identify and understand the causes, characteristics and impact of post-Cold War conflicts. While acknowledging the emergence of the new techno-wars of 'shock and awe', the 'new wars' literature (and this chapter) focuses more on the growing number of intrastate civil wars (albeit often with transborder allies), largely based in states weakened by global economic restructuring and economic neoliberalism and characterised by ethnic and religious divisions. These wars have experienced dramatic increases in civilian casualties and forced human displacement, fostered by the breakdown of public authority and the blurring of the distinction between public and private security/combatants. They have also been deeply affected by the decline of bipolar power after the Cold War, the rise of international trading networks and the diminution of state power, especially in the Global South (Newman, 2004: 174–5). In addition, international aid has been identified as an unintended ally as supplies for refugees have provided easy targets for insurgents and other groups bent on terrorising civilians and rewarding allies (Duffield, 2001; Munkler, 2005: 87–90). Thus, the emphasis has been on economic forces and identity-based motives for conflict rather than a search for ideological motives, whether political or social (Berdal, 2003).

A number of scholars have sought to test the generalisations, assumptions and implied causal connections argued by the 'new wars' literature. Newman (2004) and others question the rigid divide between 'old' and 'new' wars, arguing that post-Cold War interpretations have exaggerated criminal violence while neglecting other motivations for contemporary wars. Berdal (2003) calls for a more careful analysis of causal links between an often unproblematised interpretation of globalisation and contemporary intrastate conflicts. He is particularly skeptical of the argument that increasing poverty in developing economies and widening global inequalities are the major factors fuelling the 'new wars'. While acknowledging that many contemporary conflicts are sustained by their integration into global trade networks, both legal and illegal, Berdal cautions against overemphasising economic motives and global forces, calling for attention to historical power struggles and grievances, cultural practices, political dynamics and more subtle, often ignored factors such as 'honour, prestige, fear and pride' (ibid.: 490). Thus the claims to have discovered a new form of warfare, with dramatically intensified violence, particularly against civilians, have been (and are) hotly contested. But these criticisms are tempered by applause for the literature's engagement with the deeper forces fuelling contemporary conflicts, albeit with a call for greater attention to historical, social and cultural factors.

In her revised version of *New and Old Wars*, Mary Kaldor (2006: 2–11) defends the 'new wars' literature as an important means for highlighting the growing illegitimacy of current civil wars, and the need for a cosmopolitan political response. For Kaldor, and many others, the world is facing a contest between primordial exclusivist authoritarian systems and the possibilities for an inclusive, liberal democratic peace (often called the liberal peace) (Duffield, 2001). Acknowledging her critics, Kaldor argues that the 'new wars' do indeed reflect a new reality, one with roots in the Cold War period but shaped by a world divided between those who are able to benefit from globalisation and those who are enduring life in weakened states, with declining economies, increasing criminality and privatisation of violence. Thus, it is the disaffected, the poor and the global outsiders who are seen as primary participants of the 'new wars'. As Kaldor (2006: 4–5). points out:

> the wars epitomise a new kind of global/local divide between those members of a global class who can speak English, have access to faxes, the internet and satellite television, who use dollars or euros or credit cards, who can travel freely, and those who are excluded from global processes, who live off what they can sell or barter or what they receive in humanitarian aid, whose movement is restricted . . . and who are prey to sieges, forced famines, landmines, etc.

This link between poverty, inequalities and contemporary conflicts has resonated with many of the concerns of governments, non-governmental organisations (NGOs) and development agencies struggling to come to terms with both the conflict-ridden 1990s and the subsequent 'war on terror'. The aggrieved poor and their 'greedy' leaders are regarded as key players in this drama. Indeed, the proposition that the 'new wars' are the result of increasing poverty in developing economies and increasing global inequalities has become international orthodoxy among the major international institutions, especially the World Bank and United Nations (UN) agencies. The association of underdevelopment with a high risk of conflict (and insecurity), and the poor with rebellion as well as victim-hood, have provided a renewed purpose for development agencies long known as the 'experts' on the Global South. Indeed, the UN has promised to cut poverty in half by 2015, and development has become a new type of riot control, promising to rescue victims of poverty from the temptation of rebellion (Duffield, 2001). Soldiers willing to lay down their arms are offered reintegration programmes; those who continue fighting receive nothing but condemnation. The possibility that these rebels might have dreams for themselves and their families, communities and nations, that they might have ideas about justice and gender, has largely been ignored. Like the 'new wars' literature, the development-security complex believes it has nothing to learn from the rebellious poor and their leaders. Yet as Berdal (2003) and others suggest, other factors need to be considered, including possible links between poverty, greed, gendered practices and contemporary conflicts.

The 'new wars', poverty and gender
For the most part, the gendered aspects of the 'new wars' are only mentioned in passing; most authors prefer to focus on global forces and war economies, with their reliance on looting and pillage as well as expanding connections to international resource markets (Duffield, 2001). Munkler (2005: 74–9) is one of the few 'new wars' proponents who has commented on the impact of masculine practices, particularly on young male recruits. He points out that the new wars are 'downright cheap', requiring only light weapons, pick-ups rather than armoured vehicles, cell phones rather than computers and the clothing of choice – sunglasses, jeans and T-shirts or camouflage uniforms. Above all, they are cheap because young unemployed men are a permanent source of recruitment for the war entrepreneurs. As Munkler (2005: 78) articulates: 'Their exclusion from regular economic activity, their hunger and their lack of peacetime social prospects automatically drive them into the arms of the warring parties.'

Thus poverty does play a pivotal role in the recruitment of young men and some young women, who provide cheap, fearless foot soldiers for the leaders of the 'new wars'. Picking up a gun and joining local warlords promises at least a kind of livelihood. In the Congo, for example, warfare has become one of the best (and often only) ways to make a living. Consequently, many young recruits, along with their leaders, have no desire to stop the war, given the economic benefits gained from looting and resource sales to international companies. Many of the poorly paid government soldiers have abandoned their posts to join the militias, because they offer better pay and more possibilities for looting. Baaz and Stern (2008) discovered that combatants on both sides of the Congo struggles rationalise their participation in violence, including sexual violence, on the basis of the suffering and frustration they have endured due to poverty and neglect. In Uganda, the ongoing war in the north of the country has decimated the local economy, leaving few opportunities for young unemployed men to earn a living other than by joining the rebel forces (Dolan, 2002). These cases, and many others, support the assertion that poverty is a key element fuelling contemporary conflicts.

However, other factors are at play; poverty alone cannot explain the large-scale recruitment of young soldiers into the 'new wars'. As Berdal (2003) and others argue, the desire for social recognition and prestige is equally important. In war economies, which have seen the destruction of opportunities for the independent livelihoods necessary to achieve adult manhood, with its associated authority, economic autonomy and access to sex, picking up a gun and joining local warlords promises not only a kind of livelihood but also a way of achieving social recognition that would never be accorded young men if they did not have a gun in their hand. Even if the respect is based merely on fear, it is more than most young recruits can achieve on their own (Munkler, 2005: 78). In northern Uganda, the war has largely destroyed traditional paths to adult manhood in a region that prides itself on its militant masculine prowess. Consequently, grabbing a rifle and joining the rebels has been one of the few paths for achieving manhood and the status it confers. Indeed, those very guns and the loot they offer provide the material goods to attract women, to terrorise male competitors and even to find a bride (Dolan, 2002). Baaz and Stern (2008) discovered similar patterns in the Congo.

In general, the masculinity spawned by war and terror is resolutely patriarchal, emphasising male authority over women as well as hierarchies among men. While the ideals of global masculinity perpetuated by Western media and based on wealth, urbanity, professional credentials and family life may have some purchase with young recruits (Baaz and Stern, 2008: 71), these more peaceful versions of masculinity and manliness are for the most part crowded out by militant masculinity, often accompanied by extreme sexual violence produced and legitimated through war. Indeed, most rapes are group rapes, providing sites for performing one's masculinity and proving one's credentials as 'real' men. Government forces are equally apt to use rape to display their masculine prowess (Dolan, 2002: 72–6). Yet although both rebel soldiers and government troops in the Congo have resorted to sexual violence on a large scale, female soldiers in the country often emphasise 'male traits' and claim to be tougher than the men. As one young woman soldier reported, 'many of the men are afraid, more afraid than us women'. At the same time, these young women accept patriarchal authority in the home (Baaz and Stern, 2008: 68–9, 78). Militant masculinity thus remains the litmus test of power, authority and respectability. If anything, contemporary conflicts have intensified the link between militant masculinity and power, overwhelming alternative ways of being masculine, both for men and ambitious women. Moreover, the widespread acceptance of traditional gender hierarchies in the private sphere also strengthen the legitimacy of militant masculinity throughout society (Baaz and Stern, 2008: 68–70; Dolan, 2002).

However, the foot soldiers of the 'new wars' also have ideas about what their communities and nations should become. The world these soldiers often seek is one which is free of corruption, poor governance and lack of education. Yet at the same time, the degree to which these aspirations include a strong desire for gender justice seems rather limited. In the Congo and Uganda, for example, where men complain of women getting all the good jobs and advantages, the vision is not one of gender equality (see Baaz and Stern, 2008: 71–2; Dolan, 2002). Similarly, Taliban fighters call for respect, education and good governance – but mainly for men. One has only to look at the legacy of civil conflict in South Africa, where one of the most gender-balanced constitutions and highest number of women in Parliament have not been able to stop the epidemic of rapes in the country. Thus the legacy of warfare seems to run against gender equality. Nevertheless, it is important to realise that the young recruits in the 'new wars', despite their complicity in many violent atrocities, especially against women, also believe they are fighting for a better world, albeit one where women are supposed to be kept in their place (Baaz and Stern, 2008: 78).

Unlike their foot soldiers, the leaders of the 'new wars' are not driven by poverty, as they have made enormous amounts of money from the war economies. Between 1990 and 1994 the Liberian warlord, Charles Taylor, made roughly US$75 million per year levying taxes on Liberian exports, including rubber, timber and diamonds, primarily sold to legitimate international firms (Berdal, 2003: 485). Between 1992 and 1998, the Angolan rebel group UNITA, led by Jonas Savimbi, raked in US$3.7 billion dollars from illicit diamond sales (Duffield, 2001: 196–7). Indeed, while devastating for local civilians, the 'new wars' have proven highly profitable ventures for participants. Greed rather than poverty are regarded as driving the leaders of the 'new wars', an explanation that allows many scholars, policymakers and development practitioners to ignore the possibility that some rebel leaders may have political and social agendas which could be crucial for establishing a lasting peace (Duffield, 2001). As Berdal (2003) points out, the focus on greed alone ignores key elements in struggles for power, particularly the belief in the legitimacy of one's campaign and the search for wider acceptance. Jonas Savimbi, for example, had a messianic sense of destiny and purpose, and 'was driven less by greed than by a deep conviction that he was fated to rule the whole of Angola' (ibid.: 491). The Chechen independence movement has been more a romantic project of independence than a search for personal enrichment (ibid.: 491–2), and the Taliban are fighting both for economic autonomy and an ideal 'pure' Islamic state. Most of these visions are patriarchal, and also fundamentally opposed to many of the assumptions embedded in notions of a liberal peace, yet we ignore them at our peril.

Conclusion

Poverty alone cannot explain contemporary conflicts. Malawi, for example, is one of the poorest countries in the world, but it has not been riven by insurgencies and conflict. In contrast, Sierra Leone, with its diamonds, and the Congo, with its rich mineral resources, have been engulfed in civil war for decades, and even during 'peacetime' conflict is endemic, particularly gender-based conflict. The ability to sell valuable goods in increasingly global resource markets, with criminal as well as legal networks, is certainly a key element enabling the 'new wars'. State weakness, valuable and saleable resources, vulnerable civilians and divided communities that can be inflamed by privatised security forces are also key factors. In such situations, war economies can become goals in themselves, made possible by poverty-stricken foot soldiers, but organised and led by wealthy warlords, often in collaboration with local and international elites (Berdal, 2003).

Yet other factors clearly matter. As Berdal (2003) points out, while warlords and their followers are indeed inspired by material goals, participation in the collective search for power and pride often overrides or at least sweeps aside economic calculations, being 'no less profound impulses than the desire for worldly goods' (ibid.: 491). And this search is often cast in masculinist terms, affirming the pride and privileges of men who find little affirmation in the global economic and political systems. Ignoring these complaints and the forces they are spawning is a dangerous game, for many of these complaints will have to be attended to if a liberal peace, with its promise of well-being, inclusivity and tolerance is to be achieved. A 'peace' based on deliberate ignorance of the views and voices of those prosecuting the 'new wars' is bound to fail everyone, including those who believe in social justice and gender equality.

Select bibliography

Baaz, Maria and Maria Stern (2008) 'Making sense of violence: voices of soldiers in the Congo (DRC)', *Journal of Modern African Studies*, **46** (1), 57–86.

Berdal, Mats (2003) 'How "new" are "new wars"? Global economic changes and the study of civil war', *Global Governance*, **9**, 477–502.
Dolan, Chris (2002) 'Collapsing masculinities and weak states: a case study of northern Uganda', in Frances Cleaver (ed.), *Masculinities Matter! Men, Gender and Development*, London: Zed Books, pp. 57–83.
Duffield, Mark (2001) *Global Governance and the New Wars: The Merging of Development and Security*, London: Zed.
Kaldor, Mary (2006) *New and Old Wars: Organised Violence in a Global Era*, 2nd edn, Stanford, CA: Stanford University Press.
Munkler, Herfried (2005) *The New Wars*, translation of original 2002 edition by Patrick Camillier, Cambridge: Polity Press.
Newman, Edward (2004) 'The "new wars" debate: a historical perspective is needed', *Security Dialogue*, **35** (2), 173–89.

Index

aboriginal women *see* women
ADB (Asian Development Bank) 461; *see also* finance; World Bank
adolescence 278–83; *see also* youth
adultery 84–92
advanced economies 153–8
AEC *see* South Africa
affirmative action 123–8
Afghanistan 78–9, 83, 315, 545–6, 549
Africa
   African GDI *see* gender-related measures
   African Union (AU-Plan) 215
   sub-Saharan 16, 76, 176, 215–19, 290, 327, 329–31, 465, 472–7, 500
African-Americans 324, 561
ageing
   economic security 195–200
   and gender 115, 123, 127, 195–200, 215–16, 219–25, 232, 236, 424
   HAI (HelpAge International) 215
   MIPAA (Madrid International Plan of Action on Ageing) 215–16
   older persons 195–200, 215–19, 220–25, 226–31, 232–8
agency 105–10
agriculture *see* development, rural
aid
   architecture 497–503
   effectiveness 497–503
   HLF3 (The Third High Level Forum on Aid Effectiveness) 498
   humanitarian 405, 538, 675
   quality of 541–7
   relations 510–15
AIDS *see* HIV/AIDS
Albania 20–21, 661–6
alcoholism 84–92
alternate currencies 557–62
alternative economies *see* economies
alternatives *see* gender
Amazon, the 192
ANANDI *see* India
Angola 56, 678
anthropology 25, 40, 122, 161, 253, 259, 295, 514–15
anti-poverty
   interventions 618–24
   legislation 638–43

Argentina 112, 231, 490, 493
arranged marriages *see* marriage
Asia
   Asia-Pacific countries 116
   Asians 272–7
   gender and poverty 184–90, 424–9, 462–5, 637–9, 641–5
asset(s)
   accumulation of 391–8
   approach based on 347–52
   control of 162–6
   empowerment 601–10
   gender inequality 347–52
   land 360–63
   livelihood strategies 297–8
   overview of approaches 1–26
   poor households 101–2, 347–51
   productive 250–51
   social capital 385–9
   sub-Saharan Africa 473–4
assimilation 257, 267
Australia 10, 53, 154, 241–7, 282, 524–7
autonomy 575–80
AWID (Association for Women's Rights in Development) *see* rights

Balkans, the 663, 666
Baltic Cygnets 278–83
Bangladesh
   BRAC (Bangladesh Rural Advancement Committee) 551, 552, 581, 604
   gender and poverty 35–40, 162–4, 241, 422, 441, 459, 523–4, 549–53, 581, 584–5, 595, 604–5, 669–70
Barbados 129–34
bargaining power 161–6, 347–52
Beijing Platform for Action (BPFA) 1–26, 43–4, 101, 111, 337, 498–9, 501, 511, 530, 541, 546, 618, 655, 673
Belize 256
Beveridge model 227, 231, 234
bisexual *see* sexuality
BME *see* United Kingdom
BMI (Body Mass Index) 48
Bolivia
   CreCER (Credit with Rural Education) 569–74
   gender and microfinance 569–74

indigenous women 258–9
migrants from 260–65
Bono (Paul David Hewson) 504–9
Botswana 218–20, 327, 367–72
BPFA *see* Beijing, Platform for Action
BPL *see* India
BRAC *see* Bangladesh
Brazil
  Brasilia 23–5, 116, 214, 494
  gender 24, 112, 162, 194, 231, 254–9, 297, 321, 427–33, 465, 487, 490, 493, 523
breadwinner *see* male, breadwinner paradigm
Britain *see* United Kingdom
BSP *see* pensions
budgeting *see* gender budgeting; *see also* gender-related measures
Burkina Faso 163, 315
buzzwords 24, 497, 515

Cambodia
  CMN (Cambodian Men's Network) 462
  gender 14, 24, 241, 422, 458–62
Canada
  CWB (Community Well-Being Index) 244
  INAC (Indian and Northern Affairs) 244, 247
  gender 8, 10, 83, 133, 153–8, 241, 244–7, 282, 413
capabilities
  Capability Index (CI) 71–6
  Capability Poverty Measure (CPM) 61–2
  and gender 47–52, 71–6, 436–9, 484–5
capital *see* human capital; social capital
care credits *see* caring
Caribbean, the
  afrodescendants compared 254–8
  gender 123–34, 315, 348–50, 356, 390, 426, 439, 655–60
  poverty studies 120
  and race 273–7
caring
  carework 333–8, 434–9
  childcare 147–52
  credits 232–8
  daycare 430, 650
  general discussion 232–8
  global care chains 472–7
  labour *see* caring, carework
  UCW (Unpaid Carework) 491
  see also work, unpaid
cash transfers 1, 103, 115, 248–53, 403–5, 516, 521, 548; *see also* microfinance
Caucasus, the 184, 189

CCM (Country Coordinating Mechanism) 505–6
CCT *see* cash transfers; *see also* microfinance
CEDAW (Convention on the Elimination of All Forms of Discrimination Against Women) 43–4, 65–70, 337–8, 527–9, 541, 546
celebrities 504–9
Central America
  CAWN (Central American Women's Network) 424–6, 502–3
  Central Americans 266–71
  see also Costa Rica; Guatemala; Honduras; Mexico; Nicaragua
Central Asia 184–9; *see also* CIS; Kazakhstan; Kyrgyz Republic; Soviet Union; Uzbekistan
CGAP *see* poverty
chains *see* commodity chains; global value chains
Chávez, Hugo 650–54
child poverty *see* poverty, child
childcare *see* caring
childhood 157, 169, 192, 196, 249, 278, 281, 342–3
Chile
  AUGE (Acceso Universal con Garantías Explicitas en Salud) 311–14
  CPD (Coalition of Parties for Democracy) 227–8
  FONASA (Fondo Nacional de Salud) 311
  gender 9–10, 11–12, 24, 46, 112, 226–31, 309–14, 441, 465, 489–90, 493, 534
  ISAPRES (Institutos de Salud Previsional) 311
  PASIS (Programa de Pensiones Asistenciales) 227–8
  SPS (Sistema de Pensiones Solidarias) 228
China 29–34, 123, 126, 220, 422–6, 441–3, 445, 451, 670
Christianity *see* religion
church *see* religion
CIDA (Canadian International Development Agency) model 619, 620
CIDDEF (Algerian Centre for Information and Documentation of the Rights of Children and Women) 78
cigarette smoking 339–44
cities 153–8; *see also* urban
citizenship 272–7
civil war *see* violence
class (social class) 141–7, 225, 340, 410, 429, 652
climate change 1–26, 296–300, 538, 666

Index 683

collective models of the household *see* households
Colombia 15, 112, 194, 255, 260–65, 297, 388–90, 465, 485–8
colonialism 124, 129–30, 254, 255, 257, 258, 262, 284, 301–6, 328, 508, 513, 559, 571, 656
colonies 123, 273, 612, 617, 644
colonisation 255–6
commodity chains 310, 475–7; *see also* global value chains
Commonwealth, the 25, 46, 70, 483, 527
community
    CDD (community-driven development) 596
    change, led 84–92
    cohesion *see* multiculturalism
    community-based action teams *see* Ghana, COMBATS
    CSO (Civil Society Organisation) 353, 359, 497, 501, 517
    development 612–17
    organisations 379–84
    well-being index *see* Canada
conditional cash transfers *see* microfinance
conflicts 21, 57, 140, 353, 370, 403–4, 528, 674–8
Congo 674–9
construction workers 458–62
Consumer Price Index (CPI) *see* CPI
consumers 504–9
control
    over loans 599–605
    power 575–80
conventions
    of the International Labour Organisation 65–70
    see also ILO
    on the Elimination of All Forms of Discrimination Against Women *see* CEDAW
cooperative conflicts 47–52
Copenhagen
    Second World Conference on Women, 1980 618
    World Summit for Social Development, 1995 530
corporate labour codes *see* labour, codes
Costa Rica
    CCSS (Caja Costarricense de Seguro Social) 228, 231
    CMF (Centro Nacional del Desarrollo de la Mujer y de la Familia) 529–30
    CONASOL (Comisión Nacional de Solidaridad y Desarrollo Humano) 531
    FODESAF (Fondo de Desarrollo Social y Asignaciones Familiares) 528, 531
    gender 69–70, 111–17, 226–31, 257–8, 442, 465–6, 528–9, 533–4
    IDA (Instituto de Desarrollo Agrario) 532
    IMAS (Instituto Mixto de Ayuda Social) 528, 531–3
    INAMU (Instituto Nacional de las Mujeres) 529, 532–4
    NPM (New Public Management) 530
    PLN (Partido Liberación Nacional) 530
    PNCP (Plan Nacional de Combate a la Pobreza) 529–30
    PNS (Plan Nacional de Solidaridad) 529
    PUSC (Partido Unidad Social Cristiana) 529–31
    RNC (Régimen No-contributivo) 229
CPI (Consumer Price Index) 53–8
CPM *see* capabilities
craftworkers 575–80
credit circles 584; *see also* microfinance
credit *see* microfinance; microfinance, microcredit
crime
    crimes 502, 670
    criminal networks 674–9
    criminalisation 273, 671
    criminality 274, 675
    criminals 32
Croatia 79, 666
CSO *see* community
CT (Cash Transfer) *see* microfinance
Cuba
    FCW (Federation of Cuban Women/ Federación de Mujeres Cubanas) 124, 259
    gender 7, 70, 123–8, 131, 133, 256–9, 315, 320, 426, 652
culture
    cultural analysis 20, 47–52, 154, 183, 272–3, 384, 413, 558, 628, 638–9, 643
    cultural difference 141–6

DAC (OECD Development Assistance Committee) 43–5
data, use of *see* methodology
DAWN *see* Development Alternatives with Women for a New Era
debt
    crisis 253, 650
    high indebtedness 118, 123
    HIPC and HIPC II (Heavily Indebted Poor Countries) 1, 498, 516–17

and microcredit repayment 19, 566–8
and migration 32
see also feminisation of responsibility
decentralisation 633–7
decision-making 373–8
decomposition 452–7
democracy 227–9, 302, 509, 523, 527, 574, 634–7, 643, 656, 663
  democratic accountability 638–43
desertion (of women, by men) 103, 137, 173, 371, 394, 458–62
developing economies 339–44
development
  Asian 25
  Development Alternatives with Women for a New Era (DAWN) 1–26
  discourses 510–15
  economic 77–83
  human 24, 61–2, 83
  international 17, 24, 29, 91, 110, 132, 190, 306, 317, 334, 385, 504–5, 511, 518, 535, 542–7, 550, 587, 604, 617, 628, 632–3, 637, 673
  policy 535–40
  practice 535–40
  projects 618–24
  regional 632
  rural 569–74
  security (development-security complex) 674–9
  social 24–6, 480
  world 11, 21, 25–6, 52, 64, 83, 405
DFID *see* United Kingdom
diaspora 123–8, 194, 212, 257–8
dichotomous thinking 105–10
disasters
  conflict and 536
  ISDR International Strategy for Disaster Reduction 627
  poverty and 627–32
  risk reduction 516–21
  vulnerability to 77, 129
discourse
  analysis 41–6, 105–10
  development *see* development
  organisational 535–40
discrimination 25–6, 41–6, 60–69, 78–84, 90, 115–16, 220–26, 254–5, 261, 273–4, 399–403, 418–19, 440–45, 455–6, 490–91, 542–3, 565–7, 668–70
dislocation 278–83
displacement
  dispersement 633
  displaced people 16, 137, 222, 278, 280–83, 458, 674, 663
  displaced persons camps 278–83
  forced 358
  labour 436
diversity 536, 660
divorce 101–4
DOE *see* empowerment
domestic labour, division of 178–83
domestic violence *see* violence, domestic
Dominica
  DHS (Demographic and Health Survey) 125
  donors (aid) 606–11
  and gender 7, 123, 125–8, 130–33, 257–8, 297, 490–93
Dominican Republic
  CAFTA-DR (Central American Free Trade Area – Dominican Republic) 126
  diasporas, afrodescendant 257–8
  female-headed households 123–8
  gender 297, 490, 493
  households and poverty 130–33
  IEPD (Instituto de Estudios de Población y Desarrollo) 125

early marriage *see* marriage
earnings and poverty *see* poverty, earnings
earthquakes 21
ECERP *see* Nicaragua
ECLAC (Economic Commission for Latin America and the Caribbean) 1, 24, 46, 65
eco-justice *see* rights
ECO/PN *see* Senegal
economics
  assumptions 667–9
  and development *see* development
  and demography 225
  feminist 473
  feminist as 'smart' 301, 516, 520
  macroeconomic institutions 472–7
  market reform 452–7
  markets 429–33
    growth 47–52
    inequalities 528
  restructuring 472–7
  risk 399–406
economies
  advanced *see* advanced economies
  alternative 29–34
Ecuador
  asset accumulation 391–7
  gender 260–65, 315–18, 352–3
  Guayaquil 13–14, 387, 391–8
  Guayas 391, 395–7
  Indio Guayas 391–8
  neoliberalism 649–54

education
  of daughters 103
  female 546
  formal 75, 90, 417, 531
  of girls 59, 80, 173, 511
  health 81, 102, 124, 135, 242, 273, 425
  lack of 583
  levels of 130, 141–6, 250, 317, 397, 401
  pre-school 149, 185
  public 104, 652
  rural 176
  school 337, 548, 553
  secondary 45, 250, 640
  sex 329, 521
  tertiary 130, 454, 459
  vocational 652
  of women 164, 318, 435, 580
EEM *see* gender-related measures
Egypt
  ADEW (Association for the Development and Enhancement of Women) 581–6
  Cairo 44, 216, 558, 562, 583, 586
  gender 19, 143, 297, 466, 581–93
  MOSA (Ministry of Social Affairs) 583
  PFP (Productive Family Programme) 583–5
El Salvador 66, 270, 422, 466, 490, 493
Elson, Diane 449–51, 474–5
employment 1–26
  and earning strategies 458–62
  public 522–7
  status 478–83
empowerment
  degrees of (DOE) 619
  Empowerment Evaluation Model (EEM) 620–24
  empowerment measures *see* gender-related measures (EEM)
  evaluation 618–24
    see also gender-related measures
  feminist 575–80
  and gender 1–26, 89, 527, 540, 568, 580, 593, 596, 598, 605, 618, 619, 624, 647, 661, 663
  TTR (Three Types of Results) 622
  women's 77–83
engenderment 83, 116, 400
enterprise development 606–11
entitlements 333–8
entrepreneurship 612–17
EOI (Export-oriented Industrialisation) 453
EPZ (Export Processing Zone) 423
ESI (Employees' State Insurance) *see* pensions; United Kingdom
ethics
  and development 424, 440–45, 505, 639, 668

ETI (Ethical Trading Initiative) 424, 442–5
  TUC (Trade Union Congress) (UK) 442
Ethiopia
  Addis Ababa 575–80
  and gender 18, 19, 162–4, 520, 544–5, 575–80
ethnicity 49, 65–70, 108–9, 123–8, 129–30, 147, 156, 196, 248–53, 254–9, 263–4, 272–7, 292, 297, 315–19, 401–2, 429, 477, 487, 510, 644
ethnology 295
ETI *see* United Kingdom
EU (European Union) 154, 155, 158, 167, 181, 237, 300, 410, 414–20, 488, 501–3, 546
Europe 153–8, 184, 189, 211–13, 254, 264–5, 280–83, 340–41, 415–19, 510, 523, 557–60, 655
evaluation
  gendered 357
  methodology 618–24
  of microcredit 611, 614
  monitoring 532, 545
  processes 402
  work 480–88
exchanges 379–84
exclusion *see* social exclusion
expenditure 161–6

factor loadings 71–6
faith
  Faith-Based Development Organisation (FBDO) 661–6
  WFDD (World Faiths Development Dialogue) 662
  see also religion
family
  alternative 654
  assets 393–7
  care *see* caring
  composition 51, 98
  desertion 103, 137, 173, 250, 371, 394, 460
  'happy' 84–92
  life 33, 142, 150, 152, 190, 461, 486, 561, 677
  matrifocal system 141–6
  nuclear model 126–8, 142–3, 196, 362, 368, 394, 510, 520, 667
  relations 141–6
  structure 122
  support 195–200
  see also households
family planning
  access to 517–18, 623, 670
  delivery 551
  and PEWH 623

Index

FAO (Food and Agriculture Organisation)
FBDO *see* religion
FDI (Foreign Direct Investment 222–3)
female casual labour 440–45
female-headed households 7, 20, 24, 35, 69, 84, 93, 95–101, 105–8, 111–16, 120–29, 131–3, 135–40, 142, 155–8, 165, 180, 184, 226–31, 259, 286, 288, 347, 351, 355, 364 368–9, 370–73, 387, 390–93, 394–5, 401, 438, 460–63, 469, 474, 511, 514, 528, 581–4, 610, 628–9, 642, 667, 673; *see also* households
female labour force 490–94
female masculinity 190–94
female poverty 95–100
feminisation
  of family responsibility 117–22
    see also feminisation of responsibility
  of HIV/AIDS 333–8
  of international migration 260–65
  of labour 421–6
  of policy 548–54
  of poverty 1–26, 35, 47, 57, 68–70, 95–100, 104, 105–10, 111–16, 129–35, 153–8, 178–80, 216, 232, 260–65, 284, 391, 427, 437–8, 510, 519, 582, 628–9, 631
  of survival 29–34
feminisation of responsibility (and/or obligation) 7, 20, 60, 113–15, 117–22, 260, 516, 549, 629–31; *see also* feminisation, of poverty
feminists 77, 301, 535–7, 571, 652, 655–7
fertility 2, 69, 81, 130, 131, 134, 244, 285–8, 319, 461, 517, 551, 595, 621–3, 667
FGM (Female Genital Mutilation) 78, 81, 205, 668–70
FHH (Female-headed Households) *see* female-headed households
fieldwork 618–24
finance
  financial capital 391–8
  financialisation 548–54
  financing 2, 23, 30, 32–3, 223, 373–5, 497–8, 501–4, 526–7, 531–3, 540, 552
  IFI (International Financial Institutions) 17, 477, 516–20, 618
  loan-use 599–605
  see also cash transfers; debt; HIPC; ICFFD; microfinance
Finland 155, 234, 413, 416
First Nations 241–7
FMC *see* Cuba, FCW
FODESAF *see* Costa Rica
Folbre, Nancy 361, 374, 411, 435–9
Fourth World 1, 101, 111, 530, 618

Fourth World Conference on Women (FWCW) 1–26, 101, 111, 530
fragmentation 140, 263, 267, 276, 363, 542
free trade
  FTZ (Free Trade Zone) 125–6
  initiatives 650
  and tourism 517
  see also economics, markets; neoliberalism
freedoms 26, 68, 71, 76, 96, 293, 376, 439, 639, 641, 663
functionings 71–6
FWCW *see* Fourth World Conference on Women

GAD *see* gender, and development
GALS *see* Gender Action Learning System
GALZ *see* Zimbabwe, Gays and Lesbians
The Gambia
  ADWAC (Agency for the Development of Women and Children) 612–17
  Banjul 201, 209, 213, 612
  DoSFEA (Department of State for Finance and Economic Affairs) 207, 213
  feminisation of poverty in 111–17
  microcredit and entrepreneurs 612–17
  sexuality and youth 201–14
garment trade 29–34, 422–4, 441, 444–7
gay identity *see* self; sexuality, LBGT
GBA *see* gender-related measures
GDI *see* gender-related measures
GDP (Gross Domestic Product) 54–6, 61, 124, 130, 184, 296, 459
GEM *see* gender-related measures
gender
  alternatives (strategic gendering) 29–34
  budget analysis *see* gender-related measures
  budgeting 333–8, 522–7
    see also gender budgeting
  class 409–14
  conflict 399–406, 497–503
  Development Index (GDI) 53–8, 59–64
  division of labour 141–6
  Empowerment Measure (GEM) 59–64
  equality 535–40
  equity 226–31
  GAD (Gender and Development) 1–26, 41, 43, 105, 115, 503, 535–9, 587–93
  GADU (Gender and Development Unit, Oxfam GB) 535
  general structural model of 594–8
  identity 190–94
  indices 1–26
    see also gender-related measures
  inequality 77–83, 360–66

lens 105–10
mainstreaming 418, 535–40, 655–9
migration 296–300
models 35–40
pay gap 415–20
policy 458–62
poverty 563–8
  see also feminisation of poverty
power dynamics 201–6
privilege 41–6
relations 367–72
segmentation 472–7
sensitivity 59–64
statistics 77–83
strategic 29–34
and violence *see* violence
wage gap 178–83
Gender Action Learning System (GALS) 84–92
gender budgeting
  practical needs 171–2, 595, 630
  strategic needs 171–2
  tools 333–8, 522–7
  see also gender-related measures, GBA; gender, budgeting
gender-based violence *see* violence
gender-related measures
  African Gender and Development Index 59–64
  EEM (Empowerment Evaluation Model) 620, 622–4
  GBA (Gender Budget Analysis) 336, 522–7
    see also gender budgeting
  GDI (Gender-related Development Index) 54–6, 61–2, 459, 663
  GEM (Gender Empowerment Measure) 62, 459
  Gender Pay Gap (GPG) 415–20
  measurement 1–26
  SIGI (social Institutions and Gender Index) 77–83
  statistics *see* gender, statistics
Gender-responsive Budgeting (GRB) *see* gender, budgeting
generations *see* intergenerational support
genital cutting/mutilation *see* FGM
geography (geographies) 30–34, 128, 153–6, 200, 265, 271, 378, 445, 593
Germany 11, 26, 116, 154–5, 231, 278–83, 413, 417
Ghana
  Amedzofe 117–22
  COMBATS (Community Based Action Teams) 543–4

general 7, 9, 117–22, 163–4, 200, 214–19, 304, 403, 466, 505, 543, 544
Ghana Living Standards Survey (GLSS) *see* poverty-related measures
ghettoisation 207–14
Gini coefficient *see* poverty-related measures
global
  care chains *see* caring
  city, the 220–25
  crisis, the (global economic slow down) 220–25
  Global Fund, the 504–09
  north and North and South 29–34
  value chains (GVT) 16, 440–45
    see also commodity chains
  women's strike 655–60
global care chains 472–7
global–local nexus 105–10
globalisation 5, 7, 14, 24, 26, 29–34, 40, 57, 105–10, 116, 128, 132, 146, 195, 212, 296–7, 304, 394, 413, 421, 437–9, 451, 457, 472–7, 484, 486–7, 527, 648, 654–8, 674–5
GLSS *see* poverty-related measures
GNI *see* poverty-related measures
GNP *see* poverty-related measures
governance 633–7
  AIDS 506
  and drought relief 642
  global economic 477
  good 677
  as government 581–6
  land 353
  local 13, 20, 633–7
  neoliberal 302, 647, 649
    see also neoliberalism
  Nigeria 536
  participatory 618
  self-governance 639
  and social protection 405
government *see* governance
Grameen Bank 548–54, 569–73, 581–3, 597, 606, 612
grassroots
  activism 522–3, 641–8, 655–60
  effects 117
  empowerment 596, 624
  and microfinance 610, 614
  needs 331
  and NGOs 513–15
  organisations 379–84
GRB *see* gender, budgeting
Grenada 129–34
Grenadines 132

688 *Index*

Guatemala
  ENCOVI (Encuesta Nacional sobre Condiciones de Vida) 73–6
  gender 66, 69–76, 266–71, 348–9
Guinea 76, 403
Guyana
  gender 131, 133, 527, 655–60
  GWAR (Guyanese Women Across Race) 658
  Red Thread (Guyana) 655–60
GVC *see* global, value chains

Haiti 21, 129–34, 257, 297, 315, 659
haq 638–43
HDI *see* Human Development Index
health
  care 321–6
  maternal *see* Latin America, maternal health
  rights 309–14, 446–51
heteronormativity 190–94
hidden poverty *see* poverty, hidden
high-income countries (HIC) 339–44
HIPC and HIPC II (Heavily Indebted Poor Countries) 1, 498, 516–17; *see also* debt
HIV/AIDS
  AIDS (Acquired Immunodeficiency Syndrome) 205–6, 295, 321–38, 362, 504–9, 513–15, 538, 543, 582, 672
  ART (Anti-Retroviral Therapy/Treatment) 12, 334, 338, 507
  ARV (Anti-Retroviral Medication) 12, 334, 338, 507
  HIV (Human Immunodeficiency Virus) 7, 12, 38, 45, 129–34, 165, 194, 205–6, 295, 321–2, 324–38, 362, 504–9, 513, 538, 543, 67
  PEPFAR (US President's Emergency Plan for AIDS Relief) 329
  PLWHA (People Living With HIV/AIDS) 12
homeworkers 421–6, 464–6, 479, 482
homosexuality 107, 192, 206; *see also* sexuality
Honduras
  gender 24, 65–6, 69, 256, 259, 266–71, 297, 348, 503, 517, 521, 593, 618–24, 629
  PEWH (Promotion of Self-managed Enterprises Project of Women in Rural Areas) 623
households
  boundaries of 141–6
  collective behavioural models 161–6
  composition 135–40, 141–6
  headship 391–8

male-headed 583
and money flows 141–6
overview 1–26
processes 599–605
structure 385–90
women-headed *see* female-headed households
housing
  and home 667–73
  finance 379–84
  markets 367–72
  ownership by sex (Latin America) 347–52
  rental housing 367–72
  subsidy 373–8
HPI *see* poverty-related measures
HRP *see* United Kingdom
human capital 161–6
Human Development Index (HDI) 54–6, 61–2, 458–9; *see also* poverty-related measures
human rights 65–70
humanitarian aid 538, 675
humanitarianism 508
hunger 518–20, 576, 642, 676
hurricanes 129–34
HWW (HomeWorkers Worldwide) 424; *see also* homeworkers; work

IADB (Inter American Development Bank) 65, 70
ICESCR (International Covenant of Economic, Social and Cultural Rights) 65–70, 309–12, 319
ICFFD (International Conference on Financing for Development) 497
ICLS (International Conference of Labour Statisticians) 464, 471
ICPD (International Conference on Population and Development) 65–70, 316, 319
ICT (Information and Communications Technology) 14, 422
identity
  ethnic *see* ethnicity
  multiple 37, 49, 108
  national 2, 10, 49, 108, 123–8, 213, 229, 242, 254–9, 261, 274–7, 283, 425, 487, 551
  politics of 38, 194, 255–9, 538, 639, 654
  racial 123–8
  religious 49, 63, 108, 129, 272–4, 401–2, 661–6
IDP (Internally Displaced Person) *see* displacement
IFI (International Financial Institutions) 17, 477, 516–20, 618; *see also* finance; IMF; World Bank

IFPRI (International Food Policy and Research Institute) 166
IGVGD (Income Generating Vulnerable Group Development Programme) 604
ILO (International Labour Organisation) 254–5, 421–2, 440–45, 463–4, 475–8, 482, 487–9, 501, 581, 619
ILSP (Improving Living Standards Project, Paraguay) 621–3
images (picturing) 301–6
IMF (International Monetary Fund) 9, 29–34, 117, 517, 651, 663
immigration
  immigrants 31, 266–71
impact
  assessment 594–8
  paradox 599–605
  social 248–53
Import Substitution Industrialisation (ISI) 453
income
  deprivation 95–100
  diversification 284–9
  generation 569–74
  pooling 427–33
  poverty *see* poverty
  transfers 522–7
India
  agrarian poverty and gender 431–2
  ANANDI (Area Networking and Development Initiatives) 87, 91, 306
  Andhra Pradesh 599–605
  Bangalore 369, 370
  Bengal 523
  BPL (Below the Poverty Line) 221, 223
  citizenship 638–43
  decentralisation and rights 633–7
  Delhi 23, 24, 52, 100, 116, 225, 265, 333–8, 398, 471, 670
  educational comparison 551
  employment 481–3
  ETI Impact Assessment 442
  feminisation of labour 446–51
  GALS 84–7
  gender budgeting 523
  gender inequality and poverty 47–52
  Gujarat 480, 483
  health and education 101
  HIV/AIDS and carework 333–7
  household decision-making 162–5
  informal employment and economy 464–6, 478–9
  land, access to 355–9
  microcredit 599–605
  NACO National AIDS Control Organisation (India) 333–4
  NREGA (National Rural Employment Guarantee Act) 638–43
  NSDF (National Slum Dwellers' Federation) 380
  PDS (Public Distribution System) 642
  poverty and ageing 220–25
  PWN (Positive Women's Network) 337
  Rajasthan 638–43
  Self Help Group Bank Linkage Programme 594–98
  Self Help Group programme (SHG) 18–19, 594, 597–605
  SHPA Self Help Promotion Agent (India) 597
  SPARC (Society for the Promotion of Area Resources) 379–80, 384
  slums 381
    see also India, NSDF
  Tiruppur 14, 446–51
indigenous
  peoples 321–6
    see also rights, indigenous
  women 569–74
Indonesia
  WRI (Women's Research Institute, Indonesia) 524
industrial districts 446–51
inequality 347–52
  Inuit 241–7
informality
  employment 77–83, 220–25, 421–6, 309–14, 463–71
  and poverty 463–71
  settlements 353–9
    see also WIEGO
infrastructure 71–6
inheritance 353–9
insecurity 147–52
institutional processes 472–7
intergenerational support 195–200, 296–300
internal migration *see* migration
International Labour Organisation *see* ILO
internet 193, 313, 613, 675
intersectionality 105–10
intra-household
  allocation 161–6
  analysis 360–66
  bargaining 373–8
  distribution 391–8
  dynamics 399–406
investors 606–11
IPL (International Poverty Line) *see* poverty-related measures

Islam *see* religion
ITUC (International Trade Union Confederation) 442

Jamaica 129–34
job-seeking 167–72

Kabeer, Naila 23, 41–2, 62, 68, 552–3, 567, 575, 592, 595–7, 600, 618, 669–70, 673
Kazakhstan 79, 185, 297
Kenya
  GALCK (Gay and Lesbian Coalition) 673
  gender 164, 201, 297, 338, 382, 431–2, 441, 465, 475, 671–3
Kerala 450
Kigali 137, 507
Korea 401, 413, 427–33
Kyrgyzstan 184–9

labour
  codes 440–45
  markets 101–4, 167–72, 463–71
  non-wage benefits 421–6
  participation 284–9
  unpaid 434–9
  see also economics; work
land
  landlord–tenant relations 367–72
  ownership by sex 347–52
  redistribution 135–40
  rights 360–66
  see also development, rural; urban
Latin America
  AIDS 324
  female-headed households 123–8
  feminisation of poverty 99, 112
  housing 353–6
  housing assets 348–51
  housing markets 368
  immigrants to the US 270
  income comparisons 286
  indigenous movements 254–9
  inequality 347–52
  informality 464–5, 645
  labour market deregulation 310
  marriage legislation 529
  maternal mortality 315–20
  microfinance 549
  migrants in London 260–65
  neoliberalism 649–54
  overview 1–26
  PAHO (Pan-American Health Organisation) 315
  Proyecto MesoAmérica 65–70, 315
  PRSP process 517–20
  rights and equality 65–70
  SIGI 79
  social policy 248–53
  stereotyping 669
  street lives 196
  urban poverty 190–94
  vulnerable workforce 441
  work quality 484–94
Latin America and the Caribbean Countries (LAC) 315–20
Latinos 128, 266–71, 324–5, 326, 489, 628
Latvia 11, 154, 278–83, 416
law
  access to the 353–9
  legal status 266–71
lending *see* microfinance
lesbian *see* sexuality
Lesotho 14, 218, 399–406, 505
liberal peace 674–9
liberation 549, 665
Liberia 677–8
life course 232–8
life expectancy 178–83
Lithuania 153–8
livelihoods
  filial support 220–25
  and poverty 220–25
  strategies 290–95
  and work 667–73
Living Standard Measurement Surveys (LSMS) 347–52
loan societies 557–62
loans *see* microfinance
localisation 633–7
lone
  mothers 147–52
    see also female-headed households; feminisation of poverty
  parents 409–14
longitudinal research 391–8
low-income
  countries 339–44
  households 581–6, 594–8
  low pay 147–52
  settlements 190–94
LSMS *see* poverty-related measures

machismo 262, 530, 628
macroeconomic institutions *see* economics
Malawi 35–40
male
  bias 41–6
  breadwinner paradigm 105–10
  domination 141–6

youth unemployment 207–14
see also households; masculinity
Mali, mobility 296–300
Maoris 241–7
markets *see* caring; economics; gender; labour
marriage
  arranged marriages 207–14
  early marriage 77–83
  marriage 48–9, 80, 145, 210–11, 357, 448, 539, 567, 640, 670
Marxism 106, 446–51, 657, 666
masculinity
  crisis of 178–83
  female 190–94
  in India 47–52
  masculinisation 51, 98, 112–15, 198, 411–12, 422, 452, 678
  masculinism 104, 449, 550, 678
  masculinities 23, 26, 48, 52, 190, 194, 593, 679
  and poverty 674–9
  and sexuality 671
  working with (men) 84–92
  see also sexuality
matrifocality *see* family
means-testing 232–8
measurements 41–6; *see also* gender-related measures; poverty-related measures
medical profiling 321–6
men *see* masculinity
Men Who Have Sex with Men *see* MSM; *see also* sexuality
mestizo or *mestizaje* (non-indigenous) 123–8, 249–51, 254–9, 322, 571
methodology
  asset-based 391–8
  capabilities gender 71–6
  data (methodologies) 59–64
  economic 391–8
  equality/equity 77–83, 491–5
  GAD 588
  gender-sensitive 59–64
  indices 53–8
  learning systems 84–92
  microfinance 596, 606–7
  poverty 104
  qualitative/quantitative 150, 618–24
  SDI 380–83
  subjectivity 35–40
  transition 184–8, 452–5
Mexico
  COESIDA (Consejo Estatal para la Prevención del VIH/SIDA) 322
  CONAPO (Consejo Nacional de Población) 288–9
  gender 11–13, 24–5, 46, 65–70, 112, 146, 195, 196–9, 200, 248–53, 270, 284–9, 315–17, 321–5, 348, 366–9, 385–9, 422, 464, 490–93, 497, 521, 526, 553, 559, 659
  INEGI (Instituto Nacional de Estadística, Geografía e Informática) 286, 289
  migration to the USA 287
  Oaxaca 321–6
  PROGRESA (Programa de Educación, Salud y Alimentación) 25, 104, 248, 253, 289, 462, 518, 553
MFIs *see* microfinance
MHH (Male-headed household) *see* households
microenterprise 484–9
microfinance
  ACCION International 563
  business case 606–11
  Conditional Cash Transfer programmes (CCT) 1–26, 104, 111–16, 249, 403, 516–18
  and empowerment 563–8
  FINCA International (village banking pioneer) 551
  gender focus 549–52
  gender practices 557–62
  housing 373–7
  institutions (MFIs) 606–11
  intervention 606–15
  microcredit 301–6, 563–8, 581–6
  MFIs (Microfinance Institutions) 19, 551, 569–73, 594, 606–11
  NBFI (Non-bank Financial Institutions) *see* informality
  overview 1–26, 555–617
  pawnbroking 557–62
  rotating savings and credit circles 557–62
  savings 561–2
  Self Help Bank Linkage Programme 594–8
  and social capital 569–74
  see also finance; loan societies
MICS *see* Tajikistan
migration
  and gender 1–26
  internal 296–300
  migrant workers 260–65
  rural–rural 296–300
  rural–urban 290–95, 300
  see also immigration
Millennium Development Goals (MDGs) 1–26, 41–5, 59, 77, 129, 133, 242, 315, 361–3, 478–9, 497–8, 502, 518, 548, 618, 640, 668
MNC (Multinational Corporation) 476
mobility 296–300

692 *Index*

Molyneux, Maxine 459, 578
Momsen, Janet 7
monetisation 557–62
morality 290–95
mortality
 maternal 65–7
 MMR (Maternal Mortality Rate) 12, 315–17
 ratio 65–70
MOSA *see* Egypt
Mozambique
 gender 8, 101–4, 173–7
 MRLS (Mozambican Rural Labour Survey) 173–5
MSI (Multi-stakeholder Initiative) 442
MSM (Men Who Have Sex with Men) 333, 670; *see also* sexuality
multiculturalism 272–7; *see also* culture; immigration
Muslims 272–7; *see also* religion

nationality *see* identity, national
needs
 basic 36, 65–8, 96, 99, 114, 193–4, 221, 229, 461, 511
 practical 595, 630
 strategic 171
 see also methodology; policy
neoliberalism 301–6; *see also* structural adjustment
Nepal 220, 552
New Labour 232–8
new wars 674–9
New Zealand 10, 241–7, 413
NGDO (Non-Governmental Development Organisation) 535
NGOs (Non-Governmental Organisations) 3, 18, 23, 53–6, 115, 176, 215, 255, 301–6, 365, 371, 382, 440, 442–5, 505, 512–13, 522–5, 531–2, 541–3, 547–9, 551, 571, 581–2, 585, 597, 606, 613, 618, 641–2, 658, 663, 675
Nicaragua
 ECERP (Estrategia Reforzada de Crecimiento Económico y Reducción de Pobreza) 517
 FSLN (Frente Sandinista de Liberación Nacional) 518
 gender and poverty 63–6, 229, 255, 348–9, 351, 422, 516–21, 627–32
 PLC (Partido Liberal Constitucionalista) 517
 PND (Plan Nacional de Desarrollo) 517–18
 PNDH (National Plan for Human Development) 517–18
 RPS (Red de Protección Social) 518–19

Niger 315
Nigeria 11, 118, 208, 290–95, 297–300, 476, 536, 671
non-wage benefits 421–6; *see also* informality
NREGA *see* India

obedience 201–6
occupation 278–83
ODA (Overseas Development Assistance/ Official Development Assistance) 43
OECD (Organisation for Economic Co-operation and Development) 77–83
openness (of the economy) 452–7; *see also* economics, markets; neoliberalism
Organisation for Economic Co-operation and Development *see* OECD
organisational discourse *see* discourse
orthodoxies 105–10
othering 167–72
Oxfam (GB) 535–40

Pakistan
 Baluchistan 85–9
 communities 638–9
  see also haq; religion, Islam
 and PALS 84–90, 459
Pakistani families (in the UK) 170, 273–7
PALS (Participatory Action Learning System) 84, 89–91; *see also* participation; Uganda
Paraguay
 and empowerment 620–23
 gender 19, 79, 297, 490, 493, 618–24
 ICVP (Increasing Consumption of Vegetables Project) 620
 JICA (Japan International Cooperation Agency)
 MAG (Ministerio de Agricultura y Ganadería) 620
parallel lives 272–7
parenting 8, 142–3, 154, 157, 167–72, 290, 295, 342; *see also* poverty, child
Paris Declaration on Aid Effectiveness *see* aid, effectiveness
participation
 active 205, 536
 approach 167–72
 citizen 228
 economic 68
 female labour 124–6, 178, 258–9, 279, 369, 493
 informal economic 473–6
 methods 84–92
 Participatory Poverty Assessment (PPA) 459
 political 230, 538, 542, 546–8, 647

Index 693

and poverty 244, 376, 538, 573–4, 623, 630, 647, 657, 668
social 595
see also PALS; Uganda
partnership 541–7
patriarchy
  behaviour 48
  and globalisation 106
  in absentia 131
  and land 360–66
  latent 48
  microfinance 552, 566
  poverty 49–50
  religion 21
  values 44
PCA (Principal Components Analysis) 73
PCP (Private Consumption Poverty) 47
Pearce, Diana 6, 97, 153, 155, 457
pensions
  basic state 232–8
  BSP, Basic State Pension (UK) 235, 236
  gender and poverty 9, 10, 16, 148–52, 180, 195–200, 220–28, 230–37, 311, 337, 347–8, 351, 405, 435, 524, 659
  private 232–8
  reform 232–8
  system design 232–8
Peru 9, 84–5, 190–94, 297, 545
philanthropy 504–9
Philippines, the 7, 23–4, 111–15, 117, 144–6, 163, 297, 401
PLC see Nicaragua
PLWHA see HIV/AIDS
PNCP see Costa Rica
PND see Nicaragua
PNDH see Nicaragua
Poland 153–8
police 191, 195–7, 275, 279, 281, 380–82, 449, 641, 671
police stations 379–84
policy
  driving of 545
  formation 276, 360, 364–6
  fracture points in 360–66
  and gender 220–25, 226–31
  makers 22, 42, 45, 52–3, 56, 57, 70, 171, 208, 213, 276, 312, 360–67, 410, 413, 463, 470, 476, 490, 520, 546, 585, 617, 650–58, 678
  making 208, 228, 235, 372, 464, 512, 530
  orientation 190, 194
political will 327–32
politics 449–51, 633–9, 643–5, 654–9, 669
population control
  birth control 284

contraceptives 10, 143, 205, 621
IUD (Intra-uterine Device) 130
pornography 208
post-
  apartheid 38, 328, 644–6
  Beijing (BPFCA) 111
  Cold War 21, 674–5
  colonial 497, 550, 553
  colonialism 510–15
  communism 578, 663
  conflict 13–14, 135–40, 462, 500
  disaster 628–30
  feminism 305
  Fordism 423
  genocide 135, 140
  hurricane 24, 133, 629–32
  independence 52
  industrial societies 339–44
  industrialism 275
  marriage 363
  migration 263
  neoliberalism 649, 652–4
  reconstruction 630
  reform 643
  retirement 179
  revolution 259
  slavery 131
  Soviet 8, 9
  war 282–3
  Washington Consensus 248, 673
  welfare 646
poverty
  CGAP Consultative Group for Assisting the Poor 606
  child 167–72
  earnings and 409–14
  feminisation of see feminisation
  hidden 167–72
  income-based poverty 59–64
  index see poverty-related measures
  line see poverty-related measures
  management 167–72
  measurement 1–26, 59–64
    see also poverty-related measures
  multidimensional 59–64
  New Poverty Agenda (NPA) 516, 548
  PRSP (Poverty Reduction Strategy Papers) 1, 17, 497–503
  reduction strategies 458–62
  and single motherhood 141–6
    see also feminisation of poverty; lone mothers
  working poor, the 427–33
poverty-related measures
  CPM (Capability Poverty Measure) 61

694   Index

see also capabilities
Gini coefficient, the 65, 409, 652
GLSS (Ghana Living Standards Survey) 117, 119, 121
GNI (Gross National Income) 135
GNP (Gross National Product) 65, 118
HDI (Human Development Index) 53–8, 59–64
HPI (Human Poverty Index) 61, 459
IPL (International Poverty Line) 53–8
ISITO (Russian household survey) 180
LSMS (Living Standards Measurement Survey) 348
Poverty Index 95–100
Poverty Line (PL) 6, 53, 65–6, 69, 75, 99, 492
well-being index see Canada
power relations
  and gender 41–6, 399–406
  powerlessness 85, 113, 317, 449, 588
PPP (Purchasing Power Parity) 53–8
PRGF (Poverty Reduction and Growth Facility) 520
privatisation 227, 302, 310, 314, 321, 409, 524, 618, 634–6, 644–8
production, global politics of 446–51
productive work 516–21
profiling 321, 325, 507; see also medical profiling
property ownership 84–92; see also asset(s)
PRSP (Poverty Reduction Strategy Paper/Process) 1, 17, 498, 516–18, 520–21, 667
public employment see employment
public services 522–7
Puerto Rico 7, 123–9, 258
Purchasing Power Parity see PPP

Qatar 498
qualitative/quantitative methodology 618–24; see also methodology
Quito Consensus 65–70
quotas 256, 402

race
  agency 301–6
  racialisation 655–60
  racism 301–6
reconstruction 516–21
Red Thread see Guyana
redistribution 38–9, 123–8, 162, 226, 230–31, 254–7, 259, 302, 410, 486, 649, 650–53
regularisation 353–9

religion
  in Albania 661–6
  Catholicism 24, 45, 130, 192, 228, 520–21, 530, 559, 662
  Christianity 661–6
  Church, the 89, 130, 192–3, 228, 393, 395, 517–18, 520–21, 530
  evangelical 21, 661–3
  FBDO (Faith-Based Development Organisations) 21, 661–6
  and inequality 55
  Islam 90, 201–6, 590–93, 638–9, 662, 678
  prayer 661–6
  see also identity
remittances 123–8
rental housing see housing
representation 301–6, 504–9
reproduction
  and care see caring
  reproductive bargain 421–6
  reproductive burden 69
  reproductive health 12, 44–5, 71–3, 206, 225, 249, 252, 313–19, 403, 425, 506, 519, 655, 668, 673
  reproductive labour 385–90
  reproductive rights 43–5, 194, 313–19, 623
    see also rights
  reproductive roles 516–21
  reproductive work 71, 75, 249, 386–7, 411–13, 444, 630
  see also caring
research, longitudinal 391–8
resilience 167–72
resource allocation 360–66, 674–9
results-based management 497–503
revenue 522–7
right to food campaign 638–43
rights
  AWID (Association for Women's Rights in Development) 500–502
  eco-justice 246
  indigenous 65–70
  land 360–66
  RBA (Rights-Based Approach) 636
  reproductive see reproduction
  rights-based approaches 633–7
  vernacular 638–43
  of women, funding for 497–503
  see also human rights
riots 272–7
risk reduction 472–7
rural development 101–4
Russia
  gender 8, 77, 178–83, 189, 279–81, 280–81, 341–3

Russian Longitudinal Monitoring Survey (RLMS) 180
see also CIS; Soviet Union
Rwanda
  ADRA (Adventist Development and Relief Agency) 138–40
  gender 7, 13, 131, 135–40, 360–65, 505, 507

SAC *see* South African Countries
safe sex 201–6
Salvadorans 266–71
sanitation
  access to 155, 249, 367, 428
  basic needs 66, 96
  and participation 523–4
  sewage 72, 155, 645
SAPRIN (Structural Adjustment Participatory Review International Network) *see* structural adjustment
savings 379–84
  SAC (Savings and Credit Association, Ethiopia) 576–9
  savings culture 557–62
  see also microcredit; microfinance
schooling levels 248–53
schools 6, 41–2, 46, 78, 81, 104, 120, 213, 249–52, 278, 383, 396, 428, 521–3, 551–2, 583, 640, 658
science *see* technology
SEAGA (Socio-Economic and Gender Analysis), 619–20
segmentation 434–9
segregation 272–7
self (subjectivity) 35–40
self-employment, informal 463–71; *see also* labour
self-help *see* India
SELFINA *see* Tanzania
Sen, Amartya 47–52, 60, 65–7, 70–76, 79, 171, 181, 186, 243
Senegal
  ECO/PN (L'Espace de Concertation et d'Orientation de Pikine Nord) 613
  female household heads 354
  microcredit 612–17
  trading networks 476
sex
  and exchange 201–6, 667–73
  ratio 47–52
  tourism 207–14
  work, commercial 290–95
sex work 290–95
sexual activities 201–6
sexual connection 207–14

sexual conservatism 201–6
sexual economy 290–95
sexual exchange 35–40, 201–6, 667–73
sexual freedom 190–94
sexual relationships 290–95
sexuality
  and AIDS/HIV 322
  female 9, 206, 291, 324
  IGLHRC (International Gay and Lesbian Human Rights Commission) 669
  LGBT (Lesbian, Gay, Bisexual and Transgender) 194, 668–9, 671–3
  LGBT action plan (Sida) 668
  LGBTI (Lesbian, Gay, Bisexual, Transgender and Inter-sex) 192
  male 9, 104, 206, 322–4, 667
  and poverty 2, 9, 21–2, 35–40, 85, 104, 108, 190–94, 290–91
  research and agency 190–95
  transgender persons 190, 334, 671, 668–70
  and youth 201–6
  see also heteronormativity; youth
SHBLP *see* microfinance
SHG *see* India
Sida (Swedish International Development Agency) 17, 18, 300, 322, 510–15, 568, 598, 668, 673
SIDS (Small Island Developing States) 129
Sierra Leone 79, 538, 540, 678
SIGI *see* gender-related measures
single mothers *see* lone mothers
single parents *see* lone parents
skilled birth attendance 65–70
SLF (Sustainable Livelihoods Framework) *see* livelihoods
slums
  and gender 13, 379–84, 561
  SDI (Shack/Slum Dwellers International) 379–84
  see also India
social agents 510–15
social assistance 399–406
social capital 13, 18, 76, 163, 166, 246, 253, 347, 385–90, 394–6, 401–2, 566, 569–74, 577, 594
social change 195–200
social class 339–44
social cohesion 260–65, 273, 276
social democracy 429
social disadvantage 339–44
social exclusion 2, 69–70, 197, 237, 260–65, 276, 399, 401–3, 427, 670
social indicators 95–100
social inequalities 35–40, 339–44
social networks 141–6

social policy
  evaluation 248–53
  general 248–53
  social programmes 248–53
  social protection 16, 66–8, 81, 184, 199–200, 227–31, 391, 399–406, 435, 440, 464, 482–5, 488, 518
    see also cash transfers
  social services 266–71
  social support 141–6
social reproduction 644–8
social risk 399–406
social sciences 140, 164, 219, 225
social transfer see cash transfer
socialisation 207–14, 213, 577, 588, 668
socialism 7, 123–4, 106, 127, 230, 257, 278, 451, 646, 649–53
socio-economic status 385–90
sociocultural norms 117–22
sociology 158, 271, 568, 639
soldiers 674–9
South Africa
  AEC (Anti-Eviction Campaign) 647–8
  Cape Town 373, 378, 384, 527, 644–8
  Durban 219, 256
  gender 35–40, 321, 327–8, 330–32, 354, 359, 373, 375–8, 383, 633–7, 644–8, 669, 672, 677
  TAC (Treatment Action Campaign) 332
  Western Cape Anti-Eviction Campaign 644–8
  WILSA (Women in Law in South Africa) 539
South Asia 35, 79, 103, 224, 425, 480, 638–41
Soviet Union 11, 124, 178–86, 189, 278–83
SPARC see India
SRHH (Sexual and Reproductive Health and Rights) 668; see also reproduction; rights
SRI (Socially Responsible Investment) 606
SSA (Sub-Saharan Africa) see Africa, sub-Saharan
St Vincent 129–34
stakeholders 236, 424, 442, 533
statistics 58–9, 96–9, 116–17, 150–55, 242–4, 464–7, 470–72, 513–14, 655–7
STI (Sexually Transmitted Infection) stigmatisation 141–6
strategic gendering see gender, strategic
structural adjustment
  and neoliberalism 301–6, 645, 650–51
  policies and priorities 284–5, 511, 581, 655–9
  post (structural adjustment) 117–22
  SAPs (Structural Adjustment Programme) 285, 329, 422–3, 436, 530, 655–9
subjectivity (and identity) 35–40

subversion 189, 265, 643
Sudan 79, 84–90
SUF (Slum Upgrading Facility) see India
survival strategies 190–94
sustainability 606–11
Sweden 154, 155, 167, 413, 416, 510–15

Tajikistan
  Dushanbe 186
  gender 8–9, 184–9
  MICS (Multiple Indicator Cluster Survey) 186
Taliban 83, 546, 677, 678
Tamil 51, 52, 220–22, 337, 598
Tanzania
  gender 11, 19, 296–7, 298, 296–300, 522–6, 563–7
  PRIDE (Promotion of Rural Initiatives and Development Enterprises, Tanzania) 563–8
  SELFINA (Sero Lease and Finance Company Limited) 563–8
Tanzania
  TGNP (Tanzania Gender Networking Programme) 522–4
tax credits 147–52
taxation 522–7
technology 266, 394, 418, 488, 567
television 66, 393, 509, 659, 675
tenants 367–72
tenure
  customary 353–9, 363–4
    see also land
  housing 149, 353, 367
    see also housing
  job 437
  security of 377, 383
    see also housing, rental
territorial 125, 254, 255, 256, 258
TFEGE (Taskforce on Education and Gender Equality) 16–17
TFR (Total Fertility Rate) 131
Thailand 23, 162, 297, 421–6
Third Reich, the 278–83
time
  time poor 167–72
  time poverty 71–6
  time use (survey) 655–60
Tobago 129–34
Tonkiss, Fran 8, 111, 121
trafficking 29–34
transactional sex see sexual exchange
transgender persons see sexuality
transitions 278–83
transnationalisation 34, 133

Trinidad 129–34
triple burden (women's) 474
Turkey 670

UBN (Unmet Basic Needs) 66; *see also* needs
UCW *see* caring
Uganda 13, 84–90, 137, 360–66, 523, 676–7
UK *see* United Kingdom
UN *see* United Nations
underclass, Muslim 272–7
United Kingdom (UK)
   BME (Black and Minority Ethnic communities) 272, 273, 274, 276, 277
   CRE (Commission for Racial Equality) 272
   DCLG (Department for Communities and Local Government) 273, 274, 276, 277
   DFID (Department for International Development) 300, 317, 334, 385, 462, 503, 511, 514, 587, 589, 628
   Ethical Trading Initiative (ETI) 440–45
   gender 10–11, 23–4, 146–9, 150–52, 153–8, 167–8, 232–8, 272–7, 282–3, 303–6, 340–43, 411–14, 424–6, 502–9, 511, 525–6, 659, 662, 666, 673
   HRP Home Responsibilities Protection (UK) 235
   London 260–65
   Muslims in 272–7
United Nations
   UN CSW (Commission on the Status of Women) 544
   UN Declaration on the Rights of Indigenous People 65–70
   UN-DESA (United Nations Department of Economic and Social Affairs) 2, 26
   UN-HABITAT (United Nations Human Settlements Programme) 137, 356, 359
   UNAIDS (Joint United Nations Programme on HIV/AIDS) 194, 508
   UNCHS (United Nations Centre for Human Settlements) *see* UN-HABITAT
   UNDAW (United Nations Division for the Advancement of Women) 2, 26, 43
   UNDP (United Nations Development Programme) 1, 6, 23–6, 44–6, 53–8, 61–2, 116, 132–4, 459, 462, 511, 662–3, 666
   UNECE (United Nations Economic Commission for Europe) 184–5
   UNESCO (United Nations Economic, Scientific and Cultural Organisation) 177
   UNFPA (United Nations Fund for Population Activities) 43, 215
   UNICEF (United Nations Children's Fund) 186, 315, 318, 320, 391, 585, 671
   UNIFEM (United Nations Development Fund for Women) 4, 16, 26, 43, 116, 133, 338, 439, 459–62, 466–7, 469, 471, 483, 500–503, 523, 526
   UNMP (United Nations Millennium Project) 16, 26
   UNPD (United Nations Population Division) 215, 296, 297, 300
   UNPFII (United Nations Permanent Forum on Indigenous Issues) 241–7
United States (of America) (US/USA)
   gender 1–26, 64, 70, 100, 110, 116, 123, 126, 133, 146, 153–8 183–5, 206, 241, 282–9, 341, 390, 413, 534, 617
   IIRIRA (Illegal Immigration Reform and Immigrant Responsibility Act) 267
   PEPFAR *see* HIV/AIDS
unpaid work *see* work
urban
   housing 367–72
   planning 220–25
   policy 367–72
   poverty 153–8
Uruguay 231, 490–93
US/USA *see* United States
USAID (United States Agency for International Development) 132, 472–5, 55–51
user charges 522–7
Uzbekistan 184–9

Venezuela 20, 112, 325, 518, 649–54, 659
vernacular rights 638–43
Vietnam
   gender 11, 14, 77, 296–300, 422, 442–3, 452–7
   living standards surveys 452–7
village banking 551, 597; *see also* microfinance
village, the 117–22
violence
   civil wars 674–9
   domestic 201–6
   gender-based violence 84–92
   new wars 674–9
   Partnership Against Domestic Violence, Australia (PADV) 524
   structural 327–32
   VAW (Violence Against Women) 502
visibility 16, 21, 32, 223, 256, 260, 364–6, 411, 470, 476, 640, 655, 667, 669
voice (women's) 1–26, 44, 90, 366, 538, 667–73
vulnerabilities 33–5, 38, 40, 135–6, 333–8, 400–405

WAD (Women and Development) 106
wage
  discrimination 490–94
  inequality 452–7
  institutions 415–20
  structure 415–20
  systems 399–406
  wages 101–4
  work 385–90
war *see* violence
Washington Consensus, the 65, 248
WB *see* World Bank
wealth measures 347–52
WEF (World Economic Forum) 62, 563
welfare
  benefits 141–6
  reforms 141–6
well-being 35–40
WFP (World Food Programme) 404
WID (Women in Development) 106, 650
widows 123–7, 135–7, 140–47, 220–25, 229, 337, 348, 355–7, 362–3, 394, 402, 591–3
WIEGO (Women in informal Employment: Globalising and Organising) 464–6, 471, 476–7
WOMANKIND Worldwide 17–18, 541–7
women
  aboriginal 153–8
  afrodescendant 123–8
  agency 190–94
  CEDAW 65–70
  domestic thrift 557–62
  empowerment *see* empowerment
  entrepreneurs 612–17
  groups 661–6
  savings banks 557–62

women-headed households *see* households, female-headed
work
  decent work 478–83
  quality 484–9
  unpaid 434–9
  see also caring, carework; livelihoods
working poor *see* poverty
World Bank (WB) 25–6, 29–34, 41–5, 53–5, 65–6, 69–70, 117, 176–7, 185–6, 223, 301, 317–18, 321, 479
World Health Organisation (WHO) 667–73
World Summit for Social Development 65–70
WRI *see* Indonesia
WTO (World Trade Organization) 57, 498

xenophobia 425, 656

youth
  associations 207–14
  sexuality 201–6
  street 195–200
  survival 207–14

Zambia
  CETZAM Christian Enterprise Trust of Zambia 609
  microfinance 606–11
  Oxfam 539
  women in the labour force 475, 507
Zimbabwe
  Gays and Lesbians of Zimbabwe (GALZ) 670
  gender 379–84
Zuma, Jacob 328; *see also* South Africa